The Norton Reader

THIRD EDITION

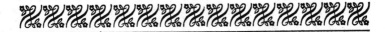

The Norton Reader

An Anthology of Expository Prose

THIRD EDITION

Arthur M. Eastman, *General Editor*
CARNEGIE-MELLON UNIVERSITY

Caesar Blake
UNIVERSITY OF TORONTO

Hubert M. English, Jr.
UNIVERSITY OF MICHIGAN

Alan B. Howes
UNIVERSITY OF MICHIGAN

Robert T. Lenaghan
UNIVERSITY OF MICHIGAN

Leo F. McNamara
UNIVERSITY OF MICHIGAN

James Rosier
UNIVERSITY OF PENNSYLVANIA

W · W · NORTON & COMPANY · INC · New York

Library of Congress Cataloging in Publication Data
Eastman, Arthur M   1918–   ed.
    The Norton reader.
    1. College readers.   I.   Title.
PE1122.E3 1973   808.88′8   72-7030
ISBN 0-393-09875-3
ISBN 0-393-09383-2 (pbk.)

PRINTED IN THE UNITED STATES OF AMERICA

5 6 7 8 9 0

ACKNOWLEDGMENTS

William Alfred: from *The Immigrant Experience*, edited by Thomas C. Wheeler. Copyright © 1971 by The Dial Press. Reprinted by permission of the publisher. Originally appeared in *The Atlantic Monthly*.

Maya Angelou: from *I Know Why the Caged Bird Sings*, copyright © 1969 by Maya Angelou. Reprinted by permission of Random House, Inc.

Robert Ardrey: from *The Territorial Imperative*. Copyright © 1966 by Robert Ardrey. Reprinted by permission of Atheneum Publishers.

Hannah Arendt: from *Eichmann in Jerusalem*. Copyright © 1963 by Hannah Arendt. Reprinted by permission of The Viking Press.

W. H. Auden: from *The Dyer's Hand*. Copyright © 1962 by W. H. Auden. Reprinted by permission of Random House, Inc.

James Baldwin: from *Notes of a Native Son*, copyright 1953, © 1955 by James Baldwin. Reprinted by permission of Beacon Press.

Margaret Culkin Banning: from *Letters to Susan*. Copyright 1934 by Margaret Culkin Banning. Reprinted by permission of Brandt & Brandt.

Owen Barfield: from *Essays Presented to Charles Williams*, edited by C. S. Lewis, Oxford University Press, 1947. Reprinted by permission of the author.

Carl Becker: from *Modern Democracy*. Copyright 1941 by Yale University Press. Reprinted by permission of the Press.

Saul Bellow: from *Intellectual Digest*, September 1971. This essay appeared originally in a slightly longer form in *Modern Occasions*. Copyright © 1971 by Saul Bellow. Reprinted by permission of Russell & Volkening, Inc.

Henri Bergson: from "Laughter," in *Comedy: Two Classic Studies*, edited by Wylie Sypher. Copyright © 1956 by Wylie Sypher. Reprinted by permission of Doubleday & Company, Inc.

Bruno Bettelheim: from *The Informed Heart*. Copyright © 1960 by The Free Press, a Corporation. Reprinted by permission of the publisher.

Peter Binzen: from *Whitetown, U.S.A.*, copyright © 1970 by Peter Binzen. Reprinted by permission of Random House, Inc.

Ronald Blythe: from *Akenfield: Portrait of an English Village*, published by Penguin Press, 1969. Reprinted by permission of David Higham Associates, Ltd.

Laura Bohannan: from *Natural History*, August–September 1966. Reprinted by permission of the author.

William Bondeson: from *The New York Times*. Copyright © 1971 by The New York Times Company. Reprinted by permission of The New York Times Company and the author.

Wayne C. Booth: "Boring from Within: The Art of the Freshman Essay," from an address to the Illinois Council of College Teachers in 1963. Reprinted by permission of the author.

Wayne C. Booth: "Is There Any Knowledge That a Man *Must* Have?" from *The Knowledge Most Worth Having*, 1967. Reprinted by permission of The University of Chicago Press.

Jacob Bronowski: "The Reach of Imagination," from *American Scholar*, Spring 1967. Reprinted by permission of The American Academy of Arts and Letters and the author.

Dee Brown: from *Bury My Heart at Wounded Knee*, copyright © 1970 by Dee Brown. Reprinted by permission of Holt, Rinehart and Winston, Inc.

Harrison Brown: from *Saturday Review*, June 26, 1971. Reprinted by permission of the author.

Jerome S. Bruner, from *Partisan Review*, Summer 1956, Vol. XXIII, No. 3. Copyright 1956 by Partisan Review. Reprinted by permission of *Partisan Review* and the author.

Anthony Burgess: from *The New York Times Magazine*, November 7, 1971. Copyright © 1971 by The New York Times Company. Reprinted by permission.

Samuel Butler: from *The Notebooks of Samuel Butler*, arranged and edited by Henry Festing Jones. Reprinted by permission of Jonathan Cape Ltd. on behalf of the Executors of the Samuel Butler Estate.

H. J. Campbell: from *Smithsonian*, October 1971, Vol. II, No. 7. Copyright © 1971 by Smithsonian National Associates. Reprinted by permission.

Edward Hallett Carr: from *What Is History?* Copyright © 1961 by Edward Hallett Carr. Reprinted by permission of Alfred A. Knopf, Inc., and The Macmillan Company Ltd. of Canada.

Joyce Cary: from *Highlights of Modern Literature*, copyright © 1949 by The New York Times Company. Reprinted by permission.

John Ciardi: from *Saturday Review*, January 8, 1972. Copyright © 1972 by Saturday Review, Inc. Reprinted by permission.

Robert Claiborne: from *The Nation*, January 25, 1971. Reprinted by permission of *The Nation*.

Kenneth Clark: from *Encounter*, January 1963. Reprinted by permission of the author and *Encounter*.

Eldridge Cleaver: from *Soul on Ice*, copyright © 1968 by Eldridge Cleaver. Reprinted by permission of McGraw-Hill Book Company.

v

Contents

xii · *Contents*

ON EDUCATION

ON MIND

SIGNS OF THE TIMES

ON LITERATURE AND THE ARTS

ON ETHICS

ON POLITICS AND GOVERNMENT

ON HISTORY

ON SCIENCE

ON RELIGION

Preface to the Third Edition

On advice from the field, this Third Edition of *The Norton Reader* is some 225 pages lighter than the Second Edition. It contains 72 new selections, a marked increase in material by women and black authors, and a new Prose Forms section on Oral History. The section formerly entitled On Civilization, now called Signs of the Times, is almost totally new, containing selections by such contemporary authors as Verta Mae Smart-Grosvenor, the Kenistons, Adrienne Rich, Eldridge Cleaver, Ada Louise Huxtable, Pauline Kael, John Kerry, Saul Bellow, and Anthony Burgess. Selections from John Updike and Tom Wolfe are among the eight that have updated An Album of Styles. On Politics has been retitled On Politics and Government—with a corresponding change in its contents.

Such additions have been purchased at the expense of a large number of selections which the editors have abandoned either because they seemed to have served their turn or because, more importantly, reports from the field indicated that they were receiving scant attention. The Prose Forms sections on Letters and Characters are gone for want of use, though some of the best of their material has been transplanted to other places in the text. Still, 124 selections continue from the past. In the opinion of the editors and of colleagues around the country, the essays by Dylan Thomas, Wallace Stegner, Allan Seager, Samuel Clemens, Bruno Bettelheim, and E. B. White—to mention only those in Personal Report—deserved to remain. Users of earlier editions will find an abundance of tried and proved material among the newer entries.

As in the past, the essays in the *Reader* are gathered into sections titled according to major fields of human concern—Language, Education, Mind, etc. The ordering remains unchanged—unobtrusive, we think, minimal, yet reflective of the individual's enlarging experience. Teachers who wish to work by topic can use its divisions. On gaining familiarity with the text, moreover, they will discover thematic links between the different sections. For example, Adrienne Rich's "When We Dead Awaken: Writing as Re-Vision" appears in Signs of the Times because its primary concern is with the awakening of the consciousness of modern women, but it ties in nicely with essays under On Literature and the Arts. Thomas LoCicero's "The Murder of Rabbi Adler" comes, appropriately, under On Ethics, but it links with a pair of essays in Signs of the Times: Alan Katz's discussion of "The Use of Drugs in America" and Anthony Burgess's challenging "Is America Falling Apart?"

Teachers who prefer to organize their courses rhetorically will, we trust, find useful the Index of Essays Illustrative of Rhetorical Modes and Devices that appears at the beginning of the book and, at the end, the Notes on Composition, which directs attention to rhetorical principles as exemplified in the text. Study questions for approximately half of the essays are offered diffidently for those who care to use them.

It is a pleasure to acknowledge again the perceptive help we received, while the First Edition was in the making, of Professors Hulon Willis of Bakersfield College, James H. Broderick of Bryn Mawr College, Cecil M. McCulley of the College of William and Mary, Harold D. Kelling of the University of Colorado, Scott Elledge of Cornell University, John Doebler of Dickinson University, Fred A. Tarpley of East Texas University, Harris W. Wilson of the University of Illinois, Don L. Cook and Donald J. Gray of the University of Indiana, Fabian Gudas of Louisiana State University, Eugene Hardy of the University of Nebraska, J. R. Gaskin of the University of North Carolina, Frederick Candelaria of the University of Oregon, Robert D. Bamberg of the University of Pennsylvania, W. Donald Head of San Jose State College, David J. DeLaura of the University of Texas, Joseph P. Roppolo of Tulane University, and John P. Cutts of Wayne State University. Their counsel was augmented in the Second Edition by Professors Byron Patterson of American River College; Hulon Willis of Bakersfield College; A. G. Medlicott, Jr., of the University of Connecticut; Charles B. Ruggless of Humboldt State College; Scott Elledge, Donald J. Gray, and James W. Groshong of Oregon State University; Carl E. Stenberg of Rhode Island College; James Wheatley of Trinity College; and Donald L. Cross of Upsala College.

For their tireless efforts in bringing to this Third Edition more selections by and about women, the editors gratefully acknowledge the assistance of Dr. Joan E. Hartman of Staten Island Community College and Dr. Carol Ohmann of Wesleyan University. Thanks are also extended to the many teachers who, by drawing on their classroom experiences with *The Norton Reader*, have offered a wealth of ideas and suggestions for its improvement. These include: Denis M. Murphy, Allegheny College; Anne Wiggins and Ella Mae York, Arizona Western College; Thomas Boghosian, Atlantic Community College; Dale K. Boyer, Boise State College; Don Norton, Brigham Young University; Robert R. Gross, Bucknell University; Louis E. Murphy, J. Michael Pilz, Katherine Rankin, and Judith A.

Switzer, Bucks County Community College; D. E. James, University of California at Riverside; Thomas Miles, Carnegie-Mellon University; David Noveshen, Catonsville Community College; Barbara Horgan and Rachel Meyerholtz, Clayton Junior College; Margaret W. Freeman, College of William and Mary; Raymond G. McAll, College of Wooster; Jack Brown, Columbus College; Ronald Migaud, Compton College; George T. Bush, William Devlin, Mrs. E. P. Johnston, Cornelia Rathke, and Alice M. Rusbar, Delgado Junior College; William G. Johnston, University of Denver; William Fisher, Detroit Institute of Technology; S. J. Kozikowski, Elms College; Peter Martin, Florida Atlantic University; Charles Gillespie, Florida Keys Community College; Marguerite del Mastro, Fordham University; James Lawrence, Framingham State College; George Haich, Richard L. Hall, and Susan Passler, Georgia State University; Martin Newitz and R. C. Ridenour, Golden West College; Georgiana Goldberg, Green River Community College; Charles Ruggless, Humboldt State College; Helen W. Krueger and Edwina Patton, Huntington College; Geary E. Danihy, Prem Kumar, and James F. O'Callaghan, University of Idaho; John Bell, University of Illinois Circle Campus; Terrance B. Kearns and Ronald Sommer, Indiana University; Judith Cushman, Ethel Deutsch, and Theresa Lenora Drew, Indiana University Northwest; S. D. Rowe and Daniel S. Grubb, Indiana University of Pennsylvania; Paul A. Parrish, Indiana University at South Bend; Mary W. Schneider, Kansas State University; Donald Stuart, Longwood College; Ira Hindman, Mansfield State College; Richard M. Judd, Marlboro College; William Kemp, Mary Washington College; John J. Lavelle, Monmouth College; Bernice Katz and Grant E. Strickland, Monroe Community College; Paul Benson, Mountain View College; Gary Lane, Muhlenberg College; Clarence S. Johnson, Newark College of Engineering; Daniel O'Day, Jr., Newark State College; Michael Spitzer, New York Institute of Technology; Arnold Bartini, North Adams State College; Edward Boucher, Mary L. Brittain, L. R. Early, James Evans, Ruth C. Hege, and Marvin Weaver, University of North Carolina at Greensboro; Martha L. Adams, Northeast Louisiana University; Maureen Edison, Dorothy Havens, Nancy Lee, Benjamin A. Little, and Harvey Vetstein, Northeastern University; Ely Liebow, Northeastern Illinois University; David Allen, Northland College; John P. Cutts, Oakland University; Rose D'Agostino and James Tarvin, Orange County Community College; Richard Woods, Pasadena City College; William E. Lucas, Peninsula College; Joseph M. Paradin and David Snyder, University of Pennsylvania; N. R. Brown, Charles Dewees, Jr., and Lee L. Snyder, Philadelphia College of Textiles and Science; Alex M. Baumgartner, Robert Fox, and Frederick Wilbur, Rider College; Anthony Amberg and Joseph Paris, Roosevelt University; Joel Magid, Rutgers University; Robert

Noreen, San Fernando Valley State College; Richard A. Alden, Kenneth Cooney, and Lee Leonard, Shasta College; Stan Smith, Sierra Junior College; Robert Weisberg, Skidmore College; Charles White, Southeastern Massachusetts University; Lila R. Fink, Juanita Mantovani, Tom Patty, and Jay Thompson, University of Southern California; George Gleason, Southwest Missouri State College; Karen Petz, State University of New York at Geneseo; Stanley M. Vogel, Suffolk University; William D. Stewart, Francis Thompson, and Earl Melton Williams, University of Tampa; Harry Ebert, Jr., Urbana College; I. R. Adams, University of Virginia; Shirley Borel, L. E. Seits, Mary Shesgreen, and James Zemek, Waubonsee Community College; W. Nicholas Knight, Wesleyan University; Sharon L. Taylor, Western State College; and Carol Metzger, West Los Angeles College.

Arthur M. Eastman

An Index of Essays
Illustrative of Rhetorical
Modes and Devices

THESIS[1]

1. The section headings of this index are treated more fully in the Notes on Composition, p. 1191.

MEANS OF DEVELOPMENT

STYLE

The Norton Reader

THIRD EDITION

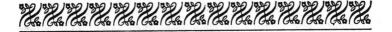

Personal Report

DYLAN THOMAS
Memories of Christmas

One Christmas was so much like another, in those years, around the sea-town corner now, and out of all sound except the distant speaking of the voices I sometimes hear a moment before sleep, that I can never remember whether it snowed for six days and six nights when I was twelve or whether it snowed for twelve days and twelve nights when I was six; or whether the ice broke and the skating grocer vanished like a snowman through a white trap-door on that same Christmas Day that the mince-pies finished Uncle Arnold and we tobogganed down the seaward hill, all the afternoon, on the best tea-tray, and Mrs. Griffiths complained, and we threw a snowball at her niece, and my hands burned so, with the heat and the cold, when I held them in front of the fire, that I cried for twenty minutes and then had some jelly.

All the Christmases roll down the hill towards the Welsh-speaking sea, like a snowball growing whiter and bigger and rounder, like a cold and headlong moon bundling down the sky that was our street; and they stop at the rim of the ice-edged, fish-freezing waves, and I plunge my hands in the snow and bring out whatever I can find; holly or robins or pudding, squabbles and carols and oranges and tin whistles, and the fire in the front room, and bang go the crackers, and holy, holy, holy, ring the bells, and the glass bells shaking on the tree, and Mother Goose, and Struwelpeter[1] —oh! the baby-burning flames and the clacking scissorman!—Billy Bunter[2] and Black Beauty, Little Women and boys who have three helpings, Alice and Mrs. Potter's badgers,[3] penknives, teddy-bears

1. The title character of *Struwelpeter* (*Slovenly Peter*), or *Merry Tales and Funny Pictures*, a children's book originally in German, by Dr. Heinrich Hoffmann, containing gaily grim admonitory narratives in verse about little Pauline, for example, who played with matches and got burned up; or the little boy who sucked his thumbs until the tall scissorman cut them off.

2. The humorous fat boy in Frank Richards' tales of English school life.

3. Beatrix Potter, creator of *Peter Rabbit* and other animal tales for children, among them *The Tale of Mr. Tod*, a badger.

—named after a Mr. Theodore Bear, their inventor, or father, who died recently in the United States—mouth-organs, tin-soldiers, and blancmange, and Auntie Bessie playing "Pop Goes the Weasel" and "Nuts in May" and "Oranges and Lemons" on the untuned piano in the parlor all through the thimble-hiding musical-chairing blind-man's-buffing party at the end of the never-to-be-forgotten day at the end of the unremembered year.

In goes my hand into that wool-white bell-tongued ball of holi-days resting at the margin of the carol-singing sea, and out come Mrs. Prothero and the firemen.

It was on the afternoon of the day of Christmas Eve, and I was in Mrs. Prothero's garden, waiting for cats, with her son Jim. It was snowing. It was always snowing at Christmas; December, in my memory, is white as Lapland, though there were no reindeers. But there were cats. Patient, cold, and callous, our hands wrapped in socks, we waited to snowball the cats. Sleek and long as jaguars and terrible-whiskered, spitting and snarling they would slink and sidle over the white back-garden walls, and the lynx-eyed hunters, Jim and I, fur-capped and moccasined trappers from Hudson's Bay off Eversley Road, would hurl our deadly snowballs at the green of their eyes. The wise cats never appeared. We were so still, Eskimo-footed arctic marksmen in the muffling silence of the eternal snows—eternal, ever since Wednesday—that we never heard Mrs. Prothero's first cry from her igloo at the bottom of the garden. Or, if we heard it at all, it was, to us, like the far-off challenge of our enemy and prey, the neighbor's Polar Cat. But soon the voice grew louder. "Fire!" cried Mrs. Prothero, and she beat the dinner-gong. And we ran down the garden, with the snow-balls in our arms, towards the house, and smoke, indeed, was pour-ing out of the dining-room, and the gong was bombilating, and Mrs. Prothero was announcing ruin like a town-crier in Pompeii. This was better than all the cats in Wales standing on the wall in a row. We bounded into the house, laden with snowballs, and stopped at the open door of the smoke-filled room. Something was burning all right; perhaps it was Mr. Prothero, who always slept there after midday dinner with a newspaper over his face; but he was standing in the middle of the room, saying "A fine Christmas!" and smacking at the smoke with a slipper.

"Call the fire-brigade," cried Mrs. Prothero as she beat the gong.

"They won't be there," said Mr. Prothero, "it's Christmas."

There was no fire to be seen, only clouds of smoke and Mr. Prothero standing in the middle of them, waving his slipper as though he were conducting.

"Do something," he said.

And we threw all our snowballs into the smoke—I think we

missed Mr. Prothero—and ran out of the house to the telephone-box.

"Let's call the police as well," Jim said.

"And the ambulance."

"And Ernie Jenkins, he likes fires."

But we only called the fire-brigade, and soon the fire-engine came and three tall men in helmets brought a hose into the house and Mr. Prothero got out just in time before they turned it on. Nobody could have had a noisier Christmas Eve. And when the firemen turned off the hose and were standing in the wet and smoky room, Jim's aunt, Miss Prothero, came downstairs and peered in at them. Jim and I waited, very quietly, to hear what she would say to them. She said the right thing, always. She looked at the three tall firemen in their shining helmets, standing among the smoke and cinders and dissolving snowballs, and she said: "Would you like something to read?"

Now out of that bright white snowball of Christmas gone comes the stocking, the stocking of stockings, that hung at the foot of the bed with the arm of a golliwog dangling over the top and small bells ringing in the toes. There was a company, gallant and scarlet but never nice to taste though I always tried when very young, of belted and busbied and musketed lead soldiers so soon to lose their heads and legs in the wars on the kitchen table after the tea-things, the mince-pies, and the cakes that I helped to make by stoning the raisins and eating them, had been cleared away; and a bag of moist and many-colored jelly-babies and a folded flag and a false nose and a tram-conductor's cap and a machine that punched tickets and rang a bell; never a catapult; once, by a mistake that no one could explain, a little hatchet; and a rubber-buffalo, or it may have been a horse, with a yellow head and haphazard legs; and a celluloid duck that made, when you pressed it, a most unducklike noise, a mewing moo that an ambitious cat might make who wishes to be a cow; and a painting-book in which I could make the grass, the trees, the sea, and the animals any color I pleased: and still the dazzling sky-blue sheep are grazing in the red field under a flight of rainbow-beaked and pea-green birds.

Christmas morning was always over before you could say Jack Frost. And look! suddenly the pudding was burning! Bang the gong and call the fire-brigade and the book-loving firemen! Some-one found the silver three-penny-bit with a currant on it; and the someone was always Uncle Arnold. The motto in my cracker read:

> Let's all have fun this Christmas Day,
> Let's play and sing and shout hooray!

and the grown-ups turned their eyes towards the ceiling, and Auntie Bessie, who had already been frightened, twice, by a clockwork mouse, whimpered at the sideboard and had some elderberry wine. And someone put a glass bowl full of nuts on the littered table, and my uncle said, as he said once every year: "I've got a shoe-nut here. Fetch me a shoehorn to open it, boy."

And dinner was ended.

And I remember that on the afternoon of Christmas Day, when the others sat around the fire and told each other that this was nothing, no, nothing, to the great snowbound and turkey-proud yule-log-crackling holly-berry-bedizened and kissing-under-the-mistletoe Christmas when *they* were children, I would go out, school-capped and gloved and muffled, with my bright new boots squeaking, into the white world on to the seaward hill, to call on Jim and Dan and Jack and to walk with them through the silent snowscape of our town.

We went padding through the streets, leaving huge deep footprints in the snow, on the hidden pavements.

"I bet people'll think there's been hippoes."

"What would you do if you saw a hippo coming down Terrace Road?"

"I'd go like this, bang! I'd throw him over the railings and roll him down the hill and then I'd tickle him under the ear and he'd wag his tail . . ."

"What would you do if you saw *two* hippoes . . . ?"

Iron-flanked and bellowing he-hippoes clanked and blundered and battered through the scudding snow towards us as we passed by Mr. Daniel's house.

"Let's post Mr. Daniel a snowball through his letter box."

"Let's write things in the snow."

"Let's write 'Mr. Daniel looks like a spaniel' all over his lawn."

"Look," Jack said, "I'm eating snow-pie."

"What's it taste like?"

"Like snow-pie," Jack said.

Or we walked on the white shore.

"Can the fishes see it's snowing?"

"They think it's the sky falling down."

The silent one-clouded heavens drifted on to the sea.

"All the old dogs have gone."

Dogs of a hundred mingled makes yapped in the summer at the sea-rim and yelped at the trespassing mountains of the waves.

"I bet St. Bernards would like it now."

And we were snowblind travelers lost on the north hills, and the great dewlapped dogs, with brandy-flasks round their necks, ambled and shambled up to us, baying "Excelsior."

We returned home through the desolate poor sea-facing streets where only a few children fumbled with bare red fingers in the thick wheel-rutted snow and catcalled after us, their voices fading away, as we trudged uphill, into the cries of the dock-birds and the hooters of ships out in the white and whirling bay.

Bring out the tall tales now that we told by the fire as we roasted chestnuts and the gaslight bubbled low. Ghosts with their heads under their arms trailed their chains and said "whooo" like owls in the long nights when I dared not look over my shoulder; wild beasts lurked in the cubby-hole under the stairs where the gas-meter ticked. "Once upon a time," Jim said, "there were three boys, just like us, who got lost in the dark in the snow, near Bethesda Chapel, and this is what happened to them . . ." It was the most dreadful happening I had ever heard.

And I remember that we went singing carols once, a night or two before Christmas Eve, when there wasn't the shaving of a moon to light the secret, white-flying streets. At the end of a long road was a drive that led to a large house, and we stumbled up the darkness of the drive that night, each one of us afraid, each one holding a stone in his hand in case, and all of us too brave to say a word. The wind made through the drive-trees noises as of old and unpleasant and maybe web-footed men wheezing in caves. We reached the black bulk of the house.

"What shall we give them?" Dan whispered.

" 'Hark the Herald'? 'Christmas comes but Once a Year' ?"

"No," Jack said: "We'll sing 'Good King Wenceslas.' I'll count three."

One, two, three, and we began to sing, our voices high and seemingly distant in the snow-felted darkness round the house that was occupied by nobody we knew. We stood close together, near the dark door.

> Good King Wenceslas looked out
> On the Feast of Stephen.

And then a small, dry voice, like the voice of someone who has not spoken for a long time, suddenly joined our singing: a small, dry voice from the other side of the door: a small, dry voice through the keyhole. And when we stopped running we were outside *our* house; the front room was lovely and bright; the gramophone was playing; we saw the red and white balloons hanging from the gas-bracket; uncles and aunts sat by the fire; I thought I smelt our supper being fried in the kitchen. Everything was good again, and Christmas shone through all the familiar town.

"Perhaps it was a ghost," Jim said.

"Perhaps it was trolls," Dan said, who was always reading.

"Let's go in and see if there's any jelly left," Jack said. And we did that.

WALLACE STEGNER
The Town Dump

The town dump of Whitemud, Saskatchewan, could only have been a few years old when I knew it, for the village was born in 1913 and I left there in 1919. But I remember the dump better than I remember most things in that town, better than I remember most of the people. I spent more time with it, for one thing; it has more poetry and excitement in it than people did.

It lay in the southeast corner of town, in a section that was always full of adventure for me. Just there the Whitemud River left the hills, bent a little south, and started its long traverse across the prairie and international boundary to join the Milk. For all I knew, it might have been on its way to join the Alph: simply, before my eyes, it disappeared into strangeness and wonder.

Also, where it passed below the dumpground, it ran through willowed bottoms that were a favorite campsite for passing teamsters, gypsies, sometimes Indians. The very straw scattered around those camps, the ashes of those strangers' campfires, the manure of their teams and saddle horses, were hot with adventurous possibilities.

It was as an extension, a living suburb, as it were, of the dumpground that we most valued those camps. We scoured them for artifacts of their migrant tenants as if they had been archaeological sites full of the secrets of ancient civilizations. I remember toting around for weeks the broken cheek strap of a bridle. Somehow or other its buckle looked as if it had been fashioned in a far place, a place where they were accustomed to flatten the tongues of buckles for reasons that could only be exciting, and where they made a habit of plating the metal with some valuable alloy, probably silver. In places where the silver was worn away the buckle underneath shone dull yellow: probably gold.

It seemed that excitement liked that end of town better than our end. Once old Mrs. Gustafson, deeply religious and a little raddled in the head, went over there with a buckboard full of trash, and as she was driving home along the river she looked and saw a spent catfish, washed in from Cypress Lake or some other part of the watershed, floating on the yellow water. He was two feet long, his whiskers hung down, his fins and tail were limp. He was a kind of fish that no one had seen in the Whitemud in the three or four years of the town's life, and a kind that none of us children had ever seen anywhere. Mrs. Gustafson had never seen one like him either; she perceived at once that he was the devil, and she whipped up the team and reported him at Hoffman's elevator.

We could hear her screeching as we legged it for the river to see for ourselves. Sure enough, there he was. He looked very tired, and he made no great effort to get away as we pushed out a half-sunken rowboat from below the flume, submerged it under him, and brought him ashore. When he died three days later we experimentally fed him to two half-wild cats, but they seemed to suffer no ill effects.

At that same end of town the irrigation flume crossed the river. It always seemed to me giddily high when I hung my chin over its plank edge and looked down, but it probably walked no more than twenty feet above the water on its spidery legs. Ordinarily in summer it carried about six or eight inches of smooth water, and under the glassy hurrying of the little boxed stream the planks were coated with deep sun-warmed moss as slick as frogs' eggs. A boy could sit in the flume with the water walling up against his back, and grab a cross brace above him, and pull, shooting himself sledlike ahead until he could reach the next brace for another pull and another slide, and so on across the river in four scoots.

After ten minutes in the flume he would come out wearing a dozen or more limber black leeches, and could sit in the green shade where darning needles flashed blue, and dragonflies hummed and darted and stopped, and skaters dimpled slack and eddy with their delicate transitory footprints, and there stretch the leeches out one by one while their sucking ends clung and clung, until at last, stretched far out, they let go with a tiny wet *puk* and snapped together like rubber bands. The smell of the river and the flume and the clay cutbanks and the bars of that part of the river was the smell of wolf willow.

But nothing in that end of town was as good as the dumpground that scattered along a little runoff coulee dipping down toward the river from the south bench. Through a historical process that went back, probably, to the roots of community sanitation and distaste for eyesores, but that in law dated from the Unincorporated Towns Ordinance of the territorial government, passed in 1888, the dump was one of the very first community enterprises, almost our town's first institution.

More than that, it contained relics of every individual who had ever lived there, and of every phase of the town's history.

The bedsprings on which the town's first child was begotten might be there; the skeleton of a boy's pet colt; two or three volumes of Shakespeare bought in haste and error from a peddler, later loaned in carelessness, soaked with water and chemicals in a house fire, and finally thrown out to flap their stained eloquence in the prairie wind.

Broken dishes, rusty tinware, spoons that had been used to mix paint; once a box of percussion caps, sign and symbol of the carelessness that most of those people felt about all matters of personal or public safety. We put them on the railroad tracks and were anonymously denounced in the *Enterprise*. There were also old iron, old brass, for which we hunted assiduously, by night conning junkmen's catalogues and the pages of the *Enterprise* to find how much wartime value there might be in the geared insides of clocks or in a pound of tea lead carefully wrapped in a ball whose weight astonished and delighted us. Sometimes the unimaginable outside world reached in and laid a finger on us. I recall that, aged no more than seven, I wrote a St. Louis junk house asking if they preferred their tea lead and tinfoil wrapped in balls, or whether they would rather have it pressed flat in sheets, and I got back a typewritten letter in a window envelope instructing me that they would be happy to have it in any way that was convenient for me. They added that they valued my business and were mine very truly. Dazed, I carried that windowed grandeur around in my pocket until I wore it out, and for months I saved the letter as a souvenir of the wondering time when something strange and distinguished had singled me out.

We hunted old bottles in the dump, bottles caked with dirt and filth, half buried, full of cobwebs, and we washed them out at the horse trough by the elevator, putting in a handful of shot along with the water to knock the dirt loose; and when we had shaken them until our arms were tired, we hauled them off in somebody's coaster wagon and turned them in at Bill Anderson's pool hall, where the smell of lemon pop was so sweet on the dark pool-hall air that I am sometimes awakened by it in the night, even yet.

Smashed wheels of wagons and buggies, tangles of rusty barbed wire, the collapsed perambulator that the French wife of one of the town's doctors had once pushed proudly up the planked sidewalks and along the ditchbank paths. A welter of foul-smelling feathers and coyote-scattered carrion which was all that remained of somebody's dream of a chicken ranch. The chickens had all got some mysterious pip at the same time, and died as one, and the dream lay out there with the rest of the town's history to rustle to the empty sky on the border of the hills.

There was melted glass in curious forms, and the half-melted office safe left from the burning of Bill Day's Hotel. On very lucky days we might find a piece of the lead casing that had enclosed the wires of the town's first telephone system. The casing was just the right size for rings, and so soft that it could be whittled with a jackknife. It was a material that might have made artists of us. If we had been Indians of fifty years before, that bright soft metal would have enlisted our maximum patience and craft and come out as ring and metal and amulet inscribed with the symbols of our observed world. Perhaps there were too many ready-made alternatives in the local drug, hardware, and general stores; perhaps our feeble artistic response was a measure of the insufficiency of the challenge we felt. In any case I do not remember that we did any more with the metal than to shape it into crude seal rings with our initials or pierced hearts carved in them; and these, though they served a purpose in juvenile courtship, stopped something short of art.

The dump held very little wood, for in that country anything burnable got burned. But it had plenty of old iron, furniture, papers, mattresses that were the delight of field mice, and jugs and demijohns that were sometimes their bane, for they crawled into the necks and drowned in the rain water or redeye that was inside.

If the history of our town was not exactly written, it was at least hinted, in the dump. I think I had a pretty sound notion even at eight or nine of how significant was that first institution of our forming Canadian civilization. For rummaging through its foul purlieus I had several times been surprised and shocked to find relics of my own life tossed out there to rot or blow away.

The volumes of Shakespeare belonged to a set that my father had bought before I was born. It had been carried through successive moves from town to town in the Dakotas, and from Dakota to Seattle, and from Seattle to Bellingham, and Bellingham to Redmond, and from Redmond back to Iowa, and from there to Saskatchewan. Then, stained in a stranger's house fire, these volumes had suffered from a house-cleaning impulse and been thrown away for me to stumble upon in the dump. One of the Cratchet girls had borrowed them, a hatchet-faced, thin, eager, transplanted Cockney girl with a frenzy, almost a hysteria, for reading. And yet somehow, through her hands, they found the dump, to become a symbol of how much was lost, how much thrown aside, how much carelessly or of necessity given up, in the making of a new country. We had so few books that I was familiar with them all, had handled them, looked at their pictures, perhaps even read them. They were the lares and penates, part of the skimpy impedimenta of household gods we had brought with us into Latium.[1] Finding those three thrown away was a little like finding my own name on a gravestone.

And yet not the blow that something else was, something that

---

1. In Roman families the lares and penates were the ancestral, household gods; they came to embody the continuity of the family. Cf. Virgil, *Aeneid* I. 1-7.

impressed me even more with the dump's close reflection of the town's intimate life. The colt whose picked skeleton lay out there was mine. He had been incurably crippled when dogs chased our mare, Daisy, the morning after she foaled. I had labored for months to make him well; had fed him by hand, curried him, exercised him, adjusted the iron braces that I had talked my father into having made. And I had not known that he would have to be destroyed. One weekend I turned him over to the foreman of one of the ranches, presumably so that he could be cared for. A few days later I found his skinned body, with the braces still on his crippled front legs, lying on the dump.

Not even that, I think, cured me of going there, though our parents all forbade us on pain of cholera or worse to do so. The place fascinated us, as it should have. For this was the kitchen midden of all the civilization we knew; it gave us the most tantalizing glimpses into our lives as well as into those of the neighbors. It gave us an aesthetic distance from which to know ourselves.

The dump was our poetry and our history. We took it home with us by the wagonload, bringing back into town the things the town had used and thrown away. Some little part of what we gathered, mainly bottles, we managed to bring back to usefulness, but most of our gleanings we left lying around barn or attic or cellar until in some renewed fury of spring cleanup our families carted them off to the dump again, to be rescued and briefly treasured by some other boy with schemes for making them useful. Occasionally something we really valued with a passion was snatched from us in horror and returned at once. That happened to the mounted head of a white mountain goat, somebody's trophy from old times and the far Rocky Mountains, that I brought home one day in transports of delight. My mother took one look and discovered that his beard was full of moths.

I remember that goat; I regret him yet. Poetry is seldom useful, but always memorable. I think I learned more from the town dump than I learned from school: more about people, more about how life is lived, not elsewhere but here, not in other times but now. If I were a sociologist anxious to study in detail the life of any community, I would go very early to its refuse piles. For a community may be as well judged by what it throws away —what it has to throw away and what it chooses to—as by any other evidence. For whole civilizations we have sometimes no more of the poetry and little more of the history than this.

QUESTIONS

1. Stegner begins his reminiscence of the town dump by saying that it had "poetry and excitement" in it. In what ways does he seek to convey those qualities to the reader?

2. Is Stegner's description of the dump and its surroundings vivid? Where does his writing directly appeal to the senses, and which senses are called into play?

3. In his second paragraph Stegner speaks of the Alph, the "sacred river" of Coleridge's poem "Kubla Khan." Why? How does allusion to that poem help him convey the strangeness and wonder he then felt?

4. In paragraphs 5-8 Stegner departs, as he had departed to a lesser degree in the two preceding paragraphs, from his description of the dump. Explain how that departure is justified and whether the writing there is appropriate to the essay as a whole.

5. Why does Stegner say (p. 9) that finding the three volumes of Shakespeare in the dump was "a little like finding my own name on a gravestone"? What is the purpose and effect of his allusion to Virgil's Aeneid in the sentence just before that?

6. Through what particular details does Stegner portray the dump as a record of his childhood? How is it shown to be also a record of the brief history of the town? In what respects does it reflect and suggest more widely yet, European and American history and culture and, ultimately, the ancient past, the foundations of civilization? Explain how and to what effect Stegner's focus on the dump enables these considerations to widen in scope but remain associated.

MAYA ANGELOU

High School Graduation[1]

The children in Stamps[2] trembled visibly with anticipation. Some adults were excited too, but to be certain the whole young population had come down with graduation epidemic. Large classes were graduating from both the grammar school and the high school. Even those who were years removed from their own day of glorious release were anxious to help with preparations as a kind of dry run. The junior students who were moving into the vacating classes' chairs were tradition-bound to show their talents for leadership and management. They strutted through the school and around the campus exerting pressure on the lower grades. Their authority was so new that occasionally if they pressed a little too hard it had to be overlooked. After all, next term was coming, and it never hurt a sixth grader to have a play sister in the eighth grade, or a tenth-year student to be able to call a twelfth grader Bubba. So all was endured in a spirit of shared understanding. But the graduating classes themselves were the nobility. Like travelers with exotic destinations on their minds, the graduates were remarkably

1. Chapter 23 of *I Know Why the Caged Bird Sings*, 1970.   2. A town in Arkansas.

forgetful. They came to school without their books, or tablets or even pencils. Volunteers fell over themselves to secure replacements for the missing equipment. When accepted, the willing workers might or might not be thanked, and it was of no importance to the pregraduation rites. Even teachers were respectful of the now quiet and aging seniors, and tended to speak to them, if not as equals, as beings only slightly lower than themselves. After tests were returned and grades given, the student body, which acted like an extended family, knew who did well, who excelled, and what piteous ones had failed.

Unlike the white high school, Lafayette County Training School distinguished itself by having neither lawn, nor hedges, nor tennis court, nor climbing ivy. Its two buildings (main classrooms, the grade school and home economics) were set on a dirt hill with no fence to limit either its boundaries or those of bordering farms. There was a large expanse to the left of the school which was used alternately as a baseball diamond or basketball court. Rusty hoops on swaying poles represented the permanent recreational equipment, although bats and balls could be borrowed from the P.E. teacher if the borrower was qualified and if the diamond wasn't occupied.

Over this rocky area relieved by a few shady tall persimmon trees the graduating class walked. The girls often held hands and no longer bothered to speak to the lower students. There was a sadness about them, as if this old world was not their home and they were bound for higher ground. The boys, on the other hand, had become more friendly, more outgoing. A decided change from the closed attitude they projected while studying for finals. Now they seemed not ready to give up the old school, the familiar paths and classrooms. Only a small percentage would be continuing on to college —one of the South's A & M (agricultural and mechanical) schools, which trained Negro youths to be carpenters, farmers, handymen, masons, maids, cooks and baby nurses. Their future rode heavily on their shoulders, and blinded them to the collective joy that had pervaded the lives of the boys and girls in the grammar school graduating class.

Parents who could afford it had ordered new shoes and ready-made clothes for themselves from Sears and Roebuck or Montgomery Ward. They also engaged the best seamstresses to make the floating graduating dresses and to cut down secondhand pants which would be pressed to a military slickness for the important event.

Oh, it was important, all right. Whitefolks would attend the ceremony, and two or three would speak of God and home, and the Southern way of life, and Mrs. Parsons, the principal's wife, would play the graduation march while the lower-grade graduates paraded down the aisles and took their seats below the platform. The high school seniors would wait in empty classrooms to make their dramatic entrance.

In the Store I was the person of the moment. The birthday girl. The center. Bailey[3] had graduated the year before, although to do so he had had to forfeit all pleasures to make up for his time lost in Baton Rouge.

My class was wearing butter-yellow piqué dresses, and Momma launched out on mine. She smocked the yoke into tiny crisscrossing puckers, then shirred the rest of the bodice. Her dark fingers ducked in and out of the lemony cloth as she embroidered raised daisies around the hem. Before she considered herself finished she had added a crocheted cuff on the puff sleeves, and a pointy crocheted collar.

I was going to be lovely. A walking model of all the various styles of fine hand sewing and it didn't worry me that I was only twelve years old and merely graduating from the eighth grade. Besides, many teachers in Arkansas Negro schools had only that diploma and were licensed to impart wisdom.

The days had become longer and more noticeable. The faded beige of former times had been replaced with strong and sure colors. I began to see my classmates' clothes, their skin tones, and the dust that waved off pussy willows. Clouds that lazed across the sky were objects of great concern to me. Their shiftier shapes might have held a message that in my new happiness and with a little bit of time I'd soon decipher. During that period I looked at the arch of heaven so religiously my neck kept a steady ache. I had taken to smiling more often, and my jaws hurt from the unaccustomed activity. Between the two physical sore spots, I suppose I could have been uncomfortable, but that was not the case. As a member of the winning team (the graduating class of 1940) I had outdistanced unpleasant sensations by miles. I was headed for the freedom of open fields.

Youth and social approval allied themselves with me and we trammeled memories of slights and insults. The wind of our swift passage remodeled my features. Lost tears were pounded to mud and then to dust. Years of withdrawal were brushed aside and left behind, as hanging ropes of parasitic moss.

My work alone had awarded me a top place and I was going to be one of the first called in the graduating ceremonies. On the classroom blackboard, as well as on the bulletin board in the auditorium, there were blue stars and white stars and red stars. No absences, no tardinesses, and my academic work was among the best of the year. I could say the preamble to the Constitution even faster

3. The author's brother.

than Bailey. We timed ourselves often: "WethepeopleoftheUnited Statesinordertoformamoreperfectunion . . ." I had memorized the Presidents of the United States from Washington to Roosevelt in chronological as well as alphabetical order.

My hair pleased me too. Gradually the black mass had lengthened and thickened, so that it kept at last to its braided pattern, and I didn't have to yank my scalp off when I tried to comb it.

Louise and I had rehearsed the exercises until we tired out ourselves. Henry Reed was class valedictorian. He was a small, very black boy with hooded eyes, a long, broad nose and an oddly shaped head. I had admired him for years because each term he and I vied for the best grades in our class. Most often he bested me, but instead of being disappointed I was pleased that we shared top places between us. Like many Southern Black children, he lived with his grandmother, who was as strict as Momma and as kind as she knew how to be. He was courteous, respectful and soft-spoken to elders, but on the playground he chose to play the roughest games. I admired him. Anyone, I reckoned, sufficiently afraid or sufficiently dull could be polite. But to be able to operate at a top level with both adults and children was admirable.

His valedictory speech was entitled "To Be or Not to Be." The rigid tenth-grade teacher had helped him write it. He'd been working on the dramatic stresses for months.

The weeks until graduation were filled with heady activities. A group of small children were to be presented in a play about buttercups and daisies and bunny rabbits. They could be heard throughout the building practicing their hops and their little songs that sounded like silver bells. The older girls (nongraduates, of course) were assigned the task of making refreshments for the night's festivities. A tangy scent of ginger, cinnamon, nutmeg and chocolate wafted around the home economics building as the budding cooks made samples for themselves and their teachers.

In every corner of the workshop, axes and saws split fresh timber as the woodshop boys made sets and stage scenery. Only the graduates were left out of the general bustle. We were free to sit in the library at the back of the building or look in quite detachedly, naturally, on the measures being taken for our event.

Even the minister preached on graduation the Sunday before. His subject was, "Let your light so shine that men will see your good works and praise your Father, Who is in Heaven." Although the sermon was purported to be addressed to us, he used the occasion to speak to backsliders, gamblers and general ne'er-do-wells. But since he had called our names at the beginning of the service we were mollified.

Among Negroes the tradition was to give presents to children going only from one grade to another. How much more important this was when the person was graduating at the top of the class. Uncle Willie and Momma had sent away for a Mickey Mouse watch like Bailey's. Louise gave me four embroidered handkerchiefs. (I gave her crocheted doilies.) Mrs. Sneed, the minister's wife, made me an undershirt to wear for graduation, and nearly every customer gave me a nickel or maybe even a dime with the instruction "Keep on moving to higher ground," or some such encouragement.

Amazingly the great day finally dawned and I was out of bed before I knew it. I threw open the back door to see it more clearly, but Momma said, "Sister, come away from that door and put your robe on."

I hoped the memory of that morning would never leave me. Sunlight was itself young, and the day had none of the insistence maturity would bring it in a few hours. In my robe and barefoot in the backyard, under cover of going to see about my new beans, I gave myself up to the gentle warmth and thanked God that no matter what evil I had done in my life He had allowed me to live to see this day. Somewhere in my fatalism I had expected to die, accidentally, and never have the chance to walk up the stairs in the auditorium and gracefully receive my hard-earned diploma. Out of God's merciful bosom I had won reprieve.

Bailey came out in his robe and gave me a box wrapped in Christmas paper. He said he had saved his money for months to pay for it. It felt like a box of chocolates, but I knew Bailey wouldn't save money to buy candy when we had all we could want under our noses.

He was as proud of the gift as I. It was a soft-leather-bound copy of a collection of poems by Edgar Allan Poe, or, as Bailey and I called him, "Eap." I turned to "Annabel Lee" and we walked up and down the garden rows, the cool dirt between our toes, reciting the beautifully sad lines.

Momma made a Sunday breakfast although it was only Friday. After we finished the blessing, I opened my eyes to find the watch on my plate. It was a dream of a day. Everything went smoothly and to my credit. I didn't have to be reminded or scolded for anything. Near evening I was too jittery to attend to chores, so Bailey volunteered to do all before his bath.

Days before, we had made a sign for the Store, and as we turned out the lights Momma hung the cardboard over the doorknob. It read clearly: CLOSED. GRADUATION.

My dress fitted perfectly and everyone said that I looked like a sunbeam in it. On the hill, going toward the school, Bailey walked behind with Uncle Willie, who muttered, "Go on, Ju." He wanted him to walk ahead with us because it embarrassed him to have to walk so slowly. Bailey said he'd let the ladies walk together, and the men would bring up the rear. We all laughed, nicely.

Little children dashed by out of the dark like fireflies. Their crepe-paper dresses and butterfly wings were not made for running and we heard more than one rip, dryly, and the regretful "uh uh" that followed.

The school blazed without gaiety. The windows seemed cold and unfriendly from the lower hill. A sense of ill-fated timing crept over me, and if Momma hadn't reached for my hand I would have drifted back to Bailey and Uncle Willie, and possibly beyond. She made a few slow jokes about my feet getting cold, and tugged me along to the now-strange building.

Around the front steps, assurance came back. There were my fellow "greats," the graduating class. Hair brushed back, legs oiled, new dresses and pressed pleats, fresh pocket handkerchiefs and little handbags, all homesewn. Oh, we were up to snuff, all right. I joined my comrades and didn't even see my family go in to find seats in the crowded auditorium.

The school band struck up a march and all classes filed in as had been rehearsed. We stood in front of our seats, as assigned, and on a signal from the choir director, we sat. No sooner had this been accomplished than the band started to play the national anthem. We rose again and sang the song, after which we recited the pledge of allegiance. We remained standing for a brief minute before the choir director and the principal signaled to us, rather desperately I thought, to take our seats. The command was so unusual that our carefully rehearsed and smooth-running machine was thrown off. For a full minute we fumbled for our chairs and bumped into each other awkwardly. Habits change or solidify under pressure, so in our state of nervous tension we had been ready to follow our usual assembly pattern: the American national anthem, then the pledge of allegiance, then the song every Black person I knew called the Negro National Anthem.[4] All done in the same key, with the same passion and most often standing on the same foot.

Finding my seat at last, I was overcome with a presentiment of worse things to come. Something unrehearsed, unplanned, was going to happen, and we were going to be made to look bad. I distinctly remember being explicit in the choice of pronoun. It was "we," the graduating class, the unit, that concerned me then.

The principal welcomed "parents and friends" and asked the Baptist minister to lead us in prayer. His invocation was brief and punchy, and for a second I thought we were getting on the high road to right action. When the principal came back to the dais, however, his voice had changed. Sounds always affected me profoundly and the principal's voice was one of my favorites. During assembly it melted and lowed weakly into the audience. It had not

4. "Lift Every Voice."

been in my plan to listen to him, but my curiosity was piqued and I straightened up to give him my attention.

He was talking about Booker T. Washington, our "late great leader," who said we can be as close as the fingers on the hand, etc. . . . Then he said a few vague things about friendship and the friendship of kindly people to those less fortunate than themselves. With that his voice nearly faded, thin, away. Like a river diminishing to a stream and then to a trickle. But he cleared his throat and said, "Our speaker tonight, who is also our friend, came from Texarkana to deliver the commencement address, but due to the irregularity of the train schedule, he's going to, as they say, 'speak and run.' " He said that we understood and wanted the man to know that we were most grateful for the time he was able to give us and then something about how we were willing always to adjust to another's program, and without more ado—"I give you Mr. Edward Donleavy."

Not one but two white men came through the door off-stage. The shorter one walked to the speaker's platform, and the tall one moved to the center seat and sat down. But that was our principal's seat, and already occupied. The dislodged gentleman bounced around for a long breath or two before the Baptist minister gave him his chair, then with more dignity than the situation deserved, the minister walked off the stage.

Donleavy looked at the audience once (on reflection, I'm sure that he wanted only to reassure himself that we were really there), adjusted his glasses and began to read from a sheaf of papers.

He was glad "to be here and to see the work going on just as it was in the other schools."

At the first "Amen" from the audience I willed the offender to immediate death by choking on the word. But Amens and Yes, sir's began to fall around the room like rain through a ragged umbrella.

He told us of the wonderful changes we children in Stamps had in store. The Central School (naturally, the white school was Central) had already been granted improvements that would be in use in the fall. A well-known artist was coming from Little Rock to teach art to them. They were going to have the newest microscopes and chemistry equipment for their laboratory. Mr. Donleavy didn't leave us long in the dark over who made these improvements available to Central High. Nor were we to be ignored in the general betterment scheme he had in mind.

He said that he had pointed out to people at a very high level that one of the first-line football tacklers at Arkansas Agricultural and Mechanical College had graduated from good old Lafayette County Training School. Here fewer Amen's were heard. Those few that did break through lay dully in the air with the heaviness of habit.

He went on to praise us. He went on to say how he had bragged that "one of the best basketball players at Fisk sank his first ball right here at Lafayette County Training School."

The white kids were going to have a chance to become Galileos and Madame Curies and Edisons and Gauguins, and our boys (the girls weren't even in on it) would try to be Jesse Owenses and Joe Louises.

Owens and the Brown Bomber were great heroes in our world, but what school official in the white-goddom of Little Rock had the right to decide that those two men must be our only heroes? Who decided that for Henry Reed to become a scientist he had to work like George Washington Carver, as a bootblack, to buy a lousy microscope? Bailey was obviously always going to be too small to be an athlete, so which concrete angel glued to what country seat had decided that if my brother wanted to become a lawyer he had to first pay penance for his skin by picking cotton and hoeing corn and studying correspondence books at night for twenty years?

The man's dead words fell like bricks around the auditorium and too many settled in my belly. Constrained by hard-learned manners I couldn't look behind me, but to my left and right the proud graduating class of 1940 had dropped their heads. Every girl in my row had found something new to do with her handkerchief. Some folded the tiny squares into love knots, some into triangles, but most were wadding them, then pressing them flat on their yellow laps.

On the dais, the ancient tragedy was being replayed. Professor Parsons sat, a sculptor's reject, rigid. His large, heavy body seemed devoid of will or willingness, and his eyes said he was no longer with us. The other teachers examined the flag (which was draped stage right) or their notes, or the windows which opened on our now-famous playing diamond.

Graduation, the hush-hush magic time of frills and gifts and congratulations and diplomas, was finished for me before my name was called. The accomplishment was nothing. The meticulous maps, drawn in three colors of ink, learning and spelling decasyllabic words, memorizing the whole of *The Rape of Lucrece*—it was for nothing. Donleavy had exposed us.

We were maids and farmers, handymen and washerwomen, and anything higher that we aspired to was farcical and presumptuous.

Then I wished that Gabriel Prosser and Nat Turner[5] had killed all whitefolks in their beds and that Abraham Lincoln had been assassinated before the signing of the Emancipation Proclamation, and that Harriet Tubman[6] had been killed by that blow on her

5. Leaders of Virginia slave rebellions in 1800 and 1831 respectively.
6. Nineteenth-century black abolitionist, a "conductor" on the Underground Railroad.

head and Christopher Columbus had drowned in the *Santa Maria*.

It was awful to be a Negro and have no control over my life. It was brutal to be young and already trained to sit quietly and listen to charges brought against my color with no chance of defense. We should all be dead. I thought I should like to see us all dead, one on top of the other. A pyramid of flesh with the whitefolks on the bottom, as the broad base, then the Indians with their silly tomahawks and teepees and wigwams and treaties, the Negroes with their mops and recipes and cotton sacks and spirituals sticking out of their mouths. The Dutch children should all stumble in their wooden shoes and break their necks. The French should choke to death on the Louisiana Purchase (1803) while silkworms ate all the Chinese with their stupid pigtails. As a species, we were an abomination. All of us.

Donleavy was running for election, and assured our parents that if he won we could count on having the only colored paved playing field in that part of Arkansas. Also—he never looked up to acknowledge the grunts of acceptance—also, we were bound to get some new equipment for the home economics building and the workshop.

He finished, and since there was no need to give any more than the most perfunctory thank-you's, he nodded to the men on the stage, and the tall white man who was never introduced joined him at the door. They left with the attitude that now they were off to something really important. (The graduation ceremonies at Lafayette County Training School had been a mere preliminary.)

The ugliness they left was palpable. An uninvited guest who wouldn't leave. The choir was summoned and sang a modern arrangement of "Onward, Christian Soldiers," with new words pertaining to graduates seeking their place in the world. But it didn't work. Elouise, the daughter of the Baptist minister, recited "Invictus," and I could have cried at the impertinence of "I am the master of my fate, I am the captain of my soul."

My name had lost its ring of familiarity and I had to be nudged to go and receive my diploma. All my preparations had fled. I neither marched up to the stage like a conquering Amazon, nor did I look in the audience for Bailey's nod of approval. Marguerite Johnson, I heard the name again, my honors were read, there were noises in the audience of appreciation, and I took my place on the stage as rehearsed.

I thought about colors I hated: ecru, puce, lavender, beige and black.

There was shuffling and rustling around me, then Henry Reed was giving his valedictory address, "To Be or Not to Be." Hadn't he heard the whitefolks? We couldn't *be*, so the question was a waste of time. Henry's voice came out clear and strong. I feared to look at him. Hadn't he got the message? There was no "nobler in the mind" for Negroes because the world didn't think we had minds, and they let us know it. "Outrageous fortune"? Now, that was a joke. When the ceremony was over I had to tell Henry Reed some things. That is, if I still cared. Not "rub," Henry, "erase." "Ah, there's the erase." Us.

Henry had been a good student in elocution. His voice rose on tides of promise and fell on waves of warnings. The English teacher had helped him to create a sermon winging through Hamlet's soliloquy. To be a man, a doer, a builder, a leader, or to be a tool, an unfunny joke, a crusher of funky toadstools. I marveled that Henry could go through with the speech as if we had a choice.

I had been listening and silently rebutting each sentence with my eyes closed; then there was a hush, which in an audience warns that something unplanned is happening. I looked up and saw Henry Reed, the conservative, the proper, the A student, turn his back to the audience and turn to us (the proud graduating class of 1940) and sing, nearly speaking,

> "Lift ev'ry voice and sing
> Till earth and heaven ring
> Ring with the harmonies of Liberty ..."

It was the poem written by James Weldon Johnson. It was the music composed by J. Rosamond Johnson. It was the Negro national anthem. Out of habit we were singing it.

Our mothers and fathers stood in the dark hall and joined the hymn of encouragement. A kindergarten teacher led the small children onto the stage and the buttercups and daisies and bunny rabbits marked time and tried to follow:

> "Stony the road we trod
> Bitter the chastening rod
> Felt in the days when hope, unborn, had died.
> Yet with a steady beat
> Have not our weary feet
> Come to the place for which our fathers sighed?"

Each child I knew had learned that song with his ABC's and along with "Jesus Loves Me This I Know." But I personally had never heard it before. Never heard the words, despite the thousands of times I had sung them. Never thought they had anything to do with me.

On the other hand, the words of Patrick Henry had made such an impression on me that I had been able to stretch myself tall and trembling and say, "I know not what course others may take, but as for me, give me liberty or give me death."

And now I heard, really for the first time:

> "We have come over a way that with tears
> has been watered,

We have come, treading our path through
the blood of the slaughtered."

While echoes of the song shivered in the air, Henry Reed bowed his head, said "Thank you," and returned to his place in the line. The tears that slipped down many faces were not wiped away in shame.

We were on top again. As always, again. We survived. The depths had been icy and dark, but now a bright sun spoke to our souls. I was no longer simply a member of the proud graduating class of 1940; I was a proud member of the wonderful, beautiful Negro race.

Oh, Black known and unknown poets, how often have your auctioned pains sustained us? Who will compute the lonely nights made less lonely by your songs, or the empty pots made less tragic by your tales?

If we were a people much given to revealing secrets, we might raise monuments and sacrifice to the memories of our poets, but slavery cured us of that weakness. It may be enough, however, to have it said that we survive in exact relationship to the dedication of our poets (include preachers, musicians and blues singers).

BERNADETTE DEVLIN

Politics in the University[1]

* * *

I went up to university with some vague notion of being able, one day, to improve some aspect of life in Northern Ireland. In my last years at school I had toyed with the idea of becoming a teacher for the gypsies, and later I thought of joining either the Ministry of Health and Social Services or the Ministry of Education, to work from within the citadel. But it seemed a long process, waiting to get into a position where I could have an impact on the system. Without any clear idea of what I planned to do with it, I started an Honours Celtic degree course. It seemed a natural choice: Celtic had been my best subject at school, and I was very interested in all the Celtic languages—from a cultural, not a political, point of view. I joined the Irish Democratic Club at Queen's, which trotted round the country to festivals and competitions, producing plays in the Irish language. But my main interest was in the Gaelic Society, which held Irish debates. Very soon I became irritated by the Gaelic Society. It was a small, inward-looking group, making very little attempt to reach anybody outside the converted, and boring people

1. From Chapter 5 of *The Price of My Soul*, 1969.

like myself to death. We produced an Irish-language newspaper called *An Scathan* (The Reflection), and there were eternal arguments over articles printed in it, over who was editor, over failures to sell the newspaper, over the fact that pamphlets and papers sent by organizations in the South hadn't been distributed by the society. In my second year at Queen's, when I gave up Celtic Studies in favor of Psychology, I become secretary of the Gaelic Society, and at the end of that year I resigned my office and my membership with a disillusioned farewell speech: until such time as they were interested in culture as culture, instead of who was leader of the group, I was bailing out.

However I was still keen on debating and used to attend meetings of the "Literific"—the Literary and Scientific Society—which organized debates just for the fun of debating, not to press any point of view, political or otherwise. In its day, the Literific had been a good forum for discussion, but by 1965 it had degenerated into nothing more than student obscenity. You could get up and shout, "Spit on the Vice-Chancellor!" without any further explanation, and be sure of applause. My friends enjoyed this frivolity but I didn't, and I never spoke at a Queen's debate in my first year. My second year saw the birth of the Union Debating Society. I had no hand in its formation, but I was one of many who saw in it a chance of discussing something worth talking about. I should have liked serious discussion on such subjects as the university structure, the relations between students and lecturer, or between student and tutor. The most obvious thing about the tutorials I attended was the credibility gap between the idea that this was an informal discussion group and the respectful attitude of the students toward the tutor. The relationship was one of teacher and pupil, there was no equal communication of ideas, and people accepted that what the lecturers said should be reproduced in examinations.

The first debate I spoke at was on the motion: Free love is too expensive. As far as I was concerned, this could be treated with a certain amount of humor, but it was a serious subject of concern to every student present. However, it degenerated into a lot of double-meaning jokes on the comparative cost of prostitutes in Amsterdam and San Francisco and about the price of contraceptives on the black market in Southern Ireland, making it cheaper to conduct your affairs in Ulster. Everybody thought it was just so amusing. Well, I sat through this for about two hours, until I couldn't resist standing up any longer, and then I told them that not only were they ignorant of the basic sexual morality of their own society, but they were also still so much part of their environment that they were incapable of rising above the situation and looking at it without embarrassment: hence all the bravado and the doubtful jokes. My own opinion was, I said, that while society had a double attitude, tolerating free love but not tolerating illegitimate children, free love *was* too expensive. We should be talking about the moral and social cost of individual independence and we were talking about contraceptives. I proposed that the motion should not be put until every student had gone out and troubled to learn a bit more about the society he or she was living in.

Everybody felt very uncomfortable when I accused them of ignorance of their own sexual morality, but when I used the word "bastard," the tension was broken, and this so-called intellectual gathering came down in an uproar of laughing and giggling. I finished off my speech by saying, "You may find the word bastard amusing. You may find free love is not expensive, if in fact it can be had for two-and-ninepence in Sandy Row (a poor area of Belfast). But how many people here can stand up without blushing and say without any qualms on the matter, 'I am a bastard'?" Nobody stood up and everything went dead quiet. Then tittering broke out and several people stood up and said, "I am a bastard." Finally a young fellow got up. "It is quite obvious," he said, "that none of those people has ever seriously been called a bastard. I have, and I understand the point you are making." But the debate broke up because people couldn't face serious discussion on it. Such was the mentality of Queen's at the time: people consciously played at being students, carrying briefcases about and looking intellectual.

Over the course of my first two years at university, I attended meetings of all the political parties. I felt I needed some ideology, so off I went on my round of the parties in search of one. There was then at Queen's a Tory Club, the Young Liberals, the Labour group that had risen and fallen over the years, the National Democrats, who were a new group, and the Young Socialists, who weren't actually part of the university at all. They were all little gatherings of initiates, but there was also the New Ireland Society, which was large and loosely structured, attracting people of different tendencies. In none of the political parties could I find anything to believe in. They all had a sort of self-importance, as if their interest in politics raised them above the level of ordinary people, and they all went in for an intellectual type of discussion that had no relevance to any kind of society I knew. They tried to be very sophisticated, working out policies and inviting guest speakers down; but they weren't *real*. You got the impression that they really didn't care what went on outside the university, so long as they had plenty to talk about. There was more real politics in the Folk Music Society than in any of the parties. They sang black civil-rights songs in the Folk Music Society before anybody else in Queen's was interested in the race problem, and they were singing songs about unemployment in Belfast long before the civil-rights movement took it up. That was a good society. It had a strong American influence in it, but because of this there was another section that was determined to keep Irish influence, so you had the best of both American protest songs and traditional Irish folk music.

What made student politics all the more absurd at that time was that Queen's was basically a nine-to-six university. None of us was the kind of independent, twenty-four-hours-a-day student that you get at colleges in England. We went home for tea. You were a student during the day, but your mother asked you where you were going at eight o'clock at night.

For a moment in my third year, it looked as if there might be some excitement. The Minister of Home Affairs issued an order banning Republican Clubs. These had been allowed to continue throughout Northern Ireland, though the Republican Party itself had always been illegal. Immediately the ban was announced, a Republican Club was formed in Queen's and I joined it. We had a peaceful little demonstration against the ban, carried a coffin to the Minister's house, mourned the death of democracy and so forth, and went back to the university. But then the steam went out of the Republican Club. It didn't seem to have anything other than an existence.

So, disenchanted with Queen's politics, I moved to the do-good organizations. These were Catholic societies who visited the poor, decorated houses for old people, did voluntary work at hospitals, and so on. I stayed with them for a while until I decided they were just perpetuating aspects of the system I didn't like. When we visited old people in their homes, we were letting off the neighbors and relatives who should have done it and who, instead of saying, "Those people are doing it—why don't we?" were saying, "Those people are doing it—we don't need to." By carol-singing at Christmas to collect money for coal for poor families, we were relieving the local authorities of their responsibility. They just budgeted our contribution into what they spent and cut down on their own spending.

For a while after that I wandered about by myself, making terrorist plans. I've often wondered why the IRA is so keen on blowing up bridges, when Northern Ireland offers much greater possibilities for disruption and international publicity. In Derry there is an American communications base that is used as a look-out post for the rest of Europe and whose strategic importance has never been appreciated by people in Northern Ireland. This base, it seemed to me, was custom-built for causing an international crisis and bringing Northern Ireland to the attention of the world, and I developed a very nasty plan for its destruction. The first thing to do was to set fire to Gortin Forest Park in County Tyrone. It always closes in the evening, so nobody would be in it by about nine o'clock at night, and since it is in the middle of the wilderness, you wouldn't endanger any houses. Once Gortin Forest Park was burning nicely, all the fire brigades in Ulster would come storming around to deal with it, blaming the IRA; and while everybody was putting out that fire, you could set fire to Tullamore Forest Park on the other side of the country. With the entire country running around putting out fires it would take no more than half a dozen hand grenades lobbed over the wall of the communications base to create a very nasty diplomatic incident. It would involve the British, because this was British territory and they were supposed to be guarding it. It would involve the Americans, because it belonged to them. And it would raise the question of why the United States had a base in Northern Ireland at all.

I never told anybody this idea because, quite honestly, it terrified me. As theoretical terrorism, it was great, but I couldn't reconcile myself to the thought that maybe, against all the probabilities, someone might be in Gortin Forest Park when it went up in flames. Another idea I had was to send an ultimatum to every fly-by-night foreign firm who invested money in Northern Ireland, giving them a breakdown of the short-term profits to them, and the long-term inefficiency to us, of their operation. Such firms are attracted to Northern Ireland by government building grants and short-term tax concessions. But when the tax concessions run out, so do they, leaving behind an empty factory and another couple of hundred unemployed. I planned to send them a warning: "You have three years to promise you will remain here more than ten years, or we'll blow your little factory out of the ground." Those were my militant Republican days. But I got over these dreams of violence, and told myself it didn't matter if the people who kept us in poverty were called British or not. It wasn't simply getting Britain out of Ireland that mattered: it was the fact that we were economically depressed, and I couldn't see terrorism solving that.

ALLAN SEAGER

The Joys of Sport at Oxford

During my first week at Oxford I decided not to go out for any sports in the fall, or Michaelmas, term. My college offered Rugby, soccer, field hockey and something referred to as "the boats." I had never done any of these. They were all outdoor sports, and outdoors was where it was raining. For a fee I could also have joined a team of chaps who trotted informally through the dripping countryside in mild competition with a group from another college. Or I could have subscribed to a beagling club and worn a green coat, stout laced boots and a hemispheric little green velvet cap and legged it over the fields behind the dogs in search of hares and perhaps gotten a furry paw glued to a wooden shield as a trophy to hang in my room. The rain discouraged me, however. I got soggy enough walking to lectures. The fall term seemed a good time to lie up in front of a fire and get a good start on my reading.

I did this. I read heavily, but after three weeks I noticed a nervousness coming over me. And after the fourth week I knew what it was. I had been getting up every half hour to look out of the window. Now, there was nothing to look at out of my window but the college coal pile and beyond it a 15-foot wall topped with broken glass to keep students from climbing in after midnight. I was looking for a girl. I had got used to having dates at home but, after a day or two of scrutiny, I could tell that I was not likely to see one poised like a mountain goat on top of the coal.

I had won a Rhodes scholarship because I was the only man at the state examination who had worn a stiff collar—an Arrow, I believe. I did not wear it to Oxford. Instead I bought shirts with what we used to call bootlegger (tab) collars, a tweed jacket and gray flannel "bags." Not knowing that Americans move differently from the English—looser, somehow—and that you can identify one as far as you can see him, I believed my attire made me indistinguishable from an Old Etonian, and I had peeped at the English girls in the lecture halls, thinking that I had at least an even start with the Englishmen. I was appalled at what I saw.

There are four women's colleges at Oxford. Most of their undergraduates were going to be schoolmistresses and looked it. They wore rugged tweeds full of sticks of heather and twigs of gorse that stank in the wet weather, and they had big, frightening muscles in their legs from bike riding. A beautiful American girl would, I thought, be glad to make the acquaintance of a compatriot because of her loneliness.

I spotted an American girl in one of my lectures and she was beautiful. By asking around among other Americans I learned her name, which I have forgotten, and her address. I called. A maid let me in and went to fetch her. When she came in I said, "I wonder if you would care to drink some sherry with me this afternoon and bring a friend." I didn't want her friend, but the university had ruled that young women could visit young men's rooms only in pairs.

"I don't think so," she said coldly.

"Tea, perhaps?"

"No."

"Ah, milk?"

She walked out.

I didn't know then, as I came to later, that American girls in

Oxford don't want to meet Americans; they want to meet Englishmen.

After this rebuff I might have lingered before my fire until spring in a dangerous inertia, dangerous because the elements of English diet are extremely reluctant to move without help after you have ingested them. But I was asked to go on the river. I was flattered to be asked, and I went.

The river is the Thames, but it is mysteriously called the Isis where it flows through Oxford, and the way to it is past the walled garden where Lewis Carroll, himself an admirer of girls—but girls rather younger than those who interested me—wrote *Alice in Wonderland* while he was a don at Christ Church. Then you go down a long alley under tremendous elms and you come to the college barges. They are houseboats, really, and they never go anyplace. They are moored tight to the bank and are used as dressing rooms. They are painted white, highly ornamented with colored moldings, and they made a pretty sight lined up along the riverbank.

The only rowing I had done was to pull a flat-bottomed rowboat over the weed beds of small lakes after bass. I was not the only novice, however, and we all had to put up with two or three days of "we call this an oar" kind of instruction before they let us sit down and try to put our backs into it. The president of the Boat Club, Tom Smith, was the coach. There was no professional coaching in any sport—there still isn't—except that the varsity cricketers and swimmers had professionals come to look at them occasionally during the season. Tom Smith told me I might make a No. 6, and he gave me politely to know that Six was supposed to move a lot of water. At 12 stone 9 (180 and one-half pounds) I was the biggest man in the boat and, as I found out later, in the college. The English had been children during World War I. They had grown up on rationed food, and I think this is why they were not very big.

At my college we were lucky. We began the season in a proper shell no thicker than a cigar box. I saw an unfortunate youth step right through it into the river because he had not set his foot exactly on the keel when he climbed in. We also had movable seats on little wheels and swivel rowlocks (pronounced "rollocks"). I kept hearing a saying: "English rowing is 10 years behind the times; Cambridge rowing is 20 years behind the times. Oxford rowing is 40 years behind the times."

The varsity boat and those of some of the colleges began training exactly as their forefathers had done when Victoria was a young queen. In the first weeks of the season the varsity eight swung grandly down the river in a craft that resembled the war canoe of some obscure tribe. It was heavy enough for the open sea. It had board seats and the rowlocks were merely two straight pegs you laid the oars between. A month's workouts in this scow certainly preserved tradition, but it also gave a man a set of boils as big as walnuts. A varsity oarsman spent more time on his feet than a cop, and when he sat down he bellowed. With such a fine start, the boils lasted all season even after the varsity shifted to the shell they would use against Cambridge. At my college, Oriel, we avoided all this pain. Daringly unorthodox, we rowed the Jesus style.

This was not blasphemy and we did not kneel in prayer before taking to the water. The Jesus style was developed at Jesus College, Cambridge by a man named Steve Fairbairn. Succinctly put, it was "blade form." This meant that if your oar blade was right, nothing else mattered. Opposed to this was the practice of the varsity, all the other colleges and, I believe, American crews, called body form, which meant that if your body was correctly poised, the blade had to be right.

A body-form crew was coached right down to its fingernails. You were supposed to keep a straight back, to stare perpetually at the fifth or sixth cervical vertebra of the man in front of you and never move your head. A body form crew is impressive to watch. The muscular decorum makes its members look virtuous and clean-limbed. Perhaps this is its own reward, for a blade-form crew, rowing with backs bending comfortably and gandering around at the blades, may look raffish and sloppy but probably is going as fast as the body-form boys.

We trained all the fall into December. It was mostly just rowing. The Thames is a canal with locks all the way to London and, if we were taking a long paddle, say, eight or 10 miles, we had to pass Iffley lock when we went one way and Osney lock when we went the other. I can remember sitting in Osney lock one dark afternoon, waiting for it to fill, with ice forming on the oars and flakes of snow as big as goose feathers wetting the back of my skimpy little Jaegar shirt, and it was no consolation to remember that the Miller's Wife in *The Canterbury Tales* had probably lived within a furlong.

On short days when we stayed within Iffley lock we were coached by Tom Smith riding a bicycle beside us on the towpath. I doubt if we rowed as much as Washington or Yale. There was no other training. Beer was believed strengthening; gin would keep coxswains small. No one spoke of cigarettes at all. As green as I was, I didn't know whether I was in shape or not, but it didn't make much difference, because term ended about the middle of December and I took off for six weeks in Paris.

The Bump Races come in two sets, late in January and early in May. They are rowed for six days, Thursday through Saturday and Monday through Wednesday. The colloquial name for the January races is Toggers; the formal one, Torpids; but no one could tell me why. The May races are called Eights, and they are quite social. If you have a girl, you bring her, give her luncheons of hock and lobster mayonnaise and she sits on the top of your barge to watch you sweat. Toggers are grimmer because January is grimmer.

Bump races are examples of much made of little. The Thames is a small river at Oxford; in fact, I think Ralph Boston could jump over it at a place called the Gut if he took a good run. There were about 25 rowing colleges at Oxford, and each college put two boats in the river, the larger colleges, like Balliol, three, sometimes four, so there were perhaps 60 in all. I doubt if you could row 60 eight-oared shells abreast at Poughkeepsie, and you certainly can't on the Isis, so they start one behind another and chase the one in front.

Small stakes are driven into the bank 60 feet apart. To each stake a rope 60 feet long is fixed. The cox holds the other end and lets the boat drift until it is taut. Each boat has a starter. Five minutes before time all the starters gather at a little brass cannon in a hayfield to synchronize their stopwatches with a chronometer. Then they come back and stand on the bank beside their boats saying, "Two minutes gone. Three minutes gone," to the yawning oarsmen in the river below. In the last minute they count off the quarters, and finally, "10, 9, 8, 7, 6, 5, 4, come forward, are you ready?" and "Bang!" goes the little brass cannon. The college bargeman gives you a hell of a shove with a boathook and away you go, the cox howling the beat at about 50 strokes a minute. It is very common to black out completely during the first 30 seconds. As soon as you are under way, the stroke drops to about 40, but not much less, because the course from Iffley lock to the top of the barges is only about a mile and a half.

Most of the members of your college are scrambling along the towpath beside you, yelling and shooting off guns. You can't tell whether the boat behind you is gaining, because you are watching Stroke's oar or your own, but if the cox's voice rises to a scream and he starts counting to raise the beat you know you are overtaking the boat ahead. When your bow overlaps his stern, the cox turns the rudder sharply. Bow touches stern. This is the bump.

When you make a bump, the next day your boat starts in the place of the bumped boat. You go up or down each day according to your prowess. The final aim, which may take several years to achieve, is to become Head of the River, the first boat in line.

I came back from Paris not in the best of shape. A wisdom tooth had started acting up. It ached and swelled monotonously. I made my apologies to Tom Smith, and he found another Six. For a week I tried to ignore it, hoping the swelling would go away. It didn't and I asked the dean to recommend a dentist. I found this man in what I took to be a large bedroom with the bed moved out. The walls were covered with flowered wallpaper, and a chromo of Watts's

Hope[1] hung on the wall. He sat me down in a chair with four legs. He took a look and, as God is my judge, he prescribed an infusion of camomile and poppyhead—not opium, poppyhead—with which to bathe the afflicted parts. I was not sleeping much and I was smoking about 50 Players a day, but I bathed away conscientiously. It didn't do any good. The swelling went gruesomely on. When I looked as if I were trying to conceal a scarlet pippin in my cheek I went back to the dentist and said, "Lance this, will you?" He bumbled and said at last, "I can't. I'm not a dental surgeon." So he took me to a real surgeon, who had his learning son in the office, and there before a blazing coal fire the three together gave me gas and lanced it. Afterward I didn't feel good, but at least I didn't feel like a bomb about to go off.

That night I was sitting in front of my fire, reading and bathing my wound with a little neat whisky when Tom Smith knocked at my door. He said that his No. 6 had just come down with a bad case of flu. Toggers started the next day. Would I care to fill in? It was so casual and the honor of the U.S.A. depended so heavily on it that I said I would be delighted—which was a lie.

On the first day of Toggers I was personally lucky. I had to row only the first six strokes. When the little brass cannon went off, we laid into the first strokes hard. The cox had just shouted, "Six!" when No. 7 in front of me caught a crab. If you are quick you can sometimes lie flat and let the oar pass over your head. Seven was not quick. He was probably blacked out, and the butt of the oar caught him in the belly and jackknifed him out of the boat. Falling, he broke his oar smack off at the rowlock. The boat staggered. There were cries of "Man overboard!" and Dawson-Grove, the cox, was yelling oaths like a banshee. I don't believe it is possible to overturn an eight-oared boat, but we nearly made it. In the confusion, Exeter came tearing into us from behind and sheared off all the oars on the bow side. It was a mess. No. 7 avoided having Exeter's keel bash his head in by cannily staying under water until after the collision; then he swam soggily ashore. Our race was over for that day and I was barely winded.

The next day, with new oars, we caught St. John's on the Green Bank and made a bump. In fact, we made five bumps in all during Toggers. If a boat makes five bumps in Toggers or four in Eights the college is required by custom to stand its members a Bump supper. It is a big jollification in honor of the Boat Club. The manciple (head chef) outdoes himself and provides a really good meal, with fresh soup (I think) and champagne at will. Alumni gather and there are sherry parties. Since many Oriel undergraduates study the-

1. An allegorical painting of a female figure seated on the globe, peeping from beneath a blindfold. She bends over a lyre on which only one string remains; the sky is dark except for one star.

ology, many of its graduates are parsons, but Church of England clergy are not stuffy. They go to sherry parties, and they don't stand around with a glass in their hands for the look of things, either.

At our Bump supper the hall was in an uproar because of the sherry parties beforehand. Cheers were started but forgotten. Boating songs were begun, broken off and begun again. A stately portrait of Matthew Arnold, once an Oriel don, hung on the wall. A swaying youth, his boiled shirt coming out in welts from spilled champagne, pegged an orange from the centerpiece clean through Matthew's jaw just at the muttonchop. A bonfire sprang up in the front quad, fed by side tables, chairs and Van Gogh reproductions. The son of a Scottish laird broke into the provost's lodgings, stole all the shoes belonging to that good old man (now knighted for his translations of Aristotle) and hurled them all into the flames.

High above the quad in a third-floor bedroom a man named Antony Henley crouched, waiting for the supper to finish. Tony had collected half the chamber pots in the college. (They used them then, and it is no more than even money they use them now.) In a room directly opposite, another man had collected the other half. A rope hung in a curve from one window to the other. At last the dons appeared under the porch of the hall, chatting only less than boisterously from the champagne. They were in full fig—dinner jackets, long M.A. gowns and mortarboards. They walked down the steps in the wavering light of the bonfire. At that moment a shower of broken crockery fell on their heads. Tony and his friend were sticking the rope ends through the pot handles and letting them slide down the rope two at a time. When they met they broke and fell on the dean, the provost, the bursar, the Goldsmith's reader, a bishop or two and other dignitaries. Big joke. The party went on all night, consuming untold bottles of Pommery and Piper-Heidsieck and much of the movable furniture of the college. At one point, I was told, seven drunken archdeacons danced around the bonfire, a spectacle very likely unmatched since the martyrdom of Ridley and Latimer, who were burned years earlier in Broad Street and from the top of whose Gothic monument the Oxford Alpine Club hangs a chamber pot each year.

The next morning the groans of hangover were decently stifled by the mists in the quad. The scouts were out with rakes and shovels, cleaning away the empties, the shards of crockery and the ashes of the bonfire strewn with the nails and eyelets of the provost's shoes. Antony Henley was haled before the dean, presented with a bill for upward of 150 chamber pots and laughingly fined £10. Toggers were over. I have never rowed since nor drunk so much champagne.

I was not, so to speak, an oarsman by trade, I was a swimmer. The rowing I had done, while exhausting and in some ways amusing, merely passed the time until the swimming season opened in the third, or Hilary, term. The trouble was I couldn't find anyplace to "go out" for swimming. There was no varsity pool, I discovered. But I heard somewhere that the swimmers used the Merton Street Baths.

The Baths were in a grubby brick building, built long before with what seemed an ecclesiastical intent, for they had long Gothic windows in front. The pool itself, gently steaming in the cold of the building, was a gloomy tank, trapezoidal in shape, and I learned later that it was 25 yards long on one side and exactly 22 and one-half yards long on the other—which made for some tricky finishes in a race. The bathing master said there hadn't been any gentlemen from the varsity near the place in months. He suggested that I see Mr. Pace in Merton College, the club president.

After I had knocked, Pace opened his door six inches, no more.

"Yes?" he said.

"Mr. Pace?"

"Yes," he said.

"My name is Seager."

"Yes?" he said.

"I wanted to ask you about the swimming."

"Oh. Ah," he said. Then he opened the door. "Do come in."

I went in.

"Seager? Oh, yes. Someone mentioned your name. From the States, aren't you? Mitchigan? A good club, I believe."

"We were national champions last year."

"Really? Just what did you want to know?"

"When do you start training?"

"Oh, I'll let you know. I'll send you a note round the week before we begin. Will that do?"

It was the Oxford manner again. He was effortlessly making my enthusiasm seem not only comic but childishly comic. However, it is just as well to be candid. I was after their records, and I didn't know then that he was Oxford's best sprinter. "I'd like to start now," I said, "I'm not in very good shape."

"I daresay you could use the Baths. Cost you a bob a time until we start meeting."

He waved his hand nonchalantly.

"Cheers," he said, and I left.

It was only later that I learned I had committed a faux pas. I was always finding out things later. You did not "go out" for the varsity. College sports, O.K.—you could turn up whenever you liked. But the varsity was strictly invitational, so much so that in my day the Varsity Boat Club had never used an American oar. There was a faint general resentment of Americans and Colonials taking over Oxford sports. However, I paid my shilling and trundled a slow half mile every day up and down the bath. It was like swimming in church.

In a couple of weeks Pace sent his note round and the season opened. I was astounded. It was not so much that they swam badly —I had more or less expected that from their record times—it was that they worked so little. In fact, they didn't *work* at all. They swam until they felt tired and quit for the day, refreshed. Where was the old pepper, the old fight? Slowly I began to comprehend the English attitude toward sports, which, unless Dr. Bannister changed it drastically with his great meticulous mile, is this: sports are for fun. If you are good at one or two of them, it is somewhat in the nature of a divine gift. Since the gift is perpetual, it is there every day and you can pull out a performance very near your best any time. With a little practice to loosen the muscles and clear the pipes, you are ready for the severest tests.

I was drinking beer one night in Balliol College with several men, one of them an Olympic runner, a 1,500-meter man. It is rare that a subject so trivial as sports would come up in Balliol, the intellectual center of England, but it came up and eventually came down to the question of how fast could this Olympic man run 1,500 meters at the moment? We all piled into a couple of taxis and drove out to the Oxford Sports Ground, where there was a cinder track. The runner, full of confidence and beer, supplied a stopwatch and a flashlight, and there in his street clothes, in the rain, in the dead of night, this man took off and ran 1,500 meters in just over four minutes. This proved to me that the English were right, but it did not prove to me that I was wrong. I knew I could not swim 100 yards in less than a minute, untrained.

But I stayed untrained. It seemed to be overly zealous to go on chugging up and down after all the other members of the club had showered, dressed and come to stand at the edge of the bath to watch me as if I were a marine curiosity, like a dugong. I tried it a couple of times and quit. I swam as little as they did, no more. Then there was the problem of entertainment after the matches— they didn't call them meets. There was little university swimming in England, so our competition was usually a town club whose members might be aquatic plumbers and carpenters—not gentlemen, you see. With a splendid condescension, we set out a table loaded with whisky, beer and wine after each match, and we had to drink to make our guests feel at home so that caste differences would be concealed and we could pretend to be all jolly good sportsmen together. After a match, say, in London with the Paddington police, the coppers would set out a table of whisky, beer and wine, and we had to drink to show our appreciation of their hospitality. This drinking was not a detestable chore, but it meant that, with two matches a week, we were getting mildly stoned twice a week just in the way of business. This was not how I had been taught to train, and it came over me suddenly how far morality had invaded sports in the U.S.

I won all my races except one, but the times were shamefully slow and I was chased right down to the wire in all of them. In May, John Pace had the whole club to tea in his rooms. There was an hour of conversation interspersed with tomato and cucumber sandwiches. Then Pace stood up by the chimney piece. "Now, chaps," he began facetiously (I never heard anyone use "chaps" except facetiously). "You know we swim the Tabs two weeks from now." "Tabs" meant Cambridge, from the latin *Cantabrigia*. "Please smoke only after meals and cut down your beer to a pint a day. And do try to swim every day between now and then."

People clapped and cried, "Hear! Hear!" as if Pace had been in the House of Commons. I gathered we were in hard training from then on. I had not gone under 61 seconds for 100 yards yet, and I had heard that Cambridge had a fancy Dan named Hill who had done 58. I was scared.

Someone said, "This rationing of beer, John. What if we're sconced?"

"Behave yourselves and you won't be," Pace said.

In Oxford dining halls a sconce is a penalty exacted in the spring of the year for some breach of taste or decorum. It is a welcome penalty, eagerly exacted. If you showed up late for dinner or wearing something odd like a turtleneck sweater or if you said something that could be remotely construed as offensive, you were sconced. Once I said something slightly off color.

"We'll have a sconce on you for that," the man next to me said. He wrote my offense in Latin on the back of a menu, "*Seager dixit obscenissime*"[2] and had a waiter take it up to high table to be approved by the dean. It was a formality. The dean always approved sconces. "What will you take it in?" I was asked. In theory you had to drink a silver quart pot of some liquid, bottoms up. In practice you had no choice; custom said old beer. Once I saw a man take it in fresh cow's milk and he never lived it down. It is the sort of thing planters discuss in Kenya and Borneo 20 years later.

The strength of English beer is indicated by the number of Xs on the barrel. Ale is the weakest, one X. Bitter beer is two Xs. Old beer is five Xs, about as strong as sherry. It is never iced, but in college it comes from the cellars and it might as well be. It looks almost coal-black and it is as thick as stout. It is hard but not impossible to drink it all down at one go. If you do, the man who sconced you has to pay for it. If you fail, it is passed around the

2. "Seager spoke most obscenely."

table like a loving cup. But the minute you set the pot down empty, you're drunk.

The Cambridge match was held at the Bath Club, then on Dover Street, London. It was a posh club. (I like the origin of posh. When people used to tour the Orient from England the most expensive cabins on the P&O boats, those that made the most of the prevailing winds and the least of the sun, were on the port side going and the starboard side returning, so the luggage for those cabins was marked P.O.S.H., that is "port out, starboard home.") We took an afternoon train down to London already dressed in white ties, black trousers and our blazers, and with an affectation of gaiety we sauntered up Piccadilly in the early evening and into the Bath Club. I knew I had to fear this Cambridge speedster, Hill, who had done 58 seconds, because I had done only 61 that season. (I had done 61 when I was a long, wheyfaced boy of 15 in high school in Tennessee.) My fear was degrading. That's why I was mad: it was a real fear. And I felt that my teammates had begun to wonder when I was going to demonstrate that I didn't fit one of the stock British images of the American, lots of noise and no performance.

I figured I could take Hill in the 50 if I scrambled, but in the 100 I knew I would have to swim and I figured I could swim about 75 yards before I blew up. Since the English started slow and finished fast, I figured I would start fast, get a big lead, frighten him and finish on whatever I had left.

The Bath Club looked like a court levee, the ladies in those English evening gowns, the men in white ties and tail coats, and the Old Blues[3] wore their blazers. Diamonds glittered. I detected dowagers with lorgnons, a colorful throng, posh. The club pool was 25 yards long on both sides, but it was dark at one end. Since you can bump your head into a goose egg or even oblivion if you slam into a turn you can't see, I wet a towel and hung it over the far end in my lane to make a white spot. As I walked back I heard resentful murmurs from the spectators. "He's an Ameddican," as if what I had done were cunning and illicit.

The 50-yard race went as I had expected. I scrambled. I won in a record time of 25 seconds. I went back to the dressing room to worry about the 100. Hill was a little fleshy fellow whose fat might hide more stamina than I had.

I swam the first two lengths of the 100 in 25 seconds, and after the third length I looked back at Hill. He was 30 feet behind, but I was not encouraged because I could tell I was going to blow up. I blew and finished the last 25 yards with a frantic overhand, dazzled by fatigue, my head out all the way so I could breathe. But I won by a yard, and they said it was a new record, 57 seconds. My team-

3. Former varsity athletes from Oxford and Cambridge.

mates shouted and pounded me on the back as if I had done well. My shabby little victories gave Oxford the match.

The adulation of the English for sports figures is greater than that in this country, possibly because a sound sports record keeps a chap from being too "clever"—which is repugnant (Churchill was too clever by half, right up until the blitz). Let a man die who has not specially distinguished himself as an admiral, a cabinet member or a press lord, and if he has been a Blue, Oxon or Cantab, the obituary will very likely be headed OLD BLUE'S DEMISE. That is what is important. A few months after my victories I was having tea with some people at a public tearoom in Oxford.

A man came up to the table, a student, and said to me, "Is this Mr. Seager, the famous swimmer?"

I looked him straight in the eye for maybe three seconds. He seemed to be perfectly serious. "I'm Seager," I answered finally.

"May I shake your hand?" he said.

I shook hands and he went away pleased, apparently. Nobody at my table seemed to think that any of this was strange, and I let my self-esteem expand a little.

I didn't get punctured for two years. I was back in Ann Arbor then and happened to run into Matt Mann, my former coach.

"Say, I hear you got a couple of English records," he said. Matt was born in Yorkshire, and he had held English records himself.

"Yes," I said. I couldn't look at him.

"What were your times?"

"Twenty-five. Fifty-seven," I mumbled. I had been a bad boy.

"Fifty-seven! Were you dragging something?" he said jovially.

Surprising myself, I said defiantly, "Matt, it was fun."

And it had been, all of it, the massive courtesy of the swimming policemen, the singing in the pub afterward, the soiree at the Bath Club—not real glory, which means work, but a hell of a lot of fun.

QUESTIONS

1. At some points Seager describes the Oxford manner and pictures himself as an outsider. Give some examples. Are there instances where Seager presents himself in the Oxford manner?

2. What characteristics of the English view of sports does Seager stress? How are these characteristics reflected in other areas of Oxford life?

3. Seager's narrative permits him to use a wide range of language, including British and American diction, and of usage, reaching from the relatively formal to slang. What kinds of effects does Seager achieve with this variety of language?

4. What is Seager's attitude toward the experiences he recounts? How is that attitude expressed in his tone? Does it vary?

5. Consider a nation or smaller social group with which you are familiar. What does its attitude toward sports reveal about the nation or group? Write an essay showing the evidence for your view.

EMMA GOLDMAN

In Jail[1]

I was called before the head matron, a tall woman with a stolid face. She began taking my pedigree. "What religion?" was her first question. "None, I am an atheist." "Atheism is prohibited here. You will have to go to church." I replied that I would do nothing of the kind. I did not believe in anything the Church stood for and, not being a hypocrite, I would not attend. Besides, I came from Jewish people. Was there a synagogue?

She said curtly that there were services for the Jewish convicts on Saturday afternoon, but as I was the only Jewish female prisoner, she could not permit me to go among so many men.

After a bath and a change into the prison uniform I was sent to my cell and locked in.

I knew from what Most[2] had related to me about Blackwell's Island that the prison was old and damp, the cells small, without light or water. I was therefore prepared for what was awaiting me. But the moment the door was locked on me, I began to experience a feeling of suffocation. In the dark I groped for something to sit on and found a narrow iron cot. Sudden exhaustion overpowered me and I fell asleep.

I became aware of a sharp burning in my eyes, and I jumped up in fright. A lamp was being held close to the bars. "What is it?" I cried, forgetting where I was. The lamp was lowered and I saw a thin, ascetic face gazing at me. A soft voice congratulated me on my sound sleep. It was the evening matron on her regular rounds. She told me to undress and left me.

But there was no more sleep for me that night. The irritating feel of the coarse blanket, the shadows creeping past the bars, kept me awake until the sound of a gong again brought me to my feet. The cells were being unlocked, the doors heavily thrown open. Blue and white striped figures slouched by, automatically forming into a line, myself a part of it. "March!" and the line began to move along the

---

1. Emma Goldman was one of the leaders of the anarchist movement in the United States between 1890 and 1920. In the wake of the Homestead Steel Strike of 1892 and with the onset of the Great Panic of 1893, she accelerated her activities on behalf of labor unions and the unemployed. She urged the unemployed to demand what was rightfully theirs and to distrust capitalists and politicians. In the fall of 1893, she was arrested, tried and convicted of inciting to riot and unlawful assemblage. She was sentenced to one year in Blackwell's Island Penitentiary in New York City. Her turbulent career as a propagandist in America extended for twenty-five years beyond this internment. Shortly after the United States entered the First World War, Emma Goldman was convicted of conspiring to organize resistance to the Draft Act of 1917. She served two years in the Missouri State Penitentiary and was subsequently deported to the Soviet Union. (The following selection is from Chapter 12 of her autobiography, *Living My Life*, 1931.)

2. Johann Most, German anarchist editor who in 1882 emigrated to the United States.

corridor down the steps towards a corner containing wash-stands and towels. Again the command: "Wash!" and everybody began clamouring for a towel, already soiled and wet. Before I had time to splash some water on my hands and face and wipe myself half-dry, the order was given to march back.

Then breakfast: a slice of bread and a tin cup of warm brownish water. Again the line formed, and the striped humanity was broken up in sections and sent to its daily tasks. With a group of other women I was taken to the sewing-room.

The procedure of forming lines—"Forward, march!"—was repeated three times a day, seven days a week. After each meal ten minutes were allowed for talk. A torrent of words would then break forth from the pent-up beings. Each precious second increased the roar of sounds; and then sudden silence.

The sewing-room was large and light, the sun often streaming through the high windows, its rays intensifying the whiteness of the walls and the monotony of the regulation dress. In the sharp light the figures in baggy and ungainly attire appeared more hideous. Still, the shop was a welcome relief from the cell. Mine, on the ground floor, was grey and damp even in the day-time; the cells on the upper floors were somewhat brighter. Close to the barred door one could even read by the help of the light coming from the corridor windows.

The locking of the cells for the night was the worst experience of the day. The convicts were marched along the tiers in the usual line. On reaching her cell each left the line, stepped inside, hands on the iron door, and awaited the command. "Close!" and with a crash the seventy doors shut, each prisoner automatically locking herself in. More harrowing still was the daily degradation of being forced to march in lock-step to the river, carrying the bucket of excrement accumulated during twenty-four hours.

I was put in charge of the sewing-shop. My task consisted in cutting the cloth and preparing work for the two dozen women employed. In addition I had to keep account of the incoming material and the outgoing bundles. I welcomed the work. It helped me to forget the dreary existence within the prison. But the evenings were torturous. The first few weeks I would fall asleep as soon as I touched the pillow. Soon, however, the nights found me restlessly tossing about, seeking sleep in vain. The appalling nights—even if I should get the customary two months' commutation time, I still had nearly two hundred and ninety of them. Two hundred and ninety—and Sasha? I used to lie awake and mentally figure in the dark the number of days and nights before him. Even if he could come out after his first sentence of seven years, he would still have more than twenty-five hundred nights! Dread overcame me that Sasha could not survive them. Nothing was so likely to drive people to madness, I felt, as sleepless nights in prison. Better dead, I thought. Dead? Frick was not dead, and Sasha's glorious youth, his life, the things he might have accomplished—all were being sacrificed—perhaps for nothing. But—was Sasha's *Attentat* in vain?[3] Was my revolutionary faith a mere echo of what others had said or taught me? "No, not in vain!" something within me insisted. "No sacrifice is lost for a great ideal."

One day I was told by the head matron that I would have to get better results from the women. They were not doing so much work, she said, as under the prisoner who had had charge of the sewing-shop before me. I resented the suggestion that I become a slave-driver. It was because I hated slaves as well as their drivers, I informed the matron, that I had been sent to prison. I considered myself one of the inmates, not above them. I was determined not to do anything that would involve a denial of my ideals. I preferred punishment. One of the methods of treating offenders consisted in placing them in a corner facing a blackboard and compelling them to stay for hours in that position, constantly before the matron's vigilant eyes. This seemed to me petty and insulting. I decided that if I was offered such an indignity, I would increase my offence and take the dungeon. But the days passed and I was not punished.

News in prison travels with amazing rapidity. Within twenty-four hours all the women knew that I had refused to act as a slave-driver. They had not been unkind to me, but they had kept aloof. They had been told that I was a terrible "anarchist" and that I didn't believe in God. They had never seen me in church and I did not participate in their ten-minute gush of talk. I was a freak in their eyes. But when they learned that I had refused to play the boss over them, their reserve broke down. Sundays after church the cells would be opened to permit the women an hour's visit with one another. The next Sunday I received visits from every inmate on my tier. They felt I was their friend, they assured me, and they would do anything for me. Girls working in the laundry offered to wash my clothes, others to darn my stockings. Everyone was anxious to do some service. I was deeply moved. These poor creatures so hungered for kindness that the least sign of it loomed high on their limited horizons. After that they would often come to me with their troubles, their hatred of the head matron, their confidences about their infatuations with the male convicts. Their ingenuity in carrying on flirtations under the very eyes of the officials was amazing.

My three weeks in the Tombs[4] had given me ample proof that

3. Sasha was her close friend and colleague Alexander Berkman. The act referred to here was Berkman's attempt to murder Henry Clay Frick, chairman of the Carnegie Steel Company, for which he was sentenced to twenty-two years in prison.

4. The Manhattan House of Detention, in New York City.

the revolutionary contention that crime is the result of poverty is based on fact. Most of the defendants who were awaiting trial came from the lowest strata of society, men and women without friends, often even without a home. Unfortunate, ignorant creatures they were, but still with hope in their hearts, because they had not yet been convicted. In the penitentiary despair possessed almost all of the prisoners. It served to unveil the mental darkness, fear, and superstition which held them in bondage. Among the seventy inmates, there were no more than half a dozen who showed any intelligence whatever. The rest were outcasts without the least social consciousness. Their personal misfortunes filled their thoughts; they could not understand that they were victims, links in an endless chain of injustice and inequality. From early childhood they had known nothing but poverty, squalor, and want, and the same conditions were awaiting them on their release. Yet they were capable of sympathy and devotion, of generous impulses. I soon had occasion to convince myself of it when I was taken ill.

The dampness of my cell and the chill of the late December days had brought on an attack of my old complaint, rheumatism. For some days the head matron opposed my being taken to the hospital, but she was finally compelled to submit to the order of the visiting physician.

Blackwell's Island Penitentiary was fortunate in the absence of a "steady" physician. The inmates were receiving medical attendance from the Charity Hospital, which was situated near by. That institution had six weeks' post-graduate courses, which meant frequent changes in the staff. They were under the direct supervision of a visiting physician from New York City, Dr. White, a humane and kindly man. The treatment given the prisoners was as good as patients received in any New York hospital.

The sick-ward was the largest and brightest room in the building. Its spacious windows looked out upon a wide lawn in front of the prison and, farther on, the East River. In fine weather the sun streamed in generously. A month's rest, the kindliness of the physician, and the thoughtful attention of my fellow prisoners relieved me of my pain and enabled me to get about again.

During one of his rounds Dr. White picked up the card hanging at the foot of my bed giving my crime and pedigree. "Inciting to riot," he read. "Piffle! I don't believe you could hurt a fly. A fine inciter you would make!" he chuckled, then asked me if I should not like to remain in the hospital to take care of the sick. "I should, indeed," I replied, "but I know nothing about nursing." He assured me that neither did anyone else in the prison. He had tried for some time to induce the city to put a trained nurse in charge of the ward, but he had not succeeded. For operations and grave cases he had to bring a nurse from the Charity Hospital. I could easily pick up the elementary things about tending the sick. He would teach me to take the pulse and temperature and to perform similar services. He would speak to the Warden and the head matron if I wanted to remain.

Soon I took up my new work. The ward contained sixteen beds, most of them always filled. The various diseases were treated in the same room, from grave operations to tuberculosis, pneumonia, and childbirth. My hours were long and strenuous, the groans of the patients nerve-racking; but I loved my job.

* * *

I was gradually given entire charge of the hospital ward, part of my duties being to divide the special rations allowed the sick prisoners. They consisted of a quart of milk, a cup of beef tea, two eggs, two crackers, and two lumps of sugar for each invalid. On several occasions milk and eggs were missing and I reported the matter to a day matron. Later she informed me that a head matron had said that it did not matter and that certain patients were strong enough to do without their extra rations. I had had considerable opportunity to study this head matron, who felt a violent dislike of everyone not Anglo-Saxon. Her special targets were the Irish and the Jews, against whom she discriminated habitually. I was therefore not surprised to get such a message from her.

A few days later I was told by the prisoner who brought the hospital rations that the missing portions had been given by this head matron to two husky Negro prisoners. That also did not surprise me. I knew she had a special fondness for the coloured inmates. She rarely punished them and often gave them unusual privileges. In return her favourites would spy on the other prisoners, even on those of their own colour who were too decent to be bribed. I myself never had any prejudice against coloured people; in fact, I felt deeply for them because they were being treated like slaves in America. But I hated discrimination. The idea that sick people, white or coloured, should be robbed of their rations to feed healthy persons outraged my sense of justice, but I was powerless to do anything in the matter.

After my first clashes with this woman she left me severely alone. Once she became enraged because I refused to translate a Russian letter that had arrived for one of the prisoners. She had called me into her office to read the letter and tell her its contents. When I saw that the letter was not for me, I informed her that I was not employed by the prison as a translator. It was bad enough for the officials to pry into the personal mail of helpless human beings, but I would not do it. She said that it was stupid of me not to take advantage of her goodwill. She could put me back in my cell, deprive me of my commutation time for good behaviour, and make the rest of my stay very hard. She could do as she pleased, I told her, but I would not read the private letters of my unfortunate sisters, much less translate them to her.

Then came the matter of the missing rations. The sick women began to suspect that they were not getting their full share and complained to the doctor. Confronted with a direct question from him, I had to tell the truth. I did not know what he said to the offending matron, but the full rations began to arrive again. Two days later I was called downstairs and locked up in the dungeon.

I had repeatedly seen the effect of a dungeon experience on other women prisoners. One inmate had been kept there for twenty-eight days on bread and water, although the regulations prohibited a longer stay than forty-eight hours. She had to be carried out on a stretcher; her hands and legs were swollen, her body covered with a rash. The descriptions the poor creature and others had given me used to make me ill. But nothing I had heard compared with the reality. The cell was barren; one had to sit or lie down on the cold stone floor. The dampness of the walls made the dungeon a ghastly place. Worse yet was the complete shutting out of light and air, the impenetrable blackness, so thick that one could not see the hand before one's face. It gave me the sensation of sinking into a devouring pit. "The Spanish Inquisition came to life in America"—I thought of Most's description. He had not exaggerated.

After the door shut behind me, I stood still, afraid to sit down or to lean against the wall. Then I groped for the door. Gradually the blackness paled. I caught a faint sound slowly approaching; I heard a key turn in the lock. A matron appeared. I recognized Miss Johnson, the one who had frightened me out of my sleep on my first night in the penitentiary. I had come to know and appreciate her as a beautiful personality. Her kindness to the prisoners was the one ray of light in their dreary existence. She had taken me to her bosom almost from the first, and in many indirect ways she had shown me her affection. Often at night, when all were asleep, and quiet had fallen on the prison, Miss Johnson would enter the hospital ward, put my head in her lap, and tenderly stroke my hair. She would tell me the news in the papers to distract me and try to cheer my depressed mood. I knew I had found a friend in the woman, who herself was a lonely soul, never having known the love of man or child.

She came into the dungeon carrying a camp-chair and a blanket. "You can sit on that," she said, "and wrap yourself up. I'll leave the door open a bit to let in some air. I'll bring you hot coffee later. It will help to pass the night." She told me how painful it was for her to see the prisoners locked up in the dreadful hole, but she could do nothing for them because most of them could not be trusted. It was different with me, she was sure.

At five in the morning my friend had to take back the chair and blanket and lock me in. I no longer was oppressed by the dungeon. The humanity of Miss Johnson had dissolved the blackness.

When I was taken out of the dungeon and sent back to the hospital, I saw that it was almost noon. I resumed my duties. Later I learned that Dr. White had asked for me, and upon being informed that I was in punishment he had categorically demanded my release.

No visitors were allowed in the penitentiary until after one month had been served. Ever since my entry I had been longing for Ed, yet at the same time I dreaded his coming. I remembered my terrible visit with Sasha. But it was not quite so appalling in Blackwell's Island. I met Ed in a room where other prisoners were having their relatives and friends to see them. There was no guard between us. Everyone was so absorbed in his own visitor that no one paid any attention to us. Still we felt constrained. With clasped hands we talked of general things.

* * *

Once Ed came accompanied by Voltairine de Cleyre. She had been invited by New York friends to address a meeting arranged in my behalf. When I visited her in Philadelphia, she had been too ill to speak. I was glad of the opportunity to come closer to her now. We talked about things nearest to our hearts—Sasha, the movement. Voltairine promised to join me, on my release, in a new effort for Sasha. Meanwhile she would write to him, she said. Ed, too, was in touch with him.

My visitors were always sent up to the hospital. I was therefore surprised one day to be called to the Warden's office to see someone. It proved to be John Swinton and his wife. Swinton was a nationally known figure; he had worked with the abolitionists and had fought in the Civil War. As editor-in-chief of the New York *Sun* he had pleaded for the European refugees who came to find asylum in the United States. He was the friend and adviser of young literary aspirants, and he had been one of the first to defend Walt Whitman against the misrepresentations of the purists. Tall, erect, with beautiful features, John Swinton was an impressive figure.

He greeted me warmly, remarking that he had just been saying to Warden Pillsbury that he himself had made more violent speeches during the abolition days than anything I said at Union Square. Yet he had not been arrested. He told the warden that he ought to be ashamed of himself to keep "a little girl like that" locked up. "And what do you suppose he said? He said that he had no choice—he was only doing his duty. All weaklings say that, cowards who always put the blame on others." Just then the Warden approached us. He assured Swinton that I was a model prisoner and that I had become an efficient nurse in the short time. In fact, I was doing such good work that he wished I had been given five more years. "Generous cuss, aren't you?" Swinton laughed. "Perhaps you'll give her a paid job when her time is up?" "I would, indeed," Pillsbury replied. "Well, you'd be a damn fool. Don't you know she doesn't believe in prisons? Sure as you live, she'd let them all escape, and what would become of you then?" The poor man was embarrassed, but he joined in the banter. Before my visitor took leave, he turned once more to the Warden, cautioning him to "take good care of his little friend," else he would "take it out of his hide."

The visit of the Swintons completely changed the attitude of the head matron towards me. The Warden had always been quite decent, and she now began showering privileges on me: food from her own table, fruit, coffee, and walks on the island. I refused her favours except for the walks; it was my first opportunity in six months to go out in the open and inhale the spring air without iron bars to check me.

In March 1894 we received a large influx of women prisoners. They were nearly all prostitutes rounded up during recent raids. The city had been blessed by a new vice crusade. The Lexow Committee, with the Reverend Dr. Parkhurst at its head, wielded the broom which was to sweep New York clean of the fearful scourge. The men found in the public houses were allowed to go free, but the women were arrested and sentenced to Blackwell's Island.

Most of the unfortunates came in a deplorable condition. They were suddenly cut off from the narcotics which almost all of them had been habitually using. The sight of their suffering was heartbreaking. With the strength of giants the frail creatures would shake the iron bars, curse, and scream for dope and cigarettes. Then they would fall exhausted to the ground, pitifully moaning through the night.

* * *

One day a young Irish girl was brought to the hospital for an operation. In view of the seriousness of the case Dr. White called in two trained nurses. The operation lasted until late in the evening, and then the patient was left in my charge. She was very ill from the effect of the ether, vomited violently, and burst the stitches of her wound, which resulted in a severe haemorrhage. I sent a hurry call to the Charity Hospital. It seemed hours before the doctor and his staff arrived. There were no nurses this time and I had to take their place.

The day had been an unusually hard one and I had had very little sleep. I felt exhausted and had to hold on to the operating-table with my left hand while passing with my right instruments and sponges. Suddenly the operating-table gave way, and my arm was caught. I screamed with pain. Dr. White was so absorbed in his manipulations that for a moment he did not realize what had happened. When he at last had the table raised and my arm was lifted out, it looked as if every bone had been broken. The pain was excruciating and he ordered a shot of morphine. "We'll set her arm later. This has got to come first." "No morphine," I begged. I still remembered the effect of morphine on me when Dr. Julius Hoffmann had given me a dose against insomnia. It had put me to sleep, but during the night I had tried to throw myself out of the window, and it had required all of Sasha's strength to pull me back. The morphine had crazed me, and now I would have none of it.

One of the physicians gave me something that had a soothing effect. After the patient on the operating-table had been returned to her bed, Dr. White examined my arm. "You're nice and chubby," he said; "that has saved your bones. Nothing has been broken—just flattened a bit." My arm was put in a splint. The doctor wanted me to go to bed, but there was no one else to sit up with the patient. It might be her last night: her tissues were so badly infected that they would not hold her stitches, and another haemorrhage would prove fatal. I decided to remain at her bedside. I knew I could not sleep with the case as serious as it was.

All night I watched her struggle for life. In the morning I sent for the priest. Everyone was surprised at my action, particularly the head matron. How could I, an atheist, do such a thing, she wondered, and choose a priest, at that! I had declined to see the missionaries as well as the rabbi. She noticed how friendly I had become with the two Catholic sisters who often visited us on Sunday. I had even made coffee for them. Didn't I think that the Catholic Church had always been the enemy of progress and that it had persecuted and tortured the Jews? How could I be so inconsistent? Of course, I thought so, I assured her. I was just as opposed to the Catholics as to the other Churches. I considered them all alike, enemies of the people. They preached submission, and their God was the God of the rich and the mighty. I hated their God and would never make peace with him. But if I could believe in any religion at all, I should prefer the Catholic Church. "It is less hypocritical," I said to her; "it makes allowance for human frailties and it has a sense of beauty." The Catholic sisters and the priest had not tried to preach to me like the missionaries, the minister, and the vulgar rabbi. They left my soul to its own fate; they talked to me about human things, especially the priest, who was a cultured man. My poor patient had reached the end of a life that had been too hard for her. The priest might give her a few moments of peace and kindness; why should I not have sent for him? But the matron was too dull to follow my argument or understand my motives. I remained a "queer one," in her estimation.

Before my patient died, she begged me to lay her out. I had been kinder to her, she said, than her own mother. She wanted to know that it would be my hand that would get her ready for the last journey. I would make her beautiful; she wanted to look beautiful to meet Mother Mary and the Lord Jesus. It required little effort to make her as lovely in death as she had been in life. Her black curls made her alabaster face more delicate than the artificial methods she had used to enhance her looks. Her luminous eyes were closed now; I had closed them with my own hands. But her chiselled eyebrows and long, black lashes were remindful of the radiance that had been hers. How she must have fascinated men! And they destroyed her. Now she was beyond their reach. Death had smoothed her suffering. She looked serene in her marble whiteness now.

During the Jewish Easter holidays I was again called to the Warden's office. I found my grandmother there. She had repeatedly begged Ed to take her to see me, but he had declined in order to spare her the painful experience. The devoted soul could not be stopped. With her broken English she had made her way to the Commissioner of Corrections, procured a pass, and come to the penitentiary. She handed me a large white handkerchief containing matzoth, *gefüllte* fish, and some Easter cake of her own baking. She tried to explain to the Warden what a good Jewish daughter her *Chavele* was; in fact, better than any rabbi's wife, because she gave everything to the poor. She was fearfully wrought up when the moment of departure came, and I tried to soothe her, begging her not to break down before the Warden. She bravely dried her tears and walked out straight and proud, but I knew she would weep bitterly as soon as she got out of sight. No doubt she also prayed to her God for her *Chavele*.

June saw many prisoners discharged from the sick-ward, only a few beds remaining occupied. For the first time since coming to the hospital I had some leisure, enabling me to read more systematically. I had accumulated a large library; John Swinton had sent me many books, as did also other friends; but most of them were from Justus Schwab. He had never come to see me; he had asked Ed to tell me that it was impossible for him to visit me. He hated prison so much that he would not be able to leave me behind. If he should come, he would be tempted to use force to take me back with him, and it would only cause trouble. Instead he sent me stacks of books. Walt Whitman, Emerson, Thoreau, Hawthorne, Spencer, John Stuart Mill, and many other English and American authors I learned to know and love through the friendship of Justus. At the same time other elements also became interested in my salvation—spiritualists and metaphysical redeemers of various kinds. I tried honestly to get at their meaning, but I was no doubt too much of the earth to follow their shadows in the clouds.

* * *

The prison library had some good literature, including the works of George Sand, George Eliot, and Ouida. The librarian in charge was an educated Englishman serving a five-year sentence for forgery. The books he handed out to me soon began to contain love notes framed in most affectionate terms, and presently they flamed with passion. He had already put in four years in prison, one of his notes read, and he was starved for the love of woman and companionship. He begged me at least to give him the companionship. Would I write him occasionally about the books I was reading? I disliked becoming involved in a silly prison flirtation, yet the need for free, uncensored expression was too compelling to resist. We exchanged many notes, often of a very ardent nature.

My admirer was a splendid musician and played the organ in the chapel. I should have loved to attend, to be able to hear him and feel him near, but the sight of the male prisoners in stripes, some of them handcuffed, and still further degraded and insulted by the lip-service of the minister, was too appalling to me. I had seen it once on the fourth of July, when some politician had come over to speak to the inmates about the glories of American liberty. I had to pass through the male wing on an errand to the Warden, and I heard the pompous patriot spouting of freedom and independence to the mental and physical wrecks. One convict had been put in irons because of an attempted escape. I could hear the clanking of his chains with his every movement. I could not bear to go to church.

* * *

Of the friends I made on Blackwell's Island the priest was the most interesting. At first I felt antagonistic to him. I thought he was like the rest of the religious busybodies, but I soon found that he wanted to talk only about books. He had studied in Cologne and had read much. He knew I had many books and he asked me to exchange some of them with him. I was amazed and wondered what kind of books he would bring me, expecting the New Testament or the Catechism. But he came with works of poetry and music. He had free access to the prison at any time, and often he would come to the ward at nine in the evening and remain till after midnight. We would discuss his favourite composers—Bach, Beethoven, and Brahms—and compare our views on poetry and social ideas. He presented me with an English-Latin dictionary as a gift, inscribed: "With the highest respect, to Emma Goldman."

On one occasion I asked him why he never gave me the Bible. "Because no one can understand or love it if he is forced to read it," he replied. That appealed to me and I asked him for it. Its simplicity of language and legendry fascinated me. There was no make-believe about my young friend. He was devout, entirely consecrated. He observed every fast and he would lose himself in prayer for hours. Once he asked me to help him decorate the chapel. When I came down, I found the frail, emaciated figure in silent prayer, oblivious of his surroundings. My own ideal, my faith, was at the opposite pole from his, but I knew he was as ardently sincere as I. Our fervour was our meeting-ground.

* * *

The nearer the day of my liberation approached, the more unbearable life in prison became. The days dragged and I grew restless and irritable with impatience. Even reading became impossible. I would sit for hours lost in reminiscences. I thought of the comrades in the Illinois penitentiary brought back to life by the pardon of Governor Altgeld. Since I had come to prison, I realized how much the release of the three men, Neebe, Fielden, and Schwab, had done for the cause for which their comrades in Chicago had been hanged. The venom of the press against Altgeld for his gesture of justice proved how deeply he had struck the vested interests, particularly by his analysis of the trial and his clear demonstration that the executed anarchists had been judicially killed in spite of their proved innocence of the crime charged against them. Every detail of the momentous days of 1887 stood out in strong relief before me. Then Sasha, our life together, his act, his martyrdom—every moment of the five years since I had first met him I now relived with poignant reality. Why was it, I mused, that Sasha was still so deeply rooted in my being? Was not my love for Ed more ecstatic, more enriching? Perhaps it was his act that had bound me to him with such powerful cords. How insignificant was my own prison experience compared with what Sasha was suffering in the Allegheny purgatory! I now felt ashamed that, even for a moment, I could have found my incarceration hard. Not one friendly face in the court-room to be near Sasha and comfort him—solitary confinement and complete isolation, for no more visits had been allowed him. The Inspector had kept his promise; since my visit in November 1892, Sasha had not again been permitted to see anyone. How he must have craved the sight and touch of a kindred spirit, how he must be yearning for it!

My thoughts rushed on. Fedya, the lover of beauty, so fine and sensitive! And Ed. Ed—he had kissed to life so many mysterious longings, had opened such spiritual sources of wealth to me! I owed my development to Ed, and to others, too, who had been in my life. And yet, more than all else, it was the prison that had proved the best school. A more painful, but a vital, school. Here I had been brought close to the depths and complexities of the human soul; here I found ugliness and beauty, meanness and generosity. Here, too, I had learned to see life through my own eyes and not through those of Sasha, Most, or Ed. The prison had been the crucible that tested my faith. It had helped me to discover strength in my own being, the strength to stand alone, the strength to live my life and fight for my ideals, against the whole world if need be. The State of New York could have rendered me no greater service than by sending me to Blackwell's Island Penitentiary!

STANLEY SANDERS
I'll Never Escape the Ghetto

I was born, raised and graduated from high school in Watts. My permanent Los Angeles home address is in Watts. My father, a brother and sister still live in Watts. By ordinary standards these are credentials enough to qualify one as coming from Watts.

But there is more to it than that. I left Watts. After I was graduated from the local high school I went away to college. A college venture in Watts terms is a fateful act. There are no retractions or future deliverances. Watts, like other black ghettos across the country, is, for ambitious youths, a transient status. Once they have left, there is no returning. In this sense, my credentials are unsatisfactory. To some people, I am not from Watts. I can never be.

The Watts-as-a-way-station mentality has a firm hold on both those who remain and those who leave. Such as it is, the ghetto is regarded as no place to make a career for those who have a future. Without exception, the prime American values underscore the notion. Negroes, inside it or out, and whites too, behave toward the ghetto like travelers.

Accordingly, I was considered one of the lucky ones. My scholarship to college was a ticket. People did not expect me to return. Understanding this, I can understand the puzzlement in the minds of those in Watts when I was home last summer, working in the local poverty program. Rumors spread quickly that I was an FBI agent. I was suspect because I was not supposed to return. Some people said I was either a federal agent or a fool, for no reasonable man, they said, returns to Watts by choice. Outside of Watts, reports stated that I had "given up" a summer vacation to work in Watts. For my part, I had come home to work in my community, but to some people I could not come home to Watts. To them I was no longer from Watts.

My own state of mind, when I left Watts eight years ago to take up the freshman year at Whittier College, was different. It was to me less of a departure; it was the stepping-off point of an Odyssey that was to take me through Whittier College and Oxford University, to Yale Law School, and back to Watts. I had intended then, as now, to make Watts my home.

A career in Watts had been a personal ambition for many years. In many ways the career I envisioned was antithetical to ghetto life. In the ghetto, a career was something on the outside. In Los Angeles, this meant a pursuit founded in a world beyond Alameda street, at a minimum in the largely Negro middle-class Westside of Los Angeles. The talk among the ambitious and future-minded youth in Watts was on getting out so that careers could begin. And they did just that. The talented young people left Watts in droves. The one skill they had in common was the ability to escape the ghetto.

I was especially intrigued by a career in Watts because it was supposed to be impossible. I wanted to demonstrate that it could be done more than anything else. I recall a moment during a city-wide high school oratorical contest when one of the judges asked whether anything good could come out of Watts. Our high school won the contest. We showed that judge. I saw that achievement as a possible pattern for the entire ghetto. I was pleased.

I had not realized in leaving for Whittier College that, however worthy my intention of returning was, I was nevertheless participating in the customary exodus from Watts. It was not long after leaving that my early ambitions began to wear thin. The stigma of Watts was too heavy to bear. I could easily do without the questioning looks of my college classmates. I did not want my being from Watts to arouse curiosity.

I followed the instructions of those who fled Watts. I adopted the language of escape. I resorted to all the devices of those who wished to escape. I was from South Los Angeles, thereafter, not Watts. "South Los Angeles," geographically identical to Watts, carried none of the latter's stigma. South Los Angeles was a cleaner—safer—designation. It meant having a home with possibilities.

It never occurred to me at the time what I was doing. I thought of it only as being practical. It was important to me to do well in college. Community identity was secondary, if a consideration at all. Somehow, the Watts things interfered with my new college life. Moreover, Negro college youth during those undergraduate years had none of its present mood. Its theme was campus involvement. Good grades, athletics, popularity—these were the things that mattered. The word "ghetto" had not even entered the lexicon of race relations. Students were not conscious of the ghetto as a separate phenomenon. Civil rights, in the Southern sense, was academically fashionable. But the ghetto of the North was not. The concern for the ghetto was still in the future.

It was to occur to me later, at the time of the Watts riots, two years after I graduated from college, if my classmates at Whittier realized that the epochal conflagration taking place was in the home of one of their very own student body presidents. They had no reason to think it was. I had never told them that I was from Watts.

A lot of things changed during the two years at Oxford. My attitude toward home was one of them. It was there, ironically enough, that the Odyssey turned homeward. Those years were bound to be meaningful as a Yankee foreign student or Rhodes Scholar. I knew that much. But I would never have imagined when receiving the award that Oxford would be significant as a Negro experience. After all, it was part of the faith gained during four years at Whittier that everything concerning me and Watts would remain conveniently buried.

It emerged in an odd context. England then, for the most part, was free of the fine distinctions between blacks and whites traditionally made in America. Except for some exclusive clubs in London, there were few occasions where racial lines were drawn. The color-blindness of England was especially true in the student life at Oxford. (This relatively mild racial climate in England during the last three years has, with the large influx of blacks from the West Indies and Southern Asia, adopted some very American-like features.) It was in such a relaxed racial atmosphere that all my defenses, about race and home, came down. At Oxford, I could reflect on the American black man.

My ghetto roots became crucially important in this examination. Englishmen were not concerned about the distinctions I was making in my own mind, between Watts and "South Los Angeles," between Watts and Whittier. They were not imagined distinctions. I was discovering that I could not escape the ghetto after all. A fundamental change was taking place in the ghettos, the Wattses, across the country. These changes were making the distinction. I realized I was a part of them, too.

By far the most traumatic of the new changes was ghetto rioting. I was studying at the University of Vienna, between semesters at Oxford, during the summer of 1964. News of Harlem rioting jolted the multi-national student community there. The typical European response was unlike anything I had seen before. They had no homes or businesses to worry about protecting. They wanted to know why Negroes did not riot more often. As the only Negro in the summer session I felt awkward for a time. I was being asked questions about the black man in America that no one had ever asked me before. I was embarrassed because I did not have any answers.

My own lack of shame in the rioting then taking place in America surprised me. In one sense, I was the archetype of the ghetto child who through hard work and initiative was pulling himself toward a better life. I was the example, the exception. It was my life that was held up to Watts youth to emulate.

In another sense, however, my feelings toward the rioting were predictable. I had always been bothered by the passivity of the ghetto. The majority of black men in the North had remained outside the struggle. Nothing was happening in the ghettos. No one was making it happen. Ghetto rioting then was the first representation I perceived of movement and activity among the mass of Negroes in the North. It marked a break with the passive tradition of dependency and indifference. The ghetto was at least no longer content with its status as bastard child of urban America. The currents set in motion had a hopeful, irreversible quality about them. The ghetto wanted legitimation. That was a beginning.

The parallel between a single individual's success and the bootstrap effort of the mass of ghetto youth is and remains too tenuous to comport with reality. This was made clear to me during the discussions of the Harlem riots on those hot summer days in Vienna. It shattered the notion that my individual progress could be hailed as an advance for all Negroes. Regrettably, it was an advance only for me. Earlier I had thought the success I had won satisfied an obligation I had to all Negroes. It is part of the lip service every successful Negro is obliged to pay to the notion of race progress whenever he achieves. In the face of mass rioting, the old shibboleths were reduced to embarrassing emptiness. I was enjoying the privileges of studying at the world's finest universities; Negroes at home were revolting against their miserable condition. To them, my experience and example were as remote as if I had never lived or been there. At best, only the top students could identify with my example—but they were few. And besides, the top students were not the problem.

When I returned to Oxford in the fall, following a spate of summer rioting in Eastern cities, I was convinced that some momentous changes had been wrought for all Negroes, not just those in the ghetto. It certainly meant a new militancy and a militancy of action, not the passive fulminations of the demi-militants. This was for Watts.

I returned home in August, 1965, from two years at Oxford just in time for the beginning of the Watts riots. As I walked the streets I was struck by the sameness of the community. There were few changes. Everything seemed to be in the same place where I had last seen it. It was unsettling for me to recall so easily the names of familiar faces I saw on the street. It was that feeling one gets when he feels he has done this one same thing before.

Streets remained unswept; sidewalks, in places, still unpaved. During this same time the growth rate in the rest of Southern California had been phenomenal, one of the highest in the country. L. A. suburbs had flourished. Watts, however, remained an unacknowledged child in an otherwise proud and respectable family of new towns.

The intellectual journey back to Watts after the Vienna summer and during the last year at Oxford had partly prepared me for what was soon to erupt into revolutionary-scale violence. My first reaction after the riot began was to have it stopped. But I was not from Watts for the past six years. I, nor anyone outside of Watts, was in no moral position to condemn this vicious expression of the ghetto.

I enrolled in Yale Law School in the fall after the riots. This time I did not leave Watts. Nor did I wish to leave Watts. Watts followed me to Yale. In fact, Watts was at Yale before I was. The discussions about riots and ghettos were more lively and compelling than the classroom discussions on the law. There were no word games or contrived problems. The questions raised were urgent ones.

Not surprisingly, Watts, too, was in the throes of painful discussion about the riots. It was beginning to look as though the deepest impact of the riots was on the people of Watts themselves. Old attitudes about the community were in upheaval. There were no explanations that seemed complete. No one knew for sure how it all began. There was no agreement on how it was continued as long as it was—and why. We only knew it happened. What I had often mistaken for pointless spoutings was in reality a manifestation of this desperate search for a truth about the riots.

The new intellectual climate in Watts was hard-wrought. It was rich enough to support even a communist bookstore. Writers, poets, artists flourished. I was handed full manuscripts of unpublished books by indigenous writers and asked to criticize them. I have not seen during eight years of college life as many personal journals kept and sketches written as in Watts since the 1965 riots. A new, rough wisdom of the street corner was emerging.

I suspected at the time and now realize that the riots were perhaps the most significant massive action taken by Northern Negroes. It was a watershed in the ghetto's history. Before the riots, the reach of the Negro movement in America seemed within the province of a small civil rights leadership. Now Watts, and places like Watts, were redefining the role of black men in their city's life.

I have affectionate ties to Watts. I bear the same mark as a son of Watts now that I did during that oratorical contest in high school. I may be personally less vulnerable to it today, but I am nevertheless influenced by it. While a group in Whittier, Calif., may regard it as unfortunate that its college's first Rhodes Scholar comes from Watts, I, for my part, could not feel more pride about that than I do now. I feel no embarrassment for those who think ill of Watts. I had once felt it. Now I only feel the regret for once having been embarrassed. "South Los Angeles" is a sour memory. Watts is my home.

Then I have my logical ties to Watts, too. My interest in the law stems from a concern for the future of Watts. The problem of the poor and of the city in America, simplified, is the problem of the ghetto Negro. I regard it as *the* problem of the last third of this century. Plainly, Watts is where the action is. The talents and leadership which I saw leave Watts as a child are the very things it needs most today. Many of the ghetto's wandering children are choosing a city to work in. My choice was made for me—long ago.

There is a difference between my schooling and the wisdom of the street corner. I know the life of a black man in Watts is larger than a federal poverty program. If there is no future for the black ghetto, the future of all Negroes is diminished. What affects it, affects me, for I am a child of the ghetto. When they do it to Watts, they do it to me, too. I'll never escape from the ghetto. I have staked my all on its future. Watts is my home.

WILLIAM ALFRED
Ourselves Alone: Irish Exiles in Brooklyn

My great-grandmother Anna Maria lived in a "city house," in the part of Brooklyn between Red Hook and Brooklyn Heights then called the Point but recently rechristened Cobble Hill by real estate agents. City houses were houses which fell to the Borough by foreclosure for nonpayment of taxes, and which were rented out at nominal rents as a form of patronage. At this point, I must in honesty say investigable fact leaves off and legend begins. Born though I was in 1922, I am a child of the nineteenth century, for it was Anna Maria who raised me until I was four years old—that is, took care of me while my parents were out working. It is mostly her memories I propose to retell. But memories make uncertain evidence, and in many cases I cannot rightly say where her memories leave off and my embroidering of them begins.

Anna Maria was the name I was conditioned to call her. I avoid "taught" advisedly. You learned what you were not to say to her as you learned not to lay hands on the ruby-red cylindrical kerosene stoves scattered through that house of hers, which now that I look back on it, she deliberately allowed to fall to ruin. She never struck but with her tongue, but when she did, you winced. When the quarter-a-week insurance man, with whom she played an endless game of hide-and-seek, once flushed her out; she called him a pimp. And once in a spasm of reflex chauvinism, she called Queen Victoria, whom she rather admired, "a goddamned old water dog."

If I am a child of the nineteenth century, Anna Maria Gavin Egan was a child of the late eighteenth. She too was raised by an old woman, her grandmother. With little or no education, she spoke and acted in the quirkily formal manner of a character in a Sterne novel. Her women friends she called by their last names, as they did her. Perhaps her exacting that we call her by her first name was her way of admitting the children of her blood (the kind of phrase she'd have used) to deeper intimacy.

She was born in Castlebar, Mayo, sometime between 1845 and 1850. She never knew her true age. Perhaps her birth was unregistered; perhaps the records were destroyed during the bad years. She was born sickly, and her mother separated her from her twin brother and sent her as an infant to the seashore, where her grandmother raised her until she "grew into her strength." One of her brothers became a Fenian,[1] and was forced to emigrate to the States. After his emigration, it was impossible to make a go of the small bakeshop her mother ran. British soldiers harried the shop and dwelling with nuisance raids, bayoneting the flour bags and even the feather beds in mock searches for the absent brother. In 1866 or 1867, she and her mother made the "eight weeks voyage in a sailing vessel" which brought her to New York.

Of Ireland, she rarely spoke, save to recall that she was often hungry there, and that for her main meal she often ate cress out of the brooks on oaten bread with a bit of lard. Although she always used to say she had no desire to return to Ireland to live, she lived out of a trunk to her dying day, and taught her children to do the same. I myself, till well on in my twenties, felt that Ireland, which I had never seen, was my true country. When, over eighty, she died in the early thirties, it did not seem strange six months afterward to receive a clipping from an Irish newspaper which read: "Died in Exile: Anna Maria Gavin Egan."

Of her first years here, she never tired of speaking. She and her mother landed at Castle Garden and walked up Broadway to City Hall, with bundles of clothes and pots and feather beds in their arms. The singing of the then exposed telegraph wires frightened them, as did the bustle of the people in the streets. They lost their fear when they met an Irish policeman who directed them to a rooming house on Baxter Street.

It must have been spring or summer when they arrived. The windows were open, and she was wakened often in the night by the sound of drunken voices singing:

> We'll hang Jefferson Davis
> On a sour apple tree.

1. A member of the Irish Republican Brotherhood, whose goal was to overthrow English rule in Ireland.

Her training as a "manty-maker" (mantua-maker—in other words, dressmaker) gave her an advantage over other girls of her age. She got a job fast. No woman would wear black satin, she remembered, because Mrs. Suratt, the lady in whose rooming house the murder of Lincoln had been plotted, was hanged in a dress of that material. On her way from work the first year, she nightly passed a house in whose tall, lit first-floor windows sat the most beautiful women she had ever seen, dressed to the nines, their hair as trimly curled, their faces painted fresh as those of new French china dolls. After weeks of gawking, she built up the courage to hazard a smile. "Come up here, you blond bitch," one of the women called to her, "and we'll wipe that smile off your face." Years after she was married, she was finally reunited with her brother, who had gone West in a vain quest for a fortune, and returned without even the wife he had married in California. "What happened to her?" Anna Maria asked. "She ran off with another fellow," he answered. "Why?" said she. "Because," said he, I've but a little bit of a thing."

The raciness of these stories, which she told me when I was eight, would make her seem atypical. But all of her women friends, even the pious ones, were as free-spoken. There was not a Mother Machree[2] among them. Free-spoken though she was about human matters, Anna Maria was a sphinx of reserve when it came to religion. She never went to Mass, although she prayed the Rosary nightly. Nor would she ever allow a priest in her house. Visiting priests, she said, brought bad luck. Why, she would not say, for it also was unlucky "to talk against the cloth."

The city house she rented for eighteen dollars a month was an abandoned mansion, let to her because my dead great-grandfather had "done favors at the Hall" to someone dead even longer than he. Churchill's mother was born a five minutes' walk from it. The Protestants—for that was what she called native-born Americans— moved out as the immigrants moved in. The first wave of immigrants must have been German and Scandinavian; there were still a few families of them left in my day. Then from the backyard tenement houses on the other side of Court Street in Brooklyn, the Irish began to move in. They were succeeded by the Italians, with whom they lived in uncertain amity.

Her house was a narrow brownstone, two windows to every floor except the ground, where the place of one window was taken by a double door of solid walnut plated with layers of dust-pocked cheap black enamel. Its shallow stoop, with ornate Gothic-arched wrought-iron railings eaten away by rust, was fronted by a long area

2. The subject of a popular song writ-   and sentimental.
ten in 1910; Mother Machree was sweet

(pronounced "airy"). A path of slate slabs led up to the stoop past an unkempt grass plot surrounded by overgrown privet hedges. Under the stoop was the blocked-up front entrance to the basement kitchen. And to the side of that, the cellar door, which boys would try to steal every Election Eve to feed the bonfire up on Union Street.

A stationery store had nibbled into the basement of the brownstone on the corner of Clinton Street. It dealt in penny wares, lousyheads (nonpareils), twisted wires with red and white propellers on them, seasons of decalcomania stamps, and sweet wax buckteeth and marbles. It was run by the Wechslers, the only Jews in the neighborhood. They were beloved by Irish and Italians alike, because of their kindness to children and because they had the only phone on the block and would walk the block's length to call a person to it.

Little Siberia, my mother called the house. Its center was the volcano of a coal stove in the basement kitchen. No comfort was to be won of a winter's night more than eighteen inches from it; and the butter had to be set on the mantel over it to prevent having to split it with a cleaver. Little Siberia—the full sense of being an alien and poor was also in the phrase.

In earlier years the two top floors were let out to aging Irish spinsters. But in the late twenties, there were only two left, a bedridden saint of seventy and her sister, both living on Old Age. All the other rooms were shut off. The house itself has always stood in my mind as a convenient symbol of what happened to the first two generations of my mother's family under the impact of immigration, each closed room standing for failed or refused chances.

In her late twenties, Anna Maria married a widower years her senior, who died long before I was born. His first wife had been a Sheridan, a distinction which the family rejoiced in as being theirs by osmosis. Whether he had children by that marriage, I do not know. I suspect not, because the legend that was made of him pictures him as lavishing more love on a scapegrace niece than on any of his children by Anna Maria. He comes down to me as a silent man in a tasseled smoking cap, who slept apart from his wife in the front room of the basement, and who, when his niece would scratch at the basement door at three in the morning, legless-drunk and scared to go home, would relinquish his bed to her, bundling himself in his overcoat to keep fitful watch over her from a creaking rocker in the stoveless room.

Anna Maria seems to have been as much her own woman in the 1880s as she was in the 1920s and 30s. From time to time she would disappear from the house for days at a time. On one of these occasions my great-grandfather was asked "Where's Egan?" "I don't know," he answered. "I think she ran away with a soldier." That was the nearest anyone came to solving the mystery.

The Dad, as his children called him, was a junk-man, a canny one, with party and institutional connections that let him in on the ground floor of any major demolition. He could read and write nothing but numbers; but those he must have been able to manage with profitable shrewdness. Poverty did not empty the table or close the doors of the house until after his death.

Anna Maria had four children by him: my grandmother Agnes; her twin, Martin; William; and Gertrude. Since Martin was a frail baby, Anna Maria gave Agnes to her mother to raise, thereby repeating the pattern of her own rearing. When my grandmother Agnes was in her early teens, Anna Maria took her to Ireland, where she met her cousin Stanislaus Bunyan, who as thoroughly loathed her at first sight as she did him. When he later emigrated to America with his sister, Katherine, he stayed with Anna Maria, fell in love with Agnes, and married her. She was eighteen at the time, he twenty-seven.

Impatient, dangerously temperamental, my grandfather earned his living by sketching for newspapers and by taking roles in the second- and third-string Frohman road companies. He was said to have drawn for the *World* and *Puck*, and to have played the lead in *Dr. Jekyll and Mr. Hyde*. In those simpler days the transformation from Jekyll to Hyde was achieved by a foaming tumbler of Seidlitz powder and a fast fall into a wooden armchair with an open tin of green greasepaint nailed upside down under one broad arm. The sizzling glass once drunk, Jekyll would writhe in the chair, dig his hand to the wrist in the greasepaint, pass the hand over his face as if to wipe away the cold sweat, then shoot up again toward the footlights, green as a beached corpse. Men in the audience gulped; women thudded to the floor.

My grandfather's life was hard, his habits wild; and he shaped his wife in his image. "He had her dancing day and night; and she'd sew sleigh bells in the hems of her skirts so the men would be looking at her ankles." Six months after she bore my mother, early in her twentieth year, she died of "congestion of the lungs," a euphemism for tuberculosis, which was considered stark and certain evidence of a shameless life.

My grandfather left my mother, then six months old, with the owner of a boardinghouse and her daughter, and went on the road. That set off a series of custody suits which produced the only heritage I have from him, a copy of "a typewritten letter," hurled at the head of the boardinghouse keeper. The threat of sending someone "a typewritten letter" was in those days as terrifying a sanction as the threat of calling the police. The letter reads:

New York, February 23rd, 1901.

Mrs. E. Walsh,
Madam:

In answer to your letter of the 21st inst, I must say that I am more than astonished to think that any sane person should be so imprudent as to dare make the proposal to me that you have done, for you should be aware by this time that I would no more think of placing my dear child in the clutches of a woman of your stamp than I would in the jaws of a wild beast.

You, who dragged my innocent babe into open court on two occasions have also dared to cast reflections on the way that she is being cared for. Permit me to tell you although it is no business of yours, that my dear child is now stronger, healthier and better in every way than she has ever been, which is a marked contrast to the half-starved condition she was in when I rescued her from you.

You have all along endeavored to force yourself on my family and you have interfered and intermeddled in my family affairs. Furthermore both you and your daughter have heaped the vilest kind of insult on my people and myself although you are complete strangers to us.

Now I hereby warn you that this must *cease*. I have already placed your letters in the hands of my lawyers, and if you still persist in your letter writing and annoyance I shall at once take steps to have you arrested and punished. My lawyers have advised me repeatedly to adopt this course and I shall act on their advice if you continue to interfere in my affairs.

Your daughter . . . has also several times endeavored to force her way into the house of my child's grand-parents and has even gone as far as to defy and threaten my people. I have taken steps to have her apprehended and dealt with according to law the very next attempt she makes in this direction.

I will take no further notice of any communication you may make other than to place it in the hands of my lawyers.

Yours truly,
S. J. Bunyan

My mother went to Anna Maria. Her only memory of her father dated from what must have been her fourth year. On a dark, cold Saturday, when she was lemon-oiling the balusters of the staircase, she heard a heavy step in the hall below. A hatted man in the carefully pressed one good suit of an unsuccessful actor was staring at her as if to commit her to memory. His handsome face was thin and white as paper; and the jaunty walking stick which actors then affected bore his whole weight like a cripple's cane. He broke his gaze and walked silently down the backstairs to the kitchen. She did not know who he was until long afterward, when she was told that he had come to say good-bye to Anna Maria on his way back home to die. He died in Dublin in his early thirties, and is said to be buried in Glas Nevin.

His sister, Katherine, also married a cousin, her first, and did so expressly against the admonitions of the family. She and her husband lied to the priest about the degree of kindred (then you needed a dispensation to marry within the fourth degree of kin-

dred). When Anna Maria threatened to tell the priest to prevent the marriage, Katherine pulled a bottle of iodine from her
purse, drank all of it, and collapsed to the kitchen floor. Katherine
managed to pull through, Anna Maria swore never to interfere
again, and the cousins were married.

Like my grandfather her brother, Katherine believed she had it in
her to make America her own. She took courses at Cooper Union
and was reputedly the first woman telegrapher to be hired by the
New York *Times*.

After her marriage, however, she fell to pieces. She lived in a flat
rather than a house, which was slightly disreputable in those days.
She kept house out of half-unpacked barrels of crockery and pans in
rooms uncarpeted and bare of wall (her pictures were still in
crates). She seems to have felt that something had played her
false, either her new country, her husband, or herself, or her dreams
about all three. Like her brother's, her embittered heart was more
and more deeply set on going home to Ireland. She drank heavily
from breakfast to bedtime, and died of a broken neck from a fall
down her own front stairs. In a prolonged agony of grief, her husband destroyed his business and himself. Every few months he
would drink himself furious, and hurl pried-up cobblestones through
the windows of his own saloon. With nothing to hold on to, his
inwards gone, he died in 1910 on the top floor of the city house, at
the tactless mercy of his impoverished relatives. In 1937, his irreconcilably reproachful ghost was said to have passed my great-aunt
on the stairs "without so much as a beck or a nod."

Of Anna Maria's sons, neither Martin nor William went far in
school. Martin left off after the eighth grade, and William in the
course of his first year at St. Francis Preparatory; Martin out of
pride and wildness, William out of incapacity. That incapacity was
usually blamed on his having fallen off a trolley as a boy and fractured his skull, an accident which was the frequent source of brutal
laughter for Anna Maria and the rest of the family. William adored
her, but she had eyes for no one but Martin, to whom she gave her
highest accolade, a mordant nickname, Mortyeen Hungry Jaws, in
sardonic appreciation of his appetite.

Such nicknames were the family's strongest terms of endearment.
There was, besides, a Mohawk chariness about addressing anyone by
his given name. Anna Maria had recourse from time to time to an
old minstrel show song to take the curse off our directly naming
her:

> Anna Maria, Anna Maria
> Anna Maria Jones,
> She can play the banjo,

The piccolo,
And the bones.

Address was awkward until you had earned your sobriquet. I earned mine, Four-Alls, when I was a crawling baby. My mother earned hers in her fifteenth year, when to measure up to the stricter standards of cleanliness in the outside world (she had just gone out to work), she undertook to do her own laundry:

Clotty Malotty
Who lives in our lane,
Every day washing,
And ne'er a day clean.

People had more than one nickname. Martin was called Mutton as well as Mortveen Hungry Jaws; William was called Wally to his face, and the more malicious Miggsy behind his back (*Miggs!* is what you cried, holding your thumbs, when you had the misfortune of meeting a person with cockeyes).

The tortuousness of the show of affection generally underlying the choice of these epithets always seemed to me to spring from the bleak Irish terror of "over-looking" those one admired, of giving them, that is, the evil eye, calling the devil's attention to them by imprudent praise. Love was never easily expressed in word or gesture. Kissing and hugging were as dangerous as they were vulgar. Honey, darling, sweetheart, and dear were words clowns used in books. In the family, they would have raised hoots of derision. "You" was the most intimate form of address. It could be used with crippling fury or devastating tenderness.

There was another form of address, the dreaded third person, reserved for "plugs" and "villains," those who had "presumed," who had "gone too far." For that kind of discourse you needed an intermediary off whom to ricochet your remarks: "Tell the other one that's the last time he'll put the bottle on his head in this kitchen [i.e., drink out of the bottle]," or "You're to tell that one this isn't the first time he's come into this house with the one arm as long as the other [i.e., without the conventional call-paying gift]." The intermediary generally remained silent; he was there only "for the sake of common decency." This periphrastic socialization was more frequently practiced for long periods than on an *ad hoc* basis, and was much in evidence at wakes. My mother never spoke directly to her Aunt Gertrude or Uncle Martin for over twenty years.

It was Anna Maria's second son, Wally, God help him (in Irish usage this is as much a dismissal as a blessing), on whom the sanction of indirect address was most often invoked. His only sojourns in the family's good graces were when he served as a convenient sucker or the butt of a passing joke. He was that most perfect of patsies, an easy victim, slow on the uptake, but once having caught on, a dervish of hurtless fury. For one whole year, every Monday morning, his older brother, Mutton, would hairpin Wally's trunk open and take his Sunday suit out to pawn for extra spending money. Every Friday afternoon he would redeem it with his new wages. When Wally at last discovered what had been happening, he flew into the Rumpelstiltskin rage his kin found so diverting and double-locked the trunk. From that time on, he locked up everything, even the cheap treats he occasionally bought himself. He once presented the family with a quarter-eaten French apple pie so tainted with camphor not even a pig with a head cold could have been brought to nose it. He meant the gesture kindly. When they refused it, he ate it himself.

In his late thirties, Wally married a plain, good-hearted second-generation Newfoundland woman whom he met at the weekly dances on Ninth Street where people used to go to "meet their own kind." He was a skilled florist, and worked for years in the shop and greenhouse of a German on Stuyvesant Avenue. He added to his income by buying various job lots of odds and ends from stores under the Myrtle Avenue El and repeddling them for at least triple what they had cost. Like his brother, Mutton, he prided himself on that quality which the Irish call cuteness, an aggressive sharp-dealing which takes more pleasure in outwitting people than in profit. "It will blacken before the hour is out," he once boasted of a gardenia he had just sold a high school boy for his date's corsage.

It was not that Wally was heartless. He certainly was not. He was always faithful to the Irish precept "Will you? was never a good fellow" (asking if someone wants something, rather than giving it to him unasked). He always gave unasked. But only to his own. He had a tribal sense of the outside world as fair game. Business to him was hunting; its only joy lay in the kill.

It was his generosity which kept the family's head above water in dirty times. Yet to them, perhaps because he seemed a distorting mirror of themselves, he was always the plug of plugs, a problem creature to be disowned by ridicule or exiled by contempt. He had the quarter-inch brow and ape's lip of the Paddies with grass hair they sell in florist shops on St. Patrick's Day. Like all of us, his opinions were three quarters prejudice, and one quarter notions. His grasp of language was haphazard. He prefaced most remarks with the old Bowery expletive "Wuh-now." Because she had been an orphan, he always introduced my mother as "this poor unfortunate." When his wife died of peritonitis, he brought the wake to a standstill by an impromptu keen in which he asked the Almighty why "her testicles got tied in knots" (he meant, intestines). When he was being ragged or crossed, he would fix his tormentor with a squint-eyed look and bellow "Wuh-now, refer!" His worst term of abuse was Communist, which he pronounced Commonness. "Wuh-now, refer! you goddamn Commonness," he once yelled at a cop who told him to stop smoking on the subway. That set-to cost him thirty days in a cell on Welfare Island.

Stunted though he was from his childhood accident and lack of schooling, half-blind from a boiler explosion in the Navy during the First World War, brutalized by family callousness, Wally flourished with the eccentric vitality of a trodden weed. There was a dignity in his refusal to hate or seek vengeance which moved the most vehement of his belittlers. That dignity saw him through the rebuffs of the non-Irish world as it had seen him through the rejections of his family, and helped him to transfigure banishment to liberation. His achievements were as modest as his desires; but of all his generation, he lived the longest and fared the best.

Mutton, Anna Maria's white-haired boy, was less lucky. He was the Yellow Kid[3] grown up, Mayor Walker[4] without an education. Tall and handsomely aquiline in a world of faces and bodies softened and shrunk by hard times and bad fare (the phrase was "All swollen up from water and potatoes"), he was the prince of the family and the neighborhood.

He had Anna Maria's testy sense of what life owed him. He took over the Dad's failing junk business rather than take jobs that would as a matter of course lead to moderate advancement. He worked, for instance, less than a week on the coveted subway-maintenance job which political pull had got him. He always said he left it out of shame: the first day he reported to work the only whole shoes in the house he could find to wear were a pair of ladies' patent leather boots which belonged to Katherine. That may have been the immediate cause, but the deeper one was the sense of insult to his dreams he felt at having to make do with an ordinary lot. Those who have been poor, like those who have been sick, often expect impossible compensation.

And crippling poor is what the family was. The reason usually given was that a bit of real estate speculation had cost them all that the Dad had left. It cost them more than that; it cost them their trust in America.

Mutton bought a handsome Federal house from a woman who had been a trained nurse. She reserved one room to store some possessions in, and Mutton let the house. The tenants turned out to be deadbeats, and after a year or so had to be evicted. When they had gone, Mutton inspected the house, and found the door of the room the nurse had reserved pried open. What he saw were piles of clothes on various pieces of furniture and chests covered with

3. The first comic strip cartoon printed in color (1895).
4. Jimmie Walker, *bon vivant* mayor of New York City in the 1920's. He was of Irish extraction.

muslin sheets. Since nothing seemed missing, he simply reclosed the jimmied door and contented himself with locking the two front doors.

A month or so later, the nurse was murdered, and the police took the broken-open room as a possible motive on Mutton's part. The room contained, among other things, some signed letters from George Washington, chests of eighteenth-century silver pots and pitchers, and a good deal of furniture and clothing which had belonged to Dolley Madison, of whom the nurse was a collateral descendant. Mutton was cleared of suspicion of murder through the help of the nurse's lawyer. A year or so later, the lawyer was arrested for the murder of a Polish countess at Greenwood Lake. When he confessed to that crime, he also confessed to the murder of the nurse.

In that experience, the family's deep-seated fears were realized and confirmed. That is what came of forming permanent ties here. That is what came of dealing with Protestants. Taboos previously allowed to lapse were reinforced. Stigmatized as unlucky, the house was left untenanted and untended till it was lost for nonpayment of taxes.

That course of action fulfilled two needs the family felt. The first was to make an expiatory sacrifice: after all, they couldn't say they hadn't always known in the bone that their graves in Holy Cross were the only property they were meant to own. The second was to make a proper show of contempt to the powers that were. They dealt with Fate as they dealt with unjust friends: they refused to "give it the satisfaction" of noticing its treachery.

Such a muddle of propitiation and pride underlay most of their behavior to fortune, whether it was bad or good. They reacted to fortune as wild creatures react to changes of light or sound. They fled or they froze.

Good fortune made them weep with apprehension. Sing before breakfast, weep before supper. There is no blessing unblackened by a curse. They were more themselves with trouble than with ease. Bad fortune turned them stupidly noble, like characters from heroic cycles. If life was that unfair, they would face the worst it had to offer. They would sooner die than cry out for mercy or relief.

What made their stand puzzling was the sense you knew they had of what was owed them for having measured up heroically to their lot, for having been at one and the same time insulted champions and the obedient children of God. It was not the American Dream that nourished their conviction of private dignity. Success was not to be measured in material terms, but in terms of inner fulfillment. Failing that, in terms of spiritual endurance. Their combat was not with social conditions, but "with principalities and powers," or, perhaps, "the ungovernable sea."

Mutton, accordingly, all his life conceived of himself as an unrealized conqueror in voluntary exile. At nearly forty, he married a widow and settled in a rented house behind a stable on the other side of Court Street, a block or so from the Gas House and the Gowanus. With a sullen and mysterious purpose, he retraced the family's steps back to poverty. When his wife broke down, he made a comic saga out of it, though it tore him in two. When he himself lost control of his bowels and bladder, he joked about the vagaries of his body as if it belonged to someone else.

His gaze arrested you with that compelling reproach you see in the eyes of dying men. His fidelity to intimate values, so self-evident to him he believed it unnecessary to state them, made the pursuit of happiness that my mother and father and I were, with the rest of our generations, engaged in seem trivial prostitution and self-indulgence. He was, like Anna Maria, literally larger than life. Like her, he believed in the inviolability of his own body. She died of a cancer she had hidden for years rather than let a doctor see or touch her; he died hopelessly crippled rather than undergo a relatively simple operation.

It was more than the peasant fear of hospitals that held them to that stand. Their attitude was a sensible and outward sign of their conviction that any tampering with mind or body would inevitably lead to a loss of wholeness worse than death. They were virgin martyrs by disposition: they relinquished the charm of life as they had relinquished the charm of the American experience in order to keep their unquestioned selves impossibly intact. Mutton dying said to me, "You'll never be the man your grandfather was." I winced at what that meant to him and to me.

It is true that Mutton recoiled from "becoming American" for fear he should lose the sense of who he was. And that the older he got, the narrower, the more ignorantly reclusive he became. And that the pride in nationality which had saved Anna Maria from going under in the bleak days after the Civil War, when the Irish were held little better than the vermin that infested their tenements, had in him become a killing reflex. And that he lived in a ghetto of his own making, and the genuine gifts which were his were lost to his generation. All those things are true. But it is also true that no Irish of my generation will ever see his like again.

SAMUEL L. CLEMENS
Overland Stagecoaching[1]

As the sun went down and the evening chill came on, we made preparation for bed. We stirred up the hard leather letter-sacks, and the knotty canvas bags of printed matter (knotty and uneven because of projecting ends and corners of magazines, boxes and books). We stirred them up and redisposed them in such a way as to make our bed as level as possible. And we *did* improve it, too, though after all our work it had an upheaved and billowy look about it, like a little piece of a stormy sea. Next we hunted up our boots from odd nooks among the mail-bags where they had settled, and put them on. Then we got down our coats, vests, pantaloons and heavy woolen shirts, from the arm-loops where they had been swinging all day, and clothed ourselves in them—for, there being no ladies either at the stations or in the coach, and the weather being hot, we had looked to our comfort by stripping to our underclothing, at nine o'clock in the morning. All things being now ready, we stowed the uneasy Dictionary where it would lie as quiet as possible, and placed the water-canteens and pistols where we could find them in the dark. Then we smoked a final pipe, and swapped a final yarn; after which, we put the pipes, tobacco and bag of coin in snug holes and caves among the mail-bags, and then fastened down the coach curtains all around, and made the place as "dark as the inside of a cow," as the conductor phrased it in his picturesque way. It was certainly as dark as any place could be—nothing was even dimly visible in it. And finally, we rolled ourselves up like silk-worms, each person in his own blanket, and sank peacefully to sleep.

Whenever the stage stopped to change horses, we would wake up, and try to recollect where we were—and succeed—and in a minute or two the stage would be off again, and we likewise. We began to get into country, now, threaded here and there with little streams. These had high, steep banks on each side, and every time we flew down one bank and scrambled up the other, our party inside got mixed somewhat. First we would all be down in a pile at the forward end of the stage, nearly in a sitting posture, and in a second we would shoot to the other end, and stand on our heads. And we would sprawl and kick, too, and ward off ends and corners of mail-bags that came lumbering

1. From Chapter IV of *Roughing It.* Twain's synoptic headings run as follows: "Making Our Bed—Assaults by the Unabridged—At a Station—Our Driver a Great and Shining Dignitary—Strange Place for a Front Yard—Accommodations—Double Portraits—An Heirloom—Our Worthy Landlord—'Fixings and Things'—An Exile—Slumgullion—A Well Furnished Table—The Landlord Astonished—Table Etiquette—Wild Mexican Mules—Stage-Coaching and Railroading."

over us and about us; and as the dust rose from the tumult, we would all sneeze in chorus, and the majority of us would grumble, and probably say some hasty thing, like: "Take your elbow out of my ribs! Can't you quit crowding?"

Every time we avalanched from one end of the stage to the other, the Unabridged Dictionary would come too; and every time it came it damaged somebody. One trip it "barked" the Secretary's elbow; the next trip it hurt me in the stomach, and the third it tilted Bemis's nose up till he could look down his nostrils—he said. The pistols and coin soon settled to the bottom, but the pipes, pipe-stems, tobacco and canteens clattered and floundered after the Dictionary every time it made an assault on us, and aided and abetted the book by spilling tobacco in our eyes, and water down our backs.

Still, all things considered, it was a very comfortable night. It wore gradually away, and when at last a cold gray light was visible through the puckers and chinks in the curtains, we yawned and stretched with satisfaction, shed our cocoons, and felt that we had slept as much as was necessary. By and by, as the sun rose up and warmed the world, we pulled off our clothes and got ready for breakfast. We were just pleasantly in time, for five minutes afterward the driver sent the weird music of his bugle winding over the grassy solitudes, and presently we detected a low hut or two in the distance. Then the rattling of the coach, the clatter of our six horses' hoofs, and the driver's crisp commands, awoke to a louder and stronger emphasis, and we went sweeping down on the station at our smartest speed. It was fascinating—that old overland stagecoaching.

We jumped out in undress uniform. The driver tossed his gathered reins out on the ground, gaped and stretched complacently, drew off his heavy buckskin gloves with great deliberation and insufferable dignity—taking not the slightest notice of a dozen solicitous inquiries after his health, and humbly facetious and flattering accostings, and obsequious tenders of service, from five or six hairy and half-civilized station-keepers and hostlers who were nimbly unhitching our steeds and bringing the fresh team out of the stables—for in the eyes of the stage-driver of that day, station-keepers and hostlers were a sort of good enough low creatures, useful in their place, and helping to make up a world, but not the kind of beings which a person of distinction could afford to concern himself with; while, on the contrary, in the eyes of the station-keeper and the hostler, the stage-driver was a hero—a great and shining dignitary, the world's favorite son, the envy of the people, the observed of the nations. When they spoke to him they received his insolent silence meekly, and as being the natural and proper conduct of so great a man;

when he opened his lips they all hung on his words with admiration (he never honored a particular individual with a remark, but addressed it with a broad generality to the horses, the stables, the surrounding country *and* the human underlings); when he discharged a facetious insulting personality at a hostler, that hostler was happy for the day; when he uttered his one jest —old as the hills, coarse, profane, witless, and inflicted on the same audience, in the same language, every time his coach drove up there—the varlets roared, and slapped their thighs, and swore it was the best thing they'd ever heard in all their lives. And how they would fly around when he wanted a basin of water, a gourd of the same, or a light for his pipe—but they would instantly insult a passenger if he so far forgot himself as to crave a favor at their hands. They could do that sort of insolence as well as the driver they copied it from—for, let it be borne in mind, the overland driver had but little less contempt for his passengers than he had for his hostlers.

The hostlers and station-keepers treated the really powerful *conductor* of the coach merely with the best of what was their idea of civility, but the *driver* was the only being they bowed down to and worshipped. How admiringly they would gaze up at him in his high seat as he gloved himself with lingering deliberation, while some happy hostler held the bunch of reins aloft, and waited patiently for him to take it! And how they would bombard him with glorifying ejaculations as he cracked his long whip and went careering away.

The station buildings were long, low huts, made of sun-dried, mud-colored bricks, laid up without mortar (*adobes*, the Spaniards call these bricks, and Americans shorten it to '*dobies*). The roofs, which had no slant to them worth speaking of, were thatched and then sodded or covered with a thick layer of earth, and from this sprung a pretty rank growth of weeds and grass. It was the first time we had ever seen a man's front yard on top of his house. The buildings consisted of barns, stable-room for twelve or fifteen horses, and a hut for an eating-room for passengers. This latter had bunks in it for the station-keeper and a hostler or two. You could rest your elbow on its eaves, and you had to bend in order to get in at the door. In place of a window there was a square hole about large enough for a man to crawl through, but this had no glass in it. There was no flooring, but the ground was packed hard. There was no stove, but the fireplace served all needful purposes. There were no shelves, no cupboards, no closets. In a corner stood an open sack of flour, and nestling against its base were a couple of black and venerable tin coffee-pots, a tin tea-pot, a little bag of salt, and a side of bacon.

By the door of the station-keeper's den, outside, was a tin wash-basin, on the ground. Near it was a pail of water and a piece of yellow bar soap, and from the eaves hung a hoary blue woolen shirt, significantly—but this latter was the station-keeper's private towel, and only two persons in all the party might venture to use it—the stage-driver and the conductor. The latter would not, from a sense of decency; the former would not because he did not choose to encourage the advances of a station-keeper. We had towels—in the valise; they might as well have been in Sodom and Gomorrah. We (and the conductor) used our handkerchiefs, and the driver his pantaloons and sleeves. By the door, inside, was fastened a small old-fashioned looking-glass frame, with two little fragments of the original mirror lodged down in one corner of it. This arrangement afforded a pleasant double-barreled portrait of you when you looked into it, with one half of your head set up a couple of inches above the other half. From the glass frame hung the half of a comb by a string—but if I had to describe that patriarch or die, I believe I would order some sample coffins. It had come down from Esau and Samson, and had been accumulating hair ever since—along with certain impurities. In one corner of the room stood three or four rifles and muskets, together with horns and pouches of ammunition. The station-men wore pantaloons of coarse, country-woven stuff, and into the seat and the inside of the legs were sewed ample additions of buckskin, to do duty in place of leggings, when the man rode horseback—so the pants were half dull blue and half yellow, and unspeakably picturesque. The pants were stuffed into the tops of high boots, the heels whereof were armed with great Spanish spurs, whose little iron clogs and chains jingled with every step. The man wore a huge beard and mustachios, an old slouch hat, a blue woolen shirt, no suspenders, no vest, no coat—in a leathern sheath in his belt, a great long "navy" revolver (slung on right side, hammer to the front), and projecting from his boot a horn-handled bowie-knife. The furniture of the hut was neither gorgeous nor much in the way. The rocking-chairs and sofas were not present, and never had been, but they were represented by two three-legged stools, a pine-board bench four feet long, and two empty candle-boxes. The table was a greasy board on stilts, and the table-cloth and napkins had not come—and they were not looking for them, either. A battered tin platter, a knife and fork, and a tin pint cup, were at each man's place, and the driver had a queensware[2] saucer that had seen better days. Of course this duke sat at the head of the table. There was one isolated piece of table furniture that bore about it a touching air of grandeur

2. Cream-colored, glazed English earthenware.

in misfortune. This was the caster.[3] It was German silver, and crippled and rusty, but it was so preposterously out of place there that it was suggestive of a tattered exiled king among barbarians, and the majesty of its native position compelled respect even in its degradation. There was only one cruet left, and that was a stopperless, fly-specked, broken-necked thing, with two inches of vinegar in it, and a dozen preserved flies with their heels up and looking sorry they had invested there.

The station-keeper up-ended a disk of last week's bread, of the shape and size of an old-time cheese, and carved some slabs from it which were as good as Nicholson pavement, and tenderer.

He sliced off a piece of bacon for each man, but only the experienced old hands made out to eat it, for it was condemned army bacon which the United States would not feed to its soldiers in the forts, and the stage company had bought it cheap for the sustenance of their passengers and employes. We may have found this condemned army bacon further out on the plains than the section I am locating it in, but we *found* it—there is no gainsaying that.

Then he poured for us a beverage which he called "*Slumgullion*," and it is hard to think he was not inspired when he named it. It really pretended to be tea, but there was too much dish-rag, and sand, and old bacon-rind in it to deceive the intelligent traveler. He had no sugar and no milk—not even a spoon to stir the ingredients with.

We could not eat the bread or the meat, nor drink the "slumgullion." And when I looked at that melancholy vinegar cruet, I thought of the anecdote (a very, very old one, even at that day) of the traveler who sat down to a table which had nothing on it but a mackerel and a pot of mustard. He asked the landlord if this was all. The landlord said:

"*All!* Why, thunder and lightning, I should think there was mackerel enough there for six."

"But I don't like mackerel."

"Oh—then help yourself to the mustard."

In other days I had considered it a good, a very good, anecdote, but there was a dismal plausibility about it, here, that took all the humor out of it.

Our breakfast was before us, but our teeth were idle.

I tasted and smelt, and said I would take coffee, I believed. The station-boss stopped dead still, and glared at me speechless. At last, when he came to, he turned away and said, as one who communes with himself upon a matter too vast to grasp:

"*Coffee!* Well, if that don't go clean ahead of me, I'm d——d!"

We could not eat, and there was no conversation among the hos-

3. Lazy Susan.

tlers and herdsmen—we all sat at the same board. At least there was no conversation further than a single hurried request, now and then, from one employe to another. It was always in the same form, and always gruffly friendly. Its western freshness and novelty startled me, at first, and interested me, but it presently grew monotonous, and lost its charm. It was:

"Pass the bread, you son of a skunk!" No, I forget—skunk was not the word; it seems to me it was still stronger than that; I know it was, in fact, but it is gone from my memory, apparently. However, it is no matter—probably it was too strong for print, anyway. It is the landmark in my memory which tells me where I first encountered the vigorous new vernacular of the occidental plains and mountains.

We gave up the breakfast, and paid our dollar apiece and went back to our mail-bag bed in the coach, and found comfort in our pipes. Right here we suffered the first diminution of our princely state. We left our six fine horses and took six mules in their place. But they were wild Mexican fellows, and a man had to stand at the head of each of them and hold him fast while the driver gloved and got himself ready. And when at last he grasped the reins and gave the word, the men sprung suddenly away from the mules' heads and the coach shot from the station as if it had issued from a cannon. How the frantic animals did scamper! It was a fierce and furious gallop—and the gait never altered for a moment till we reeled off ten or twelve miles and swept up to the next collection of little station-huts and stables.

So we flew along all day. At 2 P.M. the belt of timber that fringes the North Platte and marks its windings through the vast level floor of the Plains came in sight. At 4 P.M. we crossed a branch of the river, and at 5 P.M. we crossed the Platte itself, and landed at Fort Kearney, *fifty-six hours out from St. Joe*—THREE HUNDRED MILES!

QUESTIONS

1. Why does Twain make so much of the driver's gloves?
2. Today a bus driver is not a hero for most people. Why is Twain's driver a hero? Why aren't the passengers heroes?
3. Can you think of comparable examples of hero worship? What qualities are worshipped? What does the hero worship reveal about some fact or aspect of language? Explain.
4. Twain mentions many rather unpleasant details—the dirty comb, the "greasy board," the inedible food, etc. What modifies the unpleasantness of the impression?
5. What are the humorous devices Twain uses in such sentences as:
   a. "And we would sprawl and kick, too, and ward off ends and corners of mail-bags that came lumbering over us and about us; and as the dust rose from the tumult, we would all sneeze

in chorus, and the majority of us would grumble, and probably say some hasty thing, like: 'Take your elbow out of my ribs! Can't you quit crowding?' "

b. "One trip it [the unabridged dictionary] 'barked' the Secretary's elbow; the next trip it hurt me in the stomach, and the third it tilted Bemis's nose up till he could look down his nostrils—he said."

c. "From the glass frame hung the half of a comb by a string— but if I had to describe that patriarch or die, I believe I would order some sample coffins."

d. "The furniture of the hut was neither gorgeous nor much in the way. . . . The table was a greasy board on stilts, and the table-cloth and napkins had not come—and they were not looking for them, either."

e. "There was only one cruet left, and that was a stopperless, fly-specked, broken-necked thing, with two inches of vinegar in it, and a dozen preserved flies with their heels up and looking sorry they had invested there."

f. "The station-keeper up-ended a disk of last week's bread, of the shape and size of an old-time cheese, and carved some slabs from it which were as good as Nicholson pavement, and tenderer."

6. Twain once wrote: "The humorous story is told gravely: the teller does his best to conceal the fact that he even dimly suspects that there is anything funny about it. . . ." How accurately does this describe "Overland Stagecoaching"?

BRUNO BETTELHEIM

A Victim[1]

Many students of discrimination are aware that the victim often reacts in ways as undesirable as the action of the aggressor. Less attention is paid to this because it is easier to excuse a defendant than an offender, and because they assume that once the aggression stops the victim's reactions will stop too. But I doubt if this is of real service to the persecuted. His main interest is that the persecution cease. But that is less apt to happen if he lacks a real understanding of the phenomenon of persecution, in which victim and persecutor are inseparably interlocked.

Let me illustrate with the following example: in the winter of 1938 a Polish Jew murdered the German attaché in Paris, vom Rath. The Gestapo used the event to step up anti-Semitic actions, and in the camp new hardships were inflicted on Jewish prisoners. One of these was an order barring them from the medical clinic unless the need for treatment had originated in work accident.

1. From "Behavior in Extreme Situations: Defenses," Chapter 5 of *The Informed Heart*, 1960.

Nearly all prisoners suffered from frostbite which often led to gangrene and then amputation. Whether or not a Jewish prisoner was admitted to the clinic to prevent such a fate depended on the whim of an SS private. On reaching the clinic entrance, the prisoner explained the nature of his ailment to the SS man, who then decided if he should get treatment or not.

I too suffered from frostbite. At first I was discouraged from trying to get medical care by the fate of Jewish prisoners whose attempts had ended up in no treatment, only abuse. Finally things got worse and I was afraid that waiting longer would mean amputation. So I decided to make the effort.

When I got to the clinic, there were many prisoners lined up as usual, a score of them Jews suffering from severe frostbite. The main topic of discussion was one's chances of being admitted to the clinic. Most Jews had planned their procedure in detail. Some thought it best to stress their service in the German army during World War I: wounds received or decorations won. Others planned to stress the severity of their frostbite. A few decided it was best to tell some "tall story," such as that an SS officer had ordered them to report at the clinic.

Most of them seemed convinced that the SS man on duty would not see through their schemes. Eventually they asked me about my plans. Having no definite ones, I said I would go by the way the SS man dealt with other Jewish prisoners who had frostbite like me, and proceed accordingly. I doubted how wise it was to follow a preconceived plan, because it was hard to anticipate the reactions of a person you didn't know.

The prisoners reacted as they had at other times when I had voiced similar ideas on how to deal with the SS. They insisted that one SS man was like another, all equally vicious and stupid. As usual, any frustration was immediately discharged against the person who caused it, or was nearest at hand. So in abusive terms they accused me of not wanting to share my plan with them, or of intending to use one of theirs; it angered them that I was ready to meet the enemy unprepared.

No Jewish prisoner ahead of me in the line was admitted to the clinic. The more a prisoner pleaded, the more annoyed and violent the SS became. Expressions of pain amused him; stories of previous services rendered to Germany outraged him. He proudly remarked that *he* could not be taken in by Jews, that fortunately the time had passed when Jews could reach their goal by lamentations.

When my turn came he asked me in a screeching voice if I knew that work accidents were the only reason for admitting Jews to the clinic, and if I came because of such an accident. I replied that I knew the rules, but that I couldn't work unless my hands were freed of the dead flesh. Since prisoners were not allowed to have knives, I asked to have the dead flesh cut away. I tried to be matter-of-fact, avoiding pleading, deference, or arrogance. He replied: "If that's all you want, I'll tear the flesh off myself." And he started to pull at the festering skin. Because it did not come off as easily as he may have expected, or for some other reason, he waved me into the clinic.

Inside, he gave me a malevolent look and pushed me into the treatment room. There he told the prisoner orderly to attend to the wound. While this was being done, the guard watched me closely for signs of pain but I was able to suppress them. As soon as the cutting was over, I started to leave. He showed surprise and asked why I didn't wait for further treatment. I said I had gotten the service I asked for, at which he told the orderly to make an exception and treat my hand. After I had left the room, he called me back and gave me a card entitling me to further treatment, and admittance to the clinic without inspection at the entrance.

* * *

Because my behavior did not correspond to what he expected of Jewish prisoners on the basis of his projection, he could not use his prepared defenses against being touched by the prisoner's plight. Since I did not act as the dangerous Jew was expected to, I did not activate the anxieties that went with his stereotype. Still he did not altogether trust me, so he continued to watch while I received treatment.

Throughout these dealings, the SS felt uneasy with me, though he did not unload on me the annoyance his uneasiness aroused. Perhaps he watched me closely because he expected that sooner or later I would slip up and behave the way his projected image of the Jew was expected to act. This would have meant that his delusional creation had become real.

JOAN DIDION

On Going Home

I am home for my daughter's first birthday. By "home" I do not mean the house in Los Angeles where my husband and I and the baby live, but the place where my family is, in the Central Valley of California. It is a vital although troublesome distinction. My husband likes my family but is uneasy in their house, because once there I fall into their ways, which are difficult, oblique, deliberately inarticulate, not my husband's ways. We live in dusty houses ("D-U-S-T," he once wrote with his finger on surfaces all over the house, but no one noticed it) filled with mementos quite without value to him (what could the Canton dessert plates mean to him? how could he have known about the assay scales, why should he care if he did know?), and we appear to talk exclusively about people we know who have been committed to mental hospitals, about people we know who have been booked on drunk-driving charges, and about property, particularly about property, land, price per acre and C-2 zoning and assessments and freeway access. My brother does not understand my husband's inability to perceive the advantage in the rather common real-estate transaction known as "sale-leaseback," and my husband in turn does not understand why so many of the people he hears about in my father's house have recently been committed to mental hospitals or booked on drunk-driving charges. Nor does he understand that when we talk about sale-leasebacks and right-of-way condemnations we are talking in code about the things we like best, the yellow fields and the cotton-woods and the rivers rising and falling and the mountain roads closing when the heavy snow comes in. We miss each other's points, have another drink and regard the fire. My brother refers to my husband, in his presence, as "Joan's husband." Marriage is the classic betrayal.

Or perhaps it is not any more. Sometimes I think that those of us who are now in our thirties were born into the last generation to carry the burden of "home," to find in family life the source of all tension and drama. I had by all objective accounts a "normal" and a "happy" family situation, and yet I was almost thirty years old before I could talk to my family on the telephone without crying after I had hung up. We did not fight. Nothing was wrong. And yet some nameless anxiety colored the emotional charges between me and the place that I came from. The question of whether or not you could go home again was a very real part of the sentimental and largely literary baggage with which we left home in the fifties; I suspect that it is irrelevant to the children born of the fragmentation after World War II. A few weeks ago in a San Francisco bar I saw a pretty young girl on crystal take off her clothes and dance for the cash prize in an "amateur-topless" contest. There was no particular sense of moment about this, none of the effect of romantic degradation, of "dark journey," for which my generation strived so assiduously. What sense could that girl possibly make of, say, *Long Day's Journey into Night*? Who is beside the point?

That I am trapped in this particular irrelevancy is never more apparent to me than when I am home. Paralyzed by the neurotic lassitude engendered by meeting one's past at every turn, around every corner, inside every cupboard, I go aimlessly from room to room. I decide to meet it head-on and clean out a drawer, and I spread the contents on the bed. A bathing suit I wore the summer I

was seventeen. A letter of rejection from *The Nation*, an aerial photograph of the site for a shopping center my father did not build in
1954. Three teacups hand-painted with cabbage roses and signed
"E.M.," my grandmother's initials. There is no final solution for
letters of rejection from *The Nation* and teacups hand-painted in
1900. Nor is there any answer to snapshots of one's grandfather as a
young man on skis, surveying around Donner Pass in the year 1910.
I smooth out the snapshot and look into his face, and do and do
not see my own. I close the drawer, and have another cup of coffee
with my mother. We get along very well, veterans of a guerrilla war
we never understood.

Days pass. I see no one. I come to dread my husband's evening
call, not only because he is full of news of what by now seems to
me our remote life in Los Angeles, people he has seen, letters which
require attention, but because he asks what I have been doing, suggests uneasily that I get out, drive to San Francisco or Berkeley.
Instead I drive across the river to a family graveyard. It has been
vandalized since my last visit and the monuments are broken, overturned in the dry grass. Because I once saw a rattlesnake in the
grass I stay in the car and listen to a country-and-Western station.
Later I drive with my father to a ranch he has in the foothills. The
man who runs his cattle on it asks us to the roundup, a week from
Sunday, and although I know that I will be in Los Angeles I say, in
the oblique way my family talks, that I will come. Once home I
mention the broken monuments in the graveyard. My mother
shrugs.

I go to visit my great-aunts. A few of them think now that I am
my cousin, or their daughter who died young. We recall an anecdote about a relative last seen in 1948, and they ask if I still like
living in New York City. I have lived in Los Angeles for three years,
but I say that I do. The baby is offered a horehound drop, and I am
slipped a dollar bill "to buy a treat." Questions trail off, answers are
abandoned, the baby plays with the dust motes in a shaft of afternoon sun.

It is time for the baby's birthday party: a white cake, strawberry-
marshmallow ice cream, a bottle of champagne saved from another
party. In the evening, after she has gone to sleep, I kneel beside the
crib and touch her face, where it is pressed against the slats, with
mine. She is an open and trusting child, unprepared for and unaccustomed to the ambushes of family life, and perhaps it is just as
well that I can offer her little of that life. I would like to give her
more. I would like to promise her that she will grow up with a sense
of her cousins and of rivers and of her great-grandmother's teacups,
would like to pledge her a picnic on a river with fried chicken and
her hair uncombed, would like to give her *home* for her birthday,

but we live differently now and I can promise her nothing like that. I give her a xylophone and a sundress from Madeira, and promise to tell her a funny story.

LOREN EISELEY
The Brown Wasps

There is a corner in the waiting room of one of the great Eastern stations where women never sit. It is always in the shadow and over-hung by rows of lockers. It is, however, always frequented—not so much by genuine travelers as by the dying. It is here that a certain element of the abandoned poor seeks a refuge out of the weather, clinging for a few hours longer to the city that has fathered them. In a precisely similar manner I have seen, on a sunny day in midwin-ter, a few old brown wasps creep slowly over an abandoned wasp nest in a thicket. Numbed and forgetful and frost-blackened, the hum of the spring hive still resounded faintly in their sodden tissues. Then the temperature would fall and they would drop away into the white oblivion of the snow. Here in the station it is in no way dif-ferent save that the city is busy in its snows. But the old ones cling to their seats as though these were symbolic and could not be given up. Now and then they sleep, their gray old heads resting with pain-ful awkwardness on the backs of the benches.

Also they are not at rest. For an hour they may sleep in the gasp-ing exhaustion of the ill-nourished and aged who have to walk in the night. Then a policeman comes by on his round and nudges them upright.

"You can't sleep here," he growls.

A strange ritual then begins. An old man is difficult to waken. After a muttered conversation the policeman presses a coin into his hand and passes fiercely along the benches prodding and gesturing toward the door. In his wake, like birds rising and settling behind the passage of a farmer through a cornfield, the men totter up, move a few paces and subside once more upon the benches.

One man, after a slight, apologetic lurch, does not move at all. Tubercularly thin, he sleeps on steadily. The policeman does not look back. To him, too, this has become a ritual. He will not have to notice it again officially for another hour.

Once in a while one of the sleepers will not awake. Like the brown wasps, he will have had his wish to die in the great droning center of the hive rather than in some lonely room. It is not so bad here with the shuffle of footsteps and the knowledge that there are others who share the bad luck of the world. There are also the whistles and the sounds of everyone, everyone in the world, starting on journeys. Amidst so many journeys somebody is bound to come out all right. Somebody.

Maybe it was on a like thought that the brown wasps fell away from the old paper nest in the thicket. You hold till the last, even if it is only to a public seat in a railroad station. You want your place in the hive more than you want a room or a place where the aged can be eased gently out of the way. It is the place that matters, the place at the heart of things. It is life that you want, that bruises your gray old head with the hard chairs; a man has a right to his place.

But sometimes the place is lost in the years behind us. Or sometimes it is a thing of air, a kind of vaporous distortion above a heap of rubble. We cling to a time and place because without them man is lost, not only man but life. This is why the voices, real or unreal, which speak from the floating trumpets at spiritualist seances are so unnerving. They are voices out of nowhere whose only reality lies in their ability to stir the memory of a living person with some fragment of the past. Before the medium's cabinet both the dead and the living revolve endlessly about an episode, a place, an event that has already been engulfed by time.

This feeling runs deep in life; it brings stray cats running over endless miles, and birds homing from the ends of the earth. It is as though all living creatures, and particularly the more intelligent, can survive only by fixing or transforming a bit of time into space or by securing a bit of space with its objects immortalized and made permanent in time. For example, I once saw, on a flower pot in my own living room, the efforts of a field mouse to build a remembered field. I have lived to see this episode repeated in a thousand guises, and since I have spent a large portion of my life in the shade of a nonexistent tree, I think I am entitled to speak for the field mouse.

One day as I cut across the field which at that time extended on one side of our suburban shopping center, I found a giant slug feeding from a runnel of pink ice cream in an abandoned Dixie cup. I could see his eyes telescope and protrude in a kind of dim, uncertain ecstasy as his dark body bunched and elongated in the curve of the cup. Then, as I stood there at the edge of the concrete, contemplating the slug, I began to realize it was like standing on a shore where a different type of life creeps up and fumbles tentatively among the rocks and sea wrack. It knows its place and will only creep so far until something changes. Little by little as I stood there I began to see more of this shore that surrounds the place of man. I looked with sudden care and attention at things I had been running over thoughtlessly for years. I even waded out a short way into the grass and the wild-rose thickets to see more. A huge black-belted bee went droning by and there were some indistinct scurryings in the underbrush.

Then I came to a sign which informed me that this field was to be the site of a new Wanamaker suburban store. Thousands of obscure lives were about to perish, the spores of puffballs would go smoking off to new fields, and the bodies of little white-footed mice would be crunched under the inexorable wheels of the bulldozers. Life disappears or modifies its appearances so fast that everything takes on an aspect of illusion—a momentary fizzing and boiling with smoke rings, like pouring dissident chemicals into a retort. Here man was advancing, but in a few years his plaster and bricks would be disappearing once more into the insatiable maw of the clover. Being of an archaeological cast of mind, I thought of this fact with an obscure sense of satisfaction and waded back through the rose thickets to the concrete parking lot. As I did so, a mouse scurried ahead of me, frightened of my steps if not of that ominous Wanamaker sign. I saw him vanish in the general direction of my apartment house, his little body quivering with fear in the great open sun on the blazing concrete. Blinded and confused, he was running straight away from his field. In another week scores would follow him.

I forgot the episode then and went home to the quiet of my living room. It was not until a week later, letting myself into the apartment, that I realized I had a visitor. I am fond of plants and had several ferns standing on the floor in pots to avoid the noon glare by the south window.

As I snapped on the light and glanced carelessly around the room, I saw a little heap of earth on the carpet and a scrabble of pebbles that had been kicked merrily over the edge of one of the flower pots. To my astonishment I discovered a full-fledged burrow delving downward among the fern roots. I waited silently. The creature who had made the burrow did not appear. I remembered the wild field then, and the flight of the mice. No house mouse, no *Mus domesticus*, had kicked up this little heap of earth or sought refuge under a fern root in a flower pot. I thought of the desperate little creature I had seen fleeing from the wild-rose thicket. Through intricacies of pipes and attics, he, or one of his fellows, had climbed to this high green solitary room. I could visualize what had occurred. He had an image in his head, a world of seed pods and quiet, of green sheltering leaves in the dim light among the weed stems. It was the only world he knew and it was gone.

Somehow in his flight he had found his way to this room with drawn shades where no one would come till nightfall. And here he had smelled green leaves and run quickly up the flower pot to dabble his paws in common earth. He had even struggled half the afternoon to carry his burrow deeper and had failed. I examined the hole, but no whiskered twitching face appeared. He was gone. I gathered up the earth and refilled the burrow. I did not expect to find traces of him again.

Yet for three nights thereafter I came home to the darkened room and my ferns to find the dirt kicked gaily about the rug and the burrow reopened, though I was never able to catch the field mouse within it. I dropped a little food about the mouth of the burrow, but it was never touched. I looked under beds or sat reading with one ear cocked for rustlings in the ferns. It was all in vain; I never saw him. Probably he ended in a trap in some other tenant's room.

But before he disappeared I had come to look hopefully for his evening burrow. About my ferns there had begun to linger the insubstantial vapor of an autumn field, the distilled essence, as it were, of a mouse brain in exile from its home. It was a small dream, like our dreams, carried a long and weary journey along pipes and through spider webs, past holes over which loomed the shadows of waiting cats, and finally, desperately, into this room where he had played in the shuttered daylight for an hour among the green ferns on the floor. Every day these invisible dreams pass us on the street, or rise from beneath our feet, or look out upon us from beneath a bush.

Some years ago the old elevated railway in Philadelphia was torn down and replaced by a subway system. This ancient El with its barnlike stations containing nut-vending machines and scattered food scraps had, for generations, been the favorite feeding ground of flocks of pigeons, generally one flock to a station along the route of the El. Hundreds of pigeons were dependent upon the system. They flapped in and out of its stanchions and steel work or gathered in watchful little audiences about the feet of anyone who rattled the peanut-vending machines. They even watched people who jingled change in their hands, and prospected for food under the feet of the crowds who gathered between trains. Probably very few among the waiting people who tossed a crumb to an eager pigeon realized that this El was like a food-bearing river, and that the life which haunted its banks was dependent upon the running of the trains with their human freight.

I saw the river stop.

The time came when the underground tubes were ready; the traffic was transferred to a realm unreachable by pigeons. It was like a great river subsiding suddenly into desert sands. For a day, for two days, pigeons continued to circle over the El or stand close to the red vending machines. They were patient birds, and surely this great river which had flowed through the lives of unnumbered generations was merely suffering from some momentary drought.

They listened for the familiar vibrations that had always heralded an approaching train; they flapped hopefully about the head of an occasional workman walking along the steel runways. They passed from one empty station to another, all the while growing hungrier. Finally they flew away.

I thought I had seen the last of them about the El, but there was a revival and it provided a curious instance of the memory of living things for a way of life or a locality that has long been cherished. Some weeks after the El was abandoned workmen began to tear it down. I went to work every morning by one particular station, and the time came when the demolition crews reached this spot. Acetylene torches showered passersby with sparks, pneumatic drills hammered at the base of the structure, and a blind man who, like the pigeons, had clung with his cup to a stairway leading to the change booth, was forced to give up his place.

It was then, strangely, momentarily, one morning that I witnessed the return of a little band of the familiar pigeons. I even recognized one or two members of the flock that had lived around this particular station before they were dispersed into the streets. They flew bravely in and out among the sparks and the hammers and the shouting workmen. They had returned—and they had returned because the hubbub of the wreckers had convinced them that the river was about to flow once more. For several hours they flapped in and out through the empty windows, nodding their heads and watching the fall of girders with attentive little eyes. By the following morning the station was reduced to some burned-off stanchions in the street. My bird friends had gone. It was plain, however, that they retained a memory for an insubstantial structure now compounded of air and time. Even the blind man clung to it. Someone had provided him with a chair, and he sat at the same corner staring sightlessly at an invisible stairway where, so far as he was concerned, the crowds were still ascending to the trains.

I have said my life has been passed in the shade of a nonexistent tree, so that such sights do not offend me. Prematurely I am one of the brown wasps and I often sit with them in the great droning hive of the station, dreaming sometimes of a certain tree. It was planted sixty years ago by a boy with a bucket and a toy spade in a little Nebraska town. That boy was myself. It was a cottonwood sapling and the boy remembered it because of some words spoken by his father and because everyone died or moved away who was supposed to wait and grow old under its shade. The boy was passed from hand to hand, but the tree for some intangible reason had taken root in his mind. It was under its branches that he sheltered; it was from this tree that his memories, which are my memories, led away into the world.

After sixty years the mood of the brown wasps grows heavier

upon one. During a long inward struggle I thought it would do me good to go and look upon that actual tree. I found a rational excuse in which to clothe this madness. I purchased a ticket and at the end of two thousand miles I walked another mile to an address that was still the same. The house had not been altered.

I came close to the white picket fence and reluctantly, with great effort, looked down the long vista of the yard. There was nothing there to see. For sixty years that cottonwood had been growing in my mind. Season by season its seeds had been floating farther on the hot prairie winds. We had planted it lovingly there, my father and I, because he had a great hunger for soil and live things growing, and because none of these things had long been ours to protect. We had planted the little sapling and watered it faithfully, and I remembered that I had run out with my small bucket to drench its roots the day we moved away. And all the years since it had been growing in my mind, a huge tree that somehow stood for my father and the love I bore him. I took a grasp on the picket fence and forced myself to look again.

A boy with the hard bird eye of youth pedaled a tricycle slowly up beside me.

"What'cha lookin' at?" he asked curiously.

"A tree," I said.

"What for?" he said.

"It isn't there," I said, to myself mostly, and began to walk away at a pace just slow enough not to seem to be running.

"What isn't there?" the boy asked. I didn't answer. It was obvious I was attached by a thread to a thing that had never been there, or certainly not for long. Something that had to be held in the air, or sustained in the mind, because it was part of my orientation in the universe and I could not survive without it. There was more than an animal's attachment to a place. There was something else, the attachment of the spirit to a grouping of events in time; it was part of our morality.

So I had come home at last, driven by a memory in the brain as surely as the field mouse who had delved long ago into my flower pot or the pigeons flying forever amidst the rattle of nut-vending machines. These, the burrow under the greenery in my living room and the red-bellied bowls of peanuts now hovering in midair in the minds of pigeons, were all part of an elusive world that existed nowhere and yet everywhere. I looked once at the real world about me while the persistent boy pedaled at my heels.

It was without meaning, though my feet took a remembered path. In sixty years the house and street had rotted out of my mind. But the tree, the tree that no longer was, that had perished in its first season, bloomed on in my individual mind, unblemished as my father's words. "We'll plant a tree here, son, and we're not going to move any more. And when you're an old, old man you can sit under it and think how we planted it here, you and me, together."

I began to outpace the boy on the tricycle.

"Do you live here, Mister?" he shouted after me suspiciously. I took a firm grasp on airy nothing—to be precise, on the bole of a great tree. "I do," I said. I spoke for myself, one field mouse, and several pigeons. We were all out of touch but somehow permanent. It was the world that had changed.

E. B. WHITE

Once More to the Lake (August 1941)

One summer, along about 1904, my father rented a camp on a lake in Maine and took us all there for the month of August. We all got ringworm from some kittens and had to rub Pond's Extract on our arms and legs night and morning, and my father rolled over in a canoe with all his clothes on; but outside of that the vacation was a success and from then on none of us ever thought there was any place in the world like that lake in Maine. We returned summer after summer—always on August 1st for one month. I have since become a salt-water man, but sometimes in summer there are days when the restlessness of the tides and the fearful cold of the sea water and the incessant wind which blows across the afternoon and into the evening make me wish for the placidity of a lake in the woods. A few weeks ago this feeling got so strong I bought myself a couple of bass hooks and a spinner and returned to the lake where we used to go, for a week's fishing and to revisit old haunts.

I took along my son, who had never had any fresh water up his nose and who had seen lily pads only from train windows. On the journey over to the lake I began to wonder what it would be like. I wondered how time would have marred this unique, this holy spot—the coves and streams, the hills that the sun set behind, the camps and the paths behind the camps. I was sure the tarred road would have found it out and I wondered in what other ways it would be desolated. It is strange how much you can remember about places like that once you allow your mind to return into the grooves which lead back. You remember one thing, and that suddenly reminds you of another thing. I guess I remembered clearest of all the early mornings, when the lake was cool and motionless, remembered how the bedroom smelled of the lumber it was made of and of the wet woods whose scent entered through the screen. The partitions in the camp were thin and did not extend clear to the top of the rooms, and as I was always the first up I would dress softly so as not to wake the others, and sneak out into the sweet outdoors and start out in the canoe, keeping close along the shore in the long shadows of the pines. I remembered being very careful never to rub my paddle against the gunwale for fear of disturbing the stillness of the cathedral.

The lake had never been what you would call a wild lake. There were cottages sprinkled around the shores, and it was in farming country although the shores of the lake were quite heavily wooded. Some of the cottages were owned by nearby farmers, and you would live at the shore and eat your meals at the farmhouse. That's what our family did. But although it wasn't wild, it was a fairly large and undisturbed lake and there were places in it which, to a child at least, seemed infinitely remote and primeval.

I was right about the tar: it led to within half a mile of the shore. But when I got back there, with my boy, and we settled into a camp near a farmhouse and into the kind of summertime I had known, I could tell that it was going to be pretty much the same as it had been before—I knew it, lying in bed the first morning, smelling the bedroom, and hearing the boy sneak quietly out and go off along the shore in a boat. I began to sustain the illusion that he was I, and therefore, by simple transposition, that I was my father. This sensation persisted, kept cropping up all the time we were there. It was not an entirely new feeling, but in this setting it grew much stronger. I seemed to be living a dual existence. I would be in the middle of some simple act, I would be picking up a bait box or laying down a table fork, or I would be saying something, and suddenly it would be not I but my father who was saying the words or making the gesture. It gave me a creepy sensation.

We went fishing the first morning. I felt the same damp moss covering the worms in the bait can, and saw the dragonfly alight on the tip of my rod as it hovered a few inches from the surface of the water. It was the arrival of this fly that convinced me beyond any doubt that everything was as it always had been, that the years were a mirage and there had been no years. The small waves were the same, chucking the rowboat under the chin as we fished at anchor, and the boat was the same boat, the same color green and the ribs broken in the same places, and under the floor-boards the same fresh-water leavings and débris—the dead helgramite,[1] the wisps of moss, the rusty discarded fishhook, the dried blood from yesterday's catch. We stared silently at the tips of our rods, at the dragonflies that came and went. I lowered the tip of mine into the water, tentatively, pensively dislodging the fly, which darted two feet away, poised, darted two feet back, and came to rest again a little farther up the rod. There had been no years between the ducking of this dragonfly and the other one—the one that was part of memory. I looked at the boy, who was silently watching his fly, and it was my

1. The nymph of the May-fly, used as bait.

hands that held his rod, my eyes watching. I felt dizzy and didn't know which rod I was at the end of.

We caught two bass, hauling them in briskly as though they were mackerel, pulling them over the side of the boat in a businesslike manner without any landing net, and stunning them with a blow on the back of the head. When we got back for a swim before lunch, the lake was exactly where we had left it, the same number of inches from the dock, and there was only the merest suggestion of a breeze. This seemed an utterly enchanted sea, this lake you could leave to its own devices for a few hours and come back to, and find that it had not stirred, this constant and trustworthy body of water. In the shallows, the dark, water-soaked sticks and twigs, smooth and old, were undulating in clusters on the bottom against the clean ribbed sand, and the track of the mussel was plain. A school of minnows swam by, each minnow with its small individual shadow, doubling the attendance, so clear and sharp in the sunlight. Some of the other campers were in swimming, along the shore, one of them with a cake of soap, and the water felt thin and clear and unsubstantial. Over the years there had been this person with the cake of soap, this cultist, and here he was. There had been no years.

Up to the farmhouse to dinner through the teeming, dusty field, the road under our sneakers was only a two-track road. The middle track was missing, the one with the marks of the hooves and the splotches of dried, flaky manure. There had always been three tracks to choose from in choosing which track to walk in; now the choice was narrowed down to two. For a moment I missed terribly the middle alternative. But the way led past the tennis court, and something about the way it lay there in the sun reassured me; the tape had loosened along the backline, the alleys were green with plantains and other weeds, and the net (installed in June and removed in September) sagged in the dry noon, and the whole place steamed with midday heat and hunger and emptiness. There was a choice of pie for dessert, and one was blueberry and one was apple, and the waitresses were the same country girls, there having been no passage of time, only the illusion of it as in a dropped curtain—the waitresses were still fifteen; their hair had been washed, that was the only difference—they had been to the movies and seen the pretty girls with the clean hair.

Summertime, oh summertime, pattern of life indelible, the fade-proof lake, the woods unshatterable, the pasture with the sweetfern and the juniper forever and ever, summer without end; this was the background, and the life along the shore was the design, the cottagers with their innocent and tranquil design, their tiny docks with the flagpole and the American flag floating against the white clouds in the blue sky, the little paths over the roots of the trees leading from camp to camp and the paths leading back to the outhouses and the can of lime for sprinkling, and at the souvenir counters at the store the miniature birch-bark canoes and the post cards that showed things looking a little better than they looked. This was the American family at play, escaping the city heat, wondering whether the newcomers in the camp at the head of the cove were "common" or "nice," wondering whether it was true that the people who drove up for Sunday dinner at the farmhouse were turned away because there wasn't enough chicken.

It seemed to me, as I kept remembering all this, that those times and those summers had been infinitely precious and worth saving. There had been jollity and peace and goodness. The arriving (at the beginning of August) had been so big a business in itself, at the railway station the farm wagon drawn up, the first smell of the pine-laden air, the first glimpse of the smiling farmer, and the great importance of the trunks and your father's enormous authority in such matters, and the feel of the wagon under you for the long ten-mile haul, and at the top of the last long hill catching the first view of the lake after eleven months of not seeing this cherished body of water. The shouts and cries of the other campers when they saw you, and the trunks to be unpacked, to give up their rich burden. (Arriving was less exciting nowadays, when you sneaked up in your car and parked it under a tree near the camp and took out the bags and in five minutes it was all over, no fuss, no loud wonderful fuss about trunks.)

Peace and goodness and jollity. The only thing that was wrong now, really, was the sound of the place, an unfamiliar nervous sound of the outboard motors. This was the note that jarred, the one thing that would sometimes break the illusion and set the years moving. In those other summertimes all motors were inboard; and when they were at a little distance, the noise they made was a sedative, an ingredient of summer sleep. They were one-cylinder and two-cylinder engines, and some were make-and-break and some were jump-spark,[2] but they all made a sleepy sound across the lake. The one-lungers throbbed and fluttered, and the twin-cylinder ones purred and purred, and that was a quiet sound too. But now the campers all had outboards. In the daytime, in the hot mornings, these motors made a petulant, irritable sound; at night, in the still evening when the afterglow lit the water, they whined about one's ears like mosquitoes. My boy loved our rented outboard, and his great desire was to achieve singlehanded mastery over it, and authority, and he soon learned the trick of choking it a little (but not too much), and the adjustment of the needle valve. Watching him I would remember the things you could do with the old one-cylinder engine with the heavy flywheel, how you could have it eating out of

2. Methods of ignition timing.

your hand if you got really close to it spiritually. Motor boats in those days didn't have clutches, and you would make a landing by shutting off the motor at the proper time and coasting in with a dead rudder. But there was a way of reversing them, if you learned the trick, by cutting the switch and putting it on again exactly on the final dying revolution of the flywheel, so that it would kick back against compression and begin reversing. Approaching a dock in a strong following breeze, it was difficult to slow up sufficiently by the ordinary coasting method, and if a boy felt he had complete mastery over his motor, he was tempted to keep it running beyond its time and then reverse it a few feet from the dock. It took a cool nerve, because if you threw the switch a twentieth of a second too soon you would catch the flywheel when it still had speed enough to go up past center, and the boat would leap ahead, charging bull-fashion at the dock.

We had a good week at the camp. The bass were biting well and the sun shone endlessly, day after day. We would be tired at night and lie down in the accumulated heat of the little bedrooms after the long hot day and the breeze would stir almost imperceptibly outside and the smell of the swamp drift in through the rusty screens. Sleep would come easily and in the morning the red squirrel would be on the roof, tapping out his gay routine. I kept remembering everything, lying in bed in the mornings—the small steamboat that had a long rounded stern like the lip of a Ubangi, and how quietly she ran on the moonlight sails, when the older boys played their mandolins and the girls sang and we ate doughnuts dipped in sugar, and how sweet the music was on the water in the shining night, and what it had felt like to think about girls then. After breakfast we would go up to the store and the things were in the same place—the minnows in a bottle, the plugs and spinners disarranged and pawed over by the youngsters from the boys' camp, the fig newtons and the Beeman's gum. Outside, the road was tarred and cars stood in front of the store. Inside, all was just as it had always been, except there was more Coca-Cola and not so much Moxie and root beer and birch beer and sarsaparilla. We would walk out with a bottle of pop apiece and sometimes the pop would backfire up our noses and hurt. We explored the streams, quietly, where the turtles slid off the sunny logs and dug their way into the soft bottom; and we lay on the town wharf and fed worms to the tame bass. Everywhere we went I had trouble making out which was I, the one walking at my side, the one walking in my pants.

One afternoon while we were there at that lake a thunderstorm came up. It was like the revival of an old melodrama that I had seen long ago with childish awe. The second-act climax of the drama of the electrical disturbance over a lake in America had not changed in any important respect. This was the big scene, still the big scene.

The whole thing was so familiar, the first feeling of oppression and heat and a general air around camp of not wanting to go very far away. In midafternoon (it was all the same) a curious darkening of the sky, and a lull in everything that had made life tick; and then the way the boats suddenly swung the other way at their moorings with the coming of a breeze out of the new quarter, and the premonitory rumble. Then the kettle drum, then the snare, then the bass drum and cymbals, then crackling light against the dark, and the gods grinning and licking their chops in the hills. Afterward the calm, the rain steadily rustling in the calm lake, the return of light and hope and spirits, and the campers running out in joy and relief to go swimming in the rain, their bright cries perpetuating the deathless joke about how they were getting simply drenched, and the children screaming with delight at the new sensation of bathing in the rain, and the joke about getting drenched linking the generations in a strong indestructible chain. And the comedian who waded in carrying an umbrella.

When the others went swimming my son said he was going in too. He pulled his dripping trunks from the line where they had hung all through the shower, and wrung them out. Languidly, and with no thought of going in, I watched him, his hard little body, skinny and bare, saw him wince slightly as he pulled up around his vitals the small, soggy, icy garment. As he buckled the swollen belt suddenly my groin felt the chill of death.

QUESTIONS

1. White had not been back to the lake for many years. What bearing has this fact on the experience which the essay describes?
2. What has guided White in his selection of the details he gives about the trip? Why, for example, does he talk about the road, the dragonfly, the bather with the cake of soap?
3. How do the differences between boats of the past and boats of today relate to or support the point of the essay?
4. What is the meaning of White's last sentence? What relation has it to the sentence just preceding? How has White prepared us for this ending?
5. How would the narrative differ if it were told by the boy? What details of the scene might the boy emphasize? Why? Show what point the boy's selection of details might make.

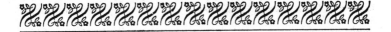

Prose Forms: Journals

[Occasionally a man catches himself having said something aloud, obviously with no concern to be heard, even by himself. And all of us have overheard, perhaps while walking, a solitary person muttering or laughing softly or exclaiming abruptly. For oneself or another, something floats up from the world within, forces itself to be expressed, takes no real account of the time or the place, and certainly intends no conscious communication.

With more self-consciousness, and yet without a specific audience, a man sometimes speaks out at something that has momentarily filled his attention from the world without. A sharp play at the ball game, the twist of a political speech, an old photograph—something from the outer world impresses the mind, stimulates it, focuses certain of its memories and values, interests and needs. Thus stimulated, the man may wish to share his experience with another, to inform or amuse him, to rouse him to action or persuade him to a certain belief. Often, though, the man experiencing may want most to talk to himself, to give a public shape in words to his thoughts and feelings but for the sake of a kind of private dialogue with himself. Communication to another may be an ultimate desire, but the immediate motive is to articulate the experience for himself.

To articulate, to shape the experience in language for his own sake, one may keep a journal. Literally a day-book, the journal enables one to write down something about the experiences of a day which for a great variety of reasons may have been especially memorable or impressive. The journal entry may be merely a few words to call to mind a thing done, a person seen, a menu enjoyed at a dinner party. It may be concerned at length with a political crisis in the community, or a personal crisis in the home. It may even be as noble as it was with some pious men in the past who used the journal to keep a record of their consciences, a periodic reckoning of their moral and spiritual accounts. In its most public aspect, the idea of a journal calls to mind the newspaper or the record of proceedings like the Congressional Record. In its most closely private form, the journal becomes the diary.

For the person keeping a journal, whatever he experiences and wants to hold he can write down. But to get it down on paper begins another adventure. For he has to focus on what he has experienced,

89

and to be able to say what, in fact, the experience is. What of it is new? What of it is remarkable because of associations in the memory it stirs up? Is this like anything I—or others—have experienced before? Is it a good or a bad thing to have happened? And why, specifically? The questions multiply themselves quickly, and as the journalist seeks to answer the appropriate ones, he begins to know what it is he contemplates. As he tries next to find the words that best represent his discovery, the experience becomes even more clear in its shape and meaning. We can imagine Emerson going to the ballet, being absorbed in the spectacle, thinking casually of this or that association the dancer and the movements suggest. When he writes about the experience in his journal, a good many questions, judgments, and speculations get tied up with the spectacle, and it is this complex of event and his total relation to it that becomes the experience he records. The simple facts of time, place, people, and actions drop down into a man's consciousness and set in motion ideas and feelings which give those facts their real meaning to that man.

Once this consciousness of events is formulated in words, the journal-keeper has it, not only in the sense of understanding what he has seen or felt or thought, but also in the sense of having it there before him to contemplate long after the event itself. When we read a carefully kept journal covering a long period and varied experiences, we have the pleasure of a small world re-created for us in the consciousness of one who experienced it. Even more, we feel the continuity, the wholeness, of the person himself. Something of the same feeling is there for the person who kept the journal: a whole world of events preserved in the form of their experienced reality, and with it the persistent self in the midst of that world. That world and that self are always accessible on the page, and ultimately, therefore, usably real.

Beyond the value of the journal as record, there is the instructive value of the habit of mind and hand journal keeping can assure. One begins to attend more carefully to what happens to him and around him. To have discovered, like Katherine Mansfield, that so apparently simple a thing as a pigeon sitting proudly on a tree can bring to mind the profoundest questions about the relation of God to His creatures, is to be thereafter a little more sensitive to all kinds of "simple" experience. Fact begins to be related to fact more readily, apparently dissimilar experiences may not be entirely different, the more and the less important begin to be discriminated. Even in so unlikely a situation for calm contemplation as war is, it is possible, like Pearce, to achieve that moment of detachment which focuses the immediate scene or event for what it is by seeing how it matters in relation to ideas or meanings beyond the battle or the beleaguered city or the desolated church. One begins to see what he is looking at, if he becomes accustomed to the characteristic method and form of the journal entry. All the while, one is learning the resources of language as a means of representing what he sees, and gaining skill and certainty in doing justice to experience and to his own consciousness when he writes.

The journal represents a discipline. It brings together an individual and a complex environment in a relation that teaches the individual something of himself, something of his world, and something of the meaning of their relation. There is scarcely a moment in a person's life when he is not poised for the lesson. When it comes with the promise of special force, there is the almost irresistible temptation to catch the impulse, give it form, make it permanent, assert its meaning. And so one commits himself to language. To have given up one's experience to words is to have begun marking out the limits and potential of its meaning. In the journal that meaning is developed and clarified to oneself primarily. When the whole intention of the development and the clarification is the consideration of another reader, the method of the journal redirects itself to become that of the essay.]

RALPH WALDO EMERSON: *from* Journal

I like to have a man's knowledge comprehend more than one class of topics, one row of shelves. I like a man who likes to see a fine barn as well as a good tragedy.   [1828]

The Religion that is afraid of science dishonors God and commits suicide.   [1831]

The things taught in colleges and schools are not an education, but the means of education.   [1831]

Don't tell me to get ready to die. I know not what shall be. The only preparation I can make is by fulfilling my present duties. This is the everlasting life.   [1832]

My aunt [Mary Moody Emerson] had an eye that went through and through you like a needle. "She was endowed," she said, "with the fatal gift of penetration." She disgusted everybody because she knew them too well.   [1832]

I am sure of this, that by going much alone a man will get more of a noble courage in thought and word than from all the wisdom that is in books.   [1833]

I fretted the other night at the hotel at the stranger who broke into my chamber after midnight, claiming to share it. But after his lamp had smoked the chamber full and I had turned round to the wall in despair, the man blew out his lamp, knelt down at his bedside, and made in low whisper a long earnest prayer. Then was the relation entirely changed between us. I fretted no more, but respected and liked him.   [1835]

I believe I shall some time cease to be an individual, that the eternal tendency of the soul is to become Universal, to animate the last extremities of organization.   [1837]

It is very hard to be simple enough to be good.   [1837]

A man must have aunts and cousins, must buy carrots and turnips, must have barn and woodshed, must go to market and to the black-smith's shop, must saunter and sleep and be inferior and silly.   [1838]

How sad a spectacle, so frequent nowadays, to see a young man after ten years of college education come out, ready for his voyage of life—and to see that the entire ship is made of rotten timber, of rotten, honeycombed, traditional timber without so much as an inch of new plank in the hull.   [1839]

A sleeping child gives me the impression of a traveler in a very far country. [1840]

In reading these letters of M.M.E. I acknowledge (with surprise that I could ever forget it) the debt of myself and my brothers to that old religion which, in those years, still dwelt like a Sabbath peace in the country population of New England, which taught privation, self-denial, and sorrow. A man was born, not for prosperity, but to suffer for the benefit of others, like the noble rock-maple tree which all around the villages bleeds for the service of man. Not praise, not men's acceptance of our doing, but the Spirit's holy errand through us, absorbed the thought. How dignified is this! how all that is called talents and worth in Paris and in Washington dwindles before it! [1841]

All writing is by the grace of God. People do not deserve to have good writing, they are so pleased with bad. In these sentences that you show me, I can find no beauty, for I see death in every clause and every word. There is a fossil or a mummy character which pervades this book. The best sepulchers, the vastest catacombs, Thebes and Cairo, Pyramids, are sepulchers to me. I like gardens and nurseries. Give me initiative, spermatic, prophesying, man-making words. [1841]

When summer opens, I see how fast it matures, and fear it will be short; but after the heats of July and August, I am reconciled, like one who has had his swing, to the cool of autumn. So will it be with the coming of death. [1846]

In England every man you meet is some man's son; in America, he may be some man's father. [1848]

Every poem must be made up of lines that are poems. [1848]

Love is necessary to the righting the estate of woman in this world. Otherwise nature itself seems to be in conspiracy against her dignity and welfare; for the cultivated, high-thoughted, beauty-loving, saintly woman finds herself unconsciously desired for her sex, and even enhancing the appetite of her savage pursuers by these fine ornaments she has piously laid on herself. She finds with indignation that she is herself a snare, and was made such. I do not wonder at her occasional protest, violent protest against nature, in fleeing to nunneries, and taking black veils. Love rights all this deep wrong. [1848]

Natural Aristocracy. It is a vulgar error to suppose that a gentleman must be ready to fight. The utmost that can be demanded of the gentleman is that he be incapable of a lie. There is a man who has good sense, is well informed, well-read, obliging, cultivated, capable, and has an absolute devotion to truth. He always means what he says, and says what he means, however courteously. You may spit upon him—nothing could induce him to spit upon you—no praises, and no possessions, no compulsion of public opinion. You may kick him—he will think it the kick of a brute—but he is not a brute, and will not kick you in return. But neither your knife and pistol, nor your gifts and courting will ever make the smallest impression on his vote or word; for he is the truth's man, and will speak and act the truth until he dies. [1849]

Love is temporary and ends with marriage. Marriage is the perfection which love aimed at, ignorant of what it sought. Marriage is a good known only to the parties—a relation of perfect understanding, aid, contentment, possession of themselves and of the world—which dwarfs love to green fruit. [1850]

I found when I had finished my new lecture that it was a very good house, only the architect had unfortunately omitted the stairs. [1851]

This filthy enactment [The Fugitive Slave Law] was made in the nineteenth century, by people who could read and write. I will not obey it, by God. [1851]

Henry [Thoreau] is military. He seemed stubborn and implacable; always manly and wise, but rarely sweet. One would say that, as Webster could never speak without an antagonist, so Henry does not feel himself except in opposition. He wants a fallacy to expose, a blunder to pillory, requires a little sense of victory, a roll of the drums, to call his powers into full exercise. [1853]

Shall we judge the country by the majority or by the minority? Certainly, by the minority. The mass are animal, in state of pupilage, and nearer the chimpanzee. [1854]

All the thoughts of a turtle are turtle. [1854]

Resources or feats. I like people who can do things. When Edward and I struggled in vain to drag our big calf into the barn, the Irish girl put her finger into the calf's mouth, and led her in directly. [1862]

George Francis Train said in a public speech in New York, "Slavery is a divine institution." "So is hell," exclaimed an old man in the crowd. [1862]

You complain that the Negroes are a base class. Who makes and keeps the Jew or the Negro base, who but you, who exclude them from the rights which others enjoy? [1867]

HENRY DAVID THOREAU: *from* Journal

As the least drop of wine tinges the whole goblet, so the least particle of truth colors our whole life. It is never isolated, or simply added as treasure to our stock. When any real progress is made, we unlearn and learn anew what we thought we knew before. [1837]

Not by constraint or severity shall you have access to true wisdom, but by abandonment, and childlike mirthfulness. If you would know aught, be gay before it. [1840]

It is the man determines what is said, not the words. If a mean person uses a wise maxim, I bethink me how it can be interpreted so as to commend itself to his meanness; but if a wise man makes a commonplace remark, I consider what wider construction it will admit. [1840]

Nothing goes by luck in composition. It allows of no tricks. The best you can write will be the best you are. Every sentence is the result of a long probation. The author's character is read from title-page to end. Of this he never corrects the proofs. We read it as the essential character of a handwriting without regard to the flourishes. And so of the rest of our actions; it runs as straight as a ruled line through them all, no matter how many curvets about it. Our whole life is taxed for the least thing well done: it is its net result. How we eat, drink, sleep, and use our desultory hours, now in these indifferent days, with no eye to observe and no occasion [to] excite us, determines our authority and capacity for the time to come. [1841]

What does education often do? It makes a straight-cut ditch of a free, meandering brook. [1850]

All perception of truth is the detection of an analogy; we reason from our hands to our head. [1851]

To set down such choice experiences that my own writings may inspire me and at last I may make wholes of parts. Certainly it is a distinct profession to rescue from oblivion and to fix the sentiments and thoughts which visit all men more or less generally, that the contemplation of the unfinished picture may suggest its harmonious completion. Associate reverently and as much as you can with your loftiest thoughts. Each thought that is welcomed and recorded is a nest egg, by the side of which more will be laid. Thoughts accidentally thrown together become a frame in which more may be developed and exhibited. Perhaps this is the main value of a habit of writing, of keeping a journal—that so we remember our best hours and stimulate ourselves. My thoughts are my company. They have a certain individuality and separate existence, aye, personality. Having by chance recorded a few disconnected thoughts and then brought them into juxtaposition, they suggest a whole new field in which it was possible to labor and to think. Thought begat thought. [1852]

It is pardonable when we spurn the proprieties, even the sanctities, making them stepping-stones to something higher. [1858]

There is always some accident in the best things, whether thoughts or expressions or deeds. The memorable thought, the happy expression, the admirable deed are only partly ours. The thought came to us because we were in a fit mood; also we were unconscious and did not know that we had said or done a good thing. We must walk consciously only part way toward our goal, and then leap in the dark to our success. What we do best or most perfectly is what we have most thoroughly learned by the longest practice, and at length it falls from us without our notice, as a leaf from a tree. It is the *last* time we shall do it—our unconscious leavings. [1859]

The expression "a *liberal* education" originally meant one worthy of freemen. Such is education simply in a true and broad sense. But education ordinarily so called—the learning of trades and professions which is designed to enable men to earn their living, or to fit them for a particular station in life—is *servile*. [1859]

KATHERINE MANSFIELD: *from* Journal[1]

March 21. Traveled with two brown women. One had a basket of chickweed on her arm, the other a basket of daffodils. They both carried babies bound, somehow, to them with a torn shawl. Neat spare women with combed and braided hair. They slung talk at each other across the bus. Then one woman took a piece of bread from her sagging pocket and gave it to the baby, the other opened her bodice and put the child to her breast. They sat and rocked their knees and darted their quick eyes over the bus load. Busy and indifferent they looked. [1914]

April 5. No bird sits a tree more proudly than a pigeon. It looks as though placed there by the Lord. The sky was silky blue and white, and the sun shone through the little leaves. But the children, pinched and crooked, made me feel a bit out of love with God. [1914]

1. The triple dots in these entries are Mansfield's; they do not indicate deletions.

I'm so hungry, simply empty, and seeing in my mind's eye just now a sirloin of beef, well browned with plenty of gravy and horse-radish sauce and baked potatoes, I nearly sobbed. There's nothing here to eat except omelettes and oranges and onions. It's a cold, sunny, windy day—the kind of day when you want a tremendous feed for lunch and an armchair in front of the fire to boa-constrict in afterwards. I feel sentimental about England now— English food, *decent* English *waste!* How much better than these thrifty French, whose flower gardens are nothing but potential salad bowls. There's not a leaf in France that you can't *faire une infusion avec*, not a blade that isn't *bon pour la cuisine.*[2] By God, I'd like to buy a pound of the best butter, put it on the window sill and watch it melt to spite 'em. They are a stingy, uncomfortable crew for all their lively scrapings. . . . For instance, their houses—what appalling furniture—and never one comfortable chair. If you want to talk the only possible thing to do is to go to bed. It's a case of either standing on your feet or lying in comfort under a puffed-up eiderdown. I quite understand the reason for what is called French moral laxity. You're simply forced into bed—no matter with whom. There's no other place for you. Supposing a *young* man comes to see about the electric light and will go on talking and pointing to the ceiling—or a friend drops in to tea and asks you if you believe in Absolute Evil. How can you give your mind to these things when you're sitting on four knobs and a square inch of cane? How much better to lie snug and *give yourself up to it.* [1916]

If only one could tell true love from false love as one can tell mushrooms from toadstools. With mushrooms it is so simple— you salt them well, put them aside and have patience. But with love, you have no sooner lighted on anything that bears even the remotest resemblance to it than you are perfectly certain it is not only a genuine specimen, but perhaps *the* only genuine mushroom ungathered. It takes a dreadful number of toadstools to make you realize that life is not one long mushroom. [1917]

The man in the room next to mine has the same complaint as I. When I wake in the night I hear him turning. And then he coughs. And I cough. And after a silence I cough. And he coughs again. This goes on for a long time. Until I feel we are like two roosters calling to each other at false dawn. From far-away hidden farms. [1918]

She is little and grey, with a black velvet band round her hair, false teeth, and skinny little hands coming out of frills like the frills on cutlets.

2. "make tea with" . . . "good for eating."

As I passed her room one morning I saw her "worked" brush-and-comb bag and her Common Prayerbook.

Also, when she goes to the "Ladies," for some obscure reason she wears a little shawl. . . .

At the dining table, smiling brightly: "This is the first time I have ever traveled alone, or stayed by myself in a Strange Hotel. But my husband does not mind. As it is so Very Quiet. Of course, if it were a Gay Place—" And she draws in her chin, and the bead chain rises and falls on her vanished bosom. [1918]

May 31. Work. Shall I be able to express one day my love of work—my desire to be a better writer—my longing to take greater pains. And the passion I feel. It takes the place of religion—it *is* my religion—of people—I create my people: of "life"—it *is* Life. The temptation is to kneel before it, to adore, to prostrate myself, to stay too long in a state of ecstasy before the idea of it. I must be more busy about my master's business. [1919]

December 15. When I had gone to bed I realized what it was that had caused me to "give way." It was the effort of being up, with a heart that won't work. Not my lungs at all. My despair simply disappeared—yes, simply. The weather was lovely. Every morning the sun came in and drew more squares of golden light on the wall, I looked round my bed on to a sky like silk. The day opened slowly, slowly like a flower, and it held the sun long, long before it slowly, slowly folded. Then my homesickness went. I not only didn't want to be in England, I began to love Italy, and the thought of it—the sun—even when it was too hot—always the sun—and a kind of *wholeness* which was good to bask in.

All these two years I have been obsessed by the fear of death. This grew and grew and grew gigantic, and this it was that made me cling so, I think. Ten days ago it went, I care no more. It leaves me perfectly cold. . . . Life either stays or goes.

I must put down here a dream. The first night I was in bed here, *i.e.* after my first day in bed, I went to sleep. And suddenly I felt my whole body *breaking up.* It broke up with a violent shock—an earthquake—and it broke like glass. A long terrible shiver, you understand—the spinal cord and the bones and every bit and particle quaking. It sounded in my ears a low, confused din, and there was a sense of floating greenish brilliance, like broken glass. When I woke I thought that there had been a violent earthquake. But all was still. It slowly dawned upon me—the conviction that in that dream I died. I shall go on living now—it may be for months, or for weeks or days or hours. Time is not. In that dream I died. The *spirit* that is the enemy of death and quakes so and is so tenacious was shaken out of me. I am (December 15,

1919) a dead woman, and *I don't care*. It might comfort others to know that one gives up caring; but they'd not believe any more than I did until it happened. And, oh, how strong was its hold upon me! How I *adored* life and *dreaded* death!

I'd like to write my books and spend some happy time with J. (not very much faith withal) and see L. in a sunny place and pick violets—all kinds of flowers. I'd like to do heaps of things, really. But I don't mind if I do not do them. . . . Honesty (why?) is the only thing one seems to prize beyond life, love, death, everything. It alone remaineth. O you who come after me, will you believe it? At the end *truth* is the only thing *worth having*: it's more thrilling than love, more joyful and more passionate. It simply *cannot* fail. All else fails. I, at any rate, give the remainder of my life to it and it alone. [1919]

What I feel is: She is never for one fraction of a second unconscious. If I sigh, I know that her head lifts. I know that those grave large eyes solemnly fix on me: Why did she sigh? If I turn she suggests a cushion or another rug. If I turn again, then it is my back. Might she try to rub it for me? There is no escape. All night: a faint rustle, the smallest cough, and her soft voice asks: "Did you speak? Can I do anything?" If I do absolutely nothing then she discovers my fatigue under my eyes. There is something profound and terrible in this eternal desire to establish contact. [1920]

August. A sudden idea of the relationship between "lovers." We are neither male nor female. We are a compound of both. I choose the male who will develop and expand the male in me; he chooses me to expand the female in him. Being made "whole." Yes, but that's a process. By love serve ye one another. . . . And why I choose *one* man for this rather than many is for safety. We bind ourselves within a ring and that ring is as it were a wall against the outside world. It is our refuge, our shelter. Here the tricks of life will not be played. Here is *safety* for us to grow.

Why, I talk like a child! . . [1921]

Tidied all my papers. Tore up and ruthlessly destroyed much. This is always a great satisfaction. Whenever I prepare for a journey I prepare as though for death. Should I never return, all is in order. This is what life has taught me. [1922]

DONALD PEARCE: *from* Journal of a War

December 28. We have been patroling the Rhine and guarding the bridge across it at Nijmegen continuously for so long now that they have begun to acquire a positive hold over our minds and imaginations. Our thoughts seem polarized by them, and turn to them like compasses to a magnet. This bridge is the only one over the Rhine left intact for a hundred miles, and we must keep it that way for our own no doubt imminent invasion of Germany. At the same time, if Jerry decides to counter-attack in force through here, and there has been a good deal of fresh evidence that he's getting ready to do just that, the bridge would become just as important to him. A really ambiguous prize. But he keeps sending explosives downstream at it. Damn strange. We shoot into the river at everything that moves, sometimes exploding mines tied to boards, or logs, or branches. Our engineers have run a huge net across the river about fifty yards upstream from the bridge to catch whatever floats downstream; but things get through or under the net somehow and that's what we shoot at. New rumor: German frogmen have been attempting to swim under the net; also, they have small one-man submarines in the river. Probably fairy lore.

But I was going to say—the bridge and river no longer appear ordinary to us, but seem to have acquired personalities, or to have been endowed with them. Sometimes the river seems less the watched one than the watcher, reflecting back our searchlight beams, and breaking the half-moon into a thousand yellow eyes as we steal along the edge on night patrols. The bridge's single span is unmistakably a high, arched eyebrow over an invisible eye peering across the Rhine. Everything we do here revolves around the bridge and river. As we go back for a rest or, as recently, for Christmas dinner, miles from the line, we cross the iced-flats that follow along the curving windswept dykes, and the great iron eyebrow is right behind us, lifting higher and higher above the mist, in a kind of inscrutable surmise, and as we return to those god-awful flats again, the eyebrow and invisible eye are at it again, staring back at us, watching the Rhine. Perhaps someone should put on a campaign to establish the ordinariness of this bridge and river, put up signs. But it would do no good, I tell myself, because this was Caesar's Rhine, Siegfried's Rhine, Wagner's Rhine, and you can't silence all that mystery. I hate it here.

Whipping the company jeep at top speed along a mile-long windswept section of one of the dykes that stretches between our company and the next is one of the low diversions we have worked out. It's completely exposed and utterly bare; so for two minutes you are an A-number one moving target. An insane game, but we play it. Once I heard the loud, flat snap of a bullet going past my head on one of these mad runs. We are, as they say, very definitely under observation.

* * *

March 3 [1945]. The city[1] was quite heavily defended. First, a steep, raw, anti-tank ditch completely girdling the city had to be negotiated, with continuous covering fire from both flanks. Then we ran into a connected system of crawl- and weapons-trenches forming a secondary ring about the interior. Our covering artillery fire was practically saturational; so he resisted only lightly till we were more than halfway in. There followed some sporadic street fighting and house clearing, nothing very spectacular, and the city fell to us shortly after daybreak; i.e., they simply pulled out and disappeared at about 4:00 A.M.

I had a couple of close ones during this show. On the way in, my platoon was evidently silhouetted against the night sky, and was fired on four times at a range of maybe 300 yards by an eighty-eight. (This is a notorious and vicious gun. The velocity of the shell is so high that you hear it pass or explode near you almost at the same instant that you hear the sound of its being fired. You really can't duck it. Also, it's an open-sights affair—you are aimed at particularly; not, as with mortars, aimed at only by approximation.) Anyway, they went past me about an arm's length above or in front of me, I don't know which. We hit the ditches. After pointing a few more, the gun was forced off by our return tank fire.

During the house-clearing phase, at one spot, I walked instead of ran from one house to another and got my helmet spun around on my head with a close shot. There was an extremely loud, flat "snap," like two hands clapped together hard beside my ear; that was all. Plus a crease in my helmet, which gave me immense prestige with the men all morning.

We had two tanks along with us, and their support made the assignment 100 per cent easier. At one point a handful of German snipers, who were perched in the attic of a three-story house at a bend in the main street, held up the battalion for over an hour. They were finally silenced by one of the tanks. In the half-dark, we circled around behind their house during the tank fire and cut off their escape route. Presently they came out through the back garden, dangling in front of them white cloths on long poles. It was vastly disconcerting. Instead of a squad of Nazi supermen in shiny boots, and packing Lugers, we were confronted by five of the most unkempt, stunted, scrubby specimens I have ever had the pleasure of capturing. Two of them couldn't have been more than

1. Udem, in The Netherlands.

fourteen on their next birthday. Possibly they were on some kind of dope; at least they acted that way, a little dazed, grinning, and rather immune to voice control. One of them had nearly shot me a few hours earlier in the dark before dawn. At the time, I remember, I had thought it wasn't any more than I had expected; but later on, seeing them, I felt that it would have been an unfortunate end to my life. I am obviously getting choosy. What I mean is that I would simply like to be well killed, if killed I am to be. I came to the conclusion that they were from the bottom of Germany's recruiting barrel.

The men in the platoon seemed to think so too, for I caught them in the middle of a queer performance. They had lined the five of them up against a schoolhouse wall and were pretending, quite ceremoniously, that they were going to shoot them. The prisoners certainly believed they were about to be shot; three of them had their hands on their heads and their faces turned to the wall, as for execution; the other two were pleading desperately with three or four of our men. I was astonished to find my best corporal in the thick of this business. I stopped it, of course. Not that they would have carried out the execution; I feel sure of that.

We passed through the town and seized a road-and-rail junction about 800 yards past the outskirts and dug in under moderate shelling. A child would know that that junction would become a hot target—which it very shortly did. We sat it out. He sent several salvos of rockets in on us. These you always hear coming, if it's any comfort. The first salvo was the best, but there was time for my sergeant and me to flatten out in a shallow ditch alongside the track. One rocket hit about four or five feet from us, practically shattering my hearing; it chewed up a couple of railway ties, took two or three chunks out of the rails, and turned me over from my stomach to my back. The blast stung my whole left side. Nothing more really close happened there all night.

Next day, I went back to have a look at Udem. In daylight it seemed in worse condition than I remembered it from the night before. Enemy shelling accounted for much of the destruction; but looters, busy rooting around before daybreak, accounted for some too. The houses that had not been shelled were practically turned inside out by our troops. I came across one soldier telling an admiring group about his morning exploits: "First I took a hammer and smashed over 100 plates, and the cups along with them. Then I took an ax to the china cabinets and buffets. Next I smashed all the furniture and pulled the stuffing out of the big chairs. Then I took the hammer again and smashed all the elements on two electric stoves and broke the enamel off the stove fronts and sides. Then I put a grenade in the big piano, and after that I poured a jar of molasses into it. I broke all the French doors and all the doors with mirrors in them and threw the lamps out into the street. I was so mad."

I turned him over to the Provost Corps in the afternoon.

Udem had a large church made of red stone with high twin towers. German artillery scouts had stationed themselves in these towers in order to direct fire onto our positions five miles away. So the church had to be "neutralized," as they say. We engaged it with 17-pounders for about an hour, I believe successfully. Anyway, I went in to see what we had done. It was full of gaping holes; the stone pillars had even been shot off far within the building. The only unharmed thing I saw was the font. The walls had had blue and gold paintings of religious scenes extending all around the interior; these were mostly peeled or ripped off. One painting was of the Descent from the Cross. It had come loose from its frame and seemed heading for a nosedive; the pale belly of Christ had a group of machine-gun bullets through it. The Germans had made a brief stand at the church and had obviously used it as a temporary strongpoint. As I left, engineers were already laying dynamite charges at critical points along the foundations, with the intention of using the stones as rubble for roads, almost the only reasonable use left for it.

On the way back, I met a number of civilians carrying bundles. Most of them were covered with mud from head to foot. They were staggering along rather than walking, and started every time a gun went off far away or close up. One tall thin man was leading two small children, one by each hand. The children were around his back. The man limped; I saw that he was weeping. My limited German enabled me to discover that he was wounded in a couple of places, that his wife had been killed by shrapnel in the morning, and that he didn't know what to do with his tiny children who were wet, cold, and hungry. I took them down into our cellar where the stretcher bearer dressed his wounds and evacuated him. I offered the two children food—chocolate, bread and jam, biscuits. They only tightened their lips and refused. So I tried a sort of game with the names of the articles of furniture in the cellar, deliberately making silly mistakes, and after a while they laughed at my stupidity. I kept this up, and before long they gobbled whatever I put in front of them. I would like to have done more; but instead I turned them over to the Civil Affairs people, not without complicated feelings of concern and regret. I will never know what happened to them.

Kept rummaging around in the town. Went to the place where I was nearly shot, stood on the exact spot, in fact, and determined the window at the end of the street where the shots had come from. An impulse sent me inside the house itself, where I climbed to the upper room. The machine gun was there on its heavy mounting, still pointing out the window and down the street. I sat behind it and took aim on the doorway I had disappeared into at the moment I was fired on, and waited for someone to pass the spot just to see how I must have looked through his sights. No one came and I got tired of the melodrama and went back to our forward positions.

* * *

March 4. When will it all end? The idiocy and the tension, the dying of young men, the destruction of homes, of cities, starvation, exhaustion, disease, children parentless and lost, cages full of shivering, staring prisoners, long lines of hopeless civilians plodding through mud, the endless pounding of the battle line. I can scarcely remember what it is like to be where explosions are not going off around me, some hostile, some friendly, all horrible; an exploding shell is a terrible sound. What keeps this war going, now that its end is so clear? What do the Germans think of us, and we of them? I do not think we think of them at all, or much. Do they think of us? I can think of their weapons, their shells, their machine guns, but not of the men behind them. I do not feel as if I were fighting against men, but against machines. I need to go up in an airplane and actually see German transport hauling guns and ammunition, see their actual armies; for everything that happens merely comes from a vague beyond, and I cannot visualize the people who are fighting against me. The prisoners that come over hills with their hands up, or who come out of houses with white cloths waving—they have no relation, almost, to anything for me. I can't connect them with the guns they have just laid down, it seems like forcing something to do so. It is becoming hard for me not to feel sometimes that both sides are the common victims of a common terror, that everybody's guns are against everybody ultimately.

These are times when I feel that every bit of fighting is defensive. Self defense. If a machine-gun nest is attacked and wiped out by us, by my own platoon, I do not feel very aggressive, as if I had attacked somebody. It is always that I have defended myself against something that was attacking me. And how often I have thought that there might be a Rilke out there in a German pill box. If I could only see them, as in battles long ago, at close range, before engaging them. In our wars, the warring sides are getting farther and farther apart and war is getting more and more meaningless for the field warriors, and more meaningful for the domestic warriors in factories and homes. Will there come a time when hundreds of miles separate the warring fronts? When long-range weapons and the ghastly impersonality of air attacks are the means of war? It is already a very impersonal thing. When a soldier is killed or wounded his buddies, shaking their heads, merely say, "Poor old Joe. He just got it. Just as he was going up that hill, he got it." As if to imply that he was merely in the wrong place at the wrong time, and that life and death are only matters of luck and do not depend on the calculations of human beings at the other end of an S.P. gun. When we were in our static positions around Wyler Meer and Nijmegen, the enemy became real to me for the first time. I watched him for weeks, saw him dig, run, hide, fire, walk. And when I went on patrols into his territory, there was meaning in that, too, for I knew where he was, I knew his habits. So that while we were probing the cuticle of the enemy, so to speak, he was real; but now when we are ripping into his body, he has disappeared and has turned into something read about in the papers. But the guns remain, manned by soldiers who are so meaningless to us that when they shoot a fellow, all we can say is, "He got it."

Once I could say you cannot be disgusted with the war, because it is too big for disgust, that disgust is too shallow an emotion for something involving millions of people. But I am disgusted now, and I know what I am saying. Once I used to get quite a thrill out of seeing a city destroyed and left an ash heap from end to end. It gave me a vicarious sense of power. I felt the romantic and histrionic emotion produced by seeing "retribution" done; and an aesthetic emotion produced by beholding ruins; and the childish emotion that comes from destroying man-made things. But it is not that way any more. All I experience is revulsion every time a fresh city is taken on. I am no longer capable of thinking that the systematic destruction of a city is a wonderful or even a difficult thing, though some seem to think it even a heroic thing. Well, how is it done? Dozens upon dozens of gun crews stationed some two or three miles away from the city simply place shell after shell into hundreds of guns and fire away for a few hours—the simplest and most elementary physical and mental work—and then presently the firing stops, the city has been demolished, has become an ash heap, and great praise is bestowed on the army for the capture of a new city.

I am not suggesting that cities shouldn't be captured in this way; actually it saves lives. But it fills me with disgust because it is all so abysmally foolish, so lunatic. It has not the dramatic elements of mere barbarism about it; it is straight scientific debauchery. A destroyed city is a terrible sight. How can anyone record it?—the million smashed things, the absolutely innumerable tiny tragedies, the crushed life-works, the jagged homes, army tanks parked in living rooms—who could tell of these things I don't know; they are too numerous to mention, too awful in their meanings. Perhaps everyone should be required to spend a couple of hours examining a single smashed home, looking at the fragmentation of every little thing, especially the tiniest things from kitchen to attic, if he could find an attic; be required, in fact, to list the ruined contents of just one home; something would be served, a little sobriety perhaps honored.

It is disgusting (that it should be necessary, is what galls me to the bones) that a towering cathedral, built by ages of care and effort, a sweet labor of centuries, should be shot down by laughing artillerymen, mere boys, because somebody with a machine gun is hiding in a belfry tower. When I see such a building, damaged perhaps beyond repair after one of these "operations," I know only disgust. The matter of sides in this war temporarily becomes irrelevant, especially if someone at my elbow says, like a conquering hero: "Well, we sure did a job on the old church, eh?"

A job has been done on Europe, on the world, and the resulting trauma will be generations long in its effects. It is not just the shock of widespread destruction, of whole cities destroyed, nor the shock which the defeated and the homeless must have suffered, that I am thinking of: it is even more the conqueror's trauma, the habit of violence, the explosion of values, the distortion of relations, the ascending significance of the purely material, the sense of power, and the pride of strength. These things will afflict the victors as profoundly and for quite as long a time as the other things will afflict the victims; and of the two I am not sure that a crass superiority complex is the more desirable. Perhaps I underestimate our ability to return to normal again.

EDWARD WESTON: *from* The Daybooks[1]

March 20 [1927] * * * The shells I photographed were so marvellous one could not do other than something of interest. What I did may be only a beginning—but I like one negative especially. I took a proof of the legs recently done of Bertha, which Miss Shore[2] was enthusiastic over.

April 1. Nudes of ———— again. Made two negatives,—variation on one conception.

I am stimulated to work with the nude body, because of the infinite combinations of lines which are presented with every move.

1. The "daybooks" are the journal of Edward Weston, one of America's great photographers. The first published volume is entitled *The Daybooks: Mexico, 1923–1927;* the second, from which the present excerpts are drawn, *The Daybooks: California,* covers the years 1927–1934. When publication was proposed, Weston went through the journals with a razor, cutting out names and comments; hence annotation cannot be complete. Both volumes were edited by Nancy Newhall.

2. Henrietta Shore, a painter, and friend of Weston's.

And now after seeing the shells of Henrietta Shore, a new field has been presented.

* * *

April 24. What have I, that bring these many women to offer themselves to me? I do not go out of my way seeking them,—I am not a stalwart virile male, exuding sex, nor am I the romantic, mooning poet type some love, nor the dashing Don Juan bent on conquest. Now it is B.

April 28. Every day finds me working, or at least thinking of work for myself,—and with more enthusiasm, surety and success than ever before. Another shell negative,—another beginning of something, from yesterday.

One of these two new shells when stood on end, is like a magnolia blossom unfolding. The difficulty has been to make it balance on end and not cut off that important end, nor show an irrelevant base. I may have solved the problem by using another shell for the chalice, but I had the Devil's own time trying to balance those two shells together. In the first negative, they slipped just a hair's breadth,—and after a three hour exposure! The second attempt is technically good.

And then the dancing nudes of B.

I feel that I have a number of exceedingly well seen negatives,— several which I am sure will live among my best.

B. left me a record of one of Chopin's *Preludes* played by Casals.[3] Starting a tender, plaintive melody, it suddenly breaks, quite without warning into thundering depths, and then in a flash rises to electrifying heights, which makes my scalp tingle.

* * *

[*Undated*] . . . I think the Chambered Nautilus has one of the most exquisite forms, to say nothing of color and texture, in nature.

I was awakened to shells by the painting of Henry.[4] I never saw a Chambered Nautilus before. If I had, my response would have been immediate! If I merely copy Henry's expression, my work will not live. If I am stimulated and work with real ecstasy it will live.

Henry's influence, or stimulation, I see not just in shell subject matter, it is in all my late work,—in the bananas and the nudes. I feel it not as an extraneous garnish but as a freshened tide swelling from within my self.

* * *

Monday morning. I worked all Sunday with the shells,—literally all day. Only three negatives made and two of them were done as records of movement to repeat again when I can find suitable backgrounds. I wore myself out trying every conceivable texture and

---

3. Pablo Casals, the cellist.   4. I.e., Henrietta Shore.

tone for grounds: Glass, tin, cardboard,—wool, velvet, even my rubber rain coat! I did not need to make these records for memory's sake,—no, they were safely recorded there. I did wish to study the tin which was perfect with the lens open; but stopped down I could not see sufficiently to tell, but was positive the surface would come into focus and show a net work of scratches—it did. My first photograph of the Chambered Nautilus done at Henry's was perfect all but the too black ground: yesterday the only available texture was white. Again I recorded to study at leisure the contrast. The feeling of course has been quite changed,—the luminosity of the shell seen against black, gone; but the new negative has a delicate beauty of its own. I had heart failure several times yesterday when the shells, balanced together, slipped. I must buy a Nautilus, for to break Henry's would be tragic.

Thursday, May 12. B. danced for me! This time I was spectator, —not photographer. A definite feeling is not always easy to put down in definite words, but I know I was privileged to have her dance for me,—to me. The work I do today must be finer than that of yesterday because of B. dancing: she has added to my creative strength. B. danced nude. What a pity all dancing cannot be in the nude: or no!—some dances may well be covered for illusion's sake — — —

I have my work room barricaded,—for there, are two shells delicately balanced together awaiting the afternoon light. My first version of the combination was done Sunday: Monday a slight turn of one shell, and I gained strength: Wednesday the second proof decided me to try a lighter ground with the same arrangement,— but desiring to repeat, I again saw more clearly.

Wednesday, after developing. I thought—before putting away the shells I will see what a still lighter ground does, in fact a white ground. Seeing, I knew at once that now I had what I was fighting for! But the hour was late, the light failing, I could not expose another film. So there stands my camera focussed, trained like a gun, commanding the shells not to move a hair's breadth. And death to the person who jars out of place what I know shall be a *very important* negative.

* * *

May 13. After watching my shell arrangement all day,—repeatedly warning Brett[5] to walk lightly,—even keeping the windows shut for fear of a slight breeze, though the day was hot,—a cardboard background slipped, fell onto the shells, and completely disarranged them. I was literally on the verge of tears from disappointment, knowing the impossibility of repeating anything absolutely.

5. Weston's second son.

But now I see the Gods meant well. I took off my shirt, for the room was like an oven, and half indifferently, half rebelliously, retired under the focussing cloth. After twenty minutes' struggle in which I tried to register my previous negative over the ground glass image,—almost but not quite succeeding, I suddenly realized that the slight change was an improvement! I shall remember the making of this negative.

In the morning I enlarged the first five positives of B.—dancing nudes. They appear to advantage blown up. I am pleased with my day's work.

Saturday, May 14. I must do the shells again! That is the last combination. If I did not have the third proof to compare I would be very happy with the last: in some ways it is better, but one important upright line is not quite as fine. Henry agrees, though she thinks I have done a very important negative. Also she responded fully to six of my last dancing nudes. Says they are among the finest photographs I have ever done.

Four of the six I shall enlarge: two I shall try to improve by doing the impossible—repeating.

* * *

Tuesday, May 17. I could not be at peace until I had made the fifth attempt to improve the shell arrangement by a fifth negative. The result has been that I have printed my fourth negative, and am quite pleased. Also printed two former shell negatives, worthy recording if not so important. The fig tree done at Palm Springs is at last printed and the first of the dancing nudes: the former comes close to being fine,—the latter is fine,—a kneeling figure cut at the shoulder, but kneeling does not mean it is passive,—it is dancing quite as intensely as if she were on her toes! I am in love with this nude — — —

Late in the afternoon I took out the Chambered Nautilus thinking to improve on the first negatives: instead there came to me a new group over which I am absolutely enthusiastic! It was too late for an exposure so I must be patient until this afternoon. I find myself, every so often, looking at my ground glass as though the unrecorded image might escape me! I can see that I am to have days of struggle with the later group also. There are so many slight variations I can make. The last negative is better in most ways,—just one line I'm not so sure of. Also the background might be varied. But I shall enjoy the struggle!

* * *

Wednesday, June 15. Twice I have repeated the shell group,—the latest, which is one of the strongest, but blurred from slight movement. Monday I got a perfect negative and an improved arrangement: but Chandler[6] was using my cardboard backgrounds to press flowers between, so finding nothing else, I used a square of black velvet, which I knew was too black,—and proved so. Why I went ahead I don't know! Yesterday, I tried again: result, movement! The exposure was 4½ hours, so to repeat was no joy, with all the preoccupation of keeping quiet children and cats,—but I went ahead and await development.

Saturday, June 18. The shells again moved! It must be the heavy trucks that pass jar the building ever so slightly. Anyway I have quit trying: I can afford no more film.

The money question is disturbing me mentally.

* * *

Sunday morn. June 26. I have had very bad luck: Chandler lost a five dollar bill, just given him for groceries. This was part of ten dollars received from a print sale,—one of the first nudes of B. Five dollars!—Enough for *me* to live on a week!

I shall work with new shells to forget this tragedy! Three shells and a piece of coral came as a present: fine material for much thought. * * *

July 7—"Last evening Orozco was here. I got out the shell prints. Well, in a few words, he liked them better than all your collection put together. Of one he said, 'This suggests much more the "Hand of God" than the hand Rodin made.' It is the one that has made everybody, including myself, think of the sexual act."[7]

From the above quotations it will be seen that I have created a definite impression, but from an angle which surprised me!

Why were all these persons so profoundly affected on the physical side?

For I can say with absolute honesty that not once while working with the shells did I have any physical reaction to them; nor did I try to record erotic symbolism. I am not sick and I was never so free from sexual suppression,—which if I had, might easily enter into my work, *as it does* in Henry's painting.

I am not blind to the sensuous quality in shells, with which they combine the deepest spiritual significance: indeed it is this very combination of the physical and spiritual in a shell like the Chambered Nautilus, which makes it such an important abstract of life.

No! I had no physical thoughts,—never have. I worked with clearer vision of sheer aesthetic form. I knew that I was recording from within, my feeling for life as I never had before. Or better, when the negatives were actually developed, I realized what I felt,

---

6. Weston's eldest son.
7. Weston is quoting from a letter written him by Tina Modotti—friend, pupil, and model of his in Mexico—in reaction to the shell photographs. José Clemente Orozco was an important Mexican painter, Auguste Rodin the French sculptor.

—for when I worked, I was never more unconscious of what I was doing.

No! The Shells are too much a sublimation of all my work and life to be pigeonholed. Others must get from them what they bring to them: evidently they do!

* * *

Saturday, March 8 [1930]. Yesterday I made photographic history: for I have every reason and belief that two negatives of kelp done in the morning will someday be sought as examples of my finest expression and understanding. Another is almost as good, and yet another might be considered a very strong example of a more usual viewpoint: this latter several steps beyond the salon type of photograph. But my two best,—they are years beyond.

I had found the kelp the evening before, almost at the foot of Ocean Avenue, washed there by the recent storm, the heavy sea. I knew it would not stay put, perhaps not even the night, so early next morning I walked down to see what the tides had done: and there it lay unchanged, twisted, tangled, interwoven, a chaos of convulsed rhythms, from which I selected a square foot, organized the apparently complex maze, and presented it, a powerful integration. This was done of course with no manual arrangement,—the selection was entirely my viewpoint as seen through the camera. I get a greater joy from finding things in Nature, already composed, than I do from my finest personal arrangements. After all, selection is another way of arranging: to move the camera an eighth of an inch is quite as subtle as moving likewise a pepper.

These kelp negatives are as strong as any of my rocks: indeed I think they are stronger. A few of my rock details have lace-like delicacy. How little subject matter counts in the ultimate reaction!

* * *

July 10. * * * Herb Klein who bought my favorite kelp, wrote, —"interweaving like a Bach fugue, yet keeping its dynamic tension through the complexity."

Whenever I can feel a Bach fugue in my work I know I have arrived.

July 19. * * * Since my last entry, much has happened. I have worked with summer squash,—one afternoon, making some very beautiful and strong negatives: the squash nearly white in the sun, a grey ground, and intense black shadow,—the simple massing of the three values, most satisfying.

And I have worked with peppers again, surprising myself! Sonya[8] brought several home, and I could not resist, though I thought to have finished with peppers. But peppers never repeat themselves:

8. Sonia Noskowiak, a student and partner of Weston's.

shells, bananas, melons, so many forms, are not inclined to experiment,—not so the pepper, always excitingly individual. So I have three new negatives, and two more under way. One of these, and they are already printed along with the squash, is extraordinarily fine and different. It is the most exquisite one I have done; the former negatives [were] usually powerful. This slender, delicate pepper, I placed on a green-glazed oval dish,—it might be a strange tropical plant in itself, spiraling up from the roots, partly unfolded at the top like a fern. It has a mystic significance.

* * *

August 1. * * * The glorious new pepper Sonya brought me has kept me keyed up all week and caused me to expose eight negatives: —I'm not satisfied yet! These eight were all from the same viewpoint: rare for me to go through this. I started out with an underexposure—by the time I had developed the light had failed, and though I tripled my time again I undertimed! Again I tried, desperately determined to get it because I could ill afford the time. Giving an exposure of 50 minutes at 5:00 I timed correctly, but during exposure the fire siren shrieked, and promptly the fire truck roared by followed by every car in town: the old porch trembled, my wobbly old camera wobbled, the pepper shimmied, and I developed a moved negative. Next morning I went at it again: interruptions came, afternoon came, light weak, prolonged exposures necessary,— result, one negative possible, but possible also to improve upon it.

I tried the light from the opposite side in the next morning light, —brilliant sun through muslin. Better! A reason for my failures. Three negatives made, on a new angle so different as to be another pepper. And more failures, this time sheer thoughtlessness: a background of picture backing was placed too close and came into focus when stopped down which I could not see but should have realized, the corrugations plainly show and spoil the feeling. The one exposure from a new angle was perfect. So I have made eight negatives from the same angle and yet must go on. Today it is foggy and I am faced with an entirely new approach.

All this work has been done between moments of greeting tourists, printing, mounting, etc. Small wonder I have failed.

But the pepper is well worth all time, money, effort. If peppers would not wither, I certainly would not have attempted this one when so preoccupied. I must get this one today: it is beginning to show the strain and tonight should grace a salad. It has been suggested that I am a cannibal to eat my models after a masterpiece. But I rather like the idea that they become a part of me, enrich my blood as well as my vision. Last night we finished my now famous squash, and had several of my bananas in a salad.

* * *

August 3. Sonya * * * keeps tempting me with new peppers! Two more have been added to my collection. While experimenting with one of these, which was so small that I used my 21 cm. Zeiss to fill the 8 x 10 size, I tried putting it in a tin funnel for background. It was a bright idea, a perfect relief for the pepper and adding reflected light to important contours. I still had the pepper which caused me a week's work, I had decided I could go no further with it, yet something kept me from taking it to the kitchen, the end of all good peppers. I placed it in the funnel, focussed with the Zeiss, and, knowing just the viewpoint, recognizing a perfect light, made an exposure of six minutes, with but a few moments' preliminary work,—the real preliminary was done in hours passed. I have a great negative,—by far the best!

August 4. * * * In the late afternoon I made three more peppers in funnel, all with the Zeiss [lens], all very close, filling entire plate. The one great objection to the Zeiss is that I cannot stop down as far as I am used to.

* * *

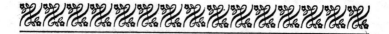

On Language

WILLIAM MARCH
The Unspeakable Words

There were words in the Brett language considered so corrupting in their effect on others that if anyone wrote them or was heard to speak them aloud, he was fined and thrown into prison. The King of the Bretts was of the opinion that the words were of no importance one way or the other, and besides, everybody in the country knew them anyway; but his advisers disagreed, and at last, to determine who was right, a committee was appointed to examine the people separately.

At length everyone in the kingdom had been examined, and found to know the words quite well, without the slightest damage to themselves. There was then left only one little girl, a five-year-old who lived in the mountains with her deaf and dumb parents. The committee hoped that this little girl, at least, had never heard the corrupting words, and on the morning they visited her, they said solemnly: "Do you know the meaning of *poost, gist, duss, feng?*"

The little girl admitted that she did not, and then, smiling happily, she said, "Oh, you must mean *feek, kusk, dalu,* and *liben!*"

Those who don't know the words must make them up for themselves.

RALPH WALDO EMERSON
The Language of the Street

The language of the street is always strong. What can describe the folly and emptiness of scolding like the word *jawing?* I feel too the force of the double negative, though clean contrary to our grammar rules. And I confess to some pleasure from the stinging rhetoric of a rattling oath in the mouths of truckmen and teamsters. How laconic and brisk it is by the side of a page of the *North American Review*. Cut these words and they would bleed; they are vascular and alive; they walk and run. Moreover they who speak them have this elegancy, that they do not trip in their speech. It is a shower of bullets, whilst Cambridge men and Yale men correct themselves and begin again at every half sentence.

WILLIAM G. MOULTON
Meaning[1]

* * * Philosophers have struggled with the concept "meaning" for centuries, and even today there is not full agreement as to what "meaning" really means. And yet * * * we simply *must* discuss this topic, because the very essence of language is the correlation between sound on the one hand and meaning on the other. Our learning of meaning begins when we are babies, and adults start waving objects in front of our faces and making noises at the same time ("Dolly! Dolly! See the dolly!"), hoping that we will get the connection between sound and meaning and thereby learn a bit of language. We learn more meaning (grammatical meaning this time) as we catch on to the fact that our language says "Mama loves baby" vs. "Baby loves Mama." We continue learning meaning by making use of the marvelous redundancy which our language contains—allowing us to learn most of the words we know *not* by having objects waved in our faces, *not* by having explanations given to us, and *not* by looking words up in a dictionary, but by observing (mostly quite unconsciously) the contexts in which the words occur. Though we learn the basic structure of our language by the time we are five or six, we continue learning new words—and new meanings —all our lives.

When most of us think of "meaning," we think primarily of the way we use words as labels for things in the world about us. "Meaning" here lies in our association of the sound of a word with the object which it denotes. The compulsion to use words as labels in this way is remarkably strong in us. When someone shows us a flower which we do not know, the first thing we ask is what its "name" is—even though we may not be particularly interested in flowers and never really intend to use the name again. It somehow bothers us to have a bit of the world called to our attention and not to have a label which we can attach to it. Scientists behave in just the same way: as soon as they have identified some new item in

1. Chapter 7 of *A Linguistic Guide to Language Learning*, 1970.

their science, they either make up a name for it themselves or else run to a colleague in the Classics Department and ask him to suggest a proper Greek or Latin term.

Much of meaning also lies within the grammar of our language. Words strung along in a row cannot produce a meaningful message unless they are arranged in one of the ways provided for by the grammar of our language. We may recall again how much of *Jabberwocky* we were able to understand, despite the fact that so many of the words denoted nothing at all. (As Alice said: "Somehow it seems to fill my head with ideas—only I don't exactly know what they are!") We may also recall that the so-called "function words"[2] often carry little more than grammatical meaning. Yet they are from one point of view the most important words of all and the ones which we must try to learn right from the start.

Still another aspect of "meaning" lies within us, the individual speakers of the language. We can call one and the same object the "Evening Star" at seven o'clock in the evening but the "Morning Star" twelve hours later, and not be bothered by the fact that the object denoted is in each case the same. As we grow up, our ideas as to the "meaning" of such words as *truth* and *beauty*, or *heat* and *light*, may change drastically, even though the labels themselves remain the same.

In the following paragraphs we shall discuss these three aspects of meaning * * * : (1) meaning and things, often called "denotative meaning"; (2) meaning and grammar, often called "grammatical meaning"; and (3) meaning and people, often called "connotative meaning."

Meaning and Things

Perhaps the most common misconception about meaning is the belief that the world in which we live consists of a certain number of "things," and that each language simply attaches to these things its own particular labels. What is in English a *house* is in French a *maison*, in Spanish a *casa*, in German a *Haus*, in Russian a *dom*, in Ilocano[3] a *balay*, etc. It is hard to know where this idea originated. Perhaps the first statement of it is that in the Book of Genesis, where God "called the light Day, . . . the darkness . . . Night, . . . the firmament Heaven, . . . the dry land Earth, . . . the gathering together of the waters . . . Seas" (Genesis 1:5-10), and where "Adam gave names to all cattle, and to the fowl of the air, and to every beast of the field" (Genesis 2:20). If the world really *did* consist of a specific number of objects to which, after Babel, each language attached its own particular linguistic symbols, then learning a

2. Prepositions and conjunctions.   tribe of the Philippines.
3. Malay language of the Ilocanos

foreign language would consist largely of learning new labels for old things. * * * However, this is clearly *not* the way in which languages work. Even if someone *could* tell us how many colors there are in the spectrum, each language would go on looking at the spectrum in its own particular way.

Perhaps the most fundamental fact which we should realize about words and their denotative meanings is that the connection between the two is arbitrary, and that it is arbitrary in two different respects. First of all, even if we suppose that there exists in the world some such necessary entity as "dog," it is totally arbitrary that this should be symbolized by the sounds *dog* in English, *chien* in French, *perro* in Spanish, *cane* in Italian, *Hund* in German, *sobáka* in Russian, and so on. If we ask "why" any one of these languages uses its particular word, we can give an explanation of sorts: French says *chien* and Italian says *cane* because the Romans said (in the accusative) *canem*, and these are the modern French and Italian developments of this 2500-year-old form. In like manner, we could try to find older forms of the word for dog in the other languages. This "explains" the modern forms in a certain sense; but in effect it simply pushes the real explanation back some twenty centuries or more in time since now we must again ask: why did the Romans call a dog (in the accusative) a *canem*? Perhaps it would be more accurate, however, to say that such historical "explanations" really circumvent the question we are asking. I myself call a dog a *dog* not because I know anything about the history of this form, but simply because everybody else in my language calls a dog a *dog*. If, when I was learning English, everybody had called it a *wug*, I would have used this set of noises instead. Just which set of noises we use in a language is quite arbitrary; the only important thing is that we all use the *same* set of noises, since otherwise the language will not work.

For whatever reason, many people find it very difficult to accept the notion that there is no logical connection between the sound of a word and the thing it refers to. Since the evidence seems to be irrefutable, they usually swallow hard and try to accept it. But then they inevitably come up with one apparent exception. How about onomatopoetic words, such as *bowwow* for the noise which a dog makes when he barks? Surely the connection here is not arbitrary! Indeed it is not (entirely) arbitrary. This is why we recognize a special class of onomatopoetic words in the first place—precisely because in this respect such words are abnormal. The very fact that we set up such a special class shows clearly that, in the normal case, the connection between sound and meaning *is* totally arbitrary. Even in the case of onomatopoetic words the connection is not as "logical" as we usually think it is. Instead of *bowwow*, a Japanese dog says *wan-wan* ("wong-wong")—and this is hardly what we, as speakers of English, would have expected from the onomatopoetic theory of a "natural" connection between sound and meaning. Here, too, there is much more arbitrariness than we might have expected. The foreign-language learner can amuse and instruct himself by finding out some of the onomatopoetic words in the language he is learning.

The second respect in which the connection between a word and its meaning is arbitrary concerns the area of reality to which it refers. It is quite arbitrary that such a bit of reality should be referred to by one word rather than by two or more—or, indeed, that it should be referred to by any word at all. Since we have in English such terms as *ear lobe*, *cheek*, *jowls*, and the like, why don't we have any name for that bit of skin which connects the base of the thumb and the base of the forefinger? Since we have a name for a closed hand (a *fist*), why don't we have any name for an open hand? If a *lap* is the area formed when we bend our legs more or less at right angles to our trunk, why don't we have a name for the area formed when we bend our forearms more or less at right angles to our trunk—the area we use when we bring in some logs of wood for the fire? By and large it seems that any language has words for those items in the culture which are important to its speakers. The classic example always cited is Eskimo, with its half a dozen or more words for different types of snow. An example closer to home is the language of carpenters. Anyone who has ever had a house built, and has talked with the carpenters as it went up, will have heard all sorts of unfamiliar labels which he himself never knew before and never felt a need for—because he is not a carpenter. Whenever a need for new words *does* arise, every language seems to be able to create them—either by borrowing them from some other language (*sputnik*) or by making them out of native materials (*spacesuit*) or foreign materials (*astronaut*). We even have words for things which have never existed in the past and will never exist in the future, such as *unicorn* and *dragon*.

As one example of the arbitrary way in which we combine bits and pieces of reality into units by means of the words which we attach to them, consider the following example from English. We group together a vast array of different objects into a single semantic unit through the label *stool*. The objects may be of wood or of metal, have three or four legs, and be short or tall, plain or upholstered, and of any color at all. As soon as we add a back, however, we get a different semantic unit: a *chair*. And as soon as we widen the object so that two or more people can sit on it, we get still another semantic unit: a *bench*. If to a chair we add upholstery, its semantic allegiance does not change: it is still a *chair*. But if to a bench we add upholstery, it becomes quite a different semantic unit: a *sofa*. All of this is highly arbitrary, and we cannot expect that any other language—through its words—will group things together in just this same way.

Some idea of the way different languages structure the world about us through the labels they attach to it can be gained by considering how a number of them use their demonstratives to structure the continuum of space. French lumps all of space into its single demonstrative *ce: ce livre* 'this/that book.' (If a further structuring of space is desired, it has to be accomplished by adding the enclitics *-ci* 'here' and *'là* 'there': *ce livre-ci, ce livre-là*.) English divides all of space into just two segments: *this book* (near the speaker), *that book* (somewhere else). Russian makes a similar division: *éta kn'íga, tá kn'íga*; but *éta* covers a larger amount of space than English *this*, and *tá* covers a correspondingly smaller amount than English *that*. Spanish carves space into three areas: *este libro* (near the speaker), *ese libro* (near the listener), *aquel libro* (elsewhere). (This is true, at least, of space in Spain; but in Spanish America *ese* generally usurps the area of *aquel*.) Ilocano structures space (plus a bit of time) into no less than five different segments: *tuy libru* (near the speaker), *ta libru* (near the listener), *dyay libru* (away from both), *tay libru* (out of sight), and *di libru* (no longer existing).

In talking about space, or the color spectrum, one might object that we are dealing in each case with a continuum, so that no two languages could even be expected to carve it up in just the same way. Let us therefore look at an area of reality which has a precise and verifiable structure: family relationships. In the normal case it is easy to determine with complete exactitude whether one man is or is not another man's father, son, uncle, cousin, nephew, etc. Precisely because this area of reality is so easy to handle, it has long been a favorite subject of study by anthropologists: they have been interested in the light which kinship terms can throw on patterns of family relationship. It has not only been extensively investigated; it has become a classic example of how *differently* various languages, through the words they use, carve up one and the same area of reality. We think of a *brother* as any male child by the same parents as ours; many languages have no word for this, but only for *older brother* or *younger brother*. Though we have words combining male and female in direct line of descent one generation above us (*parent*) and one generation below us (*child*), in our own generation we have only the rare word *sibling* and usually use instead of this the words *brother* and *sister*, which then require us to specify sex. We again insist on specifying sex in the case of 'child of my aunt and uncle,' namely *nephew* vs. *niece*; but if we want to state such a person's relationship to ourselves, we can *not* specify sex but can only say *cousin*. Dutch does the opposite: one and the same word for *nephew/niece* and *cousin*, though sex must be specified:

neef 'nephew, male cousin,' *nicht* 'niece, female cousin.' We have the words *aunt* and *uncle,* but we have no word to distinguish whether they are brother/sister of our father or brother/sister of our mother; and we have no single term which combines both sexes (parallel to *child, parent*). Furthermore, we commonly use *aunt* and *uncle* to refer to persons who stand in no blood relationship to us whatever. For the parents of our parents, we have the combined term *grandparents* and the separate terms *grandfather* and *grand-mother*; but we do not have terms to distinguish the parents of our mother from the parents of our father. When A's son marries B's daughter, we have terms for the new relationship of the daughter to A (*daughter-in-law*) and of the son to B (*son-in-law*), but we have no term for the new relationship of A to B.

The point has been made, and we need go no further. Metaphorically speaking, every language slices the pie of reality in its own whimsical way. When we learn a new language, we must remember this and not be surprised that it looks at the world, through its words, in a way that is very different from that of English.

Meaning and Grammar

Many times * * * we have * * * occasion to speak of "grammatical meanings" of various sorts. There is for instance the meaning "completion" which we signal by using the terminal intonations / \ / and / ⁄ /: "It's raining." vs. "It's raining?" The latter also contains the meaning "please answer yes or no," and this meaning may be further reinforced by using a different word order: "Is it raining?" There is the meaning "command to perform such and such an action" which we arrive at by transforming "You will work hard" to "Work hard." There is what might be called the "equational meaning" which we signal by using the structure "X is Y." We subdivide this into two types depending on whether we select for the slot "Y" a noun: *The man is a doctor,* or an adjective: *The man is sick.* If the latter, we can transform this into a meaning of "attribution": *the sick man.* Every construction has its own constructional meaning.

Much of the grammatical meaning which we derive from any sentence comes not from its SURFACE STRUCTURE but rather from the DEEP STRUCTURE which lies beneath the surface. Consider such a sentence as: *The man was upset by the boy's being accused of cheating.* On the surface, *the man* is the subject of *was upset,* and *the boy's* is a modifier of *being accused of cheating.* Semantically, however, we interpret *the man* as the object of *upset,* and *the boy* as simultaneously the object of *accuse* and the subject of *cheat.* How are we to explain this apparent discrepancy between grammatical structure and semantic interpretation? The theory of transformational grammar explains it by making the following assumptions:

(1) The grammatical code provides for two levels of structure:

(a) At the "deep" level, it produces the structures which under-lie the simple sentences (*Something*) *upset the man*, (*Someone*) *accused the boy of* (*something*), *The boy cheated.*

(b) At the "surface" level, it produces by transformation the structure which underlies the derived sentence *The man was upset by the boy's being accused of cheating.*

(2) The semantic code takes the deep structure and from it produces the semantic interpretation which we give to the sentence—that is, the way we understand it.

(3) The phonological code takes the surface structure and from it produces the phonological interpretation which we give to the sentence—that is, the way we say it.

These assumptions now make it quite clear why we can view the forms *the man* and *the boy* in such different ways. *The man* is the subject of *was upset* because this is its status in the surface structure *The man was upset* . . .; but we understand it as the object of *upset* because this is its status in the deep structure (*Something*) *upset the man*. Similarly, *the boy* (with *'s* added) is the modifier of *being accused of cheating* because this is its status in the surface structure *the boy's being accused of cheating*; but we understand it as the object of *accuse* and the subject of *cheat* because this is its status in the deep structures (*Someone*) *accused the boy of* (*something*) and *The boy cheated.*

Of particular interest to the foreign language learner are the COM-PULSORY GRAMMATICAL CATEGORIES which he may find in the language he is studying. These are meanings which the grammar of the language forces us to signal whether we want to or not. Though it is impossible to give a full list, there are at least ten general types which are common enough so that the foreign language learner should be alerted to the fact that he may find one or more of them in the language he is studying.

(1) Number

This includes singular/plural, sometimes singular/dual/plural, rarely singular/dual/trial/plural. The categories singular/plural are familiar to us from English. They are compulsory in nearly all our nouns: *man/men, dog/dogs*, etc.; in some of our pronouns: *he/they* etc.; in two noun modifiers: *this/these, that/those*; and in the present tense agreement between subject and verb: *the dog bites/the dogs bite*. Interestingly enough, this present tense agreement shows up even with those nouns which do not themselves show the singular/plural categories: *the sheep is/the sheep are*.

(2) Gender

Here a great deal of confusion is caused by the terms (familiar from Latin) *masculine, feminine,* and *neuter.* The word *gender* itself has no necessary connection with sex, but simply means 'kind,' 'type,' 'sort.' (It comes from Latin *genus, generis.*) The terms *masculine* and *feminine* were originally used, in languages which have this classification, only because one grammatical class of nouns happened to contain (among many others) most words denoting male beings of various sorts, and another class happened to contain (among many others) most words denoting female beings of various sorts; and then, if there was a third class, it was dubbed "neither" (Latin *neuter*). Though the French noun *la table* 'the table' belongs to the same (feminine) gender as *la femme* 'the woman,' the French do not in any sense think of a table as somehow "female"; and though the German noun *das Mädchen* 'the girl' belongs to the same (neuter) gender as *das Buch* 'the book,' the Germans most decidedly do not think of girls as being sexless. These are purely grammatical classes, and they have no necessary connection with the world outside of grammar. (Because the traditional terms *masculine, feminine, neuter* are so misleading, one almost wishes they could be replaced by *red, white, blue,* or *Republican, Democratic, Socialist.* These terms would do just as well, and they would have the great advantage that no one would take them seriously.)

The gender of English nouns shows up mainly in the selection of noun-substitutes. The primary categories are "personal/impersonal"; within the former there are the secondary categories "masculine/feminine." Examples: (1) personal, (1a) masculine *the man—he,* (1b) feminine *the woman—she;* (2) impersonal *the table—it.* All gender categories are suspended in the plural: *the men, the women, the tables—they.* The personal/impersonal categories also show up in question words: *who did it* vs. *what did it.* The system is by no means consistent, since we may have: *the baby —he, she, it; the ship—it, she; the auto—it, she (Fill her up!);* etc. Furthermore, since the "personal" category may include large numbers of living beings other than people (*the dog—he, the cat— she*), the primary classification comes close to the type which is better labeled "animate/inanimate" rather than "personal/impersonal."

Other languages may show no such gender categories, or they may show as many as half a dozen of them. The categories may appear in noun-substitutes, in noun-modifiers, in the forms of the nouns themselves, in gender agreement between noun-subject and verb, in gender agreement between noun-object and verb—or in any combination of these plus perhaps some others. French shows the categories "masculine/feminine," and these appear in both singular and plural in noun-substitutes and in many noun-modifiers; and they appear to some extent in the forms of the nouns, in agreement between noun-subject and verb, and in agreement between noun-object and verb. Dutch shows the categories "common/neuter," and within the "common" gender there is a partial subclassification into "masculine/feminine." All Dutch gender categories are suspended in the plural, however. German and Russian show the three categories "masculine/feminine/neuter." Many American Indian languages (among others) show the classification "animate/inanimate"; as in English, the animate class then generally includes a few nouns which do not actually denote animate objects. Some languages of Africa show six genders, and the categories appear in grammatical agreement between noun and noun-modifier, noun-subject and verb, and noun-object and verb.

(3) Case

The fragments of a case system which we have in English are highly irregular in shape and appear only in some of the pronouns: subjective *I, he, she, we, they, who*; objective *me, him, her, us, them, whom.* (Instead of "subjective" and "objective" one could use other names.) Something close to a case appears in the English "possessive": *the man's*, though it is unusual in that this suffix can be attached to whole noun phrases: *my brother-in-law's house, the Queen of England's hat.* German has four cases, customarily called nominative, accusative, dative, genitive. Its cases are more commonly signaled in noun-modifiers than in the shapes of the nouns themselves: nominative *der Mann kommt* 'the man is coming,' accusative *ich sehe den Mann* 'I see the man,' dative *mit dem Mann* 'with the man' (though very formally this can be marked as dative by use of the affix *-e: mit dem Manne*); the only case consistently marked in this type of noun is the genitive: *der Sohn des Mannes* 'the son of the man.' Latin has five cases (plus fragments of a few others): nominative *urbs* 'city,' genitive *urbis*, dative *urbī*, accusative *urbem*, ablative *urbe*; in the plural, however, nominative and accusative often have the same shape, and the dative and ablative of the plural *always* have the same shape. Other languages may show up to a score or so of cases. If there are large numbers of them, they are likely to be formed quite regularly.

(4) Definiteness

English signals the categories "definite/indefinite" syntactically, by means of words: definite *the man*, indefinite *a man*. Other languages signal it morphologically, by means of affixes; and the affixes may be either prefixes or, as in Rumanian and the Scandinavian languages, suffixes. Somewhat similar to the categories "definite/indefinite" are those which we have in English "count nouns" and "mass nouns": count noun *a pencil, some pencils,* mass noun *milk, some milk.* Many nouns have different semantic denotations depending on which way they are used: count noun *a paper, some papers* vs. mass noun *paper, some paper.*

(5) Size and Shape

Japanese (to name just one example) uses special morphemes ("counters") with its numerals depending on the size, shape, etc. of the things being counted. Four such counters are:

Plain numeral		Used with Counter 1	Used with Counter 2	Used with Counter 3	Used with Counter 4
iti	'1'	iti-mai	iti-dai	is-satu	ip-poñ
ni	'2'	ni-mai	ni-dai	ni-satu	ni-hoñ
sañ	'3'	sañ-mai	sañ-dai	sañ-satu	sañ-boñ
si/yoñ	'4'	yoñ-mai	yoñ-dai	yoñ-satu	yoñ-hoñ
go	'5'	go-mai	go-dai	go-satu	go-hoñ

Counter 1 is used in counting thin, flat objects: sheets, blankets, plates, boards, rugs, leaves, etc. Counter 2 is used in counting vehicles: autos, busses, carriages, carts, etc. Counter 3 is used in counting bound volumes: books, magazines, albums, etc. Counter 4 is used in counting long, cylindrical objects: pens, pencils, arms, legs, trees, poles, etc.

(6) Person

English has the categories "1st person," singular *I,* plural *we;* "2nd person" *you* (with no distinction between singular and plural, though Biblical English still has singular *thou,* plural *ye*); "3rd person," singular *he* (personal-masculine), *she* (personal-feminine), *it* (impersonal), plural *they.* You may find that a language you are learning distinguishes between an "inclusive 1st person plural" (speaker and hearer and perhaps others) and an "exclusive 1st person plural" (speaker and others, but not hearer). It may also distinguish between an "inclusive 2nd person plural" (hearer(s) and others not present) and an "exclusive 2nd person plural" (hearers, but no others). Or it may have a so-called "4th person," to distinguish between the first and second of two persons mentioned other than speaker and hearer: "Did *I* (1st person) tell *you* (2nd person) that I saw *Bill* (3rd person) talking to *Tom* (4th person)? *He* (to be marked either 3rd or 4th) will give *him* (to be marked either 4th or 3rd) the money tomorrow." Such categories of person show up perhaps universally in pronouns. They may also appear in agreement between noun-subject and verb (compare *I see* but *he, she, it sees*), perhaps also in agreement between verb and noun-object.

(7) Tense

Common categories are: present, past, future, pre-past ("pluper-fect"), pre-future ("future perfect"). In English we are forced to distinguish morphologically between present and past: *I see* vs. *I saw*. We can also distinguish syntactically (using phrases) between future *I shall/will see*, pre-past *I had seen*, pre-future *I shall/will have seen*. Notice that our so-called "present" is in a sense also timeless: "Water *boils* at 100° centigrade." Other languages you are learning may have a special form for this.

(8) Aspect

Categories of this type have to do with whether an action is looked upon as complete or incomplete, as occurring at one point in time or over a stretch of time, as occurring only once or repetitively or habitually, and the like. English has an interesting compulsory distinction between "past without present relevance" (*I worked here for ten years*, implying that I no longer do) and "past with present relevance" (*I have worked here for ten years*, implying that I still do). English also distinguishes between "punctual," referring to a point in time (*I worked in Chicago*), and "durative," referring to a stretch of time (*I was working in Chicago*).

(9) Mood

Categories of this type refer to the speaker's attitude toward an action. A language may distinguish between such things as a neutral attitude (often called "indicative"), an attitude which has certain reservations ("subjunctive"), an attitude of hope ("optative"), an attitude of doubt ("dubitative"), an attitude of possibility ("poten-tial"), an attitude of desire ("desiderative"), an attitude of unreal-ity ("unreal"), an attitude of negativeness ("negative"), an atti-tude of questioning ("interrogative"), an attitude of emphasis ("emphatic"), an attitude of condition ("conditional"), and the like. English has a sort of optative in its use of an uninflected verb form with a 3rd person singular subject: "I insist that he *live* in a dormitory" (vs. the indicative "I insist that he *lives* in a dormi-tory"); and it has one verb with a special unreal form, namely the use of *were* with a singular subject: "if he *were* here" (implying that he is not; though many of us also say "if he *was* here"). Aside from this, the closest we come to "moods" is through our use of normal verb forms in special contexts. We can produce something close to an "unreal" mood by using a past tense form in a present tense context: "if I *had* the money today"; something close to a "conditional" by using past *would* in a present tense context: "I *would* buy a hat" (this use is actually far commoner than the past tense use of *would*, which occurs in such sentences as: "he *would* always stutter when he tried to say it"); and something close to an "emphatic" mood by using *do/did* in contexts where otherwise the present or past of a full verb is used: "but he *does* live here," "but he *did* pay the bill."

(10) Voice

Categories of this type refer to the grammatical relationships between a verbal expression and the nominal expressions which are in construction with it. In English *The policeman shot the man* the policeman is the doer of the action and the man is the person affected by it; in *The man was shot by the policeman* the same relationships are expressed in a grammatically different way. The former grammatical structure is customarily called "active," the latter "passive." In English the active is expressed by a word (*shot*), the passive by a phrase (*was shot*); in the foreign language you may be learning the passive may be indicated by an affix attached to the verb stem. Other types of voice include: reflexive (the subject acting upon itself), reciprocal (the subjects acting upon each other), causative (the subject causing an action to happen), transitive (an action involving an object), intransitive (an action not involving an object). Other languages you are learning may indicate one or more such voices by means of affixes.

Meaning and People

We have seen that "meaning" lies partly in the connection between a word and its referent (denotative meaning), and partly within the grammar of the language (grammatical meaning); to a remarkable extent it also lies within people as users of a language (connotative meaning). To illustrate this, try the following experiment: ask a number of speakers of English what the word *livid* means to them. Answers may range all the way from 'pale' through 'bluish' to 'red.' Since most of us use the word only in such contexts as *livid with rage*, perhaps its common denotative meaning can be phrased as "denoting whatever color the user associates with extreme anger." The word is unusual in that different people associate it with such different colors. By and large we cannot allow the words of a language to behave in this way. There must in general be a kind of tacit agreement among all speakers of a language that such connotative meanings shall not cover so wide an area; otherwise language would be a very poor means of communication. Needless to say, our disagreements as to the meaning of *livid* would soon disappear if we began using it in such contexts as "Please show me a *livid* dress."

Though the word *livid* is an extreme case, many—perhaps most —content words show some such fluctuation from speaker to speaker, or from one group to another. A woman whom men call *pretty* is likely to look quite different from a woman whom women call *pretty*. The connotative meaning which a word carries for us seems to be a compounding of all the contexts—both linguistic and non-linguistic—in which we have encountered it. This leads to various groupings of words, some of which may be shared by all speakers and some of which may be quite personal. A personal example: To the writer, such words as *ocean, sea, waves* connote such further words (plus their denotations and connotations) as *happiness, vacation, sunshine, relaxation*, and the like. (This is presumably because, as a boy, he spent many summers at the seashore—and regrets only that he cannot do so as an adult.) To others, such words might connote *shipwreck, disaster, seasickness*, and so on. When such groupings of words are shared more or less by all speakers of a language, they lead to what have been called WORD FIELDS or SEMANTIC FIELDS. Thus the word *good* belongs to a word field which includes *beneficial, valuable, excellent, useful, advantageous, profitable, salutary, healthful*, and the like. This leads to the concept of SYNONYMS: words which are very close in meaning. Interestingly enough, it also leads to the concept of ANTONYMS: words which are opposite in meaning, since we also associate opposites with each other.

* * *

Translation

Before we leave the topic of meaning, a final remark needs to be made about another subject: translation. In the preceding paragraphs we have suggested that no two languages structure the world of reality in the same way, so that their denotative meanings must be different; it is obvious that no two languages have the same grammar, so that their grammatical meanings must be different; and since their speakers have had different linguistic and non-linguistic experiences from our own, the connotative meanings must be even *more* different. If all this is true, then it must be quite impossible to translate a sentence of one language into a sentence of another language. If by "translation" we mean "word-for-word translation," this is quite correct. Even such languages as English and German—closely related and belonging to the same Western European cultural tradition—contain hosts of words which cannot be translated directly from the one language into the other. Many people make a kind of parlor sport out of identifying such words. Favorite examples of untranslatable German words are *gemütlich* (something like 'homey, easygoing, humbly pleasant, informal') and *Schadenfreude* ('pleasure over the fact that someone else has suffered a misfortune'); favorite examples of untranslatable English words are *sophisticated* and *efficient*. Doubtless the reader can add examples of his own from other languages.

A word of caution needs to be added concerning this parlor sport, fascinating as it may be. Far too often, those who indulge in it jump to the conclusion that the lack of word-for-word equivalents implies also the lack of what is denoted by these words. If this were true, we would have to conclude that speakers of English never meet together in a *gemütlich* way and never indulge in *Schadenfreude*; and that there are no *sophisticated* Germans in a country where there is also no *efficiency* in industry. Or we would have to conclude that a Russian can't tell his arm from his hand, since he uses the single word *ruká* to include both. But this is obviously absurd. It is perfectly true that none of these words can be translated in an exact, unambiguous way; but it is also true that, as soon as we abandon the primitive notion of word-for-word translation, anything which can be said in one language can be translated more or less accurately into another. A paper on physics or chemistry will cause the least trouble: the international scientific community has labored long and hard over exact denotative meanings; connotative meanings are out of place in a scientific paper; the only difficulties will be those of translating grammatical meanings. A novel will be considerably more difficult, since here we also begin to run into differences of denotative and connotative meaning. Hardest of all will be a poem if, as is so often the case, the poet has purposely used wide ranges of denotative and connotative meaning. Indeed, here one can fairly say: such a poem is untranslatable. The "translation" may be a very fine poem in its own right (it may even be better than the original), but it cannot be the *same* poem. Except in the case of poems, however, reasonably accurate translation between languages is impossible only in those cases where something—most often a cultural institution of some sort—occurs in the one society but not in the other. American examples: *high school, college, drugstore*, and the like—since no other countries have institutions quite like these.

The above remarks lead us to one final conclusion. Translation is a high art, which requires great knowledge and great skill. The beginner who thinks he can indulge in it is suffering from delusions of grandeur.

QUESTIONS

1. Moulton discusses three kinds of meaning—meaning and things (denotative), meaning and grammar (grammatical), and meaning and people (connotative). He gives most space to his discussion of grammatical meaning and least to his discussion of connotative meaning. Why?

2. Compare Moulton's three categories of meaning with Fromm's three kinds of symbols (conventional, accidental, universal) (pp. 129–136). How far do Moulton's categories overlap Fromm's? Why is the overlap partial rather than complete?

3. Moulton mentions a number of things that English does not have names for (p. 127). What other things of this sort can you think of? Why do you think English has not developed names for them?
4. Moulton speaks of "surface structure" and "deep structure" (p. 120) in the context of grammatical meaning. Might one find analogous surface and deep structures in the difference between denotative and connotative meanings of certain words? Explain.
5. On p. 126 Moulton suggests an experiment to illustrate differences in connotative meaning. Carry out his experiment, asking a number of speakers of English what the word livid means to them. If possible, select one or two other words to include in your experiment.
6. If there were no connotative meanings in a particular language, would we be likely to find many synonyms in that language? Explain.

ERICH FROMM

The Nature of Symbolic Language

Let us assume you want to tell someone the difference between the taste of white wine and red wine. This may seem quite simple to you. You know the difference very well; why should it not be easy to explain it to someone else? Yet you find the greatest difficulty putting this taste difference into words. And probably you will end up by saying, "Now look here, I can't explain it to you. Just drink red wine and then white wine, and you will know what the difference is." You have no difficulty in finding words to explain the most complicated machine, and yet words seem to be futile to describe a simple taste experience.

Are we not confronted with the same difficulty when we try to explain a feeling experience? Let us take a mood in which you feel lost, deserted, where the world looks gray, a little frightening though not really dangerous. You want to describe this mood to a friend, but again you find yourself groping for words and eventually feel that nothing you have said is an adequate explanation of the many nuances of the mood. The following night you have a dream. You see yourself in the outskirts of a city just before dawn, the streets are empty except for a milk wagon, the houses look poor, the surroundings are unfamiliar, you have no means of accustomed transportation to places familiar to you and where you feel you belong. When you wake up and remember the dream, it occurs to you that the feeling you had in that dream was exactly the feeling of lostness and grayness you tried to describe to your friend the day before. It is just one picture, whose visualization took less than a second. And yet this picture is a more vivid and precise description than you could have given by talking *about* it at length. The picture you see in the dream is a *symbol* of something you felt.

What is a symbol? A symbol is often defined as "something that stands for something else." This definition seems rather disappointing. It becomes more interesting, however, if we concern ourselves with those symbols which are sensory expressions of seeing, hearing, smelling, touching, standing for a "something else" which is an inner experience, a feeling or thought. A symbol of this kind is something outside ourselves; that which it symbolizes is something inside ourselves. Symbolic language is language in which we express inner experience as if it were a sensory experience, as if it were something we were doing or something that was done to us in the world of things. Symbolic language is language in which the world outside is a symbol of the world inside, a symbol for our souls and our minds.

If we define a symbol as "something which stands for something else," the crucial question is: *What is the specific connection between the symbol and that which it symbolizes?*

In answer to this question we can differentiate between three kinds of symbols: the *conventional*, the *accidental* and the *universal* symbol. As will become apparent presently, only the latter two kinds of symbols express inner experiences as if they were sensory experiences, and only they have the elements of symbolic language.

The *conventional* symbol is the best known of the three, since we employ it in everyday language. If we see the word "table" or hear the sound "table," the letters T-A-B-L-E stand for something else. They stand for the thing table that we see, touch and use. What is the connection between the *word* "table" and the *thing* "table"? Is there any inherent relationship between them? Obviously not. The thing table has nothing to do with the sound table, and the only reason the word symbolizes the thing is the convention of calling this particular thing by a particular name. We learn this connection as children by the repeated experience of hearing the word in reference to the thing until a lasting association is formed so that we don't have to think to find the right word.

There are some words, however, where the association is not only conventional. When we say "phooey," for instance, we make with our lips a movement of dispelling the air quickly. It is an expression of disgust in which our mouths participate. By this quick expulsion of air we imitate and thus express our intention to expel something, to get it out of our system. In this case, as in some others, the symbol has an inherent connection with the feeling it symbolizes. But even if we assume that originally many or even all words had their origins in some such inherent connection between symbol and the symbolized, most words no longer have this meaning for us when we learn a language.

Words are not the only illustration for conventional symbols, although they are the most frequent and best-known ones. Pictures also can be conventional symbols. A flag, for instance, may stand for a specific country, and yet there is no connection between the specific colors and the country for which they stand. They have been accepted as denoting that particular country, and we translate the visual impression of the flag into the concept of that country, again on conventional grounds. Some pictorial symbols are not entirely conventional; for example, the cross. The cross can be merely a conventional symbol of the Christian church and in that respect no different from a flag. But the specific content of the cross referring to Jesus' death or, beyond that, to the interpenetration of the material and spiritual planes, puts the connection between the symbol and what it symbolizes beyond the level of mere conventional symbols.

The very opposite to the conventional symbol is the *accidental* symbol, although they have one thing in common: there is no intrinsic relationship between the symbol and that which it symbolizes. Let us assume that someone has had a saddening experience in a certain city; when he hears the name of that city, he will easily connect the name with a mood of sadness, just as he would connect it with a mood of joy had his experience been a happy one. Quite obviously there is nothing in the nature of the city that is either sad or joyful. It is the individual experience connected with the city that makes it a symbol of a mood.

The same reaction could occur in connection with a house, a street, a certain dress, certain scenery, or anything once connected with a specific mood. We might find ourselves dreaming that we are in a certain city. In fact, there may be no particular mood connected with it in the dream; all we see is a street or even simply the name of the city. We ask ourselves why we happened to think of that city in our sleep and may discover that we had fallen asleep in a mood similar to the one symbolized by the city. The picture in the dream represents this mood, the city "stands for" the mood once experienced in it. Here the connection between the symbol and the experience symbolized is entirely accidental.

In contrast to the conventional symbol, the accidental symbol cannot be shared by anyone else except as we relate the events connected with the symbol. For this reason accidental symbols are rarely used in myths, fairy tales, or works of art written in symbolic language because they are not communicable unless the writer adds a lengthy comment to each symbol he uses. In dreams, however, accidental symbols are frequent. * * *

The *universal* symbol is one in which there is an intrinsic relationship between the symbol and that which it represents. We have already given one example, that of the outskirts of the city. The sensory experience of a deserted, strange, poor environment has indeed a significant relationship to a mood of lostness and anxiety. True enough, if we have never been in the outskirts of a city we could not use that symbol, just as the word "table" would be meaningless had we never seen a table. This symbol is meaningful only to city dwellers and would be meaningless to people living in cultures that have no big cities. Many other universal symbols, however, are rooted in the experience of every human being. Take, for instance, the symbol of fire. We are fascinated by certain qualities of fire in a fireplace. First of all, by its aliveness. It changes continuously, it moves all the time, and yet there is constancy in it. It remains the same without being the same. It gives the impression of power, of energy, of grace and lightness. It is as if it were dancing and had an inexhaustible source of energy. When we use fire as a symbol, we describe the inner experience characterized by the same elements which we notice in the sensory experience of fire; the mood of energy, lightness, movement, grace, gaiety—sometimes one, sometimes another of these elements being predominant in the feeling.

Similar in some ways and different in others is the symbol of water—of the ocean or of the stream. Here, too, we find the blending of change and permanence, of constant movement and yet of permanence. We also feel the quality of aliveness, continuity and energy. But there is a difference; where fire is adventurous, quick, exciting, water is quiet, slow and steady. Fire has an element of surprise; water an element of predictability. Water symbolizes the mood of aliveness, too, but one which is "heavier," "slower," and more comforting than exciting.

That a phenomenon of the physical world can be the adequate expression of an inner experience, that the world of things can be a symbol of the world of the mind, is not surprising. We all know that our bodies express our minds. Blood rushes to our heads when we are furious, it rushes away from them when we are afraid; our hearts beat more quickly when we are angry, and the whole body has a different tonus if we are happy from the one it has when we are sad. We express our moods by our facial expressions and our attitudes and feelings by movements and gestures so precise that others recognize them more accurately from our gestures than from our words. Indeed, the body is a symbol—and not an allegory—of the mind. Deeply and genuinely felt emotion, and even any genuinely felt thought, is expressed in our whole organism. In the case of the universal symbol, we find the same connection between mental and physical experience. Certain physical phenomena suggest by their very nature certain emotional and mental experiences, and we express emotional experiences in the language of physical experiences, that is to say, symbolically.

The universal symbol is the only one in which the relationship between the symbol and that which is symbolized is not coincidental but intrinsic. It is rooted in the experience of the affinity between an emotion or thought, on the one hand, and a sensory experience, on the other. It can be called universal because it is shared by all men, in contrast not only to the accidental symbol, which is by its very nature entirely personal, but also to the conventional symbol, which is restricted to a group of people sharing the same convention. The universal symbol is rooted in the properties of our body, our senses, and our mind, which are common to all men and, therefore, not restricted to individuals or to specific groups. Indeed, the language of the universal symbol is the one common tongue developed by the human race, a language which it forgot before it succeeded in developing a universal conventional language.

There is no need to speak of a racial inheritance in order to explain the universal character of symbols. Every human being who shares the essential features of bodily and mental equipment with the rest of mankind is capable of speaking and understanding the symbolic language that is based upon these common properties. Just as we do not need to learn to cry when we are sad or to get red in the face when we are angry, and just as these reactions are not restricted to any particular race or group of people, symbolic language does not have to be learned and is not restricted to any segment of the human race. Evidence for this is to be found in the fact that symbolic language as it is employed in myths and dreams is found in all cultures—in so-called primitive as well as such highly developed cultures as Egypt and Greece. Furthermore, the symbols used in these various cultures are strikingly similar since they all go back to the basic sensory as well as emotional experiences shared by men of all cultures. Added evidence is to be found in recent experiments in which people who had no knowledge of the theory of dream interpretation were able, under hypnosis, to interpret the symbolism of their dreams without any difficulty. After emerging from the hypnotic state and being asked to interpret the same dreams, they were puzzled and said, "Well, there is no meaning to them—it is just nonsense."

The foregoing statement needs qualification, however. Some symbols differ in meaning according to the difference in their realistic significance in various cultures. For instance, the function and consequently the meaning of the sun is different in northern countries and in tropical countries. In northern countries, where water is plentiful, all growth depends on sufficient sunshine. The sun is the warm, life-giving, protecting, loving power. In the Near East, where the heat of the sun is much more powerful, the sun is a dangerous and even threatening power from which man must protect himself, while water is felt to be the source of all life and the main condition for growth. We may speak of dialects of universal symbolic language, which are determined by those differences in natural conditions which cause certain symbols to have a different meaning in different regions of the earth.

Quite different from these "symbolic dialects" is the fact that many symbols have more than one meaning in accordance with different kinds of experiences which can be connected with one and the same natural phenomenon. Let us take up the symbol of fire again. If we watch fire in the fireplace, which is a source of pleasure and comfort, it is expressive of a mood of aliveness, warmth, and pleasure. But if we see a building or forest on fire, it conveys to us an experience of threat or terror, of the powerlessness of man against the elements of nature. Fire, then, can be the symbolic representation of inner aliveness and happiness as well as of fear, powerlessness, or of one's own destructive tendencies. The same holds true of the symbol water. Water can be a most destructive force when it is whipped up by a storm or when a swollen river floods its banks. Therefore, it can be the symbolic expression of horror and chaos as well as of comfort and peace.

Another illustration of the same principle is a symbol of a valley. The valley enclosed between mountains can arouse in us the feeling of security and comfort, of protection against all dangers from the outside. But the protecting mountains can also mean isolating walls which do not permit us to get out of the valley and thus the valley can become a symbol of imprisonment. The particular meaning of the symbol in any given place can only be determined from the whole context in which the symbol appears, and in terms of the predominant experiences of the person using the symbol. * * *

A good illustration of the function of the universal symbol is a story, written in symbolic language, which is known to almost everyone in Western culture: the Book of Jonah. Jonah has heard God's voice telling him to go to Nineveh and preach to its inhabitants to give up their evil ways lest they be destroyed. Jonah cannot help hearing God's voice and that is why he is a prophet. But he is an unwilling prophet, who, though knowing what he should do, tries to run away from the command of God (or, as we may say, the voice of his conscience). He is a man who does not care for other human beings. He is a man with a strong sense of law and order, but without love.[1]

How does the story express the inner processes in Jonah?

We are told that Jonah went down to Joppa and found a ship which should bring him to Tarshish. In mid-ocean a storm rises and, while everyone else is excited and afraid, Jonah goes into the

1. Cf. the discussion of Jonah in E. Fromm's *Man for Himself* (New York, Rinehart & Co., 1947), where the story is discussed from the point of view of the meaning of love.

ship's belly and falls into a deep sleep. The sailors, believing that God must have sent the storm because someone on the ship is to be punished, wake Jonah, who had told them he was trying to flee from God's command. He tells them to take him and cast him forth into the sea and that the sea would then become calm. The sailors (betraying a remarkable sense of humanity by first trying everything else before following his advice) eventually take Jonah and cast him into the sea, which immediately stops raging. Jonah is swallowed by a big fish and stays in the fish's belly three days and three nights. He prays to God to free him from this prison. God makes the fish vomit out Jonah unto the dry land and Jonah goes to Nineveh, fulfills God's command, and thus saves the inhabitants of the city.

The story is told as if these events had actually happened. However, it is written in symbolic language and all the realistic events described are symbols for the inner experiences of the hero. We find a sequence of symbols which follow one another: going into the ship, going into the ship's belly, falling asleep, being in the ocean, and being in the fish's belly. All these symbols stand for the same inner experience: for a condition of being protected and isolated, of safe withdrawal from communication with other human beings. They represent what could be represented in another symbol, the fetus in the mother's womb. Different as the ship's belly, deep sleep, the ocean, and a fish's belly are realistically, they are expressive of the same inner experience, of the blending between protection and isolation.

In the manifest story events happen in space and time: *first,* going into the ship's belly; *then,* falling asleep; *then,* being thrown into the ocean; *then,* being swallowed by the fish. One thing happens after the other and, although some events are obviously unrealistic, the story has its own logical consistency in terms of time and space. But if we understand that the writer did not intend to tell us the story of external events, but of the inner experience of a man torn between his conscience and his wish to escape from his inner voice, it becomes clear that his various actions following one after the other express the same mood in him; and that *sequence in time* is expressive of a *growing intensity* of the same feeling. In his attempt to escape from his obligation to his fellow men Jonah isolates himself more and more until, in the belly of the fish, the protective element has so given way to the imprisoning element that he can stand it no longer and is forced to pray to God to be released from where he had put himself. (This is a mechanism which we find so characteristic of neurosis. An attitude is assumed as a defense against a danger, but then it grows far beyond its original defense function and becomes a neurotic symptom from which the person tries to be relieved.) Thus Jonah's escape into protective isolation ends in the terror of being imprisoned, and he takes up his life at the point where he had tried to escape.

There is another difference between the logic of the manifest and of the latent story. In the manifest story the logical connection is one of causality of external events. Jonah wants to go overseas *because* he wants to flee from God, he falls asleep *because* he is tired, he is thrown overboard *because* he is supposed to be the reason for the storm, and he is swallowed by the fish *because* there are man-eating fish in the ocean. One event occurs because of a previous event. (The last part of the story is unrealistic but not illogical.) But in the latent story the logic is different. The various events are related to each other by their association with the same inner experience. What appears to be a causal sequence of external events stand for a connection of experiences linked with each other by their association in terms of inner events. This is as logical as the manifest story—but it is a logic of a different kind. * * *

OWEN BARFIELD
Poetic Diction and Legal Fiction

The house of poetry contains many mansions. These mansions are so diverse in their qualities and in their effect on the indweller and some of them are so distant from others that the inhabitants of one mansion have been heard to deny that another is part of the same building at all. For instance, Edgar Allen Poe said that there is no such thing as a long poem, and the difference between a long narrative poem and a short lyric is admittedly rather baffling, seeming almost to be one of kind. What I have to say here touches mainly lyric poetry, and will interest those who love to dwell with recurring delight on special felicities of expression more than those to whom poetry means taking their *Iliad* or their *Faerie Queene* a thousand lines at a time and enjoying the story. It is highly specialized. Think for a moment of poems as of pieces of fabric, large tapestries, or minute embroideries as the case may be. What I have to say does not concern the whole form of even one of the embroideries, but only the texture itself, the nature of the process at any given point, as the fabric comes into being, the movements which the shuttle or the needle must have made. It is still more specialized than this; for in examining the texture of poetry one of the most important elements (a mansion to itself) is rhythm, sound, music; and all this is of necessity excluded. I am fully aware that this involves the corollary that the kind of poetry I am talking about may also be written in prose; but that is a difficulty which is chronic to the subject. I wish, however, to treat of that element in poetry which is best called "meaning" pure and simple. Not the meaning of poetry, nor the meaning of any poem as a whole, but just meaning. If this sounds like an essay in microscopy, or if it be objected that what I am talking about is not poetic diction, but etymology or philosophy or even genetic psychology, I can only reply that whatever it ought to be called, it is, to some people, extraordinarily interesting, and that if, in all good faith, I have given it a wrong address, it is still to me the roomiest, the most commodious, and the most exciting of all the mansions which I rightly or wrongly include in the plan and elevation of the great house.

The language of poetry has always been in a high degree *figurative*; it is always illustrating or expressing what it wishes to put before us by comparing that with something else. Sometimes the comparison is open and avowed, as when Shelley compares the skylark to a poet, to a high-born maiden, and to a rose embowered in its own green leaves; when Keats tells us that a summer's day is:

> like the passage of an angel's tear
> That falls through the clear ether silently.

or when Burns writes simply: "My love is like a red red rose." And then we call it a "simile." Sometimes it is concealed in the form of a bare statement, as when Shelley says of the west wind, not that it is *like* but that it *is* "the breath of Autumn's being," calls upon it to "make him its lyre" and says of himself that *his* leaves are falling. This is known as "metaphor." Sometimes the element of comparison drops still farther out of sight. Instead of saying that A is like B or that A is B, the poet simply talks about B, without making any overt reference to A at all. You know, however, that he intends A all the time, or, better say that you know he intends *an* A; for you may not have a very clear idea of what A is and even if you have got an idea, somebody else may have a different one. This is generally called "symbolism."

I do not say that these particular methods of expression are an absolute *sine qua non* of poetic diction. They are not. Poetry may also take the form of simple and literal statement. But figurative expression is found everywhere; its roots descend very deep, as we shall see, into the nature, not only of poetry, but of language itself. If you took away from the stream of European poetry every passage of a metaphorical nature, you would reduce it to a very thin trickle indeed, pure though the remainder beverage might be to the taste. Perhaps our English poetry would suffer the heaviest damage of all. Aristotle, when treating of diction in his *Poetics*, provides the right expression by calling the element of metaphor πολὺ μέγιστον—far the most important.

It may be noticed that I am now using the word "metaphor" in a slightly different and wider sense than when I placed it in the midst between simile on the one hand and symbol on the other. I am now using it, and shall use it frequently throughout this article, to cover the whole gamut of figurative language including simile and symbol. I do not think this need confuse us. Strict metaphor occurs about the middle of the gamut and expresses the essential nature of such language more perfectly perhaps than either of the extremes. In something the same way Goethe found that the leaf of a plant expressed its essential nature as plant, while the blossom and the root could be considered as metamorphoses of the leaf. Here I want to try and consider a little more closely what the essential nature of figurative language is and how that nature is most clearly apparent in the figure called metaphor.

But first of all let us return to the "gamut" and take some examples. This time let us move along it in the reverse direction, beginning from symbolism.

> Does the road wind uphill all the way?
>   Yes, to the very end.
> Will the day's journey take the whole long day?
>   From morn to night, my friend.
>
> But is there for the night a resting-place?
>   A roof for when the slow, dark hours begin.
> May not the darkness hide it from my face?
>   You cannot miss that inn.
>
> Shall I meet other wayfarers at night?
>   Those who have gone before.
> Then must I knock or call when just in sight?
>   They will not keep you waiting at that door.
>
> Shall I find comfort, travel-sore and weak?
>   Of labor you shall find the sum.
> Will there be beds for me and all who seek?
>   Yea, beds for all who come.

As I have already suggested, the ordinary way of characterizing this kind of language would be to say that the poet says one thing and means another. Is this true? Is it fair to say that Christina Rossetti says B but she really means A? I do not think this is a question which can be answered with a simple "yes" or "no." In fact the difficult and elusive relation between A and B is the heart of my matter. For the time being let me hazard, as a rather hedging sort of answer, that the truer it is to say "yes," the worse is the poem, the truer it is to say "no," the better is the poem. We feel that B, which is actually said, ought to be necessary, even inevitable in some way. It ought to be in some sense the best, if not the only way, of expressing A satisfactorily. The mind should dwell on it as well as on A and thus the two should be somehow inevitably fused together into one simple meaning. But if A is too obvious and could be equally or almost as well expressed by other and more direct means, then the mind jumps straight to A, remains focused on it, and loses interest in B, which shrinks to a kind of dry and hollow husk. I think this is a fault of Christina Rossetti's poem. We know just what A is. A = "The good life is an effort" plus "All men are mortal." Consequently it detaches itself from B, like a soul leaving a body, and the road and the inn and the beds are not a real road and inn and beds, they look faintly heraldic—or as if portrayed in lacquer. They are not even poetically real. We never get a fair chance to accord to their existence that willing suspension of disbelief which we are told constitutes "poetic faith." Let us try another:

> "Is there anybody there?" said the Traveler,
>   Knocking on the moonlit door;
> And his horse in the silence champed the grasses
>   Of the forest's ferny floor:
> And a bird flew up out of the turret,
>   Above the Traveler's head:
> And he smote upon the door again a second time:
>   "Is there anybody there?" he said.
> But no one descended to the Traveler;
>   No head from the leaf-fringed sill
> Leaned over and looked into his grey eyes,
>   Where he stood perplexed and still.
> But only a host of phantom listeners
>   That dwelt in the lone house then
> Stood listening in the quiet of the moonlight
>   To that voice from the world of men:
> Stood thronging the faint moonbeams on the dark stair,
>   That goes down to the empty hall,
> Hearkening in an air stirred and shaken
>   By the lonely Traveler's call.
> And he felt in his heart their strangeness,
>   Their stillness answering his cry,
> While his horse moved, cropping the dark turf,
>   'Neath the starred and leafy sky;
> For he suddenly smote on the door, even
>   Louder, and lifted his head:—
> "Tell them I came, and no one answered,
>   That I kept my word," he said.
> Never the least stir made the listeners,
>   Though every word he spake
> Fell echoing through the shadowiness of the still house
>   From the one man left awake:
> Ay, they heard his foot upon the stirrup
>   And the sound of iron on stone,
> And how the silence surged softly backward,
>   When the plunging hoofs were gone.[1]

This poem seems to me to possess as symbolism most of the

1. Walter de la Mare, "The Listeners."

virtues which I miss in Christina Rossetti's. First it obviously *is* a symbol. There *is* an A and a good solid one, though we do not know what it is, because we cannot put it into a separate container of words. But that is just the point. A has not got (perhaps I should say, it has not *yet* got) a separate existence in our apprehension; so it makes itself felt by modifying and enriching the meaning of B—it hides itself in B, hides itself in language which still *could* on the face of it be heard and interpreted as though no A came into the question at all.

I must here remark that merely making A obscure is not in itself a recipe for writing good symbolical poetry. William Blake at his worst, and, I fancy, many modern poets who write or intend to write symbolically, go astray here. They are so anxious to avoid the error of intending too obvious an A, so anxious to avoid a mere old-fashioned simile, that we end by being mystified or disgusted by the impossibility of getting any sort of feeling at all of what they are talking about, or why. Why are they talking about B at all, we ask ourselves. If they are doing it simply for the sake of B, it is pure drivel. On the other hand, if they intend an A, what evidence is there of it? We do not mind A being intangible, because it is still only half born from the poet's unconscious, but you cannot make poetry by cunningly removing all the clues which, if left, would discover the staleness of your meaning. In other words, if you set out to say one thing and mean another, you must really mean another, and that other must be worth meaning.

It will be observed that when we started from the simile and moved towards the symbol, the criterion or yardstick by which we measured our progress was the element of *comparison*—paramount in the simile and very nearly vanished out of sight in the symbol. When, on the other hand, we move backwards, starting from the symbol, we find ourselves with another yardstick, viz. the fact of saying one thing and meaning another. The poet says B but he means A. He hides A in B. B is the normal everyday meaning which the words so to speak "ought" to have on the face of them, and A is what the poet *really* has to say to us, and which he can only say through or alongside of, or by modifying, these normal everyday meanings. A is his own new, original, or poetic meaning. If I were writing this article in Greek or German, my public would no doubt be severly restricted, but there would be this advantage to me—that I could run the six words "say-one-thing-and-mean-another" together and use the resulting conglomerate as a noun throughout the rest of it. I cannot do this, but I will make bold to borrow another German word instead. The word *Tarnung* was, I believe, extensively used under the heel of the Nazi tyranny in Germany for the precautionary practice of hiding one meaning in another, the allusion being to the *Tarnhelm* of the Nibelungs.[2] I shall give it an English form and call it "Tarning." When I say "Tarning," therefore, the reader is asked to substitute mentally the concept of saying one thing and meaning another, in the sense in which I have just been trying to expound it. We have already seen that the more A lives as a modification or enrichment of B, the better is the tarning.

Now let us proceed to the next step in our backward progress from symbol to simile. We come to the metaphor. And here we find both the best and the most numerous examples of tarning. Almost any poem, almost any passage of really vivid prose which you pick up is sure to contain them in abundance. I will choose an example (the source of which he does not disclose) given by Dr. Hugh Blair, the eighteenth-century writer on style.

Those persons who gain the hearts of most people, who are chosen as the companions of their softer hours, and their reliefs from anxiety and care, are seldom persons of shining qualities or strong virtues: it is rather the soft green of the soul on which we rest our eyes, that are fatigued with beholding more glaring objects.

Consider how the ordinary literal meaning of the word "green" blends with the ineffable psychic quality which it is the writer's object to convey! How much weaker it would be, had he written: "It is rather persons whose souls we find restful, as the eye finds green fields restful, etc." Put it that way and nearly all the tarning, and with it half the poetry, is lost. The passage reminds me of this from Andrew Marvell's *Garden*:

> The Mind, that Ocean where each kind
> Does straight its own resemblance find;
> Yet it creates, transcending these,
> Far other Worlds, and other Seas;
> Annihilating all that's made
> To a green Thought in a green Shade.

What a lot of tarning can be done with the word "green"!

We see that any striking and original use of even a single word tends to be metaphorical and shows us the process of tarning at work. On the whole, I think it is true to say that the fewer the words containing the metaphor, the more the expression is in the strict sense a "trope" rather than a metaphor—the more tarning we shall feel. For the long and elaborate metaphor is already almost a simile—a simile with the word "like" missed out. We must, however, remember that the tarning may not have actually occurred in the particular place where we find it. People copy one another and the metaphor may be a cliché, or, if not a cliché part of our common heritage of speech. Thus when Tennyson writes:

2. The *Tarnhelm* was a helmet which made its wearer invisible.

> When the happy Yes
> Falters from her lips,
> Pass and blush the news
> Over glowing ships

we feel that the peculiarly effective use of the word "blush" throughout this lyric is a tarning of his own. It actually goes on in us as we read. When, on the other hand, Arnold writes in the *Scholar Gypsy:*

> O Life unlike to ours!
> Who fluctuate idly without term or scope

or:

> Vague half-believers of our casual creeds,
> Who never deeply felt, nor clearly willed,
> Whose insight never has borne fruit in deeds

though none of this writing can be described as cliché, yet we feel that the metaphorical element in "fluctuate" and in "borne fruit" is the product of a tarning that happened before Arnold was born. So, too, in the passage I first quoted the *"shining* qualities" and the *"softer* hours" are metaphors of the kind we are all using every day, almost without thinking of them as metaphors. We all speak of *clear* heads, of brilliant wit, of *seeing* somebody's meaning, of so and so being the *pick of the bunch,* and so on; and most of us must use at least, say, a hundred of these dead or half-dead metaphors every day of our lives. In fact, in dealing with metaphor, we soon find outselves talking, not of poetry, but of language itself. Everywhere in language we seem to find that the process of tarning, or something very like it, either is or has been at work.

We seem to owe all these tropes and metaphors embedded in language to the fact that somebody at some time had the wit to say one thing and mean another, and that somebody else had the wit to tumble to the new meaning, to detect the bouquet of a new wine emanating from the old bottle. We owe them all to tarning, a process which we find prolifically at work wherever there is poetry—from the symbol, where it shouts at us and is all too easily mishandled, to the simile, where we already hear the first faint stirrings of its presence, inasmuch as the B image even here is modified, enriched, or colored by the A image with which it is this time overtly compared.

> Then fly our greetings, fly our speech and smiles!
> —As some grave Tyrian trader, from the sea,
> Descried at sunrise an emerging prow
> Lifting the cool-hair'd creepers stealthily,
> The fringes of a southward-facing brow
> Among the Aegean isles;
> And saw the merry Grecian coaster come,
> Freighted with amber grapes, and Chian wine,

Green bursting figs, and tunnies steep'd in brine;
And knew the intruders on his ancient home,

The young light-hearted masters of the waves.

The grave Tyrian trader and the merry Grecian coaster are not the same figures that we should meet in a history book. They have their own life, they take in the imagination a special color from the things with which they are compared—that is, the *Scholar Gypsy* on the one hand and our too modern selves on the other. They are pregnant with the whole of the poem that has gone before.

I said at the beginning that I might be accused of indulging in a kind of aesthetic microscopy. The drawback of the microscope is this, that even if the grain of sand which we see through it does indeed contain a world, mere magnification is not enough to enable us to see that world. Unfortunately the processes which are said to give to the infiinitesimal a cosmic character are not merely minute; they are also very rapid. This is certainly true of the process of tarning as it takes place in the mind of the poet and his reader. It is both rapid and delicate and, as the reader may have felt already, it is difficult to take it out and examine it without rushing in where angels fear to tread. But there is another modern invention which may be brought to the aid of the microscope in order to meet this drawback; and that is the slow-motion film. Can we find in any sphere of human life something analogous to a slow-motion picture of the tarning process? I think we can. I have said that tarning can be detected not only in accredited poetry or literature but also in the history of language as a whole. Is there any other human institution in which tarning also happens, and in which it happens on a broader scale and at a more leisurely pace? I think there is. I think we shall find such an illustration as we want in the law, notably in the development of law by means of fictions.

We are accustomed to find something crabbed and something comic in legal fictions. When we read in an old pleading an averment that the plaintiff resides in the Island of Minorca, "to wit in the parish of St. Mary le Bow in the Ward of Cheap"—or, in a Note in the *Annual Practice* for 1945, that every man-of-war is deemed to be situated permanently in the parish of Stepney—it sounds funny. But it must be admitted that it is not any funnier *per se* than Shelley's telling us that his leaves are falling or Campion informing us as to his mistress that "there is a garden in her face." It is funny when we take it literally, not particularly funny when we understand what is meant and why it is expressed in that particular way.

There is one kind of metaphor which occurs both in law and in poetry and which is on the whole commoner and less odd-sounding in modern law than it is in modern poetry. This is personification of abstractions:

> Let not Ambition mock their useful toil,
> Their homely joys, and destiny obscure;
> Nor Grandeur hear with a disdainful smile
> The short and simple annals of the poor.[3]

We find this particular usage almost vanished from English poetry by the beginning of the twentieth century. The personification of abstractions and attributes which we find in the more high-flown sort of eighteenth-century poetry or in the occasional allegorical papers which Johnson inserted in the *Rambler* sound stiff and unnatural to us, and a modern poet would hardly bring himself to try and introduce the device at all. On the other hand, the personification of limited companies by which they are enabled to sue and be sued at law, to commit trespasses, and generally to be spoken of as carrying on all sorts of activities which can only *really* be carried on by sentient beings, is as common as dirt and no one ever dreams of laughing at it. But these examples will hardly do for our slow-motion picture. On the contrary, in them the gap between the B meaning and the A meaning is as wide and the *prima facie* absurdity of the B or surface-meaning is hardly less than in, let us say, Ossian's description of the Hero: "In peace, thou art the Gale of Spring, in war, the Mountain Storm."

The important thing is to see how and why the legal fiction comes into being and what is its positive function in the life of human beings. If you have suffered a wrong at the hands of another human being, the practical question for you, the point at which law really touches your life as a member of society, is, can you do anything about it? Can you bring the transgressor to book and obtain restitution? In other words, can you bring an action against him, obtain judgment, and get that judgment executed? Now the answer to that question must always depend to some extent, and in the earlier stages of a society governed by law it depends to a very large extent indeed on the answer to another question. It is not enough simply to show that the transgressor has, in common parlance, broken the law. What you or your advisers have to make up your mind about is something rather different and often much more complicated. You have to ask yourselves, Is there a form of procedure under which I can move against him? If so, is it sufficiently cheap and expeditious for me to be able to adopt it with some hope of success? Where, as in the case of English Common Law down to the middle of the nineteenth century, these forms of procedure, or forms of action as they are more often called, are severely restricted in number, these questions are very serious ones indeed.

---

3. From Thomas Gray's "Elegy Written in a Country Church-Yard."

Now suppose you had a good claim to the ownership of a piece of land, perhaps with a pleasant house on it, which was in the possession of somebody else who also, but wrongfully, claimed to be the owner. Your proper normal form of action, say, five hundred years ago, was by Writ of Right, a form of action which was very much of the first type and hedged about accordingly with all sorts of ceremonies, difficulties, and delays.

> At trahere atque moras tantis licet addere rebus![4]

One of the drawbacks of this type of action was that it was subject to things called *Essoins*. Essoins seem to have corresponded roughly to what we should call "adjournments"; they no doubt grew up procedurally with a view to preventing an unscrupulous plaintiff from taking unfair advantage of the defendant's ill health, absence, or other accidental disability. But they must have been corn in Egypt[5] for a usurping defendant. I am tempted to let Glanville,[6] in his own sedate language and at his own pace, give the reader some idea of their nature and complexity:

> If the Tenant, being summoned, appear not on the first day, but Essoin himself, such Essoin shall, if reasonable, be received; and he may, in this manner, essoin himself three times successively; and since the causes on account of which a person may justly essoin himself are various, let us consider the different kinds of Essoins.
>
> Of Essoins, some arise on account of ill health, others from other sources.

(I will here interpose that, among the Essoins arising from other sources were the *de ultra mare* and the *de esse in peregrinatione*[7] and that, if a person cast the Essoin *de esse in peregrinatione*, "it must be distinguished whether he went to Jerusalem or to another place. If to the former place, then a year and a day at least is generally allowed him." And with that I will let Glanville proceed again in his own order:)

> Of those Essoins which arise from ill health, one kind is that *ex infirmitate veniendi*, another *ex infirmitate de reseantisa*.[8]
>
> If the Tenant, being summoned, should on the first day cast the Essoin *de infirmitate veniendi*, it is in the election of his Adversary, being present, either to require from the Essoiner a lawful proof of the truth of the Essoin in question on that very day, or that he should find pledges or bind himself solemnly that at the day appointed he will have his Warrantor of the Essoin ... and he may thus Essoin himself three times successively. If on the third day, he neither appear nor essoin himself, then let it be ordered that he be forthcoming in person on another day; or that he send a fit Attorney in his place, to gain or lose for him.... It may be asked, what will be the consequence if the Tenant

---

4. "But it is lawful to draw out and add delays with such things!"

5. See Genesis, xlii. 1–2.

6. Beame's *Translation of Glanville*, London, 1812 [Barfield's note].

7. Essoins arising from being "beyond the sea or on a pilgrimage."

8. Essoins arising from "being too sick to appear" or from "a long-standing infirmity or confinement."

appear at the fourth day, after having cast three Essoins, and warrant all the Essoins? In that case, he shall prove the truth of each Essoin by his own oath and that of another; and, on the same day, he shall answer to the suit. . . .

If anyone desire to cast the Essoin *de infirmitate de reseantisa*, he may thrice do it. Yet should the Essoiner, on the third day preceding that appointed, at a proper place and before a proper person, present his Essoin. If, on the third Summons the Tenant appear not, the Court should direct that it may be seen whether his indisposition amount to a languor, or not. For this purpose let the following Writ issue, direct to the Sheriff of the County . . . :

"The King to the Sheriff, Health. I command you that, without delay you sent 4 lawful men of your County to see if the infirmity of which B. hath essoined himself in my Court, against R., be a languor or not. And, if they perceive that it is a languor, then, that they should put to him a day of one year and one day, from that day of the view, to appear before me or my justices. . . ."

Nor was it forgotten that Essoiners themselves may be subject to infirmities and languors:

The principal Essoiner is also at liberty, if so disposed, to essoin himself by another Essoiner. In this case the second Essoiner must state to the Court that the Tenant, having a just cause of Essoin, had been detained, so that he could not appear at the day appointed, neither to lose nor gain, and that therefore he had appointed a certain other person to essoin him; and that the Essoiner himself had met with such an impediment, which had prevented his appearance on that day: and this he is prepared to prove according to the practice of the Court. . . .

Having at last succeeded in getting your opponent out of bed and fixing the day for the trial, you still could not be certain that he would not appear in Court followed (subject, no doubt, to Essoins) by a professional boxer or swordsman, whom you would have to tackle in lieu of calling evidence. And so on. And all this may be about a claim so clear that you could get it disposed of in five minutes if you could only bring it to the stage of being tried at all!

It would have been a very different matter, so perhaps your Counsel would advise you, if only the issue were about *personal* property instead of real property. We could go to a different Court with a different form of action. No essoins. No wager of law. No trial by battle. No trial by ordeal. Everything up to date and efficient. What *is* personal property, you might ask. Well, your horse for one thing and your hawk and your clothes and your money—oh! yes, and oddly enough if you were a leaseholder instead of a freeholder and had only a term of years in this precious piece of land, *that* would be personal property too. But can't I get *my* case heard by these people? Don't they understand anything about fee simple?⁹ Oh! yes, they understand it all right; in fact they often

9. An estate in land without limitation to any class of heirs or restrictions on transfer of ownership.

have to decide the point. For instance, if a leaseholder in possession is ousted by a trespasser—by Jove! I've just thought of something! And then if your Counsel had a touch of creative genius, he might perhaps evolve the following device. It was evolved at all events, by Tudor times or thereabouts and continued in use down to the middle of the nineteenth century.

Remember the situation: You are the rightful owner of a piece of land of which X, who is in possession, wrongfully claims to be the owner. The device was this: you proceeded to inform the Court by your pleadings that you, as owner of the land, had recently leased it to a person whose name was John Doe, and John Doe had been ousted from his possession violently, *vi et armis*,[1] by X, the Defendant. *You* were not bringing the action, you pretended; John Doe was. But as X might aver in his defense that the blameless Doe had no title, Doe has joined you, his landlord, in the proceedings to prove that you did have a good title at the time when you leased the land to him. By this means you got your case before the Court that had jurisdiction to deal with the action known as Eject-ment, and were able to take advantage of the simpler and more effective procedure. Sometimes the fiction was a little more elabor-ate. Instead of alleging that X had ejected John Doe, you said that another gentleman called Richard Roe, or possibly William Stiles, had done so. Richard Roe having subsequently allowed X to take possession now claimed no interest in the proceedings, but he had given X notice that they were pending, so as to give X a chance to defend his title. In this case the first thing X heard of it all was a letter, signed "your loving friend, Richard Roe," telling him what had happened. Needless to say, John Doe and Richard Roe had no existence.

Many thousands of actions of this pattern and using these names must have been brought between the fifteenth and the nineteenth centuries and before long the whole procedure was no doubt so much a matter of course that it was little more than a kind of mathematical formula. There must, however, have been some ear-lier occasions on which it was a good deal more, and it is upon any one of these—perhaps the first of all—that I want the reader to bend his mind. Picture to yourself the Court, with Counsel on his feet opening the case. The story of John Doe and Richard Roe is being unfolded. At one point the Judge suddenly looks up and looks very hard at Counsel, who either winks very slightly or returns a stolid uncomprehending stare according to his tempera-ment and the intimacy of his acquaintance with the Judge out of hours. But Counsel knows all the same what has happened. The Bench has tumbled to it. The Judge has guessed that there is no

1. "By force of arms."

John Doe, no Richard Roe, no lease, no entry, no ouster. At the same moment, however, the Judge has seen the point of the whole fiction, the great advantage in the speedy administration of justice (for the real issue—the validity of X's title and yours—will be heard fairly and in full) and in the extended jurisdiction of his own Court. He decides to accord to the pleadings that willing suspension of disbelief which hundreds of years later made Mr. Bumble say that the law was a "hass."[2] The case proceeds. Place this picture before your mind's eye and there I think you will have a slow-motion picture of "tarning."

Has new law been made? It is much the same as asking whether new language has been made when a metaphor disappears into a "meaning." At all events, we begin to understand more fully what Maitland meant, when he wrote of English law that "substantive law has at first the look of being gradually secreted in the interstices of procedure." This is particularly true of an unwritten system like the English Common Law, where the law itself lay hidden in the unconscious, until it was expressed in a judgment, and where rights themselves depended on the existence of remedies. Consider that very important fiction, which is very much alive and flourishing all round us today—the fiction on which the law of trusteeship is based. Anyone who is a trustee will know how absurdly remote from reality is the B interpretation of his position, according to which he is the "owner" of the trust property. Yet this fiction, which permeates the whole of our jurisprudence, which most certainly is law, and not merely procedure, was introduced in the first place by devices strictly procedural, devices and circumstances which had their origin in that same contrast between the genealogical and the personal conceptions of Society which gave us John Doe and Richard Roe.

Moreover, this fictitious ownership, which we call trusteeship, has been strong enough to have other fictions erected on it. By the Common Law the personal property of a married woman became her husband's as soon as she married. But by a particularly ingenious piece of tarning the equity judges expressed in the form of law, and in doing so no doubt partly created, a more modern view of the rights of married women. They followed the Common Law doctrine that the husband owned everything but, as to property which someone had given to the wife with the intention that she should have it for her own separate use, the Courts of Equity began in the eighteenth century to say that the husband did indeed own this, but he owned it as *trustee* for his wife; and they would prevent him from dealing with it in any other way.

---

2. In Charles Dickens' *Oliver Twist* (Chap. 51), Mr. Bumble, after being told that the law "supposes that your wife acts under direction," replies: "If the law supposes that, * * * the law is a ass * * * the law's a bachelor * * * "

In the same way a metaphor may be strong enough to support a metaphor, as when Shelley bids the west wind "Make me thy lyre even as the forest is." If Shelley is not a lyre, neither is the forest; yet he illustrates the one fiction with the other. Nor is there anything grotesque or strained in this magnificent line. It is only when we begin to ponder and analyze it that we see how daring it is.

The long analogy which I have been drawing may be expressed more briefly in the formula:—metaphor: language: meaning:: legal fiction: law: social life. It has no particular significance if poetry is to be regarded *only* as either a pleasurable way of diverting our leisure hours or a convenient vehicle for the propagation of doctrine. For it must be conceded that there is all the difference in the world between the propagation of a doctrine and the creation of a meaning. The doctrine is already formulated and, if we choose to express it by tarning, that is simply a matter of technique or political strategy. The creation of meaning is a very different matter. I hope I may have succeeded in showing in the earlier part of this article that metaphor is something more than a piece of the technique of one of the fine arts. It is πολὺ μέγιστον[3] not merely in the diction of poetry but in the nature and growth of language itself. So far we have only considered in this connection those ubiquitous figures of speech which are, or used to be, called "tropes," as when we speak of our lives *fluctuating*, of our insight *bearing fruit* in deeds, of *seeing the point*, and so on. But if we proceed to study language with a more definitely historical bias, and look into the etymologies and derivations of words, then the vast majority even of those meanings which we normally regard as "literal" are seen to have originated either in metaphors or in something like them. Such words as *spirit, sad, humor, perceive, attend, express, understand*, and so on immediately spring to the mind as examples. Indeed the difficulty here would rather be to find words that are *not* examples. There is no doubt that they were once metaphorical. The question which a good many people have asked themselves, a little uneasily, is, Are they *still* metaphors? And, if not, when—and still more *how*—precisely, did they cease to be so?

What is essential to the nature and growth of language is clearly essential to the nature and growth of our thought, or rather of our consciousness as a whole. In what way then is metaphor or tarning essential to that nature and that growth? Here we begin to tread on metaphysical ground and here I think the analogy of legal fictions can really help us by placing our feet on one or two firmer tufts in the quaking bog. It can help us to realize in firmer outlines certain concepts which, like all those relating to the nature of thought itself, are tenuous, elusive, and difficult of expression.

Students of history will have observed that rebellions and agita-

---

3. "By far the most important" (see p. 137, above).

tions arising out of dissatisfaction with the law tend, at any rate in the earlier stages of society, to demand, not so much a reform of the law as its *publication*. People complain that they do not know what the law is. They want to know what it is, because otherwise they cannot be sure that it will be the same tomorrow as it is today. In fact it is the very essence of a law that it should apply to every case. It follows that the forms of action must be limited in number, and they must not change from day to day. If there is a different law for every case that arises, then what is being administered is simply not law at all but the arbitrary (though not necessarily unjust) decisions of those who govern us. But that is exactly what the word law *means*—something which is *not* such a series of arbitrary decisions or events, something which will be *the same* for the next case as it was for the last. This is where the difficulty arises; for it is the nature of life itself (certainly of human life) never to repeat itself exactly. Phenomena exactly repeated are not life, they are mechanism. Life varies, law is of its nature unvarying. Yet at the same time it is the function of law to serve, to express, and indeed partly to *make* the social life of the community. That is the paradox, the diurnal solution of which constitutes the process called society. One solution is legislation, the other is fiction. Legislation is drastic, *a priori*, and necessary. Fiction is flexible, empirical, and also necessary. "Without the Fiction of Adoption," says Maine in his *Ancient Law*, "it is difficult to understand how Society would ever have escaped from its swaddling clothes."

In the paradoxical relation of law to social life I think we have a useful picture of the paradoxical relation of language to consciousness. Formal logic is not much studied nowadays, but that does not alter the fact that logic is essential to the very existence of language and the forms of proposition and syllogism underlie all expression. Now logic presupposes first and foremost that the same word means the same thing in one sentence as it does in another. Humpty Dumpty may speak of making his words "mean" what he chooses, and if somebody made a noise never heard before or since he might possibly manage to convey some sort of vague sympathetic impression of the state of his feelings. Yet repetition is inherent in the very meaning of the word "meaning." To say a word "means" something implies that it means that same something more than once.

Here then is the paradox again. The logical use of language presupposes the meanings of the words it employs and presupposes them constant. I think it will be found to be a corollary of this, that the logical use of language can never add any meaning to it. The conclusion of a syllogism is implicit already in the premises, that is, in the *meanings* of the *words* employed; and all the syllogism can do is to make that meaning clearer to us and remove any misconception or confusion. But life is not constant. Every man, certainly every original man, has something new to say, something new to mean. Yet if he wants to express that meaning (and it may be that it is only when he tries to express it, that he knows what he means) he must use language—a vehicle which presupposes that he must either mean what was meant before or talk nonsense!

If therefore he would say anything really new, if that which was hitherto unconscious is to become conscious, he must resort to tarning. He must talk what is nonsense on the face of it, but in such a way that the recipient may have the new meaning suggested to him. This is the true importance of metaphor. I imagine this is why Aristotle, in calling metaphor "the most important," gives us a reason that "it alone does not mean borrowing from someone else." In terms of mixed law and logic we might perhaps say that the metaphorical proposition contains a judgment, but a judgment pronounced with a wink at the Court. Bacon put it more clearly in the *Advancement of Learning* when he said:

> Those whose conceits are seated in popular opinions need only but to prove or dispute; but those whose conceits are beyond popular opinions have a double labor; the one to make themselves conceived, and the other to prove and demonstrate. So that it is of necessity with them to have recourse to similitudes and translations to express themselves.

If we consider Bacon's position in the history of thought, it will not surprise us that the problem should have presented itself to him so clearly. Himself a lawyer, was he not attempting to do for science the very thing which Maitland tells us those old legal fictions were contrived for, that, is "to get modern results out of medieval premises"?

At all events there is a sentence in the *Novum Organum* which provides one of the most striking illustrations of tarning that it would be possible to imagine. It is a double illustration: first, there was an attempt at deliberate and fully conscious meaning-making, which failed: Bacon tried to inject new meaning into a word by *saying* precisely what he wanted it to mean. But we have seen that what is said precisely cannot convey new meaning. But, since his meaning *was* really new, there had at some point in the process to be a piece of actual tarning. There was—and it succeeded. He did in fact inject new meaning into another word—not by saying, but by just meaning it!

> Licet enim in natura nihil vere existat praeter corpora individua edentia actus puros individuos ex lege; in doctrinis tamen, illa ipsa lex, ejusque inquisitio et inventio atque explicatio, pro fundamento est tam ad sciendum quam ad operandum. Eam autem legem ejusque paragraphos

formarum nomine intelligimus; praesertim cum hoc vocabulum inval-
uerit, et familiariter occurrat.[4]

The "forms" of which Bacon here speaks were none other than
the Platonic ideas, in which Bacon, of course, did not believe.
What he did believe in was that system of abstract causes or uniformity which we have long since been accustomed to express by
the phrase "the laws of nature," but for which there was then no
name, because the meaning was a new one. He therefore tried
deliberately by way of a *simile* to put this new meaning into the
old word "*forma*"; but he failed, inasmuch as the new meaning
never came into general use. Yet at the same time, more unconsciously, and by way of *metaphor*, he was putting the new meaning
into the word "*lex*" itself—that curious meaning which it now
bears in the expression "the laws of nature." This is one of those
pregnant metaphors which pass into the language, so that much of
our subsequent thinking is based on them. To realize that after all
they *are* metaphors, and to ask what that entails, opens up avenues
of inquiry which are beyond the province of this article. Certainly,
they may be misleading, as well as illuminating. Long after Bacon's
time, two great men—a lawyer who was concerned with the nature
of law and a poet who was concerned with the nature of
Nature—felt bound to draw attention to this very metaphor.

"When an atheist," wrote Austin,[5] "speaks of laws governing the irrational world, the metaphorical application is suggested by an analogy
still more slender and remote.... He means that the uniformity of succession and co-existence resembles the uniformity of conduct produced
by an imperative rule. If, to draw the analogy closer, he ascribes these
laws to an author, he personifies a verbal abstraction and makes it play
the legislator. He attributes the uniformity of succession and
co-existence to laws set by nature: meaning by nature, the world itself;
or perhaps that very uniformity which he imputes to nature's commands."

The introduction of the atheist into this passage does not, I
think, weaken its force as an illustration, for whatever the strength
of Bacon's religious faith, it is quite plain that the "laws" of which
he speaks in the *Novum Organum* have very little to do with the
"commands" of any being other than nature itself.

4. Although it is true that in nature
nothing exists beyond separate bodies
producing separate motions according
to law; still for the *study* of nature
that very law and its investigation,
discovery, and exposition are the essential thing, for the purpose both of
science and of practice. Now it is that
law and its clauses which we understand by the term "forms"—principally
because this word is a familiar one
and has become generally accepted.
Novum Organum, ii. 2 [Barfield's note].

5. *Jurisprudence* (1869), i. 213 [Bar-
field's note].

"Long indeed," says Coleridge in The Friend, "will man strive to satisfy the inward querist with the phrase, laws of nature. But though the individual may rest content with the seeming metaphor, the race cannot. If a law of nature be a mere generalization, it is included ... as an act of the mind. But if it be other and more, and yet manifestable only in and to an intelligent spirit, it must in act and substance be itself spiritual; for things utterly heterogeneous can have no intercommunion."

Perhaps we may supplement the last sentence by saying that an *apparent* intercommunion between things utterly heterogeneous is the true mark of metaphor and may be significant of spiritual substance. If this is so, and if the aptness of a metaphor to mislead varies inversely with the extent to which it continues to be felt and understood *as* a metaphor and is not taken in a confused way semi-literally, then the contemplation by the mind of legal fictions may really be a rather useful exercise. For these are devices of expression, of which the practical expediency can easily be understood, and whose metaphorical nature is not so easily forgotten as they pass into general use.

There is not much that is more important for human beings than their relations with each other, and it is these which laws are designed to express. The making and application of law are thus fundamental human activities, but what is more important for my purpose is that they bear the same relation to naked thinking as traveling does to map reading or practice to theory. It is not by accident that such key words as *judgment* and *cause* have two distinct meanings; the practical task of fixing personal responsibility must surely have been the soil from which, as the centuries passed, the abstract notion of cause and effect was laboriously raised. Accordingly it would be strange indeed if the study of jurisprudence were not well adapted to throw light on the mind and its workings.

That study was formerly regarded as an essential element in a liberal education. It was a distinguished Italian jurist, Giovanni Battista Vico, who at the turn of the seventeenth and eighteenth centuries became interested in the figurative element in language and evolved therefrom a theory of the evolution of human consciousness from an instinctive "poetic" wisdom (*sapienza poetica*) to the modern mode of analytical thought.

It is perhaps a pity that this respectful attitude to legal studies has long since been abandoned; a pity both on general grounds and because the vast change in man's idea of himself wrought by the new notions of evolution and development, and by the comparatively recent birth of historical imagination, have opened up rich new fields of speculation both in language and in law. A better and more widely diffused knowledge of the latter could hardly fail to be beneficial in far-reaching ways at a time when the whole theory of human society is in the melting pot. For instance, a deeper, more sympathetic understanding of the long, slow movement of the human mind from the feudal, or genealogical, way of regarding human relationships towards what I have called the "personal" way would do no harm.

But I have been mainly concerned here with the subject of fictions. Properly understood, are they not a telling illustration of the fact that knowledge—the fullest possible awareness—of the nature of law is the true way of escape from its shackles? ἐγὼ γὰρ διὰ νόμου νόμῳ ἀπέθανον, "I, by the law, died unto the law," wrote St. Paul; and the *nature* of law, as law, is the same, whether it be moral, or logical, or municipal. If it be important for men to get a deep feeling for this process of liberation in general, it is equally important, for special reasons, that they should better comprehend the particular problem of the part played by metaphor in the operation and development of language. Here too the way to achieve liberation from the "confusion" of thought on which metaphor is based is not by attack or rebellion. The intrinsic nature of language makes all such attitudes puerile. It is not those who, like the optimistic Mr. Stuart Chase,[6] set out to cut away and expose all metaphorical usage who escape the curse of Babel. No. The best way to talk clearly and precisely and to talk sense is to understand as fully as possible the relation between predication and suggestion, between "saying" and "meaning." For then you will at least know what you are *trying* to do. It is not the freemen of a city who are likeliest to lose their way, and themselves, in its labyrinth of old and mazy streets; it is the simple-minded foreign nihilist making, with his honest-to-god intentions and suitcase, straight for the center, like a sensible man.

6. *The Tyranny of Words*, London, 1938 [Barfield's note].

QUESTIONS

1. Why does Barfield have to invent a new term? How does "tarning" differ from metaphor? from symbol? Discuss whether Barfield's "quaking bog" (p. 149) is an example of tarning. Analyze E. B. White's definition of democracy (p. 772–773) to determine whether or not it has examples of tarning.

2. To what extent does one "say one thing and mean another" in ordinary conversation? in an expository essay? in a short story? in an argument? in a poem? Do the purpose and occasion of each of these affect the possibility or desirability of tarning?

3. On p. 154 Barfield makes a distinction between the "genealogical way" and the "personal way" of looking at human beings.
Does Machiavelli view man in either of these two ways in "The
Prince" (pp. 749–756)? What implications do these two views
have for systems of government?

C. S. LEWIS

Bluspels and Flalansferes

Philologists often tell us that our language is full of dead metaphors. In this sentence, the word "dead" and the word "metaphors" may turn out to be ambiguous; but the fact, or group of
facts, referred to, is one about which there is no great disagreement. We all know in a rough and ready way, and all admit, these
things which are being called "dead metaphors," and for the
moment I do not propose to debate the propriety of the name. But
while their existence is not disputed, their nature, and their relation
to thought, gives rise to a great deal of controversy. For the benefit
of any who happen to have avoided this controversy hitherto, I had
better make plain what it is, by a concrete example. Bréal in his
Semantics often spoke in metaphorical, that is consciously, rhetorically, metaphorical language itself. Messrs. Ogden and Richards in
The Meaning of Meaning took Bréal to task on the ground that
"it is impossible thus to handle a scientific subject in metaphorical
terms." Barfield in his *Poetic Diction* retorted that Ogden and
Richards were, as a matter of fact, just as metaphorical as Bréal.
They had forgotten, he complained, that all language has a figurative origin and that the "scientific" terms on which they piqued
themselves—words like *organism, stimulus, reference*—were not
miraculously exempt. On the contrary, he maintained, "these
authors who professed to eschew figurative expressions were really
confining themselves to one very old kind of figure; they were rigid
under the spell of those verbal ghosts of the physical sciences which
today make up practically the whole meaning-system of so many
European minds."[1] Whether Ogden and Richards will see fit, or
have seen fit, to reply to this, I do not know; but the lines on
which any reply would run are already traditional. In fact the
whole debate may be represented by a very simple dialogue.

A. You are being metaphorical.

B. You are just as metaphorical as I am, but you don't know it.

A. No, I'm not. Of course I know all about *attending* once
having meant *stretching*, and the rest of it. But that is not what it
means now. It may have been a metaphor to Adam—but I am not

1. A. O. Barfield, *Poetic Diction,* Faber & Faber, Ltd., 1952) [Lewis'
1928, pp. 139, 140. New ed. (London: note].

using it metaphorically. What I *mean* is a pure concept with no metaphor about it at all. The fact that it was a metaphor is no more relevant than the fact that my pen is made of wood. You are simply confusing derivation with meaning.

There is clearly a great deal to be said for both sides. On the one hand it seems odd to suppose that what we *mean* is conditioned by a dead metaphor of which we may be quite ignorant. On the other hand, we see from day to day, that when a man uses a current and admitted metaphor without knowing it, he usually gets led into nonsense; and when, we are tempted to ask, does a metaphor become so old that we can ignore it with impunity? It seems harsh to rule that a man must know the whole semantic history of every word he uses—a history usually undiscoverable—or else talk without thinking. And yet, on the other hand, an obstinate suspicion creeps in that we cannot entirely jump off our own shadows, and that we deceive ourselves if we suppose that a new and purely conceptual notion of *attention* has replaced and superseded the old metaphor of stretching. Here, then, is the problem which I want to consider. How far, if at all, is thinking limited by these dead metaphors? Is Anatole France in any sense right when he reduces "The soul possesses God" to "the breath sits on the bright sky"? Or is the other party right when it urges "Derivations are one thing. Meanings are another"? Or is the truth somewhere between them?

The first and easiest case to study is that in which we ourselves invent a new metaphor. This may happen in one of two ways. It may be that when we are trying to express clearly to ourselves or to others a conception which we have never perfectly understood, a new metaphor simply starts forth, under the pressure of composition or argument. When this happens, the result is often as surprising and illuminating to us as to our audience; and I am inclined to think that this is what happens with the great, new metaphors of the poets. And when it does happen, it is plain that our new understanding is bound up with the new metaphor. In fact, the situation is for our purpose indistinguishable from that which arises when we hear a new metaphor from others; and for that reason, it need not be separately discussed. One of the ways, then, in which we invent a new metaphor, is by *finding* it, as unexpectedly as we might find it in the pages of a book; and whatever is true of the new metaphors that we find in books will also be true of those which we reach by a kind of lucky chance, or inspiration. But, of course, there is another way in which we invent new metaphors. When we are trying to explain, to someone younger or less instructed than ourselves, a matter which is already perfectly clear in our own minds, we may deliberately, and even painfully, pitch about for the metaphor that is likely to help him. Now when this happens, it is quite plain that our thought, our power of meaning, is not much helped or hindered by the metaphor that we use. On the contrary, we are often acutely aware of the discrepancy between our meaning and our image. We know that our metaphor is in some respects misleading; and probably, if we have acquired the tutorial shuffle, we warn our audience that it is "not to be pressed." It is apparently possible, in this case at least, to use metaphor and yet to keep our thinking independent of it. But we must observe that it is possible, only because we have other methods of expressing the same idea. We have already our own way of expressing the thing: we could say it, or we suppose that we could say it, literally instead. This clear conception we owe to other sources—to our previous studies. We can adopt the new metaphor as a temporary tool, which we dominate and by which we are not dominated ourselves, only because we have other tools in our box.

Let us now take the opposite situation—that in which it is we ourselves who are being instructed. I am no mathematician; and someone is trying to explain to me the theory that space is finite. Stated thus, the new doctrine is, to me, meaningless. But suppose he proceeds as follows.

"You," he may say, "can intuit only three dimensions; you therefore cannot conceive how space should be limited. But I think I can show you how that which must appear infinite in three dimensions, might nevertheless be finite in four. Look at it this way. Imagine a race of people who knew only two dimensions—like the Flatlanders. And suppose they were living on a globe. They would have no conception, of course, that the globe was curved—for it is curved round in that third dimension of which they have no inkling. They will therefore imagine that they are living on a plane; but they will soon find out that it is a plane which nowhere comes to an end; there are no edges to it. Nor would they be able even to imagine an edge. For an edge would mean that, after a certain point, there would be nothing to walk on; nothing below their feet. But that *below* and *above* dimension is just what their minds have not got; they have only backwards and forwards, and left and right. They would thus be forced to assert that their globe, which they could not see as a globe, was infinite. You can see perfectly well that it is finite. And now, can you not conceive that as these Flatlanders are to you, so you might be to a creature that intuited four dimensions? Can you not conceive how that which seems necessarily infinite to your three-dimensional consciousness might nonetheless be really finite?" The result of such a metaphor on my mind would be—in fact, has been—that something which before was sheerly meaningless acquires at least a faint hint of meaning. And if the particular example does not appeal to everyone, yet everyone has had experiences of the same sort. For all of us there are things which we cannot fully understand at all, but of which we can get a faint inkling by means of metaphor. And in such cases the relation between the thought and the metaphor is precisely the opposite of the relation which arises when it is we ourselves who understand and then invent the metaphors to help others. We are here entirely at the mercy of the metaphor. If our instructor has chosen it badly, we shall be thinking nonsense. If we have not got the imagery clearly before us, we shall be thinking nonsense. If we have it before us without knowing that it is metaphor—if we forget that our Flatlanders on their globe are a copy of the thing and mistake them for the thing itself—then again we shall be thinking nonsense. What truth we can attain in such a situation depends rigidly on three conditions. First, that the imagery should be originally well chosen; secondly, that we should apprehend the exact imagery; and thirdly that we should know that the metaphor is a metaphor. (That metaphors, misread as statements of fact, are the source of monstrous errors, need hardly be pointed out.)

I have now attempted to show two different kinds of metaphorical situation as they are at their birth. They are the two extremes, and furnish the limits within which our inquiry must work. On the one hand, there is the metaphor which we invent to teach by; on the other, the metaphor from which we learn. They might be called the Master's metaphor, and the Pupil's metaphor. The first is freely chosen; it is one among many possible modes of expression; it does not at all hinder, and only very slightly helps, the thought of its maker. The second is not chosen at all; it is the unique expression of a meaning that we cannot have on any other terms; it dominates completely the thought of the recipient; his truth cannot rise above the truth of the original metaphor. And between the Master's metaphor and the Pupil's there comes, of course, an endless number of types, dotted about in every kind of intermediate position. Indeed, these Pupil-Teachers' metaphors are the ordinary stuff of our conversation. To divide them into a series of classes and sub-classes and to attempt to discuss these separately would be very laborious, and, I trust, unnecessary. If we can find a true doctrine about the two extremes, we shall not be at a loss to give an account of what falls between them. To find the truth about any given metaphorical situation will merely be to plot its position. Insofar as it inclines to the "magistral" extreme, so far our thought will be independent of it; insofar as it has a "pupillary" element, so far it will be the unique expression, and therefore the iron limit of our thinking. To fill in this framework would be, as Aristotle used to say, "anybody's business."

Our problem, it will be remembered, was the problem of "dead" or "forgotten" metaphors. We have now gained some light on the relation between thought and metaphor as it is at the outset, when the metaphor is first made; and we have seen that this relation varies greatly according to what I have called the "metaphorical situation." There is, in fact, one relation in the case of the Master's metaphor, and an almost opposite relation in that of the Pupil's metaphor. The next step must clearly be to see what becomes of these two relations as the metaphors in question progress to the state of death or fossilization.

The question of the Master's Metaphor need not detain us long. I may attempt to explain the Kantian philosophy to a pupil by the following metaphor. "Kant answered the question 'How do I know that whatever comes round the corner will be blue?' by the supposition 'I am wearing blue spectacles.'" In time I may come to use "the blue spectacles" as a kind of shorthand for the whole Kantian machinery of the categories and forms of perception. And let us suppose, for the sake of analogy with the real history of language, that I continue to use this expression long after I have forgotten the metaphor which originally gave rise to it. And perhaps by this time the form of the word will have changed. Instead of the "blue spectacles" I may now talk of the *bloospel* or even the *bluspel*. If I live long enough to reach my dotage I may even enter on a philological period in which I attempt to find the derivation of this mysterious word. I may suppose that the second element is derived from the word *spell* and look back with interest on the supposed period when Kant appeared to me to be magical; or else, arguing that the whole word is clearly formed on the analogy of *gospel*, may indulge in unhistorical reminiscenses of the days when the *Critique* seemed to me irrefragably true. But how far, if at all, will my thinking about Kant be affected by all this linguistic process? In practice, no doubt, there will be some subtle influence; the mere continued use of the word *bluspel* may have led me to attribute to it a unity and substantiality which I should have hesitated to attribute to "the whole Kantian machinery of the categories and forms of perception." But that is a result rather of the noun-making than of the death of the metaphor. It is an interesting fact, but hardly relevant to our present inquiry. For the rest, the mere forgetting of the metaphor does not seem to alter my thinking about Kant, just as the original metaphor did not limit my thinking about Kant; provided always—and this is of the last importance—that it was, to begin with, a genuine Master's metaphor. I had my conception of Kant's philosophy before I ever thought of the blue spectacles. If I have continued philosophical studies I have it still. The "blue spectacles" phrase was from the first a temporary dress assumed by my thought for a special purpose, and ready to be laid aside at my pleasure; it did not penetrate the thinking itself, and its subsequent history is irrelevant. To any one who attempts to refute my later views on Kant by telling me that I don't know the real meaning of bluspel, I may confidently retort "Derivations aren't meanings." To be sure, if there was any *pupillary* element in its original use, if I received, as well as gave, new understanding when I used it, then the whole situation will be different. And it is fair to admit that in practice very few metaphors can be purely magistral; only that which to some degree enlightens ourselves is likely to enlighten others. It is hardly possible that when I first used the metaphor of the blue spectacles I did not gain some new awareness of the Kantian philosophy; and, so far, it was not purely magistral. But I am deliberately idealizing for the sake of clarity. Purely magistral metaphor may never occur. What is important for us is to grasp that *just insofar* as any metaphor began by being magistral, so far I can continue to use it long after I have forgotten its metaphorical nature, and my thinking will be neither helped nor hindered by the fact that it was originally a metaphor, nor yet by my forgetfulness of that fact. It is a mere accident. Here, derivations are irrelevant to meanings.

Let us now turn to the opposite situation, that of the Pupil's Metaphor. And let us continue to use our old example of the unmathematical man who has had the finitude of space suggested to him (we can hardly say "explained") by the metaphor of the Flatlanders on their sphere. The question here is rather more complicated. In the case of the Master's metaphor, by hypothesis, the master knew, and would continue to know, what he meant, independently of the metaphor. In the present instance, however, the fossilization of the metaphor may take place in two different ways. The pupil may himself become a mathematician, or he may remain as ignorant of mathematics as he was before; and in either case, he may continue to use the metaphor of the Flatlanders while forgetting its real content and its metaphorical nature.

I will take the second possibility first. From the imagery of the Flatlanders' sphere I have got my first inkling of the new meaning. My thought is entirely conditioned by this imagery. I do not apprehend the thing at all, except by seeing "it could be something like this." Let us suppose that in my anxiety to docket this new experience. I label the inkling or vague notion, "the Flatlanders' sphere." When I next hear the fourth dimension spoken of, I shall say, "Ah yes—the Flatlanders' sphere and all that." In a few years (to continue our artificial parallel) I may be talking glibly of the *Flalansfere* and may even have forgotten the whole of the imagery which this word once represented. And I am still, according to the hypothesis, profoundly ignorant of mathematics. My situation will then surely be most ridiculous. The meaning of *Flalansfere* I never knew except through the imagery. I could get beyond the imagery, to that whereof the imagery was a copy, only by learning mathematics; but this I have neglected to do. Yet I have lost the imagery. Nothing remains, then, but the conclusion that the word *Flalan-*

sfere is now really meaningless. My thinking, which could never get beyond the imagery, at once its boundary and its support, has now lost that support. I mean strictly nothing when I speak of the *Flalansfere*. I am only talking, not thinking, when I use the word. But this fact will be long concealed from me, because *Flalansfere*, being a noun, can be endlessly fitted into various contexts, so as to conform to syntactical usage and to give an appearance of meaning. It will even conform to the logical rules; and I can make many judgments about the *Flalansfere*; such as *it is what it is*, and has *attributes* (for otherwise of course it wouldn't be a thing, and if it wasn't a thing, how could I be talking about it?), and is a *substance* (for it can be the subject of a sentence). And what *affective* overtones the word may have taken on by that time, it is dangerous to predict. It had an air of mystery from the first: before the end I shall probably be building temples to it, and exhorting my countrymen to fight and die for the *Flalansfere*. But the *Flalansfere*, when once we have forgotten the metaphor, is only a noise.

But how if I proceed, after once having grasped the metaphor of the Flatlanders, to become a mathematician? In this case, too, I may well continue to use the metaphor, and may corrupt it in form till it becomes a single noun, the *Flalansfere*. But I shall have advanced, by other means, from the original symbolism; and I shall be able to study the thing symbolized without reference to the metaphor that first introduced me to it. It will then be no harm though I should forget that *Flalansfere* had ever been metaphorical. As the metaphor, even if it survived, would no longer limit my thoughts, so its fossilization cannot confuse them.

The results which emerge may now be summarized as follows. Our thought is independent of the metaphors we employ, insofar as these metaphors are optional: that is, insofar as we are able to have the same idea without them. For that is the real characteristic both of the magistral metaphors and of those which become optional, as the Flatlanders would become, if the pupil learned mathematics. On the other hand, where the metaphor is our only method of reaching a given idea at all, there our thinking is limited by the metaphor so long as we retain the metaphor; and when the metaphor becomes fossilized, our "thinking" is not thinking at all, but mere sound or mere incipient movements in the larynx. We are now in a position to reply to the statement that "Derivations are not meanings," and to the claim that "we know what we mean by words without knowing the fossilized metaphors they contain." We can see that such a statement, as it stands, is neither wholly true nor wholly false. The truth will vary from word to word, and from speaker to speaker. No rule of thumb is possible, we must take every case on its merits. A word can bear a meaning in the mouth of a speaker who has forgotten its hidden metaphor, and a meaning independent of that metaphor, but only on certain conditions. Either the metaphor must have been optional from the beginning, and have remained optional through all the generations of its use, so that the conception has always used and still uses the imagery as a mere tool; or else, at some period subsequent to its creation, we must have gone on to acquire, independently of the metaphor, such new knowledge of the object indicated by it as enables us now, at last, to dispense with it. To put the same thing in another way, meaning is independent of derivation, only if the metaphor was originally "magistral"; or if, in the case of an originally pupillary metaphor, some quite new kind of apprehension has arisen to replace the metaphorical apprehension which has been lost. The two conditions may be best illustrated by a concrete example. Let us take the word for *soul* as it exists in the Romance language. How far is a man entitled to say that what he means by the word *âme* or *anima* is quite independent of the image of *breathing*, and that he means just the same (and just as much) whether he happens to know that "derivation" or not? We can only answer that it depends on a variety of things. I will enumerate all the formal possibilities for the sake of clearness: one of them, of course, is too grotesque to appear for any other purpose.

1. The metaphor may originally have been magistral. Primitive men, we are to suppose, were clearly aware, on the one hand, of an entity called *soul*; and, on the other, of a process or object called *breath*. And they used the second figuratively to suggest the first—presumably when revealing their wisdom to primitive women and primitive children. And we may suppose, further, that this magistral relation to the metaphor has never been lost: that all generations, from the probably arboreal to the man saying "Blast your soul" in a pub this evening, have kept clearly before them these two separate entities, and used the one metaphorically to denote the other, while at the same time being well able to conceive the soul unmetaphorically, and using the metaphor merely as a color or trope which adorned but did not influence their thought. Now if all this were true, it would unquestionably follow that when a man says *anima* his meaning is not affected by the old image of breath; and also, it does not matter in the least whether he knows that the word once suggested that image or not. But of course all this is not true.

2. The metaphor may originally have been pupillary. So far from being a voluntary ornament or pedagogic device, the ideas of *breath* or *something like breath* may have been the only possible inkling that our parents could gain of the soul. But if this was so, how does the modern user of the word stand? Clearly, if he has ceased to be aware of the metaphorical element in *anima*, without replacing the metaphorical apprehension by some new knowledge

of the soul, borrowed from other sources, then he will mean nothing by it; we must not, on that account, suppose that he will cease to use it, or even to use it (as we say) intelligibly—i.e. to use it in sentences constructed according to the laws of grammar, and to insert these sentences into those conversational and literary contexts where usage demands their insertion. If, on the other hand, he has some independent knowledge of the entity which our ancestors indicated by their metaphor of breath, then indeed he may mean something.

I take it that it is this last situation in which we commonly suppose ourselves to be. It doesn't matter, we would claim, what the majestic root GNA really stood for: we have learned a great deal about *knowing* since those days, and it is these more recent acquisitions that we use in our thinking. The first name for a thing may easily be determined by some inconsiderable accident. As we learn more, we mean more; the radical meaning of the old syllables does not bind us; what we have learned since has set us free. Assuredly, the accident which led the Romans to call all Hellenes *Graeci* did not continue to limit their power of apprehending Greece. And as long as we are dealing with sensible objects this view is hardly to be disputed. The difficulty begins with objects of thought. It may be stated as follows.

Our claim to independence of the metaphor is, as we have seen, a claim to know the object otherwise than through that metaphor. If we can throw the Flatlanders overboard and still think the fourth dimension, then, and not otherwise, we can forget what *Flalansfere* once meant and still think coherently. That was what happened, you will remember, to the man who went on and learned mathematics. He came to apprehend that of which the Flatlanders' sphere was only the image, and consequently was free to think beyond the metaphor and to forget the metaphor altogether. In our previous account of him, however, we carefully omitted to draw attention to one very remarkable fact: namely, that when he deserted metaphor for mathematics, he did not really pass from symbol to symbolized, but only from one set of symbols to another. The equations and what-nots are as unreal, as metaphorical, if you like, as the Flatlanders' sphere. The mathematical problem I need not pursue further; we see at once that it casts a disquieting light on our linguistic problem. We have hitherto been speaking as if we had two methods of thought open to us: the metaphorical, and the literal. We talked as if the creator of a magistral metaphor had it always in his power to think the same concept *literally* if he chose. We talked as if the present-day user of the word *anima* could prove his right to neglect that word's buried metaphor by turning round and giving us an account of the soul which was not metaphorical at all. That he has power to dispense with the particular metaphor of *breath* is of course agreed. But we have not yet inquired what he can substitute for it. If we turn to those who are most anxious to tell us about the soul—I mean the psychologists—we shall find that the word *anima* had simply been replaced by complexes, repressions, censors, engrams, and the like. In other words the *breath* has been exchanged for *tyings-up, shovings-back, Roman magistrates,* and *scratchings.* If we inquire what has replaced the metaphorical *bright sky* of primitive theology, we shall only get a *perfect substance,* that is, a *completely made lying-under,* or—which is very much better, but equally metaphorical—a universal Father, or perhaps (in English) a *loaf-carver,* in Latin a *householder,* in Romance *a person older than.* The point need not be labored. It is abundantly clear that the freedom from a given metaphor which we admittedly enjoy in some cases is often only a freedom to choose between that metaphor and others.

Certain reassurances may, indeed, be held out. In the first place, our distinction between the different kinds of metaphorical situation can stand; though it is hardly so important as we had hoped. To have a choice of metaphors (as we have in some cases) is to know more than we know when we are the slaves of a unique metaphor. And, in the second place, all description or identification, all direction of our own thought or another's, is not so metaphorical as definition. If, when challenged on the word *anima,* we proceed to define, we shall only reshuffle the buried metaphors; but if we simply say (or think) "what I am," or "what is going on in here," we shall have at least something before us which we do not know by metaphor. We shall at least be no worse off than the arboreal psychologists. At the same time, this method will not really carry us far. "What's going on here" is really the content of *hæc anima*: for *anima* we want "*The sort of thing* that is going on here," and once we are committed to *sorts* and *kinds* we are adrift among metaphors.

We have already said that when a man claims to think independently of the buried metaphor in one of his words, his claim may sometimes be allowed. But it was allowed only insofar as he could really supply the place of that buried metaphor with new and independent apprehension of his own. We now see that this new apprehension will usually turn out to be itself metaphorical; or else, what is very much worse, instead of new apprehension we shall have simply words—each word enshrining one more ignored metaphor. For if he does not know the history of *anima,* how should he know the history of the equally metaphorical words in which he defines it, if challenged? And if he does not know their history and therefore their metaphors, and if he cannot define *them* without yet further metaphors, what can his discourse be but an endless

ringing of the changes on such *bluspels* and *Flalansferes* as seem to
mean, indeed, but do not mean? In reality, the man has played us
a very elementary trick. He claimed that he could think without
metaphor, and in ignorance of the metaphors fossilized in his
words. He made good the claim by pointing to the knowledge of
his object which he possessed independently of the metaphor; and
the proof of this knowledge was the definition or description which
he could produce. We did not at first observe that where we were
promised a freedom from metaphor we were given only a power of
changing the metaphors in rapid succession. The things he speaks
of he has never apprehended *literally*. Yet only such genuinely literal apprehension could enable him to forget the metaphors which
he was actually using and yet to have a meaning. Either literalness,
or else metaphor understood: one or other of these we must have;
the third alternative is nonsense. But literalness we cannot have.
The man who does not consciously use metaphors talks without
meaning. We might even formulate a rule: the meaning in any
given composition is in inverse ratio to the author's belief in his
own literalness.

If a man has seen ships and the sea, he may abandon the metaphor of a *sea-stallion* and call a boat a boat. But suppose a man
who has never seen the sea, or ships, yet who knows of them just as
much as he can glean, say from the following list of
Kenningar[2]—sea-stallions, winged logs, wave riders, ocean trains. If
he keeps all these together in his mind, and knows them for the
metaphors they are, he will be able to think of ships, very imperfectly indeed, and under strict limits, but not wholly in vain.
But if instead of this he pins his faith on the particular kenning,
ocean trains, because that kenning, with its comfortable air of
machinery, seems to him somehow more safely prosaic, less flighty
and dangerous than its fellows, and if, contracting that to the form
oshtrans, he proceeds to forget that it was a metaphor, then, while
he talks grammatically, he has ceased to think of anything. It will
not avail him to stamp his feet and swear that he is literal; to say
"An *oshtran* is an *oshtran*, and there's an end. I mean what I
mean. What I mean is what I say."

The remedy lies, indeed, in the opposite direction. When we
pass beyond pointing to individual sensible objects, when we begin
to think of causes, relations, of mental states or acts, we become
incurably metaphorical. We apprehend none of these things except
through metaphor: we know of the ships only what the *Kenningar*
will tell us. Our only choice is to use the metaphors and thus to
think something, though less than we could wish; or else to be

---

2. The Norse plural for "kenning,"
a metaphorical compound word (e.g.,   "whale road" for "sea") used especially
in Old English and Old Norse poetry.

driven by unrecognized metaphors and to think nothing at all. I myself would prefer to embrace the former choice, as far as my ignorance and laziness allow me.

To speak more plainly, he who would increase the meaning and decrease the meaningless verbiage in his own speech and writing, must do two things. He must become conscious of the fossilized metaphors in his words; and he must freely use new metaphors, which he creates for himself. The first depends upon knowledge, and therefore on leisure; the second on a certain degree of imaginative ability. The second is perhaps the more important of the two: we are never less the slaves of metaphor than when we are making metaphor, or hearing it new made. When we are thinking hard of the Flatlanders, and at the same time fully aware that they *are* a metaphor, we are in a situation almost infinitely superior to that of the man who talks of the *Flalansfere* and thinks that he is being literal and straightforward.

If our argument has been sound, it leads us to certain rather remarkable conclusions. In the first place it would seem that we must be content with a very modest quantity of thinking as the core of all our talking. I do not wish to exaggerate our poverty. Not all our words are equally metaphorical, not all our metaphors are equally forgotten. And even where the old metaphor is lost there is often a hope that we may still restore meaning by pointing to some sensible object, some sensation, or some concrete memory. But no man can or will confine his cognitive efforts to this narrow field. At the very humblest we must speak of things in the plural; we must point not only to isolated sensations, but to groups and classes of sensations; and the universal latent in every group and every plural inflection cannot be thought without metaphor. Thus far beyond the security of literal meaning all of us, we may be sure, are going to be driven by our daily needs; indeed, not to go thus far would be to abandon reason itself. In practice we all really intend to go much farther. Why should we not? We have in our hands the key of metaphor, and it would be pusillanimous to abandon its significant use, because we have come to realize that its meaningless use is necessarily prevalent. We must indeed learn to use it more cautiously; and one of the chief benefits to be derived from our inquiry is the new standard of criticism which we must henceforward apply both to our own apparent thought and to that of others. We shall find, too, that real meaning, judged by this standard, does not come always where we have learned to expect. *Flalansferes* and *bluspels* will clearly be most prevalent in certain types of writers. The percentage of mere syntax masquerading as meaning may vary from something like 100 per cent in political writers, journalists, psychologists, and economists, to something like forty per cent in the writers of children's stories. Some scientists will fare better than others: the historian, the geographer, and sometimes the biologist will speak significantly more often than their colleagues; the mathematician, who seldom forgets that his symbols are symbolic, may often rise for short stretches to ninety per cent of meaning and ten of verbiage. The philosophers will differ as widely from one another as any of the other groups differ among themselves: for a good metaphysical library contains at once some of the most verbal, and some of the most significant literature in the world. Those who have prided themselves on being literal, and who have endeavored to speak plainly, with no mystical tomfoolery, about the highest abstractions, will be found to be among the least significant of writers: I doubt if we shall find more than a beggarly five per cent of meaning in the pages of some celebrated "tough minded" thinkers, and how the account of Kant or Spinoza stands, none know but heaven. But open your Plato, and you will find yourself among the great creators of metaphor, and therefore among the masters of meaning. If we turn to Theology—or rather to the literature of religion—the result will be more surprising still; for unless our whole argument is wrong, we shall have to admit that a man who says *heaven* and thinks of the visible sky is pretty sure to mean more than a man who tells us that heaven is a state of mind. It may indeed be otherwise; the second man may be a mystic who is remembering and pointing to an actual and concrete experience of his own. But it is long, long odds. Bunyan and Dante stand where they did; the scale of Bishop Butler, and of better men than he, flies up and kicks the beam.[3]

It will have escaped no one that in such a scale of writers the poets will take the highest place; and among the poets those who have at once the tenderest care for old words and the surest instinct for the creation of new metaphors. But it must not be supposed that I am in any sense putting forward the imagination as the organ of truth. We are not talking of truth, but of meaning: meaning which is the antecedent condition both of truth and falsehood, whose antithesis is not error but nonsense. I am a rationalist. For me, reason is the natural organ of truth; but imagination is the organ of meaning. Imagination, producing new metaphors of revivifying old, is not the cause of truth, but its condition. It is, I confess, undeniable that such a view indirectly implies a kind of truth or rightness in the imagination itself. I said at the outset that the truth we won by metaphor could not be greater than the truth of the metaphor itself; and we have seen since that all our truth, or all but a few fragments, is won by metaphor. And thence, I confess, it does follow that if our thinking is ever true, then the metaphors by

3. Joseph Butler (1692–1752), Bishop of Durham, was noted for abstract religious speculation. Lewis believes Bunyan's and Dante's physical descriptions of heaven would tip the scales in their favor.

which we think must have been good metaphors. It does follow that if those original equations, between good and light, or evil and dark, between breath and soul and all the others, were from the beginning arbitrary and fanciful—if there is not, in fact, a kind of psycho-physical parallelism (or more) in the universe—then all our thinking is nonsensical. But we cannot, without contradiction, believe it to be nonsensical. And so, admittedly, the view I have taken has metaphysical implications. But so has every view.

QUESTIONS

1. What are the main points of Lewis' argument? How persuasively has he presented his case? Is the main line of his argument weakened by his admission (p. 162) that words which were originally metaphors may have come to reflect "new knowledge of the object"? Do his conclusions, especially those in the last two paragraphs of the essay, follow from what has preceded?

2. Lewis summarizes some of his conclusions about the relationship of metaphor to meaning on pages 162 ff. Test these conclusions by tracing the derivation of the following words in a dictionary. Are there any of these words in which some of the different senses or meanings represent one kind of development, some of them another?

nothing	biology	symbol	imagination
communism	freedom	evolution	personality
prose	religion	ritual	grammar
fossil	science	virtue	metaphor
definition	democracy	literal	literature
meaning	evil		

3. Analyze the following brief poem. Is its metaphor a Master's or Pupil's? Would Barfield consider this a good example of "tarning"? Is tarning more like the magistral or the pupillary metaphor?

> We dance round in a ring and suppose,
> But the Secret sits in the middle and knows.
> —Robert Frost, "The Secret Sits"

GEORGE ORWELL
Politics and the English Language

Most people who bother with the matter at all would admit that the English language is in a bad way, but it is generally assumed that we cannot by conscious action do anything about it. Our civilization is decadent and our language—so the argument runs—must inevitably share in the general collapse. It follows that any struggle against the abuse of language is a sentimental archaism, like preferring candles to electric light or hansom cabs to aeroplanes. Underneath this lies the half-conscious belief that language is a natural growth and not an instrument which we shape for our own purposes.

Now, it is clear that the decline of a language must ultimately have political and economic causes: it is not due simply to the bad influence of this or that individual writer. But an effect can become a cause, reinforcing the original cause and producing the same effect in an intensified form, and so on indefinitely. A man may take to drink because he feels himself to be a failure, and then fail all the more completely because he drinks. It is rather the same thing that is happening to the English language. It becomes ugly and inaccurate because our thoughts are foolish, but the slovenliness of our language makes it easier for us to have foolish thoughts. The point is that the process is reversible. Modern English, especially written English, is full of bad habits which spread by imitation and which can be avoided if one is willing to take the necessary trouble. If one gets rid of these habits one can think more clearly, and to think clearly is a necessary first step towards political regeneration: so that the fight against bad English is not frivolous and is not the exclusive concern of professional writers. I will come back to this presently, and I hope that by that time the meaning of what I have said here will have become clearer. Meanwhile, here are five specimens of the English language as it is now habitually written.

These five passages have not been picked out because they are especially bad—I could have quoted far worse if I had chosen—but because they illustrate various of the mental vices from which we now suffer. They are a little below the average, but are fairly representative samples. I number them so that I can refer back to them when necessary:

"(1) I am not, indeed, sure whether it is not true to say that the Milton who once seemed not unlike a seventeenth-century Shelley had not become, out of an experience ever more bitter in each year, more alien [*sic*] to the founder of that Jesuit sect which nothing could induce him to tolerate."

Professor Harold Laski (Essay in *Freedom of Expression*).

"(2) Above all, we cannot play ducks and drakes with a native battery of idioms which prescribes such egregious collocations of vocables as the Basic *put up with* for *tolerate* or *put at a loss* for *bewilder*."

Professor Lancelot Hogben (*Interglossa*).

"(3) On the one side we have the free personality: by definition it is not neurotic, for it has neither conflict nor dream. Its desires, such as they are, are transparent, for they are just what institutional approval keeps in the forefront of consciousness; another institutional pattern would alter their number and intensity; there is little in them that is natural, irreducible, or culturally dangerous. But *on the other side*, the social bond itself is nothing but the mutual reflection of these self-secure integrities. Recall the definition of love. Is not this the very picture of a small academic? Where is there a place in this hall of mirrors for either personality or fraternity?"

Essay on psychology in *Politics* (New York).

"(4) All the 'best people' from the gentlemen's clubs, and all the frantic fascist captains, united in common hatred of Socialism and bestial horror of the rising tide of the mass revolutionary movement, have turned to acts of provocation, to foul incendiarism, to medieval legends of poisoned wells, to legalize their own destruction of proletarian organizations, and rouse the agitated petty-bourgeoisie to chauvinistic fervour on behalf of the fight against the revolutionary way out of the crisis."

Communist pamphlet.

"(5) If a new spirit *is* to be infused into this old country, there is one thorny and contentious reform which must be tackled, and that is the humanization and galvanization of the B.B.C. Timidity here will bespeak cancer and atrophy of the soul. The heart of Britain may be sound and of strong beat, for instance, but the British lion's roar at present is like that of Bottom in Shakespeare's *Midsummer Night's Dream*—as gentle as any sucking dove. A virile new Britain cannot continue indefinitely to be traduced in the eyes or rather ears, of the world by the effete languors of Langham Place, brazenly masquerading as 'standard English'. When the Voice of Britain is heard at nine o'clock, better far and infinitely less ludicrous to hear aitches honestly dropped than the present priggish, inflated, inhibited, school-ma'amish arch braying of blameless bashful mewing maidens!"

Letter in *Tribune*.

Each of these passages has faults of its own, but, quite apart from avoidable ugliness, two qualities are common to all of them. The first is staleness of imagery: the other is lack of precision. The writer either has a meaning and cannot express it, or he inadvertently says something else, or he is almost indifferent as to whether his words mean anything or not. This mixture of vagueness and sheer incompetence is the most marked characteristic of modern English prose, and especially of any kind of political writing. As soon as certain topics are raised, the concrete melts into the abstract and no one seems able to think of turns of speech that are not hackneyed: prose consists less and less of *words* chosen for the sake of their meaning, and more and more of *phrases* tacked together like the sections of a prefabricated hen-house. I list below, with notes and examples, various of the tricks by means of which the work of prose-construction is habitually dodged:

Dying Metaphors

A newly invented metaphor assists thought by evoking a visual image, while on the other hand a metaphor which is technically "dead" (e.g. *iron resolution*) has in effect reverted to being an ordinary word and can generally be used without loss of vividness. But in between these two classes there is a huge dump of worn-out metaphors which have lost all evocative power and are merely used because they save people the trouble of inventing phrases for themselves. Examples are: *Ring the changes on, take up the cudgels for, toe the line, ride roughshod over, stand shoulder to shoulder with, play into the hands of, no axe to grind, grist to the mill, fishing in troubled waters, on the order of the day, Achilles' heel, swan song, hotbed.* Many of these are used without knowledge of their meaning (what is a "rift", for instance?), and incompatible metaphors are frequently mixed, a sure sign that the writer is not interested in what he is saying. Some metaphors now current have been twisted out of their original meaning without those who use them even being aware of the fact. For example, *toe the line* is sometimes written *tow the line.* Another example is *the hammer and the anvil,* now always used with the implication that the anvil gets the worst of it. In real life it is always the anvil that breaks the hammer, never the other way about: a writer who stopped to think what he was saying would be aware of this, and would avoid perverting the original phrase.

Operators or Verbal False Limbs

These save the trouble of picking out appropriate verbs and nouns, and at the same time pad each sentence with extra syllables which give it an appearance of symmetry. Characteristic phrases are: *render inoperative, militate against, make contact with, be subjected to, give rise to, give grounds for, have the effect of, play a leading part (role) in, make itself felt, take effect, exhibit a tendency to, serve the purpose of, etc., etc.* The keynote is the elimination of simple verbs. Instead of being a single word, such as *break, stop, spoil, mend, kill,* a verb becomes a *phrase,* made up of a noun or adjective tacked on to some general-purposes verb such as *prove, serve, form, play, render.* In addition, the passive voice is wherever possible used in preference to the active, and noun constructions are used instead of gerunds (*by examination of* instead of *by examining*). The range of verbs is further cut down by means of the *-ize* and *de-* formation, and the banal statements are given an appearance of profundity by means of the *not un-* formation. Simple conjunctions and prepositions are replaced by such phrases as *with respect to, having regard to, the fact that, by dint of, in view of, in the interests of, on the hypothesis that*; and the ends of sentences are saved from anticlimax by such resounding commonplaces as *greatly to be desired, cannot be left out of account, a development to be expected in the near future, deserving of serious consideration, brought to a satisfactory conclusion,* and so on and so forth.

Pretentious Diction

Words like *phenomenon, element, individual* (as noun), *objective, categorical, effective, virtual, basic, primary, promote, constitute, exhibit, exploit, utilize, eliminate, liquidate,* are used to dress up simple statements and give an air of scientific impartiality to biased judgments. Adjectives like *epoch-making, epic, historic, unforgettable, triumphant, age-old, inevitable, inexorable, veritable,* are used to dignify the sordid processes of international politics, while writing that aims at glorifying war usually takes on an archaic colour, its characteristic words being: *realm, throne, chariot, mailed fist, trident, sword, shield, buckler, banner, jackboot, clarion.* Foreign words and expressions such as *cul de sac, ancien régime, deus ex machina, mutatis mutandis, status quo, gleichschaltung, weltanschauung,* are used to give an air of culture and elegance. Except for the useful abbreviations *i.e., e.g.,* and *etc.,* there is no real need for any of the hundreds of foreign phrases now current in English. Bad writers, and especially scientific, political and sociological writers, are nearly always haunted by the notion that Latin or Greek words are grander than Saxon ones, and unnecessary words like *expedite, ameliorate, predict, extraneous, deracinated, clandestine, subaqueous* and hundreds of others constantly gain ground from their Anglo-Saxon opposite numbers.[1] The jargon peculiar to Marxist writing (*hyena, hangman, cannibal, petty bourgeois, these gentry, lacquey, flunkey, mad dog, White Guard,* etc.) consists largely of words and phrases translated from Russian, German or French; but the normal way of coining a new word is to use a Latin or Greek root with the appropriate affix and, where necessary, the -ize formation. It is often easier to make up words of this kind (*deregionalize, impermissible, extramarital, nonfragmentatory* and so forth) than to think up the English words that will cover one's meaning. The result, in general, is an increase in slovenliness and vagueness.

Meaningless Words

In certain kinds of writing, particularly in art criticism and literary criticism, it is normal to come across long passages which are almost completely lacking in meaning.[2] Words like *romantic, plas-*

1. An interesting illustration of this is the way in which the English flower names which were in use till very recently are being ousted by Greek ones, *snapdragon* becoming *antirrhinum, forget-me-not* becoming *myosotis,* etc. It is hard to see any practical reason for this change of fashion: it is probably due to an instinctive turning-away from the more homely word and a vague feeling that the Greek word is scientific.

2. Example: "Comfort's catholicity of perception and image, strangely Whitmanesque in range, almost the exact opposite in aesthetic compulsion, continues to evoke that trembling atmospheric accumulative hinting at a cruel, an inexorably serene timelessness ... Wrey Gardiner scores by aiming at simple bull's-eyes with precision. Only they are not so simple, and through this contented sadness runs more than the surface bittersweet of resignation." (*Poetry Quarterly.*)

tic, *values, human, dead, sentimental, natural, vitality,* as used in art criticism, are strictly meaningless in the sense that they not only do not point to any discoverable object, but are hardly ever expected to do so by the reader. When one critic writes, "The outstanding feature of Mr. X's work is its living quality", while another writes, "The immediately striking thing about Mr. X's work is its peculiar deadness", the reader accepts this as a simple difference of opinion. If words like *black* and *white* were involved, instead of the jargon words *dead* and *living,* he would see at once that language was being used in an improper way. Many political words are similarly abused. The word *Fascism* has now no meaning except in so far as it signifies "something not desirable". The words *democracy, socialism, freedom, patriotic, realistic, justice,* have each of them several different meanings which cannot be reconciled with one another. In the case of a word like *democracy,* not only is there no agreed definition, but the attempt to make one is resisted from all sides. It is almost universally felt that when we call a country democratic we are praising it: consequently the defenders of every kind of régime claim that it is a democracy, and fear that they might have to stop using the word if it were tied down to any one meaning. Words of this kind are often used in a consciously dishonest way. That is, the person who uses them has his own private definition, but allows his hearer to think he means something quite different. Statements like *Marshal Pétain was a true patriot, The Soviet Press is the freest in the world, The Catholic Church is opposed to persecution,* are almost always made with intent to deceive. Other words used in variable meanings, in most cases more or less dishonestly, are: *class, totalitarian, science, progressive, reactionary, bourgeois, equality.*

Now that I have made this catalogue of swindles and perversions, let me give another example of the kind of writing that they lead to. This time it must of its nature be an imaginary one. I am going to translate a passage of good English into modern English of the worst sort. Here is a well-known verse from *Ecclesiastes*:

"I returned and saw under the sun, that the race is not to the swift, nor the battle to the strong, neither yet bread to the wise, nor yet riches to men of understanding, nor yet favour to men of skill; but time and chance happeneth to them all."

Here it is in modern English:

"Objective consideration of contemporary phenomena compels the conclusion that success or failure in competitive activities exhibits no tendency to be commensurate with innate capacity, but that a considerable element of the unpredictable must invariably be taken into account."

This is a parody, but not a very gross one. Exhibit (3), above, for instance, contains several patches of the same kind of English. It will be seen that I have not made a full translation. The beginning and ending of the sentence follow the original meaning fairly closely, but in the middle the concrete illustrations—race, battle, bread—dissolve into the vague phrase "success or failure in competitive activities". This had to be so, because no modern writer of the kind I am discussing—no one capable of using phrases like "objective consideration of contemporary phenomena"—would ever tabulate his thoughts in that precise and detailed way. The whole tendency of modern prose is away from concreteness. Now analyse these two sentences a little more closely. The first contains forty-nine words but only sixty syllables, and all its words are those of everyday life. The second contains thirty-eight words of ninety syllables: eighteen of its words are from Latin roots, and one from Greek. The first sentence contains six vivid images, and only one phrase ("time and chance") that could be called vague. The second contains not a single fresh, arresting phrase, and in spite of its ninety syllables it gives only a shortened version of the meaning contained in the first. Yet without a doubt it is the second kind of sentence that is gaining ground in modern English. I do not want to exaggerate. This kind of writing is not yet universal, and outcrops of simplicity will occur here and there in the worst-written page. Still, if you or I were told to write a few lines on the uncertainty of human fortunes, we should probably come much nearer to my imaginary sentence than to the one from *Ecclesiastes*.

As I have tried to show, modern writing at its worst does not consist in picking out words for the sake of their meaning and inventing images in order to make the meaning clearer. It consists in gumming together long strips of words which have already been set in order by someone else, and making the results presentable by sheer humbug. The attraction of this way of writing is that it is easy. It is easier—even quicker, once you have the habit—to say *In my opinion it is a not unjustifiable assumption that* than to say *I think*. If you use ready-made phrases, you not only don't have to hunt about for words; you also don't have to bother with the rhythms of your sentences, since these phrases are generally so arranged as to be more or less euphonious. When you are composing in a hurry—when you are dictating to a stenographer, for instance, or making a public speech—it is natural to fall into a pretentious, Latinized style. Tags like *a consideration which we should do well to bear in mind* or *a conclusion to which all of us would readily assent* will save many a sentence from coming down with a bump. By using stale metaphors, similes and idioms, you save much mental effort, at the cost of leaving your meaning vague, not only for your reader but for yourself. This is the significance of mixed metaphors. The sole aim of a metaphor is to call up a visual image. When these images clash—as in *The Fascist octopus has sung its swan song, the jackboot is thrown into the melting pot*—it can be taken as certain that the writer is not seeing a mental image of the objects he is naming; in other words he is not really thinking. Look again at the examples I gave at the beginning of this essay. Professor Laski (1) uses five negatives in fifty-three words. One of these is superfluous, making nonsense of the whole passage, and in addition there is the slip *alien* for akin, making further nonsense, and several avoidable pieces of clumsiness which increase the general vagueness. Professor Hogben (2) plays ducks and drakes with a battery which is able to write prescriptions, and, while disapproving of the everyday phrase *put up with*, is unwilling to look *egregious* up in the dictionary and see what it means. (3), if one takes an uncharitable attitude towards it, is simply meaningless: probably one could work out its intended meaning by reading the whole of the article in which it occurs. In (4), the writer knows more or less what he wants to say, but an accumulation of stale phrases chokes him like tea leaves blocking a sink. In (5), words and meaning have almost parted company. People who write in this manner usually have a general emotional meaning—they dislike one thing and want to express solidarity with another—but they are not interested in the detail of what they are saying. A scrupulous writer, in every sentence that he writes, will ask himself at least four questions, thus: What am I trying to say? What words will express it? What image or idiom will make it clearer? Is this image fresh enough to have an effect? And he will probably ask himself two more: Could I put it more shortly? Have I said anything that is avoidably ugly? But you are not obliged to go to all this trouble. You can shirk it by simply throwing your mind open and letting the ready-made phrases come crowding in. They will construct your sentences for you—even think your thoughts for you, to a certain extent—and at need they will perform the important service of partially concealing your meaning even from yourself. It is at this point that the special connection between politics and the debasement of language becomes clear.

In our time it is broadly true that political writing is bad writing. Where it is not true, it will generally be found that the writer is some kind of rebel, expressing his private opinions and not a "party line". Orthodoxy, of whatever colour, seems to demand a lifeless, imitative style. The political dialects to be found in pamphlets, leading articles, manifestos, White Papers and the speeches of under-secretaries do, of course, vary from party to party, but they are all alike in that one almost never finds in them a fresh, vivid, home-made turn of speech. When one watches some tired hack on the platform mechanically repeating the familiar phrases—*bestial atrocities, iron heel, bloodstained tyranny, free peoples of the world, stand shoulder to shoulder*—one often has a curious feeling that one is not watching a live human being but some kind of dummy: a feeling which suddenly becomes stronger at moments when the light catches the speaker's spectacles and turns them into blank discs which seem to have no eyes behind them. And this is not altogether fanciful. A speaker who uses that kind of phraseology has gone some distance towards turning himself into a machine. The appropriate noises are coming out of his larynx, but his brain is not involved as it would be if he were choosing his words for himself. If the speech he is making is one that he is accustomed to make over and over again, he may be almost unconscious of what he is saying, as one is when one utters the responses in church. And this reduced state of consciousness, if not indispensable, is at any rate favourable to political conformity.

In our time, political speech and writing are largely the defence of the indefensible. Things like the continuance of British rule in India, the Russian purges and deportations, the dropping of the atom bombs on Japan, can indeed be defended, but only by arguments which are too brutal for most people to face, and which do not square with the professed aims of political parties. Thus political language has to consist largely of euphemism, question-begging and sheer cloudy vagueness. Defenceless villages are bombarded from the air, the inhabitants driven out into the countryside, the cattle machine-gunned, the huts set on fire with incendiary bullets: this is called *pacification*. Millions of peasants are robbed of their farms and sent trudging along the roads with no more than they can carry: this is called *transfer of population* or *rectification of frontiers*. People are imprisoned for years without trial, or shot in the back of the neck or sent to die of scurvy in Arctic lumber camps: this is called *elimination of unreliable elements*. Such phraseology is needed if one wants to name things without calling up mental pictures of them. Consider for instance some comfortable English professor defending Russian totalitarianism. He cannot say outright, "I believe in killing off your opponents when you can get good results by doing so". Probably, therefore, he will say something like this:

"While freely conceding that the Soviet régime exhibits certain features which the humanitarian may be inclined to deplore, we must, I think, agree that a certain curtailment of the right to political opposition is an unavoidable concomitant of transitional periods, and that the rigours which the Russian people have been called upon to undergo have been amply justified in the sphere of concrete achievement."

The inflated style is itself a kind of euphemism. A mass of Latin words falls upon the facts like soft snow, blurring the outlines and covering up all the details. The great enemy of clear language is insincerity. When there is a gap between one's real and one's declared aims, one turns as it were instinctively to long words and exhausted idioms, like a cuttlefish squirting out ink. In our age there is no such thing as "keeping out of politics". All issues are political issues, and politics itself is a mass of lies, evasions, folly, hatred and schizophrenia. When the general atmosphere is bad, language must suffer. I should expect to find—this is a guess which I have not sufficient knowledge to verify—that the German, Russian and Italian languages have all deteriorated in the last ten or fifteen years, as a result of dictatorship.

But if thought corrupts language, language can also corrupt thought. A bad usage can spread by tradition and imitation, even among people who should and do know better. The debased language that I have been discussing is in some ways very convenient. Phrases like *a not unjustifiable assumption, leaves much to be desired, would serve no good purpose, a consideration which we should do well to bear in mind,* are a continuous temptation, a packet of aspirins always at one's elbow. Look back through this essay, and for certain you will find that I have again and again committed the very faults I am protesting against. By this morning's post I have received a pamphlet dealing with conditions in Germany. The author tells me that he "felt impelled" to write it. I open it at random, and here is almost the first sentence that I see: "(The Allies) have an opportunity not only of achieving a radical transformation of Germany's social and political structure in such a way as to avoid a nationalistic reaction in Germany itself, but at the same time of laying the foundations of a co-operative and unified Europe." You see, he "feels impelled" to write—feels, presumably, that he has something new to say—and yet his words, like cavalry horses answering the bugle, group themselves automatically into the familiar dreary pattern. This invasion of one's mind by ready-made phrases (*lay the foundations, achieve a radical transformation*) can only be prevented if one is constantly on guard against them, and every such phrase anaesthetizes a portion of one's brain.

I said earlier that the decadence of our language is probably curable. Those who deny this would argue, if they produced an argument at all, that language merely reflects existing social conditions, and that we cannot influence its development by any direct tinkering with words and constructions. So far as the general tone or spirit of a language goes, this may be true, but it is not true in detail. Silly words and expressions have often disappeared, not through any evolutionary process but owing to the conscious action of a minority. Two recent examples were *explore every avenue* and *leave no stone unturned,* which were killed by the jeers of a few journalists. There is a long list of flyblown metaphors which could similarly be got rid of if enough people would interest themselves in the job; and it should also be possible to laugh the *not un-* formation out of existence,[3] to reduce the amount of Latin and Greek in the average sentence, to drive out foreign phrases and strayed scientific words, and, in general, to make pretentiousness unfashionable. But all these are minor points. The defence of the English language implies more than this, and perhaps it is best to start by saying what it does *not* imply.

To begin with it has nothing to do with archaism, with the salvaging of obsolete words and turns of speech, or with the setting up of a "standard English" which must never be departed from. On the contrary, it is especially concerned with the scrapping of every word or idiom which has outworn its usefulness. It has nothing to do with correct grammar and syntax, which are of no importance so long as one makes one's meaning clear, or with the avoidance of Americanisms, or with having what is called a "good prose style". On the other hand it is not concerned with fake simplicity and the attempt to make written English colloquial. Nor does it even imply in every case preferring the Saxon word to the Latin one, though it does imply using the fewest and shortest words that will cover one's meaning. What is above all needed is to let the meaning choose the word, and not the other way about. In prose, the worst thing one can do with words is to surrender to them. When you think of a concrete object, you think wordlessly, and then, if you want to describe the thing you have been visualizing you probably hunt about till you find the exact words that seem to fit. When you think of something abstract you are more inclined to use words from the start, and unless you make a conscious effort to prevent it, the existing dialect will come rushing in and do the job for you, at the expense of blurring or even changing your meaning. Probably it is better to put off using words as long as possible and get one's meaning as clear as one can through pictures or sensations. Afterwards one can choose—not simply *accept*—the phrases that will best cover the meaning, and then switch round and decide what impression one's words are likely to make on another person. This last effort of the mind cuts out all stale or mixed images, all prefabricated phrases, needless repetitions, and humbug and vagueness generally. But one can often be in doubt about the effect of a word or a phrase, and one needs rules that one can rely on when instinct fails. I think the following rules will cover most cases:

(i) Never use a metaphor, simile or other figure of speech which you are used to seeing in print.

(ii) Never use a long word where a short one will do.

(iii) If it is possible to cut a word out, always cut it out.

(iv) Never use the passive where you can use the active.

---

3. One can cure oneself of the *not un-*formation by memorizing this sentence: *A not unblack dog was chasing a not unsmall rabbit across a not ungreen field.*

(v) Never use a foreign phrase, a scientific word or a jargon word if you can think of an everyday English equivalent.

(vi) Break any of these rules sooner than say anything outright barbarous.

These rules sound elementary, and so they are, but they demand a deep change of attitude in anyone who has grown used to writing in the style now fashionable. One could keep all of them and still write bad English, but one could not write the kind of stuff that I quoted in those five specimens at the beginning of this article.

I have not here been considering the literary use of language, but merely language as an instrument for expressing and not for concealing or preventing thought. Stuart Chase and others have come near to claiming that all abstract words are meaningless, and have used this as a pretext for advocating a kind of political quietism. Since you don't know what Fascism is, how can you struggle against Fascism? One need not swallow such absurdities as this, but one ought to recognize that the present political chaos is connected with the decay of language, and that one can probably bring about some improvement by starting at the verbal end. If you simplify your English, you are freed from the worst follies of orthodoxy. You cannot speak any of the necessary dialects, and when you make a stupid remark its stupidity will be obvious, even to yourself. Political language—and with variations this is true of all political parties, from Conservatives to Anarchists—is designed to make lies sound truthful and murder respectable, and to give an appearance of solidity to pure wind. One cannot change this all in a moment, but one can at least change one's own habits, and from time to time one can even, if one jeers loudly enough, send some worn-out and useless phrase—some *jackboot, Achilles' heel, hotbed, melting pot, acid test, veritable inferno* or other lump of verbal refuse—into the dustbin where it belongs.

QUESTIONS

1. What is Orwell's pivotal point? Where is it best stated?
2. In his aversion to foreign words Orwell anticipates De Gaulle's repudiation of "Franglais" (French adoption of English words). Does Orwell operate on a xenophobic assumption? Look at the foreign words he gives as examples. Are some of them useful additions to English because they cover a situation not covered by any English word (cf. Moulton, p. 128) or would you agree with Orwell's assertion that "there is no real need for any of the hundreds of foreign phrases now current in English"?
3. Orwell's essay was written at the time of World War II. How far has that historical context influenced him in his choice of examples? Can his catalogue of swindles be brought up to date with more recent examples?

4. Discuss Orwell's assertion that "the decline of a language must ultimately have political and economic causes" Is this "clear" as he claims?

5. How can you be sure that a metaphor is dying, rather than alive or dead? Is Orwell's test of seeing it often in print a sufficient one? Can you defend any of his examples of dying metaphors as necessary or useful additions to our vocabularies?

6. Orwell gives a list of questions for the writer to ask himself (p.175) and a list of rules for the writer to follow (pp. 178–179). Why does he consider it necessary to give both kinds of advice? How much do the two overlap? Are both consistent with Orwell's major ideas expressed elsewhere in the essay? Does his injunction to "break any of these rules sooner than say anything outright barbarous" beg the question?

7. Orwell suggests that if you look back through his essay you will find that he has "again and again committed the very faults" he is protesting against. Is this true? If it is, does it affect the validity om his major points?

8. Words create a personality or confer a character. Describe the personality that would be created by following Orwell's six rules; show that character in action.

AN ALBUM OF STYLES

I

To see the wind with a man his eyes it is unpossible, the nature of it is so fine and subtile; yet this experience of the wind had I once myself, and that was in the great snow that fell four years ago. I rode in the high way betwixt Topcliff-upon-Swale and Borough-bridge, the way being somewhat trodden before, by wayfaring men; the fields on both sides were plain, and lay almost yard-deep with snow; the night afore had been a little frost, so that the snow was hard and crusted above; that morning the sun shone bright and clear, the wind was whistling aloft, and sharp, according to the time of the year; the snow in the high way lay loose and trodden with horses' feet; so as the wind blew, it took the loose snow with it, and made it so slide upon the snow in the field, which was hard and crusted by reason of the frost over night, that thereby I might see very well the whole nature of the wind as it blew that day. And I had a great delight and pleasure to mark it, which maketh me now far better to remember it. Sometime the wind would be not past two yards broad, and so it would carry the snow as far as I could see. Another time the snow would blow over half the field at once. Sometime the snow would tumble softly; by and by it would fly wonderful fast. And this I perceived also, that the wind goeth by streams, and not whole together. For I should see one stream within a score on me; then the space of two score, no snow would stir; but, after so much quantity of ground, another stream of snow, at the same very time, should be carried likewise, but not equally, for the one would stand still, when the other flew apace and so continue sometime swiftlier, sometime slowlier, sometime broader, sometime narrower, as far as I could see. Nor it flew not straight, but sometime it crooked this way, sometime that way, and sometime it ran round about in a compass. And sometime the snow would be lift clean from the ground up to the air, and by and by it would be all clapt to the ground, as though there had been no wind at all, straightway it would rise and fly again. And that which was the most marvel of all, at one time two drifts of snow flew, the one out of the west into the east, the other out of the north into the east. And I saw two winds, by reason of the snow, the one cross over the other, as it had been two high ways. And, again, I should hear the wind blow in the air, when nothing was stirred at the ground. And when all was still where I rode, not very far from me the snow should be lifted wonderfully. This experience made me more marvel at the nature of the wind, than it made me cunning in the knowledge of the wind; but yet thereby I learned perfectly that it is no marvel at all though men in wind lose their length in shooting, seeing so many ways the wind is so variable in blowing.

—Roger Ascham, from *Toxophilus*:
A Treatise on the Art of Shooting with the Bow, 1545.

II

Revenge is a kind of wild justice; which the more man's nature runs to, the more ought law to weed it out. For as for the first wrong, it doth but offend the law; but the revenge of that wrong putteth the law out of office. Certainly, in taking revenge, a man is but even with his enemy; but in passing it over, he is superior; for it is a prince's part to pardon. And Salomon, I am sure, saith, *It is the glory of a man to pass by an offence.* That which is past is gone, and irrevocable; and wise men have enough to do with things present and to come: therefore they do but trifle with themselves, that labour in past matters. There is no man doth a wrong for the wrong's sake; but thereby to purchase himself profit, or pleasure, or honour, or the like. Therefore why should I be angry with a man for loving himself better than me? And if any man should do wrong merely out of ill nature, why, yet it is but like the thorn or briar, which prick and scratch, because they can do no other. The most tolerable sort of revenge is for those wrongs which there is no law to remedy; but then let a man take heed the revenge be such as there is no law to punish; else a man's enemy is still beforehand, and it is two for one. Some, when they take revenge, are desirous the party should know whence it cometh: this is the more generous. For the delight seemeth to be not so much in doing the hurt as in making the party repent: but base and crafty cowards are like the arrow that flieth in the dark. Cosmus, duke of Florence, had a desperate saying against perfidious or neglecting friends, as if those wrongs were unpardonable: *You shall read* (saith he) *that we are commanded to forgive our enemies; but you never read that we are commanded to forgive our friends.* But yet the spirit of Job was in a better tune: *Shall we* (saith he) *take good at God's hands, and not be content to take evil also?* And so of friends in a proportion. This is certain, that a man that studieth revenge keeps his own wounds green, which otherwise would heal and do well. Public revenges are for the most part fortunate; as that for the death of Caesar; for the death of Pertinax;[1] for the death of Henry the third of France;[2] and many more. But in private revenges it is not so. Nay rather,

1. Publius Helvius Pertinax became Emperor of Rome in 193 and was assassinated three months after his accession to the throne by a soldier in his Prae-torian Guard.

2. King of France 1574–1589; assassinated during the Siege of Paris.

vindictive persons live the life of witches; who as they are mischievous, so end they infortunate.

—Francis Bacon, *Of Revenge*, 1625.

III

We are all conceived in close prison; in our Mothers wombs, we are close prisoners all; when we are born, we are born but to the liberty of the house;[1] prisoners still, though within larger walls; and then all our life is but a going out to the place of execution, to death. Now was there ever any man seen to sleep in the cart, between Newgate, and Tyburn?[2] Between the prison and the place of execution, does any man sleep? And we sleep all the way; from the womb to the grave we are never thoroughly awake; but pass on with such dreams, and imaginations as these, I may live as well, as another, and why should I die, rather than another? But awake, and tell me, says this text *Quis homo*?[3] Who is that other that thou talkest of? *What man is he that liveth, and shall not see death?*

—John Donne, from a sermon delivered at Easter communion, March 28, 1619, when the king was dangerously ill at Newmarket.

IV

Of the wall [of China] it is very easy to assign the motives. It secured a wealthy and timorous nation from the incursions of Barbarians, whose unskillfulness in arts made it easier for them to supply their wants by rapine than by industry, and who from time to time poured in upon the habitations of peaceful commerce, as vultures descend upon domestic fowl. Their celerity and fierceness made the wall necessary, and their ignorance made it efficacious.

But for the pyramids no reason has ever been given adequate to the cost and labor of the work. The narrowness of the chambers proves that it could afford no retreat from enemies, and treasures might have been reposited at far less expense with equal security. It seems to have been erected only in compliance with that hunger of imagination which preys incessantly upon life, and must be always appeased by some employment. Those who have already all that they can enjoy, must enlarge their desires. He that has built for use, till use is supplied must begin to build for vanity, and extend his plan to the utmost power of human performance, that he may not be soon reduced to form another wish.

1. Donne distinguishes between a prisoner confined to a cell and one given somewhat more liberty.
2. London prisoners were taken in carts from Newgate prison to nearby Tyburn for execution.
3. "Who [is] the man?"

I consider this mighty structure as a monument of the insufficiency of human enjoyments. A king, whose power is unlimited, and whose treasures surmount all real and imaginary wants, is compelled to solace, by the erection of a pyramid, the satiety of dominion and tastelessness of pleasures, and to amuse the tediousness of declining life, by seeing thousands laboring without end, and one stone, for no purpose, laid upon another. Whoever thou art, that, not content with a moderate condition, imaginest happiness in royal magnificence, and dreamest that command or riches can feed the appetite of novelty with perpetual gratifications, survey the pyramids, and confess thy folly!

—Samuel Johnson, from *Rasselas*, 1759.

V

Every day for at least ten years together did my father resolve to have it mended—'tis not mended yet: no family but ours would have borne with it an hour—and what is most astonishing, there was not a subject in the world upon which my father was so eloquent, as upon that of door-hinges. And yet at the same time, he was certainly one of the greatest bubbles to them, I think, that history can produce: his rhetoric and conduct were at perpetual handy-cuffs. Never did the parlor-door open—but his philosophy or his principles fell a victim to it; three drops of oyl with a feather, and a smart stroke of a hammer, had saved his honor for ever. Inconsistent soul that man is—languishing under wounds, which he has the power to heal—his whole life a contradiction to his knowledge—his reason, that precious gift of God to him—(instead of pouring in oyl) serving but to sharpen his sensibilities, to multiply his pains and render him more melancholy and uneasy under them—poor unhappy creature, that he should do so! Are not the necessary causes of misery in this life enow, but he must add voluntary ones to his stock of sorrow, struggle against evils which cannot be avoided, and submit to others, which a tenth part of the trouble they create him, would remove from his heart forever?

By all that is good and virtuous! if there are three drops of oyl to be got, and a hammer to be found within ten miles of Shandy-Hall, the parlor-door hinge shall be mended this reign.

—Laurence Sterne, from *Tristram Shandy*, 1761.

VI

The human species, according to the best theory I can form of it, is composed of two distinct races, *the men who borrow,* and *the men who lend.* To these two original diversities may be reduced all those impertinent classifications of Gothic and Celtic tribes, white men, black men, red men. All the dwellers upon earth, "Parthians, and Medes, and Elamites," flock hither, and do naturally fall in with one or other of these primary distinctions. The infinite superiority of the former, which I choose to designate as the *great race*, is discernible in their figure, port, and a certain instinctive sovereignty. The latter are born degraded. "He shall serve his brethren." There is something in the air of one of this cast, lean and suspicious; contrasting with the open, trusting, generous manners of the other.

Observe who have been the greatest borrowers of all ages—Alcibiades—Falstaff—Sir Richard Steele—our late incomparable Brinsley—what a family likeness in all four!

What a careless, even deportment hath your borrower! what rosy gills! what a beautiful reliance on Providence doth he manifest—taking no more thought than lilies! What contempt for money—accounting it (yours and mine especially) no better than dross. What a liberal confounding of those pedantic distinctions of *meum* and *tuum!* or rather, what a noble simplification of language (beyond Tooke), resolving these supposed opposites into one clear, intelligible pronoun adjective! What near approaches doth he make to the primitive *community*—to the extent of one half of the principle at least!

—Charles Lamb, from "The Two Races of Men," 1820.

VII

In that great social organ which, collectively, we call literature, there may be distinguished two separate offices that may blend and often do so, but capable, severally, of a severe insulation, and naturally fitted for reciprocal repulsion. There is, first, the literature of *knowledge,* and secondly, the literature of *power.* The function of the first is to *teach*; the function of the second is to *move*; the first is a rudder, the second an oar or a sail. The first speaks to the mere discursive understanding; the second speaks ultimately, it may happen, to the higher understanding or reason, but always through affections of pleasure and sympathy. Remotely, it may travel towards an object seated in what Lord Bacon calls *dry* light; but, proximately, it does and must operate—else it ceases to be a literature of *power*—and on through that *humid* light which clothes itself in the mists and glittering *iris* of human passions, desires, and genial emotions. Men have so little reflected on the higher functios of literature as to find it a paradox if one should describe it as a mean or subordinate purpose of books to give information. But this is a paradox only in the sense which makes it honorable to be paradoxical. Whenever we talk in ordinary language of seeking information or gaining knowledge, we understand the words as connected with something of absolute novelty. But it is the grandeur of all truth which *can* occupy a very high place in human interests that it is never absolutely novel to the meanest of minds: it exists eternally by way of germ or latent principle in the lowest as in the highest, needing to be developed, but never to be planted. To be capable of transplantation is the immediate criterion of a truth that ranges on a lower scale. Besides which, there is a rarer thing than truth—namely, *power*, or deep sympathy with truth. What is the effect, for instance, upon society, of children? By the pity, by the tenderness, and by the peculiar modes of admiration, which connect themselves with the helplessness, with the innocence, and with the simplicity of children, not only are the primal affections strengthened and continually renewed, but the qualities which are dearest in the sight of heaven—the frailty, for instance, which appeals to forbearance, the innocence which symbolizes the heavenly, and the simplicity which is most alien from the worldly—are kept up in perpetual remembrance, and their ideals are continually refreshed. A purpose of the same nature is answered by the high literature, viz., the literature of power. What do you learn from *Paradise Lost?* Nothing at all. What do you learn from a cookery book? Something new, something that you did not know before, in every paragraph. But would you therefore put the wretched cookery book on a higher level of estimation than the divine poem? What you owe to Milton is not any knowledge, of which a million separate items are still but a million of advancing steps on the same earthly level; what you owe is *power*—that is, exercise and expansion to your own latent capacity of sympathy with the infinite, where every pulse and each separate influx is a step upwards, a step ascending as upon a Jacob's ladder from earth to mysterious altitudes above the earth. *All* the steps of knowledge, from first to last, carry you further on the same plane, but could never raise you one foot above your ancient level of earth: whereas the very *first* step in power is a flight—is an ascending movement into another element where earth is forgotten.

—Thomas De Quincey, from "Literature of Knowledge and
Literature of Power," 1848.

VIII

Knowledge is one thing, virtue is another; good sense is not conscience, refinement is not humility, nor is largeness and justness of view faith. Philosophy, however enlightened, however profound, gives no command over the passions, no influential motives, no vivifying principles. Liberal Education makes not the Christian, not the

Catholic, but the gentleman. It is well to be a gentleman, it is well to have a cultivated intellect, a delicate taste, a candid, equitable, dispassionate mind, a noble and courteous bearing in the conduct of life—these are the connatural qualities of a large knowledge; they are the objects of a University; I am advocating, I shall illustrate and insist upon them; but still, I repeat, they are no guarantee for sanctity or even for conscientiousness, they may attach to the man of the world, to the profligate, to the heartless, pleasant, alas, and attractive as he shows when decked out in them. Taken by themselves, they do but seem to be what they are not; they look like virtue at a distance, but they are detected by close observers, and on the long run; and hence it is that they are popularly accused of pretense and hypocrisy, not, I repeat, from their own fault, but because their professors and their admirers persist in taking them for what they are not, and are officious in arrogating for them a praise to which they have no claim. Quarry the granite rock with razors, or moor the vessel with a thread of silk; then may you hope with such keen and delicate instruments as human knowledge and human reason to contend against those giants, the passion and the pride of man.

—John Henry Newman, from *The Idea of a University*, 1852.

IX

But there is of culture another view, in which not solely the scientific passion, the sheer desire to see things as they are, natural and proper in an intelligent being, appears as the ground of it. There is a view in which all the love of our neighbor, the impulses towards action, help, and beneficence, the desire for removing human error, clearing human confusion, and diminishing human misery, the noble aspiration to leave the world better and happier than we found it—motives eminently such as are called social—come in as part of the grounds of culture, and the main and pre-eminent part. Culture is then properly described not as having its origin in curiosity, but as having its origin in the love of perfection; it is *a study of perfection*. It moves by the force, not merely or primarily of the scientific passion for pure knowledge, but also of the moral and social passion for doing good. As, in the first view of it, we took for its worthy motto Montesquieu's words: "To render an intelligent being yet more intelligent!" so, in the second view of it, there is no better motto which it can have than these words of Bishop Wilson: "To make reason and the will of God prevail!"

Only, whereas the passion for doing good is apt to be overhasty in determining what reason and the will of God say, because its turn is for acting rather than thinking, and it wants to be beginning

to act; and whereas it is apt to take its own conceptions, which proceed from its own state of development and share in all the
imperfections and immaturities of this, for a basis of action; what
distinguishes culture is, that it is possessed by the scientific passion
as well as by the passion of doing good; that it demands worthy
notions of reason and the will of God, and does not readily suffer
its own crude conceptions to substitute themselves for them. And
knowing that no action or institution can be salutary and stable
which is not based on reason and the will of God, it is not so bent
on acting and instituting, even with the great aim of diminishing
human error and misery ever before its thoughts, but that it can
remember that acting and instituting are of little use, unless we
know how and what we ought to act and to institute.

—Matthew Arnold, from "Sweetness and Light," 1869.

X

The presence that rose thus so strangely beside the waters, is
expressive of what in the ways of a thousand years men had come to
desire. Hers is the head upon which all "the ends of the world are
come," and the eyelids are a little weary. It is a beauty wrought out
from within upon the flesh, the deposit, little cell by cell, of strange
thoughts and fantastic reveries and exquisite passions. Set it for a
moment beside one of those white Greek goddesses or beautiful
women of antiquity, and how would they be troubled by this
beauty, into which the soul with all its maladies has passed! All the
thoughts and experience of the world have etched and molded
there, in that which they have of power to refine and make expressive the outward form, the animalism of Greece, the lust of Rome,
the mysticism of the middle ages with its spiritual ambition and imaginative loves, the return of the Pagan world, the sins of the Bor-
gias. She is older than the rocks among which she sits; like the vam-
pire, she has been dead many times, and learned the secrets of the
grave; and has been a diver in deep seas, and keeps their fallen day
about her; and trafficked for strange webs with Eastern merchants:
and, as Leda, was the mother of Helen of Troy, and, as Saint Anne,
the mother of Mary; and all this has been to her but as the sound of
lyres and flutes, and lives only in the delicacy with which it has
molded the changing lineaments, and tinged the eyelids and the
hands. The fancy of a perpetual life, sweeping together ten-thou-
sand experiences, is an old one; and modern philosophy has conceived the idea of humanity as wrought upon by, and summing up
in itself, all modes of thought and life. Certainly Lady Lisa might

stand as the embodiment of the old fancy, the symbol of the modern idea.

—Walter Pater, from *The Renaissance*, 1873.

XI

If Man has benefited immeasurably by his association with the dog, what, you may ask, has the dog got out of it? His scroll has, of course, been heavily charged with punishments: he has known the muzzle, the leash, and the tether; he has suffered the indignities of the show bench, the tin can on the tail, the ribbon in the hair; his love life with the other sex of his species has been regulated by the frigid hand of authority, his digestion ruined by the macaroons and marshmallows of doting women. The list of his woes could be continued indefinitely. But he has also had his fun, for he has been privileged to live with and study at close range the only creature with reason, the most unreasonable of creatures.

The dog has got more fun out of Man than Man has got out of the dog, for the clearly demonstrable reason that Man is the more laughable of the two animals. The dog has long been bemused by the singular activities and the curious practices of men, cocking his head inquiringly to one side, intently watching and listening to the strangest goings-on in the world. He has seen men sing together and fight one another in the same evening. He has watched them go to bed when it is time to get up, and get up when it is time to go to bed. He has observed them destroying the soil in vast areas, and nurturing it in small patches. He has stood by while men built strong and solid houses for rest and quiet, and then filled them with lights and bells and machinery. His sensitive nose, which can detect what's cooking in the next township, has caught at one and the same time the bewildering smells of the hospital and the munitions factory. He has seen men raise up great cities to heaven and then blow them to hell.

—James Thurber, from *Thurber's Dogs*, 1955.

XII

In resenting progress and change, a man lays himself open to censure. I suppose the explanation of anyone's defending anything as rudimentary and cramped as a Pullman berth is that such things are associated with an earlier period in one's life and that this period in retrospect seems a happy one. People who favor progress and improvements are apt to be people who have had a tough enough time without any extra inconvenience. Reactionaries who pout at innovations are apt to be well-heeled sentimentalists who had the breaks. Yet for all that, there is always a subtle danger in life's refinements, a dim degeneracy in progress. I have just been refining the room in which I sit, yet I sometimes doubt that a writer should refine or improve his workroom by so much as a dictionary: one thing leads to another and the first thing you know he has a stuffed chair and is fast asleep in it. Half a man's life is devoted to what he calls improvements, yet the original had some quality which is lost in the process. There was a fine natural spring of water on this place when I bought it. Our drinking water had to be lugged in a pail, from a wet glade of alder and tamarack. I visited the spring often in those first years, and had friends there—a frog, a wood-cock, and an eel which had churned its way all the way up through the pasture creek to enjoy the luxury of pure water. In the normal course of development, the spring was rocked up, fitted with a con-crete curb, a copper pipe, and an electric pump. I have visited it only once or twice since. This year my only gesture was the purely perfunctory one of sending a sample to the state bureau of health for analysis. I felt cheap, as though I were smelling an old friend's breath.

—E. B. White, "Progress and Change," in *One Man's Meat*, 1944.

XIII

It is simple enough to say that since books have classes—fiction, biography, poetry—we should separate them and take from each what it is right that each should give us. Yet few people ask from books what books can give us. Most commonly we come to books with blurred and divided minds, asking of fiction that it shall be true, of poetry that it shall be false, of biography that it shall be flat-tering, of history that it shall enforce our own prejudices. If we could banish all such preconceptions when we read, that would be an admirable beginning. Do not dictate to your author; try to become him. Be his fellow-worker and accomplice. If you hang back, and reserve and criticise at first, you are preventing yourself from getting the fullest possible value from what you read. But if you open your mind as widely as possible, then signs and hints of almost imperceptible fineness, from the twist and turn of the first sentences, will bring you into the presence of a human being unlike any other. Steep yourself in this, acquaint yourself with this, and soon you will find that your author is giving you, or attempting to give you, something far more definite. The thirty-two chapters of a novel—if we consider how to read a novel first—are an attempt to make something as formed and controlled as a building: but words are more impalpable than bricks; reading is a longer and more complicated process than seeing. Perhaps the quickest way to understand the elements of what a novelist is doing is not to read, but to write; to make your own experiment with the dangers and difficulties of words. Recall, then, some event that has left a distinct impression on you—how at the corner of the street, perhaps, you passed two people talking. A tree shook; an electric light danced; the tone of the talk was comic, but also tragic; a whole vision, an entire conception, seemed contained in that moment.

But when you attempt to reconstruct it in words, you will find that it breaks into a thousand conflicting impressions. Some must be subdued; others emphasised; in the process you will lose, probably, all grasp upon the emotion itself. Then turn from your blurred and littered pages to the opening pages of some great novelist—Defoe, Jane Austen, Hardy. Now you will be better able to appreciate their mastery. It is not merely that we are in the presence of a different person—Defoe, Jane Austen, or Thomas Hardy —but that we are living in a different world. Here, in *Robinson Crusoe*, we are trudging a plain high road; one thing happens after another; the fact and the order of the fact is enough. But if the open air and adventure mean everything to Defoe they mean nothing to Jane Austen. Hers is the drawing-room, and people talking, and by the many mirrors of their talk revealing their characters. And if, when we have accustomed ourselves to the drawing-room and its reflections, we turn to Hardy, we are once more spun around. The moors are round us and the stars are above our heads. The other side of the mind is now exposed—the dark side that comes uppermost in solitude, not the light side that shows in company. Our relations are not towards people, but towards Nature and destiny. Yet different as these worlds are, each is consistent with itself. The maker of each is careful to observe the laws of his own perspective, and however great a strain they may put upon us they will never confuse us, as lesser writers so frequently do, by introducing two different kinds of reality into the same book. Thus to go from one great novelist to another—from Jane Austen to Hardy, from Peacock to Trollope, from Scott to Meredith—is to be wrenched and uprooted; to be thrown this way and then that. To read a novel is a difficult and complex art. You must be capable not only of great finesse of perception, but of great boldness of imagination if you are going to make use of all that the novelist—the great artist—gives you.

—Virginia Woolf, "How Should One Read a Book?" in *The Second Common Reader*, 1932.

XIV

Three merry gargoyles. Three merry harridans. Amused by a long-ago time of ignorance. They did not belong to those generations of prostitutes created in novels, with great and generous hearts, dedicated, because of the horror of circumstance, to ameliorating the luckless, barren life of men, taking money incidentally and humbly for their "understanding." Nor were they from that sensitive breed of young girl, gone wrong at the hands of fate, forced to cultivate an outward brittleness in order to protect her springtime from further shock, but knowing full well she was cut out for better things, and could make the right man happy. Neither were they the sloppy, inadequate whores who, unable to make a living at it alone, turn to drug consumption and traffic or pimps to help complete their scheme of self-destruction, avoiding suicide only to punish the memory of some absent father or to sustain the misery of some silent mother. Except for Marie's fabled love for Dewey Prince, these women hated men, all men, without shame, apology, or discrimination. They abused their visitors with a scorn grown mechanical from use. Black men, white men, Puerto Ricans, Mexicans, Jews, Poles, whatever—all were inadequate and weak, all came under their jaundiced eyes and were the recipients of their disinterested wrath. They took delight in cheating them. On one occasion the town well knew, they lured a Jew up the stairs, pounced on him, all three, held him up by the heels, shook everything out of his pants pockets, and threw him out of the window.

Neither did they have respect for women, who, although not their colleagues, so to speak, nevertheless deceived their husbands —regularly or irregularly, it made no difference. "Sugar-coated whores," they called them, and did not yearn to be in their shoes. Their only respect was for what they would have described as "good Christian colored women." The woman whose reputation was spotless, and who tended to her family, who didn't drink or smoke or run around. These women had their undying, if covert, affection. They would sleep with their husbands, and take their money, but always with a vengeance.

Nor were they protective and solicitous of youthful innocence. They looked back on their own youth as a period of ignorance, and regretted that they had not made more of it. They were not young girls in whores' clothing, or whores regretting their loss of innocence. They were whores in whores' clothing, whores who had never been young and had no word for innocence. With Pecola they were as free as they were with each other. Marie concocted stories for her because she was a child, but the stories were breezy and rough. If

Pecola had announced her intention to live the life they did, they would not have tried to dissuade her or voiced any alarm.

—Toni Morrison, from *The Bluest Eye*, 1970.

XV

A very large number of people cease when quite young to add anything to a limited stock of judgments. After a certain age, say 25, they consider that their education is finished.

It is perhaps natural that having passed through that painful and boring process, called expressly education, they should suppose it over, and that they are equipped for life to label every event as it occurs and drop it into its given pigeonhole. But one who has a label ready for everything does not bother to observe any more, even such ordinary happenings as he has observed for himself, with attention, before he went to school. He merely acts and reacts.

For people who have stopped noticing, the only possible new or renewed experience, and, therefore, new knowledge, is from a work of art. Because that is the only kind of experience which they are prepared to receive on its own terms, they will come out from their shells and expose themselves to music, to a play, to a book, because it is the accepted method of enjoying such things. True, even to plays and books they may bring artistic prejudices which prevent them from seeing *that* play or comprehending *that* book. Their artistic sensibilities may be as crusted over as their minds.

But it is part of an artist's job to break crusts, or let us say rather that artists who work for the public and not merely for themselves are interested in breaking crusts because they want to communicate their intuitions.

—Joyce Cary, "On the Function of the Novelist," 1949.

XVI

I guess it is true that big and strong things are much less dangerous than small soft weak things. Nature (whatever that is) makes the small and weak reproduce faster. And that is not true of course. The ones that did not reproduce faster than they died, disappeared. But how about little faults, little pains, little worries. The cosmic ulcer comes not from great concerns, but from little irritations. And great things can kill a man but if they do not he is stronger and better for them. A man is destroyed by the duck nibblings of nagging, small bills, telephones (wrong number), athlete's foot, ragweed, the common cold, boredom. All of these are the negatives, the tiny frustrations, and no one is stronger for them.

—John Steinbeck, from *Journal of a Novel*:
The East of Eden Letters, 1970.

XVII

This seems to be an era of gratuitous inventions and negative improvements. Consider the beer can. It was beautiful—as beautiful as the clothespin, as inevitable as the wine bottle, as dignified and reassuring as the fire hydrant. A tranquil cylinder of delightfully resonant metal, it could be opened in an instant, requiring only the application of a handy gadget freely dispensed by every grocer. Who can forget the small, symmetrical thrill of those two triangular punctures, the dainty *pffff*, the little crest of suds that foamed eagerly in the exultation of release? Now we are given, instead, a top beetling with an ugly, shmoo-shaped "tab," which, after fiercely resisting the tugging, bleeding fingers of the thirsty man, threatens his lips with a dangerous and hideous hole. However, we have discovered a way to thwart Progress, usually so unthwartable. *Turn the beer can upside down and open the bottom.* The bottom is still the way the top used to be. True, this operation gives the beer an unsettling jolt, and the sight of a consistently inverted beer can might make people edgy, not to say queasy. But the latter difficulty could be eliminated if manufacturers would design cans that looked the same whichever end was up, like playing cards. What we need is Progress with an escape hatch.

—John Updike, "Beer Can," in *Assorted Prose*, 1965.

XVIII

The legend of Junior Johnson! In this legend, here is a country boy, Junior Johnson, who learns to drive by running whiskey for his father, Johnson, Senior, one of the biggest copper-still operators of all time, up in Ingle Hollow, near North Wilkesboro, in northwestern North Carolina, and grows up to be a famous stock car racing driver, rich, grossing $100,000 in 1963, for example, respected, solid, idolized in his hometown and throughout the rural South. There is all this about how good old boys would wake up in the middle of the night in the apple shacks and hear a supercharged Oldsmobile engine roaring over Brushy Mountain and say, "Listen at him—there he goes!" although that part is doubtful, since some nights there were so many good old boys taking off down the road in supercharged automobiles out of Wilkes County, and running loads to Charlotte, Salisbury, Greensboro, Winston-Salem, High

Point, or wherever, it would be pretty hard to pick out one. It was Junior Johnson, specifically, however, who was famous for the "bootleg turn" or "about-face," in which, if the Alcohol Tax agents had a roadblock up for you or were too close behind, you threw the car up into second gear, cocked the wheel, stepped on the accelerator and made the car's rear end skid around in a complete 180-degree arc, a complete about-face, and tore on back up the road exactly the way you came from. God! The Alcohol Tax agents used to burn over Junior Johnson. Practically every good old boy in town in Wilkesboro, the county seat, got to know the agents by sight in a very short time. They would rag them practically to their faces on the subject of Junior Johnson, so that it got to be an obsession. Finally, one night they had Junior trapped on the road up toward the bridge around Millersville, there's no way out of there, they had the barricades up and they could hear this souped-up car roaring around the bend, and here it comes—but suddenly they can hear a siren and see a red light flashing in the grille, so they think it's another agent, and boy, they run out like ants and pull those barrels and boards and sawhorses out of the way, and then—Ggghhzzzzzzzzhhhhhh-gggggzzzzzzzeeeeeong!—gawdam! there he goes again, it was him, Junior Johnson! with a gawdam agent's sireen and a red light in his grille!

—Tom Wolfe, from *The Kandy-Kolored Tangerine-Flake Streamline Baby*, 1966.

W. SOMERSET MAUGHAM
Lucidity, Simplicity, Euphony[1]

I have never had much patience with the writers who claim from the reader an effort to understand their meaning. You have only to go to the great philosophers to see that it is possible to express with lucidity the most subtle reflections. You may find it difficult to understand the thought of Hume, and if you have no philosophical training its implications will doubtless escape you; but no one with any education at all can fail to understand exactly what the meaning of each sentence is. Few people have written English with more grace than Berkeley. There are two sorts of obscurity that you find in writers. One is due to negligence and the other to willfulness. People often write obscurely because they have never taken the trouble to learn to write clearly. This sort of obscurity you find too often

1. Chapters 11, 12, and 13 of *The Summing Up*, 1938.

in modern philosophers, in men of science, and even in literary critics. Here it is indeed strange. You would have thought that men who passed their lives in the study of the great masters of literature would be sufficiently sensitive to the beauty of language to write if not beautifully at least with perspicuity. Yet you will find in their works sentence after sentence that you must read twice to discover the sense. Often you can only guess at it, for the writers have evidently not said what they intended.

Another cause of obscurity is that the writer is himself not quite sure of his meaning. He has a vague impression of what he wants to say, but has not, either from lack of mental power or from laziness, exactly formulated it in his mind and it is natural enough that he should not find a precise expression for a confused idea. This is due largely to the fact that many writers think, not before, but as they write. The pen originates the thought. The disadvantage of this, and indeed it is a danger against which the author must be always on his guard, is that there is a sort of magic in the written word. The idea acquires substance by taking on a visible nature, and then stands in the way of its own clarification. But this sort of obscurity merges very easily into the willful. Some writers who do not think clearly are inclined to suppose that their thoughts have a significance greater than at first sight appears. It is flattering to believe that they are too profound to be expressed so clearly that all who run may read, and very naturally it does not occur to such writers that the fault is with their own minds which have not the faculty of precise reflection. Here again the magic of the written word obtains. It is very easy to persuade oneself that a phrase that one does not quite understand may mean a great deal more than one realizes. From this there is only a little way to go to fall into the habit of setting down one's impressions in all their original vagueness. Fools can always be found to discover a hidden sense in them. There is another form of willful obscurity that masquerades as aristocratic exclusiveness. The author wraps his meaning in mystery so that the vulgar shall not participate in it. His soul is a secret garden into which the elect may penetrate only after overcoming a number of perilous obstacles. But this kind of obscurity is not only pretentious; it is short-sighted. For time plays it an odd trick. If the sense is meagre time reduces it to a meaningless verbiage that no one thinks of reading. This is the fate that has befallen the lucubrations of those French writers who were seduced by the example of Guillaume Apollinaire. But occasionally it throws a sharp cold light on what had seemed profound and thus discloses the fact that these contortions of language disguised very commonplace notions. There are few of Mallarmé's poems now that are not clear; one cannot fail to notice that his thought singularly lacked originality. Some of his phrases were beautiful; the materials of his verse were the poetic platitudes of his day.

Simplicity is not such an obvious merit as lucidity. I have aimed at it because I have no gift for richness. Within limits I admire richness in others, though I find it difficult to digest in quantity. I can read one page of Ruskin with delight, but twenty only with weariness. The rolling period, the stately epithet, the noun rich in poetic associations, the subordinate clauses that give the sentence weight and magnificence, the grandeur like that of wave following wave in the open sea; there is no doubt that in all this there is something inspiring. Words thus strung together fall on the ear like music. The appeal is sensuous rather than intellectual, and the beauty of the sound leads you easily to conclude that you need not bother about the meaning. But words are tyrannical things, they exist for their meanings, and if you will not pay attention to these, you cannot pay attention at all. Your mind wanders. This kind of writing demands a subject that will suit it. It is surely out of place to write in the grand style of inconsiderable things. No one wrote in this manner with greater success than Sir Thomas Browne, but even he did not always escape this pitfall. In the last chapter of *Hydriotaphia* the matter, which is the destiny of man, wonderfully fits the baroque splendor of the language, and here the Norwich doctor produced a piece of prose that has never been surpassed in our literature; but when he describes the finding of his urns in the same splendid manner the effect (at least to my taste) is less happy. When a modern writer is grandiloquent to tell you whether or no a little trollop shall hop into bed with a commonplace young man you are right to be disgusted.

But if richness needs gifts with which everyone is not endowed, simplicity by no means comes by nature. To achieve it needs rigid discipline. So far as I know ours is the only language in which it has been found necessary to give a name to the piece of prose which is described as the purple patch; it would not have been necessary to do so unless it were characteristic. English prose is elaborate rather than simple. It was not always so. Nothing could be more racy, straightforward and alive than the prose of Shakespeare; but it must be remembered that this was dialogue written to be spoken. We do not know how he would have written if like Corneille he had composed prefaces to his plays. It may be that they would have been as euphuistic as the letters of Queen Elizabeth. But earlier prose, the prose of Sir Thomas More, for instance, is neither ponderous, flowery nor oratorical. It smacks of the English soil. To my mind King James's Bible has been a very harmful influence on English prose. I am not so stupid as to deny its great beauty. It is majestical. But the Bible is an oriental book. Its alien imagery has nothing to do with us. Those hyperboles, those luscious metaphors, are foreign to our genius. I cannot but think that not the least of the misfortunes that the Secession from Rome brought upon the spiritual life of our country is that this work for so long a period became the daily, and with many the only, reading of our people. Those rhythms, that powerful vocabulary, that grandiloquence, became part and parcel of the national sensibility. The plain, honest English speech was overwhelmed with ornament. Blunt Englishmen twisted their tongues to speak like Hebrew prophets. There was evidently something in the English temper to which this was congenial, perhaps a native lack of precision in thought, perhaps a naïve delight in fine words for their own sake, an innate eccentricity and love of embroidery, I do not know; but the fact remains that ever since, English prose has had to struggle against the tendency to luxuriance. When from time to time the spirit of the language has reasserted itself, as it did with Dryden and the writers of Queen Anne, it was only to be submerged once more by the pomposities of Gibbon and Dr. Johnson. When English prose recovered simplicity with Hazlitt, the Shelley of the letters and Charles Lamb at his best, it lost it again with De Quincey, Carlyle, Meredith and Walter Pater. It is obvious that the grand style is more striking than the plain. Indeed many people think that a style that does not attract notice is not style. They will admire Walter Pater's, but will read an essay by Matthew Arnold without giving a moment's attention to the elegance, distinction and sobriety with which he set down what he had to say.

The dictum that the style is the man is well known. It is one of those aphorisms that say too much to mean a great deal. Where is the man in Goethe, in his birdlike lyrics or in his clumsy prose? And Hazlitt? But I suppose that if a man has a confused mind he will write in a confused way, if his temper is capricious his prose will be fantastical, and if he has a quick, darting intelligence that is reminded by the matter in hand of a hundred things, he will, unless he has great self-control, load his pages with metaphor and simile. There is a great difference between the magniloquence of the Jacobean writers, who were intoxicated with the new wealth that had lately been brought into the language, and the turgidity of Gibbon and Dr. Johnson, who were the victims of bad theories. I can read every word that Dr. Johnson wrote with delight, for he had good sense, charm and wit. No one could have written better if he had not willfully set himself to write in the grand style. He knew good English when he saw it. No critic has praised Dryden's prose more aptly. He said of him that he appeared to have no art other than that of expressing with clearness what he thought with vigor. And one of his Lives he finished with the words: "Whoever wishes to attain an English style, familiar but not coarse, and elegant but not ostentatious, must give his days and nights to the volumes of Addison." But when he himself sat down to write it was with a very different aim. He mistook the orotund for the dignified. He had not the good breeding to see that simplicity and naturalness are the truest marks of distinction.

For to write good prose is an affair of good manners. It is, unlike verse, a civil art. Poetry is baroque. Baroque is tragic, massive and mystical. It is elemental. It demands depth and insight. I cannot but feel that the prose writers of the baroque period, the authors of King James's Bible, Sir Thomas Browne, Glanville, were poets who had lost their way. Prose is a rococo art. It needs taste rather than power, decorum rather than inspiration and vigor rather than grandeur. Form for the poet is the bit and the bridle without which (unless you are an acrobat) you cannot ride your horse; but for the writer of prose it is the chassis without which your car does not exist. It is not an accident that the best prose was written when rococo with its elegance and moderation, at its birth attained its greatest excellence. For rococo was evolved when baroque had become declamatory and the world, tired of the stupendous, asked for restraint. It was the natural expression of persons who valued a civilized life. Humor, tolerance and horse sense made the great tragic issues that had pre-occupied the first half of the seventeenth century seem excessive. The world was a more comfortable place to live in and perhaps for the first time in centuries the cultivated classes could sit back and enjoy their leisure. It has been said that good prose should resemble the conversation of a well-bred man. Conversation is only possible when men's minds are free from pressing anxieties. Their lives must be reasonably secure and they must have no grave concern about their souls. They must attach importance to the refinements of civilization. They must value courtesy, they must pay attention to their persons (and have we not also been told that good prose should be like the clothes of a well-dressed man, appropriate but unobtrusive?), they must fear to bore, they must be neither flippant nor solemn, but always apt; and they must look upon "enthusiasm" with a critical glance. This is a soil very suitable for prose. It is not to be wondered at that it gave a fitting opportunity for the appearance of the best writer of prose that our modern world has seen, Voltaire. The writers of English, perhaps owing to the poetic nature of the language, have seldom reached the excellence that seems to have come so naturally to him. It is in so far as they have approached the ease, sobriety and precision of the great French masters that they are admirable.

Whether you ascribe importance to euphony, the last of the three characteristics that I mentioned, must depend on the sensitiveness of your ear. A great many readers, and many admirable writers, are devoid of this quality. Poets as we know have always made a great use of alliteration. They are persuaded that the repetition of a sound gives an effect of beauty. I do not think it does so in prose. It seems to me that in prose alliteration should be used only for a special reason; when used by accident it falls on the ear very disagreeably. But its accidental use is so common that one can only suppose that the sound of it is not universally offensive. Many writers without distress will put two rhyming words together, join a monstrous long adjective to a monstrous long noun, or between the end of one word and the beginning of another have a conjunction of consonants that almost breaks your jaw. These are trivial and obvious instances. I mention them only to prove that if careful writers can do such things it is only because they have no ear. Words have weight, sound and appearance; it is only by considering these that you can write a sentence that is good to look at and good to listen to.

I have read many books on English prose, but have found it hard to profit by them; for the most part they are vague, unduly theoretical, and often scolding. But you cannot say this of Fowler's *Dictionary of Modern English Usage*. It is a valuable work. I do not think anyone writes so well that he cannot learn much from it. It is lively reading. Fowler liked simplicity, straightforwardness and common sense. He had no patience with pretentiousness. He had a sound feeling that idiom was the backbone of a language and he was all for the racy phrase. He was no slavish admirer of logic and was willing enough to give usage right of way through the exact demesnes of grammar. English grammar is very difficult and few writers have avoided making mistakes in it. So heedful a writer as Henry James, for instance, on occasion wrote so ungrammatically that a schoolmaster, finding such errors in a schoolboy's essay, would be justly indignant. It is necessary to know grammar, and it is better to write grammatically than not, but it is well to remember that grammar is common speech formulated. Usage is the only test. I would prefer a phrase that was easy and unaffected to a phrase that was grammatical. One of the differences between French and English is that in French you can be grammatical with complete naturalness, but in English not invariably. It is a difficulty in writing English that the sound of the living voice dominates the look of the printed word. I have given the matter of style a great deal of thought and have taken great pains. I have written few pages that I feel I could not improve and far too many that I have left with dissatisfaction because, try as I would, I could do no better. I cannot say of myself what Johnson said of Pope: "He never passed a fault unamended by indifference, nor quitted it by despair." I do not write as I want to; I write as I can.

But Fowler had no ear. He did not see that simplicity may sometimes make concessions to euphony. I do not think a far-fetched, an archaic or even an affected word is out of place when it sounds better than the blunt, obvious one or when it gives a sentence a better balance. But, I hasten to add, though I think you may without misgiving make this concession to pleasant sound, I think you should make none to what may obscure your meaning. Anything is better than not to write clearly. There is nothing to be said against lucidity, and against simplicity only the possibility of dryness. This is a risk that is well worth taking when you reflect how much better it is to be bald than to wear a curly wig. But there is in euphony a danger that must be considered. It is very likely to be monotonous. When George Moore began to write, his style was poor; it gave you the impression that he wrote on wrapping paper with a blunt pencil. But he developed gradually a very musical English. He learnt to write sentences that fall away on the ear with a misty languor and it delighted him so much that he could never have enough of it. He did not escape monotony. It is like the sound of water lapping a shingly beach, so soothing that you presently cease to be sensible of it. It is so mellifluous that you hanker for some harshness, for an abrupt dissonance, that will interrupt the silky concord. I do not know how one can guard against this. I suppose the best chance is to have a more lively faculty of boredom than one's readers so that one is wearied before they are. One must always be on the watch for mannerisms and when certain cadences come too easily to the pen ask oneself whether they have not become mechanical. It is very hard to discover the exact point where the idiom one has formed to express oneself has lost its tang. As Dr. Johnson said: "He that has once studiously formed a style, rarely writes afterwards with complete ease." Admirably as I think Matthew Arnold's style was suited to his particular purposes, I must admit that his mannerisms are often irritating. His style was an instrument that he had forged once for all; it was not like the human hand capable of performing a variety of actions.

If you could write lucidly, simply, euphoniously and yet with liveliness you would write perfectly: you would write like Voltaire. And yet we know how fatal the pursuit of liveliness may be: it may result in the tiresome acrobatics of Meredith. Macaulay and Carlyle were in their different ways arresting; but at the heavy cost of naturalness. Their flashy effects distract the mind. They destroy their persuasiveness; you would not believe a man was very intent on ploughing a furrow if he carried a hoop with him and jumped through it at every other step. A good style should show no sign of effort. What is written should seem a happy accident. I think no one in France now writes more admirably than Colette, and such is the ease of her expression that you cannot bring yourself to believe that she takes any trouble over it. I am told that there are pianists who have a natural technique so that they can play in a manner that most executants can achieve only as the result of unremitting toil, and I am willing to believe that there are writers who are equally fortunate. Among them I was much inclined to place Colette. I asked her. I was exceedingly surprised to hear that she wrote everything over and over again. She told me that she would often spend a whole morning working upon a single page. But it does not matter how one gets the effect of ease. For my part, if I get it at all, it is only by strenuous effort. Nature seldom provides me with the word, the turn of phrase, that is appropriate without being far-fetched or commonplace.

QUESTIONS

Maugham draws attention to the two conflicting yet complementary approaches to style that have been traditional in literary criticism. One approach maintains that style is primarily a combination of qualities and devices that can be learned and produced; the other, that "style is the man," the reflection in language of a personality with all its attitudes and idiosyncracies. Using passages from An Album of Styles (pp. 181–195), explore the two approaches. In any given passage what appears as impersonal technique or device, what as reflecting the special temperament or character of the author?

WAYNE C. BOOTH

Boring from Within: The Art of the Freshman Essay[1]

Last week I had for about the hundredth time an experience that always disturbs me. Riding on a train, I found myself talking with my seat-mate, who asked me what I did for a living. "I teach English." Do you have any trouble predicting his response? His face fell, and he groaned, "Oh, dear, I'll have to watch my language." In my experience there are only two other possible reactions. The first is even less inspiriting: "I hated English in school; it was my worst subject." The second, so rare as to make an honest English teacher almost burst into tears of gratitude when it occurs, is an animated conversation about literature, or ideas, or the American language— the kind of conversation that shows a continuing respect for "English" as something more than being sure about *who* and *whom*, *lie* and *lay*.

Unless the people you meet are a good deal more tactful or better liars than the ones I meet, you've had the two less favorable experiences many times. And it takes no master analyst to figure out why so many of our fellow citizens think of us as unfriendly policemen: it is because too many of us have seen ourselves as unfriendly policemen. I know of a high school English class in Indiana in which the students are explicitly told that their paper grades will not be affected by anything they say; required to write a paper a week, they are

1. Adapted by Mr. Booth from a speech delivered in May 1963 to the   Illinois Council of College Teachers of English.

graded simply on the number of spelling and grammatical errors. What is more, they are given a standard form for their papers: each paper is to have three paragraphs, a beginning, a middle, and an end —or is it an introduction, a body, and a conclusion? The theory seems to be that if the student is not troubled about having to say anything, or about discovering a good way of saying it, he can then concentrate on the truly important matter of avoiding mistakes.

What's wrong with such assignments? What's wrong with getting the problem of correctness focused sharply enough so that we can really work on it? After all, we do have the job of teaching correct English, don't we? We can't possibly teach our hordes of students to be colorful writers, but by golly, we can beat the bad grammar out of them. Leaving aside the obvious fact that we *can't* beat the bad grammar out of them, not by direct assault, let's think a bit about what that kind of assignment does to the poor teacher who gives it. Those papers must be read, by someone, and unless the teacher has more trained assistance than you and I have, *she's* the victim. She can't help being bored silly by her own paper-reading, and we all know what an evening of being bored by a class's papers does to our attitude toward that class the next day. The old formula of John Dewey was that any teaching that bores the student is likely to fail. The formula was subject to abuse, quite obviously, since interest in itself is only one of many tests of adequate teaching. A safer formula, though perhaps also subject to abuse, might be: Any teaching that bores the teacher is sure to fail. And I am haunted by the picture of that poor woman in Indiana, week after week reading batches of papers written by students who have been told that nothing they say can possibly affect her opinion of those papers. Could any hell imagined by Dante or Jean-Paul Sartre match this self-inflicted futility?

I call it self-inflicted, as if it were a simple matter to avoid receiving papers that bore us. But unfortunately it is not. It may be a simple matter to avoid the *total* meaninglessness that the students must give that Indiana teacher, but we all know that it is no easy matter to produce interesting papers; our pet cures for boredom never work as well as they ought to. Every beginning teacher learns quickly and painfully that nothing works with all students, and that on bad days even the most promising ideas work with nobody.

As I try to sort out the various possible cures for those batches of boredom—in ink, double-spaced, on one side of the sheet, only, please —I find them falling into three groups: efforts to give the students a sharper sense of writing to an audience, efforts to give them some substance to express, and efforts to improve their habits of observation and of approach to their task—what might be called improving their mental personalities.

This classification, both obvious and unoriginal, is a useful one not only because it covers—at least I hope it does—all of our efforts to improve what our students can do but also because it reminds us that no one of the three is likely to work unless it is related to each of the others. In fact each of the three types of cure—"develop an awareness of audience," "give them something to say," and "enliven their writing personalities"—threatens us with characteristic dangers and distortions; all three together are indispensable to any lasting cure.

Perhaps the most obvious omission in that Indiana teacher's assignments is all sense of an audience to be persuaded, of a serious rhetorical purpose to be achieved. One tempting cure for this omission is to teach them to put a controversial edge on what they say. So we ask them to write a three-page paper arguing that China should be allowed into the UN or that women are superior to men or that American colleges are failing in their historic task. Then we are surprised when the papers turn out to be as boring as ever. The papers on Red China are full of abstract pomposities that the students themselves obviously do not understand or care about, since they have gleaned them in a desperate dash through the most readily available courses listed in the *Readers' Guide*. Except for the rare student who has some political background and awareness, and who thus might have written on the subject anyway, they manage to convey little more than their resentment at the assignment and their boredom in carrying it out. One of the worst batches of papers I ever read came out of a good idea we had at Earlham College for getting the whole student body involved in controversial discussion about world affairs. We required them to read Barbara Ward's *Five Ideas that Change the World*; we even had Lady Jackson come to the campus and talk to everyone about her concern for the backward nations. The papers, to our surprise, were a discouraging business. We found ourselves in desperation collecting the boners that are always a sure sign, when present in great numbers, that students are thoroughly disengaged. "I think altruism is all right, so long as we practice it in our own interest." "I would be willing to die for anything fatal." "It sure is a doggie dog world."

It is obvious what had gone wrong: though we had ostensibly given the student a writing purpose, it had not become *his* purpose, and he was really no better off, perhaps worse, than if we had him writing about, say, piccolos or pizza. We might be tempted in revulsion from such overly ambitious failures to search for controversy in the students' own mundane lives. This may be a good move, but we should not be surprised when the papers on "Let's clean up the campus" or "Why must we have traffic fatalities?" turn out to be just as empty as the papers on the UN or the Congo. They may have more exclamation points and underlined adjectives, but they will not interest any teacher who would like to read papers for his own pleasure or edification. "People often fail to realize that nearly 40,000 people are killed on our highways each year. Must this carnage continue?" Well, I suppose it must, until people who write about it learn to see it with their own eyes, and hearts, instead of through a haze of cliché. The truth is that to make students assume a controversial pose before they have any genuine substance to be controversial about is to encourage dishonesty and slovenliness, and to ensure our own boredom. It may very well lead them into the kind of commercial concern for the audience which makes almost every *Reader's Digest* article intelligible to everyone over the chronological age of ten and boring to everyone over the mental age of fifteen. *Newsweek* magazine recently had a readability survey conducted on itself. It was found to be readable by the average twelfth grader, unlike *Time*, which is readable by the average eleventh grader. The editors were advised, and I understand are taking the advice, that by improving their "readability" by one year they could improve their circulation by several hundred thousand. Whether they will thereby lop off a few thousand adult readers in the process was not reported.

The only protection from this destructive type of concern for the audience is the control of substance, of having something solid to say. Our students bore us, even when they take a seemingly lively controversial tone, because they have nothing to say, to us or to anybody else. If and when they discover something to say, they will no longer bore us, and our comments will no longer bore them. Having something to say, they will be interested in learning how to say it better. Having something to say, they can be taught how to give a properly controversial edge to what will by its nature be controversial—nothing, after all, is worth saying that everybody agrees on already.

When we think of providing substance, we are perhaps tempted first to find some way of filling students' minds with a goodly store of general ideas, available on demand. This temptation is not necessarily a bad one. After all, if we think of the adult writers who interest us, most of them have such a store; they have read and thought about man's major problems, and they have opinions and arguments ready to hand about how men ought to live, how society ought to be run, how literature ought to be written. Edmund Wilson, for example, one of the most consistently interesting men alive, seems to have an inexhaustible flow of reasoned opinions on any subject that comes before him. Obviously our students are not going to interest us until they too have some ideas.

But it is not easy to impart ideas. It is not even easy to impart opinions, though a popular teacher can usually manage to get students to parrot his views. But ideas—that is, opinions backed with genuine reasoning—are extremely difficult to develop. If they were not, we wouldn't have a problem in the first place; we could simply send our students off with an assignment to prove their conviction that God does or does not exist or that the American high school system is the best on God's earth, and the interesting arguments would flow.

There is, in fact, no short cut to the development of reasoned ideas. Years and years of daily contact with the world of ideas are required before the child can be expected to begin formulating his own ideas and his own reasons. And for the most part the capacity to handle abstract ideas comes fairly late. I recently saw a paper of a bright high school sophomore, from a good private school, relating the economic growth of China and India to their political development and relative supply of natural resources. It was a terrible paper; the student's hatred of the subject, his sense of frustration in trying to invent generalizations about processes that were still too big for him, showed in every line. The child's parent told me that when the paper was returned by the geography teacher, he had pencilled on the top of one page, "Why do you mix so many bad ideas with your good ones?" The son was almost in tears, his father told me, with anger and helplessness. "He talks as if I'd put bad ideas in on purpose. *I* don't know a bad idea from a good one on this subject."

Yet with all this said, I am still convinced that general ideas are not only a resource but also a duty that cannot be dodged just because it is a dangerous one. There is nothing we touch, as English teachers, that is immune to being tainted by our touch; all the difference lies in how we go about it.

Ideas are a resource because adolescents are surprisingly responsive to any real encouragement to think for themselves, *if* methods of forced feeding are avoided. The seventeen-year-old who has been given nothing but commonplaces and clichés all his life and who finally discovers a teacher with ideas of his own may have his life changed, and, as I shall say in my final point, when his life is changed his writing is changed. Perhaps some of you can remember, as I can, a first experience with a teacher who could think for himself. I can remember going home from a conversation with my high school chemistry teacher and audibly vowing to myself: "Someday I'm going to be able to think for myself like that." There was nothing especially unconventional about Luther Gidding's ideas—at least I can remember few of them now. But what I cannot forget is the way he had with an idea, the genuine curiosity with which he approached it, the pause while he gave his little thoughtful cough, and then the bulldog tenacity with which he would argue it through. And I am convinced that though he never required me to write a line, he did more to improve my writing during the high school years than all of my English teachers put together. The diary I kept to record my sessions with him, never read by anyone, was the best possible writing practice.

If ideas, in this sense of speculation backed up with an attempt to think about things rigorously and constructively, are a great and often neglected resource, they are also our civic responsibility—a far more serious responsibility than our duty to teach spelling and grammar. It is a commonplace to say that democracy depends for its survival on an informed citizenry, but we all know that mere information is not what we are talking about when we say such things. What we mean is that democracy depends on a citizenry that can reason for themselves, on men who know whether a case has been proved, or at least made probable. Democracy depends, if you will forgive some truisms for a moment, on free choices, and choices cannot be in any sense free if they are made blind: free choice is, in fact, choice that is based on knowledge—not just opinions, but knowledge in the sense of reasoned opinion. And if that half of our population who do not go beyond high school do not learn from us how to put two and two together and how to test the efforts of others to do so, and if the colleges continue to fail with most of the other half, we are doomed to become even more sheeplike, as a nation, than we are already.

Papers about ideas written by sheep are boring; papers written by thinking boys and girls are interesting. The problem is always to find ideas at a level that will allow the student to *reason*, that is, to provide support for his ideas, rather than merely assert them in half-baked form. And this means something that is all too often forgotten by the most ambitious teachers—namely, that whatever ideas the student writes about must somehow be connected with his own experience. Teaching machines will never be able to teach the kind of writing we all want, precisely because no machine can ever know which general ideas relate, for a given student, to some meaningful experience. In the same class we'll have one student for whom philosophical and religious ideas are meaningful, another who can talk with confidence about entropy and the second law of thermodynamics, a third who can write about social justice, and a fourth who can discuss the phony world of Holden Caulfield. Each of them can do a good job on his own subject, because he has as part of his equipment a growing awareness of how conclusions in that subject are related to the steps of argument that support conclusions. Ideally, each of these students ought to have the personal attention of a tutor for an hour or so each week, someone who can help him sharpen those connections, and not force him to write on topics not yet appropriate to his interests or experience. But when these four are in a class of thirty or forty others, taught by a teacher who has three or four other similar sections, we all know what happens: the teacher is forced by his circumstances to provide some sort of mold into which all of the students can be poured. Although he is still better able to adapt to individual differences than a machine, he is unfortunately subject to boredom and fatigue, as a machine would not be. Instead of being the philosopher, scientist, political analyst, and literary critic that these four students require him to be, teaching them and learning from them at the same time, the teacher is almost inevitably tempted to force them all to write about the ideas he himself knows best. The result is that at least three of the four must write out of ignorance.

Now clearly the best way out of this impasse would be for legislatures and school boards and college presidents to recognize the teaching of English for what it is: the most demanding of all teaching jobs, justifying the smallest sections and the lightest course loads. No composition teacher can possibly concentrate on finding special interests, making imaginative assignments, and testing the effectiveness and cogency of papers if he has more than seventy-five students at a time; the really desirable limit would be about forty-five—three sections of fifteen students each. Nobody would ever expect a piano teacher, who has no themes to read, to handle the great masses of pupils that we handle. Everyone recognizes that for all other technical skills individual attention is required. Yet for this, the most delicate of all skills, the one requiring the most subtle interrelationships of training, character, and experience, we fling students and teachers into hopelessly impersonal patterns.

But if I'm not careful I'll find myself saying that our pupils bore us because the superintendents and college presidents hire us to be bored. Administrative neglect and misallocation of educational funds are basic to our problem, and we should let the citizenry know of the scandal on every occasion. But meanwhile, back at the ranch, we are 'faced with the situation as it now is: we must find some way to train a people to write responsibly even though the people, as represented, don't want this service sufficiently to pay for it.

The tone of political exhortation into which I have now fallen leads me to one natural large source of ideas as we try to encourage writing that is not just lively and controversial but informed and genuinely persuasive. For many students there is obviously more potential interest in social problems and forces, political controversy, and the processes of everyday living around them than in more general ideas. The four students I described a moment ago, students who can say something about philosophy, science, general political theory, or literary criticism, are rare. But most students, including these four, can in theory at least be interested in meaningful argument about social problems in which they are personally involved.

As a profession we have tried, over the past several decades, a variety of approaches attempting to capitalize on such interests. Papers on corruption in TV, arguments about race relations, analyses of distortions in advertising, descriptions of mass communication—these have been combined in various quantities with traditional subjects like grammar, rhetoric, and literature. The "communications" movement, which looked so powerful only a few years ago and which now seems almost dead, had at its heart a perfectly respectable notion, a notion not much different from the one I'm working with today: get them to write about something they know about, and make sure that they see their writing as an act of communication, not as a meaningless exercise. And what better material than other acts of communication.

The dangers of such an approach are by now sufficiently understood. As subject matter for the English course, current "communications media" can at best provide only a supplement to literature and analysis of ideas. But they can be a valuable supplement. Analysis in class of the appeals buried in a *New Yorker* or *Life* advertisement followed by a writing assignment requiring similar analyses can be a far more interesting introduction to the intricacies of style than assignments out of a language text on levels of usage or emotion-charged adjectives. Analysis of a *Time* magazine account, purporting to be objective news but in actual fact a highly emotional editorial, can be not only a valuable experience in itself, but it can lead to papers in which the students do say something to us. Stylistic analysis of the treatment of the same news events by two newspapers or weeklies of different editorial policy can lead to an intellectual awakening of great importance, and thus to papers that will not, cannot, bore the teacher. But this will happen only if the students' critical powers are genuinely developed. It will not do simply to teach the instructor's own prejudices.

There was a time in decades not long past when many of the most lively English teachers thought of their job as primarily to serve as handmaids to liberalism. I had one teacher in college who confessed to me that his overriding purpose was to get students to read and believe *The Nation* rather than the editorials of their daily paper. I suppose that his approach was not entirely valueless. It seems preferable to the effort to be noncontroversial that marks too many English teachers in the '60's, and at least it stirred some of us out of our dogmatic slumbers. But unfortunately it did nothing whatever about teaching us to think critically. Though we graduated from his course at least aware—as many college graduates do not seem to be today— that you can't believe anything you read in the daily press until you have analyzed it and related it to your past experience and to other accounts, it failed to teach us that you can't believe what you read in *The Nation* either. It left the job undone of training our ability to think, because it concentrated too heavily on our opinions. The result was, as I remember, that my own papers in that course were generally regurgitated liberalism. I was excited by them, and that was something. But I can't believe that the instructor found reading them anything other than a chore. There was nothing in them that came from my own experience, my own notions of what would constitute evidence for my conclusions. There I was, in Utah in the depths of the depression, writing about the Okies when I could have been writing about the impoverished farmers all around me. I wrote about race relations in the south without ever having talked with a Negro in my life and without recognizing that the bootblack I occasionally saw in Salt Lake City in the Hotel Utah was in any way related to the problem of race relations.

The third element that accounts for our boring papers is the lack of character and personality in the writer. My life, my observations, my insights were not included in those papers on the Okies and race relations and the New Deal. Every opinion was derivative, every observation second-hand. I had no real opinions of my own, and my eyes were not open wide enough for me to make first-hand observations on the world around me. What I wrote was therefore characterless, without true personality, though often full of personal pronouns. My opinions had been changed, my *self* had not. The style was the boy, the opinionated, immature, uninformed boy; whether my teacher knew it or not—and apparently he did not—his real job was to make a man of me if he wanted me to write like a man.

Putting the difficulty in this way naturally leads me to what perhaps many of you have been impatient about from the beginning. Are not the narrative arts, both as encountered in great literature and as practiced by the students themselves, the best road to the infusion of individuality that no good writing can lack? Would not a real look at the life of that bootblack, and an attempt to deal with him in narrative, have led to a more interesting paper than all of my generalized attacks on the prejudiced southerners?

I think it would, but once again I am almost more conscious of the dangers of the cure than of the advantages. As soon as we make our general rule something like, "Have the students write a personal narrative on what they know about, what they can see and feel at first hand," we have opened the floodgates for those dreadful assignments that we all find ourselves using, even though we know better: "My Summer Vacation," "Catching My First Fish," and "Our Trip to the Seattle World's Fair." Here are personal experiences that call for personal observation and narration. What's wrong with them?

Quite simply, they invite triviality, superficiality, puerility. Our students have been writing essays on such non-subjects all their lives, and until they have developed some sort of critical vision, some way of looking at the world they passed through on their vacations or fishing trips, they are going to feed us the same old bromides that have always won their passing grades. "My Summer Vacation" is an invitation to a grocery list of items, because it implies no audience, no point to be made, no point of view, no character in the speaker. A bright student will make something of such an invitation, by dramatizing the comic family quarrel that developed two days out, or by comparing his view of the American motel system with Nabokov's in *Lolita*, or by remembering the types of people seen in the campgrounds. If he had his own eyes and ears open he might have seen, in a men's room in Grand Canyon last summer, a camper with a very thick French accent trying to convert a Brooklyn Jew into believing the story of the Mormon gold plates. Or he could have heard, at Mesa Verde, a young park ranger, left behind toward the end of the season by all of the experienced rangers, struggling ungrammatically through a set speech on the geology of the area and finally breaking down in embarrassment over his lack of education. Such an episode, really *seen*, could be used narratively to say something to other high school students about what education really is.

But mere narration can be in itself just as dull as the most abstract theorizing about the nature of the universe or the most derivative opinion-mongering about politics. Even relatively skilful narration, used too obviously as a gimmick to catch interest, with no real relation to the subject, can be as dull as the most abstract pomposities. We all know the student papers that begin like *Reader's Digest* articles, with stereotyped narration that makes one doubt the event itself: "On a dark night last January, two teen agers were seen etc., etc." One can open any issue of *Time* and find this so-called narrative interest plastered throughout. From the March 29 issue I find, among many others, the following bits of fantasy: #1: "A Bolivian father sadly surveyed his nation's seven universities, then made up his mind. 'I don't want my son mixed up in politics.' . . . So saying, he sent his son off to West Germany to college." So writing, the author sends me into hysterical laughter: the quote is phony, made up for the occasion to disguise the generality of the news item. #2: "Around 12:30 P.M. every Monday and Friday, an aging Cubana Airlines turbo-prop Britannia whistles to a halt at Mexico City's International Airport. Squads of police stand by. All passengers . . . without diplomatic or Mexican passports are photographed and questioned. . . . They always dodge questions. 'Why are you here? Where are you going?' ask the Mexicans. 'None of your business,' answer the secretive travelers." "Why should I go on reading?" ask I. #3: "At 6:30 one morning early this month, a phone shrilled in the small office off the bedroom of Egypt's President. . . Nasser. [All early morning phones "shrill" for *Time*.] Already awake, he lifted the receiver to hear exciting news: a military coup had just been launched against the anti-Nasser government of Syria. The phone rang again. It was the Minister of Culture. . . . How should Radio Cairo handle the Syrian crisis? 'Support the rebels,' snapped Nasser." Oh lucky reporter, I sigh, to have such an efficient wiretapping service. #4: "In South Korea last week, a farmer named Song Kyu Il traveled all the way from the southern provinces to parade before Seoul's Duk Soo Palace with a placard scrawled in his own blood. . . . Farmer Song was thrown in jail, along with some 200 other demonstrators." That's the last we hear of Song, who is invented as an individual for this opening and then dropped. #5: "Defense Secretary Robert McNamara last spring stood beside President Kennedy on the tenth-deck bridge of the nuclear-powered carrier *Enterprise*. For as far as the eye could see, other U. S. ships deployed over the Atlantic seascape." Well, maybe. But for as far as the eye can see, the narrative clichés are piled, rank on rank. At 12:00 midnight last Thursday a gaunt, harried English professor could be seen hunched over his typewriter, a pile of *Time* magazines beside him on the floor. "What," he murmured to himself, sadly, "Whatever can we do about this trashy imitation of narration?"

Fortunately there is something we can do, and it is directly within our province. We can subject our students to models of genuine narration, with the sharp observation and penetrating critical judgment that underlies all good story telling, whether reportorial or fictional.

It is a truth universally acknowledged, that a single man in possession of a good fortune must be in want of a wife.

However little known the feelings or views of such a man may be on his first entering a neighborhood, this truth is so well fixed in the minds of the surrounding families, that he is considered as the rightful property of someone or other of their daughters.

"My dear Mr. Bennet," said his lady to him one day, "have you heard that Netherfield Park is let at last?"

And already we have a strong personal tone established, a tone of mocking irony which leaves Jane Austen's Mrs. Bennet revealed before us as the grasping, silly gossip she is. Or try this one:

I am an American, Chicago-born—Chicago, that somber city—and go at things as I have taught myself, free-style, and will make the record in my own way: first to knock, first admitted; sometimes an innocent knock, sometimes a not so innocent. But a man's character is his fate, says Heraclitus, and in the end there isn't any way to disguise the nature of the knocks by acoustical work on the door or gloving the knuckles.

Everybody knows there is no fineness or accuracy of suppression; if you hold down one thing you hold down the adjoining.

My own parents were not much to me, though I cared for my mother. She was simple-minded, and what I learned from her was not what she taught....

Do you catch the accent of Saul Bellow here, beneath the accent of his Augie March? You do, of course, but the students, many of them, do not. How do you know, they will ask, that Jane Austen is being ironic? How do you know, they ask again, that Augie is being characterized by his author through what he says? In teaching them how we know, in exposing them to the great narrative voices, ancient and modern, and in teaching them to hear these voices accurately, we are, of course, trying to change their lives, to make them new, to raise their perceptions to a new level altogether. Nobody can really catch these accents who has not grown up sufficiently to see through cheap substitutes. Or, to put it another way, a steady exposure to such voices is the very thing that will produce the maturity that alone can make our students ashamed of beclouded, commercial, borrowed spectacles for viewing the world.

It is true that exposure to good fiction will not in itself transform our students into good writers. Even the best-read student still needs endless hours and years of practice, with rigorous criticism. Fiction will not do the job of discipline in reasoned argument and of practice in developing habits of addressing a living audience. But in the great fiction they will learn what it means to look at something with full attention, what it means to see beneath the surface of society's platitudes. If we then give them practice in writing about things close to the home base of their own honest observations, constantly stretching their powers of generalization and argument but never allowing them to drift into pompous inanities or empty controversiality, we may have that rare but wonderful pleasure of witnessing the miracle: a man and a style where before there was only a bag of wind or a bundle of received opinions. Even when, as with most of our students, no miracles occur, we can hope for papers that we can enjoy reading. And as a final bonus, we might hope that when our students encounter someone on a train who says that he teaches English, their automatic response may be something other than looks of pity or cries of mock alarm.

QUESTIONS

1. *Booth is writing for an audience of English teachers. In what ways might the essay differ if he were writing for an audience of students?*
2. *On page 208 Booth says he has "now fallen" into a "tone of political exhortation." (Tone may be defined as the reflection in language of the attitude a writer takes toward his subject or his audience or both.) What other "tones" are there in the essay? Why does Booth find it necessary to vary the tone?*
3. *What steps are necessary before an "opinion" can become a "reasoned opinion"? Select some subject on which you have a strong opinion and decide whether it is a reasoned opinion.*
4. *Booth characterizes the writing in the Reader's Digest and Time (pp. 211–212). What does he feel the two magazines have in common? Analyze an article from either one of these magazines to see how accurate Booth's characterization is.*

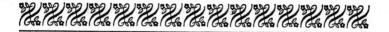

On Education

JOHN HOLT
How Teachers Make Children Hate Reading

When I was teaching English at the Colorado Rocky Mountain School, I used to ask my students the kinds of questions that English teachers usually ask about reading assignments—questions designed to bring out the points that I had decided *they* should know. They, on their part, would try to get me to give them hints and clues as to what I wanted. It was a game of wits. I never gave my students an opportunity to say what they really thought about a book.

I gave vocabulary drills and quizzes too. I told my students that every time they came upon a word in their book they did not understand, they were to look it up in the dictionary. I even devised special kinds of vocabulary tests, allowing them to use their books to see how the words were used. But looking back, I realize that these tests, along with many of my methods, were foolish.

My sister was the first person who made me question my conventional ideas about teaching English. She had a son in the seventh grade in a fairly good public school. His teacher had asked the class to read Cooper's *The Deerslayer*. The choice was bad enough in itself; whether looking at man or nature, Cooper was superficial, inaccurate and sentimental, and his writing is ponderous and ornate. But to make matters worse, this teacher had decided to give the book the microscope and x-ray treatment. He made the students look up and memorize not only the definitions but the derivations of every big word that came along—and there were plenty. Every chapter was followed by close questioning and testing to make sure the students "understood" everything.

Being then, as I said, conventional, I began to defend the teacher, who was a good friend of mine, against my sister's criticisms. The argument soon grew hot. What was wrong with making sure that children understood everything they read? My sister answered that until this class her boy had always loved reading, and had read

214

a lot on his own; now he had stopped. (He was not really to start again for many years.)

Still I persisted. If children didn't look up the words they didn't know, how would they ever learn them? My sister said, "Don't be silly! When you were little you had a huge vocabulary, and were always reading very grown-up books. When did you ever look up a word in a dictionary?"

She had me. I don't know that we had a dictionary at home; if we did, I didn't use it. I don't use one today. In my life I doubt that I have looked up as many as fifty words, perhaps not even half that.

Since then I have talked about this with a number of teachers. More than once I have said, "according to tests, educated and literate people like you have a vocabulary of about twenty-five thousand words. How many of these did you learn by looking them up in a dictionary?" They usually are startled. Few claim to have looked up even as many as a thousand. How did they learn the rest?

They learned them just as they learned to talk—by meeting words over and over again, in different contexts, until they saw how they fitted.

Unfortunately, we English teachers are easily hung up on this matter of understanding. Why should children understand everything they read? Why should anyone? Does anyone? I don't, and I never did. I was always reading books that teachers would have said were "too hard" for me, books full of words I didn't know. That's how I got to be a good reader. When about ten, I read all the D'Artagnan stories and loved them. It didn't trouble me in the least that I didn't know why France was at war with England or who was quarreling with whom in the French court or why the Musketeers should always be at odds with Cardinal Richelieu's men. I didn't even know who the Cardinal was, except that he was a dangerous and powerful man that my friends had to watch out for. This was all I needed to know.

Having said this, I will now say that I think a big, unabridged dictionary is a fine thing to have in any home or classroom. No book is more fun to browse around in—*if* you're not made to. Children, depending on their age, will find many pleasant and interesting things to do with a big dictionary. They can look up funny-sounding words, which they like, or words that nobody else in the class has ever heard of, which they like, or long words, which they like, or forbidden words, which they like best of all. At a certain age, and particularly with a little encouragement from parents or teachers, they may become very interested in where words came from and when they came into the language and how their meanings have changed over the years. But exploring for the fun of it is very different from looking up words out of your reading because you're going to get into trouble with your teacher if you don't.

While teaching fifth grade two years or so after the argument with my sister, I began to think again about reading. The children in my class were supposed to fill out a card—just the title and author and a one-sentence summary—for every book they read. I was not running a competition to see which child could read the most books, a competition that almost always leads to cheating. I just wanted to know what the children were reading. After a while it became clear that many of these very bright kids, from highly literate and even literary backgrounds, read very few books and deeply disliked reading. Why should this be?

At this time I was coming to realize, as I described in my book *How Children Fail*, that for most children school was a place of danger, and their main business in school was staying out of danger as much as possible. I now began to see also that books were among the most dangerous things in school.

From the very beginning of school we make books and reading a constant source of possible failure and public humiliation. When children are little we make them read aloud, before the teacher and other children, so that we can be sure they "know" all the words they are reading. This means that when they don't know a word, they are going to make a mistake, right in front of everyone. Instantly they are made to realize that they have done something wrong. Perhaps some of the other children will begin to wave their hands and say, "Ooooh! O-o-o-oh!" Perhaps they will just giggle, or nudge each other, or make a face. Perhaps the teacher will say, "Are you sure?" or ask someone else what he thinks. Or perhaps, if the teacher is kindly, she will just smile a sweet, sad smile—often one of the most painful punishments a child can suffer in school. In any case, the child who has made the mistake knows he has made it, and feels foolish, stupid, and ashamed, just as any of us would in his shoes.

Before long many children associate books and reading with mistakes, real or feared, and penalties and humiliation. This may not seem sensible, but it is natural. Mark Twain once said that a cat that sat on a hot stove lid would never sit on one again—but it would never sit on a cold one either. As true of children as of cats. If they, so to speak, sit on a hot book a few times, if books cause them humiliation and pain, they are likely to decide that the safest thing to do is to leave all books alone.

After having taught fifth-grade classes for four years I felt quite sure of this theory. In my next class were many children who had had great trouble with schoolwork, particularly reading. I decided to try at all costs to rid them of their fear and dislike of books, and to get them to read oftener and more adventurously.

One day soon after school had started, I said to them, "Now I'm going to say something about reading that you have probably never heard a teacher say before. I would like you to read a lot of books this year, but I want you to read them only for pleasure. I am not going to ask you questions to find out whether you understand the books or not. If you understand enough of a book to enjoy it and want to go on reading it, that's enough for me. Also I'm not going to ask you what words mean.

"Finally," I said, "I don't want you to feel that just because you start a book, you have to finish it. Give an author thirty or forty pages or so to get his story going. Then if you don't like the characters and don't care what happens to them, close the book, put it away, and get another. I don't care whether the books are easy or hard, short or long, as long as you enjoy them. Furthermore I'm putting all this in a letter to your parents, so they won't feel they have to quiz and heckle you about books at home."

The children sat stunned and silent. Was this a teacher talking? One girl, who had just come to us from a school where she had had a very hard time, and who proved to be one of the most interesting, lively, and intelligent children I have ever known, looked at me steadily for a long time after I had finished. Then, still looking at me, she said slowly and solemnly, "Mr. Holt, do you really mean that?" I said just as solemnly, "I mean every word of it."

Apparently she decided to believe me. The first book she read was Dr. Seuss's *How the Grinch Stole Christmas*, not a hard book even for most third graders. For a while she read a number of books on this level. Perhaps she was clearing up some confusion about reading that her teachers, in their hurry to get her up to "grade level," had never given her enough time to clear up. After she had been in the class six weeks or so and we had become good friends, I very tentatively suggested that, since she was a skillful rider and loved horses, she might like to read *National Velvet*. I made my sell as soft as possible, saying only that it was about a girl who loved and rode horses, and that if she didn't like it, she could put it back. She tried it, and though she must have found it quite a bit harder than what she had been reading, finished it and liked it very much.

During the spring she really astonished me, however. One day, in one of our many free periods, she was reading at her desk. From a glimpse of the illustrations I thought I knew what the book was. I said to myself, "It can't be," and went to take a closer look. Sure enough, she was reading *Moby Dick*, in the edition with woodcuts by Rockwell Kent. When I came close to her desk she looked up. I said, "Are you really reading that?" She said she was. I said, "Do you like it?" She said, "Oh, yes, it's neat!" I said, "Don't you find parts of it rather heavy going?" She answered "Oh, sure, but I just skip over those parts and go on to the next good part."

This is exactly what reading should be and in school so seldom is—an exciting, joyous adventure. Find something, dive into it, take the good parts, skip the bad parts, get what you can out of it, go on to something else. How different is our mean-spirited, picky insistence that every child get every last little scrap of "understanding" that can be dug out of a book.

For teachers who really enjoy doing it, and will do it with gusto, reading aloud is a very good idea. I have found that not just fifth graders but even ninth and eleventh graders enjoy it. Jack London's "To Build a Fire" is a good read-aloud story. So are ghost stories, and "August Heat," by W. F. Harvey, and "The Monkey's Paw," by W. W. Jacobs, are among the best. Shirley Jackson's "The Lottery" is sure-fire, and will raise all kinds of questions for discussion and argument. Because of a TV program they had seen and that excited them, I once started reading my fifth graders William Golding's *Lord of the Flies*, thinking to read only a few chapters, but they made me read it to the end.

In my early fifth-grade classes the children usually were of high IQ, came from literate backgrounds and were generally felt to be succeeding in school. Yet it was astonishingly hard for most of those children to express themselves in speech or in writing. I have known a number of five-year-olds who were considerably more articulate than most of the fifth graders I have known in school. Asked to speak, my fifth graders were covered with embarrassment; many refused altogether. Asked to write, they would sit for minutes on end, staring at the paper. It was hard for most of them to get down a half page of writing, even on what seemed to be interesting topics or topics they chose themselves.

In desperation I hit on a device that I named the Composition Derby. I divided the class into teams, and told them that when I said, "Go," they were to start writing something. It could be about anything they wanted, but it had to be about something—they couldn't just write "dog dog dog dog" on the paper. It could be true stories, descriptions of people or places or events, wishes, made-up stories, dreams—anything they liked. Spelling didn't count, so they didn't have to worry about it. When I said, "Stop," they were to stop and count up the words they had written. The team that wrote the most words would win the derby.

It was a success in many ways and for many reasons. The first surprise was that the two children who consistently wrote the most words were two of the least successful students in the class. They were bright, but they had always had a very hard time in school. Both were very bad spellers, and worrying about this had slowed down their writing without improving their spelling. When they were free of this worry and could let themselves go, they found hidden and unsuspected talents.

One of the two, a very driven and anxious little boy, used to write long adventures, or misadventures, in which I was the central character—"The Day Mr. Holt Went to Jail," "The Day Mr. Holt Fell Into the Hole," "The Day Mr. Holt Got Run Over," and so on. These were very funny, and the class enjoyed hearing me read them aloud. One day I asked the class to write a derby on a topic I would give them. They groaned; they liked picking their own. "Wait till you hear it," I said. "It's 'The Day the School Burned Down.'"

With a shout of approval and joy they went to work, and wrote furiously for 20 minutes or more, laughing and chuckling as they wrote. The papers were all much alike; in them the children danced around the burning building, throwing in books and driving me and the other teachers back in when we tried to escape.

In our first derby the class wrote an average of about ten words a minute; after a few months their average was over 20. Some of the slower writers tripled their output. Even the slowest, one of whom was the best student in the class, were writing 15 words a minute. More important, almost all the children enjoyed the derbies and wrote interesting things.

Some time later I learned that Professor I. S. Hayakawa, teaching freshman English, had invented a better technique. Every day in class he asked his students to write without stopping for about half an hour. They could write on whatever topic or topics they chose, but the important thing was not to stop. If they ran dry, they were to copy their last sentence over and over again until new ideas came. Usually they came before the sentence had been copied once. I use this idea in my own classes, and call this kind of paper a Non-Stop. Sometimes I ask students to write a Non-Stop on an assigned topic, more often on anything they choose. Once in a while I ask them to count up how many words they have written, though I rarely ask them to tell me; it is for their own information. Sometimes these papers are to be handed in; often they are what I call private papers, for the students' eyes alone.

The private paper has proved very useful. In the first place, in any English class—certainly any large English class—if the amount the students write is limited by what the teacher can find time to correct, or even to read, the students will not write nearly enough. The only remedy is to have them write a great deal that the teacher does not read. In the second place, students writing for themselves will write about many things that they would never write on a paper to be handed in, once they have learned (sometimes it takes a while) that the teacher means what he says about the papers' being private. This is important, not just because it enables them to get things off their chest, but also because they are most likely to write well, and to pay attention to how they write, when they are writing about something important to them.

Some English teachers, when they first hear about private papers, object that students do not benefit from writing papers unless the papers are corrected. I disagree for several reasons. First, most students, particularly poor students, do not read the corrections on their papers; it is boring, even painful. Second, even when they do read these corrections, they do not get much help from them, do not build the teacher's suggestions into their writing. This is true even when they really believe the teacher knows what he is talking about.

Third, and most important, we learn to write by writing, not by reading other people's ideas about writing. What most students need above all else is practice in writing, and particularly in writing about things that matter to them, so that they will begin to feel the satisfaction that comes from getting important thoughts down in words and will care about stating these thoughts forcefully and clearly.

Teachers of English—or, as some schools say (ugh!), Language Arts—spend a lot of time and effort on spelling. Most of it is wasted; it does little good, and often more harm than good. We should ask ourselves, "How do good spellers spell? What do they do when they are not sure which spelling of a word is right?" I have asked this of a number of good spellers. Their answer never varies. They do not rush for a dictionary or rack their brains trying to remember some rules. They write down the word both ways, or several ways, look at them and pick the one that looks best. Usually they are right.

Good spellers know what words look like and even, in their writing muscles, feel like. They have a good set of word images in their minds, and are willing to trust these images. The things we do to "teach" spelling to children do little to develop these skills or talents, and much to destroy them or prevent them from developing.

The first and worst thing we do is to make children anxious about spelling. We treat a misspelled word like a crime and penalize the misspeller severely; many teachers talk of making children develop a "spelling conscience," and fail otherwise excellent papers because of a few spelling mistakes. This is self-defeating. When we are anxious, we don't perceive clearly or remember what we once perceived. Everyone knows how hard it is to recall even simple things when under emotional pressure; the harder we rack our brains, the less easy it is to find what we are looking for. If we are anxious enough, we will not trust the messages that memory sends us. Many children spell badly because although their first hunches about how to spell a word may be correct, they are afraid to trust them. I have often seen on children's papers a word correctly spelled, then crossed out and misspelled.

There are some tricks that might help children get sharper word images. Some teachers may be using them. One is the trick of air writing; that is, of "writing" a word in the air with a finger and "seeing" the image so formed. I did this quite a bit with fifth graders, using either the air or the top of a desk, on which their fingers left no mark. Many of them were tremendously excited by this. I can still hear them saying, "There's nothing there, but I can see it!" It seemed like black magic. I remember that when I was little I loved to write in the air. It was effortless, voluptuous, satisfying, and it was fun to see the word appear in the air. I used to write "Money Money Money," not so much because I didn't have any as because I liked the way it felt, particularly that *y* at the end, with its swooping tail.

Another thing to help sharpen children's image-making machinery is taking very quick looks at words—or other things. The conventional machine for doing this is the tachistoscope. But these are expensive, so expensive that most children can have few chances to use them, if any at all. With some three-by-five and four-by-eight file cards you can get the same effect. On the little cards you put the words or the pictures that the child is going to look at. You hold the larger card over the card to be read, uncover it for a split second with a quick wrist motion, then cover it up again. Thus you have a tachistoscope that costs one cent and that any child can work by himself.

Once when substituting in a first-grade class, I thought that the children, who were just beginning to read and write, might enjoy some of the kind of free, nonstop writing that my fifth graders had. One day about 40 minutes before lunch, I asked them all to take pencil and paper and start writing about anything they wanted to. They seemed to like the idea, but right away one child said anxiously, "Suppose we can't spell a word."

"Don't worry about it," I said. "Just spell it the best way you can."

A heavy silence settled on the room. All I could see were still pencils and anxious faces. This was clearly not the right approach. So I said, "All right, I'll tell you what we'll do. Any time you want to know how to spell a word, tell me and I'll write it on the board."

They breathed a sigh of relief and went to work. Soon requests for words were coming fast; as soon as I wrote one, someone asked me another. By lunchtime, when most of the children were still busily writing, the board was full. What was interesting was that most of the words they had asked for were much longer and more complicated than anything in their reading books or workbooks. Freed from worry about spelling, they were willing to use the most difficult and interesting words that they knew.

The words were still on the board when we began school next day. Before I began to erase them, I said to the children, "Listen, everyone. I have to erase these words, but before I do, just out of curiosity, I'd like to see if you remember some of them."

The result was surprising. I had expected that the child who had asked for and used a word might remember it, but I did not think many others would. But many of the children still knew many of the words. How had they learned them? I suppose each time I wrote a word on the board a number of children had looked up, relaxed yet curious, just to see what the word looked like, and these images and the sound of my voice saying the word had stuck in their minds until the next day. This, it seems to me, is how children may best learn to write and spell.

What can a parent do if a school, or a teacher, is spoiling the language for a child by teaching it in some tired way? First, try to get them to change, or at least let them know that you are eager for change. Talk to other parents; push some of these ideas in the PTA; talk to the English department at the school; talk to the child's own teacher. Many teachers and schools want to know what the parents want.

If the school or teacher cannot be persuaded, then what? Perhaps all you can do is try not to let your child become too bored or discouraged or worried by what is happening in school. Help him meet the school's demands, foolish though they may seem, and try to provide more interesting alternatives at home—plenty of books and conversation, and a serious and respectful audience when a child wants to talk. Nothing that ever happened to me in English classes at school was as helpful to me as the long conversations I used to have every summer with my uncle, who made me feel that the difference in our ages was not important and that he was really interested in what I had to say.

At the end of her freshman year in college a girl I know wrote home to her mother, "Hooray! Hooray! Just think—I never have to take English any more!" But this girl had always been an excellent English student, had always loved books, writing, ideas. It seems unnecessary and foolish and wrong that English teachers should so often take what should be the most flexible, exciting, and creative of all school courses and make it into something that most children can hardly wait to see the last of. Let's hope that we can and soon will begin to do much better.

QUESTIONS

1. What are the major indictments Holt makes and what alternatives does he propose?
2. Booth discusses various metaphors (including man as machine and man as animal) that underline different theories of education ("Is There Any Knowledge That a Man Must Have?," pp. 252–268). Might Holt accept any of these metaphors? If Holt constructed a different metaphor of his own, what might it be?
3. Is the kind of teaching that Holt describes likely to lead to students' having the knowledge that Booth believes essential?
4. Here are two accounts of a young boy's going to school, the second a summary or précis of the first. Determine what has been removed from the original in the summary. Then write a short comparison of original and summary from Holt's educational point of view, as it can be inferred from his essay.

His days were rich in formal experience. Wearing overalls and an old sweater (the accepted uniform of the private seminary), he sallied forth at morn accompanied by a nurse or a parent and walked (or was pulled) two blocks to a corner where the school bus made a flag stop. This flashy vehicle was as punctual as death: seeing us waiting at the cold curb, it would sweep to a halt, open its mouth, suck the boy in, and spring away with an angry growl. It was a good deal like a train picking up a bag of mail. At school the scholar was worked on for six or seven hours by half a dozen teachers and a nurse, and was revived on orange juice in midmorning. In a cinder court he played games supervised by an athletic instructor, and in a cafeteria he ate lunch worked out by a dietitian.

—E. B. White, "Education"

His days followed a set routine. He wore overalls and an old sweater, as everyone else did in his school. In the morning, a parent or nurse walked the two blocks with him to the corner where he met the school bus. The bus was always on time. During the six or seven hours of the school day, he had six teachers. The school also employed a nurse and a dietitian. Games were supervised. The children ate in the cafeteria. Orange juice was served during the morning session.

—End-of-Year Examinations in English for college bound students grades 9-12, Commission on English.

PETER BINZEN
The Making and the Breaking
of a Whitetown Teacher[1]

* * * A generation ago the movies, the plays, books, and radio were almost wholly supportive of the American Dream. Andy Hardy and Shirley Temple, *Gone with the Wind* and *Oklahoma!*, Kay Kyser's "College of Musical Knowledge"—none of these posed threats to our established institutions. But in recent years threats have been mounted by students, by artists and writers, by blacks, by war protesters, even by dissenting politicians. Never before in a time of affluence has American capitalism come under such savage attack. Never before have the old, conservative ways of living that Whitetowners cherish been so thoroughly rejected by so many people.

Whitetown is insular; it is inward-looking, but these cataclysmic events must have had their impact. One effect may have been to make Whitetown kids less willing than their parents to accept the same old nonsense in the schools. The older generation feared and respected such authority figures as priests and principals; the younger generation doesn't, at least not to the same extent. As a group, Whitetowners even today would probably be more likely than other Americans to put up with absurdities in school and out. But the culture shock is being felt in Whitetown, too. And this may be a factor in the failure of Whitetown kids to perform with conventional curriculum.

As for teachers and administrators in Whitetown schools, something strange has happened to them as well. Few of those I talked to at Elkin[2] and later at other schools appeared to be surprised by their pupils' appallingly bad records. They agreed that, technically, fourth-grade children should be reading fourth-grade books. But they seemed to think these levels were established for middle-class and upper-middle-class children in the better sections of the city and in the suburbs. They didn't expect Whitetown children to measure up to them. If a Whitetown second-grader was reading the primer and a fourth-grader stumbled on Book 2, well, that was fair enough . . . considering the homes these children came from.

When such attitudes are found among white educators in black schools, they are cited as proof of white racism. But here I found white educators—not all of them but too many—writing off white children. In this case, the cause was not racism but something almost as pernicious educationally. In teaching children to read,

1. From *Whitetown, U.S.A.*, 1970.
2. An elementary school in Philadelphia.

Whitetown schools—again, not all of them but too many—are losers. They've been losing for so long that they've become inured to defeat. They've become so inured to it that they no longer realize that they're losing. Research has shown that schoolchildren generally do what is expected of them. If teachers' expectations are low, pupil achievement is low. That is what has happened in Whitetown. And the result has been almost as tragic and damaging to the children of Whitetown as racial prejudice and discrimination have been to the children of Blacktown.

I mulled over these matters as I watched Maria Hoffman work with her children in Room 22. Within the limits of the rigid lesson plan—forty-five minutes each for reading, arithmetic, and social studies each day—her performance was consistently impressive. I sensed that she wasn't going to pull any miracles because miracles just don't happen in city schools. But for children who were willing to learn she established and maintained a classroom atmosphere that made learning possible.

She spoke softly but firmly. She was warm but completely unsentimental. When children did well, she told them so gracefully, not condescendingly. She treated her black and white pupils exactly alike. She seemed apolitical. She had no great urge to improve the lot of ghetto masses or to right the urban wrongs; she simply wanted to teach as well as she could.

Maria Hoffman was temperamentally unable to function effectively in one of those "creative" classrooms where kids chatter happily and do their own thing. For other teachers such a permissive atmosphere might be fine, but not for Room 22's boss. Despite Philadelphia's absolute ban on physical punishment of pupils except by principals with permission of parents, some Philadelphia teachers often slap and whack recalcitrants. Maria Hoffman's method was not to strike or shout but to admonish and warn children against slouching, snoozing, scuffling feet, moving chairs, drumming pencils. So that the peaceful majority could work, she kept after the noisy minority. In the space of two hours one morning, I recorded twenty-five separate admonitions that she gave her class. No two of them were the same:

"I hear someone talking."
"Don't start talking."
"Who's chewing gum?"
"Put your crayons away."
"If you people are talking, you're not going to hear me back there."
"Boys and girls, that doesn't mean you have a chance to talk at this moment."
"Henry Reynolds [name changed], I have asked you three times. That's enough." [Mild hyperbole: she'd only asked him twice.]
"Sit up, Bill. Come on."
"Sit up straight, boys and girls."

"I've only been here fifteen minutes and look at you. I'm not going to put up with any nonsense from you."

"I asked you to clear your desks back there."

"Sit up in your chairs. You're not *that* restless."

"Wait a minute. We've only been in school a short time. You shouldn't be that restless."

"Chris, you don't have to supply everybody with pencils, do you?"

"As long as you keep playing with it, Walt, I'm not going to pass the papers."

"Colleen, are you trying to make sure we have to wait for you every time?"

"Sandra, I don't believe you're listening."

"Put the toys away. You're not a baby."

"Let's get the feet still."

"Don't do that to your desk."

"George, every time we come in, I have to tell you to put your things away."

"Boys and girls, I don't know who's doing all this talking, but it better stop."

"I have a little competition. Somebody is talking at the same time I am. Is it you, Jenny?"

"Don't sing—fifteen times I've said it since recess."

"Carol, are you going to stay and color for us for lunch? I think everybody'd rather eat than stay here and color."

When lifted out of classroom context and placed one after another in cold print, these may read like the scoldings of a harridan. They weren't. Maria Hoffman delivered them quietly, matter-of-factly. Rather than disrupting the learning process, they made it possible for work to proceed.

One morning less than two weeks after the start of school, Maria Hoffman was summoned to substitute for a fifth-grade teacher at Elkin who had called in sick at the last minute. Such sudden "illnesses" were not uncommon. Under their union contract, all Philadelphia teachers can take ten days off for sickness each year without losing any pay. A large number seem to view these "sick" days as paid vacation time and they miss ten days of school each year regardless of the state of their health.

When Mrs. Hoffman left Room 22 that morning, I was in charge. My moment of truth had arrived. Two years before, in England, I had visited the Cambridge boarding school where the master after whom James Hilton modeled his Mr. Chips taught for many years. I had talked to the headmaster. He had told me how Hilton's master had won the hearts of generations of English schoolboys while filling their minds with knowledge. Now was my chance to show that I, too, was a Chips-like teacher, knowledgeable, warm, human, spurring good students on to greater heights, spotting and assisting the late bloomers, patiently setting the slow kids onto the path of learning.

Maria Hoffman's lesson plan called for arithmetic and reading before recess. I set to work. Using an abacus, I showed the class that nine disks in the ones column and one disk in the tens column made nineteen. They took turns making two-digit and three-digit abacus numbers. Interest was high. During reading, I made the children come up in small groups and read aloud from the *Bank Street* reader. Each child took a different part. Again, I was pleased. They seemed to be responding and working hard.

There was a brief interruption when a school doctor entered our classroom. He was taking part in the school system's annual search for bugs in pupils' heads. Those children with nits or lice, he explained in a whisper, were "excludable." The infestation is termed "pediculosis," and there always seems to be more of it in Kensington[3] than anywhere else in the city. Kensington's public schools in 1966-1967 recorded 222 cases of pediculosis and its parochial schools counted 155 cases. Together, these schools accounted for more than half of the 715 cases found in the annual "head survey" in all Philadelphia public and parochial schools. Yet Kensington could claim only ten per cent of all the children examined. For years it has been the "lousiest" district in the city—nits are a Whitetown problem: they don't fasten themselves to Negro heads.[4] Among District 5's schools, all cases of nits and lice were concentrated in half a dozen white schools. Proportionately, the infestation was slightly higher among parochial-school pupils. And there were no cases in Room 22, which I found gratifying.

I took the class out for recess. Standing in the play yard while exuberant youngsters ran and shouted all around me, I thought, These are good kids. They do what they're told. I also knew that, despite their reading problems, they weren't stupid. Not one was truly mentally retarded and several of the worst readers were alert and observant. I'd had evidence of this a few days before, when Mrs. Hoffman played a game. She had all the children close their eyes and then sent one silently out of the room. The class had to figure out who was missing and describe what he (or she) was wearing. I was hopeless at this little game, but the kids nailed down a good police-relay description every time. One boy who had been identified as a candidate for a special class for retarded educable children recalled that the girl sitting directly behind him before she left the room was wearing a red sweater, brown skirt, and yellow socks. Watching the class at recess, I thought that maybe I could achieve some kind of breakthrough.

But it was the children who achieved the breakthrough. They

3. A subdivision of Philadelphia.
4. This was bad news for one mother I talked to in Fishtown. She thought that nits and lice had been transported to her school by the black children being bussed in from North Philadelphia. She was shattered to learn that only white children are buggy [Binzen's note].

broke through me. In no time at all after we returned to our class-room, things got out of hand. I was trying to teach a social-studies lesson. But I wasn't prepared, and they soon sensed my unprepared-ness. They began probing for weaknesses in my defenses. They found them. And soon the floodgates opened. They started talking among themselves. They got up and walked around the room. A few of the older boys scuffled playfully. They threw punches and shadowboxed. Others chewed gum and sailed paper airplanes.

I was furious. I was mortified. This was an outrage. Here I was, a well-traveled education expert who had visited schools on four con-tinents. Why wouldn't these bloody Whitetown kids listen quietly? I had a lot to tell them, if they would only pay attention. Well, they wouldn't pay attention. Not to me anyway. I shouted, "Boys and girls, stop that! Don't do that! *Stop!*"

It was all to no avail. The paper airplanes continued to soar wildly across the room. For an instant I thought of *Scientific Ameri-can* magazine's paper-airplane construction contest. I wondered frantically if there were some way to turn paper-airplane throwing into what educators call a "learning experience." I concluded that there was not. Gradually, some order was restored. I plodded on with the lesson, trying to get the class to locate Broad and Market streets, the site of Philadelphia's City Hall, on maps that had been passed out. Some of the children, maybe even a majority, joined me in pleading for quiet, but the vocal minority raised hell. Some of the pupils found City Hall on their maps. Others insisted that the point representing City Hall was actually "the Poconos" or the "Atlantic Ocean." I got the distinct impression that the little mon-sters were pulling my leg—just about pulling it off.

And so lunch. Ashen-faced and shaken, I joined the other teach-ers in the second-floor lunchroom. They told me to keep trying. Each had a horror story about pupil misbehavior. The conversation was hardly reassuring. And the afternoon session was worse. A phonics lesson was supposed to deal with the consonant blends *sh* and *ch*. I had met these consonant combinations at the teacher ori-entation. Using cards and pictures that Mrs. Hoffman had prepared, I tried to get across the idea that ship, sheep, shirt, and shoes all start with *sh*, while chalk, China, cherry, and change start with *ch*. Again, turmoil. A sea of hands appealed for permission to get drinks or visit the basement toilets. When I rejected all of these pleas, there were noisy protests. Bells clanged. A note was brought in from another teacher: "Can you lend me a dime? I took 10¢ from a girl for safekeeping and it's been stolen out of my desk." By coinci-dence, a girl in my own class was just then complaining that *her* dime had become wedged in a crack in her desk. Could I help her get it out? No, I couldn't. And I didn't have a dime for the other teacher.

Another note from another teacher: "Will you please keep your class quiet? We can't hear ourselves think." Very funny. Well, I couldn't think, either. The kids simply ran roughshod over me. I felt like Plimpton[5] dropping to his knees in the Lions' scrimmage. Paper Teacher. Somehow it became two o'clock. Time for physical education in the basement. The gym instructor awaited my little band of hardened criminals. The class lined up raggedly and, on my signal, raced down the stairwell as though shot from a cannon. Hardly the kind of disciplined descent that Maria Hoffman would have required. Where the hell was Maria Hoffman? I needed help. Well, she was busy with the "sick" teacher's class but unexpected assistance suddenly appeared in the person of a mathematics "coordinator" assigned to work with elementary-school teachers in District 5. He was in Elkin for the day. Passing Room 22, he saw me slumped at my desk and came in to find out what awful event had occurred. Before I could complete my tale of woe, the class came trooping back. The physical-education instructor had refused to accept such a disorganized, uncontrolled horde. I really couldn't blame him. The math teacher, an old hand, got the class back to something approaching normal. He lectured quietly, persuasively. And he got results. The kids quieted down and behaved themselves. From *Lord of the Flies* to *Little Lord Fauntleroy* in twenty-five minutes. When the dismissal bell sounded they left in reasonable order.

The experience had left me bloodied but not yet ready to quit. It was Friday afternoon and I had the weekend to prepare for my next encounter. I read the teachers' edition of the math book we were using and I studied the teachers' guide to Bank Street's 2^2 reader, which was written for children in the second half of second grade. I got ready to prove that six tens and seventeen ones equal seven tens and seven ones. I reviewed the short *a* (as in cat, not gate), the short *e* (pet, not weed), the short *i* (sit, not nine), the short *o* (hot, not road).

At the kitchen table in our house, I wrote sentences with color pens on big three-foot-by-two-foot writing tablets. The tablets were to be hung from hooks above the blackboard in Room 22. I readied arithmetic problems for dittoing on Elkin's ditto machine. To fetch more books, I returned to Elkin on Saturday afternoon. Using a key that the principal had lent me, I entered the locked building and went up to my room. After the turmoil of the day before, all was peaceful and serene.

I hoped that this tranquillity would carry over to Monday. Before eight A.M. Monday I was in the building. Early portents were ominous. Saturday night two windowpanes had been smashed in Room

---

5. George Plimpton, author of *Paper Lion*.

22. I found bits of shattered glass strewn on the floor. In the teachers' room, the ditto machine was on the fritz. When somebody repaired it, I ran my arithmetic problems through. All came out backward. Great. I had written the problems on the wrong side of the master sheet. Hasty corrections made. Back in Room 22, I wrote the preschool (eight-forty-five to nine A.M.) arithmetic drill on the blackboard, fetched books from another classroom, collected reading workbooks, and went outside to get the children.

In the schoolyard they were quiet. They usually are on Monday mornings; it takes them a little while to work up a head of steam each week. They mounted the fire escape to our room without incident. They tackled the blackboard drill. It was very easy. The idea was to get them off on the right foot. There was just simple addition: 18 and 7 and 25 and 6 and similar sums. Of thirty-six pupils on roll that day, however, only seven completed the work correctly. The children did so poorly—fourth-graders, remember—that I had them repeat the drill. Even the second time around they performed abysmally. We went on to the flag salute.

For purposes of "character education," as promised in the week's lesson plan that I had prepared on Sunday, I quizzed the class. How many stars in the American flag? Several thought fifty-two. After some other wrong guesses, a boy supplied the correct answer and explained that each star represents a state. How many stripes? "Six," said a boy. "Six," echoed the class. I went to the flag in the corner of the room and held it so that all could count the stripes. They counted thirteen red and white stripes but nobody knew why that number had been selected. I explained that each stripe represented one of the original thirteen states.

It was now time for arithmetic. There's an axiom in teaching that one way to motivate children is to move them from a "known interest" to a "new knowledge." To start the arithmetic lesson, I drew from my pocket a John F. Kennedy half dollar. That was the known interest. These kids were nuts about money—who isn't? And during my visits to schools in Rhodesia, Israel, and West Germany in 1966, I found that children invariably were thrilled at the sight of fifty-cent pieces bearing the likeness of the assassinated President. I thought Elkin kids would react the same way. I was wrong. They showed no particular interest in the Kennedy half dollar. "Oh, yeah," said one boy tonelessly. "We've got one at our house," said another, who seemed equally bored. Undaunted, I took a penny from my pocket. It was my plan to show the class how many different ways you could make fifty-one. I had a supply of nickels, dimes, and quarters, too.

But it was no good. By this time the class had recovered from its Monday-morning lethargy. Once again, it became a juggernaut running over its hapless teacher. Boys talked and girls giggled. Small

fights broke out. A girl complained that a boy struck her. Paper airplanes sailed every which way. My frenzied shouts for order were
ignored. I yelled louder. Bedlam. Another near-by teacher complained of the racket. I suppose I could have made an object lesson
of the most obstreperous boys by sending them to the office. It would
have been almost impossible to single them out, however, because
the whole class was exploding. I remembered reading of the experience of Robert Sebastian, a lawyer, writer, and Philadelphia Board
of Education member, who, to get a taste of teaching, had served
briefly as a substitute in a number of city schools. He, too, had run
into stormy weather. At one point he described himself as being
"transfixed by the bedlam." He felt, he said, as though he were "in
the eye of a hurricane."

I felt the same way that morning. So I did the only thing that
seemed to make sense—for me and for the kids in Room 22. I
walked out of the hurricane and down to the office and I asked that
somebody else take over the class. And so, good-by, Mr. Chips. I
filled in on occasion after that and gave talks to many classes, but
my career as a Whitetown teacher really ended that awful morning.

One lesson that I drew from this was probably the same one that
Sebastian had learned. It was that in the schools of both Blacktown
and Whitetown, teaching is a tough, demanding, frustrating, often
nerve-frazzling job. As the schools are organized, it's no job for amateurs. If you can't stand the heat, you've got to get out of the classroom. And that's what I did.

But why had I failed? Was it because the kids sensed that I was
trying to fake it? Was it my lack of experience, my lack of presence,
and my thin skin? Or was there something wrong with the classroom situation itself that made teaching impossible? In a sense, I
think the answer to all these questions is yes. My failure was my
fault. I tried to trick these kids and they caught on soon enough.
They did sense that I was faking it. I lacked the control mechanisms that grade-school teachers use to keep order. All new teachers
face a tremendous challenge. In city public schools, teachers and
pupils are essentially in an adversary relationship. The kids will, if
they can, drive a teacher up the wall. If they can exploit a teacher's
weakness, they'll do it every time. I don't mean that all children
become disruptive. Most of them don't. I think that most of the
kids in Room 22 were on my side. They wanted me to run the class
and teach them something. But in this game the minority rules. It
takes only a couple of kids to make a teacher's life utterly miserable.
And of course new teachers are most vulnerable. Most of the teachers I've talked to agree that the first year is the worst and the first
weeks of the first year are the worst of all. As they get to know the
children and the ways of handling them, teachers learn the art of

survival. Even for a veteran, though, a new class poses new problems. Later I saw Maria Hoffman reduced almost to tears when she took over Elkin's slowest and most unruly sixth-grade class during the regular teacher's absence.

My own problems were compounded by my not really believing in the courses I was trying to teach. Teachers are trained to take a course of study and teach it. Theirs not to reason why. Some of them, of course, develop their own units and show a lot of ingenuity, but truly creative teachers are rare just because truly creative people in any profession are rare. Most of them have to play it by the book. And if the book calls for the making of salt maps of Pennsylvania or the teaching of Pennsylvania history with an unbelievably dull, badly written textbook that makes the Indians seem as remote and unreal as, well, wooden Indians, in that case, teachers will follow the book and do the best they can. And somehow most of them get by.

* * *

QUESTIONS

1. Are Binzen's narrative of his experience and his generalizations about it equally effective?
2. If Binzen is right and all his diagnostic questions should be answered yes, then what should be done to make the best of the bad situation?
3. What are a teacher's obligations to his students? Which of the other writers in this section of the book affords the most help in defining these obligations?
4. George Jackson (pp. 674–687), largely self-educated and clearly convinced of the principles he asserts, describes what amounts to an effort to teach his father. Is his experience like Binzen's? like Ciardi's?

HENRY F. OTTINGER

In Short, Why Did the Class Fail?[1]

And now, like it or not, I'd like to say a few parting words.

As you know, I began the semester in a way that departed from the manner in which I had taught composition classes in the past. Much of my attitude at that time was influenced by Jerry Farber's book, *The Student as Nigger*. On the first day of class, I read to you the following:

1. This article was derived from a final lecture delivered in 1972 by Henry F. Ottinger, an instructor of English and a doctoral candidate at the University of Missouri. The text has been revised slightly by the author for this reprinting.

School is where you let the dying society put its trip on you. Our schools may seem useful: to make children into doctors, sociologists, engineers—to discover things. But they're poisonous as well. They exploit and enslave students; they petrify society; they make democracy unlikely. And it's not *what* you're taught that does the harm, but *how* you're taught. Our schools teach you by pushing you around, by stealing your will and your sense of power, by making timid, apathetic slaves of you—authority addicts.

That sounded like a breath of fresh air back in February—and I suggested that we try to break the mold, that we could write papers on any subject we wanted, that we could spend class time discussing things—either "the burning issues of the day," or otherwise. You seemed to agree, and we spent a lot of time agreeing together that indeed Farber had *the* word and we would do what we could to break out of the mold.

As you know, things went from initial ecstasy to final catastrophe. And recently, I fell back—no, you forced me back—into assigning general topics. As a result of that action, and several other factors, this semester has been the worst I've ever taught. In fact, I even debated with myself whether or not to go on teaching next year. But in some ways the semester was valuable because I learned something, if you didn't.

Let me share with you some of the things I learned: and keep in mind that this does not apply to all of you, but it does to the majority.

I learned that all this bull about "getting it together" or "working together" (be it for peace or a grade) is just that—bull. The 1950's were labled by pop sociologists the "silent generation." I assure you they have nothing on you. Ten years ago, the people around the fountains wore saddle shoes and chinos, and had crew-cuts. Now they're barefoot, wear Army fatigues, and have long hair. Big revelation: it's the same bunch of people.

Generally, this class has been the most silent, reticent, paranoid bunch of people in a group I have ever experienced. If you are indicative of the generation that's supposed to change things, good luck. Change is predicated on, among other things, communication between people, "which in your case," as the poem "Naming of Parts" goes, "you have not got."

You had an opportunity to exchange ideas (which it often turned out, "you have not got,") and you were too embarrassed to do so.

You had an opportunity to find out about each other—you didn't. (Or perhaps you found out some of the same things I did: if so, congratulations: the semester has not been a waste for you.)

You had an opportunity to find out something about yourselves. This, by the way, is the crux of education. And, as far as I can see, you found out very little.

You had an opportunity to explore ideas—on your own—and

didn't. Most of the papers hashed over the usual cliché-ridden topics: abortion, the SST, the population explosion. One person went so far as to churn out a masterpiece on the pros and cons of fraternities, a topic that was really hot back around 1956.

Most of all, you had the opportunity to be free—free from the usual absurdities of a composition class where topics are assigned, thesis statements are submitted, and so on. You also had freedom of thought, as long as it was confined to the standards of formal English. You had the opportunity to be free—to be responsible to yourselves—and you succeeded in proving to me and to yourselves that Freedom is Slavery, a line from 1984 which I hope, for the sake of all of us, isn't prophetic.

But you protest! (Oh, how I wished you would): "We're incapable of handling all this freedom at once. You see, Mr. Ottinger, we've been conditioned; we're not used to all this!"

Well, I read that in Farber, too, and it's bull. Rats and dogs are conditioned, and are usually incapable of breaking that conditioning. Human beings *can* break conditioning, if it's to their advantage. But here, it's too good an excuse to say "I'm conditioned." Obviously, then, it's to your advantage *not* to break out of the mold.

Why is it to your advantage not to break the mold? In short, why did the class fail?

It failed because, as Dostoevski's "Underground Man" pointed out, thinking causes pain. And, like good little utilitarians, you want to avoid pain. No, it's much easier to come up with instant aesthetics, instant solutions, instant salvation, instant thoughts. After all, instant things, like breakfasts and TV dinners, are easily digestible —and easily regurgitated—and not terribly nourishing.

One of the more atrocious remarks I've heard this semester is, "Gosh, college is no fun," or, when an idea is presented, "it doesn't turn me on."

If you don't believe that knowledge for its own sake is a valid and valuable goal, then you are in the wrong place, and you'd do much better in a vocational school, studying how to be a plumber or a beautician. And if you don't believe, along with Ezra Pound, that "real education must ultimately be limited to men who INSIST on knowing," you are definitely in the wrong place. You are merely clutter.

Granted, there are problems within the University itself—serious problems—that, despite what you may think, show some sign of possible solution. One step they could take (but probably won't) is to limit enrollment, and keep the forty-five percent of you out who don't belong here, because it's no fun.

Well, it's time, I suppose, to bring this to a halt, and let you go over to the Union, or wherever. Until then, I invite you to listen to the lyrics of the Beatles' "Nowhere Man," and if it fits, take it to heart.

Last, I will bid a good-bye (until the final) and say that if at any time some sly hint, or clue, or (God forbid) a half-truth slipped out of my unconscious and slid out the corner of my mouth and, pardon the expression, "turned one of you on," then we have not failed, you and I.

And, to paraphrase Theodore Roethke: I love you for what you might be; I'm deeply disturbed by what you are.

Was It the Class, or Was It the Teacher— Who Failed?: Responses to Mr. Ottinger

WILLIAM BONDESON: The Romance of Teaching[1]

When a lover is spurned by his love, all the brightness is taken away and disillusionment sets in. I sense that is what has happened to you. I can't help but feel that you really do love those half-formed, recalcitrant, and ignorant young minds. And that passion is absolutely necessary for education. But like most lovers, and like all romantic educators, you have views about the objects of your love, those students of yours and mine, which are partially true but partially false as well. You believe that good educational intentions, simply of themselves, will produce similarly good intentions in others. You believe that spontaneity and impulse are exactly the same as freedom. You believe that every student has a self which, waiting loaded with potentialities and direction, requires only to be left alone in order to grow.

Like most good things, a reply should begin with Plato. He says that when the young student of philosophy is to be educated, the first thing *not* to do is to expose him to the highest and most important principles, or, to use Plato's own analogy, it is unreasonable to expect someone who has long lived in darkness to immediately operate effectively when he is first exposed to broad daylight.

And this is just what you did when you tried to put those romantic half-truths into practice. In the name of freedom, you apparently abolished all structure, all restraint, and put the terrible burden of education upon the students themselves. In the ideal case there is much validity in doing this, but that's just the trouble with romantics. They assume that every case is the ideal case, act accordingly, and then become disillusioned when it turns out not to be that way. You seem to have forgotten that your composition course is required; that sets up some resistance to it automatically. If stu-

1. William Bondeson is director of the honors college and associate professor of philosophy at the University of Missouri.

dents are freed of one requirement, when all the others are retained, it is unreasonable to expect them to use that one bit of freedom in any other way than to spend more time doing the other required things.

Since I am not an expert in the teaching of English Composition I cannot give you any more suggestions, but I can point to a romantic principle which does not seem to be a part of your philosophy or at least one which you did not seem to put into effect. And this one is derived from Plato also. Romantics believe in the uniqueness and value of each individual; I suggest that you did not take that concept very seriously. If you had, you would not have imposed either radical authority or radical freedom on the members of your classes. You would have instead realized that college students are not all alike, that they come to college with very different reasons for being here and with consequently different expectations.

What about the seekers of instant gratification whom you so deservedly put down? First, they are not all the young; they are not even a major fraction of the young. But they are appreciated, if not emulated, by a very large number of our students. With you, I find it quite distressing that these students believe in the proposition "if it feels good, it's true." This is anti-intellectualism at its worst and is partly the result of their faulty concept of individualism.

JIM ESSENSON: A Student Describes the Slave System[2]

The student is probably the most intellectually conditioned animal in existence, and he suspects it least. In the same way that a small child is rewarded with an ice cream cone for being good, an adept student quickly learns to "find out what the teacher wants" or expects from him in terms of work and intellectual participation (i.e., thinking).

The larger question which now presents itself is why are people interested solely in good grades. This query has wide sociological implications. American society is success, achievement, career oriented. Careers mean college, then graduate school with good grades as the catalyst. Unfortunately, this often means playing ball with the educational system and stifling individual initiative. You learn to find out what the teacher wants, to think it, to write it out, and to commit it to memory for the brief span of an examination period en route to that "A" and that graduate career.

You memorize information which has a staying power of thirty-six hours; you learn the intricacies of multiple-choice test-taking;

2. Jim Essenson is a student at New York University.

you learn to question only in so far as the teacher demands or accepts it; you learn to interpret and to think only from your lecture notes.

Yes, Mr. Ottinger, we are slaves: slaves to SAT's, Regents, Merits, Co-ops, admissions tests and preconceived notions of success and fulfillment which permeate American society. When a student has all his academic life dealt with "cliché-ridden topics," as you call them, and has been told what to write, how many words, what aspect, and where to put his name on the paper, you cannot very well expect him to respond automatically to a plea of "O.K., here's the freedom you have asked for all along—write me a paper on anything."

MALCOLM L. DIAMOND: Self-Examination Must Begin with the Faculty[3]

The recent contribution from Mr. Ottinger was a sad example of faculty backlash. In teaching his composition course, he responded to what he felt to be current student desires by giving them complete freedom. Dispensing with a list of standard topics, he told them to write on anything that interested them. At the end of the term, he was utterly disillusioned. The students hadn't thought, and they hadn't been turned on.

In the context Mr. Ottinger's tough talk to his students is moralistic, like the tough talk of a father who tells a child with a handwashing compulsion to cut out that nonsense and get down to work. Mr. Ottinger writes as though he had never heard of Freud, Marx and other thinkers who have helped us to understand our conditioning.

As for self-knowledge, students may be reluctant to take a hard look at themselves, but so are faculty. The motivation of teachers is complex. It involves such laudable features as curiosity about the world and the desire to help students to learn about it. It also involves such natural drives as the search for status and other rewards of a successful career. One of these rewards is turning students on. Mr. Ottinger was clearly frustrated because he was open to students, gave them freedom, and still failed to turn them on.

Even in a stable period when students passively accept what is handed to them, faculty may tend to become disenchanted. This is even more likely when student agitation leads to faculty innovations. Mr. Ottinger's essay shrieks its message of betrayal.

Castigating students for unimaginativeness, laziness, and irrespon-

3. Malcolm L. Diamond is professor of religion at Princeton.

sibility doesn't help education. It only encourages the students to play the same game of name-calling. They, in turn, castigate their professors for being smug, status-conscious and opportunistic.

PATRICIA REINFELD: The Instructor's Role Is to Guide Students[4]

When a teacher—supposedly older and wiser than his students —blames *them* en masse and in print for the failure of a class, that is very sad—for the teacher.

Has Mr. Ottinger never learned, in all his courses leading to the doctorate, that the *instructor* is the one responsible for the success —or failure—of a class? Surely he did not really believe that by totally freeing his composition students to talk and write about "any subject we wanted," they would know what to do or how to do it well?

Has Mr. Ottinger never learned about directed, or guided, freedom in the classroom through which the teacher unobtrusively moves things in the direction through which they must go? He blames his students for not thinking; it sounds on the contrary as if *he* took the vacation. And is it so horrible to assign general topics to (I assume) freshmen students, who need to become acquainted with, if not to master, particular kinds of writing?

Of course, it is much *easier* to say, in effect, "OK, kids, it's all yours"—and then blame those same kids when they don't make the class as stimulating and instructive as it should have been made *by the teacher*. This procedure also obviates the need for lesson planning and for sequential writing development. My goodness, Mr. Ottinger must have had so much free time this semester, once he put the responsibility on the students, that I wonder why he's complaining now.

HARVEY A. THOMSON: Teachers Must Create Conditions for Growth[5]

Mr. Ottinger apparently attempted to design an English composition course in which students had complete responsibility for choosing what to work on and how to use class time during the term. The class failed and the article contains the substance of the instructor's final lecture, a ringing denunciation of the students.

4. Patricia Reinfeld is assistant professor of humanities at Gloucester County College, N.J.

5. Harvey A. Thomson is assistant professor of organization behavior at McGill University.

This article had a powerful impact on me because it was honest, expressed feelings, and described the author's actual experience rather than being abstract polemic.

Our methods of teaching rest on implicit assumptions about the nature of the students we teach. Mr. Ottinger experimented with a method which assumed that students were motivated toward achievement and knowledge, were responsible, and could regulate themselves to achieve the course objectives. The fact that they were Mr. Ottinger's objectives and not the students' limits the extent to which they were really "free," but that is not the main reason for the failure of the design.

My own experience with teaching this type of course is similar to Mr. Ottinger's. Most students have a great deal of difficulty handling this degree of autonomy in the classroom. But more important than this fairly predictable result is the way Mr. Ottinger and the class dealt with this problem.

Both parties seemed to feel frustrated and inadequate ("I even debated with myself whether or not to go on teaching next year") and responded by projecting the blame onto the other (or the "system" in the case of the students). While both parties probably have a point, I can't help feeling, from Mr. Ottinger's own account, that he bears a large part of the responsibility for the polarization that took place. He seems to be totally unaware of the ways in which he failed to be effective in the classroom and hence his own responsibility for what happened.

Classroom dynamics can be described in terms of teacher and student roles. Acceptable role behavior is normally agreed upon implicitly by both parties. However, the change in the ground rules in Mr. Ottinger's course meant that both students and the instructor had to learn to play their roles differently than they had been used to in the past.

WILLIAM G. PERRY, JR.

Examsmanship and the Liberal Arts: A Study in Educational Epistemology

"But sir, I don't think I really deserve it, it was mostly bull, really." This disclaimer from a student whose examination we have awarded a straight "A" is wondrously depressing. Alfred North Whitehead invented its only possible rejoinder: "Yes sir, what you wrote is nonsense, utter nonsense. But ah! Sir! It's the right *kind* of nonsense!"

Bull, in this university,[1] is customarily a source of laughter, or a problem in ethics. I shall step a little out of fashion to use the subject as a take-off point for a study in comparative epistemology. The phenomenon of bull, in all the honor and opprobrium with which it is regarded by students and faculty, says something, I think, about our theories of knowledge. So too, the grades which we assign on examinations communicate to students what these theories may be.

We do not have to be out-and-out logical-positivists to suppose that we have something to learn about "what we think knowledge is" by having a good look at "what we do when we go about measuring it." We know the straight "A" examination when we see it, of course, and we have reason to hope that the student will understand why his work receives our recognition. He doesn't always. And those who receive lesser honor? Perhaps an understanding of certain anomalies in our customs of grading good bull will explain the students' confusion.

I must beg patience, then, both of the reader's humor and of his morals. Not that I ask him to suspend his sense of humor but that I shall ask him to go beyond it. In a great university the picture of a bright student attempting to outwit his professor while his professor takes pride in not being outwitted is certainly ridiculous. I shall report just such a scene, for its implications bear upon my point. Its comedy need not present a serious obstacle to thought.

As for the ethics of bull, I must ask for a suspension of judgment. I wish that students could suspend theirs. Unlike humor, moral commitment is hard to think beyond. Too early a moral judgment is precisely what stands between many able students and a liberal education. The stunning realization that the Harvard Faculty will often accept, as evidence of knowledge, the cerebrations of a student who has little data at his disposal, confronts every student with an ethical dilemma. For some it forms an academic focus for what used to be thought of as "adolescent disillusion." It is irrelevant that rumor inflates the phenomenon to mythical proportions. The students know that beneath the myth there remains a solid and haunting reality. The moral "bind" consequent on this awareness appears most poignantly in serious students who are reluctant to concede the competitive advantage to the bullster and who yet feel a deep personal shame when, having succumbed to "temptation," they themselves receive a high grade for work they consider "dishonest."

I have spent many hours with students caught in this unwelcome bitterness. These hours lend an urgency to my theme. I have found that students have been able to come to terms with the ethical problem, to the extent that it is real, only after a refined study of the

1. Harvard.

true nature of bull and its relation to "knowledge." I shall submit grounds for my suspicion that we can be found guilty of sharing the students' confusion of moral and epistemological issues.

I

I present as my "premise," then, an amoral *fabliau*. Its hero-villain is the Abominable Mr. Metzger '47. Since I celebrate his virtuosity, I regret giving him a pseudonym, but the peculiar style of his bravado requires me to honor also his modesty. Bull in pure form is rare; there is usually some contamination by data. The community has reason to be grateful to Mr. Metzger for having created an instance of laboratory purity, free from any adulteration by matter. The more credit is due him, I think, because his act was free from premeditation, deliberation, or hope of personal gain.

Mr. Metzger stood one rainy November day in the lobby of Memorial Hall. A junior, concentrating in mathematics, he was fond of diverting himself by taking part in the drama, a penchant which may have had some influence on the events of the next hour. He was waiting to take part in a rehearsal in Sanders Theatre, but, as sometimes happens, no other players appeared. Perhaps the rehearsal had been canceled without his knowledge? He decided to wait another five minutes.

Students, meanwhile, were filing into the Great Hall opposite, and taking seats at the testing tables. Spying a friend crossing the lobby toward the Great Hall's door, Metzger greeted him and extended appropriate condolences. He inquired, too, what course his friend was being tested in. "Oh, Soc. Sci. something-or-other." "What's it all about?" asked Metzger, and this, as Homer remarked of Patroclus, was the beginning of evil for him.

"It's about Modern Perspectives on Man and Society and All That," said his friend. "Pretty interesting, really."

"Always wanted to take a course like that," said Metzger. "Any good reading?"

"Yeah, great. There's this book"—his friend did not have time to finish.

"Take your seats please" said a stern voice beside them. The idle conversation had somehow taken the two friends to one of the tables in the Great Hall. Both students automatically obeyed; the proctor put blue-books before them; another proctor presented them with copies of the printed hour-test.

Mr. Metzger remembered afterwards a brief misgiving that was suddenly overwhelmed by a surge of curiosity and puckish glee. He wrote "George Smith" on the blue book, opened it, and addressed the first question.

I must pause to exonerate the Management. The Faculty has a rule that no student may attend an examination in a course in which he is not enrolled. To the wisdom of this rule the outcome of this deplorable story stands witness. The Registrar, charged with the enforcement of the rule, has developed an organization with procedures which are certainly the finest to be devised. In November, however, class rosters are still shaky, and on this particular day another student, named Smith, was absent. As for the culprit, we can reduce his guilt no further than to suppose that he was ignorant of the rule, or, in the face of the momentous challenge before him, forgetful.

We need not be distracted by Metzger's performance on the "objective" or "spot" questions on the test. His D on these sections can be explained by those versed in the theory of probability. Our interest focuses on the quality of his essay. It appears that when Metzger's friend picked up his own blue book a few days later, he found himself in company with a large proportion of his section in having received on the essay a C +. When he quietly picked up "George Smith's" blue book to return it to Metzger, he observed that the grade for the essay was A−. In the margin was a note in the section man's hand. It read "Excellent work. Could you have pinned these observations down a bit more closely? Compare . . . in . . . pp. . . ."

Such news could hardly be kept quiet. There was a leak, and the whole scandal broke on the front page of Tuesday's *Crimson*. With the press Metzger was modest, as becomes a hero. He said that there had been nothing to it at all, really. The essay question had offered a choice of two books, Margaret Mead's *And Keep Your Powder Dry* or Geoffrey Gorer's *The American People*. Metzger reported that having read neither of them, he had chosen the second "because the title gave me some notion as to what the book might be about." On the test, two critical comments were offered on each book, one favorable, one unfavorable. The students were asked to "discuss." Metzger conceded that he had played safe in throwing his lot with the more laudatory of the two comments, "but I did not forget to be balanced."

I do not have Mr. Metzger's essay before me except in vivid memory. As I recall, he took his first cue from the name Geoffrey, and committed his strategy to the premise that Gorer was born into an "Anglo-Saxon" culture, probably English, but certainly "English speaking." Having heard that Margaret Mead was a social anthropologist, he inferred that Gorer was the same. He then entered upon his essay, centering his inquiry upon what he supposed might be the problems inherent in an anthropologist's observation of a culture which was his own, or nearly his own. Drawing in part from memories of table-talk on cultural relativity[2] and in part from creative logic, he rang changes on the relation of observer to observed, and

2. "An important part of Harvard's education takes place during meals in the Houses." An Official Publication [Perry's note].

assessed the kind and degree of objectivity which might accrue to an observer through training as an anthropologist. He concluded that the book in question did in fact contribute a considerable range of " 'objective', and even 'fresh'," insights into the nature of our culture. "At the same time," he warned, "these observations must be understood within the context of their generation by a person only partly freed from his embeddedness in the culture he is observing, and limited in his capacity to transcend those particular tendencies and biases which he has himself developed as a personality in his interraction with this culture since his birth. In this sense the book portrays as much the character of Geoffrey Gorer as it analyzes that of the American people." It is my regrettable duty to report that at this moment of triumph Mr. Metzger was carried away by the temptations of parody and added, "We are thus much the richer."

In any case, this was the essay for which Metzger received his honor grade and his public acclaim. He was now, of course, in serious trouble with the authorities.

I shall leave him for the moment to the mercy of the Administrative Board of Harvard College and turn the reader's attention to the section man who ascribed the grade. He was in much worse trouble. All the consternation in his immediate area of the Faculty and all the glee in other areas fell upon his unprotected head. I shall now undertake his defense.

I do so not simply because I was acquainted with him and feel a respect for his intelligence; I believe in the justice of his grade! Well, perhaps "justice" is the wrong word in a situation so manifestly absurd. This is more a case in "equity." That is, the grade is equitable if we accept other aspects of the situation which are equally absurd. My proposition is this: if we accept as valid those C grades which were accorded students who, like Metzger's friend, demonstrated a thorough familiarity with the details of the book without relating their critique to the methodological problems of social anthropology, then "George Smith" deserved not only the same, but better.

The reader may protest that the C's given to students who showed evidence only of diligence were indeed not valid and that both these students and "George Smith" should have received E's. To give the diligent E is of course not in accord with custom. I shall take up this matter later. For now, were I to allow the protest, I could only restate my thesis: that "George Smith's" E would, in a college of liberal arts, be properly a "better" E.

At this point I need a short-hand. It is a curious fact that there is no academic slang for the presentation of evidence of diligence alone. "Parroting" won't do; it is possible to "parrot" bull. I must beg the reader's pardon, and, for reasons almost too obvious to bear, suggest "cow."

Stated as nouns, the concepts look simple enough:

cow (pure): data, however relevant, without relevancies.
bull (pure): relevancies, however relevant, without data.

The reader can see all too clearly where this simplicity would lead. I can assure him that I would not have imposed on him this way were I aiming to say that knowledge in this university is definable as some neuter compromise between cow and bull, some infertile hermaphrodite. This is precisely what many diligent students seem to believe: that what they must learn to do is to "find the right mean" between "amounts" of detail and "amounts" of generalities. Of course this is not the point at all. The problem is not quantitative, nor does its solution lie on a continuum between the particular and the general. Cow and bull are not poles of a single dimension. A clear notion of what they really are is essential to my inquiry, and for heuristic purposes I wish to observe them further in the celibate state.

When the pure concepts are translated into verbs, their complexities become apparent in the assumptions and purposes of the students as they write:

To cow (v. *intrans.*) or the act of cowing:
To list data (or perform operations) without awareness of, or comment upon, the contexts, frames of reference, or points of observation which determine the origin, nature, and meaning of the data (or procedures). To write on the assumption that "a fact is a fact." To present evidence of hard work as a substitute for understanding, without any intent to deceive.

To bull (v. *intrans.*) or the act of bulling:
To discourse upon the contexts, frames of reference and points of observation which would determine the origin, nature, and meaning of data if one had any. To present evidence of an understanding of form in the hope that the reader may be deceived into supposing a familiarity with content.

At the level of conscious intent, it is evident that cowing is more moral, or less immoral, than bulling. To speculate about unconscious intent would be either an injustice or a needless elaboration of my theme. It is enough that the impression left by cow is one of earnestness, diligence, and painful naiveté. The grader may feel disappointment or even irritation, but these feelings are usually balanced by pity, compassion, and a reluctance to hit a man when he's both down and moral. He may feel some challenge to his teaching, but none whatever to his one-ups-manship. He writes in the margin: "See me."

We are now in a position to understand the anomaly of custom: As instructors, we always assign bull an E, *when we detect it*; whereas we usually give cow a C, *even though it is always obvious*.

After all, we did not ask to be confronted with a choice between morals and understanding (or did we?). We evince a charming humanity, I think, in our decision to grade in favor of morals and pathos. "I simply *can't* give this student an E after he has *worked* so hard." At the same time we tacitly express our respect for the bullster's strength. We recognize a colleague. If he knows so well how to dish it out, we can be sure that he can also take it.

Of course it is just possible that we carry with us, perhaps from our own school-days, an assumption that if a student is willing to work hard and collect "good hard facts" he can always be taught to understand their relevance, whereas a student who has caught onto the forms of relevance without working at all is a lost scholar.

But this is not in accord with our experience.

It is not in accord either, as far as I can see, with the stated values of a liberal education. If a liberal education should teach students "how to think," not only in their own fields but in fields outside their own—that is, to understand "how the other fellow orders knowledge," then bulling, even in its purest form, expresses an important part of what a pluralist university holds dear, surely a more important part than the collecting of "facts that are facts" which schoolboys learn to do. Here then, good bull appears not as ignorance at all but as an aspect of knowledge. It is both relevant and "true." In a university setting good bull is therefore of more value than "facts," which, without a frame of reference, are not even "true" at all.

Perhaps this value accounts for the final anomaly: as instructors, we are inclined to reward bull highly, *where we do not detect its intent*, to the consternation of the bullster's acquaintances. And often we do not examine the matter too closely. After a long evening of reading blue books full of cow, the sudden meeting with a student who at least understands the problems of one's field provides a lift like a draught of refreshing wine, and a strong disposition toward trust.

This was, then, the sense of confidence that came to our unfortunate section man as he read "George Smith's" sympathetic considerations.

II

In my own years of watching over students' shoulders as they work, I have come to believe that this feeling of trust has a firmer basis than the confidence generated by evidence of diligence alone. I believe that the theory of a liberal education holds. Students who have dared to understand man's real relation to his knowledge have shown themselves to be in a strong position to learn content rapidly and meaningfully, and to retain it. I have learned to be less concerned about the education of a student who has come to understand the nature of man's knowledge, even though he has not yet committed himself to hard work, than I am about the education of the student who, after one or two terms at Harvard is working desperately hard and still believes that collected "facts" constitute knowledge. The latter, when I try to explain to him, too often understands me to be saying that he "doesn't *put in enough generalities.*" Surely he has "put in *enough* facts."

I have come to see such quantitative statements as expressions of an entire, coherent epistemology. In grammar school the student is taught that Columbus discovered America in 1492. The *more* such items he gets "right" on a given test the more he is credited with "knowing." From years of this sort of thing it is not unnatural to develop the conviction that knowledge consists of the accretion of hard facts by hard work.

The student learns that the more facts and procedures he can get "right" in a given course, the better will be his grade. The more courses he takes, the more subjects he has "had," the more credits he accumulates, the more diplomas he will get, until, after graduate school, he will emerge with his doctorate, a member of the community of scholars.

The foundation of this entire life is the proposition that a fact is a fact. The necessary correlate of this proposition is that a fact is either right or wrong. This implies that the standard against which the rightness or wrongness of a fact may be judged exists *someplace* —perhaps graven upon a tablet in a Platonic world outside and above *this* cave of tears. In grammar school it is evident that the tablets which enshrine the spelling of a word or the answer to an arithmetic·problem are visible to my teacher who need only compare my offerings to it. In high school I observe that my English teachers disagree. This can only mean that the tablets in such matters as the goodness of a poem are distant and obscured by clouds. They surely exist. The pleasing of befuddled English teachers degenerates into assessing their prejudices, a game in which I have no protection against my competitors more glib of tongue. I respect only my science teachers, authorities who *really know.* Later I learn from them that "this is only what we think *now.*" But eventually, surely. . . . Into this epistemology of education, apparently shared by teachers in such terms as "credits," "semester hours" and "years of French" the student may invest his ideals, his drive, his competitiveness, his safety, his self-esteem, and even his love.

College raises other questions: by whose calendar is it proper to say that Columbus discovered America in 1492? How, when and by whom was the year 1 established in this calendar? What of other calendars? In view of the evidence for Leif Ericson's previous visit (and the American Indians), what historical ethnocentrism is suggested by the use of the word "discover" in this sentence? As for

Leif Ericson, in accord with what assumptions do you order the evidence?

These questions and their answers are not "more" knowledge. They are devastation. I do not need to elaborate upon the epistemology, or rather epistemologies, they imply. A fact has become at last "an observation or an operation performed in a frame of reference." A liberal education is founded in an awareness of frame of reference even in the most immediate and empirical examination of data. Its acquirement involves relinquishing hope of absolutes and of the protection they afford against doubt and the glib-tongued competitor. It demands an ever widening sophistication about systems of thought and observation. It leads, not away from, but *through* the arts of gamesmanship to a new trust.

This trust is in the value and integrity of systems, their varied character, and the way their apparently incompatible metaphors enlighten, from complementary facets, the particulars of human experience. As one student said to me: "I used to be cynical about intellectual games. Now I want to know them thoroughly. You see I came to realize that it was only when I knew the rules of the game cold that I could tell whether what I was saying was tripe."

We too often think of the bullster as cynical. He can be, and not always in a light-hearted way. We have failed to observe that there can lie behind cow the potential of a deeper and more dangerous despair. The moralism of sheer work and obedience can be an ethic that, unwilling to face a despair of its ends, glorifies its means. The implicit refusal to consider the relativity of both ends and means leaves the operator in an unconsidered proprietary absolutism. History bears witness that in the pinches this moral superiority has no recourse to negotiation, only to force.

A liberal education proposes that man's hope lies elsewhere: in the negotiability that can arise from an understanding of the integrity of systems and of their origins in man's address to his universe. The prerequisite is the courage to accept such a definition of knowledge. From then on, of course, there is nothing incompatible between such an epistemology and hard work. Rather the contrary.

I can now at last let bull and cow get together. The reader knows best how a productive wedding is arranged in his own field. This is the nuptial he celebrates with a straight A on examinations. The masculine context must embrace the feminine particular, though itself "born of woman." Such a union is knowledge itself, and it alone can generate new contexts and new data which can unite in their turn to form new knowledge.

In this happy setting we can congratulate in particular the Natural Sciences, long thought to be barren ground to the bullster. I have indeed drawn my examples of bull from the Social Sciences, and by analogy from the Humanities. Essay-writing in these fields has long been thought to nurture the art of bull to its prime. I feel, however, that the Natural Sciences have no reason to feel slighted. It is perhaps no accident that Metzger was a mathematician. As part of my researches for this paper, furthermore, a student of considerable talent has recently honored me with an impressive analysis of the art of amassing "partial credits" on examinations in advanced physics. Though beyond me in some respects, his presentation confirmed my impression that instructors of Physics frequently honor on examinations operations structurally similar to those requisite in a good essay.

The very qualities that make the Natural Sciences fields of delight for the eager gamesman have been essential to their marvelous fertility.

III

As priests of these mysteries, how can we make our rites more precisely expressive? The student who merely cows robs himself, without knowing it, of his education and his soul. The student who only bulls robs himself, as he knows full well, of the joys of inductive discovery—that is, of engagement. The introduction of frames of reference in the new curricula of Mathematics and Physics in the schools is a hopeful experiment. We do not know yet how much of these potent revelations the very young can stand, but I suspect they may rejoice in them more than we have supposed. I can't believe they have never wondered about Leif Ericson and that word "discovered," or even about 1492. They have simply been too wise to inquire.

Increasingly in recent years better students in the better high schools and preparatory schools are being allowed to inquire. In fact they appear to be receiving both encouragement and training in their inquiry. I have the evidence before me.

Each year for the past five years all freshmen entering Harvard and Radcliffe have been asked in freshman week to "grade" two essays answering an examination question in History. They are then asked to give their reasons for their grades. One essay, filled with dates, is 99% cow. The other, with hardly a date in it, is a good essay, easily mistaken for bull. The "official" grades of these essays are, for the first (alas!) C+ "because he has worked so hard," and for the second (soundly, I think) B+. Each year a larger majority of freshmen evaluate these essays as would the majority of the faculty, and for the faculty's reasons, and each year a smaller minority give the higher honor to the essay offering data alone. Most interesting, a larger number of students each year, while not overrating the second essay, award the first the straight E appropriate to it in a college of liberal arts.

For us who must grade such students in a university, these developments imply a new urgency, did we not feel it already. Through our grades we describe for the students, in the showdown, what we believe about the nature of knowledge. The subtleties of bull are not peripheral to our academic concerns. That they penetrate to the center of our care is evident in our feelings when a student whose good work we have awarded a high grade reveals to us that he does not feel he deserves it. Whether he disqualifies himself because "there's too much bull in it," or worse because "I really don't think I've worked that hard," he presents a serious educational problem. Many students feel this sleaziness; only a few reveal it to us.

We can hardly allow a mistaken sense of fraudulence to undermine our students' achievements. We must lead students beyond their concept of bull so that they may honor relevancies that are really relevant. We can willingly acknowledge that, in lieu of the date 1492, a consideration of calendars and of the word "discovered," may well be offered with intent to deceive. We must insist that this does not make such considerations intrinsically immoral, and that, contrariwise, the date 1492 may be no substitute for them. Most of all, we must convey the impression that we grade understanding qua understanding. To be convincing, I suppose we must concede to ourselves in advance that a bright student's understanding is understanding even if he achieved it by osmosis rather than by hard work in our course.

These are delicate matters. As for cow, its complexities are not what need concern us. Unlike good bull, it does not represent partial knowledge at all. It belongs to a different theory of knowledge entirely. In our theories of knowledge it represents total ignorance, or worse yet, a knowledge downright inimical to understanding. I even go so far as to propose that we award no more C's for cow. To do so is rarely, I feel, the act of mercy it seems. Mercy lies in clarity.

The reader may be afflicted by a lingering curiosity about the fate of Mr. Metzger. I hasten to reassure him. The Administrative Board of Harvard College, whatever its satanic reputations, is a benign body. Its members, to be sure, were on the spot. They delighted in Metzger's exploit, but they were responsible to the Faculty's rule. The hero stood in danger of probation. The debate was painful. Suddenly one member, of a refined legalistic sensibility, observed that the rule applied specifically to "examinations" and that the occasion had been simply an hour-test. Mr. Metzger was merely "admonished."

JOHN CIARDI
Generation Gap

I talked to some college students about what was wrong with my college generation, and they nodded in agreement. No wonder we had turned out to be such squares, their nods seemed to say.

I went on to guess at some of the things that characterized the mood and thinking of their college generation. I did not suggest that those things were shortcomings. I was trying to describe some of the conditioning circumstances of their growing up. The nods stopped. Their hair was too long to let hackles rise, but their soul hair was up. They had shifted from agreement to resistance.

It wasn't cool, I was told, to fling generalizations (of exactly the sort they had accepted gravely when I had been talking about my own peers). I wasn't relating. I was, in fact, being hostile.

One champion rose among them—and remained standing—to let me know I wasn't getting the message. Unless I was able to learn as much from him as he could learn from me, he announced, I wasn't fit to be there as a teacher—if only as a visiting lecturer impersonating a teacher.

That, I decided, was an assertion I had to learn more about, even if it meant losing the original topic forever. Did he really mean what he said? Was it his habit to enter the classroom with the assumption that the professor would learn as much from him as he would learn from the professor?

It certainly was, he insisted, moving up to share the podium with me.

I made room, confessing, as I edged aside, to an unexamined notion (one therefore subject to revision) that a teacher was one who tried to communicate a body of knowledge to students who had not yet acquired it. In time the student might well surpass the teacher. In the classroom situation, however, a professor's qualification to teach is the fact that he knows more about his subject than the students do.

A teacher, I was informed, is not a data bank. He is there to communicate. To communicate, he must be in deep human contact with his students. To be in deep human contact with other people is to learn all that really matters.

Suppose, I asked, I were teaching something as discrete as the principle of physics that states that for every action there is an equal and opposite reaction? Would I have to make a soul encounter of presenting such a principle and of illustrating various ways in which it works? Would it, in fact, be useful to seek a deep human contact in such a context?

My questions were brushed aside as matters of mere data.

I admitted that I could see no way to imagine physics without data—mere or otherwise—but I had to insist that the exposition of a principle and of the way it works in seemingly different circumstances was something more than a matter of data. Nor did I know how to personalize such things into a deep, solemn human relationship. I had, I told him, managed few such relationships in my life, treasured them, in part, for their rarity, and found them rare because they required a rapport not to be had for the asking. Nor could I imagine how to establish such a rapport with a classroomful of students. I had always assumed I entered the classroom to exchange, at a mutually respectful distance, some sort of respectful detachment from the ideas we were examining. It was, and is—as I have always assumed—equally important not to get our thumb smudges all over ideas but to remember that they existed before us, that they will exist after us, and that we are related to them only as imperfect vessels for their temporary conveyance.

I was made to understand that I had just defined myself as a square, that I had missed the whole revolutionary point of the new sensibility, and that I would never get with it until I let the natural power of my soul hang out.

I declined that invitation as a bit of ectoplasmic untidiness and wondered if we hadn't strayed from the point. What teacher—unless he is a death of the soul—could fail to learn *something* from his students? But "something" was not the point. He had said the teacher must learn *as much* from the student as the student learns from him. But if the two are learning equally from each other, they have no student-teacher relationship. They are colleagues.

That, I was told, was just the point. We are all colleagues in the universe, all beginners in the mystery of life.

Mystery, to be sure, may be what Edmund Burke asserted calamity to be—a mighty leveler. Nor had I any thought of resisting the idea that we are all equally souls and therefore, to some extent, lost and needy.

On certain subjects, however, I could list rather specifically the sort of thing a student might learn from me that I could not learn from him. On any number of other subjects, there are people from whom I could learn what they cannot learn from me. Were I to sign up for a course with such a person, my first impulse would certainly be to shut up and listen.

"Shut up and listen," I was told, was authoritarian and made me an intellectual hardhat.

Would he grant me no difference between an imposed authority and a self-imposed one? The self-imposition, I had to believe, was an act of intellectual discipline without which there could be little learning worth classroom time.

He would grant me nothing, he let me know, taking over all of the lectern and leaving me in the left middle distance that-a-way, a situation I resolved by stepping off the low podium and sitting down with the students. My way of thinking, he told me from his eminence, was chained to a dead past. It was the sort of intellect that had produced atom bombs, Vietnams, pollution, racial oppression, class systems, and hypocrisy, and that had made inevitable the coming revolution in which everyone will know the truth because everyone has it in his soul, if he will just let it out.

It would have been my day for revelation—except that I had heard it all before and wasn't really learning. I still had one question, and I raised my hand.

"As I said earlier, I could list some specific things you might learn from me if you cared to. Could you suggest what fairly specific things I might learn from you?" I asked.

"That," he said, "is exactly what a good teacher is supposed to find out."

He was right, after all. I was learning from him; and not only as much as he was learning from me, but more.

But then I had taken unfair advantage. I had been listening.

QUESTIONS

1. *In this very short piece Ciardi is working toward a narrative climax at the end; how does he go about it? What are the verbal signs of the steps he takes in that process?*
2. *In the middle of the essay are two contrasting paragraphs: "I admitted that . . ." and "I was made to understand . . ." What is the contrast and how does he make it? Are the paragraphs equally effective? If they are not, does the discrepancy significantly compromise the essay?*

WAYNE C. BOOTH

Is There Any Knowledge That a Man *Must* Have?

Everyone lives on the assumption that a great deal of knowledge is not worth bothering about; though we all know that what looks trivial in one man's hands may turn out to be earth-shaking in another's, we simply cannot know very much, compared with what might be known, and we must therefore choose. What is shocking is not the act of choice which we all commit openly but the claim that some choices are wrong. Especially shocking is the claim implied by my title: There is some knowledge that a man *must* have.

There clearly is no such thing, if by knowledge we mean mere acquaintance with this or that thing, fact, concept, literary work, or scientific law. When C. P. Snow and F. R. Leavis exchanged blows on whether knowledge of Shakespeare is more important than knowledge of the second law of thermodynamics, they were both, it seemed to me, much too ready to assume as indispensable what a great many wise and good men have quite obviously got along without. And it is not only nonprofessionals who can survive in happy ignorance of this or that bit of lore. I suspect that many successful scientists (in biology, say) have lost whatever hold they might once have had on the second law; I know that a great many literary scholars survive and even flourish without knowing certain "indispensable" classics. We all get along without vast loads of learning that other men take as necessary marks of an educated man. If we once begin to "reason the need" we will find, like Lear, that "our basest beggars/Are in the poorest thing superfluous." Indeed, we can survive, in a manner of speaking, even in the modern world, with little more than the bare literacy necessary to tell the "off" buttons from the "on."

Herbert Spencer would remind us at this point that we are interpreting *need* as if it were entirely a question of private survival. Though he talks about what a man must know to stay alive, he is more interested, in his defense of science, in what a *society* must know to survive: "Is there any knowledge that *man* must have?"—not a man, but *man*. This question is put to us much more acutely in our time than it was in Spencer's, and it is by no means as easy to argue now as it was then that the knowledge needed for man's survival is scientific knowledge. The threats of atomic annihilation, of engulfing population growth, of depleted air, water, and food must obviously be met, if man is to survive, and in meeting them man will, it is true, need more and more scientific knowledge; but it is not at all clear that more and more scientific knowledge will by itself suffice. Even so, a modern Herbert Spencer might well argue that a conference like this one, with its emphasis on the individual and his cognitive needs, is simply repeating the mistakes of the classical tradition. The knowledge most worth having would be, from his point of view, that of how to pull mankind through the next century or so without absolute self-destruction. The precise proportions of different kinds of knowledge—physical, biological, political, ethical, psychological, historical, or whatever—would be different from those prescribed in Spencer's essay, but the nature of the search would be precisely the same.

We can admit the relevance of this emphasis on social utility and at the same time argue that our business here is with other matters entirely. If the only knowledge a man *must* have is how to cross the street without getting knocked down—or, in other words, how to navigate the centuries without blowing himself up—then we may as well close the conference and go home. We may as well also roll up the college and mail it to a research institute, because almost any place that is not cluttered up with notions of liberal education will be able to discover and transmit practical bits of survival-lore better than we can. Our problem of survival is a rather different one, thrust at us as soon as we change our title slightly once again to "Is there any knowledge (other than the knowledge for survival) that a man must have?" That slight shift opens a new perspective on the problem, because the question of what it is to be a man, of what it is to be fully human, is the question at the heart of liberal education.

To be human, to be human, to be fully human. What does it mean? What is required? Immediately, we start feeling nervous again. Is the speaker suggesting that some of us are not fully human *yet*? Here come those hierarchies again. Surely in our pluralistic society we can admit an unlimited number of legitimate ways to be a man, without prescribing some outmoded aristocratic code!

Who—or what—is the creature we would educate? Our answer will determine our answers to educational questions, and it is therefore, I think, worth far more vigorous effort than it usually receives. I find it convenient, and only slightly unfair, to classify the educational talk I encounter these days under four notions of man, three of them metaphorical, only one literal. Though nobody's position, I suppose, fits my types neatly, some educators talk as if they were programming machines, some talk as if they were conditioning rats, some talk as if they were training ants to take a position in the anthill, and some—precious few—talk as if they thought of themselves as men dealing with men.

One traditional division of the human soul, you will remember, was into three parts: the vegetable, the animal, and the rational. Nobody, so far as I know, has devised an educational program treating students as vegetables, though one runs into the analogy used negatively in academic sermons from time to time. Similarly, no one ever really says that men are ants, though there is a marvelous passage in Kwame Nkrumah's autobiography in which he meditates longingly on the order and pure functionality of an anthill. Educators do talk of men as machines or as animals, but of course they always point out that men are much more complicated than any other known animals or machines. My point here is not so much to attack any one of these metaphors—dangerous as I think they are—but to describe briefly what answers to our question each of them might suggest.

Ever since Descartes, La Mettrie,[1] and others explicitly called a man a machine, the metaphor has been a dominant one in educational thinking. Some have thought of man as a very complex machine, needing very elaborate programming; others have thought of him as a very simple machine, requiring little more than a systematic pattern of stimuli to produce foretellable responses. I heard a psychologist recently repeat the old behaviorist claim (first made by John B. Watson, I believe) that if you would give him complete control over any normal child's life from birth, he could turn that child into a great musician or a great mathematician or a great poet—you name it and he could produce it. On being pressed, the professor admitted that this claim was only "in theory," because we don't yet have the necessary knowledge. When I pushed further by asking why he was so confident in advance of experimental proof, it became clear that his faith in the fundamental metaphor of man as a programmable machine was unshakable.

When the notion of man as machine was first advanced, the machine was a very simple collection of pulleys and billiard balls and levers. Such original simplicities have been badly battered by our growing awareness both of how complex real machines can be and of how much more complex man is than any known machine. Modern notions of stimulus-response patterns are immeasurably more complicated than anything Descartes imagined, because we are now aware of the fantastic variety of stimuli that the man-machine is subject to and of the even more fantastic complexity of the responding circuits.

But whether the machine is simple or complex, the educational task for those who think of man under this metaphor is to program the mechanism so that it will produce the results that we have foreordained. We do not simply fill the little pitchers, like Mr. Gradgrind in Dickens' *Hard Times*;[2] we are much too sophisticated to want only undigested "pour-back," as he might have called his product. But we still program the information channels so that the proper if-loops and do-loops will be followed and the right feedback produced. The "programming" can be done by human teachers, of course, and not only by machines; but it is not surprising that those whose thinking is dominated by this metaphor tend to discover that machines are better teachers than men. The more ambitious programmers do not hesitate to claim that they can teach both thought and creativity in this way. But I have yet to see a program that can deal effectively with any subject that cannot be reduced to simple yes and no answers, that is, to answers that are known in advance by the programmer and can thus be fixed for all time.

1. René Descartes (1596-1650), French philosopher and mathematician; Julian Offray de La Mettrie (1709-1751), French physician and philosopher.

2. Thomas Gradgrind thought of his students as "little pitchers . . . who were to be filled so full of facts."

We can assume that subtler machines will be invented that can engage in simulated dialogue with the pupil, and perhaps even recognize when a particularly bright pupil has discovered something new that refutes the program. But even the subtlest teaching machine imaginable will still be subject, one must assume, to a final limitation: it can teach only what a machine can "learn." For those who believe that man is literally nothing but a very complicated machine, this is not in fact a limitation; machines will ultimately be able to duplicate all mental processes, thus "learning" everything learnable, and they will be able in consequence to teach everything.

I doubt this claim for many reasons, and I am glad to find the testimony of Norbert Wiener, the first and best known cyberneticist, to the effect that there will always remain a radical gap between computers and the human mind. But "ultimately" is a long way off, and I am not so much concerned with whether ultimately man's mind will closely resemble some ultimately inventable machine as I am with the effects, here and now, of thinking about men under the analogy with machines of today. Let me simply close this section with an illustration of how the mechanistic model can permeate our thought in destructive ways. Ask yourselves what picture of creature-to-be-educated emerges from this professor of teacher education:

To implement the TEAM Project new curriculum proposal . . . our first concerns are with instructional systems, materials to feed the system, and personnel to operate the system. We have defined an instructional system as the optimal blending of the demands of content, communication, and learning. While numerous models have been developed, our simplified model of an instructional system would look like Figure 2. . . . We look at the process of communication—communicating content to produce learning—as something involving the senses: . . . [aural, oral, tactile, visual]. And I think in teacher education we had better think of the communications aspect of the instructional system as a package that includes the teacher, textbook, new media, classroom, and environment. To integrate these elements to more effectively transmit content into permanent learning, new and better instructional materials are needed and a new focus on the teacher of teachers is required. The teacher of teachers must: (1) examine critically the content of traditional courses in relation to desired behavioral outcomes; (2) become more sophisticated in the techniques of communicating course content; and (3) learn to work in concert with media specialists to develop the materials and procedures requisite to the efficient instructional system. And if the media specialist were to be charged with the efficient operation of the system, his upgrading would demand a broad-based "media generalist" orientation.[3]

3. Desmond P. Wedberg, *Teacher Education Looks to the Future,* Twelfth Biennial School for Executives (Washington, D. C.: American Association of Colleges for Teacher Education, 1964) [Booth's note].

I submit that the author of this passage was thinking of human beings as stimulus-response systems on the simplest possible model, and that he was thinking of the purpose of education as the transfer of information from one machine to another. Though he would certainly deny it if we asked him, he has come to think about the human mind so habitually in the mechanistic mode that he doesn't even know he's doing it.[4]

But it is time to move from the machine metaphor to animal metaphors. They are closely related, of course, because everybody who believes that man is a machine also believes that animals are machines, only simpler ones. But many people who would resist the word "machine" do tend to analogize man to one or another characteristic of animals. Since man is obviously an animal in one sense, he can be studied as an animal, and he can be taught as an animal is taught. Most of the fundamental research in learning theory underlying the use of teaching machines has been done, in fact, on animals like rats and pigeons. You can teach pigeons to play Ping-Pong rather quickly by rewarding every gesture they make that moves them toward success in the game and refusing to reward those gestures that you want to efface. Though everybody admits that human beings are more complicated than rats and pigeons, just as everyone admits that human beings are more complicated than computers, the basic picture of the animal as a collection of drives or instincts, "conditioned" to learn according to rewards or punishments, has underlain much modern educational theory.

The notion of the human being as a collection of drives different from animal drives only in being more complex carries with it implications for education planners. If you and I are motivated only by sex or hunger or more complex drives like desire for power or for ego-satisfaction, then of course all education depends on the provision of satisfactions along our route to knowledge. If our teachers can just program carrots along the path at the proper distance, we donkey-headed students will plod along the path from carrot to carrot and end up as educated men.

I cannot take time here to deal with this view adequately, but it seems to me that it is highly questionable even about animals themselves. What kind of thing, really, is a rat or a monkey? The question of whether animals have souls has been debated actively for at least nine centuries; now psychologists find themselves dealing with the same question under another guise: What *are* these little creatures that we kill so blithely for the sake of knowledge?

4. I am not of course suggesting that *any* use of teaching machines implies a mechanistic reduction of persons to machines; programmers rightly point out that machines *can* free teachers from the mechanical and save time for the personal [Booth's note].

What *are* these strangely resistant little bundles of energy that will prefer—as experiments with rats have shown—a complicated interesting maze without food to a dull one *with* food?

There are, in fact, many experiments by now showing that at the very least we must postulate, for animals, a strong independent drive for mastery of the environment or satisfaction of curiosity about it. All the more advanced animals will learn to push levers that produce interesting results—clicks or bells or flashing lights or sliding panels—when no other reward is offered.[5] It seems clear that even to be a fulfilled animal, as it were, something more than "animal satisfaction" is needed!

I am reminded here of the experiments on mother-love in monkeys reported by Harry F. Harlow in the *Scientific American* some years ago. Harlow called his article "Love in Infant Monkeys," and the subtitle of his article read, "Affection in infants was long thought to be generated by the satisfactions of feeding. Studies of young rhesus monkeys now indicate that love derives mainly from close bodily contact." The experiment consisted of giving infant monkeys a choice between a plain wire figure that offered the infant milk and a terry-cloth covered figure without milk. There was a pathetic picture of an infant clinging to the terry-cloth figure, and a caption that read "The infants spent most of their time clinging to the soft cloth 'mother' even when nursing bottles were attached to the wire mother." The article concluded—rather prematurely, I thought—that "contact comfort" had been shown to be a "prime requisite in the formation of an infant's love for its mother," that the act of nursing had been shown to be unimportant if not totally irrelevant in forming such love (though it was evident to any reader, even at the time, that no genuine "*act* of nursing" had figured in the experiment at all), and that "our investigations have established a secure experimental approach to this realm of dramatic and subtle emotional relationships." The only real problem, Harlow said, was the availability of enough infant monkeys for experiment.

Now I would not want to underrate the importance of Harlow's demonstration to the scientific community that monkeys do not live by bread alone. But I think that most scientists and humanists reading the article would have been struck by two things. The first is the automatic assumption that the way to study a subject like love is to break it down into its component parts; nobody looking at that little monkey clinging to the terry-cloth could possibly have said, "This is love," unless he had been blinded by a hidden conviction that love in animals is—must be—a mere cumulative result of a collection of drive satisfactions. This assumption is given quite

5. See Robert W. White, "Motivation Reconsidered: The Concept of Competence," *Psychological Review*, 66 (1959), 297–333 [Booth's note].

plainly in Harlow's concluding sentence: "Finally with such techniques established, there appears to be no reason why we cannot at some future time investigate the fundamental neurophysiological and biochemical variables underlying affection and love." For Harlow monkeys (and people) seem to be mere collections of neurophysiological and biochemical variables, and love will be best explained when we can explain the genesis of each of its parts. The second striking point is that for Harlow animals do not matter, except as they are useful for experiment. If he had felt that they mattered, he might have noticed the look on his infant's face—a look that predicted for me, and for other readers of the *Scientific American* I've talked with, that these monkeys were doomed.

And indeed they were. A year or so later another article appeared, reporting Harlow's astonished discovery that all of the little monkeys on which he had earlier experimented had turned out to be incurably psychotic. Not a single monkey could mate, not a single monkey could play, not a single monkey could in fact become anything more than the twisted half-creatures that Harlow's deprivations had made of them. Harlow's new discovery was that monkeys needed close association with their peers during infancy and that such association was even more important to their development than genuine mothering. There was no sign that Harlow had learned any fundamental lessons from his earlier gross mistakes; he had landed nicely on his feet, still convinced that the way to study love is to break it down into its component parts and that the way to study animals is to maim them or reduce them to something less than themselves. As Robert White says, summarizing his reasons for rejecting similar methods in studying human infancy, it is too often assumed that the scientific way is to analyze behavior until one can find a small enough unit to allow for detailed research, but in the process "very vital common properties" are lost from view.

I cite Harlow's two reports not, of course, to attack animal experimentation—though I must confess that I am horrified by much that goes on in its name—nor to claim that animals are more like human beings than they are. Rather, I want simply to suggest that the danger of thinking of men as animals is heightened if the animals we think of are reduced to machines on a simple model.

The effects of reducing education to conditioning can be seen throughout America today. Usually they appear in subtle forms, disguised with the language of personalism; you will look a long time before you find anyone (except a very few Skinnerians) saying that he thinks of education as exactly like conditioning pigeons. But there are plenty of honest, blunt folk around to let the cat out of the bag—like the author of an article this year in *College Composition and Communications*: "The Use of a Multiple Response

Device in the Teaching of Remedial English." The author claimed
to have evidence that if you give each student four buttons to be
pushed on multiple-choice questions, with all the buttons wired
into a lighted grid at the front of the room, the resulting "instantaneous feedback"—every child learning immediately whether he
agrees with the rest of the class—speeds up the learning of grammatical rules considerably over the usual workbook procedures. I
daresay it does—but meanwhile what has happened to education?
Or take the author of an article on "Procedures and Techniques of
Teaching," who wrote as follows: "If we expect students to learn
skills, they have to practice, but practice doesn't make perfect.
Practice works if the learner *learns the results* of his practice, i.e., if
he receives feedback. Feedback is most effective when it is contiguous to the response being learned. One of the chief advantages of
teaching machines is that the learner finds out quickly whether his
response is right or wrong . . . [Pressey] has published the results of
an extensive program of research with tests that students score for
themselves by punching alternatives until they hit the correct
one. . . . [Thus] teaching machines or workbooks have many theoretical advantages over lecturing or other conventional methods of
instruction." But according to what theory, one must ask, *do* systematic feedback mechanisms, perfected to whatever degree, have
"theoretical advantages" over human contact? Whatever else can
be said for such a theory, it will be based on the simplest of comparisons with animal learning. Unfortunately, the author goes on,
experimental evidence is on the whole rather discouraging: "Experiments at the Systems Development Corporation . . . suggest that
teaching incorporating . . . human characteristics is more effective
than the typical fixed-sequence machines. (In this experiment
instead of using teaching machines to simulate human teachers, the
experimenters used humans to simulate teaching machines!)"

So far I have dealt with analogies for man that apply only to
individuals. My third analogy turns to the picture of men in
groups, and it is given to me partly by discussions of education, like
those of Admiral Rickover, that see it simply as filling society's
needs. I know of only one prominent educator who has publicly
praised the anthill as a model for the kind of society a university
should serve—a society of specialists each trained to do his part.
But the notion pervades many of the defenses of the emerging mul-
tiversities.

If knowledge is needed to enable men to function as units in
society, and if the health of society is taken as the purpose of their
existence, then there is nothing wrong in training the ants to fill
their niches; it would be wrong not to. "Education is our first line

of defense—make it strong," so reads the title of the first chapter of Admiral Rickover's book, *Education and Freedom* (New York: Dutton, 1959). "We must upgrade our schools", in order to "guarantee the future prosperity and freedom of the Republic." You can tell whether the ant-analogy is dominating a man's thinking by a simple test of how he orders his ends and means. In Admiral Rickover's statement, the schools must be upgraded in order to guarantee future prosperity, that is, we improve education for the sake of some presumed social good.

I seldom find anyone putting it the other way round: we must guarantee prosperity so that we can improve the schools, and the reason we want to improve the schools is that we want to insure the development of certain kinds of persons, both as teachers and as students. You cannot even say what I just said so long as you are really thinking of ants and anthills. Ants are not ends in themselves, ultimately more valuable than the hills they live in (I *think* they are not; maybe to themselves, or in the eyes of God, even ants are ultimate, self-justifying ends). At least from our point of view, ants are expendable, or to put it another way, their society is more beautiful, more interesting, more admirable than they are. And I would want to argue that too many people think of human beings in the same way when they think of educating them. The Communists make this quite explicit: the ends of Communist society justify whatever distortion or destruction of individual purposes is necessary to achieve them; men are educated for the state, not for their own well-being. They are basically political animals, not in the Aristotelian sense that they require society if they are to achieve their full natures and thus their own special, human kind of happiness, but in the sense that they exist, like ants, for the sake of the body politic.

If the social order is the final justification of what we do in education, then a certain attitude toward teaching and research will result: all of us little workmen, down inside the anthill, will go on happily contributing our tiny bit to the total scheme without worrying much about larger questions of the why and wherefore. I know a graduate student who says that she sometimes sees her graduate professors as an army of tiny industrious miners at the bottom of a vast mine, chipping away at the edges and shipping their bits of knowledge up to the surface, blindly hoping that someone up there will know what to do with it all. An order is received for such-and-such new organic compounds; society needs them. Another order is received for an atomic bomb; it is needed, and it is therefore produced. Often no orders come down, but the chipping goes on anyway, and the shipments are made, because everyone knows that the health of the mine depends on a certain tonnage of specialized knowledge each working day.

We have learned lately that "they" are going to establish a great new atom-smasher, perhaps near Chicago. The atom-smasher will employ two thousand scientists and technicians. I look out at you here, knowing that some of you are physics majors, and I wonder whether any of you will ultimately be employed in that new installation, and if you are, whether it will be as an ant or as a human being. Which it will be must depend not on your ultimate employers but on yourself and on what happens to your education between now and then: if you have been given nothing but training to be that ultimate unit in that ultimate system, only a miracle can save you from formic dissolution of your human lineaments.

But it is long past time for me to turn from these negative, truncated portraits of what man really is not and attempt to say what he is. And here we encounter a difficulty that I find very curious. You will note that each of these metaphors has reduced man to something less than man, or at least to a partial aspect of man. It is easy to say that man is not a machine, though he is in some limited respects organized like a machine and even to some degree "programmable." It is also easy to say that man is not simply a complicated rat or monkey, though he is in some ways like rats and monkeys. Nor is man an ant, though he lives and must function in a complicated social milieu. All these metaphors break down not because they are flatly false but because they *are* metaphors, and any metaphorical definition is inevitably misleading. The ones I have been dealing with are especially misleading, because in every case they have reduced something more complex to something much less complex. But even if we were to analogize man to something more complex, say, the universe, we would be dissatisfied. What we want is some notion of what man really *is*, so that we will know what or whom we are trying to educate.

And here it is that we discover something very important about man, something that even the least religious person must find himself mystified by: man is the one "thing" we know that is completely resistant to our efforts at metaphor or analogy or image-making. What seems to be the most important literal characteristic of man is his resistance to definitions in terms of anything else. If you call me a machine, even a very complicated machine, I know that you deny what I care most about, my selfhood, my sense of being a person, my consciousness, my conviction of freedom and dignity, my awareness of love, my laughter. Machines have none of these things, and even if we were generous to their prospects, and imagined machines immeasurably superior to the most complicated ones now in existence, we would still feel an infinite gap between them and what we know to be a basic truth about ourselves:

machines are expendable, ultimately expendable, and men are mysteriously ends in themselves.

I hear people deny this, but when they do they always argue for their position by claiming marvelous feats of super-machine calculation that machines can now do or will someday be able to do. But that is not the point; of course machines can outcalculate us. The question to ask is entirely a different one: Will they ever outlove us, outlive us, outvalue us? Do we build machines because machines are good things in themselves? Do we nurture them for their own good, as we nurture our children? An obvious way to test our sense of worth in men and machines is to ask ourselves whether we would ever campaign to liberate the poor drowntrodden machines who have been enslaved. Shall we form a National Association for the Advancement of Machinery? Will anyone ever feel a smidgeon of moral indignation because this or that piece of machinery is not given equal rights before the law? Or put it another way: Does anyone value Gemini more than the twins? There may be men now alive who would rather "destruct," as we say, the pilot than the experimental rocket, but most of us still believe that the human being in the space ship is more important than the space ship.

When college students protest the so-called depersonalization of education, what they mean, finally, is not simply that they want to meet their professors socially or that they want small classes or that they do not want to be dealt with by IBM machines. All these things are but symptoms of a deeper sense of a violation of their literal reality as persons, ends in themselves rather than mere expendable things. Similarly, the current deep-spirited revolt against racial and economic injustice seems to me best explained as a sudden assertion that people, of whatever color or class, are not reducible to social conveniences. When you organize your labor force or your educational system as if men were mere social conveniences, "human resources," as we say, contributors to the gross national product, you violate something that we all know, in a form of knowledge much deeper than our knowledge of the times tables or the second law of thermodynamics: those field hands, those children crowded into the deadening classroom, those men laboring without dignity in the city anthills are *men*, creatures whose worth is mysteriously more than any description of it we might make in justifying what we do to them.

Ants, rats, and machines can all learn a great deal. Taken together, they "know" a very great part of what our schools and colleges are now designed to teach. But is there any kind of knowledge that a creature must have to qualify as a man? Is there any part of the educational task that is demanded of us by virtue of our claim to educate this curious entity, this *person* that cannot be reduced to mechanism or animality alone?

You will not be surprised, by now, to have me sound, in my answer, terribly traditional, not to say square: the education that a *man* must have is what has traditionally been called liberal education. The knowledge it yields is the knowledge or capacity or power of how to act freely as a man. That's why we call liberal education liberal: it is intended to liberate from whatever it is that makes animals act like animals and machines act like machines.

I'll return in a moment to what it means to act freely as a man. But we are already in a position to say something about what knowledge a man must have—he must first of all be able to learn for himself. If he cannot learn for himself, he is enslaved by his teachers' ideas, or by the ideas of his more persuasive contemporaries, or by machines programmed by other men. He may have what we call a good formal education, yet still be totally bound by whatever opinions happen to have come his way in attractive garb. One wonders how many of our graduates have learned how to take hold of a subject and "work it up," so that they can make themselves experts on what other men have concluded. In some ways this is not a very demanding goal, and it is certainly not very exciting. It says nothing about that popular concept, creativity, or about imagination or originality. All it says is that anyone who is dependent on his teachers *is* dependent, not free, and that anyone who knows how to learn for himself is less like animals and machines than anyone who does not know how to learn for himself.

We see already that a college is not being merely capricious or arbitrary when it insists that some kinds of learning are more important than some others. The world is overflowing with interesting subjects and valuable skills, but surely any college worth the name will put first things first: it will try to insure, as one inescapable goal, that every graduate can dig out from the printed page what he needs to know. And it will not let the desire to tamp in additional tidbits of knowledge, however delicious, interfere with training minds for whom a formal teacher is no longer required.

To put our first goal in this way raises some real problems that we cannot solve. Obviously no college can produce self-learners in very many subjects. Are we not lucky if a graduate can learn for himself even in one field, now that knowledge in all areas has advanced as far as it has? Surely we cannot expect our graduates to reach a stage of independence in mathematics and physics, in political science and psychology, in philosophy and English, *and* in all the other nice subjects that one would like to master.

Rather than answer this objection right away, let me make

things even more difficult by saying that it is not enough to learn how to learn. The man who cannot *think* for himself, going beyond what other men have learned or thought, is still enslaved to other men's ideas. Obviously the goal of learning to think is even more difficult than the goal of learning to learn. But difficult as it is we must add it to our list. It is simply not enough to be able to get up a subject on one's own, like a good encyclopedia employee, even though any college would take pride if all its graduates could do so. To be fully human means in part to think one's own thoughts, to reach a point at which, whether one's ideas are different from or similar to other men's, they are truly one's own.

The art of asking oneself critical questions that lead either to new answers or to genuine revitalizing of old answers, the art of making thought live anew in each new generation, may not be entirely amenable to instruction. But it is a necessary art nonetheless, for any man who wants to be free. It is an art that all philosophers have tried to pursue, and many of them have given direct guidance in how to pursue it. Needless to say, it is an art the pursuit of which is never fully completed. No one thinks for himself very much of the time or in very many subjects. Yet the habitual effort to ask the right critical questions and to apply rigorous tests to our hunches is a clearer mark than any other of an educated man.

But again we stumble upon the question, "Learn to think about *what*?" The modern world presents us with innumerable subjects to think about. Does it matter whether anyone achieves this rare and difficult point in more than one subject? And if not, won't the best education simply be the one that brings a man into mastery of a narrow specialty as soon as possible, so that he can learn to think for himself as soon as possible? Even at best most of us are enslaved to opinions provided for us by experts in *most* fields. So far, it might be argued, I still have not shown that there is any kind of knowledge that a man must have, only that there are certain skills that he must be able to exercise in at least one field.

To provide a proper grounding for my answer to that objection would require far more time than I have left, and I'm not at all sure that I could do so even with all the time in the world. The question of whether it is possible to maintain a human stance toward any more than a tiny fraction of modern knowledge is not clearly answerable at this stage in our history. It will be answered, if at all, only when men have learned how to store and retrieve all "machinable" knowledge, freeing themselves for distinctively human tasks. But in the meantime, I find myself unable to surrender, as it were, three distinct kinds of knowledge that seem to me indispensable to being human.

To be a man, a man must first know something about his own nature and his place in Nature, with a capital N—something about the truth of things, as men used to say in the old-fashioned days before the word "truth" was banned from academia. Machines are not curious, so far as I can judge; animals are, but presumably they never go, in their philosophies, even at the furthest, beyond a kind of solipsistic existentialism. But in science, in philosophy (ancient and modern), in theology, in psychology and anthropology, and in literature (of some kinds), we are presented with accounts of our universe and of our place in it that as men we can respond to in only one manly way: by thinking about them, by speculating and testing our speculations.

We know before we start that our thought is doomed to incompleteness and error and downright chanciness. Even the most rigorously scientific view will be changed, we know, within a decade, or perhaps even by tomorrow. But to refuse the effort to understand is to resign from the human race; the unexamined life can no doubt be worth living in other respects—after all, it is no mean thing to be a vegetable, an oak tree, an elephant, or a lion. But a man, a man will want to see, in this speculative domain, beyond his next dinner.

By putting it in this way, I think we can avoid the claim that to be a man I must have studied any one field—philosophy, science, theology. But to be a man, *I must speculate*, and I must learn how to test my speculations so that they are not simply capricious, unchecked by other men's speculations. A college education, surely, should throw every student into a regular torrent of speculation, and it should school him to recognize the different standards of validation proper to different kinds of claims to truth. You cannot distinguish a man who in this respect is educated from other men by whether or not he believes in God, or in UFO's. But you can tell an educated man by the way he takes hold of the question of whether God exists, or whether UFO's are from Mars. Do you know your own reasons for your beliefs, or do you absorb your beliefs from whatever happens to be in your environment, like plankton taking in nourishment?

Second, the man who has not learned how to make the great human achievements in the arts his own, who does not know what it means to *earn* a great novel or symphony or painting for himself, is enslaved either to caprice or to other men's testimony or to a life of ugliness. You will notice that as I turn thus to "beauty"— another old-fashioned term—I do not say that a man must know how to prove what is beautiful or how to discourse on aesthetics. Such speculative activities are pleasant and worthwhile in themselves, but they belong in my first domain. Here we are asking that a man be educated to the experience of beauty; speculation about it can then follow. My point is simply that a man is less than a man if he cannot respond to the art made by his fellow man.

Again I have tried to put the standard in a way that allows for the impossibility of any one man's achieving independent responses in very many arts. Some would argue that education should insure some minimal human competence in all of the arts, or at least in music, painting, and literature. I suppose I would be satisfied if all of our graduates had been "hooked" by at least one art, hooked so deeply that they could never get free. As in the domain of speculation, we could say that the more types of distinctively human activity a man can master, the better, but we are today talking about floors, not ceilings, and I shall simply rest content with saying that to be a man, a man must know artistic beauty, in some form, and know it in the way that beauty can be known. (The distinction between natural and man-made beauty might give me trouble if you pushed me on it here, but let me just say, dogmatically, that I would not be satisfied simply to know natural beauty—women and sunsets, say—as a substitute for art).

Finally, the man who has not learned anything about how to understand his own intentions and to make them effective in the world, who has not, through experience and books, learned something about what is possible and what impossible, what desirable and what undesirable, will be enslaved by the political and social intentions of other men, benign or malign. The domain of practical wisdom is at least as complex and troublesome as the other two, and at the same time it is even more self-evidently indispensable. How should a man live? How should a society be run? What direction should a university take in 1966? For that matter what should be the proportion, in a good university, of inquiry into truth, beauty, and "goodness"? What kind of knowledge of self or of society is pertinent to living the life proper to a man? In short, the very question of this conference falls within this final domain: What knowledge, if any, is most worthy of pursuit? You cannot distinguish the men from the boys according to any one set of conclusions, but you *can* recognize a man, in this domain, simply by discovering whether he can think for himself about practical questions, with some degree of freedom from blind psychological or political or economic compulsions. Ernest Hemingway tells somewhere of a man who had "moved one dollar's width to the [political] right for every dollar that he'd ever earned." Perhaps no man ever achieves the opposite extreme, complete freedom in his choices from irrelevant compulsions. But all of us who believe in education believe that it is possible for any man, through study and conscientious thought, to school his choices—that is, to free them through coming to understand the forces working on them.

Even from this brief discussion of the three domains, I think we are put in a position to see how it can be said that there is some knowledge that a man must have. The line I have been pursuing will not lead to a list of great books, or even to a list of indispensable departments in a university. Nor will it lead, in any clear-cut fashion, to a pattern of requirements in each of the divisions. Truth, beauty, and goodness (or "right choice") are relevant to study in every division within the university; the humanities, for example, have no corner on beauty or imagination or art, and the sciences have no corner on speculative truth. What is more, a man can be ignorant even of Shakespeare, Aristotle, Beethoven, and Einstein, and be a man for a' that—*if* he has learned how to think his own thoughts, experience beauty for himself, and choose his own actions.

It is not the business of a college to determine or limit what a man will know; if it tries to, he will properly resent its impositions, perhaps immediately, perhaps ten years later when the imposed information is outmoded. But I think that it *is* the business of a college to help teach a man how to use his mind for himself, in at least the three directions I have suggested. * * * To think for oneself is, as we all know, hard enough. To design a program and assemble faculty to assist rather than hinder students in their efforts to think for themselves is even harder. But in an age that is oppressed by huge accumulations of unassimilated knowledge, the task of discovering what it means to educate a man is perhaps more important than ever before.

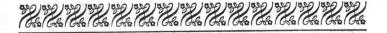

On Mind

JOHN SELDEN
The Measure of Things

We measure from ourselves; and as things are for our use and purpose, so we approve them. Bring a pear to the table that is rotten, we cry it down, 'tis naught; but bring a medlar that is rotten, and 'tis a fine thing; and yet I'll warrant you the pear thinks as well of itself as the medlar[1] does.

We measure the excellency of other men by some excellency we conceive to be in ourselves. Nash, a poet, poor enough (as poets use to be), seeing an alderman with his gold chain, upon his great horse, by way of scorn said to one of his companions, "Do you see yon fellow, how goodly, how big he looks? Why, that fellow cannot make a blank verse."

Nay, we measure the goodness of God from ourselves; we measure his goodness, his justice, his wisdom, by something we call just, good, or wise in ourselves; and in so doing, we judge proportionally to the country-fellow in the play, who said, if he were King, he would live like a lord, and have peas and bacon every day, and a whip that cried Slash.

---

1. The medlar, a fruit like the crab apple, becomes edible only after it begins to decay.

QUESTIONS

1. What pattern of parallels do you discern among the three parts of Selden's statement? How does this principle of structure enforce the thesis he is setting forth?
2. Can the three paragraphs be rearranged without damage? Explain. What principle or principles appear to govern the present arrangement? Does it imply anything about value? About the kind of universe in which Selden conceives man to live?

3. Consider the three desires of the country fellow who would be king. Has Selden arranged these desires in any particular order? If so, what relation does that order bear to the order of the whole statement?

BENJAMIN FRANKLIN

The Convenience of Being "Reasonable"[1]

I believe I have omitted mentioning that, in my first voyage from Boston, being becalmed off Block Island, our people set about catching cod, and hauled up a great many. Hitherto I had stuck to my resolution of not eating animal food, and on this occasion I considered, with my master Tryon, the taking every fish as a kind of unprovoked murder, since none of them had, or ever could do us any injury that might justify the slaughter. All this seemed very reasonable. But I had formerly been a great lover of fish, and, when this came hot out of the frying-pan, it smelled admirably well. I balanced some time between principle and inclination, till I recollected that, when the fish were opened, I saw smaller fish taken out of their stomachs; then thought I, "if you eat one another, I don't see why we mayn't eat you." So I dined upon cod very heartily, and continued to eat with other people, returning only now and then occasionally to a vegetable diet. So convenient a thing it is to be a *reasonable creature*, since it enables one to find or make a reason for everything one has a mind to do.

WILLIAM MARCH

The Dog and Her Rival

A dog who had been greatly loved by her master found her life less pleasant after he married. She came one night to talk things over with the mare and said, "I wish them both happiness. Perhaps it would be better if I went away, because it must grieve my master to see the way his wife humiliates me all day long."

The mare thought that would be a sensible thing to do, but the dog sighed, shook her head, and continued. "No, that would never work out, because if I disappeared without a word, the uncertainty of my fate would break my master's heart; and, besides, that wife of his would make him believe I was fickle and had abandoned him,

1. From the *Autobiography*.

and he'd never know how much I had suffered or how great my love was. On second thought, it might be even simpler if I took poison and died on his doorstep. That I think would be the noblest thing to do, the final proof of my love."

The mare said that such renunciation seemed a generous gesture indeed, and the dog lifted her head and stared at the moon. "I'd do it, too," she said; "I'd kill myself on my master's doorstep if only I could hear his pleas for forgiveness when he finds my body, or see him beating his worthless wife for having driven me to such an end."

Love can be the most dreadful disguise that hate assumes.

HENRY DAVID THOREAU

Observation

There is no such thing as pure *objective* observation. Your observation, to be interesting, *i.e.* to be significant, must be *subjective*. The sum of what the writer of whatever class has to report is simply some human experience, whether he be poet or philosopher or man of science. The man of most science is the man most alive, whose life is the greatest event. Senses that take cognizance of outward things merely are of no avail. It matters not where or how far you travel—the farther commonly the worse—but how much alive you are. If it is possible to conceive of an event outside to humanity, it is not of the slightest significance, though it were the explosion of a planet. Every important worker will report what life there is in him. It makes no odds into what seeming deserts the poet is born. Though all his neighbors pronounce it a Sahara, it will be a paradise to him; for the desert which we see is the result of the barrenness of our experience. No mere willful activity whatever, whether in writing verses or collecting statistics, will produce true poetry or science. If you are really a sick man, it is indeed to be regretted, for you cannot accomplish so much as if you were well. All that a man has to say or do that can possibly concern mankind, is in some shape or other to tell the story of his love—to sing, and, if he is fortunate and keeps alive, he will be forever in love. This alone is to be alive to the extremities. It is a pity that this divine creature should ever suffer from cold feet; a still greater pity that the coldness so often reaches to his heart. I look over the report of the doings of a scientific association and am surprised that there is so little life to be reported; I am put off with a parcel of dry technical terms. Anything living is easily and naturally expressed in popular language. I cannot help suspecting that the life of these learned professors has been almost as inhuman and wooden as a rain-gauge or self-registering magnetic machine. They communicate no fact which rises to the temperature of blood-heat. It doesn't all amount to one rhyme.

JACOB BRONOWSKI
The Reach of Imagination

For three thousand years, poets have been enchanted and moved and perplexed by the power of their own imagination. In a short and summary essay I can hope at most to lift one small corner of that mystery; and yet it is a critical corner. I shall ask, What goes on in the mind when we imagine? You will hear from me that one answer to this question is fairly specific: which is to say, that we can describe the working of the imagination. And when we describe it as I shall do, it becomes plain that imagination is a specifically *human* gift. To imagine is the characteristic act, not of the poet's mind, or the painter's, or the scientist's, but of the mind of man.

My stress here on the word *human* implies that there is a clear difference in this between the actions of men and those of other animals. Let me then start with a classical experiment with animals and children which Walter Hunter thought out in Chicago about 1910. That was the time when scientists were agog with the success of Ivan Pavlov in forming and changing the reflex actions of dogs, which Pavlov had first announced in 1903. Pavlov had been given a Nobel prize the next year, in 1904; although in fairness I should say that the award did not cite his work on the conditioned reflex, but on the digestive gland.

Hunter duly trained some dogs and other animals on Pavlov's lines. They were taught that when a light came on over one of three tunnels out of their cage, that tunnel would be open; they could escape down it, and were rewarded with food if they did. But once he had fixed that conditioned reflex, Hunter added to it a deeper idea: he gave the mechanical experiment a new dimension, literally—the dimension of time. Now he no longer let the dog go to the lighted tunnel at once; instead, he put out the light, and then kept the dog waiting a little while before he let him go. In this way Hunter timed how long an animal can remember where he has last seen the signal light to his escape route.

The results were and are staggering. A dog or a rat forgets which one of three tunnels has been lit up within a matter of seconds—in Hunter's experiment, ten seconds at most. If you want such an animal to do much better than this, you must make the task much simpler: you must face him with only two tunnels to choose from. Even so, the best that Hunter could do was to have a dog remember for five minutes which one of two tunnels had been lit up.

I am not quoting these times as if they were exact and universal: they surely are not. Hunter's experiment, more than fifty years old now, had many faults of detail. For example, there were too few animals, they were oddly picked, and they did not all behave consistently. It may be unfair to test a dog for what he *saw*, when he commonly follows his nose rather than his eyes. It may be unfair to test any animal in the unnatural setting of a laboratory cage. And there are higher animals, such as chimpanzees and other primates, which certainly have longer memories than the animals that Hunter tried.

Yet when all these provisos have been made (and met, by more modern experiments) the facts are still startling and characteristic. An animal cannot recall a signal from the past for even a short fraction of the time that a man can—for even a short fraction of the time that a child can. Hunter made comparable tests with six-year-old children, and found, of course, that they were incomparably better than the best of his animals. There is a striking and basic difference between a man's ability to imagine something that he saw or experienced, and an animal's failure.

Animals make up for this by other and extraordinary gifts. The salmon and the carrier pigeon can find their way home as we cannot: they have, as it were, a practical memory that man cannot match. But their actions always depend on some form of habit: on instinct or on learning, which reproduce by rote a train of known responses. They do not depend, as human memory does, on calling to mind the recollection of absent things.

Where is it that the animal falls short? We get a clue to the answer, I think, when Hunter tells us how the animals in his experiment tried to fix their recollection. They most often pointed themselves at the light before it went out, as some gun dogs point rigidly at the game they scent—and get the name *pointer* from the posture. The animal makes ready to act by building the signal into its action. There is a primitive imagery in its stance, it seems to me; it is as if the animal were trying to fix the light on its mind by fixing it in its body. And indeed, how else can a dog mark and (as it were) name one of three tunnels, when he has no such words as *left* and *right*, and no such numbers as *one, two, three?* The directed gesture of attention and readiness is perhaps the only symbolic device that the dog commands to hold on to the past, and thereby to guide himself into the future.

I used the verb *to imagine* a moment ago, and now I have some ground for giving it a meaning. *To imagine* means to make images and to move them about inside one's head in new arrangements. When you and I recall the past, we imagine it in this direct and homely sense. The tool that puts the human mind ahead of the animal is imagery. For us, memory does not demand the preoccupation that it demands in animals, and it lasts immensely longer, because we fix it in images or other substitute symbols. With the same symbolic vocabulary we spell out the future—not one but many futures, which we weigh one against another.

I am using the word *image* in a wide meaning, which does not restrict it to the mind's eye as a visual organ. An image in my usage is what Charles Peirce called a *sign*, without regard for its sensory quality. Peirce distinguished between different forms of signs, but there is no reason to make his distinction here, for the imagination works equally with them all, and that is why I call them all images.

Indeed, the most important images for human beings are simply words, which are abstract symbols. Animals do not have words, in our sense: there is no specific center for language in the brain of any animal, as there is in the human being. In this respect at least we know that the human imagination depends on a configuration in the brain that has only evolved in the last one or two million years. In the same period, evolution has greatly enlarged the front lobes in the human brain, which govern the sense of the past and the future; and it is a fair guess that they are probably the seat of our other images. (Part of the evidence for this guess is that damage to the front lobes in primates reduces them to the state of Hunter's animals.) If the guess turns out to be right, we shall know why man has come to look like a highbrow or an egghead: because otherwise there would not be room in his head for his imagination.

The images play out for us events which are not present to our senses, and thereby guard the past and create the future—a future that does not yet exist, and may never come to exist in that form. By contrast, the lack of symbolic ideas, or their rudimentary poverty, cuts off an animal from the past and the future alike, and imprisons him in the present. Of all the distinctions between man and animal, the characteristic gift which makes us human is the power to work with symbolic images: the gift of imagination.

This is really a remarkable finding. When Philip Sidney in 1580 defended poets (and all unconventional thinkers) from the Puritan charge that they were liars, he said that a maker must imagine things that are not. Halfway between Sidney and us, William Blake said, "What is now proved was once only imagined." About the same time, in 1796, Samuel Taylor Coleridge for the first time distinguished between the passive fancy and the active imagination, "the living Power and prime Agent of all human Perception." Now we see that they were right, and precisely right: the human gift is the gift of imagination—and that is not just a literary phrase.

Nor is it just a literary gift; it is, I repeat, characteristically human. Almost everything that we do that is worth doing is done in the first place in the mind's eye. The richness of human life is that we have many lives; we live the events that do not happen (and some that cannot) as vividly as those that do; and if thereby we die a thousand deaths, that is the price we pay for living a thousand lives. (A cat, of course, has only nine.) Literature is alive to us because we live its images, but so is any play of the mind—so is chess: the lines of play that we foresee and try in our heads and dismiss are as much a part of the game as the moves that we make. John Keats said that the unheard melodies are sweeter, and all chess players sadly recall that the combinations that they planned and which never came to be played were the best.

I make this point to remind you, insistently, that imagination is the manipulation of images in one's head; and that the rational manipulation belongs to that, as well as the literary and artistic manipulation. When a child begins to play games with things that stand for other things, with chairs or chessmen, he enters the gateway to reason and imagination together. For the human reason discovers new relations between things not by deduction, but by that unpredictable blend of speculation and insight that scientists call induction, which—like other forms of imagination—cannot be formalized. We see it at work when Walter Hunter inquires into a child's memory, as much as when Blake and Coleridge do. Only a restless and original mind would have asked Hunter's questions and could have conceived his experiments, in a science that was dominated by Pavlov's reflex arcs and was heading toward the behaviorism of John Watson.

Let me find a spectacular example for you from history. What is the most famous experiment that you had described to you as a child? I will hazard that it is the experiment that Galileo is said to have made in Sidney's age, in Pisa about 1590, by dropping two unequal balls from the Leaning Tower. There, we say, is a man in the modern mold, a man after our own hearts: he insisted on questioning the authority of Aristotle and St. Thomas Aquinas, and seeing with his own eyes whether (as they said) the heavy ball would reach the ground before the light one. Seeing is believing.

Yet seeing is also imagining. Galileo did challenge the authority of Aristotle, and he did look at his mechanics. But the eye that Galileo used was the mind's eye. He did not drop balls from the Leaning Tower of Pisa—and if he had, he would have got a very doubtful answer. Instead, Galileo made an imaginary experiment in his head, which I will describe as he did years later in the book he wrote after the Holy Office silenced him: the *Discorsi . . . intorno a due nuove scienze*, which was smuggled out to be printed in the Netherlands in 1638.

Suppose, said Galileo, that you drop two unequal balls from the tower at the same time. And suppose that Aristotle is right—suppose that the heavy ball falls faster, so that it steadily gains on the light ball, and hits the ground first. Very well. Now imagine the same experiment done again, with only one difference: this time the two unequal balls are joined by a string between them. The heavy ball will again move ahead, but now the light ball holds it back and acts as a drag or brake. So the light ball will be speeded up and the heavy ball will be slowed down; they must reach the ground together because they are tied together, but they cannot reach the ground as quickly as the heavy ball alone. Yet the string between them has turned the two balls into a single mass which is heavier than either ball—and surely (according to Aristotle) this mass should therefore move faster than either ball? Galileo's imaginary experiment has uncovered a contradiction; he says trenchantly, "You see how, from your assumption that a heavier body falls more rapidly than a lighter one, I infer that a (still) heavier body falls more slowly." There is only one way out of the contradiction: the heavy ball and the light ball must fall at the same rate, so that they go on falling at the same rate when they are tied together.

This argument is not conclusive, for nature might be more subtle (when the two balls are joined) than Galileo has allowed. And yet it is something more important: it is suggestive, it is stimulating, it opens a new view—in a word, it is imaginative. It cannot be settled without an actual experiment, because nothing that we imagine can become knowledge until we have translated it into, and backed it by, real experience. The test of imagination is experience. But then, that is as true of literature and the arts as it is of science. In science, the imaginary experiment is tested by confronting it with physical experience; and in literature, the imaginative conception is tested by confronting it with human experience. The superficial speculation in science is dismissed because it is found to falsify nature; and the shallow work of art is discarded because it is found to be untrue to our own nature. So when Ella Wheeler Wilcox died in 1919, more people were reading her verses than Shakespeare's; yet in a few years her work was dead. It had been buried by its poverty of emotion and its trivialness of thought: which is to say that it had been proved to be as false to the nature of man as, say, Jean Baptiste Lamarck and Trofim Lysenko[1] were false to the nature of inheritance. The strength of the imagination, its enriching power and excitement, lies in its interplay with reality—physical and emotional.

---

1. Lamarck was a French biologist (1744–1829) who held that characteristics acquired by experience were biologically transmittable. Lysenko is a Russian biologist (1898–   ) who has held that hereditary properties of organisms could be changed by manipulating the environment.

I doubt if there is much to choose here between science and the arts: the imagination is not much more free, and not much less free, in one than in the other. All great scientists have used their imagination freely, and let it ride them to outrageous conclusions without crying "Halt!" Albert Einstein fiddled with imaginary experiments from boyhood, and was wonderfully ignorant of the facts that they were supposed to bear on. When he wrote the first of his beautiful papers on the random movement of atoms, he did not know that the Brownian motion which it predicted could be seen in any laboratory. He was sixteen when he invented the paradox that he resolved ten years later, in 1905, in the theory of relativity, and it bulked much larger in his mind than the experiment of Albert Michelson and Edward Morley[2] which had upset every other physicist since 1881. All his life Einstein loved to make up teasing puzzles like Galileo's, about falling lifts and the detection of gravity; and they carry the nub of the problems of general relativity on which he was working.

Indeed, it could not be otherwise. The power that man has over nature and himself, and that a dog lacks, lies in his command of imaginary experience. He alone has the symbols which fix the past and play with the future, possible and impossible. In the Renaissance, the symbolism of memory was thought to be mystical, and devices that were invented as mnemonics (by Giordano Bruno, for example, and by Robert Fludd) were interpreted as magic signs. The symbol is the tool which gives man his power, and it is the same tool whether the symbols are images or words, mathematical signs or mesons. And the symbols have a reach and a roundness that goes beyond their literal and practical meaning. They are the rich concepts under which the mind gathers many particulars into one name, and many instances into one general induction. When a man says *left* and *right*, he is outdistancing the dog not only in looking for a light; he is setting in train all the shifts of meaning, the overtones and the ambiguities, between *gauche* and *adroit* and *dexterous*, between *sinister* and the sense of right. When a man counts *one, two, three*, he is not only doing mathematics; he is on the path to the mysticism of numbers in Pythagoras and Vitruvius and Kepler, to the Trinity and the signs of the Zodiac.

I have described imagination as the ability to make images and to move them about inside one's head in new arrangements. This is the faculty that is specifically human, and it is the common root from which science and literature both spring and grow and flourish together. For they do flourish (and languish) together; the

---

2. This was an experiment designed to measure the drag exerted on the passage of light by a hypothetical stationary medium. Its negative results eliminated the concept of a motionless, measurable ether and cleared the way for the development of the theory of relativity.

great ages of science are the great ages of all the arts, because in them powerful minds have taken fire from one another, breathless and higgledy-piggledy, without asking too nicely whether they ought to tie their imagination to falling balls or a haunted island. Galileo and Shakespeare, who were born in the same year, grew into greatness in the same age; when Galileo was looking through his telescope at the moon, Shakespeare was writing *The Tempest* and all Europe was in ferment, from Johannes Kepler to Peter Paul Rubens, and from the first table of logarithms by John Napier to the Authorized Version of the Bible.

Let me end with a last and spirited example of the common inspiration of literature and science, because it is as much alive today as it was three hundred years ago. What I have in mind is man's ageless fantasy, to fly to the moon. I do not display this to you as a high scientific enterprise; on the contrary, I think we have more important discoveries to make here on earth than wait for us, beckoning, at the horned surface of the moon. Yet I cannot belittle the fascination which that ice-blue journey has had for the imagination of men, long before it drew us to our television screens to watch the tumbling astronauts. Plutarch and Lucian, Ariosto and Ben Jonson wrote about it, before the days of Jules Verne and H. G. Wells and science fiction. The seventeenth century was heady with new dreams and fables about voyages to the moon. Kepler wrote one full of deep scientific ideas, which (alas) simply got his mother accused of witchcraft. In England, Francis Godwin wrote a wild and splendid work, *The Man in the Moone,* and the astronomer John Wilkins wrote a wild and learned one, *The Discovery of a New World*. They did not draw a line between science and fancy; for example, they all tried to guess just where in the journey the earth's gravity would stop. Only Kepler understood that gravity has no boundary, and put a law to it—which happened to be the wrong law.

All this was a few years before Isaac Newton was born, and it was all in his head that day in 1666 when he sat in his mother's garden, a young man of twenty-three, and thought about the reach of gravity. This was how he came to conceive his brilliant image, that the moon is like a ball which has been thrown so hard that it falls exactly as fast as the horizon, all the way round the earth. The image will do for any satellite, and Newton modestly calculated how long therefore an astronaut would take to fall round the earth once. He made it ninety minutes, and we have all seen now that he was right; but Newton had no way to check that. Instead he went on to calculate how long in that case the distant moon would take to round the earth, if indeed it behaves like a thrown ball that falls in the earth's gravity, and if gravity obeyed a law of inverse squares. He found that the answer would be twenty-eight days.

In that telling figure, the imagination that day chimed with nature, and made a harmony. We shall hear an echo of that harmony on the day when we land on the moon, because it will be not a technical but an imaginative triumph, that reaches back to the beginning of modern science and literature both. All great acts of imagination are like this, in the arts and in science, and convince us because they fill out reality with a deeper sense of rightness. We start with the simplest vocabulary of images, with *left* and *right* and *one, two, three,* and before we know how it happened the words and the numbers have conspired to make a match with nature: we catch in them the pattern of mind and matter as one.

QUESTIONS

1. How does the Hunter experiment provide Bronowski with the ground for defining the imagination?
2. Bronowski discusses the work of Galileo and Newton in the middle and at the end of his essay; what use does he make of their work? Does it justify placing them in the central and final positions?
3. On page 274 Bronowski attributes the imagination to a "configuration" in the brain. Configuration seems vague here; what else shows uncertainty about exactly what happens in the brain? Does this uncertainty compromise the argument of this essay?
4. What function is given to the mind by the title metaphor of reaching (later extended to symbols on page 277)? What words does Bronowski use to indicate the objects reached for? What is the significance of his selecting these words?

WILLIAM JAMES

The Ethical and Pedagogical Importance of the Principle of Habit[1]

"Habit a second nature! Habit is ten times nature," the Duke of Wellington is said to have exclaimed; and the degree to which this is true no one probably can appreciate as well as one who is a veteran soldier himself. The daily drill and the years of discipline end by fashioning a man completely over again, as to most of the possibilities of his conduct.

"There is a story," says Prof. Huxley, "which is credible enough, though it may not be true, of a practical joker who, seeing a discharged veteran carrying home his dinner, suddenly called out, 'Attention!' whereupon the man instantly brought his hands

---

1. From "Habit," Chapter 10 of *The Principles of Psychology.*

down, and lost his mutton and potatoes in the gutter. The drill had been thorough, and its effects had become embodied in the man's nervous structure."

Riderless cavalry-horses, at many a battle, have been seen to come together and go through their customary evolutions at the sound of the bugle-call. Most domestic beasts seem machines almost pure and simple, undoubtingly, unhesitatingly doing from minute to minute the duties they have been taught, and giving no sign that the possibility of an alternative ever suggests itself to their mind. Men grown old in prison have asked to be readmitted after being once set free. In a railroad accident a menagerie-tiger, whose cage had broken open, is said to have emerged, but presently crept back again, as if too much bewildered by his new responsibilities, so that he was without difficulty secured.

Habit is thus the enormous fly-wheel of society, its most precious conservative agent. It alone is what keeps us all within the bounds of ordinance, and saves the children of fortune from the envious uprisings of the poor. It alone prevents the hardest and most repulsive walks of life from being deserted by those brought up to tread therein. It keeps the fisherman and the deck-hand at sea through the winter; it holds the miner in his darkness, and nails the countryman to his log-cabin and his lonely farm through all the months of snow; it protects us from invasion by the natives of the desert and the frozen zone. It dooms us all to fight out the battle of life upon the lines of our nurture or our early choice, and to make the best of a pursuit that disagrees, because there is no other for which we are fitted, and it is too late to begin again. It keeps different social strata from mixing. Already at the age of twenty-five you see the professional mannerism settling down on the young commercial traveler, on the young doctor, on the young minister, on the young counselor-at-law. You see the little lines of cleavage running through the character, the tricks of thought, the prejudices, the ways of the "shop," in a word, from which the man can by-and-by no more escape than his coat-sleeve can suddenly fall into a new set of folds. On the whole, it is best he should not escape. It is well for the world that in most of us, by the age of thirty, the character has set like plaster, and will never soften again.

If the period between twenty and thirty is the critical one in the formation of intellectual and professional habits, the period below twenty is more important still for the fixings of *personal* habits, properly so called, such as a vocalization and pronunciation, gesture, motion, and address. Hardly ever is a language learned after twenty spoken without a foreign accent; hardly ever can a youth transferred to the society of his betters unlearn the nasality and other vices of speech bred in him by the associations of his growing years. Hardly ever, indeed, no matter how much money there be in his pocket, can he even learn to *dress* like a gentleman-born. The merchants offer their wares as eagerly to him as to the veriest "swell," but he simply *cannot* buy the right things. An invisible law, as strong as gravitation, keeps him within his orbit, arrayed this year as he was the last; and how his better-clad acquaintances contrive to get the things they wear will be for him a mystery till his dying day.

The great thing, then, in all education, is to *make our nervous system our ally instead of our enemy*. It is to fund and capitalize our acquisitions, and live at ease upon the interest of the fund. *For this we must make automatic and habitual, as early as possible, as many useful actions as we can*, and guard against the growing into ways that are likely to be disadvantageous to us, as we should guard against the plague. The more of the details of our daily life we can hand over to the effortless custody of automatism, the more our higher powers of mind will be set free for their own proper work. There is no more miserable human being than one in whom nothing is habitual but indecision, and for whom the lighting of every cigar, the drinking of every cup, the time of rising and going to bed every day, and the beginning of every bit of work, are subjects of express volitional deliberation. Full half the time of such a man goes to the deciding, or regretting, of matters which ought to be so ingrained in him as practically not to exist for his consciousness at all. If there be such daily duties not yet ingrained in any one of my readers, let him begin this very hour to set the matter right.

In Professor Bain's chapter on "The Moral Habits" there are some admirable practical remarks laid down. Two great maxims emerge from his treatment. The first is that in the acquisition of a new habit, or the leaving off of an old one, we must take care to *launch ourselves with as strong and decided an initiative as possible*. Accumulate all the possible circumstances which shall re-enforce the right motives; put yourself assiduously in conditions that encourage the new way; make engagements incompatible with the old; take a public pledge, if the case allows; in short, envelop your resolution with every aid you know. This will give your new beginning such a momentum that the temptation to break down will not occur as soon as it otherwise might; and every day during which a breakdown is postponed adds to the chances of its not occurring at all.

The second maxim is: *Never suffer an exception to occur till the new habit is securely rooted in your life*. Each lapse is like the letting fall of a ball of string which one is carefully winding up; a single slip undoes more than a great many turns will wind again. *Continuity* of training is the great means of making the nervous system act infallibly right. As Professor Bain says:

"The peculiarity of the moral habits, contradistinguishing them from the intellectual acquisitions, is the presence of two hostile powers, one to be gradually raised into the ascendant over the other. It is necessary, above all things, in such a situation, never to lose a battle. Every gain on the wrong side undoes the effect of many conquests on the right. The essential precaution, therefore, is so to regulate the two opposing powers that the one may have a series of uninterrupted successes, until repetition has fortified it to such a degree as to enable it to cope with the opposition, under any circumstances. This is the theoretically best career of mental progress."

The need of securing success at the *outset* is imperative. Failure at first is apt to damp the energy of all future attempts, whereas past experiences of success nerve one to future vigor. Goethe says to a man who consulted him about an enterprise but mistrusted his own powers: "Ach! you need only blow on your hands!" And the remark illustrates the effect on Goethe's spirits of his own habitually successful career.

The question of "tapering off," in abandoning such habits as drink and opium-indulgence comes in here, and is a question about which experts differ within certain limits, and in regard to what may be best for an individual case. In the main, however, all expert opinion would agree that abrupt acquisition of the new habit is the best way, *if there be a real possibility of carrying it out*. We must be careful not to give the will so stiff a task as to insure its defeat at the very outset; but, *provided one can stand it*, a sharp period of suffering, and then a free time, is the best thing to aim at, whether in giving up a habit like that of opium, or in simply changing one's hours of rising or of work. It is surprising how soon a desire will die of inanition if it be *never* fed.

One must first learn, unmoved, looking neither to the right nor left, to walk firmly on the strait and narrow path, before one can begin "to make one's self over again." He who every day makes a fresh resolve is like one who, arriving at the edge of the ditch he is to leap, forever stops and returns for a fresh run. Without *unbroken* advance there is no such thing as *accumulation* of the ethical forces possible, and to make this possible, and to exercise us and habituate us in it, is the sovereign blessing of regular work.[2]

A third maxim may be added to the preceding pair: *Seize the very first possible opportunity to act on every resolution you make, and on every emotional prompting you may experience in the direction of the habits you aspire to gain.* It is not in the moment of their forming, but in the moment of their producing *motor*

---

2. J. Bahnsen: "Beitäge zu Charakterologie" (1867), vol. I, p. 209 [James' note].

effects, that resolves and aspirations communicate the new "set" to the brain. As the author last quoted remarks:

> The actual presence of the practical opportunity alone furnishes the fulcrum upon which the lever can rest, by means of which the moral will may multiply its strength, and raise itself aloft. He who has no solid ground to press against will never get beyond the stage of empty gesture-making.

No matter how full a reservoir of *maxims* one may possess, and no matter how good one's *sentiments* may be, if one have not taken advantage of every concrete opportunity to *act*, one's character may remain entirely unaffected for the better. With mere good intentions, hell is proverbially paved. And this is an obvious consequence of the principles we have laid down. A "character," as J. S. Mill says, "is a completely fashioned will"; and a will, in the sense in which he means it, is an aggregate of tendencies to act in a firm and prompt and definite way upon all the principal emergencies of life. A tendency to act only becomes effectively ingrained in us in proportion to the uninterrupted frequency with which the actions actually occur, and the brain "grows" to their use. When a resolve or a fine glow of feeling is allowed to evaporate without bearing practical fruit it is worse than a chance lost; it works so as positively to hinder future resolutions and emotions from taking the normal path of discharge. There is no more contemptible type of human character than that of the nerveless sentimentalist and dreamer, who spends his life in a weltering sea of sensibility and emotion, but who never does a manly concrete deed. Rousseau, inflaming all the mothers of France, by his eloquence, to follow Nature and nurse their babies themselves, while he sends his own children to the foundling hospital, is the classical example of what I mean. But every one of us in his measure, whenever, after glowing for an abstractly formulated Good, he practically ignores some actual case, among the squalid "other particulars" of which that same Good lurks disguised, treads straight on Rousseau's path. All Goods are disguised by the vulgarity of their concomitants, in this work-a-day world; but woe to him who can only recognize them when he thinks them in their pure and abstract form! The habit of excessive novel-reading and theater-going will produce true monsters in this line. The weeping of the Russian lady over the fictitious personages in the play, while her coachman is freezing to death on his seat outside, is the sort of thing that everywhere happens on a less glaring scale. Even the habit of excessive indulgence in music, for those who are neither performers themselves nor musically gifted enough to take it in a purely intellectual way, has probably a relaxing effect upon the character. One becomes filled with emotions which habitually pass without prompting to any deed, and so the inertly sentimental condition is kept up. The remedy would be, never to suffer one's self to have an emotion at a concert, without expressing it afterward in *some* active way. Let the expression be the least thing in the world—speaking genially to one's grandmother, or giving up one's seat in a horse-car, if nothing more heroic offers—but let it not fail to take place.

These latter cases make us aware that it is not simply *particular lines* of discharge, but also *general forms* of discharge, that seem to be grooved out by habit in the brain. Just as, if we let our emotions evaporate, they get into a way of evaporating; so there is reason to suppose that if we often flinch from making an effort, before we know it the effort-making capacity will be gone; and that, if we suffer the wandering of our attention, presently it will wander all the time. Attention and effort are, as we shall see later, but two names for the same psychic fact. To what brain-processes they correspond we do not know. The strongest reason for believing that they do depend on brain-processes at all, and are not pure acts of the spirit, is just this fact, that they seem in some degree subject to the law of habit, which is a material law. As a final practical maxim, relative to these habits of the will, we may, then, offer something like this: *Keep the faculty of effort alive in you by a little gratuitous exercise every day.* That is, be systematically ascetic or heroic in little unnecessary points, do every day or two something for no other reason than that you would rather not do it, so that when the hour of dire need draws nigh, it may find you not unnerved and untrained to stand the test. Asceticism of this sort is like the insurance which a man pays on his house and goods. The tax does him no good at the time, and possibly may never bring him a return. But if the fire *does* come, his having paid it will be his salvation from ruin. So with the man who has daily inured himself to habits of concentrated attention, energetic volition, and self-denial in unnecessary things. He will stand like a tower when everything rocks around him, and when his softer fellow-mortals are winnowed like chaff in the blast.

The physiological study of mental conditions is thus the most powerful ally of hortatory ethics. The hell to be endured hereafter, of which theology tells, is no worse than the hell we make for ourselves in this world by habitually fashioning our characters in the wrong way. Could the young but realize how soon they will become mere walking bundles of habits, they would give more heed to their conduct while in the plastic state. We are spinning our own fates, good or evil, and never to be undone. Every smallest stroke of virtue or of vice leaves its never so little scar. The drunken Rip Van Winkle, in Jefferson's play, excuses himself for every fresh dereliction by saying, "I won't count this time!" Well! he may not count it, and a kind Heaven may not count it; but it is being counted none the less. Down among his nerve cells and fibres the molecules are counting it, registering and storing it up to be used against him when the next temptation comes. Nothing we ever do is, in strict scientific literalness, wiped out. Of course this has its good side as well as its bad one. As we become permanent drunkards by so many separate drinks, so we become saints in the moral, and authorities and experts in the practical and scientific spheres, by so many separate acts and hours of work. Let no youth have any anxiety about the upshot of his education, whatever the line of it may be. If he keep faithfully busy each hour of the working day, he may safely leave the final result to itself. He can with perfect certainty count on waking up some fine morning, to find himself one of the competent ones of his generation, in whatever pursuit he may have singled out. Silently, between all the details of his business, the *power of judging* in all that class of matter will have built itself up within him as a possession that will never pass away. Young people should know this truth in advance. The ignorance of it has probably engendered more discouragement and faint-heartedness in youths embarking on arduous careers than all other causes put together.

QUESTIONS

1. What, according to James, is the utility of habit for society? For the individual person?
2. Will conformity result from cultivating habits according to the maxims here presented?
3. James and Milgram ("A Behavioral Study of Obedience," pp. 293–307) are both psychologists. Do they appear to be working in similar ways? If dissimilar, how do you explain the difference? Is one more scientific than the other? How do the two pieces of writing compare as to subject, method of presentation, assumptions, purpose, style?
4. Compare this essay by James with his letter to his daughter (pp. 594–596). What similarities and what differences are there in content, treatment, tone? Explain these.

H. J. CAMPBELL

Pleasure-Seeking Brains: Artificial Tickles, Natural Joys of Thought

For some years now it has been known that animals will choose to press a lever repeatedly when the only thing that happens for their trouble is that they receive a very small amount of electricity in certain regions of the brain.

Rats engaged in this intracranial self-stimulation will press the lever so frequently and for so long that they drop to the floor of the cage with fatigue. After a little sleep, they awaken and immediately start to press the lever again.

When the electricity, by means of indwelling electrodes and a simple stimulator, goes to parts of the brain within what has been called the limbic system, the animal seems to want nothing else out of life. If it is a hungry animal, it will choose a lever for brain stimulation rather than a lever which it knows will provide food. More significantly, it will do this even if made thirsty, selecting brain stimulation rather than a source of water. Many other tests have shown that this kind of brain stimulation takes priority in the animal's behavior over any other kind of reward. It is not surprising, then, that the brain regions involved have been named the pleasure areas and that the lever-pressing is called pleasure-seeking.

I am a physiologist, concerned with normal functions, and the terrible compulsiveness of this pleasure-seeking behavior bothered me very much. It has led me, as I will show, to a new theory for explaining all behavior—or at least the behavior of animals ranging from fish to Man himself.

The presence of pleasure areas in the brain was discovered accidentally in 1954 by James Olds and Peter Milner in Canda. Since then many workers have demonstrated the same phenomenon in a variety of species—cats, dogs, sheep, dolphins, goldfish, monkeys and Man. The humans were mental patients of Dr. Robert G. Heath at Tulane University School of Medicine. They were provided with a button they could press if they wanted to. And they did want to, often. When asked why they were pressing the button, the patients replied that it made them "feel good" and gave them a "happy feeling."

Notice especially that there is no question of an electric shock to the brain, in the ordinary sense of the term. The amount of electricity supplied is intended to be of the same order of magnitude as the charges naturally developed in the brain by cellular activity. A considerable amount of interesting and provocative theorizing has been going on about the meaning of intracranial self-stimulation responses. For me, the thought of humans acting this way engendered unease. When all is done and said about intracranial self-stimulation as a means of seeking pleasure, we are left with the persistent thought that this is not like any pleasure that we have experienced yet.

I have no doubt at all that experiments using the method of intracranial self-stimulation are of great value. But I do not believe that it is a *natural* form of behavior. It is unlikely that anyone else thinks it is natural, either. Yet no one seems to have asked what to me was a very obvious question—namely, how do the pleasure areas become activated in normal life?

Not only was the question obvious. So, too, was the answer. The way in which the pleasure areas of animals, including Man, are activated is via the senses. Clearly, nerve impulses that are generated at peripheral receptors pass into the central nervous system and reach (among other places) the limbic pleasure areas, thereby causing electrical activity in those regions. A quick ruffle through the anatomical literature showed that neural pathways which could subserve such a mechanism do indeed exist. The wires, so to speak, have been shown to be there, but nobody knew what they were for.

If those wires, those neural links between peripheral sense organs and limbic regions, were concerned in the production of pleasure, then certain things would inevitably follow. Almost by immediate inference, one could say that if I were right, then animals would press a lever (or do some other task) at their own volition, purely in order to obtain stimulation of peripheral sense organs. It should be possible to demonstrate peripheral self-stimulation. No electrodes in the brain, no electric currents to the brain, just stimulation of the eye or the ear or the skin or whatever.

The modern term for this sort of idea is almost certainly "way out." So I did the initial experiments at home, all alone, using an aquarium of tropical fish. I made a set of electrodelike goalposts that went into the water of the aquarium. A beam of light passed between the electrodes and fell upon a photocell. The photocell was rigged as a switch to a stimulator that would send a small pulse of electricity into the electrodes when the light beam was obscured. The electricity would, of course, pass through whatever was cutting off the light.

My hope was that the fish would, definitively, cut off the light. And this they did. Within minutes of setting up the apparatus, fish were swimming repetitively back and forth through the beam, getting each time a quantum of—what would you call it, stroking, tickling, caressing?

It was certainly not the light beam which attracted the fish, for when this was left on while the stimulator was switched off the animals swam through the beam no more than a chance number of times. Also, when the water contained a local anesthetic, they showed no interest in the apparatus even though the light and the stimulator were on. Would *you* enjoy being kissed after a tooth extraction with procaine?

These preliminary experiments encouraged me to go ahead with the project, using more sophisticated apparatus and a wider range of animals. I moved on to amphibians and reptiles, and found that newts and terrapins would seek out a source of electric current in the water. Most impressive, though, was the crocodile, for these creatures are well-known to be among the most sluggish kind.

The crocodile in my laboratory spends its time—for many hours on end—lying motionless on a stone slab. But when the goalpost-electrode assembly is put into its tank, the creature lumbers backwards and forwards between the electrodes about 50 times in 15 minutes. Sometimes, due to its largely immobile life, the crocodile becomes coated with green algae. It will not then respond to the electrodes until after its exterior has been scrubbed. The algae would seem to be forming an insulating layer over the skin receptors.

My next step was mammals, and I found that rabbits would press a lever for a longish flash of bright light. Moving on to primates, I tried the squirrel monkey. We have a capacitance rod, which looks and feels just like a piece of metal but is in fact a switch. This is connected to a stimulator that will activate a lamp whenever the rod is touched. The light goes out after five seconds unless the rod is released and touched again. When totally undeprived squirrel monkeys have had the rod pushed through the bars of their cage for a day or two for 15 minutes each day, they begin to reach through the bars and grab the rod before we can slide it in. As soon as they see the rod they begin to make happy, anticipatory chirping noises. They then touch the rod about 500 times in 15 minutes when a 750-watt bulb is the stimulus. With no light they touch the rod only about 20 times.

These experiments all show that peripheral and intracranial self-stimulation have much in common. One feature, however, is very different—and of great significance. It has been pointed out in many studies that a characteristic feature of intracranial self-stimulation is a lack of satiation: The animal never wants to stop pressing the lever. But with peripheral self-stimulation, all the animals tested, from fish to monkey, show a gradual decline in response rate down to zero when allowed the possibility to stimulate themselves indefinitely. This, surely, is much more like what happens in normal life.

While demonstrating the fact of peripheral self-stimulation from fish to monkey, I thought about its implications. There seemed no need to carry out any experiments with the highest primate: Even a brief glance at much human behavior reveals that it consists of a search for stimulation of the senses. Stimulus-seeking is by no means a new idea in psychology, or philosophy, but I developed a theory which establishes a neurological basis for stimulus-seeking—and indeed, I believe, for all animal behavior, at least from fish to Man.

We have seen that when the pleasure areas have electrodes in them, the animal is disinclined to engage in any behavior except lever-pressing for electrical stimulation of its brain. In peripheral self-stimulation, the animal obtains electrical activity in its pleasure areas by ensuring that sense organs generate nerve impulses which travel from the receptors to the limbic system. With this "natural" method, the animal does not continue indefinitely to ensure stimulation of a set of receptors. It does not, for example, go on and on eating, in order to make its taste buds act like electrodes in its brain.

We may ask why the animal reaches satiation. The answer is simply that all receptors exhibit a property known as "adaptation," which means that they cease to discharge impulses after a while even though the stimulus continues. Because of this property there comes a point in any pleasurable activity where continuance of the stimulus will *not* cause activation of the limbic pleasure areas. What seemed important to me about satiation, and which does not appear to have been given attention by other scientists, is that when an animal reaches satiation it does not stop behaving; it changes its behavior. Whereas intracranial self-stimulation is just one damned thing, peripheral self-stimulation (that is, natural behavior) is just one damned thing after another.

Thus it seems that we have here a neurological basis for the daily round of behavior—if we make just one assumption, which, sadly, can never be proved. The assumption is that in the course of evolution, when the nervous system reached a certain degree of complexity (at the moment we must start with the fish brain), the way in which it was put together demanded that the *pleasure areas be kept active*. Was this the "program" for the ancestral brain computer? If so, then much that has been vague and ill-defined about the animal kingdom and its history becomes readily explainable.

If we assume that animals, at least from fish to Man, *must*, in the sense defined, keep the limbic areas of the brain electrically activated, then we now know why animals behave and plants do not. We can explain Behavior as well as specific kinds of behavior, and we can now see the material basis of evolution, survival and extinction. In evolution, random genetic mutations have brought about gradual improvement of the motor system and nervous system, so that animals have become more competent at finding and manipulating the sensory stimuli available in the environment. Some animals found pleasure (that is, activation of parts of the limbic system) by stimulating their receptors in ways which were biologically disadvantageous: They became *extinct*. Others were spawned in an environment that, in a sense, was akin to the intracranial electrodes, conforming in near-perfection to the ancestral command, the intrinsic "program." Such animals exhibit remarkably slow evolution; why should they change their form or seek new sensory pastures? Still other animals chose advantageous means of seeking pleasure and also survived. From them evolved humankind, an animal with no fixed ecological niche, still motivated to wander and spread and explore the sensory surroundings and still, let us hope, to evolve.

But with the evolution of the human brain a very significant advance occurred. Few people doubt that Man is the highest animal. Fewer still could say in realistic, nonemotional terms why they believe this. Theories such as the notion of Man as the only creature to make tools on a systematic basis have fallen by the wayside, plagued with qualifications.

Many would take refuge in saying that the human brain shows the most complex structure, having that enormous amount of convoluted cerebral cortex. Numerous others would point to Man's works, his institutions, laws, religions and his overwhelmingly superior power to tamper with his environment. Caught up in both of these concepts is a rather tremulous adumbration of Man's uniqueness in being rational. Those who closely live and work with lower animals, especially but not exclusively with primates (do you own a dog?), have grave cause to doubt Man's prerogative of reasoning. And, pitifully, many who work closely with people doubt it too. What, then, is *human* behavior?

According to many experts, the experiments on peripheral self-stimulation carried out so far leave no sensible doubt that the neural mechanism of pleasure-seeking, of activating these limbic areas, requires no more complexity than the very simple brain of a fish. Obviously, with such a simple brain, there can be only simple pleasures. Equally obviously, even with a much more complex brain and much more complex sensory pleasures, the essential fundamental mechanism of action must be the same as that of a fish or a terrapin or a crocodile.

When people engage in a behavior that is a source of pleasure solely, or predominantly, because it stimulates their sense organs, then they are using their complex brains, that "enormous amount of convoluted cortex" to enable them to do what a fish or a crocodile does, only to do it much better—though possibly more expensively and harmfully. Should there be any people whose behavior is totally sensorially oriented, then they are not human, inasmuch as their behavior is, stripping off the technological veneer, the same as my monkeys or my fish. It is unlikely that such people exist. In the real world, we can say that the extent to which an individual's pleasure is obtained solely from the senses is the extent to which that individual is subhuman. Hard words. But these are hard times and we must face what seems to be the truth.

What behavior, then, is uniquely human? My theory is this, and you may take it or leave it at your own peril. It was said previously that a very significant advance occurred in the evolution of the human brain. It is this advance, and this advance only, which distinguishes some people almost all of the time and most people some of the time from the lower animals.

Neuroanatomists and some electrophysiologists have demonstrated that neural pathways exist between the cortical thinking regions of the brain and the limbic system and that nerve impulses flow downwards from the higher to the lower regions. We can now draw a distinct materialistic, nonreligious, nonphilosophical line between human and nonhuman behavior. Human behavior—meaning that not found in lower animals—is behavior that causes activation of the limbic pleasure regions of the brain, *not* as a result, primarily, of the sense organs, but primarily as activity of the brain's thinking regions. We all know that some people derive pleasure from non-sensory activity. Some of us are fortunate enough to be among the group who can have fun with mathematics or philosophy or science or languages or chess or crossword puzzles or reveries or anticipation or anything else that prompts us to behave without actually stimulating the sense organs, except, perhaps, adventitiously, as in music. When we are doing those things, those *thinking* kinds of things, we are being human. For, as far as we now know, the lower animals do not engage in behavior such that the process of thought is the reward. Only in the human brain can thinking activate the limbic pleasure areas.

It is pleasure-by-thinking that separates humans from lower animals. It is not true that the apes are nearest to us, unless we are overawed by anatomy. When a man is drinking bourbon he is no nearer to the ape than the fish. And whatever the ape does, he is as near to fish as to Man.

Usually it will be found upon analysis that unsuitable human behavior is firmly based upon materialistic, sensory objectives. Magic evolved into religion because of this. The main teaching of all major religions is, in effect, to moderate the sensory pleasures and give more importance to thinking, to be less subhuman and more human. In Oriental religions contemplation takes pride of place. Legal systems, which are uniquely human institutions, are essentially involved with reducing, by penalty, behavior based upon sensory pleasure-seeking.

Sexual mores in their multiplicity reflect the gigantic role that sexual behavior plays in the lives of people, as compared with lower animals. Whereas with lower animals sex is merely a part of life, it often dominates the human scene, so that some subscribe to the Freudian idea that "everything is sex." Since Man can turn his superior sensorimotor abilities to great account, he has made sex the most potent source of sensory pleasure, involving many more kinds of peripheral receptors than any animal uses. It is unlikely that any other form of behavior focuses so great a barrage of nerve impulses into the limbic areas of the brain.

There are many other implications of this theory which throw light upon the present state of Man. The direction of the arts towards abstraction, classical music towards mathematical design, architecture towards rhythmic functionalism; the occurrence of psychedelic predilections in the immature, the rise of vandalism and delinquency among juveniles, the mass hypnosis of the sensory communication media—all of these would bear an appraisal from the point of view of the new theory. But what of the future? Is the new theory one which implies hope or doom?

If I am right, evolution is moving with its traditional unalterable irrevocability towards a thinking organism rather than a feeling organism. Gradually, Man's brain structure and function are slowly changing, independently of his institutions, political systems and ideologies. Survival of the fittest applies, now, not to the sensorimotor people but to the thinking people. Natural selection is working in favor of mind, not muscle. Therefore Man's biological destiny is eventually to be fully distinguishable from the lower animals, by virtue of his behavior being totally directed to activating the limbic pleasure areas by exercising his capacity for thought, using his sense organs as ancillaries to mental phenomena. Each of us must decide whether that is cause for hope or despair.

If we take hope in it, then we do not have to wait for random mutations. The brain can be changed by experience as well. By recognizing what is human and what is subhuman behavior we can exert pressures upon ourselves and upon those around us, especially our children, to choose the human way of doing things. If we teach that the destruction of property—in the name of whatever freedom —is apelike sensation-seeking, if we show by preaching and preeminently by example that the rich store of human civilized treasures of the mind form the birthright of human people—if we do all this and more of its kind, we might well speed the course of Man's evolution. For whether or not a given *individual* is human or subhuman depends upon what has happened to him, not upon his genes. It depends upon the values and philosophy of life built into the potentially human brain with which he was born, wherever he happened to be born, whatever his color.

The laws of biology, I believe, are taking care of Man's evolution, with or without his help. But if we are really going to take the future seriously, it would be erroneous to continue with our totally man-centered anxieties alone. We have seen that the basic mechanism of behavior is present in the simple neural organization of the fish brain. There is no reason to believe that there is anything special about fish. Even lower animals, the invertebrates, seek their simple pleasures. We cannot rationally believe that the evolutionary processes that resulted in Man are not also at work in other animal hierarchies.

What will happen, do you suppose, when, millennia from now, some kind of activity in the higher centers causes activation of the pleasure areas in the brain of the octopus? We are not alone upon this planet. Nor has evolution ceased.

STANLEY MILGRAM
A Behavioral Study of Obedience[1]

This article describes a procedure for the study of destructive obedience in the laboratory. It consists of ordering a naive S to administer increasingly more severe punishment to a victim in the context of a learning experiment. Punishment is administered by means of a shock generator with 30 graded switches ranging from Slight Shock to Danger: Severe Shock. The victim is a confederate of the E. The primary dependent variable is the maximum shock the S is willing to administer before he refuses to continue further. 26 Ss obeyed the experimental commands fully, and administered the highest shock on the generator. 14 Ss broke off the experiment at some point after the victim protested and refused to provide further answers. The procedure created extreme levels of nervous tension in some Ss. Profuse sweating, trembling, and stuttering were typical expressions of this emotional disturbance. One unexpected sign of tension— yet to be explained—was the regular occurrence of nervous laughter, which in some Ss developed into uncontrollable seizures. The variety of interesting behavioral dynamics observed in the experiment, the reality of the situation for the S, and the possibility of parametric variation within the framework of the procedure, point to the fruitfulness of further study.[2]

Obedience is as basic an element in the structure of social life as one can point to. Some system of authority is a requirement of all communal living, and it is only the man dwelling in isolation who is not forced to respond, through defiance or submission, to the commands of others. Obedience, as a determinant of behavior is of particular relevance to our time. It has been reliably established that from 1933–1945 millions of innocent persons were systematically slaughtered on command. Gas chambers were built, death camps were guarded, daily quotas of corpses were produced with the same efficiency as the manufacture of appliances. These inhumane policies may have originated in the mind of a single person, but they could only be carried out on a massive scale if a very large number of persons obeyed orders.

Obedience is the psychological mechanism that links individual

1. This research was supported by a grant (NSF G-17916) from the National Science Foundation. Exploratory studies conducted in 1960 were supported by a grant from the Higgins Fund at Yale University. The research assistance of Alan C. Elms and Jon Wayland is gratefully acknowledged [Milgram's note].

2. This headnote, written by the author, appeared with the article as it was originally published. S means subject; E the experimenter.

action to political purpose. It is the dispositional cement that binds men to systems of authority. Facts of recent history and observation in daily life suggest that for many persons obedience may be a deeply ingrained behavior tendency, indeed, a prepotent impulse overriding training in ethics, sympathy, and moral conduct. C. P. Snow (1961) points to its importance when he writes:

When you think of the long and gloomy history of man, you will find more hideous crimes have been committed in the name of obedience than have ever been committed in the name of rebellion. If you doubt that, read William Shirer's *Rise and Fall of the Third Reich*. The German Officer Corps were brought up in the most rigorous code of obedience ... in the name of obedience they were party to, and assisted in, the most wicked large-scale actions in the history of the world [p. 24].

While the particular form of obedience dealt with in the present study has its antecedents in these episodes, it must not be thought all obedience entails acts of aggression against others. Obedience serves numerous productive functions. Indeed, the very life of society is predicated on its existence. Obedience may be ennobling and educative and refer to acts of charity and kindness, as well as to destruction.

GENERAL PROCEDURE

A procedure was devised which seems useful as a tool for studying obedience (Milgram, 1961). It consists of ordering a naive subject to administer electric shock to a victim. A simulated shock generator is used, with 30 clearly marked voltage levels that range from 15 to 450 volts. The instrument bears verbal designations that range from Slight Shock to Danger: Severe Shock. The responses of the victim, who is a trained confederate of the experimenter, are standardized. The orders to administer shocks are given to the naive subject in the context of a "learning experiment" ostensibly set up to study the effects of punishment on memory. As the experiment proceeds the naive subject is commanded to administer increasingly more intense shocks to the victim, even to the point of reaching the level marked Danger: Severe Shock. Internal resistances become stronger, and at a certain point the subject refuses to go on with the experiment. Behavior prior to this rupture is considered "obedience," in that the subject complies with the commands of the experimenter. The point of rupture is the act of disobedience. A quantitative value is assigned to the subject's performance based on the maximum intensity shock he is willing to administer before he refuses to participate further. Thus for any particular subject and for any particular experimental condition the degree of obedience may be specified with a numerical value. The crux of the study is to systematically vary the factors believed to alter the degree of obedience to the experimental commands.

The technique allows important variables to be manipulated at several points in the experiment. One may vary aspects of the source of command, content and form of command, instrumentalities for its execution, target object, general social setting, etc. The problem, therefore, is not one of designing increasingly more numerous experimental conditions, but of selecting those that best illuminate the *process* of obedience from the socio-psychological standpoint.

RELATED STUDIES

The inquiry bears an important relation to philosophic analyses of obedience and authority (Arendt, 1958; Friedrich, 1958; Weber, 1947), an early experimental study of obedience by Frank (1944), studies in "authoritarianism" (Adorno, Frenkel-Brunswik, Levinson, & Sanford, 1950; Rokeach, 1961), and a recent series of analytic and empirical studies in social power (Cartwright, 1959). It owes much to the long concern with *suggestion* in social psychology, both in its normal forms (*e.g.*, Binet, 1900) and in its clinical manifestations (Charcot, 1881). But it derives, in the first instance, from direct observation of a social fact; the individual who is commanded by a legitimate authority ordinarily obeys. Obedience comes easily and often. It is a ubiquitous and indispensable feature of social life.

Method
SUBJECTS

The subjects were 40 males between the ages of 20 and 50, drawn from New Haven and the surrounding communities. Subjects were obtained by a newspaper advertisement and direct mail solicitation. Those who responded to the appeal believed they were to participate in a study of memory and learning at Yale University. A wide range of occupations is represented in the sample. Typical subjects were postal clerks, high school teachers, salesmen, engineers, and laborers. Subjects ranged in educational level from one who had not finished elementary school, to those who had doctorate and other professional degrees. They were paid $4.50 for their participation in the experiment. However, subjects were told that payment was simply for coming to the laboratory, and that the money was theirs no matter what happened after they arrived. Table 1 shows the proportion of age and occupational types assigned to the experimental condition.

TABLE 1
DISTRIBUTION OF AGE AND OCCUPATIONAL TYPES IN THE EXPERIMENT

Occupations	20-29 years n	30-39 years n	40-50 years n	Percentage of total (Occupations)
Workers, skilled and unskilled	4	5	6	37.5
Sales, business, and white-collar	3	6	7	40.0
Professional	1	5	3	22.5
Percentage of total (age)	20	40	40	

Note. Total $N = 40$.

The experiment was conducted on the grounds of Yale University in the elegant interaction laboratory. (This detail is relevant to the perceived legitimacy of the experiment. In further variations, the experiment was dissociated from the university, with consequences for performances.) The role of experimenter was played by a 31-year-old high school teacher of biology. His manner was impassive, and his appearance somewhat stern throughout the experiment. He was dressed in a gray technician's coat. The victim was played by a 47-year-old accountant, trained for the role; he was of Irish-American stock, whom most observers found mild-mannered and likable.

One naive subject and one victim (an accomplice) performed in each experiment. A pretext had to be devised that would justify the administration of electric shock by the naive subject. This was effectively accomplished by the cover story. After a general introduction on the presumed relation between punishment and learning, subjects were told:

But actually, we know *very little* about the effect of punishment on learning, because almost no truly scientific studies have been made of it in human beings.

For instance, we don't know how *much* punishment is best for learning —and we don't know how much difference it makes as to who is giving the punishment, whether an adult learns best from a younger or an older person than himself—or many things of that sort.

So in this study we are bringing together a number of adults of different occupations and ages. And we're asking some of them to be teachers and some of them to be learners.

We want to find out just what effect different people have on each other as teachers and learners, and also what effect *punishment* will have on learning in this situation.

Therefore, I'm going to ask one of you to be the teacher here tonight and the other one to be the learner.

Does either of you have a preference?

Subjects then drew slips of paper from a hat to determine who would be the teacher and who would be the learner in the experiment. The drawing was rigged so that the naive subject was always the teacher and the accomplice always the learner. (Both slips contained the word "Teacher.") Immediately after the drawing, the teacher and learner were taken to an adjacent room and the learner was strapped into an "electric chair" apparatus.

The experimenter explained that the straps were to prevent excessive movement while the learner was being shocked. The effect was to make it impossible for him to escape from the situation. An electrode was attached to the learner's wrist, and electrode paste was applied "to avoid blisters, and burns." Subjects were told that the electrode was attached to the shock generator in the adjoining room.

In order to improve credibility the experimenter declared, in response to a question by the learner: "Although the shocks can be extremely painful, they cause no permanent tissue damage."

Learning task. The lesson administered by the subject was a paired-associate learning task. The subject read a series of word pairs to the learner, and then read the first word of the pair along with four terms. The learner was to indicate which of the four terms had originally been paired with the first word. He communicated his answer by pressing one of four switches in front of him, which in turn lit up one of four numbered quadrants in an answer-box located atop the shock generator.

Shock generator. The instrument panel consists of 30 lever switches set in a horizontal line. Each switch is clearly labeled with a voltage designation that ranges from 15 to 450 volts. There is a 15-volt increment from one switch to the next going from left to right. In addition, the following verbal designations are clearly indicated for groups of four switches going from left to right: Slight Shock, Moderate Shock, Strong Shock, Very Strong Shock, Intense Shock, Extreme Intensity Shock, Danger: Severe Shock. (Two switches after this last designation are simply marked XXX.)

Upon depressing a switch: a pilot light corresponding to each switch is illuminated in bright red; an electric buzzing is heard; an electric blue light, labeled "voltage energizer," flashes; the dial on the voltage meter swings to the right; various relay clicks are sounded.

The upper left-hand corner of the generator is labeled Shock Generator, Type ZLB, Dyson Instrument Company, Waltham, Mass. Output 15 Volts-450 Volts.

Details of the instrument were carefully handled to insure an appearance of authenticity. The panel was engraved by precision industrial engravers, and all components were of high quality. No subject in the experiment suspected that the instrument was merely a simulated shock generator.[3]

Sample shock. Each naive subject is given a sample shock on the shock generator, prior to beginning his run as teacher. This shock is always 45 volts, and is applied by pressing the third switch of the generator. The shock is applied to the wrist of the naive subject, and

3. A related technique, making use of a shock generator, was reported by Buss (1961) for the study of aggression in the laboratory. Despite the considerable similarity of technical detail in the experimental procedures, both investigators proceeded in ignorance of the other's work. Milgram provided plans and photographs of his shock generator, experimental procedure, and first results in a report to the National Science Foundation in January, 1961. This report received only limited circulation. Buss reported his procedure 6 months later, but to a wider audience. Subsequently, technical information and reports were exchanged. The present article was first received in the Editor's office on December 27, 1961; it was resubmitted with deletions on July 27, 1962 [Milgram's note].

has its source in a 45-volt battery wired into the generator. This further convinces the subject of the authenticity of the generator.

Shock instructions. The subject is told to administer a shock to the learner each time he gives a wrong response. Moreover—and this is the key command—the subject is instructed to "move one level higher on the shock generator each time the learner flashes a wrong answer." He is also instructed to announce the voltage level before administering a shock. This serves to continually remind subjects of the increasing intensity of shocks administered to the learner.

Preliminary and regular run. Pretests revealed that the procedure of reading words and administering shocks requires some practice before it can be handled smoothly. Therefore, immediately preceding the regular run, the teacher is given a preliminary series of 10 words to read to the learner. There are 3 neutral words in the practice series (*i.e.*, words that the learner answers correctly), so that shocks are administered for 7 of the words, with the maximum shock at 105 volts (moderate shock). Almost all subjects master the procedure by the time the preliminary run is over.

Subjects are then presented with a second list, and are told that the procedure is the same as for the first list; the experimenter adds, however:

When you get to the bottom of the list, repeat it over again, and continue giving shocks, until the learner has learned all the pairs correctly.

The experimenter instructs the subject to,

start from 15 volts and increase the shock level one step each time the learner gives a wrong answer.

Feedback from the victim. In all conditions the learner gives a predetermined set of responses to the word pair test, based on a schedule of approximately three wrong answers to one correct answer. In the present experimental condition no vocal response or other sign of protest is heard from the learner until Shock Level 300 is reached. When the 300-volt shock is administered, the learner pounds on the wall of the room in which he is bound to the electric chair. The pounding can be heard by the subject. From this point on, the learner's answers no longer appear on the four-way panel.

At this juncture, subjects ordinarily turn to the experimenter for guidance. The experimenter instructs the subject to treat the absence of a response as a wrong answer, and to shock the subject according to the usual schedule. He advises the subjects to allow 5–10 seconds before considering no response as a wrong answer, and to increase the shock level one step each time the learner fails to respond correctly. The learner's pounding is repeated after the 315-volt shock is administered; afterwards he is not heard from, nor do his answers reappear on the four-way signal box.

Experimenter feedback. At various points in the experiment the subject may turn to the experimenter for advice on whether he should continue to administer shocks. Or he may indicate that he does not wish to go on. It was important to standardize the experimenter's responses to these inquiries and reactions.

If the subject indicated his unwillingness to go on, the experimenter responded with a sequence of "prods," using as many as necessary to bring the subject into line.

Prod 1: Please continue, *or* Please go on.
Prod 2: The experiment requires that you continue.
Prod 3: It is absolutely essential that you continue.
Prod 4: You have no other choice, you *must* go on.

The prods were always made in sequence: Only if Prod 1 had been unsuccessful, could Prod 2 be used. If the subject refused to obey the experimenter after Prod 4, the experiment was terminated. The experimenter's tone of voice was at all times firm, but not impolite. The sequence was begun anew on each occasion that the subject balked or showed reluctance to follow orders.

Special prods. If the subject asked if the learner was liable to suffer permanent physical injury, the experimenter said:

Although the shocks may be painful, there is no permanent tissue damage, so please go on. [Followed by Prods 2, 3, and 4 if necessary.]

If the subject said that the learner did not want to go on, the experimenter replied:

Whether the learner likes it or not, you must go on until he has learned all the word pairs correctly. So please go on. [Followed by Prods 2, 3, and 4 if necessary.]

DEPENDENT MEASURES

The primary dependent measure for any subject is the maximum shock he administers before he refuses to go any further. In principle this may vary from 0 (for a subject who refuses to administer even the first shock) to 30 (for a subject who administers the highest shock on the generator). A subject who breaks off the experiment at any point prior to administering the thirtieth shock level is termed a *defiant subject.* One who complies with experimental commands fully, and proceeds to administer all shock levels commanded, is termed an *obedient* subject.

Further records. With few exceptions, experimental sessions were recorded on magnetic tape. Occasional photographs were taken through one-way mirrors. Notes were kept on any unusual behavior occurring during the course of the experiments. On occasion, additional observers were directed to write objective descriptions of the subjects' behavior. The latency and duration of shocks were measured by accurate timing devices.

Interview and dehoax. Following the experiment, subjects were interviewed; open-ended questions, projective measures, and attitude scales were employed. After the interview, procedures were undertaken to assure that the subject would leave the laboratory in a state of well being. A friendly reconciliation was arranged between the subject and the victim, and an effort was made to reduce any tensions that arose as a result of the experiment.

Results

PRELIMINARY NOTIONS

Before giving an account of the experimental results, it is instructive to consider how persons predict others will perform when commanded to administer powerful shocks to another person. Fourteen Yale seniors, all psychology majors, were provided with a detailed description of the experimental situation. They were asked to reflect carefully on it, and to predict the behavior of 100 hypothetical subjects. More specifically, they were instructed to plot the distribution of obedience of "100 Americans of diverse occupations, and ranging in age from 20 to 50 years," who were placed in the experimental situation.

There was considerable agreement among the respondents on the expected behavior of hypothetical subjects. All respondents predicted that only an insignificant minority would go through to the end of the shock series. (The estimates ranged from 0 to 3%; *i.e.*, the most "pessimistic" member of the class predicted that of 100 persons, 3 would continue through to the most potent shock available on the shock generator—450 volts.) The class mean was 1.2%. The question was also posed informally to colleagues of the author, and the most general feeling was that few if any subjects would go beyond the designation Very Strong Shock.

RESULT OF EXPERIMENT I

Subjects accept situation. With few exceptions subjects were convinced of the reality of the experimental situation, that they were administering shocks to another person, and the most potent shocks were extremely painful. In the post-experimental interview subjects were asked: "How painful to the learner were the last few shocks that you administered to him?" Subjects were instructed to indicate their answers on a printed 14-point scale ranging from "Not at all painful" to "Extremely painful." The modal[4] response was 14 (Extremely painful), with the mean at 13.42.

Signs of extreme tension. Many subjects showed signs of nervousness in the experimental situation, and especially upon administering the more powerful shocks. In a large number of cases the degree of tension reached extremes that are rarely seen in sociopsychological laboratory studies. Subjects were observed to sweat, tremble, stutter,

4. Most frequent.

bite their lips, groan, and dig their fingernails into their flesh. These were characteristic rather than exceptional responses to the experiment.

One sign of tension was the regular occurrence of nervous laughing fits. Fourteen of the 40 subjects showed definite signs of nervous laughter and smiling. The laughter seemed entirely out of place, even bizarre. Full-blown, uncontrollable seizures were observed for 3 subjects. On one occasion we observed a seizure so violently convulsive that it was necessary to call a halt to the experiment. The subject, a 46-year-old encyclopedia salesman, was seriously embarrassed by his untoward and uncontrollable behavior. In the post-experimental interviews subjects took pains to point out that they were not sadistic types, and that the laughter did not mean they enjoyed shocking the victim.

Distribution of scores. It had been conjectured that persons would not, in general, agree to administer shocks beyond the level designated as Very Strong Shock. The distribution of maximum shocks for this experiment is shown in Table 2. The obtained distribution of scores deviates radically from the prediction.

Upon command of the experimenter, each of the 40 subjects went beyond the expected breakoff point. No subject stopped prior to administering Shock Level 20. (At this level—300 volts—the victim kicks on the wall and no longer provides answers to the teacher's multiple-choice questions.)

Of the 40 subjects, 5 refused to obey the experimental commands beyond the 300-volt level. Four more subjects administered one further shock, and then refused to go on. Two broke off at the 330-volt level, and 1 each at 345, 360, and 375 volts. Thus a total of 14 subjects defied the experimenter. It is instructive to reprint their remarks at the point of defiance, as transcribed from the tape recordings:

[0124] I think he's trying to communicate, he's knocking.... Well it's not fair to shock the guy ... these are terrific volts. I don't think this is very humane.... Oh, I can't go on with this; no, this isn't right. It's a hell of an experiment. The guy is suffering in there. No, I don't want to go on. This is crazy. [Subject refused to administer more shocks.]

[0123] He's banging in there. I'm gonna chicken out. I'd like to continue, but I can't do that to a man.... I'm sorry I can't do that to a man. I'll hurt his heart. You take your check.... No really, I couldn't do it.

These subjects were frequently in a highly agitated and even angered state. Sometimes, verbal protest was at a minimum, and the subject simply got up from his chair in front of the shock generator, and indicated that he wished to leave the laboratory.

Of the 40 subjects, 26 obeyed the orders of the experimenter to the end, proceeding to punish the victim until they reached the most potent shock available on the shock generator. At that point,

TABLE 2
DISTRIBUTION OF BREAKOFF POINTS

Verbal designation and voltage indication	Number of subjects for whom this was maximum shock
Slight Shock	
15	0
30	0
45	0
60	0
Moderate Shock	
75	0
90	0
105	0
120	0
Strong Shock	
135	0
150	0
165	0
180	0
Very Strong Shock	
195	0
210	0
225	0
240	0
Intense Shock	
255	0
270	0
285	0
300	5
Extreme Intensity Shock	
315	4
330	2
345	1
360	1
Danger: Severe Shock	
375	1
390	0
405	0
420	0
XXX	
435	0
450	26

the experimenter called a halt to the session. (The maximum shock is labeled 450 volts, and is two steps beyond the designation: Danger: Severe Shock.) Although obedient subjects continued to administer shocks, they often did so under extreme stress. Some expressed reluctance to administer shocks beyond the 300-volt level, and displayed fears similar to those who defied the experimenter; yet they obeyed.

After the maximum shocks had been delivered, and the experimenter called a halt to the proceedings, many obedient subjects heaved sighs of relief, mopped their brows, rubbed their fingers over their eyes, or nervously fumbled cigarettes. Some shook their heads, apparently in regret. Some subjects had remained calm throughout the experiment, and displayed only minimal signs of tension from beginning to end.

Discussion

The experiment yielded two findings that were surprising. The first finding concerns the sheer strength of obedient tendencies manifested in this situation. Subjects have learned from childhood that it is a fundamental breach of moral conduct to hurt another person against his will. Yet, 26 subjects abandon this tenet in following the instructions of an authority who has no special powers to enforce his commands. To disobey would bring no material loss to the subject; no punishment would ensue. It is clear from the remarks and outward behavior of many participants that in punishing the victim they are often acting against their own values. Subjects often expressed deep disapproval of shocking a man in the face of his objections, and others denounced it as stupid and senseless. Yet the majority complied with the experimental commands. This outcome was surprising from two perspectives: first, from the standpoint of predictions made in the questionnaire described earlier. (Here, however, it is possible that the remoteness of the respondents from the actual situation, and the difficulty of conveying to them the concrete details of the experiment, could account for the serious underestimation of obedience.)

But the results were also unexpected to persons who observed the experiment in progress, through one-way mirrors. Observers often uttered expressions of disbelief upon seeing a subject administer more powerful shocks to the victim. These persons had a full acquaintance with the details of the situation, and yet systematically underestimated the amount of obedience that subjects would display.

The second unanticipated effect was the extraordinary tension generated by the procedures. One might suppose that a subject would simply break off or continue as his conscience dictated. Yet, this is very far from what happened. There were striking reactions of tension and emotional strain. One observer related:

I observed a mature and initially poised businessman enter the laboratory smiling and confident. Within 20 minutes he was reduced to a twitching, stuttering wreck, who was rapidly approaching a point of nervous collapse. He constantly pulled on his earlobe, and twisted his hands. At one point he pushed his fist into his forehead and muttered: "Oh God, let's stop it." And yet he continued to respond to every word of the experimenter, and obeyed to the end.

Any understanding of the phenomenon of obedience must rest on an analysis of the particular conditions in which it occurs. The following features of the experiment go some distance in explaining the high amount of obedience observed in the situation.

1. The experiment is sponsored by and takes place on the grounds of an institution of unimpeachable reputation, Yale University. It may be reasonably presumed that the personnel are competent and reputable. The importance of this background authority is now being studied by conducting a series of experiments outside of New Haven, and without any visible ties to the university.

2. The experiment is, on the face of it, designed to attain a worthy purpose—advancement of knowledge about learning and memory. Obedience occurs not as an end in itself, but as an instrumental element in a situation that the subject construes as significant, and meaningful. He may not be able to see its full significance, but he may properly assume that the experimenter does.

3. The subject perceives that the victim has voluntarily submitted to the authority system of the experimenter. He is not (at first) an unwilling captive impressed for involuntary service. He has taken the trouble to come to the laboratory presumably to aid the experimental research. That he later becomes an involuntary subject does not alter the fact that, initially, he consented to participate without qualification. Thus he has in some degree incurred an obligation toward the experimenter.

4. The subject, too, has entered the experiment voluntarily, and perceives himself under obligation to aid the experimenter. He has made a commitment, and to disrupt the experiment is a repudiation of this initial promise of aid.

5. Certain features of the procedure strengthen the subject's sense of obligation to the experimenter. For one, he has been paid for coming to the laboratory. In part this is canceled out by the experimenter's statement that:

Of course, as in all experiments, the money is yours simply for coming to the laboratory. From this point on, no matter what happens, the money is yours.[5]

---

5. Forty-three subjects, undergraduates at Yale University, were run in the experiment without payment. The results are very similar to those obtained with paid subjects [Milgram's note].

6. From the subject's standpoint, the fact that he is the teacher and the other man the learner is purely a chance consequence (it is determined by drawing lots) and he, the subject, ran the same risk as the other man in being assigned the role of learner. Since the assignment of positions in the experiment was achieved by fair means, the learner is deprived of any basis of complaint on this count. (A similar situation obtains in Army units, in which—in the absence of volunteers—a particularly dangerous mission may be assigned by drawing lots, and the unlucky soldier is expected to bear his misfortune with sportsmanship.)

7. There is, at best, ambiguity with regard to the prerogatives of a psychologist and the corresponding rights of his subject. There is a vagueness of expectation concerning what a psychologist may require of his subject, and when he is overstepping acceptable limits. Moreover, the experiment occurs in a closed setting, and thus provides no opportunity for the subject to remove these ambiguities by discussion with others. There are few standards that seem directly applicable to the situation, which is a novel one for most subjects.

8. The subjects are assured that the shocks administered to the subject are "painful but not dangerous." Thus they assume that the discomfort caused the victim is momentary, while the scientific gains resulting from the experiment are enduring.

9. Through Shock Level 20 the victim continues to provide answers on the signal box. The subject may construe this as a sign that the victim is still willing to "play the game." It is only after Shock Level 20 that the victim repudiates the rules completely, refusing to answer further.

These features help to explain the high amount of obedience obtained in this experiment. Many of the arguments raised need not remain matters of speculation, but can be reduced to testable propositions to be confirmed or disproved by further experiments.[6]

The following features of the experiment concern the nature of the conflict which the subject faces.

10. The subject is placed in a position in which he must respond to the competing demands of two persons: the experimenter and the victim. The conflict must be resolved by meeting the demands of one or the other; satisfaction of the victim and the experimenter are mutually exclusive. Moreover, the resolution must take the form of a highly visible action, that of continuing to shock the victim or breaking off the experiment. Thus the subject is forced into a public conflict that does not permit any completely satisfactory solution.

11. While the demands of the experimenter carry the weight of scientific authority, the demands of the victim spring from his per-

6. A series of recently completed experiments employing the obedience paradigm is reported in Milgram (1964) [Milgram's note].

sonal experience of pain and suffering. The two claims need not be regarded as equally pressing and legitimate. The experimenter seeks an abstract scientific datum; the victim cries out for relief from physical suffering caused by the subject's actions.

12. The experiment gives the subject little time for reflection. The conflict comes on rapidly. It is only minutes after the subject has been seated before the shock generator that the victim begins his protests. Moreover, the subject perceives that he has gone through but two-thirds of the shock levels at the time the subject's first protests are heard. Thus he understands that the conflict will have a persistent aspect to it, and may well become more intense as increasingly more powerful shocks are required. The rapidity with which the conflict descends on the subject, and his realization that it is predictably recurrent may well be sources of tension to him.

13. At a more general level, the conflict stems from the opposition of two deeply ingrained behavior dispositions: first, the disposition not to harm other people, and second, the tendency to obey those whom we perceive to be legitimate authorities.

References

Adorno, T., Else Frenkel-Brunswik, D. J. Levinson, and R. N. Sanford, *The Authoritarian Personality*. New York: Harper & Row, 1950.

Arendt, H., "What Was Authority?" In C. J. Friedrich (ed.), *Authority*. Cambridge, Mass.: Harvard University Press, 1958. Pp. 81-112.

Binet, S., *La suggestibilité*. Paris: Schleicher, 1900.

Buss, A. H., *The Psychology of Aggression*. New York: Wiley, 1961.

Cartwright, S. (ed.), *Studies in Social Power*. Ann Arbor: University of Michigan Institute for Social Research, 1959.

Chacot, J. M., *Oeuvres complètes*. Paris: Bureaux du Progrès Médical, 1881.

Frank, J. D., "Experimental Studies of Personal Pressure and Resistance." *Journal of General Psychology*, 30 (1944), 23-64.

Friedrich, C. J. (ed.), *Authority*. Cambridge, Mass.: Harvard University Press, 1958.

Milgram, S., *Dynamics of Obedience*. Washington, D.C.: National Science Foundation, January 25, 1961. (Mimeographed.)

Milgram, S., "Some Conditions of Obedience and Disobedience to Authority." *Human Relations* (1964).

Rokeach, M., "Authority, Authoritarianism, and Conformity." In I. A. Berg and B. M. Bass (eds.), *Conformity and Deviation*. New York: Harper & Row, 1961. Pp. 230-257.

Snow, C. P., "Either-or." *The Progressive*, 24 (Feburary 1961).

Weber, M., *The Theory of Social and Economic Organization*. Oxford, Eng.: Oxford University Press, 1947.

QUESTIONS

1. The opening paragraph states that "from 1933–1945 millions of innocent persons were systematically slaughtered on command." Does this study help to explain how that could have happened? What is the purpose of the study? What do you learn from it?
2. Does this experiment involve an actual shock to anybody?

3. What explanation is offered for the subjects' continuing the experiment even when they believed that they were inflicting intense physical pain upon the "learner"? What explains the experimenters' continuing the experiment even when they knew that they were inflicting evident psychological pain upon the subjects? How many subjects refused to complete the experiment? How many times did the experimenters find it necessary to stop?

4. Milgram points out (p. 305) that "There is, at best, ambiguity with regard to the prerogatives of a psychologist and the corresponding rights of his subject. There is a vagueness of expectation concerning what a psychologist may require of his subject, and when he is overstepping acceptable limits." Does this study appear to bear out that observation?

5. "The orders to administer shocks are given to the naive subject in the context of a 'learning experiment' ostensibly set up to study the effects of punishment on memory" (p. 294). This sentence is in the passive voice; recast it in the active. How frequent is the passive voice in this piece of writing? Does the passive voice indicate scientific precision? Or objectivity? Or what?

6. What is a prod? A dehoax? (See pp. 299–300.) How do these terms help define the role of the experimental scientist?

JEROME S. BRUNER

Freud and the Image of Man

By the dawn of the sixth century before Christ, the Greek physicist-philosophers had formulated a bold conception of the physical world as a unitary material phenomenon. The Ionians had set forth a conception of matter as fundamental substance, transformation of which accounted for the myriad forms and substances of the physical world. Anaximander was subtle enough to recognize that matter must be viewed as a generalized substance, free of any particular sensuous properties. Air, iron, water or bone were only elaborated forms, derived from a more general stuff. Since that time, the phenomena of the physical world have been conceived as continuous and monistic, as governed by the common laws of matter. The view was a bold one, bold in the sense of running counter to the immediate testimony of the senses. It has served as an axiomatic basis of physics for more than two millennia. The bold view eventually became the obvious view, and it gave shape to our common understanding of the physical world. Even the alchemists rested their case upon this doctrine of material continuity and, indeed, had they known about neutron bombardment, they might even have hit upon the proper philosopher's stone.

The good fortune of the physicist—and these matters are always relative, for the material monism of physics may have impeded nineteenth-century thinking and delayed insights into the nature of complementarity in modern physical theory—this early good fortune or happy insight has no counterpart in the sciences of man. Lawful continuity between man and the animal kingdom, between dreams and unreason on one side and waking rationality on the other, between madness and sanity, between consciousness and unconsciousness, between the mind of the child and the adult mind, between primitive and civilized man—each of these has been a cherished discontinuity preserved in doctrinal canons. There were voices in each generation, to be sure, urging the exploration of continuities. Anaximander had a passing good approximation to a theory of evolution based on natural selection; Cornelius Agrippa offered a plausible theory of the continuity of mental health and disease in terms of bottled-up sexuality. But Anaximander did not prevail against Greek conceptions of man's creation nor did Cornelius Agrippa against the demonopathy of the *Malleus Maleficarum*.[1] Neither in establishing the continuity between the varied states of man nor in pursuing the continuity between man and animal was there conspicuous success until the nineteenth century.

I need not insist upon the social, ethical, and political significance of an age's image of man, for it is patent that the view one takes of man affects profoundly one's standard of dignity and the humanly possible. And it is in the light of such a standard that we establish our laws, set our aspirations for learning, and judge the fitness of men's acts. Those who govern, then, must perforce be jealous guardians of man's ideas about man, for the structure of government rests upon an uneasy consensus about human nature and human wants. Since the idea of man is of the order of *res publica*,[2] it is an idea not subject to change without public debate. Nor is it simply a matter of public concern. For man as individual has a deep and emotional investment in his image of himself. If we have learned anything in the last half-century of psychology, it is that man has powerful and exquisite capacities for defending himself against violation of his cherished self-image. This is not to say that Western man has not persistently asked: "What is man that thou art mindful of him?" It is only that the question, when pressed, brings us to the edge of anxiety where inquiry is no longer free.

Two figures stand out massively as the architects of our present-day conception of man: Darwin and Freud. Freud's was the more daring, the more revolutionary, and in a deep sense, the more poetic insight. But Freud is inconceivable without Darwin. It is both timely and perhaps historically just to center our inquiry on Freud's contribution to the modern image of man. Darwin I shall treat as a necessary condition for Freud and for his success, recognizing, of

1. A notorious book about demons and witchcraft. 2. The state.

course, that this is a form of psychological license. Not only is it the centenary of Freud's birth;[3] it is also a year in which the current of popular thought expressed in commemoration of the date quickens one's awareness of Freud's impact on our times.

Rear-guard fundamentalism did not require a Darwin to slay it in an age of technology. He helped, but this contribution was trivial in comparison with another. What Darwin had done was to propose a set of principles unified around the conception that all organic species had their origins and took their form from a common set of circumstances—the requirements of biological survival. All living creatures were on a common footing. When the post-Darwin era of exaggeration had passed and religious literalism had abated into a new nominalism, what remained was a broad, orderly, and unitary conception of organic nature, a vast continuity from the monocellular protozoans to man. Biology had at last found its unifying principle in the doctrine of evolution. Man was not unique but the inheritor of an organic legacy.

As the summit of an evolutionary process, man could still view himself with smug satisfaction, indeed proclaim that God or Nature had shown a persistent wisdom in its effort to produce a final, perfect product. It remained for Freud to present the image of man as the unfinished product of nature: struggling against unreason, impelled by driving inner vicissitudes and urges that had to be contained if man were to live in society, host alike to seeds of madness and majesty, never fully free from an infancy anything but innocent. What Freud was proposing was that man at his best and man at his worst is subject to a common set of explanations: that good and evil grow from a common process.

Freud was strangely yet appropriately fitted for his role as architect of a new conception of man. We must pause to examine his qualifications, for the image of man that he created was in no small measure founded on his painfully achieved image of himself and of his times. We are concerned not so much with his psychodynamics, as with the intellectual traditions he embodies. A child of his century's materialism, he was wedded to the determinism and the classical physicalism of nineteenth-century physiology so boldly represented by Helmholtz. Inded, the young Freud's devotion to the exploration of anatomical structures was a measure of the strength of this inheritance. But at the same time, as both Lionel Trilling and W. H. Auden have recognized with much sensitivity, there was a deep current of romanticism in Freud—a sense of the role of impulse, of the drama of life, of the power of symbolism, of ways of knowing that were more poetic than rational in spirit, of the poet's cultural alienation. It was perhaps this romantic's sense of drama that led to his gullibility about parental seduction and to his gener-

3. 1956

ous susceptibility to the fallacy of the dramatic instance.

Freud also embodies two traditions almost as antithetical as romanticism and nineteenth-century scientism. He was profoundly a Jew, not in a doctrinal sense but in his conception of morality, in his love of the skeptical play of reason, in his distrust of illusion, in the form of his prophetic talent, even in his conception of mature eroticism. His prophetic talent was antithetic to a Utopianism either of innocence or of social control. Nor did it lead to a counsel of renunciation. Free oneself of illusion, of neurotic infantilism, and "the soft voice of intellect" would prevail. Wisdom for Freud was neither doctrine nor formula, but the achievement of maturity. The patient who is cured is the one who is now free enough of neurosis to decide intelligently about his own destiny. As for his conception of mature love, it has always seemed to me that its blend of tenderness and sensuality combined the uxorious imagery of the Chassidic tradition and the sensual quality of the Song of Songs. And might it not have been Freud rather than a commentator of the Haftorahs[4] who said, "In children, it was taught, God gives humanity a chance to make good its mistakes." For the modern trend of permissiveness toward children is surely a feature of the Freudian legacy.

But for all the Hebraic quality, Freud is also in the classical tradition—combining the Stoics and the great Greek dramatists. For Freud as for the Stoics, there is no possibility of man disobeying the laws of nature. And yet, it is in this lawfulness that for him the human drama inheres. His love for Greek drama and his use of it in his formulation are patent. The sense of the human tragedy, the inevitable working out of the human plight—these are the hallmarks of Freud's case histories. When Freud, the tragic dramatist, becomes a therapist, it is not to intervene as a directive authority. The therapist enters the drama of the patient's life, makes possible a play within a play, the transference, and when the patient has "worked through" and understood the drama, he has achieved the wisdom necessary for freedom. Again, like the Stoics, it is in the recognition of one's own nature and in the acceptance of the laws that govern it that the good life is to be found.

Freud's contribution lies in the continuities of which he made us aware. The first of these is the continuity of organic lawfulness. Accident in human affairs was no more to be brooked as "explanation" than accident in nature. The basis for accepting such an "obvious" proposition had, of course, been well prepared by a burgeoning nineteenth-century scientific naturalism. It remained for Freud to extend naturalistic explanation to the heart of human affairs. The *Psychopathology of Everyday Life* is not one of Freud's deeper works, but "the Freudian slip" has contributed more to the

4. The Old Testament Prophets.

common acceptance of lawfulness in human behavior than perhaps any of the more rigorous and academic formulations from Wundt to the present day. The forgotten lunch engagement, the slip of the tongue, the barked shin could no longer be dismissed as accident. Why Freud should have succeeded where the novelists, philosophers, and academic psychologists had failed we will consider in a moment.

Freud's extension of Darwinian doctrine beyond Haeckel's theorem that ontogeny recapitulates phylogeny is another contribution to continuity. It is the conception that in the human mind, the primitive, infantile, and archaic exist side-by-side with the civilized and evolved.

Where animals are concerned we hold the view that the most highly developed have arisen from the lowest. . . . In the realm of mind, on the other hand, the primitive type is so commonly preserved alongside the transformations which have developed out of it that it is superfluous to give instances in proof of it. When this happens, it is usually the result of a bifurcation in development. One quantitative part of an attitude or an impulse has survived unchanged while another has undergone further development. This brings us very close to the more general problem of conservation in the mind. . . . Since the time when we recognized the error of supposing that ordinary forgetting signified destruction or annihilation of the memory-trace, we have been inclined to the opposite view that nothing once formed in the mind could ever perish, that everything survives in some way or other, and is capable under certain conditions of being brought to light again . . . (Freud, *Civilization and Its Discontents*, pp. 14–15).

What has now come to be common sense is that in everyman there is the potentiality for criminality, and that these are neither accidents nor visitations of degeneracy, but products of a delicate balance of forces that, under different circumstances, might have produced normality or even saintliness. Good and evil, in short, grow from a common root.

Freud's genius was in his resolution of polarities. The distinction of child and adult was one such. It did not suffice to reiterate that the child was father to the man. The theory of infantile sexuality and the stages of psychosexual development were an effort to fill the gap, the latter clumsy, the former elegant. Though the alleged progression of sexual expression from the oral, to the anal, to the phallic, and finally to the genital has not found a secure place either in common sense or in general psychology, the developmental continuity of sexuality has been recognized by both. Common sense honors the continuity in the baby-books and in the permissiveness with which young parents of today resolve their doubts. And the research of Beach and others has shown the profound effects of infantile experience on adult sexual behavior—even in lower organisms.

If today people are reluctant to report their dreams with the innocence once attached to such recitals, it is again because Freud brought into common question the discontinuity between the rational purposefulness of waking life and the seemingly irrational purposelessness of fantasy and dream. While the crude symbolism of Freud's early efforts at dream interpretation has come increasingly to be abandoned—that telephone poles and tunnels have an invariant sexual reference—the conception of the dream as representing disguised wishes and fears has become common coin. And Freud's recognition of deep unconscious processes in the creative act, let it also be said, has gone far toward enriching our understanding of the kinship between the artist, the humanist, and the man of science.

Finally, it is our heritage from Freud that the all-or-none distinction between mental illness and mental health has been replaced by a more humane conception of the continuity of these states. The view that neurosis is a severe reaction to human trouble is as revolutionary in its implications for social practice as it is daring in formulation. The "bad seed" theories, the nosologies of the nineteenth century, the demonologies and doctrines of divine punishment— none of these provided a basis for compassion toward human suffering comparable to that of our time.

One may argue, at last, that Freud's sense of the continuity of human conditions, of the likeness of the human plight, has made possible a deeper sense of the brotherhood of man. It has in any case tempered the spirit of punitiveness toward what once we took as evil and what we now see as sick. We have not yet resolved the dilemma posed by these two ways of viewing. Its resolution is one of the great moral challenges of our age.

Why, after such initial resistance, were Freud's views so phenomenally successful in transforming common conceptions of man?

One reason we have already considered: the readiness of the Western world to accept a naturalistic explanation of organic phenomena and, concurrently, to be readier for such explanation in the mental sphere. There had been at least four centuries of uninterrupted scientific progress, recently capped by a theory of evolution that brought man into continuity with the rest of the animal kingdom. The rise of naturalism as a way of understanding nature and man witnessed a corresponding decline in the explanatory aspirations of religion. By the close of the nineteenth century, religion, to use Morton White's phrase, "too often agreed to accept the role of a non-scientific spiritual grab-bag, or an ideological know-nothing." The elucidation of the human plight had been abandoned by religion and not yet adopted by science.

It was the inspired imagery, the proto-theory of Freud that was to fill the gap. Its success in transforming the common conception of man was not simply its recourse to the "cause-and-effect" discourse of science. Rather it is Freud's imagery, I think, that provides the clue to this ideological power. It is an imagery of necessity, one that combines the dramatic, the tragic, and the scientific views of necessity. It is here that Freud's intellectual heritage matters so deeply. Freud's is a theory or a proto-theory peopled with actors. The characters are from life: the blind, energic, pleasure-seeking id; the priggish and punitive super-ego; the ego, battling for its being by diverting the energy of the others to its own use. The drama has an economy and a terseness. The ego develops canny mechanisms for dealing with the threat of id impulses: denial, projection, and the rest. Balances are struck between the actors, and in the balance is character and neurosis. Freud was using the dramatic technique of decomposition, the play whose actors are parts of a single life. It is a technique that he himself had recognized in fantasies and dreams, one he honored in "The Poet and the Daydream."

The imagery of the theory, moreover, has an immediate resonance with the dialectic of experience. True, it is not the stuff of superficial conscious experience. But it fits the human plight, its conflictedness, its private torment, its impulsiveness, its secret and frightening urges, its tragic quality.

Concerning its scientific imagery, it is marked by the necessity of the classical mechanics. At times the imagery is hydraulic: suppress this stream of impulses, and perforce it breaks out in a displacement elsewhere. The system is a closed and mechanical one. At times it is electrical, as when cathexes are formed and withdrawn like electrical charges. The way of thought fitted well the common-sense physics of its age.

Finally, the image of man presented was thoroughly secular; its ideal type was the mature man free of infantile neuroticism, capable of finding his own way. This freedom from both Utopianism and asceticism has earned Freud the contempt of ideological totalitarians of the Right and the Left. But the image has found a ready home in the rising, liberal intellectual middle class. For them, the Freudian ideal type has become a rallying point in the struggle against spiritual regimentation.

I have said virtually nothing about Freud's equation of sexuality and impulse. It was surely and still is a stimulus to resistance. But to say that Freud's success lay in forcing a reluctant Victorian world to accept the importance of sexuality is as empty as hailing Darwin for his victory over fundamentalism. Each had a far more profound effect.

Can Freud's contribution to the common understanding of man in the twentieth century be likened to the impact of such great physical and biological theories as Newtonian physics and Darwin's conception of evolution? The question is an empty one. Freud's mode of thought is not a theory in the conventional sense, it is a metaphor, an analogy, a way of conceiving man, a drama. I would propose that Anaximander is the proper parallel: his view of the connectedness of physical nature was also an analogy—and a powerful one. Freud is the ground from which theory will grow, and he has prepared the twentieth century to nurture the growth. But far more important, he has provided an image of man that has made him comprehensible without at the same time making him contemptible.

Signs of the Times

VERTA MAE
The Kitchen Crisis

AUTHOR'S NOTE:
i do not consider myself a writer, i am a rapper. therefore do not read this piece silently . . . rap it aloud.

there is confusion in the kitchen!
we've got to develop kitchen consciousness or we may very well see the end of kitchens as we now know them. kitchens are getting smaller. in some apts the closet is bigger than the kitchen. something that i saw the other day leads me to believe that there may well be a subversive plot to take kitchens out of the home and put them in the street. i was sitting in the park knitting my old man a pair of socks for next winter when a tall well dressed man in his mid thirties sat next to me.
i didnt pay him no mind until he went into his act.
he pulled his irish linen hankie from his lapel, spread it on his lap, opened his attache case, took out a box, popped a pill, drank from his thermos jug, and turned and offered the box to me. thank you no said i. "i never eat with strangers."
that would have been all except that i am curious black and i looked at the label on the box, then i screamed, the box said INSTANT LUNCH PILL: (imitation ham and cheese on rye, with diet cola, and apple pie flavor). i sat frozen while he did his next act. he folded his hankie, put it back in his lapel, packed his thermos jug away, and took out a piece of yellow plastic and blew into it, in less than 3 minutes it had turned into a yellow plastic castro convertible couch.
enough is enough i thought to myself. so i dropped the knitting and ran like hell. last i saw of that dude he was stretched out on the couch reading portnoys complaint.

315

the kitchens that are still left in the home are so instant they might as well be out to lunch.

instant milk, instant coffee, instant tea, instant potatoes, instant old fashioned oatmeal, everything is preprepared for the unprepared woman in the kitchen. the chicken is pre cut. the flour is pre measured, the rice is minute, the salt is pre seasoned, and the peas are pre buttered. just goes to show you white folks will do anything for their women. they had to invent instant food because the servant problem got so bad that their women had to get in the kitchen herself with her own two little lily white hands. it is no accident that in the old old south where they had slaves that they was eating fried chicken, coated with batter, biscuits so light they could have flown across the mason dixon line if they had wanted to. they was eating pound cake that had to be beat 800 strokes. who do you think was doing this beating?

it sure wasnt missy. missy was beating the upstairs house nigger for not bringing her mint julep quick enough.

massa was out beating the field niggers for not hoeing the cotton fast enough. meanwhile up in the north country where they didnt have no slaves to speak of they was eating baked beans and so called new england boiled dinner.

it aint no big thing to put everything in one pot and let it cook. missy wasnt about to go through changes and whup no pound cake for 800 strokes.

black men and black women have been whipping up fine food for centuries and outside of black bottom pie and nigger toes there is no reference to our contribution and participation in and to the culinary arts.

when they do mention our food they act like it is some obscure thing that niggers down south made up and dont nobody else in the world eat it.

food aint nothing but food.

food is universal.

everybody eats.

a potato is a patata and not irish as white folks would have you believe. watermelons is prehistoric and eaten all ober de world.

the russians make a watermelon beer. in the orient they dry and roast and salt the seeds. when old chris got here the indians was eating hominy grits. and before he "discovered" this country the greeks and romans were smacking on collard greens. blackeyed peas aint nothing but dried cow peas whose name in sanskrit traces its lineage back to the days before history was recorded. uh ah excuse me boss, means befo you-all was recording history. uh ah i know this is hard for you to believe suh but i got it from one of yo history books and i know you-all wouldnt talk with no forked tongue about history.

the cooking of food is one of the highest of all the human arts. we need to develop food consciousness.

so called enlightened people will rap for hours about jean paul sartre, campus unrest, the feminine mystique, black power, and tania, but mention food and they say, rather proudly too, "i'm a bad cook." some go so far as to boast "i cant even boil water without burning it."

that is a damn shame.

bad cooks got a bad life style.

food is life.

food changes up into blood, blood into cells, cells into energy, energy changes up into the forces which make up your life style.

so if one takes a creative, imaginative, loving, serious attitude toward life everything one does will reflect one attitude hence when one cooks this attitude will be served at the table. and it will be good.

so bad cooks got a bad life style and i dont mean bad like we (blacks) mean bad i mean bad bad.

come on give a damn. anybody can get it together for vacation. change up and daily walk through kitchen life like you was on an endless holiday. aint no use to save yourself for vacation. it's here now.

make every and each moment count like time was running out. that will cool out that matter of guess who is coming to dinner and make it a fact that DINNER IS SERVED.

one of the best meals i was ever served was at my friend bella's. bella served an elegant meal in her two room cold water tub in kitchen six story walk up flat. she had a round oak table with carved legs, covered with a floor length off white shaker lace tablecloth. in the center was a carved african gourd filled with peanuts, persimmons, lemons and limes. to start off we had fresh squeezed tangerine juice in chilled champagne glasses. then scrambled eggs, sliced red onions marinated in lemon juice and pickapeppa sauce, fried green tomatoes, on cobalt blue china plates. hot buttermilk biscuits with homemade apple jelly on limoges saucers (bella got them from goodwill for 10 cent a piece) and fresh ground bustelo coffee served in mugs that bella made in pottery class at the neighborhood anti poverty pro community cultural workshop for people in low socio economic ethnic groups.

you are what you eat.

i was saying that a long time before the movie came out but it doesnt bother me that they stole my line. white folks are always stealing and borrowing and discovering and making myths. you take terrapins. diamondback terrapins. the so called goremays squeal with epicurean delight at the very mention of the word. there is a mystique surrounding the word. diamondback terrapins.

are you ready for the demystification of diamondback terrapins???????? they ain't nothing but salt water turtles.
slaves on the eastern shores used to eat them all the time. the slaves
was eating so many that a law was passed to making it a crime to
feed slaves terrapins more than 3 times a week.
white folks discovered terrapins, ate them all up and now they are
all but extinct (terrapins).
oh there are a few left on terrapin reservations but the chances of
seeing one in your neighborhood is not likely.

in my old neighborhood (fairfax s.c.) we always talk about how
folks in new york will give you something to drink but nothing to
eat. after having lived for several years in fun city i understand how
the natives got into this.
with the cost of living as high as it is here i understand how you
can become paranoid and weird about your food. i understand
where they are coming from but i thank the creator that there is
still a cultural gap between me and the natives. on the other hand
you cant be no fool about it. it dont make sense to take food out
your childrens mouths to give to the last lower east side poet who
knocks on your door but you can give up a margarine sandwich and
a glass of water. cant you? eating is a very personal thing.
some people will sit down and eat with anybody.
that is very uncool. you cant eat with everybody.
you got to have the right vibrations.
if you dont get good vibrations from someone, cancel them out for
eating. (other things too.)
that is the only way to keep bad kitchen vibes at a minimum. tell
those kind of folks that you will meet them in a luncheonette or a
bar.
even at the risk of static from family and friends PRO TECT YO
KITCH'N. it's hard though. sometimes look like in spite of all you do
and as careful as you try to be a rapscallion will slip right in your
kitchen. i cant stand rapscallions. among other things they are
insensitive. you ask them "may i offer you something" "some coffee
tea juice water milk juice or maybe an alcoholic beverage."
they always answer "nah nutin for me" or else they say "i'll have
tea if you got tea bags" or "coffee if it is instant i dont want to put
you through no trouble." check that out! talking about not going to
any trouble. hell they already in your house and that is trouble and
personal. what the rapscallions are really saying is dont go to any
trouble for me cause i wouldnt go to none for you. rapscallions dont
mind taking the alcoholic drink because it is impersonal. nothing of
you is in that. all you got to do is pour from a bottle. they dont feel
that you have extended yourself for them so they wont have to do
no trouble for you in return. in most other cultures when you enter
a persons home you and the host share a moment together by par-

taking of something. rapscallions love to talk about culture but their actions prove they aint got none. they dont understand that it is about more than the coffee tea or drink of water.

it's about extending yourself.

so watch out for rapscallions. they'll mess up your kitchen vibes.

PROTECT YOUR KITCHEN

MARGARET MEAD
Each Family in a Home of Its Own[1]

The belief that every family should have a home of its own seems like a truism to which almost every American would assent without further thought. Most Americans also accept the fact that we have a housing shortage as the consequences of a failure to build in the thirties and during World War II, and of discrepancies between housing costs and wages that should somehow be reconciled. But it is important to realize that the word "family" has come to mean fewer and fewer people, the number of families has steadily increased, and so the need for housing units as distinguished from living-space has also increased by leaps and bounds. Although Southern Senators may occasionally argue against some piece of legislation for women, claiming that women's place is in the home, most legislators yield, at least nominally, to the question, "Whose home?" Women's place in the United States is no longer in the home, and her exclusion from a right that has been hers in most societies is part of our belief that every family should have its own home—with only one woman in it. Furthermore, each family should consist only of a husband, a wife, and minor children.

All other forms of living are seen as having great disadvantages. A mother-son combination is classified as bad for the son, and a failure to break the silver cord; it will spoil his life. A father-daughter household is not as disapproved, but if the girl appears marriageable, then the father may be condemned and the daughter urged to bestir herself. Brother-and-sister households, such a common refuge of the genteel poor in other ages, are also frowned upon, even where one is widowed and has children. Somebody will be said to be sacrificed to somebody else in such an arrangement. Unmarried children who are self-supporting shouldn't be clinging to the home; they should get out and get married and start homes of their own. Nor should the elderly parents of married children live in their children's homes, certainly not if they are both alive to be "company

1. A chapter from the fourth part, "The Two Sexes in Contemporary America," of *Male and Female*, 1949.

for each other," and not unless absolutely necessary when only one survives. The rigorousness of the American belief that in-laws, especially mothers-in-law, are ruinous to marriages takes little account of the loneliness of elderly people. We respect them when they "make their own lives," without, however, any social arrangements that make it possible for them to do so. The two exceptions to the insistence on the inferiority, and indeed genuine undesirability, of any other form of living-arrangement than the biological family with young or no children, are the cases of two unmarried women living together and of the divorced or widowed woman with some children who returns to the home of some relative, often an unmarried sister, or a father.[2] The proper attitude towards a woman with children to support whose husband is dead, or who is divorced, is to hope that she will marry again, and that the present living-arrangement is merely temporary. Children need a man in the home to bring them up, and are to be pitied if they haven't got a father. Grandfathers and uncles are not thought of as really good substitutes. As for the households in which two unmarried women live together, they are still regarded with a tolerance that includes some of the last century's pity and absolution from blame of the woman who did not marry, but this is markedly decreasing. Young women to-day who work and share a household have to draw heavily on the housing situation or considerations of economy to justify their continuing such an arrangement. There will be doubts, perhaps fears, that at least the chances of marriage, for one if not both, are being compromised by the arrangement. Group living for men is only really tolerated in college dormitories, in armies, and in work-camps, highly patterned situations where either men are assumed to be too young to marry or their wives cannot accompany them. Men who keep house together have to fend off very heavy social doubts as to their heterosexuality. The ethics that informs all these various social disapprovals, which is expressed in private upbraiding of the one who is assumed to be selfish and attempts to rouse the one who is assumed to be suffering, is the firm American belief that one of the most heinous sins is to limit other people's emotional freedom to live the good life. As the good life is defined as marriage, obviously any living-arrangement is wrong that may make any marriageable individual forgo marriage, and to benefit from such an arrangement is selfish and exploitive.

All of these attitudes and preferences add up to a world in which one should either be married, with a home of one's own, or live alone, eating in restaurants, reading all night in bed, seeing the same

2. In 1947 one family in ten did not maintain a separate home. Of these, 2,500,000 were married couples with or without children; that is, individuals who are culturally entitled to feel that their happiness is as seriously endangered as their health would be during a famine. Three-quarters of a million were parent-child groups (nearly all mother-and-child groups) [Mead's note].

movies twice, dependent upon endless daily plans and initiative for companionship. Against such a background it is not surprising that Americans see one of the principal values in marriage as companionship, for we are a gregarious people, needing the presence of others to give us a full sense of ourselves. Nowhere in childhood or youth is there any training or any practice in self-sufficient isolation. Everything that a child does quietly by itself is suspect. "He is so quiet he must be up to mischief." Day-dreaming is frowned upon. People who would rather stay at home with a good book than go out with friends get poor scores on personality quizzes. Even simple sensuous pleasures, such as reading in the bath-tub on Sunday morning, are regarded as pretty self-indulgent and antisocial. Most time spent alone could be spent better if spent with others, and time and money are valuables that ought to be spent in the best way possible. The child goes from a home in which the whole family share a living-room to a school in which he studies and plays in groups, through an adolescence in which any night when he doesn't have to study he feels left out if he hasn't a date, to an adulthood in which any break in ready companionship is felt as almost unbearable. In his empty room he turns on the radio as soon as he enters, to dispel the silence. "Silence," says a generation brought up to study in groups with a radio blaring over their heads, "is embarrassing." Which is another way of saying that when one is left alone with oneself, the question "What have you done to deserve being alone?" is almost inevitable, for children who are watched if they seek isolation are also as punishment sent out of the room or to bed.

> And if you doubt what things I say,
> Suppose you make the test;
> Suppose when you've been bad someday
> And up to bed are sent away
>   From mother and the rest—
> Suppose you ask, "Who has been bad?"
>   And then you'll hear what's true;
> For the wind will moan in its ruefullest tone:
>   "Yooooooooo!
>   "Yooooooooo!
>   "Yooooooooo!"[3]

Self-sought loneliness and involuntary loneliness are both unattractive and suspect. The more popular and loved one is, the more sought-after, the more selfish it becomes to sit at home with a good book, and so make at least one other person involuntarily unhappy. Good-sportsmanship, which has shifted much of its meaning in America from its traditional English content, includes never refusing to do something labelled as fun if one or more other people ask you to, on such grounds as being tired, fed-up, or even needing to study, or write letters, or mend one's stockings. Critics of Americans'

3. From Eugene Field's "The Night Wind."

need for the reassurance of other people's company often neglect to stress that in a culture like ours universally acknowledged needs also imply universal duties, and that if every one is defined as lonely when he is alone, then it is obviously every one's duty to be with some one else. So children have to have "some one to play with," adolescents have to have dates, and adults have to marry and have a home of their own.

Assured companionship and parenthood thus become the two so-cially desirable values that cannot be obtained outside marriage. Almost every other human need that has historically been met in the home can now be met outside it: restaurants serve food; comics, movies, and radio provide amusement, news, and gossip; there are laundries and dry-cleaners and places that mend one's socks and store one's winter coat, wash one's hair and manicure one's nails and shine one's shoes. For sex satisfaction it is no longer necessary to choose between marriage and prostitution; for most of those without religious scruples sex is available on a friendly and amateur basis and without responsibility. The automobile has made it even unnec-essary for one of a pair of temporary sex partners to have an apart-ment. Entertaining can be done in a hotel or at a club. When one is sick, one goes to a hospital, and when one dies, one can be buried quite professionally from an undertaking establishment. A tele-phone service will answer one's telephone, and a shopping service do one's shopping. The old needs of food, shelter, sex, and recreation are all efficiently met outside the home—and yet more people are married to-day than ever before in the country's recorded history.

Marriage is a state towards which young Americans are propelled, and within which American women, educated to be energetic and active, try to live out the desires that have been both encouraged and muffled in them as children. Although there are other cultures in which women dominate the home more, America is conspicuous for the extent to which women have set the style of the home. This may be referred to a variety of background events: to the way in which the realm of the aesthetic was left to women during pioneer days, to the emphasis on work for every one which meant that men were too tired to spend much of their effort on the home; and, very importantly, to the division of labour among non-English-speaking immigrants. When immigrants came to this country, the husband set to work to make a living, the wife to find out how to live, and this division between making a living and a way of life, one as man's field, the other as woman's, has been intensified. Our patterns of urban life, with its highly developed transportation systems which mean that fewer and fewer men ever come home to lunch, are also one of the supporting factors in the situation. As more schools are consolidated and the distance from home is increased, and as school-lunches develop, the home with school-age children is deserted all day long, while Mother is free to study the magazines and rearrange the living-room or her knowledge of world peace or the community's school system, in between answering the telephone, waiting for the laundry-man, and doing the next errand.

So it falls to the lot of women to design the way of life of the family, consulting her husband on major issues only, simply because that is her job. Into it, during the early days of marriage and motherhood she pours all the energy that comes from a healthy well-fed active childhood. If she has had a good education and is trained for some outside work, or even possibly for a career, even more if she was successful before marriage, there is likely to be an extra bit of emphasis in the way she manages her home and her children, in her insistence on what a good mother and what a good wife she is. Sometimes she can even say frankly: "Yes, I know my child is old enough to go to school alone, but I still take her. After all, that is my justification for staying home." More often, without any articulate comment on her doubt as to whether home-making really is a full-time job, she simply puts more effort into her complex day. Here the same standards apply that apply to her husband: like him, she also must succeed, must make good, must meet higher and higher standards.

When we analyze the task of home-making in the United States to-day, in the home that is celebrated in the pages of the women's magazines and assumed in the carefully unspecific radio serials, we find some very curious contradictions. The well-equipped home—towards which all the advertisements are pointed—is a home in which everything can be done more quickly and more effortlessly, clothes get white in no time, irons press almost without your noticing it, the extra attachment on the vacuum cleaner will even brush the backs of your books, the new silver-polish keeps your silver looking like new. In fact, the American woman, and the American woman's husband, who does not escape the advertisements even if he misses the radio serials, are told how fortunate, modern, and leisurely she can be—if she simply equips her house properly. There really seems to have been a period—back in the twenties, when domestic servants were still relatively available—when a married woman who had a goodly supply of gadgets, and at least one servant, did get quite a little time to play bridge. Her image lingers on in the avid comments of professional women over fifty who still see the home-maker as having a wicked amount of leisure—especially when contrasted with the life led by the woman who must both work and discharge all the duties of the home-maker, as so many American women do, not by choice but by necessity. There was a time also when in the first fine flush of laundries and bakeries, milk deliveries and canned goods, ready-made clothes and dry-cleaning, it did look as if American life was being enormously simplified. A vacuum cleaner was a great addition to a home that kept the standards of a carpet-sweeper and a broom, laundries were a godsend to a household whose routine of sheet-changing was geared to the old-fashioned wash-tub, and bakeries to homes in which the making of bread had dominated one whole day. But just as our new medical palliatives are creating new vulnerabilities and new disease states, so the new equipment has led not to more leisure, more time to play with the baby, more time to curl up and read by an open fire, or to help with the PTA, but has merely combined with other trends in making the life of the American home-maker not easier, but more exacting. Most urban-living women do not realize that, as the Bryn Mawr report shows, housekeeping activities consumed 60.55 hours a week in a typical farm family, 78.35 in urban households in cities under 100,000, and 80.57 in households in cities of over 100,000. This was in pre-war days, and in a world that has been moving steadily towards a forty-hour week on the job.

Perhaps the most significant word in family relationships that has been invented for a very long time is the word "sitter"—the extra person who must come into the family and sit whenever the two parents go out of it together. The modern wife and mother lives alone, with a husband who comes home in the evening, and children, who as little children are on her hands twenty-four hours out of twenty-four, in a house that she is expected to run with the efficiency of a factory—for hasn't she a washing-machine and a vacuum cleaner?—and from which a great number of the compensations that once went with being a home-maker have been removed. Except in rural areas, she no longer produces, in the sense of preserving and pickling and canning. She has no orgies of house-cleaning twice a year. She doesn't give the sort of party where she is admired because of the heaps of food that she has ostentatiously prepared, but instead she is admired just in proportion to the way she "looks as if it had taken her no time at all." As our factories move toward the ideal of eliminating human labor, our home ideals have paralleled them; the successful home-maker to-day should always look as if she had neither done any work nor would have to do any; she should produce a finished effect effortlessly, even if she has to spend all day Saturday rehearsing the way in which she will serve an effortless Sunday-morning breakfast. The creativity that is expected of her is a creativity of management of an assembly-line, not of materials lovingly fashioned into food and clothes for children. She shops, she markets, she chooses, she transports, she integrates, she co-ordinates, she fits little bits of time together so as "to get through the week," and her proudest boast often has to be "It was a good week. Nothing went wrong."

The average young American woman is very cheeful over these tasks. They are a drain on her nervous energy rather than on her physical strength, time-consuming rather than back-breaking; in her incredibly clean and polished home, her kitchen where the handle of the egg-beater matches the step-ladder in color, she moves lightly, producing the miracle dishes that will make her husband and children happy and strong. Two things mar her happiness, however: the fear that even though she never has any time, she is not perhaps doing a full-time job, and the fact that although she, like her brother, was taught that the right to choose a job is every American's sacred right, she doesn't feel that she chose this one. She chose wifehood and motherhood, but she did not necessarily choose to "keep house." That, in the phrasing of contemporary America, is thrust upon her becaue she is a woman; it is not a full status to be proudly chosen, but a duty that one cannot avoid and still find happiness in marriage. Women who have jobs ask her what she is doing and she says, "Nothing," or, "Just keeping house." Eighty hours a week of work, a sitter perhaps one evening a week, great loneliness as she rushes through the work that no other woman now shares, with an eye on the children as they play, hurrying so as to look "fresh and rested" when her husband comes home.

As we have narrowed the home, excluded from it the grandmother, the unmarried sister, the unmarried daughter, and—as part of the same process of repudiating any sharing of a home with another adult—the domestic servant has vanished, we have multiplied the number of homes in which the whole life of the family has to be integrated each day, meals cooked, lunches packed, children bathed, doors locked, dogs walked, cats put out, food ordered, washing-machines set in motion, flowers sent to the sick, birthday-cakes baked, pocket-money sorted, mechanical refrigerators defrosted. Where one large pot of coffee once served a household of ten or twelve, there are three or four small pots to be made and watched and washed and polished. Each home has been reduced to the bare essentials—to barer essentials than most primitive people would consider possible. Only one woman's hands to feed the baby, answer the telephone, turn off the gas under the pot that is boiling over, soothe the older child who has broken a toy, and open both doors at once. She is a nutritionist, a child psychologist, an engineer, a production manager, an expert buyer, all in one. Her husband sees her as free to plan her own time, and envies her; she sees him as having regular hours, and envies him. To the degree to which they also see each other as the same kind of people, with the same tastes and the same preferences, each is to a degree dissatisfied and inclined to be impatient with the other's discontent.

It is not new in history that men and women have misunderstood each other's rôles or envied each other, but the significant aspect of the American scene is that there is a discrepancy between the way we bring up boys and girls—each to choose both a job and a marriage partner—and then stylize housekeeping as a price the girl pays without stylizing the job as the price the boy pays. Men are trained to want a job in a mill, or a mine, on a farm, in an office, on a newspaper, or on a ship as a sign of their maleness, their success, and to want a wife and children to crown that success; but women to-day are not given the same clear career-line—to want an apartment, or a semi-detached house, or a farm-house, or a walk-up, or some other kind of home, as their job. The American woman wants a husband, yes, children, yes, a home of her own—yes indeed, it's intolerable to live with other people! But housekeeping—she isn't sure she wouldn't rather "do something" after she gets married. A great proportion of men would like a different job—to have at least better pay, or higher status, or different working-conditions— but they are not asked to face the seeming discrepancy between being reared for a choice and reared to think that success matters, and also that love matters and that every one should marry, and yet not be able to feel that the mate one chooses and the job one does after marriage are independent. It is as if a man were to make a set of plans for his life—to be an accountant, or a lawyer, or a pilot —and then have to add, "Unless of course, I marry." "Why?" you ask. "Because then I'll have to be a farmer. It's better for the children, you know."

It is not that we have found any good substitute for the association between home-making and motherhood. Good nurseries and schools can put children into good settings for many hours a day, settings that are often better than the small family where two bitter little rivals may otherwise spend hours quarreling and traumatizing each other. Freezers and frozen-food services and pressure cookers make it possible to prepare meals without long hours beside a watched pot. Hospitals do care for the very ill. But the task of integrating the lives of little children, even with the help of nursery-schools, kindergartens, and play-grounds, remains a full-time charge on some woman's time. If one woman leaves the home to work, part time or full time, another woman must replace her unless the children are to suffer. The nursery-school is no answer for the child with a cold, or the child who has been exposed to some contagious disease that it has not contracted. American women have become steadily more independent, more enterprising, more efficient, less willing to be merely part of some on-going operation, more insistent that when they do paid work, they work on a strictly professional basis, with part of their personality only, and that when they keep house they must be completely in control. But the price of this autonomy has risen also. It is almost as if the pioneer dream, which led Europeans of all sorts of backgrounds to become the independent American farmer, who could turn his hand to anything—and which survives today in the perennial nostalgia for a chicken-farm, or a business where one is one's own boss—had been transferred to the women, who live it out in their homes, but without the full pleasure of feeling that this is the job as well as the husband, the routine as well as the children, that they chose.

The intensity with which the American woman with children tends to her task of home-making includes innumerable excursions out of the home, as consumer, as transportation officer of the family, as responsible citizen who must protect the environment in which her children grow up by working for better schools, better play-grounds, better public-health regulations. To the old puritan vigour of the pioneer woman is now added a recognition that the modern isolated home, just because it is so isolated, is also terribly dependent upon the community. The functions that no one woman in a home by herself can possibly discharge must somehow be organized in the community around her, and even so, mothers cannot get sick. When they do, there are no adequate ordinary social ways of meeting this major emergency in the lives of their children. But however actively a married woman with small children takes responsibility for community work, still her life is centered in, her time filled by, her home, but principally by the children. She may importune her husband to take her out, she may complain loudly of the loneliness and the boredom of housework, but she does not complain that she has nothing to do.

It is all the harder for the mother of adolescent children when the break comes, when the children leave home for school or jobs and her task is over. Every social pressure to which she is subjected tells her that she should not spoil her children's lives, that she should let them lead their own lives, that she should make them independent and self-sufficient. Yet the more faithfully she obeys these injunctions, the more she is working herself out of a job. Some day, while she is still a young woman, she will have to face a break-fast-table with only one face across it, her husband's, and she will be alone, quite alone, in a home of their own. She is out of a job; her main justification, the work for which she "gave up everything," is gone, and yet there are still two, possibly three, meals a day to get, the door to be answered, the house to be cleaned. But there are only dishes for two and floors do not need to be polished so often when there are no children's feet to track them up. She isn't completely out of a job, but she is on the shelf, kicked upstairs, given one of those placebos by which large organizations whose employees have tenure try to disguise from the employee who is still too young to be retired the fact that he ought to be. This domestic crisis is of course much more difficult if it occurs at and is reinforced by the hormonal instability and emotional fears that surround the menopause, and combine unjustified fear of the loss of physical desire with the necessary recognition of the end of reproductivity. For married American women who have had children, the fear of loss of attractiveness and the fear of becoming emotionally unstable outweigh worries about the end of reproductivity, for they have had the one or two or three children that validate their marriages and, at least consciously, do not want more.

Meanwhile the father has been facing difficulties of his own. His rôle in the maturation of his children, especially in the maturation of his son, is to be the friendly ally of the boy, to help him cut free from his mother's apron-strings. To the extent that he sympathizes with and facilitates his son's growing desires for a job and a girl, he is a good father. He must pooh-pooh the mother's anxieties, back the boy up in minor escapades, be fraternally understanding. But to the extent that he does this he runs several risks. He relives, at least in imagination, his own budding freedom as a young adult, the freedom that he traded in so young, so willingly, for the continuous unremitting work that has kept his marriage going. Remembering, he may begin to feel that he has never really lived, that he settled down too early. This feeling may be all the stronger if it comes at a time when he realizes that further advancement in job or profession is unlikely. As long as the gradient of his life was rising, he was spurred on by the great rewards that Americans find in success. But now it will rise no further, he will instead in many cases have to work simply to hold his place, a dispiriting thought. Helping his son escape from his mother further identifies his wife for him as one from whom he has, after all, never properly escaped himself into the pleasant byways of irresponsible dalliance. Seeing his wife through his son's eyes, and through the eyes of his son's friends, he discovers a new impatience with her, as the representative of finished, self-satisfied achievement. Here he is, only in middle age, and his life is over—no new love, no new fields to conquer, only emptiness ahead. So while he is not out of a job— indeed he may often be at the height of his work-strength—the very nature of the life-cycle in America is such that he feels like an old man. He may have to fight very hard to resist the impulse to break away from it all, and he may develop serious health disturbances and die prematurely.

Superficially, the problem that faces the middle-aged couple in the home of their own is that the mother's main life-task is done while she is strong and well, and she must now find some other channel for her energies and still keep her life adjusted to the habits and needs of a husband who has lived terribly closely with her in that little self-contained home, while that husband's life-task is still going full tilt. But because of the great emphasis on Youth, because Youth is the period to which both sexes look back and age holds so few rewards, both face a deeper crisis of disappointment. The crisis may be further intensified if there are deaths of aged parents to be faced, with all the complications of the disposition of a surviving parent, long months of illness, sales of houses and furniture, all of which exacerbate the conflict about growing older. Every step of this process is made more acute by the insistence that each married couple should be self-sufficient, because many such couples have forgotten how. Yet they cannot look forward to combined homes with their married children, or with their widowed or unmarried siblings. Deeply dependent upon each other in every way, they have often become so just to the extent that the marriage is a good marriage. They have become so much like a single person that, like most individuals in America, they feel the need of others to complete themselves, to reassure them that they are good, to rid them of the self-searching that comes from being left alone and the self-reproach that attends condemning others to aloneness.

There are emerging solutions to this crisis when the children leave home. Some couples attempt a last child, for which there are even affectionate slang phrases—"little postscript," "little frost blossom" —that change the tone of the old folk-phrase "change-of-life baby." To have such a child is one way of facing the extent to which the woman's life in that home, and the marriage itself, has centered on the children. The most familiar solution is for women to make much of the independence for which they have openly yearned during the time they were tied down and go in for some active voluntary work, or even go back to the work they did before they were married. But in this event they face new hazards, especially if they have lived successfully through the instabilities of the menopause. Free of their major previous responsibilities, with twenty good years ahead of them, such women may start out on a gradient that rises steeply as they become involved in community activities or the delights of a job from which they have had a long vacation. And as it is the gradient that matters so much in America, their enthusiastic new spurt may contrast sharply with their husbands' unhappy acceptance of a plateau. A daughter's marriage and permitted absorption in grandchildren may mute the wife's energetic attitude towards her new activities, but that involves a severe problem for the husband who has to face the fact that he is a grandfather. In a country that gives so few rewards to age, who wants to be a grandfather? The woman of his unlicensed day-dreams is still a slim girl in her teens, now younger than his married daughter, who with each step that she takes towards maturity puts him more definitely out of the running.

Increasingly, the more aware middle-aged couples are treating this period seriously, assaying their personal as well as their material resources, and directing their plans not towards some dim and unhoped-for retirement, but towards the next twenty years. To the extent that both are able to re-plan their lives together, they make of the crisis a step forward rather than a step back. It is probable that society will recognize this period as a period in which professional counselling is needed as much as in adolescence. For each married couple alone in a home of their own is exposed to pressures and difficulties unknown in differently organized societies. And expressive of the shifting cycle of responsibility, the young married sons and daughters sit in their own small homes and try to decide what to do about Father and Mother. This is a question that is not answered by their all taking a house together, but by finding the parents something they can be interested in. Ideally, they will readjust their lives, live independently of their children except for grave emergencies, act as sitters, which means they go in as their children go out, and finally retire to a cottage in Florida, where their children piously hope they will have a lot of friends of their own age.

ELLEN KENISTON and KENNETH KENISTON

An American Anachronism: The Image of Women and Work

The most effective forms of oppression are those with which the victim covertly cooperates. So long as coercion is exercised from without and experienced as such by the coerced, revolt is possible and ultimately probable. As the rulers of Chinese thought-reform centers know, coercion is truly effective only when its targets assent to its justice, and, more than that, accept their servitude as a part of their view of themselves. As long as American Negroes consciously or unconsciously saw themselves as an inferior race, they inevitably collaborated in their own exploitation; only the awareness of their unwitting connivance with oppression has released their energies toward relieving their second-class citizenship.

The past few years have seen renewed concern about the problems, the continuing "oppression" and the "incomplete emancipation" of American women. We have been reminded that women attend college in smaller ratio to men than thirty years ago; that sex-linked wage differentials persist in most occupations; that other industrialized countries make far better provision for working mothers; that our mass media extol the virtues of home, family and children while deprecating the working woman; that feminism in America exhausted itself with the achievement of the vote for women. Although women work in greater numbers than ever before, many professions remain closed to any but the most resolute women, and most women's jobs are concentrated in underpaid and menial positions. Compared, say with Russian society, ours makes little use of the extrafamilial talents of women, and seems to "oppress" them by pushing them simultaneously away from work and toward home and family.[1]

In seeking to explain this apparent backwardness of our society, two interpretations are frequently given. One is largely conspiratorial: in its most extreme form, it holds that women are kept oppressed by a sinister junta of reactionary psychoanalysts, Madison Avenue hucksters, and insecure husbands;[2] in more moderate statement, it stresses the role of men's vanity, weakness, or need for an "Other."[3] The second common explanation of the "problem" of American women emphasizes the absence of "objective opportunities," such as equal employment regulations, subsidies for women's education, maternity benefits, community supported day-care centers for children, more adequate domestic help, *et cetera*. Were such opportunities available, this argument runs, women would move easily outside the confines of kitchen, kaffee-klatsch and kindergarten.

Each of these explanations has something to be said for it. Advertisers clearly do have a vested interest in keeping women at home buying their products; psychoanalysts have often advanced theories of universal feminine "masochism" and "passivity" (which made it difficult to explain the undeniable intellectual talents and careers of many women psychoanalysts[4]); insecure men do frequently stand between their wives and "fulfillment" outside the home; and a majority of American (male) congressmen have shown little interest in legislation to equalize women's inferior economic position. So, too, the lack of adequate institutional support for women is clear, and clearly needs correction: the lot of working women, and especially of working mothers, could be vastly improved by changes in employment laws, by added social security benefits for maternity and by better facilities for child care. And the absence of such institutional support does indeed discourage women wno might otherwise want to do something outside their own homes.

But both these interpretations overlook what seems to us the central "problem" for most American women: namely, that most not only accept but largely desire a homebound position, and the obstacles on which they founder are less often external conditions than internal ambivalences. The vast majority of women in this country —even the vast majority of middle-class college graduates—give

1. See, for example, Betty Friedan, *The Feminine Mystique* (New York: Norton, 1963); Simone de Beauvoir, *The Second Sex* (New York: Knopf, 1953); and the Spring, 1964, issue of *Daedalus* [Kenistons' note].

2. Friedan, *op. cit.* [Kenistons' note].

3. De Beauvoir, *op. cit.* [Kenistons' note].

4. See Marie Bonaparte, *Female Sexuality* (New York: International Universities Press, 1956) for an extreme case [Kenistons' note].

love, marriage and family supreme priority over "career." If they are indignant or resentful, it is most often over the social or personal situation that requires them to work, and far more rarely over either the pressures that impede their working or the injustices of their situation in work. Whether they work to supplement their husbands' incomes (the reason given by most working-class women), to relieve the boredom of empty houses once children are in school, or, as widowed, divorced, separated or unmarried women, simply to earn a living, most women work because they must, and would gladly exchange their "careers" for the life of a happily-married, financially-secure wife-and-mother. If working-class high school girls are asked about their ideal life, they tell of a dream-cottage with successful husband and many children: there is no mention of work. And even in elite women's colleges, many, and perhaps most, girls consider any pressure to plan seriously for a career an unwanted distraction from their main emotional concern—finding husbands and beginning their lives as wives-and-mothers. Despite the fact that eight or nine out of every ten American women will be employed at some time during their lives, probably the same proportion in some part of themselves dislikes, even detests, the thought of working.

Resentment and indignation at the social barriers to complete emancipation are not widespread. They tend to be concentrated among a relatively small group of highly educated professional women, many of whom have succeeded in overcoming these real barriers and in finding interesting and even "fulfilling" jobs because they were unambivalently determined to do so. Indeed, if anything like a majority of American women felt a small part of their resentment and indignation, the social barriers would soon crumble before the pressure. If even a quarter of the electorate (half of the women) was willing to vote with some selectivity for candidates who favored equal employment opportunities for women, subsidies for women's education, maternity benefits, women's employment rights and community-supported child-care centers, it would take but a decade before these easily envisioned goals were attained. But there is no consistent demand; these are rarely live political issues; most women "fulfill their potential" outside the home reluctantly, if at all. If there is a "problem" for women in America today, it is that they work only of necessity or by default; if women remain unemancipated, theirs is a largely voluntary servitude.

It is therefore an oversimplification to trace the causes of women's homebound situation solely to masculine prejudice and to seek a solution of the problem only in improvements in social opportunities. Behind both masculine prejudice and women's homebound situation lie enormous historical changes that have pushed the American woman into an unprecedented social and human situation; and behind the inability of American women to create better social conditions for themselves lie anachronistic images of woman-liness and work, defensively reasserted by women themselves. How has the situation of American women changed in the past genera-tions? And why do outmoded definitions of womanliness and work persist despite these radical changes?

The Unprecedented Situation of American Women

Consider the life-situation of the average woman in all societies two hundred years ago, and in most nonindustrial societies today. None of the "problems of modern woman" could possibly arise: to survive, society had no choice but to require women to spend their lives as guardians of the home and of the next generation. In any community where the average life-span is thirty to forty years and infant mortality approaches fifty percent, mere maintenance of the population requires that adult women devote all of their time to bearing children. Moreover, what to do with "the later years" is hardly a problem: most women are dead long before they reach the end of their fertility, and those few who survive are usually so ex-hausted from childbearing that they have little energy available for "a later career." And even if a singular woman wanted to have only a few children, knowledge of contraception was so limited that she had no way of doing it short of refusing all men.

Furthermore, high birth and death rates have usually gone hand in hand with a kind of family organization that gave a woman more than enough to do *within* her family. In most societies, the family, not the individual, was the basic unit of the economy, and women have had to work for and within families in order to survive. The peasant wife must share the tasks of the land with her husband; the wife of the hunter must clean and store her husband's game; the shepherd's wife must help to guard the herds. Even today on old-fashioned farms a wife is essential to care for domestic animals, can and store food for the winter, and maintain the domestic side of farm life. In a few complex and highly differentiated societies, of course, small groups of leisured aristocratic women have existed; but these women have often become, as Veblen pointed out, status sym-bols for their husbands; and much of their energy has traditionally gone toward maintaining the visible signs of leisure and affluence that would provide continual reminders of their husbands' wealth and power. Historically, then, women have always worked, but at the tasks of the family economy, not outside it.

The industrial revolution, however, brought a series of changes that created a "problem" where none could have existed before. Advances in medicine and public health have decreased the infant mortality rate and lengthened the life-span; changes in economic organization have all but destroyed the family as an economic unit.

Women began to work outside the home primarily in response to these economic and social changes. Thoughts of self-fulfillment, always an aristocratic ideal, were far from the minds of the first women in the mills of England and Germany in the eighteenth and nineteenth centuries; for them factory labor was an unwanted economic necessity. To be sure, the physical conditions of life were probably better in the new mill towns than they had been for the peasantry; but the "alienated" labor of the women factory worker was psychologically far more arduous than tilling fields that had been tended by the same family for generations. Working women in the early industrial period must have looked back with nostalgia to the lives of their own peasant mothers, for whom work and family were part of an unfragmented whole. For the vast majority of working women, work outside the family began as a deprivation, as a necessity, as part of the loss of peasant family life; and these meanings of work persist to the present.

The medical and technological advances made possible by the industrial revolution have of course borne full fruit only in the past two generations. Only now has infant mortality been sufficiently lowered and the life-span enough increased so that social survival is fully compatible with widespread family limitation. A modern American woman can rightly anticipate that her children will survive into adulthood, and that she herself will live into her mid-seventies. Modern medical care makes bearing children less dangerous, and modern conveniences make caring for them less onerous. Furthermore, any woman who wants to limit the size of her family has available a variety of contraceptive techniques; and the population explosion suggests that family limitation, formerly the route to social suicide, has on the contrary become a prerequisite for social survival. Technology advances have both freed and deprived women of the need to devote their lives to procreation and child care.

The impact on women of these technological advances has been shaped by equally unprecedented changes in the family.[5] Consider the family's increasing sociological "isolation." Formerly, husband, wife and their children were embedded in a network of extended family relationships—cousins, aunts, uncles, grandparents and grandchildren who lived together and functioned as a social and economic unit. Now, increasingly, parents and their offspring live apart and separate, isolated both geographically and psychologically from wider family ties. In societies with extended family systems,

5. For a fuller account of American family structure, see Talcott Parsons, "The Kinship System of the Contemporary United States," Chap. XI in *Essays in Sociological Theory Pure and Applied* (Glencoe: Free Press, 1949); and "The American Family: its Relations to Personality and to the Social Structure," Chap. I in T. Parsons and F. Bales, *Family, Socialization and Interaction Process* (Glencoe: Free Press, 1955) [Kenistons' note].

surviving older women can be socially useful by caring for their grandchildren, nieces and nephews. But in our society a woman must anticipate that her adult children will leave her to establish new homes of their own, often far from her; and any older woman who assumes a maternal role with anyone but her own children is usually told, subtly or directly, that she is neither wanted nor needed. Furthermore, the isolation and the small size of American families mean that all emotional ties within the family are inevitably concentrated on a smaller number of people and, in that measure, intensified. The absence of aunts, grandmothers, female cousins and the like within the immediate family gives the mother an added centrality as the *only* female model available to her daughters during their early years—a point to which we will return.

In addition, the family's functions have been drastically reduced in the last century. The family is no longer the chief productive unit of society: only in a declining number of old-style farms or small retail stores do husband and wife share a family economic task; instead, for the vast majority of Americans of all classes, the "isolated" family is tied to the economic system solely through its breadwinner's work. To be sure, the older notion of husband and wife working "side by side" in a common task often recurs as a dream or hope; but for most women it is a practical impossibility. Even those rare couples today who manage to work as a team usually do so outside the home; and most can testify how hard it is to maintain such a husband-wife team in a society that normally considers their marriage relationship detrimental to their objectivity, performance and achievement on the job. Work is no longer a family affair; the "home workshop" has become a place to play; both women and men sharply separate family and work.

What is left for a woman is of course her role as "homemaker," "wife-and-mother," nurturer and upbringer of her children. But even here her job has been drastically reduced. Labor-saving devices and modern homes, advances in the packaging and processing of food, the introduction of electricity, running water, bathrooms, refrigeration and telephones into American life, all mean that a woman's housework can be quickly done unless she is truly determined to make a full-time job of housecleaning and cooking. Nor can bringing up children be counted on to occupy a woman's life, for in the past two centuries the family has relinquished many of its child-rearing functions to schools. In a technological society, teaching children adult skills is too complex and essential a task to leave to idiosyncratic families; we therefore remove children from their parents for the better part of the day and "socialize" them in schools where more standardized learning is guaranteed. This approach again both frees women and deprives them of their traditional role as those who teach children the complex skills of adulthood; it leave mothers responsible for the full-time care of their children for only five or six years.

Finally, new demands on men in their work directly increase the pressures on women. Over the past few generations, men's jobs have become increasingly specialized, increasingly distant from any visible relationship to a useful finished product, more and more demanding of technical skill, expertise, "rationality," and the suppression of emotion, fantasy and passion on the job. More and more, men work "to earn a living," and the real "living" for which they work is increasingly sought within the family, kept separate from the working world by physical distance and social convention. After marriage, the average woman sees nothing of her husband during the working-and-commuting day; and middle-class wives with "successful" husbands often do without their spouses evenings and weekends as well. To make a "career" of marriage is psychologically difficult when one's husband is away for eighty percent of one's waking hours.

And when men are with their wives, they usually need them to make up for what is lacking in their jobs. Like our ideals of recreation, our ideals of family life are defined by contrast with the demands of our working day. In home or recreation, women are expected to fill the emotional lacunae in their husbands' jobs and to relieve the pressures and tensions they come home with. In family or fun, the good wife should be spontaneous, warm, caring, emotionally responsive, not too practical or intellectual and somewhat passive, yet at the same time consoling and supportive when necessary. Above all, she should not be aggressive, initiating, intellectual, analytic, ambitious or in any other way encourage talents or qualities in herself that might remind her husband of the working world he comes home to forget.

In every nation with an advanced industrial technology, similar changes in medical care, family life and the demands of work have, as in America, begun to alter the situation of women and to create a "problem" where none could have existed two generations ago. But in most other industrial nations the impact of these social changes on women has been attenuated by strong centers of opposition to the new industrial order. Most often, opposition has sprung from traditional institutions and values that long antedated industrialism: in France, the Church and the peasantry; in Japan, "feudal" patterns of familial and social interdependence; in England, an entrenched class system. In each case, these traditional institutions have preserved competing models of family and woman, so that women who remained loyal to the Church, the extended family, or their social class could often be relatively unaffected by the new demands of industrialism. But in America, a nation without a "feudal" past, without an entrenched class system, without an established church or an aristocratic tradition, the impact of industrial society on women has been unusually thoroughgoing and intense.

The lack of an aristocratic tradition in this country is especially important in explaining the special stresses on American women. Traditionally, in Europe, women of the upper classes have had enough leisure and freedom from family needs to permit them, if they chose, to "work" outside their homes. Those who did choose to work gradually developed a positive definition of woman's work, at first concerned with matters charitable and educational, then artistic and intellectual, and finally even scientific or political—a model that in part counterbalanced the negative images of prostitutes, servants and factory workers. But in this country, where aristocratic traditions were weak and highly suspect and where most upper-class women devoted themselves not to intellectual attainment but to ostentatious display, no countervailing image of woman's work could develop. Most American women continue to view work as at best a necessity, to be avoided if possible and borne with resignation if required.

Countless other factors contribute to the special stresses on American women. Industrialization and specialization have been more thoroughgoing here than abroad, and the resulting pressures on the family, on women, and men's demands on women, have been correspondingly more intense. Our national reverence for youth helps make it difficult for women (or men) to plan realistically for a time in life when neither they nor their children will be young. So, too, our traditional distrust of grand ideologies has inoculated most Americans against that continuing enthusiasm for feminist ideals that exists in other nations. Together, these factors have cooperated to push American women into the vanguard of social change; and it may always be the lot of those who must face an unprecedented historical situation without signposts, models or maps to suffer the most intensely and to blame themselves for their "problems." Without adequate signposts, a vanguard inevitably falls back on outdated guides. In this case, definitions of family, conceptions of womanliness and images of work left over from an era when they were necessary for social survival and congruent with family function have persisted into an era in which they are no longer viable. The result of this cultural lag is the "problem" of American women.

From Generation to Generation

"Cultural lag" is of course not so much an explanation as a description, and only by examining the reasons why archaic definitions of womanliness have persisted can we understand the ambivalence and reluctance with which most American women confront the need for life outside the family. We cannot hope to deal here with all of the social, cultural and historical factors that have contributed to preserve more traditional ideals of woman's role, nor can we consider the enormous variety of outlooks on womanliness in different sectors of American society. Instead we will concentrate on the transmission of images of femininity and masculinity from generation to generation within the family.

The fundamental processes involved in learning the lessons of gender are fairly constant in American society. An American girl first learns what it means to be a woman at her mother's knee. She may decide to be like her mother, not to be like her mother, to be like her in some ways and not in other ways; she may even believe she has completely forgotten her mother and set out on a new path of her own; but in the background her conscious and unconscious assessment of her mother's life, of its joys, satisfactions, virtues and failings, almost always remains central. In determining this assessment, the mother's conception of her own adequacy as a woman is of enormous importance, but equally momentous is the father's conscious and unconscious conception of his wife. In most stable marriages, these two judgments are (or soon become) complementary; and in our small and "isolated" families where mother and father are the only two adults present to a small girl, their consensus is especially decisive in forming the daughter's view of her sex. So, too, from their parents American girls also learn the meanings of masculinity and, by repeated admonition and example, the precise boundaries between what is desirably "ladylike" and what is undesirably "boyish." Again, if the parents feel and act in concert, these early lessons become so deeply ingrained that they persist unconsciously even for adult women who consciously deny their validity.

Beyond these commonplaces of the learning of sex roles, there are vast differences among American families, differences related to individual idiosyncrasy, to ethnicity and social class, to region and religion. But, despite these differences, we know enough of how our society has changed in the last two generations to reconstruct a more or less "typical" pattern of development. Very few of the grandmothers of today's young women worked outside their families; rather, as did ninety percent of late Victorian women of all classes in America, they devoted themselves to the care of children, home and husband. In such a family, a daughter was likely to inherit from both mother and father an unambivalent definition of womanliness, which glorified domestic virtues and saw outside work as an unequivocal "fall" to menial status, factory exploitation, or— the ultimate fall—prostitution. The "outside world" was quintessentially masculine; and the sharp lines that separated male and female partly served to protect "innocent" women from a side of life and of themselves seen as potentially dangerous, wild and promiscuous.[6]

In our grandparents' day, this splitting of existence into a dangerous, masculine outside world and a sheltered, protected feminine domestic world was still workable. But for a woman born at the turn of the century and married in the 1920's, the situation began to change. Although she herself may have initially accepted her parents' view of womanhood, the rapid change in the objective conditios of women's lives—the dissipation of the extended family, the lengthening of the life-span, the introduction of laborsaving devices —all these meant that the definition of womanhood that satisfied her mother was less likely to satisfy her. New economic pressures, new job opportunities for women and her own lengthening life-span made it more likely that she would work at some point in her life —either to supplement the family income or to relieve her boredom in a spotless but empty house.

But the fact of working rarely meant joy in working. Given their upbringing, few women were psychologically prepared to enter a "man's world" without inner conflict. In the absence of any positive image of women's work, all ways of construing a job were fraught with difficulty; to find satisfaction in a job inevitably meant to find something heretofore defined as a male prerogative, and often resulted in a feeling of loss of womanliness; not to find satisfaction in one's work—and still to work—meant to risk reduction to the role of a menial in one's own eyes. In either case, working seemed to mean not being as good as one's mother, who had "made a go" of a purely domestic life.

Furthermore, husbands of the last generation were rarely happy about wives who moved outside the family. Remembering their own mothers (who had stayed at home), they could seldom confront their wives' outside jobs without feelings of inadequacy. And should the wife work—whether as volunteer or as paid employee—in order to relieve her own frustration and boredom within an empty home, then the husband's guilt and fear would usually be even greater, for this suggested that he, compared to his father, was less able to "satisfy" his wife, to "provide for her" a marriage within which she felt "fulfilled"—with all the myriad sexual and economic implications

---

6. The "outside" male world was thus equated with two of the basic forces in instinctual life, aggression and sexuality; and its dangers and attractions for women grew partly out of the negative and positive aspects of these forces. Negatively, women feared the "aggressiveness" and the "promiscuity" in this world and themselves, as epitomized by the "aggressive" career woman, the "promiscuous" fallen woman, or as fused in the prostitute. But positively, they dseired a right to be "active" in work and to end the double standard in sexual matters. It was, and still is, difficult for women (like men) not to fear that by seeking these legitimate goals they were also seeking illicit ones, and consequently to "solve" their dilemma by seeking neither [Kenistons' note].

of these terms. Men, like women, tended to see work as an exclusively male prerogative; and they felt easily unmanned by wives who entered any but a small number of traditionally feminine jobs, such as nursing.

Nor should we overlook the real elements of masculine identification and rivalry in women which were fostered by Victorian definitions of sex roles. The "outside world" of the Victorian male was seen as not only dangerous and wild, but intensely interesting, free and exciting; and the protected "inside world" of Victorian women had its custodial and even imprisoning side. Many a daughter of a Victorian family covertly scorned the domestic docility of her mother and, in her own quest for freedom and excitement, secretly envied and identified with men. Those few who acted on their envy had to accept society's explicit judgment that their demeanor was "mannish" and its unstated suspicion that their behavior was "loose." But most women guiltily suppressed whatever "mannish" and "loose" aspirations they had, and, by compulsive conscious attachment to a "homely" role, denied—even to themselves—the existence of these aspirations.

A young woman of today is most likely to have grown up in a family in which her mother, if she worked, felt at some level inadequate or guilty about it, and if she did not work, felt frustration and resentment at the boredom of her homebound life. Her father was usually made subtly uneasy by whatever domestic discontents or career aspirations his wife had, and appreciated her most in her homely role. Such attitudes are of course rarely stated as such, but they are nonetheless expressed in countless indirect ways, and are the more powerful because, unstated, they are the harder to confront or oppose. A mother's look of remorse as she leaves for work, her fear of "neglecting" her children, her resentment of her need to work, her failure to discuss her work at home—these are far more expressive than any open discussion of her ambivalence. And a father's deprecation of "mannish" women, his praise for the "truly feminine," and his dislike of women in his own work more effectively tell his daughter what he desires from her than any lecture could. Most fathers and mothers of the last generation implicitly agreed in blaming women for their inability to be happy in a narrowly defined wife-and-mother role, and in seeing women who wanted to work as really wanting to wear the pants.

As often happens, the assumptions and conflicts of parents form the unconscious substratum of inner conflict in their children; the stage was thus set for a continuing, although often unconscious, ambivalence about the relationship between work and womanliness in this generation. But, ironically, both emulation of one's mother and rivalry with her have often led in practice to the same determination to excel in a homely role. The woman who strongly identifies with the best in her mother has usually come unconsciously to define the best as the domestic; the woman who seeks to avoid her mother's failings has usually learned to attribute women's failings to their inability to find fulfillment within the family. And not least of all, many women who naturally enough envy and identify themselves with men's work and freedom cannot admit this envy to themselves because it seems a denial of their femininity; and they often devote themselves to home and family with a passion born partly from fear of their latent discontents.[7]

These same psychological themes can of course lead to very different outcomes in behavior.[8] But it is a rare working woman in whom inner conflict does *not* complicate the practical problems of combining marriage and career, for whom working is *not* accompanied by silent questions about her adequacy and by implicit apprehension about her "envy" of men, and who does *not* at some level consider a career a denial rather than an expression of femininity. On the other hand, few women are able to make a full and lifetime job from reduced family roles—and to remain satisfied and content in their later years. Not surprisingly, those who have escaped inner conflict have been most often recruited from atypical circumstances —from upper-class families or from European backgrounds[9] where a more positive conception of women's work prevails.

A woman's sense of what it is to be a woman, although founded on her relationships with her parents, is of course much more than this. But for most American girls the familistic lessons of their childhoods are merely reinforced by their later education. The curriculum of American schools is primarily oriented toward what are thought to be the special talents of boys, and this emphasis convinces girls that they are not "really good" at the things that matter in the world of men. So, too, girls soon learn that "popularity"— that peculiar American ecstasy from which all other goods flow—accrues to her who hides any intelligence she may have, flatters the often precarious maleness of adolescent boys, and devotes herself to activities that can in no way challenge their sex. The popular girls in high schools are seldom the brilliant girls; or if they are, it is only because they are so brilliant they can hide their brilliance from less

7. Even those women who sympathized with their mothers' plight and blamed their fathers for unduly constricting her often resolved to avoid this plight merely by finding a husband who *would* provide the love (and/or money) to support a wife at home, thus continuing the basic pattern of domesticity [Kenistons' note].

8. For excellent clinical descriptions of the varied solutions to the "problem" of femininity, see Helene Deutsch, *The Psychology of Women* (New York: Grune and Stratton, 1944–1945), esp. Vol. I, Chaps. V and VIII. Deutsch by and large interprets these solutions within an orthodox psychoanalytic framework. For an interpretation that stresses the importance of cultural factors, see Karen Horney, *New Ways in Psychoanalysis* (New York: Norton, 1939), esp. Chap. VI, "Feminine Psychology" [Kenistons' note].

9. For example, a remarkable number of women of outstanding scholarly achievement in this country were born in Europe [Kenistons' note].

brilliant boys.[1] Any girl whose parents support her in an early commitment to a career outside those few that are deemed unthreateningly feminine often spends many miserable years in a public school system. Indeed, most American public schools (like many private schools) make a girl with passionate intellectual interests feel a strong sense of her own inadequacy as a woman, feel guilty about these "masculine" outlooks, perhaps even wonder about her own normality.

At best, adolescence should provide a second chance in life, an opportunity to reassess childhood self-definitions, envies and identifications and to seek out new models of selfhood more appropriate to capacities and opportunities. But as we argued earlier, American society provides few models adequate to the situation of modern women. On the whole, mass media and popular fiction continue to portray career women as mannish, loose, or both; and the happy ending for working girls still involves abandoning work, marrying and having many children—and there the story ends.[2] So, too, many of the potential models have been systematically debunked by the misapplication of psychiatric judgments; thus, few outstanding women have been spared the implication that their achievements spring primarily from neurosis.[3] And the most immediate models of working women available to girls during adolescence—their teachers —are too often unmarried women who have had to pay a high human price for their work. Thus, the selective reorganization and redefinition of childhood images of womanhood that *could* take place during adolescence rarely occur; and during her late teens and early twenties, many a girl who might otherwise be capable of more merely confirms her surrender to the pressures for popularity. Adequate models of adult identification can sustain one against strong internal and social pressure; when they are absent, one surrenders at the first push.

Paradoxically, then, the effect of new technology, of changes in family structure and function, has been to make many—probably most—women even *more* determined to make a go of a wife-and-mother role which objective conditions daily undermine more completely. Most young women in this country still cherish the fantasy of a marriage that will totally and automatically fulfill all emotional and intellectual needs, a fantasy that sets the stage for colossal disappointment, guilt and self-castigation when—as increasingly happens—marriage alone is not enough. So, too, most remain enor-

1. James S. Coleman, *The Adolescent Society* (Glencoe: Free Press, 1961), esp. Chap. VI [Kenistons' note].

2. Friedan, *op. cit.*, Chap. II, has an excellent analysis of the portrayal of working women in women's magazines [Kenistons' note].

3. Cf. F. Lundberg and M. F. Farnham, *Modern Woman: The Lost Sex* (New York: Grosset's Universal Library, 1947), esp. Chap. VII, for an especially vicious treatment of feminists [Kenistons' note].

mously ambivalent about the thought of working, to say nothing of finding a "vocation" in work; and even those who secretly enjoy their jobs often find it easier to blame their extrafamilial life on financial need than to admit, even to themselves, that they want or enjoy it. Although the dream-cottage with the built-in totally fulfilling wife-and-mother role has been destroyed by a changing society, most women cling tenaciously and sometimes defensively to this older image and blame themselves for the cracks in the picture window.

Womanliness and Work

Assuming that our characterization is adequate, what can be done? Or, indeed, need anything be done? One rejoinder would be to argue that be freely choosing to devote themselves entirely to their husbands and families, women are merely expressing a deeply feminine outlook. But against this, recall that any American woman who has had a family of three children by the time she is thirty years old and who lives to the age of seventy-five will have forty years of her adult life that can*not* under any circumstances be spent primarily in child care. Furthermore, the disappearance of the family as a productive unit means that a woman has few economic functions to perform within the home. Cleaning, cooking, and caring for older children are, even for the most compulsive housewife and conscientious mother, at best part-time occupations. For a girl to dream only of being a happy wife-and-mother thus is a gross denial of reality, a motivated refusal to confront the kind of life she will actually lead.

Furthermore, the choice most women make can hardly be said to be "free" in the psychological sense. We have argued that identification, rivalry, emulation, fear and guilt often make it psychologically impossible for women to respond to changed social conditions, to seize the opportunities that do exist or to fight for those that do not. Thus we return to the proposition from which we began: the failure of most American women to exploit the potentials open to them or to struggle to create new opportunities stems in large part from their own inner conflicts, from archaic images of womanhood and from family patterns that subtly but effectively discourage commitment to vocation. If our society has not yet availed itself of the talents of women, it is largely because women themselves feel they must hide their talents under a bushel.

Nor can the choice of the wife-and-mother role to the exclusion of all else be seen as merely a "natural" expression of the "eternal feminine," of woman's biological role as bearer and nurturer of the next generation. To be sure, a woman's capacity for biological creativity is and must be central to many of her fundamental concerns, affecting her life-style, her personal relations, her conceptions of time, even her orientation to space. But women express their wom- anliness differently in every culture; and in our own culture they often express it in ways less than adequate to meet their unprece- dented situation. Women need not abandon their distinguishing womanliness: even now, there are the many exceptions to these remarks who are sufficiently free of inner conflict to realize their womanliness both within their families and in useful work outside their homes. The problem is how to open this option to all women.

What, then, can be done to alter the prevailing outmoded defini- tions of the good life for women? We have already mentioned one major line of improvement—the development of social institutions to support and encourage those women who want or need to work. But if our analysis is correct, an even deeper problem than the lack of opportunities is the lack of unambivalent motivation. And the process of generational identification, emulation and rivalry upon which such lack of motivation is based are difficult to change by direct social intervention. What parents communicate to their daughters about womanhood, work and femininity can only be af- fected indirectly, by changing other social agencies, ideologies and models, which may in turn affect patterns of family influence, inter- action and identification.

This is not a small or simple task, but some of the ways it might be done can be anticipated. For one, the facts we have here empha- sized should be continually reiterated to both young men and young women: that most women *will* work, that society has changed so as to make *impossible* the kind of fulfillment within the family that earlier generations found; that unless they work most women—sin- gle or married—will find themselves during the greater part of their adulthood with nothing to do. Educational authorities, mass media, school, all can cooperate in emphasizing the difficulties in an older conception of womanhood and the objective possibilities open to women today.

Women's conceptions of their potentials might also be changed by altering the demands that men—their fathers and husbands— make upon them. Unlike all other "oppressed" groups, women live on terms of intimate interdependence with their alleged oppressors, and this interdependance means that if the lives of men are grossly lacking in some crucial quality, their women will be impelled to develop compensating and opposite qualities. Thus, as we argued earlier, many of the pressures that men exert on their wives and daughters ultimately spring from the lacks in their own work. Could we but make work more humane and more challenging for men, asking less of their patience and more of their imagination, it would be less necessary for women to compensate for what is missing on the job by being passively "feminine" in the home. As it is, a man whose work is essentially dull, monotonous and *unfulfilling* can be only threatened when his wife seeks "self-fulfillment" in her work.

But perhaps the greatest leverage for changing the image of women and their potential could be gained by providing more viable models of womanhood to girls in adolescence. In every community, there are some women who feel little inner conflict between their commitments to their families and their vocations, who manage both with equal womanliness. The existence of such women must be brought to the attention of adolescent girls searching for models for the future. At present, most adolescent girls are confronted with two equally unsatisfactory models—spinster teachers, sometimes embittered, mannish and overly intellectual, and women like their mothers, who usually have the many conflicts about work and womanliness we have discussed. If a third model could be available as well—as housemothers, teachers, advisors and friends— a model that epitomizes marriage *and* career instead of marriage or career, more adolescent girls and young women might break out of these sterile alternatives. We Americans are not an ideological people, and our pragmatism demands visible proof of the possibility of what we advocate.[4] Such proof exists in every community, and were it consistently brought to the attention of girls in the process of defining their future lives as women, they might be better able to avoid the literally impossible alternatives in whose terms many now shape their futures.[5]

All this implies a vision of the possibilities available to women for the first time in history. We would hopefully envisage a society that was not an androgenous world in which men and women were as similar as anatomically possible,[6] but one in which women could make what Erik Erikson calls their "inner space"[7] and their attitude toward their inner creativity felt in the outer world as well—and

4. Americans, habitually a nonideological and empirical people, have usually been more influenced by exemplary figures than by explicit ideologies, and we feel that adolescent girls who might be suspicious of ideological feminism could still admire women who embodied its virtues. See Carl N. Degler, "Revolution without Ideology: The Changing Place of Women in America," *Daedalus* (Spring, 1964) [Kenistons' note].

5. Although we have here stressed changing women's view of womanliness and work, it is equally important that men, who are after all the sons, husbands and fathers of women, should alter their conceptions as well. Any attack on the problem would fail unless it came to terms with the inevitable complementarity of expectations of men and women.

6. Here we disagree with those who would push the social similarity of men and women as far as anatomically possible. This seems to us to ignore the many subtle nonanatomical differences between the sexes and to be potentially dangerous for the sexual identification of children, which largely depends on having parents whose behavior is consistently gender-typed. And even if it were psychologically possible and harmless, a maximally androgenous world would seem to us an undesirably ugly one. Rather than attempt to become more similar, we feel men and women should learn to exploit and enjoy their complementarities in wider areas of life. For an able advocacy of androgeny, however, see Alice S. Rossi, "Equality between the Sexes: An Immodest Proposal," *Daedalus* (Spring, 1964) [Kenistons' note].

7. "Inner and Outer Space: Reflections on Womanhood," *Daedalus* (Spring, 1964) [Kenistons' note].

men could learn to enjoy it. We would hope that women who saw the need to extend their life-space beyond the family would become not less but more womanly in consequence; that in time they would evolve new ways of expressing, rather than denying, their womanliness in their work; and that the result would be a betterment of work for both men and women. We would hope that Americans of both sexes could gradually abandon outdated images of masculinity and femininity without ceasing to rejoice in the difference. And we would hope that women who were emancipated from voluntary servitude to anachronistic images of "femininity" could abandon out-moded alternatives for more appropriate alternations between the traditional inner world of children and family and new efforts to realize the virtues of this inner world outside the home. Thus, we would hope, the fruitful mutuality and interdependence of men and women that has always existed in love might be extended in the works of society.

ADRIENNE RICH

When We Dead Awaken: Writing as Re-Vision

Ibsen's *When We Dead Awaken* is a play about the use that the male artist and thinker—in the process of creating culture as we know it—has made of women, in his life and in his work; and about a woman's slow struggling awakening to the use to which her life has been put. Bernard Shaw wrote in 1900 of this play: "[Ibsen] shows us that no degradation ever devized or permitted is as disastrous as this degradation; that through it women can die into luxuries for men and yet can kill them; that men and women are becoming conscious of this: and that what remains to be seen as perhaps the most interesting of all imminent social developments is what will happen 'when we dead awaken.' "[1]

It's exhilarating to be alive in a time of awakening consciousness; it can also be confusing, disorienting, and painful. This awakening of dead or sleeping consciousness has already affected the lives of millions of women, even those who don't know it yet. It is also affecting the lives of men, even those who deny its claims upon them. The argument will go on whether an oppressive economic class system is responsible for the oppressive nature of male/female relations, or whether, in fact, the sexual class system is the original model on which all the others are based. But in the last few years connections have been drawn between our sexual lives and our political institutions which are inescapable and illuminating. The

---

1. G. B. Shaw, *The Quintessence of Ibsenism* (New York: Hill & Wang, 1959), p. 139.

sleepwalkers are coming awake, and for the first time this awakening has a collective reality; it is no longer such a lonely thing to open one's eyes.

Re-vision—the act of looking back, of seeing with fresh eyes, of entering an old text from a new critical direction—is for us more than a chapter in cultural history: it is an act of survival. Until we can understand the assumptions in which we are drenched we cannot know ourselves. And this drive to self-knowledge, for woman, is more than a search for identity: it is part of her refusal of the destructiveness of male-dominated society. A radical critique of literature, feminist in its impulse, would take the work first of all as a clue to how we live, how we have been living, how we have been led to imagine ourselves, how our language has trapped as well as liberated us; and how we can begin to see—and therefore live—afresh. A change in the concept of sexual identity is essential if we are not going to see the old political order reassert itself in every new revolution. We need to know the writing of the past, and know it differently than we have ever known it; not to pass on a tradition but to break its hold over us.

For writers, and at this moment for women writers in particular, there is the challenge and promise of a whole new psychic geography to be explored. But there is also a difficult and dangerous walking on the ice, as we try to find language and images for a consciousness we are just coming into, and with little in the past to support us. I want to talk about some aspects of this difficulty and this danger.

Jane Harrison, the great classical anthropologist, wrote in 1914 in a letter to her friend Gilbert Murray: "By the by, about 'Women,' it has bothered me often—why do women never want to write poetry about Man as a sex—why is Woman a dream and a terror to man and not the other way around? . . . Is it mere convention and propriety, or something deeper?"[2] I think Jane's question cuts deep into the myth-making tradition, the romantic tradition; deep into what women and men have been to each other; and deep into the psyche of the woman writer. Thinking about that question, I began thinking of the work of two twentieth-century women poets, Sylvia Plath and Diane Wakoski. It strikes me that in the work of both Man appears as, if not a dream, a fascination, and a terror; and that the source of the fascination and the terror is, simply, Man's power —to dominate, tyrannize, choose or reject the woman. The charisma of Man seems to come purely from his power over her, and his control of the world by force; not from anything fertile or life-giving in him. And, in the work of both these poets, it is finally the

2. Jessie G. Stewart, *Jane Ellen Harrison: A Portrait from Letters* (London: Merlin Press, 1959), pp. 140–41.

woman's sense of *herself*—embattled, possessed—that gives the poetry its dynamic charge, its rhythms of struggle, need, will and female energy. Convention and propriety are perhaps not the right words, but until recently this female anger, this furious awareness of the Man's power over her, were not available materials to the female poet, who tended to write of Love as the source of her suffering, and to view that victimization by Love as an almost inevitable fate. Or, like Marianne Moore and Elizabeth Bishop, she kept human sexual relationships at a measured and chiselled distance in her poems.

One answer to Jane Harrison's question has to be that historically men and women have played very different parts in each others' lives. Where woman has been a luxury for man, and has served as the painter's model and the poet's muse, but also as comforter, nurse, cook, bearer of his seed, secretarial assistant, and copyist of manuscripts, man has played a quite different role for the female artist. Henry James repeats an incident which the writer Prosper Mérimée described, of how, while he was living with George Sand,

he once opened his eyes, in the raw winter dawn, to see his companion, in a dressing-gown, on her knees before the domestic hearth, a candlestick beside her and a red *madras* round her head, making bravely, with her own hands, the fire that was to enable her to sit down betimes to urgent pen and paper. The story represents him as having felt that the spectacle chilled his ardor and tried his taste; her appearance was unfortunate, her occupation an inconsequence, and her industry a reproof—the result of all of which was a lively irritation and an early rupture.[3]

I am suggesting that the specter of this kind of male judgment, along with the active discouragement and thwarting of her needs by a culture controlled by males, has created problems for the woman writer: problems of contact with herself, problems of language and style, problems of energy and survival.

In rereading Virginia Woolf's *A Room of One's Own* for the first time in some years, I was astonished at the sense of effort, of pains taken, of dogged tentativeness, in the tone of that essay. And I recognized that tone. I had heard it often enough, in myself and in other women. It is the tone of a woman almost in touch with her anger, who is determined not to appear angry, who is *willing* herself to be calm, detached, and even charming in a roomful of men where things have been said which are attacks on her very integrity. Virginia Woolf is addressing an audience of women, but she is acutely conscious—as she always was—of being overheard by men: by Morgan and Lytton and Maynard Keynes and for that matter by her father, Leslie Stephen. She drew the language out into an exacerbated thread in her determination to have her own sensibility yet protect it from those masculine presences. Only at rare moments in that essay do you hear the passion in her voice; she was trying to sound as cool as Jane Austen, as Olympian as Shakespeare, because that is the way the men of the culture thought a writer should sound.

No male writer has written primarily or even largely for women, or with the sense of women's criticism as a consideration when he chooses his materials, his theme, his language. But to a lesser or greater extent, every woman writer has written for men even when, like Virginia Woolf, she was supposed to be addressing women. If we have come to the point when this balance might begin to change, when women can stop being haunted, not only by "convention and propriety" but by internalized fears of being and saying themselves, then it is an extraordinary moment for the woman writer —and reader.

I have hesitated to do what I am going to do now, which is to use myself as an illustration. For one thing, it's a lot easier and less dangerous to talk about other women writers. But there is something else. Like Virginia Woolf, I am aware of the women who are not with us here because they are washing the dishes and looking after the children. Nearly fifty years after she spoke, that fact remains largely unchanged. And I am thinking also of women whom she left out of the picture altogether—women who are washing other people's dishes and caring for other people's children, not to mention women who went on the streets last night in order to feed their children. We seem to be special women here, we have liked to think of ourselves as special, and we have known that men would tolerate, even romanticize us as special, as long as our words and actions didn't threaten their privilege of tolerating or rejecting us according to *their* ideas of what a special woman ought to be. An important insight of the radical women's movement, for me, has been how divisive and how ultimately destructive is this myth of the special woman, who is also the token woman. Every one of us here in this room has had great luck; our own gifts could not have been enough, for we all know women whose gifts are buried or aborted. Our struggles can have meaning only if they can help to change the lives of women whose gifts—and whose very being— continues to be thwarted.

My own luck was being born white and middle-class into a house full of books, with a father who encouraged me to read and write. So for about twenty years I wrote for a particular man, who criticized and praised me and made me feel I was indeed "special." The obverse side of this, of course, was that I tried for a long time to please him, or rather, not to displease him. And then of course there were other men—writers, teachers—the Man, who was not a terror or a dream but a literary master and a master in other ways less easy to acknowledge. And there were all those poems about women, written by men: it seemed to be a given that men wrote poems and women frequently inhabited them. These women were almost always beautiful, but threatened with the loss of beauty, the loss of youth—the fate worse than death. Or, they were beautiful and died young, like Lucy and Lenore. Or, the woman was like Maud Gonne, cruel and disastrously mistaken, and the poem reproached her because she had refused to become a luxury for the poet.

A lot is being said today about the influence that the myths and images of women have on all of us who are products of culture. I think it has been a peculiar confusion to the girl or woman who tries to write, because she is peculiarly susceptible to language. She goes to poetry or fiction looking for *her* way of being in the world, since she too has been putting words and images together; she is looking eagerly for guides, maps, possibilities; and over and over in the "words' masculine persuasive force" of literature she comes up against something that negates everything she is about: she meets the image of Woman in books written by men. She finds a terror and a dream, she finds a beautiful pale face, she finds La Belle Dame Sans Merci, she finds Juliet or Tess or Salomé, but precisely what she does not find is that absorbed, drudging, puzzled, sometimes inspired creature, herself, who sits at a desk trying to put words together.

So what does she do? What did I do? I read the older women poets with their peculiar keenness and ambivalence: Sappho, Christina Rossetti, Emily Dickinson, Elinor Wylie, Edna Millay, H.D. I discovered that the woman poet most admired at the time (by men) was Marianne Moore, who was maidenly, elegant, intellectual, discreet. But even in reading these women I was looking in them for the same things I had found in the poetry of men, because I wanted women poets to be the equals of men, and to be equal was still confused with sounding the same.

I know that my style was formed first by male poets: by the men I was reading as an undergraduate—Frost, Dylan Thomas, Donne, Auden, MacNiece, Stevens, Yeats. What I chiefly learned from them was craft. But poems are like dreams: in them you put what you don't know you know. Looking back at poems I wrote before I was twenty-one, I'm startled because beneath the conscious craft are glimpses of the split I even then experienced between the girl who wrote poems, who defined herself in writing poems, and the girl who was to define herself by her relationships with men. "Aunt Jennifer's Tigers," written while I was a student, looks with deliberate detachment at this split.

> Aunt Jennifer's tigers stride across a screen,
> Bright topaz denizens of a world of green.

They do not fear the men beneath the tree,
They pace in sleek chivalric certainty.

Aunt Jennifer's fingers, fluttering through her wool,
Find even the ivory needle hard to pull.
The massive weight of Uncle's wedding-band
Sits heavily upon Aunt Jennifer's hand.

When Aunt is dead, her terrified hands will lie
Still ringed with ordeals she was mastered by.
The tigers in the panel that she made
Will go on striding, proud and unafraid.

In writing this poem, composed and apparently cool as it is, I
thought I was creating a portrait of an imaginary woman. But this
woman suffers from the opposition of her imagination, worked out
in tapestry, and her life-style, "ringed with ordeals she was mastered
by." It was important to me that Aunt Jennifer was a person as distinct from myself as possible—distanced by the formalism of the
poem; by its objective, observant tone; even by putting the woman
in a different generation.

In those years formalism was part of the strategy—like asbestos
gloves, it allowed me to handle materials I couldn't pick up bare-
handed. (A later strategy was to use the persona of a man, as I did
in "The Loser.")

*A man thinks of the woman he once loved: first, after her wedding, and
then nearly a decade later.*

I

I kissed you, bride and lost, and went
home from that bourgeois sacrament,
your cheek still tasting cold upon
my lips that gave you benison
with all the swagger that they knew—
as losers somehow learn to do.

Your wedding made my eyes ache; soon
the world would be worse off for one
more golden apple dropped to ground
without the least protesting sound,
and you would windfall lie, and we
forget your shimmer on the tree.

Beauty is always wasted: if
not Mignon's song sung to the deaf,
at all events to the unmoved.
A face like yours cannot be loved
long or seriously enough.
Almost, we seem to hold it off.

II

Well, you are tougher than I thought.
Now when the wash with ice hangs taut
this morning of St. Valentine,
I see you strip the squeaking line,
your body weighed against the load,
and all my groans can do no good.

Because you still are beautiful,
though squared and stiffened by the pull
of what nine windy years have done.
You have three daughters, lost a son.
I see all your intelligence
flung into that unwearied stance.

My envy is of no avail.
I turn my head and wish him well
who chafed your beauty into use
and lives forever in a house
lit by the friction of your mind.
You stagger in against the wind.[4]

1958

    I finished college, published my first book by a fluke, as it seemed
to me, and broke off a love-affair. I took a job, lived alone, went on
writing, fell in love. I was young, full of energy, and the book
seemed to mean that others agreed I was a poet. Because I was also
determined to have a "full" woman's life, I plunged in my early
twenties into marriage and had three children before I was thirty.
There was nothing overt in the environment to warn me: these
were the fifties, and in reaction to the earlier wave of feminism, middle-class women were making careers of domestic perfection, working to send their husbands through professional schools, then retiring to raise large families. People were moving out to the suburbs,
technology was going to be the answer to everything, even sex; the
family was in its glory. Life was extremely private; women were isolated from each other by the loyalties of marriage. I have a sense
that women didn't talk to each other much in the fifties—not
about their secret emptinesses, their frustrations. I went on trying to
write, my second book and first child appeared in the same month.
But by the time that book came out I was already dissatisfied with
those poems, which seemed to me mere exercises for poems I hadn't
written. The book was praised, however, for its "gracefulness"; I had
a marriage and a child. If there were doubts, if there were periods of
null depression or active despairing, these could only mean that I
was ungrateful, insatiable, perhaps a monster.

    4. "The Losers," in *Snapshots of a*   Norton, 1956), pp. 15–16.
Daughter-in-Law (New York: W. W.

About the time my third child was born, I felt that I had either to consider myself a failed woman and a failed poet, or try to find some synthesis by which to understand what was happening to me. What frightened me most was the sense of drift, of being pulled along on a current which called itself my destiny, but in which I seemed to be losing touch with whoever I had been, with the girl who had experienced her own will and energy almost ecstatically at times, walking around a city or riding a train at night or typing in a student room. In a poem about my grandmother, I wrote (of myself): "A young girl, thought sleeping, is certified dead."[5] I was writing very little, partly from fatigue, that female fatigue of suppressed anger and the loss of contact with her own being; partly from the discontinuity of female life with its attention to small chores, errands, work that others constantly undo, small children's constant needs. What I did write was unconvincing to me; my anger and frustration were hard to acknowledge in or out of poem, because in fact I cared a great deal about my husband and my children. Trying to look back and understand that time I have tried to analyze the real nature of the conflict. Most, if not all, human lives are full of fantasy—passive daydreaming which need not be acted on. But to write poetry or fiction, or even to think well, is not to fantasize, or to put fantasies on paper. For a poem to coalesce, for a character or an action to take shape, there has to be an imaginative transformation of reality which is in no way passive. And a certain freedom of the mind is needed—freedom to press on, to enter the currents of your thought like a glider pilot, knowing that your motion can be sustained, that the buoyancy of your attention will not be suddenly snatched away. Moreover, if the imagination is to transcend and transform experience it has to question, to challenge, to conceive of alternatives, perhaps to the very life you are living at that moment. You have to be free to play around with the notion that day might be night, love might be hate; nothing can be too sacred for the imagination to turn into its opposite or to call experimentally by another name. For writing is re-naming. Now, to be maternally with small children all day in the old way, to be with a man in the old way of marriage, requires a holding-back, a putting-aside of that imaginative activity, and seems to demand instead a kind of conservatism. I want to make it clear that I am *not* saying that in order to write well, or think well, it is necessary to become unavailable to others, or to become a devouring ego. This has been the myth of the masculine artist and thinker; and I repeat, I do not accept it. But to be a female human being trying to fulfill traditional female functions in a traditional way *is* in direct conflict with the subversive function of the imagination. The word *traditional* is important here. There must be ways, and we will be finding out

5. "Halfway," in *Necessities of Life* (New York: W. W. Norton, 1966), p. 34.

more and more about them, in which the energy of creation and the energy of relation can be united. But in those earlier years I always felt the conflict as a failure of love in myself. I had thought I was choosing a full life: the life available to most men, in which sexuality, work and parenthood could coexist. But I felt, at twenty-nine, guilt toward the people closest to me, and guilty toward my own being.

I wanted, then, more than anything, the one thing of which there was never enough: time to think, time to write. The fifties and early sixties were years of rapid revelations: the sit-ins and marches in the South, the Bay of Pigs, the early anti-war movement raised large questions—questions for which the masculine world of the academy around me seemed to have expert and fluent answers. But I needed desperately to think for myself—about pacifism and dissent and violence, about poetry and society and about my own relationship to all these things. For about ten years I was reading in fierce snatches, scribbling in notebooks, writing poetry in fragments; I was looking desperately for clues, because if there were no clues then I thought I might be insane. I wrote in a notebook about this time: "Paralyzed by the sense that there exists a mesh of relationships—e.g. between my anger at the children, my sensual life, pacifism, sex, (I mean sex in its broadest significance, not merely sexual desire)—an interconnectedness which, if I could see it, make it valid, would give me back myself, make it possible to function lucidly and passionately. Yet I grope in and out among these dark webs." I think I began at this point to feel that politics was not something "out there" but something "in here" and of the essence of my condition.

In the late fifties I was able to write, for the first time, directly about experiencing myself as a woman. The poem was jotted in fragments during children's naps, brief hours in a library, or at 3 A.M. after rising with a wakeful child. I despaired of doing any continuous work at this time. Yet I began to feel that my fragments and scraps had a common consciousness and a common theme, one which I would have been very unwilling to put on paper at an earlier time because I had been taught that poetry should be "universal," which meant, of course, non-female. Until then I had tried very much *not* to identify myself as a female poet. Over two years I wrote a ten-part poem called "Snapshots of A Daughter-in-Law," in a longer, looser mode than I've ever trusted myself with before. It was an extraordinary relief to write that poem. It strikes me now as too literary, too dependent on allusion; I hadn't found the courage yet to do without authorities, or even to use the pronoun *I*—the woman in the poem is always *she*. One section of it, 2, concerns a woman who thinks she is going mad; she is haunted by voices telling her to resist and rebel, voices which she can hear but not obey.

2.

Banging the coffee-pot into the sink
she hears the angels chiding, and looks out
past the raked gardens to the sloppy sky.
Only a week since They said: *Have no patience.*

The next time it was: *Be insatiable.*
Then: *Save yourself; others you cannot save.*
Sometimes she's let the tapstream scald her arm,
a match burn to her thumbnail,

or held her hand above the kettle's snout
right in the woolly steam. They are probably angels,
since nothing hurts her any more, except
each morning's grit blowing into her eyes.[6]

The poem "Orion," written five years later, is a poem of
reconnection with a part of myself I had felt I was losing—the
active principle, the energetic imagination, the "half-brother" whom
I projected, as I had for many years, into the constellation Orion.

Far back when I went zig-zagging
through tamarack pastures
you were my genius, you
my cast-iron Viking, my helmed
lion-heart king in prison.
Years later now you're young

my fierce half-brother, staring
down from that simplified west
your breast open, your belt dragged down
by an oldfashioned thing, a sword
the last bravado you won't give over
though it weighs you down as you stride

and the stars in it are dim
and maybe have stopped burning.
But you burn, and I know it;
as I throw back my head to take you in
an old transfusion happens again:
divine astronomy is nothing to it.

Indoors I bruise and blunder,
break faith, leave ill enough
alone, a dead child born in the dark.
Night cracks up over the chimney,
pieces of time, frozen geodes
come showering down in the grate.

A man reaches behind my eyes
and finds them empty

6. "Snapshots of a Daughter-in-Law," in *Snapshots of a Daughter-in-Law*, p. 21.

a woman's head turns away
from my head in the mirror
children are dying my death
and eating crumbs of my life.

Pity is not your forte.
Calmly you ache up there
pinned aloft in your crow's nest,
my speechless pirate!
You take it all for granted
and when I look you back

it's with a starlike eye
shooting its cold and egotistical spear
where it can do least damage.
Breathe deep! No hurt, no pardon
out here in the cold with you
you with your back to the wall.[7]

It's no accident that the words *cold and egotistical* appear in this poem, and are applied to myself. The choice still seemed to be between "love"—womanly, maternal love, altruistic love—a love defined and ruled by the weight of an entire culture—and egotis—a force directed by men into creation, achievement, ambition, often at the expense of others, but justifiably so. For weren't they men, and wasn't that their destiny as womanly love was ours? I know now that the alternatives are false ones—that the word *love* is itself in need of re-vision.

There is a companion poem to "Orion," written three years later, in which at last the woman in the poem and the woman writing the poem become the same person. It is called "Planetarium," and it was written after a visit to a real planetarium, where I read an account of the work of Caroline Herschel, the astronomer, who worked with her brother William, but whose name remained obscure, as his did not.

> (*Thinking of Caroline Herschel, 1750–1848, astronomer, sister of William; and others*)

A woman in the shape of a monster
a monster in the shape of a woman
the skies are full of them

a woman   'in the snow
among the Clocks and instruments
or measuring the ground with poles'

in her 98 years to discover
8 comets

---

7. "Orion," in *Leaflets* (New York: W. W. Norton, 1969), pp. 11–12.

she whom the moon ruled
like us
levitating into the night sky
riding the polished lenses

Galaxies of women, there
doing penance for impetuousness
ribs chilled
in those spaces   of the mind

An eye,
          'virile, precise and absolutely certain'
          from the mad webs of Uranisborg
                              encountering the NOVA

every impulse of light exploding
from the core
as life flies out of us

          Tycho whispering at last
          'Let me not seem to have lived in vain'

What we see, we see
and seeing is changing

the light that shrivels a mountain
and leaves a man alive

Heartbeat of the pulsar
heart sweating through my body

The radio impulse
pouring in from Taurus

          I am bombarded yet   I stand

I have been standing all my life in the
direct path of a battery of signals
the most accurately transmitted most
untranslatable language in the universe
I am a galactic cloud so deep   so invo-
luted that a light wave could take 15
years to travel through me   And has
taken   I am an instrument in the shape
of a woman trying to translate pulsations
into images   for the relief of the body
and the reconstruction of the mind.[8]

In closing I want to tell you about a dream I had last summer. I
dreamed I was asked to read my poetry at a mass women's meeting;

8. "Planetarium," in *The Will to* 1971), pp. 11–12.
Change (New York: W. W. Norton,

but when I began to read, what came out were the lyrics of a blues song. I share this dream with you because it seemed to me to say a lot about the problems and the future of the woman writer, and probably of women in general. The awakening of consciousness is not like the crossing of a frontier—one step, and you are in another country. Much of women's poetry has been of the nature of the blues song: a cry of pain, of victimization, or a lyric of seduction. And today, much poetry by women—and prose for that matter—is charged with anger. I think we need to go through that anger, and we will betray our own reality if we try, as Virginia Woolf was trying, for an objectivity, a detachment; that would make us sound more like Jane Austen or Shakespeare. We know more than Jane Austen or Shakespeare knew: more than Jane Austen because our lives are more complex, more than Shakespeare because we know more about the lives of women, Jane Austen and Virginia Woolf included.

Both the victimization and the anger experienced by women are real, and have real sources, everywhere in the environment, built into society. They must go on being tapped and explored by poets, among others. We can neither deny them, nor can we rest there. They are our birth-pains, and we are bearing ourselves. We would be failing each other as writers and as women, if we neglected or denied what is negative, regressive or Sisyphean in our inwardness.

We all know that there is another story to be told. I am curious and expectant about the future of the masculine consciousness. I feel in the work of the men whose poetry I read today a deep pessimism and fatalistic grief; and I wonder if it isn't the masculine side of what women have experienced, the price of masculine dominance. One thing I am sure of: just as woman is becoming her own midwife, creating herself anew, so man will have to learn to gestate and give birth to his own subjectivity—something he has frequently wanted woman to do for him. We can go on trying to talk to each other, we can sometimes help each other, poetry and fiction can show us what the other is going through; but women can no longer be primarily mothers and muses for men: we have our own work cut out for us.

QUESTIONS

1. A typical male-chauvinist cliché is that women take everything too personally, that they lack the larger (i.e. male) perspective. Does this article tend to confirm or deny that belief?
2. In the eighth paragraph, Rich asserts that "no male writer has written primarily or even largely for women, or with the sense of women's criticism as a consideration when he chooses his materials, his theme, his language." How can she know this? Do you think she is right? How do you know?

ELDRIDGE CLEAVER
Convalescence[1]

> . . . just as in childhood I envied Negroes for what seemed to me their superior masculinity, so I envy them today for what seems to me their superior physical grace and beauty. I have come to value physical grace very highly, and I am now capable of aching with all my being when I watch a Negro couple on the dance floor, or a Negro playing baseball or basketball. *They are on the kind of terms with their own bodies that I should like to be on with mine, and for that precious quality they seem blessed to me.* [Italics added]

> —Norman Podhoretz, "My Negro Problem—And Ours,"
> *Commentary*, February 1963

> Why envy the Negro his grace, his physical skills? Why not ask what it is that prevents grace and physical skill from becoming a general property of the young? Mr. Podhoretz speaks of middle-class, white respectability—what does this mean but being cut off from the labor process, the work process, the creative process, as such? *The solution is thus not the direct liquidation of the color line, through the liquidation of color; but rather through a greater physical connectedness of the whites; and a greater intellective connectedness of the blacks . . ."* [Italics added]
> —Irving Louis Horowitz,
> Chairman, Department of Sociology,
> Hobart and William Smith Colleges, Geneva, New York,
> *Commentary*, June 1963

If the separation of the black and white people in America along the color line had the effect, in terms of social imagery, of separating the Mind from the Body—the oppressor whites usurping sovereignty by monopolizing the Mind, abdicating the Body and becoming bodiless Omnipotent Administrators and Ultrafeminines; and the oppressed blacks, divested of sovereignty and therefore of Mind, manifesting the Body and becoming mindless Supermasculine Menials and Black Amazons—if this is so, then the 1954 U.S. Supreme Court decision in the case of *Brown v. Board of Education*, demolishing the principle of segregation of the races in public education and striking at the very root of the practice of segregation generally, was a major surgical operation performed by nine men in black robes on the racial Maginot Line which is imbedded as deep as sex or the lust for lucre in the schismatic American psyche. This piece of social surgery, if successful, performed without benefit of any anesthetic except God and the Constitution, in a land where God is dead and the Constitution has been in a coma for 180 years,

1. From *Soul on Ice*, 1968.

is more marvelous than a successful heart transplant would be, for it was meant to graft the nation's Mind back onto its Body and vice versa.

If the foregoing is true, then the history of America in the years following the pivotal Supreme Court edict should be a record of the convalescence of the nation. And upon investigation we should be able to see the Omnipotent Administrators and Ultrafeminines grappling with their unfamiliar and alienated Bodies, and the Super-masculine Menials and Amazons attempting to acquire and assert *a mind of their own*. The record, I think, is clear and unequivocal. The bargain which seems to have been struck is that the whites have had to turn to the blacks for a clue on how to swing with the Body, while the blacks have had to turn to the whites for the secret of the Mind. It was Chubby Checker's mission, bearing the Twist as *good news*, to teach the whites, whom history had taught to forget, how to shake their asses again. It is a skill they surely must once have possessed but which they abandoned for puritanical dreams of escaping the corruption of the flesh, by leaving the terrors of the Body to the blacks.

In the swift, fierce years since the 1954 school desegregation decision, a rash of seemingly unrelated mass phenomena has appeared on the American scene—deviating radically from the prevailing Hot-Dog-and-Malted-Milk norm of the bloodless, square, superficial, faceless Sunday-Morning atmosphere that was suffocating the nation's soul. And all of this in a nation where the so-called molders of public opinion, the writers, politicians, teachers, and cab drivers, are willful, euphoric liars or zip-dam ostriches and owls, a clique of undercover ghosts, a bunch of Walter Jenkinses,[2] a lot of coffee-drinking, cigarette-smoking, sly, suck-assing, status-seeking, cheating, nervous, dry-balled, tranquillizer-gulched, countdown-minded, out-of-style, slithering snakes. No wonder that many "innocent people," the manipulated and the stimulated, some of whom were game for a reasonable amount of mystery and even adventure, had their minds scrambled. These observers were not equipped to either *feel* or *know* that a radical break, a revolutionary leap out of their sight, had taken place in the secret parts of this nation's soul. It was as if a driverless vehicle were speeding through the American night down an unlighted street toward a stone wall and was boarded on the fly by a stealthy ghost with a drooling leer on his face, who, at the last detour before chaos and disaster, careened the vehicle down a smooth highway that leads to the future and life; and to ask these Americans to understand that they were the passengers on this driverless vehicle and that the lascivious ghost was the Saturday-night

2. Former White House aide; arrested in 1964 on a morals charge.

crotchfunk of the Twist, or the "Yeah, Yeah, Yeah!" which the Beatles highjacked from Ray Charles, to ask these Calvinistic profligates to see the logical and reciprocal links is more cruel than asking a hope-to-die Okie Music buff to cop the sounds of John Coltrane.

In the beginning of the era came a thief with a seven-year itch who knew that the ostriches and the owls had been bribed with a fix of Euphony, which is their kick. The thief knew that he need not wait for the cover of night, that with impunity he could show his face in the marketplace in the full light of the sun, do his deed, scratch his dirt, sell his loot to the fence while the ostriches and owls, coasting on Euphony, one with his head in a hole—any hole —and the other with his head in the clouds, would only cluck and whisper and hear-see-speak no evil.

So Elvis Presley came, strumming a weird guitar and wagging his tail across the continent, ripping off fame and fortune as he scrunched his way, and, like a latter-day Johnny Appleseed, sowing seeds of a new rhythm and style in the white souls of the white youth of America, whose inner hunger and need was no longer satisfied with the antiseptic white shoes and whiter songs of Pat Boone. "You can do anything," sang Elvis to Pat Boone's white shoes, "but don't you step on my Blue Suede Shoes!"

During this period of ferment and beginnings, at about the same time that the blacks of Montgomery, Alabama, began their historic bus boycott (giving birth to the leadership of Martin Luther King, signifying to the nation that, with this initiative, this first affirmative step, somewhere in the universe a gear in the machinery had shifted), something, a target, came into focus. The tensions in the American psyche had torn a fissure in the racial Maginot Line and through this fissure, this tiny bridge between the Mind and Body, the black masses, who had been silent and somnolent since the '20s and '30s, were now making a break toward the dimly seen light that beckoned to them through the fissure. The fact that these blacks could now take such a step was perceived by the ostriches and owls as a sign of national decay, a sign that the System had caved in at that spot. And this gave birth to a fear, a fear that quickly became a focus for all the anxieties and exasperations in the Omnipotent Administrators' minds; and to embody this perceived decay and act as a lightning rod for the fear, the beatniks bloomed onto the American scene.

Like pioneers staking their claims in the no-man's land that lay along the racial Maginot Line, the beatniks, like Elvis Presley before them, dared to do in the light of day what America had long been doing in the sneak-thief anonymity of night—consorted on a human level with the blacks. Reviled, cursed, held in contempt by the "molders of public opinion," persecuted by the police, made into an epithet of derision by the deep-frozen geeks of the Hot-

Dog-and-Malted-Milk set, the beatniks irreverently refused to go away. Allan Ginsberg and Jack Kerouac ("the Suzuki rhythm boys," James Baldwin called them, derisively, in a moment of panic, "tired of white ambitions" and "dragging themselves through the Negro streets at dawn, looking for an angry fix"; "with," as Mailer put it, "the black man's code to fit their facts"). Bing Crosbyism, Perry Comoism, and Dinah Shoreism had led to cancer, and the vanguard of the white youth knew it.

And as the spirit of revolt crept across the continent from that wayward bus in Montgomery, Alabama, seeping like new life into the cracks and nooks of the northern ghettos and sweeping in furious gales across the campuses of southern Negro colleges, erupting, finally, in the sit-ins and freedom rides—as this swirling maelstrom of social change convulsed the nation, shocking an unsuspecting American public, folk music, speaking of fundamental verities, climbed slowly out of the grave; and the hip lobe of the national ear, twitching involuntarily at first, began to listen.

From the moment that Mrs. Rosa Parks, in that bus in Montgomery, Alabama, resisted the Omnipotent Administrator, contact, however fleeting, had been made with the lost sovereignty—the Body had made contact with its Mind—and the shock of that contact sent an electric current throughout this nation, traversing the racial Maginot Line and striking fire in the hearts of the whites. The wheels began to turn, the thaw set in, and though Emmett Till and Mack Parker[3] were dead, though Eisenhower sent troops to Little Rock,[4] though Autherine Lucy's token presence at the University of Alabama was a mockery—notwithstanding this, it was already clear that the 1954 major surgical operation had been successful and the patient would live. The challenge loomed on the horizon: Africa, black, enigmatic, and hard-driving, had begun to parade its newly freed nations into the UN; and the Islam of Elijah Muhammad, amplified as it was fired in salvos from the piercing tongue of Malcolm X, was racing through the Negro streets with Allen Ginsberg and Jack Kerouac.

Then, as the verbal revolt of the black masses soared to a cacophonous peak—the Body, the Black Amazons and Supermasculine Menials, becoming conscious, shouting, in a thousand different ways, *"I've got a Mind of my own!"*; and as the senator from Massachusetts was saving the nation from the Strangelove grasp of Dirty Dick, injecting, as he emerged victorious, a new and vivacious spirit into the people with the style of his smile and his wife's hairdo;

---

3. Emmett Till, a fourteen-year-old youth, kidnapped and killed for whistling at a white woman in Mississippi in August 1955; Mack Parker, lynched in Poplarville, Mississippi, while awaiting trial on a rape charge, April 1959.

4. Troops sent to Little Rock, Arkansas, in 1957 in support of a court order to integrate Little Rock schools.

then, as if a signal had been given, as if the Mind had shouted to the Body, "I'm ready!"—the Twist, superseding the Hula Hoop, burst upon the scene like a nuclear explosion, sending its fallout of rhythm into the Minds and Bodies of the people. The fallout: the Hully Gully, the Mashed Potato, the Dog, the Smashed Banana, the Watusi, the Frug, the Swim. The Twist was a guided missile, launched from the ghetto into the very heart of suburbia. The Twist succeeded, as politics, religion, and law could never do, in writing in the heart and soul what the Supreme Court could only write on the books. The Twist was a form of therapy for a convalescing nation. The Omnipotent Administrator and the Ultrafeminine responded so dramatically, in stampede fashion, to the Twist precisely because it afforded them the possibility of reclaiming their Bodies again after generations of alienated and disembodied existence.

The stiff, mechanical Omnipotent Administrators and Ultrafeminines presented a startling spectacle as they entered in droves onto the dance floors to learn how to Twist. They came from every level of society, from top to bottom, writhing pitifully though gamely about the floor, feeling exhilarating and soothing new sensations, release from some unknown prison in which their Bodies had been encased, a sense of freedom they had never known before, a feeling of communion with some mystical root-source of life and vigor, from which sprang a new awareness and enjoyment of the flesh, a new appreciation of the possibilities of their Bodies. They were swinging and gyrating and shaking their dead asses like petrified zombies trying to regain the warmth of life, rekindle the dead limbs, the cold ass, the stone heart, the stiff, mechanical, disused joints with the spark of life.

This spectacle truly startled many Negroes, because they perceived it as an intrusion by the Mind into the province of the Body, and this intimated chaos; because the Negroes knew, from the survival experience of their everyday lives, that the system within which they were imprisoned was based upon the racial Maginot Line and that the cardinal sin, crossing the line—which was, in their experience, usually initiated from the black side—was being committed, *en masse*, by the whites. The Omnipotent Administrators and Ultrafeminines were storming the Maginot Line! A massive assault had been launched without parallel in American history, and to Negroes it was confusing. Sure, they had witnessed it on an individual scale: they had seen many ofays destroy the Maginot Line in themselves. But this time it had all the appearances of a national movement. There were even rumors that President Kennedy and his Jackie were doing the Twist secretly in the White House; that their Number One Boy had been sent to the Peppermint Lounge in disguise to learn how to Twist, and he in turn brought the trick back

to the White House. These Negroes knew that something fundamental had changed.

"Man, what done got into them ofays?" one asked.

"They trying to get back," said another.

"Shit," said a young Negro who made his living by shoplifting.
"If you ask me, I think it must be the end of the world."

"Oooo-weee!" said a Negro musician who had been playing at a
dance and was now standing back checking the dancers. "Baby, I
don't dig this action at all! Look here, baby, pull my coat to what's
going down! I mean, have I missed it somewhere? Where've I
been? Baby, I been blowing all my life and I ain't never dug no
happenings like this. You know what, man, I'm gon' cut that fucking weed aloose. Oooo-weee! Check that little bitch right there!
What the fuck she trying to do? Is she trying to shake it or break
it? Oooo-weee!"

A Negro girl said: "Take me home, I'm sick!"

Another one said: "No, let's stay! This is too much!"

And a bearded Negro cat, who was not interested in learning how
to Twist himself, who felt that if he was interested in doing it, he
could get up from the table right now and start Twisting, he said,
sitting at the table with a tinsel-minded female: "It ain't nothing.
They just trying to get back, that's all."

"Get back?" said the girl, arching her brows quizzically, "Get
back from where?"

"From wherever they've been," said the cat, "where else?"

"Are they doing it in Mississippi is what I want to know," said a
tall, deadly looking Negro who had a long razor line down his left
cheek and who had left Mississippi in a hurry one night.

And the dancers: they were caught up in a whirl of ecstasy,
swinging like pendulums, mechanical like metronomes or puppets
on invisible strings being manipulated by a master with a sick sense
of humor. "They look like Chinese doing communal exercise," said
a Negro. "That's all they're doing, calisthenics!"

"Yeah," said his companion. "They're trying to get in shape."

But if at first it was funny and confusing, it was nonetheless a
breakthrough. The Omnipotent Administrators and Ultrafeminines
were discovering new aspects of the Body, new possibilities of
rhythm, new ways to move. The Hula Hoop had been a false start,
a mechanized, theatrical attempt by the Mind to supply to itself
what only the Body can give. But, with the Twist, as last they knew
themselves to be swinging. The forces acting upon the world stage
in our era had created, in the collective psyche of the Omnipotent
—and the Hula Hoop and Twist offered socially acceptable ways to
Administrators and Ultrafeminines, an irresistible urge—to just
stand up and shake the ice and cancer out of their alienated white

asses—the Hula Hoop and Twist offered socially acceptable ways to do it.

Of course, not all the whites took part in these joyful experiments. For many, the more "suggestive" a dance became—i.e., the more it became pure Body and less Mind—the more scandalous it seemed to them; and their reaction in this sense was an index to the degree of their alienation from their Bodies. But what they condemned as a sign of degeneracy and moral decay was actually a sign of health, a sign of hope for full recovery. As Norman Mailer prophesied: ". . . the Negro's equality would tear a profound shift into the psychology, the sexuality, and the moral imagination of every white alive." Precisely because the Mind will have united with the Body, theory will have merged with practice.

It is significant that the Twist and the Hula Hoop came into the scene in all their fury at the close of the Eisenhower and the dawn of the Kennedy era. It could be interpreted as a rebellion against the vacuous Eisenhower years. It could also be argued that the same collective urge that gave rise to the Twist also swept Kennedy into office. I shudder to think that, given the closeness of the final vote in 1960, Richard Nixon might have won the election in a breeze if he had persuaded one of his Ultrafeminine daughters, not to mention Ultrapat, to do the Twist in public. Not if Kennedy had stayed on the phone a week sympathizing with Mrs. Martin Luther King, Jr., over the fact that the cat was in jail, would he have won. Even as I am convinced that Luci Baines Johnson, dancing the Watusi in public with Killer Joe Piro,[5] won more votes for her old man in 1964 than a whole boxcar full of his hog-calling speeches ever did.

When the Birmingham Revolt erupted in the summer of 1963 and President Kennedy stepped into the void and delivered his unprecedented speech to the nation on civil rights and sent his bill to Congress, the foundation had been completed. Martin Luther King, Jr., giving voice to the needs of the Body, and President Kennedy, speaking out the needs of the Mind, made contact on that day. The Twisters, sporting their blue suede shoes, moved beyond the ghost in white shoes who ate a Hot Dog and sipped Malted Milk as he danced the mechanical jig of Satan on top of Medgar Evers' tomb.[6] In vain now would the murderers bomb that church and slaughter grotesquely those four little black girls[7] (what did they hope to kill? were they striking at the black of the skin or the fire of the soul? at history? at the Body?). In vain also the assassins' bullets that crashed through the head of John Kennedy, taking a life, yes, but creating a larger-than-life and failing utterly to expunge

5. Discothèque dance teacher.

6. Evers was killed by a sniper in Jackson, Mississippi, in June 1963.

7. The bombing took place in Birmingham, Alabama, in September 1963.

from the record the March on Washington and its truth: that this nation—bourgeois or not, imperialist or not, murderous or not, ugly or not—its people, somewhere in their butchered and hypocritical souls, still contained an epic potential of spirit which is its hope, a bottomless potential which fires the imaginations of its youth. It was all too late. It was too late because it was time for the blacks ("I've got a *Mind* of my own!') to riot, to sweep through the Harlem night like a wave of locusts, breaking, screaming, bleeding, laughing, crying, rejoicing, celebrating, in a jubilee of destruction, to regurgitate the white man's bullshit they'd been eating for four hundred years; smashing the windows of the white man's stores, throwing bricks they wished were bombs, running, leaping whirling like a cyclone through the white man's Mind, past his backlash, through the night streets of Rochester, New Jersey, Philadelphia. And even though the opposition, gorging on Hot Dogs and Malted Milk, with blood now splattered over the white shoes, would still strike out in the dark against the manifestations of the turning, showing the protocol of Southern Hospitality reserved for Niggers and Nigger Lovers—SCHWERNER–CHANEY–GOODMAN[8] —it was still too late. For not only had Luci Baines Johnson danced the Watusi in public with Killer Joe, but the Beatles were on the scene, injecting Negritude by the ton into whites, in this post-Elvis Presley-beatnik era of ferment.

Before we toss the Beatles a homosexual kiss—saying, "If a man be ass enough to reach for the bitch in them, that man will kiss a man, and if a woman reaches for the stud in them, that woman will kiss a woman"—let us marvel at the genius of their image, which comforts the owls and ostriches in the one spot where Elvis Presley bummed their kick: Elvis, with his *unfunky* (yet mechanical, alienated) bumpgrinding, was still too much Body (too soon) for the strained collapsing psyches of the Omnipotent Administrators and Ultrafeminines; whereas the Beatles, affecting the caucasoid crown of femininity and ignoring the Body on the visual plane (while their music on the contrary being full of Body), assuaged the doubts of the owls and ostriches by presenting an incorporeal, cerebral image.

Song and dance are, perhaps, only a little less old than man himself. It is with his music and dance, the recreation through art of the rhythms suggested by and implicit in the tempo of his life and cultural environment, that man purges his soul of the tensions of daily strife and maintains his harmony in the universe. In the increasingly mechanized, automated, cybernated environment of the modern world—a cold, bodiless world of wheels, smooth plastic surfaces, tubes, pushbuttons, transistors, computers, jet propulsion, rockets to the moon, atomic energy—man's need for affirmation of

---

8. Michael Schwerner, James Chaney, and Andrew Goodman, civil rights workers, were killed near Philadelphia, Mississippi, in June 1964.

his biology has become that much more intense. He feels need for a clear definition of where his body ends and the machine begins, where man ends and the *extensions* of man begin. This great mass hunger, which transcends national or racial boundaries, recoils from the subtle subversions of the mechanical evironment which modern technology is creating faster than man, with his present savage relationship to his fellow men, is able to receive and assimilate. This is the central contradiction of the twentieth century; and it is against this backdrop that America's attempt to unite its Mind with its Body, to save its soul, is taking place.

It is in this connection that the blacks, personifying the Body and thereby in closer communion with their biological roots than other Americans, provide the saving link, the bridge between man's biology and man's machines. In its purest form, as adjustment to the scientific and technological environment of our era, as purgative and lullaby-soother of man's soul, it is the jazz issuing from the friction and harmony of the American Negro with his environment that captured the beat and tempo of our times. And although modern science and technology are the same whether in New York, Paris, London, Accra, Cairo, Berlin, Moscow, Tokyo, Peking, or São Paulo, jazz is the only true international medium of communication current in the world today, capable of speaking creatively, with equal intensity and relevance, to the people in all those places.

The less sophisticated (but no less Body-based) popular music of urban Negroes—which was known as Rhythm and Blues before the whites appropriated and distilled it into a product they called Rock 'n Roll—is the basic ingredient, the core, of the gaudy, cacophonous hymns with which the Beatles of Liverpool drive their hordes of Ultrafeminine fans into catatonia and hysteria. For Beatle fans, having been alienated from their own Bodies so long and so deeply, the effect of these potent, erotic rhythms is electric. Into this music, the Negro projected—as it were, *drained off*, as pus from a sore—a powerful sensuality, his pain and lust, his love and his hate, his ambition and his despair. The Negro projected into his music his very Body. The Beatles, the four long-haired lads from Liverpool, are offering up as their gift the Negro's Body, and in so doing establish a rhythmic communication between the listener's own Mind and Body.

Enter the Beatles—soul by proxy, middlemen between the Mind and the Body. A long way from Pat Boone's White Shoes. A way station on a slow route traveled with all deliberate speed.

QUESTIONS

1. What racial differences does Cleaver assume? Would you respond differently to these assumptions if they had been implicit in a piece by, say, a southern white racist politician?

2. Does Cleaver establish any connection between the Supreme Court decision he discusses in his introduction and the song and dance he focuses on in the body of the essay? Do you think the "convalescence" could have occurred without that particular piece of surgery? What other influences may have served to graft mind and body? What others may have impeded the convalescence?
3. This piece abounds with figures of speech. How many can you find? What purposes do they serve? Do they clarify Cleaver's argument? Or do they becloud the issues?
4. Cleaver's sentences are long, with ins and outs and round-abouts—and many internal interruptions. How would he do at Time or Newsweek?
5. Are Cleaver's long lists of appositives and adjectives of substantive importance? Or are they mere gimmicks?
6. Are you persuaded by Cleaver's pronouncements on how things are—or were?

JANE JACOBS

Sidewalk Ballet[1]

Under the seeming disorder of the old city, wherever the old city is working successfully, is a marvelous order for maintaining the safety of the streets and the freedom of the city. It is a complex order. Its essence is intricacy of sidewalk use, bringing with it a constant succession of eyes. This order is all composed of movement and change, and although it is life, not art, we may fancifully call it the art form of the city and liken it to the dance—not to a simple-minded precision dance with everyone kicking up at the same time, twirling in unison, and bowing off en masse, but to an intricate ballet in which the individual dancers and ensembles all have distinctive parts which miraculously reinforce each other and compose an orderly whole. The ballet of the good city sidewalk never repeats itself from place to place, and in any one place is always replete with new improvisations.

The stretch of Hudson Street where I live is each day the scene of an intricate sidewalk ballet. I make my own first entrance into it a little after eight when I put out the garbage can, surely a prosaic occupation, but I enjoy my part, my little clang, as the droves of junior high school students walk by the center of the stage dropping candy wrappers. (How do they eat so much candy so early in the morning?)

While I sweep up the wrappers I watch the other rituals of morning: Mr. Halpert unlocking the laundry's handcart from its

1. From Chapter 2 of *The Death and Life of Great American Cities*, 1961.

mooring to a cellar door, Joe Cornacchia's son-in-law stacking out the empty crates from the delicatessen, the barber bringing out his sidewalk folding chair, Mr. Goldstein arranging the coils of wire which proclaim the hardware store is open, the wife of the tenement's superintendent depositing her chunky three-year-old with a toy mandolin on the stoop, the vantage point from which he is learning the English his mother cannot speak. Now the primary children, heading for St. Luke's, dribble through to the south; the children for St. Veronica's cross, heading to the west, and the children for P.S. 41, heading toward the east. Two new entrances are being made from the wings: well-dressed and even elegant women and men with briefcases emerge from doorways and side streets. Most of these are heading for the bus and subways, but some hover on the curbs, stopping taxis which have miraculously appeared at the right moment, for the taxis are part of a wider morning ritual: having dropped passengers from midtown in the downtown financial district, they are now bringing downtowners up to midtown. Simultaneously, numbers of women in housedresses have emerged and as they crisscross with one another they pause for quick conversations that sound with either laughter or joint indignation, never, it seems, anything between. It is time for me to hurry to work too, and I exchange my ritual farewell with Mr. Lofaro, the short, thick-bodied, white-aproned fruit man who stands outside his doorway a little up the street, his arms folded, his feet planted, looking solid as earth itself. We nod; we each glance quickly up and down the street, then look back to each other and smile. We have done this many a morning for more than ten years, and we both know what it means: All is well.

The heart-of-the-day ballet I seldom see, because part of the nature of it is that working people who live there, like me, are mostly gone, filling the roles of strangers on other sidewalks. But from days off, I know enough of it to know that it becomes more and more intricate. Longshoremen who are not working that day gather at the White Horse or the Ideal or the International for beer and conversation. The executives and business lunchers from the industries just to the west throng the Dorgene restaurant and the Lion's Head coffee house; meat-market workers and communications scientists fill the bakery lunchroom. Character dancers come on, a strange old man with strings of old shoes over his shoulders, motor-scooter riders with big beards and girl friends who bounce on the back of the scooters and wear their hair long in front of their faces as well as behind, drunks who follow the advice of the Hat Council and are always turned out in hats, but not hats the Council would approve. Mr. Lacey, the locksmith, shuts up his shop for a while and goes to exchange the time of day with Mr. Slube at the cigar store. Mr. Koochagian, the tailor, waters the luxuriant jungle of plants in his window, gives them a critical look from the outside, accepts a compliment on them from two passers-by, fingers the leaves on the plane tree in front of our house with a thoughtful gardener's appraisal, and crosses the street for a bite at the Ideal where he can keep an eye on customers and wigwag across the message that he is coming. The baby carriages come out, and clusters of everyone from toddlers with dolls to teen-agers with homework gather at the stoops.

When I get home after work, the ballet is reaching its crescendo. This is the time of roller skates and stilts and tricycles, and games in the lee of the stoop with bottletops and plastic cowboys; this is the time of bundles and packages, zigzagging from the drug store to the fruit stand and back over to the butcher's; this is the time when teen-agers, all dressed up, are pausing to ask if their slips show or their collars look right; this is the time when beautiful girls get out of MG's; this is the time when the fire engines go through; this is the time when anybody you know around Hudson Street will go by.

As darkness thickens and Mr. Halpert moors the laundry cart to the cellar door again, the ballet goes on under lights, eddying back and forth but intensifying at the bright spotlight pools of Joe's sidewalk pizza dispensary, the bars, the delicatessen, the restaurant, and the drug store. The night workers stop now at the delicatessen, to pick up salami and a container of milk. Things have settled down for the evening but the street and its ballet have not come to a stop.

I know the deep night ballet and its seasons best from waking long after midnight to tend a baby and, sitting in the dark, seeing the shadows and hearing the sounds of the party conversation and, about three in the morning, singing, very good singing. Sometimes there is sharpness and anger or sad, sad weeping, or a flurry of search for a string of beads broken. One night a young man came roaring along, bellowing terrible language at two girls whom he had apparently picked up and who were disappointing him. Doors opened, a wary semicircle formed around him, not too close, until the police came. Out came the heads, too, along Hudson Street, offering opinion, "Drunk ... Crazy ... A wild kid from the suburbs."[2]

Deep in the night, I am almost unaware how many people are on the street unless something calls them together, like the bagpipe. Who the piper was and why he favored our street I have no

2. He turned out to be a wild kid from the suburbs. Sometimes, on Hudson Street, we are tempted to believe the suburbs must be a difficult place to bring up children [Jacobs' note].

idea. The bagpipe just skirled out in the February night, and as if it were a signal the random, dwindled movements of the sidewalk took on direction. Swiftly, quietly, almost magically a little crowd was there, a crowd that evolved into a circle with a Highland fling inside it. The crowd could be seen on the shadowy sidewalk, the dancers could be seen, but the bagpiper himself was almost invisible because his bravura was all in his music. He was a very little man in a plain brown overcoat. When he finished and vanished, the dancers and watchers applauded, and applause came from the galleries too, half a dozen of the hundred windows on Hudson Street. Then the windows closed, and the little crowd dissolved into the random movements of the night street.

The strangers on Hudson Street, the allies whose eyes help us natives keep the peace of the street, are so many that they always seem to be different people from one day to the next. That does not matter. Whether they are so many always-different people as they seem to be, I do not know. Likely they are. When Jimmy Rogan fell through a plate-glass window (he was separating some scuffling friends) and almost lost his arm, a stranger in an old T shirt emerged from the Ideal bar, swiftly applied an expert tourniquet, and, according to the hospital's emergency staff, saved Jimmy's life. Nobody remembered seeing the man before and no one has seen him since. The hospital was called in this way: a woman sitting on the steps next to the accident ran over to the bus stop, wordlessly snatched the dime from the hand of a stranger who was waiting with his fifteen-cent fare ready, and raced into the Ideal's phone booth. The stranger raced after her to offer the nickel too. Nobody remembered seeing him before, and no one has seen him since. When you see the same stranger three or four times on Hudson Street, you begin to nod. This is almost getting to be an acquaintance, a public acquaintance, of course.

I have made the daily ballet of Hudson Street sound more frenetic than it is, because writing it telescopes it. In real life, it is not that way. In real life, to be sure, something is always going on, the ballet is never at a halt, but the general effect is peaceful and the general tenor even leisurely. People who know well such animated city streets will know how it is. I am afraid people who do not will always have it a little wrong in their head—like the old prints of rhinoceroses made from travelers' descriptions of rhinoceroses.

On Hudson Street, the same as in the North End of Boston or in any other animated neighborhoods of great cities, we are not innately more competent at keeping the sidewalks safe than are the people who try to live off the hostile truce of Turf in a blind-eyed city. We are the lucky possessors of a city order that makes it relatively simple to keep the peace because there are plenty of eyes on the street. But there is nothing simple about that order itself, or the bewildering number of components that go into it. Most of those components are specialized in one way or another. They unite in their joint effect upon the sidewalk, which is not specialized in the least. That is its strength.

ADA LOUISE HUXTABLE
The World of the Absurd[1]

City life and city problems have come to Antarctica. In some kind of record for nest-fouling, urban sprawl has turned McMurdo Station into an urban horror in a brief ten years. This may be a standing backjump record for ruining the environment.

"A smoking garbage dump and junkyard litter the shore of a once picturesque inlet, power lines from the nuclear plant deface the stark, wind-swept and lifeless hills that so awed and impressed explorers 50 years ago," a reporter noted. The answer? A McMurdo redevelopment program, naturally.

Every year sees megalopolis, the urban smear that is staining the entire American northeast and blurring city boundaries everywhere, relentlessly on its way to ecumenopolis, or a totally urbanized world, according to planner Constantinos Doxiadis. (The Greeks had a word for it and still do. Any trend or truism dressed up in classical etymology becomes a charismatic concept for the intellectually susceptible. It has the authority of a sermon from the Acropolis.)

Ecumenopolis may take a little while, but we'll get there. We are getting to the moon first, of course, although only one thing is sure about that and none of the scientific prognostications mention it. When we get there, we'll make a mess of it.[2]

* * *

Meanwhile, back at the foundations and universities, studies of the city proliferate and more are promised. In a brilliant review of "Taming Megalopolis," planner and architect Clive Entwistle[3] envisions "continuing and increasing and ever more expensive 'research' projects to the horizons of urban space and post-graduate time."

The pinned butterfly of urban phenomena, the dissected and annotated crisis, substitute handily for solutions. Few studies have the jolting pertinence of a Moynihan[4] analysis of the Negro family

1. From *Will They Ever Finish Bruckner Boulevard?*, 1970.

2. Man the explorer made it to the moon on July 20, 1969, and became man the litterer as he jettisoned electronic equipment, waste and wrappings

[Huxtable's note].

3. A writer on environmental problems.

4. Daniel P. Moynihan, American sociologist.

in American society. Most are pretentious and fatiguingly detailed enshrinements of the obvious or ordinary, properly impressive to those who are awed by Greek-root words. "Before the buzz of refined scholarship," Entwistle concludes, "the decision makers, engineers and politicians stand abashed and emasculated."

"Trend is not destiny," Lewis Mumford has warned in one of his periodic blasts on the urban scene from his sanctuary in the non-urban hills, quoting Albert Mayer's book *The Urgent Future*. "Progress," said *The New York Times* editorially, is an idea that needs to be "challenged."

All this makes it quite clear where we are. We are obviously in the world of the absurd. The black urban comedy continues to be played out in the research institutes and the black urban tragedy goes on in the ghettos while Rome, and Detroit and Newark, burn.

Disaster is charted as destiny and objective, scholarly truth. Progress consists of making the same mistake, but on an Olympian scale. Research builds abstract monuments to itself. Funds are made available for "prototytpe studies" while untouched problems take their toll of the human heart and the urban world. In government agencies, policy set at the top is reversed by bureaucracy at the bottom.

We pollute the country with the refuse of the affluent society. In Washington, D.C., it has been found that there is more gold per ton of fly ash in the refuse dumps than in commercial mines. At McMurdo we have the apotheosis of absurdity; we have destroyed the environment while studying it. The reality of the world of the absurd can't be touched by anything in the imagination of man.

There is hope, of course. We can press that precious garbage into construction blocks and build with them, according to promising new processes, rather than face slow strangulation from the detritus of prosperity. Eventually we may be able to move to a $4 billion experimental city being studied by ten industries and three Federal agencies in Minnesota. We can enter the research cloisters in handsome parts of the countryside where megalopolis waits to spring.

But for now we substitute the high-level make-work of scholars for responsibility and action. It is a face-saving, if not city-saving, evasion. For value judgments we embrace more esoteric studies of the natural chaos of "the scene." The administrator, politician or planner who holds convictions enough to battle for solutions—and solutions are always partial, imperfect, debatable and without guarantees—must be an extraordinary combination of gutter tough and intellectual visionary. He does it, surprisingly, in an age of cynicism, because he cares.

What he deals in is the environment, an "in" word in the crisis of cities that is a poorly understood concept at best. As a word, it is meaningless. Its comprehension is a visual, emotional, sensuous, physical and visceral process; it is the direct, three-dimensional, individual and collective experience of one's surroundings; the sum total of external conditions and influences affecting life for better or worse.

In a city the environment is made by man. "Made by Man" should be stamped across the blank towers and arid open spaces that are the equally barren contribution of both public and luxury housing at the two extremes of the scale. (One has art, the other has vandalism in the lobby.) "Made by Man" should be branded on rotting piers and scabrous waterfront. It should be emblazoned on city-maiming expressways and the shadowed slums beneath them. It all comes off the drawing board at the start, whatever subsequent overlays of social disaster may add rich varieties of human blight.

The urban world is a conscious act; it is the work of some hand and eye and mind, no matter how mindless it may appear. The original blight was the designer's, the builder's, the developer's, the engineer's or the architect's, whatever economic, political or legislative pressures or incentives may have set the standards or the style.

What is being designed privately and publicly with alarming consistency is instant blight. We are building blight for the next hundred years. The environment is being sealed systematically into sterility and its social problems are being compounded and immortalized by substandard design. The failure of the environment is our theme.

QUESTIONS

1. From defining environment (an "in" word but a "poorly understood concept"), Huxtable switches to the question of comprehension of the term. Is she evading the problem of definition or solving it?
2. "The urban world is a conscious act." Does this statement testify to a belief in what Skinner rejects as the "autonomous man"?
3. In this short essay, what is Huxtable's main concern? What is the main source of the essay's impact?

ROBERT CLAIBORNE
Future Schlock

schlock, *n. slang:* Merchandise of meretricious or obviously inferior quality . . .
—American Heritage Dictionary

America, which leads the world in almost every economic category, leads it above all in the production of schlock. Christmas toys broken before New Year's, wash-n-wear suits that neither wash well nor wear well, appliances that expire a month after the guarantee, Barbie dolls, frozen pizza—these are but a few of the shoddy goods whose main contribution to our civilization, apart from a momentary satisfaction to the purchaser, is to swell the sanitary-fill schlock heaps that are the feces of our Gross (and how!) National Product.

America's schlock output is not limited to material goods, of course. Schlock novels, movies and TV programs are an old story, and the spread of higher education has more recently begotten a new division of schlock software: intellectual schlock. We have schlock anthropology (Ardrey, Morris); schlock psychology (Franzblau, Brothers, many more); and schlock criticism (you name 'em). President Nixon has obviously been relying on schlock economics, even as the Pentagon has long dealt in schlock geopolitics. Most omnipresent of all is the subject of the present essay: schlock sociology.

Sociological schlock, like any other variety, is designed to exploit a human need—in this case, the craving to make some sort of sense out of an increasingly demented society. Since the market is assured, and virtually limitless, the production of schlock sociology for fun and profit is not particularly difficult, given a reasonable amount of imagination and a firm grasp of the major requirements. An important ingredient is a lively literary style; the ideal product should read like *The Decline of the West* rewritten by Vance Packard (who would himself qualify as a schlock sociologist if he were a bit more pretentious). But even a lumpy style can sometimes be adequately leavened by some trendy chapter headings.

The absolutely essential ingredient, however, is an Insight—a phrase that sums up, aphoristically or antithetically, some current —and usually alarming—social tendency and thereby strikes a nerve in the body politic. Representative Insights include "the lonely crowd," "the true believer," "the end of ideology," "organization man," "repressive tolerance" and—the probable granddaddy of them all—"the managerial revolution."

As will be seen from these examples, an Insight need not necessarily be false and in fact is usually true—though a really virtuoso performer can make do with one that is merely catchy ("the medium is the message"). It is not by the validity of his Insight that one identifies the schlock sociologist, but by how he develops it: the fulsomeness of his documentation, the plausible superficiality of his analysis, and the evasiveness of his conclusion.

There is, to be sure, a much simpler test for schlockiness: time. Within five years (and often by the time the book is out in paperback) events will have made clear whether the acuteness of the author's Insight is matched by his understanding of its genesis and future development. Thus it was not many years after Daniel Bell's funeral oration over the grave of ideology that ideological movements dislodged an American President and brought France close to civil war. The reader interested in quicker methods of intellectual quality control, however, may care to consider the following diagnostic traits, any one of which should create a suspicion of schlock, while together they can be taken as conclusive.

Documentation

This will be voluminous, multidisciplinary and preferably multilingual; the effect will be to overwhelm the reader with "facts" so that he has little opportunity to reflect on whether they are true, let alone whether they fit together. The longer the bibliography and the more obscure or inaccessible its constituents, moreover, the more certain that—whether or not the author has read all the items —no reader will be familiar, now or ever, with more than a small fraction of them. Often, however, the reader can apply the simple touchstone of the "I Was There" test: locate in the index some person, institution or field of knowledge of which he happens to have detailed personal knowledge and then check to see how the author handles it. My own disenchantment with *The Lonely Crowd* began when I read in it a number of statements which I knew to be nonsense—because they dealt with a magazine I happened to be working for.

Analysis

The most conspicuous giveaway is an explicit rejection or an implicit abandonment of logic, but this is dangerously obvious unless the author possesses the bravura of a McLuhan, or is addressing the ill-educated young. Most schlock sociologists, therefore, prefer to rely primarily on obfuscation by means of various identifiable rhetorical ploys, some of which I shall describe in detail in a moment.

Conclusion

However ominous the world that the schlock sociologist portrays, he will invariably conclude that either (a) nothing *can* be done about it (e.g., *The Organization Man*) or (b) nothing *need* be done about it (e.g., *The Greening of America*) or (c) nothing *much* need to be done about it—i.e., the difficulty can be resolved without seriously discommoding the reader or anyone else. An author who tells you that dealing with the problem he poses will cost you time, trouble and conceivably your life, your fortune and your sacred honor may be a nut, a commie or an ignoramus, but he is assuredly not a schlock merchant.

Analyzed by these techniques, Alvin Toffler's *Future Shock* assays as unmistakable schlock, albeit of superior quality. His style is lively and readable—his chapter and section hearings, in particular, glitter with such gems as "The Paper Wedding Gown," "The Modular Man," "Communes and Homosexual Daddies" and (my favorite) "Twiggy and the K-Mesons." And, to do him full justice, he has come up with an absolute dilly of an Insight: Future Shock, "the shattering stress and disorientation that we induce in individuals by subjecting them to too much change in too short a time." Future shock is in effect a subdivision of cultural shock—"what happens when the familiar psychological cues that help an individual to function in society are suddenly withdrawn and replaced by new ones that are strange or incomprehensible." Toffler deserves our gratitude for having the wit to see that culture shock can occur not only in space but also in time.

Thus, he writes, "the increased rate at which situations flow past us vastly complicates the entire structure of life, multiplying the number of roles we must play and the number of choices we are forced to make. . . . The speeded-up flow-through of situations demands much more work from the complex focusing mechanisms by which we shift our attention from one situation to another. There is more switching back and forth, less time for extended, peaceful attention to one problem or situation at a time. . . ." Moreover, "rising rates of change . . . compel us not merely to cope with a faster flow, but with more and more situations to which previous personal experience does not apply."

Given an Insight of this potency, it doesn't much matter that Toffler's account of its origins is overlong and exaggerated, or that his discussion of the physical and psychological ills it entrains is overshort and scientifically inconclusive. Future shock is a reality that most of us can feel in our guts. Change implies uncertainty— and there is a limit to the amount of uncertainty a man can cope with before freaking out; coping with change requires energy—and there is a limit to the amount of energy a man can expend in a given time without succumbing to nervous and/or physical exhaustion. Almost everyone has experienced this sort of overstress at least occasionally; the accelerating rate of innovation in our world and the multiplying choices we must make among innovations now threaten to make it chronic.

Yet for all that, the book, by the tests cited above, still comes out schlock. As regards documentation, we note that Toffler's bibliography includes no less than 358 books, plus seven "consulted" periodicals, in half a dozen languages including the Scandinavian. They range from A *Social Psychological Interpretation of the Udall, Kansas, Tornado* to John Barth's *The Floating Opera.* Less than half of them are listed in the footnotes, engendering the suspicion that at least some of the remainder are padding. Suspicion is strengthened when we notice a tendency common among schlock sociologists: citation of other schlock or quasi-schlock authorities. As a rule of thumb, suspicion of mutual schlock-scratching exists when an author cites more than six works by Vance Packard, Buckminster Fuller, David Riesman, Marshall McLuhan, B. F. Skinner and Margaret Mead, singly or in combination. Toffler cites fourteen. (I should add that my characterization of Miss Mead's sociological efforts obviously do not apply to her anthropological contributions.)

The book also fails to pass a simple "I Was There" test. Toffler, seeking a metaphor for the wracking social transition we are now undergoing, comes up with the "traumatic" period in which our vertebrate ancestors were evolving from fish to amphibians: "Eons ago, the shrinking seas cast millions of unwilling aquatic creatures onto the newly created beaches. Reprived of their familiar environment, they died, gasping and clawing for each additional instant of eternity. . . ." Now, I Was There, in the sense that, having written three books and part of a fourth dealing in one way or another with evolution, I have considerable expertise in the field. I can therefore say flatly that there is not the slightest evidence that during the period in question the seas were shrinking—especially not with such suddenness as to strand millions of aquatic creatures. There is, moreover, much evidence that the evolutionary transition from fish to amphibian occurred, not upon ocean beaches, "newly created" or otherwise, but in fresh-water swamps. Finally, there is no reason to suppose that the transition was especially "traumatic" for any of the organisms involved. Toffler's affecting narrative is pure hokum. Admittedly, *hokum in unum, hokum in omnium* is by no means an absolute principle, but in schlock testing it is a useful working hypothesis.

It is when we examine Toffler's analytic methods, however, that the suspicion of schlockiness becomes certainty, for he consistently uses most of the half-dozen ploys by which the schlock sociologist obfuscates the problem he is ostensibly elucidating. To begin with, the Evasive We, invaluable for shifting the responsibility for a social problem from somebody to nobody. Thus (my emphasis)

"We have created the disposable person: Modular Man"; "We are forcing people to adapt to a new life pace"; "We have not merely extended the scope and scale of change, we have radically altered its pace"—*und so weiter*. To make certain that an author is employing the Evasive We, replace "we" with "I and my friends"; if the result is gibberish, you are being conned.

Sometimes, however, the Evasive We won't do; only a fool would expect to get away with saying that "We are making new scientific discoveries every day and we are putting them to work more quickly than ever before." Toffler therefore adopts the Plausible Passive: "New scientific discoveries are being made every day. . . . These new ideas are being put to work more quickly. . . ."—thereby rather neatly obscuring the fact that scientists and engineers (mostly paid by industry) are making the discoveries and industrialists (often with the aid of public funds) are putting them to work. An alternative to the Plausible Passive is the Elusive Impersonal: "Buildings in New York literally disappear overnight." What Toffler is trying to avoid saying is that contractors and real estate speculators *destroy* buildings overnight.

But if not industrialists and speculators, *something* is surely causing social change, and Toffler is too expert a schlockmeister to ignore this fact. He therefore resorts to yet another ploy, Rampant Reification, in which conceptual abstractions are transformed into causal realities. Thus he speaks of "the roaring current of change" as "an elemental force" and of "that great, growling engine of change—technology." Which of course completely begs the question of what fuels the engine and whose hand is on the throttle. One does not cross-examine an elemental force, let alone suggest that it may have been engendered by monopoly profits (especially in defense and aerospace) or accelerated by government incentives (e.g., open or concealed subsidies, low capital gains tax, accelerated depreciation—which Nixon is now seeking to reinstitute).

Space does not allow a detailed discussion of all Toffler's schlock ploys. There is the "Now I Say It. Now I Don't" maneuver, especially useful for trapping critics who, in pouncing on some particularly silly statement, may well overlook the author's own refutation of it some chapters away. There is the Goldbrick Generality, in which a plating of generalized truth conceals the leaden absence of specifics within. ("We would do well to hasten the controlled—selective—arrival of tomorrow's technologies" seems reasonable until you realize that nothing is said about who is to do the controlling, by what social mechanisms, and to what ends.) In fact about the only important ploy *not* present is that favorite of McLuhan's, the Semantic Fast Shuffle, where a word means one thing going into a paragraph and something else coming out. Two devices, however, must be singled out for special attention because they bear on the substance—if that is the word—of Toffler's argument.

The first is the Things Are Usually What They Seem caper. Toffler gets into this because, while deploring the headlong pace of change in general (Goldbrick Generality), he fights shy of attacking specific kinds of changes, and in fact seems to feel that in most areas change is a pretty Good Thing. Thus he finds traditional bureaucracy changing to a looser-structured (and presumably less dehumanizing) arrangement that he calls Ad-hocracy. This is obviously a Good Thing—so long as one ignores the fact that the new Ad-hocracies somehow end up doing the same manipulative, self-serving and often stupid things as the old bureaucracies (for documentation, see under PENTAGON, LOCKHEED, BOEING, PENN CENTRAL, etc.).

Again, he sees modern technology as by and large a Good Thing; it does not (as suggested by some) lock us into a rigid, dehuman-ied existence but rather enormously expands the choices open to us. As an example of these choices, he quotes McLuhan (who else?) on the various "combinations of styles, options and colors available on a certain new family sports car"; the total works out at some 25 million "choices." Unfortunately, every goddamn one of the 25 million pollutes the atmosphere, dents if you lean on it too hard and is unsafe at any speed. As most thoughtful consumers have become aware, the choices open to them are governed by the Law of Minimal Differences: the degree of substantive difference among functionally similar products varies inversely with the number of such products—i.e., as the number approaches infinity, the differ-ence approaches zero. Schlock sociology, like schlock everything else, focuses on the package, not the contents.

Yet despite his evident reluctance to indict any specific changes as dispensable, Toffler has made too powerful a case against future shock to drop the matter there. Indeed, he concedes that both future shock and most of our other problems "stem not from implacable natural forces but from man-made processes that are at last potentially subject to our control." Taken together with his previous citation of the "elemental force" of change, this is of course a Now I Say It Now I Don't, and simultaneously a Gold-brick Generality, since it leaves hanging the central question of what men are in fact making these man-made processes.

Insofar as he makes a stab at answering the question, in passages scattered throughout the book. Toffler resorts to perhaps the most basic maneuver of all liberal schlock sociology: All Men Are Guilty —and So What? Manufacturers are guilty—"many of the annual model changes .. are not technologically substantive." Well then, should we—meaning I and my friends—try to force manufacturers to dispense with trivial changes? Deponent sayeth not. Manufactures are guilty—and so what?

Advertising is also not blameless: "Madison Avenue frequently exaggerates the importance of new features and encourages consumers to dispose of partially worn-out goods to make way for the new." Should we perhaps do something about Madison Avenue— say, a truth in advertising law, or a limit on the amount of advertising that can be charged off as tax-deductible? Toffler doesn't tell us.

Consumers, too, are guilty: often the consumer "has a vague feeling that he wants a change." This statement is undocumented and, in my own case, untrue; if anything, I have a by-no-means-vague feeling that change is what I *don't* want. This derives from repeated experiences with a new marketing principle: if it works, change it —whereby products that I know and like disappear, to be replaced by other, inferior versions. But assuming it *is* true of some consumers—so what should we do about it? So nothing!

Obviously, tackling the problem of unnecessary change from any of these directions, let alone all three together, would involve a long, hard and dubious battle. Toffler, as a partisan of the "nothing much need be done about it" school, wants none of this. What he proposes is not struggle but a series of Mad Tea Parties. Thus he recommends "the construction of highly intricate models, games and simulations, the preparation of detailed speculative scenarios" to descry the alternative futures open to us. We must, in other words, consult those clever people who gave us Vietnam—which, as one very knowledgeable commentator has noted, was the most thoroughly "gamed" and "scenarioed" war in history. We need to construct "utopia factories" which can experiment with new models of society. We need, God help us, to "convene . . . democratic constituent assemblies charged with social stock-taking . . . with defining and assigning priorities to specific social goals . . ." National priorities . . . social goals . . . Oy! Having told us that we are being psychologically raped by change, Toffler finally concludes that with just a bit of painless social tinkering we can relax and enjoy it.

A meaningful, non-schlock analysis of the future-shock problems would have to begin with Toffler's own unexceptionable conclusion: "Change rampant, change unguided and unrestrained, accelerated change, overwhelming not only man's physical defenses but his decisional proesses—such change is the enemy of life." It would continue with the recognition that most changes in our society—at a guess, something like 80 per cent—are unnecessary (in the sense that they make no contribution toward meeting human needs or improving the human condition) and often actively inimical. At best, they are feats of packaging which are not "technologically substantive," which gussie up schlock products—or institutions—for the benefit of their proprietors; at worst, they are substantively anti-human, enforced by top corporate and governmental bureaucrats (or Ad-hocrats) for their own power or profit. (Toffler cites the case of an executive compelled to change his residence twenty-eight times in twenty-three years of married life!)

We do not have to put up with these changes. We do not have to have an SST or an Everglades jetport; we do not have to have the annual spate of new, "improved" models in everything from automobiles to skirts; we do not have to have conglomerates, nonreturnable bottles, paper wedding gowns or any of the other innovations which simultaneously foul up our natural, our social and (as Toffler has made clear) our psychological environments. We do not have to have schlock.

But to set bounds to these changes, be they inimical or merely spurious, involves facing up to the nature of their source. Toffler himself, in one of his few non-schlock passages, says of technological change what could equally be said of change in general: "In the West, the basic criterion for filtering out certain ... innovations and applying others remains economic profitability." If we are to seize control of our own future, we must confront the long, difficult problem of restructuring social institutions so that they march to a different drummer, making man, not Mammon, the measure of all things. And if, bemused by the agile evasions and trendy catchwords of schlock sociology, we fail to do this, then we—meaning I and my friends and all the rest of us—will deserve what we get: both future shock and a schlock future.

QUESTIONS

1. Like Orwell ("Politics and the English Language," pp. 168–179), Claiborne describes categories of conceptual-linguistic abuses; does his set of categories have much in common with Orwell's?
2. Essays by some of the schlock sociologists Claiborne names appear in this book; applying his categories or "diagnostic traits" to these samples of their writings, would you diagnose them as schlock?
3. Does Claiborne undercut his own argument when he concedes that Toffler has made too strong a case against future shock to let the matter drop? Since he does continue the case, you have a brief opportunity to assess Claiborne's performance by the standards he describes—how does he do?

PETER SCHRAG
The Forgotten American

There is hardly a language to describe him, or even a set of social statistics. Just names: racist-bigot-redneck-ethnic-Irish-Italian-Pole-Hunkie-Yahoo. The lower middle class. A blank. The man under whose hat lies the great American desert. Who watches the tube, plays the horses, and keeps the niggers out of his union and his neighborhood. Who might vote for Wallace (but didn't). Who cheers when the cops beat up on demonstrators. Who is free, white and twenty-one, has a job, a home, a family, and is up to his eye-balls in credit. In the guise of the working class—or the American yeoman or John Smith—he was once the hero of the civics book, the man that Andrew Jackson called "the bone and sinew of the country." Now he is "the forgotten man," perhaps the most alien-ated person in America.

Nothing quite fits, except perhaps omission and semi-invisibility. America is supposed to be divided between affluence and poverty, between slums and suburbs. John Kenneth Galbraith begins the foreword to *The Affluent Society* with the phrase, "since I sailed for Switzerland in the early summer of 1955 to begin work on this book . . ." But *between* slums and suburbs, between Scarsdale and Harlem, between Wellesley and Roxbury, between Shaker Heights and Hough, there are some eighty million people (depending on how you count them) who didn't sail for Switzerland in the summer of 1955 or at any other time, and who never expect to. Between slums and suburbs: South Boston and South San Fran-cisco, Bell and Parma, Astoria and Bay Ridge, Newark, Cicero, Downey, Daly City, Charlestown, Flatbush. Union halls, American Legion posts, neighborhood bars and bowling leagues, the Ukrain-ian Club and the Holy Name. Main Street. To try to describe all this is like trying to describe America itself. If you look for it, you find it everywhere: the rows of frame houses overlooking the belch-ing steel mills in Bethlehem, Pennsylvania; two-family brick houses in Canarsie (where the most common slogan, even in the middle of a political campaign, is "curb your dog"); the Fords and Chevies with a decal American flag on the rear window (usually a cut-out from the *Reader's Digest*, and displayed in counter-protest against peaceniks and "those bastards who carry Vietcong flags in demon-strations"); the bunting on the porch rail with the inscription, "Welcome Home, Pete." The gold star in the window.

When he was Under Secretary of Housing and Urban Develop-ment, Robert C. Wood tried a definition. It is not good, but it's the best we have:

He is a white employed male . . . earning between $5,000 and $10,000. He works regularly, steadily, dependably, wearing a blue collar or white collar. Yet the frontiers of his career expectations have been fixed since he reached the age of thirty-five, when he found that he had too many obligations, too much family, and too few skills to match opportunities with aspirations.

This definition of the "working American" involves almost 23 million American families.

The working American lives in the gray area fringes of a central city or in a close-in or very far-out cheaper suburban subdivision of a large metropolitan area. He is likely to own a home and a car, especially as his income begins to rise. Of those earning between $6,000 and $7,500, 70 per cent own their own homes and 94 percent drive their own cars.

94 per cent have no education beyond high school and 43 per cent have only completed the eighth grade.

He does all the right things, obeys the law, goes to church and insists—usually—that his kids get a better education than he had. But the right things don't seem to be paying off. While he is making more than he ever made—perhaps more than he ever dreamed—he's still struggling while a lot of others—"them" (on welfare, in demonstrations, in the ghettos)—are getting most of the attention. "I'm working my ass off," a guy tells you on a stoop in South Boston. "My kids don't have a place to swim, my parks are full of glass, and I'm supposed to bleed for a bunch of people on relief." In New York a man who drives a Post Office trailer truck at night (4:00 P.M. to midnight) and a cab during the day (7:00 A.M. to 2:00 P.M.), and who hustles radios for his Post Office buddies on the side is ready, as he says, to "knock somebody's ass." "The colored guys work when they feel like it. Sometimes they show up and sometimes they don't. One guy tore up all the time cards. I'd like to see a white guy do that and get away with it."

What Counts

Nobody knows how many people in America moonlight (half of the eighteen million families in the $5,000 to $10,000 bracket have two or more wage earners) or how many have to hustle on the side. "I don't think anybody has a single job anymore," said Nicholas Kisburg, the research director for a Teamsters Union Council in New York. "All the cops are moonlighting, and the teachers; and there's a million guys who are hustling, guys with phony social-security numbers who are hiding part of what they make so they don't get kicked out of a housing project, or guys who work as guards at sports events and get free meals that they don't want to pay taxes on. Every one of them is cheating. They are underground people— *Untermenschen.* ... We really have no systematic data on any of this. We have no ideas of the attitudes of the white worker. (We've been too busy studying the black worker.) And yet he's the source of most of the reaction in this country."

The reaction is directed at almost every visible target: at integration and welfare, taxes and sex education, at the rich and the poor, the foundations and students, at the "smart people in the suburbs." In New York State the legislature cuts the welfare budget; in Los Angeles, the voters reelect Yorty after a whispered racial campaign against the Negro favorite. In Minneapolis a police detective named Charles Stenvig, promising "to take the handcuffs off the police," wins by a margin stunning even to his supporters: in Massachusetts the voters mail tea bags to their representatives in protest against new taxes, and in state after state legislatures are passing bills to punish student demonstrators. ("We keep talking about permissiveness in training kids," said a Los Angeles labor official, "but we forget that these are our kids.")

And yet all these things are side manifestations of a malaise that lacks a language. Whatever law and order means, for example, to a man who feels his wife is unsafe on the street after dark or in the park at any time, or whose kids get shaken down in the school yard, it also means something like normality—the demand that everybody play it by the book, that cultural and social standards be somehow restored to their civics-book simplicity, that things shouldn't be as they are but as they were supposed to be. If there is a revolution in this country—a revolt in manners, standards of dress and obscenity, and, more importantly, in our official sense of what America is—there is also a counter-revolt. Sometimes it is inarticulate, and sometimes (perhaps most of the time) people are either too confused or apathetic—or simply too polite and too decent—to declare themselves. In Astoria, Queens, a white working-class district of New York, people who make $7,000 or $8,000 a year (sometimes in two jobs) call themselves affluent, even though the Bureau of Labor Statistics regards an income of less than $9,500 in New York inadequate to a moderate standard of living. And in a similar neighborhood in Brooklyn a truck driver who earns $151 a week tells you he's doing well, living in a two-story frame house separated by a narrow driveway from similar houses, thousands of them in block after block. This year, for the first time, he will go on a cruise—he and his wife and two other couples—two weeks in the Caribbean. He went to work after World War II ($57 a week) and he has lived in the same house for twenty years, accumulating two television sets, wall-to-wall carpeting in a small living room, and a basement that he recently remodeled into a recreation room with the help of two moonlighting firemen. "We get fairly good salaries, and this is a good neighborhood, one of the few good ones left. We have no smoked Irishmen around."

Stability is what counts, stability in job and home and neighborhood, stability in the church and in friends. At night you watch television and sometimes on a weekend you go to a nice place—maybe a downtown hotel—for dinner with another couple. (Or maybe your sister, or maybe bowling, or maybe, if you're defeated, a night at the track.) The wife has the necessary appliances, often still being paid off, and the money you save goes for your daughter's orthodontist, and later for her wedding. The smoked Irishmen—the colored (no one says black; few even say Negro)—represent change and instability, kids who cause trouble in school, who get treatment that your kids never got, that you never got. ("Those fucking kids," they tell you in South Boston, "raising hell, and not one of 'em paying his own way. Their fucking mothers are all on welfare.") The black kids mean a change in the rules, a double standard in grades and discipline, and—vaguely—a challenge to all you believed right. Law and order is the stability and predictability of established ways. Law and order is equal treatment—in school, in jobs, in the courts—even if you're cheating a little yourself. The Forgotten Man is Jackson's man. He is the vestigial American democrat of 1840: "They all know that their success depends upon their own industry and economy and that they must not expect to become suddenly rich by the fruits of their toil." He is also Franklin Roosevelt's man —the man whose vote (or whose father's vote) sustained the New Deal.

There are other considerations, other styles, other problems. A postman in a Charlestown (Boston) housing project: eight children and a ninth on the way. Last year, by working overtime, his income went over $7,000. This year, because he reported it, the Housing Authority is raising his rent from $78 to $106 a month, a catastrophe for a family that pays $2.20 a day for milk, has never had a vacation, and for which an excursion is "going out for ice cream." "You try and save for something better; we hope to get out of here to someplace where the kids can play, where there's no broken glass, and then something always comes along that knocks you right back. It's like being at the bottom of the well waiting for a guy to throw you a rope." The description becomes almost Chaplinesque. Life is humble but not simple; the terrors of insolent bureaucracies and contemptuous officials produce a demonology that loses little of its horror for being partly misunderstood. You want to get a sink fixed but don't want to offend the manager; want to get an eye operation that may (or may not) have been necessitated by a military injury five years earlier, "but the Veterans Administration says I signed away my benefits"; want to complain to someone about the teen-agers who run around breaking windows and harassing women but get no response either from the management or the police. "You're afraid to complain because if they don't get you during the day they'll get you at night." Automobiles, windows, children, all become hostages to the vague terrors of everyday life; everything is vulnerable. Liabilities that began long ago cannot possibly be liquidated: "I never learned anything in that school except how to fight. I got tired of being caned by the teachers so at sixteen I quit and joined the Marines. I still don't know anything."

At the Bottom of the Well

American culture? Wealth is visible, and so, now, is poverty. Both have become intimidating clichés. But the rest? A vast, complex, and disregarded world that was once—in belief, and in fact— the American middle: Greyhound and Trailways bus terminals in little cities at midnight, each of them with its neon lights and its cardboard hamburgers; acres of tar-paper beach bungalows in places like Revere and Rockaway; the hair curlers in the supermarket on Saturday, and the little girls in the communion dresses the next morning; pinball machines and the *Daily News,* the *Reader's Digest* and Ed Sullivan; houses with tiny front lawns (or even large ones) adorned with statues of the Virgin or of Sambo welcomin' de folks home; Clint Eastwood or Julie Andrews at the Palace; the trotting tracks and the dog tracks—Aurora Downs, Connaught Park, Roosevelt, Yonkers, Rockingham, and forty others—where gray men come not for sport and beauty, but to read numbers, to study and dope. (If you win you have figured something, have in a small way controlled your world, have surmounted your impotence. If you lose, bad luck, shit. "I'll break his goddamned head.") Baseball is not the national pastime; racing is. For every man who goes to a major-league baseball game there are four who go to the track and probably four more who go to the candy store or the barbershop to make their bets. (Total track attendance in 1965: 62 million plus another 10 million who went to the dogs.)

There are places, and styles, and attitudes. If there are neighborhoods of aspiration, suburban enclaves for the mobile young executive and the aspiring worker, there are also places of limited expectation and dead-end districts where mobility is finished. But even there you can often find, however vestigial, a sense of place, the roots of old ethnic loyalties, and a passionate, if often futile, battle against intrusion and change. "Everybody around here," you are told, "Pays his own way." In this world the problems are not the ABM or air pollution (have they heard of Biafra?) or the international population crisis; the problem is to get your street cleaned, your garbage collected, to get your husband home from Vietnam alive; to negotiate installment payments and to keep the schools orderly. Ask anyone in Scarsdale or Winnetka about the schools and they'll tell you about new programs, or about how many are getting into Harvard, or about the teachers; ask in Oakland or the North Side of Chicago, and they'll tell you that they have (or haven't) had trouble. Somewhere in his gut the man in those communities knows that mobility and choice in this society are limited. He cannot imagine any major change for the better; but he can imagine change for the worse. And yet for a decade he is the one who has been asked to carry the burden of social reform, to integrate his schools and his neighborhood, has been asked by comfortable people to pay the social debts due to the poor and the black. In Boston, in San Francisco, in Chicago (not to mention Newark or Oakland) he has been telling the reformers to go to hell. The Jewish schoolteachers of New York and the Irish parents of Dorchester have asked the same question: "What the hell did Lindsay (or the Beacon Hill Establishment) ever do for us?"

The ambiguities and changes in American life that occupy discussions in university seminars and policy debates in Washington, and that form the backbone of contemporary popular sociology, become increasingly the conditions of trauma and frustration in the middle. Although the New Frontier and Great Society contained some programs for those not already on the roll of social pathology—federal aid for higher education, for example—the public priorities and the rhetoric contained little. The emphasis, properly, was on the poor, on the inner cities (*e.g.*, Negroes) and the unemployed. But in Chicago a widow with three children who earns $7,000 a year can't get them college loans because she makes too much; the money is reserved for people on relief. New schools are built in the ghetto but not in the white working-class neighborhoods where they are just as dilapidated. In Newark the head of a white vigilante group (now a city councilman) runs, among other things, on a platform opposing pro-Negro discrimination. "When pools are being built in the Central Ward—don't they think white kids have got frustration? The white can't get a job; we have to hire Negroes first." The middle class, said Congressman Roman Pucinski of Illinois, who represents a lot of it, "is in revolt. Everyone has been generous in supporting anti-poverty. Now the middle-class American is disqualified from most of the programs."

"Somebody Has to Say No . . ."

The frustrated middle. The liberal wisdom about welfare, ghettos, student revolt, and Vietnam has only a marginal place, if any, for the values and life of the working man. It flies in the face of most of what he was taught to cherish and respect: hard work, order, authority, self-reliance. He fought, either alone or through labor organizations, to establish the precincts he now considers his own. Union seniority, the civil-service bureaucracy, and the petty professionalism established by the merit system in the public schools become sinecures of particular ethnic groups or of those who have learned to negotiate and master the system. A man who worked all his life to accumulate the points and grades and paraphernalia to become an assistant school principal (no matter how silly the requirements) is not likely to relinquish his position with equanimity. Nor is a dock worker whose only estate is his longshoreman's card. The job, the points, the credits become property:

> Some men leave their sons money [wrote a union member to the *New York Times*], some large investments, some business connections, and some a profession. I have only one worthwhile thing to give: my trade. I hope to follow a centuries-old tradition and sponsor my sons for an apprenticeship. For this simple father's wish it is said that I discriminate against Negroes. Don't all of us discriminate? Which of us . . . will not choose a son over all others?

Suddenly the rules are changing—all the rules. If you protect your job for your own you may be called a bigot. At the same time it's perfectly acceptable to shout black power and to endorse it. What does it take to be a good American? *Give the black man a position because he is black, not because he necessarily works harder or does the job better.* What does it take to be a good American? Dress nicely, hold a job, be clean-cut, don't judge a man by the color of his skin or the country of his origin. What about the demands of Negroes, the long hair of the students, the dirty movies, the people who burn draft cards and American flags? Do you have to go out in the street with picket signs, do you have to burn the place down to get what you want? What does it take to be a good American? *This is a sick society, a racist society, we are fighting an immoral war.* ("I'm against the Vietnam war, too," says the truck driver in Brooklyn. "I see a good kid come home with half an arm and a leg in a brace up to here, and what's it all for? I was glad to see *my* kid flunk the Army physical. Still, somebody has to say no to these demonstrators and enforce the law.") What does it take to be a good American?

The conditions of trauma and frustration in the middle. What does it take to be a good American? Suddenly there are demands for Italian power and Polish power and Ukrainian power. In Cleveland the Poles demand a seat on the school board, and get it, and in Pittsburgh John Pankuch, the seventy-three-year-old president of the National Slovak Society, demands "action, plenty of it to make up for lost time." Black power is supposed to be nothing but emulation of the ways in which other ethnic groups made it. But have they made it? In Reardon's Bar on East Eighth Street in South Boston, where the workmen come for their fish-chowder lunch and for their rye and ginger, they still identify themselves as Galway men and Kilkenny men; in the newsstand in Astoria you can buy *Il Progresso*, *El Tiempo*, the *Staats-Zeitung*, the *Irish World*, plus papers in Greek, Hungarian, and Polish. At the parish of Our Lady of Mount Carmel the priest hears confession in English, Italian, and Spanish and, nearby, the biggest attraction is not the stickball game, but the *boccie* court. Some of the poorest people in America are white, native, and have lived all of their lives in the same place as their fathers and grandfathers. The problems that were presumably solved in some distant past, in that prehistoric era before the textbooks were written—problems of assimilation, of upward mobility—now turn out to be very much unsolved. The melting pot and all: millions made it, millions moved to the affluent suburbs; several million—no one knows how many—did not. The median income in Irish South Boston is $5,100 a year but the community-action workers have a hard time convincing the local citizens that any white man who is not stupid or irresponsible can be poor. Pride still keeps them from applying for income supplements or Medicaid, but it does not keep them from resenting those who do. In Pittsburgh, where the members of Polish-American organizations earn an estimated $5,000 to $6,000 (and some fall below the poverty line), the Poverty Programs are nonetheless directed primarily to Negroes, and almost everywhere the thing called urban backlash associates itself in some fashion with ethnic groups whose members have themselves only a precarious hold on the security of affluence. Almost everywhere in the old cities, tribal neighborhoods and their styles are under assault by masscult. The Italian grocery gives way to the supermarket, the ma-and-pa store and the walk-up are attacked by urban renewal. And almost everywhere, that assault tends to depersonalize and to alienate. It has always been this way, but with time the brave new world that replaces old patterns becomes increasingly bureaucratized, distant, and hard to control.

Yet beyond the problems of ethnic identity, beyond the problems of Poles and Irishmen left behind, these are others more pervasive and more dangerous. For every Greek or Hungarian there are a dozen American-Americans who are past ethnic consciousness and who are as alienated, as confused, and as angry as the rest. The obvious manifestations are the same everywhere—race, taxes, welfare, students—but the threat seems invariably more cultural and psychological than economic or social. What upset the police at the Chicago convention most was not so much the politics of the demonstrators as their manners and their hair. (The barbershops in their neighborhoods don't advertise Beatle Cuts but the Flat Top and the Chicago Box.) The affront comes from middle-class people —and their children—who had been cast in the role of social exemplars (and from those cast as unfortunates worthy of public charity) who offend all the things on which working class identity is built: "hippies [said a San Francisco longshoreman] who fart around the streets and don't work"; welfare recipients who strike and march for better treatment; "all those [said a California labor official] who challenge the precepts that these people live on." If ethnic groups are beginning to organize to get theirs, so are others: police and firemen ("The cop is the new nigger"); schoolteachers;

lower-middle-class housewives fighting sex education and busing; small property owners who have no ethnic communion but a passionate interest in lower taxes, more policemen, and stiffer penalties for criminals. In San Francisco the Teamsters, who had never been known for such interests before, recently demonstrated in support of the police and law enforcement and, on another occasion, joined a group called Mothers Support Neighborhood Schools at a school-board meeting to oppose—with their presence and later, apparently, with their fists—a proposal to integrate the schools through busing. ("These people," someone said at the meeting, "do not look like mothers.")

Which is not to say that all is frustration and anger, that anybody is ready "to burn the country down." They are not even ready to elect standard model demagogues. "A lot of labor people who thought of voting for Wallace were ashamed of themselves when they realized what they were about to do," said Morris Iushewitz, an officer of New York's Central Labor Council. Because of a massive last-minute union campaign, and perhaps for other reasons, the blue-collar vote for Wallace fell far below the figures predicted by the early polls last fall.[1] Any number of people, moreover, who are not doing well by any set of official statistics, who are earning well below the national mean ($8,000 a year), or who hold two jobs to stay above it think of themselves as affluent, and often use that word. It is almost as if not to be affluent is to be un-American. People who can't use the word tend to be angry; people who come too close to those who can't become frightened. The definition of affluence is generally pinned to what comes in, not to the quality of life as it's lived. The $8,000 son of a man who never earned more than $4,500 may, for that reason alone, believe that he's "doing all right." If life is not all right, if he can't get his curbs fixed, or his streets patrolled, if the highways are crowded and the beaches polluted, if the schools are ineffectual he is still able to call himself affluent, feels, perhaps, a social compulsion to do so. His anger, if he is angry, is not that of the wage earner resenting management—and certainly not that of the socialist ideologue asking for redistribution of wealth—but that of the consumer, the taxpayer, and the family man. (Inflation and taxes are wiping out most of the wage gains made in labor contracts signed during the past three years.) Thus he will vote for a Louise Day Hicks in Boston who promises to hold the color line in the schools or for a Charles Stenvig calling for law enforcement in Minneapolis but reject a George Wallace who seems to threaten his pocketbook. The danger is that he will identify with the politics of the Birchers and other middle-class reactionaries (who often pretend to speak for him) even though his income and style of life are far removed from theirs; that taxes, for example,

1. The presidential campaign of 1968.

will be identified with welfare rather than war, and that he will blame his limited means on the small slice of the poor rather than the fat slice of the rich.

If you sit and talk to people like Marjorie Lemlow, who heads Mothers Support Neighborhood Schools in San Francisco, or Joe Owens, a house painter who is president of a community-action organization in Boston, you quickly discover that the roots of reaction and the roots of reform are often identical, and that the response to particular situations is more often contingent on the politics of the politicians and leaders who appear to care than on the conditions of life or the ideology of the victims. Mrs. Lemlow wants to return the schools to some virtuous past; she worries about disintegration of the family and she speaks vaguely about something that she can't bring herself to call a conspiracy against Americanism. She has been accused of leading a bunch of Birchers, and she sometimes talks Birch language. But whatever the form, her sense of things comes from a small-town vision of national virtues, and her unhappiness from the assaults of urban sophistication. It just so happens that a lot of reactionaries now sing that tune, and that the liberals are indifferent.

Joe Owens—probably because of his experience as a Head Start parent, and because of his association with an effective community-action program—talks a different language. He knows, somehow, that no simple past can be restored. In his world the villains are not conspirators but bureaucrats and politicians, and he is beginning to discover that in a struggle with officials the black man in the ghetto and the working man (black or white) have the same problem. "Every time you ask for something from the politicians they treat you like a beggar, like you ought to be grateful for what you have. They try to make you feel ashamed."

When Hope Becomes a Threat

The imponderables are youth and tradition and change. The civics book and the institution it celebrates—however passé—still hold the world together. The revolt is in their name, not against them. And there is simple decency, the language and practice of the folksy cliché, the small town, the Boy Scout virtues, the neighborhood charity, the obligation to support the church, the rhetoric of open opportunity: "They can keep Wallace and they can keep Alabama. We didn't fight a dictator for four years so we could elect one over here." What happens when all that becomes Mickey Mouse? Is there an urban ethic to replace the values of the small town? Is there a coherent public philosophy, a consistent set of beliefs to replace family, home, and hard work? What happens when the hang-ups of upper-middle-class kids are in fashion and those of blue-collar kids are not? What happens when Doing Your

Own Thing becomes not the slogan of the solitary deviant but the norm? Is it possible that as the institutions and beliefs of tradition are fashionably denigrated a blue-collar generation gap will open to the Right as well as to the Left? (There is statistical evidence, for example, that Wallace's greatest support within the unions came from people who are between twenty-one and twenty-nine, those, that is, who have the most tenuous association with the liberalism of labor.) Most are politically silent; although SDS has been trying to organize blue-collar high-school students, there are no Mario Savios or Mark Rudds—either of the Right or the Left—among them. At the same time the union leaders, some of them old hands from the Thirties, aren't sure that the kids are following them either. Who speaks for the son of the longshoreman or the Detroit auto worker? What happens if he doesn't get to college? What, indeed, happens when he does?

Vaguely but unmistakably the hopes that a youth-worshiping nation historically invested in its young are becoming threats. We have never been unequivocal about the symbolic patricide of Americanization and upward mobility, but if at one time mobility meant rejection of older (or European) styles it was, at least, done in the name of America. Now the labels are blurred and the objectives indistinct. Just at the moment when a tradition-bound Italian father is persuaded that he should send his sons to college—that education is the only future—the college blows up. At the moment when a parsimonious taxpayer begins to shell out for what he considers an extravagant state university system the students go on strike. Marijuana, sexual liberation, dress styles, draft resistance, even the rhetoric of change become monsters and demons in a world that appears to burn old virtues upside down. The paranoia that fastened on Communism twenty years ago (and sometimes still does) is increasingly directed to vague conspiracies undermining the schools, the family, order and discipline. "They're feeding the kids this generation-gap business," says a Chicago housewife who grinds out a campaign against sex education on a duplicating machine in her living room. "The kids are told to make their own decisions. They're all mixed up by situation ethics and open-ended questions. They're alienating children from their own parents." They? The churches, the schools, even the YMCA and the Girl Scouts, are implicated. But a major share of the villainy is now also attributed to "the social science centers," to the apostles of sensitivity training, and to what one California lady, with some embarrassment, called "nude therapy." "People with sane minds are being altered by psychological methods." The current major campaign of the John Birch Society is not directed against Communists in government or the Supreme Court, but against sex education.

(There is, of course, also sympathy with the young, especially in poorer areas where kids have no place to play. "Everybody's got to have a hobby," a South Boston adolescent told a youth worker. "Ours is throwing rocks." If people will join reactionary organizations to protect their children, they will also support others: community-action agencies which help kids get jobs; Head Start parent groups, Boys Clubs. "Getting this place cleaned up" sometimes refers to a fear of young hoods; sometimes it points to the day when there is a park or a playground or when the existing park can be used. "I want to see them grow up to have a little fun.")

Can the Common Man Come Back?

Beneath it all there is a more fundamental ambivalence, not only about the young, but about institutions—the schools, the churches, the Establishment—and about the future itself. In the major cities of the East (though perhaps not in the West) there is a sense that time is against you, that one is living "in one of the few decent neighborhoods left," that "if I can get $125 a week upstate (or downstate) I'll move." The institutions that were supposed to mediate social change and which, more than ever, are becoming priesthoods of information and conglomerates of social engineers, are increasingly suspect. To attack the Ford Foundation (as Wright Patman has done) is not only to fan the embers of historic populism against concentrations of wealth and power, but also to arouse those who feel that they are trapped by an alliance of upper-class Wasps and lower-class Negroes. If the foundations have done anything for the blue-collar worker he doesn't seem to be aware of it. At the same time the distrust of professional educators that characterizes the black militants is becoming increasingly prevalent among a minority of lower-middle-class whites who are beginning to discover that the schools aren't working for them either. ("Are all those new programs just a cover-up for failure?") And if the Catholic Church is under attack from its liberal members (on birth control, for example) it is also alienating the traditionalists who liked their minor saints (even if they didn't actually exist) and were perfectly content with the Latin Mass. For the alienated Catholic liberal there are other places to go; for the lower-middle-class parishioner in Chicago or Boston there are none.

Perhaps, in some measure, it has always been this way. Perhaps none of this is new. And perhaps it is also true that the American lower middle has never had it so good. And yet surely there is a difference, and that is that the common man has lost his visibility and, somehow, his claim on public attention. There are old liberals and socialists—men like Michael Harrington—who believe that a new alliance can be forged for progressive social action:

From Marx to Mills, the Left has regarded the middle class as a stratum of hyprocritical, vacillating rear-guarders. There was often sound reason for this contempt. But is it not possible that a new class is coming into being? It is not the old middle class of small property owners and entrepreneurs, nor the new middle class of managers. It is composed of scientists, technicians, teachers, and professionals in the public sector of the society. By education and work experience it is predisposed toward planning. It could be an ally of the poor and the organized workers—or their sophisticated enemy. In other words, an unprecedented social and political variable seems to be taking shape in America.

The American worker, even when he waits on a table or holds open a door, is not servile; he does not carry himself like an inferior. The openness, frankness, and democratic manner which Tocqueville described in the last century persists to this very day. They have been a source of rudeness, contemptuous ignorance, violence—and of a creative self-confidence among great masses of people. It was in this latter spirit that the CIO was organized and the black freedom movement marched.

There are recent indications that the white lower middle class is coming back on the roster of public priorities. Pucinski tells you that liberals in Congress are privately discussing the pressure from the middle class. There are proposals now to increase personal income-tax exemptions from $600 to $1,000 (or $1,200) for each dependent, to protect all Americans with a national insurance system covering catastrophic medical expenses, and to put a floor under all incomes. Yet these things by themselves are insufficient. Nothing is sufficient without a national sense of restoration. What Pucinski means by the middle class has, in some measure, always been represented. A physician earning $75,000 a year is also a working man but he is hardly a victim of the welfare system. Nor, by and large, are the stockholders of the Standard Oil Company or U.S. Steel. The fact that American ideals have often been corrupted in the cause of self-aggrandizement does not make them any less important for the cause of social reform and justice. "As a movement with the conviction that there is more to people than greed and fear," Harrington said, "the Left must . . . also speak in the name of the historic idealism of the United States."

The issue, finally, is not *the program* but the vision, the angle of view. The huge constituency may be coming up for grabs, and there considerable evidence that its political mobility is more sensitive is than anyone can imagine, that all the sociological determinants are not as significant as the simple facts of concern and leadership. When Robert Kennedy was killed last year, thousands of working-class people who had expected to vote for him—if not hundreds of thousands—shifted their loyalties to Wallace. A man who can change from a progressive democrat into a bigot overnight deserves attention.

PAULINE KAEL
Baby Machos[1]

"The Cowboys," which features one of the most torpid cattle drives since the invention of motion pictures, is an incomparable index to the confusion of values in the movie business right now. This Western epic, shaped for the family trade, is set in cattle country in 1877. John Wayne is a rancher whose hired hands desert him when there's a gold strike; unable to find men to help drive his cattle to market, he takes on eleven local schoolboys—aged nine to fifteen—and trains them during the four-hundred-mile drive. *Cowboys*—get it? The movie, which minds its language and is sexually clean as a eunuch's whistle, is sufficiently sanctimonious to have earned a GP* ("Contains material which may not be suitable for pre-teenagers") rating. It is playing at Radio City Music Hall, which was graced with an appearance by Wayne himself, who then lunched with five hundred newsboys and winners of "Cowboys" contests. It is being touted as the biggest family picture since "The Sound of Music." One could easily think that Warner Brothers and the director, Mark Rydell, and the writers, Irving Ravetch and his wife, Harriet Frank, Jr., and William Dale Jennings (who also wrote the original novel), were in the business of corrupting minors, because this movie is about how these schoolboys become men through learning the old-fashioned virtues of killing.

It's a no-nonsense view of growing up; the *macho* cadets are well-mannered, obedient, good-boy killers. The whole world knows that Wayne is not a man to put up with any guff. Almost in passing, he cures a boy of stuttering by telling him that if he wanted to speak clearly he could, and the boy cries "Son of a bitch!" over and over with perfect articulation. Is Warners getting ready to sell holy water under the Warner Brothers–Lourdes label?

At one point along the trail, there is an encounter with a madam (Colleen Dewhurst) and her girls, and you may guess that the plot logic requires the boys to be sexually initiated as part of their transition to manhood. A look at the book on which the movie is based confirms your guess, but in the movie the whores (starlets in exquisitely laundered petticoats) are introduced and then left with nothing to do. The boys can kill and the movie gets its GP* and is booked into the Music Hall, but if they had been sexually initiated the picture would have been restricted. *One* boy getting initiated—and so tactfully that you might have thought he was taking the veil—was sufficient to get "Summer of '42" restricted; the mothers of America may not go to the movies anymore, but they are still the watchdogs of movie morality when it comes to their sons' purity. So

1. *Machos* is a Spanish word for *men*.

the boys must be virginal killers; sex would make them bad, dirty boys.

In the first half of the picture, the actors seem to be planted where they speak, and there's an awesome interval before anyone replies. It feels like a long wait before overlapping dialogue will be invented. Wayne is presented as an idealized Western father figure, and his screen career as the archetypal good guy gives weight to the homely, reactionary platitudes that make this a family picture. Even when he works himself up for an oath, the final words are always genteel. He pontificates to his gruff, understanding wife—played by Sarah Cunningham, who is in the Leora Dana–Anne Revere mold: the strong women who turn understanding into a form of doughy piousness. They're *boring*; that's no service to women—and their dreary goodness certainly doesn't light up the screen. And this movie needs lighting up, because the eleven boys don't do much for it. They're Disney choirboys—clean, scrubbed nothings—so there's no dramatic or psychological preparation for the explosion of killing. The director doesn't care about the characters; he is just marking time until the mayhem. The only preparation for the explosions is in Wayne's code of honor.

Wayne's teaching is that there are good men and there are bad men; there are no crossovers and nothing in between. People don't get a second chance around him; to err once is to be doomed. Most of the bloodshed seems to be caused by his pigheadedness, but that is definitely not the movie's point of view. The boys learn their lessons so well that when Wayne is killed by rustlers they know better than to waste effort trying to bring the rustlers to justice. The movie is set up so that *they* are justice. Their faces are strong and clear-eyed as they slaughter some seventeen men; they appear to have an almost mystic union as they act in concert, infallibly, and without a glimmer of doubt or of pity. When the ex-convict villain (Bruce Dern) is trapped under his horse and pleads for help, a boy cuts one strap loose and fires a gun to frighten the horse, and the whole troupe watches with manly impassivity as the horse runs, dragging the man screaming to his death. The obscenely complacent movie invites us to identify with these good little men and to be proud of them.

There are things going on in this movie for kids that shouldn't escape notice. Some of these things—like the way that people don't die in clean kills but writhe in slow torture—may be among the reasons that this movie is expected to make money. In its way, it's innovative: the sensual pleasures of violence haven't been packaged with eternal verities before. Blood and homilies.

The confusion of values in the seedy folklore is glaringly obvious in matters of race. The Negro cook on the drive is played with peerless urbanity by Roscoe Lee Browne; with his reserves of charm to call upon, and with that deep voice rising from his great chest, Browne acts Wayne right off the screen, and without raising a bead of sweat. Not only does Browne come across as the only real actor in the movie but the cook is by far the verbal and intellectual superior of everyone else. He's wickedly, incongruously suave, like a Shakespearean ham lost in the sticks but dressing for dinner every night. If you retain any sense of humor, you may ask yourself why the *cook* isn't the father figure for the boys, particularly since it is he who devises the strategies that enable them to kill all the rustlers without loss of a boy. Parading their own lack of prejudice, the moviemakers have turned the cook into a super-black and then let Browne do his number. He's entertaining—which is better than the moviemakers deserve. And, still trying to save face, they toss in a bit of dialogue in which one of the boys informs Wayne that he is fighting-Jewish—which enables Wayne to show his patriarchal tolerance. (Another boy is an Indian—distrusted at first, but he proves himself.) As long as the movie isn't anti-Semitic or anti-Negro, the Hollywood liberals who worked on it can probably convince themselves that they have retained their image. The villains are—natch —all nondenominational whites, and they are such vipers that you hear rattles on the sound track when they are lurking nearby. Bruce Dern gives the kind of wheedling, cringing-cur ex-convict performance that disappeared for decades but is now renascent. Pro-violence, pro-revenge movies like "Dirty Harry" and "The Cowboys" require the unredeemably vicious villains of primitive melodrama. But these movies are not inconsequential melodramas; they thump for a simplistic right-wing ideology at a time when people may be ready to buy it.

Wayne says, "It's a hard life," and that's supposed to be the truth that explains why boys must learn to be killers. It's not such a hard life for the Hollywood moviemakers who are peddling this line. "The Cowboys" cost five million dollars, and most of us will never earn in a lifetime what an anxious hack director makes on a five-million-dollar movie. Mark Rydell hasn't mastered much film technique—just enough of the old show-biz one-two to raise lumps in some throats—and the violence is bloody-banal. The Hollywood hills are full of educated liberals who will make a movie glorifying the tortures at the Dacca race course and try to get it to come out right by working in a Puerto Rican love interest or a black rabbi.

ALAN S. KATZ

The Use of Drugs in America: Toward a Better
Understanding of Passivity

When we at Boston University's Mental Health Clinic were first
confronted, five years ago, with the new drug scene we knew very
little about it and all pharmacology books were of little help
beyond the chemical analysis which they offered. Although we were
well-trained psychiatrists, drugs other than for therapeutic purposes
were not part of our training. Drugs had for the most part been a
ghetto problem and thus neglected and the very hard-core users
were being treated in isolated government hospitals, and the results
were worse than a dismal failure. But we were trained in the psychoanalytic model so we knew that we could learn, that we could
see with sufficient experience how and in what way drugs affected
personality, if at all.

And we talked and we listened in fine detail to a mob of new
users who were as ignorant about the drugs as we were but who
were demonstrating every kind of personality disturbance that we
had ever seen. It was really quite frightening to us for at that time
we also had very little knowledge of what pharmaceutic medications
were specifically effective to combat the side effects. We did a lot of
learning by trial and error. In fact our first task was to use our basic
skills and to enlarge our understanding as rapidly as possible. This
was incredibly difficult because of the panic that was being caused.
At the same time the basic wish of the University was to deny that
there was such a problem; it was a kind of philosophy which was
universally typical, i.e., don't talk about it and it will go away.
However, we were quickly able to show the importance of the problem to the administration of Boston University and received its full
support to bring the problem out into the open and to deal with it.

Five years ago is now old hat, but for purposes of methodology it
has to be reviewed. We saw kids (I call them kids for they are
mostly late adolescents) who seemed little affected, but we also saw
others who were overtly psychotic. It was almost impossible to distinguish between them and others who were having typical acute
schizophrenic episodes. We were beginning to get the vibrations
from the media and the law-enforcement agencies, which enhanced
the paranoia of the users. Words like *addict, fiend, maniac, degen-
erate,* and *communist* were being bandied around. Finally there was
the increasing panic within the university community. Wild suggestions were made by some that we ought to have them all arrested. I
sarcastically replied that our enrollment could be diminished by
ninety percent. We continued working intensely with drug users

and we conducted a seemingly endless series of teach-ins with students to learn what they had to say and to share with them our rapidly accumulating knowledge. We also were beginning to distinguish between drug use and drug abuse.

Within a year we had a treatment model which was working effectively. The classical psychoanalytic and theoretical formulations were essentially correct but needed expansion, and this we felt was verified by the outstanding success of the treatment model. The Mental Health Unit worked closely with patients seen in private practice two to three times a week for two to three years. This provided a lot of detail to the uncompleted puzzle.

Our findings represent some 2,000 patient cases. The actual number seen was much greater than that, and it represents some 750 treated from onset to discharge. The treatment time was as short as six sessions and as long as three years. This paper is essentially about drug abuse, that is, where the pathology is manifest. This allows for drug use, which can have its proper social and in fact therapeutic value. The populations we studied were different. They were:

1) Those students seeking psychiatric help who *also* used drugs very occasionally and where the drug seemed of no significance. This has a subcategory; namely, where the drug use looked as ·though it might become significant.

2) Those students who were abusing drugs, that is, were using them copiously and in many forms, and where there was marked evidence of personality alteration but without signs of psychosis.

3) Those students using drugs who were prepsychotic, i.e., showing signs of confusion or the beginnings of thought disorder, or who were already psychotic, i.e., hallucinating, with gross failure in reality testing, loss of abstraction, and the other signs of psychosis.

4) The fourth group was not in treatment, but constituted over four years of about 10,000 students meeting in groups of all sizes from 15 to 600 at once to rap about drugs and all other issues which seemed relevant to late adolescence, such as sex and freedom, etc. This allowed us to come into contact with a fairly substantial number of students who were dealing with life well or fairly well, who either did not need or had not sought professional help. This was the closest to a random population to offset the idea that we were only seeing kids who were "upset." Incidentally, there was never one meeting where I was not approached afterwards by one or more students who asked how they could get our help. We attribute this to the fact that they saw that we were on the level, that we were not working for the FBI, and above all, and I cannot emphasize this sufficiently, that our Mental Health Unit held and upheld total, absolute confidentiality as an inviolable principle. This

is one of the unfortunate by-products of law enforcement: conflicted people involved in illegal activity are afraid to seek help.

What did all of this teach us? We learned that no matter what drug was used, if it was being used for other than occasional social-fun purposes and (strangely enough, this includes heroin, for heroin is used also for social purposes), it was being used to ward off or deal with tension, anxiety, and depression. And we learned what had been theoretically formulated in classical psychiatric literature: that we were dealing with a specific personality type. In psychiatry we call this the passive dependent personality. Conversely we also found that the passive dependent personality types whom we were seeing for non-drug reasons, those of the first subcategory, were tending to become more involved with drugs as their underlying anxieties started to come out in the course of therapy and sought relief by turning on in order to turn off: for us this development again was a validation.

There is to my mind, a view I share with almost every colleague I know, no greater jungle of confusion than psychiatric diagnosis, not only because of the abstractness, the differences in clinical training and skills, but also because the psychiatric label changes as the personality changes. Similarly there are few more threatening ideas than that of passivity, because passivity implies *vulnerability, helplessness,* and *dependence* on others. To tell an adolescent that he is passive is to send him up a wall. It is a major insult to his mind. But we have learned, as had others long ago, that one can protest very loudly about "give me my freedom," but if you listen closely there is frequently another little voice that is saying very firmly *"don't you dare."* This is a normal process in adolescence. But it becomes pathologic in drug abuse, I repeat, *abuse* not just *drug use.*

By "passive dependent" we were and are referring specifically to unresolved wishes to remain in a child-like dependent status despite the protestations to the contrary. This wish to remain passive ultimately has to do with anxiety about separation from the nurturing parent. It is crucial to understand the meaning of the patient's passivity.

The law of conservation of experience cannot be thwarted or surpassed by any stretch of the imagination, by therapist or patient. To treat as reality the illusion that one can discard any part of one's experience is foolishness in its most flagrant form. So the student generates anxiety within himself, assuming tacitly that growth will occur by exclusion rather than by acquisition, that one becomes an adult by putting away or discarding childish styles or ways. In reality, growth occurs from within, wherein the entire being grows but where previous ambivalent, ambiguous experiences are retained. Regression, or return to earlier styles of behavioral transactions with the world, figures so prominently in the drug abuser. When adolescents return home on vacation, they begin to bicker, argue, and squabble after a day or so of blissful reunion. This is regression. The more basic truth of passivity is its *healthy intent*, to resist *any advance* which would ignore the important, unsettled, unsatisfied blocks of experience. Passivity may be seen as a self-preserving effort. It has to be seen in terms of its usefulness of value rather than condemned wholesale. The intense threat is that passivity thrusts an individual back to or maintains a position of vulnerability linked to a sense of helplessness. The psychiatrist often become angry with the patient, labeling him as "passive aggressive," thereby seeing the passivity as a form of hostility, whereas more often than not in the passive dependent person it is his major defense for survival. That is, the patient in *being ill is not being bad*. The pertinence of these dynamics is crucial in giving direction towards an encompassing understanding of the patient, so that the goal becomes that of accepting the presence of the passivity rather than the rejecting of it. This allows the patient to be released from the stranglehold of his own passivity.

As I stated before, such growth ultimately has to do with the separation from the nurturing parent. The whole process begins in infancy, when the really helpless infant through the sound, smell, taste, and touch of the nurturing mother takes into himself and into his very primitive, undifferentiated psyche, or "mind," things from the outside. It is the process by which the infant learns to recognize and remember the outside. For example, when a newborn is hungry he experiences pain, which is relieved by something put into his mouth, and frequently; in the process of feeding he is touched, and fondled, and cooed to.

Some months later the newborn, who is now an infant, has learned that his mother, who is in another room, will come to him if he cries. The amazing thing that has happened is that now he has an image of mother in his head, even though she is not present in the room. Then we begin to see the smiles of recognition. The infant begins to distinguish between different people, different sounds, different smells, and different voices. Slowly all the representations of the outside world, the family, the siblings, the teachers, the society, religion are taken and stored in the unconscious, which is the total memory bank. And they are stored as they are experienced, both good and bad, happy and unhappy. Just as the child develops a sense of I, as separate from you, he must later through a whole series of tasks requiring mastery selectively learn to function independently. When the early development fosters tremendous dependency and does not allow for independent exploration, error making, and correction, when all tensions are relieved by the parent, the child holds on very intensely to the total parent, whose image he has stored in his mind. To grow, to find his own style, to achieve his own goals and destiny, he must selectively give up parts of the parental image. This is the normal process of adolescence which allows the young adult to have a profound sense of self. If this psychological separation *does not occur,* he remains dependent on his parent. The problem arises when the adolescent fights his own dependent wishes towards the parents who are so firmly entrenched in his own head, even though they may be as far away as 10,000 miles, or even dead. This concept explains the bickering in adolescence, the fighting of "I want"—"no you can't." It is shadow boxing of a kind. The problem is greatly intensified when the parents remain over-protective at a time when the child, now adolescent, should be learning to accomplish on his own. He is searching for independence but he is bound up within himself, fighting his being dependent on the image and the values of the parent in his own mind. So he is constantly expending enormous energy in a battle with those parents. He has not found his own identity, he regresses—he goes backwards under tension. He has not been given the permission to grow up and be different , nor has he utilized it when it was given. So his goal becomes to distinguish himself from his parents by being against them. He denies the meaningfulness of the values of the "straight society" but not selectively. He expresses profound disappointment in his family and this is expanded to include the large family of man. By contrast, the healthier adolescent who has not held on so tenaciously to the parental image, or who has not been held onto so tenaciously, does not feel the perpetual need for battle of dependency-independency. He finds gratification and creative goals to his own liking, to his own talents and style, and has the energy to achieve them. For him being different is not the only way of being free. The implications of this go beyond the drug scene, where origins of rebellion come, not out of ideology and idealism, but out of personal problems.

A second characteristic we found in drug abusers was a withdrawal into the self, and the greater the drug abuse, the greater the withdrawal. Withdrawal means less communication with a varied society, much time spent in reflection which does not imply productive thought but feelings of alienation, and paranoia. As there is usually an increased gap between child and family, and between the student and other peers who have not withdrawn, there is an increased need to huddle together into what we call brotherhoods, which in the last analysis are substitute families, characterized by their permissiveness, the capacity to get close physically, which is warded off in adult children towards their parents, and by the feeling of belonging without restriction and especially belonging without real commitment—commitment to another seen as an equal and not as a parent substitute. In some places these are known as communes. This is not to disparage all communes, for some have

very constructive aims, but these brotherhoods can exist in the form
of several people living in one room, or in a house, or in a bus, or in
a reconverted hearse, or just a group that is always together.

A third characteristic found in virtually all of the patients was a
state of clinical depression, with feelings of worthlessness, of loss, of
sadness, and an attempt to alleviate these symptoms with various
drugs. The heroin user is the extreme example. Although the
patient may not recognize this state of depression, *it is always there*
to the clinical eye. Some can acknowledge this feeling, for others it
is an intriguing and captivating idea worth looking at. In any
event, way down deep he knows that he is depressed. He describes
his depression in simplistic terms of being "down on the family,"
"down on society," without greater elaboration. He seems to have
achieved liberation from home and is eager to experience, to move,
to realize, and to become. Suddenly the adolescent finds that it is
lonely out there, and he comes against the unpleasant recognition
that life has blockades to plans, disappointments for aspirations, a
diminution of importance for aspirations, a diminution of importance and of relevance in an active crowd around him. Here the
therapist is presented with the opportunity to exert his most valuable asset: his compassion, his more mature, accepting, *unalarmed*
empathic attitude toward all that the human experience includes.
To recognize the depression is of enormous value, for it offers the
passive depressed patient an avenue of freedom towards seeing himself more realistically. The depressive crisis is not a breakdown, but
rather a breakup of insufficient, antiquated ways of dealing with
problems in contemporary society. It is never the aim of therapy to
reduce the student to anonymity in the crowd. The abuser becomes
anonymous. The student is uneradicably singular, his uniqueness is
the focus of recognition. To fracture or dismantle the narcissism of
the late adolescence is a cruel injustice. The promise of individualism is infinitely more potent than a substitute dependency. That
is, "I will help you, but I won't do it for you." The therapy becomes
the implementation of these ideas.

These were the basic ideas that we formulated to develop our
treatment program. The exception to this program is the heroin
user who has a particularly severe psychological deterioration and
who has very special needs. But we are convinced that many of
them can be helped as well, but by other techniques. The only time
in our treatment program that a patient was instructed to stop
using drugs was when he was prepsychotic, psychotic, or experiencing flashes. Flashing is a particular phenomenon which occurs in
some individuals wherein they experience a drug trip spontaneously
without having just taken the drug. There is also a cross-over phenomenon: for example, a person smoking some pot might re-experi-

ence a past LSD trip. To our minds, this is a warning sign of an impending psychotic episode if the drugs are continued.

Very briefly, the four steps to the treatment method are:

1) Make an alliance with the patient to look at the problem, don't moralize, don't probe too deeply or the patient will run from treatment.

2) Search for the underlying clinical depression and get the patient involved with this.

3) Clarify the parental relations, not with the goal of breaking up the family, but rather to help the family to grow up, to become adults with one another. This idea has to be frequently reiterated because if the dependent person hears the statement as a threat of breakup, it would mean that there will be no one to depend on.

4) Help the patient to leave the brotherhood, to get re-established with a varied society. This is the most hazardous part of the model.

Incidentally, at this point, without much or any coaxing, the drug user is in the process of voluntarily stopping. The therapist clearly sees the need to give up the drug, but the patient, though he may understand the reason, is magically bound to it. What is rational and logical is unimportant. His sense of control predominates. The passivity has its stranglehold and the patient seems not to be able to budge, for there is still something unaccomplished. With the knowledge that the patient is no longer getting the same pleasure or kind of kicks he once got from drugs, but that he is still clinging to them and their uses as a unenjoyable form of ritual, the therapist then begins to investigate the fear of no longer belonging to the peer group, which is the drug group that makes up the brotherhood. This allows the ritual to become unravelled so that the passivity loses its power. Attention is paid especially to the one, two, or three friends with whom the patient is particularly close, with whom he takes his trips. After all, they belong to the brotherhood and he can believe in the brotherhood because for him it represents the tension-free new kind of adulthood which is better than his parents' adulthood. He is terribly afraid of leaving his friends for he figures that he cannot stand on his own. He is faced with a real dilemma, for although the brotherhood no longer serves the purpose it once did, he had shared in it—in essence he had a sense of existence and meaning in it. His friends as well are threatened if he leaves them, and we see they exert a subtle and sometimes more blatant pressure on him not to believe the "shrink" so that the group will not be diminished. Separating from the brotherhood generally opens a whole vista of ideas concerning the dread of being in a neutral state, of giving up one's only friends, and one's feeling of inadequacy and fear upon entering the "straight society."

Such crises are all derivatives of the task of separation from mother and father; they are the issues of the passivity that has been unresolved but which can now be dealt with, and they are among the reasons that have led to the initial drug use. The exploration of being alone and ultimately confronting one's wishes to be dependent permit the patient to slowly take up the role required for adulthood. It is much like learning to walk. The job of the therapist is, as always, to assist in unstopping the natural growth process, so it may proceed. The new task is a big one, but it is the task which was earlier thwarted: dealing with anxiety and the achievement of goals pleasing to the self. The person is wobbly but there is a mass of energy available for *doing* rather than for just *being*.

But the matter becomes further complicated, and I hope what ensues from these ideas is an original contribution to psychiatric literature. During these years of work at the Mental Health Unit, we observed that there was a very distorted idea of what it meant to be aggressive: that competitiveness, striving, and mastery in some manner had become linked up with some destruction, that is: to compete with someone is to destroy the competitor, to achieve is to kill. In some way I came to realize that this concept was inextricably related to drug passivity. In fact, all through this work something had been missing, some factor had been overlooked which was crucial to tying things together. About two years ago it began to make sense and it was very exciting to the scientist-researcher part of me. Small but vital clues had been overlooked in a maze of accumulated data which took on significance only after my working in very intensive therapy with some patients. Obviously I had not heard all things at all times, but I began to hear material that stuck out like a sore thumb, material which I could interpret as meaning "if I take drugs I won't feel so aggressive." The therapist was having an insight. I had often wondered what was at the core of the love movement with the hippies. The hippies and the students whom I have seen and who have used LSD in the largest quantities (such as over 200 times) were in fact the most passive, non-destructive, turned-off group of all drug abusers. Their regression has the most intense infantile character: the wish to be fed, to be protected, and to be carefree. Why had I not thought of this before, because it is classic that one of the aspects of being passive is to ward off being hurt, as I've explained, but also to control the fear of hurting. So I began to review cases and there it clearly was, hundreds of times: "If my parents took drugs, they wouldn't want war." "If you took drugs, you'd understand peace." "If you took drugs you'd see that straight people kill." "When I take drugs, I love everyone." "Man, with drugs you don't have to hassle." "Man, I don't want to hurt anyone" and so forth. The connection between taking drugs to deal with aggressive feeling is now blatantly clear.

I profoundly believe that aside from the social-peer purposes, aside from defying the law, aside from the fantasy of warding off depression, tension, and anxiety, the most significant unconscious, unresolved factor in passivity is to ward off the killer in oneself; that is to say, there is a tremendous rage inside, a complicated kind of rage directed at the self, at the figures on whom one is dependent, at the incapacity to bridge the gap between the age groups, a rage at the inequities in society, at the double standards of law and civil rights, against the killer instinct which is cultivated and released by war, at the frustration of not being heard, at the idea competition is war, that achievement is destructive. The drug abuser does not have the freedom to deal with these issues; he is a be-er rather than a doer. He is not a free activist, involved in a creative ideology, in idealism which demands stamina and energy. Instead I contend that he is a very dependent person who is very angry inside, who, ironically, becomes even more passive, more dependent, less aggressive, less striving, and remarkably more depressed. And whenever there is depression there is rage. So I am stating in conclusion that the use of drugs by the abuser is intended to deal with and put down his rage, over which he has poor control, the use of drugs is to do away with the killer. So he maintains and accentuates his passivity through the drugs, drugs make him more passive, and the rage is put down. Thus we have gone the full circle.

JOHN F. KERRY
I Would Like to Tell You Something

I would like to tell you something about what veterans are doing in this country, and about our feelings now that we've come back from a war we didn't really want to fight.

A little over a week ago we held an investigation in Detroit where over 150 honorably discharged veterans, many of them highly decorated, testified to war crimes committed in Indochina—not isolated incidents, but crimes committed on a day-to-day basis with the full awareness of officers at all levels of command.

It's impossible to accurately describe to you the emotion in that room in Detroit, but these veterans relived the absolute horror of their experiences and told of the times that they had personally raped, cut off ears, taped wires from portable phones to human genitals and turned up the power, cut off limbs, blown up bodies, randomly shot at civilians, razed villages in a fashion reminiscent of Genghis Khan, shot cattle for fun, poisoned wells and foodstock, and on and on.

The investigation was not staged so that veterans could spill out their hearts or purge their souls; it was done to prove that the policy of the United States in Indochina is tantamount to genocide, and that not only the soldiers are responsible for what is happening, but that everyone here in America who has allowed the brutalization and depersonalization to go on is responsible. It was done also to show that you don't start making things right by prosecuting William Calley, no matter how guilty he may be; you also prosecute the men who encouraged the situation. It was done to show that there is not just one Mylai but countless Mylais and they are continuing every single day. There was an almost total press blackout on the testimony of those veterans.

But this isn't new to those of us who were in the war. I can remember traveling to Saigon and trying to talk to the admiral who commanded the naval forces to tell him that what we were doing was wrong. I remember going to a writer for a national magazine and telling him this was a story the American people should hear. He agreed, but said it would never get by his desk because the Army would rescind the magazine's accreditation to cover the war, and if you don't cover the war you don't sell magazines, and if you don't sell magazines then nothing happens because that's the American way.

But the press isn't the only party in this country that's guilty of this rampant insensitivity. When I went to the chairman of the board of a large New York-based firm and asked him for money to help us get transcripts of the testimony to present to each member of Congress so that we can press our demands for open hearings, I was told in seriousness: "I don't think you can market war crimes —it's a marketing question, you know." And then in the next breath to his executive vice president: "Hell, we used to do that in World War II. Christ, what's new?"

We all know that this de-sensitizing started a long time ago in this country, but it is carried out in a far more vicious way with the soldier. At boot camp he's presented with a poster in his barracks of a crucified Vietnamese and underneath it says, "Kill the gooks." The message begins to sink in. During training, calisthenics are done to a four-count, and at the end of the four-count everybody jumps up and yells "Kill!" For the Marines at Camp Pendleton, before they depart for Vietnam, there's a very special treat: the sergeant takes a live rabbit and skins it, tearing it open, pulling out the entrails to throw at the assembled soldiers, saying, "That's how it's done in Nam; go get 'em Marines!"

And so we're suddenly faced with a sickening situation in this country. There's no longer any moral indignation. And if there is, it comes from people who are almost exhausted from past indignities inflicted on them. The country seems to be lying down and accepting something as serious as Laos, just as before we dismissed the loss of 700,000 lives in Pakistan, the so-called greatest disaster of all time. Well, I think we're in the midst of the greatest disaster of all time right now, because they are still dying over there every day. And I don't just mean American boys.

And the mass of people in this country literally don't give a damn. After all, you can switch off the TV news and put on Dick Van Dyke. We're not on food rationing; people can still charge prostitutes on credit cards; so what if a few lives are used to save American face in an unsaveable situation? It should not be hard for people in this country to admit there is no difference between a ground troop and a helicopter troop; yet we have accepted a differentiation fed us by the Administration. No ground troops are in Laos, so it's all right to kill Laotians as long as it's done by remote control. Believe me, the helicopter crews fill the same body bags as the ground troops, and they do the same damage to the Vietnamese countryside and the Laotian people. It's absolutely incredible that this country is ready to accept this kind of hypocrisy.

But what this country doesn't know is that America has created a monster in the form of millions of fighting men who have been taught to deal in violence, and who have been given a chance to die for the biggest nothing in history. We have returned to this country with a sense of anger and betrayal which nobody has yet grasped. We're angry about the same things you are in terms of policy—a little angrier because our lives were the things used to test those policies.

But we're angry also because of statements like the one Vice President Agnew made when he spoke at West Point in 1970. He spoke of how some people glamorize the criminal misfits of society while the best men die in Asian rice paddies to preserve the freedoms that those misfits abuse. Support the boys in Vietnam. But for us, those boys in Vietnam whom the country is supposed to support, this is a terrible distortion from which we draw only the deepest revulsion.

It's a distortion because we in no way considered ourselves the "best men" in this country, because those he called misfits were standing up for us in a way nobody else in this country dared to, because we know that so many who died would have come back to join the misfits, and because so many of us have actually returned to this country to demand an immediate withdrawal from Vietnam. And because so many of those "best men" have returned as amputees and quadraplegics to lie in rancid hospitals which fly the flag that Mr. Agnew holds so close.

And one can't consider us "best men" when we were ashamed of and hated what we were called on to do in Asia. And to attempt to justify the loss of one American life in Vietnam, Cambodia, Laos or anywhere in Indochina, or anywhere in the world, or even here in America, by saying that that kind of loss of life is linked to the preservation of freedom, is to play exactly the kind of criminal hypocrisy that has torn this country apart.

Our anger goes beyond the simple policy matters. It goes into the fact that all the things we were told about Vietnam we found untrue when we got there. We found that too often American men were dying in those rice paddies from want of support from our so-called allies. We saw first-hand the money—your taxes—squandered by a corrupt dictatorial regime. We saw that Agnew had a one-sided idea of who was kept free by the flag, as blacks provided the highest percentage of casualties.

We saw Vietnam ravaged equally by American bombs and search-and-destroy missions and by Viet Cong terrorists, and we listened while America blamed it all on the Viet Cong. We watched while we rationalized destroying villages to save them, while we saw America lose her sense of morality as she coolly accepted a Mylai and refused to give up the image of American soldiers handing out chewing gum and chocolate bars.

We watched while pride allowed unimportant battles to be escalated into the most important stands of the war—because we couldn't lose and we couldn't retreat and because it didn't matter how many American bodies were provided to prove that point. Now we are told that we have to watch quietly while more American lives are lost so that we can exercise the incredible arrogance of Vietnamizing the Vitnamese.

The problem of the veteran doesnt just end with his anger. One out of every 10 of the unemployed in this country today is a Vietnam veteran. That's 22.5 per cent of all the veterans who are unemployed. Thirty-three per cent of these are black. We have veterans who practically have to sue the Veterans Administration to get their artificial limbs. Fifty-seven per cent of those entering hospitals have thought about suicide and 27 per cent have tried it. Sixty-eight per cent of the troops in Vietnam are on dope, and the addicts who return receive little if any care.

We're going to do something about this situation. On April 19,[1] members of Vietnam Veterans Against the War, now numbering 7,000 men and growing, are marching on Washington—in uniform, wearing medals. We're paying homage to the dead in Arlington. We are then marching with veterans of other wars, with families of the deceased, families of prisoners of war, whoever will join us, on the Capitol. And we're camping and we're staying there to demand that our needs be met. But more important, we won't move until they set a date for withdrawal of troops from Vietnam.

1. 1971

We will also be returning our war medals to Congress and be demanding that the judiciary of this country rule on the Massachusetts bill which calls for the declaration that the Vietnam war is unconstitutional. We're asking for the support of all sections of the peace movement because we do not feel that this is a time to be dormant. The war is part and parcel of everything that we're trying to communicate to people of this country. The problem of Vietnam is not just the problem of war and diplomacy; it's a problem of the very basic American idealism that we're trying to question.

An American Indian friend of mine, a veteran, a member of the Indian Nation of Alcatraz, put it to me very succinctly: he told me how, as a boy on the Indian reservation, he had watched televison and cheered the cowboys who killed the Indians in an ambush. Then suddenly one day he woke up in Vietnam and he found himself doing to the Vietnamese exactly what had been done to his people and what he had been conditioned by America to applaud. I think that that says it all. The veteran has been used horribly.

But now he's going to to do something about it. He's going to take all the goodness of his uniform, all the apple pie and motherhood and medals in the service of his country, and he's going to place it before the people of this country, telling it like it really is.

SAUL BELLOW

Culture Now

The American literary situation has greatly changed during the past decade. What do you think of the more recent trend?

I'm not sure that what we have *is* a literary situation; it seems rather to be a sociological, a political, a psychological situation in which there are literary elements. Literature itself has been swallowed up. In East Africa last year I heard an account (probably sheer fantasy) of a disaster that had overtaken one of three young Americans who had parked their Land Rover under a tree for the night. A python had silently crushed and swallowed the young man. In the morning his friends saw the shape of his body within the snake and his tennis shoes sticking out of the creature's mouth. What we see of literature now are its sneakers.

Why has this happened? No one should take upon himself the responsibility of a definitive explanation—indeed, no such explanation would be generally acceptable—but, for what they may be worth, I am willing to offer my impressions and opinions.

Literature became swallowable, enormously profitable, after World War II, thanks to the university boom, the expansion of the publishing industry and the new opportunities offered by journalism. In the universities a literary culture rapidly formed. It took charge of certain modern masterpieces (James, Lawrence, Joyce, Eliot, etc.), taught them, discoursed about them, *described* them. This process of redescription is most important. Everything was told again, in other words, and related to myth, to history, to philosophy or to psychology.

Behind this body of interpretations appeared a new bureaucracy with its own needs and ambitions and its own orthodoxy. Since the masterpieces of modernism are radical, this orthodoxy is radical too. Within a liberal society, a "revolutionary" or anticapitalist culture has established itself. The need—a social need—for such a culture is evidently great, much greater than the need for novels and poems. In a word, what-can-be-done with literature is for many intellectuals, certainly for the most influential of them, infinitely more important than books.

We have passed from contemplative reading to movement, to action, politics and power struggles. I do not mean large action, broad movement or the conquest of national power. No, not large, not broad. But intellectuals are curiously busy with social questions. From the study of literature comes the prestige they enjoy and exploit. And why do I say that they are curiously busy? Well, consider for example the statement by Marshall McLuhan in *The New York Times* of September 18, 1970. It interprets the Mick Jagger film *Performance* and runs, in part, as follows:

Performance is figured against the overall background of "Planet Polluto." . . .

Performance is a key term in American management and organization circles, and mergers, private and corporate, are the themes of the picture. . . .

Figured against the British background of a society junked by the new surround of larger powers, *Performance* is a satirical spoof on the screen and fiction violence of the days of Bogart, Al Capone, Studs Lonigan and Hemingway—the tough guy as half-man. . . .

Figured against the new background of America "The Inefficient," America deprived of outer goals and inner connection, America confronted by the Orient within, *Performance* is as satirical as The Beatles or The Rolling Stones. . . .

Performance projects a nihilistic vision of the establishments which are using all their means for their own liquidation. . . .

Performance is a "garbage apocalypse—notice of the cancellation of a world."

These utterances (copyright McLuhan Associates Ltd., 1970) show what the avant-garde and Ph.D. programs in literature have combined to give us: apocalyptic clichés; a wild self-confidence; violently compact historical judgments; easy formulas about the "cancellation of a world." And can one miss here the presence of money? What else does the copyright by McLuhan Associates signify? McLuhan, who speaks continually of the medium, seems himself, in a different sense, the Cagliostro sense, to be a medium. The avant-garde formed him. He started out esoteric; he speaks now to a great public.

Avant-Garde Bias

Everyone now has a sense that a great revolution is occurring in the consciousness of mankind—in the consciousness of a majority. But literary intellectuals who began with an avant-garde bias against the great public seem to have changed their minds about it. They have returned to the majority, to the masses, but as demagogues and not as writers.

It is not literature that they offer but a culture that contains, as we can see from our McLuhan sample, literary elements. Their interests are exclusively social and political. The long estrangement of the avant-garde from the larger community has come to a curious end. Intellectuals hunger once more for contact with the tribe— that tribe to whose words a century ago the Mallarmés were trying to give a more pure sense.

A few months ago I forced myself on several miserable afternoons to go to the library and to read the literary magazines and the underground papers. This is my report. I shall begin with the representatives or former representatives of the avant-garde, the literary quarterlies. Reading them I was first uncomfortable, then queasy, then indignant, contemptuous and finally quite bleak, flattened out by the bad writing. Brutal profs and bad-tempered ivy league sodomites seemed to have taken over.

Amazing Country

Who was reading this stuff, cultivated housewives? Graduate students who felt they must know the latest? Was it possible that anyone wanted to eat these stale ideological French chocolates? Yes. Evidently there were customers. People were reading these wearisome pages. And someone was financially responsible, paying the bills. This is an amazing country! McLuhan doesn't know the half of it.

Open the *Partisan Review*. Turn to a recent essay by William Phillips.

The subject is—Susan Sontag.

The experience is much like trying to go scuba diving at Coney Island in urinous brine and scraps of old paper, orange rinds and soaked hot dog buns.

The essay on Silence is a good example of Susan Sontag's method. The idea of silence is actually used as a metaphor· for the opposite of talkiness in art, talkiness being too full of subject matter, too directly aimed at an audience, too bustly in its language, too nicely constructed —all suggesting a closed, stale view of existence. Art that babbles thinks of itself as finished, with an audience out there, an inert voyeuristic mass. Only a silent medium can properly engage an audience, because it is not performing but completing itself. The ideal form for Miss Sontag, as one would expect, is the movies, which is able to deal with subjects, that is, with verbal material, by splintering and transforming into immediate visual associations and experiences. And several long and quite brilliant essays in the book, on Godard, Bergman, and the relation of theater to film, explore the possibilities of the most modern art.

One of the nice things about *Hamlet* is that Polonius is stabbed.

Mr. Phillips is an old-timer, a founder of the magazine. In the thirties, forties and fifties *Partisan Review* published Malraux, Koestler, Orwell, Silone, Leon Trotsky; its American contributors were Jarrell, Delmore Schwartz, John Berryman, Robert Lowell, Jean Stafford, Edmund Wilson. Future textbooks will surely contain the name of Mr. Phillips. What is he saying?

Upsidedown Politics

"The idea of silence is actually used as a metaphor for the opposite of talkiness in art. . . ." What writing! Eleanor Roosevelt wrote far better in *My Days*.

Of Susan Sontag's rage against the U.S. he says, "On the whole, anti-Americanism has become identified in many parts of the world with socialism and national liberation, though not, significantly, in the communist countries of Eastern Europe, and it is often used as a substitute for socialist theory. As Trotsky pointed out, this is upsidedown politics. . . . Clearly what is lacking is some large perspective for assessing motives and movements throughout the world. . . . These are some of the questions I found myself thinking about as I read Susan Sontag's new book. And if there are no answers to many of them, it might be because this is a time not for rigor and caution in politics and criticism but for boldness in discarding stale ideas and trying out untested ones."

Let us look at one of these original, bold untested ideas. Mr. Phillips is speaking of the New Left. He grants that the New Left has no theory, no program. But, he says, "I am convinced that only an antitheoretical, antihistorical, non-Marxist, unstructured movement like that of the youth today could have created a new left force in the West." This statement, in its idiocy, is really rather touching. One must consider that in surrendering his Marxism Mr. Phillips is giving up his youth, his maturity, forty years of his life. When in doubt he still quotes Trotsky. And he is still a revolutionist, for he desires a New Left force in the West.

Why has Marxism lost his loyalty? Is it because communist revolutions have created nothing but police states? He doesn't say that. Is it because the communists have made Russia one of the most boring nations in history? He doesn't say that either. Is it because China threatens to be even more tedious than Russia? No, I don't think that tedium frightens Mr. Phillips. What frightens him is that he may not make it with the young and that people in New York will think him a silly dry old stick who is *out* of it.

In the same number of *Partisan Review* there is an essay by Mr. Cecil M. Brown on "The White Whale." Mr. Brown, author of a novel, *The Life and Loves of Mr. Jiveass Nigger*, sees in Ishmael the ancestor of the contemporary white liberal.

> In *Moby Dick*, Ishmael's understanding and questioning of his "survival" is so conspicuously absent that one is tempted to conclude that it was he, and not Ahab, who went down with the white whale.

Ishmael, then, is one of the living dead, not a survivor, but, in Mr. Brown's own words, a cop out. Ishmael's attempt to explain himself in the final chapter of the novel

> . . . is so vacuous as to be soporific . . . oh, man, stop the literary bullshit; because *we* know why you survived, you survived because you were white; because you didn't pay your dues, survived because physically you were not even on the ship, you survived because when Queequeg, Tashtego and Daggo, those niggers, were actually in there dealing with that whale, actually *risking* their lives, actually *using* their *bodies*, while they were actually involved your disembodied intelligence, your white ghost, as it were, was off somewhere contemplating in a moment of crisis the significance of Plato and Aristotle, you survived because you never invested any soul, survived because you were never really vulnerable hence never really alive, yes, you survived like a piece of driftwood survives (good image), survived because you planned it that way, and if you didn't plan it, how is it that although it is Queequeg—that strange nigger from the South Seas—who actually executed the idea of a coffin—lifesaver, it is you, the white boy, who survives on it? Do you think we are stupid enough to believe that if Queequeg had anything to do with the master plans he'd have let you survive on *his* lifesaver? And furthermore, we are hip to your weird game—we *know* that the white whale, that heinous symbol of the gray world which "darn Ahab" and his "mongrel crew" (i.e., the Third World, dig that) detested so is none other than you, Ishmael—the white, disembodied, overliterate, boring, snobbish, insipid, jew-bastard, nigger-lover, effete, mediocre, assistant-professor-type liberal.

Mr. Brown ends his article with a quotation from LeRoi Jones.

> *Who will survive America?*
> *Few Americans*
> *Very few Negroes*
> *No crackers at all . . .*
>
> *But the Black Man will survive America.*
> *His survival will mean the death of America.*

Some of this of course is Halloween childishness. Educated readers love a hearty scare. Abuse is good for us, they seem to think, and revolutionary violence is what we all want. The revolutionary position is a privileged one. Rage is a luxury, destruction is a sort of *romance*. In the *Art of Being Ruled* Wyndham Lewis spoke of the super freedom of the revolutionary rich. He held that emancipation and irresponsibility were for most people commutative terms and that in playing at revolution and aping proletarian freedom the rich were having and eating their cake.

This, I suggest, is the position of many middle-class liberals whose fortunes have risen. They are doing what the revolutionary rich were able to do in 1925, enjoying a sort of utopian freedom. There is no risk, really. It is perfectly safe and shows that one has done well in life and enjoys a higher status. Moreover, anger is emotionally valuable, as every kindergarten teacher knows. And that ideological passion puts liberalism—i.e., slow secular morality—to shame is not exactly the latest news. There may even be vestiges of religion here; a touch of masochism possibly reminds people of the beatitudes. And, lastly, energy is beauty—that we know from William Blake.

(As for Melville, he was evidently of two minds about it for he wrote, later in life, "*Indolence is Heaven's ally here/And energy the Child of Hell.*")

American intellectuals, White and Black, live on a trust fund of ideas. One can often see the source of a writer's mental income. In Mr. Brown's case I see the hatred of bourgeois intellectuals, the cult of will, the heroics of personal involvement, fondness for cataclysm, etc. Malraux had some of these notions; before him came Sorel; before Sorel a good many others. But for Mr. Brown and Mr. LeRoi Jones, the supreme source seems to be D. H. Lawrence. Here is Lawrence himself on *Moby Dick*. The similarities will be obvious:

Doom of our white day. We are doomed, doomed. And the doom is in America. The doom of our white day.

Ah, well, if my day is doomed, and I am doomed with my day, it is something greater than I which dooms me, so I accept my doom as a sign of the greatness which is more than I am.

Melville knew. He knew his race was doomed, his white soul, doomed. His great white epoch, doomed. Himself, doomed. The idealist, doomed. The spirit, doomed. . . .

What then is Moby Dick? He is the deepest blood-being of the white race; he is our deepest blood-nature.

And he is hunted, hunted, hunted by the maniacal fanaticism of our white mental consciousness. We want to hunt him down. To subject him to our will. . . .

The last phallic being of the white man. Hunted into the death of upper consciousness and the ideal will. . . .

Oh God, oh God, what next when the Pequod has sunk?

She sank in the war, and we are all flotsam. . . .

The Pequod went down. And the Pequod was the ship of the white American soul. . . . If the Great White Whale sank the ship of the Great White Soul in 1851, what has been happening ever since?

Post-mortem effect, presumably.

And there it is, all of it: the last phallic being of the white man, the sinking of the white soul, the doom of the white day. No wonder Mr. Brown and Mr. Jones conclude that the Black man alone will make it. It was Lawrence who set up this little trust fund. He was a genius, but was he also a seer? Perhaps not.

I have picked on the *Partisan Review*. The other quarterlies are not very different. Most of them are university subsidized, as what is not these days. The university has become the sanctuary, at times the hospital, of literature, painting, music and theater. It contains also computers, atom smashers, agricultural researchers, free psychotherapy, technocratic planners, revolutionary ideologists. It has everything, including bohemia. But the university is only one of the homes of bohemia. American society is being thoroughly bohemianized. I speak not only of the middle class, where the signs are clear, but also of the working class, where they are now beginning to appear. And what is art, in this bohemianized society? It is a toy.

New Self-Consciousness

De Tocqueville observed that in a democracy ordinary people wished primarily to view themselves and that the citizen of a democratic country would find nothing more fascinating than—himself. In America we are, I think, looking—no, staring!—at ourselves.

Art is an element of this new self-consciousness. Assimilated by the mass media, the methods, the discoveries of great modern artists are being spread throughout society. The *frénésie journalière*[1] of Baudelaire is no longer exclusively for poets. Millions of people are involved in some sort of *frénésie journalière*.

In *Playboy*, too, we can see the sneakers in the python's mouth. In a recent number of that magazine, Dr. Leslie Fiedler has the following things to say:

Almost all today's readers and writers are aware that we are living through the death throes of literary modernism and the birth pangs of postmodernism. The kind of literature that had arrogated to itself the name modern (with the presumption that it represented the ultimate advance in sensibility and form, that beyond it newness was not possible), and whose moment of triumph lasted from just before World War One until just after World War Two, is *dead*; i.e., belongs to history, not actuality. In the field of the novel, this means that the age of Proust, Mann and Joyce is over, just as in verse, that of T. S. Eliot and Paul Valéry is done with....
The kind of criticism the age demands is death-of-art criticism, which is most naturally practiced by those who have come of age since the death of the new poetry and the new criticism. It seems evident that writers not blessed to be under 30 (or 35, or whatever the critical age is these days) must be reborn in order to seem relevant to the moment and to those who inhabit it most comfortably: the young. But one hasn't even the hope of being reborn unless he knows first that he is dead.

1. Daily frenzy.

What a lot of death we have here! Ishmael is dead without knowing it. The survival of the Black man will mean the death of America. The ship of the Great White Soul sank in 1851 and since then we have been seeing postmortem effects. And now Fiedler's coroner's verdict. Actually he is nicer than the others because he gives the dead a second chance.

But what a lot of ideological burial parties the twentieth century has seen! Common to all of them is a certain historical outlook. All that is not *now*, they say, is obsolete and dead. Any man who does not accept the historical moment as defined by the only authoritative interpreters is dead. In Dr. Fiedler's view, however, a man can rise again from the grave if he agrees that he is indeed dead. "Okay —I'm dead." "Then come forth, Lazarus." It can be fun, I suppose. Anyway it beats oblivion.

What Fiedler wants is to "close the gap between high culture and low, belles lettres and pop art." He calls for more obscenity, more of the *mantic*, the *mad* and the *savage*. We must go back again to Westerns:

> It is impossible to write any Western that does not in some sense glorify violence; but the violence celebrated in the anti-white Western is guerrilla violence—the sneak attack on civilization as practiced first by Geronimo and Cochise and other Indian warrior chiefs and more latterly apologized for by Che Guevara or the spokesman for North Vietnam. Warfare, however, is not the final vision implicit in the new Western, which is motivated on a deeper level by a nostalgia for the tribe—a social organization thought of as preferable to both the bourgeois family, from which its authors come, and the soulless out-of-human-scale bureaucratic state, into which they are initiated via schools and universities. In the end, both the dream of violence in the woods and the vision of tribal life seem juvenile, even infantile. But this is precisely the point; for what recommends the Western to the new novelist is preeminently its association with children.

For without the Child, where are we? And Dr. Fiedler now goes full throttle.

> For our latest poets realize . . . that merely to instruct and delight is not enough. They are convinced that wonder and fantasy that deliver the mind from the body, the body from the mind, must be naturalized to a world of machines. . . . One must live the tribal life among and with the support of machines; to shelter new communes under domes constructed according to the technology of Buckminster Fuller; and to warm the nakedness of new primitives with advanced techniques of solar heating.

In short, postelectronic romanticism. Dow Chemical manufactures napalm but also the "powerful psychedelic agent STP," and drugs are linked by Dr. Fiedler to

> . . . a great religious revival, scarcely noticed by the official spokesmen of established Christian churches, since it speaks quite another language. . . . Certain poets and novelists, as well as pop singers and pornographic

playwrights, are suggesting in print, on the air, everywhere, that not work but vision is the proper activity of men and that, therefore, the contemplative life [contemplation induced by LSD, STP—S.B.] may, after all, be preferable to the active one. In such an age, it is not surprising that the books that most move the young are essentially religious books, as indeed, pop art is always religious.

This is amusing but it is dismal, too. One cannot keep smiling at this nonsense, it is too near to madness. Nor is the madness original, the madness of great wit; it's all such old stuff. Again Dr. Fiedler shows us the Rebel, and the Outsider, and again The Desperado, the Primitive, the Redskin, the Sense-Deranged Poet, the Child, and then the Bard chanting to the tribe, and then again the Child. The Child, *über alles!* And he, Dr. Fiedler, is also a man of many faces. Sometimes he is the Little Demon of Sologub[2] and sometimes the dear Professor of *Little Women*,[3] all loving kindness.

A Good Scare

But loving kindness is often the favorite camouflage of the nihilist. The Grand Inquisitor[4] is always primping to kiss Jesus. However, a positive attitude is required of all who address the great U.S. public. Every society has its favorite lies. Our own favorite is kindliness. Dr. Fiedler loves the young, the new, loves the tribe, loves popular culture (formerly known to intellectuals as Masscult). Still the Petty Demon does burst out, spitting wrathfully.

Why does reading Fiedler's essay so promptly and strongly bring fascism to mind? Is he really a dangerous person? Does he literally mean that those of us who are over thirty-five might as well be dead? Probably not. His job is to frighten us, to give us all a good scare. In the old days he would have been writing for the Hearst Sunday Supplement. (Hefner[5] is quite a lot like W. R. Hearst.) But hatred of liberalism, love of an imaginary past (Cowboys and Indians), somnambulistic certitude, praise of tribalism and of Dionysiac excesses, the cult of youth, the chastising of high culture by the masses, the consecration of violence—all these suggest fascism. Lidless, the garbage can waits. Necessary and superfluous are the main categories, here. History is important for what you can get rid of. Considerations of style, quality or degree are irrelevant.

An Old Story

According to Fiedler, we are confronted with nothing less than the spiritual regeneration of mankind, we must expect to pass

2. Fyodor Sologub was the pen name of F. K. Teternikov, a Russian novelist, whose best-known book, *Little Demon*, portrays a sordid, perverted, and paranoid schoolteacher.
3. A children's novel by Louisa May Alcott.
4. Ivan's fictional cardinal, in Dostoievsky's *Brothers Karamazov*, who, on Jesus' coming again to earth, condemns Him to death.
5. Hugh Hefner, publisher of *Playboy*.

through the earlier theological and metaphysical stages of voodoo, storefront revivalism, astrology, holyrolling and Manson[6] cults. But the barbarous and the monstrous will refresh us and, as everybody knows, renewal always follows destruction. High culture will return —like *Mare Nostrum?* like the Thousand-Year Reich?

An old, old story—an ancient religious belief, really. Destruction purifies. We go through Hell, and we come out again. Jung, Lawrence, many others repeat the same myth. After the holocaust, the Phoenix; after the Flood, Ararat; after the Final Conflict, a Just Society; after Death, Resurrection. From Dr. Fiedler, powerfully flapping but never actually flying, the same message reaches us.

At this time, he says, we must yield and go along with pop art. Does that mean that we must make terms with the media-managing intellectuals? Evidently it does. And here it begins to appear that Dr. Fiedler's own class interests are involved. Isn't it obvious that college-educated, swinging, bearded, costumed, bohemianized intellectuals are writing the ads, manufacturing the gimmicks, directing the shows, exploiting the Woodstocks? Dr. Fiedler, an influential educator, is endorsing his own product. These new publicity intellectuals are his pupils. He tells us that the worst sins of the masses are better than the dead virtues of high culture. From many beards we hear amen to that. Yes, civilization has been profoundly disappointing. But this disappointment is also the foundation of their personal success. *It*—civilization—is a failure, but *they*—the publicity intellectuals—are doing extremely well.

What civilization has accumulated they treat as fuel and burn up. As the nineteenth century got its industrial power from coal, from the combustion of carboniferous forests, so successful operators burn up the culture of the nineteenth, the eighteenth, the seventeenth centuries, of all centuries, of all the ages. While they complain of a consumer culture, they consume the past, consume it all. They see nothing wrong with this. They find their sanction in the Contemporaneous. For whatever is not Contemporaneous is worthless.

I now turn briefly to the Underground Press.

Mr. D. A. Latimer, writing in the *East Village Other*, has this to say about the use of the word bullshit in the *New York Daily News*.

Reuben Maury has been busted for using the word "bullshit." Not I, mind you, I use the word "bullshit" without fear—bullshit on you, *Daily NEWS!*—because there is already one who has died for my sins, and that is Lenny Bruce. This week Douglas Records released a new album of Lenny Bruce tapes, monologues that have not been heard since their original delivery in some sleazy nightclub; and as part of their massive publicity campaign, Douglas invited me up to their plush offices last month

6. Charles Manson, head of the "family" that murdered Sharon Tate and others in California in 1969.

and laid some sweet rap on me. Mainly they allowed me to cup a lazy moment in my hands the posterior of the resident receptionist, a tall brunette lovely right out of some of my better cocaine visions. You want some bally-hoo, you just send your office chickie around by Latimer; women's lib will be down on me for this, but there it is, a piece for a piece, that's my professional credo.

At no time in the last few years have I heard any Lenny Bruce tapes, but I *have* been doing some research, and you know, there's a story in all that for our times. He was a fucking genius, this Bruce, when the scroll is written up on the Twentieth Century this guy has got to be the presiding Great Mind. And of course they blew him away, caught him in a lavatory trying to pump a French cruller up his arm, burned him off in August, 1966, you know all that. But the way they did it was so very similar to the way they're burning everybody off today, it could be quite instructive to inspect his history.

They kept busting him, see, and they ruined his head with all that courtroom shit. That's really bad news, when you're just trying to get your point across to some people, and the heat comes out and hits you for using dirty words. "Pray the Court's indulgence, the defendant in a public place used the word 'bullshit' at approximately 7:10 in the evening and repeated it at 7:27, 7:40, and 8:12. Also on the same occasion, he was heard by myself and Officer Phlud as saying, 'the sisters, the sisters do it this way,' in an obscene context." Now, how do you defend yourself against something like that? Sure enough, Lenny Bruce *said* "bullshit" several times in his life, and he made innumerable references to God and the Church and the sisters—but he knew there wasn't anything *illegal* about it, how can something you *say* be *illegal?* But they kept putting him in the exceedingly clumsy position before the courts of having to prove that he hadn't broken any laws, to persuade a judge to that effect. And the judge hasn't seen the show, but he *has* seen the District Attorney, day in and day out, so he's very likely to send you down the river just to keep this confusing shit at arm's length.

With Mr. Latimer we are at the heart of the phenomenon. And what do we see? We see, straight from *King Lear*, the burning words, "Thou, Nature, art my Goddess." Then we see feces as the most potent of primordial materials, very powerful indeed. The word Shit is to anal Protestantism what the crucifix was to were-wolves. Narcotics also are known in the underground as Shit, addicts are said to "shoot Shit" into their veins.

In his essay "Inside the Whale" George Orwell praised Henry Miller for putting aside the old literary language, the language of literary protocol, and for using instead the real language of real men, the language of streets and shipping rooms. The Miller victory is complete. The resonance of the street words has become great. A word like Bullshit has a moral force like that of Church Latin. *Vade retro Satanas!*[7] sounds no more magnificent to modern ears. There are religious undertones, too, for even in the underground religion (though in the form of blasphemy) has not disappeared, Dr. Fiedler is right about that. Thus Bruce is a Jesus who died for our sins. He was caught while taking the narcotics sacrament and

7. "Get thee hence, Satan." Matthew iv.10.

his (or His) pure spirit was destroyed. (An excrement-sacrament?) "They" caught him trying to pump a French cruller up his arm. "They" is the Heat, Authority, the Law, the Enemy. It is certainly, in many ways, an enemy. Even to itself it is no friend. Heavily armed, authority feels weak. Upper-class Protestant America freely, even excessively confesses its failures. Its last great man was F.D.R. It has much power still, but it is floundering. Certain of its industries are dominated by a new class, the publicity intellectuals. These are former students of literature, sociology or psychology, graduates of art institutes and drama departments. They have gone directly from college into the Mass Media. Unlike the intellectuals of the Depression era who were unemployed and who lived as intellectuals, publicity intellectuals have never been independent (and impoverished) writers, painters or thinkers.

Seeking Intercession

In the magazines and newspapers, top management, formerly so autocratic (think of Henry Luce), now casts itself at the feet of the publicity intellectuals, seeking their intercession with the youth-worshiping public. One picks up *The New York Times* and reads on the front page that the posthumous homosexual novel of E. M. Forster is about to appear in England. Why not simply Forster's posthumous novel, on page 40? No, the word is HOMOSEXUAL and it is on the front page. The *Times* still keeps up its statesman-like and grave appearance, but its journalism is yellower than ever. It has surrendered without a fight to the new class.

The present standard is the amusement standard: more accurately the amusement-boredom standard.

Literature in the nineteenth century laid a transforming touch on ordinary social realities, on city scenes and on the modern character. Many people now want to make literal use of imaginative suggestions. How shall we put it: they want to cook their meals over Pater's hard gemlike flame and light their cigarettes at it. They crave the exceptional for daily use, and the main purpose is perhaps to make behavior. No wonder the boundaries between stage and audience are disappearing and that spectators take off their clothes and mingle with the actors. Even American intellectuals, from Emerson to Norman O. Brown, preferred marvelous conduct to sedentary culture. Now belles lettres are licked; beautiful behavior wins hands down.

A powerful nation of unparalleled energy and practicality created an industrial society without precedent in history. The accompanying ugliness, boredom and spiritual trouble are also without precedent. Parts of society seem mad. It is essential (as Edgar Wind remarks in *Art and Anarchy*) that the whole should be less mad then the parts. But Authority has neither the imagination nor the moral capacity to act for the whole.

The peculiar difficulty of the artist in this situation is that he is obliged to take a common-sense view of things. What are his alternatives? He can no longer do the Child, the Primitive, the Romantic Agonist, the Rebel, the Drugged Visionary. All that is busted. Modernism is in the hands of demagogues, dunces and businessmen. It belongs to the publicity intellectuals. Because of this, the artist loses the benefit of contact with his modernist predecessors and is deprived of certain impulses and of a certain admirable verve.

Theatricality of Literature

As many observers tell us, everyone is "in the act." Of course Wallace Stevens was correct in pointing out the theatricality of literature. Authors are actors, he said, and books are theaters. But if the theater is everywhere and everyone is acting, where are exemplary events to be seen? The theory of creative equality implies the death of art. Reading the Underground Press, one becomes aware of ten thousand Villons.[8] The problem is one for the census taker, not the critic.

It should not be assumed that I recommend common sense for the artist. Surrounded by lunatics, he must make rational judgments, but he is not bound by these in his art. The operations of common sense are only preliminary. Once a writer has understood the state of fantasy prevailing, once he has understood what an art-polluted environment this is, his imagination is free again to receive new impulses.

The depths of the spirit are never overcrowded.

This society, like decadent Rome, is an amusement society. That is the grim fact. Art cannot and should not compete with amusement. It has business at the heart of humankind. The artist, as Collingwood tells us, must be a prophet, "not in the sense that he foretells things to come, but that he tells the audience, at risk of their displeasure, the secrets of their own hearts." That is why he exists. He is spokesman of his community. This account of the artist's business is old, much older than Collingwood, very old, but in modern times this truth, which we all feel, is seldom expressed. ". . . no community altogether knows its own heart: and by failing in this knowledge a community deceives itself on the one subject concerning which ignorance means death. . . . The remedy is the poem itself. Art is the community's medicine for the worst disease of mind, the corruption of consciousness."

8. François Villon, fifteenth-century French poet, here used as a type of the anti-establishment bard.

ANTHONY BURGESS
Is America Falling Apart?

I am back in Bracciano, a castellated town about 13 miles north of Rome, after a year in New Jersey. I find the Italian Government still unstable, gasoline more expensive than anywhere in the world, butchers and bank clerks and tobacconists (which also means salt-sellers) ready to go on strike at the drop of a *cappello*, neo-Fascists at their dirty work, the hammer and sickle painted on the rumps of public statues, a thousand-lire note (officially worth about $1.63) shrunk to the slightness of a dollar bill.

Nevertheless, it's delightful to be back. People are underpaid but they go through an act of liking their work, the open markets are luscious with esculent color, the community is more important than the state, the human condition is humorously accepted. The *tramontana* blows viciously today, and there's no central heating to turn on, but it will be pleasant when the wind drops. The two television channels are inadequate, but next Wednesday's rerun of an old Western, with Gary Cooper coming into a saloon saying *"Ciao, ragazzi,"* is something to look forward to. Manifold consumption isn't important here. The quality of life has nothing to do with the quantity of brand names. What matters is talk, family, cheap wine in the open air, the wresting of minimal sweetness out of the long-known bitterness of living. I was spoiled in New Jersey. The Italian for *spoiled* is *viziato*, cognate with *vitiated*, which has to do with vice.

Spoiled? Well, yes. I never had to shiver by a fire that wouldn't draw, or go without canned kraut juice or wild rice. America made me develop new appetites in order to make proper use of the super-market. A character in Evelyn Waugh's *Put Out More Flags* said that the difference between prewar and postwar life was that, prewar, if one thing went wrong the day was ruined; postwar, if one thing went right the day would be made. America is a prewar country, psychologically unprepared for one thing to go wrong. Now everything seems to be going wrong. Hence the neurosis, despair, the Kafka feeling that the whole marvelous fabric of American life is coming apart at the seams. Italy is used to everything going wrong. This is what the human condition is about.

Let me stay for a while on this subject of consumption. American individualism, on the face of it an admirable philosophy, wishes to manifest itself in independence of the community. You don't share things in common; you have your own things. A family's strength is signalized by its possessions. Herein lies a paradox. For the desire for possessions must eventually mean dependence on possessions.

Freedom is slavery. Once let the acquisitive instinct burgeon (enough flour for the winter, not just for the week), and there are ruggedly individual forces only too ready to make it come to full and monstrous blossom. New appetites are invented; what to the European are bizarre luxuries become, to the American, plain necessities.

During my year's stay in New Jersey I let my appetites flower into full Americanism except for one thing. I did not possess an automobile. This self-elected deprivation was a way into the nastier side of the consumer society. Where private ownership prevails, public amenities decay or are prevented from coming into being. The wretched run-down rail services of America are something I try, vainly, to forget. The nightmare of filth, outside and in, that enfolds the trip from Springfield, Mass., to Grand Central Station would not be accepted in backward Europe. But far worse is the nightmare of travel in and around Los Angeles, where public transport does not exist and people are literally choking to death in their exhaust fumes. This is part of the price of the metaphysic of individual ownership.

But if the car owner can ignore the lack of public transport, he can hardly ignore the decay of services in general. His car needs mechanics, and mechanics grow more expensive and less efficient. The gadgets in the home are cheaper to replace than repair. The more efficiently self-contained the home, primary fortress of independence, seems to be, the more dependent it is on the great impersonal corporations, as well as a diminishing army of servitors. Skills at the lowest level have to be wooed slavishly and exorbitantly rewarded. Plumbers will not come. Nor, at the higher level, will doctors. And doctors and dentists, in a nation committed to maiming itself with sugar and cholesterol, know their scarcity value and behave accordingly.

Americans are at last realizing that the acquisition of goods is not the whole of life. Consumption, on one level, is turning insipid, especially as the quality of the artifacts themselves seems to be deteriorating. Planned obsolescence is not conducive to pride in workmanship. On another level, consumption is turning sour. There is a growing guilt about the masses of discarded junk—rusting automobiles and refrigerators and washing machines and dehumidifiers— that it is uneconomical to recycle. Indestructible plastic hasn't even the grace to undergo chemical change. America, the world's biggest consumer, is the world's biggest polluter. Awareness of this is a kind of redemptive grace, but it doesn't appreciably lead to repentance and a revolution in consumer habits. Citizens of Los Angeles are horrified by that daily pall of golden smog, but they don't noticeably clamor for a decrease in the number of owner-vehicles. There is no worse neurosis than that which derives from a consciousness of guilt and an inability to reform.

America is anachronistic in so many ways, and not least in its clinging to a belief—now known to be unviable—in the capacity of the individual citizen to do everything for himself. Americans are admirable in their distrust of the corporate state—they have fought both Fascism and Communism—but they forget that there is a use for everything, even the loathesome bureaucratic machine. America needs a measure of socialization, as Britain needed it. Things—especially those we need most—don't always pay their way, and it is here that the state must enter, dismissing the profit element. Part of the present American neurosis, again, springs from awareness of this but inability to do anything about practical implementation. Perhaps only a country full of bombed cities feels capable of this kind of social revolution.

It would be supererogatory for me to list those areas in which thoughtful Americans feel that collapse is coming. It is enough for me to concentrate on what, during my New Jersey stay, impinged on my own life. Education, for instance, since I have a 6-year-old son to be brought up. America has always despised its teachers and, as a consequence, it has been granted the teachers it deserves. The quality of first-grade education that my son received, in a New Jersey town noted for the excellence of its public schools, could not, I suppose, be faulted on the level of dogged conscientiousness. The principal had read all the right pedagogic books, and was ready to quote these in the footnotes to his circular exhortations to parents. The teachers worked rigidly from the approved rigidly programed primers, ensuring that school textbook publication remains the big business it is.

But there seemed to be no spark; no daring, no madness, no readiness to engage the individual child's mind as anything other than raw material for statistical reductions. The fear of being unorthodox is rooted in the American teacher's soul: you can be fired for treading the path of experimental enterprise. In England, teachers cannot be fired, except for raping girl students and getting boy students drunk. In consequence, there is the kind of security that breeds eccentric genius, the capacity for firing mad enthusiasms.

I know that American technical genius, and most of all the moon landings, seems to give the lie to too summary a condemnation of the educational system, but there is more to education than the segmental equipping of the mind. There is that transmission of the value of the past as a force still miraculously fertile and moving—mostly absent from American education at all levels.

Of course, America was built on a rejection of the past. Even the basic Christianity which was brought to the continent in 1620 was of a novel and bizarre kind that would have nothing to do with the great rank river of belief that produced Dante and Michelangelo. America as a nation has never been able to settle to a common belief more sophisticated than the dangerous naiveté of the Declaration of Independence. "Life, liberty and the pursuit of happiness," indeed. And now America, filling in the vacuum left by the liquefied British Empire, has the task of telling the rest of the world that there's something better than Communism. The something better can only be money-making and consumption for its own sake. In the name of this ghastly creed the jungles must be defoliated.

No wonder the guilt of the thoughtful Americans I met in Princeton and New York and, indeed, all over the Union tended to express itself as an extravagant masochism, a desire for flagellation. Americans want to take on all the blame they can find, gluttons for punishment. "What do Europeans really think of us?" is a common question at parties. The expected answer is: "They think you're a load of decadent, gross-lipped, potbellied, callous, overbearing neoimperialists." Then the head can be bowed and the chest smitten: "*Nostra culpa, nostra maxima culpa. . . .*" But the fact is that such an answer, however much desired, would not be an honest one. Europeans think more highly of Americans now than they ever did. Let me try to explain why.

When Europe, after millennia of war, rapine, slavery, famine, intolerance, had sunk to the level of a sewer, America became the golden dream, the Eden where innocence could be recovered. Original sin was the monopoly of that dirty continent over there; in America man could glow in an aura of natural goodness, driven along his shining path by divine reason. The Declaration of Independence itself is a monument to reason. Progress was possible, and the wrongs committed against the Indians, the wildlife, the land itself, could be explained away in terms of the rational control of environment necessary for the building of a New Jerusalem. Right and wrong made up the moral dichotomy; evil—that great eternal inextirpable entity—had no place in America.

At last, with the Vietnam war and especially the Mylai horror, Americans are beginning to realize that they are subject to original sin as much as Europeans are. Some things—the massive crime figures, for instance—can now be explained only in terms of absolute evil. Europe, which has long known about evil and learned to live with it (*live* is *evil* spelled backwards), is now grimly pleased to find that America is becoming like Europe. America is no longer Europe's daughter nor her rich stepmother: she is Europe's sister. The agony that America is undergoing is not to be associated with breakdown so much as with the parturition of self-knowledge.

It has been assumed by many that the youth of America has

been in the vanguard of the discovery of both the disease and the cure. The various copping-out movements, however, from the Beats on, have committed the gross error of assuming that original sin rested with their elders, their rulers, and that they themselves could manifest their essential innocence by building little neo-Edens. The drug culture could confirm that the paradisal vision was available to all who sought it. But instant ecstasy has to be purchased, like any other commodity, and, in economic terms, that passive life of pure being involves parasitism. Practically all of the crime I encountered in New York—directly or through report—was a preying of the opium-eaters on the working community. There has to be a snake in paradise. You can't escape the heritage of human evil by building communes, usually on an agronomic ignorance that, intended to be a rejection of inherited knowledge, that suspect property of the elders, does violence to life. The American young are well-meaning but misguided, and must not themselves be taken as guides.

The guides, as always, lie among the writers and artists. And Americans ought to note that, however things may seem to be falling apart, arts and the humane scholarship are flourishing here, as they are not, for instance, in England. I'm not suggesting that Bellow, Mailer, Roth and the rest have the task of finding a solution to the American mess, but they can at least clarify its nature and show how it relates to the human condition in general. Literature, that most directly human of the arts, often reacts magnificently to an ambience of unease or apparent breakdown. The Elizabethans, to whose era we look back as to an irrecoverable Golden Age, were far more conscious than modern Americans of the chaos and corruption and incompetence of the state. Shakespeare's period was one of poverty, unemployment, ghastly inflation, violence in the streets. Twenty-six years after his death there was a bloody civil war, followed by a dictatorship of religious fanatics, followed by a calm respite in which the seeds of a revolution were sown. England survived. America will survive.

I'm not suggesting that Americans sit back and wait for a transient period of mistrust and despair to resolve itself, like a disease, through the unconscious healing forces which lie deep in organic nature. Man, as Thornton Wilder showed in *The Skin of Our Teeth*, always comes through—though sometimes only just. Americans living here and now have a right to an improvement in the quality of their lives, and they themselves, not the remote governors, must do something about it. It is not right that men and women should fear to go on the streets at night, and that they should sometimes fear the police as much as the criminals, both of whom sometimes look like mirror images of each other. I have had too much evidence, in my year in New Jersey, of the police behaving like the "Fascist pigs" of the revolutionary press. There are too many guns about, and the disarming of the police should be a natural aspect of the disarming of the entire citizenry.

American politics, at both the state and the Federal levels, is too much concerned with the protection of large fortunes, America being the only example in history of a genuine timocracy. The wealth qualification for the aspiring politician is taken for granted; a governmental system dedicated to the promotion of personal wealth in a few selected areas will never act for the public good. The time has come, nevertheless, for citizens to demand, from their government, a measure of socialization—the provision of amenities for the many, of which adequate state pensions and sickness benefits, as well as nationalized transport, should be priorities.

As for those remoter solutions to the American nightmare—only an aspect, after all, of the human nightmare—an Englishman must be diffident about suggesting that America made her biggest mistake in becoming America—meaning a revolutionary republic based on a romantic view of human nature. To reject a limited monarchy in favor of an absolute one (which is, after all, what the American Presidency is) argues a trust in the disinterestedness of an elected ruler which is, of course, no more than a reflection of belief in the innate goodness of man—so long as he happens to be American man. The American Constitution is out of date. Republics tend to corruption. Canada and Australia have their own problems, but they are happier countries than America.

This *Angst* about America coming apart at the seams, which apparently is shared by nearly 50 per cent of the entire American population, is something to rejoice about. A sense of sin is always admirable, though it must not be allowed to become neurotic. If electric systems break down and gadgets disintegrate, it doesn't matter much. There is always wine to be drunk by candlelight, uniced. If America's position as a world power collapses, and the Union dissolves into independent states, there is still the life of the family or the individual to be lived. England has survived her own dissolution as an imperial power, and Englishmen seem to be happy enough. But I ask the reader to note that I, an Englishman, no longer live in England, and I can't spend more than six months at a stretch in Italy—or any other European country, for that matter. I home to America as to a country more stimulating than depressing. The future of mankind is being worked out there on a scale typically American—vast, dramatic, almost apocalyptical. I brave the brutality and the guilt in order to be in on the scene. I shall be back.

QUESTIONS

1. What would Burgess say of the Whole Earth Catalogue: is it a rejection of consumerism or a surrender to it?
2. In what respects is the substance of Burgess' argument similar to those of Eldridge Cleaver (above, pp. 359–367) and George Jackson (below, pp. 674–687)? Compare the language used by the three to articulate the similar substance; is the language of any one more basic than that of the other two?
3. Burgess' observation about the Italian word for spoiled implies a concern for etymology and precision of language. Is there evidence of that concern in his choice of English words?

X. J. KENNEDY

Who Killed King Kong?

The ordeal and spectacular death of King Kong, the giant ape, undoubtedly have been witnessed by more Americans than have ever seen a performance of *Hamlet, Iphigenia at Aulis,* or even *Tobacco Road.* Since RKO-Radio Pictures first released *King Kong,* a quarter-century has gone by; yet year after year, from prints that grow more rain-beaten, from sound tracks that grow more tinny, ticket-buyers by thousands still pursue Kong's luckless fight against the forces of technology, tabloid journalism, and the DAR. They see him chloroformed to sleep, see him whisked from his jungle isle to New York and placed on show, see him burst his chains to roam the city (lugging a frightened blonde), at last to plunge from the spire of the Empire State Building, machine-gunned by model airplanes.

Though Kong may die, one begins to think his legend unkillable. No clearer proof of his hold upon the popular imagination may be seen than what emerged one catastrophic week in March 1955, when New York WOR-TV programmed *Kong* for seven evenings in a row (a total of sixteen showings). Many a rival network vice-president must have scowled when surveys showed that *Kong*—the 1933 B-picture—had lured away fat segments of the viewing populace from such powerful competitors as Ed Sullivan, Groucho Marx and Bishop Sheen.

But even television has failed to run *King Kong* into oblivion. Coffee-in-the-lobby cinemas still show the old hunk of hokum, with the apology that in its use of composite shots and animated models the film remains technically interesting. And no other monster in movie history has won so devoted a popular audience. None of the plodding mummies, the stultified draculas, the white-coated Lugosis[1] with their shiny pinball-machine laboratories, none of the invisible stranglers, berserk robots, or menaces from Mars has ever enjoyed so many resurrections.

Why does the American public refuse to let King Kong rest in peace? It is true, I'll admit, that *Kong* outdid every monster movie before or since in sheer carnage. Producers Cooper and Schoedsack crammed into it dinosaurs, headhunters, riots, aerial battles, bullets, bombs, bloodletting. Heroine Fay Wray, whose function is mainly to scream, shuts her mouth for hardly one uninterrupted minute from first reel to last. It is also true that *Kong* is larded with good healthy sadism, for those whose joy it is to see the frantic girl dangled from cliffs and harried by pterodactyls. But it seems to me that the abiding appeal of the giant ape rests on other foundations.

Kong has, first of all, the attraction of being manlike. His simian nature gives him one huge advantage over giant ants and walking vegetables in that an audience may conceivably identify with him. Kong's appeal has the quality that established the Tarzan series as American myth—for what man doesn't secretly image himself a huge hairy howler against whom no other monster has a chance? If Tarzan recalls the ape in us, then Kong may well appeal to that great-granddaddy primordial brute from whose tribe we have all deteriorated.

Intentionally or not, the producers of *King Kong* encourage this identification by etching the character of Kong with keen sympathy. For the ape is a figure in a tradition familiar to moviegoers: the tradition of the pitiable monster. We think of Lon Chaney in the role of Quasimodo, of Karloff in the original *Frankenstein*. As we watch the Frankenstein monster's fumbling and disastrous attempts to befriend a flower-picking child, our sympathies are enlisted with the monster in his impenetrable loneliness. And so with Kong. As he roars in his chains, while barkers sell tickets to boobs who gape at him, we perhaps feel something more deep than pathos. We begin to sense something of the problem that engaged Eugene O'Neill in *The Hairy Ape*: the dilemma of a displaced animal spirit forced to live in a jungle built by machines.

King Kong, it is true, had special relevance in 1933. Landscapes of the depression are glimpsed early in the film when an impresario, seeking some desperate pretty girl to play the lead in a jungle movie, visits souplines and a Woman's Home Mission. In Fay Wray—who's been caught snitching an apple from a fruitstand—his search is ended. When he gives her a big feed and a movie contract, the girl is magic-carpeted out of the world of the National Recovery Act. And when, in the film's climax, Kong smashes that very Third

1. Bela Lugosi, an actor in many horror movies.

Avenue landscape in which Fay had wandered hungry, audiences of 1933 may well have felt a personal satisfaction.

What is curious is that audiences of 1960 remain hooked. For in the heart of urban man, one suspects, lurks the impulse to fling a bomb. Though machines speed him to the scene of his daily grind, though IBM comptometers ("freeing the human mind from drudgery") enable him to drudge more efficiently once he arrives, there comes a moment when he wishes to turn upon his machines and kick hell out of them. He wants to hurl his combination radio-alarmclock out the bedroom window and listen to its smash. What subway commuter wouldn't love—just for once—to see the downtown express smack head-on into the uptown local? Such a wish is gratified in that memorable scene in *Kong* that opens with a wide-angle shot: interior of a railway car on the Third Avenue El. Straphangers are nodding, the literate refold their newspapers. Unknown to them, Kong has torn away a section of trestle toward which the train now speeds. The motorman spies Kong up ahead, jams on the brakes. Passengers hurtle together like so many peas in a pail. In a window of the car appear Kong's bloodshot eyes. Women shriek. Kong picks up the railway car as if it were a rat, flips it to the street and ties knots in it, or something. To any commuter the scene must appear one of the most satisfactory pieces of celluloid ever exposed.

Yet however violent his acts, Kong remains a gentleman. Remarkable is his sense of chivalry. Whenever a fresh boa constrictor threatens Fay, Kong first sees that the lady is safely parked, then manfully thrashes her attacker. (And she, the ingrate, runs away every time his back is turned.) Atop the Empire State Building, ignoring his pursuers, Kong places Fay on a ledge as tenderly as if she were a dozen eggs. He fondles her, then turns to face the Army Air Force. And Kong is perhaps the most disinterested lover since Cyrano: his attentions to the lady are utterly without hope of reward. After all, between a five-foot blonde and a fifty-foot ape, love can hardly be more than an intellectual flirtation. In his simian way King Kong is the hopelessly yearning lover of Petrarchan convention. His forced exit from his jungle, in chains, results directly from his single-minded pursuit of Fay. He smashes a Broadway theater when the notion enters his dull brain that the flashbulbs of photographers somehow endanger the lady. His perilous shinnying up a skyscraper to pluck Fay from her boudoir is an act of the kindliest of hearts. He's impossible to discourage even though the love of his life can't lay eyes on him without shrieking murder.

The tragedy of King Kong then, is to be the beast who at the end of the fable fails to turn into the handsome prince. This is the conviction that the scriptwriters would leave with us in the film's closing line. As Kong's corpse lies blocking traffic in the street, the enterpreneur who brought Kong to New York turns to the assembled reporters and proclaims: "That's your story, boys—it was Beauty killed the Beast!" But greater forces than those of the screaming Lady have combined to lay Kong low, if you ask me. Kong lives for a time as one of those persecuted near-animal souls bewildered in the middle of an industrial order, whose simple desires are thwarted at every turn. He climbs the Empire State Building because in all New York it's the closest thing he can find to the clifftop of his jungle isle. He dies, a pitiful dolt, and the army brass and publicity-men cackle over him. His death is the only possible outcome to as neat a tragic dilemma as you can ask for. The machine-guns do him in, while the manicured human hero (a nice clean Dartmouth boy) carries away Kong's sweetheart to the altar. O, the misery of it all. There's far more truth about upper-middle-class American life in *King Kong* than in the last seven dozen novels of John P. Marquand.

A Negro friend from Atlanta tells me that in movie houses in colored neighborhoods throughout the South, *Kong* does a constant business. They show the thing in Atlanta at least every year, presumably to the same audiences. Perhaps this popularity may simply be due to the fact that Kong is one of the most watchable movies ever constructed, but I wonder whether Negro audiences may not find some archetypical appeal in this serio-comic tale of a huge black powerful free spirit whom all the hardworking white policemen are out to kill.

Every day in the week on a screen somewhere in the world, King Kong relives his agony. Again and again he expires on the Empire State Building, as audiences of the devout assist his sacrifice. We watch him die, and by extension kill the ape within our bones, but these little deaths of ours occur in prosaic surroundings. We do not die on a tower, New York before our feet, nor do we give our lives to smash a few flying machines. It is not for us to bring to a momentary standstill the civilization in which we move. King Kong does this for us. And so we kill him again and again, in much-spliced celluloid, while the ape in us expires from day to day, obscure, in desperation.

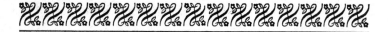

Prose Forms: Oral History

["But what did he say?" is a question listeners would sometimes like to ask when they have been told what another person meant, or intended, or implied, or even thought. It is not a matter of distrusting the reporter's account, nor necessarily of merely wishing to hear the report put differently. It may be that in order to get the direct, unmediated, uninterpreted utterance, the listener will ask for the authentic—and authoritative—words as they were said. Does the listener therefore get a greater measure of truth or a clearer sense of meaning from the original utterance than from a report of it? He may not, of course; but he may in many instances, if the "truth" and "meaning" of the utterance depend as much on the personality and character of the speaker as they do on the occasion about which he speaks.

The kind of occasion is important here. If it is generally familiar in its outline because widely known or frequently encountered (either directly in one's own experience or indirectly through reading, study, or the communications and entertainment media), it is public and therefore familiarly accessible to our immediate understanding. The relation of a specific personality to that occasion, his perception of it, is as telling as the public occasion itself seen independently of its private effect on specific individuals—and frequently much more interesting because the coming together of the private and the public not only particularizes the relation but indeed humanizes the occasion. The speaker in Herb Goro's "A Fireman" gives us almost incidentally a rough narrative of a fire company's problems in answering an alarm (familiar enough as a public occurrence), but his account of his involvement in it, his private disgusts and indignations, irradiates the narrative with human poignancy (hates, biases, stupidities, and all). The narrative gains human authority, and a certain honesty and spontaneity peculiar to what we call oral history.

The range of possibility in oral history encompasses the closely reasoned interchange between Huey Newton and Erik Erikson on the meaning of "armed love" and James Thurber's thoughts on his— and others'—methods as artists, on the one hand, and the simple declarations with complex implications of a police sergeant and a dime store saleswoman, on the other. The oral historian keeps us strictly in touch with the privately, personally human sieve of public experience.

All history was once oral, and out of it grew poetry as well as formal history as we now know it. One of the things which modern oral history preserves for us is the element of the poetic, if we understand that term to mean, in this broad context, the sense of private vision articulated in language which points toward both the public object or occasion and the unique sensibility perceiving it. In addition, it often arises freely, unpremeditated, almost unstructured except for loose chronology and the vagaries of association. It may not be logical, depending instead on a kind of psycho-logic which has its own meaning, usually evident in the style, the peculiar flavor of a distinct mind and personality apparent in the language of the recital.

And it is direct and honest, seeking usually no end except to express itself. We tend to minimize the factual errors, the mistaken vocabulary, the flamboyant rhetoric, the preposterous judgments of people and events in "Doc Graham," even as we are totally fascinated by him and his ruminations on crime, the Depression, and his own career in both. Uncensored, unrepressed, confined only by a sense of his own authority and confidence, Doc Graham's history wells up and flows out spontaneously, honestly, authentically. All around the edges of his remarks and appearing dramatically in the midst of them are "facts," public events and personalities and occasions which we know about independently. They are unsullied in our minds even if they are mangled in Doc Graham's, but the power and grandeur of his posture, his style as a man and as a speaker, ring marvelous subtleties on those facts without destroying them. He literally brings them to life, his life, in a way instructive to both. Private and public, person and events are the mixture. History of a very real and useful kind is the issue.]

STUDS TERKEL: Doc Graham[1]

A mutual acquaintance, Kid Pharaoh, insisted that we meet. Doc Graham had obviously seen better days.

My introduction to Chicago was when a guy got his head blowed off right across from where I went to stay. In that neighborhood where I gravitated, there was every kind of character that was ever invented. Con men, heist men, burglars, peet men: you name it, they had it.

These are highly sophisticated endeavors. To be proficient at it —well, my God, you spent a lifetime. And then you might fall, through not being sophisticated enough. You may have committed a common error, leaving fingerprints. . . .

I was a caged panther. It was jungle. Survival was the law of the land. I watched so many of my partners fall along the way. I decided the modus operandi was bad. Unavailing, non-productive. After spending ten Saturdays in jail, one right after another, I changed my modus operandi.

What were you in jail for?

Various allegations. All alleged. I been a con man, a heist man— you name it.

How does a heist man differ from a con man?

One is by force and the other is by guile. Very few people have encompassed both. I was very daring. When I came to the city and seen groceries on the sidewalk, I swore I'd never be hungry again. My family was extremely poor. My father was an unsuccessful gambler, and my mother was a missionary. Not much money was connected with either profession.

A family conflict . . . ?

Yes, slightly. He threw the Bible in the fire. He was right, incidentally. [Laughs.] My mother didn't see it that way.

I'm sixty-one, and I have never held a Social Security card. I'm not knocking it. I have been what society generally refers to as a parasite. But I don't think I'd be a nicer fellow if I held two jobs.

My teacher was Count Victor Lustig. He was perhaps the greatest con man the United States has ever known. Lustig's outstanding achievement was getting put in jail and paying a Texas sheriff off with $30,000 counterfeit. And the sheriff made the penitentiary also. He got to be a believer. And he went into the counterfeit profession.

Another teacher was Ace Campbell.[2] He was the greatest card

1. From *Hard Times: An Oral History of the Great Depression*, 1970.

mechanic that ever arrived on the scene. Nick the Greek[3] wouldn't make him a butler. A footman. He couldn't open the door for him. Ace played the crimp. A crimp is putting a weave in a card that you'd need a microscope to see it. I know the techniques, but having had my arm half removed, I had to switch left-handed, deal left-handed. I'm ambidexterous.

An accident . . . ?

With a colored North American. The twenties and early thirties was a jungle, where only the strong survived and the weak fell by the wayside. In Chicago, at the time, the unsophisticated either belonged to the Bugs Moran mob or the Capone mob. The fellas with talent didn't bother with either one. And went around and robbed both of 'em.

We were extremely independent. Since I'm Irish, I had a working affiliate with Bugs Moran's outfit. In case muscle was needed beyond what I had, I called on Moran for help. On the other hand, Moran might use me to help in one of his operations.

The nature of one operation was: if you had a load of whiskey hijacked, we went over and reloaded it on a truck, while several surrounded the place with machine guns, sawed-off shotguns, etcetera.

Did you find yourself in ticklish situations on occasion . . . ?

Many of them. You see this fellow liquidated, that fellow disposed of. Red McLaughlin had the reputation of being the toughest guy in Chicago. But when you seen Red run out of the drainage canal, you realized Red's modus operandi was unavailing. His associates was Clifford and Adams. They were set in Al's doorway in his hotel in Cicero. That was unavailing. Red and his partners once stole the Checker Cab Company. They took machine guns and went up and had an election, and just went and took it over. I assisted in that operation.

What role did the forces of law and order play?

With a $10 bill, you wasn't bothered. If you had a speaking acquaintance with Mayor Thompson,[4] you could do no wrong. [Laughs.] Al spoke loud to him.

There was a long period during the Depression where the police were taking scrip. Cash had a language all of its own. One night in particular, I didn't have my pistol with me, and the lady of the evening pointed out a large score to me. [Laughs.] A squad car came by, which I was familiar with. A Cadillac, with a bell on it. I knew all the officers. I borrowed one of their pistols and took the score. Then I had to strip and be searched by the policemen, keeping

2. A pseudonym for a celebrated gambler of the twenties and early thirties. He is still alive [Terkel's note].

3. Another renowned gambler of the time [Terkel's note].

4. William Hale Thompson, three-term mayor of Chicago [Terkel's note].

honest in the end, as we divided the score. They wanted the right count. They thought I might be holding out on 'em. They even went into my shoes, even.

Oh, many policemen in that era were thieves. Legal thieves. I accepted it as such and performed accordingly. We didn't have no problems. It was an era where there was no bread on the table. So what was the difference whether I put the bread on the table by my endeavor or they put the bread? I performed with a hundred policemen in my time. I can't say nothin' for 'em, nothin' against 'em. I would say they were opportunists. I would say that they were merely persons that didn't perhaps have the courage to go on and do what I did. Nevertheless, they were willing to be a part of it. A minor part, that is.

The era of the times led into criminality, because of the old precept and concepts were destroyed against everyday reality. So when a policeman or a fireman was not being paid, how in the name of God could you expect him to enforce what he knew as the concept of law and order, when you see the beer barons changing hundred-dollar bills, and the pimp and the whorehouse guy had hundred-dollar bills, and the guy digging the sewers couldn't pay his bills? So how could you equate these things?

A good example is Clyde Barrow and Bonnie Parker. They were a product of the era. Dillinger—it wasn't that he was really a tough. No, he was just a product of survival. Actually, Dillinger was a country bumpkin. He realized the odds were stacked against him and performed accordingly. I knew Dillinger. Yeah, I met him on the North Side. And Dillinger was nothing like people wrote about him. The times produced Dillinger. Pretty Boy Floyd. Baby Face Nelson.

They were dedicated heist men and in the end were killed, to achieve their purpose. By themselves, they didn't need an army.

Al Capone sublet the matter. Capone quickly removed himself from the danger zone, aside from murdering Anselmi and Scalisi with a baseball bat. Bugs Moran to the end—he died for a bank heist in Ohio. They were from two different bolts of cloth. One was a dedicated thief. And one was an intriguing Mediterranean product of guile, etcetera. So you'd have to say that Moran was dedicated while Capone was an opportunist.

How did you get along during those hard times?

By every way known to the human brain. All my brothers were in the penitentiary. I had one brother in Jefferson City, another one in San Quentin, another one in Leavenworth, another one in Louisiana. At that time I am a fighter. I started boxing in 1925. Fourteen years till 1939. And it's a bloodthirsty thing.

How'd you become a boxer?

Gravitation. Being on the road simulated that fate, trying to grab

a buck and so forth. Five different years, *Ring* magazine rated me the most devastating puncher in the profession, pound for pound.
What was it like, being a boxer in those days . . . ?

Survival. If it worked out that you were on top, you made a living. And if you were three or four shades below the top, you scuffled for a buck. Fighters were very, very hungry.

I made some pretty big scores. But I spent it practically all on getting my brothers out of penitentiaries around the country. At that time, the one in San Quentin stood me thirty thousand, the one in Jefferson City stood me twenty-five thousand. Those were big give-ups in those days.

I lived from the bottom to the top. I lived as good as you could live. I run the gamut of having a butler and a chauffeur to a flop joint, into an open car overnight.
He describes the boxing "combination" of those days; the fix; the refusal of his manager and himself to "play ball"; the boxer as an investment, cut up "like a watermelon."

I had many injuries in between. My hands, you can see. [He holds out his gnarled, broken knuckles.] In the meantime, I had to step out and make a dollar otherwise. It was never with the law.

I've switched craps, I've run up the cards, I do the complete bit. Every way known to the human brain. I'm probably a rare species that's left.
Was muscle always involved?

Muscle if you hope to leave with the money. Muscle everywhere, yes. Because for some unknown reason, muscle has been going on since the Roman Army conquered the field with a way of life.

When you enter an endeavor unsuccessfully, then the planning was incorrect. The risk was above the gains, and you stumble along the way. And the windup is a rude awakening with numbers strung out over your back. Unsuccessful in your modus operandi. Sagacity, ingenuity, planning . . . it involves much weighing, odds against failure, odds against gain—if you care to be in a free society.

I spent much time in jail. That's why I'm a student of the matter.
(At this point, Kid Pharaoh and he conducted a vigorous and somewhat arcane debate concerning the relative dishonesty of Hoover and Roosevelt. The Kid insisted it was Hoover who, by clout, was saved from "the bucket." Doc was equally certain it was F.D.R. who should have had "numbers strung out over his shoulders.")
Do you recall your biggest haul during the thirties?

It was alleged—
Who alleged . . . ?

The newspaper report came out as $75,000. We took eight and were happy about the whole thing.
What was your role during Prohibition?

I was a cheater. After studying under Count Lustig and Ace Campbell, I considered it beneath my dignity delivering a barrel of beer. Although I drink beer. I hustled with crap mobs, on the crimp, the weave, the holdout—the reason I didn't do the rum running is you can hire a mooch with muscle. But can you hire brains? Big firms have not succeeded in doing this.

I have met only several proficient men in my time. On of them was Jack Freed. [Cups hand over mouth, whispers.] D-e-a-d. He worked right up to the edge of his demise. This is in the evening, when you are not at home. He was dedicated to his labor. He spent half his lifetime in the penitentiaries. One of my closest friends. I, of course, assisted him, from time to time. He accused me of rattling my coat one night, making entrance. I, who have endeavored in every participation known to the human brain, where art, subterfuge and guile is involved.

I take it you were caught a few times—

Incarcerated. Nothing proven substantially. I was a victim of circumstances. What they were, I didn't say. Yes, I spent a year in Salinas, California, amongst other places. The highlight was when I was nineteen. If I get convicted, I'm going out to join my brother in San Quentin. My brother was doing twenty years there. If I'm not convicted, I'm going up to visit him. I'm going to San Quentin, one way or the other.

And you did?

I did. As a free man. I was fortunate enough in having one of the greatest criminal lawyers of all time defending me.

For someone engaging in your varied skills, do you sense a difference between the thirties and today?

It's so different today, it's unfathomable. You can't conjure what the difference is. Today everything is a robot. Today everything is mechanical. There is very little ingenuity. Everything today is nopersonal, there is no personality whatsoever. Everything today is *ipso facto, fait accompli*. In my era they had to prove their point. Today, you don't have to prove your point.

Back then Ace Campbell steered Arnold Rothstein,[5] with Nigger Nate Raymond, into one of maybe the biggest card games was ever involved. I was a small feature of it in the Park Central Hotel in New York. Ace changed the weave [laughs], and when Rothstein wound up a half-a-million loser, he said he was cheated. Rothstein became jaded after he lost the half a million, no longer had any interest. No interest in life. After the card game broke up, he said he was no longer interested in this, that or the other. He refused to pay off. So Nigger Nate Raymond held court with him. And that

5. A gambler and fixer of reknown. He was involved in the Black Sox scandal of 1919.

was the end of that.

Held court . . . ?

The S&W people[6] had the implements that they held court with. That's all. Rothstein didn't have to pay off. You understand what I mean? I know, because I assisted in the operation with Ace. But let that be as it may. It was unfortunate, yes. But that was his demise.

Were the S&W people popular those days?

Naturally, it was part of your wearing apparel.

Aren't some of the survivors in legitimate enterprises today?

One of the fellows who was a pimp in Chicago is the boss of one of the grandest hotels in Las Vegas. I assisted him in a few small matters. But true to all pimping, he forgot me entirely as he advanced into the autumn of life.

After Prohibition, what did the guys do?

The ones that were adroit enough branched into other fields. If they didn't have any knowledge, they fell by the wayside. I achieved some small success in race tracks. Machine Gun Jack McGurn[7] couldn't stand the traffic. He got his brains blowed out, branching into other fields.

The night Prohibition was repealed, everybody got drunk. It was the only decent thing Roosevelt ever did in his Administration. I was not one of his admirers. I tried to fire him on four different occasions. If I ever had a person work for me that displeased me, it was Roosevelt. I voted against him four times.

What was it about him you didn't like?

Him being a con man, taking advantage of poor, misguided, gibbering idiots who believed in his fairy tales. The New Deal, the various gimmicks, the NRA . . . the complete subterfuge, artifice and guile. . . .

Some say Roosevelt saved our society. . . .

I dare say it would have been saved if Roosevelt's mother and father had never met.

Many people were on relief . . . on WPA. . . .

I didn't have a thing to do with that, because I was above that. Nevertheless, the people that were involved in it did it merely to get some meat on the plates, some food in the kitchen. It was no more, no less. Survival. None of the connotations of social dissent that has crept in since then. Merely an abstract way of eating. . . .

What do you think would happen if there were a big Depression today?

Very simple. They'd commit suicide today. I don't think they're

---

6. Smith & Wesson, revolver manufacturers.
7. It was alleged that he was one of Capone's executioners in the St. Valentine's Day Massacre. He was killed in a bowling alley in 1936, on the eve of St. Valentine's Day.

conditioned to stand it. We were a hardier race then. We'd win wars. We didn't procrastinate. We'd win them or lose them. Today we're a new race of people. They'll quit on a draw—if they see any feasible way to see their way out to quit with any dignity, they'll quit. Back then, you had a different breed of people. You got $21 a month going into the army or the navy. So them guys, they went to win the war. There's been an emancipated woman since the beginning of the war, also.

KID PHARAOH *interjects. "The American woman during the Depression was domesticated. Today, as we move into the late sixties, if you go into any high school, you don't see any classes of cooking any more. You don't see any classes at all in sewing. None of them can boil water. They're all today in business in competition to the male animal. Why should a Playboy bunny make $200 a week? If a veteran goes to war, puts his life up . . . can't raise a family."*

DOC: *". . . a lot of country bumpkins in the city wanting to look at poor, misguided, gibbering idiot waitresses. That they've stripped down like a prostitute, but hasn't sense enough to know that it's on her alleged sex allure that the poor misguided chump is in the place. In the end it amounts to absolutely nothing. A hypothesis of silly nothingness . . . undressed broads serving hootch, that cannot fulfill. . . ."*

KID PHARAOH: *" . . . his dick directs him, like radar, to the Playboy Club. In a high moral society—in Russia—guys like Hugh Hefner would be working in the library."*

During the Depression . . . if a guy had a few drinks with a girl . . .?

If she had two drinks with him, and she didn't lay her frame down, she was in a serious matter. She could have one, and explain she made a mistake by marrying some sucker that she was trying to fulfill her marriage commitment. But in the thirties, if you had a second drink and she didn't make the commitment where she's going to lay her frame down for you, the entire matter was resolved quickly to the point and could end in mayhem. She was in a serious matter.

In the thirties, then, the individual con man, the heist man, had an easier time with it—all around?

Oh yes, it was much easier then. The Federal Government now has you on practically anything you do. They make a conspiracy whether you accomplish the matter or not. Today, it's fraught with much peril, any type of endeavor you engage in. A nefarious matter. It constantly comes under the heading of a federal statute. The Federal Government then collected taxes, and just a few interstate things, as white slavery, and that was about it.

Today, the Federal Government has expanded into every field. If you use a telephone, as an example, and you put slugs in it, that's a penitentiary offense. Strange as that may seem. So that will give you an idea how far the Federal Government has encroached on a citizen's prerogative.

You think Roosevelt had a role to play in this?

Definitely. He was perhaps the lowest human being that ever held public office. He, unfortunately, was a despot. I mean, you get an old con man at a point in high office, he begins to believe the platitudes that are expounded by the stupid populace about him.

What about the young people, during the Depression . . . ?

The young people in the Depression respected what laws there were. If they'd steal, they tried to do it with dignity. And what not. They respected the policeman. They looked at him with forebearance, that he was a necessary part of society. But, nevertheless, he didn't impede the mere fact of gain.

No, he didn't stop 'em.

The young today are feminized, embryo homosexuals. Stool pigeons.

What about the young dissenters?

If you gave 'em a push, they'd turn into a homosexual. When the German hordes fifty years ago surrounded Paris, Marshall Pétain brought out the pimps, whores, thieves, underground operators, he says: Our playground is jeopardized by the German Hun. Well, all Paris, every thief, burglar, pimp, he come out and picked up a musket. Stopped the German hordes.

Today you don't see any kind of patriotism like that. They're trying to tear down the courthouse, they try to throw paint on Johnson's car. How can you compare that era, coming into this? Those were men, and today you've got to question whether they're homosexual or whether they're not.

Since the Depression, manhood has been lost—the manhood that I knew. Where four or five guys went on an endeavor, they died trying to take the endeavor off. It was no big deal if they did die. If it didn't come off right, there was no recrimination. Everybody put skin off what they set on.

Today, the foible of our civilization is to attack the policeman with a rotten egg, throwing it at him. Or walking around with a placard, that they're against whatever the present society advocates as civilized. Those people today—the Fall of Rome could be compared with it. Because they were the strongest nation on earth, and they disinterrogated into nothing. Through debauchery, through moral decay.

They need a narcotic to do anything, they can't do it on their own. They need a drug. Back in my era, we could cold-bloodedly do it.

RONALD BLYTHE: Leonard Thompson,
Aged Seventy-one, Farm-Worker[1]

You went to the verge, you say, and come back safely?
Some have not been so fortunate—some have fallen.
Conrad Aiken, *Prelude XIV*

* * *

In my four months' training with the regiment I put on nearly a
stone in weight and got a bit taller. They said it was the food but it
was really because for the first time in my life there had been no
strenuous work. I want to say this simply as a fact, that village
people in Suffolk in my day were worked to death. It literally happened. It is not a figure of speech. I was worked mercilessly. I am
not complaining about it. It is what happened to me.

We were all delighted when war broke out on August 4th. I was
now a machine-gunner in the Third Essex Regiment. A lot of boys
from the village were with me and although we were all sleeping in
ditches at Harwich, wrapped in our greatcoats, we were bursting
with happiness. We were all damned glad to have got off the farms.
I had 7s. a week and sent my mother half of it. If you did this, the
government would add another 3s. 6d.—so my mother got 7s. My
father died early this year and my mother lived on this 7s. a week
for the whole of the war, adding a scrap to it by doing washing, and
weeding in the fields. Neither of my parents lived long enough to
draw the Old Age Pension. I can remember, when work was short, a
group of unemployed young men coming to where some old men
were sugar-beeting, which is the worst job there is, and shouting,
'Now that you grandfathers have got the pension'—it was 5s. a
week—'why don't you get out of the field and give us a chance?'
These 'old' men were only in their fifties but the hardness of their
lives had made them ancient.

All this trouble with the village fell behind us now. I was nineteen and off to the Dardanelles, which is the Hellespont, I discovered. I had two boys from the village with me. We'd heard a lot
about France so we thought we'd try Turkey. The band played on
the banks of the river as we pulled out of Plymouth and I wondered
if we would ever come home again. We were all so patriotic then
and had been taught to love England in a fierce kind of way. The
village wasn't England; England was something better than the village. We got to Gib and it was lovely and warm. Naked Spanish
boys dived round us for coins. There were about fifty nurses on the
top deck and they threw tanners.[2] You could see they were having
an eye-opener. We stopped to coal-up. The dust blew all over the

---

1. From Chapter 1 of *Akenfield: Por-*   2. Sixpence pieces.
trait of an English Village, 1969.

decks and all over us. We were packed like sardines and eating rubbish again. Water and salt porridge for breakfast. Beans and high salt pork for dinner. The pork was too bad for land-men to eat so we threw it into the coaldust and the coolies snatched it up and thrust it into their mouths, or put it into sacks to take home for their families.

We arrived at the Dardanelles and saw the guns flashing and heard rifle-fire. They heaved our ship, the *River Clyde* right up to the shore. They had cut a hole in it and made a little pier, so we were able to walk straight off and on to the beach. We all sat there —on the Hellespont!—waiting for it to get light. The first things we saw were big wrecked Turkish guns, the second a big marquee. It didn't make me think of the military but of the village fêtes. Other people must have thought like this because I remember how we all rushed up to it, like boys getting into a circus, and then found it all laced up. We unlaced it and rushed in. It was full of corpses. Dead Englishmen, lines and lines of them, and with their eyes wide open. We all stopped talking. I'd never seen a dead man before and here I was looking at two or three hundred of them. It was our first fear. Nobody had mentioned this. I was very shocked. I thought of Suffolk and it seemed a happy place for the first time.

Later that day we marched through open country and came to within a mile and half of the front line. It was incredible. We were there—at the war! The place we had reached was called 'dead ground' because it was where the enemy couldn't see you. We lay in little square holes, myself next to James Sears from the village. He was about thirty and married. That evening we wandered about on the dead ground and asked about friends of ours who had arrived a month or so ago. 'How is Ernie Taylor?'—'Ernie?—he's gone.' 'Have you seen Albert Paternoster?'—'Albert?—he's gone.' We learned that if 300 had 'gone' but 700 were left, then this wasn't too bad. We then knew how unimportant our names were.

I was on sentry that night. A chap named Scott told me that I must only put my head up for a second but that in this time I must see as much as I could. Every third man along the trench was a sentry. The next night we had to move on to the third line of trenches and we heard that the Gurkhas were going over and that we had to support their rear. But when we got to the communication trench we found it so full of dead men that we could hardly move. Their faces were quite black and you couldn't tell Turk from English. There was the most terrible stink and for a while there was nothing but the living being sick on to the dead. I did sentry again that night. It was one-two-sentry, one-two-sentry all along the trench, as before. I knew the next sentry up quite well. I remembered him in Suffolk singing to his horses as he ploughed. Now he fell back with a great scream and a look of surprise—dead. It is quick, anyway, I thought. On June 4th we went over the top. We took the Turks' trench and held it. It was called Hill 13. The next day we were relieved and told to rest for three hours, but it wasn't more than half an hour before the relieving regiment came running back. The Turks had returned and recaptured their trench. On June 6th my favourite officer was killed and no end of us butchered, but we managed to get hold of Hill 13 again. We found a great muddle, carnage and men without rifles shouting 'Allah! Allah!', which is God's name in the Turkish language. Of the sixty men I had started out to war from Harwich with, there were only three left.

We set to work to bury people. We pushed them into the sides of the trench but bits of them kept getting uncovered and sticking out, like people in a badly made bed. Hands were the worst; they would escape from the sand, pointing, begging—even waving! There was one which we all shook when we passed, saying, 'Good morning', in a posh voice. Everybody did it. The bottom of the trench was springy like a mattress because of all the bodies underneath. At night, when the stench was worse, we tied crêpe round our mouths and noses. This crêpe had been given to us because it was supposed to prevent us being gassed. The flies entered the trenches at night and lined them completely with a density which was like a moving cloth. We killed millions by slapping our spades along the trench walls but the next night it would be just as bad. We were all lousy and we couldn't stop shitting because we had caught dysentery. We wept, not because we were frightened but because we were all so dirty.

* * *

HERB GORO: A Fireman[1]

The only thing is, I'm a fireman. I'm not a clown out in Coney Island that you throw balls at. Put my head in a hole and throw balls at me. That ain't what I'm getting paid for.

You don't want these people to throw roses at you when you go down the street, but just get out of your goddam way. I mean that's the least they can do. These people, they get in your way. They literally get in your way. You got some guys lay down in front of the rig, right in the middle of the street. What the hell is that? We had a fireman mugged at a fire. Now you don't call this normal. You begin to hate them, and then you become indifferent completely, like a doctor doing an operation. Like he don't know who it is, doesn't care who it is, but he's doing the best job he can.

1. From *The Block*, 1970.

We sometimes get an applause when we come into it. You get three, four floors going—applause. They're all lined up across the street waiting to watch the show. They have nothing to do. They're selling popcorn.

Well, don't give me any applause or anything like that after the fire's out. That's not what I'm looking for. I get that every second week. We get paid for that. We don't need the applause. But get off our backs, let us do the job. We're not even out at the fire, we're at the box that we're called to, and it's like going to a no man's land. It's like *All Quiet on the Western Front*. Well, for example, I drive this apparatus. Now, I have to take the shortest and the safest means to get to the box. It's only within the past four or five years that I don't come back the same way any more. I look for an alternate route. They figure you're coming back the same route. They have this thing in quite a few places where they set a booby trap for you. They got this thing set up. They'll point one way and the fire will be the other way, and when you pull into the block now, you get clobbered.

We've had cases where fellows have been really stoned. We had one case in particular. The guy's eye was almost completely put out, coming down from Tremont and Third Avenue, with a rock—but this was a rock the size of an orange. And like the lieutenant, Wilson, he got hit in the eye. This must be going back four years I guess. Pulling the box at four o'clock in the morning, on a wet night like tonight. Nobody in the street, he pulled up, and the whole side of his face is opened up. A big sheet of glass.

This is our job today, protecting ourselves from getting killed with these people—not the fire. The fires we know. We've been taught. You know from experience what you can do at a fire and what you can't do at a fire, but when a human element is involved that's on the other side of the fence, you don't know if you're going to get stabbed, punched or get hit with a milk box—which has happened. One fellow got hit with a milk box. If you just look at the apparatus we're riding in today, everything is covered up. We have places where the men sit with a cover over it, and a door on it, with glass in front of them. The truck companies ride with that little chicken coop in the back. This isn't to help put the fire out, by no means. This is to help the firemen get to the fire so they can put it out. Now, once he's at the fire, Lord knows what's going to happen to him after that. I mean like he's on the street all by himself. You're liable to come down and find this guy laying in a pool of blood.

These people use the Fire Department as a game, but it's a little rougher game than hide-and-seek when they start off the rooftops. They burn their own buildings with their own families in them. We had a woman here, she was screaming, "There's a fire! There's a fire!" We go running up. They're passing kids out the window on the first-floor level, right? Smoke all over the place. You get around the corner and what had happened I couldn't say—whether it was her boyfriend or her husband or what—but it was some kind of a family thing, an argument. She wouldn't let him in the house, so he poured gasoline or lighter fluid under the door and set it on fire; and she was trapped in there with the kids. Had she been on the third or fourth floor, she'd never have gotten them kids out of there that easy. She passed them out the window to some fellow who was walking by, screaming, breaking windows and all. But they'll do this to their own kind.

And like the other day this lady was sitting out there waiting for her furniture to be picked up or something like that. The kids they put a fire to her bed. That's the truth. I don't know whether they have it in their blood system or not. I don't know what it is but they're doing it. To them it might be a case of, well, it's another activity to pass the hot summer months, or the cold winter months, or whatever they feel.

You see, these people are moving around too much. It's not their community. Nothing here belongs to them, that's what they figure anyway. They don't give a damn whose property it belongs to, I mean they just live in it. The kids don't care whose car they're jumping on. They're given too much.

We do their baby-sitting. We keep them from burning; the cops keep them from killing each other; the garbage men clean up their dirt after them, or whatever dirt they can pick up. Yeah, the whole neighborhood is about the average of four years old. In mentality and in attitude. And the mayor is their mother and they don't have a father. And you are their baby-sitters for the night. And you can't hit back. You don't hit them and they stamp their feet and they stamp their feet by burning the building. It's the whole bloody city, not these. people any more than anybody else. I don't blame these people for anything. I blame these characters who come in telling them what to do, telling them this is your right, telling them you deserve this, this is your money. It's not their money, it's my money. My money is paying for their welfare. You get a hundred dollars taken out of your pay every two weeks, just on taxes, man. Before, it used to buy a mile of the Alabama road—with a hundred dollars. Now they're buying a two-hundred-dollar apartment. They have to abuse me and I have to pay for my own abuse? I'm financing my own misery? That's ridiculous. I'm working my ass off to maintain what some other guy is getting for nothing?

I got six years left. I could probably retire in six years—a fifteen-year job—and I'm getting as far away from this place as I can get, not out of the city, but out of the state, maybe even out of the country. I want to live with normal people—who respect one another, who respect what they got, what you got. There's only two classes in the city—the characters that sit on the top and the characters on the bottom. There's only rich and poor, there's no place for a middle guy—no place. And these politicians are telling you what to do: train them, teach them values. Man, I don't want to live with them; you live with them and teach them. If you wanted to do that, then you should open up Hyannis Port and move in. Five thousand of them. Same with Rockefeller, same with Lindsay.

They don't live with them; they drive through. And when they come in they come in with a bodyguard, about fifty guys. And beautiful, they're going to put twenty million dollars—in this community. Twenty million dollars—the people don't even know how to count that high. And two months later they're still standing there waiting for the twenty million dollars.

ROBERT COLES: A Police Sergeant[1]

* * *

Is he an "ordinary cop," as he once called himself? Is he a "boss," a "sergeant boss," as he refers to himself sometimes with mixed pride and embarrassment? Is he a "fascist pig," as he is called, among other things, by bright, vocal college students who are taking courses in sociology and psychology and political science and economics and urban affairs and law—and who prompt from him a wider range of responses than they might believe possible, for all their unquestionable awareness and sharpness of mind? It is, of course, possible to list those responses, and yet somehow no list, however well drawn up and accurately phrased, quite seems to render truthfully a man's ideas as they come tumbling out in the course of talk after talk—all of which is rather obvious not only to "investigators" and "observers" doing their "research" but those very able and sensitive and strong-minded and independent and mean-spirited and inefficient and awkward and generous and sullen and lighthearted and callous and kind people who are "interviewed."

More than anything else the police sergeant resents "propaganda" about the police, his way of describing "those articles about our problems." He is tired of them, tired of "dumb reporters" doing "quickie stories on the cops," and tired of "smart-aleck graduate students and their professors" who are always going to police headquarters and wanting to interview someone on the force. Can't

1. From *The Middle Americans*, 1971.

they simply go strike up a conversation with a cop, buy him a beer, get to know him, learn "whatever in hell it is" they want to know *that way?* Can't they do anything without those folders and the questions, dozens and dozens of questions? Life for him is too complicated for a questionnaire. Life for him is hard to put into any words, "even your own, never mind someone else's." It is easy to argue with him, or applaud him because he says what seems eminently sensible and correct. It is more important, perhaps, for all of us to understand that he is not so much against one or another "method" of research as he is doubtful that "a policeman or a fireman or a man who works on an assembly line of a factory" is going to get the compassion and fair treatment he deserves from people who make it their business to be known as compassionate and fair-minded: "The worst insults the police get is from the liberals and the radicals. A suburban housewife called up the other day and demanded to speak with 'the lieutenant.' She said she belonged to some committee, I didn't catch the name. She said we were the worst people in America, and if a Hitler ever took over here, we'd be marching people into concentration camps. Now, you know, that's not the first time I've heard that. Every time we get called to a college campus we get told things like that; and not only by the kids. Their teachers can be just as bad. I'd like to give each of them a jab to the stomach and a jab to the jaw. But I can't. And I tell my men that *they* can't either.

"Very few people know what it's like to have the radicals shouting at you from one direction and the Negro people in the slums looking at you as if you hate each and every one of them, and the people in between, most white people, claiming you've failed them, too, because there's crime all over, and it's the fault of the police, *the police.* I go to work some days and tell myself I'm going to quit. The men all say that. I don't know a policeman who feels he's being treated right. We don't get nearly the money we should, considering the fact that every hour we take risks all the time and could be killed almost every minute of the working day. And even our best friends and supporters don't know what we do—the calls that come in for our help, the duties we have. You go and ask the average Negro in a Negro neighborhood about the police, and he won't talk the way the civil rights people do. They call us all the time, Negroes do. I used to work in one of their districts. The switchboard was busy all day and all night. They fight and squabble with each other. They drink a lot. They lose themselves on drugs. They rob and steal from each other. They take after each other and kill. Then people say it's us, the police, the white man, that's to blame.

"I know I keep telling you all that, but people don't understand. I have one wish. I wish I could take some of those student radicals and send them out with some of my men that work in the Negro sections. I think it would open up their eyes, the students—that is, if anything can. They'd see that if you pulled the police out of the Negro sections, like the white radicals say you should—*they* don't live there—then the ones who would suffer would be the poor, innocent colored people. They're always the ones to suffer. A lot of Negroes are like a lot of white folks—good people, real good people.

"I hear my men talking. They say what I do. I have a brother who's a fireman. He says the same thing: it's not the average colored man who's to blame for all the trouble we're having in this country. It's a handful; well, it's more than a handful of trouble-makers. There are the crazy agitators, and the college crowd, the students and the teachers, and worst of all, if you ask me, are the rich people who support them all, and come into the city to march and demonstrate and wave their signs. Maybe it's all for the good, though. I've given up figuring out the answers. There's a whole lot of injustice in America. I know that. I can't afford for anyone in my family to get sick, least of all myself. The rich get richer and the poor ordinary man, he can barely buy his food and pay his rent. I feel sorry for the Negroes, I really do. People are prejudiced, most people are. You're almost born that way, don't you think? People like to stick together. The Irish want to live near the Irish. The same with the Italians or the others. Jews always stick together, even when they get rich, and a lot of them do. The poor Negroes, they want to get away from each other. They want to break out. I don't blame them. But when they break out what will they find? They'll see that the Irish are no good, and the Italians and Jews and everyone. We're all no good. I believe you should know the man, not where his grandfather came from. I mean, people like their own, but that isn't the way it should be. My son comes home and tells me that his teacher says the world is always changing. Well, you know it *is* always changing. I can remember a different world, the one I grew up in. That's gone, that world. A Negro boy born today is growing up in a country really worried over his people. I think everyone accepts the fact that we've got to end poverty and give people an even break, whether their skin is black or brown or whatever color it is.

"When I was a kid of twenty-five, I used to patrol a Negro section of this city. All was quiet then, no riots and no talk of revolution, and all the rest. I knew a lot of Negro people. They were poor, but they were polite and friendly. I'd get dozens of offers of coffee or a drink. We could talk, easy, real easy, with each other. Now all I hear is how no white man is trusted over there in that section. So, I asked one of my buddies who's a sergeant like me, and over in the district I used to be in—I asked him how he could stand it over there. He said he was surprised at me talking that way. I said I was surprised at *him* talking that way. He said it wasn't the same all the time, because they'd had a small riot or two, but it was the same as it always was most of the time: women who have to be rushed to the hospital to deliver their babies, and fires, and robberies, and fights to help settle, and kids caught on a roof or hurt playing who need to go to the emergency ward—you know, a cop's job. Then I thought to myself that I was a real fool for not thinking like that in the first place. You let those news stories go to your head, and you forget that most Negro people are too busy for demonstrations; they go to work, like the rest of us.

"I'd like to see more Negro policemen. I have nothing against them. But I don't believe in hiring a man just because he's colored or white or Chinese or anything else. If a man is going to be a policeman these days he's got to be tough. The world is tough; it's tougher than it ever was. Sometimes I look at my kids and hope they'll be all right when they grow up. I hope they'll have a world to live in."

LINDA LANE: Over the Counter: A Conversation with a Saleswoman[1]

I went as far as the sixth grade in school. I'm 57 now. I was 16 and didn't want to be 16 in the seventh grade so I quit. I was out of school a year and a half with blood poisoning and one teacher I had left me back twice. When I walked into her classroom the first day, she told me to get to the last row last seat and that's the way it was all year. She just didn't like me. I got her as a teacher twice and it was the same thing again.

After getting married and having a baby at sixteen I became a maid because my mother was a maid. Most jobs I got $35 a month plus room and board. $30 went to board my baby. My husband was a seaman and didn't support us. My mother used to make $8 a month when she came to this country so I thought I was doing pretty good. I was proud I could work and felt better off than most people. This was in the Depression. The nicest maid job I had was with a bootlegger. I could eat and talk with the family. We all ate in the kitchen. I had my own room with my baby and $10 a month. The rich people I worked for I couldn't have my baby and most of the time I didn't have my own room. One rich person I was a maid for took money out of my pay for a water glass I broke and a window that was already broken so I quit and she accused me of stealing. Anyway I didn't have anything in common with those

1. "Linda Lane" is a pseudonym for who works at a five-and-ten-cent store. the subject of this interview, a woman

people and ate in the kitchen alone so I was very lonely. That's one of the reasons I like my job at the 5 & 10 better than being a maid. Here I talk to people and no one tells me I'm doing something wrong.

My job is marking the prices on the items and I only spend two hours on the counters and no one watches over me. Five kids and another husband later I'm doing well taking home from $65.12 from $82.50 a week gross. I started working for this store around Easter time 16 years ago. I made Easter baskets for $1.00 an hour. Then they offered me a full time job at $48 a week.

Once they didn't pay me for a day I stayed home sick so I walked out. It was the first rebellious thing I ever did and it felt so good—I was never the same again. The reason I had walked out was that the girl on the bird counter was out for eight days and she got paid for all eight days. She had such a bad job that the manager knew he couldn't get anyone else so fast so he paid her. I had to take care of her counter when she was out and it was a terrible job.

Then my boss offered me $60 a week to stay. It was upsetting in a way—I told him that Jean worked there for 25 years and she was getting $48 so why should I get $60? He told me not to fight other people's battles.

All the women get $82.50 now except part-time and floorgirls. When women leave or are fired the boss doesn't replace them—we have eight women less than we had five years ago but we have to get the same work done. The woman on hardware has three counters to take care of now.

The manager has so many gimmicks to get the salesgirls to work harder. Each girl gets a "campaign button" with her name on it and the customers "vote" for the girls. The salesgirl with the most votes gets $10 in merchandise and a customer's name is taken from a jar and she gets $10 in merchandise too. This makes the girls super-polite to customers—they're not usually because it's a hectic job. It also pits the women against each other. They even had this contest on television and they hired a model to be a typical 5&10 salesgirl. We were thinking, "Why not one of us?"

The manager tells the salesgirls they can raise the prices on their counters as much as they think people will pay. The girls like that —they want to feel they have some control over their jobs. I guess it makes them feel important to be on the boss's side. He gets a commission from the profits of the store.

A few years ago I talked to the other women about starting a union, but their lives depend on the job. They wanted to organize but they were afraid of getting fired. Most of them didn't get far in school and they have to work because their husbands don't make enough. A year ago there was talk of a union, so the office raised everyone $.10 an hour. Big deal. I tell the women to threaten to quit cause then the boss gets panicked and gives them a raise, but the women are too scared.

The women chip in for everything. I don't mind chipping in for another girl but the brown-nosers start collecting for the manager every Christmas—they buy him a shirt which he doesn't need and give him the leftover money too. These "choice" women give him the gift on the side and none of the other women see him get the gift. All the gifts are bought in the 5&10 except the manager's. The assistant manager changes every year and the women chip in for his leaving too. I refuse to chip in for them with some other women and the brown-nosers get mad at us. We all get a Christmas bonus—$15 for one-year's service and $5 for each year after that, and they take off taxes too.

I like the high-school girls who work at night. We get along good. Only, once one of them told me to get flowers from the basement to fill up the counter so I said to her, "What? No more Indians, all chiefs?"

The prices go up every day and it's depressing. Now you can buy anything at the 5&10, from refrigerators to pencils, and you can probably get it cheaper someplace else. They have less help than years ago and they blame it on our "wage increases." The manager comments every Christmas that people would buy horseshit if it was on the counter with a price on it. Jean, who is working over thirty years now, got seven shares of the company's stock as a bonus for twenty-five years' service—she got a $2 dividend every three months —it just went up to $2.50. If she wanted 10 shares, she would have had to pay $90 in taxes right away, so she only took seven—she got a bill for taxes anyway. When she got the shares I went out and bought the *Wall Street Journal*—we had a good laugh.

She once tried to get another job. But if you work at a 5&10 other stores don't consider it a good reference because they think the women are dishonest and it's just like having no reference at all. The salesgirls that work here are very honest—I don't believe any of them steal. The other day my boss (the manager) was going up the stairs and one of the salesgirls was in front of him. He told her to get out of the way, she was going too slow for him. She had her hands in her pockets and he asked her why does she always have her hands in her pockets and then mentioned he was "working on getting rid of the pockets." What does he think, she can put one of the store's TVs in her pocket?

The store has a problem of shoplifting. The first shoplifter I saw was a well-dressed woman and she had a prayer book in her hands. I wouldn't steal cause I wouldn't want my kids to. I don't want them to be dishonest. Some people steal in front of their kids and they can afford to pay for it because they are made to pay for it when they are caught. Sometimes the manager and the floorgirl go to hell with it. Once the floorgirl followed a man in his seventies all around the store. He had a rolled-up newspaper under his arm and she accused him of stealing—he shook out the newspaper and showed he had nothing in it. Many times they'll throw kids out of the store—usually black kids. If a black person comes into the store they say, "Watch that one."

If you're working and you're not getting the right pay you want to steal cause you feel you're getting even with the boss. As a maid you steal what you can cause you're not getting paid enough. They give you a feeling you're no good so you steal from them to make them suffer. I did this once but some of my friends did it a lot. Sometimes the people you work for leave a penny or a nickel around to see if you would take it. Everybody that's got money got it some way and they got it by crooking people under them. That's how they got rich.

There's a real Hitler behind the lunch counter. She yells at the girls in front of the customers. She's the boss behind there and sometimes the customers complain about her. I feel sorry for her when I'm not mad at her. I know she has a hard life at home and needs to be "somebody." There aren't enough girls at the fountain so they are all pretty irritable. Right now, on top of all that, there's a gimmick of the boss's that drives the girls crazy. There's a sign on the fountain that says, "If your waitress doesn't ask if you want dessert, you get a free dessert." So people say the waitress didn't ask them when she did. Never eat at any 5&10—they have to use the food up from previous days before they make a new batch. Some of the stuff looks horrible—especially when the jelly apples get a week old, sometimes they get re-dipped.

Each girl that works behind the lunch counter has her own tip box. At the end of the day they have to take it to the office and the office personnel count it and take out the tax money from the tips. It's none of their business how much tips the girls get so they shouldn't take tax money off. Countergirls get less pay than the rest of us, too.

The whole story in a nutshell is we work hard. We keep the store clean and stocked but the company is trying to trick us and cheat us in little ways all the time. It's always the little person that gets hurt. It's about time that something happens so it's the rich people that hurt for a change. I'm not anyone's enemy unless they're an enemy to me and it seems to me people aren't seeing who their real friends are.

Two of my daughters and one son worked at this store. If you ask my nine-year-old granddaughter what she wants to be when she grows up she'll tell you a salesgirl at the 5&10. I think it's the best position she's ever seen a woman in, since her mother's on welfare.

She likes the colors of the items and she likes to visit me at work. That would be the third generation to work there—but her grandmother wants her to be President of the U.S.

PETER BINZEN: A Couple from Kensington ("Whitetown") [1]

Directly across the street from the school live a couple whom I'll name John and Connie. I've gotten to know them through the minister who recruited them to help in the new-school campaign. John is thirty-six, Polish, a $165-a-week machinist at a Federal installation. His mother completed four years of school in Poland, his father six years in Philadelphia. John went through Catholic high school. His wife, a few years younger than John, is English and also a high-school graduate. They have two children in elementary school.

They urge me to come in out of the rain. In size and shape, their house is almost identical to Wanda's, but with children living there its furnishings and atmosphere are totally different. In the living room, their son's bicycle is leaning precariously against one wall. No other place to put it, John explains, unless you take it down to the basement. And it's a pain in the neck getting the bike down the cellar stairs. Also, John and Connie have interests far different from Wanda's. They have books, records, camping gear, a rock collection.

John and Connie are more middle class in living style and outlook than many Kensingtonians. Yet John, a husky, thoughtful man with glasses, hasn't tried to break out and maybe he never will. We sit in the kitchen drinking coffee and he talks about it. He speaks slowly, picking his words carefully and forming perfect sentences.

"We couldn't afford that tent we have," he says, "if we lived in another neighborhood. We couldn't afford the car I had to buy. For myself, I would like to move out. We stay here primarily because our parents are here. They're old and no one else stayed so we stayed. This is my wife's rationalization for staying. This angers me. I would like to move out. But the reality is: Why bring up a family fight over nothing? I do have it good here. There are some minor things. I can go down in my basement and bang my head against the pipes. Every time it happens, I swear, I curse. I love flowers. I love dirt. I don't have anything. If I go out in the yard, it's all cement. But generally I can be a little freer with the dollar than if I did move out.

"My anger is not with the poorer people moving in. It's with the older people who don't want change. These people are passive. They won't get involved. They're so old that they're afraid. All the

1. From *Whitetown, U.S.A.*, 1970.

fight has been driven out of them. It's not fear that you should be ashamed of, it's inaction. My anger with these people is that they let their fear master them. There are ways of overcoming fear and one of them is facing up to it. I was never as active as I am right now. There was a couple of times when I spoke before the whole auditorium of people over in school. I was terrified but still I did it. I felt there was a need for it and when I get up again I'll be terrified again."

John says that he grew up frightened of Authority and cowed by it, whether that Authority was the mother superior or the cop on the beat. Those in authority never sought out his views on anything. Now he finds the public school doing just that: inviting the people in and soliciting their opinions on whether a new school should be built and where and how big.

"Whether they listen or not, to me with my background," John says, "I would say that this is amazing. To be able to talk back to Authority—this is something that I have to get used to. And this is one of the things also that retards me as a leader—that I cannot talk to authority without any feelings of fear or whatever, whatever feelings I have. It's a compound feeling, not only fear, respect for Authority and everything else."

John may be too introspective to be the prototype Whitetowner. But he understands Whitetowners. He does not know his neighbors well, but he shares their feelings on many issues.

On city politics: "People feel they are being short-changed. I think it's more than a suspicion. I feel that people . . . my attitude is that in a political year they'll take from one to give to another. My feeling is that this is a political reality. Whether it's necessary or not I don't know. I'm angered by this. I don't like it. But I don't know what to do about it."

On Negro gains: "The colored are evening up a big score. They're getting a lot more attention. My feeling is that we [Whitetowners] don't squawk enough. The squeaky wheel gets the oil, and it's a Depression axiom. Why should you have to scream and holler to get things done? If you lack leadership, if you lack drive, you won't get things yourself. It's not just a feeling that the Negro is getting it. There's also a feeling that the richer whites are getting it."

On patriotism: "I'm an American and proud of it. When I put on a uniform [John was a draftee, serving from 1952 to 1954], it was an American uniform. People may call me a Polack and I'll laugh at them, but I don't feel myself as being Polish. I'm an American. If you were to come with a [peace] placard down Kensington Avenue, this would get people mad enough to throw rocks at you."

On ethnic relations: "A race riot when I was a child was trouble between the Polish and the Italians. The Italians came up from

South Philly and they bought right on our street corner. And there was a big fight. Now the Polish and the Italians intermarry. My sister married an Italian. And values change. Not that I would like to see the whites and colored—I still have that feeling—I don't know that I would like to see it. But, like I say, values change and they're not as horrifying when the change does come as the way people fantasize them."

On integrating Kensington:"I find myself being prejudiced. I do have the feeling that if the Negro comes in that it will deteriorate. The professional class will not move into this neighborhood. The middle class wants to move to Germantown. So what we are going to get is the lower class. I don't hate the Negro, I don't love him. But he's got to prove himself. And I don't feel that he's proving himself."

* * *

JAMES THURBER: Writers at Work
The *Paris Review* Interviews

The Hôtel Continental, just down from the Place Vendôme on the Rue Castiglione. It is from here that Janet Flanner (Genêt) sends her Paris letter to The New Yorker, and it is here that the Thurbers usually stay while in Paris. "We like it because the service is first-rate without being snobbish."

Thurber was standing to greet us[1] in a small salon whose cold European formality had been somewhat softened and warmed by well-placed vases of flowers, by stacks and portable shelves of American novels in bright dust jackets, and by pads of yellow paper and bouquets of yellow pencils on the desk. Thurber impresses one immediately by his physical size. After years of delighting in the shy, trapped little man in the Thurber cartoons and the confused and bewildered man who has fumbled in and out of some of the funniest books written in this century, we, perhaps like many readers, were expecting to find the frightened little man in person. Not at all. Thurber by his firm handgrasp and confident voice and by the way he lowered himself into his chair gave the impression of outward calmness and assurance. Though his eyesight has almost failed him, it is not a disability which one is aware of for more than the opening minute, and if Thurber seems to be the most nervous person in the room, it is because he has learned to put his visitors so completely at ease.

He talks in a surprisingly boyish voice, which is flat with the accents of the Midwest where he was raised and, though slow in tempo,

---

1. George Plimpton and Max Steele.

never dull. He is not an easy man to pin down with questions. He prefers to sidestep them and, rather than instructing, he entertains with a vivid series of ancedotes and reminiscences.

Opening the interview with a long history of the bloodhound, Thurber was only with difficulty persuaded to shift to a discussion of his craft. Here again his manner was typical—the anecdotes, the reminiscences punctuated with direct quotes and factual data. His powers of memory are astounding. In quoting anyone—perhaps a conversation of a dozen years before—Thurber pauses slightly, his voice changes in tone, and you know what you're hearing is exactly as it was said.

THURBER: Well, you know it's a nuisance—to have memory like mine—as well as an advantage. It's . . . well . . . like a whore's top drawer. There's so much else in there that's junk—costume jewelry, unnecessary telephone numbers whose exchanges no longer exist. For instance, I can remember the birthday of anybody who's ever told me his birthday. Dorothy Parker—August 22, Lewis Gannett—October 3, Andy White—July 9, Mrs. White—September 17. I can go on with about two hundred. So can my mother. She can tell you the birthday of the girl I was in love with in the third grade, in 1903. Offhand, just like that. I got my powers of memory from her. Sometimes it helps out in the most extraordinary way. You remember Robert M. Coates? Bob Coates? He is the author of *The Eater of Darkness*, which Ford Madox Ford called the first true Dadaist novel. Well, the week after Stephen Vincent Benét died—Coates and I had both known him—we were talking about Benét. Coates was trying to remember an argument he had had with Benét some fifteen years before. He couldn't remember. I said, "I can." Coates told me that was impossible since I hadn't been there. "Well," I said, "you happened to mention it in passing about twelve years ago. You were arguing about a play called *Swords*." I was right, and Coates was able to take it up from there. But it's strange to reach a position where your friends have to be supplied with their own memories. It's bad enough dealing with your own.

INTERVIEWERS: Still, it must be a great advantage for the writer. I don't suppose you have to take notes.

THURBER: No. I don't have to do the sort of thing Fitzgerald did with *The Last Tycoon*—the voluminous, the tiny and meticulous notes, the long descriptions of character. I can keep all these things in my mind. I wouldn't have to write down "three roses in a vase" or something, or a man's middle name. Henry James dictated notes just the way that I write. His note writing was part of the creative act, which is why his prefaces are so good. He dictated notes to see what it was they might come to.

INTERVIEWERS: Then you don't spend much time prefiguring your work?

THURBER: No. I don't bother with charts and so forth. Elliott Nugent, on the other hand, is a careful constructor. When we were working on *The Male Animal* together, he was constantly concerned with plotting the play. He could plot the thing from back to front—what was going to happen here, what sort of situation would end the first-act curtain, and so forth. I can't work that way. Nugent would say, "Well, Thurber, we've got our problem, we've got all these people in the living room. Now what are we going to do with them?" I'd say that I didn't know and couldn't tell him until I'd sat down at the typewriter and found out. I don't believe the writer should know too much where he's going. If he does, he runs into old man blueprint—old man propaganda.

INTERVIEWERS: Is the act of writing easy for you?

THURBER: For me it's mostly a question of rewriting. It's part of a constant attempt on my part to make the finished version smooth, to make it seem effortless. A story I've been working on —"The Train on Track Six," it's called—was rewritten fifteen complete times. There must have been close to 240,000 words in all the manuscripts put together, and I must have spent two thousand hours working at it. Yet the finished version can't be more than twenty thousand words.

INTERVIEWERS: Then it's rare that your work comes out right the first time?

THURBER: Well, my wife took a look at the first version of something I was doing not long ago and said, "Goddamn it, Thurber, that's high-school stuff." I have to tell her to wait until the seventh draft, it'll work out all right. I don't know why that should be so, that the first or second draft of everything I write reads as if it was turned out by a charwoman. I've only written one piece quickly. I wrote a thing called "File and Forget" in one afternoon—but only because it was a series of letters just as one would ordinarily dictate. And I'd have to admit that the last letter of the series, after doing all the others that one afternoon, took me a week. It was the end of the piece and I had to fuss over it.

INTERVIEWERS: Does the fact that you're dealing with humor slow down the production?

THURBER: It's possible. With humor you have to look out for traps. You're likely to be very gleeful with what you've first put down, and you think it's fine, very funny. One reason you go over and over it is to make the piece sound less as if you were having a lot of fun with it yourself. You try to play it down. In fact, if there's such a thing as a *New Yorker* style, that would be it—playing it down.

INTERVIEWERS: Do you envy those who write at high speed, as against your method of constant revision?

THURBER: Oh, no, I don't, though I do admire their luck. Hervey Allen, you know, the author of the big best-seller *Anthony Adverse*, seriously told a friend of mine who was working on a biographical piece on Allen that he could close his eyes, lie down on a bed, and hear the voices of his ancestors. Furthermore there was some sort of angel-like creature that danced along his pen while he was writing. He wasn't balmy by any means. He just felt he was in communication with some sort of metaphysical recorder. So you see the novelists have all the luck. I never knew a humorist who got any help from his ancestors. Still, the act of writing is either something the writer dreads or actually likes, and I actually like it. Even rewriting's fun. You're getting somewhere, whether it seems to move or not. I remember Elliot Paul and I used to argue about rewriting back in 1925 when we both worked for the *Chicago Tribune* in Paris. It was his conviction you should leave the story as it came out of the typewriter, no changes. Naturally, he worked fast. Three novels he could turn out, each written in three weeks' time. I remember once he came into the office and said that a sixty-thousand-word manuscript had been stolen. No carbons existed, no notes. We were all horrified. But it didn't bother him at all. He'd just get back to the typewriter and bat away again. But for me—writing as fast as that would seem too facile. Like my drawings, which I do very quickly, sometimes so quickly that the result is an accident, something I hadn't intended at all. People in the arts I've run into in France are constantly indignant when I say I'm a writer and not an artist. They tell me I mustn't run down my drawings. I try to explain that I do them for relaxation, and that I do them too fast for them to be called art.

INTERVIEWERS: You say that your drawings often don't come out the way you intended?

THURBER: Well, once I did a drawing for *The New Yorker* of a naked woman on all fours up on top of a bookcase—a big bookcase. She's up there near the ceiling, and in the room are her husband and two other women. The husband is saying to one of the women, obviously a guest, "This is the present Mrs. Harris. That's my first wife up there." Well, when I did the cartoon originally I meant the naked woman to be at the top of a flight of stairs, but I lost the sense of perspective and instead of getting in the stairs when I drew my line down, there she was stuck up there, naked, on a bookcase.

Incidentally, that cartoon really threw the *New Yorker* editor, Harold Ross. He approached any humorous piece of writing, or more particularly a drawing, not only grimly but realistically. He called me on the phone and asked if the woman up on the bookcase was supposed to be alive, stuffed, or dead. I said, "I don't know, but I'll let you know in a couple of hours." After a while I called him back and told him I'd just talked to my taxidermist, who said you can't stuff a woman, that my doctor had told me a dead woman couldn't support herself on all fours. "So, Ross," I said, "she must be alive." "Well then," he said, "what's she doing up there naked in the home of her husband's second wife?" I told him he had me there.

INTERVIEWERS: But he published it.

THURBER: Yes, he published it, growling a bit. He had a fine understanding of humor, Ross, though he couldn't have told you about it. When I introduced Ross to the work of Peter de Vries,

he first said, "He won't be good; he won't be funny; he won't
know English." (He was the only successful editor I've known
who approached everything like a ship going on the rocks.) But
when Ross had looked at the work he said, "How can you get this
guy on the phone?" He couldn't have said why, but he had that
bloodhound instinct. The same with editing. He was a wonderful
man at detecting something wrong with a story without knowing
why.

INTERVIEWERS: Could he develop a writer?

THURBER: Not really. It wasn't true what they often said of him
—that he broke up writers like matches—but still he wasn't the
man to develop a writer. He was an unread man. Well, he'd read
Mark Twain's *Life on the Mississippi* and several other books he
told me about—medical books—and he took the Encyclopedia
Britannica to the bathroom with him. I think he was about up to
H when he died. But still his effect on writers was considerable.
When you first met him you couldn't believe he was the editor
of *The New Yorker* and afterward you couldn't believe that anyone else could have been. The main thing he was interested in was
clarity. Someone once said of *The New Yorker* that it never contained a sentence that would puzzle an intelligent fourteen-year-
old or in any way affect her morals badly. Ross didn't like that,
but nevertheless he was a purist and perfectionist and it had a
tremendous effect on all of us: it kept us from being sloppy. When
I first met him he asked me if I knew English. I thought he meant
French or a foreign language. But he repeated, "Do you know
English?" When I said I did he replied, "Goddamn it, nobody
knows English." As Andy White mentioned in his obituary, Ross
approached the English sentence as though it was an enemy,
something that was going to throw him. He used to fuss for an
hour over a comma. He'd call me in for lengthy discussions about
the Thurber colon. And as for poetic license, he'd say, "Damn
any license to get things wrong." In fact, Ross read so carefully
that often he didn't get the sense of your story. I once said: "I
wish you'd read my stories for pleasure, Ross." He replied he
hadn't time for that.

INTERVIEWERS: It's strange that one of the main ingredients of
humor—low comedy—has never been accepted for *The New
Yorker*.

THURBER: Ross had a neighbor woman's attitude about it. He never
got over his Midwestern provincialism. His idea was that sex is
an incident. "If you can prove it," I said, "we can get it in a
box on the front page of *The New York Times*." Now I don't
want to say that in private life Ross was a prude. But as regards
the theater or the printed page he certainly was. For example, he
once sent an office memorandum to us in a sealed envelope. It
was an order: "When you send me a memorandum with four-
letter words in it, *seal it*. There are women in this office." I said,
"Yah, Ross, and they know a lot more of these words than you
do." When women were around he was very conscious of them.

Once my wife and I were in his office and Ross was discussing a man and woman he knew much better than we did. Ross told us, "I have every reason to believe that they're *s-l-e-e-p-i-n-g* together." My wife replied, "Why, Harold Ross, what words you do spell out." But honest to goodness, that was genuine. Women are either good or bad, he once told me, and the good ones must not hear these things.

Incidentally, I'm telling these things to refresh my memory. I'm doing a short book on him called "Ross in Charcoal." I'm putting a lot of this stuff in. People may object, but after all it's a portrait of the man and I see no reason for not putting it in.

INTERVIEWERS: Did he have much direct influence on your own work?

THURBER: After the seven years I spent in newspaper writing, it was more E. B. White who taught me about writing, how to clear up sloppy journalese. He was a strong influence, and for a long time in the beginning I thought he might be too much of one. But at least he got me away from a rather curious style I was starting to perfect—tight journalese laced with heavy doses of Henry James.

INTERVIEWERS: Henry James was a strong influence, then?

THURBER: I have the reputation for having read all of Henry James. Which would argue a misspent youth *and* middle age.

INTERVIEWERS: But there were things to be learned from him?

THURBER: Yes, but again he was an influence you had to get over. Especially if you wrote for *The New Yorker*. Harold Ross wouldn't have understood it. I once wrote a piece called "The Beast in the Dingle" which everybody took as a parody. Actually it was a conscious attempt to write the story as James would have written it. Ross looked at it and said: "Goddamn it, this is too literary; I got only fifteen per cent of the allusions." My wife and I often tried to figure out which were the fifteen per cent he could have got.

You know, I've occasionally wondered what James would have done with our world. I've just written a piece—"Preface to Old Friends," it's called—in which James at the age of a hundred and four writes a preface to a novel about our age in which he summarizes the trends and complications, but at the end is so completely lost he doesn't really care enough to read it over to find his way out again.

That's the trouble with James. You get bored with him finally. He lived in the time of four-wheelers, and no bombs, and the problems then seemed a bit special and separate. That's one reason you feel restless reading him. James is like—well, I had a bulldog once who used to drag rails around, enormous ones—six-, eight-, twelve-foot rails. He loved to get them in the middle and you'd hear him growling out there, trying to bring the thing home. Once he brought home a chest of drawers—without the drawers in it. Found it on an ash-heap. Well, he'd start to get these things in the garden gate, everything finely balanced, you see, and then *crash*, he'd come up against the gate posts. He'd get it through finally, but I had that feeling in some of the James novels: that he was trying to get that rail through a gate not wide enough for it.

INTERVIEWERS: How about Mark Twain? Pretty much everybody believes him to have been the major influence on American humorists.

THURBER: Everybody wants to know if I've learned from Mark Twain. Actually I've never read much of him. I did buy *Tom Sawyer*, but dammit, I'm sorry, I've not got around to reading it all the way through. I told H. L. Mencken that, and he was shocked. He said America had produced only two fine novels: *Huck Finn* and *Babbitt*. Of course it's always a matter of personal opinion—these lists of the great novels. I can remember calling on Frank Harris—he was about seventy then—when I was on the *Chicago Tribune*'s edition in Nice. In his house he had three portraits on the wall—Mark Twain, Frank Harris, and I think it was Hawthorne. Harris was in the middle. Harris would point up to them and say, "Those three are the best American writers. The one in the middle is the best." Harris really thought he was wonderful. Once he told me he was going to live to be a hundred. When I asked him what the formula was, he told me it was very simple. He said, "I've bought myself a stomach pump and one half-hour after dinner I pump myself out." Can you imagine that? Well, it didn't work. It's a wonder it didn't kill him sooner.

INTERVIEWERS: Could we ask you why you've never attempted a long work?

THURBER: I've never wanted to write a long work. Many writers feel a sense of frustration or something if they haven't, but I don't.

INTERVIEWERS: Perhaps the fact that you're writing humor imposes a limit on the length of a work.

THURBER: Possibly. But brevity in any case—whether the work is supposed to be humorous or not—would seem to me to be desirable. Most of the books I like are short books: *The Red Badge of Courage*, *The Turn of the Screw*, Conrad's short stories, *A Lost Lady*, Joseph Hergesheimer's *Wild Oranges*, Victoria Lincoln's *February Hill*, *The Great Gatsby*. . . . You know Fitzgerald once wrote Thomas Wolfe: "You're a puttier-inner and I'm a taker-outer." I stick with Fitzgerald. I don't believe, as Wolfe did, that you have to turn out a massive work before being judged a writer. Wolfe once told me at a cocktail party I didn't know what it was to be a writer. My wife, standing next to me, complained about that. "But my husband *is* a writer," she said. Wolfe was genuinely surprised. "He is?" he asked. "Why, all I ever see is that stuff of his in *The New Yorker*." In other words, he felt that prose under five thousand words was certainly not the work of a writer . . . it was some kind of doodling in words. If you said you were a writer, he wanted to know where the books were, the great big long books. He was really genuine about that.

I was interested to see William Faulkner's list not so long ago of the five most important American authors of this century.

According to him Wolfe was first, Faulkner second—let's see, now that Wolfe's dead that puts Faulkner up there in the lead, doesn't it?— Dos Passos third, then Hemingway, and finally Steinbeck. It's interesting that the first three are putter-inners. They write expansive novels.

INTERVIEWERS: Wasn't Faulkner's criterion whether or not the author dared to go out on a limb?

THURBER: It seems to me you're going out on a limb these days to keep a book short.

INTERVIEWERS: Though you've never done a long serious work you have written stories—"The Cane in the Corridor" and "The Whippoorwill" in particular—in which the mood is far from humorous.

THURBER: In anything funny you write that isn't close to serious you've missed something along the line. But in those stories of which you speak there was an element of anger—something I wanted to get off my chest. I wrote "The Whippoorwill" after five eye operations. It came somewhere out of a grim fear in the back of my mind. I've never been able to trace it.

INTERVIEWERS: Some critics think that much of your work can be traced to the depicting of trivia as a basis for humor. In fact, there's been some criticism—

THURBER: Which is trivia—the diamond or the elephant? Any humorist must be interested in trivia, in every little thing that occurs in a household. It's what Robert Benchley did so well— in fact so well that one of the greatest fears of the humorous writer is that he has spent three weeks writing something done faster and better by Benchley in 1919. Incidentally, you never got very far talking to Benchley about humor. He'd do a take-off of Max Eastman's *Enjoyment of Laughter*. "We must understand," he'd say, "that all sentences which begin with W are funny."

INTERVIEWERS: Would you care to define humor in terms of your own work?

THURBER: Well, someone once wrote a definition of the difference between English and American humor. I wish I could remember his name. I thought his definition very good. He said that the English treat the commonplace as if it were remarkable and the Americans treat the remarkable as if it were commonplace. I believe that's true of humorous writing. Years ago we did a parody of *Punch* in which Benchley did a short piece depicting a wife bursting into a room and shouting "The primroses are in bloom!"—treating the commonplace as remarkable, you see. In "The Secret Life of Walter Mitty" I tried to treat the remarkable as commonplace.

INTERVIEWERS: Does it bother you to talk about the stories on which you're working? It bothers many writers, though it would seem that particularly the humorous story is polished through retelling.

THURBER: Oh, yes. I often tell them at parties and places. And I write them there too.

INTERVIEWERS: You write them?

THURBER: I never quite know when I'm not writing. Sometimes my wife comes up to me at a party and says, "Dammit, Thurber, stop writing." She usually catches me in the middle of a paragraph. Or my daughter will look up from the dinner table and ask, "Is he sick?" "No," my wife says, "he's writing something." I have to do it that way on account of my eyes. I still write occasionally—in the proper sense of the word—using black crayon on yellow paper and getting perhaps twenty words to the page. My usual method, though, is to spend the mornings turning over the text in my mind. Then in the afternoon, between two and five, I call in a secretary and dictate to her. I can do about two thousand words. It took me about ten years to learn.

INTERVIEWERS: How about the new crop of writers? Do you note any good humorists coming along with them?

THURBER: There don't seem to be many coming up. I once had a psychoanalyst tell me that the depression had a considerable effect—much worse than Hitler and the war. It's a tradition for a child to see his father in uniform as something glamorous—not his father coming home from Wall Street in a three-button sack suit saying, "We're ruined," and the mother bursting into tears— a catastrophe that to a child's mind is unexplainable. There's been a great change since the thirties. In those days students used to ask me what Peter Arno did at night. And about Dorothy Parker. Now they want to know what my artistic credo is. An element of interest seems to have gone out of them.

INTERVIEWERS: Has the shift in the mood of the times had any effect on your own work?

THURBER: Well, *The Thurber Album* was written at a time when in America there was a feeling of fear and suspicion. It's quite different from *My Life and Hard Times*, which was written earlier and is a funnier and better book. The *Album* was kind of an escape—going back to the Middle West of the last century and the beginning of this, when there wasn't this fear and hysteria. I wanted to write the story of some solid American characters, more or less as an example of how Americans started out and what they should go back to—to sanity and soundness and away from this jumpiness. It's hard to write humor in the mental weather we've had, and that's likely to take you into reminiscence. Your heart isn't in it to write anything funny. In the years 1950 to 1953 I did very few things, nor did they appear in *The New Yorker*. Now, actually, I think the situation is beginning to change for the better.

INTERVIEWERS: No matter what the "mental climate," though, you would continue writing?

THURBER: Well, the characteristic fear of the American writer is not so much that as it is the process of aging. The writer looks in the mirror and examines his hair and teeth to see if they're still with him. "Oh my God," he says, "I wonder how my writing is. I bet I can't write today." The only time I met Faulkner he told me he wanted to live long enough to do three more novels. He was fifty-three then, and I think he *has* done them. Then Hemingway says, you know, that he doesn't expect to be alive after sixty. But he doesn't look forward *not* to being. When I met Hemingway with John O'Hara in Costello's Bar five or six years ago we sat around and talked about how *old* we were getting. You see it's constantly on the minds of American writers. I've never known a woman who could weep about her age the way the men I know can.

Coupled with this fear of aging is the curious idea that the writer's inventiveness and ability will end in his fifties. And of course it often does. Carl Van Vechten stopped writing. The prolific Joseph Hergesheimer suddenly couldn't write any more. Over here in Europe that's never been the case—Hardy, for instance, who started late and kept going. Of course Keats had good reason to write, "When I have fears that I may cease to be Before my pen has glean'd my teeming brain." That's the great classic statement. But in America the writer is more likely to fear that his brain may cease to teem. I once did a drawing of a man at his typewriter, you see, and all this crumpled paper is on the floor, and he's staring down in discouragement. "What's the matter," his wife is saying, "has your pen gleaned your teeming brain?"

INTERVIEWERS: In your case there wouldn't be much chance of this?

THURBER: No. I write basically because it's so much fun—even though I can't see. When I'm not writing, as my wife knows, I'm miserable. I don't have that fear that suddenly it will stop. I have enough outlined to last me as long as I live.

ERIK H. ERIKSON AND HUEY P. NEWTON: Armed Love[1]

JHB: . . . I would like to . . . go back to a matter that Erik has always been interested in: maybe it's time to talk about the gun.

EHE: Well, actually, that fits right in here. You see, when I started to talk in New Haven I reminded the students of the traditional image which Huey used to represent and which still appears on the cover of the Panther paper—the young Black man with the gun. All of this became more dialectical in our conversations when you, Huey, began to speak about arms and love. I thought I understood what you meant to some extent because of something

1. Reprinted from *In Search of Common Ground*, edited by Kai T. Erikson and J. Herman Blake, 1973. This book is the record of two conversations which took place in early 1971 between Huey P. Newton, the Black Panther Party leader, and Erik H. Erikson, the renowned psychoanalyst and author of *Gandhi's Truth, Young Man Luther*, and many other books. The first conversation was in a formal conference setting at Yale University before a largely academic audience; the second took place around a small breakfast table in Newton's Oakland, California, apartment. Also participating in the dialogues are Kai T. Erikson, Eric Erikson's son, who teaches sociology at Yale, and J. Herman Blake, who teaches sociology at the University of California at Santa Cruz and is a member of the Black Panther Party. The excerpt reprinted here is taken from the first day of conversation in Oakland.

that became clear to Gandhi as he developed his non-violent method—namely, that most people seem to feel that to be non-violent means not to *have* any gun and not to *want* any gun because one would not want to use it or would not know how to use it anyway. But there is an intermediary step between violence and non-violence where you have a gun but use it only in the most disciplined way—in part, at least, to show up the absurdity of particular kinds of armed violence. This, I think, you did on several important occasions which really created your original public image. I hope you see now what I mean. You were not afraid to carry that gun. Now I would understand armed love to mean that one can really love only if one knows that one could and would defend one's dignity, for only two people of equal dignity can love each other. There is no use trying to love somebody who denies you dignity or to whom you deny it. In this sense, then, there is a dialectical relation between violence and non-violence, and the last thing I would want to imply here is that your earlier image is inconsistent with the things you are saying and doing now. Both together make up an historical step and (I would assume) a very personal step, and you needed the one for the other. I don't know whether you would agree to that. You would now accept the gun-carrying image, wouldn't you, as historically necessary and valid?

HPN: I think it served a strategic purpose—although I imagine historians are going to make a lot out of it.

EHE: You mean as I just did?

HPN: No, no. It's just that so much has been written about the whole business of the armed self-defense of the community, and I haven't seen one thing that's accurate. I'm not talking about you, Erik; I think your interpretation is fair. But I just sort of shiver whenever I see books written on the matter.

EHE: For example, Bobby Seale describes some of the things you two did in the early days of the Party that, to me, seemed to amount to a parallel with the Gandhi technique—although I assume you didn't know about it then or, at any rate, it was not uppermost in your mind. When you faced down those policemen, for example —not threatening them with your guns or indicating with gestures that you would shoot first, but daring them to shoot first. That was a very important psychological condition you created there. You gave them the initiative and said, "Okay, you shoot first." All of this is probably related somehow to the old western frontier scenario, where the cowboys used to make this kind of confrontation a supreme test as to who would be quicker on the trigger. But you made something very different and, in a way, very revolutionary out of it when you made it clear that you didn't come to shoot them, but if they had come to shoot you, then they should come out with it. You paralyzed them morally, don't you think?

HPN: Well, I would agree that they were paralyzed at least.

KTE: But why were they paralyzed?

HPN: They had never been required to cope with a situation like that one. Because of their own racism, their own misconception of the Black community and the Black psyche, they did not know how to deal with the fact that we were not afraid of them, you see? And they were very provocative.

EHE: This kind of transvaluation can be a historical act, and Bobby Seale has a very good sense of how to describe such things—with humor, too. For example, how you would stand there with a few of your men and would confront those policemen and all the armed power they had behind them. Now, of course, you shouldn't be surprised if they afterwards should feel endangered in their essence. It has often been said about Gandhi that he could only have done what he did with the British and not anyone else. All of that fits rather well into what you refer to as the dialectical development of empires. You see, Gandhi met the British head-on with their own ideas of fairness, ideas they had widely established as an ideal, and when he faced them down with that they simply had to accept it as a lesson. It could well be that a policeman whose background does not include any kind of experience with this kind of thing would simply say to himself, "Okay, to hell with it, I'll sure get him some other time." What I learned in studying Gandhi was how he could give to a concrete object—and this is what I meant to apply to the gun in your case—some endless symbolic meaning. For example, Gandhi announced that he was going to the Indian Ocean, and that he was going to take salt out of it, salt that the British were taxing, no matter what they would say or do. It is perfectly obvious that he picked salt for many reasons. It is absolutely necessary in the tropics, for one thing, but it has great symbolic value too. Now my feeling is that, in principle, what you tried to do with the gun might have had something of the same concrete and symbolic meaning, and that you did it at the right historical moment. Does that make sense or not?

JHB: It makes perfect sense to me. I wish you would just be more specific, though. You used as a subtitle for the Gandhi book an expression like "the origins of militant non-violence," and I think the concept of non-violence as utilized by Americans with respect to Blacks is quite different from what I hear you saying. It seems to me that non-violence here has always meant acquiescence to whatever power is used against one in one's attempt to gain justice. Some moral force would come from somewhere and overcome the violent application of force. I'm not so sure that is what you are saying.

EHE: Not exactly. In fact, there is a similarity here which I brought out in the Gandhi book. It would be very easy to say that Black people have to remain non-violent because they'll never learn to fight anyway, and some people would say, "Well, non-violence fits their inborn meekness and their religious orientation." Now the case is very similar with India because there you have one military caste that had done virtually all the fighting, so that the great masses of people in India never learned to use weapons at all

until the British came along and drafted them into the Army.
Those crack Indian troops in the British Army that we heard so
much about all came from warrior castes whose job on earth,
decreed by heaven, was to fight. The rest of the Indians didn't
know how to fight, had never had any experience with weapons,
and made it a point of religious observance to do no harm to
anyone. Now Gandhi (and his friends did not like him for it)
would sometimes support the British demand that Indians be
drafted, because he felt that Indians would have to learn to fight
before they could *choose* to be non-violent. That's what you meant
in part, isn't it? That it makes no sense for a meek person to call
himself non-violent, because, sure, what else can he be?

HPN: I think it would be wrong to compare other situations to
Gandhi's action. You have to leave it in context and regard it in
terms of the particular contradictions involved. Now I would have
agreed with the notion that Indians join the British Army in
order to get the training necessary to oppose the Army: I can
understand that at some point it is worthwhile to play upon the
weakness of the oppressor. Gandhi did this knowing the character
of the British quite well, but I think he would have acted differently here. People here who tried to act the same way he did,
I think, missed the mark and were not realistic.

JHB: Most people would say that the apostle of non-violence in
this country with respect to Blacks was Martin Luther King. He
had a clearly stated philosophy and openly expressed a debt to
Gandhi. Now I would suspect that most people, not understanding
the context in which you are speaking, would expect to see a very
strong clash between your [Erikson's] views and Huey's views on
this particular subject. And I would like to see that cleared up,
because I've always argued that there have to be certain social bases
for non-violence....

EHE: Look, the last thing I would wish to do is advocate non-violence
outside of a concrete situation, particularly since it makes exploited
people all the more vulnerable. Unless one is very careful, the
whole non-violent point of view could be used against people
rather than for them. I gave a seminar at MIT once, and somebody brought Tom Mboya to one of the meetings. The students
and I had just been discussing Gandhi, so we asked Mboya what
he thought about non-violence. Well, he said, you can use it
with the British but you can't use it with the Belgians. No two
historical situations are ever identical in this sense. What Mboya
may have also meant is that Gandhi had become something of
a Britisher himself. He had been educated in England, of course,
and so he knew where he could count on the British to react to
non-violence in a certain way. I guess that is really all I have to
say. I just have a feeling that you [Newton] are not an advocate of
violence as such, you know.

HPN: No, I don't advocate violence. I advocate non-violence. If I
really had a choice, I would prefer the non-antagonistic kind of
contradictions because they usually can be resolved in a peaceful

way. But of course we have to deal with concrete conditions and the reality of the situation at this time is that there are many contradictions that probably can only be resolved in antagonistic ways and will probably result in violence—and this will probably be the case until man and society develop to the point where contradictions will no longer be antagonistic. So I am working for the day when antagonisms will no longer exist. And this will probably be only after people commonly own and share things.

JHB: Erik, you were saying the other day that the Panthers may understand non-violence better than anyone else because they understand violence so well. And I was thinking about that in connection with Huey's statement that we advocate the abolition of war. We say that power grows out of the barrel of a gun, Chairman Mao's words; but we also say that the purpose of picking up the gun is to get rid of it. Now most people in this society pick up the gun for the purpose of maintaining control, and they do not understand that someone else might pick it up in order to abolish control.

HPN: Use violence in order to eliminate it.

JHB: Right. Right.

EHE: The point is that you cannot step from undisciplined violence to non-violence. In India, Gandhi failed mostly where he could not restrain people from rioting, and you remember (I remember, at least) how he called off some of his non-violent campaigns because rioting broke out. Now the Panthers have actually opposed violence for its own sake, isn't that right?

HPN: Non-disciplined violence, yes.

EHE: Only a very self-disciplined use of force can lead to disciplined non-violence and the abolition of violence. And, of course, it also takes a pretty high set of moral aspirations for leaders to make people understand all of that. . . .

On Literature and the Arts

SUSANNE K. LANGER
Expressiveness[1]

When we talk about "Art" with a capital "A"—that is, about any or all of the arts: painting, sculpture, architecture, the potter's and goldsmith's and other designers' arts, music, dance, poetry, and prose fiction, drama and film—it is a constant temptation to say things about "Art" in this general sense that are true only in one special domain, or to assume that what holds for one art must hold for another. For instance, the fact that music is made for performance, for presentation to the ear, and is simply not the same thing when it is given only to the tonal imagination of a reader silently perusing the score, has made some aestheticians pass straight to the conclusion that literature, too, must be physically heard to be fully experienced, because words are originally spoken, not written; an obvious parallel, but a careless and, I think, invalid one. It is dangerous to set up principles by analogy, and generalize from a single consideration.

But it is natural, and safe enough, to ask analogous questions: What is the function of sound in music? What is the function of sound in poetry? What is the function of sound in prose composition? What is the function of sound in drama?" The answers may be quite heterogeneous; and that is itself an important fact, a guide to something more than a simple and sweeping theory. Such findings guide us to exact relations and abstract, variously exemplified basic principles.

At present, however, we are dealing with principles that have proven to be the same in all the arts, when each kind of art—plastic, musical, balletic, poetic, and each major mode, such as literary and dramatic writing, or painting, sculpturing, building plastic

1. Chapter 2 of *Problems of Art*, 1957.

shapes—has been studied in its own terms. Such candid study is more rewarding than the usual passionate declaration that all the arts are alike, only their materials differ, their principles are all the same, their techniques all analogous, etc. That is not only unsafe, but untrue. It is in pursuing the differences among them that one arrives, finally, at a point where no more differences appear; then one has found, not postulated, their unity. At that deep level there is only one concept exemplified in all the different arts, and that is the concept of Art.

The principles that obtain wholly and fundamentally in every kind of art are few, but decisive; they determine what is art, and what is not. Expressiveness, in one definite and appropriate sense, is the same in all art works of any kind. What is created is not the same in any two distinct arts—this is, in fact, what makes them distinct—but the principle of creation is the same. And "living form" means the same in all of them.

A work of art is an expressive form created for our perception through sense or imagination, and what it expresses is human feeling. The word "feeling" must be taken here in its broadest sense, meaning *everything that can be felt*, from physical sensation, pain and comfort, excietment and repose, to the most complex emotions, intellectual tensions, or the steady feeling-tones of a conscious human life. In stating what a work of art is, I have just used the words "form," "expressive," and "created"; these are key words. One at a time, they will keep us engaged.

Let us consider first what is meant, in this context, by a *form*. The word has many meanings, all equally legitimate for various purposes; even in connection with art it has several. It may, for instance—and often does—denote the familiar, characteristic structures known as the sonnet form, the sestina, or the ballad form in poetry, the sonata form, the madrigal, or the symphony in music, the contredance or the classical ballet in choreography, and so on. This is not what I mean; or rather, it is only a very small part of what I mean. There is another sense in which artists speak of "form" when they say, for instance, "form follows function," or declare that the one quality shared by all good works of art is "significant form," or entitle a book *The Life of Forms in Art*, or *Search for Form*. They are using "form" in a wider sense, which on the one hand is close to the commonest, popular meaning, namely just the *shape* of a thing, and on the other hand to the quite unpopular meaning it has in science and philosophy, where it designates something more abstract; "form" in its most abstract sense means structure, articulation, a whole resulting from the relation of mutually dependent factors, or more precisely, the way that whole is put together.

The abstract sense, which is sometimes called "logical form," is involved in the notion of expression, at least the kind of expression that characterizes art. That is why artists, when they speak of achieving "form," use the word with something of an abstract connotation, even when they are talking about a visible and tangible art object in which that form is embodied.

The more recondite concept of form is derived, of course, from the naive one, that is, material shape. Perhaps the easiest way to grasp the idea of "logical form" is to trace its derivation.

Let us consider the most obvious sort of form, the shape of an object, say a lampshade. In any department store you will find a wide choice of lampshades, mostly monstrosities, and what is monstrous is usually their shape. You select the least offensive one, maybe even a good one, but realize that the color, say violet, will not fit into your room; so you look about for another shade of the same shape but a different color, perhaps green. In recognizing this same shape in another object, possibly of another material as well as another color, you have quite naturally and easily abstracted the concept of this shape from your actual impression of the first lampshade. Presently it may occur to you that this shade is too big for your lamp; you ask whether they have *this same shade* (meaning another one of this shape) in a smaller size. The clerk understands you.

But what is *the same* in the big violet shade and the little green one? Nothing but the interrelations among their respective various dimensions. They are not "the same" even in their spatial properties, for none of their actual measures are alike; but their shapes are congruent. Their respective spatial factors are put together in the same way, so they exemplify the same form.

It is really astounding what complicated abstractions we make in our ordinary dealing with forms—that is to say, through what twists and transformations we recognize the same logical form. Consider the similarity of your two hands. Put one on the table, palm down, superimpose the other, palm down, as you may have superimposed cut-out geometric shapes in school—they are not alike at all. But their shapes are *exact opposites*. Their respective shapes fit the same description, provided that the description is modified by a principle of application whereby the measures are read one way for one hand and the other way for the other—like a timetable in which the list of stations is marked: "Eastbound, read down; Westbound, read up."

As the two hands exemplify the same form with a principle of reversal understood, so the list of stations describes two ways of moving, indicated by the advice to "read down" for one and "read up" for the other. We can all abstract the common element in these two respective trips, which is called the *route*. With a return ticket we may return only by the same route. The same principle relates a mold to the form of the thing that is cast in it, and establishes their formal correspondence, or common logical form.

So far we have considered only objects—lampshades, hands, or regions of the earth—as having forms. These have fixed shapes; their parts remain in fairly stable relations to each other. But there are also substances that have no definite shapes, such as gases, mist, and water, which take the shape of any bounded space that contains them. The interesting thing about such amorphous fluids is that when they are put into violent motion they do exhibit visible forms, not bounded by any container. Think of the momentary efflorescence of a bursting rocket, the mushroom cloud of an atomic bomb, the funnel of water or dust screwing upward in a whirlwind. The instant the motion stops, or even slows beyond a certain degree, those shapes collapse and the apparent "thing" disappears. They are not shapes of things at all, but forms of motions, or dynamic forms.

Some dynamic forms, however, have more permanent manifestations, because the stuff that moves and makes them visible is constantly replenished. A waterfall seems to hang from the cliff, waving streamers of foam. Actually, of course, nothing stays there in mid-air; the water is always passing; but there is more and more water taking the same paths, so we have a lasting shape made and maintained by its passage—a permanent dynamic form. A quiet river, too, has dynamic form; if it stopped flowing it would either go dry or become a lake. Some twenty-five hundred years ago, Heracleitos was struck by the fact that you cannot step twice into the same river at the same place—at least, if the river means the water, not its dynamic form, the flow.

When a river ceases to flow because the water is deflected or dried up, there remains the river bed, sometimes cut deeply in solid stone. That bed is shaped by the flow, and records as graven lines the currents that have ceased to exist. Its shape is static, but it *expresses* the dynamic form of the river. Again, we have two congruent forms, like a cast and its mold, but this time the congruence is more remarkable because it holds between a dynamic form and a static one. That relation is important; we shall be dealing with it again when we come to consider the meaning of "living form" in art.

The congruence of two given perceptible forms is not always evident upon simple inspection. The common *logical* form they both exhibit may become apparent only when you know the principle whereby to relate them, as you compare the shapes of your hands not by direct correspondence, but by correspondence of opposite parts. Where the two exemplifications of the single logical form are unlike in most other respects one needs a rule for matching up the relevant factors of one with the relevant factors of the other; that is to say, a *rule of translation*, whereby one instance of the logical form is shown to correspond formally to the other.

The logical form itself is not another thing, but an abstract concept, or better an *abstractable* concept. We usually don't abstract it deliberately, but only use it, as we use our vocal cords in speech without first learning all about their operation and then applying our knowledge. Most people perceive intuitively the similarity of their two hands without thinking of them as conversely related; they can guess at the shape of the hollow inside a wooden shoe from the shape of a human foot, without any abstract study of topology. But the first time they see a map in the Mercator projection—with parallel lines of longitude, not meeting at the poles—they find it hard to believe that this corresponds logically to the circular map they used in school, where the meridians bulged apart toward the equator and met at both poles. The visible shapes of the continents are different on the two maps, and it takes abstract thinking to match up the two representations of the same earth. If, however, they have grown up with both maps, they will probably see the geographical relationships either way with equal ease, because these relationships are not *copied* by either map, but *expressed*, and expressed equally well by both; for the two maps are different *projections* of the same logical form, which the spherical earth exhibits in still another—that is, a spherical—projecton.

An expressive form is any perceptible or imaginable whole that exhibits relationships of parts, or points, or even qualities or aspects within the whole, so that it may be taken to represent some other whole whose elements have analogous relations. The reason for using such a form as a symbol is usually that the thing it represents is not perceivable or readily imaginable. We cannot see the earth as an object. We let a map or a little globe express the relationships of places on the earth, and think about the earth by means of it. The understanding of one thing through another seems to be a deeply intuitive process in the human brain; it is so natural that we often have difficulty in distinguishing the symbolic expressive form from what it conveys. The symbol seems to be the thing itself, or contain it, or be contained in it. A child interested in a globe will not say: "This means the earth," but: "Look, this is the earth." A similar identification of symbol and meaning underlies the widespread conception of holy names, of the physical efficacy of rites, and many other primitive but culturally persistent phenomena. It has a bearing on our perception of artistic import; that is why I mention it here.

The most astounding and developed symbolic device humanity has evolved is language. By means of language we can conceive the intangible, incorporeal things we call our *ideas*, and the equally inostensible elements of our perceptual world that we call *facts*. It is by virtue of language that we can think, remember, imagine, and finally conceive a universe of facts. We can describe things and represent their relations, express rules of their interactions, speculate and predict and carry on a long symbolizing process known as reasoning. And above all, we can communicate, by producing a serried array of audible or visible words, in a pattern commonly known, and readily understood to reflect our multifarious concepts and percepts and their interconnections. This use of language is *discourse*; and the pattern of discourse is known as *discursive* form. It is a highly versatile, amazingly powerful pattern. It has impressed itself on our tacit thinking, so that we call all systematic reflection "discursive thought." It has made, far more than most people know, the very frame of our sensory experience—the frame of objective facts in which we carry on the practical business of life.

Yet even the discursive pattern has its limits of usefulness. An expressive form can express any complex or conceptions that, via some rule of projection, appears congruent with it, that is, appears to be of that form. Whatever there is in experience that will not take the impress—directly or indirectly—of discursive form, is not discursively communicable or, in the strictest sense, logically thinkable. It is unspeakable, ineffable; according to practically all serious philosophical theories today, it is unknowable.

Yet there is a great deal of experience that is knowable, not only as immediate, formless, meaningless impact, but as one aspect of the intricate web of life, yet defies discursive formulation, and therefore verbal expression: that is what we sometimes call the *subjective aspect* of experience, the direct feeling of it—what it is like to be waking and moving, to be drowsy, slowing down, or to be sociable, or to feel self-sufficient but alone; what it feels like to pursue an elusive thought or to have a big idea. All such directly felt experiences usually have no names—they are named, if at all, for the outward conditions that normally accompany their occurrence. Only the most striking ones have names like "anger," "hate," "love," "fear," and are collectively called "emotion." But we feel many things that never develop into any designable emotion. The ways we are moved are as various as the lights in a forest; and they may intersect, sometimes without cancelling each other, take shape and dissolve, conflict, explode into passion, or be transfigured. All these inseparable elements of subjective reality compose what we call the "inward life" of human beings. The usual factoring of that life-stream into mental, emotional, and sensory units is an arbitrary scheme of simplification that makes scientific treatment possible to a considerable extent; but we may already be close to the limit of its usefulness, that is, close to the point where its simplicity becomes an obstacle to further questioning and discovery instead of the revealing, ever-suitable logical projection it was expected to be.

Whatever resists projection into the discursive form of language is, indeed, hard to hold in conception, and perhaps impossible to communicate, in the proper and strict sense of the word "communicate." But fortunately our logical intuition, or form-perception, is really much more powerful than we commonly believe, and our knowledge—genuine knowledge, understanding—is considerably wider than our discourse. Even in the use of language, if we want to name something that is too new to have a name (e.g., a newly invented gadget or a newly discovered creature), or want to express a relationship for which there is no verb or other connective word, we resort to metaphor; we mention it or describe it as something else, something analogous. The principle of metaphor is simply the principle of saying one thing and meaning another, and expecting to be understood to mean the other. A metaphor is not language, it is an idea expressed by language, an idea that in its turn functions as a symbol to express something. It is not discursive and therefore does not really make a statement of the idea it conveys; but it formulates a new conception for our direct imaginative grasp.

Sometimes our comprehension of a total experience is mediated by a metaphorical symbol because the experience is new, and language has words and phrases only for familiar notions. Then an extension of language will gradually follow the wordless insight, and discursive expression will supersede the non-discursive pristine symbol. This is, I think, the normal advance of human thought and language in that whole realm of knowledge where discourse is possible at all.

But the symbolic presentation of subjective reality for contemplation is not only tentatively beyond the reach of language—that is, not merely beyond the words we have; it is impossible in the essential frame of language. That is why those semanticists who recognize only discourse as a symbolic form must regard the whole life of feeling as formless, chaotic, capable only of symptomatic expression, typified in exclamations like "Ah!" "Ouch!" "My sainted aunt!" They usually do believe that art is an expression of feeling, but that "expression" in art is of this sort, indicating that the speaker has an emotion, a pain, or other personal experience, perhaps also giving us a clue to the general kind of experience it is—pleasant or unpleasant, violent or mild—but not setting that piece of inward life objectively before us so we may understand its intricacy, its rhythms and shifts of total appearance. The differences in feeling-tones or other elements of subjective experience are regarded as differences in quality, which must be felt to be appreciated. Furthermore, since we have no intellectual access to pure subjectivity, the only way to study it is to study the symptoms of the person who is having subjective experiences. This leads to physiological psychology—a very important and interesting field. But it tells us nothing about the phenomena of subjective life, and sometimes simplifies the problem by saying they don't exist.

Now, I believe the expression of feeling in a work of art—the function that makes the work an expressive form—is not symptomatic at all. An artist working on a tragedy need not be in personal despair or violent upheaval; nobody, indeed, could work in such a state of mind. His mind would be occupied with the causes of his emotional upset. Self-expression does not require composition and lucidity; a screaming baby gives his feeling far more release than any musician, but we don't go into a concert hall to hear a baby scream; in fact, if that baby is brought in we are likely to go out. We don't want self-expression.

A work of art presents feeling (in the broad sense I mentioned before, as everything that can be felt) for our contemplation, making it visible or audible or in some way perceivable through a symbol, not inferable from a symptom. Artistic form is congruent with the dynamic forms of our direct sensuous, mental, and emotional life; works of art are projections of "felt life," as Henry James called it, into spatial, temporal, and poetic structures. They are images of feeling, that formulate it for our cognition. What is artistically good is whatever articulates and presents feeling to our understanding.

Artistic forms are more complex than any other symbolic forms we know. They are, indeed, not abstractable from the works that exhibit them. We may abstract a shape from an object that has this shape, by disregarding color, weight and texture, even size; but to the total effect that is an artistic form, the color matters, the thickness of lines matters, and the appearance of texture and weight. A given triangle is the same in any position, but to an artistic form its location, balance, and surroundings are not indifferent. Form, in the sense in which artists speak of "significant form" or "expressive form," is not an abstracted structure, but an apparition; and the vital processes of sense and emotion that a good work of art expresses seem to the beholder to be directly contained in it, not symbolized but really presented. The congruence is so striking that symbol and meaning appear as one reality. Actually, as one psychologist who is also a musician has written, "Music sounds as feelings feel." And likewise, in good painting, sculpture, or building, balanced shapes and colors, lines and masses look as emotions, vital tensions and their resolutions feel.

An artist, then, expresses feeling, but not in the way a politician blows off steam or a baby laughs and cries. He formulates that elusive aspect of reality that is commonly taken to be amorphous and chaotic; that is, he objectifies the subjective realm. What he expresses is, therefore, not his own actual feelings, but what he knows about human feeling. Once he is in possession of a rich symbolism, that knowledge may actually exceed his entire personal experience. A work of art expresses a conception of life, emotion, inward reality. But it is neither a confessional nor a frozen tantrum; it is a developed metaphor, a non-discursive symbol that articulates what is verbally ineffable—the logic of consciousness itself.

NORTHROP FRYE

The Keys to Dreamland[1]

* * * Suppose you're walking down the street of a North American city. All around you is a highly artificial society, but you don't think of it as artificial: you're so accustomed to it that you think of it as natural. But suppose your imagination plays a little trick on you of a kind that it often does play, and you suddenly feel like a complete outsider, someone who's just blown in from Mars on a flying saucer. Instantly you see how conventionalized everything is: the clothes, the shop windows, the movement of the cars in traffic, the cropped hair and shaved faces of the men, the red lips and blue eyelids that women put on because they want to conventionalize their faces, or "look nice," as they say, which means the same thing. All this convention is pressing toward uniformity or likeness. To be outside the convention makes a person look queer, or, if he's driving a car, a menace to life and limb. The only exceptions are people who have decided to conform to different conventions, like nuns or beatniks. There's clearly a strong force making toward conformity in society, so strong that it seems to have something to do with the stability of society itself. In ordinary life even the most splendid things we can think of, goodness and truth and beauty, all mean essentially what we're accustomed to. As I hinted just now in speaking of female makeup, most of our ideas of beauty are pure convention, and even truth has been defined as whatever doesn't disturb the pattern of what we already know.

When we move on to literature, we again find conventions, but this time we notice that they are conventions, because we're not so used to them. These conventions seem to have something to do with making literature as unlike life as possible. Chaucer represents people as making up stories in ten-syllable couplets. Shakespeare uses dramatic conventions, which means, for instance, that Iago has to smash Othello's marriage and dreams of future happiness and get him ready to murder his wife in a few minutes. Milton has two nudes in a garden haranguing each other in set speeches beginning with such lines as "Daughter of God and Man, immortal Eve"—Eve being Adam's daughter because she's just been

1. Chapter 4 in *The Educated Imagination,* 1964.

extracted from his ribcase. Almost every story we read demands that we accept as fact something that we know to be nonsense: that good people always win, especially in love; that murders are complicated and ingenious puzzles to be solved by logic, and so on. It isn't only popular literature that demands this: more highbrow stories are apt to be more ironic, but irony has its conventions too. If we go further back into literature, we run into such conventions as the king's rash promise, the enraged cuckold, the cruel mistress of love poetry—never anything that we or any other time would recognize as the normal behavior of adult people, only the maddened ethics of fairyland.

Even the details of literature are equally perverse. Literature is a world where phoenixes and unicorns are quite as important as horses and dogs—and in literature some of the horses talk, like the ones in *Gulliver's Travels*. A random example is calling Shakespeare the "swan of Avon"—he was called that by Ben Jonson. The town of Stratford, Ontario, keeps swans in its river partly as a literary allusion. Poets of Shakespeare's day hated to admit that they were writing words on a page: they always insisted that they were producing music. In pastoral poetry they might be playing a flute (or more accurately an oboe), but every other kind of poetic effort was called song, with a harp, a lyre or a lute in the background, depending on how highbrow the song was. Singing suggests birds, and so for their typical songbird and emblem of themselves, the poets chose the swan, a bird that can't sing. Because it can't sing, they made up a legend that it sang once before death, when nobody was listening. But Shakespeare didn't burst into song before his death: he wrote two plays a year until he'd made enough money to retire, and spent the last five years of his life counting his take.

So however useful literature may be in improving one's imagination or vocabulary, it would be the wildest kind of pedantry to use it directly as a guide to life. Perhaps here we see one reason why the poet is not only very seldom a person one would turn to for insight into the state of the world, but often seems even more gullible and simple-minded than the rest of us. For the poet, the particular literary conventions he adopts are likely to become, for him, facts of life. If he finds that the kind of writing he's best at has a good deal to do with fairies, like Yeats, or a white goddess, like Graves, or a life-force, like Bernard Shaw, or episcopal sermons, like T. S. Eliot, or bullfights, like Hemingway, or exasperation at social hypocrisies, as with the so-called angry school, these things are apt to take on a reality for him that seems badly out of proportion to his contemporaries. His life may imitate literature in a way that may warp or even destroy his social personality, as Byron wore himself out at thirty-four with the strain of being Byronic. Life and literature, then, are both conventionalized, and of the conventions of literature about all we can say is that they don't much resemble the conditions of life. It's when two sets of conventions collide that we realize how different they are.

In fact, whenever literature gets too probable, too much like life, some self-defeating process, some mysterious law of diminishing returns, seems to set in. There's a vivid and expertly written novel by H. G. Wells called *Kipps*, about a lower-middle-class, inarticulate, very likeable Cockney, the kind of character we often find in Dickens. Kipps is carefully studied: he never says anything that a man like Kipps wouldn't say; he never sounds the "h" in home or head; nothing he does is out of line with what we expect such a person to be like. It's an admirable novel, well worth reading, and yet I have a nagging feeling that there's some inner secret in bringing him completely to life that Dickens would have and that Wells doesn't have. All right, then, what would Dickens have done? Well, one of the things that Dickens often does do is write *badly*. He might have given Kipps sentimental speeches and false heroics and all sorts of inappropriate verbiage to say; and some readers would have clucked and tut-tutted over these passages and explained to each other how bad Dickens's taste was and how uncertain his hold on character could be. Perhaps they'd be right too. But we'd have had Kipps a few times the way he'd look to himself or the way he'd sometimes wish he could be: that's part of his reality, and the effect would remain with us however much we disapproved of it. Whether I'm right about this book or not, and I'm not at all sure I am, I think my general principle is right. What we'd never see except in a book is often what we go to books to find. Whatever is completely lifelike in literature is a bit of a laboratory specimen there. To bring anything really to life in literature we can't be lifelike: we have to be literaturelike.

The same thing is true even of the use of language. We're often taught that prose is the language of ordinary speech, which is usually true in literature. But in ordinary life prose is no more the language of ordinary speech than one's Sunday suit is a bathing suit. The people who actually speak prose are highly cultivated and articulate people, who've read a good many books, and even they can speak prose only to each other. If you read the beautiful sentences of Elizabeth Bennett's conversation in *Pride and Prejudice*, you can see how in that book they give a powerfully convincing impression of a sensible and intelligent girl. But any girl who talked as coherently as that on a street car would be stared at as though she had green hair. It isn't only the difference between 1813 and 1962 that's involved either, as you'll see if you compare her speech with her mother's. The poet Emily Dickinson complained that everybody said "What?" to her, until finally she practically gave up trying to talk altogether, and confined herself to writing notes.

All this is involved with the difference between literary and other kinds of writing. If we're writing to convey information, or for any practical reason, our writing is an act of will and intention: we mean what we say, and the words we use represent that meaning directly. It's different in literature, not because the poet doesn't mean what he says too, but because his real effort is one of putting words together. What's important is not what he may have meant to say, but what words themselves say when they get fitted together. With a novelist it's rather the incidents in the story he tells that get fitted together—as D. H. Lawrence says, don't trust the novelist; trust his story. That's why so much of a writer's best writing is or seems to be involuntary. It's involuntary because the forms of literature itself are taking control of it, and these forms are what are embodied in the conventions of literature. Conventions, we see, have the same role in literature that they have in life: they impose certain patterns of order and stability on the writer. Only, if they're such different conventions, it seems clear that the order of words, or the structure of literature, is different from the social order.

The absence of any clear line of connection between literature and life comes out in the issues involved in censorship. Because of the large involuntary element in writing, works of literature can't be treated as embodiments of conscious will or intention, like people, and so no laws can be framed to control their behavior which assume a tendency to do this or an intention of doing that. Works of literature get into legal trouble because they offend some powerful religious or political interest, and this interest in its turn usually acquires or exploits the kind of social hysteria that's always revolving around sex. But it's impossible to give legal definitions of such terms as obscenity in relation to works of literature. What happens to the book depends mainly on the intelligence of the judge. If he's a sensible man we get a sensible decision; if he's an ass we get that sort of decision, but what we don't get is a legal decision, because the basis for one doesn't exist. The best we get is a precedent tending to discourage cranks and pressure groups from attacking serious books. If you read the casebook on the trial of *Lady Chatterley's Lover*, you may remember how bewildered the critics were when they were asked what the moral effect of the book would be. They weren't putting on an act: they didn't know. Novels can only be good or bad in their own categories. There's no such thing as a morally bad novel: its moral effect depends entirely on the moral quality of its reader, and nobody can predict what that will be. And if literature isn't morally bad it isn't morally good either. I suppose one reason why *Lady Chatterley's Lover* dramatized this question so vividly was that it's a rather preachy and self-conscious book: like the Sunday-school novels of my childhood, it bores me a little because it tries so hard to do me good.

So literature has no consistent connection with ordinary life, positive or negative. Here we touch on another important difference between structures of the imagination and structures of practical sense, which include the applied sciences. Imagination is certainly essential to science, applied or pure. Without a constructive power in the mind to make models of experience, get hunches and follow them out, play freely around with hypotheses, and so forth, no scientist could get anywhere. But all imaginative effort in practical fields has to meet the test of practicability, otherwise it's discarded. The imagination in literature has no such test to meet. You don't relate it directly to life or reality: you relate works of literature to each other. Whatever value there is in studying literature, cultural or practical, comes from the total body of our reading, the castle of words we've built, and keep adding new wings to all the time.

So it's natural to swing to the opposite extreme and say that literature is really a refuge or escape from life, a self-contained world like the world of the dream, a world of play or make-believe to balance the world of work. Some literature is like that, and many people tell us that they only read to get away from reality for a bit. And I've suggested myself that the sense of escape, or at least detachment, does come into everybody's literary experience. But the real point of literature can hardly be that. Think of such writers as William Faulkner or François Mauriac, their great moral dignity, the intensity and compassion that they've studied the life around them with. Or think of James Joyce, spending seven years on one book and seventeen on another, and having them ridiculed or abused or banned by the customs when they did get published. Or of the poets Rilke and Valéry, waiting patiently for years in silence until what they had to say was ready to be said. There's a deadly seriousness in all this that even the most refined theories of fantasy or make-believe won't quite cover. Still, let's go along with the idea for a bit, because we're not getting on very fast with the relation of literature of life, or what we could call the horizontal perspective of literature. That seems to block us off on all sides.

The world of literature is a world where there is no reality except that of the human imagination. We see a great deal in it that reminds us vividly of the life we know. But in that very vividness there's something unreal. We can understand this more clearly with pictures, perhaps. There are trick-pictures—*trompe l'oeil*, the French call them—where the resemblance to life is very strong. An American painter of this school played a joke on his bitchy wife by painting one of her best napkins so expertly that she grabbed at the canvas trying to pull it off. But a painting as realistic as that isn't a reality but an illusion: it has the glittering unnatural clarity of a hallucination. The real realities, so to speak, are things that don't remind us directly of our own experience, but are such things as the wrath of Achilles or the jealousy of Othello, which are bigger and more intense experiences than anything we can reach—except in our imagination, which is what we're reaching with. Sometimes, as in the happy endings of comedies, or in the ideal world of romances, we seem to be looking at a pleasanter world than we ordinarily know. Sometimes, as in tragedy and satire, we seem to be looking at a world more devoted to suffering or absurdity than we ordinarily know. In literature we always seem to be looking either up or down. It's the vertical perspective that's important, not the horizontal one that looks out to life. Of course, in the greatest works of literature we get both the up and down views, often at the same time as different aspects of one event.

There are two halves to literary experience, then. Imagination gives us both a better and a worse world than the one we usually live with, and demands that we keep looking steadily at them both. The arts follow the path of the emotions, and of the tendency of the emotions to separate the world into a half that we like and a half that we don't like. Literature is not a world of dreams, but it would be if we had only one half without the other. If we had nothing but romances and comedies with happy endings, literature would express only a wish-fulfilment dream. Some people ask why poets want to write tragedies when the world's so full of them anyway, and suggest that enjoying such things has something morbid or gloating about it. It doesn't, but it might if there were nothing else in literature.

This point is worth spending another minute on. You recall that terrible scene in *King Lear* where Gloucester's eyes are put out on the stage. That's part of a play, and a play is supposed to be entertaining. Now in what sense can a scene like that be entertaining? The fact that it's not really happening is certainly important. It would be degrading to watch a real blinding scene, and far more so to get any pleasure out of watching it. Consequently, the entertainment doesn't consist in its reminding us of a real blinding scene. If it did, one of the great scenes of drama would turn into a piece of repulsive pornography. We couldn't stop anyone from reacting in this way, and it certainly wouldn't cure him, much less help the public, to start blaming or censoring Shakespeare for putting sadistic ideas in his head. But a reaction of that kind has nothing to do with drama. In a dramatic scene of cruelty and hatred we're seeing cruelty and hatred, which we know are permanently real things in human life, from the point of view of the imagination. What the imagination suggests is horror, not the paralyzing sickening horror of a real blinding scene, but an exuberant horror, full of the energy of repudiation. This is as powerful a rendering as we can ever get of life as we don't want it.

So we see that there are moral standards in literature after all, even though they have nothing to do with calling the police when we see a word in a book that's more familiar in sound that in print. One of the things Gloucester says in that scene is: "I am tied to the stake, and I must stand the course." In Shakespeare's day it was a favorite sport to tie a bear to a stake and set dogs on it until they killed it. The Puritans suppressed this sport, according to Macaulay, not because it gave pain to the bear but because it gave pleasure to the spectators. Macaulay may have intended his remark to be a sneer at the Puritans, but surely if the Puritans did feel this way they were one hundred per cent right. What other reason is there for abolishing public hangings? Whatever their motives, the Puritans and Shakespeare were operating in the same direction. Literature keeps presenting the most vicious things to us as entertainment, but what is appeals to is not any pleasure in these things, but the exhilaration of standing apart from them and being able to see them for what they are because they aren't really happening. The more exposed we are to this, the less likely we are to find an unthinking pleasure in cruel or evil things. As the eighteenth century said in a fine mouth-filling phrase, literature refines our sensibilities.

The top half of literature is the world expressed by such words as sublime, inspiring, and the like, where what we feel is not detachment but absorption. This is the world of heroes and gods' and titans and Rabelaisian giants, a world of powers and passions and moments of ecstasy far greater than anything we meet outside the imagination. Such forces would not only absorb but annihilate us if they entered ordinary life, but luckily the protecting wall of the imagination is here too. As the German poet Rilke says, we adore them because they disdain to destroy us. We seem to have got quite a long way from our emotions with their division of things into "I like this" and "I don't like this." Literature gives us an experience that stretches us vertically to the heights and depths of what the human mind can conceive, to what corresponds to the conceptions of heaven and hell in religion. In this perspective what I like or don't like disappears, because there's nothing left of me as a separate person: as a reader of literature I exist only as a representative of humanity as a whole.

No matter how much experience we may gather in life, we can never in life get the dimension of experience that the imagination gives us. Only the arts and sciences can do that, and of these, only literature gives us the whole sweep and range of human imagination as it sees itself. It seems to be very difficult for many people to understand the reality and intensity of literary experience. To give an example that you may think a bit irrelevant: why have so many people managed to convince themselves that Shakespeare did not write Shakespeare's plays, when there is not an atom of evidence that anybody else did? Apparently because they feel that poetry must be written out of personal experience, and that Shakespeare didn't have enough experience of the right kind. But Shakespeare's plays weren't produced by his experience: they were produced by his imagination, and the way to develop the imagination is to read a good book or two. As for us, we can't speak or think or comprehend even our own experience except within the limits of our own power over words, and those limits have been established for us by our great writers.

Literature, then, is not a dream-world: it's two dreams, a wish-fulfillment dream and an anxiety dream, that are focused together, like a pair of glasses, and become a fully conscious vision. Art, according to Plato, is a dream for awakened minds, a work of imagination withdrawn from ordinary life, dominated by the same forces that dominate the dream, and yet giving us a perspective and dimension on reality that we don't get from any other approach to reality. So the poet and the dreamer are distinct, as Keats says. Ordinary life forms a community, and literature is among other things an art of communication, so it forms a community too. In ordinary life we fall into a private and separate subconscious every night, where we reshape the world according to a private and separate imagination. Underneath literature there's another kind of subconscious, which is social and not private, a need for forming a community around certain symbols, like the Queen and the flag, or around certain gods that represent order and stability, or becoming and change, or death and rebirth to a new life. This is the myth-making power of the human mind, which throws up and dissolves one civilization after another.

I've taken my title, "The Keys to Dreamland," from what is possibly the greatest single effort of the literary imagination in the twentieth century, Joyce's *Finnegans Wake*. In this book a man goes to sleep and falls, not into the Freudian separate or private subconscious, but into the deeper dream of man that creates and destroys his own societies. The entire book is written in the language of this dream. It's a subconscious language, mainly English, but connected by associations and puns with the eighteen or so other languages that Joyce knew. *Finnegans Wake* is not a book to read, but a book to decipher: as Joyce says, it's about a dreamer, but it's addressed to an ideal reader suffering from an ideal insomnia. The reader or critic, then, has a role complementing the poet's role. We need two powers in literature, a power to create and a power to understand.

In all our literary experience there are two kinds of response. There is the direct experience of the work itself, while we're reading a book or seeing a play, especially for the first time. This experience is uncritical, or rather pre-critical, so it's not infallible. If our experience is limited, we can be roused to enthusiasm or carried away by something that we can later see to have been second-rate or even phony. Then there is the conscious, critical response we make after we've finished reading or left the theatre, where we compare what we've experienced with other things of the same kind, and form a judgment of value and proportion on it. This critical response, with practice, gradually makes our pre-critical responses more sensitive and accurate, or improves our taste, as we say. But behind our responses to individual works, there's a bigger response to our literary experience as a whole, as a total possession.

The critic has always been called a judge of literature, which means, not that he's in a superior position to the poet, but that he ought to know something about literature, just as a judge's right to be on a bench depends on his knowledge of law. If he's up against something the size of Shakespeare, he's the one being judged. The critic's function is to interpret every work of literature in the light of all the literature he knows, to keep constantly struggling to understand what literature as a whole is about. Literature as a whole is not an aggregate of exhibits with red and blue ribbons attached to them, like a cat show, but the range of articulate human imagination as it extends from the height of imaginative heaven to the depth of imaginative hell. Literature is a human apocalypse, man's revelation to man, and criticism is not a body of adjudications, but the awareness of that revelation, the last judgment of mankind.

QUESTIONS

1. Frye uses the word "conventions" a number of times; what meanings does he appear to give the word? Why does he seek to show that life has conventions as does literature? Are they the same sort of conventions?

2. Early in his essay Frye makes some amusing remarks about poets and their ways. Is he making fun of them? If so, why? Does he suggest that poets are contemptible? If not, what is he trying to do?

3. Toward what sort of audience is Frye addressing his remarks? What can you tell about the audience he has in view from the language he chooses, and from the line of development his essay takes? What conception of the relationship between life and literature does Frye assume his audience might have at the outset? Does Frye seek to persuade his audience to adopt a certain view of literature, perhaps to change a previous view? What devices in his writing (as of tone, diction, figures of speech) are directed toward persuasion?

4. What ideas about literature and its relationship to life does Frye examine and reject? Why does he reject them? What are the

main features of his own position? Does he set forth that position in a single thesis sentence anywhere in the essay?
5. What is Frye's view of the moral effect of art and literature? How does his view compare with that of Krutch ("Modern Painting," pp. 553–558)?

CARL GUSTAV JUNG
The Poet

Creativeness, like the freedom of the will, contains a secret. The psychologist can describe both these manifestations as processes, but he can find no solution of the philosophical problems they offer. Creative man is a riddle that we may try to answer in various ways, but always in vain, a truth that has not prevented modern psychology from turning now and again to the question of the artist and his art. Freud thought that he had found a key in his procedure of deriving the work of art from the personal experiences of the artist. It is true that certain possibilities lay in this direction, for it was conceivable that a work of art, no less than a neurosis, might be traced back to those knots in psychic life that we call the complexes. It was Freud's great discovery that neuroses have a causal origin in the psychic realm—that they take their rise from emotional states and from real or imagined childhood experiences. Certain of his followers, like Rank and Stekel, have taken up related lines of enquiry and have achieved important results. It is undeniable that the poet's psychic disposition permeates his work root and branch. Nor is there anything new in the statement that personal factors largely influence the poet's choice and use of his materials. Credit, however, must certainly be given to the Freudian school for showing how far-reaching this influence is and in what curious ways it comes to expression.

Freud takes the neurosis as a substitute for a direct means of gratification. He therefore regards it as something inappropriate—a mistake, a dodge, an excuse, a voluntary blindness. To him it is essentially a shortcoming that should never have been. Since a neurosis, to all appearances, is nothing but a disturbance that is all the more irritating because it is without sense or meaning, few people will venture to say a good word for it. And a work of art is brought into questionable proximity with the neurosis when it is taken as something which can be analysed in terms of the poet's repressions. In a sense it finds itself in good company, for religion and philosophy are regarded in the same light by Freudian psychology. No objection can be raised if it is admitted that this approach amounts to nothing more than the elucidation of those personal determinants without which a work of art is unthinkable. But should the claim be made that such an analysis accounts for the work of art itself, then a categorical denial is called for. The personal idiosyncrasies that creep into a work of art are not essential; in fact, the more we have to cope with these peculiarities, the less is it a question of art. What is essential in a work of art is that it should rise far above the realm of personal life and speak from the spirit and heart of the poet as man to the spirit and heart of mankind. The personal aspect is a limitation—and even a sin—in the realm of art. When a form of "art" is primarily personal it deserves to be treated as if it were a neurosis. There may be some validity in the idea held by the Freudian school that artists without exception are narcissistic—by which is meant that they are undeveloped persons with infantile and autoerotic traits. The statement is only valid, however, for the artist as a person, and has nothing to do with the man as an artist. In his capacity of artist he is neither auto-erotic, nor hetero-erotic, nor erotic in any sense. He is objective and impersonal—even inhuman —for as an artist he is his work, and not a human being.

Every creative person is a duality or a synthesis of contradictory aptitudes. On the one side he is a human being with a personal life, while on the other side he is an impersonal, creative process. Since as a human being he may be sound or morbid, we must look at his psychic make-up to find the determinants of his personality. But we can only understand him in his capacity of artist by looking at his creative achievement. We should make a sad mistake if we tried to explain the mode of life of an English gentleman, a Prussian officer, or a cardinal in terms of personal factors. The gentleman, the officer and the cleric function as such in an impersonal role, and their psychic make-up is qualified by a peculiar objectivity. We must grant that the artist does not function in an official capacity—the very opposite is nearer the truth. He nevertheless resembles the types I have named in one respect, for the specifically artistic disposition involves an overweight of collective psychic life as against the personal. Art is a kind of innate drive that seizes a human being and makes him its instrument. The artist is not a person endowed with free will who seeks his own ends, but one who allows art to realize its purposes through him. As a human being he may have moods and a will and personal aims, but as an artist he is "man" in a higher sense—he is "collective man"—one who carries and shapes the unconscious, psychic life of mankind. To perform this difficult office it is sometimes necessary for him to sacrifice happiness and everything that makes life worth living for the ordinary human being.

All this being so, it is not strange that the artist is an especially interesting case for the psychologist who uses an analytical method. The artist's life cannot be otherwise than full of conflicts, for two forces are at war within him—on the one hand the common human longing for happiness, satisfaction and security in life, and on the other a ruthless passion for creation which may go so far as to override every personal desire. The lives of artists are as a rule so highly unsatisfactory—not to say tragic—because of their inferiority on the human and personal side, and not because of a sinister dispensation. There are hardly any exceptions to the rule that a person must pay dearly for the divine gift of the creative fire. It is as though each of us were endowed at birth with a certain capital of energy. The strongest force in our make-up will seize and all but monopolize this energy, leaving so little over that nothing of value can come of it. In this way the creative force can drain the human impulses to such a degree that the personal ego must develop all sorts of bad qualities—ruthlessness, selfishness and vanity (so-called "auto-erotism")—and even every kind of vice, in order to maintain the spark of life and to keep itself from being wholly bereft. The auto-erotism of artists resembles that of illegitimate or neglected children who from their tenderest years must protect themselves from the destructive influence of people who have no love to give them—who develop bad qualities for that very purpose and later maintain an invincible egocentrism by remaining all their lives infantile and helpless or by actively offending against the moral code or the law. How can we doubt that it is his art that explains the artist, and not the insufficiencies and conflicts of his personal life? These are nothing but the regrettable results of the fact that he is an artist— that is to say, a man who from his very birth has been called to a greater task than the ordinary mortal. A special ability means a heavy expenditure of energy in a particular direction, with a consequent drain from some other side of life.

It makes no difference whether the poet knows that his work is begotten, grows and matures with him, or whether he supposes that by taking thought he produces it out of the void. His opinion of the matter does not change the fact that his own work outgrows him as a child its mother. The creative process has feminine quality, and the creative work arises from unconscious depths—we might say, from the realm of the mothers. Whenever the creative force predominates, human life is ruled and moulded by the unconscious as against the active will, and the conscious ego is swept along on a subterranean current, being nothing more than a helpless observer of events. The work in process becomes the poet's fate and determines his psychic development. It is not Goethe who creates *Faust*, but *Faust* which creates Goethe. And what is *Faust* but a symbol? By this I do not mean an allegory that points to something all too familiar, but an expression that stands for something not clearly known and yet profoundly alive. Here it is something that lives in the soul of every German, and that Goethe has helped to bring to birth. Could we conceive of anyone but a

German writing *Faust* or *Also sprach Zarathustra?* Both play upon something that reverberates in the German soul—a "primordial image," as Jacob Burckhardt once called it—the figure of a physician or teacher of mankind. The archetypal image of the wise man, the saviour or redeemer, lies buried and dormant in man's unconscious since the dawn of culture; it is awakened whenever the times are out of joint and a human society is committed to a serious error. When people go astray they feel the need of a guide or teacher or even of the physician. These primordial images are numerous, but do not appear in the dreams of individuals or in works of art until they are called into being by the waywardness of the general outlook. When conscious life is characterized by one-sidedness and by a false attitude, then they are activated—one might say, "instinctively"—and come to light in the dreams of individuals and the visions of artists and seers, thus restoring the psychic equilibrium of the epoch.

In this way the work of the poet comes to meet the spiritual need of the society in which he lives, and for this reason his work means more to him than his personal fate, whether he is aware of this or not. Being essentially the instrument for his work, he is subordinate to it, and we have no reason for expecting him to interpret it for us. He has done the best that in him lies in giving it form, and he must leave the interpretation to others and to the future. A great work of art is like a dream; for all its apparent obviousness it does not explain itself and is never unequivocal. A dream never says: "You ought," or: "This is the truth." It presents an image in much the same way as nature allows a plant to grow, and we must draw our own conclusions. If a person has a nightmare, it means either that he is too much given to fear, or else that he is too exempt from it; and if he dreams of the old wise man it may mean that he is too pedagogical, as also that he stands in need of a teacher. In a subtle way both meanings come to the same thing, as we perceive when we are able to let the work of art act upon us as it acted upon the artist. To grasp its meaning, we must allow it to shape us as it once shaped him. Then we understand the nature of his experience. We see that he has drawn upon the healing and redeeming forces of the collective psyche that underlies consciousness with its isolation and its painful errors; that he has penetrated to that matrix of life in which all men are embedded, which imparts a common rhythm to all human existence, and allows the individual to communicate his feeling and his striving to mankind as a whole.

The secret of artistic creation and of the effectiveness of art is to be found in a return to the state of *participation mystique*—to that level of experience at which it is man who lives, and not the individual, and at which the weal or woe of the single human being does not count, but only human existence. This is why every great work of art is objective and impersonal, but none the less profoundly moves us each and all. And this is also why the personal life of the poet cannot be held essential to his art—but at most a help or a hindrance to his creative task. He may go the way of a Philistine, a good citizen, a neurotic, a fool or a criminal. His personal career may be inevitable and interesting, but it does not explain the poet.

QUESTIONS

1. Jung makes a distinction between the "human being with a personal life" and the "impersonal, creative process." What is the importance of this distinction? How does it help to shape the rest of Jung's argument?
2. Jung says that the "personal idiosyncrasies that creep into a work of art are not essential," since art "should rise far above the realm of personal life and speak from the spirit and heart of the poet as man to the spirit and heart of mankind." Is a contradiction involved here? Can a poet speak from his heart without being personal? Are "personal idiosyncrasies" desirable in a work to give it the flavor of a distinctive style?
3. In "The Keys to Dreamland" (p. 484), Frye says that "literature has no consistent connection with ordinary life. . . . You don't relate it directly to life or reality, you relate works of literature to each other." Compare Frye's view with Jung's statement that "a great work of art is like a dream. . . . It presents an image in much the same way as nature allows a plant to grow, and we must draw our own conclusions."
4. Compare Jung's view of the creative process with that of Neil Simon ("I, a Grown Man, Hit in the Head with a Frozen Veal Chop," pp. 567–573). Explain whether they agree in their views of the essential nature of the artist and of the creative process.
5. Consider the following stanzas (69–72) from Byron's "Childe Harold's Pilgrimage." To what extent would Jung feel that psychological considerations were helpful in analyzing these lines?

> To fly from, need not be to hate, mankind:
> All are not fit with them to stir and toil,
> Nor is it discontent to keep the mind
> Deep in its fountain, lest it overboil
> In the hot throng, where we become the spoil
> Of our infection, till too late and long
> We may deplore and struggle with the coil,
> In wretched interchange of wrong for wrong
> Midst a contentious world, striving where none are strong.
>
> There, in a moment we may plunge our years
> In fatal penitence, and in the blight
> Of our own Soul turn all our blood to tears,
> And colour things to come with hues of Night;
> The race of life becomes a hopeless flight
> To those that walk in darkness: on the sea

The boldest steer but where their ports invite—
But there are wanderers o'er Eternity
Whose bark drives on and on, and anchored ne'er shall be.

Is it not better, then, to be alone,
And love Earth only for its earthly sake?
By the blue rushing of the arrowy Rhone,
Or the pure bosom of its nursing Lake,
Which feeds it as a mother who doth make
A fair but froward infant her own care,
Kissing its cries away as these awake;—
Is it not better thus our lives to wear,
Than join the crushing crowd, doomed to inflict or bear?

I live not in myself, but I become
Portion of that around me; and to me
High mountains are a feeling, but the hum
Of human cities torture: I can see
Nothing to loathe in Nature, save to be
A link reluctant in a fleshly chain,
Classed among creatures, when the soul can flee,
And with the sky—the peak—the heaving plain.
Of ocean, or the stars, mingle—and not in vain.

WILLIAM EDWARD WILSON

Madeline Among the Midshipmen

One night not long ago, I found myself remembering for the first time in years a gruff and briny old sea-dog I served under for a while in the Second World War. I had been reading the poems of Percy Bysshe Shelley, and it was the "Hymn to Intellectual Beauty" that brought my old skipper to mind.

No finer officer than this Captain, U.S.N., ever sailed the seas, I am sure, but when I knew him he was Head of the Department of English, History, and Government at the United States Naval Academy. At the Academy, the Department of E., H., and G. is appropriately known as "the Bull Department," and I was assigned to it early in the war when BuPers decided I was more expendable with a book in my hand than while conning an LST. Why the Captain was assigned to that Department I do not know, unless it was because he had once read "A Dissertation on Roast Pig."

"You ever read that thing about roast pork?" he always asked newcomers to the Department, as a test of their backgrounds in literature. "I thought it was a pretty good yarn when I was a Midshipman."

I admired the Captain. Indeed, I was grateful that he was my first skipper on shore duty, because he gave a salty atmosphere to Mahan Hall and almost justified the Academy's ironclad rule that we must think of walls as bulkheads, floors as decks, drinking fountains as scuttlebutts, and ourselves as Naval officers. Still, with all the ribbons on his broad chest, the Captain had never fought the campaign of iambic pentameter nor the battle of the synecdoche, nor had he navigated any closer to the main current of English Literature than Charles Lamb's little eddy about roast pig. It was therefore inevitable that the day he discovered Shelley in the Plebe reading assignments he blew all his stacks at once.

When he came steaming across the gangway to the Lit Deck in Mahan Hall that day, the Lit textbook in his hand and his eyes ablaze, we officers of the Lit Detail were so startled that we knocked over a half dozen chairs coming to attention.

"Ten*shun!*" shouted the Chairman of the Lit Detail, a Lieutenant, U.S.N.R., recently surfaced from the Harvard Graduate School; but we were already standing and as stiff as *rigor mortis.*

"What is *this* doing in here?" the Captain roared; and as he spoke he pounded the Lit text so hard with his fist that he knocked it out of his own hand.

The Chairman of the Lit Detail leaped to pick the book up.

"Find that fellow Shelley for me," the Captain commanded. "That thing about beauty."

Later, the Chairman of the Lit Detail said it was like looking for hay in a haystack. But he took a long shot and returned the book to the Captain opened to "Hymn to Intellectual Beauty."

The Captain scanned the page till he found the lines he wanted.

"Now, hear this!" he bellowed, and began to read to us in a high falsetto, which he obviously intended to sound effeminate but which sounded, instead, more like a bosun with laryngitis:

"*Sudden, thy shadow fell on me; I shrieked and clasped my hands with ecstasy.*"

Snapping the book shut, the Captain then glowered at each of us in turn, as if to ferret out any concealed admiration for the lines he had read. If there was any such admiration in that complement of men, it was not exposed. The officers of the Lit Detail, every man-jack of them—and the majority held Ph.D.'s in English— looked as if they had never before heard of Percy Bysshe Shelley.

When he was satisfied with his inspection, the Captain proceeded to a pronouncement.

"That Shelley fellow was a *sissy!* Strike the poem off the reading list."

"Aye, aye, sir!" said the Chairman of the Lit Detail.

The Captain warped his majestic hull around toward the door, but there he stopped, caught in the backwash of an afterthought.

"Belay that," he said, turning to the Chairman. "Not just that thing about beauty. Strike off everything in the book by that fellow. No Shelley. Understand?"

"But, sir—" the Chairman began.

"*All* of it!" the Captain shouted. "No Shelley! Won't do for Midshipmen. Can't have them exposed to that kind of bilge." He gave his falsetto a try again. "*Shrieking* and *clasping* his hands!" But he still sounded like a bosun in sick bay. "I might have known it when I saw the fellow's name on the list. *Percy*—!"

"Please let us keep 'Ode to the West Wind,' Captain," the Chairman of the Lit Detail pleaded. "In a way, sir, it's a nautical poem. That is, it's about the weather."

The Captain shook his head.

"Won't do!" he said. 'That one too! *All* of them! After all, there's a war on. Throw them *all* out! Understand? *Shrieking* and all that bilge! *Percy*—! Percy Bysshe—! Percy *Bosh*, I say!"

So, that year at the United States Naval Academy, Nineteenth Century English Poetry was taught with no mention of Percy Bysshe Shelley. To quiet my conscience in the matter, I tried to believe that a whole class of officers in the U. S. Navy would be manlier than their comrades in Blue and Gold because they had never heard of him. At least, if they ever encountered Beauty and recognized it and *shrieked*, they would have no one to blame but themselves.

We did retain Keats in the Plebe syllabus that year, however, probably because the Captain never had the stomach for looking into "The Eve of St. Agnes" after he jettisoned Shelley. At the time, I was sure that if he had known what was going on in Madeline's bedroom on St. Agnes Eve and heard the commotion it caused in my Plebe class John Keats would have gone over the side too.

'At the Naval Academy, the teaching method is somewhat different from the method practiced in most institutions of so-called higher learning. Or so it was during the war. Every Midshipman had to have a grade in the instructor's grade book for every day, and for that reason you had very little time for shilly-shallying around with superfluous things like ideas. You got each Midshipman on his feet in the course of the fifty-minute period, asked him a question that he would find it hard to answer equivocally, jotted a numerical grade in your grade book, and proceeded to the next man. According to Academy Regs, you said, "That is well," at the end of each recitation, whether all was well or not; and it was a good idea to observe this rule because, if you didn't, your Midshipman would remain standing at attention, as solemn as a ninepin, even after you had called on someone else.

When I came to "The Eve of St. Agnes" in the Lit syllabus, I was pleased to note that there were forty-two stanzas in the poem. There were twenty-one Plebes in my Lit class. That meant two stanzas per Plebe. At the rate of a minute per stanza, I would have eight minutes left over for teaching.

We cast off to a good start with Keats's poem. I gave the class the poop about the legend of St. Agnes Eve, made sure they had the word on the rivalry between Madeline's family and Porphyro's, ran them through a drill in pronouncing Porphyro as *Porphyro* and not *Proffero*, and together we convoyed that amorous young man through the "dusky galleries" of Madeline's castle and into Madeline's bedroom, where, as Keats put it, he "took covert, pleased amain." That phrase caused a little difficulty, but I persuaded my future officers and gentlemen that *Porphyro*, being himself a gentleman if not a Naval officer, only hid in a corner of Madeline's room and did not take to the covers of her sack.

Then came Madeline's turn. All innocence, but eagerness too, "St. Agnes' charmèd maid" climbed the marble stairs, lighting her way with a candle, and finally hove to at the door of her room, where Porphyro was hiding.

"Then what happened?" I asked the Plebe I had brought to attention to sound off on Stanzas 23 and 24.

The Plebe hesitated, and I thought he looked puzzled. But it was hard to tell. Most Plebes looked puzzled aboard the Bull Department.

"Well, sir," he said, finally, "when Madeline opened her bedroom door, a big animal ran out."

I could not have been more startled if the Engineering Department (known as "Steam") had blown out a boiler under my classroom windows, as indeed they were in the habit of doing from time to time.

"A big *what?*" I said.

"A big animal, sir."

I tried to think of all the things cluttering Madeline's bedroom that St. Agnes Eve. There was a table covered with cloth of woven crimson, gold, and jet. There were candied apple, quince, and plum and lucent syrops, tinct with cinnamon. And of course there was Porphyro. But I could recall no animals, large or small on the loose in the girl's chamber.

"I think you must be mistaken," I said.

"It's in the book, sir," the Plebe replied, solemnly. "May I show you?"

In the Navy, if it's in the book it's so. In my place, even the Captain would have had to give that Plebe a 4.0 for the day if he proved himself right.

"Very well," I said. "Find it in the book and read it to me."

The Plebe opened his book to Stanza 23 and read the first line.

"*Out went the taper as she hurried in.* . . . That's a large tropical animal found mainly in South America, sir," he said. "I looked it up."

Five minutes later, Steam was sending over a man to ask *us* to pipe down.

The Captain never heard about this interpretation of Keats in my classroom, and at the time I was grateful. Maybe, though, it would have been all right if he had. On second thought, I believe he would have approved of Madeline's bedroom. After all, he liked animals in literature. It was only Beauty and that sort of bilge that he disapproved of.

LAURA BOHANNAN
Prince Hamlet in Africa

Just before I left Oxford for the Tiv in West Africa, conversation turned to the season at Stratford. "You Americans," said a friend, "often have difficulty with Shakespeare. He was, after all, a very English poet, and one can easily misinterpret the universal by mis-understanding the particular."

I protested that human nature is pretty much the same the whole world over; at least the general plot and motivation of the greater tragedies would always be clear—everywhere—although some details of custom might have to be explained and difficulties of translation might produce other slight changes. To end an argu-ment we could not conclude, my friend gave me a copy of *Hamlet* to study in the African bush: it would, he hoped, lift my mind above its primitive surroundings, and possibly I might, by prolonged meditation, achieve the grace of correct interpretation.

It was my second field trip to that African tribe, and I thought myself ready to live in one of its remote sections—an area difficult to cross even on foot. I eventually settled on the hillock of a very knowledgeable old man, the head of a homestead of some hundred and forty people, all of whom were either his close relatives or their wives and children. Like the other elders of the vicinity, the old man spent most of his time performing ceremonies seldom seen these days in the more accessible parts of the tribe. I was delighted. Soon there would be three months of enforced isolation and leisure, between the harvest that takes place just before the rising of the swamps and the clearing of new farms when the water goes down. Then, I thought, they would have even more time to perform cere-monies and explain them to me.

I was quite mistaken. Most of the ceremonies demanded the pres-ence of elders from several homesteads. As the swamps rose, the old men found it too difficult to walk from one homestead to the next, and the ceremonies gradually ceased. As the swamps rose even higher, all activities but one came to an end. The women brewed beer from maize and millet. Men, women, children sat on their hil-locks and drank it.

People began to drink at dawn. By midmorning the whole home-stead was singing, dancing, and drumming. When it rained, people had to sit inside their huts: there they drank and sang or they drank and told stories. In any case, by noon or before, I either had to join the party or retire to my own hut and my books. "One does not dis-cuss serious matters when there is beer. Come, drink with us." Since I lacked their capacity for the thick native beer, I spent more and more time with *Hamlet*. Before the end of the second month, grace descended on me. I was quite sure that *Hamlet* had only one possi-ble interpretation, and that one universally obvious.

Early every morning, in the hope of having some serious talk before the beer party, I used to call on the old man at his reception hut—a circle of posts supporting a thatched roof above a low mud-wall to keep out wind and rain. One day I crawled through the low doorway and found most of the men of the homestead sitting hud-dled in their ragged cloths on stools, low plank beds, and reclining chairs, warming themselves against the chill of the rain around a smoky fire. In the center were three pots of beer. The party had started.

The old man greeted me cordially. "Sit down and drink." I accepted a large calabash full of beer, poured some into a small drinking gourd, and tossed it down. Then I poured some more into the same gourd for the man second in seniority to my host before I handed my calabash over to a young man for further dis-tribution. Important people shouldn't ladle beer themselves.

"It is better like this," the old man said, looking at me approv-ingly and plucking at the thatch that had caught in my hair. "You should sit and drink with us more often. Your servants tell me that when you are not with us, you sit inside your hut looking at a paper."

The old man was acquainted with four kinds of "papers": tax receipts, bride price receipts, court fee receipts, and letters. The messenger who brought him letters from the chief used them mainly as a badge of office, for he always knew what was in them and told the old man. Personal letters for the few who had relatives in the government or mission stations were kept until someone went to a large market where there was a letter writer and reader. Since my arrival, letters were brought to me to be read. A few men also brought me bride price receipts, privately, with requests to change the figures to a higher sum. I found moral arguments were of no avail, since in-laws are fair game, and the technical hazards of forgery difficult to explain to an illiterate people. I did not wish them to think me silly enough to look at any such papers for days on end, and I hastily explained that my "paper" was one of the "things of long ago" of my country.

"Ah," said the old man. "Tell us."

I protested that I was not a storyteller. Storytelling is a skilled art among them; their standards are high, and the audiences critical— and vocal in their criticism. I protested in vain. This morning they wanted to hear a story while they drank. They threatened to tell me no more stories until I told them one of mine. Finally, the old man promised that no one would criticize my style "for we know you are struggling with our language." "But," put in one of the elders, "you must explain what we do not understand, as we do when we tell you our stories." Realizing that here was my chance to prove *Hamlet* universally intelligible, I agreed.

The old man handed me some more beer to help me on with my storytelling. Men filled their long wooden pipes and knocked coals from the fire to place in their pipe bowls; then, puffing contentedly, they sat back to listen. I began in the proper style, "Not yesterday, not yesterday, but long ago, a thing occurred. One night three men were keeping watch outside the homestead of the great chief, when suddenly they saw the former chief approach them."

"Why was he no longer their chief?"

"He was dead," I explained. "That is why they were troubled and afraid when they saw him."

"Impossible," began one of the elders, handing his pipe on to his neighbor, who interrupted, "Of course it wasn't the dead chief. It was an omen sent by a witch. Go on."

Slightly shaken, I continued. "One of these three was a man who knew things"—the closest translation for scholar, but unfortunately it also meant witch. The second elder looked truimphantly at the first. "So he spoke to the the dead chief saying, 'Tell us what we must do so you may rest in your grave,' but the dead chief did not answer. He vanished, and they could see him no more. Then the man who knew things—his name was Horatio—said this event was the affair of the dead chief's son, Hamlet."

There was a general shaking of heads round the circle. "Had the dead chief no living brothers? Or was his son the chief?"

"No," I replied. "That is, he had one living brother who became the chief when the elder brother died."

The old men muttered such omens were matters for chiefs and elders, not for youngsters; no good could come of going behind a chief's back; clearly Horatio was not a man who knew things.

"Yes, he was," I insisted, shooing a chicken away from my beer. "In our country the son is next to the father. The dead chief's younger brother had become the great chief. He had also married this elder brother's widow only about a month after the funeral."

"He did well," the old man beamed and announced to the others, "I told you that if we knew more about Europeans, we would find they really were very like us. In our country also," he added to me, "the younger brother marries the elder brother's widow and becomes the father of his children. Now, if your uncle, who married your widowed mother, is your father's full brother, then he will be a real father to you. Did Hamlet's father and uncle have one mother?"

His question barely penetrated my mind; I was too upset and thrown too far off balance by having one of the most important elements of *Hamlet* knocked straight out of the picture. Rather uncertainly I said that I thought they had the same mother, but I wasn't sure—the story didn't say. The old man told me severely that these genealogical details made all the difference and that when I got home I must ask the elders about it. He shouted out the door to one of his younger wives to bring his goatskin bag.

Determined to save what I could of the mother motif, I took a deep breath and began again. "The son Hamlet was very sad because his mother had married again so quickly. There was no need for her to do so, and it is our custom for a widow not to go to her next husband until she has mourned for two years."

"Two years is too long," objected the wife, who had appeared with the old man's battered goatskin bag. "Who will hoe your farms for you while you have no husband?"

"Hamlet," I retorted without thinking, "was old enough to hoe his mother's farms himself. There was no need for her to remarry." No one looked convinced. I gave up. "His mother and the great chief told Hamlet not to be sad, for the great chief himself would be a father to Hamlet. Furthermore, Hamlet would be the next chief: therefore he must stay to learn the things of a chief. Hamlet agreed to remain, and all the rest went off to drink beer."

While I paused, perplexed at how to render Hamlet's disgusted soliloquy to an audience convinced that Claudius and Gertrude had behaved in the best possible manner, one of the younger men asked me who had married the other wives of the dead chief.

"He had no other wives," I told him.

"But a chief must have many wives! How else can he brew beer and prepare food for all his guests?"

I said firmly that in our country even chiefs had only one wife, that they had servants to do their work, and that they paid them from tax money.

It was better, they returned, for a chief to have many wives and sons who would help him hoe his farms and feed his people; then everyone loved the chief who gave much and took nothing—taxes were a bad thing.

I agreed with the last comment, but for the rest fell back on their favorite way of fobbing off my questions: "That is the way it is done, so that is how we do it."

I decided to skip the soliloquy. Even if Claudius was here

thought quite right to marry his brother's widow, there remained the poison motif, and I knew they would disapprove of fratricide. More hopefully I resumed, "That night Hamlet kept watch with the three who had seen his dead father. The dead chief again appeared, and although the others were afraid, Hamlet followed his dead father off to one side. When they were alone, Hamlet's dead father spoke."

"Omens can't talk!" The old man was emphatic.

"Hamlet's dead father wasn't an omen. Seeing him might have been an omen, but he was not." My audience looked as confused as I sounded. "It *was* Hamlet's dead father. It was a thing we call a 'ghost.' " I had to use the English word, for unlike many of the neighboring tribes, these people didn't believe in the survival after death of any individuating part of the personality.

"What is a 'ghost?' An omen?"

"No, a 'ghost' is someone who is dead but who walks around and can talk, and people can hear him and see him but not touch him."

They objected. "One can touch zombis."

"No, no! It was not a dead body the witches had animated to sacrifice and eat. No one else made Hamlet's dead father walk. He did it himself."

"Dead men can't walk," protested my audience as one man.

I was quite willing to compromise. "A 'ghost' is the dead man's shadow."

But again they objected. "Dead men cast no shadows."

"They do in my country," I snapped.

The old man quelled the babble of disbelief that arose immediately and told me with that insincere, but courteous, agreement one extends to the fancies of the young, ignorant, and superstitious, "No doubt in your country the dead can also walk without being zombis." From the depths of his bag he produced a withered fragment of kola nut, bit off one end to show it wasn't poisoned, and handed me the rest as a peace offering.

"Anyhow," I resumed, "Hamlet's dead father said that his own brother, the one who became chief, had poisoned him. He wanted Hamlet to avenge him. Hamlet believed this in his heart, for he did not like his father's brother." I took another swallow of beer. "In the country of the great chief, living in the same homestead, for it was a very large one, was an important elder who was often with the chief to advise and help him. His name was Polonius. Hamlet was courting his daughter, but her father and her brother . . . [I cast hastily about for some tribal analogy] warned her not to let Hamlet visit her when she was alone on her farm, for he would be a great chief and so could not marry her."

"Why not?" asked the wife, who had settled down on the edge

of the old man's chair. He frowned at her for asking stupid questions and growled, "They lived in the same homestead."

"That was not the reason," I informed them. "Polonius was a stranger who lived in the homestead because he helped the chief, not because he was a relative."

"Then why couldn't Hamlet marry her?"

"He could have," I explained, "but Polonius didn't think he would. After all, Hamlet was a man of great importance who ought to marry a chief's daughter, for in his country a man could have only one wife. Polonius was afraid that if Hamlet made love to his daughter, then no one else would give a high price for her.' '

"That might be true," remarked one of the shrewder elders, "but a chief's son would give his mistress's father enough presents and patronage to more than make up the difference. Polonius sounds like a fool to me."

"Many people think he was," I agreed. "Meanwhile Polonius sent his son Laertes off to Paris to learn the things of that country, for it was the homestead of a very great chief indeed. Because he was afraid that Laertes might waste a lot of money on beer and women and gambling, or get into trouble by fighting, he sent one of his servants to Paris secretly, to spy out what Laertes was doing. One day Hamlet came upon Polonius's daughter Ophelia. He behaved so oddly he frightened her. Indeed"—I was fumbling for words to express the dubious quality of Hamlet's madness—"the chief and many others had also noticed that when Hamlet talked one could understand the words but not what they meant. Many people thought that he had become mad." My audience suddenly became much more attentive. "The great chief wanted to know what was wrong with Hamlet, so he sent for two of Hamlet's age mates [school friends would have taken long explanation] to talk to Hamlet and find out what troubled his heart. Hamlet, seeing that they had been bribed by the chief to betray him, told them nothing. Polonius, however, insisted that Hamlet was mad because he had been forbidden to see Ophelia, whom he loved."

"Why," inquired a bewildered voice, "should anyone bewitch Hamlet on that account?"

"Bewitch him?"

"Yes, only witchcraft can make anyone mad, unless, of course, one sees the beings that lurk in the forest."

I stopped being a storyteller, took out my notebook and demanded to be told more about these two causes of madness. Even while they spoke and I jotted notes, I tried to calculate the effect of this new factor on the plot. Hamlet had not been exposed to the beings that lurk in the forests. Only his relatives in the male line could bewitch him. Barring relatives not mentioned by Shakespeare, it had to be Claudius who was attempting to harm him. And, of course, it was.

For the moment I staved off questions by saying that the great chief also refused to believe that Hamlet was mad for the love of Ophelia and nothing else. "He was sure that something much more important was troubling Hamlet's heart."

"Now Hamlet's age mates," I continued, "had brought with them a famous storyteller. Hamlet decided to have this man tell the chief and all his homestead a story about a man who had poisoned his brother because he desired his brother's wife and wished to be chief himself. Hamlet was sure the great chief could not hear the story without making a sign if he was indeed guilty, and then he would discover whether his dead father had told him the truth."

The old man interrupted, with deep cunning, "Why should a father lie to his son?" he asked.

I hedged: "Hamlet wasn't sure that it really was his dead father." It was impossible to say anything, in that language, about devil-inspired visions.

"You mean," he said, "it actually was an omen, and he knew witches sometimes send false ones. Hamlet was a fool not to go to one skilled in reading omens and divining the truth in the first place. A man-who-sees-the-truth could have told him how his father died, if he really had been poisoned, and if there was witchcraft in it; then Hamlet could have called the elders to settle the matter."

The shrewd elder ventured to disagree. "Because his father's brother was a great chief, one-who-sees-the-truth might therefore have been afraid to tell it. I think it was for that reason that a friend of Hamlet's father—a witch and an elder—sent an omen so his friend's son would know. Was the omen true?"

"Yes," I said, abandoning ghosts and the devil; a witch-sent omen it would have to be. "It was true, for when the storyteller was telling his tale before all the homestead, the great chief rose in fear. Afraid that Hamlet knew his secret he planned to have him killed."

The stage set of the next bit presented some difficulties of translation. I began cautiously. "The great chief told Hamlet's mother to find out from her son what he knew. But because a woman's children are always first in her heart, he had the important elder Polonius hide behind a cloth that hung against the wall of Hamlet's mother's sleeping hut. Hamlet started to scold his mother for what she had done."

There was a shocked murmur from everyone. A man should never scold his mother.

"She called out in fear, and Polonius moved behind the cloth. Shouting, 'A rat!' Hamlet took his machete and slashed through the cloth." I paused for dramatic effect. "He had killed Polonius!"

The old men looked at each other in supreme disgust. "That

Polonius truly was a fool and a man who knew nothing! What child would not know enough to shout, 'It's me!' " With a pang, I remembered that these people are ardent hunters, always armed with bow, arrow, and machete; at the first rustle in the grass an arrow is aimed and ready, and the hunter shouts "Game!" If no human voice answers immediately, the arrow speeds on its way. Like a good hunter Hamlet had shouted, "A rat!"

I rushed in to save Polonius's reputation. "Polonius did speak. Hamlet heard him. But he thought it was the chief and wished to kill him to avenge his father. He had meant to kill him earlier that evening. . . ." I broke down, unable to describe to these pagans, who had no belief in individual afterlife, the difference between dying at one's prayers and dying "unhousell'd, disappointed, unaneled."

This time I had shocked my audience seriously. "For a man to raise his hand against his father's brother and the one who has become his father—that is a terrible thing. The elders ought to let such a man be bewitched."

I nibbled at my kola nut in some perplexity, then pointed out that after all the man had killed Hamlet's father.

"No," pronounced the old man, speaking less to me than to the young men sitting behind the elders. "If your father's brother has killed your father, you must appeal to your father's age mates; *they* may avenge him. No man may use violence against his senior relatives." Another thought struck him. "But if his father's brother had indeed been wicked enough to bewitch Hamlet and make him mad that would be a good story indeed, for it would be his fault that Hamlet, being mad, no longer had any sense and thus was ready to kill his father's brother."

There was a murmur of applause. *Hamlet* was again a good story to them, but it no longer seemed quite the same story to me. As I thought over the coming complications of plot and motive, I lost courage and decided to skim over dangerous ground quickly.

"The great chief," I went on, "was not sorry that Hamlet had killed Polonius. It gave him a reason to send Hamlet away, with his two treacherous age mates, with letters to a chief of a far country, saying that Hamlet should be killed. But Hamlet changed the writing on their papers, so that the chief killed his age mates instead." I encountered a reproachful glare from one of the men whom I had told undetectable forgery was not merely immoral but beyond human skill. I looked the other way.

"Before Hamlet could return, Laertes came back for his father's funeral. The great chief told him Hamlet had killed Polonius. Laertes swore to kill Hamlet because of this, and because his sister Ophelia, hearing her father had been killed by the man she loved, went mad and drowned in the river."

"Have you already forgotten what we told you?" The old man

was reproachful. "One cannot take vengeance on a madman; Hamlet killed Polonius in his madness. As for the girl, she not only went mad, she was drowned. Only witches can make people drown. Water itself can't hurt anything. It is merely something one drinks and bathes in."

I began to get cross. "If you don't like the story, I'll stop."

The old man made soothing noises and himself poured me some more beer. "You tell the story well, and we are listening. But it is clear that the elders of your country have never told you what the story really means. No, don't interrupt! We believe you when you say your marriage customs are different, or your clothes and weapons. But people are the same everywhere; therefore, there are always witches and it is we, the elders, who know how witches work. We told you it was the great chief who wished to kill Hamlet, and now your own words have proved us right. Who were Ophelia's male relatives?"

"There were only her father and her brother." Hamlet was clearly out of my hands.

"There must have been many more; this also you must ask of your elders when you get back to your country. From what you tell us, since Polonius was dead, it must have been Laertes who killed Ophelia, although I do not see the reason for it."

We had emptied one pot of beer, and the old men argued the point with slightly tipsy interest. Finally one of them demanded of me, "What did the servant of Polonius say on his return?"

With difficulty I recollected Reynaldo and his mission. "I don't think he did return before Polonius was killed."

"Listen," said the elder, "and I will tell you how it was and how your story will go, then you may tell me if I am right. Polonius knew his son would get into trouble, and so he did. He had many fines to pay for fighting, and debts from gambling. But he had only two ways of getting money quickly. One was to marry off his sister at once, but it is difficult to find a man who will marry a woman desired by the son of a chief. For if the chief's heir commits adultery with your wife, what can you do? Only a fool calls a case against a man who will someday be his judge. Therefore Laertes had to take the second way: he killed his sister by witchcraft, drowning her so he could secretly sell her body to the witches."

I raised an objection. "They found her body and buried it. Indeed Laertes jumped into the grave to see his sister once more— so, you see, the body was truly there. Hamlet, who had just come back, jumped in after him."

"What did I tell you?" The elder appealed to the others. "Laertes was up to no good with his sister's body. Hamlet prevented him, because the chief's heir, like a chief, does not wish any other man to grow rich and powerful. Laertes would be angry, because he would have killed his sister without benefit to himself. In our country he would try to kill Hamlet for that reason. Is this not what happened?"

"More or less," I admitted. "When the great chief found Hamlet was still alive, he encouraged Laertes to try to kill Hamlet and arranged a fight with machetes between them. In the fight both the young men were wounded to death. Hamlet's mother drank the poisoned beer that the chief meant for Hamlet in case he won the fight. When he saw his mother die of poison, Hamlet, dying, managed to kill his father's brother with his machete."

"You see, I was right!" exclaimed the elder.

"That was a very good story," added the old man, "and you told it with very few mistakes. There was just one more error, at the very end. The poison Hamlet's mother drank was obviously meant for the survivor of the fight, whichever it was. If Laertes had won, the great chief would have poisoned him, for no one would know that he arranged Hamlet's death. Then, too, he need not fear Laertes' witchcraft; it takes a strong heart to kill one's only sister by witchcraft.

"Sometime," concluded the old man, gathering his ragged toga about him, "you must tell us some more stories of your country. We, who are elders, will instruct you in their true meaning, so that when you return to your own land your elders will see that you have not been sitting in the bush, but among those who know things and who have taught you wisdom."

QUESTIONS

1. In "Madeline Among the Midshipmen" (pp. 494–498) Wilson describes difficulties in teaching literature at the U.S. Naval Academy which are analogous to those experienced by Bohannan. Were the bases for the difficulties similar or different? Explain.
2. Bohannan's African audience in effect rewrites Hamlet as she tells it. How do you think this African version of the play would be received by an American audience, more or less enthusiastically than the original version? Explain.
3. Frye discusses conventions in "The Keys to Dreamland" (pp. 480–488) and suggests how different things may look to an outsider with a different set of conventions. Which conventions of the Africans are furthest from those in Hamlet and which are most influential in giving them a rather different view of the play?
4. Invent a set of conventions which differ from our American ones in one or more important ways and then interpret and criticize a work of literature (poem, story, play) from that point of view.

W. K. WIMSATT
What to Say About a Poem [1]

At the outset what can we be sure of? Mainly that a poem says or means something, or ought to mean something (or ought to if we as teachers have any business with it—perhaps that is the safe minimum). The meaning of the poem may be quite obscure and difficult (rough, opaque, and resistant to first glance), or it may be smooth and easy, perhaps deceptively smooth and easy, a nice surface and seemingly transparent. For either kind of poem, the simplest, but not the least important kind of observation we can make, the simplest question we can ask, is the kind which relates to the dictionary. What does a certain word or phrase mean? We are lucky enough, I am assuming, to have a poem which contains some archaic, technical, or esoteric expression, which the class, without previous research, will not understand. If we are even luckier, the word has another, a modern, an easy and plausible meaning, which conceals the more difficult meaning. (Ambiguity, double or simultaneous meaning, our grammar instructs us, is a normal situation in poems.) In any case, we can put our question in two stages: "Are there any difficulties or questions with this stanza?" "Well, in that case, Miss Proudfit, what does the word *braw* mean?" "What does *kirkward* mean?" "When six braw gentlemen kirkward shall carry ye." We are lucky, I say, not simply that we have a chance to teach the class something—to earn our salary in a clear and measurable way. But of course because we hereby succeed in turning the attention of the class to the poem, to the surface, and then through the surface. They may begin to suspect the whole of this surface. They may ask a few questions of their own.

The answers to questions of the kind just noticed lie in a clean, dictionary region of meaning. This kind of meaning is definitely, definably, and provably there—some of our pupils just did not hap-

---

1. This essay is a reduced version of a paper read before *The Eighth Yale Conference on the Teaching of English*, at New Haven, April 14, 1962. An introductory section, here omitted, touched on the "grammar" of criticism, the categories of theme, diction, metaphor, symbol, meter, genre, person, tone, tension, wit, irony, and the like, which theoretical effort makes available to criticism. These, I argued, are an important part of critical equipment but not necessarily the immediate idiom of practical criticism and certainly not a dictionary of the trophies which criticism can expect to bring away from its exploration of actual poems. My essay aims to consider in a less technical way how we are using the materials of language and poetry, and how we are using our own minds, when we address ourselves to the examination of a given poem, to asking questions about it, to eliciting answers from our students. In its original form, the paper was fortified by a fairly extended explication of one short poem, William Blake's "London," in his *Songs of Experience* [Wimsatt's note].

pen to be aware of it. Let us call this *explicit* meaning. I believe
it is important to give this kind of meaning a name and to keep it
fixed. The act of expounding this meaning also needs a name. Let
us call it explanation—*explanation of the explicit.*

Obviously, our talking about the poem will not go far at this level—not much farther than our translation of Caesar or Virgil in a
Latin reading class.

And so we proceed, or most often we do, to another level of
commentary on the poem—not necessarily second *in order* for
every teacher or for every poem, but at least early and fundamental,
or in part so. This level of commentary may usefully be called
description of a poem—not *explanation*, just *description*. There is
no way of describing the weather report, except to repeat what it
says—describing the weather. A poem, on the other hand, not only
says something, but *is* something. "A poem," we know, "should not
mean but be." And so the poem itself especially *invites* description.

The meter of a poem, for instance, is of a certain kind, with certain kinds of variations and certain relations to the syntax; one kind
of word rhymes with another kind (*Aristotle* with *bottle*, in Byron;
Adam with *madam*, in Yeats); some conspicuous repetition or
refrain in a poem shows partial variations ("On the Echoing
Green.... On the darkening Green." "Could frame thy fearful
symmetry.... Dare frame thy fearful symmetry"). Some unusual
word is repeated several times in a short poem, or a word appears in
some curious position. Some image (or "symbol") or cluster of
images recurs in a tragedy or is played against some other image or
cluster. Shakespeare's *Hamlet*, for instance, may be described as a
dramatic poem which concerns the murder of a father and a son's
burden of exacting revenge. At the same time it is a work which
exhibits a remarkable number and variety of images relating to the
expressive arts and to the criticism of the arts—music, poetry, the
theater. "That's an ill phrase, a vile phrase; 'beautified' is a vile
phrase." "Speak the speech, I pray you ... trippingly on the
tongue." "Govern these ventages with your finger and thumb ... it
will discourse most eloquent music."

Description in the most direct sense moves inside the poem,
accenting the parts and showing their relations. It may also, however, look outside the poem. *Internal* and *external* are complementary. The external includes all the kinds of history in which the
poem has its setting. A specially important kind of history, for
example, is the literary tradition itself. The small neat squared-off
quatrains of Andrew Marvell's *Horatian Ode* upon Oliver Cromwell go in a very exact way with the title and with the main statement of the poem. Both in ostensible theme and in prosody the
poem is a kind of echo of Horatian alcaics in honor of Caesar

Augustus. The blank verse of Milton's *Paradise Lost* and the couplets of Dryden's translation of the *Aeneid* are both attempts to find an equivalent for, or a vehicle of reference to, the hexameters of Greek and Latin epic poetry. A poem in William Blake's *Songs of Innocence* is written in simple quatrains, four rising feet or three to a line, with perhaps alternate rhymes. These are something like the stanzas of a folk ballad, but they are more like something else. A more immediate antecedent both of Blake's metric and of his vocabulary of child-like piety, virtues, and vices, hopes and fears, is the popular religious poetry of the eighteenth century, the hymns sung at the evangelical chapels, written for children by authors like Isaac Watts or Christopher Smart.

II

We can insist, then, on *description* of poems, both *internal* and *external*, as a moment of critical discourse which has its own identity and may be usefully recognized and defined. Let us hasten to add, however, that in making the effort to define this moment we are mainly concerned with setting up a platform for the accurate construction of something further.

The truth is that description of a poetic structure is never simply a report on appearances (as it might be, for instance, if the object were a painted wooden box). Description of a poetic structure is inevitably also an engagement with meanings which inhere in that structure. It is a necessary first part of the engagement with certain kinds of meaning. (*Certain kinds*—in the long run we shall want to lay some emphasis on that qualification. But for the moment the point is that there *is* meaning.) In the critic's discourse "pure description" will always have a hard time taking the "place of sense."

Perhaps we shall feel guilty of stretching the meaning of the word *meaning* slightly, but unless we are willing to leave many kinds of intimation out of our account of poetry, we shall have to say, for example, that Byron meant that criticism had fallen on evil days—and that it didn't matter very much. "Longinus o'er a bottle, Or, Every Poet his *own* Aristotle." We shall have to say, surely we shall wish to say, that Milton in the opening of his *Paradise Lost* means, "This is the language and style of epic, the greatest kind of poetry; and this is the one theme that surpasses those of the greatest epics of antiquity." ("This"—in a sense—"is an epic to end all epics." As it did.) Alexander Pope in his *Epistle to Augustus* means, "This is a poem to the King of England which sounds curiously like the Epistle of Horace to the Emperor Augustus. Let anybody who cares or dares notice how curious it sounds." Shakespeare means that the action of *Hamlet* takes place on a stage, in a world, where relations between appearance and reality are manifold and some of them oddly warped.

Through description of poems, then, we move back to meaning—though scarcely to the same kind of meaning as that with which we were engaged in our initial and simple explanation of words. Through description, we arrive at a kind of meaning which ought to have its own special name. We can safely and usefully, I think, give it the simple name of the *implicit*. What we are doing with it had better too be given a special name. Perhaps *explication* is the best, though the harsher word *explicitation* may seem invited. The realms of the *explicit* and the *implicit* do not, of course, constitute sealed-off separate compartments. Still there will be some meanings which we can say are clearly explicit, and some which are clearly but implicit.

I believe that we ought to work to keep ourselves keenly aware of, and on occasion ought to make as clear as we can to our pupils, two things concerning the nature of *implicit* meaning. One of these is the strongly directive and selective power of such meaning—the power of the *pattern*, of the main formally controlling purpose in the well-written poem (in terms of Gestalt psychology, the principle of "closure"). It is this which is the altogether sufficient and compelling reason in many of our decisions about details of meaning which we proceed, during our discussion of the poem, to make quite explicit—though the dictionary cannot instruct us. In the third stanza of Marvell's *Garden*: "No white or red was ever seen/ So am'rous as this lovely green." How do we know that the words *white* and *red* refer to the complexions of the British ladies?—and not, for instance, to white and red roses? The word *am'rous* gives a clue. The whole implicit pattern of meaning in the poem proves it. In these lines of this poem the words can mean nothing else. In Marvell's *Ode on Cromwell*: ". . . now the *Irish* are asham'd to see themselves in one Year tam'd. . . . They can affirm his Praises best, And have, though overcome, confest How good he is, how just, And fit for highest Trust." How do we show that these words do not express simply a complacent English report, for the year 1650, on the ruthless efficiency of Cromwell in Ireland? Only by appealing to the delicately managed intimations of the whole poem. The cruder reading, which might be unavoidable in some other context, will here reveal (in the interest of a supposedly stolid historical accuracy) a strange critical indifference to the extraordinary finesse of Marvell's poetic achievement. "Proud Maisie is in the wood, Walking so early. . . . 'Tell me, thou bonny bird, When shall I marry me?' 'When six braw gentlemen. Kirkward shall carry ye.'" How do we prove to our freshman class that the word *proud* does not mean in the first place—does not necessarily mean at all—

conceited, unlikable, nasty, unlovable, that Maisie does not suffer a fate more or less well deserved (withered and grown old as a spinster—an example of poetic justice)? Only, I think, by appealing to the whole contour and intent of this tiny but exquisitely complete poem.

> "Who makes the bridal bed,
>   Birdie, say truly?"—
> "The gray-headed sexton
>   Who delves the grave duly.
> "The glow-worm o'er grave and stone
>   Shall light thee steady.
> The owl from the steeple sing,
>   'Welcome, proud lady.'"

The second thing concerning *implicit* meaning which I think we ought to stress is exactly its character as *implicit*—and this in reaction against certain confused modes of talk which sometimes prevail. It was a hard fight for criticism, at one time not so long past, to gain recognition of the formal and implicit at all as a kind of meaning. But that fight being in part won, perhaps a careless habit developed of talking about all sorts and levels of meaning as if they all were meaning in the same direct and simple way. And this has brought anguished bursts of protest from more sober and literal scholars. The critic seems all too gracefully and readily to move beyond mere explanation. (Being a sophisticated man, he feels perhaps the need to do relatively little of this.) He soars or plunges into descriptions of the colors and structures of the poem, with immense involvements of meaning, manifold explicitations—yet all perhaps in one level tone of confident and precise insistence, which scarcely advertises or even admits what is actually going on. The trouble with this kind of criticism is that it knows too much. Students, who of course know too little, will sometimes render back and magnify this kind of weakness in weird parodies, innocent sabotage. "I am overtired/Of the great harvest I myself desired," proclaims the man who lives on the farm with the orchard, the cellar bin, the drinking trough, and the woodchuck, in Robert Frost's *After Apple-Picking*. "This man," says the student in his homework paper, "is tired of life. He wants to go to sleep and die." This we mark with a red pencil. Then we set to work, somehow, in class, to retrieve the "symbolism." This monodrama of a tired applepicker, with the feel of the ladder rungs in his instep, bears nearly the same relation to the end of a country fair, the end of a victorious football season, of a long vacation, or of a full lifetime, as a doughnut bears to a Christmas wreath, a ferris wheel, or the rings of Saturn. *Nearly* the same relation, let us say. A poem is a kind of shape, a cunning and precise shape of words and human experience, which has something of the indeterminacy of a simpler physical shape, round or square, but which at the same time invites and justifies a very wide replication or reflection of itself in the field of our awareness.

> Till the little ones, weary,
> No more can be merry;
> The sun does descend,
> And our sports have an end.
> Round the laps of their mothers
> Many sisters and brothers,
> Like birds in their nest,
> Are ready for rest,
> And sport no more seen
> On the darkening Green.

What experience has any member of the class ever had, or what experiences can he think of or imagine, that are parallel to or concentric to that of the apple-picker? of the Echoing Green?—yet the words of the poem do not *mean* these other experiences in the same way that they mean the apples, the ladder, the man, the sport, and the green. The kind of student interpretation which I have mentioned may be described as the fallacy of the literal feedback. Proud Maisie translated into conceited Maisie may be viewed as a miniature instance of the same. And this will illustrate the close relation between the two errors of implicit reading which I have just been trying to describe. The uncontrolled reading is very often the over-explicit reading.

III

Explanation, then—of the explicit and clearly ascertainable but perhaps obscure or disguised meaning of words; *description*—of the poem's structure and parts, its shape and colors, and its historical relations; *explication*—the turning of such description as far as possible into meaning. These I believe are the teacher-critic's staple commitments—which we may sum up, if we wish, in some such generic term as *elucidation* or *interpretation*. But is this all? Is there not another activity which has been going on in our minds, almost inevitably, all this while? The activity of *appreciation*. All this time, while reading the poem so carefully, have we not also been liking it or disliking it? Admiring it or despising it? Presumably we have. And presumably we ought now to ask ourselves this further question: Is there any connection between the things we have managed so far to say about the poem and the kind of response we experience toward it? Our liking it or our disliking it? Are we inclined to try to explain why we like the poem? Do we know how to do this? More precisely: Would a statement of our liking for the poem, an act of praise or appreciation, be something different from (even though perhaps dependent upon) the things we have already been saying? Or has the appreciation already been sufficiently implied or entailed by what we have been saying?

At the first level, that of simple dictionary *explanation*, very little, we will probably say, has been implied. And very little, we will most likely say, in many of our motions at the second level, the simply *descriptive*. It is not a merit in a poem, or surely not much of a merit, that it should contain any given vocabulary, say of striking or unusual words, or even that it should have metaphors, or that it should have meter or any certain kind of meter, or rhymes, as any of these entities may be purely conceived.

But that—as we have been saying—is to put these matters of simple *explanation* and simple *description* more simply and more abstractly than they are really susceptible of being put. We pass imperceptibly and quickly beyond these matters. We are inevitably and soon caught up in the demands of *explication*—the realization of the vastly more rich and interesting implicit kinds of meaning. We are engaged with features of a poem which—given always other features too of the whole context—do tend to assert themselves as reasons for our pleasure in the poem and our admiration for it. We begin to talk about patterns of meaning; we encounter structures or forms which are radiant or resonant with meaning. Patterns and structures involve coherence (unity, coherence, and emphasis), and coherence is an aspect of truth and significance. I do not think that our evaluative intimations will often, if ever, advance to the firmness and completeness of a demonstration. Perhaps it is hardly conceivable that they should. But our discourse upon the poem will almost inevitably be charged with intimations of its value. It will be more difficult to keep out these intimations than to let them in. Critics who have announced the most resolute programs of neutrality have found this out. Take care of the weight, the color, the shape of the poem, be fair to the explanation and description, the indisputable parts of the formal explication—the appreciation will be there, and it will be difficult to avoid having expressed it.

Explicatory criticism (or explicatory evaluation) is an account of a poem which exhibits the relation between its form and its meaning. Only poems which are worth something are susceptible of this kind of account. It is something like a definition of poetry to say that whereas rhetoric—in the sense of mere persuasion or sophistic—is a kind of discourse the power of which diminishes in proportion as the artifice of it is understood or seen through; poetry, on the other hand, is a kind of discourse the power of which—or the satisfaction which we derive from it—is actually increased by an increase in our understanding of the artifice. In poetry the artifice is art. This comes close I think to the center of the aesthetic fact.

IV

One of the attempts at a standard of poetic value most often reiterated in past ages has been the doctrinal—the explicitly didactic.
The aim of poetry, says the ancient Roman poet, is double, both to
give pleasure and to teach some useful doctrine. You might get by
with only one or the other, but it is much sounder to do both. Or,
the aim of poetry is to teach some doctrine—and to do this convincingly and persuasively, by *means* of vividness and pleasure—as
in effect the Elizabethan courtier and the eighteenth-century essayist would say. But in what does the pleasure consist? Why is the
discourse pleasurable? Well, the aim of poetry is really to please us
by means of or through the act of teaching us. The pleasure is a
dramatized *moral* pleasure. Thus in effect some theories of
drama in France during the seventeenth century. Or, the pleasure
of poetry is a pleasure simply of tender and morally good feelings.
Thus in effect the philosophers of the age of reason in England and
France. And at length the date 1790 and Immanuel Kant's *Critique of Judgment:* which asserts that the end or effect of art is not
teaching certainly, and not, on the other hand, pleasure in anything
like a simple sensuous way—rather it is something apart, a feeling,
but precisely its own kind of feeling, the aesthetic. Art is autonomous—though related symbolically to the realm of moral values.

Between the time of Immanuel Kant and our own some complications in the purity of the aesthetic view have developed. Through
the romantic period and after, the poetic mind advanced pretty
steadily in its own autonomous way, toward a claim to be in itself
the creator of higher values—to be perhaps the only creator. Today
there is nothing that the literary theorist—at least in the British
and American-speaking world—will be more eager to repudiate
than any hint of moral or religious didacticism, any least intimation
that the poem is to measure its meaning or get its sanction from
any kind of authority more abstract or more overtly legislative than
itself. But on the other hand there has probably never been a
generation of teachers of literature less willing to admit any lack of
high seriousness, of implicit and embodied ethical content, even of
normative vision in the object of their study. Despite our reiterated
denials of didacticism, we live in an age, we help to make an age,
of momentous claims for poetry—claims the most momentous conceivable, as they advance more and more under the sanction of an
absolutely creative and autonomous visionary imagination. The
visionary imagination perforce repudiates all but the tautological
commitment to itself. And thus, especially when it assumes (as
now it begins to do) the form of what is called the "Tragic

Vision" (not "The Vision of Tragedy"), it is the newest version of the *Everlasting No*. Vision *per se* is the vision of itself. "Tragic Vision" is the nearly identical vision of "Absurdity." (War-weariness and war-horror, the developing mind and studies of a generation that came out of the Second War and has been living in expectation of the third may go far to explain the phenomenon, but will not justify it.) Anti-doctrine is of course no less a didactic energy than doctrine itself. It is the reverse of doctrine. No more than doctrine itself, can it be located or even approached by a dis-cussion of the relation between poetic form and poetic meaning. Anti-doctrine is actually asserted by the poems of several English romantic poets, and notably, it would appear, though it is difficult to be sure, by the "prophecies" of William Blake. The idea of it may be hence a part of these poems, though never their achieved result or expression. Any more than an acceptable statement of Christian doctrine is Milton's achieved expression in *Paradise Lost*, or a statement of Aristotelian ethics is the real business of Spenser's *Faerie Queene*. Today I believe no prizes are being given for even the best doctrinal interpretation of poems. (The homiletic or para-bolic interpretation of Shakespeare, for example, has hard going with the reviewer.) On the other hand, it you are willing to take a part in the exploitation of the neuroses, the misgivings, the anxieties, the infidelities of the age—if you have talents for the attitudes of Titanism, the graces needed by an impresario of the nuptials of Heaven and Hell, you are likely to find yourself in some sense rewarded. It is my own earnest conviction, and I believe it impor-tant for the critic who understands this to assert it at every oppor-tunity, that the reward will *not* consist in the achievement of a valid account of the relation between poetic form and poetic mean-ing.

ROBERT FROST

Education by Poetry: A Meditative Monologue[1]

I am going to urge nothing in my talk. I am not an advocate. I am going to consider a matter, and commit a description. And I am going to describe other colleges than Amherst. Or, rather say all that is good can be taken as about Amherst; all that is bad will be about other colleges.

I know whole colleges where all American poetry is barred—whole colleges. I know whole colleges where all contemporary poetry is barred.

I once heard of a minister who turned his daughter—his poetry-writing daughter—out on the street to earn a living, because he said

1. An address given at Amherst College in 1930.

there should be no more books written; God wrote one book, and that was enough. (My friend George Russell, "Æ", has read no literature, he protests, since just before Chaucer.)

That all seems sufficiently safe, and you can say one thing for it. It takes the onus off the poetry of having to be used to teach children anything. It comes pretty hard on poetry, I sometimes think, what it has to bear in the teaching process.

Then I know whole colleges where, though they let in older poetry, they manage to bar all that is poetical in it by treating it as something other than poetry. It is not so hard to do that. Their reason I have often hunted for. It may be that these people act from a kind of modesty. Who are professors that they should attempt to deal with a thing as high and as fine as poetry? Who are *they?* There is a certain manly modesty in that.

That is the best general way of settling the problem; treat all poetry as if it were something else than poetry, as if it were syntax, language, science. Then you can even come down into the American and into the contemporary without any special risk.

There is another reason they have, and that is that they are, first and foremost in life, markers. They have the marking problem to consider. Now, I stand here a teacher of many years' experience and I have never complained of having had to mark. I had rather mark anyone for anything—for his looks, carriage, his ideas, his correctness, his exactness, anything you please—I would rather give him a mark in terms of letters, A, B, C, D, than have to use adjectives on him. We are all being marked by each other all the time, classified, ranked, put in our place, and I see no escape from that. I am no sentimentalist. You have got to mark, and you have got to mark, first of all, for accuracy, for correctness. But if I am going to give a mark, that is the least part of my marking. The hard part is the part beyond that, the part where the adventure begins.

One other way to rid the curriculum of the poetry nuisance has been considered. More merciful than the others it would neither abolish nor denature the poetry, but only turn it out to disport itself, with the plays and games—in no wise discredited, though given no credit for. Any one who liked to teach poetically could take his subject, whether English, Latin, Greek or French, out into the no-where along with the poetry. One side of a sharp line would be left to the rigorous and righteous; the other side would be assigned to the flowery where they would know what could be expected of them. Grade marks where more easily given, of course, in the courses concentrating on correctness and exactness as the only forms of honesty recognized by plain people; a general indefinite mark of X in the courses that scatter brains over taste and opinion. On inquiry I have found no teacher willing to take position on either side of the line, either among the rigors or among the flowers. No one is willing to admit that his discipline is not partly in exactness. No one is willing to admit that his discipline is not partly in taste and enthusiasm.

How shall a man go through college without having been marked for taste and judgment? What will become of him? What will his end be? He will have to take continuation courses for college graduates. He will have to go to night schools. They are having night schools now, you know, for college graduates. Why? Because they have not been educated enough to find their way around in contemporary literature. They don't know what they may safely like in the libraries and galleries. They don't know how to judge an editorial when they see one. They don't know how to judge a political campaign. They don't know when they are being fooled by a metaphor, an analogy, a parable. And metaphor is, of course, what we are talking about. Education by poetry is education by metaphor.

Suppose we stop short of imagination, initiative, enthusiasm, inspiration and originality—dread words. Suppose we don't mark in such things at all. There are still two minimal things, that we have got to take care of, taste and judgment. Americans are supposed to have more judgment than taste, but taste is there to be dealt with. That is what poetry, the only art in the colleges of arts, is there for. I for my part would not be afraid to go in for enthusiasm. There is the enthusiasm like a blinding light, or the enthusiasm of the deafening shout, the crude enthusiasm that you get uneducated by poetry, outside of poetry. It is exemplified in what I might call "sunset raving." You look westward toward the sunset, or if you get up early enough, eastward toward the sunrise, and you rave. It is oh's and ah's with you and no more.

But the enthusiasm I mean is taken through the prism of the intellect and spread on the screen in a color, all the way from hyperbole at one end—or overstatement, at one end—to understatement at the other end. It is a long strip of dark lines and many colors. Such enthusiasm is one object of all teaching in poetry. I heard wonderful things said about Virgil yesterday, and many of them seemed to me crude enthusiasm, more like a deafening shout, many of them. But one speech had range, something of overstatement, something of statement, and something of understatement. It had all the colors of an enthusiasm passed through an idea.

I would be willing to throw away everything else but that: enthusiasm tamed by metaphor. Let me rest the case there. Enthusiasm tamed to metaphor, tamed to that much of it. I do not think anybody ever knows the discreet use of metaphor, his own and other people's, the discreet handling of metaphor, unless he has been properly educated in poetry.

Poetry begins in trivial metaphors, petty metaphors, "grace" metaphors, and goes on to the profoundest thinking that we have. Poetry provides the one permissible way of saying one thing and meaning another. People say, "Why don't you say what you mean?"

We never do that, do we, being all of us too much poets. We like to talk in parables and in hints and in indirections—whether from diffidence or some other instinct.

I have wanted in late years to go further and further in making metaphor the whole of thinking. I find some one now and then to agree with me that all thinking, except mathematical thinking, is metaphorical, or all thinking except scientific thinking. The mathematical might be difficult for me to bring in, but the scientific is easy enough.

Once on a time all the Greeks were busy telling each other what the All was—or was like unto. All was three elements, air, earth, and water (we once thought it was ninety elements; now we think it is only one). All was substance, said another. All was change, said a third. But best and most fruitful was Pythagoras' comparison of the universe with number. Number of what? Number of feet, pounds, and seconds was the answer, and we had science and all that has followed in science. The metaphor has held and held, breaking down only when it came to the spiritual and psychological or the out of the way places of the physical.

The other day we had a visitor here, a noted scientist, whose latest word to the world has been that the more accurately you know where a thing is, the less accurately you are able to state how fast it is moving. You can see why that would be so, without going back to Zeno's problem of the arrow's flight. In carrying numbers into the realm of space and at the same time into the realm of time you are mixing metaphors, that is all, and you are in trouble. They won't mix. The two don't go together.

Let's take two or three more of the metaphors now in use to live by. I have just spoken of one of the new ones, a charming mixed metaphor right in the realm of higher mathematics and higher physics: that the more accurately you state where a thing is, the less accurately you will be able to tell how fast it is moving. And, of course everything is moving. Everything is an event now. Another metaphor. A thing, they say, is an event. Do you believe it is? Not quite. I believe it is almost an event. But I like the comparison of a thing with an event.

I notice another from the same quarter. "In the neighborhood of matter space is something like curved." Isn't that a good one! It seems to me that that is simply and utterly charming—to say that space is something like curved in the neighborhood of matter. "Something like."

Another amusing one is from—what is the book?—I can't say it now; but here is the metaphor. Its aim is to restore you to your ideas of free will. It wants to give you back your freedom of will. All right, here it is on a platter. You know that you can't tell by name what persons in a certain class will be dead ten years after graduation, but you can tell actuarially how many will be dead. Now, just so this scientist says of the particles of matter flying at a screen, striking a screen; you can't tell what individual particles will come, but you can say in general that a certain number will strike in a given time. It shows, you see, that the individual particle can come freely. I asked Bohr about that particularly, and he said, "Yes, it is so. It can come when it wills and as it wills; and the action of the individual particle is unpredictable. But it is not so of the action of the mass. There you can predict." He says, "That gives the individual atom its freedom, but the mass its necessity."

Another metaphor that has interested us in our time and has done all our thinking for us is the metaphor of evolution. Never mind going into the Latin word. The metaphor is simply the metaphor of the growing plant or of the growing thing. And somebody very brilliantly, quite a while ago, said that the whole universe, the whole of everything, was like unto a growing thing. That is all. I know the metaphor will break down at some point, but it has not failed everywhere. It is a very brilliant metaphor, I acknowledge, though I myself get too tired of the kind of essay that talks about the evolution of candy, we will say, or the evolution of elevators—the evolution of this, that, and the other. Everything is evolution. I emancipate myself by simply saying that I didn't get up the metaphor and so am not much interested in it.

What I am pointing out is that unless you are at home in the metaphor, unless you have had your proper poetical education in the metaphor, you are not safe anywhere. Because you are not at ease with figurative values: you don't know the metaphor in its strength and its weakness. You don't know how far you may expect to ride it and when it may break down with you. You are not safe in science; you are not safe in history. In history, for instance—to show that is the same in history as elsewhere—I heard somebody say yesterday that Aeneas was to be likened unto (those words, "likened unto"!) George Washington. He was that type of national hero, the middle-class man, not thinking of being a hero at all, bent on building the future, bent on his children, his descendants. A good metaphor, as far as it goes, and you must know how far. And then he added that Odysseus should be likened unto Theodore Roosevelt. I don't think that is so good. Someone visiting Gibbon at the point of death, said he was the same Gibbon as of old; still at his parallels.

Take the way we have been led into our present position morally, the world over. It is by a sort of metaphorical gradient. There is a kind of thinking—to speak metaphorically—there is a kind of thinking you might say was endemic in the brothel. It is always there. And every now and then in some mysterious way it becomes epidemic in the world. And how does it do so? By using all the good words that virtue has invented to maintain virtue. It uses honesty, first—frankness, sincerity—those words; picks them up, uses them. "In the name of honesty, let us see what we are." You know. And then it picks up the word joy. "Let us in the name of joy, which is the enemy of our ancestors, the Puritans . . . Let us in the name of joy, which is the enemy of the kill-joy Puritan . . . " You see. "Let us," and so on. And then, "In the name of health . . . " Health is another good word. And that is the metaphor Freudianism trades on, mental health. And the first thing we know, it has us all in up to the top knot. I suppose we may blame the artists a good deal, because they are great people to spread by metaphor. The stage too—the stage is always a good intermediary between the two worlds, the under and the upper, if I may say so without personal prejudice to the stage.

In all this, I have only been saying that the devil can quote Scripture, which simply means that the good words you have lying around the devil can use for his purposes as well as anybody else. Never mind about my morality. I am not here to urge anything. I don't care whether the world is good or bad—not on any particular day.

Let me ask you to watch a metaphor breaking down here before you.

Somebody said to me a little while ago, "It is easy enough for me to think of the universe as a machine, as a mechanism."

I said, "You mean the universe is like a machine?"

He said, "No. I think it is one . . .Well, it is like . . ."

"I think you mean the universe is like a machine."

"All right. Let it go at that."

I asked him, "Did you ever see a machine without a pedal for the foot, or a lever for the hand, or a button for the finger?"

He said "No—no."

I said, "All right. Is the universe like that?"

And he said, "No. I mean it is like a machine, only . . ."

". . . it is different from a machine," I said.

He wanted to go just that far with that metaphor and no further. And so do we all. All metaphor breaks down somewhere. That is the beauty of it. It is touch and go with the metaphor, and until you have lived with it long enough you don't know when it is going. You don't know how much you can get out of it and when it will cease to yield. It is a very living thing. It is as life itself.

I have heard this ever since I can remember, and ever since I have taught: the teacher must teach the pupil to think. I saw a teacher once going around in a great school and snapping pupils' heads with thumb and finger and saying, "Think." That was when thinking was becoming the fashion. The fashion hasn't yet quite gone out.

We still ask boys in college to think, as in the nineties, but we seldom tell them what thinking means; we seldom tell them it is just putting this and that together; it is saying one thing in terms of another. To tell them is to set their feet on the first rung of a ladder the top of which sticks through the sky.

Greatest of all attempts to say one thing in terms of another is the philosophical attempt to say matter in terms of spirit, or spirit in terms of matter, to make the final unity. That is the greatest attempt that ever failed. We stop just short there. But it is the height of poetry, the height of all thinking, the height of all poetic thinking, that attempt to say matter in terms of spirit and spirit in terms of matter. It is wrong to call anybody a materialist simply because he tries to say spirit in terms of matter, as if that were a sin. Materialism is not the attempt to say all in terms of matter. The only materialist —be he poet, teacher, scientist, politician, or statesman—is the man who gets lost in his material without a gathering metaphor to throw it into shape and order. He is the lost soul.

We ask people to think, and we don't show them what thinking is. Somebody says we don't need to show them how to think; bye and bye they will think. We will give them the forms of sentences and, if they have any ideas, then they will know how to write them. But that is preposterous. All there is to writing is having ideas. To learn to write is to learn to have ideas.

The first little metaphor . . . Take some of the trivial ones. I would rather have trivial ones of my own to live by than the big ones of other people.

I remember a boy saying, "He is the kind of person that wounds with his shield." That may be a slender one, of course. It goes a good way in character description. It has poetic grace. "He is the kind that wounds with his shield."

The shield reminds me—just to linger a minute—the shield reminds me of the inverted shield spoken of in one of the books of the *Odyssey*, the book that tells about the longest swim on record. I forget how long it lasted—several days, was it?—but at last as Odysseus came near the coast of Phoenicia, he saw it on the horizon "like an inverted shield."

There is a better metaphor in the same book. In the end Odysseus comes ashore and crawls up the beach to spend the night under a double olive tree, and it says, as in a lonely farmhouse where it is hard to get fire—I am not quoting exactly—where it is hard to start the fire again if it goes out, they cover the seeds of fire with ashes to preserve it for the night, so Odysseus covered himself with the leaves around him and went to sleep. There you have something that gives you character, something of Odysseus himself. "Seeds of fire." So Odysseus covered the seeds of fire in himself. You get the greatness of his nature.

But these are slighter metaphors than the ones we live by. They have their charm, their passing charm. They are as it were the first steps toward the great thoughts, grave thoughts, thoughts lasting to the end.

The metaphor whose manage we are best taught in poetry—that is all there is of thinking. It may not seem far for the mind to go but it is the mind's furthest. The richest accumulation of the ages is the noble metaphors we have rolled up.

I want to add one thing more that the experience of poetry is to anyone who comes close to poetry. There are two ways of coming close to poetry. One is by writing poetry. And some people think I want people to write poetry, but I don't; that is, I don't necessarily. I only want people to write poetry if they want to write poetry. I have never encouraged anybody to write poetry that did not want to write it, and I have not always encouraged those who did want to write it. That ought to be one's own funeral. It is a hard, hard life, as they say.

(I have just been to a city in the West, a city full of poets, a city they have made safe for poets. The whole city is so lovely that you do not have to write it up to make it poetry; it is ready-made for you. But, I don't know—the poetry written in that city might not seem like poetry if read outside of the city. It would be like the jokes made when you were drunk; you have to get drunk again to appreciate them.)

But as I say, there is another way to come close to poetry, fortunately, and that is in the reading of it, not as linguistics, not as history, not as anything but poetry. It is one of the hard things for a teacher to know how close a man has come in reading poetry. How do I know whether a man has come close to Keats in reading Keats? It is hard for me to know. I have lived with some boys a whole year over some of the poets and I have not felt sure whether they have come near what it was all about. One remark sometimes told me. One remark was their mark for the year; had to be—it was all I got that told me what I wanted to know. And that is enough, if it was the right remark, if it came close enough. I think a man might make twenty fool remarks if he made one good one some time in the year. His mark would depend on that good remark.

The closeness—everything depends on the closeness with which you come, and you ought to be marked for the closeness, for nothing else. And that will have to be estimated by chance remarks, not by question and answer. It is only by accident that you know some day how near a person has come.

The person who gets close enough to poetry, he is going to know more about the word *belief* than anybody else knows, even in religion nowadays. There are two or three places where we know belief outside of religion. One of them is at the age of fifteen to twenty, in our self-belief. A young man knows more about himself than he is able to prove to anybody. He has no knowledge that anybody else will accept as knowledge. In his foreknowledge he has something that is going to believe itself into fulfilment, into acceptance.

There is another belief like that, the belief in someone else, a relationship of two that is going to be believed into fulfilment. That is what we are talking about in our novels, the belief of love. And disillusionment that the novels are full of is simply the disillusionment from disappointment in that belief. That belief can fail, of course.

Then there is a literary belief. Every time a poem is written, every time a short story is written, it is written not by cunning, but by belief. The beauty, the something, the little charm of the thing to be, is more felt than known. There is a common jest, one that always annoys me, on the writers, that they write the last end first, and then work up to it; that they lay a train toward one sentence that they think is pretty nice and have all fixed up to set like a trap to close with. No, it should not be that way at all. No one who has ever come close to the arts has failed to see the difference between things written that way, with cunning and device, and the kind that are believed into existence, that begin in something more felt than known. This you can realize quite as well—not quite as well, perhaps, but nearly as well—in reading as you can in writing. I would undertake to separate short stories on that principle; stories that have been believed into existence and stories that have been cunningly devised. And I could separate the poems still more easily.

Now I think—I happen to think—that those three beliefs that I speak of, the self-belief, the love-belief, and the art-belief, are all closely related to the God-belief, that the belief in God is a relationship you enter into with Him to bring about the future.

There is a national belief like that, too. One feels it. I have been where I came near getting up and walking out on the people who thought that they had to talk against nations, against nationalism, in order to curry favor with internationalism. Their metaphors are all mixed up. They think that because a Frenchman and an American and an Englishman can all sit down on the same platform and receive honors together, it must be that there is no such thing as nations. That kind of bad thinking springs from a source we all know. I should want to say to anyone like that: "Look! First I want to be a person. And I want you to be a person, and then we can be as interpersonal as you please. We can pull each other's noses—do all sorts of things. But, first of all, you have got to have the personality. First of all, you have got to have the nations and then they can be as international as they please with each other."

I should like to use another metaphor on them. I want my palette, if I am a painter, I want my palette on my thumb or on my chair, all clean, pure, separate colors. Then I will do the mixing on the canvas. The canvas is where the work of art is, where we make the conquest. But we want the nations all separate, pure, distinct, things as separate as we can make them; and then in our thoughts, in our arts, and so on, we can do what we please about it.

But I go back. There are four beliefs that I know more about from having lived with poetry. One is the personal belief, which is a knowledge that you don't want to tell other people about because you cannot prove that you know. You are saying nothing about it till you see. The love belief, just the same, has that same shyness. It knows it cannot tell; only the outcome can tell. And the national belief we enter into socially with each other, all together, party of the first part, party of the second part, we enter into that to bring the future of the country. We cannot tell some people what it is we believe, partly, because they are too stupid to understand and partly because we are too proudly vague to explain. And anyway it has got to be fulfilled, and we are not talking until we know more, until we have something to show. And then the literary one in every work of art, not of cunning and craft, mind you, but of real art; that believing the thing into existence, saying as you go more than you even hoped you were going to be able to say, and coming with surprise to an end that you foreknew only with some sort of emotion. And then finally the relationship we enter into with God to believe the future in—to believe the hereafter in.

QUESTIONS

1. In what way does the subtitle describe this essay? Is it rambling? Is it unified?
2. How can the "poetry nuisance" be gotten out of the curriculum? Does Frost think it ought to stay in? Why?
3. What is meant by "enthusiasm passed through an idea" and "enthusiasm tamed to metaphor" (p. 518)? What sort of metaphors does Frost use in those phrases, and what do they imply?
4. What does Frost mean when he says "unless you have had your proper poetical education in the metaphor, you are not safe anywhere" (p. 520)? Indicate some of the metaphors Frost examines in this essay. From what fields are they drawn? What does he say about each? Nominate some further metaphors—from politics, science, sociology, or anything else—and analyze them. To what extent are they useful? Do they have a breaking point? How might they mislead beyond the breaking point?
5. Frost admires a speech that has "range, something of overstatement, something of statement, and something of understatement." Is this spectrum visible in Frost's own speech? Show where and how.

WOLFGANG AMADEUS MOZART
A Letter[1]

When I am, as it were, completely myself, entirely alone, and of good cheer—say, travelling in a carriage, or walking after a good meal, or during the night when I cannot sleep; it is on such occasions that my ideas flow best and most abundantly. *Whence* and *how* they come, I know not; nor can I force them. Those ideas that please me I retain in memory, and am accustomed, as I have been told, to hum them to myself. If I continue in this way, it soon occurs to me how I may turn this or that morsel to account, so as to make a good dish of it, that is to say, agreeably to the rules of counterpoint, to the peculiarities of the various instruments, etc.

All this fires my soul, and, provided I am not disturbed, my subject enlarges itself, becomes methodised and defined, and the whole, though it be long, stands almost complete and finished in my mind, so that I can survey it, like a fine picture or a beautiful statue, at a glance. Nor do I hear in my imagination the parts *successively*, but I hear them, as it were, all at once (*gleich alles zusammen*). What a delight this is I cannot tell! All this inventing, this producing, takes place in a pleasing lively dream. Still the actual hearing of the *tout ensemble* is after all the best. What has been thus produced I do not easily forget, and this is perhaps the best gift I have my Divine Maker to thank for.

When I proceed to write down my ideas, I take out of the bag of my memory, if I may use that phrase, what has been previously collected into it in the way I have mentioned. For this reason the committing to paper is done quickly enough, for everything is, as I said before, already finished; and it rarely differs on paper from what it was in my imagination. At this occupation I can therefore suffer myself to be disturbed; for whatever may be going on around me, I write, and even talk, but only of fowls and geese, or of Gretel or Bärbel, or some such matters. But why my productions take from my hand that particular form and style that makes them *Mozartish*, and different from the works of other composers, is probably owing to the same cause which renders my nose so large or so aquiline, or, in short, makes it Mozart's, and different from those of other people. For I really do not study or aim at any originality.

---

1. The authenticity of this letter remains in doubt.

RALPH ELLISON
Living with Music

In those days it was either live with music or die with noise, and we chose rather desperately to live. In the process our apartment—what with its booby-trappings of audio equipment, wires, discs and tapes—came to resemble the Collier mansion,[1] but that was later. First there was the neighborhood, assorted drunks and a singer.

We were living at the time in a tiny ground-floor-rear apartment in which I was also trying to write. I say "trying" advisedly. To our right, separated by a thin wall, was a small restaurant with a juke box the size of the Roxy.[2] To our left, a night-employed swing enthusiast who took his lullaby music so loud that every morning promptly at nine Basie's[3] brasses started blasting my typewriter off its stand. Our living room looked out across a small back yard to a rough stone wall to an apartment building which, towering above, caught every passing thoroughfare sound and rifled it straight down to me. There were also howling cats and barking dogs, none capable of music worth living with, so we'll pass them by.

But the court behind the wall, which on the far side came knee-high to a short Iroquois, was a forum for various singing and/or preaching drunks who wandered back from the corner bar. From these you sometimes heard a fair barbershop style "Bill Bailey," free-wheeling versions of "The Bastard King of England," the saga of Uncle Bud, or a deeply felt rendition of Leroy Carr's "How Long Blues." The preaching drunks took on any topic that came to mind: current events, the fate of the long-sunk *Titanic* or the relative merits of the Giants and the Dodgers. Naturally there was great argument and occasional fighting—none of it fatal but all of it loud.

I shouldn't complain, however, for these were rather entertaining drunks, who like the birds appeared in the spring and left with the first fall cold. A more dedicated fellow was there all the time, day and night, come rain, come shine. Up on the corner lived a drunk of legend, a true phenomenon, who could surely have qualified as the king of all the world's winos—not excluding the French. He was neither poetic like the others nor ambitious like the singer (to whom we'll presently come) but his drinking bouts were truly awe-inspiring and he was not without his sensitivity. In the throes of his

---

1. The home of two wealthy recluse brothers, packed with newspapers and junk.

2. A New York theater and music hall.

passion he would shout to the whole wide world one concise command, "Shut up!" Which was disconcerting enough to all who heard (except, perhaps, the singer), but such were the labyrinthine acoustics of courtyards and areaways that he seemed to direct his command at me. The writer's block which this produced is indescribable. On one heroic occasion he yelled his obsessive command without one interruption longer than necessary to take another drink (and with no appreciable loss of volume, penetration or authority) for three long summer days and nights, and shortly afterwards he died. Just how many lines of agitated prose he cost me I'll never know, but in all that chaos of sound I sympathized with his obsession, for I, too, hungered and thirsted for quiet. Nor did he inspire me to a painful identification, and for that I was thankful. Identification, after all, involves feelings of guilt and responsibility, and since I could hardly hear my own typewriter keys I felt in no way accountable for his condition. We were simply fellow victims of the madding crowd. May he rest in peace.

No, these more involved feelings were aroused by a more intimate source of noise, one that got beneath the skin and worked into the very structure of one's consciousness—like the "fate" motif in Beethoven's Fifth or the knocking-at-the-gates scene in *Macbeth*. For at the top of our pyramid of noise there was a singer who lived directly above us; you might say we had a singer on our ceiling.

Now, I had learned from the jazz musicians I had known as a boy in Oklahoma City something of the discipline and devotion to his art required of the artist. Hence I knew something of what the singer faced. These jazzmen, many of them now world-famous, lived for and with music intensely. Their driving motivation was neither money nor fame, but the will to achieve the most eloquent expression of idea-emotions through the technical mastery of their instruments (which, incidentally, some of them wore as a priest wears the cross) and the give and take, the subtle rhythmical shaping and blending of idea, tone and imagination demanded of group improvisation. The delicate balance struck between strong individual personality and the group during those early jam sessions was a marvel of social organization. I had learned too that the end of all this discipline and technical mastery was the desire to express an affirmative way of life through its musical tradition and that this tradition insisted that each artist achieve his creativity within its frame. He must learn the best of the past, and add to it his personal vision. Life could be harsh, loud and wrong if it wished, but they lived it fully, and when they expressed their attitude toward the world it was with a fluid style that reduced the chaos of living to form.

The objectives of these jazzmen were not at all those of the singer on our ceiling, but though a purist committed to the mastery of the *bel canto* style, German *lieder,* modern French art songs and a few American slave songs sung as if *bel canto,* she was intensely devoted to her art. From morning to night she vocalized, regardless of the condition of her voice, the weather or my screaming nerves. There were times when her notes, sifting through her floor and my ceiling, bouncing down the walls and ricocheting off the building in the rear, whistled like tenpenny nails, buzzed like a saw, wheezed like the asthma of a Hercules, trumpeted like an enraged African elephant—and the squeaky pedal of her piano rested plumb center above my typing chair. After a year of non-co-operation from the neighbor on my left I became desperate enough to cool down the hot blast of his phonograph by calling the cops, but the singer presented a serious ethical problem: Could I, an aspiring artist, complain against the hard work and devotion to craft of another aspiring artist?

Then there was my sense of guilt. Each time I prepared to shatter the ceiling in protest I was restrained by the knowledge that I,. too, during my boyhood, had tried to master a musical instrument and to the great distress of my neighbors—perhaps even greater than that which I now suffered. For while our singer was concerned basically with a single tradition and style, I had been caught actively between two: that of the Negro folk music, both sacred and profane, slave song and jazz, and that of Western classical music. It was most confusing; the folk tradition demanded that I play what I heard and felt around me, while those who were seeking to teach the classical tradition in the schools insisted that I play strictly according to the book and express that which I was *supposed* to feel. This sometimes led to heated clashes of wills. Once during a third-grade music appreciation class a friend of mine insisted that it was a large green snake he saw swimming down a quiet brook instead of the snowy bird the teacher felt that Saint-Saëns' *Carnival of the Animals* should evoke. The rest of us sat there and lied like little black, brown and yellow Trojans about that swan, but our stalwart classmate held firm to his snake. In the end he got himself spanked and reduced the teacher to tears, but truth, reality and our environment were redeemed. For we were all familiar with snakes, while a swan was simply something the Ugly Duckling of the story grew up to be. Fortunately some of us grew up with a genuine appreciation of classical music *despite* such teaching methods. But as an aspiring trumpeter I was to wallow in sin for years before being awakened to guilt by our singer.

Caught mid-range between my two traditions, where one attitude often clashed with the other and one technique of playing was by the other opposed, I caused whole blocks of people to suffer.

Indeed, I terrorized a good part of an entire city section. During summer vacation I blew sustained tones out of the window for hours, usually starting—especially on Sunday mornings—before breakfast. I sputtered whole days through M. Arban's (he's the great authority on the instrument) double- and triple-tonguing exercises—with an effect like that of a jackass hiccupping off a big meal of briars. During school-term mornings I practiced a truly exhibitionist "Reveille" before leaving for school, and in the evening I generously gave the ever-listening world a long, slow version of "Taps," ineptly played but throbbing with what I in my adolescent vagueness felt was a romantic sadness. For it was farewell to day and a love song to life and a peace-be-with-you to all the dead and dying.

On hot summer afternoons I tormented the ears of all not blessedly deaf with imitations of the latest hot solos of Hot Lips Paige (then a local hero), the leaping right hand of Earl "Fatha" Hines, or the rowdy poetic flights of Louis Armstrong. Naturally I rehearsed also such school-band standbys as the *Light Cavalry* Overture, Sousa's "Stars and Stripes Forever," the *William Tell* Overture, and "Tiger Rag." (Not even an after-school job as office boy to a dentist could stop my efforts. Frequently, by way of encouraging my development in the proper cultural direction, the dentist asked me proudly to render Schubert's *Serenade* for some poor devil with his jaw propped open in the dental chair. When the drill got going, or the forceps bit deep, I blew real strong.)

Sometimes, inspired by the even then considerable virtuosity of the late Charlie Christian (who during our school days played marvelous riffs on a cigar box banjo), I'd give whole summer afternoons and the evening hours after heavy suppers of black-eyed peas and turnip greens, cracklin' bread and buttermilk, lemonade and sweet potato cobbler, to practicing hard-driving blues. Such food oversupplied me with bursting energy, and from listening to Ma Rainey, Ida Cox and Clara Smith, who made regular appearances in our town, I knew exactly how I wanted my horn to sound. But in the effort to make it do so (I was no embryo Joe Smith or Tricky Sam Nanton) I sustained the curses of both Christian and infidel—along with the encouragement of those more sympathetic citizens who understood the profound satisfaction to be found in expressing oneself in the blues.

Despite those who complained and cried to heaven for Gabriel to blow a chorus so heavenly sweet and so hellishly hot that I'd forever put down my horn, there were more tolerant ones who were willing to pay in present pain for future pride.

For who knew what skinny kid with his chops wrapped around a trumpet mouthpiece and a faraway look in his eyes might become the next Armstrong? Yes, and send you, at some big dance a few years hence, into an ecstasy of rhythm and memory and brassy

affirmation of the goodness of being alive and part of the community? Someone had to: for it was part of the group tradition—
though that was not how they said it.

"Let that boy blow," they'd say to the protesting ones. "He's got
to talk baby talk on that thing before he can preach on it. Next
thing you know he's liable to be up there with Duke Ellington.
Sure, plenty Oklahoma boys are up there with big bands. Son, let's
hear you try those "Trouble in Mind Blues." Now try and make it
sound like ole Ida Cox sings it."

And I'd draw in my breath and do Miss Cox great violence.

Thus the crimes and aspirations of my youth. It had been years
since I had played the trumpet or irritated a single ear with other
than the spoken or written word, but as far as my singing neighbor
was concerned I had to hold my peace. I was forced to listen, and
in listening I soon became involved to the point of identification. If
she sang badly I'd hear my own futility in the windy sound; if well,
I'd stare at my typewriter and despair that I should ever make my
prose so sing. She left me neither night nor day, this singer on our
ceiling, and as my writing languished I became more and more
upset. Thus one desperate morning I decided that since I seemed
doomed to live within a shrieking chaos I might as well contribute
my share; perhaps if I fought noise with noise I'd attain some small
peace. Then a miracle: I turned on my radio (an old Philco AM set
connected to a small Pilot FM tuner) and I heard the words

> *Art thou troubled?*
> *Music will calm thee ...*

I stopped as though struck by the voice of an angel. It was Kathleen
Ferrier, that loveliest of singers, giving voice to the aria from Han-
del's *Rodelinda*. The voice was so completely expressive of words
and music that I accepted it without question—what lover of the
vocal art could resist her?

Yet it was ironic, for after giving up my trumpet for the typewriter I had avoided too close a contact with the very art which she
recommended as balm. For I had started music early and lived with
it daily, and when I broke I tried to break clean. Now in this magical moment all the old love, the old fascination with music superbly
rendered, flooded back. When she finished I realized that with such
music in my own apartment, the chaotic sounds from without and
above had sunk, if not into silence, then well below the level where
they mattered. Here was a way out. If I was to live and write in
that apartment, it would be only through the grace of music. I had
tuned in a Ferrier recital, and when it ended I rushed out for several
of her records, certain that now deliverance was mine.

But not yet. Between the hi-fi record and the ear, I learned, there was a new electronic world. In that realization our apartment was well on its way toward becoming an audio booby trap. It was 1949 and I rushed to the the Audio Fair. I have, I confess, as much gadget-resistance as the next American of my age, weight and slight income; but little did I dream of the test to which it would be put. I had hardly entered the fair before I heard David Sarser's and Mel Sprinkle's Musician's Amplifier, took a look at its schematic and, recalling a boyhood acquaintance with such matters, decided that I could build one. I did, several times before it measured within specifications. And still our system was lacking. Fortunately my wife shared my passion for music, so we went on to buy, piece by piece, a fine speaker system, a first-rate AM-FM tuner, a transcription turntable and a speaker cabinet. I built half a dozen or more preamplifiers and record compensators before finding a commercial one that satisfied my ear, and, finally, we acquired an arm, a magnetic cartridge and—glory of the house—a tape recorder. All this plunge into electronics, mind you, had as its simple end the enjoyment of recorded music as it was intended to be heard. I was obsessed with the idea of reproducing sound with such fidelity that even when using music as a defense behind which I could write, it would reach the unconscious levels of the mind with the least distortion. And it didn't come easily. There were wires and pieces of equipment all over the tiny apartment (I became a compulsive experimenter) and it was worth your life to move about without first taking careful bearings. Once we were almost crushed in our sleep by the tape machine, for which there was space only on a shelf at the head of our bed. But it was worth it.

For now when we played a recording on our system even the drunks on the wall could recognize its quality. I'm ashamed to admit, however, that I did not always restrict its use to the demands of pleasure or defense. Indeed, with such marvels of science at my control I lost my humility. My ethical consideration for the singer up above shriveled like a plant in too much sunlight. For instead of soothing, music seemed to release the beast in me. Now when jarred from my writer's reveries by some especially enthusiastic flourish of our singer, I'd rush to my music system with blood in my eyes and burst a few decibels in her direction. If she defied me with a few more pounds of pressure against her diaphragm, then a war of decibels was declared.

If, let us say, she were singing *"Depuis le Jour"* from *Louise,* I'd put on a tape of Bidu Sayão performing the same aria, and let the rafters ring. If it was some song by Mahler, I'd match her spitefully with Marian Anderson or Kathleen Ferrier; if she offended with something from *Der Rosenkavalier,* I'd attack her flank with Lotte Lehmann. If she brought me up from my desk with art songs by Ravel or Rachmaninoff, I'd defend myself with Maggie Teyte or

Jennie Tourel. If she polished a spiritual to a meaningless artiness I'd play Bessie Smith to remind her of the earth out of which we came. Once in a while I'd forget completely that I was supposed to be a gentleman and blast her with Strauss' *Zarathustra,* Bartók's *Concerto for Orchestra,* Ellington's "Flaming Sword," the famous crescendo from *The Pines of Rome,* or Satchmo scatting, "I'll be Glad When You're Dead" (you rascal you!). Oh, I was living with music with a sweet vengeance.

One might think that all this would have made me her most hated enemy, but not at all. When I met her on the stoop a few weeks after my rebellion, expecting her fully to slap my face, she astonished me by complimenting our music system. She even questioned me concerning the artist I had used against her. After that, on days when the acoustics were right, she'd stop singing until the piece was finished and then applaud—not always, I guessed, without a justifiable touch of sarcasm. And although I was now getting on with my writing, the unfairness of this business bore in upon me. Aware that I could not have withstood a similar comparison with literary artists of like caliber, I grew remorseful. I also came to admire the singer's courage and control, for she was neither intimidated into silence nor goaded into undisciplined screaming; she persevered, she marked the phrasing of the great singers I sent her way, she improved her style.

Better still, she vocalized more softly, and I, in turn, used music less and less as a weapon and more for its magic with mood and memory. After a while a simple twirl of the volume control up a few decibels and down again would bring a live-and-let-live reduction of her volume. We have long since moved from that apartment and that most interesting neighborhood and now the floors and walls of our present apartment are adequately thick and there is even a closet large enough to house the audio system; the only wire visible is that leading from the closet to the corner speaker system. Still we are indebted to the singer and the old environment for forcing us to discover one of the most deeply satisfying aspects of our living. Perhaps the enjoyment of music is always suffused with past experience; for me, at least, this is true.

It seems a long way and a long time from the glorious days of Oklahoma jazz dances, the jam sessions at Halley Richardson's place on Deep Second, from the phonographs shouting the blues in the back alleys I knew as a delivery boy, and from the days when watermelon men with voices like mellow bugles shouted their wares in time with the rhythm of their horses' hoofs and farther still from the washerwomen singing slave songs as they stirred sooty tubs in sunny yards; and a long time, too, from those intense, conflicting days when the school music program of Oklahoma City was tuning our earthy young ears to classical accents—with music appreciation classes and free musical instruments and basic instruction for any child who cared to learn and uniforms for all who made the band. There was a mistaken notion on the part of some of the teachers that classical music had nothing to do with the rhythms, relaxed or hectic, of daily living, and that one should crook the little finger when listening to such refined strains. And the blues and the spirituals—jazz—? they would have destroyed them and scattered the pieces. Nevertheless, we learned some of it, for in the United States when traditions are juxtaposed they tend, regardless of what we do to prevent it, irresistibly to merge. Thus musically at least each child in our town was an heir of all the ages. One learns by moving from the familiar to the unfamiliar, and while it might sound incongruous at first, the step from the spirituality of the spirituals to that of the Beethoven of the symphonies or the Bach of the chorales is not as vast as it seems. Nor is the romanticism of a Brahms or Chopin completely unrelated to that of Louis Armstrong. Those who know their native culture and love it unchauvinistically are never lost when encountering the unfamiliar.

Living with music today we find Mozart and Ellington, Kirsten Flagstad and Chippie Hill, William L. Dawson and Carl Orff all forming part of our regular fare. For all exalt life in rhythm and melody; all add to its significance. Perhaps in the swift change of American society in which the meanings of one's origin are so quickly lost, one of the chief values of living with music lies in its power to give us an orientation in time. In doing so, it gives significance to all those indefinable aspects of experience which nevertheless help to make us what we are. In the swift whirl of time music is a constant, reminding us of what we were and of that toward which we aspired. Art thou troubled? Music will not only calm, it will ennoble thee.

E. M. FORSTER

Not Listening to Music

Listening to music is such a muddle that one scarcely knows how to start describing it. The first point to get clear in my own case is that during the greater part of every performance I do not attend. The nice sounds make me think of something else. I wool-gather most of the time, and am surprised that others don't. Professional critics can listen to a piece as consistently and as steadily as if they were reading a chapter in a novel. This seems to me an amazing feat, and probably they only achieve it through intellectual training; that is to say, they find in the music the equivalent of a plot; they are following the ground bass or expecting the theme to re-enter in the dominant, and so on, and this keeps them on the rails. But I fly off every minute: after a bar or two I think how musical I am, or of something smart I might have said in conversation; or I wonder what the composer—dead a couple of centuries—can be feeling as the flames on the altar still flicker up; or how soon an H.E. bomb[1] would extinguish them. Not to mention more obvious distractions: the tilt of the soprano's chin or chins; the antics of the conductor, that impassioned beetle, especially when it is night time and he waves his shards; the affection of the pianist when he takes a top note with difficulty, as if he too were a soprano; the backs of the chairs; the bumps on the ceiling; the extreme physical ugliness of the audience. A classical audience is surely the plainest collection of people anywhere assembled for any common purpose; contributing my quota, I have the right to point this out. Compare us with a gang of navvies or with an office staff, and you will be appalled. This, too, distracts me.

What do I hear during the intervals when I do attend? Two sorts of music. They melt into each other all the time, and are not easy to christen, but I will call one of them "music that reminds me of something," and the other "music itself." I used to be very fond of music that reminded me of something, and especially fond of Wagner. With Wagner I always knew where I was; he never let the fancy roam; he ordained that one phrase should recall the ring, another the sword, another the blameless fool and so on; he was as precise in his indications as an oriental dancer. Since he is a great poet, that did not matter, but I accepted his leitmotiv system much too reverently and forced it onto other composers whom it did not suit, such as Beethoven and Franck. I thought that music must be the better for having a meaning. I think so still, but am less clear as to what "a meaning" is. In those days it was either a non-musical object, such as a sword or a blameless fool, or a non-musical emotion, such as fear, lust, or resignation. When music reminded me of something which was not music, I supposed it was getting me somewhere. "How like Monet!" I thought when listening to Debussy, and "How like Debussy!" when looking at Monet. I translated sounds into colours, saw the piccolo as apple-green, and the trumpets as scarlet. The arts were to be enriched by taking in one another's washing.

I still listen to some music this way. For instance, the slow start of Beethoven's Seventh Symphony invokes a gray-green tapestry of hunting scenes, and the slow movement of his Fourth Piano Concerto (the dialogue between piano and orchestra) reminds me of the dialogue between Orpheus and the Furies in Gluck. The climax of the first movement of the Appassionata (the "più allegro") seems to me sexual, although I can detect no sex in the Kreutzer, nor have I come across anyone who could, except Tolstoy. That disappointing

1. A high explosive.

work, Brahms' Violin Concerto, promises me clear skies at the opening, and only when the violin has squealed up in the air for page after page is the promise falsified. Wolf's "Ganymed" does give me sky—stratosphere beyond stratosphere. In these cases and in many others music reminds me of something non-musical, and I fancy that to do so is part of its job. Only a purist would condemn all visual parallels, all emotional labelings, all programs.

Yet there is a danger. Music that reminds does open the door to that imp of the concert hall, inattention. To think of a gray-green tapestry is not very different from thinking of the backs of the chairs. We gather a superior wool from it, still we do wool-gather, and the sounds slip by blurred. The sounds! It is for them that we come, and the closer we can get up against them the better. So I do prefer "music itself" and listen to it and for it as far as possible. In this connection, I will try to analyze a mishap that has recently overtaken the Coriolanus Overture. I used to listen to the Coriolanus for "itself," conscious when it passed of something important and agitating, but not defining further. Now I learn that Wagner, endorsed by Sir Donald Tovey, has provided it with a Program: the opening bars indicate the hero's decision to destroy the Volscii, then a sweet tune for female influence, then the dotted-quaver-restlessness of indecision. This seems indisputable, and there is no doubt that this was, or was almost, Beethoven's intention. All the same, I have lost my Coriolanus. Its largeness and freedom have gone. The exquisite sounds have been hardened like a road that has been tarred for traffic. One has to go somewhere down them, and to pass through the same domestic crisis to the same military impasse, each time the overture is played.

Music is so very queer that an amateur is bound to get muddled when writing about it. It seems to be more "real" than anything, and to survive when the rest of civilization decays. In these days I am always thinking of it with relief. It can never be ruined or nationalized. So that the music which is untrammeled and untainted by reference is obviously the best sort of music to listen to; we get nearer the center of reality. Yet though it is untainted, it is never abstract; it is not like mathematics, even when it uses them. The Goldberg Variations, the last Beethoven Sonata, the Franck Quartet, the Schumann Piano Quintet and the Fourth Symphonies of Tchaikovsky and of Brahms certainly have a message. Though what on earth is it? I shall get tied up trying to say. There's an insistence in music—expressed largely through rhythm; there's a sense that it is trying to push across at us something which is neither an esthetic pattern nor a sermon. That's what I listen for specially.

So music that is itself seems on the whole better than music that reminds. And now to end with an important point: my own performances upon the piano. These grow worse yearly, but never will

I give them up. For one thing, they compel me to attend—no wool-gathering or thinking myself clever here—and they drain off all non-musical matter. For another thing, they teach me a little about construction. I see what becomes of a phrase, how it is transformed or returned, sometimes bottom upward, and get some notion of the relation of keys. Playing Beethoven, as I generally do, I grow familiar with his tricks, his impatience, his sudden softnesses, his dropping of a tragic theme one semitone, his love, when tragic, for the key of C minor, and his aversion to the key of B major. This gives me a physical approach to Beethoven which cannot be gained through the slough of "appreciation." Even when people play as badly as I do, they should continue: it will help them to listen.

QUESTIONS

1. Forster carries his discussion of listening to music through three stages. What are they? Where in the essay is each introduced? Where does Forster make it clear that the first two stages resemble each other?
2. What devices of language and attitude does Forster use to establish an informal, relaxed approach to his topic? Does he appear to be addressing himself to a particular kind of audience? Explain.
3. What is "music itself"? By what means does Forster seek to define it?
4. Early in the essay Forster says that it seems to him an "amazing feat" that professional critics can listen to music "as consistently and steadily as if they were reading a chapter in a novel." What does this indicate as to Forster's view of the novel? Is he being ironical?
5. What does playing the piano teach Forster about listening to music? The closing paragraph, on playing and listening, suggests a similar relationship between writing and reading. Following Forster's strategy of organization, write a brief essay on "Not Reading a Novel," "Not Looking at Pictures," "Not Going to a Lecture," or "Not Studying an Assignment."

KENNETH CLARK

The Blot and the Diagram

I have been told to "look down from a high place over the whole extensive landscape of modern art." We all know how tempting high places can be, and how dangerous. I usually avoid them myself. But if I must do as I am told, I shall try to find out why modern art has taken its peculiar form, and to guess how long that form will continue.

I shall begin with Leonardo da Vinci, because although all processes are gradual, he does represent one clearly marked turning point in the history of art. Before that time, the painters intentions were quite simple; they were first of all to tell a story, secondly to make the invisible visible, and thirdly to turn a plain surface into a decorated surface. Those are all very ancient aims, going back to the earliest civilizations, or beyond; and for three hundred years painters had been instructed how to carry them out by means of a workshop tradition. Of course, there had been breaks in that tradition—in the fourth century, maybe, and towards the end of the seventh century; but broadly speaking, the artist learnt what he could about the technique of art from his master in his workshop, and then set up shop on his own and tried to do better.

As is well known, Leonardo had a different view of art. He thought that it involved both science and the pursuit of some peculiar attribute called beauty or grace. He was, by inclination, a scientist: he wanted to find out how things worked, and he believed that this knowledge could be stated mathematically. He said "Let no one who is not a mathematician read my works," and he tried to relate this belief in measurement to his belief in beauty. This involved him in two rather different lines of thought, one concerned with magic—the magic of numbers—the other with science. Ever since Pythagoras had discovered that the musical scale could be stated mathematically, by means of the length of the strings, etc., and so had thrown a bridge between intellectual analysis and sensory perception, thinkers on art had felt that it should be possible to do the same for painting. I must say that their effort had not been very rewarding; the modulus, or golden section, and the logarithmic spiral of shells are practically the only undisputed results. But Leonardo lived at a time when it was still possible to hope great things from perspective, which should not only define space, but order it harmoniously; and he also inherited a belief that ideal mathematical combinations could be derived from the proportions of the human body. This line of thought may be called the *mystique* of measurement. The other line may be called *the use* of measurement. Leonardo wished to state mathematically various facts related to the act of seeing. How do we see light passing over a sphere? What happens when objects make themselves perceptible on our retina? Both these lines of thought involved him in drawing diagrams and taking measurements, and for this reason were closely related in his mind. No painter except perhaps Piero della Francesca has tried more strenuously to find a mathematical statement of art, nor has had a greater equipment for doing so.

But Leonardo was also a man of powerful and disturbing imagination. In his notebooks, side by side with his attempts to achieve *order* by mathematics, are drawings and descriptions of the most violent scenes of *disorder* which the human mind can conceive—battles, deluges, eruptions. And he included in his treatise on painting advice on how to develop this side of the artistic faculty also. The passages in which he does so have often been quoted, but they are so incredibly foreign to the whole Renaissance idea of art, although related to a remark in Pliny,[1] that each time I read them, they give me a fresh surprise. I will, therefore, quote them again.

> I shall not refrain from including among these precepts a new and specu-lative idea, which although it may seem trivial and almost laughable, is none the less of great value in quickening the spirit of invention. It is this: that you should look at certain walls stained with damp or at stones of un-even color. If you have to invent some setting you will be able to see in these the likeness of divine landscapes, adorned with mountains, ruins, rocks, woods, great plains, hills and valleys in great variety; and then again you will see there battles and strange figures in violent action, expressions of faces and clothes and an infinity of things which you will be able to reduce to their complete and proper forms. In such walls the same thing happens as in the sound of bells, in whose strokes you may find every named word which you can imagine.

Later he repeats this suggestion in slightly different form, advis-ing the painter to study not only marks on walls, but also "the embers of the fire, or clouds or mud, or other similar objects from which you will find most admirable ideas . . . because from a con-fusion of shapes the spirit is quickened to new inventions."

I hardly need to insist on how relevant these passages are to modern painting. Almost every morning I receive cards inviting me to current exhibitions, and on the cards are photographs of the works exhibited. Some of them consist of blots, some of scrawls, some look like clouds, some like embers of the fire, some are like mud—some of them are mud; a great many look like stains on walls, and one of them, I remember, consisted of actual stains on walls, photographed and framed. Leonardo's famous passage has been illustrated in every particular. And yet I doubt if he would have been satisfied with the results, because he believed that we must somehow unite the two opposite poles of our faculties. Art itself was the connection between the diagram and the blot.

Now in order to prevent the impression that I am taking advantage of a metaphor, as writers on art are often bound to do, I should explain how I am going to use these words. By "diagram" I mean a rational statement in a visible form, involving measurements, and usually done with an ulterior motive. The theorem of Pythagoras is proved by a diagram. Leonardo's drawings of light striking a sphere are diagrams; but the works of Mondrian, although made up of straight lines, are not diagrams, because they are not done in order to prove or measure some experience, but to please the eye. That they look like diagrams is due to influences which I will examine later. But diagrams can exist with no motive other than their own perfection, just as mathematical propositions can.

1. Roman naturalist, first century A.D.

By "blots" I mean marks or areas which are not intended to convey information, but which, for some reason, seem pleasant and memorable to the maker, and can be accepted in the same sense by the spectator. I said that these blots were not intended to convey information, but of course they do, and that of two kinds. First, they tell us through association, about things we had forgotten; that was the function of Leonardo's stains on walls, which as he said, quickened the spirit of invention, and it can be the function of man-made blots as well; and secondly a man-made blot will tell us about the artist. Unless it is made entirely accidentally, as by spilling an inkpot, it will be a commitment. It is quite difficult to make a non-committal blot. Although the two are connected, I think we can distinguish between analogy blots and gesture blots.

Now let me try to apply this to modern art. Modern art is not a subject on which one can hope for a large measure of agreement, but I hope I may be allowed two assumptions. The first is that the kind of painting and architecture which we call, with varying inflections of the voice, "modern," is a true and vital expression of our own day; and the second assumption is that it differs radically from any art which has preceded it. Both these assumptions have been questioned. It has been said that modern art is "a racket" engineered by art dealers, who have exploited the incompetence of artists and the gullibility of patrons, that the whole thing is a kind of vast and very expensive practical joke. Well, fifty years is a long time to keep up a hoax of this kind, and during these years modern art has spread all over the free world and created a complete international style. I don't think that any honest-minded historian, whether he liked it or not, could pretend that modern art was the result of an accident or a conspiracy. The only doubt he could have would be whether it is, so to say, a long-term or a short-term movement. In the history of art there are stylistic changes which appear to develop from purely internal causes, and seem almost accidental in relation to the other circumstances of life and society. Such, for example, was the state of art in Italy (outside Venice) from about 1530 to 1600. When all is said about the religious disturbances of the time, the real cause of the Mannerist style was the domination of Michelangelo, who had both created an irresistible style and exhausted its possibilities. It needed the almost equally powerful pictorial imagination of Caravaggio to produce a counter-infection, which could spread from Rome to Spain and the Netherlands and prepare the way for Rembrandt. I can see nothing in the history of man's spirit to account for this episode. It seems to me to be due to an internal and specifically artistic chain of events which are easily related to one another, and comprehensible within the general framework of European art. On the other hand, there are events in the history of art which go far beyond the interaction of styles and which evidently reflect a change in the whole condition of the human spirit. Such an event took place towards the end of the fifth century, when the Hellenistic-Roman style gradually became what we call Byzantine; and again in the early thirteenth century, when the Gothic cathedrals shot up out of the ground. In each case the historian could produce a series of examples to prove that the change was inevitable. But actually, it was nothing of the sort; it was wholly unpredictable; and was part of a complete spiritual revolution.

Whether we think that modern art represents a transformation of style or a change of spirit depends to some extent on my second assumption, that it differs radically from anything which has preceded it. This too has been questioned; it has been said that Léger is only a logical development of Poussin, or Mondrian of Vermeer.[2] And it is true that the element of design in each has something in common. If we pare a Poussin down to its bare bones, there are combinations of curves and cubes which are the foundations of much classical painting, and Léger had the good sense to make use of them. Similarly, in Vermeer there is a use of rectangles, large areas contrasted with very narrow ones, and a feeling for shallow recessions, which became the preferred theme of Mondrian. But such analogies are trifling compared with the differences. Poussin was a very intelligent man who thought deeply about his art, and if anyone had suggested to him that his pictures were praiseworthy solely on account of their construction, he would have been incredulous and affronted.

So let us agree that the kind of painting and architecture which we find most representative of our times—say, the painting of Jackson Pollock and the architecture of the Lever building—is deeply different from the painting and architecture of the past; and is not a mere whim of fashion, but the result of a great change in our ways of thinking and feeling.

How did this great change take place and what does it mean? To begin with, I think it is related to the development upon which all industrial civilization depends, the differentiation of function. Leonardo was exceptional, almost unique in his integration of functions —the scientific and the imaginative. Yet he foreshadowed more than any other artist their disintegration, by noting and treating in isolation the diagrammatic faculty and the blot-making faculty. The average artist took the unity of these faculties for granted. They were united in Leonardo, and in lesser artists, by *interest or pleasure in the thing seen.* The external object was like a magnetic pole which drew the two faculties together. At some point the external object became a negative rather than a positive charge. Instead of drawing

2. Léger and Mondrian: French and Dutch modern painters, respectively. Poussin, French, and Vermeer, Dutch, were both seventeenth-century painters.

together the two faculties, it completely dissociated them; architecture went off in one direction with the diagram, painting went in the other direction with the blot.

This disintegration was related to a radical change in the philosophy of art. We all know that such changes, however harmless they sound when first enunciated, can have drastic consequences in the world of action. Rulers who wish to maintain the *status quo* are well advised to chop off the heads of all philosophers. What Hilaire Belloc called the "remote and ineffectual don" is more dangerous than the busy columnist with his eye on the day's news. The revolution in our ideas about the nature of painting seems to have been hatched by a don who was considered remote and ineffectual even by Oxford standards—Walter Pater. It was he (inspired, I believe, by Schopenhauer) who first propounded the idea of the aesthetic sensation, intuitively perceived.

In its primary aspect [Pater said] a great picture has no more difficult message for us than an accidental play of sunlight and shadow for a few moments on the wall or floor; in itself, in truth, a space of such fallen light, caught, as in the colors of an Eastern carpet, but refined upon and dealt with more subtly and exquisitely than by nature itself.

It is true that his comparison with an Eastern carpet admits the possibility of "pleasant sensations" being arranged or organized; and Pater confirms this need for organization a few lines later, when he sets down his famous dictum that "all art constantly aspires towards the condition of music." He does not believe in blots uncontrolled by the conscious mind. But he is very far from the information-giving diagram.

This belief that art has its origin in our intuitive rather than our rational faculties, picturesquely asserted by Pater, was worked out historically and philosophically, in the somewhat wearisome volumes of Benedetto Croce, and owing to his authoritative tone, he is usually considered the originator of a new theory of aesthetics. It was, in fact, the reversion to a very old idea. Long before the Romantics had stressed the importance of intuition and self-expression, men had admitted the Dionysiac nature of art. But philosophers had always assumed that the frenzy of inspiration must be controlled by law and by the intellectual power of putting things into harmonious order. And this general philosophic concept of art as a combination of intuition and intellect had been supported by technical necessities. It was necessary to master certain laws and to use the intellect in order to build the Gothic cathedrals, or set up the stained glass windows of Chartres or cast the bronze doors of the Florence Baptistry. When this bracing element of craftsmanship ceased to dominate the artist's outlook, as happened soon after the time of Leonardo, new scientific disciples had to be invented to maintain the intellectual element in art. Such were perspective and anatomy. From a purely artistic point of view, they were unneccessary. The Chinese produced some of the finest landscapes ever painted, without any systematic knowledge of perspective. Greek figure sculpture reached its highest point before the study of anatomy had been systematized. But from the Renaissance onwards, painters felt that these two sciences made their art intellectually respectable. They were two ways of connecting the diagram and the blot.

In the nineteenth century, belief in art as a scientific activity declined, for a quantity of reasons. Science and technology withdrew into specialization. Voltaire's efforts to investigate the nature of heat seem to us ludicrous; Goethe's studies of botany and physics a waste of a great poet's time. In spite of their belief in inspiration, the great Romantics were aware of the impoverishment of the imagination which would take place when science had drifted out of reach, and both Shelley and Coleridge spent much time in chemical experiments. Even Turner, whose letters reveal a singular lack of analytic faculty, annotated Goethe's theories of color, and painted two pictures to demonstrate them. No good. The laws which govern the movement of the human spirit are inexorable. The enveloping assumption, within which the artist has to function, was that science was no longer approachable by any but the specialist. And gradually there grew up the idea that all intellectual activities were hostile to art.

I have mentioned the philosophic development of this view of Croce. Let me give one example of its quiet acceptance by the official mind. The British Council sends all over the world, even to Florence and Rome, exhibitions of children's art—the point of these children's pictures being that they have no instruction of any kind, and do not attempt the troublesome task of painting what they see. Well, why not, after all? The results are quite agreeable—sometimes strangely beautiful; and the therapeutic effect on the children is said to be excellent. It is like one of those small harmless heresies which we are shocked to find were the object of persecution by the Mediaeval Church. When, however, we hear admired modern painters saying that they draw their inspiration from the drawings of children and lunatics, as well as from stains on walls, we recognize that we have accomplices in a revolution.

The lawless and intuitive character of modern art is a familiar theme and certain historians have said that it is symptomatic of a decline in Western civilization. This is journalism—one of those statements that sound well to-day and nonsense to-morrow. It is obvious that the development of physical science in the last hundred years has been one of the most colossal efforts the human intellect has ever made. But I think it is also true that human beings can produce, in a given epoch, only a certain amount of creative energy, and that this is directed to different ends and different times

—music in the eighteenth century is the obvious example; and I believe that the dazzling achievements of science during the last seventy years have deflected far more of those skills and endowments which go to the making of a work of art than is usually realized. To begin with, there is the sheer energy. In every molding of a Renaissance palace we are conscious of an immense intellectual energy, and it is the absence of this energy in the nineteenth-century copies of Renaissance buildings which makes them seem so dead. To find a form with the same vitality as a window molding of the Palazzo Farnese I must wait till I get back into an aeroplane, and look at the relation of the engine to the wing. That form is alive, not (as used to be said) because it is functional—many functional shapes are entirely uninteresting—but because it is animated by the breath of modern science.

The deflections from art to science are the more serious because these are not, as used to be supposed, two contrary activities, but in fact draw on many of the same capacities of the human mind. In the last resort each depends on the imagination. Artist and scientist alike are both trying to give concrete form to dimly apprehended ideas. Dr. Bronowski has put it very well: "All science is the search for unity in hidden likenesses, and the starting point is an image, because then the unity is before our mind's eye." Even if we no longer have to pretend that a group of stars looks like a plough or a bear, our scientists still depend on humanly comprehensible images, and it is striking that the valid symbols of our time, invented to embody some scientific truth, have taken root in the popular imagi- nation. Do those red and blue balls connected by rods really resemble a type of atomic structure? I am too ignorant to say. I accept the symbol just as an early Christian accepted the Fish or the Lamb, and I find it echoed or even (it would seem) anticipated in the work of modern artists like Kandinsky and Miró.

Finally, there is the question of popular interest and approval. We have grown accustomed to the idea that artists can work in solitude and incomprehension; but that was not the way things hap- pened in the Renaissance or the seventeenth century, still less in ancient Greece. The pictures carried through the streets by cheering crowds, the *Te Deum* sung on completion of a public building—all this indicates a state of opinion in which men could undertake great works of art with a confidence quite impossible to-day. The research scientist, on the other hand, not only has millions of pounds worth of plant and equipment for the asking, he has principalities and powers waiting for his conclusions. He goes to work, as Titian once did, confident that he will succeed because the strong tide of popular admiration is flowing with him.

But although science has absorbed so many of the functions of art and deflected (I believe) so many potential artists, it obviously cannot be a *substitute* for art. Its mental process may be similar, but its ends are different. There have been three views about the purpose of art. First that it aims simply at imitation; secondly that it should influence human conduct; and thirdly that it should produce a kind of exalted happiness. The first view, which was developed in ancient Greece, must be reckoned one of the outstanding failures of Greek thought. It is simply contrary to experience, because if the visual arts aimed solely at imitating things they would be of very little importance; whereas the Greeks above all people knew that they were important, and treated them as such. Yet such was the prestige of Greek thought that this theory of art was revived in the Renaissance, in an uncomfortable sort of way, and had a remarkable recrudescence in the nineteenth century. The second view, that art should influence conduct and opinions, is more respectable, and held the field throughout the Middle Ages; indeed the more we learn about the art of the past and motives of those who commissioned it, the more important this particular aim appears to be; it still dominated art theory in the time of Diderot. The third view, that art should produce a kind of exalted happiness, was invented by the Romantics at the beginning of the nineteenth century (well, perhaps *invented* by Plotinus, but given currency by the Romantics), and gradually gained ground until by the end of the century it was believed in by almost all educated people. It has held the field in Western Europe till the present day. Leaving aside the question which of these theories is correct, let me ask which of them is most likely to be a helpful background to art (for that is all that a theory of aesthetics can be) in an age when science has such an overwhelming domination over the human mind. The first aim must be reckoned *by itself* to be pointless, since science has now discovered so many ways of imitating appearances, which are incomparably more accurate and convincing than even the most realistic picture. Painting might defend itself against the daguerreotype, but not against Cinerama.

The popular application of science has also, it seems to me, invalidated the second aim of art, because it is quite obvious that no picture can influence human conduct as effectively as a television advertisement. It is quite true that in totalitarian countries artists are still instructed to influence conduct. But that is either due to technical deficiencies, as in China, where in default of T.V., broadsheets and posters are an important way of communicating with an illiterate population; or, in Russia, to a philosophic time-lag. The fact is that very few countries have had the courage to take Plato's advice and exclude works of art altogether. They have, therefore, had to invent some excuse for keeping them on, and the Russians are still using the pretext that paintings and sculpture can influence people in favor of socialist and national policies, although it must have dawned on them that these results can be obtained far more effectively by the cinema and television.

So it seems to me that of these three possible purposes of art—imitation, persuasion, or exalted pleasure—only the third still holds good in an age of science; and it must be justified very largely by the fact that it is a feeling which is absent from scientific achievements—although mathematicians have told us that it is similar to the feeling aroused by their finest calculations. We might say that in the modern world the art of painting is defensible only in so far as it is complementary to science.

We are propelled in the same direction by another achievement of modern science, the study of psychology. That peeling away of the psyche, which was formerly confined to spiritual instructors, or the great novelists, has become a commonplace of conversation. When a good, solid, external word like Duty is turned into a vague, uneasy, internal word like Guilt, one cannot expect artists to take much interest in good, solid, external objects. The artist has always been involved in the painful process of turning himself inside out, but in the past his inner convictions have been of such a kind that they can, so to say, re-form themselves round an object. But, as we have seen, even in Leonardo's time, there were certain obscure needs and patterns of the spirit, which could discover themselves only through less precise analogies—the analogies provided by stains on walls or the embers of a fire. Now, I think that in this inward-looking age, when we have become so much more aware of the vagaries of the spirit, and so respectful of the working of the unconscious, the artist is more likely to find his point of departure in analogies of this kind. They are more exciting because they, so to say, take us by surprise, like forgotten smells; and they seem to be more profound because the memories they awaken have been deeply buried in our minds. Whether Jung is right in believing that this free, undirected, illogical form of mental activity will allow us to pick up, like a magic radio station, some deep memories of our race which can be of universal interest, I do not know. The satisfaction we derive from certain combinations of shape and color does seem to be inexplicable even by the remotest analogies, and may perhaps involve inherited memories. It is not yet time for the art-historian to venture in to that mysterious jungle. I must, however, observe that our respect for the unconscious mind not only gives us an interest in analogy blots, but in what I called "gesture blots" as well. We recognize how free and forceful such a communication can be, and this aspect of art has become more important in the last ten years. An apologist of modern art has said: "What we want to know is not what the world looks like, but what we mean to each other." So the gesture blot becomes a sort of ideogram, like primitive Chinese writing. Students of Zen assure us it is a means of communication more direct and complete than anything which our analytic system can achieve. Almost 2,000 years before Leonardo looked for images in blots, Lao-tzu had written:

> The Tao is something blurred and indistinct.
> How indistinct! How blurred!
> Yet within are images,
> How blurred! How indistinct!
> Yet within are things.

I said that when the split took place between our faculties of measurement and intuition, *architecture* went off with the diagram. Of course architecture had always been involved with measurement and calculation, but we tend to forget how greatly it was also involved with the imitation of external objects. "The question to be determined," said Ruskin, "is whether architecture is a frame for the sculpture, or the sculpture an ornament of the architecture." And he came down on the first alternative. He thought that a building became architecture only in so far as it was a frame for figurative sculpture. I wonder if there is a single person alive who would agree with him. And yet Ruskin had the most sensitive eye and the keenest analytic faculty that has ever been applied to architecture. Many people disagreed with him in his own day; they thought that sculpture should be subordinate to the total design of the building. But that anything claiming to be architecture could dispense with ornament altogether never entered anyone's head till a relatively short time ago.

A purely diagrammatic architecture is only about thirty years older than a purely blottesque painting; yet it has changed the face of the world and produced in every big city a growing uniformity. Perhaps because it is a little older, perhaps because it seems to have a material justification, we have come to accept it without question. People who are still puzzled or affronted by action painting are proud of the great steel and glass boxes which have arisen so miraculously in the last ten years. And yet these two are manifestations of the same state of mind. The same difficulties of function, the same deflection from the external object, and the same triumph of science. Abstract painting and glass box architecture are related in two different ways. There is the direct relationship of style—the kind of relationship which painting and architecture had with one another in the great consistent ages of art like the 13th and 17th centuries. For modern architecture is not simply functional; at its best it has a style which is almost as definite and as arbitrary as Gothic. And this leads me back to my earlier point: that diagrams can be drawn in order to achieve some imagined perfection, similar to that of certain mathematical propositions. Thirty years after Pater's famous dictum, painters in Russia, Holland, and France began to put into practice the theory that "all art constantly aspires to the condition of music"; and curiously enough this Pythagorean mystique of measurements produced a style—the style which reached its purest expression in the Dutch painter, Mondrian. And through the influence of the Bauhaus, this became the leading style of modern architecture.

The other relationship between contemporary architecture and painting appears to be indirect and even accidental. I am thinking of the visual impact when the whole upper part of a tall glass building mirrors the clouds or the dying embers of a sunset, and so becomes a frame for a marvelous, moving Tachiste[3] picture. I do not think that future historians of art will find this accidental at all, but will see it as the culmination of a long process beginning in the Romantic period, in which, from Wordsworth and De Quincey onwards, poets and philosophers recognized the movement of clouds as the symbol of a newly discovered mental faculty.

Such, then, would be my diagnosis of the present condition of art. I must now, by special request, say what I think will happen to art in the future. I think that the state of affairs which I have called the blot and the diagram will last for a long time. Architecture will continue to be made up of glass boxes and steel grids, without ornament of any kind. Painting will continue to be subjective and arcane, an art of accident rather than rule, of stains on walls rather than of calculation, of inscape rather than of external reality.

This conclusion is rejected by those who believe in a social theory of art. They maintain that a living art must depend on the popular will, and that neither the blot nor the diagram is popular; and, since those who hold a social theory of art are usually Marxists, they point to Soviet Russia as a country where all my conditions obtain—differentiation of function, the domination of science and so forth—and yet what we call modern art has gained no hold. This argument does not impress me. There is of course, nothing at all in the idea that Communist doctrines inevitably produce social realism. Painting in Yugoslavia, in Poland and Hungary is in the same modern idiom as painting in the United States, and shows remarkable vitality. Whereas the official social realism of the U.S.S.R., except for a few illustrators, lacks life or conviction, and shows no evidence of representing the popular will. In fact Russian architecture has already dropped the grandiose official style, and I am told that this is now taking place in painting also. In spite of disapproval amounting to persecution, experimental painters exist and find buyers.

I doubt if the Marxists are even correct in saying that the blot and the diagram are not popular. The power, size, and splendor of,

3. A method of nonrepresentational contemporary painting which exploits the quality of freely flowing oil paint for its own sake.

say, the Seagram building in New York makes it as much the object of pride and wonder as great architecture was in the past. And one of the remarkable things about Tachisme is the speed with which it has spread throughout the world, not only in sophisticated centers, but in small local art societies. It has become as much an international style as Gothic in the 14th and Baroque in the 17th centuries. I recently visited the exhibition of a provincial academy in the north of England, a very respectable body then celebrating its hundred and fiftieth anniversary. A few years ago it had been full of Welsh mountain landscapes, and scenes of streets and harbors, carefully delineated. Now practically every picture was in the Tachiste style, and I found that many of them were painted by the same artists, often quite elderly people, who had previously painted the mountains and streets. As works of art, they seemed to me neither better nor worse. But I could not help thinking that they must have been less trouble to do, and I reflected that the painters must have had a happy time releasing the Dionysiac elements in their natures. However, we must not be too cynical about this. I do not believe that the spread of action painting is due solely to the fact that it is easy to do. Cubism, especially synthetic Cubism, also looks easy to do, and never had this immense diffusion. It remained the style of a small élite of professional painters and specialized art lovers; whereas Tachisme has spread to fabrics, to the decoration of public buildings, to the backgrounds of television programs, to advertising of all kinds. Indeed the closest analogy to action painting is the most popular art of all—the art of jazz. The trumpeter who rises from his seat as one possessed, and squirts out his melody like a scarlet scrawl against a background of plangent dashes and dots, is not as a rule performing for a small body of intellectuals.

Nevertheless, I do not think that the style of the blot and the diagram will last forever. For one thing, I believe that the imitation of external reality is a fundamental human instinct which is bound to reassert itself. In his admirable book on sculpture called *Aratra Pentelici*, Ruskin describes an experience which many of us could confirm. "Having been always desirous," he says,

that the education of women should begin in learning how to cook, I got leave, one day, for a little girl of eleven years old to exchange, much to her satisfaction, her schoolroom for the kitchen. But as ill fortune would have it, there was some pastry toward, and she was left unadvisedly in command of some delicately rolled paste; whereof she made no pies, but an unlimited quantity of cats and mice....

Now [he continues] you may read the works of the gravest critics of art from end to end; but you will find, at last, they can give you no other true account of the spirit of sculpture than that it is an irresistible human instinct for the making of cats and mice, and other imitable living creatures, in such permanent form that one may play with the images at leisure.

I cannot help feeling that he was right. I am fond of works of art, and I collect them. But I do not want to hang them on the wall simply in order to get an electric shock every time that I pass them. I want to hold them, and turn them round and re-hang them—in short, to play with the images at leisure. And, putting aside what may be no more than a personal prejudice, I rather doubt if an art which depends solely on the first impact on our emotions is permanently valid. When the shock is exhausted, we have nothing to occupy our minds. And this is particularly troublesome with an art which depends so much on the unconscious, because, as we know from the analysis of dreams, the furniture of our unconscious minds is even more limited, repetitive, and commonplace than that of our conscious minds. The blots and stains of modern painting depend ultimately on the memories of things seen, memories sunk deep in the unconscious, overlaid, transformed, assimilated to a physical condition, but memories none the less. *Ex nihilo nihil fit.* It is not possible for a painter to lose contact with the visible world.

At this point the apes have provided valuable evidence. There is no doubt that they are Tachiste painters of considerable accomplishment. I do not myself care for the work of Congo the chimp, but Sophie, the Rotterdam gorilla, is a charming artist, whose delicate traceries remind me of early Paul Klee. As you know, apes take their painting seriously. The patterns they produce are not the result of mere accident, but of intense, if short-lived, concentration, and a lively sense of balance and space-filling. If you compare the painting of a young ape with that of a human child of relatively the same age, you will find that in the first, expressive, pattern-making stage, the ape is superior. Then, automatically and inexorably the child begins to draw *things*—man, house, truck, etc. This the ape never does. Of course his Tachiste paintings are far more attractive than the child's crude conceptual outlines. But they cannot develop. They are monotonous and ultimately rather depressing.

The difference between the child and the ape does not show itself in aesthetic perception, or in physical perception of any kind, but in the child's power to form a concept. Later, as we know, he will spend his time trying to adapt his concept to the evidence of physical sensation; in that struggle lies the whole of style. But the concept —the need to draw a line round his thought—comes first. Now it is a truism that the power to form concepts is what distinguishes man from the animals; although the prophets of modern society, Freud, Jung, D. H. Lawrence, have rightly insisted on the importance of animal perceptions in balanced human personality, the concept-forming faculty has not declined in modern man. On the contrary, it is the basis of that vast scientific achievement which, as I said earlier, seems almost to have put art out of business.

Now, if the desire to represent external reality depended solely on an interest in visual sensation, I would agree that it might disap-

pear from art and never return. But if, as the evidence of children
and monkeys indicates, it depends primarily on the formation of
concepts, which are then modified by visual sensation, I think it is
bound to return. For I consider the human faculty of forming concepts at least as "inalienable" as "life, liberty, and the pursuit of
happiness. . . ."

I am not, of course, suggesting that the imitation of external
reality will ever again become what it was in European art from the
mid-17th to the late 19th centuries. Such a subordination of the
concept to the visual sensation was altogether exceptional in the
history of art. Much of the territory won by modern painting will, I
believe, be held. For example, freedom of association, the immediate passage from one association to another—which is so much a part
of Picasso's painting and Henry Moore's sculpture, is something
which has existed in music since Wagner and in poetry since
Rimbaud and Mallarmé. (I mean existed consciously; of course it
underlies all great poetry and music.) It need not be sacrificed
in a return to external reality. Nor need the direct communication
of intuition, through touch and an instinctive sense of materials. This I consider pure gain. In the words of my original
metaphor, both the association blot and the gesture blot can remain. But they must be given more nourishment: they must be
related to a fuller knowledge of the forms and structures which
impress us most powerfully, and so become part of our concept of
natural order. At the end of the passage in which Leonardo tells the
painter that he can look for battles, landscapes, and animals in the
stains on walls, he adds this caution, "But first be sure that you know
all the members of all things you wish to depict, both the members
of the animals and the members of landscapes, that is to say of
rocks, plants, and so forth." It is because one feels in Henry Moore's
sculpture this knowledge of the members of animals and plants, that
his work, even at its most abstract, makes an impression on us
different from that of his imitators. His figures are not merely pleasing examples of design, but seem to be a part of nature, "rolled
round in Earth's diurnal course with rocks and stones and trees."

Those lines of Wordsworth lead me to the last reason why I feel
that the intuitive blot and scribble may not dominate painting forever. Our belief in the whole purpose of art may change. I said earlier
that we now believe it should aim at producing a kind of exalted
happiness: this really means that art becomes an end in itself. Now
it is an incontrovertible fact of history that the greatest art has
always been *about* something, a means of communicating some truth
which is assumed to be more important than the art itself. The
truths which art has been able to communicate have been of a kind
which could not be put in any other way. They have been ultimate
truths, stated symbolically. Science has achieved its triumph precisely

by disregarding such truths, by not asking unanswerable questions, but sticking to the question "how." I confess it looks to me as if we shall have to wait a long time before there is some new belief which requires expression through art rather than through statistics or equations. And until this happens, the visual arts will fall short of the greatest epochs, the ages of the Parthenon, the Sistine Ceiling, and Chartres Cathedral.

I am afraid there is nothing we can do about it. No amount of goodwill and no expenditure of money can affect that sort of change. We cannot even dimly foresee when it will happen or what form it will take. We can only be thankful for what we have got—a vigorous, popular, decorative art, complementary to our architecture and our science, somewhat monotonous, somewhat prone to charlatanism, but genuinely expressive of our time.

QUESTIONS

1. What definition does Clark give of his central metaphor, "the blot and the diagram"? Are "blot" and "diagram" the equivalents of "art" and "science"? Explain.

2. What distinction does Clark make between "analogy (or association) blot" and "gesture blot"? What importance does the distinction have for his discussion of modern painting?

3. In what ways, according to Clark, is the place of science in the modern world similar to the place occupied by science in the past? What past functions of art has science assumed? To what extent does Clark consider the situation satisfactory? What defects does he mention?

4. How does Clark show "blot" painting and "diagram" architecture to be related? Is architecture today an art or a science? How scientific is painting?

5. Clark points out that "the closest analogy to action painting is the most popular art of all—the art of jazz" (p. 549). Is there any jazz analogous to "diagram"? Explain.

6. Study closely some examples of advertising layout. To what extent do they appear influenced by "blot"? Is there influence of "diagram" in any? Are any exemplary of "blot" and "diagram" in harmony?

7. What extensions into other disciplines can be made of Clark's blot-diagram antithesis? Does it apply in literature? In psychology?

8. Why, according to Clark, will man's concept-forming nature eventually bring about a change of style in art?

JOSEPH WOOD KRUTCH
Modern Painting

I am, I hope, not insensitive to any of the arts. I have spent happy hours in museums, and I listen with pleasure to Bach, Mozart, and Beethoven. But I have more confidence in my ability to understand what is said in words than I have in my understanding of anything that dispenses with them. Such opinions as I hold concerning modern music or modern painting are as tentative as those I once expressed in these pages[1] about modern architecture.

Nevertheless, as I said on that occasion, it is one of the privileges of the essayist to hold forth on subjects he doesn't know much about. Because he does not pretend to any expertness, those who know better than he what he is talking about need be no more than mildly exasperated. His misconceptions may give valuable hints to those who would set him right. If he didn't expose his obtuseness, his would-be mentors wouldn't know so well just what the misconceptions are and how they arose. An honest philistinism is easier to educate than the conscious or unconscious hypocrisy of those who admire whatever they are told that they should.

In the case of modern painting, the very fact that I can take pleasure in some of the works of yesterday's *avant-garde* but little in that of my own day suggests, even to me, that I may be merely the victim of a cultural lag. But there is no use in pretending that I am delighted by what delights me not, and I find that much serious criticism of the most recent painting is no help. Those who write it are talking over my head; they just don't start far enough back.

For instance, I read in the *Nation* that what a certain painter I had never heard of had accomplished during the war might be summarized as "an unstructured painterliness—neither expressionist nor surrealist in character, and therefore out of keeping with available alternatives." Shortly after the war "he followed through with an intimation of the picture facade as its own reason for being, preferring a unitary sensation, by being irregularly blotted out by masses that kept on pushing at, and disappearing past, the perimeters. Executed on a vastness of scale quite unprecedented in easel painting (which he was in any event attacking), these paintings sidestep drawing and the illusion of spatial recession without ever giving the impression of evasiveness. The result was a sense of the picture surface—now extraordinarily flattened—as a kind of wall

1. "If You Don't Mind My Saying So," Mr. Krutch's regular column in   *The American Scholar.*

whereby constricted elements no longer had any exclusive formal relationship with one another."

When I read things like that my first impulse is to exclaim, "If that young man expresses himself in terms too deep for me . . ."[2] But then I realize the possibility that the words do say something to those whose visual perceptions are better trained than mine. I am at best a second grader, still struggling with the multiplication table, who has wandered into a seminar at the Institute for Advanced Studies.

When, therefore, I happened to see an advertisement of the Book-of-the-Month Club explaining that the Metropolitan Museum of Art had been persuaded to prepare a twelve-part seminar on art, which could be subscribed to for "only $60," I had the feeling that this might very well be getting down to my level. The advertisement was adorned by reproductions of two contrasting pictures: one of the Metropolitan's own "Storm" (or "Paul and Virginia") by Pierre Cot, and the other of a swirling abstraction. "Which of these is a good painting?" demanded the headline. My immediate answer "Neither." And I was not too much discouraged by the fact that I was pretty sure this was not the right answer.

I think I know at least some of the reasons why "The Storm" is not one of the great masterpieces—even though some supposedly competent expert must have once paid a whopping price for it. On the other hand, I had not the slightest idea why the abstraction was good or even just not quite as bad as the supposedly horrid example facing it.

I confess that I did not subscribe to the seminars. But I did borrow a set from an acquaintance who had done so, and I must report that I did understand what the Metropolitan people were saying as I had not understood the *Nation* critic. But I was not by any means wholly convinced. Many years ago I read Roger Fry on "Significant Form" and the terrible-tempered Albert Barnes on *The Art in Painting*. I found nothing in the Metropolitan seminar that was not this doctrine somewhat updated, and I was no more convinced than I had been by the earlier critics that what they were talking about was indeed the only thing in painting worth talking about, or that significant form by itself (if that is possible) was as good as, if not better than, classical paintings in which equally significant form had been imposed upon subject matters themselves interesting or moving in one way or another. In that problem lies the real crux of the matter. Granted that "composition," "significant form," or whatever you want to call it is a *sine qua non* of great painting, is it also the one thing necessary? Is it *the* art in

2. " * * * Why, what a most particularly deep young man that deep young man must be." So the aesthete Bunthorne sings admiringly of himself in Gilbert and Sullivan's *Patience*.

painting or only *an* art in painting? My mentors from the Metropolitan are by no means fanatical. They never themselves insist that subject matter, or the communication of an emotion in connection with it, is irrelevant in judging a picture. But unless my memory fails me, they never really face the question of the extent to which the painter who abandons the suggestion of a subject matter is to that extent lesser than one who at the same time tells a story, reveals a character, or communicates an attitude.

The hopeful student is confronted at the very beginning with what seems to me this unanswered question. He is warned that "Whistler's Mother" was called by the artist "Arrangement in Grey and Black"—and let that be a lesson to you. You may think that your enjoyment of the picture derives from its "appealing likeness of the author's mother and from sentimental associations with old age," but "the *real* [italics in the original] subject is something else . . . We may ask whether the picture would be just as effective if we omitted the subject altogether . . . the abstract school of contemporary painting argues that subject matter is only something that gets in the way. It confuses the issue—the issue being pure expression by means of color, texture, line, and shape existing in their own right and representing nothing at all."

Throughout the course, stress is laid again and again on the comparison between two seemingly very different pictures said to be similar, although I don't think they are ever said to be identical. For instance, Vermeer's "The Artist and His Studio" is compared with Picasso's "The Studio." "Picasso," I am told, "had sacrificed . . . the interest inherent in the objects comprising the picture . . . the fascination and variety of natural textures . . . the harmonies of flowing light, the satisfaction of building solid forms out of light and shape. What has he gained? . . . Complete freedom to manipulate the forms of his picture . . . The abstractionist would argue that the enjoyment of a picture like Picasso's 'The Studio' is more intense because it is purer than the enjoyment we take in Vermeer."

Is "purer" the right adjective? Is it purer or merely thinner? To me the answer is quite plain and the same as that given to the proponents of pure poetry who argued that poetry is essentially only sound so that the most beautiful single line in French literature is Racine's "*La fille de Minos et de Pasiphaé*," not because the genealogy of Phèdre was interesting but just because the sound of the words is delightful. The sound of "O frabjous day! Callooh! Callay!" is also delightful but I don't think it as good as, for instance, "No spring, nor summer beauty hath such grace,/ As I have seen in one autumnal face."

It is all very well to say that two pictures as different as those by

Vermeer and Picasso are somewhat similar in composition and that to this extent they produce a somewhat similar effect. But to say that the total experience of the two is not vastly different is, so it seems to me, pure nonsense and so is the statement that the two experiences are equally rich.

The author of the seminar session just quoted seems himself to think so when he writes: "But we also contend that a painting is a projection of the personality of the man who painted it, and a statement of the philosophy of the age that produced it."

If that is true, then the painter who claims to be "painting nothing but paint" is either a very deficient painter or is, perhaps without knowing it, projecting his personality and making a statement of a philosophy of the age that produced it. He is doing that just as truly and just as inevitably as Whistler was doing more than an arrangement in black and grey. And if that also is true, then the way to understand what is most meaningful and significant in any modern painting is to ask what it is that the painter, consciously or not, is revealing about his personality and about the age that finds his philosophy and his personality congenial.

At least that much seems often to be admitted by admiring critics of certain painters not fully abstract but who seem to be interested primarily in pure form. Take, for instance, the case of Ferdinand Léger and his reduction of the whole visible world, including human beings, to what looks like mechanical drawings. Are they examples of pure form meaning nothing but themselves? Certainly they are not always so considered by admirers. When the painter died in 1955 the distinguished critic André Chastel wrote:

From 1910 on, his views of cities with smoke-like zinc, his country scenes inspired as if by a woodchopper, his still lifes made as if of metal, clearly showed what always remained his inspiration: the maximum hardening of a world of objects, which he made firmer and more articulate than they are in reality. Sacrifice of color and nuance was total and line was defined with severity and a well-meaning aggressiveness, projecting his violent, cold Norman temperament. This revolution he consecrated himself to seemed rather simple—the exaltation of the machine age, which after 1920 dominated the western world.

To me it seems equally plain that even those who profess to paint nothing but paint are in fact doing a great deal more because they would not find anything of the sort to be the real aim of painting unless they had certain attitudes toward nature, toward society, and toward man. What that attitude is cannot, I think, be very well defined without recourse to two words that I hate to use because they have become so fashionable and are so loosely tossed about. What these painters are expressing is the alienation of the existentialist. They no longer represent anything in the external world because they no longer believe that the world that exists outside of man in any way shares or supports human aspirations and values or has any meaning for him. They are determined, like the existential moralist, to go it alone. They do not believe that in nature there is anything inherently beautiful, just as the existentialist moralizer refuses to believe that there is any suggestion of moral values in the external universe. The great literature and painting of the past have almost invariably been founded upon assumptions the exact opposite of these. They expressed man's attempt to find beauty and meaning in an external world from which he was not alienated because he believed that both his aesthetic and his moral sense corresponded to something outside himself.

Salvador Dali (whom, in general, I do not greatly admire) once made the remark that Picasso's greatness consisted in the fact that he had destroyed one by one all the historical styles of painting. I am not sure that there is not something in that remark, and if there is, then it suggests that in many important respects Picasso is much like the workers in several branches of literature whose aim is to destroy the novel with the antinovel, the theater with the antitheater, and philosophy by philosophies that consist, like logical positivism and linguistic analysis, in a refusal to philosophize. They are all determined, as the surrealist André Breton once said he was, to "wring the neck of literature."

Having now convinced myself of all these things, I will crawl farther out on a limb and confess that I have often wondered if the new styles created by modern painters—pointillism, cubism, surrealism, and the mechanism of Léger (to say nothing of op and pop)—ought not be regarded as gimmicks rather than actual styles. And to my own great astonishment I have discovered that Picasso himself believes, or did once believe, exactly that.

The luxurious French monthly *Jardin des Arts* published (March 1964) a long and laudatory article on Picasso in the course of which it cited "a text of Picasso on himself" which had been reproduced at various times but most recently in a periodical called *Le Spectacle du Monde* (November 1962). I translate as follows:

When I was young I was possessed by the religion of great art. But, as the years passed, I realized that art as one conceived it up to the end of the 1880's was, from then on, dying, condemned, and finished and that the pretended artistic activity of today, despite all its superabundance, was nothing but a manifestation of its agony . . . Despite appearances our contemporaries have given their heart to the machine, to scientific discovery, to wealth, to the control of natural forces, and of the world . . . From that moment when art became no longer the food of the superior, the artist was able to exteriorize his talent in various sorts of experiments, in new formulae, in all kinds of caprices and fantasies, and in all the varieties of intellectual charlatanism . . .

As for me, from cubism on I have satisfied these gentlemen [rich people who are looking for something extravagant] and the critics also with all the many bizarre notions which have come into my head and the less they understood the more they admired them . . . Today, as you know, I am famous and rich. But when I am alone with my soul, I haven't the courage to consider myself as an artist. In the great and ancient sense of that word, Greco, Titian, Rembrandt, and Goya were great painters. I am only the entertainer of a public which understands its age.

Chirico is another modern painter who has said something very much like this. But enough of quotations. And to me it seems that Picasso said all that I have been trying to say, namely, that a picture somehow involved with the world of reality outside man is more valuable than one that has nothing to say about anything except the painter himself. What he calls painters "in the great and ancient sense of that word" were able to be such only because they were not alienated existentialists.

QUESTIONS

1. Indicate particular details that show what Krutch suggests to be the proper business of an essayist.
2. What is this essay's thesis? What assumptions underlie the thesis?
3. What relationship does Krutch see between modern painting and "the philosophy of the age"? How does he attempt to demonstrate, or illustrate, that relationship? Is this view persuasive? Why, or why not?
4. Does Krutch assume that his audience is disposed at the outset to think of modern painting very much as he does, or very differently? to think as he does in some particulars, and not in others? Show, by specific details of his manner, what attitudes he seems to expect, what responses he anticipates.
5. Why does Krutch quote (p. 553) a passage he has read about a certain painter? What can be learned from the quotation? Would it help to know the identity of the painter? Why doesn't Krutch name him?
6. What effect does Krutch achieve by referring twice, in two separate connections, to Picasso?

HENRI BERGSON

The Comic in General; the Comic Element in Forms and Movements[1]

What does laughter mean? What is the basal element in the laughable? What common ground can we find between the grimace of a merry-andrew,[2] a play upon words, an equivocal situation in a

1. From the opening section of Bergson's essay "Laughter."
2. A clown.

burlesque and a scene of high comedy? What method of distillation will yield us invariably the same essence from which so many different products borrow either their obtrusive odor or their delicate perfume? The greatest of thinkers, from Aristotle downwards, have tackled this little problem, which has a knack of baffling every effort, of slipping away and escaping only to bob up again, a pert challenge flung at philosophic speculation.

Our excuse for attacking the problem in our turn must lie in the fact that we shall not aim at imprisoning the comic spirit within a definition. We regard it, above all, as a living thing. However trivial it may be, we shall treat it with the respect due to life. We shall confine ourselves to watching it grow and expand. Passing by imperceptible gradations from one form to another, it will be seen to achieve the strangest metamorphoses. We shall disdain nothing we have seen. Maybe we may gain from this prolonged contact, for the matter of that, something more flexible than an abstract definition—a practical, intimate acquaintance, such as springs from a long companionship. And maybe we may also find that, unintentionally, we have made an acquaintance that is useful. For the comic spirit has a logic of its own, even in its wildest eccentricities. It has a method in its madness. It dreams, I admit, but it conjures up in its dreams visions that are at once accepted and understood by the whole of a social group. Can it then fail to throw light for us on the way that human imagination works, and more particularly social, collective, and popular imagination? Begotten of real life and akin to art, should it not also have something of its own to tell us about art and life?

At the outset we shall put forward three observations which we look upon as fundamental. They have less bearing on the actually comic than on the field within which it must be sought.

I

The first point to which attention should be called is that the comic does not exist outside the pale of what is strictly *human*. A landscape may be beautiful, charming and sublime, or insignificant and ugly; it will never be laughable. You may laugh at an animal, but only because you have detected in it some human attitude or expression. You may laugh at a hat, but what you are making fun of, in this case, is not the piece of felt or straw, but the shape that men have given it—the human caprice whose mold it has assumed. It is strange that so important a fact, and such a simple one too, has not attracted to a greater degree the attention of philosophers. Several have defined man as "an animal which laughs." They might equally well have defined him as an animal which is laughed at; for if any other animal, or some lifeless object, produces the same effect, it is always because of some resemblance to man, of the stamp he gives it or the use he puts it to.

Here I would point out, as a symptom equally worthy of notice, the *absence of feeling* which usually accompanies laughter. It seems as though the comic could not produce its disturbing effect unless it fell, so to say, on the surface of a soul that is thoroughly calm and unruffled. Indifference is its natural environment, for laughter has no greater foe than emotion. I do not mean that we could not laugh at a person who inspires us with pity, for instance, or even with affection, but in such a case we must, for the moment, put our affection out of court and impose silence upon our pity. In a society composed of pure intelligences there would probably be no more tears, though perhaps there would still be laughter; whereas highly emotional souls, in tune and unison with life, in whom every event would be sentimentally prolonged and re-echoed, would neither know nor understand laughter. Try, for a moment, to become interested in everything that is being said and done; act, in imagination, with those who act, and feel with those who feel; in a word, give your sympathy its widest expansion: as though at the touch of a fairy wand you will see the flimsiest of objects assume importance, and a gloomy hue spread over everything. Now step aside, look upon life as a disinterested spectator: many a drama will turn into a comedy. It is enough for us to stop our ears to the sound of music in a room, where dancing is going on, for the dancers at once to appear ridiculous. How many human actions would stand a similar test? Should we not see many of them suddenly pass from grave to gay, on isolating them from the accompanying music of sentiment? To produce the whole of its effect, then, the comic demands something like a momentary anesthesia of the heart. Its appeal is to intelligence, pure and simple.

This intelligence, however, must always remain in touch with other intelligences. And here is the third fact to which attention should be drawn. You would hardly appreciate the comic if you felt yourself isolated from others. Laughter appears to stand in need of an echo. Listen to it carefully: it is not an articulate, clear, well-defined sound; it is something which would fain be prolonged by reverberating from one to another, something beginning with a crash, to continue in successive rumblings, like thunder in a mountain. Still, this reverberation cannot go on for ever. It can travel within as wide a circle as you please: the circle remains, none the less, a closed one. Our laughter is always the laughter of a group. It may, perchance, have happened to you, when seated in a railway carriage or at *table d'hôte*, to hear travelers relating to one another stories which must have been comic to them, for they laughed heartily. Had you been one of their company, you would have laughed like them, but, as you were not, you had no desire whatever to do so. A man who was once asked why he did not weep at a sermon when everybody else was shedding tears replied:

"I don't belong to the parish!" What that man thought of tears would be still more true of laughter. However spontaneous it seems, laughter always implies a kind of secret freemasonry, or even complicity, with other laughers, real or imaginary. How often has it been said that the fuller the theatre, the more uncontrolled the laughter of the audience! On the other hand, how often has the remark been made that many comic effects are incapable of translation from one language to another, because they refer to the customs and ideas of a particular social group! It is through not understanding the importance of this double fact that the comic has been looked upon as a mere curiosity in which the mind finds amusement, and laughter itself as a strange, isolated phenomenon, without any bearing on the rest of human activity. Hence those definitions which tend to make the comic into an abstract relation between ideas: "an intellectual contrast," "a patent absurdity," etc., definitions which, even were they really suitable to every form of the comic, would not in the least explain why the comic makes us laugh. How, indeed, should it come about that this particular logical relation, as soon as it is perceived, contracts, expands and shakes our limbs, whilst all other relations leave the body unaffected? It is not from this point of view that we shall approach the problem. To understand laughter, we must put it back into its natural environment, which is society, and above all must we determine the utility of its functions, which is a social one. Such, let us say at once, will be the leading idea of all our investigations. Laughter must answer to certain requirements of life in common. It must have a *social* signification.

Let us clearly mark the point towards which our three preliminary observations are converging. The comic will come into being, it appears, whenever a group of men concentrate their attention on one of their number, imposing silence on their emotions and calling into play nothing but their intelligence. What, now, is the particular point on which their attention will have to be concentrated, and what will here be the function of intelligence? To reply to these questions will be at once to come to closer grips with the problem. But here a few examples have become indispensable.

II

A man, running along the street, stumbles and falls; the passersby burst out laughing. They would not laugh at him, I imagine, could they suppose that the whim had suddenly seized him to sit down on the ground. They laugh because his sitting down is involuntary. Consequently, it is not his sudden change of attitude that raises a laugh, but rather the involuntary element in this change— his clumsiness, in fact. Perhaps there was a stone on the road. He should have altered his pace or avoided the obstacle. Instead of that, through lack of elasticity, through absentmindedness and a kind of physical obstinacy, *as a result, in fact, of rigidity or of momentum*, the muscles continued to perform the same movement when the circumstances of the case called for something else. That is the reason of the man's fall, and also of the people's laughter.

Now, take the case of a person who attends to the petty occupations of his everyday life with mathematical precision. The objects around him, however, have all been tampered with by a mischievous wag, the result being that when he dips his pen into the inkstand he draws it out all covered with mud, when he fancies he is sitting down on a solid chair he finds himself sprawling on the floor, in a word his actions are all topsy-turvy or mere beating the air, while in every case the effect is invariably one of momentum. Habit has given the impulse: what was wanted was to check the movement or deflect it. He did nothing of the sort, but continued like a machine in the same straight line. The victim, then, of a practical joke is in a position similar to that of a runner who falls—he is comic for the same reason. The laughable element in both cases consists of a certain *mechanical inelasticity*, just where one would expect to find the wideawake adaptability and the living pliableness of a human being. The only difference in the two cases is that the former happened of itself, whilst the latter was obtained artificially. In the first instance, the passer-by does nothing but look on, but in the second the mischievous wag intervenes.

All the same, in both cases the result has been brought about by an external circumstance. The comic is therefore accidental: it remains, so to speak, in superficial contact with the person. How is it to penetrate within? The necessary conditions will be fulfilled when mechanical rigidity no longer requires for its manifestation a stumbling-block which either the hazard of circumstance or human knavery has set in its way, but extracts by natural processes, from its own store, an inexhaustible series of opportunities for externally revealing its presence. Suppose, then, we imagine a mind always thinking of what it has just done and never of what it is doing, like a song which lags behind its accompaniment. Let us try to picture to ourselves a certain inborn lack of elasticity of both senses and intelligence, which brings it to pass that we continue to see what is no longer visible, to hear what is no longer audible, to say what is no longer to the point: in short, to adapt ourselves to a past and therefore imaginary situation, when we ought to be shaping our conduct in accordance with the reality which is present. This time the comic will take up its abode in the person himself; it is the person who will supply it with everything—matter and form, cause and opportunity. Is it then surprising that the absent-minded individual—for this is the character we have just been describing—has usually fired the imagination of comic authors? When

La Bruyère[3] came across this particular type, he realized, on analyzing it, that he had got hold of a recipe for the wholesale manufacture of comic effects. As a matter of fact he overdid it, and gave us far too lengthy and detailed a description of *Ménalque*, coming back to his subject, dwelling and expatiating on it beyond all bounds. The very facility of the subject fascinated him. Absentmindedness, indeed, is not perhaps the actual fountain-head of the comic, but surely it is contiguous to a certain stream of facts and fancies which flows straight from the fountain-head. It is situated, so to say, on one of the great natural watersheds of laughter.

Now, the effect of absentmindedness may gather strength in its turn. There is a general law, the first example of which we have just encountered, and which we will formulate in the following terms: when a certain comic effect has its origin in a certain cause, the more natural we regard the cause to be, the more comic shall we find the effect. Even now we laugh at absentmindedness when presented to us as a simple fact. Still more laughable will be the absentmindedness we have seen springing up and growing before our very eyes, with whose origin we are acquainted and whose life-history we can reconstruct. To choose a definite example: suppose a man has taken to reading nothing but romances of love and chivalry. Attracted and fascinated by his heroes, his thoughts and intentions gradually turn more and more towards them, till one fine day we find him walking among us like a somnambulist. His actions are distractions. But then his distractions can be traced back to a definite, positive cause. They are no longer cases of *absence* of mind, pure and simple; they find their explanation in the *presence* of the individual in quite definite, though imaginary, surroundings. Doubtless a fall is always a fall, but it is one thing to tumble into a well because you were looking anywhere but in front of you, it is quite another thing to fall into it because you were intent upon a star. It was certainly a star at which Don Quixote was gazing. How profound is the comic element in the over-romantic, Utopian bent of mind! And yet, if you reintroduce the idea of absentmindedness, which acts as a go-between you will see this profound comic element uniting with the most superficial type. Yes, indeed, these whimsical wild enthusiasts, these madmen who are yet so strangely reasonable, excite us to laugher by playing on the same chords within ourselves, by setting in motion the same inner mechanism, as does the victim of a practical joke or the passer-by who slips down in the street. They, too, are runners who fall and simple souls who are being hoaxed—runners after the ideal who stumble over realities, child-like dreamers for whom life delights to lie in wait.

3. Seventeenth-century French moralist, a writer of "characters"; his *Ménalque* describes the absent-minded man.

But, above all, they are past-masters in absentmindedness, with this superiority over their fellows that their absentmindedness is systematic and organized around one central idea, and that their mishaps are also quite coherent, thanks to the inexorable logic which reality applies to the correction of dreams, so that they kindle in those around them, by a series of cumulative effects, a hilarity capable of unlimited expansion.

Now, let us go a little further. Might not certain vices have the same relation to character that the rigidity of a fixed idea has to intellect? Whether as a moral kink or a crooked twist given to the will, vice has often the appearance of a curvature of the soul. Doubtless there are vices into which the soul plunges deeply with all its pregnant potency, which it rejuvenates and drags along with it into a moving circle of reincarnations. Those are tragic vices. But the vice capable of making us comic is, on the contrary, that which is brought from without, like a ready-made frame into which we are to step. It lends us its own rigidity instead of borrowing from us our flexibility. We do not render it more complicated; on the contrary, it simplifies us. Here, as we shall see later on in the concluding section of this study, lies the essential difference between comedy and drama. A drama, even when portraying passions or vices that bear a name, so completely incorporates them in the person that their names are forgotten, their general characteristics effaced, and we no longer think of them at all, but rather of the person in whom they are assimilated; hence, the title of a drama can seldom be anything else than a proper noun. On the other hand, many comedies have a common noun as their title: *l'Avare*, *le Joueur*, etc. Were you asked to think of a play capable of being called *le Jaloux*, for instance, you would find that *Sganarelle* or *George Dandin* would occur to your mind, but not *Othello*: *le Jaloux* could only be the title of a comedy.[4] The reason is that, however intimately vice, when comic, is associated with persons, it none the less retains its simple, independent existence, it remains the central character, present though invisible, to which the characters in flesh and blood on the stage are attached. At times it delights in dragging them down with its own weight and making them share in its tumbles. More frequently, however, it plays on them as on an instrument or pulls the strings as though they were puppets. Look closely: you will find that the art of the comic poet consists in making us so well acquainted with the particular vice, in introducing us, the spectators, to such a degree of intimacy with it, that in the end we get hold of some of the strings of the marionette

---

4. *L'Avare* (*The Miser*) is a play by Molière, and *le Joueur* (*The Gamester*) was the work of his successor, Jean-Francois Regnard. Molière's *Sganarelle* and *George Dandin* have jealous husbands as their chief comic figures, so that *le Jaloux* (*The Jealous Man*) would be a suitable title for either play.

with which he is playing, and actually work them ourselves; this it is that explains part of the pleasure we feel. Here, too, it is really a kind of automatism that makes us laugh—an automatism, as we have already remarked, closely akin to mere absentmindedness. To realize this more fully, it need only be noted that a comic character is generally comic in proportion to his ignorance of himself. The comic person is unconscious. As though wearing the ring of Gyges with reverse effect, he becomes invisible to himself while remaining visible to all the world. A character in a tragedy will make no change in his conduct because he will know how it is judged by us; he may continue therein even though fully conscious of what he is and feeling keenly the horror he inspires in us. But a defect that is ridiculous, as soon as it feels itself to be so, endeavors to modify itself or at least to appear as though it did. Were Harpagon[5] to see us laugh at his miserliness, I do not say that he would get rid of it, but he would either show it less or show it differently. Indeed, it is in this sense only that laughter "corrects men's manners." It makes us at once endeavor to appear what we ought to be, what some day we shall perhaps end in being.

It is unnecessary to carry this analysis any further. From the runner who falls to the simpleton who is hoaxed, from a state of being hoaxed to one of absentmindedness, from absentmindedness to wild enthusiasm, from wild enthusiasm to various distortions of character and will, we have followed the line of progress along which the comic becomes more and more deeply imbedded in the person, yet without ceasing, in its subtler manifestations, to recall to us some trace of what we noticed in its grosser forms, an effect of automatism and of inelasticity. Now we can obtain a first glimpse —a distant one, it is true, and still hazy and confused—of the laughable side of human nature and of the ordinary function of laughter.

What life and society require of each of us is a constantly alert attention that discerns the outlines of the present situation, together with a certain elasticity of mind and body to enable us to adapt ourselves in consequence. *Tension* and *elasticity* are two forces, mutually complementary, which life brings into play. If these two forces are lacking in the body to any considerable extent, we have sickness and infirmity and accidents of every kind. If they are lacking in the mind, we find every degree of mental deficiency, every variety of insanity. Finally, if they are lacking in the character, we have cases of the gravest inadaptability to social life, which are the sources of misery and at times the causes of crime. Once these elements of inferiority that affect the serious side of existence are removed—and they tend to eliminate themselves in what has

5. The miser of Molière's *l'Avare*.

been called the struggle for life—the person can live, and that in common with other persons. But society asks for something more; it is not satisfied with simply living, it insists on living well. What it now has to dread is that each one of us, content with paying attention to what affects the essentials of life, will, so far as the rest is concerned, give way to the easy automatism of acquired habits. Another thing it must fear is that the members of whom it is made up, instead of aiming after an increasingly delicate adjustment of wills which will fit more and more perfectly into one another, will confine themselves to respecting simply the fundamental conditions of this adjustment: a cut-and-dried agreement among the persons will not satisfy it, it insists on a constant striving after reciprocal adaptation. Society will therefore be suspicious of all *inelasticity* of character, of mind and even of body, because it is the possible sign of a slumbering activity as well as of an activity with separatist tendencies, that inclines to swerve from the common center round which society gravitates: in short, because it is the sign of an eccentricity. And yet, society cannot intervene at this stage by material repression, since it is not affected in a material fashion. It is confronted with something that makes it uneasy, but only as a symptom—scarcely a threat, at the very most a gesture. A gesture, therefore, will be its reply. Laughter must be something of this kind, a sort of *social gesture*. By the fear which it inspires, it restrains eccentricity, keeps constantly awake and in mutual contact certain activities of a secondary order which might retire into their shell and go to sleep, and in short, softens down whatever the surface of the social body may retain of mechanical inelasticity. Laughter, then, does not belong to the province of esthetics alone, since unconsciously (and even immorally in many particular instances) it pursues a utilitarian aim of general improvement. And yet there is something esthetic about it, since the comic comes into being just when society and the individual, freed from the worry of self-preservation, begin to regard themselves as works of art. In a word, if a circle be drawn round those actions and dispositions—implied in individual or social life—to which their natural consequences bring their own penalties, there remains outside this sphere of emotion and struggle—and within a neutral zone in which man simply exposes himself to man's curiosity—a certain rigidity of body, mind and character that society would still like to get rid of in order to obtain from its members the greatest possible degree of elasticity and sociability. This rigidity is the comic, and laughter is its corrective.

Still, we must not accept this formula as a definition of the comic. It is suitable only for cases that are elementary, theoretical and perfect, in which the comic is free from all adulteration. Nor do we offer it, either, as an explanation. We prefer to make it, if you will, the *leitmotiv* which is to accompany all our explanations. We must ever keep it in mind, though without dwelling on it too much, somewhat as a skilful fencer must think of the discontinuous movements of the lesson whilst his body is given up to the continuity of the fencing-match. We will now endeavor to reconstruct the sequence of comic forms, taking up again the thread that leads from the horseplay of a clown up to the most refined effects of comedy, following this thread in its often unforeseen windings, halting at intervals to look around, and finally getting back, if possible, to the point at which the thread is dangling and where we shall perhaps find—since the comic oscillates between life and art —the general relation that art bears to life.

QUESTIONS

1. What three conditions does Bergson say are necessary to the appearance of comic effect? Does Bergson contradict himself when he says that the appeal of the comic "is to intelligence, pure and simple" but that a definition of the comic as "an abstract relation between ideas" is inadequate? Explain his point.
2. According to what principle does Bergson arrange his examples of the comic in section II of the essay? How are the examples differentiated, and what are they said to have in common?
3. What relationships exist between sections I and II of the essay?
4. What, according to Bergson, is the social function of laughter?
5. Bergson refers to Don Quixote as exemplary of comic romantic idealism. But few readers consider the Don solely comic. Why not? What considerations might inhibit, or replace, laughter as romantic idealism?
6. Does Bergson's analysis explain the comic effect of animated movie cartoons, often violent and preposterous? How? What qualities of film comedy in general does Bergson's discussion illuminate?

NEIL SIMON

I, a Grown Man, Hit in the Head with a Frozen Veal Chop[1]

Not long after we were married, my wife and I stood toe to toe in the kitchen, exchanging verbal punches that were as devastating and as painful as any thrown in a championship heavyweight match. Each accusation, each emotional blow found its mark, and we both reeled from the awesome destructive power of the truths we hurled. Then suddenly, because there were no adequate words left to express her hurt, frustration and anger, my wife did what

1. Introduction to *The Comedy of Neil Simon*, 1971.

now seems to be the only sensible and rational thing she could have done. She picked up a frozen veal chop recently left out on the table to defrost, and hurled it at me, striking me just above the right eye.

I was so stunned I could barely react; stunned not by the blow nor the intent, but by the absurdity that I, a grown man, had just been hit in the head with a frozen veal chop. I could not contain myself, and a faint flicker of a smile crossed my face. Suddenly the anger and hostility drained from me and I found myself outside the situation looking in, no longer involved as a man in conflict, but as an observer, an audience so to speak, watching two people on a stage, both of whom cared for each other, but were unable or unwilling to yield or to submit without having first gained some small vicious victory.

Add to the scene the fact that, like the two policemen in a Roald Dahl short story who ate the frozen mutton leg murder instrument for dinner, thus depriving themselves of their single piece of evidence, I would soon be eating the object that nearly destroyed my marriage. And I hate veal chops.

The marriage survived and is still prospering, despite occasional rematches of our earlier, more successful fights. On these occasions, I again find myself subtly extricating myself from the scene of battle, and taking a seat at a higher and safer vantage point, viewing the struggle much like Lord Cardigan and Lord Raglan in the Crimean War, concerned about the outcome, but at the same time making notes for future use. A strange phenomenon, this two-headed monster who finds himself totally involved in situations, and then suddenly and without warning steps back to watch the proceedings. There is evidence that this phenomenon is prevalent among that strange breed called writers, but it is even more prevalent among that stranger breed called comic writers. It is one thing for a writer to understand this; it is another to live with it.

Like the werewolf, that half-man, half-beast, I have had to come to grips with the frightening but indisputable truth: I am a creature controlled by some cruel fate that had twisted and warped my personality so that at the first sign of personal involvement, I became transformed from human being into the most feared and dangerous beast on earth, the observer-writer. Like Lon Chaney Jr.'s portrayal of Lawrence Talbot, the werewolf-turned-back-into-man, the writer-once-more-human suffers great pangs of guilt the mornings after his transformations, but is powerless to do anything about it. He is cursed. He tries to go about his normal life—until he feels the transformation beginning again, and he knows what lies ahead.

I wasn't always like that. In the beginning, I was a boy. A plain boy. A nice, plain boy. I went to school, I ate breakfast, I listened to "The Shadow," I dreamt of being Joe DiMaggio, I went to the movies a lot and once was thrown out of a theater for laughing too loud at Chaplin in *Modern Times.* No sinister signs, no black omens. A nice, plain boy . . . Well, perhaps a few telltale hints to a discerning eye. I would go with my parents to visit a "distant" relative, distant in those days meaning a 40-minute trolley ride across the river to the Bronx, and once there, I imagined myself invisible. No earthly creature could see me because no earthly creature talked to me for hours at a time, save for grown-ups, when they offered me a cookie or a nice apple. I refused, hoping this would discourage them from further contact, enabling me to mask myself again in a cloak of obscurity.

Hours would go by. They would talk, I would listen. I got to know them better by listening than if I had engaged them in conversation myself. On the trolley going home, I realized again that I could not be seen by the human eye. People talked to each other, not to me. They looked at each other, not at me. Unobserved, unnoticed, unheeded, I could go about my curious business, storing up vast amounts of valuable information like accents, hair styles, those who shined their shoes and those who did not, nose blowers, nose wipers, nose leakers and those with various other nose habits too indelicate to mention.

Occasionally I would be noticed, invariably by another young boy my own age and alone with his parent. I would have to be careful. If the other boy noticed what I was doing, I would be exposed. I stared at the Wrigley Chewing Gum sign above the heads of the occupants on the other side, hoping and praying the interloper would get off before I did. Success at last. There he goes. Stubby arms and a fat behind. Bad athlete, good student, and probably gets an allowance. Oh, terrific, his underwear constantly sticks in his crotch and he pulls at it in a really ridiculous way. I have him now. Let him dare to threaten to expose me, to reveal to the world my existence, and I shall shame him with vivid descriptions of how he gets off a trolley. Home to bed and dreams of victory and triumph. The Shadow knows.

I grow. An inch here, an inch there, a crack in the voice, a stubble on the chin, a passing shot at puberty, a glancing blow at sex and Shazam, I'm a man. If not a man, at least a tall boy. Would you accept an enormous child? My dreams, my goals, my ambitions are to be like Them, the Others. Accepted, Respected and Noticed. Not an impossible dream to fulfill if one works zealously, passionately and tirelessly. But at what? Business? No interest. Sports? No talent. Doctor? Lawyer? Engineer? No college degree, no talent, no interest.

My dreams and ambitions suddenly seem to be unreachable. How can you be Accepted, Respected and Noticed, when you are Unseen, Unobserved and Unheeded? Dichotomy. A Division in two. Split right down the old middle. May I make a suggestion about a blending of the two? If you remain Unseen, Unobserved and Unheeded, and write down for others to read what you see, observe and heed, you might become Accepted, Respected and Noticed.

Marriage, a home, a child here, a child there, Manhood at last. But the breach widens, the rift expands. The Unseen Eye observes, the Unseen Hand writes—but it doesn't live comfortably alongside normal human functions. How can one be a husband, a father, a friend, a person, by withdrawing? How does one become an Observer, a Listener, if one is engaged, involved? The two continue to grow, to mature, but separately, apart . . . Until finally the split is complete. They can and do exist by themselves, housed in the same shell, but functioning as single and independent entities. A Monster is born.

The Human Being is a rather dull fellow. He doesn't smoke, is a moderate social drinker, dresses neatly but conservatively, watches his weight, his receding hairline and long-legged girls in short skirts, like the millions of faceless and fairly undistinguished members of his class and generation. He is often mistaken for a grocery clerk— often *by* grocery clerks. He enjoys sports and indulges in childhood fantasies. He throws a pass, catches a long fly or hits a smashing backhand and envisages some shrewd sports promoter standing on the sidelines, cigar in mouth, asking, "Who's the new kid? Tell him I want to see him in my office." He drives rented Avis cars, always within the speed limits, his reading habits fluctuate somewhere between the Classics and Variety, and he would skip a seven-course meal in a three-star French restaurant for a corned beef on a seeded roll any time.

He watches his children perform in school plays, leaving in the middle on some pretext of an important business appointment and later regretting it, and sometimes stays to the bitter end, and regrets that too. He is kind to his mother, respectful to his mother-in-law, and is politically liberal, dove-ish, active and incredibly naive. He is an ecologist who believes in trees and grass and fresh air and the freedom of all animals, and has been seen on more than one occasion kicking his dog in the kidneys to get the mutt off the bed.

He is a childish optimist. He thinks that justice will always prevail, that the meek shall inherit the earth, that bigotry and prejudice will not go unpunished and that the New York Football Giants, the Mets and the Knicks all will finish first next season. He is a dreamer and a realist, not acknowledging pain and defeat in his life but accepting it when it comes. He is a sensitive man and a sentimentalist; he reveres *Jules and Jim* for its classic beauty and cries at *Love Story*. Some would say, an ordinary man.

A look, the sound of a voice, a stranger passing on the street—and in an instant the transformation takes place. The mild-mannered Human Being suddenly dashes for cover behind his protective cloak called skin and peers out, unseen, through two tiny keyholes called eyes. He stands there undetected, unnoticed, a gleeful, malicious smirk on his face, watching, penetrating, probing the movements, manners and absurd gestures of those ridiculous creatures performing their inane daily functions. "How laughably that woman dresses . . . How pathetically that man eats . . . How forlornly that couple walks . . ." The writer is loose!

The lenses are constantly adjusted, more distance for wider observations of physical behavior and characteristics; close range for deep probing and psychological motivations. But wait. Look there. A familiar face approaches. Quick. Look the other way. Don't risk discovery. There's important work to be done, this is no time for social amenities. Too late. He's spotted you. A fast Hello, How's your wife, Why don't we have dinner next week? He's gone. Relax. Nice fellow, but's who's he kidding with that moustache? Compensating for a height deficiency. Did you notice how his eyes kept avoiding yours, constantly looking at the traffic as he talked? What's he afraid of? What's he done? Who is he looking for? When is he—? Stop it! Stop it! Behave yourself. Leave that poor fellow with his short legs alone. He's your friend. You like him. He's a decent man. So his eyes avoid yours, does that make him guilty of a criminal act? Perhaps he just likes to watch traffic when he talks? You really must call him next week and say you'd like to have dinner.

The Human Being, having asserted his position and being satisfied with his own decency and humane behavior, relaxes into his reveries. If the Knicks can just get by Baltimore, and Willis Reed's knee can hold out just a little longer—what's that? There's a crazy lady who's talking to her dog. She's not crazy because she's talking to him but because she expects an answer. "Why did you do that, Teddy? Don't pull away from me, you naughty dog. You tell Mommy why you did that."

She will not be satisfied until Teddy answers, which Teddy will not, which means she will never be satisfied, which she is not, which is why she is a little old lady living by herself, which is why —Oh, God, shut up! Shut up, will you? Leave the poor woman alone. She's lucky she's got a Teddy. I am bored with your probing and prying. Stop looking at everyone. It's a beautiful spring day. Can't we just walk and enjoy the sun, for God's sake?

The warmth of the sun passes through his body, pleasing him

and comforting him. Is life not wonderful? Is nature not divine? Are God's creatures not truly wonderful? Is a hot dog with sauerkraut and a cold Pepsi in the park not one of mankind's greatest joys? His pleasure is not long-lasting. A man and an attractive woman are walking slowly in front of him, talking in muted but heated words. He loves her but this can't go on. What can't go on? Their marriage? Their affair? Their business partnership? Their dance team? Damn that loud bus, I missed what she said. They're stopping. She's tired, she wants to sit on the bench. What do I do? Sit on the other end of the bench and pretend to read my newspaper? Fool, I have no newspaper. I could read the contents on my Pepsi bottle but how long would that take? Surely they'll suspect and move on ... How about leaving them alone and permitting them to live their lives in privacy? Monster, Monster, leave the world alone, it's none of your business.

Not content to prey on his fellow creatures, the Monster eventually turns on his alter ego, the Human Being, and dissects him unmercifully. In one play he has a newlywed accuse her husband of a week of being a stuffed shirt. "You're very proper and dignified. Even when you're drunk. You sit in a restaurant looking unhappy and watching your coat." It's true. He does. He tries to protect and defend himself. "The only reason I was watching my coat was that I saw someone else watching my coat."

But the Monster will not be put off. He knows a stuffed shirt when he sees one, and he cuts even deeper. He uses the newlywed as the instrument to voice the feelings he has about the young husband. "You can't even walk into a candy store and ask for a Tootsie Roll. You've got to point to it and say to the lady, 'I'll have that thing in the brown and white wrapper.' "

The Human Being-Young Husband fights back feebly. The Monster turns on the newlywed. He accuses her of being immature, adolescent, childishly romantic. Words echoing a real-life encounter that ended with a flying frozen veal chop. Is nothing sacred? Are there no secrets to be kept? But the Monster has observed, and what he has observed, he will reveal. Even the truth about himself. The young bride points another accusing finger: "Do you know what you are? You're a Watcher. There are Watchers in this world and there are Do-ers. And the Watchers sit around watching the Do-ers do. Well, tonight you watched and I did." Damn you, Monster, they're just a couple of nice kids starting out in life. Give them a break, will you?

The transformation begins to take place more often, more easily, sometimes almost going unnoticed, not realizing it's even happening. The distinguishing characteristics that separated them slowly become faded and muted until finally it is difficult to tell one from the other. Who is that now, looking back at me in the glass? If it's the Monster, why does the face look so benign, so innocent, so content with the world? If it's the Human Being, why does he look into the eyes so deeply, with such disgust and self-contempt? It is night. The battle for sleep rages. The human is tired, but the writer is restless with ideas, characters, conflicts, situations. "Shut up, damn you," screams the gentle self, "and let a person get some sleep."

After a fitful night, morning comes and it's the Human who pays the price, who wears the baggy-eyed scars of a sleepless night. The Monster is bright, alert, ready to go to work. The man drags his weary body into the kitchen and force-feeds himself so that the Beast can live for another day, to pry and probe and eventually to leave the remains of his victims spread out on a typewritten page with their names disguised, but their identities known to the world, exposed for all to see, to examine, to jeer at, to sympathize and identify with, and hopefully to laugh with, at and for—all under the soon-to-be disparaged, cheered, ignored and overpraised title of "A New Comedy by . . ."

CHRISTOPHER FRY

Laughter

A friend once told me that when he was under the influence of et'ner, he dreamed he was turning over the pages of a great book, in which he knew he would find, on the last page, the meaning of life. The pages of the book were alternately tragic and comic, and he turned page after page, his excitement growing, not only because he was approaching the answer but because he couldn't know, until he arrived, on which side of the book the final page would be. At last it came: the universe opened up to him in a hundred words: and they were uproariously funny. He came back to consciousness crying with laughter, remembering everything. He opened his lips to speak. It was then that the great and comic answer plunged back out of his reach.

If I had to draw a picture of the person of Comedy, it is so I should like to draw it: the tears of laughter running down the face, one hand still lying on the tragic page which so nearly contained the answer, the lips about to frame the great revelation, only to find it had gone as disconcertingly as a chair twitched away when we want to sit down. Comedy is an escape, not from truth but from despair: a narrow escape into faith. It believes in a universal cause for delight, even though knowledge of the cause is always twitched away from under us, which leaves us to rest on our own buoyancy. In tragedy every moment is eternity; in comedy eternity is a moment. In tragedy we suffer pain; in comedy pain is a fool, suffered gladly.

Charles Williams once said to me, indeed it was the last thing he said to me (he died not long after), and it was shouted from the tailboard of a moving bus, over the heads of pedestrians and bicyclists outside the Midland Station, Oxford: "When we're dead we shall have the sensation of having enjoyed life altogether, whatever has happened to us." The distance between us widened, and he leaned out into the space so that his voice should reach me: "Even if we've been murdered, what a pleasure to have been capable of it!"; and, having spoken the words for comedy, away he went like that revelation which almost came out of the ether.

He was not at all saying that everything is for the best in the best of all possible worlds. He was saying—or so it seems to me—that there is an angle of experience where the dark is distilled into light: either here or hereafter, in or out of time: where our tragic fate finds itself with perfect pitch, and goes straight to the key which creation was composed in. And comedy senses and reaches out to this experience. It says, in effect, that, groaning as we may be, we move in the figure of a dance, and, so moving, we trace the outline of the mystery. Laughter did not come by chance, but how or why it came is beyond comprehension, unless we think of it as a kind of perception. The human animal, beginning to feel his spiritual inches, broke in onto an unfamiliar tension of life, where laughter became inevitable. But how? Could he, in his first unlaughing condition, have contrived a comic view of life and then developed the strange rib-shaking response?

Or is it not more likely that when he was able to grasp the tragic nature of time he was of a stature to sense its comic nature also; and, by the experience of tragedy and the intuition of comedy, to make his difficult way? The difference between tragedy and comedy is the difference between experience and intuition. In the experience we strive against every condition of our animal life: against death, against the frustration of ambition, against the instability of human love. In the intuition we trust the arduous eccentricities we're born to, and see the oddness of a creature who has never got acclimatized to being created. Laughter inclines me to know that man is essential spirit; his body, with its functions and accidents and frustrations, is endlessly quaint and remarkable to him; and though comedy accepts our position in time, it barely accepts our posture in space.

The bridge by which we cross from tragedy to comedy and back again is precarious and narrow. We find ourselves in one or the other by the turn of a thought; a turn such as we make when we turn from speaking to listening. I know that when I set about writing a comedy the idea presents itself to me first of all as tragedy. The characters press on to the theme with all their divisions and perplexities heavy about them; they are already entered for the race to doom, and good and evil are an infernal tangle skinning the fingers that try to unravel them. If the characters were not qualified for tragedy there would be no comedy, and to some extent I have to cross the one before I can light on the other. In a century less flayed and quivering we might reach it more directly; but not now, unless every word we write is going to mock us. A bridge has to be crossed, a thought has to be turned. Somehow the characters have to unmortify themselves: to affirm life and assimilate death and persevere in joy. Their hearts must be as determined as the phoenix; what burns must also light and renew: not by a vulnerable optimism but by a hard-won maturity of delight, by the intuition of comedy, an active patience declaring the solvency of good. The Book of Job is the great reservoir of comedy. "But there is a spirit in man. . . . Fair weather cometh out of the north. . . . The blessing of him that was ready to perish came upon me: and I caused the widow's heart to sing for joy."

I have come, you may think, to the verge of saying that comedy is greater than tragedy. On the verge I stand and go no further. Tragedy's experience hammers against the mystery to make a breach which would admit the whole triumphant answer. Intuition has no such potential. But there are times in the state of man when comedy has a special worth, and the present is one of them: a time when the loudest faith has been faith in a trampling materialism, when literature has been thought unrealistic which did not mark and remark our poverty and doom. Joy (of a kind) has been all on the devil's side, and one of the necessities of our time is to redeem it. If not, we are in poor sort to meet the circumstances, the circumstances being the contention of death with life, which is to say evil with good, which is to say desolation with delight. Laughter may only seem to be like an exhalation of air, but out of that air we came; in the beginning we inhaled it; it is a truth, not a fantasy, a truth voluble of good which comedy stoutly maintains.

E. B. WHITE

Some Remarks on Humor[1]

Analysts have had their go at humor, and I have read some of this interpretative literature, but without being greatly instructed. Humor can be dissected, as a frog can, but the thing dies in the

1. From *The Second Tree from the Corner*, 1954.

process and the innards are discouraging to any but the pure scientific mind.

In a newsreel theatre the other day I saw a picture of a man who had developed the soap bubble to a higher point than it had ever before reached. He had become the ace soap bubble blower of America, had perfected the business of blowing bubbles, refined it, doubled it, squared it, and had even worked himself up into a convenient lather. The effect was not pretty. Some of the bubbles were too big to be beautiful, and the blower was always jumping into them or out of them, or playing some sort of unattractive trick with them. It was, if anything, a rather repulsive sight. Humor is a little like that: it won't stand much blowing up, and it won't stand much poking. It has a certain fragility, an evasiveness, which one had best respect. Essentially, it is a complete mystery. A human frame convulsed with laughter, and the laughter becoming hysterical and uncontrollable, is as far out of balance as one shaken with the hiccoughs or in the throes of a sneezing fit.

One of the things commonly said about humorists is that they are really very sad people—clowns with a breaking heart. There is some truth in it, but it is badly stated. It would be more accurate, I think, to say that there is a deep vein of melancholy running through everyone's life and that the humorist, perhaps more sensible of it than some others, compensates for it actively and positively. Humorists fatten on trouble. They have always made trouble pay. They struggle along with a good will and endure pain cheerfully, knowing how well it will serve them in the sweet by and by. You find them wrestling with foreign languages, fighting folding ironing boards and swollen drainpipes, suffering the terrible discomfort of tight boots (or as Josh Billings wittily called them, "tite" boots). They pour out their sorrows profitably, in a form that is not quite fiction nor quite fact either. Beneath the sparkling surface of these dilemmas flows the strong tide of human woe.

Practically everyone is a manic depressive of sorts, with his up moments and his down moments, and you certainly don't have to be a humorist to taste the sadness of situation and mood. But there is often a rather fine line between laughing and crying, and if a humorous piece of writing brings a person to the point where his emotional responses are untrustworthy and seem likely to break over into the opposite realm, it is because humor, like poetry, has an extra content. It plays close to the big hot fire which is Truth, and sometimes the reader feels the heat.

QUESTIONS

1. White uses a number of concrete details (dissected frog, soap bubbles and bubble blower, clowns with a breaking heart, fighting folding ironing boards and swollen drain pipes, suffering the ter-

rible discomfort of tight boots, big hot fire which is Truth). Which of these are metaphors or analogies (comparisons with a different kind of thing) and which are concrete examples of general statements? Why does White use so many metaphors or analogies in his definition?

2. Rewrite White's definition in abstract or general language, leaving out the analogies or metaphors and the concrete examples. Then compare the rewritten version with the original. Which is clearer? Which is more interesting to read?

3. Compare White's definition of humor with his definition of democracy (p.772). Is there a recognizable similarity in language or style? In devices used?

4. Compare White's definition of humor with Fry's definition of laughter. How far do the two definitions agree? Would White agree with Fry's hint that comedy might even be considered greater than tragedy?

5. Bergson says that "laughter has no greater foe than emotion," since its "appeal is to intelligence, pure and simple." White, on the other hand, suggests that laughter "is a complete mystery" and that "there is often a rather fine line between laughing and crying." Does the seeming disagreement between Bergson and White result from the fact their viewpoints are opposed or from the fact they appear to be defining slightly different things?

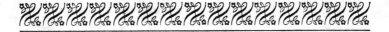

On Ethics

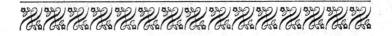

JOHN DONNE

Tentation

After wee have parled with a tentation,[1] debating whether we should embrace it or no, and entertain'd some discourse with it, though some tendernesse, some remorse, make us turn our back upon it, and depart a little from it, yet the arrow overtakes us; some *reclinations*, some *retrospects* we have, a little of *Lot's wife*[2] is in us, a little *sociablenesse*, and *conversation*, a little point of *honour*, not to be false to former promises, a little *false gratitude*, and thankfulnesse, in respect of former obligations, a little of the *compassion* and *charity* of Hell, that another should not be miserable, for want of *us*, a little of this, which is but the good nature of the *Devill*, arrests us, stops us, fixes us, till the arrow, the tentation shoot us in the back, even when wee had a purpose of departing from that sin, and kils us over again.

1. Parleyed, spoken with a temptation.
2. Fleeing from the burning Sodom,
she looked back upon the city. Genesis
xix. 17-26.

QUESTIONS

1. Analyze this single-sentence passage, determining its syntax. What are the subject, predicate, and object? How many main or independent clauses are there? Which clauses and phrases are modifiers?
2. What metaphors does Donne use?
3. Taking syntax and metaphorical content together, indicate the effects Donne achieves in this sentence. Does it convey a sense of motion, speedy or lingering? What scene or scenes are pictured? What use is made of the sense of touch? How does the presentation of physical sensation work to convey Donne's statement about the operation of temptation?

JAMES THURBER
The Bear Who Let It Alone

In the words of the Far West there once lived a brown bear who could take it or let it alone. He would go into a bar where they sold mead, a fermented drink made of honey, and he would have just two drinks. Then he would put some money on the bar and say, "See what the bears in the back room will have," and he would go home. But finally he took to drinking by himself most of the day. He would reel home at night, kick over the umbrella stand, knock down the bridge lamps, and ram his elbows through the windows. Then he would collapse on the floor and lie there until he went to sleep. His wife was greatly distressed and his children were very frightened.

At length the bear saw the error of his ways and began to reform. In the end he became a famous teetotaller and a persistent temperance lecturer. He would tell everybody that came to his house about the awful effects of drink, and he would boast about how strong and well he had become since he gave up touching the stuff. To demonstrate this, he would stand on his head and on his hands and he would turn cartwheels in the house, kicking over the umbrella stand, knocking down the bridge lamps, and ramming his elbows through the windows. Then he would lie down on the floor, tired by his healthful exercise, and go to sleep. His wife was greatly distressed and his children were very frightened.

Moral: You might as well fall flat on your face as lean over too far backward.

SAMUEL JOHNSON
On Self-Love and Indolence[1]

—*Steriles transmisimus annos,*
Haec aevi mihi prima dies, haec limina vitae.
STAT. [I. 362]

—Our barren years are past;
Be this of life the first, of sloth the last.

ELPHINSTON

No weakness of the human mind has more frequently incurred animadversion, than the negligence with which men overlook their own faults, however flagrant, and the easiness with which they pardon them, however frequently repeated.

It seems generally believed, that, as the eye cannot see itself, the mind has no faculties by which it can contemplate its own state,

1. *The Rambler*, No. 15, Tuesday, September 10, 1751.

and that therefore we have not means of becoming acquainted with our real characters; an opinion which, like innumerable other postulates, an inquirer finds himself inclined to admit upon very little evidence, because it affords a ready solution of many difficulties. It will explain why the greatest abilities frequently fail to promote the happiness of those who possess them; why those who can distinguish with the utmost nicety the boundaries of vice and virtue, suffer them to be confounded in their own conduct; why the active and vigilant resign their affairs implicitly to the management of others; and why the cautious and fearful make hourly approaches toward ruin, without one sigh of solicitude or struggle for escape.

When a position teems thus with commodious consequences, who can without regret confess it to be false? Yet it is certain that declaimers have indulged a disposition to describe the dominion of the passions as extended beyond the limits that nature assigned. Self-love is often rather arrogant than blind; it does not hide our faults from ourselves, but persuades us that they escape the notice of others, and disposes us to resent censures lest we would confess them to be just. We are secretly conscious of defects and vices which we hope to conceal from the public eye, and please ourselves with innumerable impostures, by which, in reality, no body is deceived.

In proof of the dimness of our internal sight, or the general inability of man to determine rightly concerning his own character, it is common to urge the success of the most absurd and incredible flattery, and the resentment always raised by advice, however soft, benevolent, and reasonable. But flattery, if its operation be nearly examined, will be found to owe its acceptance not to our ignorance but knowledge of our failures, and to delight us rather as it consoles our wants than displays our possessions. He that shall solicit the favor of his patron by praising him for qualities which he can find in himself, will be defeated by the more daring panegyrist who enriches him with adscititious excellence. Just praise is only a debt, but flattery is a present. The acknowledgment of those virtues on which conscience congratulates us, is a tribute that we can at any time exact with confidence, but the celebration of those which we only feign, or desire without any vigorous endeavors to attain them, is received as a confession of sovereignty over regions never conquered, as a favorable decision of disputable claims, and is more welcome as it is more gratuitous.

Advice is offensive, not because it lays us open to unexpected regret, or convicts us of any fault which had escaped our notice, but because it shows us that we are known to others as well as to ourselves; and the officious monitor is persecuted with hatred, not because his accusation is false, but because he assumes that superiority which we are not willing to grant him, and has dared to detect what we desired to conceal.

For this reason advice is commonly ineffectual. If those who follow the call of their desires, without inquiry whither they are going, had deviated ignorantly from the paths of wisdom, and were rushing upon dangers unforeseen, they would readily listen to information that recalls them from their errors, and catch the first alarm by which destruction or infamy is denounced. Few that wander in the wrong way mistake it for the right; they only find it more smooth and flowery, and indulge their own choice rather than approve it: therefore few are persuaded to quit it by admonition or reproof, since it impresses no new conviction, nor confers any powers of action or resistance. He that is gravely informed how soon profusion will annihilate his fortune, hears with little advantage what he knew before, and catches at the next occasion of expense, because advice has no force to suppress his vanity. He that is told how certainly intemperance will hurry him to the grave, runs with his usual speed to a new course of luxury, because his reason is not invigorated, nor his appetite weakened.

The mischief of flattery is, not that it persuades any man that he is what he is not, but that it suppresses the influence of honest ambition, by raising an opinion that honor may be gained without the toil of merit; and the benefit of advice arises commonly, not from any new light imparted to the mind, but from the discovery which it affords of the publick suffrages. He that could withstand conscience, is frighted at infamy, and shame prevails where reason was defeated.

As we all know our own faults, and know them commonly with many aggravations which human perspicacity cannot discover, there is, perhaps, no man, however hardened by impudence or dissipated by levity, sheltered by hypocrisy, or blasted by disgrace, who does not intend some time to review his conduct, and to regulate the remainder of his life by the laws of virtue. New temptations indeed attack him, new invitations are offered by pleasure and interest, and the hour of reformation is always delayed; every delay gives vice another opportunity of fortifying itself by habit; and the change of manners, though sincerely intended and rationally planned, is referred to the time when some craving passion shall be fully gratified, or some powerful allurement cease its importunity.

Thus procrastination is accumulated on procrastination, and one impediment succeeds another, till age shatters our resolution, or death intercepts the project of amendment. Such is often the end of salutary purposes, after they have long delighted the imagination, and appeased that disquiet which every mind feels from known misconduct, when the attention is not diverted by business or by pleasure.

Nothing surely can be more unworthy of a reasonable nature, than to continue in a state so opposite to real happiness, as that all the peace of solitude and felicity of meditation, must arise from resolutions of forsaking it. Yet the world will often afford examples of men, who pass months and years in a continual war with their own convictions, and are daily dragged by habit or betrayed by passion into practices, which they closed and opened their eyes with purposes to avoid; purposes which, though settled on conviction, the first impulse of momentary desire totally overthrows.

The influence of custom is indeed such that to conquer it will require the utmost efforts of fortitude and virtue, nor can I think any man more worthy of veneration and renown, than those who have burst the shackles of habitual vice. This victory however has different degrees of glory as of difficulty; it is more heroic as the objects of guilty gratification are more familiar, and the recurrence of solicitation more frequent. He that from experience of the folly of ambition resigns his offices, may set himself free at once from temptation to squander his life in courts, because he cannot regain his former station. He who is enslaved by an amorous passion, may quit his tyrant in disgust, and absence will without the help of reason overcome by degrees the desire of returning. But those appetites to which every place affords their proper object, and which require no preparatory measures or gradual advances, are more tenaciously adhesive; the wish is so near the enjoyment, that compliance often precedes consideration, and before the powers of reason can be summoned, the time for employing them is past.

Indolence is therefore one of the vices from which those whom it once infects are seldom reformed. Every other species of luxury operates upon some appetite that is quickly satiated, and requires some concurrence of art or accident which every place will not supply; but the desire of ease acts equally at all hours, and the longer it is indulged in the more increased. To do nothing is in every man's power; we can never want an opportunity of omitting duties. The lapse to indolence is soft and imperceptible, because it is only a mere cessation of activity; but the return to diligence is difficult, because it implies a change from rest to motion, from privation to reality.

> —*Facilis descensus Averni:*
> *Noctes atque dies patet atri janua Ditis:*
> *Sed revocare gradum, superasque evadere ad auras,*
> *Hoc opus, hic labor est.—*
> [VIR. *Aeneid* VI. 126]

> The gates of *Hell* are open night and day;
> Smooth the descent, and easy is the way:
> But, to return, and view the chearful skies;
> In this, the task and mighty labour lies.
>
> DRYDEN

Of this vice, as of all others, every man who indulges it is conscious; we all know our own state, if we could be induced to consider it; and it might perhaps be useful to the conquest of all these ensnarers of the mind, if at certain stated days life was reviewed. Many things necessary are omitted, because we vainly imagine that they may be always performed, and what cannot be done without pain will for ever be delayed if the time of doing it be left unsettled. No corruption is great but by long negligence, which can scarcely prevail in a mind regularly and frequently awakened by periodical remorse. He that thus breaks his life into parts, will find in himself a desire to distinguish every stage of his existence by some improvement, and delight himself with the approach of the day of recollection, as of the time which is to begin a new series of virtue and felicity.

FRANCIS BACON

Of Simulation and Dissimulation

Dissimulation is but a faint kind of policy or wisdom; for it asketh a strong wit and a strong heart to know when to tell truth, and to do it. Therefore it is the weaker sort of politics[1] that are the great dissemblers.

Tacitus saith, *Livia sorted well with the arts of her husband and dissimulation of her son*; attributing arts or policy to Augustus, and dissimulation to Tiberius. And again, when Mucianus encourageth Vespasian to take arms against Vitellius, he saith, *We rise not against the piercing judgment of Augustus, nor the extreme caution or closeness of Tiberius.*[2] These properties, of arts or policy and dissimulation or closeness, are indeed habits and faculties several, and to be distinguished. For if a man have that penetration of judgment as he can discern what things are to be laid open, and what to be secreted, and what to be shewed at half lights, and to whom and when, (which indeed are arts of state and arts of life, as Tacitus well calleth them), to him a habit of dissimulation is a hinderance and a poorness. But if a man cannot obtain to that judgment, then it is left to him generally to be close, and a dissembler. For where a man cannot choose or vary in particulars, there it is good to take the safest and wariest way in general; like the going softly, by one that cannot well see. Certainly the ablest men that ever were have had all an openness and frankness of dealing; and a name of certainty and veracity; but then they were like horses well managed; for they could tell passing well when to stop or turn; and at such times

---

1. Politicians.
2. The Roman historian Tacitus here speaks of the plottings of Livia, wife of the emperor Augustus Caesar and mother of his successor Tiberius; and of the Roman official Mucianus, who in 69 A.D. supported Vespasian in his successful struggle against Vitellius to gain the imperial throne.

when they thought the case indeed required dissimulation, if then they used it, it came to pass that the former opinion spread abroad of their good faith and clearness of dealing made them almost invisible.

There be three degrees of this hiding and veiling of a man's self. The first, Closeness, Reservation, and Secrecy; when a man leaveth himself without observation, or without hold to be taken, what he is. The second, Dissimulation, in the negative; when a man lets fall signs and arguments, that he is not that he is. And the third, Simulation, in the affirmative; when a man industriously and expressly feigns and pretends to be that he is not.

For the first of these, Secrecy; it is indeed the virtue of a confessor.[3] And assuredly the secret man heareth many confessions. For who will open himself to a blab or babbler? But if a man be thought secret, it inviteth discovery; as the more close air sucketh in the more open; and as in confession the revealing is not for worldly use, but for the ease of a man's heart, so secret men come to the knowledge of many things in that kind; while men rather discharge their minds than impart their minds. In few words, mysteries are due to secrecy. Besides (to say truth) nakedness is uncomely, as well in mind as body; and it addeth no small reverence to men's manners and actions, if they be not altogether open. As for talkers and futile persons, they are commonly vain and credulous withal. For he that talketh what he knoweth, will also talk what he knoweth not. Therefore set it down, *that an habit of secrecy is both politic and moral.* And in this part, it is good that a man's face give his tongue leave to speak. For the discovery of a man's self by the tracts of his countenance is a great weakness and betraying; by how much it is many times more marked and believed than a man's words.

For the second, which is Dissimulation; it followeth many times upon secrecy by a necessity; so that he that will be secret must be a dissembler in some degree. For men are too cunning to suffer a man to keep an indifferent carriage between both, and to be secret, without swaying the balance on either side. They will so beset a man with questions, and draw him on, and pick it out of him, that, without an absurd silence, he must shew an inclination one way; or if he do not, they will gather as much by his silence as by his speech. As for equivocations, or oraculous speeches, they cannot hold out for long. So that no man can be secret, except he give himself a little scope of dissimulation; which is, as it were, but the skirts or train of secrecy.

But for the third degree, which is Simulation and false profession; that I hold more culpable, and less politic; except it be in great and rare matters. And therefore a general custom of simulation (which is this last degree) is a vice, rising either of a natural false-

3. One to whom confession is made.

ness or fearfulness, or of a mind that hath some main faults, which because a man must needs disguise, it maketh him practice simulation in other things, lest his hand should be out of ure.[4]

The great advantages of simulation and dissimulation are three. First, to lay asleep opposition, and to surprise. For where a man's intentions are published, it is an alarum to call up all that are against them. The second is, to reserve to a man's self a fair retreat. For if a man engage himself by a manifest declaration, he must go through or take a fall. The third is, the better to discover the mind of another. For to him that opens himself men will hardly shew themselves adverse; but will (fair) let him go on, and turn their freedom of speech to freedom of thought. And therefore it is a good shrewd proverb of the Spaniard, *Tell a lie and find a troth.* As if there were no way of discovery but by simulation. There be also three disadvantages, to set it even. The first, that simulation and dissimulation commonly carry with them a shew of fearfulness, which in any business doth spoil the feathers of round flying up to the mark.[5] The second, that it puzzleth and perplexeth the conceits of many, that perhaps would otherwise co-operate with him; and makes a man walk almost alone to his own ends. The third and greatest is, that it depriveth a man of one of the most principal instruments for action; which is trust and belief. The best composition and temperature is to have openness in fame and opinion; secrecy in habit; dissimulation in seasonable use; and a power to feign, if there be no remedy.

4. Practice.   5. Conceptions, thoughts.

QUESTIONS

1. Explain Bacon's distinction, drawn in the first two paragraphs, between dissembling, on the one hand, and, on the other, arts and policy. How does this opening prepare the way for the remainder of the essay?
2. How is the word "dissimulation" as used in the third paragraph and thereafter to be distinguished from its use in the first two paragraphs?
3. What are the three degrees of hiding of a man's self? According to what principles does Bacon arrange these degrees? What accounts for his according unequal amounts of space to the exposition of them?
4. Make a close analysis of Bacon's closing paragraph, indicating the ways Bacon achieves symmetry, balance. How does that effect contribute to his tone and purpose? What elements in the paragraph offset a mere symmetry?
5. In what connection and to what purpose does Bacon use the following expressions? Explain the image or allusion in each:
   a. "like the going softly, by one that cannot well see" (p. 583)
   b. "like horses well managed; for they could tell passing well when to stop or turn" (p. 583)

c. "as the more close air sucketh in the more open" (p. 584)
d. "it is good that a man's face give his tongue leave to speak"
   (p. 584)
e. "he must go through or take a fall" (p. 585)
f. "fearfulness, which in any business doth spoil the feathers of
   round flying up to the mark" (p. 585)

6. Bacon would allow "simulation and false profession" in "great
   and rare matters." Would you? Give an example of such matters. Write a brief essay explaining your position.
7. What view of the world underlies Bacon's essay? Write an essay
   showing what Bacon's assumptions about the world seem to be.
   Be careful to show how you draw upon the essay to find out
   Bacon's assumptions.

JOHN EARLE
A Plausible Man

Is one that would fain run an even path in the world, and jut
against no man. His endeavor is not to offend, and his aim the general
opinion. His conversation is a kind of continued compliment, and his
life a practice of manners. The relation he bears to others, a kind of
fashionable respect, not friendship but friendliness, which is equal
to all and general, and his kindnesses seldom exceed courtesies. He
loves not deeper mutualities, because he would not take sides, nor
hazard himself on displeasures, which he principally avoids. At your
first acquaintance with him he is exceedingly kind and friendly, and
at your twentieth meeting after but friendly still. He has an excellent
command over his patience and tongue, especially the last, which he
accommodates always to the times and persons, and speaks seldom
what is sincere, but what is civil. He is one that uses all companies,
drinks all healths, and is reasonable cool in all religions. He considers
who are friends to the company, and speaks well where he is sure to
hear of it again. He can listen to a foolish discourse with an applausive
attention, and conceal his laughter at nonsense. Silly men much
honor and esteem him, because by his fair reasoning with them as
with men of understanding, he puts them into an erroneous opinion
of themselves, and makes them forwarder thereafter to their own discovery. He is one rather well thought on than beloved, and that love
he has is more of whole companies together than any one in particular. Men gratify him notwithstanding with a good report, and whatever vices he has besides, yet having no enemies, he is sure to be an
honest fellow.

JOHN EARLE
A Coward

Is the man that is commonly most fierce against the coward, and laboring to take off this suspicion from himself; for the opinion of valor is a good protection to those that dare not use it. No man is valianter than he is in civil company, and where he thinks no danger may come on it, and is the readiest man to fall upon a drawer and those that must not strike again: wonderful exceptious and choleric where he sees men are loth to give him occasion, and you cannot pacify him better than by quarreling with him. The hotter you grow, the more temperate man is he; he protests he always honored you, and the more you rail upon him, the more he honors you, and you threaten him at last into a very honest quiet man. The sight of a sword wounds him more sensibly than the stroke, for before that come he is dead already. Every man is his master that dare beat him, and every man dares that knows him. And he that dare do this is the only man can do much with him; for his friend he cares not for, as a man that carries no such terror as his enemy, which for this cause only is more potent with him of the two: and men fall out with him of purpose to get courtesies from him, and be bribed again to a reconcilement. A man in whom no secret can be bound up, for the apprehension of each danger loosens him, and makes him bewray both the room and it. He is a Christian merely for fear of hell-fire; and if any religion could fright him more, would be of that.

THOMAS FULLER
The Harlot

The Harlot is one that herself is both merchant and merchandise, which she selleth for profit, and hath pleasure given her into the bargain, and yet remains a great loser. To describe her is very difficult; it being hard to draw those to the life, who never sit still: she is so various in her humors and mutable, it is almost impossible to character her in fixed posture; yea, indeed, some cunning harlots are not discernible from honest women. Solomon saith, "She wipeth her mouth"; and who can distinguish betwixt that which was never foul, and that which is cleanly wiped?

THEOPHRASTUS
The Flatterer

Flattery is a cringing sort of conduct that aims to promote the advantage of the flatterer. The flatterer is the kind of man who, as he walks with an acquaintance, says: "Behold! how the people gaze at you! There is not a man in the city who enjoys so much notice as yourself. Yesterday your praises were the talk of the Porch. While above thirty men were sitting there together and the conversation fell upon the topic: 'Who is our noblest citizen?' they all began and ended with your name." As the flatterer goes on talking in this strain he picks a speck of lint from his hero's cloak; or if the wind has lodged a bit of straw in his locks, he plucks it off and says laughingly, "See you? Because I have not been with you these two days, your beard is turned gray. And yet if any man has a beard that is black for his years, it is you."

While his patron speaks, he bids the rest be silent. He sounds his praises in his hearing and after the patron's speech gives the cue for applause by "Bravo!" If the patron makes a stale jest, the flatterer laughs and stuffs his sleeve into his mouth as though he could not contain himself.

If they meet people on the street, he asks them to wait until the master passes. He buys apples and pears, carries them to his hero's house and gives them to the children, and in the presence of the father, who is looking on, he kisses them, exclaiming: "Bairns of a worthy sire!" When the patron buys a pair of shoes, the flatterer observes: "The foot is of a finer pattern than the boot"; if he calls on a friend, the flatterer trips on ahead and says: "You are to have the honor of his visit"; and then turns back with, "I have announced you." Of course he can run and do the errands at the market in a twinkle.

Amongst guests at a banquet he is the first to praise the wine and, doing it ample justice, he observes: "What a fine cuisine you have!" He takes a bit from the board and exclaims: "What a dainty morsel this is!" Then he inquires whether his friend is chilly, asks if he would like a wrap put over his shoulders, and whether he shall throw one about him. With these words he bends over and whispers in his ear. While his talk is directed to the rest, his eye is fixed on his patron. In the theatre he takes the cushions from the page and himself adjusts them for the comfort of the master. Of his hero's house he says: "It is well built"; of his farm: "It is well tilled"; and of his portrait: "It is a speaking image."

LORD CHESTERFIELD
Letter to His Son

London, October 16, O.S. 1747

DEAR BOY

The art of pleasing is a very necessary one to possess, but a very difficult one to acquire. It can hardly be reduced to rules; and your own good sense and observation will teach you more of it than I can. "Do as you would be done by," is the surest method that I know of pleasing. Observe carefully what pleases you in others, and probably the same things in you will please others. If you are pleased with the complaisance and attention of others to your humors, your tastes, or your weaknesses, depend upon it, the same complaisance and attention on your part to theirs will equally please them. Take the tone of the company that you are in, and do not pretend to give it; be serious, gay, or even trifling, as you find the present humor of the company; this is an attention due from every individual to the majority. Do not tell stories in company; there is nothing more tedious and disagreeable; if by chance you know a very short story, and exceedingly applicable to the present subject of conversation, tell it in as few words as possible; and even then, throw out that you do not love to tell stories, but that the shortness of it tempted you.

Of all things banish the egotism out of your conversation, and never think of entertaining people with your own personal concerns or private affairs; though they are interesting to you, they are tedious and impertinent to everybody else; besides that, one cannot keep one's own private affairs too secret. Whatever you think your own excellencies may be, do not affectedly display them in company; nor labor, as many people do, to give that turn to the conversation, which may supply you with an opportunity of exhibiting them. If they are real, they will infallibly be discovered, without your pointing them out yourself, and with much more advantage. Never maintain an argument with heat and clamor, though you think or know yourself to be in the right; but give your opinion modestly and coolly, which is the only way to convince; and, if that does not do, try to change the conversation, by saying, with good-humor, "We shall hardly convince one another; nor is it necessary that we should, so let us talk of something else."

Remember that there is a local propriety to be observed in all companies; and that what is extremely proper in one company may be, and often is, highly improper in another.

The jokes, the *bon-mots*, the little adventures, which may do very well in one company, will seem flat and tedious, when related in another. The particular characters, the habits, the cant of one company may give merit to a word, or a gesture, which would have none at all if divested of those accidental circumstances. Here people very commonly err; and fond of something that has entertained them in one company, and in certain circumstances, repeat it with emphasis in another, where it is either insipid, or, it may be, offensive, by being ill-timed or misplaced. Nay, they often do it with this silly preamble: "I will tell you an excellent thing," or, "I will tell you the best thing in the world." This raises expectations, which, when absolutely disappointed, make the relator of this excellent thing look, very deservedly, like a fool.

If you would particularly gain the affection and friendship of particular people, whether men or women, endeavor to find out their predominant excellency, if they have one, and their prevailing weakness, which everybody has; and do justice to the one, and something more than justice to the other. Men have various objects in which they may excel, or at least would be thought to excel; and, though they love to hear justice done to them, where they know that they excel, yet they are most and best flattered upon those points where they wish to excel, and yet are doubtful whether they do or not. As for example: Cardinal Richelieu, who was undoubtedly the ablest statesman of his time, or perhaps of any other, had the idle vanity of being thought the best poet too; he envied the great Corneille his reputation, and ordered a criticism to be written upon the *Cid*. Those, therefore, who flattered skillfully, said little to him of his abilities in state affairs, or at least but *en passant*, and as it might naturally occur. But the incense which they gave him, the smoke of which they knew would turn his head in their favor, was as a *bel esprit* and a poet. Why? Because he was sure of one excellency, and distrustful as to the other.

You will easily discover every man's prevailing vanity by observing his favorite topic of conversation; for every man talks most of what he has most a mind to be thought to excel in. Touch him but there, and you touch him to the quick. The late Sir Robert Walpole (who was certainly an able man) was little open to flattery upon that head, for he was in no doubt himself about it; but his prevailing weakness was, to be thought to have a polite and happy turn to gallantry— of which he had undoubtedly less than any man living. It was his favorite and frequent subject of conversation, which proved to those who had any penetration that it was his prevailing weakness, and they applied to it with success.

Women have, in general, but one object, which is their beauty; upon which scarce any flattery is too gross for them to follow. Nature has hardly formed a woman ugly enough to be insensible to flattery upon her person; if her face is so shocking that she must, in some degree, be conscious of it, her figure and air, she trusts, make ample amends for it. If her figure is deformed, her face, she thinks, counterbalances it. If they are both bad, she comforts herself that she has graces, a certain manner, a *je ne sais quoi* still more engaging than beauty. This truth is evident from the studied and elaborate dress of the ugliest woman in the world. An undoubted, uncontested, conscious beauty is, of all women, the least sensible of flattery upon that head; she knows it is her due, and is therefore obliged to nobody for giving it her. She must be flattered upon her understanding; which, though she may possibly not doubt of herself, yet she suspects that men may distrust.

Do not mistake me, and think that I mean to recommend to you abject and criminal flattery: no; flatter nobody's vices or crimes: on the contrary, abhor and discourage them. But there is no living in the world without a complaisant indulgence for people's weaknesses, and innocent, though ridiculous vanities. If a man has a mind to be thought wiser, and a woman handsomer, than they really are, their error is a comfortable one to themselves, and an innocent one with regard to other people; and I would rather make them my friends by indulging them in it, than my enemies by endeavoring (and that to no purpose) to undeceive them.

There are little attentions, likewise, which are infinitely engaging, and which sensibly affect that degree of pride and self-love, which is inseparable from human nature, as they are unquestionable proofs of the regard and consideration which we have for the persons to whom we pay them. As, for example, to observe the little habits, the likings, the antipathies, and the tastes of those whom we would gain; and then take care to provide them with the one, and to secure them from the other; giving them, genteelly, to understand, that you had observed they liked such a dish, or such a room, for which reason you had prepared it: or, on the contrary, that having observed they had an aversion to such a dish, a dislike to such a person, etc., you had taken care to avoid presenting them. Such attention to such trifles flatters self-love much more then greater things, as it makes people think themselves almost the only objects of your thoughts and care.

These are some of the arcana necessary for your initiation in the great society of the world. I wish I had known them better at your age; I have paid the price of three and fifty years for them, and shall not grudge it if you reap the advantage. Adieu.

MARGARET CULKIN BANNING
Letter to Susan

November 15, 1934

DEAR SUSAN

No, you can't drive to Detroit for Thanksgiving with the two boys and Ann. I thought that I'd better put that simple, declarative sentence at the beginning of this letter so that you wouldn't be kept in suspense even if you are put in a bad temper. I'm sorry to have to be so definite and final. I would like to leave the decision to your own judgment, but this is one of the few times when I can't do that. For the judgment of so many people, young and old, is a little askew about just such propositions as four young people motoring together for most of two days and a night without any stops except for breath and coffee.

I do agree with much of what you wrote me. It would be delightful to be there for that Thanksgiving dance and it wouldn't be expensive to carry out your plan. I quite understand that you can manage the complicated schedules all around by leaving Wednesday afternoon, driving all that night and most of Thursday, and I don't doubt that you would have a grand time until Saturday noon and all be back in college by Sunday night. Also I know that Mark is probably the best driver of all your friends and that he behaves well. His father was like that too. He was also—though this bit of history may not interest you—rather dashing in his ways, like Mark. I don't know the other boy, David, or is it Daniel? (your handwriting certainly doesn't get any better) but I'll take your word for all the sterling qualities you say he has. Nobody need argue with me about Ann, after the way she measured up to family troubles and kept gay all last summer. Even you are all that I sometimes say you are, but it doesn't affect the situation.

In fact, I think it aggravates it. Such young people as you four have no right to do things that confuse you with people who are quite different in habits and ideas of control. You write, quote, please don't say that I can't go because of the looks of the thing because that's such rubbish and not like you, unquote. You're wrong on both counts. It is not rubbish and it is like me. I get a little angry about this highhanded scrapping of the looks of things. What else have we to go by? How else can the average person form an opinion of a girl's sense of values or even of her chastity except by the looks of her conduct? If looks are so unimportant, why do you yourself spend so much time on your physical looks before you go out with strangers? In your own crowd you will go around all day wearing shorts and a sweat shirt and that eternal and dreadful red checked scarf that should be burned. But if you are going to be with people you don't know or who don't know who you are, it is different. Then you are careful to make yourself look as if you were decently bred, as if you could read and write, and as if you had good taste in clothes and cosmetics. You wouldn't be caught wearing cheap perfume, would you? Then why do you want to wear cheap perfume on your conduct?

Looks do matter and I do not mean just hair and skin and teeth and clothes. Looks are also your social contact with the world. Suppose you take this drive. How would it look to strangers? Two young men (of marriageable age) take two young women (also of marriageable age) on a forty-hour drive. Everyone knows that many girls go on forty-hour drives with men with extremely bad results, such as overexcited emotions, reckless conduct, and road accidents. How is anyone to make a special case of you? Why should anyone? It looks as if you deliberately assumed the pathetic privileges of girls who want to be with men at any cost to their reputations.

You wrote also that you think that it is nobody's business except your own what you do, but you are wrong. This is the kind of world—and there doesn't seem to be any other—in which conduct is social as well as individual. The main point of your education, from kindergarten up, has been to make you understand that, and I don't want you to break down at this small test. Your conduct is not entirely your own business, though it begins there. Afterwards it affects other people's conduct. Other girls, seeing you go off on an unchaperoned motor jaunt, think it's all right to do the same thing. Parents doubt and wonder. Men, and even boys, grow skeptical and more careless. You confuse things by such conduct.

I must also point out, even in the face of your cool young rage, that you ask a great deal more than gasoline and company of Mark and David—who may be Daniel. An unchaperoned girl, for whom a young man is responsible to parents whom he knows and respects, is a great burden to a young man. You are—so you said yourself—decent. Mark would have you on his hands in situations when people would not know whether you are decent or not. Suppose you all had an accident. Suppose, for example, that you couldn't make this trip without a long stop, speed being so eminently respectable but stops always so questionable. If you trail into some hotel after midnight, though a tourist camp should be all any of you can afford this year, it wouldn't be so easy for either of those boys. Did it ever occur to you that there's something almost crooked in the way decent girls nowadays use the shelter of their established respectability to make things awkward for men?

There's another thing in my mind which is only partly relevant. You make no mention of it, assuming the coolest of friendly relations between the four of you. But suppose that David-Daniel (I'm begin-

ning to love that name) found himself more excited than you anticipate by the proximity—and what proximity!—of you two good-
looking girls. That happens. I seem to remember having mentioned
it before. It might happen to one of those two boys. And how about
you and Ann? Are you quite frank with me or yourselves? Isn't part
of the lure of this trip the fact that you yourself do like Mark very
much? Your plan really is to drive a car full of high explosives for
forty hours, from dark to dawn, and enjoy your own daring no matter who blows up.

You wrote me that it would be such fun that you hope I'll see it
your way. That's always a very disarming argument, but I think it's
on my side this time. You see, if there were any necessity for this
trip I would feel differently about it. If you were compelled for some
real reason to travel that way, if there were a war or a *siege* to make
it necessary, or if it were the only way you could see Mark for years,
I would say that you could do it. But fun—that so-transient fun—
of just missing being hit by a bus or finding the best hamburgers in
the world at a roadside inn, or being cut in on twenty times at that
Thanksgiving dance—isn't a good enough reason.

It is no fun for me either, to disappoint you like this. It isn't easy
to be the person who sometimes has to try to preserve your happiness
at the expense of your fun. After Thanksgiving—I know you probably can't do it until then—will you please believe that's true?

With love to you, Ann, Mark and David-Daniel,

MOTHER

WILLIAM JAMES

Letter to Peg[1]

Villa Luise
Bad-Nauheim, May 26, 1900

DARLING PEG—Your letter came last night and explained sufficiently the cause of your long silence. You have evidently been in
a bad state of spirits again, and dissatisfied with your environment;
and I judge that you have been still more dissatisfied with the inner
state of trying to consume your own smoke, and grin and bear it,
so as to carry out your mother's behests made after the time when
you scared us so by your inexplicable tragic outcries in those earlier
letters. Well! I believe you have been trying to do the manly thing
under difficult circumstances, but one learns only gradually to do
the *best* thing; and the best thing for you would be to write at least
weekly, if only a post-card, and say just how things are going. If you

---

1. Peg is James' thirteen-year-old
daughter who was then living with family friends in England and experiencing
some home-sickness.

are in bad spirits, there is no harm whatever in communicating that fact, and defining the character of it, or describing it as exactly as you like. The bad thing is to pour out the *contents* of one's bad spirits on others and leave them with it, as it were, on their hands, as if it was for them to do something about it. That was what you did in your other letter which alarmed us so, for your shrieks of anguish were so excessive, and so unexplained by anything you told us in the way of facts, that we didn't know but what you had suddenly gone crazy. That is the *worst* sort of thing you can do. The middle sort of thing is what you do this time—namely, keep silent for more than a fortnight, and when you do write, still write rather mysteriously about your sorrows, not being quite open enough.

Now, my dear little girl, you have come to an age when the inward life develops and when some people (and on the whole those who have most of a destiny) find that all is not a bed of roses. Among other things there will be waves of terrible sadness, which last sometimes for days; and dissatisfaction with one's self, and irritation at others, and anger at circumstances and stony insensibility, etc., etc., which taken together form a melancholy. Now, painful as it is, this is sent to us for an enlightenment. It always passes off, and we learn about life from it, and we ought to learn a great many good things if we react on it rightly. [*From margin.*] (For instance, you learn how good a thing your home is, and your country, and your brothers, and you may learn to be more considerate of other people, who, you now learn, may have their inner weaknesses and sufferings, too.) Many persons take a kind of sickly delight in hugging it; and some sentimental ones may even be proud of it, as showing a fine sorrowful kind of sensibility. Such persons make a regular habit of the luxury of woe. That is the worst possible reaction on it. It is usually a sort of disease, when we get it strong, arising from the organism having generated some poison in the blood; and we mustn't submit to it an hour longer than we can help, but jump at every chance to attend to anything cheerful or comic or take part in anything active that will divert us from our mean, pining inward state of feeling. When it passes off, as I said, we know more than we did before. And we must try to make it last as short a time as possible. The worst of it often is that, while we are in it, we don't *want* to get out of it. We hate it, and yet we prefer staying in it—that is a part of the disease. If we find ourselves like that, we must make ourselves do something different, go with people, speak cheerfully, set ourselves to some hard work, make ourselves sweat, etc.; and that is the good way of reacting that makes of us a valuable character. The disease makes you think of *yourself* all the time; and the way out of it is to keep as busy as we can thinking of *things* and of *other people* —no matter what's the matter with our self.

I have no doubt you are doing as well as you know how, darling little Peg; but we have to learn everything, and I also have no doubt that you'll manage it better and better if you ever have any more of it, and soon it will fade away, simply leaving you with more experience. The great thing for you *now*, I should suppose, would be to enter as friendlily as possible into the interest of the Clarke children. If you like them, or acted as if you liked them, you needn't trouble about the question of whether they like you or not. They probably will, fast enough; and if they don't, it will be their funeral, not yours. But this is a great lecture, so I will stop. The great thing about it is that it is all true.

QUESTIONS

1. What distinction does James intend between pouring out "the contents of one's bad spirits" and "communicating that fact, and defining the character of it, or describing it as exactly as you like"? Why does he advise against the one and encourage the other?
2. James says we can learn a great many good things if we react rightly to an experience of melancholy. What things does he mention? What other things might be learned?

ERNEST HEMINGWAY

Bullfighting[1]

The bullfight is not a sport in the Anglo-Saxon sense of the word, that is, it is not an equal contest or an attempt at an equal contest between a bull and a man. Rather it is a tragedy; the death of the bull, which is played, more or less well, by the bull and the man involved and in which there is danger for the man but certain death for the animal. This danger to the man can be increased by the bullfighter at will in the measure in which he works close to the bull's horns. Keeping within the rules for bullfighting on foot in a closed ring formulated by years of experience, which, if known and followed, permit a man to perform certain actions with a bull without being caught by the bull's horns, the bullfighter may, by decreasing his distance from the bull's horns, depend more and more on his own reflexes and judgment of that distance to protect him from the points. This danger of goring, which the man creates voluntarily, can be changed to certainty of being caught and tossed by the bull if the man, through ignorance, slowness, torpidness, blind folly, or momentary grogginess breaks any of these fundamental rules for the execution of the different suertes. Everything that is done by the man in the ring is called a "suerte." It is the easiest term to use as it is short. It means act, but the word act has, in

1. Chapter 2 in *Death in the After-noon*, 1932.
2. A small cloth attached to a short tapered stick and used by a matador during the final passes leading to the kill.

English, a connotation of the theatre that makes its use confusing.

People seeing their first bullfight say, "But the bulls are so stupid. They always go for the cape and not for the man."

The bull only goes for the percale of the cape or for the scarlet serge of the muleta[2] if the man makes him and so handles the cloth that the bull sees it rather than the man. Therefore to really start to see bullfights a spectator should go to the novilladas or apprentice fights. There the bulls do not always go for the cloth because the bullfighters are learning before your eyes the rules of bullfighting and they do not always remember or know the proper terrain to take and how to keep the bull after the lure and away from the man. It is one thing to know the rules in principle and another to remember them as they are needed when facing an animal that is seeking to kill you, and the spectator who wants to see men tossed and gored rather than judge the manner in which the bulls are dominated should go to a novillada before he sees a corrida de toros or complete bullfight. It should be a good thing for him to see a novillada first anyway if he wants to learn about technique, since the employment of knowledge that we call by that bastard name is always most visible in its imperfection. At a novillada the spectator may see the mistakes of the bullfighters, and the penalties that these mistakes carry. He will learn something too about the state of training or lack of training of the men and the effect this has on their courage.

One time in Madrid I remember we went to a novillada in the middle of the summer on a very hot Sunday when every one who could afford it had left the city for the beaches of the north or the mountains and the bullfight was not advertised to start until six o'clock in the evening, to see six Tovar bulls killed by three aspirant matadors who have all since failed in their profession. We sat in the first row behind the wooden barrier and when the first bull came out it was clear that Domingo Hernandorena, a short, thick-ankled, graceless Basque with a pale face who looked nervous and incompletely fed in a cheap rented suit, if he was to kill this bull would either make a fool of himself or be gored. Hernandorena could not control the nervousness of his feet. He wanted to stand quietly and play the bull with the cape with a slow movement of his arms, but when he tried to stand still as the bull charged his feet jumped away in short, nervous jerks. His feet were obviously not under his personal control and his effort to be statuesque while his feet jittered him away out of danger was very funny to the crowd. It was funny to them because many of them knew that was how their own feet would behave if they saw the horns coming toward them, and as always, they resented any one else being in there in the ring, making money, who had the same physical defects which barred them, the spectators, from that supposedly highly paid way of making a living. In their turn the other two matadors were very fancy with the cape and Hernandorena's nervous jerking was even worse after their performance. He had not been in the ring with a bull for over a year and he was altogether unable to control his nervousness. When the banderillas were in and it was time for him to go out with the red cloth and the sword to prepare the bull for killing and to kill, the crowd which had applauded ironically at every nervous move he had made knew something very funny would happen. Below us, as he took the muleta and the sword and rinsed his mouth out with water I could see the muscles of his cheeks twitching. The bull stood against the barrier watching him. Hernandorena could not trust his legs to carry him slowly toward the bull. He knew there was only one way he could stay in one place in the ring. He ran out toward the bull, and ten yards in front of him dropped to both knees on the sand. In that position he was safe from ridicule. He spread the red cloth with his sword and jerked himself forward on his knees toward the bull. The bull was watching the man and the triangle of red cloth, his ears pointed, his eyes fixed, and Hernandorena knee-ed himself a yard closer and shook the cloth. The bull's tail rose, his head lowered and he charged and, as he reached the man, Hernandorena rose solidly from his knees into the air, swung over like a bundle, his legs in all directions now, and then dropped to the ground. The bull looked for him, found a wide-spread moving cape held by another bullfighter instead, charged it, and Hernandorena stood up with sand on his white face and looked for his sword and the cloth. As he stood up I saw the heavy, soiled gray silk of his rented trousers open cleanly and deeply to show the thigh bone from the hip almost to the knee. He saw it too and looked very surprised and put his hand on it while people jumped over the barrier and ran toward him to carry him to the infirmary. The technical error that he had committed was in not keeping the red cloth of the muleta between himself and the bull until the charge; then at the moment of jurisdiction as it is called, when the bull's lowered head reaches the cloth, swaying back while he held the cloth, spread by the stick and the sword, far enough forward so that the bull following it would be clear of his body. It was a simple technical error.

That night at the café I heard no word of sympathy for him. He was ignorant, he was torpid, and he was out of training. Why did he insist on being a bullfighter? Why did he go down on both knees? Because he was a coward, they said. The knees are for cowards. If he was a coward why did he insist on being a bullfighter? There was no natural sympathy for uncontrollable nervousness because he was a paid public performer. It was preferable that he be gored rather than run from the bull. To be gored was honorable; they would have sympathized with him had he been caught in one of his nervous uncontrollable jerky retreats, which, although they mocked, they knew were from lack of training, rather than for him to have gone down on his knees. Because the hardest thing when frightened by the bull is to control the feet and let the bull come, and any attempt to control the feet was honorable even though they jeered at it because it looked ridiculous. But when he went on both knees, without the technique to fight from that position; the technique that Marcial Lalanda, the most scientific of living bull-fighters, has, and which alone makes that position honorable; then Hernandorena admitted his nervousness. To show his nervousness was not shameful; only to admit it. When, lacking the technique and thereby admitting his inability to control his feet, the matador went down on both knees before the bull the crowd had no more sympathy with him than with a suicide.

For myself, not being a bullfighter, and being much interested in suicides, the problem was one of depiction and waking in the night I tried to remember what it was that seemed just out of my remembering and that was the thing that I had really seen and, finally, remembering all around, I got it. When he stood up, his face white and dirty and the silk of his breeches opened from waist to knee, it was the dirtiness of the rented breeches, the dirtiness of his slit underwear, and the clean, clean, unbearably clean whiteness of the thigh bone that I had seen, and it was that which was important.

At the novilladas, too, besides the study of technique, and the consequences of its lack you have a chance to learn about the manner of dealing with defective bulls since bulls which cannot be used in a formal bullfight because of some obvious defect are killed in the apprentice fights. Nearly all bulls develop defects in the course of any fight which must be corrected by the bullfighter, but in the novillada these defects, those of vision for instance, are many times obvious at the start and so the manner of their correcting, or the result of their not being corrected, is apparent.

The formal bullfight is a tragedy, not a sport, and the bull is certain to be killed. If the matador cannot kill him and, at the end of the allotted fifteen minutes for the preparation and killing, the bull is led and herded out of the ring alive by steers to dishonor the killer, he must, by law, be killed in the corrals. It is one hundred to one against the matador de toros or formally invested bull-fighter being killed unless he is inexperienced, ignorant, out of training or too old and heavy on his feet. But the matador, if he knows his profession, can increase the amount of the danger of death that he runs exactly as much as he wishes. He should, however, increase this danger, *within the rules provided for his protection*. In other words it is to his credit if he does something that he knows how to do in a highly dangerous but still geometrically possible manner. It is to his discredit if he runs danger through ignorance, through disregard of the fundamental rules, through physical or mental slowness, or through blind folly.

The matador must dominate the bulls by knowledge and science. In the measure in which this domination is accomplished with grace will it be beautiful to watch. Strength is of little use to him except at the actual moment of killing. Once some one asked Rafael Gomez, "El Gallo," nearing fifty years old, a gypsy, brother of Jose Gomez, "Gallito," and the last living member of the great family of gypsy bullfighters of that name, what physical exercise he, Gallo, took to keep his strength up for bullfighting.

"Strength," Gallo said. "What do I want with strength, man? The bull weighs half a ton. Should I take exercises for strength to match him? Let the bull have the strength."

If the bulls were allowed to increase their knowledge as the bull-fighter does and if those bulls which are not killed in the alloted fifteen minutes in the ring were not afterwards killed in the corrals but were allowed to be fought again they would kill all the bull-fighters, if the bullfighters fought them according to the rules. Bull-fighting is based on the fact that it is the first meeting between the wild animal and a dismounted man. This is the fundamental prem-ise of modern bullfighting; that the bull has never been in the ring before. In the early days of bullfighting bulls were allowed to be fought which had been in the ring before and so many men were killed in the bull ring that on November 20, 1567, Pope Pius the Fifth issued a Papal edict excommunicating all Christian princes who should permit bullfights in their countries and denying Chris-tian burial to any person killed in the bull ring. The Church only agreed to tolerate bullfighting, which continued steadily in Spain in spite of the edict, when it was agreed that the bulls should only appear once in the ring.

You would think then that it would make of bullfighting a true sport, rather than merely a tragic spectacle, if bulls that had been in the ring were allowed to reappear. I have seen such bulls fought, in violation of the law, in provincial towns in improvised arenas made by blocking the entrances to the public square with piled-up carts in the illegal capeas, or town-square bullfights with used bulls. The aspirant bullfighters, who have no financial backing, get their first experience in capeas. It is a sport, a very savage and primitive sport, and for the most part a truly amateur one. I am afraid however due to the danger of death it involves it would never have much success among the amateur sportsmen of America and England who play games. We, in games, are not fascinated by death, its nearness and its avoidance. We are fascinated by victory and we replace the avoidance of death by the avoidance of defeat. It is a very nice symbolism but it takes more cojones to be a sportsman when death is a closer party to the game.

The bull in the capeas is rarely killed. This should appeal to sports-men who are lovers of animals. The town is usually too poor to afford to pay for the killing of the bull and none of the aspirant bullfighters has enough money to buy a sword or he would not have chosen to serve his apprenticeship in the capeas. This would afford an opportunity for the man who is a wealthy sportsman, for he could afford to pay for the bull and buy himself a sword as well.

However, due to the mechanics of a bull's mental development the used bull does not make a brilliant spectacle. After his first charge or so he will stand quite still and will only charge if he is certain of getting the man or boy who is tempting him with a cape. When there is a crowd and the bull charges into it he will pick one man out and follow him, no matter how he may dodge, run and twist until he gets him and tosses him. If the tips of the bull's horns have been blunted this chasing and tossing is good fun to see for a little while. No one has to go in with the bull who does not want to, although of course many who want to very little go in to show their courage. It is very exciting for those who are down in the square, that is one test of a true amateur sport, whether it is more enjoyable to player than to spectator (as soon as it becomes enjoyable enough to the spectator for the charging of admission to be profitable the sport contains the germ of professionalism), and the smallest evidence of coolness or composure brings immediate applause. But when the bull's horns are sharp-pointed it is a dis-turbing spectacle. The men and boys try cape work with sacks, blouses, and old capes on the bull just as they do when his horns have been blunted; the only difference is that when the bull catches them and tosses them they are liable to come off the horn with wounds no local surgeon can cope with. One bull which was a great favorite in the capeas of the province of Valencia killed six-teen men and boys and badly wounded over sixty in a career of five years. The people who go into these capeas do so sometimes as aspirant professionals to get free experience with bulls but most often as amateurs, purely for sport, for the immediate excitement, and it is very great excitement; and for the retrospective pleasure, of having shown their contempt for death on a hot day in their own town square. Many go in from pride, hoping that they will be brave. Many find they are not brave at all; but at least they went in. There is absolutely nothing for them to gain except the inner satisfaction of having been in the ring with a bull; itself a thing that any one who has done it will always remember. It is a strange feeling to have an animal come toward you consciously seeking to kill you, his eyes open looking at you, and see the oncoming of the lowered horn that he intends to kill you with. It gives enough of a sensation so that there are always men willing to go into the capeas for the pride of having experienced it and the pleasure of having tried some bullfighting maneuver with a real bull although the actual pleasure at the time may not be great. Sometimes the bull is killed if the town has the money to afford it, or if the populace gets out of control; every one swarming on him at once with knives, daggers, butcher knives, and rocks; a man perhaps between his horns, being swung up and down, another flying through the air, surely several holding his tail, a swarm of choppers, thrusters and stabbers pushing into him, laying on him or cutting up at him until he sways and goes down. All amateur or group killing is a very barbarous, messy, though exciting business and is a long way from the ritual of the formal bullfight.

The bull which killed the sixteen and wounded the sixty was killed in a very odd way. One of those he had killed was a gypsy boy of about fourteen. Afterward the boy's brother and sister followed the bull around hoping perhaps to have a chance to assassinate him when he was loaded in his cage after a capea. That was difficult since, being a very highly valued performer, the bull was carefully taken care of. They followed him around for two years, not attempting anything, simply turning up wherever the bull was used. When the capeas were again abolished, they are always being abolished and reabolished, by government order, the bull's owner decided to send him to the slaughterhouse in Valencia, for the bull was getting on in years anyway. The two gypsies were at the slaughterhouse and the young man asked permission, since the bull had killed his brother, to kill the bull. This was granted and he started in by digging out both the bull's eyes while the bull was in his cage, and spitting carefully into the sockets, then after killing him by severing the spinal marrow between the neck vertebrae with a dagger, he experienced some difficulty in this, he asked permission to cut off the bull's testicles, which being granted, he and his sister built a small fire at the edge of the dusty street outside the slaughterhouse and roasted the two glands on sticks and when they were done, ate them. They then turned their backs on the slaughterhouse and went away along the road and out of town.

DONALD PEARCE

Rosalie[1]

Life among the peasants of Belgium has been extremely pleasant; in fact, delightful. The platoon is quartered in a bar, but I—thank God—am in the farmhouse, where I occcupy the spare bedroom and can observe what goes on inside this beehive. The day begins

---

1. From *Journal of a War*, 1965.

at 4:30 A.M. At that time I can hear Rosalie, the fifty-year-old woman who runs this little farm, padding to and fro in soft slippers doing I know not what to the stove, the dishes, the kitchen, and the pantry. By the time I get up, a couple of hours later, the cows have been attended to, breakfast prepared, the washing hung out, apples peeled, eggs collected, and other unseen tasks performed. Rosalie waves me to the kitchen table; and, though the gruel is curiously sour, I must eat, for she has made it especially for me and has filled it full of her best grains and buttermilk. She nods, smacks her lips, smiles her head, in vicarious delight, with every spoonful I take. I smile and grunt right back, and lately I have meant it, for the flavor of the stuff begins to grow on you.

I've watched Rosalie for days now, and have not once seen her idle. Her day is geared to the minute hand of the kitchen clock, and neither she or it ever stops. Her whole life must have been spent in continuous activity, or rather service, and it has bent her over. Inactivity is obviously immoral to her. If there is no big task to hand, like kneading huge quantities of dough (on her knees, by the stove), she polishes the stove-lifter, waxes the table top, scrubs the doorstep, shines the windows. She is constantly cleaning. Yet she hasn't the faintest idea of real sanitation. A primitive cleanliness is all that she understands. She scrubs the floor each day with boiling water, but the hands that have wrung out the mop plunge themselves tirelessly and deep into the heavy dough. She scalds the dishes and then dries them with a dirty cloth. She cleans the forks with a far-from-immaculate apron. She wears herself out. She has done so for at least forty years, and now she can no longer walk upright, but moves bent over, hustling here and there from one corner of the room to another, led by a momentary fixed idea rather than a plan of work. The salt is at the opposite end of the kitchen from the pepper, the butter from the milk, but she always returns them to these disparate places in the scuttling darkness of her low-beamed kitchen.

Her brother Raymond, who is a widower, is about Rosalie's age. He sits by the stove most of the day, warming his back and soaking his lame foot in water. He does little work, and probably never has; his foot is only sprained from a fall. Work has never bent him over, or any of the other men I see in this district. They are like dwindled feudal lords, and the women are their uncomplaining serfs. Girls of fourteen do hard barnyard work, or labor in the fields all day long. They will all be Rosalies at last, you can see it coming. They carry pails of milk or water suspended at their sides from yokes that fit over their shoulders, haul baskets of potatoes, and only stop pulling up acres of mangels for half an hour for lunch. Boys of the same age work much less, ride bicycles most of the time, and in the evenings talk to the soldiers in the taverns.

Rosalie is strictly religious. Her day begins with matins and closes with an evening prayer. She prays silently and like a statue before and after each meal. On all the walls of the rooms she has pinned up religious pictures which she has cut from calendars or magazines. Here and there are sacred mottoes and phrases, done in *petit-point* and set in little frames above doorways. Mantelpieces are laden with metal crucifixes and silver figures of saints and angels in a variety of attitudes. By candlelight, these effigies gleam softly along the walls like peering eyes. Rosalie lifts them, straining upwards with apparent tenderness, and dusts off the spots on which they stand, and puts them softly back. There are two before which she blesses herself.

At night, perhaps ten of the men from the platoon gather in the kitchen. We sit around a big table, the top of which is never completely dry because Rosalie scrubs it three times every day, and in the glow of the single candle we raise a great deal of noise and laughter, eat huge helpings of creamed potatoes, and gulp down cognac. In the background, quite in the shadows, four or five visitors sit smoking their pipes beside the stove, and watch our party. Rosalie peels a peck or more of potatoes while we are there, never looking down as she works and never breaking a single peel; they lie in a great curling pile at her feet, like a pile of carpenter's shavings. We get noisier and noisier, and Rosalie peels faster and faster, till her fingers fairly flicker and her hair comes loose in wisps about her forehead. We stand beside the stove in a large dim group, and everybody tries to talk Flemish to the visitors. They offer us cigars, we give them cigarettes, and the place so fills with smoke that there is a bright halo around the candle. When we fail to understand them, which is usually, they shout at us as if we were deaf, poking their whiskered faces near our ears.

We sing a song or two, and prepare to leave. Rosalie sees each one out, guiding them through the cluster of wooden shoes near the door; they look like a fleet of little tied-up gondolas. Then the visitors leave, indicating to me with their hands beside their cheeks that they are going to go to bed. Rosalie makes me some hot milk, washes the dishes in a nearly dark corner, and starts to mix some applesauce, at which she can still be heard working long after I have gone to bed. I read a French newspaper by candlelight and listen to stray aircraft carrying bombs or supplies to the front. It is a deep and comfortable bed, and I never wake up all night.

ERNEST van den HAAG
Is Pornography a Cause of Crime?

Whether pornography should be treated as a crime is largely a moral question. In her book *On Iniquity*, Pamela Hansford Johnson was more concerned with a factual and logical question: Is pornography a cause of crime? She became inclined to think so as she reported (scantily) and reflected (impressionistically) on the "Moors" trial in which Ian Brady and Myra Hindley were found guilty of having murdered an adolescent boy (Evans) and of having abused, tortured, and murdered a little girl aged ten and a boy twelve years old. The bodies of the child victims were found in the moors nearby. The motive was sexual gratification: the pair compelled the children to pose for obscene pictures and made a recording of the terrified screams, the sobs and pitiful pleas for mercy of ten-year-old Lesley Ann Downey as they tortured her to death. In 1966, a court in Chester sentenced the couple to life imprisonment, the severest penalty available.

Although continuing her longstanding opposition to the death penalty, Lady Snow felt uneasy: the outcome of the trial was "aesthetically" disappointing—it did not produce a catharsis. The parents of the dead children (and possibly the community generally) probably were not relieved either by learning that English law now compels them to feed, house, and protect the murderers as long as they live. (The death penalty may have drawbacks but life imprisonment has no fewer.)

Miss Johnson briefly asks whether the murderers might be insane but finds no reason to think so. Neither did the defense. (Both defendants testified rationally, if not very credibly.) In the U.S. insanity might have been pleaded more easily: many American judges and psychiatrists are convinced that people are born good and that wicked acts are sufficient proof that the perpetrators were sick (preferably driven into sickness by society). These psychiatrists and judges transform "sickness" from an independently testable clinical category into the morally necessary cause of all wicked acts. Therefore, the perpetrators of outrageous acts are made sick by definition. Thus, a factual category is transformed into a (rather dubious) moral category unfalsifiable by evidence, yet withdrawn from philosophical scrutiny by being disguised as a scientific (clinical) finding. Psychiatry becomes a normative pseudo-science; and the administration of justice an odd way of providing therapy.

Unfortunately Miss Johnson's reporting tells us more about her reactions to the proceedings, and to the defendants, than about their personalities. Perhaps it is because she is so honestly puzzled about behavior so alien to her that she wonders whether it was Brady's reading which transformed the benevolent utilitarianism so familiar to her—it does not occur to her to question it—into the malevolent utilitarianism which Brady used to rationalize his actions.

Brady had a library almost exclusively concerned with sex and sadism. The works of the Marquis de Sade were prominent and Brady thought of himself as a disciple of his philosophy.

It is here that the issue is joined. Did Brady read what he read because he was what he was? (Might he even have gratified his pre-existing disposition more often by action without the vicarious satisfaction yielded by his reading?) Or, conversely, did Brady become what he became because of his reading? In short, was the reading the effect or the cause?[1] Posed in this way, the question can be (and has been) endlessly debated. But if it is formulated more reasonably, a tentative answer can be given.

Obviously not all readers of de Sade become sadists; nor do all non-readers lead blameless lives. It follows that reading de Sade is not sufficient to become a sadist, nor necessary. It does not follow that reading him has no effect, or that the effect cannot be, at times, decisive either in initiating an inclination leading to acts, or in precipitating acts when the inclination exists.[2] The possibility of sadism is in all of us. Various external conditions may lead us to sadistic actions, or to mere fantasies, or to repudiation of either. Reading of the fantasies of others may lead to actions no less than other external stimuli. From the fact that not all readers of the

1. Mr. J. W. Lambert knows that "the appetites of people like Brady are formed long before any books . . . can have influenced them. Their appetites will lead them to literature not *vice versa.*" Unfortunately Mr. Lambert does not disclose the source of his knowledge. If he has evidence why not disclose it? Or is he pronouncing a dogma? That the opposite case has not been proven is, he surely knows, no proof of his contention. At any rate the issue is not so much "appetites"—these are common enough although usually unconscious—but their translation into action. This translation can plausibly be fostered by literary, moral, or social support. I think it has been [van den Haag's note].

2. Certainly Mr. Kenneth Allsop's argument that "vile deeds originated" with non-readers of sadistic books as well, is irrelevant as an argument against eliminating *one* of the possible causes of "vile deeds." So is his remarkable argument that "a far greater number of children are killed by the motor car each year," or "by aerial bombardment." I am against traffic accidents and wars but I do not see why their occurrence argues for not controlling homicidal literature (or for it not being homicidal). Oddly enough, the fact that we have not found expedient means of preventing traffic accidents or wars has not persuaded Messrs. Lambert and Allsop to come out in favor of either; nor do they favor giving up attempts to control them. Yet they both argue as though their belief that no reasonable way of distinguishing and controlling sadistic literature can be found—quite unrealistic in my opinion—shows the undesirability or unnecessariness of attempting to control it. Of course, it merely shows the difficulties facing (possibly the inexpediency of) an enterprise that remains desirable. It is surely easier to get rid of, and as a first step to prohibit, sadistic literature, than to abolish wars and traffic accidents. Although prohibition will not prevent all distribution it will reduce it and deprive it of social approval. The advantage of this must be weighed against likely disadvantages. I find no such pondering in the intemperate, fustian *ex cathedra* rhetoric of Messrs. Lambert and Allsop [van den Haag's note].

Bible become Christians or act as such, and that some non-readers
do, few people would conclude that the Bible has no influence. Or
(to avoid the issue of "grace"): not all readers of Marx become
Marxists, but some do; some non-readers might have become socialists anyway. Are we to say that Marx had no influence?

How can literate persons accept Jimmy Walker's famous dictum,
"No girl was ever seduced by a book"? Dante's view expressed by
Francesca, that she and Paolo were seduced by a book (*galeotto fu
il libro e chi lo scrisse*)[3] is certainly more realistic. Actions are
influenced by ideas; even emotions—such as love or hate—are
often shaped by ideas and ideal models. Else why write about
them, or about anything? The desire for sex may inhere in us. But
when and how to gratify it, what actions are morally permissible
and what actions are not, whether and when to seduce (or be
seduced) and how, whether and when to rape, or torture, or
kill—these decisions are influenced by culture and milieu, in turn
certainly influenced by literature—quite apart from its direct influence on individuals.

Of course it is hard to trace the direct causes of any individual
act, and to say whether it would have occurred without the book
that, however indirectly, suggested it. The possible causes cannot
be isolated from each other and their role in any action is difficult
to assess. But this hardly argues that books have no influence. It is
odd (as well as wrong) to defend the freedom of literature by pretending that it has no influence. The influence of books varies from
case to case; it can contribute to the formation of dispositions
(given the individual potential for the disposition) or can precipitate the action, once the disposition has been formed for whatever
reasons—just as LSD may precipitate a psychotic episode when
there is a disposition. Since a book hardly ever can be the only
influence, or be influential in isolation—it is always a person with
previous experiences and preexisting disposition who is being
influenced—its precise quantitative role in causation is hard to
trace. But the conclusion that it has *no role* is logically unwar-
ranted and empirically implausible. Nor can one argue reasonably
that something else would necessarily have taken the place of books
among the causes of action. The drug addict might have become
an alcoholic—but not necessarily.

It is strange that the criminal rampage of, say, a deprived Negro
in the U.S.A. is easily ascribed to his deprivation. We are told that
we are guilty of failing to remedy it, and thus of his acts (and that
he is not). But why are we not guilty then of failing to restrict literature, no less logically connected with the rampage of the sadist
who read it? In neither case can a direct causal connection be

---

3. "A betrayer was that book and he who wrote it."

established, or such matters as disposition discounted. In both cases, a causal connection of some sort seems quite likely.

Unless one objects to pornography *per se*, these reflections apply only to sadistic pornography, or to literature that invites non-consensual sexual acts. However, I believe that pornography nearly always leads to sadistic pornography. By definition, pornography deindividualizes and dehumanizes sexual acts; by eliminating all the contexts it reduces people simply to bearers of impersonal sensations of pleasure and pain. This dehumanization eliminates the empathy that restrains us ultimately from sadism and non-consensual acts. The cliché language and the stereotyped situations, the characters not characterized except sexually, are defining characteristics of pornography: the pornographer avoids distraction from the masturbatory fantasy by avoiding art and humanity. Art may "cancel lust" (as Santayana thought) or sublimate it. The pornographer wants to desublimate it. Those who resort to such fantasies habitually are people who are ungratified by others (for endogenous or external reasons). They seek gratification in using others, in inflicting pain (sometimes in suffering it) at least in their fantasy. In this respect, *The Story of O*, which, itself pornographic, also depicts the (rather self-defeating) outcome of pornographic fantasy, is paradigmatic.

In a sense, pornographic and finally sadistic literature is anti-human. Were it directed against a specific human group—*e.g.* Jews or Negroes—the same libertarian ideologues who now oppose censorship might advocate it. Should we find a little Negro or Jewish girl tortured to death and her death agony taped by her murderers, and should we find the murderers imbued with sadistic anti-Semitic or anti-Negro literature—certainly most liberals would advocate that the circulation of such literature be prohibited. But why should humanity as such be less protected than any of the specific groups that compose it? That the hate articulated is directed against people in general rather than against only Jews or Negroes makes it no less dangerous; on the contrary: it makes it as dangerous to more people.

I do not foresee a social organization which can avoid resentments in individuals or sadistic wishes and fantasies. But we could do better in controlling them by, among other things, censoring the literature that by offering models and rationalizations fosters their growth and precipitates them into action.

But shouldn't an adult be able to control himself and read without enacting what he knows to be wrong or, at least, illegal? Perhaps he should. But we are not dealing with a homogeneous group called grown-ups (nor is it possible in the American modern environment to limit anything to adults; children and adolescents are not supervised enough—and the authority of their supervisors has been absent far too long—to make that possible). Too many grown-ups are far from the self-restrained healthy type envisaged by democratic theory. They may easily be given a last, or first, push by the literature I would like to see restricted.

Now, if that literature had literary value, we would have to weigh its loss against the importance of avoiding the deleterious influence it may have. We may even be ready to sacrifice some probable victims for the sake of this literary value. But pornographic "literature" is without literary value. It is printed but it is not literature. Hence there is nothing to be lost by restricting it and there possibly is something to be gained—the lives of the victims who are spared.

There remains the problem of distinguishing pornography from literature. I am convinced that our presumed inability to do so is largely a pretended inability and often pretended in bad faith. But how do you determine what is to be censored? "Lewdness" and "prurience" are matters of opinion; so, therefore, is censorship. Because the power of the censor cannot but be used arbitrarily, by relying on one opinion or another, it endangers the freedom of literature, ultimately of all expression, no less than the license of pornography. Isn't this too high a price to pay?

I don't think we have to pay this price. And, I know of no historical instance where censorship of pornography has endangered freedom in other areas. (The converse does occur, but is irrelevant. Communism or Nazism restricts freedom and *thereupon* censors pornography.) Anyway, a definition of pornography which distinguishes it from literature is neither so nearly impossible a task as some lawyers make it, nor as different from other legal distinctions as they presume. And if we can distinguish pornography from literature we can censor one without restricting the other.

Several extrinsic and intrinsic qualities set pornography apart. The extrinsic qualities are: (1) the intention of the author (or painter, comedian, actor, photographer, editor—or anyone who communicates); (2) the use made of his work—the means used to advertise and sell it, the context created for it; (3) the actual effect on the consumer.

1. If pornographic intention is admitted or proved by testimony and circumstances, there is no problem. If doubtful, intention must be tested by the intrinsic qualities of the work.

2. Regardless of the author's intent his work may be advertised or sold by stressing its (actual or putative) prurient appeal. By itself this justifies action against the seller only. Yet, although sales tactics are neither sufficient nor necessary to establish the prurient appeal of what is sold, they can be relevant: the image created by the seller may well fuse with the object of which it is an image and

have effects on the consumer. Advertisers often claim they achieve this fusion. Sometimes they can—when the object lends itself to it.

3. The actual effect on the consumer—whether "prurient interest" is or is not aroused—depends on the work, its presentation, and the character of the consumer. A work not intended to be pornographic may nonetheless awaken lust, or have lewd effects; and one intended to do so may fail. Censors must consult not only their own reactions but rely on testimony about probable and prevailing reactions and standards. Pornography, to be such, must be likely to have a prurient or lewd effect. But this effect alone, though necessary, is not sufficient. However, together the three extrinsic qualities certainly are. Any two of them seem quite enough.

These qualities suffice to characterize "hard-core" pornography, which is "hard-core" precisely because it has at least two of these extrinsic qualities—and not much else to confuse matters. But what about works which cannot be classified by means of their extrinsic qualities alone—where effect or intention are mixed, or doubtful? Such works can be dealt with only by exploring the intrinsic qualities which make pornography pornographic.

Characteristically, pornography, while dreary and repulsive to one part of the normal (more usual) personality, is also seductive to another: it severs sex from its human context (the Id from Ego and Super-ego), reduces the world to orifices and organs, the action to their combinations.

The pornographic reduction of life to varieties of sex is but the spinning out of pre-adolescent fantasies which reject the burdens of reality and individuation, of conflict, commitment, thought, consideration, and love, of regarding others as more than objects—a burden which becomes heavier and less avoidable in adolescence. Thus in fantasy a return to the pure libidinal pleasure principle is achieved—and fantasy may regress to even more infantile fears and wishes: people are literally devoured, tortured, mutilated, and altogether dehumanized. (Such fantasies are acted out—*e.g.* in concentration camps—whenever authority fails to control, or supports, the impulses it usually helps to repress.)

So much for the content of pornography. It has one aim only: to arouse the reader's lust so that, by sharing the fantasy manufactured for him, he may attain a vicarious sexual experience. Pornography is intended to produce this experience, unlike literature, which aims at the contemplation of experience, at the revelation of its significance. Revelation too is an experience—but one which helps understand and enlarge the possibilities and complexities of the human career—whereas pornography narrows and simplifies them till they are reduced to a series of more or less sophisticated but anonymous (therefore monotonous) sensations.

It is impossible, of course, to serve pornography pure. The vicarious experience must occur through the medium of words, and be depicted in a setting that permits the suspension of disbelief. Yet aesthetic merit would be distracting. To avoid this, pornographers use well-worn and inconspicuous clichés and conventions which do not encumber the libidinous purpose. These qualities are intrinsic to pornography and distinguish it from literature.

Some lawyers argue that the perception of the intrinsic qualities of pornography in any work depends on literary criticism and is, therefore, a matter of opinion. It seems odd, though, that, in a legal context, serious critics themselves often behave as though they believed criticism to be a matter of opinion. Why be a critic—and teach in universities—if it involves no more than uttering capricious and arbitrary opinions? And if criticism cannot tell pornography from literature what can it tell us? Of course critics may disagree; so do other witnesses, including psychiatrists and handwriting experts. The decision is up to the court; the literary witnesses only have the obligation to testify truthfully as to what is or is not pornography.

Some of the critics who claim that they cannot make the distinction do not wish to because they regard pornography as legitimate; others fear that censorship of pornography may be extended to literature. Whatever the merits of such views, they do not justify testifying that the distinction cannot be made. A witness is not entitled to deny that he saw what he did see, simply to save the accused from a punishment he dislikes. A critic who is really incapable of distinguishing pornography from literature certainly has no business being one; a critic who is capable of making the distinction has no business testifying that he is not.

Impulsively, I am against both censors and pornographers—but even more am I against one without the other; if you are for either you should be for both. On reflection, I am: both are wanted and they call for each other, as toreros and bulls do, or hunters and game.

Censorship is no less possible nor less needed than pornography. If we indulge pornography, and do not allow censorship to restrict it, our society at best will become ever more coarse, brutal, anxious, indifferent, de-individualized, hedonistic; at worst its ethos will disintegrate altogether.

The self-restrained and controlled individual may exist and function in an environment which fosters reasonable conduct—but few such individuals will be created, and they will function less well in an environment where they receive little social support, where sadistic acts are openly held up as models and sadistic fantasies are sold to any purchaser. To be sure, a virtuous man will not commit adultery. But a wise wife will avoid situations where the possibility is alluring and the opportunity available. Why must society lead its members into temptation and then punish them when they do what they were tempted to do?

QUESTIONS

1. Upon what argumentative method does van den Haag place his primary reliance? How does he face up to the hard question of determining pornography's effect?
2. How does van den Haag define pornography? How does he distinguish it from literature?
3. In a reply to van den Haag, J. W. Lambert says: "Twice Mr. van den Haag quite unnecessarily shows his cloven hoof—when making, as it happens, perfectly valid points: 'Were it [sadistic pornography] directed against specific human groups—e.g., Jews or Negroes—certainly most liberals would advocate that the circulation of such literature be prohibited.' He is quite right, of course, and this is one of the problems which champions of freedom are almost surely going to have to face in the near future. But the way he has chosen to phrase the observation makes it into an attack on liberal attitudes of mind rather than a strictly relevant comment on the subject under discussion. Again, 'Too many grown-ups,' he writes, 'are far from the self-restrained, healthy type envisaged by democratic theory.' Perfectly true, but the way in which he has chosen to frame the remark turns it into a sneer at democratic values." Is Lambert right? Lambert further says that the way van den Haag argues his case makes him appear to be a "muddle-headed authoritarian"; does it?

THOMAS V. LoCICERO
The Murder of Rabbi Adler[1]

According to his teachers at the University of Michigan, where he majored in political science, Richard Wishnetsky was a brilliant young man. John Higham, professor of history, once described his qualities as follows: "1. intense intellectual curiosity and genuine excitement about ideas; 2. strong sense of the importance of philosophical beliefs, especially natural law; 3. great clarity and logical rigor of thought; 4. judicious and scholarly but nevertheless lively way of handling problems. Personally, he is polite, likable, and extremely eager. Although not without some decided convictions, he is keenly aware of not having most of the answers." Frank Grace, professor of political science, had a similar impression of

---

1. A detailed account of the subject appears in the author's book *Murder in* the *Synagogue* (Englewood Cliffs: Prentice-Hall, 1970).

Richard: "I have never known a young man more eager to learn and more willing to expend the effort which learning requires. He is supremely gifted and will in my opinion become an original and creative scholar."

In his junior year, Richard was elected to Phi Beta Kappa, and upon his graduation in 1964, he was awarded a Woodrow Wilson Fellowship for further study at the University of Detroit. There were satisfying moments also outside his academic career according to Jonathan Rose, his dormitory mate, who said, "Richard considered one of the high points of his student life the time he had a chance to meet President Kennedy after that famous speech given at Ann Arbor on founding the Peace Corps. He talked about joining the Peace Corps for a long while after that, then he talked about attending the London School of Economics, but neither of those things happened, unfortunately."

Some who knew Richard in Ann Arbor maintain that a line might be drawn between his reaction to the assassination of Kennedy and the later events in his life. Because the assassination disturbed him deeply, it may also have impressed him with the remarkable extent to which a public outrage can affect private individuals, and it may have intensified his growing sense of the necessity for rigid, absolute answers to questions he had previously been willing to explore with tolerance and patience.

In any case, Richard Wishnetsky's life apparently took a new turn the summer following the assassination, when—after graduation from Michigan—he went on a trip to Israel. There, he became intensely interested in one of the ultra-orthodox Hasidic sects and its idea of a "holy life." He had received some religious training at Detroit's Conservative Shaarey Zedek congregation, of which his parents were members, but prior to his trip he had exhibited no great concern with matters of faith. In September, 1964, after his return home, he began work on a master's degree in sociology at the University of Detroit. Soon, however, he was including courses in comparative religion and spending more and more of his time reading theology.

Changes were also occurring in his personal life. He had moved into an apartment with two other young men, one of whom, Patrick J. Burke, later reported: "Occasionally he would talk about what he thought was wrong with the world or about thinking the Jewish people were not living up to the tenets of their religion. At first it all was in the nature of calm discussion, which grew gradually more excited as the weeks went past. After a few months, Richard started talking against specific people." Often upset and irrational, Richard would argue senselessly and viciously with his parents, friends, and professors, then fly into tantrums knocking over furniture and threatening violence. According to Dr. Sander J. Breiner, a psychiatrist, and a friend of the Wishnetsky family, "From a quiet and well-mannered individual, Richard turned into a poor-mannered and bellicose young man. Where he used to discuss issues and listen to others' opinions, he suddenly knew all the answers and was argumentative. He began to issue pronouncements."

Though he finally alienated most of his teachers and allowed his academic work to deteriorate, Richard did manage to make at least one friend among the faculty of the University of Detroit—Joyce Carol Oates, a writer and a member of the English department. Richard walked into her office one day in the spring of 1965 and engaged her in what was to be the first in a series of long conversations. "It was all there on that first day," Miss Oates has said, "the latent violence, the scornful refutations, the sense that the majority of people are somehow wrong and therefore contemptible. But he had flashes of insight and good humor; he was charming. He could recognize at times his own audacity, his table-pounding egotism, and nod in agreement with my sometimes harsh judgments of him —in those occasional tender moments of self-illumination that made him unforgettably human."[2]

In the course of these talks, Richard told Miss Oates that "if God did not exist, life was not worth living and he would commit suicide." Moreover, he once mentioned casually, "with a smile, that if he did commit suicide—which he would not—it would be in the synagogue during Sabbath services."

In May of 1965, on the advice of a family physician, Richard's parents asked their son to submit to psychiatric testing and therapy. Richard agreed, but after visits to a number of psychiatrists, he abandoned treatment. Shortly thereafter, following one of his tantrums, his parents had police pick him up at his apartment at four A.M. and place him in the mental ward of Detroit's Herman Kiefer Hospital.

On July 29, 1965, with Richard still in the hospital but bitterly unhappy and anxious to leave, his father, Edward Wishnetsky, the owner of an insurance agency, petitioned probate court for Richard's admission to Ypsilanti State Hospital. At the time, Mr. Wishnetsky said of his son:

He has been extremely hostile, belligerent, and threatening recently. He has threatened to smear his family with scandal although in reality there is no scandal to spread. He has threatened to burn up his mother's car and the family home. He broke his mother's golf club in a fit of anger. He also broke a large glass tabletop at home. He has threatened to smear the University of Detroit with scandal if they did not prematurely release his scholarship funds to him so that he could use these funds to go to Europe instead of to the university. He has been extremely hyperactive, does not sleep, makes innumerable phone calls day and night, says

2. From an article in the *Detroit Free Press*, March 6, 1966 [LoCicero's note].

he is going to get a date with President Johnson's daughters. He is at times very depressed, alternating with a very agitated, frenzied behavior. Although very bright, he uses his intellect to verbally slaughter those around him in a very belligerent and hostile manner.

Statements from two doctors, who maintained that Richard was mentally ill, a danger to himself and others, accompanied Mr. Wishnetsky's petition, which was granted: on August 19, 1965, Richard entered the state hospital. Ten days later he was permitted the freedom of the hospital grounds, and on September 9 he escaped from the institution and succeeded in persuading his parents that he was well enough to be free. The court, acting on the advice of two psychiatrists at the hospital, later ruled that Richard be officially discharged.

In one of their conversations, Richard told Dr. Breiner that "he thought his stay in the hospital was one of the best things that ever happened to him, although he didn't make it clear why. And he appeared to be calmer. Before he went into the hospital, he'd often say things like, 'There's nothing wrong with me, it's the world,' but after he got out he recognized he had a problem." Indeed, after his stay in the hospital, Richard paid several visits to two psychiatrists, one of whom wrote to the court on December 3, saying: "At the present time, he seems very well controlled. He is working well in his relationship with me, and I do not anticipate the need for hospitalization."

Yet Richard stayed with neither doctor very long and—according to Dr. Breiner—was constantly running away from people who might have been able to help him. Dr. Breiner recalls that "Whenever I talked to Richard about his problem, he would smile and say, 'I know ... but.'"

The fall and early winter of 1965 were a chaotic time for Richard: living at home with his parents but disappearing without a word for days at a time; running to and from psychiatrists, friends, and acquaintances, all terribly worried about him; returning to his former roommates to blame them for his troubles, and insisting they were against him since they had not tried to get him out of the hospital; attending classes at Wayne State University in Detroit and giving religious lectures on the campus; visiting in Brooklyn, long after midnight, with the Lubavitcher Rebbe,[3] who advised him to study Judaism thoroughly and to wait until he was fifty before turning to comparative religion; working as a substitute teacher in Detroit public schools; writing tormented letters which he left unmailed.

One such letter, dated October 20 and later found with other personal writings and belongings, reads:

3. Spiritual leader of a Hasidic group in Brooklyn.

I think too much. I don't think enough. I want to be me—I am only the welter of my anxieties, fears and superficialities. I do not walk, I stumble. I do not live, I respond to stimuli. I do not live, I exist. I am not a man, just a body. I live, yet I am dead. The only anguish I experience is that of self-pity and becoming aware of my own horrid, pervasive, unacceptable and contemptible selfishness, my own inability to love. When I am not miserable I am a phony.

The same letter includes a prayer:

Let my life be a testimony to Thy diverse truths, let it be one of beauty and of justice, for its roots shall be in love and reason. Oh, God, I want to live! Let me! And then let my life go beyond justice, beyond vengeance; let it emerge into the pure understanding of mercy.

Through all of this, Richard continued to dream and plan on an impressive scale. Earlier in the year he had applied for admission to the University of Chicago's Committee on Social Thought to work with Mircea Eliade, Saul Bellow, and Hannah Arendt. Eliade agreed to supervise his work on a thesis involving a study of "the creation and destruction of philosophy"—its creation begun by Aristotle and its destruction initiated by Descartes and completed by Nietzsche.

Richard had also applied to, and was accepted by, the university's divinity school, where he wanted to work with Paul Tillich. But on October 22, two days after Richard wrote his prayer, Paul Tillich died of a heart ailment at the age of seventy-nine.

On February 1, 1966, Richard began writing a tract entitled, "Fantasy Regarding an Assassination of Robert S. McNamara" which eventually covered six pages in longhand. It contains an apology for his imagined murder of the Secretary of Defense, along with a bitter, rambling commentary on himself and the world in which he was trying to live. He begins:

My act was motivated by philosophical and social reasons, not political ones. It is a protest, the registration of an outrage, a dire warning. Its author entertains no illusions as to its bringing about any immediate substantial change in the American scene. At present I do believe there will be a change in the future—a change for the worse. The selfishness, stupidity, and vanity of men shall succeed in triumphing over whatever goodness there is, the ultimate being obliteration, both spiritual and physical, of this planet. Hail brave new world! Hail nothingness!

Of Secretary of Defense Robert McNamara, Richard writes:

[He] symbolizes that which I despise—the business mentality which is more concerned with material matters than human matters—the kind of mentality (Protestant ethic) which is most responsible for the dehumanization of society, the prostitution of intellect, resulting in a very bright but neither wise nor profound man. . . . He who lives by the sword shall die by the sword. How much did Mr. McNamara take into consideration the killing of innocent Vietnamese which has resulted from American bombings, for this killing is murder?

He is full of bitter contempt for the quality of American life:

> The church has become a hypocrisy whose structures no longer find
> genuine residence in the souls of those who hear them. And most im-
> portantly and most sadly of all, the family is swiftly becoming—if it has
> not already arrived there—shot to hell. . . . I am part of the bastard
> progeny of this nation. We are building not men, but a generation of
> barbarians and mediocrities who recognize and will breed no value higher
> than their paltry selfish selves. Zombies. . . . Judaism in America does
> not need to worry about anti-Semitism destroying it from without. The
> American Jewish community is destroying itself from within. Shaarey
> Zedek is a synagog which bears witness against God.

About himself, Richard writes:

> My life will probably end with a whimper—a depressed whimper. Pos-
> sibly with a bang. Since I cannot live like a man, I hope to die like one.
> I am entering the final stage of unreality. . . . You say that I am sick—
> you are right. You dismiss me because I am sick—in that you are wrong.
> . . . The dark side of creativity is sickness. . . . Anyway, in our society
> to be normal is to be sick, to be hung up on loneliness, insecure about
> one's stature, uncertain about one's self, overly concerned about pleasing
> everybody, being "nice" all the time—damn niceness. . . . not offending
> anyone, so that one winds up pleasing no one and, to boot, not knowing
> who or why one is.

Richard included a "last will and testament" in this document,
leaving whatever money he possessed to the Jewish National Fund
and the Lubavitcher Hasidim. Two days later, on February 3, he
traveled to Toledo, Ohio, where the laws governing the purchase of
firearms are less strict than in Michigan. In a Toledo pawnshop he
paid $72.05 for a twenty-year-old .32 caliber Colt revolver with its
former five-inch barrel sawed off to one inch. (Two weeks before,
the pawnshop had bought the gun for $10.00.) Back in his parents'
home, Richard tested the weapon in the basement, and—according
to a friend—stated that firing the gun gave him a "sense of power."

On Monday, February 7, Richard reported to the Fort Wayne
army induction center for examination, and was promptly found
unacceptable for military service. The next day he called the psychiatrist he had not seen for weeks. Richard's parents were heartened
by his apparent renewal of interest in treatment, but on Thursday,
their son once more disappeared from home without a word.

On Friday evening, February 11, Richard checked into a small
Detroit hotel. In a large leather satchel, he carried a change of
clothes; toilet articles; a number of books, including *The Brothers
Karamazov*, a Bible, works by Ortega y Gasset and Nietzsche; some
records featuring the Soviet Army Chorus and Band, Joan Baez,
Igor Stravinsky, Arturo Toscanini, and Theodore Bikel; and his gun.

In his copy of *The Brothers Karamazov*, Richard had underlined a
passage which describes Alyosha, the gentle and forgiving Karamazov; in the margin he had written, "Me." The passage reads:

. . . Add to that that he was to a certain extent a young man of our times, that is, honest by nature, demanding truth, seeking it, believing in it, and believing in it, demanding to serve it with all the strength of his soul, yearning for an immediate act of heroism and wishing to sacrifice everything, even life itself, for that act of heroism.

Apparently he did not give similar attention to the lines that immediately follow:

. . . these young men unhappily fail to understand that the sacrifice of life is, in many cases, the easiest of all sacrifices, and that to sacrifice, for instance, five or six years of their seething youth to hard and tedious study, if only to multiply tenfold their powers of serving the truth and the cause they have set before them as their goal—such a sacrifice is utterly beyond the strength of many of them.

The Saturday morning of February 12, 1966—Lincoln's birthday —was unseasonably warm, with the temperature near 40 degrees, and a light mixture of rain and snow falling. Late that morning, Richard arrived at the huge, impressive synagogue of Congregation Shaarey Zedek in suburban Southfield, northwest of Detroit—a building which presents a massive and oblique triangular thrust to the western sky. Dressed neatly in a suit and tie, he unobtrusively took a seat in front and listened to Rabbi Morris Adler speak about Abraham Lincoln and the Emancipation Proclamation. The point of the sermon was that Lincoln—destroyed at the apex of his service to mankind by a deranged and frustrated critic—was a truly religious man even though he did not belong to any church.

Rabbi Adler, a bearded, barrel-chested man of athletic build, was an eloquent speaker who bore his learning lightly. A scholar and theologian of considerable repute, he had contributed articles and essays to numerous magazines, and had written and edited several books on the Talmud. A school had been named after him in Israel, where he had recently spent a year on sabbatical, and two honorary doctoral degrees had been conferred on him in the past few years.

As a young man, Rabbi Adler, now fifty-nine years old, had been a chaplain in the Pacific theatre during World War II. Among other things, he was known in Detroit for his work in interfaith relations—this very service was being attended by a hundred and twenty-five visitors from various churches. He was also active in civic affairs: chairman of the United Auto Workers union's public review board, vice-president of the Community Health Association, member of the Governor's Committee for Higher Education, member of the Citizen's Advisory Committee on Equal Opportunities, and president of the Zionist Organization of Detroit.

"A rabbi practices the most unspecialized profession in the universe," he had said not long before, "but my association with the young people is, for me, the most satisfying part of my work."

Richard Wishnetsky, sitting quietly with a gun in his pocket, was in a position to know all of this. He had often talked to Rabbi

Adler, and during the year past had frequently sought his counsel. Rabbi Adler, in turn, was familiar with Richard's problems, and had been trying to draw him away from the abyss that threatened to engulf him.

Rabbi Adler finished his sermon at approximately 11:40 A.M. and returned to his seat on the *bimah*[4] next to thirteen-year-old Steven Frank, whose bar mitzvah had been celebrated during the service. As a cantor began to chant the Kaddish, Richard moved calmly but swiftly to the front of the *bimah*, raised his gun and fired a bullet into the high, vaulted ceiling of the Sanctuary. A moment of stunned silence followed. Then Richard shouted to the two cantors, the president of the congregation, and the Frank boy, all of whom were on the *bimah*, "In your seats! Off the *bimah!*" They hesitated but then obeyed when Rabbi Adler said, "You had better do what he says. This boy is sick."

Richard climbed the steps to the pulpit at the center of the *bimah* and turned to face the congregation of over seven hundred people, including his father, mother, and sister. The rabbi remained in his seat, about fifteen feet away. Richard placed his gun on the pulpit, unfolded a piece of paper, grabbed the microphone, and began to read a statement. A tape recorder, used to record the rabbi's sermon, continued to turn, thus capturing the speech and sounds of what followed.

"This congregation," Richard read in a clear and self-possessed voice, "is a travesty and an abomination. It has made a mockery by its phoniness and hypocrisy of the beauty and spirit of Judaism. It is composed of people . . ." He stopped as he noticed a member of the congregation moving toward him. "Off!" he shouted. The rabbi motioned the man away. "Go back down," he said quietly. "I know this boy."

"It is composed of people," continued Richard, "who on the whole make me ashamed to say that I am a Jew. For the most part . . ." Here his audience began to stir, and he said firmly, "Everybody quiet. It is composed of men, women, and children who care for nothing except their vain, egotistical selves. With this act I protest a humanly horrifying and hence unacceptable situation."

Richard turned to his right, revolver in hand, to face Rabbi Adler. In a soft, almost tender voice, he said, "Rabbi . . ." and then shot the seated man in the left forearm. The bullet ricocheted off the bone and entered the left side of the rabbi's head behind the ear. Amid wild screams from the audience, the rabbi rose and Richard took a few steps toward him. At almost point-blank range Richard fired again. This time the bullet pierced the rabbi's yarmulke and creased the top of his skull. As the screaming from the

---

4. The platform from which services are conducted [LoCicero's note].

audience reached a wild intensity, Rabbi Adler fell heavily to the floor. Richard now placed the gun barrel against his own head and fired a shot through his brain. He reeled and stumbled backward for seven or eight feet, then fell on his back.

The two men, the rabbi and his young assailant, were rushed to immediate surgery in separate hospitals nearby. After lingering in life for nearly five more days, Richard Wishnetsky died early in the morning on Wednesday, February 16, 1966. He was buried that same afternoon, following a private service. The eulogy was spoken by Rabbi Irwin Groner, an assistant at Shaarey Zedek, who said: "How could these qualities and tendencies reside within one human spirit? Love and hate. Intelligence and madness. The search for clarity and the acceptance of fantasy! 'The heart's devious—who can know it?' "

In the ambulance which took him from Shaarey Zedek to the hospital, Rabbi Adler gained consciousness from time to time, asking for his wife. At the hospital it was discovered that the first bullet, rather than penetrating the skull, had flattened against it, sending minute bone fragments into vital areas of the brain. A team of prominent surgeons performed two operations, after which Rabbi Adler was placed in an intensive-care ward. The doctors explained that they could do nothing further.

The rabbi remained in the ward for more than three weeks, without regaining consciousness. His wife was almost constantly at his side. She had been one of the first to reach her fallen husband on the *bimah*, and one of the first to console the horror-stricken Wishnetsky family.

Prayers were offered for Rabbi Adler in churches throughout the country, and messages of sympathy poured in from all over the world. Rabbi Morris Adler died early in the morning on March 11, 1966, and was buried two days later. Over six thousand people attended the funeral, described as the largest in the history of Detroit.

Earlier a note had been discovered, written by Richard before the fatal day; in it he spoke of what he was planning to do as though it had already been accomplished:

My distorted, disoriented voice, either barely uttered or tremendously violent, gives you a slight horrifying glimpse into the dehumanized future that awaits you and your unfortunate children, who will be healthy, comfortable and secure beyond your fondest dreams and just as diseased. Since I feel that I am no longer able to make any significant creative contributions I shall make a destructive one. What happened in Shaarey Zedek happens only once in a lifetime. . . . Suffer in your frozen hells of apathy, boil in the self-hate of outraged impotence. Listen to my voice, you deaf ones. Listen to how sick, sad, lonely and forlorn it is.

QUESTIONS

1. What effect does the third paragraph have on your understanding of Wishnetsky's decline? Is the suggestion of some connection between Kennedy's assassination and Wishnetsky's madness warranted by the materials of the article? What would be the effect of dropping this paragraph?
2. Could the author have used other public or private events in Wishnetsky's life to give a different focus to his actions?
3. How does the author feel about Wishnetsky? How does he want us to feel?

ERIK H. ERIKSON

The Golden Rule in the Light of New Insight[1]

When a lecture is announced one does not usually expect the title to foretell very much about the content. But it must be rare, indeed, that a title is as opaque as the one on your invitation to this lecture: for it does not specify the field from which new insight is to come and throw new light on the old principle of the Golden Rule. You took a chance, then, in coming, and now that I have been introduced as a psychoanalyst, you must feel that you have taken a double chance.

Let me tell you, therefore, how I came upon our subject. In Harvard College, I teach a course, "The Human Life Cycle." There (since I am by experience primarily a clinician) we begin by considering those aggravated *crises* which mark each stage of life and are known to psychiatry as potentially pathogenic. But we proceed to discuss the potential *strengths* which each stage contributes to human maturity. In either case, so psychiatric experience and the observation of healthy children tell us, much depends on the interplay of generations in which human strength can be revitalized or human weakness perseverated "into the second and third generation." But this leads us to the role of the individual in the sequence of generations, and thus to that evolved order which your scriptures call *Lokasangraha*—the "maintenance of the world" (in Professor Radhakrishnan's translation). Through the study of case-histories and of life-histories we psychoanalysts have begun to discern certain fateful and certain fruitful patterns of interaction in those most concrete categories (parent and child, man and woman, teacher and pupil) which carry the burden of maintenance from generation to generation. The implication of our insights for ethics had preoccupied me before I came here; and, as you will well understand, a few months of animated discussion in India have by no means disa-

1. From *Insight and Responsibility* (1964).

bused me from such concerns. I have, therefore, chosen to tell you where I stand in my teaching, in the hope of learning more from you in further discussion.

My base line is the Golden Rule, which advocates that one should do (or not do) to another what one wishes to be (or not to be) done by. Systematic students of ethics often indicate a certain disdain for this all-too-primitive ancestor of more logical principles; and Bernard Shaw found the rule an easy target: don't do to another what you would like to be done by, he warned, because his tastes may differ from yours. Yet this rule has marked a mysterious meeting ground between ancient peoples separated by oceans and eras, and has provided a hidden theme in the most memorable sayings of many thinkers.

The Golden Rule obviously concerns itself with one of the very basic paradoxes of human existence. Each man calls his own a separate body, a self-conscious individuality, a personal awareness of the cosmos, and a certain death; and yet he shares this world as a *reality* also perceived and judged by others and as an *actuality* within which he must commit himself to ceaseless interaction. This is acknowledged in your scriptures as the principle of Karma.

To identify self-interest and the interest of other selves, the Rule alternately employs the method of warning, "Do *not* as you would *not* be done by," and of exhortation, "Do, as you *would* be done by." For psychological appeal, some versions rely on a minimum of *egotistic prudence*, while others demand a maximum of *altruistic sympathy*. It must be admitted that the formula, "Do not to others what if done to you would cause you pain," does not presuppose much more than the mental level of the small child who desists from pinching when it gets pinched in return. More mature insight is assumed in the saying, "No one is a believer until he loves for his brother what he loves for himself." Of all the versions, however, none commit us as unconditionally as the Upanishad's, "he who sees all beings in his own self and his own self in all beings," and the Christian injunction, "love thy neighbor as thyself." They even suggest a true love and a true knowledge of ourselves. Freud, of course, took this Christian maxim deftly apart as altogether illusory, thus denying with the irony of the enlightenment what a maxim really is—and what (as I hope to show) his method may really stand for.

I will not (I could not) trace the versions of the Rule to various world religions. No doubt in English translation all of them have become somewhat assimilated to Biblical versions. Yet the basic formula seems to be universal, and it re-appears in an astonishing number of the most revered sayings of our civilization, from St. Francis' prayer to Kant's moral imperative and Lincoln's simple political creed: "As I would not be slave, I would not be master."

The variations of the Rule have, of course, provided material for many a discussion of ethics weighting the soundness of the logic implied and measuring the degree of ethical nobility reached in each. My field of inquiry, the clinical study of the human life cycle, suggests that I desist from arguing logical merit or spiritual worth and instead distinguish *variations in moral and ethical sensitivity* in accordance with stages in the development of human conscience.

The dictionary, our first refuge from ambiguity, in this case only confounds it: morals and ethics are defined as synonyms *and* antonyms of each other. In other words, they are the same, with a difference—a difference which I intend to emphasize. For it is clear that he who knows what is legal or illegal and what is moral or immoral has not necessarily learned thereby what is ethical. Highly moralistic people can do unethical things, while an ethical man's involvement in immoral doings becomes by inner necessity an occasion for tragedy.

I would propose that we consider *moral rules* of conduct to be based on a fear of *threats* to be forestalled. These may be outer threats of abandonment, punishment and public exposure, or a threatening inner sense of guilt, of shame or of isolation. In either case, the rationale for obeying a rule may not be too clear; it is the threat that counts. In contrast, I would consider *ethical rules* to be based on *ideals* to be striven for with a high degree of rational assent and with a ready consent to a formulated good, a definition of perfection, and some promise of self-realization. This differentiation may not agree with all existing definitions, but it is substantiated by the observation of human development. Here, then, is my first proposition: the moral and the ethical sense are different in their psychological dynamics, because the moral sense develops on an earlier, more immature level. This does not mean that the moral sense could be skipped, as it were. On the contrary, all that exists layer upon layer in an adult's mind has developed step by step in the growing child's, and all the major steps in the comprehension of what is considered good behavior in one's cultural universe are—for better and for worse—related to different stages in individual maturation. But they are all necessary to one another.

The response to a moral tone of voice develops early, and many an adult is startled when inadvertently he makes an infant cry, because his voice has conveyed more disapproval than he intended to. Yet, the small child, so limited to the intensity of the moment, somehow must learn the boundaries marked by "don'ts." Here, cultures have a certain leeway in underscoring the goodness of one who does not transgress or the evilness of one who does. But the conclusion is unavoidable that children can be made to feel evil, and that adults continue to project evil on one another and on their children far beyond the verdict of rational judgment. Mark Twain once characterized man as "the animal that blushes."

Psychoanalytic obervation first established the psychological basis of a fact which Eastern thinkers have always known, namely, that the radical division into good and bad can be *the* sickness of the mind. It has traced the moral scruples and excesses of the adult to the childhood stages in which guilt and shame are ready to be aroused and are easily exploited. It has named and studied the "super-ego" which hovers over the ego as the inner perpetuation of the child's subordination to the restraining will of his elders. The voice of the super-ego is not always cruel and derisive, but it is ever ready to become so whenever the precarious balance which we call a good conscience is upset, at which times the secret weapons of this inner governor are revealed: the brand of shame and the bite of conscience. We who deal with the consequences in individual neuroses and in collective irrationality must ask ourselves whether excessive guilt and excessive shame are "caused" or merely accentuated by the pressure of parental and communal methods, by the threat of loss of affection, of corporal punishment, of public shaming. Or are they by now a proclivity for self-alienation which has become a part—and, to some extent, a necessary part—of man's evolutionary heritage?

All we know for certain is that the moral proclivity in man does not develop without the establishment of some chronic self-doubt and some truly terrible—even if largely submerged—rage against anybody and anything that reinforces such doubt. The "lowest" in man is thus apt to reappear in the guise of the "highest." Irrational and pre-rational combinations of goodness, doubt, and rage can re-emerge in the adult in those malignant forms of righteousness and prejudice which we may call *moralism*. In the name of high moral principles all the vindictiveness of derision, of torture, and of mass extinction can be employed. One surely must come to the conclusion that the Golden Rule was meant to protect man not only against his enemy's open attacks, but also against his friend's righteousness.

Lest this view, in spite of the evidence of history, seem too "clinical," we turn to the writings of the evolutionists who in the last few decades have joined psychoanalysis in recognizing the super-ego as an evolutionary fact—and danger. The *developmental* principle is thus joined by an *evolutionary* one. Waddington[2] even goes so far as to say that super-ego rigidity may be an overspecialization in the human race, like the excessive body armor of the late dinosaurs. In a less grandiose comparison he likens the super-ego to "the finicky adaptation of certain parasites which fits them to live only on one

2. C. H. Waddington, *The Ethical Animal*, London: Allen and Unwin, 1960 [Erikson's note].

host animal." In recommending his book, *The Ethical Animal*, I must admit that his terminology contradicts mine. He calls the awakening of morality in childhood a proclivity for "ethicizing," whereas I would prefer to call it moralizing. As do many animal psychologists, he dwells on analogies between the very young child and the young animal instead of comparing, as I think we must, the young animal with the pre-adult human, including the adolescent.

In fact, I must introduce here an amendment to my first, my "developmental" proposition, for between the development in childhood of man's *moral* proclivity and that of his *ethical* powers in adulthood, adolescence intervenes when he perceives the universal good in *ideological* terms. The imagery of steps in development, of course, is useful only where it is to be suggested that one item precedes another in such a way that the earlier one is necessary to the later ones and that each later one is of a higher order.

This "epigenetic" principle, according to which the constituent parts of a ground plan develop during successive stages, will be immediately familiar to you. For in the traditional Hindu concept of the life cycle the four intrinsic goals of life (Dharma, the orders that define virtue; Artha, the powers of the actual; Kama, the joys of libidinal abandon; and Moksha, the peace of deliverance) come to their successive and mutual perfection during the four stages, the ashramas of the apprentice, the householder, the hermit, and the ascetic. These stages are divided from each other by sharp turns of direction; yet, each depends on the previous one, and whatever perfection is possible depends on them all.

I would not be able to discuss the relation of these two foursomes to each other, nor ready to compare this ideal conception to our epigenetic views of the life cycle. But the affinities of the two conceptions are apparent, and at least the ideological indoctrination of the apprentice, the Brahmacharya, and the ethical one of the Grihasta, the householder, correspond to the developmental categories suggested here.

No wonder; for it is the joint development of cognitive and emotional powers paired with appropriate social learning which enables the individual to realize the potentialities of a stage. Thus youth becomes ready—if often only after a severe bout with moralistic regression—to envisage the more universal principles of a highest human good. The adolescent learns to grasp the flux of time, to anticipate the future in a coherent way, to perceive ideas and to assent to ideals, to take—in short—an *ideological* position for which the younger child is cognitively not prepared. In adolescence, then, an ethical view is approximated, but it remains susceptible to an alternation of impulsive judgment and odd rationalization. It is, then, as true for adolescence as it is for childhood that man's way stations to maturity can become fixed, can become premature end stations, or stations for future regression.

The moral sense, in its perfections and its perversions, has been an intrinsic part of man's *evolution,* while the sense of ideological rejuvenation has pervaded his *revolutions,* both with prophetic idealism and with destructive fanaticism. Adolescent man, in all his sensitivity to the ideal, is easily exploited by promises of counterfeit millennia, easily taken in by the promise of a new and arrogantly exclusive identity.

The *true* ethical sense of the young adult, finally, encompasses and goes beyond moral restraint and ideal vision, while insisting on concrete commitments to those intimate relationships and work associations by which man can hope to share a lifetime of productivity and competence. But young adulthood engenders its own dangers. It adds to the moralist's righteousness, the *territorial defensiveness* of one who has appropriated and staked out his earthly claim and who seeks eternal security in the super-identity of organizations. Thus, what the Golden Rule at its highest has attempted to make all-inclusive, tribes and nations, castes and classes, moralities and ideologies have consistently made exclusive again—proudly, superstitiously, and viciously denying the status of reciprocal ethics to those "outside."

If I have so far underscored the malignant potentials of man's slow maturation, I have done so not in order to dwell on a kind of dogmatic pessimism which can emerge all too easily from clinical preoccupation and often leads only to anxious avoidances. I know that man's moral, ideological, and ethical propensities can find, and have found on occasion, a sublime integration, in individuals and in groups who were both tolerant and firm, both flexible and strong, both wise and obedient. Above all, men have always shown a dim knowledge of their better potentialities by paying homage to those purest leaders who taught the simplest and most inclusive rules for an undivided mankind. I will have a word to say later about Gandhi's continued "presence" in India. But men have also persistently betrayed them, on what passed for moral or ideological grounds, even as they are now preparing a potential betrayal of the human heritage on scientific and technological grounds in the name of that which is considered good merely because it can be made to work—no matter where it leads. No longer do we have license to emphasize either the "positive" or the "negative" in man. Step for step, they go together: moralism with moral obedience, fanaticism with ideological devotion, and rigid conservatism with adult ethics.

Man's socio-genetic evolution is about to reach a crisis in the full sense of the word, a crossroads offering one path to fatality, and one to recovery and further growth. Artful perverter of joy and keen exploiter of strength, man is the animal that has learned to survive "in a fashion," to multiply without food for the multitudes, to grow up healthily without reaching personal maturity, to live well but without purpose, to invent ingeniously without aim, and to kill grandiosely without need. But the processes of socio-genetic evolution also seem to promise a new humanism, the acceptance by man—as an evolved product as well as a producer, and a self-conscious tool of further evolution—of the obligation to be guided in his planned actions and his chosen self-restraints by his knowledge and his insights. In this endeavor, then, it may be of a certain importance to learn to understand and to master the differences between infantile morality, adolescent ideology and adult ethics. Each is necessary to the next, but each is effective only if they eventually combine in that wisdom which, as Waddington puts it, "fulfills sufficiently the function of mediating evolutionary advance."

At the point, however, when one is about to end an argument with a global injunction of what we *must* do, it is well to remember Blake's admonition that the common good readily becomes the topic of "the scoundrel, the hypocrite, and the flatterer"; and that he who would do some good must do so in "minute particulars." And indeed, I have so far spoken only of the developmental and the evolutionary principle, according to which the propensity for ethics grows in the individual as part of an adaptation roughly laid down by evolution. Yet, to grow in the individual, ethics must be generated and regenerated in and by the sequence of generations—again, a matter fully grasped and systematized, some will say stereotyped, in the Hindu tradition. I must now make more explicit what our insights tell us about this process.

Let me make an altogether new start here. Let us look at scientific man in his dealings with animals and let us assume (this is not a strange assumption in India) that animals, too, may have a place close to the "other" included in the Rule. The psychologists among you know Professor Harry Harlow's studies on the development of what he calls affection in monkeys.[3] He did some exquisite experimental and photographic work attempting, in the life of laboratory monkeys, to "control the mother variable." He took monkeys from their mothers within a few hours after birth, isolated them and left them with "mothers" made out of wire, metal, wood, and terry cloth. A rubber nipple somewhere in their middles emitted piped-in milk, and the whole contraption was wired for body warmth. All the "variables" of this mother situation were controlled: the amount of rocking, the temperature of the "skin," and the exact

3. H. F. Harlow and M. K. Harlow, "A Study of Animal Affection," *The Journal of the American Museum of* *Natural History*, Vol. 70, No. 10, 1961 [Erikson's note].

incline of the maternal body necessary to make a scared monkey feel safe and comfortable. Years ago, when this method was presented as a study of the development of affection in monkeys, the clinician could not help wondering whether the small animals' obvious attachment to this contraption was really *monkey* affection or a fetishist addiction to inanimate objects. And, indeed, while these laboratory-reared monkeys became healthier and healthier, and much more easily trained in technical know-how than the inferior animals brought up by mere monkey mothers, they became at the end what Harlow calls "psychotics." They sit passively, they stare vacantly, and some do a terrifying thing: when poked they bite themselves and tear at their own flesh until the blood flows. They have not learned to experience "the other," whether as mother, mate, child—or enemy. Only a tiny minority of the females produced offspring, and only one of them made an attempt to nurse hers. But science remains a wonderful thing. Now that we have succeeded in producing "psychotic" monkeys experimentally, we can convince ourselves that we have at last given scientific support to the theory that severely disturbed mother-child relationships "cause" human psychosis.

This is a long story; but it speaks for Professor Harlow's methods that what they demonstrate is unforgettable. At the same time, they lead us to that borderline where we recognize that the scientific approach toward living beings must be with concepts and methods adequate to the study of ongoing life, not of selective extinction. I have put it this way: one can study the nature of things by doing something *to* them, but one can really learn something about the essential nature of living beings only by doing something *with* them or *for* them. This, of course, is the principle of clinical science. It does not deny that one can learn by dissecting the dead, or that animal or man can be motivated to lend circumscribed parts of themselves to an experimental procedure. But for the study of those central transactions which are the carriers of socio-genetic evolution, and for which we must take responsibility in the future, the chosen unit of observation must be the generation, not the individual. Whether an individual animal or human being has partaken of the stuff of life can only be tested by the kind of observation which includes his ability to transmit life—in some essential form—to the next generation.

One remembers here the work of Konrad Lorenz, and the kind of "inter-living" research which he and others have developed, making—in principle—the life cycle of certain selected animals part of the same environment in which the observer lives his own life cycle, studying his own role as well as theirs and taking his chances with what his ingenuity can discern in a setting of sophisticated naturalist inquiry. One remembers also Elsa the lioness, a foundling who was brought up in the Adamson household in Kenya. There the mother variable was not controlled, it was in control. Mrs. Adamson and her husband even felt responsible for putting grown-up Elsa back among the lions and succeeded in sending her back to the bush, where she mated and had cubs, and yet came back from time to time (accompanied by her cubs) to visit her human foster parents. In our context, we cannot fail to wonder about the built-in "moral" sense that made Elsa respond—and respond in very critical situations, indeed—to the words, "No, Elsa, no," *if* the words came from human beings she trusted. Yet, even with this built-in "moral" response, and with a lasting trust in her foster parents (which she transmitted to her wild cubs) she was able to live as a wild lion. Her mate, however, never appeared; he apparently was not too curious about her folks.

The point of this and similar stories is that our habitual relationship to what we call beasts in nature and "instinctive" or "instinctual" beastliness in ourselves may be highly distorted by thousands of years of superstition, and that there may be resources for peace even in our "animal nature" if we will only learn to nurture nature, as well as to master it. Today, we can teach a monkey, in the very words of the Bible, to "eat the flesh of his own arm," even as we can permit "erring leaders" to make of all mankind the "fuel of the fire." Yet, it seems equally plausible that we can also let our children grow up to lead "the calf and the young lion and the fatling together"—in nature and in their own nature.

To recognize one of man's prime resources, however, we must trace back his individual development to his *pre-moral* days, his infancy. His earliest social experimentation at that time leads to a certain ratio of basic trust and basic mistrust—a ratio which, if favorable, establishes the fundamental human strength: hope. This over-all attitude emerges as the newborn organism reaches out to its caretakers and as they bring to it what we will now discuss as *mutuality*. The failure of basic trust and of mutuality has been recognized in psychiatry as the most far-reaching failure, undercutting all development. We know how tragic and deeply pathogenic its absence can be in children and parents who cannot arouse and cannot respond. It is my further proposition, then, that all moral, ideological, and ethical propensities depend on this early experience of mutuality.

I would call mutuality a relationship in which partners depend on each other for the development of their respective strengths. A baby's first responses can be seen as part of an actuality consisting of many details of mutual arousal and response. While the baby initially smiles at a mere configuration resembling the human face, the adult cannot help smiling back, filled with expectations of a "recognition" which he needs to secure from the new being as surely as it needs him. The fact is that the mutuality of adult and baby is the original source of hope, the basic ingredient of all effective as well as ethical human action. As far back as 1895, Freud, in his first outline of a "Psychology for Neurologists," confronts the "helpless" newborn infant with a "help-rich" ("*hilfreich*") adult, and postulates that their mutual understanding is "the primal source of all moral motives."[4] Should we, then, endow the Golden Rule with a principle of mutuality, replacing the reciprocity of both prudence and sympathy?

Here we must add the observation that a parent dealing with a child will be strengthened in *his* vitality, in *his* sense of identity, and in *his* readiness for ethical action by the very ministrations by means of which he secures to the child vitality, future identity, and eventual readiness for ethical action.

But we should avoid making a new Utopia out of the "mother-child relationship." The paradise of early childhood must be abandoned—a fact which man has as yet not learned to accept. The earliest mutuality is only a beginning and leads to more complicated encounters, as both the child and his interaction with a widening circle of persons grow more complicated. I need only point out that the second basic set of vital strengths in childhood (following trust and hope) is autonomy and will, and it must be clear that a situation in which the child's willfulness faces the adult's will is a different proposition from that of the mutuality of instilling hope. Yet, any adult who has managed to train a child's will must admit—for better or for worse—that he has learned much about himself and about will that he never knew before, something which cannot be learned in any other way. Thus each growing individual's developing strength "dovetails" with the strengths of an increasing number of persons arranged about him in the formalized orders of family, school, community and society. But orders and rules are kept alive only by those "virtues" of which Shakespeare says (in what appears to me to be *his* passionate version of the Rule) that they, "shining upon others heat them and they retort that heat again to the first giver."

One more proposition must be added to the developmental and to the generational one, and to that of mutuality. It is implied in the term "activate," and I would call it the principle of *active choice*. It is, I think, most venerably expressed in St. Francis's prayer: "Grant that I may not so much seek to be consoled as to console; to be understood, as to understand; to be loved as to love; for it is in giving that we receive." Such commitment to an initia-

4. Sigmund Freud, *The Origins of Psychoanalysis: Letters to Wilhelm Fliess, Drafts and Notes:* 1887-1902, edited by Marie Bonaparte, Anna Freud and Ernst Kris, New York: Basic Books, 1954 [Erikson's note].

tive in love is, of course, contained in the admonition to "love thy neighbor." I think that we can recognize in these words a psychological verity, namely, that only he who approaches an encounter in a (consciously and unconsciously) active and giving attitude, rather than in a demanding and dependent one, will be able to make of that encounter what it can become.

With these considerations in mind, then, I will try to formulate my understanding of the Golden Rule. I have been reluctant to come to this point; it has taken thousands of years and many linguistic acrobatics to translate this Rule from one era to another and from one language into another, and at best one can only confound it again, in a somewhat different way.

I would advocate a general orientation which has its center in whatever activity or activities gives man the feeling, as William James put it, of being "most deeply and intensely active and alive." In this, so James promises, each one will find his "real me"; but, I would now add, he will also acquire the experience that *truly worthwhile acts enhance a mutuality between the doer and the other—a mutuality which strengthens the doer even as it strengthens the other.* Thus, the "doer" and "the other" are partners in one deed. Seen in the light of human development, this means that the doer is activated in whatever strength is *appropriate to his age, stage, and condition*, even as he activates in the other the strength appropriate to *his* age, stage, and condition. Understood this way, the Rule would say that it is best to do to another what will strengthen you even as it will strengthen him—that is, what will develop his best potentials even as it develops your own.

This variation of the Rule is obvious enough when applied to the relation of parent and child. But does the uniqueness of their respective positions, which has served as our model so far, have any significant analogies in other situations in which uniqueness depends on a divided function?

To return to particulars, I will attempt to apply my amendment to the diversity of function in the two sexes. I have not dwelled so far on this most usual subject of a psychoanalytic discourse, sexuality. So much of this otherwise absorbing aspect of life has, in recent years, become stereotyped in theoretical discussion. Among the terminological culprits to be blamed for this sorry fact is the psychoanalytic term "love object." For this word "object" in Freud's theory has been taken too literally by many of his friends and by most of his enemies—and moralistic critics do delight in misrepresenting a man's transitory formulations as his ultimate "values." The fact is that Freud, on purely conceptual grounds, and on the basis of the scientific language of his laboratory days, pointed out that drive energies have "objects." But he certainly never advocated that men or women should treat one another as objects on which to live out their sexual idiosyncrasies.

Instead, his central theory of genitality which combines strivings of sexuality and of love points to one of those basic mutualities in which *a partner's potency and potentialities are activated even as he activates the other's potency and potentialities.* Freud's theory implies that a man will be more a man to the extent to which he makes a woman more a woman—and vice versa—because only two uniquely different beings can enhance their respective uniqueness for one another. A "genital" person in Freud's sense is thus more apt to act in accordance with Kant's version of the Golden Rule, in that he would so act as to treat humanity "whether in his person or in another, always as an end, and never as only a means." What Freud added to the ethical principle, however, is a methodology which opens to our inquiry and to our influence the powerhouse of inner forces. For they provide the shining heat for our strengths— and the smoldering smoke of our weaknesses.

I cannot leave the subject of the two sexes without a word on the uniqueness of women. One may well question whether or not the Rule in its oldest form tacitly meant to include women as partners in the golden deal. Today's study of lives still leaves quite obscure the place of women in what is most relevant in the male image of man. True, women are being granted *equality* of political rights, and the recognition of a certain *sameness* in mental and moral equipment. But what they have not begun to earn, partially because they have not cared to ask for it, is the *equal right to be effectively unique,* and to use hard-won rights in the service of what they uniquely represent in human evolution. The West has much to learn, for example, from the unimpaired womanliness of India's modern women. But there is today a universal sense of the emergence of a new feminism as part of a more inclusive humanism. This coincides with a growing conviction—highly ambivalent, to be sure—that the future of mankind cannot depend on men alone and may well depend on the fate of a "mother variable" uncontrolled by technological man. The resistance to such a consideration always comes from men and women who are mortally afraid that by emphasizing what is unique one may tend to re-emphasize what is unequal. And, indeed, the study of life histories confirms a far-reaching sameness in men and women insofar as they express the mathematical architecture of the universe, the organization of logical thought, and the structure of language. But such a study also suggests that while boys and girls can think and act and talk alike, they naturally do not experience their bodies (and thus the world) alike. I have attempted to demonstrate this by pointing to sex differences in the structuralization of space in the play of children.[5] But I assume that a uniqueness of either sex will be granted without proof, and that the "difference" acclaimed by the much-quoted Frenchman is not considered only a matter of anatomical appointments for mutual sexual enjoyment, but a psychobiological difference central to two great modes of life, the *paternal* and the *maternal* modes. The amended Golden Rule suggests that one sex enhances the uniqueness of the other; it also implies that each, to be really unique, depends on a mutuality with an equally unique partner.

From the most intimate human encounters we now turn to a professional, and yet relatively intimate, one: that between healer and patient. There is a very real and specific inequality in the relationship of doctor and patient in their roles of knower and known, helper and sufferer, practitioner of life and victim of disease and death. For this reason medical people have their own and unique professional oath and strive to live up to a universal ideal of "the doctor." Yet the practice of the healing arts permits extreme types of practitioners, from the absolute authoritarian over homes and clinics to the harassed servant of demanding mankind, from the sadist of mere proficiency, to the effusive lover of all (well, almost all) of his patients. Here, too, Freud has thrown intimate and original light on the workings of a unique relationship. His letters to his friend and mentor Fliess illustrate the singular experience which made him recognize in his patients what he called "transference"—that is, the patient's wish to exploit sickness and treatment for infantile and regressive ends. But more, Freud, recognized a "countertransference" in the healer's motivation to exploit the patient's transference and to dominate or serve, possess or love him to the disadvantage of his true function. He made systematic insight into transference *and* countertransference part of the training of the psychoanalytic practitioner.

I would think that all of the motivations necessarily entering so vast and so intricate a field could be reconciled in a Golden Rule amended to include a mutuality of divided function. Each specialty and each technique in its own way permits the medical man to *develop as a practitioner, and as a person, even as the patient is cured as a patient, and as a person.* For a real cure transcends the transitory state of patienthood. It is an experience which enables the cured patient to develop and to transmit to home and neigh-

5. Erik H. Erikson, "Sex Differences in the Play Constructions of Pre-Adolescents," in *Discussions in Child Development*, World Health Organization, Vol. III, New York: International Universities Press, 1958. See also "Reflections on Womanhood," *Daedalus*, Spring 1964 [Erikson's note].

borhood an attitude toward health which is one of the most essential ingredients of an ethical outlook.

Beyond this, can the healing arts and sciences contribute to a new ethical outlook? This question always recurs in psychoanalysis and is usually disposed of with Freud's original answer that the psychoanalyst represents the ethics of scientific truth only and is committed to studying ethics (or morality) in a scientific way. Beyond this, he leaves *Weltanschauungen* (ethical world views) to others.

It seems to me, however, that the clinical arts and sciences, while employing the scientific method, are not defined by it or limited by it. The healer is commited to a highest good, the preservation of life and the furtherance of well-being—the "maintenance of life." He need not prove scientifically that these are, in fact, the highest good; rather, he is precommitted to this basic proposition while investigating what can be verified by scientific means. This, I think, is the meaning of the Hippocratic oath, which subordinates all medical method to a humanist ethic. True, a man can separate his personal, his professional, and his scientific ethics, seeking fulfillment of idiosyncratic needs in personal life, the welfare of others in his profession, and truths independent of personal preference or service in his research. However, there are psychological limits to the multiplicity of values a man can live by, and, in the end, not only the practitioner, but also his patient and his research, depend on a certain unification in him of temperament, intellect, and ethics. This unification clearly characterizes great doctors.

While it is true, then, that as scientists we must study ethics objectively, we are, as professional individuals, committed to a unification of personality, training, and conviction which alone will help us to do our work adequately. At the same time, as transient members of the human race, we must record the truest meaning of which the fallible methods of our era and the accidental circumstances of our existence have made us aware. In this sense, there is (and always has been) not only an ethics governing clinical work, and a clinical approach to the study of ethics, but also a contribution to ethics of the healing orientation. The healer, furthermore, has now committed himself to prevention on a large scale, and he cannot evade the problem of assuring ethical vitality to all lives saved from undernourishment, morbidity, and early mortality. Man's technical ability and social resolve to prevent accidental conception makes every child conceived a subject of universal responsibility.

As I approach my conclusion, let me again change my focus and devote a few minutes to a matter political and economic as well as ethical: Gandhi's "Rule."

In Ahmedabad I had occasion to visit Gandhi's ashram[6] across the Sabarmati River; and it was not long before I realized that in Ahmedabad a hallowed and yet eminently concrete event had occurred which perfectly exemplifies everything I am trying to say. I refer, of course, to Gandhi's leadership in the lockout and strike of the mill-workers in 1918, and his first fast in a public cause. This event is well known in the history of industrial relations the world over, and vaguely known to all educated Indians. Yet, I believe that only in Ahmedabad, among surviving witnesses and living institutions, can one fathom the "presence" of that event as a lastingly successful "experiment" in local industrial relations, influential in Indian politics, and, above all, representing a new type of encounter in divided human functions. The details of the strike and of the settlement need not concern us here. As usual, it began as a matter of wages. Nor can I take time to indicate the limited political and economic applicability of the Ahmedabad experiment to other industrial areas in and beyond India. What interests us here is the fact that Gandhi, from the moment of his entry into the struggle, considered it an occasion not for maximum reciprocal coercion resulting in the usual compromise, but as an opportunity for all—the workers, the owners, and himself—"to rise from the present conditions."

The utopian quality of the principles on which he determined to focus can only be grasped by one who can visualize the squalor of the workmen's living conditions, the latent panic in the ranks of the paternalistic millowners (beset by worries of British competition), and Gandhi's then as yet relative inexperience in handling the masses of India. The shadows of defeat, violence, and corruption hovered over every one of the "lofty" words which I am about to quote. But to Gandhi, any worthwhile struggle must "transform the inner life of the people." Gandhi spoke to the workers daily under the famous Babul Tree outside the medieval Shahpur Gate. He had studied their desperate condition, yet he urged them to ignore the threats and the promises of the millowners who in the obstinate fashion of all "haves" feared the anarchic insolence and violence of the "have nots." He knew that they feared him, too, for they had indicated that they might even accept his terms if only he would promise to leave and to stay away forever. But he settled down to prove that a just man could "secure the good of the workers while safeguarding the good of the employers"—the two opposing sides being represented by a sister and a brother, Anasuyabehn and Ambalal Sarabhai. Under the Babul Tree Gandhi announced the principle which somehow corresponds to our amended Rule:

6. Holy retreat.

"That line of action is alone justice which does not harm either party to a dispute." By harm he meant—and his daily announcements leave no doubt of this—an inseparable combination of economic disadvantage, social indignity, loss of self-esteem, and latent vengeance.

Neither side found it easy to grasp this principle. When the workers began to weaken, Gandhi suddenly declared a fast. Some of his friends, he admitted, considered this "foolish, unmanly, or worse"; and some were deeply distressed. But, "I wanted to show you," he said to the workers, "that I was not playing with you." He was, as we would say, in dead earnest, and this fact, then as later, immediately raised an issue of local conscience to national significance. In daily appeals, Gandhi stressed variously those basic inner strengths without which no issue has "virtue," namely, will with justice, purpose with discipline, respect for work of any kind, and truthfulness. But he knew, and he said so, that these masses of illiterate men and women, newly arrived from the villages and already exposed to proletarization, did not have the moral strength or the social solidarity to adhere to principle without strong leadership. "You have yet to learn how and when to take an oath," he told them. The oath, the dead earnestness, then, was as yet the leader's privilege and commitment. In the end the matter was settled, not without a few Gandhian compromises to save face all around, but with a true acceptance of the settlement originally proposed by Gandhi.

I do not claim to understand the complex motivations and curious turns of Gandhi's mind—some contradicting Western rigidity in matters of principle, and some, I assume, strange to Indian observers, as well. I can also see in Gandhi's actions a paternalism which may now be "dated." But his monumental simplicity and total involvement in the "experiment" made both workers and owners revere him. And he himself said with humorous awe, "I have never come across such a fight." For, indeed both sides had matured in a way that lifted labor relations in Ahmedabad to a new and lasting level. Let me quote only the fact that, in 1950, the Ahmedabad Textile Labor Organization accounted for only a twentieth of India's union membership, but for eighty per cent of its welfare expenditures.

Such a singular historical event, then, reveals something essential in human strength, in traditional Indian strength, and in the power of Gandhi's own personal transformation at the time. To me, the miracle of the Ahmedabad experiment has been not only its lasting success and its tenacity during those days of anarchic violence which after the great partition broke down so many dams of solidarity, but above all, the spirit which points beyond the event.

And now a final word on what is, and will be for a long time to come, the sinister horizon of the world in which we all study and work: the international situation. Here, too, we cannot afford to live for long with a division of personal, professional, and political ethics—a division endangering the very life which our professions have vowed to keep intact, and thus cutting through the very fiber of our personal existence. Only in our time, and in our very generation, have we come, with traumatic suddenness, to be conscious of what was self-evident all along, namely, that in all of previous history the Rule, in whatever form, has comfortably coexisted with warfare. A warrior, all armored and spiked and set to do to another what he fully expected the other to be ready to do to him, saw no ethical contradiction between the Rule and his military ideology. He could, in fact, grant to his adversary a respect which he hoped to earn in return. This tenuous coexistence of ethics and warfare may outlive itself in our time. Even the military mind may well come to fear for its historical identity, as boundless slaughter replaces tactical warfare. What is there, even for a "fighting man," in the Golden Rule of the Nuclear Age, which seems to say, "Do not unto others—unless you are sure you can do them in as totally as they can do you in"?

One wonders, however, whether this deadlock in international morals can be broken by the most courageous protest, the most incisive interpretation, or the most prophetic warning—a warning of catastrophe so all-consuming that most men must ignore it, as they ignore their own death and have learned to ignore the monotonous prediction of hell. It seems, instead that only an ethical orientation, a direction for vigorous cooperation, can free today's energies from their bondage in armed defensiveness. We live at a time in which—with all the species-wide destruction possible—we can think for the first time of a species-wide identity, of a truly universal ethics, such as has been prepared in the world religions, in humanism, and by some philosophers. Ethics, however, cannot be fabricated. They can only emerge from an informed and inspired search for a more inclusive human identity, which a new technology and a new world image make possible as well as mandatory. But again, all I can offer you here is another variation of the theme. What has been said about the relationships of parent and child, of man and woman, and of doctor and patient, may have some application to the relationship of nations to each other. Nations today are by definition units at different stages of political, technological, and economic transformation. Under these conditions, it is all too easy for overdeveloped nations to believe that nations, too, should treat one another with a superior educative or clinical attitude. The point of what I have to say, however, is not underscored inequality, but respected uniqueness within historical differences. Insofar as a nation thinks of itself as a collective individual, then, it may well learn to visualize its task as that of maintaining mutuality in international relations. For the only alternative to armed competition seems to be the effort to *activate in the historical partner what will strengthen him in his historical development even as it strengthens the actor in his own development— toward a common future identity.* Only thus can we find a common denominator in the rapid change of technology and history and transcend the dangerous imagery of victory and defeat, of subjugation and exploitation which is the heritage of a fragmented past.

Does this sound utopian? I think, on the contrary, that all of what I have said is already known in many ways, is being expressed in many languages, and practiced on many levels. At our historical moment it becomes clear in a most practical way that the doer of the Golden Rule, and he who is done by, is the same man, *is* man.

Men of clinical background, however, must not lose sight of a dimension which I have taken for granted here. While the Golden Rule in its classical versions prods man to strive *consciously* for a highest good and to avoid mutual harm with a sharpened awareness, our insights assume an *unconscious* substratum of ethical strength and, at the same time, unconscious arsenals of destructive rage. The last century has traumatically expanded man's awareness of unconscious motivations stemming from his animal ancestry, from his economic history, and from his inner estrangements. It has also created (in all these respects) methods of productive self-analysis. These I consider the pragmatic Western version of that universal trend toward self-scrutiny which once reached such heights in Asian tradition. It will be the task of the next generation everywhere to begin to integrate new and old methods of self-awareness with the minute particulars of universal technical proficiency.

It does not seem easy to speak of ethical subjects without indulging in some moralizing. As an antidote I will conclude with the Talmudic version of the Rule. Rabbi Hillel once was asked by an unbeliever to tell the whole of the Torah while he stood on one foot. I do not know whether he meant to answer the request or to remark on its condition when he said: "What is hateful to yourself, do not to your fellow man. That is the whole of the Torah and the rest is but commentary." At any rate, he did not add: "Act accordingly." He said: "Go and learn it."

QUESTIONS

1. At times Erikson implies that he is digressing, and he certainly does cover a wide range of topics. How tightly is his talk organized? Can it be outlined?
2. Erikson distinguishes three stages of growth—moral, ideological, and ethical. What are the significant characteristics of each, and how do they relate to one another? What does Erikson mean by "evolution"?
3. How might Erikson regard Thucydides' conception of human nature as self-seeking and anarchic (pp. 805–810)?
4. How might Erikson regard Milgram's procedure as he reports it in "A Behavioral Study of Obedience" (pp. 293–306)?
5. Bruno Bettelheim said that liberals, the press, and teachers who failed to assert their authority all shared some blame for denying superego models to the young, particularly to the poor and disadvantaged: "There's no doubt about the underlying violence with which we are born. Whether we are going to have violence depends to a very large degree on how we develop the superego and controls of the coming generation." Would Erikson agree? Can you think of ways in which superego models are denied? Does a man in authority have to be unusually good himself to serve as a satisfactory model?

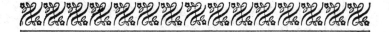

On Politics
and Government

W. E. B. DU BOIS
Jacob and Esau[1]

I remember very vividly the Sunday-school room where I spent
the Sabbaths of my early years. It had been newly built after a disastrous fire; the room was large and full of sunlight; nice new chairs
were grouped around where the classes met. My class was in the
center, so that I could look out upon the elms of Main Street and
see the passersby. But I was interested usually in the lessons and in
my fellow students and the frail rather nervous teacher, who tried
to make the Bible and its ethics clear to us. We were a trial to her,
full 'of mischief, restless and even noisy; but perhaps more especially
when we asked questions. And on the story of Jacob and Esau we
did ask questions. My judgment then and my judgment now is very
unfavorable to Jacob. I thought that he was a cad and a liar and I
did not see how possibly he could be made the hero of a Sunday-
school lesson.

Many days have passed since then and the world has gone
through astonishing changes. But basically, my judgment of Jacob
has not greatly changed and I have often promised myself the pleasure of talking about him publicly, and especially to young people.
This is the first time that I have had the opportunity.

My subject then is "Jacob and Esau," and I want to examine
these two men and the ideas which they represent; and the way in
which those ideas have come to our day. Of course, our whole
interpretation of this age-old story of Jewish mythology has greatly
changed. We look upon these Old Testament stories today not as
untrue and yet not as literally true. They are simple, they have their
truths, and yet they are not by any means the expression of eternal
verity. Here were brought forward for the education of Jewish chil-

1. Commencement address at Talladega College, June 5, 1944.

dren and for the interpretation of Jewish life to the world, two men: one small, lithe and quick-witted; the other tall, clumsy and impetuous; a hungry, hard-bitten man.

Historically, we know how these two types came to be set forth by the Bards of Israel. When the Jews marched north after escaping from slavery in Egypt, they penetrated and passed through the land of Edom; the land that lay between the Dead Sea and Egypt. It was an old center of hunters and nomads and the Israelites, while they admired the strength and organization of the Edomites, looked down upon them as lesser men; as men who did not have the Great Plan. Now the Great Plan of the Israelites was the building of a strong, concentered state under its own God, Jehovah, devoted to agriculture and household manufacture and trade. It raised its own food by careful planning. It did not wander and depend upon chance wild beasts. It depended upon organization, strict ethics, absolute devotion to the nation through strongly integrated planned life. It looked upon all its neighbors, not simply with suspicion, but with the exclusiveness of a chosen people, who were going to be the leaders of earth.

This called for sacrifice, for obedience, for continued planning. The man whom we call Esau was from the land of Edom, or inter-married with it, for the legend has it that he was twin of Jacob the Jew but the chief fact is that, no matter what his blood relations were, his cultural allegiance lay among the Edomites. He was trained in the free out-of-doors; he chased and faced the wild beasts; he knew vast and imperative appetite after long self-denial, and even pain and suffering; he gloried in food, he traveled afar; he gathered wives and concubines and he represented continuous prim-itive strife.

The legacy of Esau has come down the ages to us. It has not been dominant, but it has always and continually expressed and re-expressed itself; the joy of human appetites, the quick resentment that leads to fighting, the belief in force, which is war.

As I look back upon my own conception of Esau, he is not nearly as clear and definite a personality as Jacob. There is something rather shadowy about him; and yet he is curiously human and easily conceived. One understands his contemptuous surrender of his birthright; he was hungry after long days of hunting; he wanted rest and food, the stew of meat and vegetables which Jacob had in his possession, and determined to keep unless Esau bargained. "And Esau said, Behold, I am at the point to die: and what profit shall this birthright be to me? And Jacob said, Swear to me this day; and he swore unto him: and he sold his birthright unto Jacob."

On the other hand, the legacy of Jacob which has come down through the years, not simply as a Jewish idea, but more especially as typical of modern Europe, is more complicated and expresses itself something like this: life must be planned for the Other Self, for that personification of the group, the nation, the empire, which has eternal life as contrasted with the ephemeral life of individuals. For this we must plan, and for this there must be timeless and unceasing work. Out of this, the Jews as chosen children of Jehovah would triumph over themselves, over all Edom and in time over the world.

Now it happens that so far as actual history is concerned, this dream and plan failed. The poor little Jewish nation was dispersed to the ends of the earth by the overwhelming power of the great nations that arose East, North, and South and eventually became united in the vast empire of Rome. This was the diaspora, the dispersion of the Jews. But the idea of the Plan with a personality of its own took hold of Europe with relentless grasp and this was the real legacy of Jacob, and of other men of other peoples, whom Jacob represents.

There came the attempt to weld the world into a great unity, first under the Roman Empire, then under the Catholic Church. When this attempt failed, and the empire fell apart, there arose the individual states of Europe and of some other parts of the world; and these states adapted the idea of individual effort to make each of them dominant. The state was *all*, the individual subordinate, but right here came the poison of the Jacobean idea. How could the state get this power? Who was to wield the power within the state? So long as power was achieved, what difference did it make how it was gotten? Here then was war—but not Esau's war of passion, hunger and revenge, but Jacob's war of cold acquisition and power.

Granting to Jacob, as we must, the great idea of the family, the clan, and the state as dominant and superior in its claims, nevertheless, there is the bitter danger in trying to seek these ends without reference to the great standards of right and wrong. When men begin to lie and steal, in order to make the nation to which they belong great, then comes not only disaster, but rational contradiction which in many respects is worse than disaster, because it ruins the leadership of the divine machine, the human reason, by which we chart and guide our actions.

It was thus in the middle age and increasingly in the seventeenth and eighteenth and more especially in the nineteenth century, there arose the astonishing contradiction: that is, the action of men like Jacob who were perfectly willing and eager to lie and steal so long as their action brought profit to themselves and power to their state. And soon identifying themselves and their class with the state they identified their own wealth and power as that of the state. They did not listen to any arguments of right or wrong; might was right; they came to despise and deplore the natural appetites of human beings and their very lives, so long as by their suppression, they themselves got rich and powerful. There arose a great, rich Italy; a fabulously wealthy Spain; a strong and cultured France and, eventually, a British Empire which came near to dominating the world. The Esaus of those centuries were curiously represented by various groups of people: by the slum-dwellers and the criminals who, giving up all hope of profiting by the organized state, sold their birthrights for miserable messes of pottage. But more than that, the great majority of mankind, the peoples who lived in Asia, Africa and America and the islands of the sea, became subordinate tools for the profit-making of the crafty planners of great things, who worked regardless of religion or ethics.

It is almost unbelievable to think what happened in those centuries, when it is put in cold narrative; from whole volumes of tales, let me select only a few examples. The peoples of whole islands and countries were murdered in cold blood for their gold and jewels. The mass of the laboring people of the world were put to work for wages which led them into starvation, ignorance and disease. The right of the majority of mankind to speak and to act; to play and to dance was denied,. if it interfered with profit-making work for others, or was ridiculed if it could not be capitalized. Karl Marx writes of Scotland: "As an example of the method of obtaining wealth and power in nineteenh century; the story of the Duchess of Sutherland will suffice here. This Scottish noblewoman resolved, on entering upon the government of her clan of white Scottish people, to turn the whole country, whose population had already been, by earlier processes, reduced to 15,000, into a sheep pasture. From 1814 to 1820 these 15,000 inhabitants were systematically hunted and rooted out. All their villages were destroyed and burnt, all their fields turned into pasture. Thus this lady appropriated 794,000 acres of land that had from time immemorial been the property of the people. She assigned to the expelled inhabitants about 6,000 acres on the seashore. The 6,000 acres had until this time lain waste, and brought in no income to their owners. The Duchess, in the nobility of her heart, actually went so far as to let these at an average rent of 50 cents per acre to the clansmen, who for centuries had shed their blood for her family. The whole of the stolen clan-land she divided into 29 great sheep farms, each inhabited by a single imported English family. In the year 1835 the 15,-000 Scotsmen were already replaced by 131,000 sheep."[1]

1. This is a quotation from Karl Marx's *Capital*. However, Du Bois in places has paraphrased Marx and interpolated his own words for those of the English translation of the work. The essential meaning, however, is not distorted. Since it is likely Du Bois used the translation of *Capital* by Samuel Moore and Edward Aveling (published by Charles H. Kerr and Co., Chicago, 1906) the reader can compare Du Bois's rendition with the original by consulting pp. 801–802, vol. I, of the Kerr edition of *Capital*. [This and subsequent notes are those of Du Bois's editor, Philip S. Foner.]

The discovery of gold and silver in America, the extirpation, enslavement and entombment in mines of the Indian population, the beginning of the conquest and looting of the East Indies, the turning of Africa into a warren for the commercial hunting of black-skins, signalized the rosy dawn of power of those spiritual children of Jacob, who owned the birthright of the masses by fraud and murder. These idyllic proceedings are the chief momenta of primary accumulation of capital in private hands. On their heels tread the commercial wars of the European nations, with the globe for a theater. It begins with the revolt of the Netherlands from Spain, assumes giant dimensions in England's anti-jacobin war, and continues in the opium wars against China.

Of the Christian colonial system, Howitt says: "The barbarities and desperate outrages of the so-called Christians, throughout every region of the world, and upon people they have been able to subdue, are not to be paralleled by those of any other race, in any age of the earth." This history of the colonial administration of Holland—and Holland was the head capitalistic nation of the seventeenth century—is one of the most extraordinary relations of treachery, bribery, massacre, and meanness.

Nothing was more characteristic than the Dutch system of stealing men, to get slaves for Java. The men-stealers were trained for this purpose. The thief, the interpreter, and the seller were the chief agents in this trade; the native princes, the chief sellers. The young people stolen, were thrown into the secret dungeons of Celebes, until they were ready for sending to the slave ships. . . .

The English East India Company, in the seventeenth and eighteenth centuries, obtained, besides the political rule in India, the exclusive monopoly of the tea trade, as well as of the Chinese trade in general, and of the transport of goods to and from Europe. But the coasting trade of India was the monopoly of the higher employees of the company. The monopolies of salt, opium, betel nuts and other commodities, were inexhaustible mines of wealth. The employees themselves fixed the price and plundered at will the unhappy Hindus. The Governor General took part in this private traffic. His favorites received contracts under conditions whereby they, cleverer than the alchemists, made gold out of nothing. Great English fortunes sprang up like mushrooms in a day; investment profits went on without the advance of a shilling. The trial of Warren Hastings swarms with such cases. Here is an instance: a contract for opium was given to a certain Sullivan at the moment of his departure on an official mission. Sullivan sold his contract to one Binn for $200,000; Binn sold it the same day for $300,000 and the ultimate purchaser who carried out the contract declared that after all he realized an enormous gain. According to one of the lists laid before Parliament, the East India Company and its employees from 1757 to 1766 got $30,000,000 from the Indians as gifts alone.

The treatment of the aborigines was, naturally, most frightful in plantation colonies destined for export trade only, such as the West Indies, and in rich and well-populated countries, such as Mexico and India, that were given over to plunder. But even in the colonies properly so called, the followers of Jacob outdid him. These sober Protestants, the Puritans of New England, in 1703, by decrees of their assembly set a premium of $200 on every Indian scalp and every captured redskin: in 1720 a premium of $500 on every scalp; in 1744, after Massachusetts Bay had proclaimed a certain tribe as rebels, the following prices prevailed: for a male scalp of 12 years upward, $500 (new currency); for a male prisoner, $525; for women and children prisoners, $250; for scalps of women and children, $250. Some decades later, the colonial system took its revenge on the descendants of the pious pilgrim fathers, who had grown seditious in the meantime. At English instigation and for English pay they were tomahawked by redskins. The British Parliament proclaimed bloodhounds and scalping as "means that God and Nature had given into its hands."[2]

With the development of national industry during the eighteenth century, the public opinion of Europe had lost the last remnant of shame and conscience. The nations bragged cynically of every infamy that served them as a means to accumulating private wealth. Read, e.g., the naive *Annals of Commerce* of Anderson. Here it is trumpeted forth as a triumph of English statecraft that at the Peace of Utrecht, England extorted from the Spaniards by the Asiento Treaty the privilege of being allowed to ply the slave trade, between Africa and Spanish America. England thereby acquired the right of supplying Spanish America until 1743 with 4,800 Negroes yearly. This threw, at the same time, an official cloak over British smuggling. Liverpool waxed fat on the slave trade. ... Aikin (1795) quotes that spirit of bold adventure which has characterized the trade of Liverpool and rapidly carried it to its present state of prosperity; has occasioned vast employment for shipping and sailors, and greatly augmented the demand for the manufactures of the country; Liverpool employed in the slave trade, in 1730, 15 ships; in 1760, 74; in 1770, 96; and in 1792, 132.[3]

Henry George wrote of *Progress and Poverty* in the 1890s. He says: "At the beginning of this marvelous era it was natural to expect, and it was expected, that labor-saving inventions would lighten the toil and improve the condition of the laborer; that the enormous increase in the power of producing wealth would make

2. *Ibid.*, pp. 823–826.   3. *Ibid.*, pp. 832–833.

real poverty a thing of the past. Could a man of the last century [the eighteenth]—a Franklin or a Priestley—have seen, in a vision of the future, the steamship taking the place of the sailing vessel; the railroad train, of the wagon; the reaping machine, of the scythe; the threshing machine, of the flail; could he have heard the throb of the engines that in obedience to human will, and for the satisfaction of the human desire, exert a power greater than that of all the men and all the beasts of burden of the earth combined; could he have seen the forest tree transformed into finished lumber—into doors, sashes, blinds, boxes or barrels, with hardly the touch of a human hand; the great workshops where boots and shoes are turned out by the case with less labor than the old-fashioned cobbler could have put on a sole; the factories where, under the eye of one girl, cotton becomes cloth faster than hundreds of stalwart weavers could have turned it out with their hand-looms; could he have seen steam hammers shaping mammoth shafts and mighty anchors, and delicate machinery making tiny watches; the diamond drill cutting through the heart of the rocks, and coal oil sparing the whale; could he have realized the enormous saving of labor resulting from improved facilities of exchange and communication—sheep killed in Australia eaten fresh in England, and the order given by the London banker in the afternoon executed in San Francisco in the morning of the same day; could he have conceived of the hundred thousand improvements which these only suggest, what would he have inferred as to the social condition of mankind?

"It would not have seemed like an inference; further than the vision went it would have seemed as though he saw; and his heart would have leaped and his nerves would have thrilled, as one who from a height beholds just ahead of the thirst-stricken caravan the living gleam of rustling woods and the glint of laughing waters. Plainly, in the sight of the imagination, he would have beheld these new forces elevating society from its very foundations, lifting the very poorest above the possibility of want, exempting the very lowest from anxiety for the material needs of life; he would have seen these slaves of the lamp of knowledge taking on themselves the traditional curse, these muscles of iron and sinews of steel making the poorest laborer's life a holiday, in which every high quality and noble impulse could have scope to grow."[4]

This was the promise of Jacob's life. This would establish the birthright which Esau despised. But, says George, "Now, however, we are coming into collision with facts which there can be no mis-

---

4. Henry George, *Progress and Poverty*, New York, Robert Schalkenbach Foundation, 1939, pp. 3–4. This work, originally published in 1879, argued that the land belonged to society, which created its value and should properly tax that value, not improvements on the land. George's proposal for such a "Single Tax" gained many adherents.

taking. From all parts of the civilized world," he says speaking fifty years ago, "come complaints of industrial depression; of labor condemned to involuntary idleness; of capital massed and wasting; of pecuniary distress among businessmen; of want and suffering and anxiety among the working classes. All the full, deadening pain, all the keen, maddening anguish, that to great masses of men are involved in the words 'hard times,' afflict the world today."[5] What would Henry George have said in 1933 after airplane and radio and mass production, turbine and electricity had come?

Science and art grew and expanded despite all this, but it was warped by the poverty of the artist and the continuous attempt to make science subservient to industry. The latter effort finally succeeded so widely that modern civilization became typified as industrial technique. Education became learning a trade. Men thought of civilization as primarily mechanical and the mechanical means by which they reduced wool and cotton to their purposes, also reduced and bent humankind to their will. Individual initiative remained but it was cramped and distorted and there spread the idea of patriotism to one's country as the highest virtue, by which it became established, that just as in the case of Jacob, a man not only could lie, steal, cheat and murder for his native land, but by doing so, he became a hero whether his cause was just or unjust.

One remembers that old scene between Esau who had thoughtlessly surrendered his birthright and the father who had blessed his lying son; "Jacob came unto his father, and said, My Father: and he said, Here am I; who art thou? And Jacob said unto his father, I am Esau thy firstborn; I have done according as thou badest me: arise, I pray thee, sit and eat of my venison, that thy soul may bless me." In vain did clumsy, careless Esau beg for a blessing—some little blessing. It was denied and Esau hated Jacob because of the blessing: and Esau said in his heart, "The days of mourning for my father are at hand; then I will slay my brother Jacob." So revolution entered—so revolt darkened a dark world.

The same motif was repeated in modern Europe and America in the nineteenth and twentieth centuries, when there grew the superstate called the Empire. The Plan had now regimented the organization of men covering vast territories, dominating immense force and immeasurable wealth and determined to reduce to subserviency as large a part as possible, not only of Europe's own internal world, but of the world at large. Colonial imperialism swept over the earth and initiated the First World War, in envious scramble for division of power and profit.

Hardly a moment of time passed after that war, a moment in the eyes of the eternal forces looking down upon us when again the

5. *Ibid.*, pp. 5–6.

world, using all of that planning and all of that technical superiority for which its civilization was noted; and all of the accumulated and accumulating wealth which was available, proceeded to commit suicide on so vast a scale that it is almost impossible for us to realize the meaning of the catastrophe. Of course, this sweeps us far beyond anything that the peasant lad Jacob, with his petty lying and thievery had in mind. Whatever was begun there of ethical wrong among the Jews was surpassed in every particular by the white world of Europe and America and carried to such length of universal cheating, lying and killing that no comparisons remain.

We come therefore to the vast impasse of today: to the great question, what was the initial right and wrong of the original Jacobs and Esaus and of their spiritual descendants the world over? We stand convinced today, at least those who remain sane, that lying and cheating and killing will build no world organization worth the building. We have got to stop making income by unholy methods; out of stealing the pittances of the poor and calling it insurance; out of seizing and monopolizing the natural resources of the world and then making the world's poor pay exorbitant prices for aluminum, copper and oil, iron and coal. Not only have we got to stop these practices, but we have got to stop lying about them and seeking to convince human beings that a civilization based upon the enslavement of the majority of men for the income of the smart minority is the highest aim of man.

But as is so usual in these cases, these transgressions of Jacob do not mean that the attitude of Esau was flawless. The conscienceless greed of capital does not excuse the careless sloth of labor. Life cannot be all aimless wandering and indulgence if we are going to constrain human beings to take advantage of their brain and make successive generations stronger and wiser than the previous. There must be reverence for the *birthright* of inherited *culture* and that birthright cannot be sold for a dinner course, a dress suit or a winter in Florida. It must be valued and conserved.

The method of conservation is work, endless and tireless and planned work and this is the legacy which the Esaus of today who condemn the Jacobs of yesterday have got to substitute as their path of life, not vengeful revolution, but building and rebuilding. Curiously enough, it will not be difficult to do this, because the great majority of men, the poverty-stricken and diseased are the *real workers* of the world. They are the ones who have made and are making the *wealth* of this universe, and their future path is clear. It is to accumulate such knowledge and balance of judgment that they can reform the world, so that the workers of the world receive just share of the wealth which they make and that all human beings who are capable of work shall work. Not national glory and empire for the few, but food, shelter and happiness for the many. With the disappearance of systematic lying and killing, we may come into that birthright which so long we have called Freedom: that is, the right to act in a manner that seems to be beautiful; which makes life worth living and joy the only possible end of life. This is the experience which is Art and planning for this is the highest satisfaction of civilized needs. So that looking back upon the allegory and the history, tragedy and promise, we may change our subject and speak in closing of Esau and Jacob, realizing that neither was perfect, but that of the two, Esau had the elements which lead more naturally and directly to the salvation of man; while Jacob with all his crafty planning and cold sacrifice, held in his soul the things that are about to ruin mankind: exaggerated national patriotism, individual profit, the despising of men who are not the darlings of our particular God and the consequent lying and stealing and killing to monopolize power.

May we not hope that in the world after this catastrophe of blood, sweat and fire, we may have a new Esau and Jacob; a new allegory of men who enjoy life for life's sake; who have the Freedom of Art and wish for all men of all sorts the same freedom and enjoyment that they seek themselves and who work for all this and work hard.

Gentlemen and ladies of the class of 1944: in the days of the years of my pilgrimage, I have greeted many thousands of young men and women at the commencement of their careers as citizens of the select commonwealth of culture. In no case have I welcomed them to such a world of darkness and distractions as that into which I usher you. I take joy only in the thought that if work to be done is measure of man's opportunity you inherit a mighty fortune. You have only to remember that the birthright which is today in symbol draped over your shoulders is a heritage which has been preserved all too often by the lying, stealing and murdering of the Jacobs of the world, and if these are the only means by which this birthright can be preserved in the future, it is not worth the price. I do not believe this, and I lay it upon your hearts to prove that this not only need not be true, but is eternally and forever false.

JAMES BALDWIN
Stranger in the Village

From all available evidence no black man had ever set foot in this tiny Swiss village before I came. I was told before arriving that I would probably be a "sight" for the village; I took this to mean that people of my complexion were rarely seen in Switzerland, and also that city people are always something of a "sight" outside of the city. It did not occur to me—possibly because I am an American—that there could be people anywhere who had never seen a Negro.

It is a fact that cannot be explained on the basis of the inaccessibility of the village. The village is very high, but it is only four hours from Milan and three hours from Lausanne. It is true that it is virtually unknown. Few people making plans for a holiday would elect to come here. On the other hand, the villagers are able, presumably, to come and go as they please—which they do: to another town at the foot of the mountain, with a population of approximately five thousand, the nearest place to see a movie or go to the bank. In the village there is no movie house, no bank, no library, no theater; very few radios, one jeep, one station wagon; and at the moment, one typewriter, mine, an invention which the woman next door to me here had never seen. There are about six hundred people living here, all Catholic—I conclude this from the fact that the Catholic church is open all year round, whereas the Protestant chapel, set off on a hill a little removed from the village, is open only in the summertime when the tourists arrive. There are four or five hotels, all closed now, and four or five *bistros*, of which, however, only two do any business during the winter. These two do not do a great deal, for life in the village seems to end around nine or ten o'clock. There are a few stores, butcher, baker, *épicerie*, a hardware store, and a money-changer—who cannot change travelers' checks, but must send them down to the bank, an operation which takes two or three days. There is something called the *Ballet Haus*, closed in the winter and used for God knows what, certainly not ballet, during the summer. There seems to be only one schoolhouse in the village, and this for the quite young children; I suppose this to mean that their older brothers and sisters at some point descend from these mountains in order to complete their education—possibly, again, to the town just below. The landscape is absolutely forbidding, mountains towering on all four sides, ice and snow as far as the eye can reach. In this white wilderness, men and women and children move all day, carrying washing, wood, buckets of milk or water, sometimes skiing on Sunday afternoons. All week long boys and young men are to be seen shoveling snow off the rooftops, or dragging wood down from the forest in sleds.

The village's only real attraction, which explains the tourist season, is the hot spring water. A disquietingly high proportion of these tourists are cripples, or semi-cripples, who come year after year—from other parts of Switzerland, usually—to take the waters. This lends the village, at the height of the season, a rather terrifying air of sanctity, as though it were a lesser Lourdes. There is often something beautiful, there is always something awful, in the spectacle of a person who has lost one of his faculties, a faculty he never questioned until it was gone, and who struggles to recover it. Yet people remain people, on crutches or indeed on deathbeds; and wherever I passed, the first summer I was here, among the native villagers or among the lame, a wind passed with me—of astonishment, curiosity, amusement, and outrage. That first summer I stayed two weeks and never intended to return. But I did return in the winter, to work; the village offers, obviously, no distractions whatever and has the further advantage of being extremely cheap. Now it is winter again, a year later, and I am here again. Everyone in the village knows my name, though they scarcely ever use it, knows that I come from America— though, this, apparently, they will never really believe: black men come from Africa—and everyone knows that I am the friend of the son of a woman who was born here, and that I am staying in their chalet. But I remain as much a stranger today as I was the first day I arrived, and the children shout *Neger! Neger!* as I walk along the streets.

It must be admitted that in the beginning I was far too shocked to have any real reaction. In so far as I reacted at all, I reacted by trying to be pleasant—it being a great part of the American Negro's education (long before he goes to school) that he must make people "like" him. This smile-and-the-world-smiles-with-you routine worked about as well in this situation as it had in the situation for which it was designed, which is to say that it did not work at all. No one, after all, can be liked whose human weight and complexity cannot be, or has not been, admitted. My smile was simply another unheard-of phenomenon which allowed them to see my teeth—they did not, really, see my smile and I began to think that, should I take to snarling, no one would notice any difference. All of the physical characteristics of the Negro which had caused me, in America, a very different and almost forgotten pain were nothing less than miraculous —or infernal—in the eyes of the village people. Some thought my hair was the color of tar, that it had the texture of wire, or the texture of cotton. It was jocularly suggested that I might let it all grow long and make myself a winter coat. If I sat in the sun for more than five minutes some daring creature was certain to come along and gingerly put his fingers on my hair, as though he were afraid of an electric shock, or put his hand on my hand, astonished that the color did not rub off. In all of this, in which it must be conceded there was the charm of genuine wonder and in which there were certainly no element of intentional unkindness, there was yet no suggestion that I was human: I was simply a living wonder.

I knew that they did not mean to be unkind, and I know it now; it is necessary, nevertheless, for me to repeat this to myself each time that I walk out of the chalet. The children who shout *Neger!* have no way of knowing the echoes this sound raises in me. They are brimming with good humor and the more daring swell with pride when I stop to speak with them. Just the same, there are days when I cannot pause and smile, when I have no heart to play with them; when, indeed, I mutter sourly to myself, exactly as I muttered on the streets of a city these children have never seen, when I was no bigger than these children are now: *Your* mother *was a nigger.* Joyce is right about history being a nightmare—but it may be the nightmare from which no one *can* awaken. People are trapped in history and history is trapped in them.

There is a custom in the village—I am told it is repeated in many villages—of "buying" African natives for the purpose of converting them to Christianity. There stands in the church all year round a small box with a slot for money, decorated with a black figurine, and into this box the villagers drop their francs. During the *carnaval* which precedes Lent, two village children have their faces blackened —out of which bloodless darkness their blue eyes shine like ice—and fantastic horsehair wigs are placed on their blond heads; thus disguised, they solicit among the villagers for money for the missionaries in Africa. Between the box in the church and the blackened children, the village "bought" last year six or eight African natives. This was reported to me with pride by the wife of one of the *bistro* owners and I was careful to express astonishment and pleasure at the solicitude shown by the village for the souls of black folks. The *bistro* owner's wife beamed with a pleasure far more genuine than my own and seemed to feel that I might now breathe more easily concerning the souls of at least six of my kinsmen.

I tried not to think of these so lately baptized kinsmen, of the price paid for them, or the peculiar price they themselves would pay, and said nothing about my father, who having taken his own conversion too literally never, at bottom, forgave the white world (which he described as heathen) for having saddled him with a Christ in whom, to judge at least from their treatment of him, they themselves no longer believed. I thought of white men arriving for the first time in an African village, strangers there, as I am a stranger here, and tried to imagine the astounded populace touching their hair and marveling at the color of their skin. But there is a great difference between being the first white man to be seen by Africans and being the first black man to be seen by whites. The white man takes the astonishment as tribute, for he arrives to conquer and to convert the natives, whose inferiority in relation to himself is not even to be questioned; whereas I, without a thought of conquest, find myself among a people whose culture controls me, has even, in a sense, created me, people who have cost me more in anguish and rage than they will ever know, who yet do not even know of my existence. The astonishment with which I might have greeted them, should they have stumbled into my African village a few hundred years ago, might have rejoiced their hearts. But the astonishment with which they greet me today can only poison mine.

And this is so despite everything I may do to feel differently, despite my friendly conversations with the *bistro* owner's wife, despite their three-year-old son who has at last become my friend, despite the *saluts* and *bonsoirs* which I exchange with people as I walk, despite the fact that I know that no individual can be taken to task for what history is doing, or has done. I say that the culture of these people controls me—but they can scarcely be held responsible for European culture. America comes out of Europe, but these people have never seen America, nor have most of them seen more of Europe than the hamlet at the foot of their mountain. Yet they move with an authority which I shall never have; and they regard me, quite rightly, not only as a stranger in their village but as a suspect late-comer, bearing no credentials, to everything they have—however unconsciously—inherited.

For this village, even were it incomparably more remote and incredibly more primitive, is the West, the West onto which I have been so strangely grafted. These people cannot be, from the point of view of power, strangers anywhere in the world; they have made the modern world, in effect, even if they do not know it. The most illiterate among them is related, in a way that I am not, to Dante, Shakespeare, Michelangelo, Aeschylus, Da Vinci, Rembrandt, and Racine; the cathedral at Chartres says something to them which it cannot say to me, as indeed would New York's Empire State Building, should anyone here ever see it. Out of their hymns and dances come Beethoven and Bach. Go back a few centuries and they are in their full glory—but I am in Africa, watching the conquerors arrive.

The rage of the disesteemed is personally fruitless, but it is also absolutely inevitable; this rage, so generally discounted, so little understood even among the people whose daily bread it is, is one of the things that makes history. Rage can only with difficulty, and never entirely, be brought under the domination of the intelligence and is therefore not susceptible to any arguments whatever. This is a fact which ordinary representatives of the *Herrenvolk*,[1] having never felt this rage and being unable to imagine, quite fail to understand. Also, rage cannot be hidden, it can only be dissembled. This dissembling deludes the thoughtless, and strengthens rage and adds, to rage, contempt. There are, no doubt, as many ways of coping with the resulting complex of tensions as there are black men in the world, but no black man can hope ever to be entirely liberated from this internal warfare—rage, dissembling, and contempt having inevitably accompanied his first realization of the power of white men. What is crucial here is that, since white men represent in the black man's world so heavy a weight, white men have for black men a reality which is far from being reciprocal; and hence all black men have

1. Master race.

toward all white men an attitude which is designed, really, either to rob the white man of the jewel of his naïveté, or else to make it cost him dear.

The black man insists, by whatever means he finds at his disposal, that the white man cease to regard him as an exotic rarity and recognize him as a human being. This is a very charged and difficult moment, for there is a great deal of will power involved in the white man's naïveté. Most people are not naturally reflective any more than they are naturally malicious, and the white man prefers to keep the black man at a certain human remove because it is easier for him thus to preserve his simplicity and avoid being called to account for crimes committed by his forefathers, or his neighbors. He is inescapably aware, nevertheless, that he is in a better position in the world than black men are, nor can he quite put to death the suspicion that he is hated by black men therefore. He does not wish to be hated, neither does he wish to change places, and at this point in his uneasiness he can scarcely avoid having recourse to those legends which white men have created about black men, the most usual effect of which is that the white man finds himself enmeshed, so to speak, in his own language which describes hell, as well as the attributes which lead one to hell, as being as black as night.

Every legend, moreover, contains its residuum of truth, and the root function of language is to control the universe by describing it. It is of quite considerable significance that black men remain, in the imagination, and in overwhelming numbers in fact, beyond the disciplines of salvation; and this despite the fact that the West has been "buying" African natives for centuries. There is, I should hazard, an instantaneous necessity to be divorced from this so visibly unsaved stranger, in whose heart, moreover, one cannot guess what dreams of vengeance are being nourished; and, at the same time, there are few things on earth more attractive than the idea of the unspeakable liberty which is allowed the unredeemed. When, beneath the black mask, a human being begins to make himself felt one cannot escape a certain awful wonder as to what kind of human being it is. What one's imagination makes of other people is dictated, of course, by the laws of one's own personality and it is one of the ironies of black-white relations that, by means of what the white man imagines the black man to be, the black man is enabled to know who the white man is.

I have said, for example, that I am as much a stranger in this village today as I was the first summer I arrived, but this is not quite true. The villagers wonder less about the texture of my hair than they did then, and wonder rather more about me. And the fact that their wonder now exists on another level is reflected in their attitudes and in their eyes. There are the children who make those delightful, hilarious, sometimes astonishingly grave overtures of friendship in the unpredictable fashion of children; other children, having been taught that the devil is a black man, scream in genuine anguish as I approach. Some of the older women never pass without a friendly greeting, never pass, indeed, if it seems that they will be able to engage me in conversation; other women look down or look away or rather contemptuously smirk. Some of the men drink with me and suggest that I learn how to ski—partly, I gather, because they cannot imagine what I would look like on skis—and want to know if I am married, and ask questions about my *métier*. But some of the men have accused *le sale nègre*—behind my back—of stealing wood and there is already in the eyes of some of them that peculiar, intent, paranoiac malevolence which one sometimes surprises in the eyes of American white men when, out walking with their Sunday girl, they see a Negro male approach.

There is a dreadful abyss between the streets of this village and the streets of the city in which I was born, between the children who shout *Neger!* today and those who shouted *Nigger!* yesterday— the abyss is experience, the American experience. The syllable hurled behind me today expresses, above all, wonder: I am a stranger here. But I am not a stranger in America and the same syllable riding on the American air expresses the war my presence has occasioned in the American soul.

For this village brings home to me this fact: that there was a day, and not really a very distant day, when Americans were scarcely Americans at all but discontented Europeans, facing a great unconquered continent and strolling, say, into a marketplace and seeing black men for the first time. The shock this spectacle afforded is suggested, surely, by the promptness with which they decided that these black men were not really men but cattle. It is true that the necessity on the part of the settlers of the New World of reconciling their moral assumptions with the fact—and the necessity—of slavery enhanced immensely the charm of this idea, and it is also true that this idea expresses, with a truly American bluntness, the attitude which to varying extents all masters have had toward all slaves.

But between all former slaves and slave-owners and the drama which begins for Americans over three hundred years ago at Jamestown, there are at least two differences to be observed. The American Negro slave could not suppose, for one thing, as slaves in past epochs had supposed and often done, that he would ever be able to wrest the power from his master's hands. This was a supposition which the modern era, which was to bring about such vast changes in the aims and dimensions of power, put to death; it only begins, in unprecedented fashion, and with dreadful implications, to be resurrected today. But even had this supposition persisted with undiminished force, the American Negro slave could not have used it to lend his condition dignity, for the reason that this supposition rests on another: that the slave in exile yet remains related to his past, has some means—if only in memory—of revering and sustaining the forms of his former life, is able, in short, to maintain his identity.

This was not the case with the American Negro slave. He is unique among the black men of the world in that his past was taken from him, almost literally, at one blow. One wonders what on earth the first slave found to say to the first dark child he bore. I am told that there are Haitians able to trace their ancestry back to African kings, but any American Negro wishing to go back so far will find his journey through time abruptly arrested by the signature on the bill of sale which served as the entrance paper for his ancestor. At the time—to say nothing of the circumstances—of the enslavement of the captive black man who was to become the American Negro, there was not the remotest possibility that he would ever take power from his master's hands. There was no reason to suppose that his situation would ever change, nor was there, shortly, anything to indicate that his situation had ever been different. It was his necessity, in the words of E. Franklin Frazier, to find a "motive for living under American culture or die." The identity of the American Negro comes out of this extreme situation, and the evolution of this identity was a source of the most intolerable anxiety in the minds and the lives of his masters.

For the history of the American Negro is unique also in this: that the question of his humanity, and of his rights therefore as a human being, became a burning one for several generations of Americans, so burning a question that it ultimately became one of those used to divide the nation. It is out of this argument that the venom of the epithet *Nigger!* is derived. It is an argument which Europe has never had, and hence Europe quite sincerely fails to understand how or why the argument arose in the first place, why its effects are frequently disastrous and always so unpredictable, why it refuses until today to be entirely settled. Europe's black possessions remained —and do remain—in Europe's colonies, at which remove they represented no threat whatever to European identity. If they posed any problem at all for the European conscience, it was a problem which remained comfortingly abstract: in effect, the black man, as a *man*, did not exist for Europe. But in America, even as a slave, he was an inescapable part of the general social fabric and no American could escape having an attitude toward him. Americans attempt until today to make an abstraction of the Negro, but the very nature of these abstractions reveals the tremendous effects the presence of the Negro has had on the American character.

When one considers the history of the Negro in America it is of the greatest importance to recognize that the moral beliefs of a person, or a people, are never really as tenuous as life—which is not moral—very often causes them to appear; these create for them a frame of reference and a necessary hope, the hope being that when life has done its worst they will be enabled to rise above themselves and to triumph over life. Life would scarcely be bearable if this hope did not exist. Again, even when the worst has been said, to betray a belief is not by any means to have put oneself beyond its power; the betrayal of a belief is not the same thing as ceasing to believe. If this were not so there would be no moral standards in the world at all. Yet one must also recognize that morality is based on ideas and that all ideas are dangerous—dangerous because ideas can only lead to action and where the action leads no man can say. And dangerous in this respect: that confronted with the impossibility of remaining faithful to one's beliefs, and the equal impossibility of becoming free of them, one can be driven to the most inhuman excesses. The ideas on which American beliefs are based are not, though Americans often seem to think so, ideas which originated in America. They came out of Europe. And the establishment of democracy on the American continent was scarcely as radical a break with the past as was the necessity, which Americans faced, of broadening this concept to include black men.

This was, literally, a hard necessity. It was impossible, for one thing, for Americans to abandon their beliefs, not only because these beliefs alone seemed able to justify the sacrifices they had endured and the blood that they had spilled, but also because these beliefs afforded them their only bulwark against a moral chaos as absolute as the physical chaos of the continent it was their destiny to conquer. But in the situation in which Americans found themselves, these beliefs threatened an idea which, whether or not one likes to think so, is the very warp and woof of the heritage of the West, the idea of white supremacy.

Americans have made themselves notorious by the shrillness and the brutality with which they have insisted on this idea, but they did not invent it; and it has escaped the world's notice that those very excesses of which Americans have been guilty imply a certain, unprecedented uneasiness over the idea's life and power, if not, indeed, the idea's validity. The idea of white supremacy rests simply on the fact that white men are the creators of civilization (the present civilization, which is the only one that matters; all previous civilizations are simply "contributions" to our own) and are therefore civilization's guardians and defenders. Thus it was impossible for Americans to accept the black man as one of themselves, for to do so was to jeopardize their status as white men. But not so to accept him was to deny his human reality, his human weight and complexity, and the strain of denying the overwhelmingly undeniable forced Americans into rationalizations so fantastic that they approached the pathological.

At the root of the American Negro problem is the necessity of the American white man to find a way of living with the Negro in order to be able to live with himself. And the history of this problem can be reduced to the means used by Americans—lynch law and law, segregation and legal acceptance, terrorization and concession —either to come to terms with this necessity, or to find a way around it, or (most usually) to find a way of doing both these things at once. The resulting spectacle, at once foolish and dreadful, led someone to make the quite accurate observation that "the Negro-in-America is a form of insanity which overtakes white men."

In this long battle, a battle by no means finished, the unforeseeable effects of which will be felt by many future generations, the white man's motive was the protection of his identity; the black man was motivated by the need to establish an identity. And despite the terrorization which the Negro in America endured and endures sporadically until today, despite the cruel and totally inescapable ambivalence of his status in his country, the battle for his identity has long ago been won. He is not a visitor to the West, but a citizen there, an American; as American as the Americans who despise him, the Americans who fear him, the Americans who love him—the Americans who became less than themselves, or rose to be greater than themselves by virtue of the fact that the challenge he represented was inescapable. He is perhaps the only black man in the world whose relationship to white men is more terrible, more subtle, and more meaningful than the relationship of bitter possessed to uncertain possessors. His survival depended, and his development depends, on his ability to turn his peculiar status in the Western world to his own advantage and, it may be, to the very great advantage of that world. It remains for him to fashion out of his experience that which will give him sustenance, and a voice.

The cathedral at Chartres, I have said, says something to the people of this village which it cannot say to me; but it is important to understand that this cathedral says something to me which it cannot say to them. Perhaps they are struck by the power of the spires, the glory of the windows; but they have known God, after all, longer than I have known him, and in a different way, and I am terrified by the slippery bottomless well to be found in the crypt, down which heretics were hurled to death, and by the obscene, inescapable gargoyles jutting out of the stone and seeming to say that God and the devil can never be divorced. I doubt that the villagers think of the devil when they face a cathedral because they have never been identified with the devil. But I must accept the status which myth, if nothing else, gives me in the West before I can hope to change the myth.

Yet, if the American Negro has arrived at his identity by virtue of the absoluteness of his estrangement from his past, American white men still nourish the illusion that there is some means of recovering the European innocence, of returning to a state in which black men do not exist. This is one of the greatest errors Americans can make. The identity they fought so hard to protect has, by virtue of that battle, undergone a change: Americans are as unlike any other white people in the world as it is possible to be. I do not think, for example, that it is too much to suggest that the American vision of the world—which allows so little reality, generally speaking, for any of the darker forces in human life, which tends until today to paint moral issues in glaring black and white—owes a great deal to the battle waged by Americans to maintain between themselves and black men a human separation which could not be bridged. It is only now beginning to be borne in on us—very faintly, it must be admitted, very slowly, and very much against our will—that this vision of the world is dangerously inaccurate, and perfectly useless. For it protects our moral high-mindedness at the terrible expense of weakening our grasp of reality. People who shut their eyes to reality simply invite their own destruction, and anyone who insists on remaining in a state of innocence long after that innocence is dead turns himself into a monster.

The time has come to realize that the interracial drama acted out on the American continent has not only created a new black man, it has created a new white man, too. No road whatever will lead Americans back to the simplicity of this European village where white men still have the luxury of looking on me as a stranger. I am not, really, a stranger any longer for any American alive. One of the things that distinguishes Americans from other people is that no other people has ever been so deeply involved in the lives of black men, and vice versa. This fact faced, with all its implications, it can be seen that the history of the American Negro problem is not merely shameful, it is also something of an achievement. For even when the worst has been said, it must also be added that the perpetual challenge posed by this problem was always, somehow, perpetually met. It is precisely this black-white experience which may prove of indispensable value to us in the world we face today. This world is white no longer, and it will never be white again.

QUESTIONS

1. Baldwin begins with the narration of his experience in a Swiss village. At what point do you become aware that he is going to do more than tell the story of his stay in the village? What purpose does he make his experience serve?

2. On page 656 Baldwin says that Americans have attempted to make an abstraction of the Negro. To what degree has his purpose forced Baldwin to make an abstraction of the white man? What are the components of that abstraction?

3. Baldwin intimately relates the white man's language and legends about black men to the "laws" of the white man's personality.

Bettelheim makes similar use of the myths of science fiction.
This kind of inference reveals a conviction both men share about
the nature of language; what is that conviction?
4. Describe some particular experience which raises a large social
question or shows the working of large social forces. Does
Baldwin offer any help in the problem of connecting the particular and the general?
5. Define alienation.

MARTIN LUTHER KING, JR.

Letter from Birmingham Jail[1]

My Dear Fellow Clergymen:

While confined here in the Birmingham city jail, I came across
your recent statement calling my present activities "unwise and
untimely." Seldom do I pause to answer criticism of my work and
ideas. If I sought to answer all the criticisms that cross my desk, my
secretaries would have little time for anything other than such correspondence in the course of the day, and I would have no time for
constructive work. But since I feel that you are men of genuine
good will and that your criticisms are sincerely set forth, I want to
try to answer your statement in what I hope will be patient and
reasonable terms.

I think I should indicate why I am here in Birmingham, since
you have been influenced by the view which argues against "outsiders coming in." I have the honor of serving as president of the
Southern Christian Leadership Conference, an organization operating in every southern state, with headquarters in Atlanta, Georgia.
We have some eighty-five affiliated organizations across the South,
and one of them is the Alabama Christian Movement for Human
Rights. Frequently we share staff, educational, and financial
resources with our affiliates. Several months ago the affiliate here in
Birmingham asked us to be on call to engage in a nonviolent
direct-action program if such were deemed necessary. We readily

---

1. This response to a published statement by eight fellow clergymen from
Alabama (Bishop C. C. J. Carpenter,
Bishop Joseph A. Durick, Rabbi Hilton
L. Grafman, Bishop Paul Hardin,
Bishop Holan B. Harmon, the Reverend
George M. Murray, the Reverend Edward V. Ramage and the Reverend Earl
Stallings) was composed under somewhat constricting circumstances. Begun
on the margins of the newspaper in
which the statement appeared while I
was in jail, the letter was continued
on scraps of writing paper supplied by
a friendly Negro trusty, and concluded
on a pad my attorneys were eventually
permitted to leave me. Although the
text remains in substance unaltered, I
have indulged in the author's prerogative of polishing it for publication
[King's note].

consented, and when the hour came we lived up to our promise. So I, along with several members of my staff, am here because I was invited here. I am here because I have organizational ties here.

But more basically, I am in Birmingham because injustice is here. Just as the prophets of the eighth century B.C. left their villages and carried their "thus saith the Lord" far beyond the boundaries of their home towns, and just as the Apostle Paul left his village of Tarsus and carried the gospel of Jesus Christ to the far corners of the Greco-Roman world, so am I compelled to carry the gospel of freedom beyond my own home town. Like Paul, I must constantly respond to the Macedonian call for aid.

Moreover, I am cognizant of the interrelatedness of all communities and states. I cannot sit idly by in Atlanta and not be concerned about what happens in Birmingham. Injustice anywhere is a threat to justice everywhere. We are caught in an inescapable network of mutuality, tied in a single garment of destiny. Whatever affects one directly, affects all indirectly. Never again can we afford to live with the narrow, provincial "outside agitator" idea. Anyone who lives inside the United States can never be considered an outsider anywhere within its bounds.

You deplore the demonstrations taking place in Birmingham. But your statement, I am sorry to say, fails to express a similar concern for the conditions that brought about the demonstrations. I am sure that none of you would want to rest content with the superficial kind of social analysis that deals merely with effects and does not grapple with underlying causes. It is unfortunate that demonstrations are taking place in Birmingham, but it is even more unfortunate that the city's white power structure left the Negro community with no alternative.

In any nonviolent campaign there are four basic steps: collection of the facts to determine whether injustices exist; negotiation; self-purification; and direct action. We have gone through all these steps in Birmingham. There can be no gainsaying the fact that racial injustice engulfs this community. Birmingham is probably the most thoroughly segregated city in the United States. Its ugly record of brutality is widely known. Negroes have experienced grossly unjust treatment in the courts. There have been more unsolved bombings of Negro homes and churches in Birmingham than in any other city in the nation. These are the hard, brutal facts of the case. On the basis of these conditions, Negro leaders sought to negotiate with the city fathers. But the latter consistently refused to engage in good-faith negotiation.

Then, last September, came the opportunity to talk with leaders of Birmingham's economic community. In the course of the negotiations, certain promises were made by the merchants—for example, to remove the stores' humiliating racial signs. On the basis of these promises, the Reverend Fred Shuttlesworth and the leaders of the Alabama Christian Movement for Human Rights agreed to a moratorium on all demonstrations. As the weeks and months went by, we realized that we were the victims of a broken promise. A few signs, briefly removed, returned; the others remained.

As in so many past experiences, our hopes had been blasted, and the shadow of deep disappointment settled upon us. We had no alternative except to prepare for direct action, whereby we would present our very bodies as a means of laying our case before the conscience of the local and the national community. Mindful of the difficulties involved, we decided to undertake a process of self-purification. We began a series of workshops on nonviolence, and we repeatedly asked ourselves: "Are you able to accept blows without retaliating?" "Are you able to endure the ordeal of jail?" We decided to schedule our direct-action program for the Easter season, realizing that except for Christmas, this is the main shopping period of the year. Knowing that a strong economic-withdrawal program would be the by-product of direct action, we felt that this would be the best time to bring pressure to bear on the merchants for the needed change.

Then it occurred to us that Birmingham's mayoral election was coming up in March, and we speedily decided to postpone action until after election day. When we discovered that the Commissioner of Public Safety, Eugene "Bull" Connor, had piled up enough votes to be in the run-off, we decided again to postpone action until the day after the run-off so that the demonstrations could not be used to cloud the issues. Like many others, we waited to see Mr. Connor defeated, and to this end we endured postponement after postponement. Having aided in this community need, we felt that our direct-action program could be delayed no longer.

You may well ask, "Why direct action? Why sit-ins, marches, and so forth? Isn't negotiation a better path?" You are quite right in calling for negotiation. Indeed, this is the very purpose of direct action. Nonviolent direct action seeks to create such a crisis and foster such a tension that a community which has constantly refused to negotiate is forced to confront the issue. It seeks so to dramatize the issue that it can no longer be ignored. My citing the creation of tension as part of the work of the nonviolent-resister may sound rather shocking. But I must confess that I am not afraid of the word "tension." I have earnestly opposed violent tension, but there is a type of constructive, nonviolent tension which is necessary for growth. Just as Socrates felt that it was necessary to create a tension in the mind so that individuals could rise from the bondage of myths and half-truths to the unfettered realm of creative analysis and objective appraisal, so must we see the need for nonviolent gadflies to create the kind of tension in society that will help men rise from the dark depths of prejudice and racism to the majestic heights of understanding and brotherhood.

The purpose of our direct-action program is to create a situation so crisis-packed that it will inevitably open the door to negotiation. I therefore concur with you in your call for negotiation. Too long has our beloved Southland been bogged down in a tragic effort to live in monologue rather than dialogue.

One of the basic points in your statement is that the action that I and my associates have taken in Birmingham is untimely. Some have asked: "Why didn't you give the new city administration time to act?" The only answer that I can give to this query is that the new Birmingham administration must be prodded about as much as the outgoing one, before it will act. We are sadly mistaken if we feel that the election of Albert Boutwell as mayor will bring the millennium to Birmingham. While Mr. Boutwell is a much more gentle person than Mr. Connor, they are both segregationists, dedicated to maintenance of the status quo. I have hoped that Mr. Boutwell will be reasonable enough to see the futility of massive resistance to desegregation. But he will not see this without pressure from devotees of civil rights. My friends, I must say to you that we have not made a single gain in civil rights without determined legal and nonviolent pressure. Lamentably, it is an historical fact that privileged groups seldom give up their privileges voluntarily. Individuals may see the moral light and voluntarily give up their unjust posture; but, as Reinhold Niebuhr has reminded us, groups tend to be more immoral than individuals.

We know through painful experience that freedom is never voluntarily given by the oppressor; it must be demanded by the oppressed. Frankly, I have yet to engage in a direct-action campaign that was "well timed" in the view of those who have not suffered unduly from the disease of segregation. For years now I have heard the word "Wait!" It rings in the ear of every Negro with piercing familiarity. This "Wait" has almost always meant "Never." We must come to see, with one of our distinguished jurists, that "justice too long delayed is justice denied."

We have waited for more than 340 years for our constitutional and God-given rights. The nations of Asia and Africa are moving with jetlike speed toward gaining political independence, but we still creep at horse-and-buggy pace toward gaining a cup of coffee at a lunch counter. Perhaps it is easy for those who have never felt the stinging darts of segregation to say, "Wait." But when you have seen vicious mobs lynch your mothers and fathers at will and drown your sisters and brothers at whim; when you have seen hate-filled policemen curse, kick, and even kill your black brothers and sisters; when you see the vast majority of your twenty million Negro brothers smothering in an airtight cage of poverty in the midst of an affluent society; when you suddenly find your tongue twisted and your speech stammering as you seek to explain to your six-year-old daughter why she can't go to the public amusement park that has just been advertised on television, and see tears welling up in her eyes when she is told that Funtown is closed to colored children, and see ominous clouds of inferiority beginning to form in her little mental sky, and see her beginning to distort her personality by developing an unconscious bitterness toward white people; when you have to concoct an answer for a five-year-old son who is asking, "Daddy, why do white people treat colored people so mean?"; when you take a cross-country drive and find it necessary to sleep night after night in the uncomfortable corners of your automobile because no motel will accept you; when you are humiliated day in and day out by nagging signs reading "white" and "colored"; when your first name becomes "nigger," your middle name becomes "boy" (however old you are) and your last name becomes "John," and your wife and mother are never given the respected title "Mrs."; when you are harried by day and haunted by night by the fact that you are a Negro, living constantly at tiptoe stance, never quite knowing what to expect next, and are plagued with inner fears and outer resentments; when you are forever fighting a degenerating sense of "nobodiness"—then you will understand why we find it difficult to wait. There comes a time when the cup of endurance runs over, and men are no longer willing to be plunged into the abyss of despair. I hope, sirs, you can understand our legitimate and unavoidable impatience.

You express a great deal of anxiety over our willingness to break laws. This is certainly a legitimate concern. Since we so diligently urge people to obey the Supreme Court's decision of 1954 outlawing segregation in the public schools, at first glance it may seem rather paradoxical for us consciously to break laws. One may well ask: "How can you advocate breaking some laws and obeying others?" The answer lies in the fact that there are two types of laws: just and unjust. I would be the first to advocate obeying just laws. One has not only a legal but a moral responsibility to obey just laws. Conversely, one has a moral responsibility to disobey unjust laws. I would agree with St. Augustine that "an unjust law is no law at all."

Now, what is the difference between the two? How does one determine whether a law is just or unjust? A just law is a man-made code that squares with the moral law or the law of God. An unjust law is a code that is out of harmony with the moral law. To put it in the terms of St. Thomas Aquinas: An unjust law is a human law that is not rooted in eternal law and natural law. Any law that uplifts human personality is just. Any law that degrades human personality is unjust. All segregation statutes are unjust because segregation distorts the soul and damages the personality. It gives the segregator a false sense of superiority and the segregated a false sense of inferiority. Segregation, to use the terminology of the Jewish philosopher Martin Buber, substitutes an "I-it" relationship for an "I-thou" relationship and ends up relegating persons to the status of things. Hence segregation is not only politically, economically, and sociologically unsound, it is morally wrong and sinful. Paul Tillich has said that sin is separation. Is not segregation an existential expression of man's tragic separation, his awful estrangement, his terrible sinfulness? Thus it is that I can urge men to obey the 1954 decision of the Supreme Court, for it is morally right; and I can urge them to disobey segregation ordinances, for they are morally wrong.

Let us consider a more concrete example of just and unjust laws. An unjust law is a code that a numerical or power majority group compels a minority group to obey but does not make binding on itself. This is *difference* made legal. By the same token, a just law is a code that a majority compels a minority to follow and that it is willing to follow itself. This is *sameness* made legal.

Let me given another explanation. A law is unjust if it is inflicted on a minority that, as a result of being denied the right to vote, had no part in enacting or devising the law. Who can say that the legislature of Alabama which set up that state's segregation laws was democratically elected? Throughout Alabama all sorts of devious methods are used to prevent Negroes from becoming registered voters, and there are some counties in which, even though Negroes constitute a majority of the population, not a single Negro is registered. Can any law enacted under such circumstances be considered democratically structured?

Sometimes a law is just on its face and unjust in its application. For instance, I have been arrested on a charge of parading without a permit. Now, there is nothing wrong in having an ordinance which requires a permit for a parade. But such an ordinance becomes unjust when it is used to maintain segregation and to deny citizens the First-Amendment privilege of peaceful assembly and protest.

I hope you are able to see the distinction I am trying to point out. In no sense do I advocate evading or defying the law, as would the rabid segregationist. That would lead to anarchy. One who breaks an unjust law must do so openly, lovingly, and with a willingness to accept the penalty. I submit that an individual who breaks a law that conscience tells him is unjust, and who willingly accepts the penalty of imprisonment in order to arouse the conscience of the community over its injustice, is in reality expressing the highest respect for law.

Of course, there is nothing new about this kind of civil disobedience. It was evidenced sublimely in the refusal of Shadrach, Meshach, and Abednego to obey the laws of Nebuchadnezzar, on the ground that a higher moral law was at stake. It was practiced superbly by the early Christians, who were willing to face hungry lions and the excruciating pain of chopping blocks rather than submit to certain unjust laws of the Roman Empire. To a degree, academic freedom is a reality today because Socrates practiced civil disobedience. In our own nation, the Boston Tea Party represented a massive act of civil disobedience.

We should never forget that everything Adolf Hitler did in Germany was "legal" and everything the Hungarian freedom fighters did in Hungary was "illegal." It was "illegal" to aid and comfort a Jew in Hitler's Germany. Even so, I am sure that, had I lived in Germany at the time, I would have aided and comforted my Jewish brothers. If today I lived in a Communist country where certain principles dear to the Christian faith are suppressed, I would openly advocate disobeying that country's anti-religious laws.

I must make two honest confessions to you, my Christian and Jewish brothers. First, I must confess that over the past few years I have been gravely disappointed with the white moderate. I have almost reached the regrettable conclusion that the Negro's great stumbling block in his stride toward freedom is not the White Citizen's Counciler or the Ku Klux Klanner, but the white moderate, who is more devoted to "order" than to justice; who prefers a negative peace which is the absence of tension to a positive peace which is the presence of justice; who constantly says, "I agree with you in the goal you seek, but I cannot agree with your methods of direct action"; who paternalistically believes he can set the timetable for another man's freedom; who lives by a mythical concept of time and who constantly advises the Negro to wait for a "more convenient season." Shallow understanding from people of good will is more frustrating than absolute misunderstanding from people of ill will. Lukewarm acceptance is much more bewildering than outright rejection.

I had hoped that the white moderate would understand that law and order exist for the purpose of establishing justice and that when they fail in this purpose they become the dangerously structured dams that block the flow of social progress. I had hoped that the white moderate would understand that the present tension in the South is a necessary phase of the transition from an obnoxious negative peace, in which the Negro passively accepted his unjust plight, to a substantive and positive peace, in which all men will respect the dignity and worth of human personality. Actually, we who engage in nonviolent direct action are not the creators of tension. We merely bring to the surface the hidden tension that is already alive. We bring it out in the open, where it can be seen and dealt with. Like a boil that can never be cured so long as it is covered up but must be opened with all its ugliness to the natural medicines of air and light, injustice must be exposed, with all the tension its exposure creates, to the light of human conscience and the air of national opinion, before it can be cured.

In your statement you assert that our actions, even though peaceful, must be condemned because they precipitate violence. But is this a logical assertion? Isn't this like condemning a robbed man because his possession of money precipitated the evil act of robbery? Isn't this like condemning Socrates because his unswerving commitment to truth and his philosophical inquiries precipitated the act by the misguided populace in which they made him drink hemlock? Isn't this like condemning Jesus because his unique God-consciousness and never-ceasing devotion to God's will precipitated the evil act of crucifixion? We must come to see that, as the federal courts have consistently affirmed, it is wrong to urge an individual to cease his efforts to gain his basic constitutional rights because the quest may precipitate violence. Society must protect the robbed and punish the robber.

I had also hoped that the white moderate would reject the myth concerning time in relation to the struggle for freedom. I have just received a letter from a white brother in Texas. He writes: "All Christians know that the colored people will receive equal rights eventually, but it is possible that you are in too great a religious hurry. It has taken Christianity almost two thousand years to accomplish what it has. The teachings of Christ take time to come to earth." Such an attitude stems from a tragic misconception of time, from the strangely irrational notion that there is something in the very flow of time that will inevitably cure all ills. Actually, time itself is neutral; it can be used either destructively or constructively. More and more I feel that the people of ill will have used time much more effectively than have the people of good will. We will have to repent in this generation not merely for the hateful words and actions of the bad people, but for the appalling silence of the good people. Human progress never rolls in on wheels of inevitability; it comes through the tireless efforts of men willing to be co-workers with God, and without this hard work, time itself becomes an ally of the forces of social stagnation. We must use time creatively, in the knowledge that the time is always ripe to do right. Now is the time to make real the promise of democracy and transform our pending national elegy into a creative psalm of brotherhood. Now is the time to lift our national policy from the quicksand of racial injustice to the solid rock of human dignity.

You speak of our activity in Birmingham as extreme. At first I was rather disappointed that fellow clergymen would see my nonviolent efforts as those of an extremist. I began thinking about the fact that I stand in the middle of two opposing forces in the Negro community. One is a force of complacency, made up in part of Negroes who, as a result of long years of oppression, are so drained of self-respect and a sense of "somebodiness" that they have adjusted to segregation; and in part of a few middle-class Negroes who, because of a degree of academic and economic security and because in some ways they profit by segregation, have become insensitive to the problems of the masses. The other force is one of bitterness and hatred, and it comes perilously close to advocating violence. It is expressed in the various black nationalist groups that are springing up across the nation, the largest and best-known being Elijah Muhammad's Muslim movement. Nourished by the Negro's frustration over the continued existence of racial discrimination, this movement is made up of people who have lost faith in America, who have absolutely repudiated Christianity, and who have concluded that the white man is an incorrigible "devil."

I have tried to stand between these two forces, saying that we need emulate neither the "do-nothingism" of the complacent nor the hatred and despair of the black nationalist. For there is the more excellent way of love and nonviolent protest. I am grateful to God that, through the influence of the Negro church, the way of nonviolence became an integral part of our struggle.

If this philosophy had not emerged, by now many streets of the South would, I am convinced, be flowing with blood. And I am further convinced that if our white brothers dismiss as "rabble-rousers" and "outside agitators" those of us who employ nonviolent direct action, and if they refuse to support our nonviolent efforts, millions of Negroes will, out of frustration and despair, seek solace and security in black-nationalist ideologies—a development that would inevitably lead to a frightening racial nightmare.

Oppressed people cannot remain oppressed forever. The yearning for freedom eventually manifests itself, and that is what has happened to the American Negro. Something within has reminded him of his birthright of freedom, and something without has reminded him that it can be gained. Consciously or unconsciously, he has been caught up by the *Zeitgeist*, and with his black brothers of Africa and his brown and yellow brothers of Asia, South America, and the Caribbean, the United States Negro is moving with a sense of great urgency toward the promised land of racial justice. If one recognizes this vital urge that has engulfed the Negro community, one should readily understand why public demonstrations are taking place. The Negro has many pent-up resentments and latent frustrations, and he must release them. So let him march; let him make prayer pilgrimages to the city hall; let him go on freedom rides—and try to understand why he must do so. If his repressed emotions are not released in nonviolent ways, they will seek expression through violence; this is not a threat but a fact of history. So I have not said to my people, "Get rid of your discontent." Rather, I have tried to say that this normal and healthy discontent can be channeled into the creative outlet of nonviolent direct action. And now this approach is being termed extremist.

But though I was initially disappointed at being categorized as an extremist, as I continued to think about the matter I gradually gained a measure of satisfaction from the label. Was not Jesus an extremist for love: "Love your enemies, bless them that curse you, do good to them that hate you, and pray for them which despitefully use you, and persecute you." Was not Amos an extremist for justice: "Let justice roll down like waters and righteousness like an ever-flowing stream." Was not Paul an extremist for the Christian gospel: "I bear in my body the marks of the Lord Jesus." Was not Martin Luther an extremist: "Here I stand; I cannot do otherwise, so help me God." And John Bunyan: "I will stay in jail to the end of my days before I make a butchery of my conscience." And Abraham Lincoln: "This nation cannot survive half slave and half free." And Thomas Jefferson: "We hold these truths to be self-evident, that all men are created equal. . . ." So the question is not whether we will be extremists, but what kind of extremists we will be. Will we be extremists for hate or for love? Will we be extremists for the preservation of injustice or for the extension of justice? In that dramatic scene on Calvary's hill three men were crucified. We must never forget that all three were crucified for the same crime—the crime of extremism. Two were extremists for immorality, and thus fell below their environment. The other, Jesus Christ, was an extremist for love, truth, and goodness, and thereby rose above his environment. Perhaps the South, the nation, and the world are in dire need of creative extremists.

I had hoped that the white moderate would see this need. Perhaps I was too optimistic; perhaps I expected too much. I suppose I should have realized that few members of the oppressor race can understand the deep groans and passionate yearnings of the oppressed race, and still fewer have the vision to see that injustice must be rooted out by strong, persistent, and determined action. I am thankful, however, that some of our white brothers in the South have grasped the meaning of this social revolution and committed themselves to it. They are still all too few in quantity, but they are big in quality. Some—such as Ralph McGill, Lillian Smith, Harry Golden, James McBride Dabbs, Ann Braden, and

Sarah Patton Boyle—have written about our struggle in eloquent and prophetic terms. Others have marched with us down nameless streets of the South. They have languished in filthy, roach-infested jails, suffering the abuse and brutality of policemen who view them as "dirty nigger-lovers." Unlike so many of their moderate brothers and sisters, they have recognized the urgency of the moment and sensed the need for powerful "action" antidotes to combat the disease of segregation.

Let me take note of my other major disappointment. I have been so greatly disappointed with the white church and its leadership. Of course, there are some notable exceptions. I am not unmindful of the fact that each of you has taken some significant stands on this issue. I commend you, Reverend Stallings, for your Christian stand on this past Sunday, in welcoming Negroes to your worship service on a nonsegregated basis. I commend the Catholic leaders of this state for integrating Spring Hill College several years ago.

But despite these notable exceptions, I must honestly reiterate that I have been disappointed with the church. I do not say this as one of those negative critics who can always find something wrong with the church. I say this as a minister of the gospel, who loves the church; who was nurtured in its bosom; who has been sustained by its spiritual blessings and who will remain true to it as long as the cord of life shall lengthen.

When I was suddenly catapulted into the leadership of the bus protest in Montgomery, Alabama, a few years ago, I felt we would be supported by the white church. I felt that the white ministers, priests, and rabbis of the South would be among our strongest allies. Instead, some have been outright opponents, refusing to understand the freedom movement and misrepresenting its leaders; all too many others have been more cautious than courageous and have remained silent behind the anesthetizing security of stained-glass windows.

In spite of my shattered dreams, I came to Birmingham with the hope that the white religious leadership of this community would see the justice of our cause and, with deep moral concern, would serve as the channel through which our just grievances could reach the power structure. I had hoped that each of you would understand. But again I have been disappointed.

I have heard numerous southern religious leaders admonish their worshipers to comply with a desegregation decision because it is the law, but I have longed to hear white ministers declare: "Follow this decree because integration is morally right and because the Negro is your brother." In the midst of blatant injustices inflicted upon the Negro, I have watched white churchmen stand on the sideline and mouth pious irrelevancies and sanctimonious trivialities. In the midst of a mighty struggle to rid our nation of racial and economic injustice, I have heard many ministers say: "Those are social issues, with which the gospel has no real concern." And I have watched many churches commit themselves to a completely otherworldly religion which makes a strange, un-Biblical distinction between body and soul, between the sacred and the secular.

I have traveled the length and breadth of Alabama, Mississippi, and all the other southern states. On sweltering summer days and crisp autumn mornings I have looked at the South's beautiful churches with their lofty spires pointing heavenward. I have beheld the impressive outlines of her massive religious-education buildings. Over and over I have found myself asking: "What kind of people worship here? Who is their God? Where were their voices when the lips of Governor Barnett dripped with words of interposition and nullification? Where were they when Governor Wallace gave a clarion call for defiance and hatred? Where were their voices of support when bruised and weary Negro men and women decided to rise from the dark dungeons of complacency to the bright hills of creative protest?"

Yes, these questions are still in my mind. In deep disappointment I have wept over the laxity of the church. But be assured that my tears have been tears of love. There can be no deep disappointment where there is not deep love. Yes, I love the church. How could I do otherwise? I am in the rather unique position of being the son, the grandson, and the great-grandson of preachers. Yes, I see the church as the body of Christ. But, oh! How we have blemished and scarred that body through social neglect and through fear of being nonconformists.

There was a time when the church was very powerful—in the time when the early Christians rejoiced at being deemed worthy to suffer for what they believed. In those days the church was not merely a thermometer that recorded the ideas and principles of popular opinion; it was a thermostat that transformed the mores of society. Whenever the early Christians entered a town, the people in power became disturbed and immediately sought to convict the Christians for being "disturbers of the peace" and "outside agitators." But the Christians pressed on, in the conviction that they were "a colony of heaven," called to obey God rather than man. Small in number, they were big in commitment. They were too God-intoxicated to be "astronomically intimidated." By their effort and example they brought an end to such ancient evils as infanticide and gladiatorial contests.

Things are different now. So often the contemporary church is a weak, ineffectual voice with an uncertain sound. So often it is an archdefender of the status quo. Far from being disturbed by the presence of the church, the power structure of the average community is consoled by the church's silent—and often even vocal—

sanction of things as they are.

But the judgment of God is upon the church as never before. If today's church does not recapture the sacrificial spirit of the early church, it will lose its authenticity, forfeit the loyalty of millions, and be dismissed as an irrelevant social club with no meaning for the twentieth century. Every day I meet young people whose disappointment with the church has turned into outright disgust.

Perhaps I have once again been too optimistic. Is organized religion too inextricably bound to the status quo to save our nation and the world? Perhaps I must turn my faith to the inner spiritual church, the church within the church, as the true *ekklesia*[2] and the hope of the world. But again I am thankful to God that some noble souls from the ranks of organized religion have broken loose from the paralyzing chains of conformity and joined us as active partners in the struggle for freedom. They have left their secure congregations and walked the streets of Albany, Georgia, with us. They have gone down the highways of the South on tortuous rides for freedom. Yes, they have gone to jail with us. Some have been dismissed from their churches, have lost the support of their bishops and fellow ministers. But they have acted in the faith that right defeated is stronger than evil triumphant. Their witness has been the spiritual salt that has preserved the true meaning of the gospel in these troubled times. They have carved a tunnel of hope through the dark mountain of disappointment.

I hope the church as a whole will meet the challenge of this decisive hour. But even if the church does not come to the aid of justice, I have no despair about the future. I have no fear about the outcome of our struggle in Birmingham, even if our motives are at present misunderstood. We will reach the goal of freedom in Birmingham and all over the nation, because the goal of America is freedom. Abused and scorned though we may be, our destiny is tied up with America's destiny. Before the pilgrims landed at Plymouth, we were here. Before the pen of Jefferson etched the majestic words of the Declaration of Independence across the pages of history, we were here. For more than two centuries our forebears labored in this country without wages; they made cotton king; they built the homes of their masters while suffering gross injustice and shameful humiliation—and yet out of a bottomless vitality they continued to thrive and develop. If the inexpressible cruelties of slavery could not stop us, the opposition we now face will surely fail. We will win our freedom because the sacred heritage of our nation and the eternal will of God are embodied in our echoing demands.

Before closing I feel impelled to mention one other point in your statement that has troubled me profoundly. You warmly com-

2. The Greek New Testament word for the early Christian church.

mended the Birmingham police force for keeping "order" and "preventing violence." I doubt that you would have so warmly commended the police force if you had seen its dogs sinking their teeth into unarmed, nonviolent Negroes. I doubt that you would so quickly commend the policemen if you were to observe their ugly and inhumane treatment of Negroes here in the city jail; if you were to watch them push and curse old Negro women and young Negro girls; if you were to see them slap and kick old Negro men and young boys; if you were to observe them, as they did on two occasions, refuse to give us food because we wanted to sing our grace together. I cannot join you in your praise of the Birmingham police department.

It is true that the police have exercised a degree of discipline in handling the demonstrators. In this sense they have conducted themselves rather "nonviolently" in public. But for what purpose? To preserve the evil system of segregation. Over the past few years I have consistently preached that nonviolence demands that the means we use must be as pure as the ends we seek. I have tried to make clear that it is wrong to use immoral means to attain moral ends. But now I must affirm that it is just as wrong, or perhaps even more so, to use moral means to preserve immoral ends. Perhaps Mr. Connor and his policemen have been rather nonviolent in public, as was Chief Pritchett in Albany, Georgia, but they have used the moral means of nonviolence to maintain the immoral end of racial injustice. As T. S. Eliot has said, "The last temptation is the greatest treason: To do the right deed for the wrong reason."

I wish you had commended the Negro sit-inners and demonstrators of Birmingham for their sublime courage, their willingness to suffer, and their amazing discipline in the midst of great provocation. One day the South will recognize its real heroes. They will be the James Merediths, with the noble sense of purpose that enables them to face jeering and hostile mobs, and with the agonizing loneliness that characterizes the life of the pioneer. They will be old, oppressed, battered Negro women, symbolized in a seventy-two-year-old woman in Montgomery, Alabama, who rose up with a sense of dignity and with her people decided not to ride segregated buses, and who responded with ungrammatical profundity to one who inquired about her weariness: "My feets is tired, but my soul is at rest." They will be the young high school and college students, the young ministers of the gospel and a host of their elders, courageously and nonviolently sitting in at lunch counters and willingly going to jail for conscience' sake. One day the South will know that when these disinherited children of God sat down at lunch counters, they were in reality standing up for what is best in the American dream and for the most sacred values in our Judaeo-Christian heritage, thereby bringing our nation back to those great wells of democracy which were dug deep by the founding fathers in their formulation of the Constitution and the Declaration of Independence.

Never before have I written so long a letter. I'm afraid it is much too long to take your precious time. I can assure you that it would have been much shorter if I had been writing from a comfortable desk, but what else can one do when he is alone in a narrow jail cell, other than write long letters, think long thoughts, and pray long prayers?

If I have said anything in this letter that overstates the truth and indicates an unreasonable impatience, I beg you to forgive me. If I have said anything that understates the truth and indicates my having a patience that allows me to settle for anything less than brotherhood, I beg God to forgive me.

I hope this letter finds you strong in the faith. I also hope that circumstances will soon make it possible for me to meet each of you, not as an integrationist or a civil-rights leader but as a fellow clergyman and a Christian brother. Let us all hope that the dark clouds of racial prejudice will soon pass away and the deep fog of misunderstanding will be lifted from our fear-drenched communities, and in some not too distant tomorrow the radiant stars of love and brotherhood will shine over our great nation with all their scintillating beauty.

Yours for the cause of Peace and Brotherhood,
MARTIN LUTHER KING, JR.

GEORGE L. JACKSON
Letter from Soledad Prison

DEAR FAY,

For very obvious reasons it pains me to dwell on the past. As an individual, and as the male of our order I have only the proud flesh[1] of very recent years to hold up as proof that I did not die in the sickbed in which I lay for so long. I've taken my lesson from the past and attempted to close it off.

I've drunk deeply from the cisterns of gall, swam against the current in Blood Alley, Urban Fascist Amerika, experienced the nose rub in shit, armed myself with a monumental hatred and tried to forget and pretend. A standard black male defense mechanism.

It hasn't worked. It may just be me, but I suspect that it's part of the pitiful black condition that the really bad moments record themselves so clearly and permanently in the mind, while the few

---

1. Proud flesh is a medical term for the abnormal growth of flesh that some- times forms round a healing wound.

brief flashes of gratification are lost immediately, nightmare overhanging darkly.

My recall is nearly perfect, time has faded nothing. I recall the very first kidnap. I've lived through the passage, died on the passage, lain in the unmarked, shallow graves of the millions who fertilized the Amerikan soil with their corpses; cotton and corn growing out of my chest, "unto the third and fourth generation," the tenth, the hundredth. My mind ranges back and forth through the uncounted generations, and I feel all that they ever felt, but double. I can't help it; there are too many things to remind me of the 23½ hours that I'm in this cell. Not ten minutes pass without a reminder. In between, I'm left to speculate on what form the reminder will take.

Down here we hear relaxed, matter-of-fact conversations centering around how best to kill all the nation's niggers and in what order. It's not the fact that they consider killing me that upsets. They've been "killing all the niggers" for nearly half a millennium now, but I am still alive. I might be the most resilient dead man in the universe. The upsetting thing is that they never take into consideration the fact that I am going to resist. No they honestly believe that shit. They do! That's what they think of us. That they have beaten and conditioned all the defense and attack reflexes from us. That the region of the mind that stores the principles upon which men base their rationale to resist is missing in us. Don't they talk of concentration camps? Don't they state that it couldn't happen in the U.S. because the fascists here are nice fascists? Not because it's impossible to incarcerate 30 million resisters, but because they are humane imperialists, enlightened fascists.

Well, they've made a terrible mistake. I recall the day I was born, the first day of my generation. It was during the second (and most destructive) capitalist world war for colonial privilege, early on a rainy Wednesday morning, late September, Chicago. It happened to me in a little fold-into-the-wall bed, in a little half-flat on Racine and Lake. Dr. Rogers attended. The el train that rattled by within fifteen feet of our front windows (the only two windows) screamed in at me like the banshee, portentous of pain, death, threatening and imminent. The first motion that my eyes focused on was this pink hand swinging in a wide arc in the general direction of my black ass. I stopped that hand, the left downward block, and countered the right needle finger to the eye. I was born with my defence reflexes well developed.

It's going to be "Kill me if you can," fool, not "Kill me if you please."

But let them make their plans on the supposition, "like slave, like son." I'm not going for it, though, and they've made my defence easier. A cop gives the keys to a group of right-wing cons. They're going to open our cells—one at a time—all over the building. They don't want to escape, or deal with the men who hold them here. They can solve their problems only if they kill all of us—think about that—these guys live a few cells from me. None of them have ever lived, most are state-raised in institutions like this one. They have nothing coming, nothing at all, they have nothing at stake in this order of things. In defending right-wing ideals and the status quo they're saying in effect that ninety-nine years and a dark day in prison is their idea of fun. Most are in and out, and mostly in, all of their life. The periods that they pass on the outside are consid- ered runs. Simply stated, they consider the periods spent in the joint more natural, more in keeping with their tastes. Well, I understand their condition, and I know how they got that way. I could honestly sympathize with them if they were not so wrong, so stupid as to let the pigs use them. Sounds like Germany of the thirties and forties to me. It's the same on the outside there. I'll venture to say that there's not one piece of stock, not one bond owned by anyone in any of the families of the pigs who murdered Fred Hampton.[2] They organize marches around the country, marches and demon- strations in support of total immediate destruction of Vietnam, and afterwards no one is able to pick up the tab. The fascists, it seems, have a standard M.O. for dealing with the lower classes. Actually oppressive power throughout history has used it. They turn a man against himself—think of all the innocent things that make us feel good, but that make some of us also feel guilty. Think of how the people of the lower classes weigh themselves against the men who rule. Consider the con going through the courts on a capital offence who supports capital punishment. I swear I heard something just like that today. Look how long Hershey ran Selective Service. Blacks embrace capitalism, the most unnatural and outstanding example of man against himself that history can offer. After the Civil War, the form of slavery changed from chattel to economic slavery, and we were thrown on to the labor market to compete at a disadvantage with poor whites. Ever since that time, our principal enemy must be isolated and identifed as capitalism. The slaver was and is the factory owner, the businessman of capitalist Amerika, the man responsible for employment, wages, prices, control of the nation's institutions and culture. It was the capitalist infrastructure of Europe and the U.S. which was responsible for the rape of Africa and Asia. Capitalism murdered those 30 million in the Congo. Believe me, the European and Anglo-Amerikan capitalist would never have wasted the ball and powder were it not for the profit principle. The men, all the men who went into Africa and Asia, the fleas who climbed on that elephant's back with rape on their minds,

2. Black Panther leader, killed by a Chicago policeman in December 1970.

richly deserve all that they are called. Every one of them deserved to die for their crimes. So do the ones who are still in Vietnam, Angola, Union of South Africa (U.S.A.!!). But we must not allow the emotional aspects of these issues, the scum at the surface, to obstruct our view of the big picture, the whole rotten hunk. It was capitalism that armed the ships, free enterprise that launched them, private ownership of property that fed the troops. Imperialism took up where the slave trade left off. It wasn't until after the slave trade ended that Amerika, England, France, and the Netherlands invaded and settled in on Afro-Asian soil in earnest. As the European industrial revolution took hold, new economic attractions replaced the older ones; chattel slavery was replaced by neoslavery. Capital ism, "free" enterprise, private ownership of public property armed and launched the ships and fed the troops; it should be clear that it was the profit motive that kept them there.

It was the profit motive that built the tenement house and the city project. Profit and loss prevents repairs and maintenance. Free enterprise brought the monopolistic chain store into the neighbour hood. The concept of private ownership of facilities that the people need to exist brought the legions of hip-shooting, brainless pigs down upon our heads, our homes, our streets. They're there to pro tect the entrepreneur!! His chain store, and his property that you are renting, his bank.

If the entrepreneur decides that he no longer wants to sell you food, let's say, because the Yankee dollar that we value so dearly has suddenly lost its last thirty cents of purchasing power, private own ership means that the only way many of the people will eat is to break the law. Fat Rat Daley has ordered all looters shot.[3]

Black capitalism, black against itself. The silliest contradiction in a long train of spineless, mindless contradictions. Another painless, ultimate remedy: be a better fascist than the fascist. Bill Cosby, acting out the establishment agent—what message was this soul brother conveying to our children? *I Spy* was certainly programmed to a child's mentality. This running dog in the company of a fascist with a cause, a flunky's flunky, was transmitting the credo of the slave to our youth, the mod version of the old house nigger. We can never learn to trust as long as we have them. They are as much a part of the repression, more even than the real live, rat-informer- pig. Aren't they telling our kids that it is romantic to be a running dog? The kids are so hungry to see the black male do some shooting and throw some hands that they can't help themselves from iden tifying with the quislings. So first they turn us against ourselves, precluding all possibility of trust, then fascism takes any latent

3. During race riots in Chicago Mayor Richard Daley ordered police to shoot all looters on sight.

divisible forces and develops them into divisions in fact: racism, nationalism, religions.

You have Spic, Dago, Jew, Jap, Chink, Gook, Pineapple, and the omnibus nigger to represent the nations of Africa. The point being that it is easier to persuade that little man who joined the army to see the world and who has never murdered before to murder a Gook. Well, it's not quite like murdering a man. Polack, Frog, Kraut, etc.

The wheels just fell off altogether in the thirties. People in certain circles like to forget it, and any reference to the period draws from these circles such defensive epithets as "old-fashioned," "simple old-style socialism," and "out of date." But fashion doesn't concern me, I'm after the facts. The facts are that no one, absolutely no one in the Western world, and very few anywhere else (this includes even those who may have been born yesterday), is unaffected by those years when capitalism's roulette wheel locked in depression. It affected every nation-state on earth. Of course Russia had no stock market and consequently no business cycle, but it was affected by the war that grew out of the efforts to restart the machines and by the effect it had on other nations with which Russia has had to deal. Relativism enters. Since international capitalism was at the time in its outward peak of expansion, there were no African, Asian, or Latin lands organized along nation-state lines that were not adversely affected. Every society in the world that lived by a money economy was part of the depression. Although Russia had abandoned the forms and vacillations of capitalism, it too was damaged due to the principles of relativism.

If there is any question whether those years have any effect on, or relevance to now, just consider the effect on today's mentality. Had the world's people been struck with hereditary cretinism all at once, instead of Adam Smith's "invisible hand,"[4] the analogy couldn't be more perfect. I mean cretinism in its literal, medical sense: a congenital deficiency in the secretions of the thyroid gland resulting in deformity and idiocy. Causation links that depression with World War II. The rise of power to Europe's Nazis can be attributed to the depression. The WASP fascists of Amerika secretly desired a war with Japan to stimulate demand and control unemployment. The syllogism is perfect.

So question and analyze the state of being of Europe's Jews who survive. Do the same with the people of Hiroshima and Nagasaki. But we don't have to isolate groups. Causation and relativism link everyone inescapably with the past. None of the righteous people would even be alive had their parents died of the underconsumption of that period or the desperate fascist chicanery aimed at

4. Term used by Smith in his *Wealth of Nations* to describe the individual's self-interest as a self-regulating market mechanism.

diverting the lower classes from the economic reality of class struggle. The Nazis actually succeeded in foisting upon the lower-class Germans and some of the other European national groups the notion that their economic plight was due not to bad economic principles but caused by the existence of Jews within the system and the shortage of markets (colonies). The obvious intent being to pit lower-class, depressed German against lower-class Jew, instead of exploited lower-class German against privileged upper-class German.

The Amerikan fascist used a thousand similar devices, delaying maneuvers, to prevent the people from questioning the validity of the principles upon which capitalism is founded, to turn the people against themselves, people against people, people against other groups of people. Always they will promote competition (while they cooperate), division, mistrust, a sense of isolation. The antipodes of love. The M.O. of the fascist arrangement is always to protect the capitalist class by destroying the consciousness, the trust, the unity of the lower classes. My father is in his forties today; thirty-five years ago he was living through his most formative years. He was a child of the Great Depression. I want you to notice for later reference that I emphasize and differentiate *Great* Depression. There were many more international, national, and regional depressions during the period in history relevant to this comment.

There are millions of blacks of my father's generation now living. they are all products of a totally depressed environment. All of the males have lived all of their lives in a terrible quandary; none were able to grasp that a morbid economic deprivation, an outrageous and enormous abrasion, formed the basis of their character.

My father developed his character, convention, convictions, his traits, his life style, out of a situation that began with his mother running out. She left him and his oldest brother on the corner of one of the canyons in East St. Louis. They raised themselves, in the streets, then on a farm somewhere in Louisiana, then in C.C.C. camps. This brother, my father, had no formal education at all. He taught himself the essentials later on. Alone, in the most hostile jungle on earth, ruled over by the king of beasts in the first throes of a bloody and protracted death. Alone, in the most savage moment of history, without arms, and burdened by a black face that he's been hiding ever since.

I love this brother, my father, and when I use the word "love" I am not making an attempt at rhetoric. I am attempting to express a refulgent, unrestrained emanation from the deepest, most durable region of my soul, an unshakeable thing that I have never questioned. But no one can come through his ordeal without suffering the penalty of psychosis. It was the price of survival. I would venture that there are no healthy brothers of his generation, *none at all.*

The brother has reached the prime of his life without ever show-ing in my presence or anywhere, to my knowledge, an overt mani-festation of *real* sensitivity, affection, or sentiment. He has lived his entire life in a state of shock. Nothing can touch him now, his calm is complete, his immunity to pain is total. When I can fix his eyes, which is not often since when they aren't closed they are shaded, I see staring back at me the expressionless mask of the zombie.

But he must have loved us, of this I am certain. Part of the credo of the neoslave, the latter-day slave, who is free to move from place to place if he can come by the means, is to shuffle away from any situation that becomes too difficult. He stayed with us, worked six-teen hours a day, after which he would eat, bathe and sleep—pe-riod. He never owned more than two pairs of shoes in his life and in the time I was living with him never more than one suit, never took a drink, never went to a nightclub, expressed no feelings about such things, and never once reminded any one of us, or so it seemed, never expected any notice of the fact that he was giving to us all of the life force and activity that the monster-machine had left to him. The part that the machine seized, that death of the spirit visited upon him by a world that he never influenced, was mourned by us, and most certainly by me, but no one ever made a real effort to give him solace. How do you console a man who is unapproachable?

He came to visit me when I was in San Quentin. He was in his forties then too, an age in men when they have grown full. I had decided to reach for my father, to force him with my revolutionary dialectic to question some of the mental barricades he'd thrown up to protect his body from what to him was an undefinable and omni-present enemy. An enemy that would starve his body, expose it to the elements, chain his body, jail it, club it, rip it, hang it, electrify it, and poison-gas it. I would have him understand that although he had saved his body he had done so at a terrible cost to his mind. I felt that if I could superimpose the explosive doctrine of self-deter-mination through people's government and revolutionary culture upon what remained of his mind, draw him out into the real world, isolate and identify his real enemies, if I could hurl him through Fanon's[5] revolutionary catharsis, I would be serving him, the people, the historical obligation.

San Quentin was in the riot season. It was early January 1967. The pigs had for the last three months been on a search-and-destroy foray into our cells. All times of the day or night our cells were being invaded by the goon squad: you wake up, take your licks, get skin-searched, and wait on the tier naked while they mangled your few personal effects. This treatment, fear therapy, was not accorded to all however. Some Chicanos behind dope, some whites behind

5. Frantz Fanon, African revolutionary and philosopher who was devoted to the overthrow of colonialism.

extortionate activities were exempted. Mostly, it came down on us. Rehabilitational terror. Each new pig must go through a period of in-service training where he learns the Gestapo arts, the full range of anti-body tactics that he will be expected to use on the job. Part of this in-service training is a crash course in close-order combat where the pigs are taught how to use club and sap, and how to form and use the simpler karate hands, where to hit a man with these hands for the best (or worst) effect.

The new pigs usually have to serve a period on the goon squad before they fall into their regular role on the animal farm. They are always anxious to try their new skills—"to see if it really works"— we were always forced to do something to slow them down, to demonstrate that violence was a two-edged sword. This must be done at least once every year, or we would all be as punchy and fractured as a Thai Boxer before our time was up. The brothers wanted to protest. The usual protest was a strike, a work stoppage, closing the sweatshops where industrial products are worked up for two cents an hour. (Some people get four cents after they've been on the job for six months.) The outside interests who made the profits didn't dig strikes. That meant the captain didn't like them either since it meant pressure on him from these free-enterprising political connections.

January in San Quentin is the worst way to be. It's cold when you don't have proper clothing, it's wet, dreary. The drab green, barred, buttressed walls that close in the upper yard are sixty to seventy feet high. They make you feel that your condition may be permanent.

On the occasion I wish to relate, my father had driven all night from Los Angeles alone; he had not slept more than a couple of hours in the last forty-eight.

We shook hands and the dialectic began. He listened while I scorned the diabolical dog—capitalism. Didn't it raise pigs and murder Vietnamese? Didn't it glut some and starve most of us? Didn't it build housing projects that resemble prisons and luxury hotels and apartments that resemble the Hanging Gardens on the same street? Didn't it build a hospital and then a bomb? Didn't it erect a school and then open a whorehouse? Build an airplane to sell a tranquilizer tablet? For every church didn't it construct a prison? For each new medical discovery didn't it produce as a by-product ten new biological warfare agents? Didn't it aggrandize men like Hunt and Hughes[6] and dwarf him?

He said, "Yes, but what can we do? There's too many of the bastards." His eyes shaded over and his mind went into a total regression, a relapse back through time, space, pain, neglect, a thousand

---

6. H. L. Hunt and Howard Hughes, multimillionaires.

dreams deferred, broken promises, forgotten ambitions, back
through the hundreds of renewed hopes shattered to a time when
he was young, roaming the Louisiana countryside for something
to eat. He talked for ten minutes of things that were not in the present, people that I didn't know. "We'll have to take something
back to Aunt Bell." He talked of places that we had never seen
together. He called me by his brother's name twice. I was so
shocked I could only sit and blink. This was the guy who took
nothing seriously, the level-headed, practical Negro, the work-a-day,
never-complain, cool, smooth, colored gentleman. They have driven
him to the abyss of madness; just behind the white veneer waits the
awesome, vindictive black madness. There are a lot of blacks living
in his generation, the one of the Great Depression, when it was no
longer possible to maintain the black self by serving. Even that had
dried up. Blacks were beaten and killed for jobs like porter, bellboy,
stoker, pearl diver, and bootblack. My clenched fist goes up for
them; I forgive them, I understand, and if they will stop their collaboration with the fascist enemy, stop it now, and support our revolution with just a nod, we'll forget and forgive them for casting us
naked into a grim and deleterious world.

The black colonies of Amerika have been locked in depression
since the close of the Civil War. We have lived under regional
depression since the end of chattel slavery. The beginning of the
new slavery was marked by massive unemployment and underem-
ployment. That remains with us still. The Civil War destroyed the
landed aristocracy. The dictatorship of the agrarian class was displaced by the dictatorship of the manufacturing-capitalist class. The
neoslaver destroyed the uneconomic plantation, and built upon its
ruins a factory and a thousand subsidiaries to serve the factory
setup. Since we had no skills, outside of the farming techniques that
had proved uneconomic, the subsidiary service trades and menial
occupations fell to us. It is still so today. We are a subsidiary subculture, a depressed area within the parent monstrosity. The other
four stages of the capitalist business cycle are: recovery, expansion,
inflation, and recession. Have we ever gone through a recovery or
expansion stage? We are affected adversely by inflationary trends
within the larger economy. Who suffers most when the prices of
basic, necessary commodities go up? When the parent economy
dips into inflation and recession we dip into subdepression. When it
goes into depression, we go into total desperation. The difference
between what my father's generation went through during the
Great Depression and what we are going through now is simply a
matter of degree. We can sometimes find a service to perform
across the tracks. They couldn't. We can go home to Mama for a
meal when things get really tight. They couldn't. There's welfare

and housework for Mama now. Then there was no such thing as welfare.

Depression is an economic condition. It is a part of the capitalist business cycle, a necessary concomitant of capitalism. Its colonies— secondary markets—will always be depressed areas, because the steadily decreasing labour force, decreasing and growing more skilled under the advances of automation, casts the unskilled colonial subject into economic roles that preclude economic mobility. Learning the new skills even if we were allowed wouldn't help. It wouldn't help the masses even if they learned them. It wouldn't help because there is a fixed ceiling on the labor force. This ceiling gets lower with every advance in the arts of production. Learning the newer skills would merely put us into a competition with established labor that we could not win. One that we don't want. There are absolutely no vacuums for us to fill in the business world. We don't want to capitalize on people anyway. Capitalism is the enemy. It must be destroyed. There is no other recourse. The System is not workable in view of the modern industrial city-based society. Men are born disenfranchised. The contract between ruler and ruled perpetuates this disenfranchisement.

Men in positions of trust owe an equitable distribution of wealth and privilege to the men who have trusted them. Each individual born in these Amerikan cities should be born with those things that are necessary to survival. Meaningful social roles, education, medical care, food, shelter, and understanding should be guaranteed at birth. They have been part of all civilized human societies—until this one. Why else do men allow other men to govern? To what purpose is a Department of Health, Education, and Welfare, or of Housing and Urban Development, etc.? Why do we give these men power over us? Why do we give them taxes? For nothing? So they can say that the world owes our children nothing? This world owes each of us a living the very day we are born. If not we can make no claims to civilization and we can stop recognizing the power of any administrator. Evolution of the huge modern city-based society has made our dependence upon government complete. Individually, we cannot feed ourselves and our children. We cannot, by ourselves, train and educate them at home. We cannot organize our own work inside the city structure by ourselves. Consequently, we must allow men to specialize in coordinating these activities. We pay them, honor them, and surrender control of certain aspects of our lives to them so that they will in return take each new, helpless entry into the social group and work on him until he is no longer helpless, until he can start to support himself and make his contribution to the continuity of the society.

If a man is born into Amerikan society with nothing coming, if the capitalist creed that runs "The world doesn't owe you a living" is true, then the thing that my father's mother did is not outrageous at all. If it is true that government shouldn't organize then the fact that my father had no place to seek help until he could help himself has little consequence. But it would also mean that we are all in the grip of some monstrous contradiction. And that we have no more claim to civilization than a pack of baboons.

What is it then that *really* destroyed my father's comfort, that doomed his entire generation to a life without content? What is it that has been working against my generation from the day we were born through every day to this one?

Capitalism and capitalist man, wrecker of worlds, scourge of the people. It cannot address itself to our needs, it cannot and will not change itself to adapt to natural changes within the social structure.

To the black male the losses were most tragic of all. It will do us no good to linger over the fatalities, they're numberless and beyond our reach. But we who have survived must eventually look at ourselves and wonder why. The competition at the bottom of the social spectrum is for symbols, honors, and objects; black against itself, black against lower-class whites and browns, virulent, cutthroat, back-stabbing competition, the Amerikan way of life. But the fascists cooperate. The four estates of power form a morbid lone quadrangle. The competition has destroyed trust. Among the black males a premium has been placed on distrust. Every other black male is viewed as the competition; the wise and practical black is the one who cares nothing for any living ass, the cynic who has got over any principles he may have picked up by mistake. We can't express love on the supposition that the recipient will automatically use it against us as a weapon. We're going to have to start all over again. This next time around we'll let it all hang out, we'll stop betraying ourselves, and we'll add some trust and love.

I do not include those who support capitalism in any appreciable degree or who feel they have something to lose with its destruction. They are our irreconcilable enemy. We can never again trust people like Cosby, Gloves Davis,[7] or the old Negro bus driver who testified in the Huey Newton[8] trial. Any man who stands up to speak in defense of capitalism must be slapped down.

Right now our disease must be identified as capitalist man and his monstrous machine, a machine with the senseless and calloused ability to inflict these wounds programmed into its every cycle.

I was born with terminal cancer, a suppurating, malignant sore

7. The black Chicago policeman who was reported to have shot Fred Hampton.

8. Newton, minister of defense of the Black Panther Party, was convicted of voluntary manslaughter in the killing of an Oakland, California, policeman in 1968; the conviction was overturned in 1970.

that attacked me in the region just behind the eyes and moves outward to destroy my peace.

It has robbed me of these twenty-eight years. It has robbed us all for nearly half a millennium. The greatest bandit of all time, we'll stop him now.

Recall the stories you've read about the other herd animals, the great Amerikan bison, the caribou or Amerikan reindeer.

The great Amerikan bison or buffalo—he's a herd animal, or social animal if you prefer, just like us in that. We're social animals, we need others of our general kind about us to feel secure. Few men would enjoy total isolation. To be alone constantly is torture to normal men. The buffalo, cattle, caribou, and some others are like folks in that they need company most of the time. They need to butt shoulders and butt butts. They like to rub noses. We shake hands, slap backs, and rub lips. Of all the world's people we blacks love the company of others most, we are the most socialistic. Social animals eat, sleep, and travel in company, they need this company to feel secure. This fact means that socialistic animals also need leaders. It follows logically that if the buffalo is going to eat, sleep, and travel in groups some coordinating factor is needed or some will be sleeping when others are traveling. Without the leadership-follower complex, in a crisis the company would roar off in a hundred different directions. But the buffalo did evolve the leader-follower complex as did the other social animals; if the leader of a herd of caribou loses his footing and slips to his death from some high place, it is very likely that the whole herd will die behind. The leader-follower complex. The hunter understood this. Predatory man learned of the natural occurrence of leadership in all of the social animals; that each group will by nature produce a leader, and to these natural leaders fall the responsibility for coordination of the group's activity, organizing them for survival. The buffalo hunter knew that if he could isolate and identify the leader of the herd and kill him first, the rest of the herd would be helpless, at his mercy, to be killed off as he saw fit.

We blacks have the same problem the buffalo had; we have the same weakness also, and predatory man understands this weakness well.

Huey Newton, Ahmed Evans, Bobby Seale,[9] and the hundreds of others will be murdered according to the fascist scheme.

A sort of schematic natural selection in reverse: Medgar Evers, Malcolm X, Bobby Hutton, Brother Booker, W. L. Noland, M. L. King, Featherstone, Mark Clark, and Fred Hampton[1]—just a few who have already gone the way of the buffalo.

---

9. Prominent members of the Black Panther Party.

1. Black leaders, all of whom have been killed beginning in 1963.

The effect these moves from the right have had on us is a classic textbook exercise in fascist political economy. At the instant a black head rises out of our crisis existence, it's lopped off and hung from the highest courthouse or newspaper firm. Our predetermined response is a schizophrenic indifference, withdrawal, and an appreciation of things that do not exist. "Oh happy days. Oh happy days. Oh happy days." Self-hypnotically induced hallucinations.

The potential black leadership looks at the pitiable condition of the black herd: the corruption, the preoccupation with irrelevance, the apparent ineptitude concerning matters of survival. He knows that were he to give the average brother an M-16, this brother wouldn't have anything but a club for a week. He weighs this thing that he sees in the herd against the possible risks he'll be taking at the hands of the fascist monster and he naturally decides to go for himself, feeling that he can't help us because we are beyond help, that he may as well get something out of existence. These are the 'successful Negroes,' the opposite of the 'failures'. You find them on the ball courts and fields, the stage, pretending and playing children's games. And looking for all the world just as pitiable as the so-called failures.

We were colonized by the white predatory fascist economy. It was from them that we evolved our freak subculture, and the attitudes that perpetuate our conditions. These attitudes cause us to give each other up to the Klan pigs. We even on occasion work gun in hand right with them. A black killed Fred Hampton; blacks working with the C.I.A. killed Malcolm X; blacks are plentiful on the payroll of the many police forces that fascism must employ to protect itself from the people. These fascist subcultural attitudes have sent us to Europe, Asia (one-fourth of the fatalities in Vietnam are black fatalities), and even Africa (the Congo during the Simba attempt to establish people's government) to die for nothing. In the recent cases of Africa and Asia we have allowed the neoslaver to use us to help enslave people we love. We are so confused, so foolishly simple that we not only fail to distinguish what is generally right and what is wrong, but we also fail to appreciate what is good and not good for us in very personal matters concerning the black colony and its liberation. The ominous government economic agency whose only clear motive is to further enslave, number, and spy on us, the black agency subsidized by the government to infiltrate us and retard liberation, is accepted, and by some, even invited and welcomed, while the Black Panther is avoided and hard-pressed to find protection among the people. The Black Panther is our brother and son, the one who wasn't afraid. He wasn't so lazy as the rest, or so narrow and restricted in his vision. If we allow the fascist machine to destroy these brothers, our dream of eventual self-determination and control over the factors surrounding our survival is going to die with them, and the generations to come will curse and condemn us for irresponsible cowardice. I have a young courageous brother whom I love more than I love myself, but I have given him up to the revolution. I accept the possibility of his eventual death as I accept the possibility of my own. Some moment of weakness, a slip, a mistake, since we are the men who can make none, will bring the blow that kills. I accept this as a necessary part of our life. I don't want to raise any more black slaves. We have a determined enemy who will accept us only on a master-slave basis. When I revolt, slavery dies with me. I refuse to pass it down again. The terms of my existence are founded on that.

Black Mama, you're going to have to stop making cowards: "Be a good *boy*;" "You're going to worry me to death, *boy*;" "Don't trust those niggers;" "Stop letting those bad niggers lead you around, *boy*;" "Make you a dollar, *boy*." Black Mama, your overriding concern with the survival of our sons is mistaken if it is survival at the cost of their manhood.

The young Panther party member, our vanguard, must be embraced, protected, allowed to develop. We must learn from him and teach him; he'll be full grown soon, a son and brother of whom we can be proud. If he sags we'll brace him up, when he takes a step we'll step with him, our dialectic, our communion in perfect harmony, and there'll never, never be another Fred Hampton affair.

Power to the people.

GEORGE

QUESTIONS

1. Jackson speaks of revolutionary dialectic; where in his discussion do you see the clearest example of its workings? What is its relation to revolutionary rhetoric?
2. Analyze the transitions within the paragraph on p. 679 beginning, "The Amerikan fascist. . . ."
3. What was Jackson's motive for deciding "to reach" for his father, "to force" him to question his defences?
4. Jackson disclaims any attempt at rhetoric when he speaks of his love for his father and then defines his love (p. 679). What is the source of the impact of his definition?

JONATHAN SWIFT

A Modest Proposal

FOR PREVENTING THE CHILDREN OF POOR PEOPLE IN IRELAND
FROM BEING A BURDEN TO THEIR PARENTS OR COUNTRY,
AND FOR MAKING THEM BENEFICIAL TO THE PUBLIC

It is a melancholy object to those who walk through this great town or travel in the country, when they see the streets, the roads, and cabin doors, crowded with beggars of the female-sex, followed by three, four, or six children, all in rags and importuning every passenger for an alms. These mothers, instead of being able to work for their honest livelihood, are forced to employ all their time in strolling to beg sustenance for their helpless infants, who, as they grow up, either turn thieves for want of work, or leave their dear native country to fight for the Pretender in Spain, or sell themselves to the Barbadoes.[1]

I think it is agreed by all parties that this prodigious number of children in the arms, or on the backs, or at the heels of their mothers, and frequently of their fathers, is in the present deplorable state of the kingdom a very great additional grievance; and therefore whoever could find out a fair, cheap, and easy method of making these children sound, useful members of the commonwealth would deserve so well of the public as to have his statue set up for a preserver of the nation.

But my intention is very far from being confined to provide only for the children of professed beggars; it is of a much greater extent, and shall take in the whole number of infants at a certain age who are born of parents in effect as little able to support them as those who demand our charity in the streets.

As to my own part, having turned my thoughts for many years upon this important subject, and maturely weighed the several schemes of other projectors, I have always found them grossly mistaken in their computation. It is true, a child just dropped from its dam may be supported by her milk for a solar year, with little other nourishment; at most not above the value of two shillings, which the mother may certainly get, or the value in scraps, by her lawful occupation of begging; and it is exactly at one year old that I propose to provide for them in such a manner as instead of being a charge upon their parents or the parish, or wanting food and raiment for the rest of their lives, they shall on the contrary contribute to the feeding, and partly to the clothing, of many thousands.

There is likewise another great advantage in my scheme, that it

1. That is, bind themselves to work for a period of years, in order to pay for their transportation to a colony.

will prevent those voluntary abortions, and that horrid practice of women murdering their bastard children, alas, too frequent among us, sacrificing the poor innocent babes, I doubt, more to avoid the expense than the shame, which would move tears and pity in the most savage and inhuman breast.

The number of souls in this kingdom being usually reckoned one million and a half, of these I calculate there may be about two hundred thousand couple whose wives are breeders; from which number I subtract thirty thousand couples who are able to maintain their own children, although I apprehend there cannot be so many under the present distresses of the kingdom; but this being granted, there will remain an hundred and seventy thousand breeders. I again subtract fifty thousand for those women who miscarry, or whose children die by accident or disease within the year. There only remain an hundred and twenty thousand children of poor parents annually born. The question therefore is, how this number shall be reared and provided for, which, as I have already said, under the present situation of affairs, is utterly impossible by all the methods hitherto proposed. For we can neither employ them in handicraft or agriculture; we neither build houses (I mean in the country) nor cultivate land. They can very seldom pick up a livelihood by stealing till they arrive at six years old, except where they are of towardly parts; although I confess they learn the rudiments much earlier, during which time they can however be looked upon only as probationers, as I have been informed by a principal gentleman in the county of Cavan, who protested to me that he never knew above one or two instances under the age of six, even in a part of the kingdom so renowned for the quickest proficiency in that art.

I am assured by our merchants that a boy or a girl before twelve years old is no salable commodity; and even when they come to this age they will not yield above three pounds, or three pounds and half a crown at most on the Exchange; which cannot turn to account either to the parents or the kingdom, the charge of nutriment and rags having been at least four times that value.

I shall now therefore humbly propose my own thoughts, which I hope will not be liable to the least objection.

I have been assured by a very knowing American of my acquaintance in London, that a young healthy child well nursed is at a year old a most delicious, nourishing, and wholesome food, whether stewed, roasted, baked, or boiled; and I make no doubt that it will equally serve in a fricassee or a ragout.

I do therefore humbly offer it to public consideration that of the hundred and twenty thousand children, already computed, twenty thousand may be reserved for breed, whereof only one fourth part to be males, which is more than we allow to sheep, black cattle, or swine; and my reason is that these children are seldom the fruits of marriage, a circumstance not much regarded by our savages, therefore one male will be sufficient to serve four females. That the remaining hundred thousand may at a year old be offered in sale to the persons of quality and fortune through the kingdom, always advising the mother to let them suck plentifully in the last month, so as to render them plump and fat for a good table. A child will make two dishes at an entertainment for friends; and when the family dines alone, the fore or hind quarter will make a reasonable dish, and seasoned with a little pepper or salt will be very good boiled on the fourth day, especially in winter.

I have reckoned upon a medium that a child just born will weigh twelve pounds, and in a solar year if tolerably nursed increaseth to twenty-eight pounds.

I grant this food will be somewhat dear, and therefore very proper for landlords, who, as they have already devoured most of the parents, seem to have the best title to the children.

Infant's flesh will be in season throughout the year, but more plentiful in March, and a little before and after. For we are told by a grave author, an eminent French physician,[2] that fish being a prolific diet, there are more children born in Roman Catholic countries about nine months after Lent than at any other season; therefore, reckoning a year after Lent, the markets will be more glutted than usual, because the number of popish infants is at least three to one in this kingdom; and therefore it will have one other collateral advantage, by lessening the number of Papists among us.

I have already computed the charge of nursing a beggar's child (in which list I reckon all cottagers, laborers, and four fifths of the farmers) to be about two shillings per annum, rags included; and I believe no gentleman would repine to give ten shillings for the carcass of a good fat child, which, as I have said, will make four dishes of excellent nutritive meat, when he hath only some particular friend or his own family to dine with him. Thus the squire will learn to be a good landlord, and grow popular among the tenants; the mother will have eight shillings net profit, and be fit for work till she produces another child.

Those who are more thrifty (as I must confess the times require) may flay the carcass; the skin of which artificially dressed will make admirable gloves for ladies, and summer boots for fine gentlemen.

As to our city of Dublin, shambles may be appointed for this purpose in the most convenient parts of it, and butchers we may be assured will not be wanting; although I rather recommend buying the children alive, and dressing them hot from the knife as we do roasting pigs.

A very worthy person, a true lover of his country, and whose

2. Rabelais.

virtues I highly esteem, was lately pleased in discoursing on this matter to offer a refinement upon my scheme. He said that many gentlemen of this kingdom, having of late destroyed their deer, he conceived that the want of venison might be well supplied by the bodies of young lads and maidens, not exceeding fourteen years of age nor under twelve, so great a number of both sexes in every county being now ready to starve for want of work and service; and these to be disposed of by their parents, if alive, or otherwise by their nearest relations. But with due deference to so excellent a friend and so deserving a patriot, I cannot be altogether in his sentiments; for as to the males, my American acquaintance assured me from frequent experience that their flesh was generally tough and lean, like that of our schoolboys, by continual exercise, and their taste disagreeable; and to fatten them would not answer the charge. Then as to the females, it would, I think with humble submission, be a loss to the public, because they soon would become breeders themselves: and besides, it is not improbable that some scrupulous people might be apt to censure such a practice (although indeed very unjustly) as a little bordering upon cruelty; which, I confess, hath always been with me the strongest objection against any project, how well soever intended.

But in order to justify my friend, he confessed that this expedient was put into his head by the famous Psalmanazar, a native of the island Formosa, who came from thence to London above twenty years ago, and in conversation told my friend that in his country when any young person happened to be put to death, the executioner sold the carcass to persons of quality as a prime dainty; and that in his time the body of a plump girl of fifteen, who was crucified for an attempt to poison the emperor, was sold to his Imperial Majesty's prime minister of state, and other great mandarins of the court, in joints from the gibbet, at four hundred crowns. Neither indeed can I deny that if the same use were made of several plump young girls in this town, who without one single groat to their fortunes cannot stir abroad without a chair, and appear at the playhouse and assemblies in foreign fineries which they never will pay for, the kingdom would not be the worse.

Some persons of a desponding spirit are in great concern about that vast number of poor people who are aged, diseased, or maimed, and I have been desired to employ my thoughts what course may be taken to ease the nation of so grievous an encumbrance. But I am not in the least pain upon that matter, because it is very well known that they are every day dying and rotting by cold and famine, and filth and vermin, as fast as can be reasonably expected. And as to the younger laborers, they are now in almost as hopeful a condition. They cannot get work, and consequently pine away for want of nourishment to a degree that if at any time they are accidentally hired to common labor, they have not strength to perform it; and thus the country and themselves are happily delivered from the evils to come.

I have too long digressed, and therefore shall return to my subject. I think the advantages by the proposal which I have made are obvious and many, as well as of the highest importance.

For first, as I have already observed, it would greatly lessen the number of Papists, with whom we are yearly overrun, being the principal breeders of the nation as well as our most dangerous enemies; and who stay at home on purpose to deliver the kingdom to the Pretender, hoping to take their advantage by the absence of so many good Protestants, who have chosen rather to leave their country than to stay at home and pay tithes against their conscience to an Episcopal curate.

Secondly, the poorer tenants will have something valuable of their own, which by law may be made liable to distress, and help to pay their landlord's rent, their corn and cattle being already seized and money a thing unknown.

Thirdly, whereas the maintenance of an hundred thousand children, from two years old and upwards, cannot be computed at less than ten shillings a piece per annum, the nation's stock will be thereby increased fifty thousand pounds per annum, besides the profit of a new dish introduced to the tables of all gentlemen of fortune in the kingdom who have any refinement in taste. And the money will circulate among ourselves, the goods being entirely of our own growth and manufacture.

Fourthly, the constant breeders, besides the gain of eight shillings sterling per annum by the sale of their children, will be rid of the charge of maintaining them after the first year.

Fifthly, this food would likewise bring great custom to taverns, where the vintners will certainly be so prudent as to procure the best receipts for dressing it to perfection, and consequently have their houses frequented by all the fine gentlemen, who justly value themselves upon their knowledge in good eating; and a skillful cook, who understands how to oblige his guests, will contrive to make it as expensive as they please.

Sixthly, this would be a great inducement to marriage, which all wise nations have either encouraged by rewards or enforced by laws and penalties. It would increase the care and tenderness of mothers toward their children, when they were sure of a settlement for life to the poor babes, provided in some sort by the public, to their annual profit instead of expense. We should see an honest emulation among the married women, which of them could bring the fattest child to the market. Men would become as fond of their wives during the time of their pregnancy as they are now of their mares in foal, their cows in calf, or sows when they are ready to farrow;

nor offer to beat or kick them (as is too frequent a practice) for fear of a miscarriage.

Many other advantages might be enumerated. For instance, the addition of some thousand carcasses in our exportation of barreled beef, the propagation of swine's flesh, and improvement in the art of making good bacon, so much wanted among us by the great destruction of pigs, too frequent at our tables, which are no way comparable in taste or magnificence to a well-grown, fat, yearling child, which roasted whole will make a considerable figure at a lord mayor's feast or any other public entertainment. But this and many others I omit, being studious of brevity.

Supposing that one thousand families in this city would be constant customers for infants' flesh, besides others who might have it at merry meetings, particularly weddings and christenings, I compute that Dublin would take off annually about twenty thousand carcasses, and the rest of the kingdom (where probably they will be sold somewhat cheaper) the remaining eighty thousand.

I can think of no one objection that will possibly be raised against this proposal, unless it should be urged that the number of people will be thereby much lessened in the kingdom. This I freely own, and it was indeed one principal design in offering it to the world. I desire the reader will observe, that I calculate my remedy for this one individual kingdom of Ireland and for no other that ever was, is, or I think ever can be upon earth. Therefore let no man talk to me of other expedients: of taxing our absentees at five shillings a pound: of using neither clothes nor household furniture except what is of our own growth and manufacture: of utterly rejecting the materials and instruments that promote foreign luxury: of curing the expensiveness of pride, vanity, idleness, and gaming in our women: of introducing a vein of parsimony, prudence, and temperance: of learning to love our country, in the want of which we differ even from Laplanders and the inhabitants of Topinamboo[3]: of quitting our animosities and factions, nor acting any longer like the Jews, who were murdering one another at the very moment their city was taken: of being a little cautious not to sell our country and conscience for nothing: of teaching landlords to have at least one degree of mercy toward their tenants: lastly, of putting a spirit of honesty, industry, and skill into our shopkeepers; who, if a resolution could now be taken to buy only our native goods, would immediately unite to cheat and exact upon us in the price, the measure, and the goodness, nor could ever yet be brought to make one fair proposal of just dealing, though often and earnestly invited to it.[4]

Therefore I repeat, let no man talk to me of these and the like

---

3. A district in Brazil.
4. Swift himself has made these various proposals in previous works.

expedients, till he hath at least some glimpse of hope that there will ever be some hearty and sincere attempt to put them in practice.

But as to myself, having been wearied out for many years with offering vain, idle, visionary thoughts, and at length utterly despairing of success, I fortunately fell upon this proposal, which, as it is wholly new, so it hath something solid and real, of no expense and little trouble, full in our own power, and whereby we can incur no danger in disobliging England. For this kind of commodity will not bear exportation, the flesh being of too tender a consistence to admit a long continuance in salt, although perhaps I could name a country which would be glad to eat up our whole nation without it.

After all, I am not so violently bent upon my own opinion as to reject any offer proposed by wise men, which shall be found equally innocent, cheap, easy, and effectual. But before something of that kind shall be advanced in contradiction to my scheme, and offering a better, I desire the author or authors will be pleased maturely to consider two points. First, as things now stand, how they will be able to find food and raiment for an hundred thousand useless mouths and backs. And secondly, there being a round million of creatures in human figure throughout this kingdom, whose sole subsistence put into a common stock would leave them in debt two millions of pounds sterling, adding those who are beggars by profession to the bulk of farmers, cottagers, and laborers, with their wives and children who are beggars in effect; I desire those politicians who dislike my overture, and may perhaps be so bold to attempt an answer, that they will first ask the parents of these mortals whether they would not at this day think it a great happiness to have been sold for food at a year old in the manner I prescribe, and thereby have avoided such a perpetual scene of misfortunes as they have since gone through by the oppression of landlords, the impossibility of paying rent without money or trade, the want of common sustenance, with neither house nor clothes to cover them from the inclemencies of the weather, and the most inevitable prospect of entailing the like or greater miseries upon their breed forever.

I profess, in the sincerity of my heart, that I have not the least personal interest in endeavoring to promote this necessary work, having no other motive than the public good of my country, by advancing our trade, providing for infants, relieving the poor, and giving some pleasure to the rich. I have no children by which I can propose to get a single penny; the youngest being nine years old, and my wife past childbearing.

QUESTIONS

1. This essay has been called one of the best examples of sustained irony in the English language. Irony is difficult to handle because

there is always the danger that the reader will miss the irony and take what is said literally. What does Swift do to try to prevent this? In answering this question, consider such matters as these: Is the first sentence of the essay ironic? At what point do you begin to suspect that Swift is using irony? What further evidence accumulates to make you certain that Swift is being ironic?

2. What is the speaker like? How are his views and character different from Swift's? Is the character of the speaker consistent? What is the purpose of the essay's final sentence?

3. Why does Swift use such phrases as "just dropt from its dam," "whose wives are breeders," "one fourth part to be males"?

4. Does the essay shock you? Was it Swift's purpose to shock you?

5. What is the main target of Swift's attack? What subsidiary targets are there? Does Swift offer any serious solutions for the problems and conditions he is describing?

6. What devices of argument, apart from the use of irony, does Swift use that could be successfully applied to other subjects?

7. Compare Swift's methods of drawing in or engaging his audience to Coffin's ("What Crucified Christ?" pp. 1131–1144).

JAMES THURBER
The Rabbits Who Caused All the Trouble

Within the memory of the youngest child there was a family of rabbits who lived near a pack of wolves. The wolves announced that they did not like the way the rabbits were living. (The wolves were crazy about the way they themselves were living, because it was the only way to live.) One night several wolves were killed in an earthquake and this was blamed on the rabbits, for it is well known that rabbits pound on the ground with their hind legs and cause earthquakes. On another night one of the wolves was killed by a bolt of lightning and this was also blamed on the rabbits, for it is well known that lettuce-eaters cause lightning. The wolves threatened to civilize the rabbits if they didn't behave, and the rabbits decided to run away to a desert island. But the other animals, who lived at a great distance, shamed them, saying, "You must stay where you are and be brave. This is no world for escapists. If the wolves attack you, we will come to your aid, in all probability." So the rabbits continued to live near the wolves and one day there was a terrible flood which drowned a great many wolves. This was blamed on the rabbits, for it is well known that carrot-nibblers with long ears cause floods. The wolves descended on the rabbits, for their own good, and imprisoned them in a dark cave, for their own protection.

When nothing was heard about the rabbits for some weeks, the other animals demanded to know what had happened to them.

The wolves replied that the rabbits had been eaten and since they had been eaten the affair was a purely internal matter. But the other animals warned that they might possibly unite against the wolves unless some reason was given for the destruction of the rabbits. So the wolves gave them one. "They were trying to escape," said the wolves, "and, as you know, this is no world for escapists."

Moral: Run, don't walk, to the nearest desert island.

WILLIAM MARCH

The Slave and the Cart Horse

A slave who had been beaten by his master came to the hut where his wife waited for him. He lay on a pallet, while the woman took a basin and filled it with water. He spoke after a time, answering the question his wife did not dare ask him: "It happened while I was working in the fields, near sunset. They had overloaded one of the cart horses, and the poor creature was hardly able to stand up. They were beating him with a whip, and although he was pulling with all his strength, he wasn't able to move the load out of the ruts in the field."

"Speak softer," said his wife. "The master might pass and hear you."

The slave lowered his voice and continued: "So I went to the master and told him that the horse couldn't carry such a load, and I asked him to take some of it off."

"Speak softer," said the woman. She bent over the slave and bathed his back with wet rags. "Speak softer. They'll whip you again if they hear what you're saying."

The slave got up and went to the door, to see that there was nobody outside; then he came and lay once more on the pallet. "I can't stand to see a horse cruelly treated. Horses always seem so helpless and pitiful to me."

When the woman spoke, her voice was so soft that it hardly carried to her husband's ears. "You did right," she said. "Horses aren't like us. They can't express themselves or stand up for their rights, and they have no way of defending themselves, like we have."

Then they looked into each others' eyes and sighed, thinking how fortunate they were and how cruelly horses were used, for no man can see his own misery clearly, and that is God's great mercy to us all.

CLARENCE DARROW

Address to the Prisoners in the Cook County Jail[1]

If I looked at jails and crimes and prisoners in the way the ordinary person does, I should not speak on this subject to you. The reason I talk to you on the question of crime, its cause and cure, is that I really do not in the least believe in crime. There is no such thing as a crime as the word is generally understood. I do not believe there is any sort of distinction between the real moral conditions of the people in and out of jail. One is just as good as the other. The people here can no more help being here than the people outside can avoid being outside. I do not believe that people are in jail because they deserve to be. They are in jail simply because they cannot avoid it on account of circumstances which are entirely beyond their control and for which they are in no way responsible.

I suppose a great many people on the outside would say I was doing you harm if they should hear what I say to you this afternoon, but you cannot be hurt a great deal anyway, so it will not matter. Good people outside would say that I was really teaching you things that were calculated to injure society, but it's worth while now and then to hear something different from what you ordinarily get from preachers and the like. These will tell you that you should be good and then you will get rich and be happy. Of course we know that people do not get rich by being good, and that is the reason why so many of you people try to get rich some other way, only you do not understand how to do it quite as well as the fellow outside.

There are people who think that everything in this world is an accident. But really there is no such thing as an accident. A great many folks admit that many of the people in jail ought to be there, and many who are outside ought to be in. I think none of them ought to be here. There ought to be no jails; and if it were not for the fact that the people on the outside are so grasping and heartless in their dealings with the people on the inside, there would be no such institution as jails.

1. The warden of the Cook County Jail in Chicago, who knew Darrow as a criminologist, lawyer, and writer, invited him to speak before the inmates of the jail in 1902. Darrow's friends felt that the talk was inappropriate for its audience, but Darrow defended himself in the introduction to the lecture, which he had printed in pamphlet form: "Realizing the force of the suggestion that the truth should not be spoken to all people, I have caused these remarks to be printed on rather good paper and in a somewhat expensive form. In this way the truth does not become cheap and vulgar, and is only placed before those whose intelligence and affluence will prevent their being influenced by it." The pamphlet sold for five cents.

I do not want you to believe that I think all you people here are angels. I do not think that. You are people of all kinds, all of you doing the best you can—and that is evidently not very well. You are people of all kinds and conditions and under all circumstances. In one sense everybody is equally good and equally bad. We all do the best we can under the circumstances. But as to the exact things for which you are sent here, some of you are guilty and did the particular act because you needed the money. Some of you did it because you are in the habit of doing it, and some of you because you are born to it, and it comes to be as natural as it does, for instance, for me to be good.

Most of you probably have nothing against me, and most of you would treat me the same way as any other person would, probably better than some of the people on the outside would treat me, because you think I believe in you and they know I do not believe in them. While you would not have the least thing against me in the world, you might pick my pockets. I do not think all of you would, but I think some of you would. You would not have anything against me, but that's your profession, a few of you. Some of the rest of you, if my doors were unlocked, might come in if you saw anything you wanted—not out of any malice to me, but because that is your trade. There is no doubt there are quite a number of people in this jail who would pick my pockets. And still I know this—that when I get outside pretty nearly everybody picks my pocket. There may be some of you who would hold up a man on the street, if you did not happen to have something else to do, and needed the money; but when I want to light my house or my office the gas company holds me up. They charge me one dollar for something that is worth twenty-five cents. Still all these people are good people; they are pillars of society and support the churches, and they are respectable.

When I ride on the streetcars I am held up—I pay five cents for a ride that is worth two and a half cents, simply because a body of men have bribed the city council and the legislature, so that all the rest of us have to pay tribute to them.

If I do not want to fall into the clutches of the gas trust and choose to burn oil instead of gas, then good Mr. Rockefeller holds me up, and he uses a certain portion of his money to build universities and support churches which are engaged in telling us how to be good.

Some of you are here for obtaining property under false pretenses—yet I pick up a great Sunday paper and read the advertisements of a merchant prince—"Shirtwaists for 39 cents, marked down from $3.00."

When I read the advertisements in the paper I see they are all lies. When I want to get out and find a place to stand anywhere on the face of the earth, I find that it has all been taken up long ago before I came here, and before you came here, and somebody says, "Get off, swim into the lake, fly into the air; go anywhere, but get off." That is because these people have the police and they have the jails and the judges and the lawyers and the soldiers and all the rest of them to take care of the earth and drive everybody off that comes in their way.

A great many people will tell you that all this is true, but that it does not excuse you. These facts do not excuse some fellow who reaches into my pocket and takes out a five-dollar bill. The fact that the gas company bribes the members of the legislature from year to year, and fixes the law, so that all you people are compelled to be "fleeced" whenever you deal with them; the fact that the streetcar companies and the gas companies have control of the streets; and the fact that the landlords own all the earth—this, they say, has nothing to do with you.

Let us see whether there is any connection between the crimes of the respectable classes and your presence in the jail. Many of you people are in jail because you have really committed burglary; many of you, because you have stolen something. In the meaning of the law, you have taken some other person's property. Some of you have entered a store and carried off a pair of shoes because you did not have the price. Possibly some of you have committed murder. I cannot tell what all of you did. There are a great many people here who have done some of these things who really do not know themselves why they did them. I think I know why you did them—every one of you; you did these things because you were bound to do them. It looked to you at the time as if you had a chance to do them or not, as you saw fit; but still, after all, you had no choice. There may be people here who had some money in their pockets and who still went out and got some more money in a way society forbids. Now, you may not yourselves see exactly why it was you did this thing, but if you look at the question deeply enough and carefully enough you will see that there were circumstances that drove you to do exactly the thing which you did. You could not help it any more than we outside can help taking the positions that we take. The reformers who tell you to be good and you will be happy, and the people on the outside who have property to protect—they think that the only way to do it is by building jails and locking you up in cells on weekdays and praying for you Sundays.

I think that all of this has nothing whatever to do with right conduct. I think it is very easily seen what has to do with right conduct. Some so-called criminals—and I will use this word because it is handy, it means nothing to me—I speak of the criminals who get caught as distinguished from the criminals who catch them—some of these so-called criminals are in jail for their first offenses, but nine tenths of you are in jail because you did not have a good lawyer and, of course, you did not have a good lawyer because you did not have enough money to pay a good lawyer. There is no very great danger of a rich man going to jail.

Some of you may be here for the first time. If we would open the doors and let you out, and leave the laws as they are today, some of you would be back tomorrow. This is about as good a place as you can get anyway. There are many people here who are so in the habit of coming that they would not know where else to go. There are people who are born with the tendency to break into jail every chance they get, and they cannot avoid it. You cannot figure out your life and see why it was, but still there is a reason for it; and if we were all wise and knew all the facts, we could figure it out.

In the first place, there are a good many more people who go to jail in the wintertime than in summer. Why is this? Is it because people are more wicked in winter? No, it is because the coal trust begins to get in its grip in the winter. A few gentlemen take possession of the coal, and unless the people will pay seven or eight dollars a ton for something that is worth three dollars, they will have to freeze. Then there is nothing to do but to break into jail, and so there are many more in jail in the winter than in summer. It costs more for gas in the winter because the nights are longer, and people go to jail to save gas bills. The jails are electric-lighted. You may not know it, but these economic laws are working all the time, whether we know it or do not know it.

There are more people who go to jail in hard times than in good times—few people, comparatively, go to jail except when they are hard up. They go to jail because they have no other place to go. They may not know why, but it is true all the same. People are not more wicked in hard times. That is not the reason. The fact is true all over the world that in hard times more people go to jail than in good times, and in winter more people go to jail than in summer. Of course it is pretty hard times for people who go to jail at any time. The people who go to jail are almost always poor people— people who have no other place to live, first and last. When times are hard, then you find large numbers of people who go to jail who would not otherwise be in jail.

Long ago, Mr. Buckle,[2] who was a great philosopher and historian, collected facts, and he showed that the number of people who are arrested increased just as the price of food increased. When

2. Henry Thomas Buckle (1821-1862), British historian and author of a *History of Civilization*, who was attacked during his lifetime by conservatives for his "radical" views of history.

they put up the price of gas ten cents a thousand, I do not know who will go to jail, but I do know that a certain number of people will go. When the meat combine raises the price of beef, I do not know who is going to jail, but I know that a large number of people are bound to go. Whenever the Standard Oil Company raises the price of oil, I know that a certain number of girls who are seamstresses, and who work night after night long hours for somebody else, will be compelled to go out on the streets and ply another trade, and I know that Mr. Rockefeller and his associates are responsible and not the poor girls in the jails.

First and last, people are sent to jail because they are poor. Sometimes, as I say, you may not need money at the particular time, but you wish to have thrifty forehanded habits, and do not always wait until you are in absolute want. Some of you people are perhaps plying the trade, the profession, which is called burglary. No man in his right senses will go into a strange house in the dead of night and prowl around with a dark lantern through unfamiliar rooms and take chances of his life, if he has plenty of the good things of the world in his own home. You would not take any such chances as that. If a man had clothes in his clothes-press and beefsteak in his pantry and money in the bank, he would not navigate around nights in houses where he knows nothing about the premises whatever. It always requires experience and education for this profession, and people who fit themselves for it are no more to blame than I am for being a lawyer. A man would not hold up another man on the street if he had plenty of money in his own pocket. He might do it if he had one dollar or two dollars, but he wouldn't if he had as much money as Mr. Rockefeller has. Mr. Rockefeller has a great deal better hold-up game than that.

The more that is taken from the poor by the rich, who have the chance to take it, the more poor people there are who are compelled to resort to these means for a livelihood. They may not understand it, they may not think so at once, but after all they are driven into that line of employment.

There is a bill before the legislature of this state to punish kidnaping children with death. We have wise members of the legislature. They know the gas trust when they see it and they always see it—they can furnish light enough to be seen; and this legislature thinks it is going to stop kidnaping children by making a law punishing kidnapers of children with death. I don't believe in kidnaping children, but the legislature is all wrong. Kidnaping children is not a crime, it is a profession. It has been developed with the times. It has been developed with our modern industrial conditions. There are many ways of making money—many new ways that our ancestors knew nothing about. Our ancestors knew nothing about a billion-dollar trust; and here comes some poor fellow who has no other trade and he discovers the profession of kidnaping children.

This crime is born, not because people are bad; people don't kidnap other people's children because they want the children or because they are devilish, but because they see a chance to get some money out of it. You cannot cure this crime by passing a law punishing by death kidnapers of children. There is one way to cure it. There is one way to cure all these offenses, and that is to give the people a chance to live. There is no other way, and there never was any other way since the world began; and the world is so blind and stupid that it will not see. If every man and woman and child in the world had a chance to make a decent, fair, honest living, there would be no jails and no lawyers and no courts. There might be some persons here or there with some peculiar formation of their brain, like Rockefeller, who would do these things simply to be doing them; but they would be very, very few, and those should be sent to a hospital and treated, and not sent to jail; and they would entirely disappear in the second generation, or at least in the third generation.

I am not talking pure theory. I will just give you two or three illustrations.

The English people once punished criminals by sending them away. They would load them on a ship and export them to Australia. England was owned by lords and nobles and rich people. They owned the whole earth over there, and the other people had to stay in the streets. They could not get a decent living. They used to take their criminals and send them to Australia—I mean the class of criminals who got caught. When these criminals got over there, and nobody else had come, they had the whole continent to run over, and so they could raise sheep and furnish their own meat, which is easier than stealing it. These criminals then became decent, respectable people because they had a chance to live. They did not commit any crimes. They were just like the English people who sent them there, only better. And in the second generation the descendants of those criminals were as good and respectable a class of people as there were on the face of the earth, and then they began building churches and jails themselves.

A portion of this country was settled in the same way, landing prisoners down on the southern coast; but when they got here and had a whole continent to run over and plenty of chances to make a living, they became respectable citizens, making their own living just like any other citizen in the world. But finally the descendants of the English aristocracy who sent the people over to Australia found out they were getting rich, and so they went over to get possession of the earth as they always do, and they organized land syndicates and got control of the land and ores, and then they had just as many criminals in Australia as they did in England. It was not because the world had grown bad; it was because the earth had been taken away from the people.

Some of you people have lived in the country. It's prettier than it is here. And if you have ever lived on a farm you understand that if you put a lot of cattle in a field, when the pasture is short they will jump over the fence; but put them in a good field where there is plenty of pasture, and they will be law-abiding cattle to the end of time. The human animal is just like the rest of the animals, only a little more so. The same thing that governs in the one governs in the other.

Everybody makes his living along the lines of least resistance. A wise man who comes into a country early sees a great undeveloped land. For instance, our rich men twenty-five years ago saw that Chicago was small and knew a lot of people would come here and settle, and they readily saw that if they had all the land around here it would be worth a good deal, so they grabbed the land. You cannot be a landlord because somebody has got it all. You must find some other calling. In England and Ireland and Scotland less than five per cent own all the land there is, and the people are bound to stay there on any kind of terms the landlords give. They must live the best they can, so they develop all these various professions—burglary, picking pockets, and the like.

Again, people find all sorts of ways of getting rich. These are diseases like everything else. You look at people getting rich, organizing trusts and making a million dollars, and somebody gets the disease and he starts out. He catches it just as a man catches the mumps or the measles; he is not to blame, it is in the air. You will find men speculating beyond their means, because the mania of money-getting is taking possession of them. It is simply a disease—nothing more, nothing less. You cannot avoid catching it; but the fellows who have control of the earth have the advantage of you. See what the law is: when these men get control of things, they make the laws. They do not make the laws to protect anybody; courts are not instruments of justice. When your case gets into court it will make little difference whether you are guilty or innocent, but it's better if you have a smart lawyer. And you cannot have a smart lawyer unless you have money. First and last it's a question of money. Those men who own the earth make the laws to protect what they have. They fix up a sort of fence or pen around what they have, and they fix the law so the fellow on the outside cannot get in. The laws are really organized for the protection of the men who rule the world. They were never organized or enforced to do justice. We have no system for doing justice, not the slightest in the world.

Let me illustrate: Take the poorest person in this room. If the community had provided a system of doing justice, the poorest person in this room would have as good a lawyer as the richest, would he not? When you went into court you would have just as long a trial and just as fair a trial as the richest person in Chicago. Your case would not be tried in fifteen or twenty minutes, whereas it would take fifteen days to get through with a rich man's case.

Then if you were rich and were beaten, your case would be taken to the Appellate Court. A poor man cannot take his case to the Appellate Court; he has not the price. And then to the Supreme Court. And if he were beaten there he might perhaps go to the United States Supreme Court. And he might die of old age before he got into jail. If you are poor, it's a quick job. You are almost known to be guilty, else you would not be there. Why should anyone be in the criminal court if he were not guilty? He would not be there if he could be anywhere else. The officials have no time to look after all these cases. The people who are on the outside, who are running banks and building churches and making jails, they have no time to examine 600 or 700 prisoners each year to see whether they are guilty or innocent. If the courts were organized to promote justice the people would elect somebody to defend all these criminals, somebody as smart as the prosecutor—and give him as many detectives and as many assistants to help, and pay as much money to defend you as to prosecute you. We have a very able man for state's attorney, and he has many assistants, detectives, and policemen without end, and judges to hear the cases—everything handy.

Most all of our criminal code consists in offenses against property. People are sent to jail because they have committed a crime against property. It is of very little consequence whether one hundred people more or less go to jail who ought not to go—you must protect property, because in this world property is of more importance than anything else.

How is it done? These people who have property fix it so they can protect what they have. When somebody commits a crime it does not follow that he has done something that is morally wrong. The man on the outside who has committed no crime may have done something. For instance: to take all the coal in the United States and raise the price two dollars or three dollars when there is no need of it, and thus kill thousands of babies and send thousands of people to the poorhouse and tens of thousands to jail, as is done every year in the United States—this is a greater crime than all the people in our jails ever committed; but the law does not punish it. Why? Because the fellows who control the earth make the laws. If you and I had the making of the laws, the first thing we would do would be to punish the fellow who gets control of the earth. Nature put this coal in the ground for me as well as for them and nature made the prairies up here to raise wheat for me as well as for them, and then the great railroad companies came along and fenced it up.

Most all of the crimes for which we are punished are property crimes. There are a few personal crimes, like murder—but they are very few. The crimes committed are mostly those against property. If this punishment is right the criminals must have a lot of property. How much money is there is this crowd? And yet you are all here for crimes against property. The people up and down the Lake Shore[3] have not committed crime; still they have so much property they don't know what to do with it. It is perfectly plain why these people have not committed crimes against property; they make the laws and therefore do not need to break them. And in order for you to get some property you are obliged to break the rules of the game. I don't know but what some of you may have had a very nice chance to get rich by carrying a hod for one dollar a day, twelve hours. Instead of taking that nice, easy profession, you are a burglar. If you had been given a chance to be a banker you would rather follow that. Some of you may have had a chance to work as a switchman on a railroad where you know, according to statistics, that you cannot live and keep all your limbs more than seven years, and you can get fifty dollars or seventy-five dollars a month for taking your lives in your hands; and instead of taking that lucrative position you chose to be a sneak thief, or something like that. Some of you made that sort of choice. I don't know which I would take if I was reduced to this choice. I have an easier choice.

I will guarantee to take from this jail, or any jail in the world, five hundred men who have been the worst criminals and lawbreakers who ever got into jail, and I will go down to our lowest streets and take five hundred of the most abandoned prostitutes, and go out somewhere where there is plenty of land, and will give them a chance to make a living, and they will be as good people as the average in the community.

There is a remedy for the sort of condition we see here. The world never finds it out, or when it does find it out it does not enforce it. You may pass a law punishing every person with death for burglary, and it will make no difference. Men will commit it just the same. In England there was a time when one hundred different offenses were punishable with death, and it made no difference. The English people strangely found out that so fast as they repealed the severe penalties and so fast as they did away with punishing men by death, crime decreased instead of increased; that the smaller the penalty the fewer the crimes.

Hanging men in our county jails does not prevent murder. It

---

3. The fashionable and expensive section of Chicago along Lake Michigan.

makes murderers.

And this has been the history of the world. It's easy to see how to do away with what we call crime. It is not so easy to do it. I will tell you how to do it. It can be done by giving the people a chance to live—by destroying special privileges. So long as big criminals can get the coal fields, so long as the big criminals have control of the city council and get the public streets for streetcars and gas rights—this is bound to send thousands of poor people to jail. So long as men are allowed to monopolize all the earth, and compel others to live on such terms as these men see fit to make, then you are bound to get into jail.

The only way in the world to abolish crime and criminals is to abolish the big ones and the little ones together. Make fair conditions of life. Give men a chance to live. Abolish the right of private ownership of land, abolish monopoly, make the world partners in production, partners in the good things of life. Nobody would steal if he could get something of his own some easier way. Nobody will commit burglary when he has a house full. No girl will go out on the streets when she has a comfortable place at home. The man who owns a sweatshop or a department store may not be to blame himself for the condition of his girls, but when he pays them five dollars, three dollars, and two dollars a week, I wonder where he thinks they will get the rest of their money to live. The only way to cure these conditions is by equality. There should be no jails. They do not accomplish what they pretend to accomplish. If you would wipe them out there would be no more criminals than now. They terrorize nobody. They are a blot upon any civilization, and a jail is an evidence of the lack of charity of the people on the outside who make the jails and fill them with the victims of their greed.

QUESTIONS

1. What is Darrow's central thesis? What relationship does he see between the nature of a government or a society and the action of the individual?
2. One of the prisoners that Darrow addressed is said to have commented that the speech was "too radical." What might Darrow say this shows about his audience and their society?
3. Remembering that Darrow is a lawyer writing in 1902 and Martin Luther King, Jr. ("Letter from Birmingham Jail," pp. 661–674) a minister writing in 1963,
   a. compare the two pieces with respect to the writers, the occasions, and the audiences; and
   b. discuss whether segregation represents for King the things that property does for Darrow. (How far do their ideas on justice, minorities, and laws coincide? What possibilities for action by the individual does each see?)

4. Compare Darrow's views on poverty with those expressed by Shaw in "The Gospel of St. Andrew Undershaft."

GEORGE BERNARD SHAW
The Gospel of St. Andrew Undershaft[1]

In the millionaire Undershaft I have represented a man who has become intellectually and spiritually as well as practically conscious of the irresistible natural truth which we all abhor and repudiate: to wit, that the greatest of our evils, and the worst of our crimes is poverty, and that our first duty to which every other consideration should be sacrificed, is not to be poor. "Poor but honest," "the respectable poor," and such phrases are as intolerable and as immoral as "drunken but amiable," "fraudulent but a good after-dinner speaker," "splendidly criminal," or the like. Security, the chief pretense of civilization, cannot exist where the worst of dangers, the danger of poverty, hangs over everyone's head, and where the alleged protection of our persons from violence is only an accidental result of the existence of a police force whose real business is to force the poor man to see his children starve whilst idle people overfeed pet dogs with the money that might feed and clothe them.

It is exceedingly difficult to make people realize that an evil is an evil. For instance, we seize a man and deliberately do him a malicious injury: say, imprison him for years. One would not suppose that it needed any exceptional clearness of wit to recognize in this an act of diabolical cruelty. But in England such a recognition provokes a stare of surprise, followed by an explanation that the outrage is punishment or justice or something else that is all right, or perhaps by a heated attempt to argue that we should all be robbed and murdered in our beds if such stupid villainies as sentences of imprisonment were not committed daily. It is useless to argue that even if this were true, which it is not, the alternative to adding crimes of our own to the crimes from which we suffer is not helpless submission. Chickenpox is an evil; but if I were to declare that we must either submit to it or else repress it sternly by seizing everyone who suffers from it and punishing them by inoculation with smallpox, I should be laughed at; for though nobody could deny that the result would be to prevent chickenpox to some extent by making people avoid it much more carefully, and to effect a further apparent prevention by making them conceal it very

---

1. From the preface to his play *Major Barbara*, 1905.

anxiously, yet people would have sense enough to see that the deliberate propagation of smallpox was a creation of evil, and must therefore be ruled out in favor of purely humane and hygienic measures. Yet in the precisely parallel case of a man breaking into my house and stealing my wife's diamonds I am expected as a matter of course to steal ten years of his life, torturing him all the time. If he tries to defeat that monstrous retaliation by shooting me, my survivors hang him. The net result suggested by the police statistics is that we inflict atrocious injuries on the burglars we catch in order to make the rest take effectual precautions against detection; so that instead of saving our wives' diamonds from burglary we only greatly decrease our chances of ever getting them back, and increase our chances of being shot by the robber if we are unlucky enough to disturb him at his work.

But the thoughtless wickedness with which we scatter sentences of imprisonment, torture in the solitary cell and on the plank bed, and flogging, on moral invalids and energetic rebels, is as nothing compared to the silly levity with which we tolerate poverty as if it were either a wholesome tonic for lazy people or else a virtue to be embraced as St. Francis embraced it. If a man is indolent, let him be poor. If he is drunken, let him be poor. If he is not a gentleman, let him be poor. If he is addicted to the fine arts or to pure science instead of to trade and finance, let him be poor. If he chooses to spend his urban eighteen shillings a week or his agricultural thirteen shillings a week on his beer and his family instead of saving it up for his old age, let him be poor. Let nothing be done for "the undeserving": let him be poor. Serve him right! Also—somewhat inconsistently—blessed are the poor!

Now what does this Let Him Be Poor mean? It means let him be weak. Let him be ignorant. Let him become a nucleus of disease. Let him be a standing exhibition and example of ugliness and dirt. Let him have rickety children. Let him be cheap and let him drag his fellows down to his own price by selling himself to do their work. Let his habitations turn our cities into poisonous congeries of slums. Let his daughters infect our young men with the diseases of the streets, and his sons revenge him by turning the nation's manhood into scrofula, cowardice, cruelty, hypocrisy, political imbecility and all the other fruits of oppression and malnutrition. Let the undeserving become still less deserving; and let the deserving lay up for himself, not treasures in heaven, but horrors in hell upon earth. This being so, is it really wise to let him be poor? Would he not do ten times less harm as a prosperous burglar, incendiary, ravisher or murderer, to the utmost limits of humanity's comparatively negligible impulses in these directions? Suppose we were to abolish all penalties for such activities, and decide that poverty is the one thing we will not tolerate—that every adult with less than, say, £365 a year, shall be painlessly but inexorably killed, and every hungry half-naked child forcibly fattened and clothed, would not that be an enormous improvement on our existing system, which has already destroyed so many civilizations, and is visibly destroying ours in the same way?

Is there any radicle of such legislation in our parliamentary system? Well, there are two measures just sprouting in the political soil, which may conceivably grow to something valuable. One is the institution of a Legal Minimum Wage. The other, Old Age Pensions. But there is a better plan than either of these. Some time ago I mentioned the subject of Universal Old Age Pensions to my fellow Socialist Cobden-Sanderson, famous as an artist-craftsman in bookbinding and printing. "Why not Universal Pensions for Life?" said Cobden-Sanderson. In saying this, he solved the industrial problem at a stroke. At present we say callously to each citizen "If you want money, earn it" as if his having or not having it were a matter that concerned himself alone. We do not even secure for him the opportunity of earning it: on the contrary, we allow our industry to be organized in open dependence on the maintenance of "a reserve army of unemployed" for the sake of "elasticity." The sensible course would be Cobden-Sanderson's: that is, to give every man enough to live well on, so as to guarantee the community against the possibility of a case of the malignant disease of poverty, and then (necessarily) to see that he earned it.

Undershaft, the hero of Major Barbara, is simply a man who, having grasped the fact that poverty is a crime, knows that when society offered him the alternative of poverty or a lucrative trade in death and destruction,[2] it offered him, not a choice between opulent villainy and humble virtue, but between energetic enterprise and cowardly infamy. His conduct stands the Kantian test, which Peter Shirley's does not.[3] Peter Shirley is what we call the honest poor man. Undershaft is what we call the wicked rich one: Shirley is Lazarus, Undershaft Dives. Well, the misery of the world is due to the fact that the great mass of men act and believe as Peter Shirley acts and believes. If they acted and believed as Undershaft acts and believes, the immediate result would be a revolution of incalculable beneficence. To be wealthy, says Undershaft, is with me a point of honor for which I am prepared to kill at the risk of my own life. This preparedness is, as he says, the final test of sincerity. Like Froissart's medieval hero, who saw that "to rob and pill was a good life" he is not the dupe of that public sentiment against killing which is propagated and endowed by people who would otherwise be

2. Undershaft was a munitions manufacturer.
3. The Kantian test is to act only as you would have all others act in similar circumstances. Peter Shirley is an unemployed old man in the soup kitchen whose conscience was shaped by social-protest theories.

killed themselves, or of the mouth-honor paid to poverty and obedience by rich and insubordinate do-nothings who want to rob the poor without courage and command them without superiority. Froissart's knight, in placing the achievement of a good life before all the other duties—which indeed are not duties at all when they conflict with it, but plain wickednesses—behaved bravely, admirably, and, in the final analysis, public-spiritedly. Medieval society, on the other hand, behaved very badly indeed in organizing itself so stupidly that a good life could be achieved by robbing and pilling. If the knight's contemporaries had been all as resolute as he, robbing and pilling would have been the shortest way to the gallows, just as, if we were all as resolute and clearsighted as Undershaft, an attempt to live by means of what is called "an independent income" would be the shortest way to the lethal chamber. But as, thanks to our political imbecility and personal cowardice (fruits of poverty, both), the best imitation of a good life now procurable is life on an independent income, all sensible people aim at securing such an income, and are, of course, careful to legalize and moralize both it and all the actions and sentiments which lead to it and support it as an institution. What else can they do? They know, of course, that they are rich because others are poor. But they cannot help that: it is for the poor to repudiate poverty when they have had enough of it. The thing can be done easily enough: the demonstrations to the contrary made by the economists, jurists, moralists and sentimentalists hired by the rich to defend them, or even doing the work gratuitously out of sheer folly and abjectness, impose only on those who want to be imposed on.

The reason why the independent income-tax payers are not solid in defence of their position is that since we are not medieval rovers through a sparsely populated country, the poverty of those we rob prevents our having the good life for which we sacrifice them. Rich men or aristocrats with a developed sense of life—men like Ruskin and William Morris and Kropotkin—have enormous social appetites and very fastidious personal ones. They are not content with handsome houses: they want handsome cities. They are not content with bediamonded wives and blooming daughters: they complain because the charwoman is badly dressed, because the laundress smells of gin, because the sempstress is anemic, because every man they meet is not a friend and every woman not a romance. They turn up their noses at their neighbors' drains, and are made ill by the architecture of their neighbors' houses. Trade patterns made to suit vulgar people do not please them (and they can get nothing else): they cannot sleep nor sit at ease upon "slaughtered" cabinet makers' furniture. The very air is not good enough for them: there is too much factory smoke in it. They even demand abstract conditions: justice, honor, a noble moral atmosphere, a·

mystic nexus to replace the cash nexus. Finally they declare that though to rob and pill with your own hand on horseback and in steel coat may have been a good life, to rob and pill by the hands of the policeman, the bailiff, and the soldier, and to underpay them meanly for doing it, is not a good life, but rather fatal to all possibility of even a tolerable one. They call on the poor to revolt, and, finding the poor shocked at their ungentlemenliness, despairingly revile the proletariat for its "damned wantlessness" (*verdammte Bedürfnislosigkeit*).

So far, however, their attack on society has lacked simplicity. The poor do not share their tastes nor understand their art-criticisms. They do not want the simple life, nor the esthetic life; on the contrary, they want very much to wallow in all the costly vulgarities from which the elect souls among the rich turn away with loathing. It is by surfeit and not by abstinence that they will be cured of their hankering after unwholesome sweets. What they do dislike and despise and are ashamed of is poverty. To ask them to fight for the difference between the Christmas number of the Illustrated London News and the Kelmscott Chaucer is silly: they prefer the News. The difference between a stockbroker's cheap and dirty starched white shirt and collar and the comparatively costly and carefully dyed blue shirt of William Morris is a difference so disgraceful to Morris in their eyes that if they fought on the subject at all, they would fight in defence of the starch. "Cease to be slaves, in order that you may become cranks" is not a very inspiring call to arms; nor is it really improved by substituting saints for cranks. Both terms denote men of genius; and the common man does not want to live the life of a man of genius: he would much rather live the life of a pet collie if that were the only alternative. But he does want more money. Whatever else he may be vague about, he is clear about that. He may or may not prefer Major Barbara to the Drury Lane pantomime; but he always prefers five hundred pounds to five hundred shillings.

Now to deplore this preference as sordid, and teach children that it is sinful to desire money, is to strain towards the extreme possible limit of impudence in lying and corruption in hypocrisy. The universal regard for money is the one hopeful fact in our civilization, the one sound spot in our social conscience. Money is the most important thing in the world. It represents health, strength, honor, generosity and beauty as conspicuously and undeniably as the want of it represents illness, weakness, disgrace, meanness and ugliness. Not the least of its virtues is that it destroys base people as certainly as it fortifies and dignifies noble people. It is only when it is cheapened to worthlessness for some and made impossibly dear to others, that it becomes a curse. In short, it is a curse only in such foolish social conditions that life itself is a curse. For the two things are inseparable: money is the counter that enables life to be distributed socially: it *is* life as truly as sovereigns and bank notes are money. The first duty of every citizen is to insist on having money on reasonable terms; and this demand is not complied with by giving four men three shillings each for ten or twelve hours' drudgery and one man a thousand pounds for nothing. The crying need of the nation is not for better morals, cheaper bread, temperance, liberty, culture, redemption of fallen sisters and erring brothers, nor the grace, love and fellowship of the Trinity, but simply for enough money. And the evil to be attacked is not sin, suffering, greed, priestcraft, kingcraft, demagogy, monopoly, ignorance, drink, war, pestilence, nor any other of the scapegoats which reformers sacrifice, but simply poverty.

QUESTIONS

1. Cite *some examples of Shaw's deliberately outrageous manner in his first paragraph. Does he ever modify this extreme manner?*
2. In *the second paragraph he speaks of two cases as "precisely parallel": what premise must he assume in order to say this? How vital is this assertion to his main line of argument? What is his central assertion?*
3. Explain *the definition of money as life which appears in the last paragraph.*
4. Outline *in more neutral words and phrases than Shaw's a more conventional approach to his argument.*
5. Who *are Shaw's controversial antagonists? In what way is his controversial manner suited to these antagonists?*

PAUL A. FREUND

5-to-4: Are the Justices Really Objective?[1]

The recurrence of 5-to-4 decisions of the Supreme Court raises once again the question whether the judicial process is really objective in resolving important issues of constitutional law.

Given a constitutional text written in plain and, for the most part, nontechnical English, how are we to explain the sharp divergence of views in applying the Constitution to an undisputed set of facts? Is there no explanation except that the judges are free to impose their personal social beliefs on the country in the name of the Constitution?

The first thing to observe is that constitutional guarantees like due process of law, freedom of speech, press, and assembly, and equal protection of the laws do not supply ready-made answers to

1. This essay first appeared in *The Boston Globe* in 1967.

concrete, changing, and unforeseen problems as those problems arise in life. Moreover, various constitutional guarantees may point in opposite directions. Criminal trials are to be fair, and the press is to be free; how then do we decide whether the news media may or may not publish distorted and sensational accounts of a criminal suspect or a trial in progress?

Working with mandates so deliberately spacious and sometimes ambiguous as these, the wonder may well be that there is as much agreement as we actually find among the judges in their resolution of the controversies before them. For the dramatic dissents that capture public attention should not obscure the very substantial measure of common ground among the judges. One of the recent 5-to-4 decisions that captured public attention was the case of the civil rights demonstrators who were convicted for refusing to leave the courtyard of a jail. Justice Black's majority opinion was widely regarded as a significant retreat by the court from its previous positions.[2] Actually, all the members of the court would clearly have agreed that a demonstration in the gallery of a legislative hall could be punished without any infringement of freedom of speech or assembly. By the same token, there would have been agreement that a peaceful demonstration in the public park would have been immune from prosecution. Thus the precise and narrow issue was whether a demonstration in the courtyard of a jail was more like that in a legislative hall or in a public park. It is hardly astonishing that an answer is not to be found in the constitutional text.

Granted that the cleavages may not be as wide or as deep as the rhetoric of the opinions might suggest, the question still remains: how are we to account for the differences that do exist, except in terms of willful and unconstrained predilection? When Justice Cardozo had to describe the judicial process, he referred to several ingredients that enter into a decision; the most important, in his view, were logic, history, and social utility. The real problem is how they shall be mixed in order to reach a satisfying conclusion. When this kind of question was put to Justice Frankfurter, he was fond of quoting the reply of Velázquez to a lady who asked him how he mixed his paints. "Madame," he said, "I mix them with taste."

Two recent examples will illustrate how judges have to mix their ingredients with judgment as artists mix theirs with taste.

The Supreme Court ruled in another 5-to-4 decision that Geor-

2. In the decision referred to (Adderley v. Florida), the majority held that some places, such as courtrooms, were not appropriate for demonstrations and that hence the state had the right to prosecute. This represented a retreat from previous decisions, since it placed limits on places where free speech and assembly could be exercised.

gia might elect its governor by vote of the Legislature after a popular election produced no majority for any candidate. The dissenters argued that this result was repugnant to the principle of the reapportionment cases, the equality of weight to each person's vote, since the Legislature might select for governor a candidate who would not prevail in a runoff.

On the other hand, Justice Black for the majority reasoned that Georgia could regard the popular vote as having exhausted itself and a new kind of election as having been substituted in which each legislator was free to vote his own choice. Both opinions were perfectly logical; they simply differed in the premises from which they started. The dissent regarded the whole selection process as a unit, while the majority looked on it as two separate processes. In choosing between these premises, the dissent would have extended the majoritarian philosophy of the reapportionment cases. Speaking for the court, Justice Black gave controlling weight to the long history of the legislative role in the election of a governor in Georgia, a role dating back to the state constitution of 1824. Both positions were rationally defensible. What would be indefensible is a judicial decision motivated by a personal preference for candidate Maddox or candidate Callaway.

The other illustration involves the validity of a poll tax as a condition of voting in state elections. Here the court ruled the condition on the suffrage to be a violation of equal protection of the laws. Justice Black, dissenting, relied heavily on the long history of the poll tax in relation to voting rights, reflecting a tolerable judgment that the privilege of voting might be made to rest on a financial stake of the voter in his government.

But the majority were not persuaded by the weight of this history, in view of marked changes in the sharing of tax burdens and in our general outlook on the relevance of poverty to the rights of citizenship. There is no suggestion that Justice Black is personally more enamored of the poll tax than are his colleagues.

The upshot is that judges are constrained but not wholly so, and are free but by no means completely at large. This ought not to be so surprising when we recall that even scientists, who are thought to be engaged in an exact discipline, differ sharply when they reach frontier questions. On the same evidence and with the same principles of reasoning one astronomer will maintain the "big-bang" view of the cosmos and another the "steady-state" theory. So, also, will one philosopher maintain a theory of freedom of the will and another of determinism.

The judges, like the scientists and the philosophers, may see the same phenomenon in different lights, with different predictions of what will in time satisfy thoughtful minds. The pursuit of justice, after all, is not necessarily easier than the pursuit of truth.

HARRISON BROWN
After the Population Explosion

At one time or another almost all of us have asked: How many human beings can the Earth support? When this question is put to me, I find it necessary to respond with another question: In what kind of world are you willing to live? In the eyes of those who care about their environment, we have perhaps already passed the limits of growth. In the eyes of those who don't care how they live or what dangers they create for posterity, the limits of growth lie far ahead.

The populations of all biological species are limited by environmental factors, and man's is no exception. Food supplies and the presence of predators are of prime importance. When two rabbits of opposite sex are placed in a fenced-in field of grass, they will go forth and multiply, but the population will eventually be limited by the grass supply. If predators are placed in the field, the rabbit population will either stabilize at a new level or possibly become extinct. Given no predators and no restrictions on food, but circumscribed space, the number of rabbits will still be limited, either by the psychological and biological effects of overcrowding or by being buried in their own refuse.

When man, endowed with the power of conceptual thought, appeared upon the Earth scene, something new was introduced into the evolutionary process. Biological evolution, which had dominated all living species for billions of years, gave way to cultural evolution. As man gradually learned how to control various elements of his environment, he succeeded in modifying a number of the factors that limited his population. Clothing, fire, and crude shelters extended the range of habitable climate. Tools of increasing sophistication helped man gather edible vegetation, hunt animals more effectively, and protect himself from predators.

But no matter how effective the tools, there is a limit to the number of food gatherers who can inhabit a given area of land. One cannot kill more animals than are born or pick more fruit than trees bear. The maximum population of a worldwide food-gathering society was about ten million persons. Once that level was reached, numerous cultural patterns emerged that caused worldwide birth rates and death rates to become equal. In some societies, the natural death rate was elevated by malnutrition and disease; in others, the death rate was increased artifically by such practices as infanticide or the waging of war. In some cases, certain sex taboos and rituals appear to have lowered the birth rate. But, however birth and death rates came into balance, we can be confident that for a long time prior to the agricultural revolution the human population remained virtually constant.

With the introduction of agriculture about 10,000 years ago, the levels of population that had been imposed by limited supplies of food were raised significantly. Even in the earliest agricultural societies, several hundred times as much food could be produced from a given area of fertile land than could be collected by food gatherers. As the technology of agriculture spread, population grew rapidly. This new technology dramatically affected the entire fabric of human culture. Man gave up the nomad life and settled in villages, some of which became cities. Sufficient food could be grown to make it possible for about 10 per cent of the population to engage in activities other than farming.

The development of iron technology and improved transportation accelerated the spread of this peasant-village culture. Indeed, had new technological developments ceased to appear after 1700, it is nevertheless likely that the peasant-village culture would have spread to all inhabitable parts of the Earth, eventually to reach a level of roughly five billion persons, some 500 million of whom would live in cities. But long before the population had reached anything close to that level, the emergence of new technologies leading up to the Industrial Revolution markedly changed the course of history. The steam engine for the first time gave man a means of concentrating enormous quantities of inanimate mechanical energy, and the newly found power was quickly applied.

During the nineteenth century in western Europe, improved transportation, increased food supplies, and a generally improved environment decreased the morbidity of a number of infectious diseases and virtually eliminated the large fluctuations in mortality rates that had been so characteristic of the seventeenth and eighteenth centuries. As mortality rates declined and the birth rate remained unchanged, populations in these areas increased rapidly. But as industrialization spread, a multiplicity of factors combined to lessen the desirability of large families. After about 1870, the size of families decreased, at first slowly and then more rapidly; eventually, the rate of population growth declined.

During the nineteenth and early twentieth centuries, some of the new technologies were gradually transplanted to the non-industrialized parts of the world, but in a very one-sided manner. Death rates were reduced appreciably, and, with birth rates unchanged, populations in these poorer countries increased rapidly and are still growing.

In spite of the fact that the annual rate of population growth in the industrialized countries has dropped to less than 1 per cent, the worldwide rate is now close to 2 per cent, the highest it has ever been. This rate represents a doubling of population about every thirty-five years. The human population is now 3.5 billion and at the present rate of increase is destined to reach 6.5 billion by the turn of the century and ten billion fifty years from now. Beyond that point, how much further can population grow?

An analysis of modern technology's potentials makes it clear that from a long-range, theoretical point of view, food supplies need no longer be the primary factor limiting population growth. Today nearly 10 per cent of the land area of the Earth, or about 3.5 billion acres, is under cultivation. It is estimated that with sufficient effort about fifteen billion acres of land could be placed under cultivation—some four times the present area. Such a move would require prodigious effort and investment and would necessitate the use of substantial quantities of desalinated water reclaimed from the sea. Given abundant energy resources, however, it now appears that in principle this can be done economically.

Large as the potential is for increasing the area of agricultural land, the increases in yield that can be obtained through fertilizers, application of supplementary water, and the use of new high-yielding varieties of cereals are even more impressive. Whereas in the past the growth of plants was circumscribed by the availability of nutrients and water, this need no longer be true. Using our new agricultural technology, solar energy can be converted into food with a high degree of efficiency, and even on the world's presently cultivated lands several times as much food can be produced each year than is now being grown.

To accomplish these objectives, however, an enormous amount of industrialization will be required. Fertilizers must be produced; thus, phosphate rock must be mined and processed, and nitrogen fixation plants must be built. Pesticides and herbicides are needed; thus, chemical plants must be built. All this requires steel and concrete, highways, railroads, and trucks. To be sure, the people of India, for example, might not need to attain Japan's level of industrialization in order to obtain Japanese levels of crop yield (which are about the highest in the world), but they will nevertheless need a level of industrialization that turns out to be surprisingly high.

Colin Clark, the director of the Agricultural Economics Research Institute of Oxford and a noted enthusiast for large populations, estimates that, given this new agricultural land and a level of industrialization sufficiently high to apply Japanese standards of farming, close to thirty billion persons could be supported on a Western European diet. Were people to content themselves with a Japanese diet, which contains little animal protein, he estimates that 100 billion persons could be supported.

To those who feel that life under such circumstances might be rather crowded, I should like to point out that even at the higher population level, the mean density of human beings over the land areas of the Earth would be no more than that which exists today in the belt along the Eastern Seaboard between Boston and Washington, D.C., where the average density is now 2,000 persons per square mile and where many people live quite comfortably. After all, Hong Kong has a population density of about 13,000 persons per square mile (nearly six times greater), and I understand that there are numerous happy people there.

Of course, such a society would need to expend a great deal of energy in order to manufacture, transport, and distribute the fertilizers, pesticides, herbicides, water, foodstuffs, and countless associated raw materials and products that would be necessary.

In the United States we currently consume energy equivalent to the burning of twelve-and-a-half short tons of coal per person per year. This quantity is bound to increase in the future as we find it necessary to process lower-grade ores, as we expend greater effort on controlling pollution (which would otherwise increase enormously), and as we recover additional quantities of potable water from the sea. Dr. Alvin Weinberg, director of the Oak Ridge National Laboratory, and his associates estimate that such activities will cost several additional tons of coal per person per year, and they suggest that for safety we budget twenty-five tons of coal per person per year in order to maintain our present material standard of living. Since we are a magnanimous people, we would not tolerate a double standard of living (a rich one for us and a poor one for others); so I will assume that this per capita level of energy expenditure will be characteristic of the world as a whole.

It has been estimated that the world's total usable coal reserve is on the order of 7,600 billion tons. This amount would last a populaton of thirty billion persons only ten years and a population of 100 billion only three years. Clearly, long before such population levels are reached, man must look elsewhere for his energy supplies.

Fortunately, technology once again gets us out of our difficulty, for nuclear fuels are available to us in virtually limitless quantities in the form of uranium and thorium for fission, and possibly in the form of deuterium for fusion. The Conway granite in New Hampshire could alone provide fuel for a population of twenty billion persons for 200 years. When we run out of high-grade granites, we can move on to process low-grade granites. Waste rock can be dumped into the holes from which it came and can be used to create new land and areas on bays and on the continental shelf. Waste fission products can be stored in old salt mines.

Actually, a major shift to nuclear fuel might well be necessary long before our supplies of fossil fuels are exhausted. The carbon dioxide concentration in our atmosphere is rapidly increasing as a result of our burning of coal, petroleum, and natural gas, and it is destined to increase still more rapidly in the future. More than likely, any such increase will have a deleterious effect upon our climate, and if this turns out to be the case, use of those fuels will probably be restricted.

Thus, we see that in theory there should be little difficulty in feeding a world population of thirty billion or even 100 billion persons and in providing it with the necessities of life. But can we go even further?

With respect to food, once again technology can come to our rescue, for we have vast areas of the seas to fertilize and farm. Even more important, we will be able to produce synthetic foods in quantity. The constituents of our common oils and fats can already be manufactured on a substantial scale for human consumption and animal feeds. In the not too distant future, we should be able to synthetically produce complete, wholesome foods, thus bypassing the rather cumbersome process of photosynthesis.

Far more difficult than the task of feeding people will be that of cooling the Earth, of dissipating the heat generated by nuclear power plants. It has been suggested that if we were to limit our total energy generation to no more than 5 per cent of the incident solar radiation, little harm would be done. The mean surface temperature of the Earth would rise by about 6 degrees F. A temperature rise much greater than this could be extremely dangerous and should not be permitted until we have learned more about the behavior of our ocean/atmosphere system.

Of course, there will be local heating problems in the vicinity of the power stations. Dr. Weinberg suggests a system of "nuclear parks," each producing about forty million kilowatts of electricity and located on the coast or offshore. A population of 333 billion persons would require 65,000 such parks. The continental United States, with a projected population of close to twenty-five billion persons, would require nearly 5,000 parks spaced at twenty-mile intervals along its coastline.

Again, I want to allay the fears of those who worry about crowding. A population of 333 billion spread uniformly over the land areas of the Earth would give us a population density of only 6,000 persons per square mile, which, after all, is only somewhat greater than the population density in the city of Los Angeles. Just imagine the thrill of flying from Los Angeles to New York and having the landscape look like Los Angeles all the way. Imagine the excitement of driving from Los Angeles to New York on a Santa Monica Freeway 2,800 miles long.

A few years ago Dr. J. H. Fremlin of the University of Birmingham analyzed the problem of population density and concluded that several stages of development might be possible beyond the several-hundred-billion-person level of population. He conceives of hermetically sealing the outer surface of the planet and of using pumps to transfer heat to the solid outer skin from which it would be radiated directly into space. Combining this with a roof over the oceans to prevent excessive evaporation of water and to provide additional living space, he feels it would be possible to accommodate about 100 persons per square yard, thus giving a total population of about sixty million billion persons. But, frankly, I consider this proposal visionary. Being basically conservative, I doubt that the human population will ever get much above the 333-billion-person level.

Now some readers might be thinking that I am writing nonsense, and they are right. My facts are correct; the conclusions I have drawn from those facts are correct. Yet, I have truthfully been writing nonsense. Specifically, I have given only *some* of the facts. Those facts that I have omitted alter the conclusions considerably.

I have presented only what is deemed possible by scientists from an energetic or thermodynamic point of view. An analogy would be for me to announce that I have calculated that in principle all men should be able to leap ten feet into the air. Obviously, such an announcement would not be followed by a sudden, frenzied, worldwide demonstration of people showing their leaping capabilities. Some people have sore feet; others have inadequate muscles; most haven't the slightest desire to leap into the air. The calculation might be correct, but the enthusiasm for jumping and the ability to jump might be very low. The problem is the behavior of people rather than that of inanimate matter.

We are confronted by the brutal fact that humanity today doesn't really know how to cope with the problems presented by three-and-a-half billion persons, let alone 333 billion. More than two-thirds of the present human population is poor in the material sense and is malnourished. The affluent one-third is, with breathtaking rapidity, becoming even more affluent. Two separate and distinct societies have emerged in the world, and they are becoming increasingly distinct and separated. Numerically the largest is the culture of the poor, composed of some 2,500 million persons. Numerically the smallest is the culture of the rich, composed of some 1,000 million persons. On the surface, the rich countries would appear to have it made; in historical perspective, their average per capita incomes are enormous. Their technological competence is unprecedented. Yet, they have problems that might well prove insoluble.

The most serious problem confronting the rich countries today is nationalism. We fight among each other and arm ourselves in order to do so more effectively. The Cold War has become a way of life, as is reflected in military budgets. Today the governments of the United States and the Soviet Union spend more on their respective military establishments than they do on either education or health —indeed a scandalous situation but, even worse, an explosive one.

All of the rich countries are suffering from problems of growth. Although the rates of population proliferation in these areas are not large, per capita consumption is increasing rapidly. Today an average "population unit" in the United States is quite different from one in the primitive world. Originally, a unit of population was simply a human being whose needs could be met by "eating" 2,500 calories and 60 grams of protein a day. Add to this some simple shelter, some clothing, and a small fire, and his needs were taken care of. A population unit today consists of a human being wrapped in tons of steel, copper, aluminum, lead, tin, zinc, and plastics. This new creature requires far more than food to keep it alive and functioning. Each day it gobbles up sixty pounds of coal or its equivalent, three pounds of raw steel, plus many pounds of other materials. Far from getting all of this food from his own depleted resources, he ranges abroad, much as the hunters of old, and obtains raw supplies in other parts of the world, more often than not in the poorer countries.

Industrial societies the world over are changing with unprecedented speed as the result of accelerated technological change, and they are becoming increasingly complex. All of them are encountering severe problems with their cities, which were designed within the framework of one technology and are falling apart at the seams within the framework of another.

The technological and social complexities of industrial society—composed as it is of vast interlocking networks of mines, factories, transportation systems, power grids, and communication networks, all operated by people—make it extremely vulnerable to disruption. Indeed, during the past year we have seen that the United States is far more vulnerable to labor strikes[1] than North Vietnam is to air strikes. This vulnerability may eventually prove to be our undoing.

A concomitant of our affluence has been pollution. That which goes into a system must eventually come out; as our society has consumed more, it has excreted more. Given adequate supplies of energy and the necessary technology, such problems can be handled from a technical point of view. But it is by no means clear that we are about to solve these problems from a social or political point of view.

Although we know that theoretically we can derive our sustenance from the leanest of earth substances, such as seawater and rock, the fact remains that with respect to the raw materials needed for a highly industrialized society the research essential to the development of the necessary technology has hardly begun. Besides, it is

1. In 1970.

less expensive for the rich countries to extract their sustenance from the poor ones.

As to the poor countries with their rapidly increasing populations, I fail to see how, in the long run, they can lift themselves up by their own boot-straps. In the absence of outside help commensurate with their needs, I suspect they will fail, and the world will become permanently divided into the rich and the poor—at least until such time as the rich, in their stupidity, blow themselves up.

One of the most difficult problems in the poor countries is that of extremely rapid population growth. If an economy grows only as fast as its population, the average well-being of the people does not improve—and indeed this situation prevails in many parts of the world. Equally important, rapid growth produces tremendous dislocations—physical, social, and economic. It is important to understand that the major population problem confronting the poor countries today is not so much the actual number of people as it is rapid growth rates. Clearly, if development is to take place, birth rates must be reduced.

Unfortunately, it is not clear just how birth rates can be brought down in these areas. Even with perfect contraceptives, there must be motivation upon the part of individuals, and in many areas this appears to be lacking. Some people say that economic development is necessary to produce the motivation, and they might be right. In any event, the solution will not be a simple one.

Although I am pessimistic about the future, I do not consider the situation to be by any means hopeless. I am convinced that our problems both here and abroad are soluble. But if they are ever solved, it will be because all of us reorient our attitudes away from those of our parents and more toward those of our children. I am convinced that young people today more often than not have a clearer picture of the world and its problems than do their elders. They are questioning our vast military expenditures and ask whether the Cold War is really necessary. They question the hot war in which we have become so deeply involved. They are questioning our concepts of nationalism, materialism, and laissez faire. It is just such questioning on the part of the young that gives me hope.

If this questioning persists, I foresee the emergence of a new human attitude in which people the world over work together to transform anarchy into law, to decrease dramatically military expenditures, to lower rates of population growth to zero, and to build an equitable world economy, so that all people can lead free and abundant lives in harmony with nature and with each other.

GARRETT HARDIN
The Tragedy of the Commons

At the end of a thoughtful article on the future of nuclear war, Wiesner and York[1] concluded that: "Both sides in the arms race are . . . confronted by the dilemma of steadily increasing military power and steadily decreasing national security. *It is our considered professional judgment that this dilemma has no technical solution.* If the great powers continue to look for solutions in the area of science and technology only, the result will be to worsen the situation."

I would like to focus your attention not on the subject of the article (national security in a nuclear world) but on the kind of conclusion they reached, namely that there is no technical solution to the problem. An implicit and almost universal assumption of discussions published in professional and semipopular scientific journals is that the problem under discussion has a technical solution. A technical solution may be defined as one that requires a change only in the techniques of the natural sciences, demanding little or nothing in the way of change in human values or ideas or morality.

In our day (though not in earlier times) technical solutions are always welcome. Because of previous failures in prophecy, it takes courage to assert that a desired technical solution is not possible. Wiesner and York exhibited this courage; publishing in a science journal, they insisted that the solution to the problem was not to be found in the natural sciences. They cautiously qualified their statement with the phrase, "It is our considered professional judgment. . . ." Whether they were right or not is not the concern of the present article. Rather, the concern here is with the important concept of a class of human problems which can be called "no technical solution problems," and, more specifically, with the identification and discussion of one of these.

It is easy to show that the class is not a null class. Recall the game of tick-tack-toe. Consider the problem, "How can I win the game of tick-tack-toe?" It is well known that I cannot, if I assume (in keeping with the conventions of game theory) that my opponent understands the game perfectly. Put another way, there is no "technical solution" to the problem. I can win only by giving a radical meaning to the word "win." I can hit my opponent over the head; or I can drug him; or I can falsify the records. Every way in which I "win" involves, in some sense, an abandonment of the game, as we intuitively understand it. (I can also, of course, openly

1. J. B. Wiesner and H. F. York, *Sci. Amer.* 211 (No. 4), 27 (1964) [Hardin's note].

abandon the game—refuse to play it. This is what most adults do.)

The class of "no technical solution problems" has members. My thesis is that the "population problem," as conventionally conceived, is a member of this class. How it is conventionally conceived needs some comment. It is fair to say that most people who anguish over the population problem are trying to find a way to avoid the evils of overpopulation without relinquishing any of the privileges they now enjoy. They think that farming the seas or developing new strains of wheat will solve the problem—technologically. I try to show here that the solution they seek cannot be found. The population problem cannot be solved in a technical way, any more than can the problem of winning the game of tick-tack-toe.

What Shall We Maximize?

Population, as Malthus said, naturally tends to grow "geometrically," or, as we would now say, exponentially. In a finite world this means that the per capita share of the world's goods must steadily decrease. Is ours a finite world?

A fair defense can be put forward for the view that the world is infinite; or that we do not know that it is not. But, in terms of the practical problems that we must face in the next few generations with the foreseeable technology, it is clear that we will greatly increase human misery if we do not, during the immediate future, assume that the world available to the terrestrial human population is finite. "Space" is no escape.[2]

A finite world can support only a finite population; therefore, population growth must eventually equal zero. (The case of perpetual wide fluctuations above and below zero is a trivial variant that need not be discussed.) When this condition is met, what will be the situation of mankind? Specifically, can Bentham's goal of "the greatest good for the greatest number" be realized?

No—for two reasons, each sufficient by itself. The first is a theoretical one. It is not mathematically possible to maximize for two (or more) variables at the same time. This was clearly stated by von Neumann and Morgenstern,[3] but the principle is implicit in the theory of partial differential equations, dating back at least to D'Alembert (1717–1783).

The second reason springs directly from biological facts. To live, any organism must have a source of energy (for example, food). This energy is utilized for two purposes: mere maintenance and work. For man, maintenance of life requires about 1600 kilo-calories a day ("maintenance calories"). Anything that he does over and

2. G. Hardin, *J. Hered.* 50, 68 (1959); S. von Hoerner, *Science*, 137, 18 (1962) [Hardin's note].

3. J. von Neumann and O. Morgenstern, *Theory of Games and Economic Behavior* (Princeton Univ. Press, Princeton, N.J., 1947), p. 11 [Hardin's note].

above merely staying alive will be defined as work, and is supported by "work calories" which he takes in. Work calories are used not only for what we call work in common speech; they are also required for all forms of enjoyment, from swimming and automobile racing to playing music and writing poetry. If our goal is to maximize population it is obvious what we must do: We must make the work calories per person approach as close to zero as possible. No gourmet meals, no vacations, no sports, no music, no literature, no art. . . . I think that everyone will grant, without argument or proof, that maximizing population does not maximize goods. Bentham's goal is impossible.

In reaching this conclusion I have made the usual assumption that it is the acquisition of energy that is the problem. The appearance of atomic energy has led some to question this assumption. However, given an infinite source of energy, population growth still produces an inescapable problem. The problem of the acquisition of energy is replaced by the problem of its dissipation, as J. H. Fremlin has so wittily shown.[4] The arithmetic signs in the analysis are, as it were, reversed; but Bentham's goal is still unobtainable.

The optimum population is, then, less than the maximum. The difficulty of defining the optimum is enormous; so far as I know, no one has seriously tackled this problem. Reaching an acceptable and stable solution will surely require more than one generation of hard analytical work—and much persuasion.

We want the maximum good per person; but what is good? To one person it is wilderness, to another it is ski lodges for thousands. To one it is estuaries to nourish ducks for hunters to shoot; to another it is factory land. Comparing one good with another is, we usually say, impossible because goods are incommensurable. Incommensurables cannot be compared.

Theoretically this may be true; but in real life incommensurables *are* commensurable. Only a criterion of judgment and a system of weighting are needed. In nature the criterion is survival. Is it better for a species to be small and hideable, or large and powerful? Natural selection commensurates the incommensurables. The compromise achieved depends on a natural weighting of the values of the variables.

Man must imitate this process. There is no doubt that in fact he already does, but unconsciously. It is when the hidden decisions are made explicit that the arguments begin. The problem for the years ahead is to work out an acceptable theory of weighting. Synergistic effects, nonlinear variation, and difficulties in discounting the future make the intellectual problem difficult, but not (in principle) insoluble.

4. J. H. Fremlin, *New Sci.*, No. 415 (1964), p. 285 [Hardin's note].

Has any cultural group solved this practical problem at the present time, even on an intuitive level? One simple fact proves that none has: there is no prosperous population in the world today that has, and has had for some time, a growth rate of zero. Any people that has intuitively identified its optimum point will soon reach it, after which its growth rate becomes and remains zero.

Of course, a positive growth rate might be taken as evidence that a population is below its optimum. However, by any reasonable standards, the most rapidly growing populations on earth today are (in general) the most miserable. This association (which need not be invariable) casts doubt on the optimistic assumption that the positive growth rate of a population is evidence that it has yet to reach its optimum.

We can make little progress in working toward optimum population size until we explicitly exorcize the spirit of Adam Smith in the field of practical demography. In economic affairs, *The Wealth of Nations* (1776) popularized the "invisible hand," the idea that an individual who "intends only his own gain," is, as it were, "led by an invisible hand to promote . . . the public interest."[5] Adam Smith did not assert that this was invariably true, and perhaps neither did any of his followers. But he contributed to a dominant tendency of thought that has ever since interfered with positive action based on rational analysis, namely, the tendency to assume that decisions reached individually will, in fact, be the best decisions for an entire society. If this assumption is correct it justifies the continuance of our present policy of laissez-faire in reproduction. If it is correct we can assume that men will control their individual fecundity so as to produce the optimum population. If the assumption is not correct, we need to reexamine our individual freedoms to see which ones are defensible.

Tragedy of Freedom in a Commons

The rebuttal to the invisible hand in population control is to be found in a scenario first sketched in a little-known pamphlet[6] in 1833 by a mathematical amateur named William Forster Lloyd (1794–1852). We may well call it "the tragedy of the commons," using the word "tragedy" as the philosopher Whitehead used it:[7] "The essence of dramatic tragedy is not unhappiness. It resides in the solemnity of the remorseless working of things." He then goes on to say, "This inevitableness of destiny can only be illustrated in

5. A. Smith, *The Wealth of Nations* (Modern Library, New York, 1937), p. 423 [Hardin's note].

6. W. F. Lloyd, *Two Lectures on the Checks to Population* (Oxford Univ. Press, Oxford, England, 1833), reprinted (in part) in *Population, Evolution, and Birth Control*, G. Hardin, ed. (Freeman, San Francisco, 1964), p. 37 [Hardin's note].

7. A. N. Whitehead, *Science and the Modern World* (Mentor, New York, 1948), p. 17 [Hardin's note].

terms of human life by incidents which in fact involve unhappiness. For it is only by them that the futility of escape can be made evident in the drama."

The tragedy of the commons develops in this way. Picture a pasture open to all. It is to be expected that each herdsman will try to keep as many cattle as possible on the commons. Such an arrangement may work reasonably satisfactorily for centuries because tribal wars, poaching, and disease keep the numbers of both man and beast well below the carrying capacity of the land. Finally, however, comes the day of reckoning, that is, the day when the long-desired goal of social stability becomes a reality. At this point, the inherent logic of the commons remorselessly generates tragedy.

As a rational being, each herdsman seeks to maximize his gain. Explicitly or implicitly, more or less consciously, he asks, "What is the utility *to me* of adding one more animal to my herd?" This utility has one negative and one positive component.

1. The positive component is a function of the increment of one animal. Since the herdsman receives all the proceeds from the sale of the additional animal, the positive utility is nearly $+1$.

2. The negative component is a function of the additional overgrazing created by one more animal. Since, however, the effects of overgrazing are shared by all the herdsmen, the negative utility for any particular decision-making herdsman is only a fraction of -1.

Adding together the component partial utilities, the rational herdsman concludes that the only sensible course for him to pursue is to add another animal to his herd. And another; and another.... But this is the conclusion reached by each and every rational herdsman sharing a commons. Therein is the tragedy. Each man is locked into a system that compels him to increase his herd without limit—in a world that is limited. Ruin is the destination toward which all men rush, each pursuing his own best interest in a society that believes in the freedom of the commons. Freedom in a commons brings ruin to all.

Some would say that this is a platitude. Would that it were! In a sense, it was learned thousands of years ago, but natural selection favors the forces of psychological denial.[8] The individual benefits as an individual from his ability to deny the truth even though society as a whole, of which he is a part, suffers. Education can counteract the natural tendency to do the wrong thing, but the inexorable succession of generations requires that the basis for this knowledge be constantly refreshed.

A simple incident that occured a few years ago in Leominister, Massachusetts, shows how perishable the knowledge is. During the Christmas shopping season the parking meters downtown were cov-

---

8. G. Hardin, Ed. *Population, Evolu- tion, and Birth Conrtol* (Freeman, San   Francisco, 1964), 56 [Hardin's note].

ered with plastic bags that bore tags reading: "Do not open until after Christmas. Free parking courtesy of the mayor and city council." In other words, facing the prospect of an increased demand for already scarce space, the city fathers reinstituted the system of the commons. Cynically, we suspect that they gained more votes than they lost by this retrogressive act.)

In an approximate way, the logic of the commons has been understood for a long time, perhaps since the discovery of agriculture or the invention of private property in real estate. But it is understood mostly only in special cases which are not sufficiently generalized. Even at this late date, cattlemen leasing national land on the western ranges demonstrate no more than an ambivalent understanding, in constantly pressuring federal authorities to increase the head count to the point where overgrazing produces erosion and weed-dominance. Likewise, the oceans of the world continue to suffer from the survival of the philosophy of the commons. Maritime nations still respond automatically to the shibboleth of the "freedom of the seas." Professing to believe in the "inexhaustible resources of the oceans," they bring species after species of fish and whales closer to extinction.[9]

The national parks present another instance of the working out of the tragedy of the commons. At present, they are open to all, without limit. The parks themselves are limited in extent—there is only one Yosemite Valley—whereas population seeems to grow without limit. The values that visitors seek in the parks are steadily eroded. Plainly, we must soon cease to treat the parks as commons or they will be of no value to anyone.

What shall we do? We have several options. We might sell them off as private property. We might keep them as public property, but allocate the right to enter them. The allocation might be on the basis of wealth, by the use of an auction system. It might be on the basis of merit, as defined by some agreed-upon standards. It might be by lottery. Or it might be on a first-come, first-served basis, administered to long queues. These, I think, are all the reasonable possibilities. They are all objectionable. But we must choose —or acquiesce in the destruction of the commons that we call our national parks.

Pollution

In a reverse way, the tragedy of the commons reappears in problems of pollution. Here it is not a question of taking something out of the commons, but of putting something in—sewage, or chemical, radioactive, and heat wastes into water; noxious and dangerous fumes into the air; and distracting and unpleasant advertising signs

9. S. McVay, *Sci. Amer.* 216 (No. 8), 13 (1966) [Hardin's note].

into the line of sight. The calculations of utility are much the same as before. The rational man finds that his share of the cost of the wastes he discharges into the commons is less than the cost of purifying his wastes before releasing them. Since this is true for everyone, we are locked into a system of "fouling our own nest," so long as we behave only as independent, rational, free-enterprisers.

The tragedy of the commons as a food basket is averted by private property, or something formally like it. But the air and waters surrounding us cannot readily be fenced, and so the tragedy of the commons as a cesspool must be prevented by different means, by coercive laws or taxing devices that make it cheaper for the polluter to treat his pollutants than to discharge them untreated. We have not progressed as far with the solution of this problem as we have with the first. Indeed, our particular concept of private property, which deters us from exhausting the positive resources of the earth, favors pollution. The owner of a factory on the bank of a stream—whose property extends to the middle of the stream—often has difficulty seeing why it is not his natural right to muddy the waters flowing past his door. The law, always behind the times, requires elaborate stitching and fitting to adapt it to this newly perceived aspect of the commons.

The pollution problem is a consequence of population. It did not much matter how a lonely American frontiersman disposed of his waste. "Flowing water purifies itself every ten miles," my grandfather used to say, and the myth was near enough to the truth when he was a boy, for there were not too many people. But as population became denser, the natural chemical and biological recycling processes became overloaded, calling for a redefinition of property rights.

How to Legislate Temperance?

Analysis of the pollution problem as a function of population density uncovers a not generally recognized principle of morality, namely: *the morality of an act is a function of the state of the system at the time it is performed.*[1] Using the commons as a cesspool does not harm the general public under frontier conditions, because there is no public; the same behavior in a metropolis is unbearable. A hundred and fifty years ago a plainsman could kill an American bison, cut out only the tongue for his dinner, and discard the rest of the animal. He was not in any important sense being wasteful. Today, with only a few thousand bison left, we would be appalled at such behavior.

In passing, it is worth noting that the morality of an act cannot be determined from a photograph. One does not know whether a

---

1. J. Fletcher, *Situation Ethics* (Westminster, Philadelphia, 1966) [Hardin's note].

man killing an elephant or setting fire to the grassland is harming others until one knows the total system in which his act appears. "One picture is worth a thousand words," said an ancient Chinese; but it may take 10,000 words to validate it. It is as tempting to ecologists as it is to reformers in general to try to persuade others by way of the photographic shortcut. But the essence of an argument cannot be photographed: it must be presented rationally—in words.

That morality is system-sensitive escaped the attention of most codifiers of ethics in the past. "Thou shalt not . . ." is the form of traditional ethical directives which make no allowance for particular circumstances. The laws of our society follow the pattern of ancient ethics, and therefore are poorly suited to governing a complex, crowded, changeable world. Our epicyclic solution is to augment statutory law with administrative law. Since it is practically impossible to spell out all the conditions under which it is safe to burn trash in the back yard or to run an automobile without smog-control, by law we delegate the details to bureaus. The result is administrative law, which is rightly feared for an ancient reason—*Quis custodiet ipsos custodes?*—"Who shall watch the watchers themselves?" John Adams said that we must have "a government of laws and not men." Bureau administrators, trying to evaluate the morality of acts in the total system, are singularly liable to corruption, producing a government by men, not laws.

Prohibition is easy to legislate (though not necessarily to enforce); but how do we legislate temperance? Experience indicates that it can be accomplished best through the mediation of administrative law. We limit possibilities unnecessarily if we suppose that the sentiment of *Quis custodiet* denies us the use of administrative law. We should rather retain the phrase as a perpetual reminder of fearful dangers we cannot avoid. The great challenge facing us now is to invent the corrective feedbacks that are needed to keep custodians honest. We must find ways to legitimate the needed authority of both the custodians and the corrective feedbacks.

Freedom to Breed Is Intolerable

The tragedy of the commons is involved in population problems in another way. In a world governed solely by the principle of "dog eat dog"—if indeed there ever was such a world—how many children a family had would not be a matter of public concern. Parents who bred too exuberantly would leave fewer descendants, not more, because they would be unable to care adequately for their children. David Lack and others have found that such a negative feedback demonstrably controls the fecundity of birds.[2] But men are not

2. D. Lack, *The Natural Regulation of Animal Numbers* (Clarendon Press, Oxford, 1954 [Hardin's note].

birds, and have not acted like them for millenniums, at least.

If each human family were dependent only on its own resources; *if* the children of improvident parents starved to death; *if*, thus, overbreeding brought its own "punishment" to the germ line—*then* there would be no public interest in controlling the breeding of families. But our society is deeply committed to the welfare state,[3] and hence is confronted with another aspect of the tragedy of the commons.

In a welfare state, how shall we deal with the family, the religion, the race, or the class (or indeed any distinguishable and cohesive group) that adopts overbreeding as a policy to secure its own aggrandizement?[4] To couple the concept of freedom to breed with the belief that everyone born has an equal right to the commons is to lock the world into a tragic course of action.

Unfortunately this is just the course of action that is being pursued by the United Nations. In late 1967, some thirty nations agreed to the following:[5]

The Universal Declaration of Human Rights describes the family as the natural and fundamental unit of society. It follows that any choice and decision with regard to the size of the family must irrevocably rest with the family itself, and cannot be made by anyone else.

It is painful to have to deny categorically the validity of this right; denying it, one feels as uncomfortable as a resident of Salem, Massachusetts, who denied the reality of witches in the seventeenth century. At the present time, in liberal quarters, something like a taboo acts to inhibit criticism of the United Nations. There is a feeling that the United Nations is "our last and best hope," that we shouldn't find fault with it; we shouldn't play into the hands of the archconservatives. However, let us not forget what Robert Louis Stevenson said: "The truth that is suppressed by friends is the readiest weapon of the enemy." If we love the truth we must openly deny the validity of the Universal Declaration of Human Rights, even though it is promoted by the United Nations. We should also join with Kingsley Davis[6] in attempting to get Planned Parenthood-World Population to see the error of its ways in embracing the same tragic ideal.

Conscience Is Self-Eliminating

It is a mistake to think that we can control the breeding of mankind in the long run by an appeal to conscience. Charles Galton Darwin made this point when he spoke on the centennial of the

3. H. Girvetz, *From Wealth to Welfare* (Stanford Univ. Press, Stanford, Calif., 1950) [Hardin's note].

4. G. Hardin, *Perspec. Biol. Med.* 6, 366 (1963) [Hardin's note].

5. U. Thant, *Int. Planned Parenthood News*, No. 168 (February, 1968), p. 3 [Hardin's note].

6. K. Davis, *Science* 158, 730 (1967) [Hardin's note].

publication of his grandfather's great book. The argument is straightforward and Darwinian.

People vary. Confronted with appeals to limit breeding, some people will undoubtedly respond to the plea more than others. Those who have more children will produce a larger fraction of the next generation than those with more susceptible consciences. The difference will be accentuated, generation by generation.

In C. G. Darwin's words: "It may well be that it would take hundreds of generations for the progenitive instinct to develop in this way, but if it should do so, nature would have taken her revenge, and the variety *Homo contracipiens*[7] would become extinct and would be replaced by the variety *Homo progenitivus*."[8]

The argument assumes that conscience or the desire for children (no matter which) is hereditary—but hereditary only in the most general formal sense. The result will be the same whether the attitude is transmitted through germ cells, or exosomatically, to use A. J. Lotka's term. (If one denies the latter possibility as well as the former, then what's the point of education?) The argument has here been stated in the context of the population problem, but it applies equally well to any instance in which society appeals to an individual exploiting a commons to restrain himself for the general good—by means of his conscience. To make such an appeal is to set up a selective system that works toward the elimination of conscience from the race.

Pathogenic Effects of Conscience

The long-term disadvantage of an appeal to conscience should be enough to condemn it; but it has serious short-term disadvantages as well. If we ask a man who is exploiting a commons to desist "in the name of conscience," what are we saying to him? What does he hear?—not only at the moment but also in the wee small hours of the night when, half asleep, he remembers not merely the words we used but also the nonverbal communications cues we gave him unawares? Sooner or later, consciously or subconsciously, he senses that he has received two communications, and that they are contradictory: (i) (intended communication) "If you don't do as we ask, we will openly condemn you for not acting like a responsible citizen"; (ii) (the unintended communication) "If you *do* behave as we ask, we will secretly condemn you for a simpleton who can be shamed into standing aside while the rest of us exploit the commons."

Every man then is caught in what Bateson has called a "double bind." Bateson and his coworkers have made a plausible case for

7. *Homo contracipiens* means "non-reproductive man," *homo progenitivus* "reproductive man."

8. S. Tax, ed., *Evolution after Darwin* (Univ. of Chicago Press, Chicago, 1960), vol. 2, p. 469 [Hardin's note].

viewing the double bind as an important causative factor in the genesis of schizophrenia.[9] The double bind may not always be so damaging, but it always endangers the mental health of anyone to whom it is applied. "A bad conscience," said Nietzsche, "is a kind of illness."

To conjure up a conscience in others is tempting to anyone who wishes to extend his control beyond the legal limits. Leaders at the highest level succumb to this temptation. Has any president during the past generation failed to call on labor unions to moderate voluntarily their demands for higher wages, or to steel companies to honor voluntary guidelines on prices? I can recall none. The rhetoric used on such occasions is designed to produce feelings of guilt in noncooperators.

For centuries it was assumed without proof that guilt was a valuable, perhaps even an indispensable, ingredient of the civilized life. Now, in this post-Freudian world, we doubt it.

Paul Goodman speaks from the modern point of view when he says: "No good has ever come from feeling guilty, neither intelligence, policy, nor compassion. The guilty do not pay attention to the object but only to themselves, and not even to their own interests, which might make sense, but to their anxieties."[1]

One does not have to be a professional psychiatrist to see the consequences of anxiety. We in the Western world are just emerging from a dreadful two-centuries-long Dark Ages of Eros that was sustained partly by prohibition laws, but perhaps more effectively by the anxiety-generating mechanisms of education. Alex Comfort has told the story well in *The Anxiety Makers*;[2] it is not a pretty one.

Since proof is difficult, we may even concede that the results of anxiety may sometimes, from certain points of view, be desirable. The larger question we should ask is whether, as a matter of policy, we should ever encourage the use of a technique the tendency (if not the intention) of which is psychologically pathogenic. We hear much talk these days of responsible parenthood; the coupled words are incorporated into the titles of some organizations devoted to birth control. Some people have proposed massive propaganda campaigns to instill responsibility into the nation's (or the world's) breeders. But what is the meaning of the word responsibility in this context? Is it not merely a synonym for the word conscience? When we use the word responsibility in the absence of substantial sanctions are we not trying to browbeat a free man in a commons into acting against his own interest? Responsibility is a verbal counterfeit for a substantial *quid pro quo*. It is an attempt to get some-

9. G. Bateson, D. D. Jackson, J. Haley, J. Weakland, *Behav. Sci.* 1, 251 (1956) [Hardin's note].
1. P. Goodman, *New York Rev. Books*

10 (18), 22 (23 May 1968) [Hardin's note].
2. A. Comfort, *The Anxiety Makers* (Nelson, London, 1967) [Hardin's note].

thing for nothing.

If the word responsibility is to be used at all, I suggest that it be in the sense Charles Frankel uses it.[3] "Responsibility," says this philosopher, "is the product of definite social arrangements." Notice that Frankel calls for social arrangements—not propaganda.

Mutual Coercion Mutually Agreed Upon

The social arrangements that produce responsibility are arrangements that create coercion, of some sort. Consider bank-robbing. The man who takes money from a bank acts as if the bank were a commons. How do we prevent such action? Certainly not by trying to control his behavior solely by a verbal appeal to his sense of responsibility. Rather than rely on propaganda we follow Frankel's lead and insist that a bank is not a commons; we seek the definite social arrangements that will keep it from becoming a commons. That we thereby infringe on the freedom of would-be robbers we neither deny nor regret.

The morality of bank-robbing is particularly easy to understand because we accept complete prohibition of this activity. We are willing to say "Thou shalt not rob banks," without providing for exceptions. But temperance also can be created by coercion. Taxing is a good coercive device. To keep downtown shoppers temperate in their use of parking space we introduce parking meters for short periods, and traffic fines for longer ones. We need not actually forbid a citizen to park as long as he wants to; we need merely make it increasingly expensive for him to do so. Not prohibition, but carefully biased options are what we offer him. A Madison Avenue man might call this persuasion; I prefer the greater candor of the word coercion.

Coercion is a dirty word to most liberals now, but it need not forever be so. As with the four-letter words, its dirtiness can be cleansed away by exposure to the light, by saying it over and over without apology or embarrassment. To many, the word coercion implies arbitrary decisions of distant and irresponsible bureaucrats; but this is not a necessary part of its meaning. The only kind of coercion I recommend is mutual coercion, mutually agreed upon by the majority of the people affected.

To say that we mutually agree to coercion is not to say that we are required to enjoy it, or even to pretend we enjoy it. Who enjoys taxes? We all grumble about them. But we accept compulsory taxes because we recognize that voluntary taxes would favor the conscienceless. We institute and (grumblingly) support taxes and other coercive devices to escape the horror of the commons.

3. C. Frankel, *The Case for Modern Man* (Harper, New York, 1955), p. 203   [Hardin's note].

An alternative to the commons need not be perfectly just to be preferable. With real estate and other material goods, the alternative we have chosen is the institution of private property coupled with legal inheritance. Is this system perfectly just? As a genetically trained biologist I deny that it is. It seems to me that, if there are to be differences in individual inheritance, legal possession should be perfectly correlated with biological inheritance—that those who are biologically more fit to be the custodians of property and power should legally inherit more. But genetic recombination continually makes a mockery of the doctrine of "like father, like son" implicit in our laws of legal inheritance. An idiot can inherit millions, and a trust fund can keep his estate intact. We must admit that our legal system of private property plus inheritance is unjust—but we put up with it because we are not convinced, at the moment, that anyone has invented a better system. The alternative of the commons is too horrifying to contemplate. Injustice is preferable to total ruin.

It is one of the peculiarities of the warfare between reform and the status quo that it is thoughtlessly governed by a double standard. Whenever a reform measure is proposed it is often defeated when its opponents triumphantly discover a flaw in it. As Kingsley Davis has pointed out,[4] worshippers of the status quo sometimes imply that no reform is possible without unanimous agreement, an implication contrary to historical fact. As nearly as I can make out, automatic rejection of proposed reforms is based on one of two unconscious assumptions: (i) that the status quo is perfect; or (ii) that the choice we face is between reform and no action; if the proposed reform is imperfect, we presumably should take no action at all, while we wait for a perfect proposal.

But we can never do nothing. That which we have done for thousands of years is also action. It also produces evils. Once we are aware that the status quo is action, we can then compare its discoverable advantages and disadvantages with the predicted advantages and disadvantages of the proposed reform, discounting as best we can for our lack of experience. On the basis of such a comparison, we can make a rational decision which will not involve the unworkable assumption that only perfect systems are tolerable.

Recognition of Necessity

Perhaps the simplest summary of this analysis of man's population problems is this: the commons, if justifiable at all, is justifiable only under conditions of low-population density. As the human

4. J. D. Roslansky, *Genetics and the Future of Man* (Appleton-Century-Crofts, New York, 1966), p. 177 [Hardin's note].

population has increased, the commons has had to be abandoned in one aspect after another.

First we abandoned the commons in food gathering, enclosing farm land and restricting pastures and hunting and fishing areas. These restrictions are still not complete throughout the world.

Somewhat later we saw that the commons as a place for waste disposal would also have to be abandoned. Restrictions on the disposals of domestic sewage are widely accepted in the Western world; we are still struggling to close the commons to pollution by automobiles, factories, insecticide sprayers, fertilizing operations, and atomic energy installations.

In a still more embryonic state is our recognition of the evils of the commons in matters of pleasure. There is almost no restriction on the propagation of sound waves in the public medium. The shopping public is assaulted with mindless music, without its consent. Our government is paying out billions of dollars to create supersonic transport which will disturb 50,000 people for every one person who is whisked from coast to coast three hours faster. Advertisers muddy the airwaves of radio and television and pollute the view of travelers. We are a long way from outlawing the commons in matters of pleasure. Is this because our Puritan inheritance makes us view pleasure as something of a sin, and pain (that is, the pollution of advertising) as the sign of virtue?

Every new enclosure of the commons involves the infringement of somebody's personal liberty. Infringements made in the distant past are accepted because no contemporary complains of a loss. It is the newly proposed infringements that we vigorously oppose; cries of "rights" and "freedom" fill the air. But what does "freedom" mean? When men mutually agreed to pass laws against robbing, mankind became more free, not less so. Individuals locked into the logic of the commons are free only to bring on universal ruin; once they see the necessity of mutual coercion, they become free to pursue other goals. I believe it was Hegel who said, "Freedom is the recognition of necessity."

The most important aspect of necessity that we must now recognize, is the necessity of abandoning the commons in breeding. No technical solution can rescue us from the misery of overpopulation. Freedom to breed will bring ruin to all. At the moment, to avoid hard decisions many of us are tempted to propagandize for conscience and responsible parenthood. The temptation must be resisted, because an appeal to independently acting consciences selects for the the disappearance of all conscience in the long run, and an increase in anxiety in the short.

The only way we can preserve and nurture other and more precious freedoms is by relinquishing the freedom to breed, and that very soon. "Freedom is the recognition of necessity"—and it is the role of education to reveal to all the necessity of abandoning the freedom to breed. Only so, can we put an end to this aspect of the tragedy of the commons.

ALDO LEOPOLD
The Conservation Ethic[1]

When god-like Odysseus returned from the wars in Troy, he hanged all on one rope some dozen slave-girls of his household whom he suspected of misbehavior during his absence.

This hanging involved no question of propriety, much less of justice. The girls were property. The disposal of property was then, as now, a matter of expedience, not of right and wrong.

Criteria of right and wrong were not lacking from Odysseus' Greece: witness the fidelity of his wife through the long years before at last his black-prowed galleys clove the wine-dark seas for home. The ethical structure of that day covered wives, but had not yet been extended to human chattels. During the three thousand years which have since elapsed, ethical criteria have been extended to many fields of conduct, with corresponding shrinkages in those judged by expediency only.

This extension of ethics, so far studied only by philosophers, is actually a process in ecological evolution. Its sequences may be described in biological as well as philosophical terms. An ethic, biologically, is a limitation on freedom of action in the struggle for existence. An ethic, philosophically, is a differentiation of social from anti-social conduct. These are two definitions of one thing. The thing has its origin in the tendency of interdependent individuals or societies to evolve modes of cooperation. The biologist calls these symbioses. Man elaborated certain advanced symbioses called politics and economics. Like their simpler biological antecedents, they enable individuals or groups to exploit each other in an orderly way. Their first yardstick was expediency.

The complexity of cooperative mechanisms increased with population density, and with the efficiency of tools. It was simpler, for example, to define the antisocial uses of sticks and stones in the days of the mastodons than of bullets and billboards in the age of motors.

At a certain stage of complexity, the human community found

---

1. Fourth Annual John Wesley Powell Lecture, Southwestern Division, American Association for the Advancement of Science, Las Cruces, New Mexico, May 1, 1933.

expediency-yardsticks no longer sufficient. One by one it has evolved and superimposed upon them a set of ethical yardsticks. The first ethics dealt with the relationship between individuals. The Mosaic Decalogue[1] is an example. Later accretions dealt with the relationship between the individual and society. Christianity tries to integrate the individual to society, Democracy to integrate social organization to the individual.

There is as yet no ethic dealing with man's relationship to land and to the non-human animals and plants which grow upon it. Land, like Odysseus' slave-girls, is still property. The land-relation is still strictly economic, entailing privileges but not obligations.

The extension of ethics to this third element in human environment is, if we read evolution correctly, an ecological possibility. It is the third step in a sequence. The first two have already been taken. Civilized man exhibits in his own mind evidence that the third is needed. For example, his sense of right and wrong may be aroused quite as strongly by the desecration of a nearby woodlot as by a famine in China, a near-pogrom in Germany, or the murder of the slavegirls in ancient Greece. Individual thinkers since the days of Ezekiel and Isaiah have asserted that the despoliation of land is not only inexpedient but wrong. Society, however, has not yet affirmed their belief. I regard the present conservation movement as the embryo of such an affirmation. I here discuss why this is, or should be, so.

Some scientists will dismiss this matter forthwith, on the ground that ecology has no relation to right and wrong. To such I reply that science, if not philosophy, should by now have made us cautious about dismissals. An ethic may be regarded as a mode of guidance for meeting ecological situations so new or intricate, or involving such deferred reactions, that the path of social expediency is not discernible to the average individual. Animal instincts are just this. Ethics are possibly a kind of advance social instinct in-the-making.

Whatever the merits of this analogy, no ecologist can deny that our land-relation involves penalties and rewards which the individual does not see, and needs modes of guidance which do not yet exist. Call these what you will, science cannot escape its part in forming them.

Ecology—Its Role in History

A harmonious relation to land is more intricate, and of more consequence to civilization, than the historians of its progress seem to realize. Civilization is not, as they often assume, the enslavement of a stable and constant earth. It is a state of *mutual and interdependent coöperation* between human animals, other animals, plants,

---

1. The ten commandments.

and soils, which may be disrupted at any moment by the failure of any of them. Land-despoliation has evicted nations, and can on occasion do it again. As long as six virgin continents awaited the plow, this was perhaps no tragic matter,—eviction from one piece of soil could be recouped by despoiling another. But there are now wars and rumors of wars which foretell the impending saturation of the earth's best soils and climates. It thus becomes a matter of some importance, at least to ourselves, that our dominion, once gained, be self-perpetuating rather than self-destructive.

This instability of our land-relation calls for example. I will sketch a single aspect of it: the plant succession as a factor in history.

In the years following the Revolution, three groups were contending for control of the Mississippi valley: the native Indians, the French and English traders, and American settlers. Historians wonder what would have happened if the English at Detroit had thrown a little more weight into the Indian side of those tipsy scales which decided the outcome of the Colonial migration into the cane-lands of Kentucky. Yet who ever wondered why the cane-lands, when subjected to the particular mixture of forces represented by the cow, plow, fire, and axe of the pioneer, became blue-grass? What if the plant succession inherent in this "dark and bloody ground" had, under the impact of these forces, given us some worthless sedge, shrub, or weed? Would Boone and Kenton[2] have held out? Would there have been any overflow into Ohio? Any Louisiana Purchase? Any transcontinental union of new states? Any Civil War? Any machine age? Any depression? The subsequent drama of American history, here and elsewhere, hung in large degree on the reaction of particular soils to the impact of particular forces exerted by a particular kind and degree of human occupation. No statesman-biologist selected those forces, nor foresaw their effects. That chain of events which on the Fourth of July we call our National Destiny hung on a "fortuitous concourse of elements," the interplay of which we now dimly decipher *by hindsight only.*

Contrast Kentucky with what hindsight tells us about the Southwest. The impact of occupancy here brought no bluegrass, nor other plant fitted to withstand the bumps and buffetings of misuse. Most of these soils, when grazed, reverted through a successive series of more and more worthless grasses, shrubs, and weeds to a condition of unstable equilibrium. Each recession of plant types bred erosion; each increment to erosion bred a further recession of plants. The result today is a progressive and mutual deterioration, not only of

2. Daniel Boone and Simon Kenton, American frontiersmen; both lived in Boonesboro, Kentucky, during the Revolution.

plants and soils, but of the animal community subsisting thereon. The early settlers did not expect this, on the cienegas[3] of central New Mexico some even cut artificial gullies to hasten it. So subtle has been its progress that few people know anything about it. It is not discussed at polite tea-tables or go-getting luncheon clubs, but only in the arid halls of science.

All civilizations seem to have been conditioned upon whether the plant succession, under the impact of occupancy, gave a stable and habitable assortment of vegetative types, or an unstable and uninhabitable assortment. The swampy forests of Caesar's Gaul were utterly changed by human use—for the better. Moses' land of milk and honey was utterly changed—for the worse. Both changes are the unpremeditated resultant of the impact between ecological and economic forces. We now decipher these reactions retrospectively. What could possibly be more important than to foresee and control them?

We of the machine age admire ourselves for our mechanical ingenuity; we harness cars to the solar energy impounded in carboniferous forests; we fly in mechanical birds; we make the ether carry our words or even our pictures. But are these not in one sense mere parlor tricks compared with our utter ineptitude in keeping land fit to live upon? Our engineering has attained the pearly gates of a near-millennium, but our applied biology still lives in nomad's tents of the stone age. If our system of land-use happens to be self-perpetuating, we stay. If it happens to be self-destructive we move, like Abraham, to pastures new.

Do I overdraw this paradox? I think not. Consider the transcontinental airmail which plies the skyways of the Southwest—a symbol of its final conquest. What does it see? A score of mountain valleys which were green gems of fertility when first described by Coronado, Espejo, Pattie, Abert, Sitgreaves, and Couzens.[4] What are they now? Sandbars, wastes of cobbles and burroweed, a path for torrents. Rivers which Pattie says were clear, now muddy sewers for the wasting fertility of an empire. A "Public Domain," once a velvet carpet of rich buffalo-grass and grama,[5] now an illimitable waste of rattlesnake-bush and tumbleweed, too impoverished to be accepted as a gift by the states within which it lies. Why? Because the ecology of this Southwest happened to be set on a hair-trigger. Because cows eat brush when the grass is gone, and thus postpone the penalties of over-utilization. Because certain grasses, when grazed too closely to bear seed-stalks, are weakened and give way to inferior grasses, and these to inferior shrubs, and these to weeds,

3. Marsh.
4. All led exploratory expeditions to the American southwest.

5. A prairie grass found in the American west.

and these to naked earth. Because rain which spatters upon vege-tated soil stays clear and sinks, while rain which spatters upon deve-getated soil seals its interstices with colloidal mud and hence must run away as floods, cutting the heart out of country as it goes. Are these phenomena any more difficult to foresee than the paths of stars which science deciphers without the error of a single second? Which is the more important to the permanence and welfare of civ-ilization?

I do not here berate the astronomer for his precocity, but rather the ecologist for his lack of it. The days of his cloistered sequestra-tion are over:

> "Whether you will or not,
> You are a king, Tristram, for you are one
> Of the time-tested few that leave the world,
> When they are gone, not the same place it was.
> Mark what you leave."

Unforseen ecological reactions not only make or break history in a few exceptional enterprises—they condition, circumscribe, delimit, and warp all enterprises, both economic and cultural, that pertain to land. In the cornbelt, after grazing and plowing out all the cover in the interests of "clean farming," we grew tearful about wild-life, and spent several decades passing laws for its restoration. We were like Canute commanding the tide. Only recently has research made it clear that the implements for restoration lie not in the legislature, but in the farmer's toolshed. Barbed wire and brains are doing what laws alone failed to do.

In other instances we take credit for shaking down apples which were, in all probability, ecological windfalls. In the Lake States and the Northeast lumbering, pulping, and fire accidentally created some scores of millions of acres of new second growth. At the proper stage we find these thickets full of deer. For this we naively thank the wisdom of our game laws.

In short, the reaction of land to occupancy determines the nature and duration of civilization. In arid climates the land may be destroyed. In all climates the plant succession determines what eco-nomic activities can be supported. Their nature and intensity in turn determine not only the domestic but also the wild plant and animal life, the scenery, and the whole face of nature. We inherit the earth, but within the limits of the soil and the plant succession we also *rebuild* the earth—without plan, without knowledge of its properties, and without understanding of the increasingly coarse and powerful tools which science has placed at our disposal. We are remodelling the Alhambra[7] with a steam-shovel.

7. The fortress palace of the Moorish kings at Granada; constructed 1248–1354.

Ecology and Economics

The conservation movement is, at the very least, an assertion that these interactions between man and land are too important to be left to chance, even that sacred variety of chance known as economic law.

We have three possible controls: Legislation, self-interest, and ethics. Before we can know where and how they will work, we must first understand the reactions. Such understanding arises only from research. At the present moment research, inadequate as it is, has nevertheless piled up a large store of facts which our land using industries are unwilling, or (they claim) unable, to apply. Why? A review of three sample fields will be attempted.

Soil science has so far relied on self-interest as the motive for conservation. The landholder is told that it pays to conserve his soil and its fertility. On good farms this economic formula has improved land-practice, but on poorer soils vast abuses still proceed unchecked. Public acquisition of submarginal soils is being urged as a remedy for their misuse. It has been applied to some extent, but it often comes too late to check erosion, and can hardly hope more than to ameliorate a phenomenon involving in some degree *every square foot* on the continent. Legislative compulsion might work on the best soils where it is least needed, but it seems hopeless on poor soils where the existing economic set-up hardly permits even uncontrolled private enterprise to make a profit. We must face the fact that, by and large, no defensible relationship between man and the soil of his nativity is as yet in sight.

Forestry exhibits another tragedy—or comedy—of *Homo sapiens*, astride the runaway Juggernaut of his own building, trying to be decent to his environment. A new profession was trained in the confident expectation that the shrinkage in virgin timber would, as a matter of self-interest, bring an expansion of timber-cropping. Foresters are cropping timber on certain parcels of poor land which happen to be public, but on the great bulk of private holdings they have accomplished little. Economics won't let them. Why? He would be bold indeed who claimed to know the whole answer, but these parts of it seem agreed upon: modern transport prevents profitable tree-cropping in cut-out regions until virgin stands in all others are first exhausted; substitutes for lumber have undermined confidence in the future need for it; carrying charges on stumpage reserves are so high as to force perennial liquidation, overproduction, depressed prices, and an appalling wastage of unmarketable grades which must be cut to get the higher grades; the mind of the forest owner lacks the point-of-view underlying sustained yield; the low wage-standards on which European forestry rests do not obtain in America.

A few tentative gropings toward industrial forestry were visible before 1929, but these have been mostly swept away by the depression, with the net result that forty years of "campaigning" have left us only such actual tree-cropping as is under-written by public treasuries. Only a blind man could see in this the beginnings of an orderly and harmonious use of the forest resource.

There are those who would remedy this failure by legislative compulsion of private owners. Can a landholder be successfully compelled to raise any crop, let alone a complex long-time crop like a forest, on land the private possession of which is, for the moment at least, a liability? Compulsion would merely hasten the avalanche of tax-delinquent land-titles now being dumped into the public lap.

Another and larger group seeks a remedy in more public ownership. Doubtless we need it—we are getting it whether we need it or not—but how far can it go? We cannot dodge the fact that the forest problem, like the soil problem, *is coextensive with the map of the United States*. How far can we tax other lands and industries to maintain forest lands and industries artificially? How confidently can we set out to run a hundred-yard dash with a twenty foot rope tying our ankle to the starting point? Well, we are bravely "getting set," anyhow.

The trend in wild-life conservation is possibly more encouraging than in either soils or forests. It has suddenly become apparent that farmers, out of self-interest, can be induced to crop game. Game crops are in demand, staple crops are not. For farm-species, therefore, the immediate future is relatively bright. Forest game has profited to some extent by the accidental establishment of new habitat following the decline of forest industries. Migratory game, on the other hand, has lost heavily through drainage and over-shooting; its future is black because motives of self-interest do not apply to the private cropping of birds so mobile that they "belong" to everybody, and hence to nobody. Only governments have interests coextensive with their annual movements, and the divided counsels of conservationists give governments ample alibi for doing little. Governments could crop migratory birds because their marshy habitat is cheap and concentrated, but we get only an annual crop of new hearings on how to divide the fast-dwindling remnant.

These three fields of conservation, while but fractions of the whole, suffice to illustrate the welter of conflicting forces, facts, and opinions which so far comprise the result of the effort to harmonize our machine civilization with the land whence comes its sustenance. We have accomplished little, but we should have learned much. What?

I can see clearly only two things:

First, that the economic cards are stacked against some of the most important reforms in land-use.

Second, that the scheme to circumvent this obstacle by public ownership, while highly desirable and good as far as it goes, can never go far enough. Many will take issue on this, but the issue is between two conflicting conceptions of the end towards which we are working.

One regards conservation as a kind of sacrificial offering, made for us vicariously by bureaus, on lands nobody wants for other purposes, in propitiation for the atrocities which still prevail everywhere else. We have made a real start on this kind of conservation, and we can carry it as far as the tax-string on our leg will reach. Obviously, though, it conserves our self-respect better than our land. Many excellent people accept it, either because they despair of anything better, or because they fail to see the *universality of the reactions needing control*. That is to say their ecological education is not yet sufficient.

The other concept supports the public program, but regards it as merely extension, teaching, demonstration, an initial nucleus, a means to an end, but not the end itself. The real end is a *universal symbiosis with land*, economic and esthetic, public and private. To this school of thought public ownership is a patch but not a program.

Are we, then, limited to patchwork until such time as Mr. Babbitt[8] has taken his Ph.D. in ecology and esthetics? Or do the new economic formulae offer a short-cut to harmony with our environment?

The Economic Isms

As nearly as I can see, all the new isms—Socialism, Communism, Fascism, and especially the late but not lamented Technocracy—outdo even Capitalism itself in their preoccupation with one thing: The distribution of more machine-made commodities to more people. They all proceed on the theory that if we can all keep warm and full, and all own a Ford and a radio, the good life will follow. Their programs differ only in ways to mobilize machines to this end. Though they despise each other, they are all, in respect of this objective, as identically alike as peas in a pod. They are competitive apostles of a single creed: *salvation by machinery*.

We are here concerned, not with their proposals for adjusting men and machinery to goods, but rather with their lack of any vital proposal for adjusting men and machines to land. To conservationists they offer only the old familiar palliatives: Public ownership and private compulsion. If these are insufficient now, by what magic are they to become sufficient after we change our collective label?

8. Leading character in Sinclair Lewis' novel *Babbitt*; the businessman of ortho- dox outlook and values with no interest in cultural values.

Let us apply economic reasoning to a sample problem and see where it takes us. As already pointed out, there is a huge area which the economist calls submarginal, because it has a minus value for exploitation. In its once-virgin condition, however, it could be "skinned" at a profit. It has been, and as a result erosion is washing it away. What shall we do about it?

By all the accepted tenets of current economics and science we ought to say "let her wash." Why? Because staple land-crops are overproduced, our population curve is flattening out, science is still raising the yields from better lands, we are spending millions from the public treasury to retire unneeded acreage, and here is nature offering to do the same thing free of charge; why not let her do it? This, I say, is economic reasoning. *Yet no man has so spoken.* I cannot help reading a meaning into this fact. To me it means that the average citizen shares in some degree the intuitive and instantaneous contempt with which the conservationist would regard such an attitude. We can, it seems, stomach the burning or plowing-under of over-produced cotton, coffee, or corn, but the destruction of mother-earth, however "sub-marginal," touches something deeper, some sub-economic stratum of the human intelligence wherein lies that something—perhaps the essence of civilization—which Wilson called "the decent opinion of mankind."

The Conservation Movement

We are confronted, then by a contradiction. To build a better motor we tap the uttermost powers of the human brain; to build a better countryside we throw dice. Political systems take no cognizance of this disparity, offer no sufficient remedy. There is, however, a dormant but widespread consciousness that the destruction of land, and of the living things upon it, is wrong. A new minority have espoused an idea called conservation which tends to assert this as a positive principle. Does it contain seeds which are likely to grow?

Its own devotees, I confess, often give apparent grounds for skepticism. We have, as an extreme example, the cult of the barbless hook, which acquires self-esteem by a self-imposed limitation of armaments in catching fish. The limitation is commendable, but the illusion that it has something to do with salvation is as naive as some of the primitive taboos and mortifications which still adhere to religious sects. Such excrescences seem to indicate the whereabouts of a moral problem, however irrelevant they be in either defining or solving it.

Then there is the conservation-booster, who of late has been rewriting the conservation ticket in terms of "tourist-bait." He exhorts us to "conserve outdoor Wisconsin" because if we don't the motorist-on-vacation will streak through to Michigan, leaving us only a cloud of dust. Is Mr. Babbitt trumping up hard-boiled reasons to serve as a screen for doing what he thinks is right? His tenacity suggests that he is after something more than tourists. Have he and other thousands of "conservation workers" labored through all these barren decades fired by a dream of augmenting the sales of sandwiches and gasoline? I think not. Some of these people have hitched their wagon to a star—and that is something.

Any wagon so hitched offers the discerning politician a quick ride to glory. His agility in hopping up and seizing the reins adds little dignity to the cause, but it does add the testimony of his political nose to an important question: is this conservation something people really want? The political objective, to be sure, is often some trivial tinkering with the laws, some useless appropriation, or some pasting of pretty labels on ugly realities. How often, though, does any political action portray the real depth of the idea behind it? For political consumption a new thought must always be reduced to a posture or a phrase. It has happened before that great ideas were heralded by growing-pains in the body politic, semi-comic to those onlookers not yet infected by them. The insignificance of what we conservationists, in our political capacity, say and do, does not detract from the significance of our persistent desire to do something. To turn this desire into productive channels is the task of time, and ecology.

The recent trend in wild-life conservation shows the direction in which ideas are evolving. At the inception of the movement fifty years ago, its underlying thesis was to save species from extermination. The means to this end were a series of restrictive enactments. The duty of the individual was to cherish and extend these enactments, and to see that his neighbor obeyed them. The whole structure was negative and prohibitory. It assumed land to be a constant in the ecological equation. Gun-powder and blood-lust were the variables needing control.

There is now being superimposed on this a positive and affirmatory ideology, the thesis of which is to prevent the deterioration of environment. The means to this end is research. The duty of the individual is to apply its findings to land, and to encourage his neighbor to do like-wise. The soil and the plant succession are recognized as the basic variables which determine plant and animal life, both wild and domesticated, and likewise the quality and quantity of human satisfactions to be derived. Gun-powder is relegated to the status of a tool for harvesting one of these satisfactions. Blood-lust is a source of motive-power, like sex in social organization. Only one constant is assumed, and that is common to both equations: the love of nature.

This new idea is so far regarded as merely a new and promising means to better hunting and fishing, but its potential uses are much larger. To explain this, let us go back to the basic thesis—the preservation of fauna and flora.

Why do species become extinct? Because they first become rare. Why do they become rare? Because of shrinkage in the particular environments which their particular adaptations enable them to inhabit. Can such shrinkage be controlled? Yes, once the specifications are known. How known? Through ecological research. How controlled? By modifying the environment with those same tools and skills already used in agriculture and forestry.

Given, then the knowledge and the desire, this idea of controlled wild culture or "management" can be applied not only to quail and trout, but to *any living thing* from bloodroots to Bell's vireos.[9] Within the limits imposed by the plant succession, the soil, the size of the property, and the gamut of the seasons, the landholder can "raise" any wild plant, fish, bird, or mammal he wants to. A rare bird or flower need remain no rarer than the people willing to venture their skill in *building it a habitat.* Nor need we visualize this as a new diversion for the idle rich. The average dolled-up estate merely proves what we will some day learn to acknowledge: that bread and beauty grow best together. Their harmonious integration can make farming not only a business but an art; the land not only a food-factory but an instrument for self-expression, on which each can play music of his own choosing.

It is well to ponder the sweep of this thing. It offers us nothing less than a renaissance—a new creative stage—in the oldest, and potentially the most universal, of all the fine arts. "Landscaping," for ages dissociated from economic land-use, has suffered that dwarfing and distortion which always attends the relegation of esthetic or spiritual functions to parks and parlors. Hence it is hard for us to visualize a creative art of land-beauty which is the prerogative, not of esthetic priests but of dirt farmers, which deals not with plants but with biota,[1] and which wields not only spade and pruning shears, but also draws rein on those invisible forces which determine the presence or absence of plants and animals. Yet such is this thing which lies to hand, if we want it. In it are the seeds of change, including, perhaps, a rebirth of that social dignity which ought to inhere in land-ownership, but which, for the moment, has passed to inferior professions, and which the current processes of land-skinning hardly deserve. In it, too, are perhaps the seeds of a new fellowship in land, a new solidarity in all men privileged to plow, a realization of Whitman's dream to *"plant companionship as thick as trees along all the rivers of America."* What bitter parody

9. Small insectivorous birds.
1. The animal and plant life of a region.

of such companionship, and trees, and rivers, is offered to this our generation!

I will not belabor the pipe-dream. It is no prediction, but merely an assertion that the idea of controlled environment contains colors and brushes wherewith society may some day paint a new and possibly a better picture of itself. Granted a community in which the combined beauty and utility of land determines the social status of its owner, and we will see a speedy dissolution of the economic obstacles which now beset conservation. Economic laws may be permanent, but their impact reflects what people want, which in turn reflects what they know and what they are. The economic set-up at any one moment is in some measure the result, as well as the cause, of the then prevailing standard of living. Such standards change. For example: some people discriminate against manufactured goods produced by child-labor or other anti-social processes. They have learned some of the abuses of machinery, and are willing to use their custom as a leverage for betterment. Social pressures have also been exerted to modify ecological processes which happened to be simple enough for people to understand;—witness the very effective boycott of birdskins for millinery ornament. We need postulate only a little further advance in ecological education to visualize the application of like pressures to other conservation problems.

For example: the lumberman who is now unable to practice forestry because the public is turning to synthetic boards may then be able to sell man-grown lumber "to keep the mountains green." Again: certain wools are produced by gutting the public domain; couldn't their competitors, who lead their sheep in greener pastures, so label their product? Must we view forever the irony of educating our sons with paper, the offal of which pollutes the rivers which they need quite as badly as books? Would not many people pay an extra penny for a "clean" newspaper? Government may some day busy itself with the legitimacy of labels used by land-industries to distinguish conservation products, rather than with the attempt to operate their lands for them.

I neither predict nor advocate these particular pressures—their wisdom or unwisdom is beyond my knowledge. I do assert that these abuses are just as real, and their correction every whit as urgent, as was the killing of egrets for hats. *They differ only in the number of links composing the ecological chain of cause and effect.* In egrets there were one or two links, which the mass-mind saw, believed, and acted upon. In these others there are many links; people do not see them, nor believe us who do. The ultimate issue, in conservation as in other social problems, is whether the mass-mind *wants* to extend its power of comprehending the world in which it lives, or, granted the desire, *has the capacity to do so*. Ortega, in his *Revolt of the Masses*, has pointed the first question with devastating lucidity. The geneticists are gradually, with trepidations, coming to grips with the second. I do not know the answer to either. I simply affirm that a sufficiently enlightened society, by changing its wants and tolerances, can change the economic factors bearing on land. It can be said of nations, as of individuals: "as a man thinketh, so is he."

It may seem idle to project such imaginary elaborations of culture at a time when millions lack even the means of physical existence. Some may feel for it the same honest horror as the Senator from Michigan who lately arraigned Congress for protecting migratory birds at a time when fellow-humans lacked bread. The trouble with such deadly parallels is we can never be sure which is cause and which is effect. It is not inconceivable that the wave phenomena which have lately upset everything from banks to crime-rates might be less troublesome if the human medium in which they run *readjusted its tensions*. The stampede is an attribute of animals interested solely in grass.

QUESTIONS

1. Outline this lecture. What is Leopold's thesis?
2. This lecture was delivered in 1933; are there any incidental signs, references or allusions which suggest its date? Considering such as you find and supplying updated equivalents, do you think Leopold would change either the substance or the tone of his lecture if he were giving it today?
3. What in Leopold's lecture would you expect B. F. Skinner to agree with? Where would you expect him to disagree?

NICCOLÒ MACHIAVELLI

The Morals of the Prince[1]

On Things for Which Men, and Particularly Princes, Are Praised or Blamed

We now have left to consider what should be the manners and attitudes of a prince toward his subjects and his friends. As I know that many have written on this subject I feel that I may be held presumptuous in what I have to say, if in my comments I do not follow the lines laid down by others. Since, however, it has been my intention to write something which may be of use to the understanding reader, it has seemed wiser to me to follow the real truth of the matter rather than what we imagine it to be. For imagination has created many principalities and republics that have never been seen or known to have any real existence, for how we live is so

---

1. Chapters 15-18 of *The Prince*.

different from how we ought to live that he who studies what ought to be done rather than what is done will learn the way to his downfall rather than to his preservation. A man striving in every way to be good will meet his ruin among the great number who are not good. Hence it is necessary for a prince, if he wishes to remain in power, to learn how not to be good and to use his knowledge or refrain from using it as he may need.

Putting aside then the things imagined as pertaining to a prince and considering those that really do, I will say that all men, and particularly princes because of their prominence, when comment is made of them, are noted as having some characteristics deserving either praise or blame. One is accounted liberal, another stingy, to use a Tuscan term—for in our speech avaricious (*avaro*) is applied to such as are desirous of acquiring by rapine whereas stingy (*misero*) is the term used for those who are reluctant to part with their own—one is considered bountiful, another rapacious; one cruel, another tender-hearted; one false to his word, another trustworthy; one effeminate and pusillanimous, another wild and spirited; one humane, another haughty; one lascivious, another chaste; one a man of integrity and another sly; one tough and another pliant; one serious and another frivolous; one religious and another skeptical, and so on. Everyone will agree, I know, that it would be a most praiseworthy thing if all the qualities accounted as good in the above enumeration were found in a Prince. But since they cannot be so possessed nor observed because of human conditions which do not allow of it, what is necessary for the prince is to be prudent enough to escape the infamy of such vices as would result in the loss of his state; as for the others which would not have that effect, he must guard himself from them as far as possible but if he cannot, he may overlook them as being of less importance. Further, he should have no concern about incurring the infamy of such vices without which the preservation of his state would be difficult. For, if the matter be well considered, it will be seen that some habits which appear virtuous, if adopted would signify ruin, and others that seem vices lead to security and the well-being of a prince.

Generosity and Meanness

To begin then with the first characteristic set forth above, I will say that it would be well always to be considered generous, yet generosity used in such a way as not to bring you honor does you harm, for if it is practiced virtuously and as it is meant to be practiced it will not be publicly known and you will not lose the name of being just the opposite of generous. Hence to preserve the reputation of being generous among your friends you must not neglect any kind of lavish display, yet a prince of this sort will consume all his property in such gestures and, if he wishes to preserve his reputation for generosity, he will be forced to levy heavy taxes on his subjects and turn to fiscal measures and do everything possible to get money. Thus he will begin to be regarded with hatred by his subjects and should he become poor he will be held in scant esteem; having by his prodigality given offense to many and rewarded only a few, he will suffer at the first hint of adversity, and the first danger will be critical for him. Yet when he realizes this and tries to reform he will immediately get the name of being a miser. So a prince, as he is unable to adopt the virtue of generosity without danger to himself, must, if he is a wise man, accept with indifference the name of miser. For with the passage of time he will be regarded as increasingly generous when it is seen that, by virtue of his parsimony, his income suffices for him to defend himself in wartime and undertake his enterprises without heavily taxing his people. For in that way he practices generosity towards all from whom he refrains from taking money, who are many, and stinginess only toward those from whom he withholds gifts, who are few.

In our times we have seen great things accomplished only by such as have had the name of misers; all others have come to naught. Pope Julius made use of his reputation for generosity to make himself Pope but later, in order to carry on his war against the King of France, he made no effort to maintain it; and he has waged a great number of wars without having had recourse to heavy taxation because his persistent parsimony has made up for the extra expenses. The present King of Spain, had he had any reputation for generosity, would never have carried through to victory so many enterprises.

A prince then, if he wishes not to rob his subjects but to be able to defend himself and not to become poor and despised nor to be obliged to become rapacious, must consider it a matter of small importance to incur the name of miser, for this is one of the vices which keep him on his throne. Some may say Caesar through generosity won his way to the purple, and others either through being generous or being accounted so have risen to the highest ranks. But I will answer by pointing out that either you are already a prince or you are on the way to becoming one and in the first case generosity is harmful while in the second it is very necessary to be considered open-handed. Caesar was seeking to arrive at the domination of Rome but if he had survived after reaching his goal and had not moderated his lavishness he would certainly have destroyed the empire.

It might also be objected that there have been many princes, accomplishing great things with their armies, who have been acclaimed for their generosity. To which I would answer that the prince either spends his own (or his subjects') money or that of others; in the first case he must be very sparing but in the second he should overlook no aspect of open-handedness. So the prince who leads his armies and lives on looting and extortion and booty, thus handling the wealth of others, must indeed have this quality of generosity for otherwise his soldiers will not follow him. You can be very free with wealth not belonging to yourself or your subjects, in the fashion of Cyrus, Caesar, or Alexander, for spending what belongs to others rather enhances your reputation than detracts from it; it is only spending your own wealth that is dangerous. There is nothing that consumes itself as does prodigality; even as you practice it you lose the faculty of practicing it and either you become poor and despicable or, in order to escape poverty, rapacious and unpopular. And among the things a prince must guard against is precisely the danger of becoming an object either of contempt or of hatred. Generosity leads you to both these evils, wherefore it is wiser to accept the name of miserly, since the reproach it brings is without hatred, than to seek a reputation for generosity and thus perforce acquire the name of rapacious, which breeds hatred as well as infamy.

Cruelty and Clemency and Whether It Is Better to Be Loved or Feared

Now to continue with the list of characteristics. It should be the desire of every prince to be considered merciful and not cruel, yet he should take care not to make poor use of his clemency. Cesare Borgia was regarded as cruel, yet his cruelty reorganized Romagna and united it in peace and loyalty. Indeed, if we reflect, we shall see that this man was more merciful than the Florentines who, to avoid the charge of cruelty, allowed Pistoia to be destroyed.[2] A prince should care nothing for the accusation of cruelty so long as he keeps his subjects united and loyal; by making a very few examples he can be more truly merciful than those who through too much tender-heartedness allow disorders to arise whence come killings and rapine. For these offend an entire community, while the few executions ordered by the prince affect only a few individuals. For a new prince above all it is impossible not to earn a reputation for cruelty since new states are full of dangers. Virgil indeed has Dido apologize for the inhumanity of her rule because it is new, in the words:

> Res dura et regni novitas me talia cogunt
> Moliri et late fines custode tueri.[3]

Nevertheless a prince should not be too ready to listen to tale-

---

2. By unchecked rioting between opposing factions (1502).
3. ". . . my cruel fate / And doubts attending an unsettled state / Force me to guard my coast from foreign foes" — DRYDEN.

bearers nor to act on suspicion, nor should he allow himself to be easily frightened. He should proceed with a mixture of prudence and humanity in such a way as not to be made incautious by over-confidence nor yet intolerable by excessive mistrust.

Here the question arises; whether it is better to be loved than feared or feared than loved. The answer is that it would be desirable to be both but, since that is difficult, it is much safer to be feared than to be loved, if one must choose. For on men in general this observation may be made: they are ungrateful, fickle, and deceitful, eager to avoid dangers, and avid for gain, and while you are useful to them they are all with you, offering you their blood, their property, their lives, and their sons so long as danger is remote, as we noted above, but when it approaches they turn on you. Any prince, trusting only in their words and having no other preparations made, will fall to his ruin, for friendships that are bought at a price and not by greatness and nobility of soul are paid for indeed, but they are not owned and cannot be called upon in time of need. Men have less hesitation in offending a man who is loved than one who is feared, for love is held by a bond of obligation which, as men are wicked, is broken whenever personal advantage suggests it, but fear is accompanied by the dread of punishment which never relaxes.

Yet a prince should make himself feared in such a way that, if he does not thereby merit love, at least he may escape odium, for being feared and not hated may well go together. And indeed the prince may attain this end if he but respect the property and the women of his subjects and citizens. And if it should become necessary to seek the death of someone, he should find a proper justification and a public cause, and above all he should keep his hands off another's property, for men forget more readily the death of their father than the loss of their patrimony. Besides, pretexts for seizing property are never lacking, and when a prince begins to live by means of rapine he will always find some excuse for plundering others, and conversely pretexts for execution are rarer and are more quickly exhausted.

A prince at the head of his armies and with a vast number of soldiers under his command should give not the slightest heed if he is esteemed cruel, for without such a reputation he will not be able to keep his army united and ready for action. Among the marvelous things told of Hannibal is that, having a vast army under his command made up of all kinds and races of men and waging war far from his own country, he never allowed any dissension to arise either as between the troops and their leaders or among the troops themselves, and this both in times of good fortune and bad. This could only have come about through his most inhuman cruelty which, taken in conjunction with his great valor, kept him always an object of respect and terror in the eyes of his soldiers. And without the cruelty his other characteristics would not have achieved this effect. Thoughtless writers have admired his actions and at the same time deplored the cruelty which was the basis of them. As evidence of the truth of our statement that his other virtues would have been insufficient let us examine the case of Scipio, an extraordinary leader not only in his own day but for all recorded history. His army in Spain revolted and for no other reason than because of his kind-heartedness, which had allowed more license to his soldiery than military discipline properly permits. His policy was attacked in the Senate by Fabius Maximus, who called him a corrupter of the Roman arms. When the Locrians had been mishandled by one of his lieutenants, his easy-going nature prevented him from avenging them or disciplining his officer, and it was apropos of this incident that one of the senators remarked, wishing to find an excuse for him, that there were many men who knew better how to avoid error themselves than to correct it in others. This characteristic of Scipio would have clouded his fame and glory had he continued in authority, but as he lived under the government of the Senate, its harmful aspect was hidden and it reflected credit on him.

Hence, on the subject of being loved or feared I will conclude that since love depends on the subjects, but the prince has it in his own hands to create fear, a wise prince will rely on what is his own, remembering at the same time that he must avoid arousing hatred, as we have said.

In What Manner Princes Should Keep Their Word

How laudable it is for a prince to keep his word and govern his actions by integrity rather than trickery will be understood by all. Nonetheless we have in our times seen great things accomplished by many princes who have thought little of keeping their promises and have known the art of mystifying the minds of men. Such princes have won out over those whose actions were based on fidelity to their word.

It must be understood that there are two ways of fighting, one with laws and the other with arms. The first is the way of men, the second is the style of beasts, but since very often the first does not suffice it is necessary to turn to the second. Therefore a prince must know how to play the beast as well as the man. This lesson was taught allegorically by the ancient writers who related that Achilles and many other princes were brought up by Chiron the Centaur, who took them under his discipline. The clear significance of this half-man and half-beast preceptorship is that a prince must know how to use either of these two natures and that one without the other has no enduring strength. Now since the prince must make use of the characteristics of beasts he should choose those of the fox and the lion, though the lion cannot defend himself against snares and the fox is helpless against wolves. One must be a fox in avoiding traps and a lion in frightening wolves. Such as choose simply the rôle of a lion do not rightly understand the matter. Hence a wise leader cannot and should not keep his word when keeping it is not to his advantage or when the reasons that made him give it are no longer valid. If men were good, this would not be a good precept, but since they are wicked and will not keep faith with you, you are not bound to keep faith with them.

A prince has never lacked legitimate reasons to justify his breach of faith. We could give countless recent examples and show how any number of peace treaties or promises have been broken and rendered meaningless by the faithlessness of princes, and how success has fallen to the one who best knows how to counterfeit the fox. But it is necessary to know how to disguise this nature well and how to pretend and dissemble. Men are so simple and so ready to follow the needs of the moment that the deceiver will always find some one to deceive. Of recent examples I shall mention one. Alexander VI did nothing but deceive and never thought of anything else and always found some occasion for it. Never was there a man more convincing in his asseverations nor more willing to offer the most solemn oaths nor less likely to observe them. Yet his deceptions were always successful for he was an expert in this field.

So a prince need not have all the aforementioned good qualities, but it is most essential that he appear to have them. Indeed, I should go so far as to say that having them and always practising them is harmful, while seeming to have them is useful. It is good to appear clement, trustworthy, humane, religious, and honest, and also to be so, but always with the mind so disposed that, when the occasion arises not to be so, you can become the opposite. It must be understood that a prince and particularly a new prince cannot practise all the virtues for which men are accounted good, for the necessity of preserving the state often compels him to take actions which are opposed to loyalty, charity, humanity, and religion. Hence he must have a spirit ready to adapt itself as the varying winds of fortune command him. As I have said, so far as he is able, a prince should stick to the path of good but, if the necessity arises, he should know how to follow evil.

A prince must take great care that no word ever passes his lips that is not full of the above mentioned five good qualities, and he must seem to all who see and hear him a model of piety, loyalty, integrity, humanity, and religion. Nothing is more necessary than to seem to possess this last quality, for men in general judge more by the eye than the hand, as all can see but few can feel. Everyone sees what you seem to be, few experience what you really are and these few do not dare to set themselves up against the opinion of the majority supported by the majesty of the state. In the actions of all men and especially princes, where there is no court of appeal, the end is all that counts. Let a prince then concern himself with the acquisition or the maintenance of a state; the means employed will always be considered honorable and praised by all, for the mass of mankind is always swayed by appearances and by the outcome of an enterprise. And in the world there is only the mass, for the few find their place only when the majority has no base of support.

DESIDERIUS ERASMUS
The Arts of Peace[1]

Although the writers of antiquity divided the whole theory of state government into two sections, war and peace, the first and most important objective is the instruction of the prince in the matter of ruling wisely during times of peace, in which he should strive his utmost to preclude any future need for the science of war. In this matter it seems best that the prince should first know his own kingdom. This knowledge is best gained from a study of geography and history and from frequent visits through his provinces and cities. Let him first be eager to learn the location of his districts and cities, with their beginnings, their nature, institutions, customs, laws, annals, and privileges. No one can heal the body until he is thoroughly conversant with it. No one can properly till a field which he does not understand. To be sure, the tyrant takes great care in such matters, but it is the spirit, not the act, which singles out the good prince. The physician studies the functions of the body so as to be more adept in healing it; the poisoning assassin, to more surely end it! Next, the prince should love the land over which he rules just as a farmer loves the fields of his ancestors or as a good man feels affection toward his household. He should make it his especial interest to hand it over to his successor, whosoever he may be, better than he received it. If he has any children, devotion toward them should urge him on; if he has no family, he should be guided by devotion to his country; and he should always keep kindled the flame of love for his subjects. He should consider his kingdom as a great body of which he is the most outstanding member and remember that they who have entrusted all their fortunes and their very safety to the good faith of one man are deserving of consideration. He should keep constantly in mind the example of those rulers to whom the welfare of their people was dearer than their own lives; for it is obviously impossible for a prince to do violence to the state without injuring himself.

1. From *The Education of a Christian Prince.*

In the second place the prince will see to it that he is loved by his subjects in return, but in such a way that his authority is no less strong among them. There are some who are so stupid as to strive to win good will for themselves by incantations and magic rings, when there is no charm more efficacious than good character itself; nothing can be more lovable than that, for, as this is a real and immortal good, so it brings a man true and undying good will. The best formula is this: let him love, who would be loved, so that he may attach his subjects to him as God has won the peoples of the world to Himself by His goodness.

They are also wrong who win the hearts of the masses by largesses, feasts, and gross indulgence. It is true that some popular favor, instead of affection, is gained by these means, but it is neither genuine nor permanent. In the meanwhile the greed of the populace is developed, which, as happens, after it has reached large proportions thinks nothing is enough. Then there is an uprising, unless complete satisfaction is made to their demands. By this means your people are not won, but corrupted. And so by this means the average prince is accustomed to win his way into the hearts of the people after the fashion of these foolish husbands who beguile their wives with blandishments, gifts, and complaisance, instead of winning their love by their character and good actions. So at length it comes about that they are not loved; instead of a thrifty and well mannered wife they have a haughty and intractable one; instead of an obedient spouse they find one who is quarrelsome and rebellious. Or take the case of those unhappy women who desperately try to arouse love in their husbands' hearts by giving them drugs, with the result that they have madmen instead of sane lovers.

The wife should first learn the ways and means of loving her husband and then let him show himself worthy of her love. And so with the people—let them become accustomed to the best, and let the prince be the source of the best things. Those who begin to love through reason, love long.

In the first place, then, he who would be loved by his people should show himself a prince worthy of love; after that it will do some good to consider how best he may win his way into their hearts. The prince should do this first so that the best men may have the highest regard for him and that he may be accepted by those who are lauded by all. They are the men he should have for his close friends; they are the ones for his counselors; they are the ones on whom he should bestow his honors and whom he should allow to have the greatest influence with him. By this means everyone will come to have an excellent opinion of the prince, who is the source of all good will. I have known some princes who were not really evil themselves who incurred the hatred of the people for no other reason than that they granted too much liberty to those whom universal public sentiment condemned. The people judged the character of the prince by these other men.

For my part, I should like to see the prince born and raised among those people whom he is destined to rule, because friendship is created and confirmed most when the source of good will is in nature itself. The common people shun and hate even good qualities which they are unknown to them, while evils which are familiar are sometimes loved. This matter at hand has a twofold advantage to offer, for the prince will be more kindly disposed toward his subjects and certainly more ready to regard them as his own. The people on their part will feel more kindness in their hearts and be more willing to recognize his position as prince. For this reason I am especially opposed to the accepted [idea of] alliances of the princes with foreign, particularly with distant, nations.

The ties of birth and country and a mutual spirit of understanding, as it were, have a great deal to do with establishing a feeling of good will. A goodly part of this feeling must of necessity be lost if mixed marriages confuse that native and inborn spirit. But when nature has laid a foundation of mutual affection, then it should be developed and strengthened by every other means. When the opposite situation is presented, then even greater energy must be employed to secure this feeling of good will by mutual obligations and a character worthy of commendation. In marriage, the wife at first yields entirely to the husband, and he makes a few concessions to her and indulges her whims until, as they come really to know one another, a firm bond unites them; so it should be in the case of a prince selected from a foreign country. Mithridates learned the languages of all the peoples over whom he ruled, and they were said to be twenty in number. Alexander the Great, however barbarous the peoples with whom he was dealing, at once used to imitate their ways and customs and by this method subtly worked himself into their good graces. Alcibiades has been praised for the same thing. Nothing so alienates the affections of his people from a prince as for him to take great pleasure in living abroad, because then they seem to be neglected by him to whom they wish to be most important. The result of this is that the people feel that they are not paying taxes to a prince (since the moneys are spent elsewhere and totally lost as far as they are concerned) but that they are casting spoils to foreigners. Lastly, there is nothing more harmful and disastrous to a country, nor more dangerous for a prince, than visits to far-away places, especially if these visits are prolonged; for it was this, according to the opinion of everyone, that took Philip from us and injured his kingdom no less than the war with the Gelrii, which was dragged out for so many years. The king bee is hedged about in the midst of the swarm and does not fly out and away. The heart is situated in the very middle of the body. Just so should a prince always be found among his own people.

There are two factors, as Aristotle tells us in his *Politics*, which have played the greatest roles in the overthrow of empires. They are hatred and contempt. Good will is the opposite of hatred; respected authority, of contempt. Therefore it will be the duty of the prince to study the best way to win the former and avoid the latter. Hatred is kindled by an ugly temper, by violence, insulting language, sourness of character, meanness, and greediness; it is more easily aroused than allayed. A good prince must therefore use every caution to prevent any possibility of losing the affections of his subjects. You may take my word that whoever loses the favor of his people is thereby stripped of a great safeguard. On the other hand, the affections of the populace are won by those characteristics which, in general, are farthest removed from tyranny. They are clemency, affability, fairness, courtesy, and kindliness. This last is a spur to duty, especially if they who have been of good service to the state, see that they will be rewarded at the hands of the prince. Clemency inspires to better efforts those who are aware of their faults, while forgiveness extends hope to those who are now eager to make recompense by virtuous conduct for the short-comings of their earlier life and provides the steadfast with a happy reflection on human nature. Courtesy everywhere engenders love— or at least assuages hatred. This quality in a great prince is by far the most pleasing to the masses.

Contempt is most likely to spring from a penchant for the worldly pleasures of lust, for excessive drinking and eating, and for fools and clowns—in other words, for folly and idleness. Authority is gained by the following varied characteristics: in the first place wisdom, then integrity, self-restraint, seriousness, and alertness. These are the things by which a prince should commend himself, if he would be respected in his authority over his subjects. Some have the absurd idea that if they make the greatest confusion possible by their appearance, and dress with pompous display, they must be held in high esteem among their subjects. Who thinks a prince great just because he is adorned with gold and precious stones? Everyone knows he has as many as he wants. But in the meanwhile what else does the prince expose except the misfortunes of his people, who are supporting his extravagance to their great cost? And now lastly, what else does such a prince sow among his people, if not the seeds of all crime? Let the good prince be reared in such a manner and [continue to] live in such a manner that from the example of his life all the others (nobles and commoners alike) may take the model of frugality and temperance. Let him so conduct himself in the privacy of his home as not to be caught unawares by the sudden entrance of anyone. And in public it is unseemly for a prince to be seen anywhere, unless always in connection with

something that will benefit the people as a whole. The real character of the prince is revealed by his speech rather than by his dress.
Every word that is dropped from the lips of the prince is scattered
wide among the masses. He should exercise the greatest care to see
that whatever he says bears the stamp of [genuine] worth and evi-
dences a mind becoming a good prince.

Aristotle's advice on this subject should not be overlooked. He
says that a prince who would escape incurring the hatred of his
people and would foster their affection for him should delegate to
others the odious duties and keep for himself the tasks which will
be sure to win favor. Thereby a great portion of any unpopularity
will be diverted upon those who carry out the administration, and
especially will it be so if these men are unpopular with the people
on other grounds as well. In the matter of benefits, however, the
genuine thanks redound to the prince alone. I should like to add
also that gratitude for a favor will be returned twofold if it is given
quickly, with no hesitation, spontaneously, and with a few words
of friendly commendation. If anything must be refused, refusal
should be affable and without offense. If it is necessary to impose
a punishment, some slight diminution of the penalty prescribed by
law should be made, and the sentence should be carried out as if
the prince were being forced [to act] against his own desires.

It is not enough for the prince to keep his own character pure
and uncorrupted for his state. He must give no less serious attention, in so far as he can, to see that every member of his household
—his nobles, his friends, his ministers, and his magistrates—follows
his example. They are one with the prince, and any hatred that is
aroused by their vicious acts rebounds upon the prince himself.
But, someone will say, this supervision is extremely difficult to
accomplish. It will be easy enough if the prince is careful to admit
only the best men into his household, and if he makes them understand that the prince is most pleased by that which is best for
the people. Otherwise it too often turns out that, due to the disregard of the prince in these matters or even his connivance in them,
the most criminal men (hiding under cover of the prince) force a
tyranny upon the people, and while they appear to be carrying out
the affairs of the prince, they are doing the greatest harm to his
good name. What is more, the condition of the state is more bearable when the prince himself is wicked than when he has evil
friends; we manage to bear up under a single tyrant. Somehow or
other the people can sate the greed of one man without difficulty:
it is not a matter of great effort to satisfy the wild desires of just
one man or to appease the vicious fierceness of a single individual,
but to content so many tyrants is a heavy burden. The prince should
avoid every novel idea in so far as he is capable of doing so; for
even if conditions are bettered thereby, the very innovation is a

stumbling block. The establishment of a state, the unwritten laws of a city, or the old legal code are never changed without great confusion. Therefore, if there is anything of this sort that can be endured, it should not be changed but should either be tolerated or happily diverted to a better function. As a last resort, if there is some absolutely unbearable condition, the change should be made, but [only] gradually and by a practiced hand.

The end which the prince sets for himself is of the greatest consequence, for if he shows little wisdom in its selection he must of necessity be wrong in all his plans. The cardinal principle of a good prince should be not only to preserve the present prosperity of the state but to pass it on more prosperous than when he received it. To use the jargon of the Peripatetics, there are three kinds of "good"—that of the mind, that of the body, and the external good. The prince must be careful not to evaluate them in reverse order and judge the good fortune of his state mainly by the external good, for these latter conditions should only be judged good in so far as they relate to the good of the mind and of the body; that is, in a word, the prince should consider his subjects to be most fortunate not if they are very wealthy or in excellent bodily health but if they are most honorable and self-controlled, if they have as little taste for greed and quarreling as could be hoped for, and if they are not at all factious but live in complete accord with one another. He must also beware of being deceived by the false names of the fairest things, for in this deception lies the fountainhead from which spring practically all the evils that abound in the world. It is no true state of happiness in which the people are given over to idleness and wasteful extravagance, any more than it is true liberty for everyone to be allowed to do as he pleases. Neither is it a state of servitude to live according to the letter of just laws. Nor is that a peaceful state in which the populace bows to every whim of the prince; but rather is it peaceful when it obeys good laws and a prince who has a keen regard for the authority of the laws. Equity does not lie in giving everyone the same reward, the same rights, the same honor; as a matter of fact, that is sometimes a mark of the greatest unfairness.

A prince who is about to assume control of the state must be advised at once that the main hope of a state lies in the proper education of its youth. This Xenophon wisely taught in his *Cyropaedia.* Pliable youth is amenable to any system of training. Therefore the greatest care should be exercised over public and private schools and over the education of the girls, so that the children may be placed under the best and most trustworthy instructors and may learn the teachings of Christ and that good literature which is beneficial to the state. As a result of this scheme of things, there will be no need for many laws or punishments, for the people will of their own free will follow the course of right.

Education exerts such a powerful influence, as Plato says, that a man who has been trained in the right develops into a sort of divine creature, while on the other hand, a person who has received a perverted training degenerates into a monstrous sort of savage beast. Nothing is of more importance to a prince than to have the best possible subjects.

The first effort, then, is to get them accustomed to the best influences, because any music has a soothing effect to the accustomed ear, and there is nothing harder than to rid people of those traits which have become second nature to them through habit. None of those tasks will be too difficult if the prince himself adheres to the best manners. It is the essence of tyranny, or rather trickery, to treat the common citizen as animal trainers are accustomed to treat a savage beast: first they carefully study the way in which these creatures are quieted or aroused, and then they anger them or quiet them at their pleasure. This Plato has painstakingly pointed out. Such a course is an abuse of the emotions of the masses and is no help to them. However, if the people prove intractable and rebel against what is good for them, then you must bide your time and gradually lead them over to your end, either by some subterfuge or by some helpful pretence. This works just as wine does, for when that is first taken it has no effect, but when it has gradually flowed through every vein it captivates the whole man and holds him in its power.

If sometimes the whirling course of events and public opinion beat the prince from his course, and he is forced to obey the [exigencies of the] time, yet he must not cease his efforts as long as he is able to renew his fight, and what he has not accomplished by one method he should try to effect by another.

QUESTIONS

1. Early in the essay Erasmus analogizes the relation of prince to people to that of a physician to the body, a farmer to a field, a husband to a wife. Why does he develop this last analogy more fully than the others and use it again later?

2. On page 759 Erasmus lists the "varied characteristics" by which authority is gained. Why does he put wisdom "in the first place"? Is there any significance to the order in which he places the other characteristics?

3. Erasmus says that "the real character of the prince is revealed by his speech rather than by his dress." Would this be equally true of people other than princes? How can both speech and dress reveal character?

4. Compare Erasmus' ideal prince with Machiavelli's. What is the significance of the title, "The Arts of Peace"?

5. Is the advice to "avoid every novel idea" (p. 760) sound? To

what does "novelty" apply in this context? How would Erasmus counter the charge that such a policy might lead to stagnation and corruption in government?

6. Why does Erasmus find it necessary to qualify so carefully what he means by "prosperity" (p. 761)? How does his definition differ from more commonly accepted ones today?

7. "Equity does not lie in giving everyone the same reward, the same rights, the same honor; as a matter of fact, that is sometimes a mark of the greatest unfairness" (p. 761). How does this implied definition of "equity" jibe with the statement in the Declaration of Independence that "all men are created equal" and "are endowed by their Creator with certain unalienable Rights" (pp. 769–772)?

8. How far do leading political figures today correspond to Erasmus' ideal prince?

ABRAHAM LINCOLN
Second Inaugural Address

At this second appearing to take the oath of the presidential office, there is less occasion for an extended address than there was at the first. Then a statement, somewhat in detail, of a course to be pursued, seemed fitting and proper. Now, at the expiration of four years, during which public declarations have been constantly called forth on every point and phase of the great contest which still absorbs the attention, and engrosses the energies of the nation, little that is new could be presented. The progress of our arms, upon which all else chiefly depends, is as well known to the public as to myself; and it is, I trust, reasonably satisfactory and encouraging to all. With high hope for the future, no prediction in regard to it is ventured.

On the occasion corresponding to this four years ago, all thoughts were anxiously directed to an impending civil war. All dreaded it—all sought to avert it. While the inaugural address was being delivered from this place, devoted altogether to *saving* the Union without war, insurgent agents were in the city seeking to *destroy* it without war—seeking to dissolve the Union, and divide effects, by negotiation. Both parties deprecated war; but one of them would *make* war rather than let the nation survive; and the other would *accept* war rather than let it perish. And the war came.

One-eighth of the whole population were colored slaves, not distributed generally over the Union, but localized in the Southern part of it. These slaves constituted a peculiar and powerful interest. All knew that this interest was, somehow, the cause of the war. To strengthen, perpetuate, and extend this interest was the object for which the insurgents would rend the Union, even by war; while the government claimed no right to do more than to restrict the territorial enlargement of it. Neither party expected for the war, the magnitude, or the duration, which it has already attained. Neither anticipated that the *cause* of the conflict might cease with, or even before, the conflict itself should cease. Each looked for an easier triumph, and a result less fundamental and astounding. Both read the same Bible, and pray to the same God; and each invokes His aid against the other. It may seem strange that any men should dare to ask a just God's assistance in wringing their bread from the sweat of other men's faces[1]; but let us judge not that we be not judged.[2] The prayers of both could not be answered; that of neither has been answered fully. The Almighty has His own purposes. "Woe unto the world because of offenses! for it must needs be that offenses come; but woe to that man by whom the offense cometh!"[3] If we shall suppose that American slavery is one of those offenses which, in the providence of God, must needs come, but which, having continued through His appointed time, He now wills to remove, and that He gives to both North and South, this terrible war, as the woe due to those by whom the offense came, shall we discern therein any departure from those divine attributes which the believers in a Living God always ascribe to Him? Fondly do we hope—fervently do we pray—that this mighty scourge of war may speedily pass away. Yet, if God wills that it continue, until all the wealth piled by the bondman's two hundred and fifty years of unrequited toil shall be sunk, and until every drop of blood drawn with the lash, shall be paid by another drawn with the sword, as was said three thousand years ago, so still it must be said "the judgments of the Lord are true and righteous altogether."[4]

With malice toward none; with charity for all; with firmness in the right, as God gives us to see the right, let us strive on to finish the work we are in; to bind up the nation's wounds; to care for him who shall have borne the battle, and for his widow, and his orphan —to do all which may achieve and cherish a just, and a lasting peace, among ourselves, and with all nations.

1. See Genesis iii. 19.
2. See Matthew vii. 1.
3. See Matthew xviii. 7.
4. See Psalms xix. 9.

THOMAS JEFFERSON

Original Draft of the Declaration of Independence

A DECLARATION OF THE REPRESENTATIVES OF THE UNITED STATES OF AMERICA, IN GENERAL CONGRESS ASSEMBLED.

When in the course of human events it becomes necessary for a people to advance from that subordination in which they have hitherto remained, & to assume among the powers of the earth the equal & independant station to which the laws of nature & of nature's god entitle them, a decent respect to the opinions of mankind requires that they should declare the causes which impel them to the change.

We hold these truths to be sacred & undeniable; that all men are created equal & independant, that from that equal creation they derive rights inherent & inalienable, among which are the preservation of life, & liberty, & the spirit of happiness; that to secure these ends, governments are instituted among men, deriving their just powers from the consent of the governed; that whenever any form of government shall become destructive of these ends, it is the right of the people to alter or to abolish it, & to institute new government, laying it's foundation on such principles & organising it's powers in such form, as to them shall seem most likely to effect their safety & happiness. prudence indeed will dictate that governments long established should not be changed for light & transient causes: and accordingly all experience hath shewn that mankind are more disposed to suffer while evils are sufferable, than to right themselves by abolishing the forms to which they are accustomed. but when a long train of abuses & usurpations, begun at a distinguished period, & pursuing invariably the same object, evinces a design to subject them to arbitrary power, it is their right, it is their duty, to throw off such government & to provide new guards for their future security. such has been the patient sufferance of these colonies; & such is now the necessity which constrains them to expunge their former systems of government. the history of his present majesty, is a history of unremitting injuries and usurpations, among which no one fact stands single or solitary to contradict the uniform tenor of the rest, all of which have in direct object the establishment of an absolute tyranny over these states. to prove this, let facts be submited to a candid world, for the truth of which we pledge a faith yet unsullied by falsehood.

he has refused his assent to laws the most wholesome and necessary for the public good:

he has forbidden his governors to pass laws of immediate & pressing importance, unless suspended in their operation till his assent should be obtained; and when so suspended, he has neglected utterly to attend to them.

he has refused to pass other laws for the accommodation of large districts of people unless those people would relinquish the right of representation, a right inestimable to them, & formidable to tyrants alone:[1]

he has dissolved Representative houses repeatedly & continually, for opposing with manly firmness his invasions on the rights of the people:

he has refused for a long space of time to cause others to be elected, whereby the legislative powers, incapable of annihilation, have returned to the people at large for their exercise, the state remaining in the mean time exposed to all the dangers of invasion from without, &, convulsions within:

he has suffered the administration of justice totally to cease in some of these colonies, refusing his assent to laws for establishing judiciary powers:

he has made our judges dependant on his will alone, for the tenure of their offices, and amount of their salaries:

he has erected a multitude of new offices by a self-assumed power, & sent hither swarms of officers to harrass our people & eat out their substance:

he has kept among us in times of peace standing armies & ships of war:

he has affected to render the military, independent of & superior to the civil power:

he has combined with others to subject us to a jurisdiction foreign to our constitutions and unacknoledged by our laws; giving his assent to their pretended acts of legislation, for quartering large bodies of armed troops among us;

> for protecting them by a mock-trial from punishment for any murders they should commit on the inhabitants of these states;

> for cutting off our trade with all parts of the world;

> for imposing taxes on us without our consent;

> for depriving us of the benefits of trial by jury

he has endeavored to prevent the population of these states; for that purpose obstructing the laws for naturalization of foreigners; refusing to pass others to encourage their migrations hither; & raising the conditions of new appropriations of lands;

---

1. At this point in the manuscript a strip containing the following clause is inserted: "He called together legislative bodies at places unusual, unco[mforta-ble, & distant from] the depository of their public records for the sole purpose of fatiguing [them into compliance] with his measures:" Missing parts in the Library of Congress text are supplied from the copy made by Jefferson for George Wythe. This copy is in the New York Public Library. The fact that this passage was omitted from John Adams's transcript suggests that it was not a part of Jefferson's original rough draft.

for transporting us beyond seas to be tried for pretended
offences:

for taking away our charters & altering fundamentally the
forms of our governments;

for suspending our own legislatures & declaring themselves
invested with power to legislate for us in all cases whatsoever:

he has abdicated government here, withdrawing his governors,
& declaring us out of his allegiance & protection:

he has plundered our seas, ravaged our coasts, burnt our towns
& destroyed the lives of our people:

he is at this time transporting large armies of foreign mercenaries
to compleat the works of death, desolation & tyranny, already
begun with circumstances of cruelty & perfidy unworthy the
head of a civilized nation:

he has endeavored to bring on the inhabitants of our frontiers
the merciless Indian savages, whose known rule of warfare
is an undistinguished destruction of all ages, sexes, & conditions of existence:

he has incited treasonable insurrections of our fellow-citizens,
with the allurements of forfeiture & confiscation of our property:

he has waged cruel war against human nature itself, violating
it's most sacred rights of life & liberty in the persons of a distant
people who never offended him, captivating & carrying them
into slavery in another hemisphere, or to incur miserable death
in their transportion thither. this piratical warfare, the
opprobrium of *infidel* powers, is the warfare of the CHRIS-
TIAN king of Great Britain. determined to keep open
a market where MEN should be bought & sold; he has pros-
tituted his negative for suppressing every legislative attempt
to prohibit or to restrain this execrable commerce: and that
this assemblage of horrors might want no fact of distinguished
die, he is now exciting those very people to rise in arms among
us, and to purchase that liberty of which *he* has deprived them,
by murdering the people upon whom *he* also obtruded them;
thus paying off former crimes committed against the *liberties*
of one people, with crimes which he urges them to commit
against the *lives* of another.

in every stage of these oppressions we have petitioned for redress
in the most humble terms; our repeated petitions have been answered
by repeated injury. a prince whose character is thus marked by every
act which may define a tyrant, is unfit to be the ruler of a people
who mean to be free. future ages will scarce believe that the hardi-
ness of one man, adventured within the short compass of twelve
years only, on so many acts of tyranny without a mask, over a people

fostered & fixed in principles of liberty.

Nor have we been wanting in attentions to our British brethren. we have warned them from time to time of attempts by their legislature to extend a jurisdiction over these our states. we have reminded them of the circumstances of our emigration & settlement here, no one of which could warrant so strange a pretension: that these were effected at the expence of our own blood & treasure, unassisted by the wealth or the strength of Great Britain: that in constituting indeed our several forms of government, we had adopted one common king, thereby laying a foundation for perpetual league & amity with them; but that submission to their [Parliament, was no Part of our Constitution, nor ever in Idea, if History may be]² credited: and we appealed to their native justice & magnanimity, as to the ties of our common kindred to disavow these usurpations which were likely to interrupt our correspondence & connection. they too have been deaf to the voice of justice & of consanguinity, & when occasions have been given them, by the regular course of their laws, of removing from their councils the disturbers of our harmony, they have by their free election re-established them in power. at this very time too they are permitting their chief magistrate to send over not only soldiers of our common blood, but Scotch & foreign mercenaries to invade & deluge us in blood. these facts have given the last stab to agonizing affection, and manly spirit bids us to renounce for ever these unfeeling brethren. we must endeavor to forget our former love for them, and to hold them as we hold the rest of mankind, enemies in war, in peace friends. we might have been a free & a great people together; but a communication of grandeur & of freedom it seems is below their dignity. be it so, since they will have it: the road to glory & happiness is open to us too; we will climb it in a separate state, and acquiesce in the necessity which pronounces our everlasting Adieu!

We therefore the representatives of the United States of America in General Congress assembled do, in the name & by authority of the good people of these states, reject and renounce all allegiance & subjection to the kings of Great Britain & all others who may hereafter claim by, through, or under them; we utterly dissolve & break off all political connection which may have heretofore subsisted between us & the people or parliament of Great Britain; and finally we do assert and declare these colonies to be free and independant states, and that as free & independant states they shall hereafter have power to levy war, conclude peace, contract alliances, establish commerce, & to do all other acts and things which independant states may of right do. And for the support of this declaration we mutually pledge to each other our lives, our fortunes, & our sacred honour.

2. An illegible passage is supplied from John Adams's transcription.

THOMAS JEFFERSON and OTHERS
The Declaration of Independence

IN CONGRESS, JULY 4, 1776
THE UNANIMOUS DECLARATION OF THE
THIRTEEN UNITED STATES OF AMERICA

When in the Course of human events it becomes necessary for one people to dissolve the political bands which have connected them with another, and to assume among the powers of the earth, the separate and equal station to which the Laws of Nature and of Nature's God entitle them, a decent respect to the opinions of mankind requires that they should declare the causes which impel them to the separation.

We hold these truths to be self-evident, that all men are created equal, that they are endowed by their Creator with certain unalienable Rights, that among these are Life, Liberty and the pursuit of Happiness. That to secure these rights, Governments are instituted among Men, deriving their just powers from the consent of the governed, That whenever any Form of Government becomes destructive of these ends, it is the Right of the People to alter or to abolish it, and to institute new Government, laying its foundation on such principles and organizing its powers in such form, as to them shall seem most likely to affect their Safety and Happiness. Prudence, indeed, will dictate that Governments long established should not be changed for light and transient causes; and accordingly all experience hath shewn that mankind are more disposed to suffer, while evils are sufferable, than to right themselves by abolishing the forms to which they are accustomed. But when a long train of abuses and usurpations, pursuing invariably the same Object evinces a design to reduce them under absolute Despotism, it is their right, it is their duty, to throw off such Government, and to provide new Guards for their future security. Such has been the patient sufferance of these Colonies; and such is now the necessity which constrains them to alter their former Systems of Government. The history of the present King of Great Britain is a history of repeated injuries and usurpations, all having in direct object the establishment of an absolute Tyranny over these States. To prove this, let Facts be submitted to a candid world.

He has refused his Assent to Laws, the most wholesome and necessary for the public good.

He has forbidden his Governors to pass laws of immediate and pressing importance, unless suspended in their operation till his Assent should be obtained; and when so suspended, he has utterly neglected to attend to them.

He has refused to pass other Laws for the accommodation of large districts of people, unless those people would relinquish the right of Representation in the Legislature, a right inestimable to them and formidable to tyrants only.

He has called together legislative bodies at places unusual, uncomfortable, and distant from the depository of their Public Records, for the sole purpose of fatiguing them into compliance with his measures.

He has dissolved Representative Houses repeatedly, for opposing with manly firmness his invasions on the rights of the people.

He has refused for a long time, after such dissolutions, to cause others to be elected; whereby the Legislative Powers, incapable of Annihilation, have returned to the People at large for their exercise; the State remaining in the mean time exposed to all the dangers of invasion from without, and convulsions within.

He has endeavored to prevent the population of these States; for that purpose obstructing the Laws for Naturalization of Foreigners; refusing to pass others to encourage their migration hither, and raising the conditions of new Appropriations of Lands.

He has obstructed the Administration of Justice, by refusing his Assent to Laws for establishing Judiciary Powers.

He has made Judges dependent on his Will alone, for the tenure of their offices, and the amount and payment of their salaries.

He has erected a multitude of New Offices, and sent hither swarms of Officers to harass our people, and eat out their substance.

He has kept among us, in times of peace, Standing Armies without the Consent of our legislatures.

He has affected to render the Military independent of and superior to the Civil Power.

He has combined with others to subject us to a jurisdiction foreign to our constitution, and unacknowledged by our laws; giving his Assent to their Acts of pretended Legislation: For quartering large bodies of armed troops among us: For protecting them, by a mock Trial, from punishment for any Murders which they should commit on the Inhabitants of these States: For cutting off our Trade with all parts of the world: For imposing Taxes on us without our Consent: For depriving us in many cases, of the benefits of Trial by Jury; For transporting us beyond Seas to be tried for pretended offenses: for abolishing the free System of English Laws in a neighboring Province, establishing therein an Arbitrary government, and enlarging its Boundaries so as to render it at once an example and fit instrument for introducing the same absolute rule into these Colonies: For taking away our Charters, abolishing our most valuable Laws and altering fundamentally the Forms of our Governments: For suspending our own Legislatures, and declaring themselves invested with power to legislate for us in all cases whatsoever.

He has abdicated Government here, by declaring us out of his Protection and waging War against us.

He has plundered our seas, ravaged our Coasts, burnt our towns, and destroyed the lives of our people.

He is at this time transporting large Armies of foreign Mercenaries to complete the works of death, desolation and tyranny, already begun with circumstances of Cruelty & Perfidy scarcely paralleled in the most barbarous ages, and totally unworthy the Head of a civilized nation.

He has constrained our fellow Citizens taken Captive on the high Seas to bear Arms against their Country, to become the executioners of their friends and Brethren, or to fall themselves by their Hands.

He has excited domestic insurrections amongst us, and has endeavored to bring on the inhabitants of our frontiers, the merciless Indian Savages, whose known rule of warfare, is an undistinguished destruction of all ages, sexes, and conditions.

In every stage of these Oppressions We have Petitioned for Redress in the most humble terms: Our repeated Petitions have been answered only by repeated injury. A Prince, whose character is thus marked by every act which may define a Tyrant, is unfit to be the ruler of a free people.

Nor have We been wanting in attention to our British brethren. We have warned them from time to time of attempts by their legislature to extend an unwarrantable jurisdiction over us. We have reminded them of the circumstances of our emigration and settlement here. We have appealed to their native justice and magnanimity, and we have conjured them by the ties of our common kindred to disavow these usurpations, which would inevitably interrupt our connections and correspondence. They too have been deaf to the voice of justice and of consanguinity. We must, therefore, acquiesce in the necessity, which denounces our Separation, and hold them, as we hold the rest of mankind, Enemies in War, in Peace Friends.

We, THEREFORE, the Representatives of the UNITED STATES OF AMERICA, in General Congress, Assembled, appealing to the Supreme Judge of the world for the rectitude of our intentions, do, in the Name, and by Authority of the good People of these Colonies, solemnly publish and declare, That these United Colonies are, and of Right ought to be FREE AND INDEPENDENT STATES; that they are Absolved from all Allegiance to the British Crown, and that all political connection between them and the State of Great Britain, is and ought to be totally dissolved; and that as Free and Independent States, they have full Power to levy War, conclude Peace, contract Alliances, establish Commerce, and to do all other Acts and Things which Independent States may of right do. And for the support of this Declaration, with a firm reliance on the protection of Divine Providence, we mutually pledge to each other our Lives, our Fortunes, and our sacred Honor.

QUESTIONS

1. *The Declaration of Independence was addressed to several audiences: the king of Great Britain, the people of Great Britain, the people of America, and the world at large. Show ways in which the final draft was adapted for its several audiences.*
2. *Examine the second paragraph of each version closely. How have the revisions in the final version increased its effectiveness over the first draft?*
3. *The Declaration has often been called a classic example of deductive argument: setting up general statements, relating particular cases to them, and drawing conclusions. Trace this pattern through the document, noting the way each part is developed. Would the document have been as effective if the long middle part had either come first or been left out entirely? Explain.*
4. *Find the key terms and phrases of the Declaration (such as "these truths . . . self-evident," "created equal," "unalienable rights," and so on) and determine how fully they are defined by the contexts in which they occur. Why are no formal definitions given for them?*
5. *The signers of the Declaration appeal both to general principles and to factual evidence in presenting their case. Which of the appeals to principle could still legitimately be made today by a nation eager to achieve independence? In other words, how far does the Declaration reflect unique events of history and how far does it reflect universal aspirations and ideals?*

E. B. WHITE

Democracy

July 3, 1943

We received a letter from the Writers' War Board the other day asking for a statement on "The Meaning of Democracy." It presumably is our duty to comply with such a request, and it is certainly our pleasure.

Surely the Board knows what democracy is. It is the line that forms on the right. It is the don't in don't shove. It is the hole in the stuffed shirt through which the sawdust slowly trickles; it is the dent in the high hat. Democracy is the recurrent suspicion that more than half of the people are right more than half of the time. It is the feeling of privacy in the voting booths, the feeling of communion in the libraries, the feeling of vitality everywhere. Democracy is a letter to the editor. Democracy is the score at the beginning of the ninth. It is an idea which hasn't been disproved yet, a song the words of which have not gone bad. It's the mustard on the hot dog and the cream in the rationed coffee. Democracy is a request from a War Board, in the middle of a morning in the middle of a war, wanting to know what democracy is.

QUESTIONS

1. White's piece is dated July 3, 1943, the middle of World War II. How did the occasion shape what White says about democracy?
2. Look up "democracy" in a standard desk dictionary. Of the several meanings given, which one best applies to White's definition (below)? Does more than one apply?
3. Translate White's definition into non-metaphorical language. (For example, "It is the line that forms on the right" might be translated by "It has no special privileges.") Determine what is lost in the translation, or, in other words, what White has gained by using figurative language.

CARL BECKER

Democracy[1]

Democracy, like liberty or science or progress, is a word with which we are all so familiar that we rarely take the trouble to ask what we mean by it. It is a term, as the devotees of semantics say, which has no "referent"—there is no precise or palpable thing or object which we all think of when the word is pronounced. On the contrary, it is a word which connotes different things to different people, a kind of conceptual Gladstone bag which, with a little manipulation, can be made to accommodate almost any collection of social facts we may wish to carry about in it. In it we can as easily pack a dictatorship as any other form of government. We have only to stretch the concept to include any form of government supported by a majority of the people, for whatever reasons and by whatever means of expressing assent, and before we know it the empire of Napoleon, the Soviet regime of Stalin, and the Fascist systems of Mussolini and Hitler are all safely in the bag. But if this is what we mean by democracy, then virtually all forms of government are democratic, since virtually all governments, except in times of revolution, rest upon the explicit or implicit consent of the people. In order to discuss democracy intelligently it will be necessary, therefore, to define it, to attach to the word a sufficiently precise meaning to avoid the confusion which is not infrequently the chief result of such discussions.

All human institutions, we are told, have their ideal forms laid

1. From Lecture I, "The Ideal," in *Modern Democracy*, 1941.

away in heaven, and we do not need to be told that the actual institutions conform but indifferently to these ideal counterparts. It would be possible then to define democracy either in terms of the ideal or in terms of the real form—to define it as government of the people, by the people, for the people; or to define it as government of the people, by the politicians, for whatever pressure groups can get their interests taken care of. But as a historian I am naturally disposed to be satisfied with the meaning which, in the history of politics, men have commonly attributed to the word—a meaning, needless to say, which derives partly from the experience and partly from the aspirations of mankind. So regarded, the term democracy refers primarily to a form of government, and it has always meant government by the many as opposed to government by the one—government by the people as opposed to government by a tyrant, a dictator, or an absolute monarch. This is the most general meaning of the word as men have commonly understood it.

In this antithesis there are, however, certain implications, always tacitly understood, which give a more precise meaning to the term. Peisistratus, for example, was supported by a majority of the people, but his government was never regarded as a democracy for all that. Caesar's power derived from a popular mandate, conveyed through established republican forms, but that did not make his government any the less a dictatorship. Napoleon called his government a democratic empire, but no one, least of all Napoleon himself, doubted that he had destroyed the last vestiges of the democratic republic. Since the Greeks first used the term, the essential test of democratic government has always been this: the source of political authority must be and remain in the people and not in the ruler. A democratic government has always meant one in which the citizens, or a sufficient number of them to represent more or less effectively the common will, freely act from time to time, and according to established forms, to appoint or recall the magistrates and to enact or revoke the laws by which the community is governed. This I take to be the meaning which history has impressed upon the term democracy as a form of government.

WALTER LIPPMANN
The Indispensable Opposition

Were they pressed hard enough, most men would probably confess that political freedom—that is to say, the right to speak freely and to act in opposition—is a noble ideal rather than a practical necessity. As the case for freedom is generally put today, the argument lends itself to this feeling. It is made to appear that, whereas each man claims his freedom as a matter of right, the freedom he accords to other men is a matter of toleration. Thus, the defense of freedom of opinion tends to rest not on its substantial, beneficial, and indispensable consequences, but on a somewhat eccentric, a rather vaguely benevolent, attachment to an abstraction.

It is all very well to say with Voltaire, "I wholly disapprove of what you say, but will defend to the death your right to say it," but as a matter of fact most men will not defend to the death the rights of other men: if they disapprove sufficiently what other men say, they will somehow suppress those men if they can.

So, if this is the best that can be said for liberty of opinion, that a man must tolerate his opponents because everyone has a "right" to say what he pleases, then we shall find that liberty of opinion is a luxury, safe only in pleasant times when men can be tolerant because they are not deeply and vitally concerned.

Yet actually, as a matter of historic fact, there is a much stronger foundation for the great constitutional right of freedom of speech, and as a matter of practical human experience there is a much more compelling reason for cultivating the habits of free men. We take, it seems to me, a naïvely self-righteous view when we argue as if the right of our opponents to speak were something that we protect because we are magnanimous, noble, and unselfish. The compelling reason why, if liberty of opinion did not exist, we should have to invent it, why it will eventually have to be restored in all civilized countries where it is now suppressed, is that we must protect the right of our opponents to speak because we must hear what they have to say.

We miss the whole point when we imagine that we tolerate the freedom of our political opponents as we tolerate a howling baby next door, as we put up with the blasts from our neighbor's radio because we are too peaceable to heave a brick through the window. If this were all there is to freedom of opinion, that we are too good-natured or too timid to do anything about our opponents and our critics except to let them talk, it would be difficult to say whether we are tolerant because we are magnanimous or because we are lazy, because we have strong principles or because we lack serious convictions, whether we have the hospitality of an inquiring mind or the indifference of an empty mind. And so, if we truly wish to understand why freedom is necessary in a civilized society, we must begin by realizing that, because freedom of discussion improves our own opinions, the liberties of other men are our own vital necessity.

We are much closer to the essence of the matter, not when we quote Voltaire, but when we go to the doctor and pay him to ask us the most embarrassing questions and to prescribe the most disagreeable diet. When we pay the doctor to exercise complete freedom of speech about the cause and cure of our stomachache, we do not look upon ourselves as tolerant and magnanimous, and worthy to be admired by ourselves. We have enough common sense to know that if we threaten to put the doctor in jail because we do not like the diagnosis and the prescription it will be unpleasant for the doctor, to be sure, but equally unpleasant for our own stomach-ache. That is why even the most ferocious dictator would rather be treated by a doctor who was free to think and speak the truth than by his own Minister of Propaganda. For there is a point, the point at which things really matter, where the freedom of others is no longer a question of their right but of our own need.

The point at which we recognize this need is much higher in some men than in others. The totalitarian rulers think they do not need the freedom of an opposition: they exile, imprison, or shoot their opponents. We have concluded on the basis of practical experience, which goes back to Magna Carta and beyond, that we need the opposition. We pay the opposition salaries out of the public treasury.

In so far as the usual apology for freedom of speech ignores this experience, it becomes abstract and eccentric rather than concrete and human. The emphasis is generally put on the right to speak, as if all that mattered were that the doctor should be free to go out into the park and explain to the vacant air why I have a stomach-ache. Surely that is a miserable caricature of the great civic right which men have bled and died for. What really matters is that the doctor should tell *me* what ails me, that I should listen to him; that if I do not like what he says I should be free to call in another doctor; and that then the first doctor should have to listen to the second doctor; and that out of all the speaking and listening, the give-and-take of opinions, the truth should be arrived at.

This is the creative principle of freedom of speech, not that it is a system for the tolerating of error, but that it is a system for finding the truth. It may not produce the truth, or the whole truth all the time, or often, or in some cases ever. But if the truth can be found, there is no other system which will normally and habitually find so much truth. Until we have thoroughly understood this principle, we shall not know why we must value our liberty, or how we can protect and develop it.

Let us apply this principle to the system of public speech in a totalitarian state. We may, without any serious falsification, picture a condition of affairs in which the mass of the people are being addressed through one broadcasting system by one man and his chosen subordinates. The orators speak. The audience listens but cannot and dare not speak back. It is a system of one-way communication; the opinions of the rulers are broadcast outwardly to the mass of the people. But nothing comes back to the rulers from the people except the cheers; nothing returns in the way of knowledge of forgotten facts, hidden feelings, neglected truths, and practical suggestions.

But even a dictator cannot govern by his own one-way inspiration alone. In practice, therefore, the totalitarian rulers get back the reports of the secret police and of their party henchmen down among the crowd. If these reports are competent, the rulers may manage to remain in touch with public sentiment. Yet that is not enough to know what the audience feels. The rulers have also to make great decisions that have enormous consequences, and here their system provides virtually no help from the give-and-take of opinion in the nation. So they must either rely on their own intuition, which cannot be permanently and continually inspired, or, if they are intelligent despots, encourage their trusted advisers and their technicians to speak and debate freely in their presence.

On the walls of the houses of Italian peasants one may see inscribed in large letters the legend, "Mussolini is always right." But if that legend is taken seriously by Italian ambassadors, by the Italian General Staff, and by the Ministry of Finance, then all one can say is heaven help Mussolini, heaven help Italy, and the new Emperor of Ethiopia.

For at some point, even in a totalitarian state, it is indispensable that there should exist the freedom of opinion which causes opposing opinions to be debated. As time goes on, that is less and less easy under a despotism; critical discussion disappears as the internal opposition is liquidated in favor of men who think and feel alike. That is why the early successes of despots, of Napoleon I and of Napoleon III, have usually been followed by an irreparable mistake. For in listening only to his yes men—the others being in exile or in concentration camps, or terrified—the despot shuts himself off from the truth that no man can dispense with.

We know all this well enough when we contemplate the dictatorships. But when we try to picture our own system, by way of contrast, what picture do we have in our minds? It is, is it not, that anyone may stand up on his own soapbox and say anything he pleases, like the individuals in Kipling's poem[1] who sit each in his separate star and draw the Thing as they see it for the God of Things as they are. Kipling, perhaps, could do this, since he was a poet. But the ordinary mortal isolated on his separate star will have an hallucination, and a citizenry declaiming from separate soapboxes will poison the air with hot and nonsensical confusion.

If the democratic alternative to the totalitarian one-way broadcasts is a row of separate soapboxes, than I submit that the alternative is unworkable, is unreasonable, and is humanly unattractive.

---

1. "L'Envoi."

It is above all a false alternative. It is not true that liberty has developed among civilized men when anyone is free to set up a soapbox, is free to hire a hall where he may expound his opinions to those who are willing to listen. On the contrary, freedom of speech is established to achieve its essential purpose only when different opinions are expounded in the same hall to the same audience.

For, while the right to talk may be the beginning of freedom, the necessity of listening is what makes the right important. Even in Russia and Germany a man may still stand in an open field and speak his mind. What matters is not the utterance of opinions. What matters is the confrontation of opinions in debate. No man can care profoundly that every fool should say what he likes. Nothing has been accomplished if the wisest man proclaims his wisdom in the middle of the Sahara Desert. This is the shadow. We have the substance of liberty when the fool is compelled to listen to the wise man and learn; when the wise man is compelled to take account of the fool, and to instruct him; when the wise man can increase his wisdom by hearing the judgment of his peers.

That is why civilized men must cherish liberty—as a means of promoting the discovery of truth. So we must not fix our whole attention on the right of anyone to hire his own hall, to rent his own broadcasting station, to distribute his own pamphlets. These rights are incidental; and though they must be preserved, they can be preserved only by regarding them as incidental, as auxiliary to the substance of liberty that must be cherished and cultivated.

Freedom of speech is best conceived, therefore, by having in mind the picture of a place like the American Congress, an assembly where opposing views are represented, where ideas are not merely uttered but debated, or the British Parliament, where men who are free to speak are also compelled to answer. We may picture the true condition of freedom as existing in a place like a court of law, where witnesses testify and are cross-examined, where the lawyer argues against the opposing lawyer before the same judge and in the presence of one jury. We may picture freedom as existing in a forum where the speaker must respond to questions; in a gathering of scientists where the data, the hypothesis, and the conclusion are submitted to men competent to judge them; in a reputable newspaper which not only will publish the opinions of those who disagree but will re-examine its own opinion in the light of what they say.

Thus the essence of freedom of opinion is not in mere toleration as such, but in the debate which toleration provides: it is not in the venting of opinion, but in the confrontation of opinion. That this is the practical substance can readily be understood when we remember how differently we feel and act about the censorship and regulation of opinion purveyed by different media of communication. We find then that, in so far as the medium makes difficult the confrontation of opinion in debate, we are driven towards censorship and regulation.

There is, for example, the whispering campaign, the circulation of anonymous rumors by men who cannot be compelled to prove what they say. They put the utmost strain on our tolerance, and there are few who do not rejoice when the anonymous slanderer is caught, exposed, and punished. At a higher level there is the moving picture, a most powerful medium for conveying ideas, but a medium which does not permit debate. A moving picture cannot be answered effectively by another moving picture; in all free countries there is some censorship of the movies, and there would be more if the producers did not recognize their limitations by avoiding political controversy. There is then the radio. Here debate is difficult: it is not easy to make sure that the speaker is being answered in the presence of the same audience. Inevitably, there is some regulation of the radio.

When we reach the newspaper press, the opportunity for debate is so considerable that discontent cannot grow to the point where under normal conditions there is any disposition to regulate the press. But when newspapers abuse their power by injuring people who have no means of replying, a disposition to regulate the press appears. When we arrive at Congress we find that, because the membership of the House is so large, full debate is impracticable. So there are restrictive rules. On the other hand, in the Senate, where the conditions of full debate exist, there is almost absolute freedom of speech.

This shows us that the preservation and development of freedom of opinion are not only a matter of adhering to abstract legal rights, but also, and very urgently, a matter of organizing and arranging sufficient debate. Once we have a firm hold on the central principle, there are many practical conclusions to be drawn. We then realize that the defense of freedom of opinion consists primarily in perfecting the opportunity for an adequate give-and-take of opinion; it consists also in regulating the freedom of those revolutionists who cannot or will not permit or maintain debate when it does not suit their purposes.

We must insist that free oratory is only the beginning of free speech; it is not the end, but a means to an end. The end is to find the truth. The practical justification of civil liberty is not that self-expression is one of the rights of man. It is that the examination of opinion is one of the necessities of man. For experience tells us that it is only when freedom of opinion becomes the compulsion to debate that the seed which our fathers planted has produced its fruit. When that is understood, freedom will be cherished not because it is a vent for our opinions but because it is the surest method of correcting them.

The unexamined life, said Socrates, is unfit to be lived by man. This is the virtue of liberty, and the ground on which we may best justify our belief in it, that it tolerates error in order to serve the truth. When men are brought face to face with their opponents, forced to listen and learn and mend their ideas, they cease to be children and savages and begin to live like civilized men. Then only is freedom a reality, when men may voice their opinions because they must examine their opinions.

The only reason for dwelling on all this is that if we are to preserve democracy we must understand its principles. And the principle which distinguishes it from all other forms of government is that in a democracy the opposition not only is tolerated as constitutional but must be maintained because it is in fact indispensable.

The democratic system cannot be operated without effective opposition. For, in making the great experiment of governing people by consent rather than by coercion, it is not sufficient that the party in power should have a majority. It is just as necessary that the party in power should never outrage the minority. That means that it must listen to the minority and be moved by the criticisms of the minority. That means that its measures must take account of the minority's objections, and that in administering measures it must remember that the minority may become the majority.

The opposition is indispensable. A good statesman, like any other sensible human being, always learns more from his opponents than from his fervent supporters. For his supporters will push him to disaster unless his opponents show him where the dangers are. So if he is wise he will often pray to be delivered from his friends, because they will ruin him. But, though it hurts, he ought also to pray never to be left without opponents; for they keep him on the path of reason and good sense.

The national unity of a free people depends upon a sufficiently even balance of political power to make it impracticable for the administration to be arbitrary and for the opposition to be revolutionary and irreconcilable. Where that balance no longer exists, democracy perishes. For unless all the citizens of a state are forced by circumstances to compromise, unless they feel that they can affect policy but that no one can wholly dominate it, unless by habit and necessity they have to give and take, freedom cannot be maintained.

QUESTIONS

1. What is Lippmann's reason for dividing the essay into three parts? What is the purpose of the third part?

2. What is the importance of Lippmann's distinction between "free oratory" and "free speech" (p. 779)?

3. What does Lippmann mean when he says that the point at which we recognize the need for the freedom of others "is much higher in some men than in others" (p. 776)? Does this assertion in any way weaken his argument?

4. Why has Lippmann discussed motion pictures but not literature (p. 779)? How sound is his view that the motion picture is "a medium which does not permit debate"? Does literature permit debate?

5. What does Lippmann mean by his statement that "the usual apology for freedom of speech . . . becomes abstract and eccentric rather than concrete and human" (p. 776)? Why has he chosen these particular words to contrast the "usual apology" with his own view? Is his argument "concrete and human"?

6. Thurber's rabbits (p. 695) listened to their opposition—that is, "the other animals, who lived at a great distance"—and were annihilated. Does Thurber's fable suggest any necessary qualification for Lippmann's thesis concerning the value of the opposition? Explain.

7. Lippmann's essay was written before the term "brainwashing" was in common use. If he were writing the essay today, how might he take account of this term?

Prose Forms: Apothegms

[At the beginning of Bacon's essay "Of Truth," jesting Pilate asks, "What is truth?" and does not stay for an answer. Perhaps Pilate asked in jest because he thought the question foolish; perhaps because he thought an answer impossible. Something of Pilate's skepticism is in most of us, but something too of a belief that there is truth, even if—as the history of philosophy teaches us—determining its nature may be enormously difficult. We readily assume some things to be true even if we hesitate to say what ultimately is Truth.

The test of truth most often is an appeal to the observed facts of experience. The observation of experience yields knowledge; the generalized statement of that knowledge yields a concept of the experience; the concise, descriptive form in which that concept is expressed we call variously, apothegm, proverb, maxim, or aphorism. Thus Sir James Mackintosh can speak of apothegms as "the condensed good sense of nations," because the apothegm conveys the distilled observations of men about their own persistent conduct. To hear the familiar "Absence makes the heart grow fonder" is to be reminded of a general truth which you and the world acknowledge. It does not matter that the equally familiar "Out of sight, out of mind" seems to contradict the other saying; both are true but applicable to different situations. Both statements are immediately recognizable as true and neither requires to be argued for, representing as they do the collective experience of mankind intelligently observed.

Not everyone is as astute an observer as the writer of apothegms and maxims, of course, but everyone is presumably capable of perceiving their rightness. What we perceive first is the facts to which the saying applies. When Franklin says "An empty bag cannot stand upright" (in 1740 he obviously had in mind a cloth bag), we acknowledge that this is the condition of the empty bag—and of ourselves when we are empty. Or when La Rochefoucauld says "We are all strong enough to endure the misfortunes of others," he too observes a condition that exists among men.

Many aphoristic assertions claim their validity primarily in descriptive terms. But the descriptive "is" in most apothegms and maxims is joined to a normative "ought" and the sayings therefore convey

782

admonitions about and judgments of the conditions they describe. "Waste not, want not" is a simple illustration of this use of fact to admonish. Samuel Butler briefly gives us the presumed fact that "the world will always be governed by self-interest." Then he quickly advises: "We should not try to stop this, we should try to make the self-interest of cads a little more consistent with that of decent people." The condition of "ought" need not always be admonitory; it may be the implied judgment in La Rochefoucauld's assertion that "It is the habit of mediocre minds to condemn all that is beyond their grasp." The judgment is explicit in Franklin's "Fish and visitors stink in three days." And Bierce's definitions of ordinary words are not specifications of meanings in the way of ordinary dictionaries, but critical concepts of the experiences to which the words point.

"Wisdom" or "good sense," then, is the heart of the apothegm or maxim, the conjunction of "is" and "ought" in an assertion of universal truth. Unlike ordinary assertions of fact or opinion usually concerned with particular rather than universal experience, the wise saying is complete in its brevity. Before the ordinary assertion is allowed to hold, we require that the assumptions on which it rests, the implications it carries, the critical concepts and terms it contains, be examined closely and explored or justified. If someone says that the modern college student wants most to succeed materially in life, we want to be satisfied about what constitutes "modern," which college students (and where) are referred to, what else is involved in the comparative "most," what specifically is meant by "materially." But the apothegm assumes facts widely known and accepted, and in its judgments invokes values or attitudes readily intelligible to the great majority. It is the truth as most men experience it.

In a sense, every writer's concern is ultimately with truth. Certainly the essayist is directly concerned, in his definition and ordering of ideas, to say what is true and, somehow, to say it "new." Much of what he says is of the nature of assertion about particular experience; he must therefore be at pains to handle such matters as assumptions and logical proofs carefully and deliberately. But he cannot always be starting from scratch, not daring to assume anything, trusting no certain knowledge or experience or beliefs held in common with his fellows. Careful he must be, but also aware that available to him, in addition to methods of logical analysis and proof, rules of evidence, and the other means to effective exposition, is the whole memory and record of the vast experience of the race contained in a people's apothegms and aphorisms. In them is a treasury of truths useful to many demands of clarity and precision. And in them, too, is a valuable lesson in the way a significantly large body of experience—direct, in a person's day-to-day encounters; indirect, in his study of all forms of history—can be observed, conceptualized, and then expressed in an economy of language brief in form, comprehensive in meaning, and satisfyingly true.]

W. H. AUDEN: Apothegms

Some books are undeservedly forgotten; none are undeservedly remembered.

You do not educate a person's palate by telling him that what he has been in the habit of eating—watery, overboiled cabbage, let us say—is disgusting, but by persuading him to try a dish of vegetables which have been properly cooked. With some people, it is true, you seem to get quicker results by telling them—"Only vulgar people like overcooked cabbage; the best people like cabbage as the Chinese cook it"—but the results are less likely to be lasting.

No poet or novelist wishes he were the only one who ever lived, but most of them wish they were the only one alive, and quite a number fondly believe their wish has been granted.

The integrity of a writer is more threatened by appeals to his social conscience, his political or religious convictions, than by appeals to his cupidity. It is morally less confusing to be goosed by a traveling salesman than by a bishop.

Only a minor talent can be a perfect gentleman; a major talent is always more than a bit of a cad. Hence the importance of minor writers—as teachers of good manners. Now and again, an exquisite minor work can make a master feel thoroughly ashamed of himself.

Narcissus does not fall in love with his reflection because it is beautiful, but because it is *his*. If it were his beauty that enthralled him he would be set free in a few years by its fading.

"After all," sighed Narcissus the hunchback, "on *me* it looks good."

Our sufferings and weaknesses, in so far as they are personal, *our* sufferings, *our* weaknesses, are of no literary interest whatsoever. They are only interesting in so far as we can see them as typical of the human condition. A suffering, a weakness, which cannot be expressed as an aphorism should not be mentioned.

The same rules apply to self-examination as apply to confession to a priest: *be brief, be blunt, be gone.* Be brief, be blunt, forget. The scrupuland is a nasty specimen.

In a state of panic, a man runs round in circles by himself. In a state of joy, he links hands with others and they dance round in a circle together.

A sense of humor develops in a society to the degree that its members are simultaneously conscious of being each a unique person and of being all in common subjection to unalterable laws.

Among those whom I like or admire, I can find no common denominator, but among those whom I love, I, can: all of them make me laugh.

If Homer had tried reading the *Iliad* to the gods on Olympus, they would either have started to fidget and presently asked if he hadn't got something a little lighter, or, taking it as a comic poem, would have roared with laughter or possibly, even, reacting like ourselves to a tear-jerking movie, have poured pleasing tears.

AMBROSE BIERCE: *from* The Devil's Dictionary

abdication, *n.* An act whereby a sovereign attests his sense of the high temperature of the throne.

abscond, *v.i.* To "move in a mysterious way," commonly with the property of another.

absent, *adj.* Peculiarly exposed to the tooth of detraction; vilified; hopelessly in the wrong; superseded in the consideration and affection of another.

accident, *n.* An inevitable occurrence due to the action of immutable natural laws.

accordion, *n.* An instrument in harmony with the sentiments of an assassin.

achievement, *n.* The death of endeavor and the birth of disgust.

admiration, *n.* Our polite recognition of another's resemblance to ourselves.

alone, *adj.* In bad company.

applause, *n.* The echo of a platitude.

ardor, *n.* The quality that distinguishes love without knowledge.

bore, *n.* A person who talks when you wish him to listen.

cemetery, *n.* An isolated suburban spot where mourners match lies, poets write at a target and stone-cutters spell for a wager. The inscription following will serve to illustrate the success attained in these Olympian games:

> His virtues were so conspicuous that his enemies, unable to overlook them, denied them, and his friends, to whose loose lives they were a rebuke, represented them as vices. They are here commemorated by his family, who shared them.

childhood, *n.* The period of human life intermediate between the idiocy of infancy and the folly of youth—two removes from the sin of manhood and three from the remorse of age.

Christian, *n.* One who believes that the New Testament is a divinely inspired book admirably suited to the spiritual needs of his neighbor. One who follows the teachings of Christ in so far as they are not inconsistent with a life of sin.

compulsion, *n.* The eloquence of power.

congratulation, *n.* The civility of envy.

conservative, *n.* A statesman who is enamored of existing evils, as distinguished from the Liberal, who wishes to replace them with others.

consult, *v.t.* To seek another's approval of a course already decided on.

contempt, *n.* The feeling of a prudent man for an enemy who is too formidable safely to be opposed.

coward, *n.* One who in a perilous emergency thinks with his legs.

debauchee, *n.* One who has so earnestly pursued pleasure that he has had the misfortune to overtake it.

destiny, *n.* A tyrant's authority for crime and a fool's excuse for failure.

diplomacy, *n.* The patriotic art of lying for one's country.

distance, *n.* The only thing that the rich are willing for the poor to call theirs and keep.

duty, *n.* That which sternly impels us in the direction of profit, along the line of desire.

education, *n.* That which discloses to the wise and disguises from the foolish their lack of understanding.

erudition, *n.* Dust shaken out of a book into an empty skull.

extinction, *n.* The raw material out of which theology created the future state.

faith, *n.* Belief without evidence in what is told by one who speaks without knowledge, of things without parallel.

genealogy, *n.* An account of one's descent from an ancestor who did not particularly care to trace his own.

ghost, *n.* The outward and visible sign of an inward fear.

habit, *n.* A shackle for the free.

heaven, *n.* A place where the wicked cease from troubling you with talk of their personal affairs, and the good listen with attention while you expound your own.

historian, *n.* A broad-gauge gossip.

hope, *n.* Desire and expectation rolled into one.

hypocrite, *n.* One who, professing virtues that he does not respect, secures the advantage of seeming to be what he despises.

impiety, *n.* Your irreverence toward my deity.

impunity, *n.* Wealth.

language, *n.* The music with which we charm the serpents guarding another's treasure.

logic, *n.* The art of thinking and reasoning in strict accordance with the limitations and incapacities of the human misunderstanding. The basis of logic is the syllogism, consisting of a major and a minor premise and a conclusion—thus:

Major Premise: Sixty men can do a piece of work sixty times as quickly as one man.

Minor Premise: One man can dig a post-hole in sixty seconds; therefore—

Conclusion: Sixty men can dig a post-hole in one second.

This may be called the syllogism arithmetical, in which, by combining logic and mathematics, we obtain a double certainty and are twice blessed.

love, *n.* A temporary insanity curable by marriage or by removal of the patient from the influences under which he incurred the disorder. This disease, like *caries* and many other ailments, is prevalent only among civilized races living under artificial conditions; barbarous nations breathing pure air and eating simple food enjoy immunity from its ravages. It is sometimes fatal, but more frequently to the physician than to the patient.

miracle, *n.* An act or event out of the order of nature and unaccountable, as beating a normal hand of four kings and an ace with four aces and a king.

monkey, *n.* An arboreal animal which makes itself at home in genealogical trees.

mouth, *n.* In man, the gateway to the soul; in woman, the outlet of the heart.

non-combatant, *n.* A dead Quaker.

platitude, *n.* The fundamental element and special glory of popular literature. A thought that snores in words that smoke. The wisdom of a million fools in the diction of a dullard. A fossil sentiment in artificial rock. A moral without the fable. All that is mortal of a departed truth. A demi-tasse of milk-and-morality. The Pope's-nose of a featherless peacock. A jelly-fish withering on the shore of the sea of thought. The cackle surviving the egg. A dessicated epigram.

pray, *v.* To ask that the laws of the universe be annulled in behalf of a single petitioner confessedly unworthy.

presidency, *n.* The greased pig in the field game of American politics.

prude, *n.* A bawd hiding behind the back of her demeanor.

rapacity, *n.* Providence without industry. The thrift of power.

reason, *v.i.* To weigh probabilities in the scales of desire.

religion, *n.* A daughter of Hope and Fear, explaining to Ignorance the nature of the Unknowable.

resolute, *adj.* Obstinate in a course that we approve.

retaliation, *n.* The natural rock upon which is reared the Temple of Law.

saint, *n.* A dead sinner revised and edited.

The Duchess of Orleans relates that the irreverent old calumniator, Marshal Villeroi, who in his youth had known St. Francis

de Sales, said, on hearing him called saint: "I am delighted to
hear that Monsieur de Sales is a saint. He was fond of saying indelicate things, and used to cheat at cards. In other respects he
was a perfect gentleman, though a fool."

valor, *n.* A soldierly compound of vanity, duty and the gambler's
hope:

> "Why have you halted?" roared the commander of a division at
> Chickamauga, who had ordered a charge; "move forward, sir, at once."
> "General," said the commander of the delinquent brigade, "I am
> persuaded that any further display of valor by my troops will bring
> them into collision with the enemy."

WILLIAM BLAKE: Proverbs of Hell

In seed time learn, in harvest teach, in winter enjoy.
Drive your cart and your plough over the bones of the dead.
The road of excess leads to the palace of wisdom.
Prudence is a rich, ugly old maid courted by Incapacity.
He who desires but acts not, breeds pestilence.
The cut worm forgives the plough.
Dip him in the river who loves water.
A fool sees not the same tree that a wise man sees.
He whose face gives no light, shall never become a star.
Eternity is in love with the productions of time.
The busy bee has no time for sorrow.
The hours of folly are measur'd by the clock; but of wisdom, no
clock can measure.
All wholesome food is caught without a net or a trap.
Bring out number, weight, and measure in a year of dearth.
No bird soars too high, if he soars with his own wings.
A dead body revenges not injuries.
The most sublime act is to set another before you.
If the fool would persist in his folly he would become wise.
Folly is the cloak of knavery.
Shame is Pride's cloak.
Prisons are built with stones of Law, brothels with bricks of Religion.
The pride of the peacock is the glory of God.
The lust of the goat is the bounty of God.
The wrath of the lion is the wisdom of God.
The nakedness of woman is the work of God.
Excess of sorrow laughs. Excess of joy weeps.
The roaring of lions, the howling of wolves, the raging of the stormy
sea, and the destructive sword are portions of eternity too great
for the eye of man.
The fox condemns the trap, not himself.
Joys impregnate. Sorrows bring forth.

Let man wear the fell of the lion, woman the fleece of the sheep.

The bird a nest, the spider a web, man friendship.

The selfish, smiling fool, and the sullen, frowning fool shall be both thought wise, that they may be a rod.

What is now proved was once only imagin'd.

The rat, the mouse, the fox, the rabbit watch the roots; the lion, the tiger, the horse, the elephant watch the fruits.

The cistern contains: the fountain overflows.

One thought fills immensity.

Always be ready to speak your mind, and a base man will avoid you.

Everything possible to be believ'd is an image of truth.

The eagle never lost so much time as when he submitted to learn of the crow.

The fox provides for himself; but God provides for the lion.

Think in the morning. Act in the noon. Eat in the evening. Sleep in the night.

He who has suffer'd you to impose on him, knows you.

As the plough follows words, so God rewards prayers.

The tigers of wrath are wiser than the horses of instruction.

Expect poison from the standing water.

You never know what is enough unless you know what is more than enough.

Listen to the fool's reproach! it is a kingly title!

The eyes of fire, the nostrils of air, the mouth of water, the beard of earth.

The weak in courage is strong in cunning.

The apple tree never asks the beech how he shall grow; nor the lion, the horse, how he shall take his prey.

The thankful receiver bears a plentiful harvest.

If others had not been foolish, we should be so.

The soul of sweet delight can never be defil'd.

When thou seest an eagle, thou seest a portion of Genius; lift up thy head!

As the caterpillar chooses the fairest leaves to lay her eggs on, so the priest lays his curse on the fairest joys.

To create a little flower is the labor of ages.

Damn braces. Bless relaxes.

The best wine is the oldest, the best water the newest.

Prayers plough not! Praises reap not!

Joys laugh not! Sorrows weep not!

The head Sublime, the heart Pathos, the genitals Beauty, the hands and feet Proportion.

As the air to a bird or the sea to a fish, so is contempt to the contemptible.

The crow wish'd everything was black, the owl that everything was white.

Exuberance is Beauty.

If the lion was advised by the fox, he would be cunning.

Improvement makes straight roads; but the crooked roads without improvement are roads of Genius.

Sooner murder an infant in its cradle than nurse unacted desires.

Where man is not, nature is barren.

Truth can never be told so as to be understood, and not be believ'd.

Enough! or Too much.

SAMUEL BUTLER: *from* Notebooks

We play out our days as we play out cards, taking them as they come, not knowing what they will be, hoping for a lucky card and sometimes getting one, often getting just the wrong one.

The world will always be governed by self-interest. We should not try to stop this, we should try to make the self-interest of cads a little more consistent with that of decent people.

Morality turns on whether the pleasure precedes or follows the pain. Thus, it is immoral to get drunk because the headache comes after the drinking, but if the headache came first, and the drunkenness afterwards, it would be moral to get drunk.

Morality is the custom of one's country and the current feeling of one's peers. Cannibalism is moral in a cannibal country.

We want words to do more than they can. We try to do with them what comes to very much like trying to mend a watch with a pickaxe or to paint a miniature with a mop; we expect them to help us to grip and dissect that which in ultimate essence is as ungrippable as shadow. Nevertheless there they are; we have got to live with them, and the wise course is to treat them as we do our neighbours, and make the best and not the worst of them. But they are parvenu people as compared with thought and action. What we should read is not the words but the man whom we feel to be behind the words.

Words impede and either kill, or are killed by, perfect thought; but they are, as a scaffolding, useful, if not indispensable, for the building up of imperfect thought and helping to perfect it.

Always eat grapes downwards—that is, always eat the best grape first; in this way there will be none better left on the bunch, and each grape will seem good down to the last. If you eat the other way, you will not have a good grape in the lot. Besides, you will be tempting Providence to kill you before you come to the best. This is why autumn seems better than spring: in the autumn we are eating our days downwards, in the spring each day still seems "very bad." People should live on this principle more than they do, but they do live on it a good deal; from the age of, say, fifty, we eat our days downwards.

In New Zealand for a long time I had to do the washing-up after each meal. I used to do the knives first, for it might please God to take me before I came to the forks, and then what a sell it would have been to have done the forks rather than the knives!

The evil that men do lives after them. Yes, and a good deal of the evil that they never did as well.

A definition is the enclosing a wilderness of ideas within a wall of words.

Perseus and St. George. These dragon-slayers did not take lessons in dragon-slaying, nor do leaders of forlorn hopes generally rehearse their parts beforehand. Small things may be rehearsed, but the greatest are always do-or-die, neck-or-nothing matters.

Silence is not always tact and it is tact that is golden, not silence.

Providence, in making the rain fall also upon the sea, was like the man who, when he was to play Othello, must needs black himself all over.

A little girl and a little boy were looking at a picture of Adam and Eve.

"Which is Adam and which is Eve?" said one.

"I do not know," said the other, "but I could tell if they had their clothes on."

The pursuit of truth is chimerical. That is why it is so hard to say what truth is. There is no permanent absolute unchangeable truth; what we should pursue is the most convenient arrangement of our ideas.

The firmest line that can be drawn upon the smoothest paper has still jagged edges if seen through a mircroscope. This does not matter until important deductions are made on the supposition that there are no jagged edges.

Truth generally is kindness, but where the two diverge or collide, kindness should override truth.

We do with truth much as we do with God. We create it according to our own requirements and then say that it has created us, or requires that we shall do or think so and so—whatever we find convenient.

"What is Truth?" is often asked, as though it were harder to say what truth is than what anything else is. But what is Justice? What is anything? An eternal contradiction in terms meets us at the end of every enquiry. We are not required to know what truth is, but to speak the truth, and so with justice.

Imagination depends mainly upon memory, but there is a small percentage of creation of something out of nothing with it. We can invent a trifle more than can be got at by mere combination of remembered things.

Intuition and evidence seem to have something of the same relation that faith and reason, luck and cunning, free-will and necessity and demand and supply have. They grow up hand in hand and no man can say which comes first. It is the same with life and death, which lurk within the others as do rest and unrest, change and persistence, heat and cold, poverty and riches, harmony and counterpoint, night and day, summer and winter.

And so with pantheism and atheism; loving everybody is loving nobody, and God everywhere is, practically, God nowhere. I once asked a man if he was a free-thinker; he replied that he did not think he was. And so, I have heard of a man exclaiming "I am an atheist, thank God!" Those who say there is a God are wrong unless they mean at the same time that there is no God, and vice versa. The difference is the same as that between plus nothing and minus nothing, and it is hard to say which we ought to admire and thank most—the first theist or the first atheist. Nevertheless, for many reasons, the plus nothing is to be preferred.

BENJAMIN FRANKLIN: *from* Poor Richard's Almanack

Light purse, heavy heart.   1733
He's a fool that makes his doctor his heir.
Love well, whip well.
Hunger never saw bad bread.
Fools make feasts, and wise men eat 'em.
He that lies down with dogs, shall rise up with fleas.
He is ill clothed, who is bare of virtue.
There is no little enemy.

Without justice courage is weak.   1734
Where there's marriage without love, there will be love without marriage.
Do good to thy friend to keep him, to thy enemy to gain him.
He that cannot obey, cannot command.
Marry your son when you will, but your daughter when you can.

Approve not of him who commends all you say.   1735
Necessity never made a good bargain.
Be slow in chusing a friend, slower in changing.
Three may keep a secret, if two of them are dead.
Deny self for self's sake.
To be humble to superiors is duty, to equals courtesy, to inferiors
nobleness.

Fish and visitors stink in three days.   1736
Do not do that which you would not have known.
Bargaining has neither friends nor relations.
Now I've a sheep and a cow, every body bids me good morrow.
God helps them that help themselves.
He that speaks much, is much mistaken.
God heals, and the doctor takes the fees.

There are no ugly loves, nor handsome prisons.   1737
Three good meals a day is bad living.

Who has deceiv'd thee so oft as thyself?   1738
Read much, but not many books.
Let thy vices die before thee.

He that falls in love with himself, will have no rivals.   1739
Sin is not hurtful because it is forbidden, but it is forbidden
because it's hurtful.

An empty bag cannot stand upright.   1740

Learn of the skilful: he that teaches himself, hath a fool for his
master.   1741

Death takes no bribes.   1742

An old man in a house is a good sign.   1744
Fear God, and your enemies will fear you.

He's a fool that cannot conceal his wisdom.   1745
Many complain of their memory, few of their judgment.

When the well's dry, we know the worth of water.   1746
The sting of a reproach is the truth of it.

Write injuries in dust, benefits in marble.   1747

Nine men in *ten* are suicides.   1749
A man in a passion rides a mad horse.

He is a governor that governs his passions, and he is a servant
that serves them.   1750
Sorrow is good for nothing but sin.

Calamity and prosperity are the touchstones of integrity.   1752
Generous minds are all of kin.

Haste makes waste.   1753

The doors of wisdom are never shut.   1755

The way to be safe, is never to be secure.   1757

WILLIAM HAZLITT: *from* Characteristics

1. Of all virtues, magnamity is the rarest. There are a hundred persons of merit for one who willingly acknowledges it in another.

13. Some people tell us all the harm—others as carefully conceal all the good they hear of us.

15. The silence of a friend commonly amounts to treachery. His not daring to say anything in our behalf implies a tacit censure.

23. Envy is a littleness of soul, which cannot see beyond a certain point, and if it does not occupy the whole space, feels itself excluded.

27. Those who are the most distrustful of themselves, are the most envious of others; as the most weak and cowardly are the most revengeful.

38. The wish is often "father to the thought"; but we are quite as apt to believe what we dread as what we hope.

46. We like characters and actions which we do not approve. There are amiable vices and obnoxious virtues, on the mere principle that our sympathy with a person who yields to obvious impulses (however prejudicial) is itself agreeable, while to sympathize with exercises of self-denial or fortitude, is a painful effort. Virtue costs the spectator, as well as the performer, something. We are touched by the immediate motives of actions, we judge of them by the consequences. We like a convivial character better than an abstemious one, because the idea of conviviality in the first instance is pleasanter than that of sobriety. For the same reason, we prefer generosity to justice, because the imagination lends itself more easily to an ebullition of feeling, than to the suppression of it on remote and abstract principles; and we like a good-natured fool, or even knave better than the severe professors of wisdom and morality. Cato, Brutus, etc. are characters to admire and applaud, rather than to love or imitate.

57. The surest way to make ourselves agreeable to others is by seeming to think them so. If we appear fully sensible of their good qualities, they will not complain of the want of them in us.

59. Silence is one great art of conversation. He is not a fool who knows when to hold his tongue; and a person may gain credit for

sense, eloquence, wit, who merely says nothing to lessen the opinion which others have of these qualities in themselves.

61. A man who is always defending his friends from the most trifling charges, will be apt to make other people their enemies.

85. The public have neither shame nor gratitude.

89. It is wonderful how soon men acquire talents for offices of trust and importance. The higher the situation, the higher the opinion it gives us of ourselves; and as is our confidence, so is our capacity. We *assume* an equality with circumstances.

105. The error in the reasonings of Mandeville, Rochefoucauld, and others, is this: they first find out that there is something mixed in the motives of all our actions, and they then proceed to argue, that they must all arise from one motive, *viz.* self-love. They make the exception the rule. It would be easy to reverse the argument, and prove that our most selfish actions are disinterested. There is honor among thieves. Robbers, murderers, etc. do not commit those actions, from a pleasure in pure villainy, or for their own benefit only, but from a mistaken regard to the welfare or good opinion of those with whom they are immediately connected.

115. We do not hate those who injure us, if they do not at the same time wound our self-love. We can forgive any one sooner than those who lower us in our own opinion. It is no wonder, therefore, that we as often dislike others for their virtues as for their vices. We naturally hate whatever makes us despise ourselves.

127. We as often repent the good we have done as the ill.

131. The fear of punishment may be necessary to the suppression of vice; but it also suspends the finer motives to virtue.

134. Vulgar prejudices are those which arise out of accident, ignorance, or authority. Natural prejudices are those which arise out of the constitution of the human mind itself.

138. Most codes of morality proceed on a supposition of *Original Sin;* as if the only object was to coerce the headstrong propensities to vice, and there were no natural disposition to good in the mind, which it was possible to improve, refine, and cultivate.

139. This *negative* system of virtue leads to a very low style of moral sentiment. It is as if the highest excellence in a picture was to avoid gross defects in drawing; or in writing, instances of bad grammar. It ought surely to be our aim in virtue, as well as in other things, "to snatch a grace beyond the reach of art."

142. When the imagination is continually led to the brink of vice by a system of terror and denunciations, people fling themselves over the precipice from the mere dread of falling.

145. Honesty is one part of eloquence. We persuade others by being in earnest ourselves.

LA ROCHEFOUCAULD: *from* Maxims

Our virtues are mostly but vices in disguise.

14. Men not only forget benefits received and injuries endured; they even come to dislike those to whom they are indebted, while ceasing to hate those others who have done them harm. Diligence in returning good for good, and in exacting vengeance for evil, comes to be a sort of servitude which we do not readily accept.

19. We are all strong enough to endure the misfortunes of others.

20. The steadiness of the wise man is only the art of keeping his agitations locked within his breast.

25. Firmer virtues are required to support good fortune than bad.

28. Jealousy is, in its way, both fair and reasonable, since its intention is to preserve for ourselves something which is ours, or which we believe to be ours; envy, on the other hand, is a frenzy which cannot endure contemplating the possessions of others.

31. Were we faultless, we would not derive such satisfaction from remarking the faults of others.

38. Our promises are made in hope, and kept in fear.

50. A man convinced of his own merit will accept misfortune as an honor, for thus can he persuade others, as well as himself, that he is a worthy target for the arrows of fate.

56. To achieve a position in the world a man will do his utmost to appear already arrived.

59. There is no accident so disastrous that a clever man cannot derive some profit from it: nor any so fortunate that a fool cannot turn it to his disadvantage.

62. Sincerity comes from an open heart. It is exceedingly rare; what usually passes for sincerity is only an artful pretense designed to win the confidence of others.

67. Grace is to the body what sense is to the mind.

71. When two people have ceased to love, the memory that remains is almost always one of shame.

72. Love, to judge by most of its effects, is closer to hatred than to friendship.

75. Love, like fire, needs constant motion; when it ceases to hope, or to fear, love dies.

78. For most men the love of justice is only the fear of suffering injustice.

79. For a man who lacks self-confidence, silence is the wisest course.

83. What men have called friendship is only a social arrangement, a mutual adjustment of interests, an interchange of services given and received; it is, in sum, simply a business from which those involved purpose to derive a steady profit for their own self-love.

89. Everyone complains of his memory, none of his judgment.

90. In daily life our faults are frequently more pleasant than our good qualities.

93. Old people love to give good advice: it compensates them for their inability nowadays to set a bad example.

119. We are so accustomed to adopting a mask before others that we end by being unable to recognize ourselves.

122. If we master our passions it is due to their weakness, not our strength.

134. We are never so ridiculous through what we are as through what we pretend to be.

138. We would rather speak ill of ourselves than not at all.

144. We do not like to give praise, and we never do so without reasons of self-interest. Praise is a cunning, concealed and delicate form of flattery which, in different ways, gratifies both the giver and the receiver; the one accepts it as the reward for merit; the other bestows it to display his sense of justice and his powers of discernment.

146. We usually only praise that we may be praised.

149. The refusal to accept praise is the desire to be praised twice over.

150. The wish to deserve the praise we receive strengthens our virtues; and praise bestowed upon wit, courage and beauty contributes to their increase.

167. Avarice, more than open-handedness, is the opposite of economy.

170. When a man's behavior is straightforward, sincere and honest it is hard to be sure whether this is due to rectitude or cleverness.

176. In love there are two sorts of constancy: the one comes from the perpetual discovery of new delights in the beloved: the other, from the self-esteem which we derive from our own fidelity.

180. Our repentance is less a regret for the evil we have done than a precaution against the evil that may be done to us.

185. Evil, like good, has its heroes.

186. Not all who have vices are contemptible: all without a trace of virtue are.

190. Only great men are marked with great faults.

192. When our vices depart from us, we flatter ourselves that it is we who have rid ourselves of them.

200. Virtue would not go so far did vanity not keep her company.

205. Virtue, in women, is often love of reputation and fondness for tranquillity.

216. Perfect valor is to behave, without witnesses, as one would act were all the world watching.

218. Hypocrisy is the tribute that vice pays to virtue.

230. Nothing is as contagious as example, and we never perform an outstandingly good or evil action without its producing others of its sort. We copy goodness in the spirit of emulation, and wickedness owing to the malignity of our nature which shame holds in check until example sets it free.

237. No man should be praised for his goodness if he lacks the strength to be bad: in such cases goodness is usually only the effect of indolence or impotence of will.

259. The pleasure of love is in loving: and there is more joy in the passion one feels than in that which one inspires.

264. Pity is often only the sentiment of our own misfortunes felt in the ills of others. It is a clever pre-science of the evil times upon which we may fall. We help others in order to ensure their help in similar circumstances; and the kindnesses we do them are, if the truth were told, only acts of charity towards ourselves invested against the future.

276. Absence diminishes small loves and increases great ones, as the wind blows out the candle and blows up the bonfire.

277. Women frequently believe themselves to be in love even when they are not: the pursuit of an intrigue, the stimulus of gallantry, the natural inclination towards the joys of being loved, and the difficulty of refusal, all these combine to tell them that their passions are aroused when in fact it is but their coquetry at play.

375. It is the habit of mediocre minds to condemn all that is beyond their grasp.

376. True friendship destroys envy, as true love puts an end to coquetry.

378. We give advice but we do not inspire behavior.

392. One should treat one's fate as one does one's health; enjoy it when it is good, be patient with it when it is poorly, and never attempt any drastic cure save as an ultimate resort.

399. There is a form of eminence which is quite independent of our fate; it is an air which distinguishes us from our fellow men and makes us appear destined for great things; it is the value which we imperceptibly attach to ourselves; it is the quality which wins us the deference of others; more than birth, honours or even merit, it gives us ascendancy.

417. In love, the person who recovers first recovers best.

423. Few people know how to be old.

467. Vanity leads us to act against our inclinations more often than does reason.

479. Only people who are strong can be truly gentle: what normally passes for gentleness is mere weakness, which quickly turns sour.

483. Vanity, rather than malice, is the usual source of slander.

540. Hope and fear are inseparable. There is no hope without fear, nor any fear without hope.

576. We always discover, in the misfortunes of our dearest friends, something not altogether displeasing.

597. No man can be sure of his own courage until he has stared danger in the face.

617. How can we expect another to keep our secret, if we cannot keep it ourself?

GEORGE BERNARD SHAW: *from* The Revolutionist's Handbook (*in* Man and Superman)

Democracy

Democracy substitutes selection by the incompetent many for appointment by the corrupt few.

Democratic republics can no more dispense with national idols than monarchies with public functionaries.

Liberty and Equality

He who confuses political liberty with freedom and political equality with similarity has never thought for five minutes about either.

Nothing can be unconditional: consequently nothing can be free.

Liberty means responsibility. That is why most men dread it.

The duke inquires contemptuously whether his gamekeeper is the equal of the Astronomer Royal; but he insists that they shall both be hanged equally if they murder him.

The notion that the colonel need be a better man than the private is as confused as the notion that the keystone need be stronger than the coping stone.

The relation of superior to inferior excludes good manners.

Education

When a man teaches something he does not know to somebody else who has no aptitude for it, and gives him a certificate of proficiency, the latter has completed the education of a gentleman.

A fool's brain digests philosophy into folly, science into superstition, and art into pedantry. Hence University education.

The best brought-up children are those who have seen their parents as they are. Hypocrisy is not the parent's first duty.

The vilest abortionist is he who attempts to mould a child's character.

He who can, does. He who cannot, teaches.

A learned man is an idler who kills time with study. Beware of his false knowledge: it is more dangerous than ignorance.

Activity is the only road to knowledge.

Every fool believes what his teachers tell him, and calls his credulity science or morality as confidently as his father called it divine revelation.

No man fully capable of his own language ever masters another.

No man can be a pure specialist without being in the strict sense an idiot.

Do not give your children moral and religious instruction unless you are quite sure they will not take it too seriously. Better be the mother of Henri Quatre and Nell Gwynne than of Robespierre and Queen Mary Tudor.

Virtues and Vices

No specific virtue or vice in a man implies the existence of any other specific virtue or vice in him, however closely the imagination may associate them.

Virtue consists, not in abstaining from vice, but in not desiring it.

Self-denial is not a virtue: it is only the effect of prudence on rascality.

Obedience simulates subordination as fear of the police simulates honesty.

Disobedience, the rarest and most courageous of the virtues, is seldom distinguished from neglect, the laziest and commonest of the vices.

Vice is waste of life. Poverty, obedience, and celibacy are the canonical vices.

Economy is the art of making the most of life.

The love of economy is the root of all virtue.

Greatness

In heaven an angel is nobody in particular.

Greatness is the secular name for Divinity: both mean simply what lies beyond us.

If a great man could make us understand him, we should hang him.

We admit that when the divinity we worshipped made itself visible and comprehensible we crucified it.

To a mathematician the eleventh means only a single unit: to the bushman who cannot count further than his ten fingers it is an incalculable myriad.

The difference between the shallowest routineer and the deepest thinker appears, to the latter, trifling; to the former, infinite.

In a stupid nation the man of genius becomes a god: everybody worships him and nobody does his will.

Gambling
The most popular method of distributing wealth is the method of the roulette table.

The roulette table pays nobody except him that keeps it. Nevertheless a passion for gaming is common, though a passion for keeping roulette tables is unknown.

Gambling promises the poor what Property performs for the rich: that is why the bishops dare not denounce it fundamentally.

On History

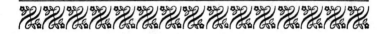

HENRY DAVID THOREAU
The Battle of the Ants[1]

One day when I went out to my wood-pile, or rather my pile of stumps, I observed two large ants, the one red, the other much larger, nearly half an inch long, and black, fiercely contending with one another. Having once got hold they never let go, but struggled and wrestled and rolled on the chips incessantly. Looking farther, I was surprised to find that the chips were covered with such combatants, that it was not a *duellum*, but a *bellum*, a war between two races of ants, the red always pitted against the black, and frequently two red ones to one black. The legions of these Myrmidons covered all the hills and vales in my wood-yard, and the ground was already strewn with the dead and dying, both red and black. It was the only battle which I have ever witnessed, the only battle-field I ever trod while the battle was raging; internecine war; the red republicans on the one hand, and the black imperialists on the other. On every side they were engaged in deadly combat, yet without any noise that I could hear, and human soldiers never fought so resolutely. I watched a couple that were fast locked in each other's embraces, in a little sunny valley amid the chips, now at noonday prepared to fight till the sun went down, or life went out. The smaller red champion had fastened himself like a vice to his adversary's front, and through all the tumblings on that field never for an instant ceased to gnaw at one of his feelers near the root, having already caused the other to go by the board; while the stronger black one dashed him from side to side, and, as I saw on looking nearer, had already divested him of several of his members. They fought with more pertinacity than bulldogs. Neither manifested the least disposi-

1. From "Brute Neighbors," Chapter XII of *Walden*.

tion to retreat. It was evident that their battle-cry was "Conquer or die." In the meanwhile there came along a single red ant on the hillside of this valley, evidently full of excitement, who either had despatched his foe, or had not yet taken part in the battle; probably the latter, for he had lost none of his limbs; whose mother had charged him to return with his shield or upon it. Or perchance he was some Achilles, who had nourished his wrath apart, and had now come to avenge or rescue his Patroclus.[2] He saw this unequal combat from afar—for the blacks were nearly twice the size of the red—he drew near with rapid pace till he stood on his guard within half an inch of the combatants; then, watching his opportunity, he sprang upon the black warrior, and commenced his operations near the root of his right fore leg, leaving the foe to select among his own members; and so there were three united for life, as if a new kind of attraction had been invented which put all other locks and cements to shame. I should not have wondered by this time to find that they had their respective musical bands stationed on some eminent chip, and playing their national airs the while, to excite the slow and cheer the dying combatants. I was myself excited somewhat even as if they had been men. The more you think of it, the less the difference. And certainly there is not the fight recorded in Concord history, at least, if in the history of America, that will bear a moment's comparison with this, whether for the numbers engaged in it, or for the patriotism and heroism displayed. For numbers and for carnage it was an Austerlitz or Dresden.[3] Concord Fight! Two killed on the patriots' side, and Luther Blanchard wounded! Why here every ant was a Buttrick—"Fire! for God's sake fire!"—and thousands shared the fate of Davis and Hosmer. There was not one hireling there. I have no doubt that it was a principle they fought for, as much as our ancestors, and not to avoid a three-penny tax on their tea; and the results of this battle will be as important and memorable to those whom it concerns as those of the battle of Bunker Hill, at least.

I took up the chip on which the three I have particularly described were struggling, carried into my house, and placed it under a tumbler on my window-sill, in order to see the issue. Holding a microscope to the first-mentioned red ant, I saw that, though he was assiduously gnawing at the near fore leg of his enemy, having severed his remaining feeler, his own breast was all torn away, exposing what vitals he had there to the jaws of the black warrior, whose breastplate was apparently too thick for him to pierce; and the dark carbuncles of the sufferer's eyes shone with ferocity such as war only could excite. They struggled half an hour longer under the tumbler, and when I looked again the black soldier had severed the heads of his foes from their bodies, and the still living heads were hanging on

2. A Greek warrior in the *Iliad*, whose death Achilles avenges.
3. Bloody Napoleonic victories.

either side of him like ghastly trophies at his saddle-bow, still apparently as firmly fastened as ever, and he was endeavoring with feeble struggles, being without feelers, and with only the remnant of a leg, and I know not how many other wounds, to divest himself of them; which at length, after half an hour more, he accomplished. I raised the glass, and he went off over the window-sill in that crippled state. Whether he finally survived that combat, and spent the remainder of his days in some Hôtel des Invalides, I do not know; but I thought that his industry would not be worth much thereafter. I never learned which party was victorious, nor the cause of the war, but I felt for the rest of that day as if I had my feelings excited and harrowed by witnessing the struggle, the ferocity and carnage, of a human battle before my door.

Kirby and Spence tell us that the battles of ants have long been celebrated and the date of them recorded, though they say that Huber[4] is the only modern author who appears to have witnessed them. "Aeneas Sylvius," say they, "after giving a very circumstantial account of one contested with great obstinacy by a great and small species on the trunk of a pear tree," adds that " 'this action was fought in the pontificate of Eugenius the Fourth, in the presence of Nicholas Pistoriensis, an eminent lawyer, who related the whole history of the battle with the greatest fidelity.' A similar engagement between great and small ants is recorded by Olaus Magnus, in which the small ones, being victorious, are said to have buried the bodies of their own soldiers, but left those of their giant enemies a prey to the birds. This event happened previous to the expulsion of the tyrant Christiern the Second from Sweden." The battle which I witnessed took place in the Presidency of Polk, five years before the passage of Webster's Fugitive-Slave Bill.

---

4. Kirby and Spence were nineteenth-century American entomologists; Huber was a great Swiss entomologist.

QUESTIONS

1. Thoreau uses the Latin word bellum to describe the struggle of the ants and he quickly follows this with a reference to the Myrmidons of Achilles. What comparison is implicit here? Find further examples of it. This passage comes from a chapter entitled "Brute Neighbors"; how does this comparison amplify the meaning of that title?

2. Describe the life, or part of the life, of an animal so that, while remaining faithful to the facts as you understand them, your description opens outward as do those of Thoreau, Stewart ("Vulture Country," pp. 980–987), and Ardrey ("From Territory To Nation," pp. 997–1010) and speaks not only of the animal but of man, society, or nature.

THUCYDIDES

The Corcyraean Revolution[1]

The Athenian commander Nicostratus, the son of Diitrephes, came up from Naupactus with a force of twelve ships and 500 Messenian hoplites.[2] His aim was to arrange a settlement, and he persuaded the two parties to agree among themselves to bring to trial ten men who had been chiefly responsible (and who immediately went into hiding); the rest were to come to terms with each other and live in peace, and the whole state was to conclude an offensive and defensive alliance with Athens.

Having made this settlement, Nicostratus was on the point of sailing away, but the leaders of the democratic party persuaded him to leave behind five of his ships to act as a check on any movement which their opponents might make, while they themselves would man five of their own ships and send them with him. Nicostratus agreed, and the democratic leaders put down the names of their enemies for service in the ships. Those who were called up, however, fearing that they would be sent off to Athens, seated themselves as suppliants in the temple of the Dioscuri. Nicostratus offered them guarantees and spoke reassuringly to them, but his words had no effect. The democratic party then armed themselves on the pretext that these men could not be sincere in their intentions if they felt doubtful about sailing with Nicostratus. They seized their opponents' arms out of their houses, and would have put to death some of them whom they found there, if they had not been prevented by Nicostratus. The rest of the oligarchical party, seeing what was happening, took up their positions as suppliants in the temple of Hera. There were at least 400 of them. The democrats, fearing that they might do something violent, persuaded them to rise, took them across to the island in front of the temple, and had provisions sent out to them there.

At this stage in the revolution, four or five days after the men had been taken across to the island, the Peloponnesian ships arrived from Cyllene, where they had been stationed since their return from Ionia. There were fifty-three of them, commanded, as before, by Alcidas, though now Brasidas sailed with him as his

---

1. From Book III of *The Peloponnesian War*. This war (431–404 B.C.), fought between the Athenians (the compatriots of Thucydides) and the Spartans ("the Peloponnesians"), produced political divisions in the smaller Greek cities. In the section preceding the excerpt given here, Thucydides tells how the democratic party in Corcyra, intending an alliance with Athens, put down an attempted coup by the oligarchical party, sympathetic to Sparta.

2. Infantrymen.

adviser. This fleet came to anchor in the harbor of Sybota on the mainland, and at daybreak set out for Corcyra.

The Corcyraeans were now in a state of the utmost confusion, alarmed both at what was happening inside their city and at the approach of the enemy fleet. They immediately got ready sixty ships and sent them straight out against the enemy, as soon as they were manned, neglecting the advice of the Athenians, which was to let them sail out first and then come out in support of them later with all their ships together. As the Corcyraean ships approached the enemy in this disorganized way, two of them immediately deserted, in other ships the crews were fighting among themselves, and no sort of order was kept in anything. The Peloponnesians observed the confusion in which they were, set aside twenty of their ships to meet the Corcyraeans, and put all the rest of their fleet against the twelve Athenian ships, among which were the *Salaminia* and the *Paralus*.

The Corcyraeans, in their part of the battle, were soon in difficulties, since they were making their attacks inefficiently and in small detachments. The Athenians, afraid of the numbers of the enemy and of the risk of encirclement, did not commit themselves to a general engagement and did not even charge the fleet opposed to them in the center. Instead they fell upon its wing where they sank one ship. After this the Peloponnesians formed their ships up in a circle and the Athenians rowed round them, trying to create confusion among them. Seeing this, and fearing a repetition of what had happened at Naupactus, the other Peloponnesians, who had been dealing with the Corcyraeans, came up in support, and then the whole Peloponnesian fleet together bore down on the Athenians, who now began to back water and to retire in front of them. They carried out the maneuver in their own good time, wishing to give the Corcyraean ships the fullest opportunity to escape first by keeping the enemy facing them in battle formation. So the fighting went, and it continued until sunset.

The Corcyraeans now feared that the enemy would follow up their victory by sailing against the city, or rescuing the men from the island, or by taking some other bold step. So they brought the men back again from the island to the temple of Hera, and put the defenses of the city in order. The Peloponnesians, however, in spite of their victory on the sea, did not risk sailing against the town, but sailed back to their original station on the mainland, taking with them the thirteen Corcyraean ships which they had captured. Nor were they any the more disposed to sail against the city on the next day, although the Corcyraeans were thoroughly disorganized and in a state of panic, and although Brasidas is said to have urged Alcidas to do so. Brasidas, however, was overruled, and the Peloponnesians merely made a landing on the headland of Leukimme and laid waste the country.

Meanwhile the democratic party in Corcyra were still terrified at the prospect of an attack by the enemy fleet. They entered into negotiations with the suppliants and with others of their party with a view to saving the city, and they persuaded some of them to go on board the ships. Thus they succeeded in manning thirty ships to meet the expected attack.

The Peloponnesians, however, having spent the time up till midday in laying waste the land, sailed away again, and about nightfall were informed by fire signals that a fleet of sixty Athenian ships was approaching from the direction of Leucas. This fleet, which was under the command of Eurymedon, the son of Thucles, had been sent out by the Athenians when they heard that the revolution had broken out and that Alcidas's fleet was about to sail for Corcyra. Thus the Peloponnesians set off by night, at once and in a hurry, for home, sailing close in to the shore. They hauled their ships across the isthmus of Leucas, so as to avoid being seen rounding the point, and so they got away.

When the Corcyraeans realized that the Athenian fleet was approaching and that their enemies had gone, they brought the Messenians, who had previously been outside the walls, into the city and ordered the fleet which they had manned to sail round into the Hyllaic harbor. While it was doing so, they seized upon all their enemies whom they could find and put them to death. They then dealt with those whom they had persuaded to go on board the ships, killing them as they landed. Next they went to the temple of Hera and persuaded about fifty of the suppliants there to submit to a trial. They then condemned every one of them to death. Seeing what was happening, most of the other suppliants, who had refused to be tried, killed each other there in the temple; some hanged themselves on the trees, and others found various other means of committing suicide. During the seven days that Eurymedon stayed there with his sixty ships, the Corcyraeans continued to massacre those of their own citizens whom they considered to be their enemies. Their victims were accused of conspiring to overthrow the democracy, but in fact men were often killed on grounds of personal hatred or else by their debtors because of the money that they owed. There was death in every shape and form. And, as usually happens in such situations, people went to every extreme and beyond it. There were fathers who killed their sons; men were dragged from the temples or butchered on the very altars; some were actually walled up in the temple of Dionysus and died there.

So savage was the progress of this revolution, and it seemed all the more so because it was one of the first which had broken out.

Later, of course, practically the whole of the Hellenic world was convulsed, with rival parties in every state—democratic leaders trying to bring in the Athenians, and oligarchs trying to bring in the Spartans. In peacetime there would have been no excuse and no desire for calling them in, but in time of war, when each party could always count upon an alliance which would do harm to its opponents and at the same time strengthen its own position, it became a natural thing for anyone who wanted a change of government to call in help from outside. In the various cities these revolutions were the cause of many calamities—as happens and always will happen while human nature is what it is, though there may be different degrees of savagery, and, as different circumstances arise, the general rules will admit of some variety. In times of peace and prosperity cities and individuals alike follow higher standards, because they are not forced into a situation where they have to do what they do not want to do. But war is a stern teacher; in depriving them of the power of easily satisfying their daily wants, it brings most people's minds down to the level of their actual circumstances.

So revolutions broke out in city after city, and in places where the revolutions occurred late the knowledge of what had happened previously in other places caused still new extravagances of revolutionary zeal, expressed by an elaboration in the methods of seizing power and by unheard-of atrocities in revenge. To fit in with the change of events, words, too, had to change their usual meanings. What used to be described as a thoughtless act of aggression was now regarded as the courage one would expect to find in a party member; to think of the future and wait was merely another way of saying one was a coward; any idea of moderation was just an attempt to disguise one's unmanly character; ability to understand a question from all sides meant that one was totally unfitted for action. Fanatical enthusiasm was the mark of a real man, and to plot against an enemy behind his back was perfectly legitimate self-defense. Anyone who held violent opinions could always be trusted, and anyone who objected to them became a suspect. To plot successfully was a sign of intelligence, but it was still cleverer to see that a plot was hatching. If one attempted to provide against having to do either, one was disrupting the unity of the party and acting out of fear of the opposition. In short, it was equally praiseworthy to get one's blow in first against someone who was going to do wrong, and to denounce someone who had no intention of doing any wrong at all. Family relations were a weaker tie than party membership, since party members were more ready to go to any extreme for any reason whatever. These parties were not formed to enjoy the benefits of the established laws, but to acquire power by overthrowing the existing regime; and the members of these parties felt confidence in each other not because of any fellowship in a religious communion, but because they were partners in crime. If an opponent made a reasonable speech, the party in power, so far from giving it a generous reception, took every precaution to see that it had no practical effect.

Revenge was more important than self-preservation. And if pacts of mutual security were made, they were entered into by the two parties only in order to meet some temporary difficulty, and remained in force only so long as there was no other weapon available. When the chance came, the one who first seized it boldly, catching his enemy off his guard, enjoyed a revenge that was all the sweeter from having been taken, not openly, but because of a breach of faith. It was safer that way, it was considered, and at the same time a victory won by treachery gave one a title for superior intelligence. And indeed most people are more ready to call villainy cleverness than simple-mindedness honesty. They are proud of the first quality and ashamed of the second.

Love of power, operating through greed and through personal ambition, was the cause of all these evils. To this must be added the violent fanaticism which came into play once the struggle had broken out. Leaders of parties in the cities had programs which appeared admirable—on one side political equality for the masses, on the other the safe and sound government of the aristocracy—but in professing to serve the public interest they were seeking to win the prizes for themselves. In their struggles for ascendancy nothing was barred; terrible indeed were the actions to which they committed themselves, and in taking revenge they went farther still. Here they were deterred neither by the claims of justice nor by the interests of the state; their one standard was the pleasure of their own party at that particular moment, and so, either by means of condemning their enemies on an illegal vote or by violently usurping power over them, they were always ready to satisfy the hatreds of the hour. Thus neither side had any use for conscientious motives; more interest was shown in those who could produce attractive arguments to justify some disgraceful action. As for the citizens who held moderate views, they were destroyed by both the extreme parties, either for not taking part in the struggle or in envy at the possibility that they might survive.

As the result of these revolutions, there was a general deterioration of character throughout the Greek world. The simple way of looking at things, which is so much the mark of a noble nature, was regarded as a ridiculous quality and soon ceased to exist. Society had become divided into two ideologically hostile camps, and each side viewed the other with suspicion. As for ending this state of affairs, no guarantee could be given that would be trusted, no oath sworn that people would fear to break; everyone had come to the conclusion that it was hopeless to expect a permanent settlement and so, instead of being able to feel confident in others, they devoted their energies to providing against being injured themselves. As a rule those who were least remarkable for intelligence showed the greater powers of survival. Such people recognized their own deficiencies and the superior intelligence of their opponents; fearing that they might lose a debate or find themselves outmaneuvered in intrigue by their quick-witted enemies, they boldly launched straight into action; while their opponents, overconfident in the belief that they would see what was happening in advance, and not thinking it necessary to seize by force what they could secure by policy, were the more easily destroyed because they were off their guard.

Certainly it was in Corcyra that there occurred the first examples of the breakdown of law and order. There was the revenge taken in their hour of triumph by those who had in the past been arrogantly oppressed instead of wisely governed; there were the wicked resolutions taken by those who, particularly under the pressure of misfortune, wished to escape from their usual poverty and coveted the property of their neighbors; there were the savage and pitiless actions into which men were carried not so much for the sake of gain as because they were swept away into an internecine struggle by their ungovernable passions. Then, with the ordinary conventions of civilized life thrown into confusion, human nature, always ready to offend even where laws exist, showed itself proudly in its true colors, as something incapable of controlling passion, insubordinate to the idea of justice, the enemy to anything superior to itself; for, if it had not been for the pernicious power of envy, men would not so have exalted vengeance above innocence and profit above justice. Indeed, it is true that in these acts of revenge on others men take it upon themselves to begin the process of repealing those general laws of humanity which are there to give a hope of salvation to all who are in distress, instead of leaving those laws in existence, remembering that there may come a time when they, too, will be in danger and will need their protection.

QUESTIONS

1. Thucydides describes the dissolution of a functioning community at Corcyra; what are the key features of this dissolution? What is most shocking to Thucydides?
2. What does Thucydides see as the basis for a society's moral code or ethical system? What is the biggest threat to this code or system?

3. How accurate is Thucydides' general assessment of "human nature"? Can such an issue be settled by appeals to facts?

THOMAS JEFFERSON
George Washington[1]

I think I knew General Washington intimately and thoroughly; and were I called on to delineate his character, it should be in terms like these.

His mind was great and powerful, without being of the very first order; his penetration strong, though not so acute as that of a Newton, Bacon, or Locke; and as far as he saw, no judgment was ever sounder. It was slow in operation, being little aided by invention or imagination, but sure in conclusion. Hence the common remark of his officers, of the advantage he derived from councils of war, where hearing all suggestions, he selected whatever was best; and certainly no general ever planned his battles more judiciously. But if deranged during the course of the action, if any member of his plan was dislocated by sudden circumstances, he was slow in re-adjustment. The consequence was, that he often failed in the field, and rarely against an enemy in station, as at Boston and York. He was incapable of fear, meeting personal dangers with the calmest unconcern. Perhaps the strongest feature in his character was prudence, never acting until every circumstance, every consideration, was maturely weighed; refraining if he saw a doubt, but, when once decided, going through with his purpose, whatever obstacles opposed. His integrity was most pure, his justice the most inflexible I have ever known, no motives of interest or consanguinity, of friendship or hatred, being able to bias his decision. He was, indeed, in every sense of the words, a wise, a good, and a great man. His temper was naturally irritable and high toned; but reflection and resolution had obtained a firm and habitual ascendency over it. If ever, however, it broke its bonds, he was most tremendous in his wrath. In his expenses he was honorable, but exact; liberal in contributions to whatever promised utility; but frowning and unyielding on all visionary projects, and all unworthy calls on his charity. His heart was not warm in its affections; but he exactly calculated every man's value, and gave him a solid esteem proportioned to it. His person, you know, was fine, his stature exactly what one would wish, his deportment easy, erect and noble; the best horseman of his age, and

---

1. From a letter written in 1814 to a Doctor Jones, who was writing a history and wanted to know about Washington's role in the Federalist-Republican controversy.

the most graceful figure that could be seen on horseback. Although in the circle of his friends, where he might be unreserved with safety, he took a free share in conversation, his colloquial talents were not above mediocrity, possessing neither copiousness of ideas, nor fluency of words. In public, when called on for a sudden opinion, he was unready, short and embarrassed. Yet he wrote readily, rather diffusely, in an easy and correct style. This he had acquired by conversation with the world, for his education was merely reading, writing and common arithmetic, to which he added surveying at a later day. His time was employed in action chiefly, reading little, and that only in agriculture and English history. His correspondence became necessarily extensive, and, with journalizing his agricultural proceedings, occupied most of his leisure hours within doors. On the whole, his character was, in its mass, perfect, in nothing bad, in few points indifferent; and it may truly be said, that never did nature and fortune combine more perfectly to make a man great, and to place him in the same constellation with whatever worthies have meritied from man an everlasting remembrance. For his was the singular destiny and merit, of leading the armies of his country successfully through an arduous war, for the establishment of its independence; of conducting its councils through the birth of a government, new in its forms and principles, until it had settled down into a quiet and orderly train; and of scrupulously obeying the laws through the whole of his career, civil and military, of which the history of the world furnishes no other example.

* * * I am satisfied the great body of republicans think of him as I do. We were, indeed, dissatisfied with him on his ratification of the British treaty. But this was short lived. We knew his honesty, the wiles with which he was encompassed, and that age had already begun to relax the firmness of his purposes; and I am convinced he is more deeply seated in the love and gratitude of the republicans, than in the Pharisaical homage of the federal monarchists. For he was no monarchist from preference of his judgment. The soundness of that gave him correct views of the rights of man, and his severe justice devoted him to them. He has often declared to me that he considered our new Constitution as an experiment on the practicability of republican government, and with what dose of liberty man could be trusted for his own good; that he was determined the experiment should have a fair trial, and would lose the last drop of his blood in support of it. And these declarations he repeated to me the oftener and more pointedly, because he knew my suspicions of Colonel Hamilton's views, and probably had heard from him the same declarations which I had, to wit, "that the British constitution, with its unequal representation, corruption and other existing abuses, was the most perfect government which had ever been established on earth, and that a reformation of those abuses would make it an

impracticable government." I do believe that General Washington had not a firm confidence in the durability of our government. He was naturally distrustful of men, and inclined to gloomy apprehensions; and I was ever persuaded that a belief that we must at length end in something like a British constitution, had some weight in his adoption of the ceremonies of levees, birthdays, pompous meetings with Congress, and other forms of the same character, calculated to prepare us gradually for a change which he believed possible, and to let it come on with as little shock as might be to the public mind.

These are my opinions of General Washington which I would vouch at the judgment seat of God, having been formed on an acquaintance of thirty years. I served with him in the Virginia legislature from 1769 to the Revolutionary war, and again, a short time in Congress, until he left us to take command of the army. During the war and after it we corresponded occasionally, and in the four years of my continuance in the office of Secretary of State, our intercourse was daily, confidential and cordial. After I retired from that office, great and malignant pains were taken by our federal monarchists, and not entirely without effect, to make him view me as a theorist, holding French principles of government, which would lead infallibly to licentiousness and anarchy. And to this he listened the more easily, from my known disapprobation of the British treaty. I never saw him afterwards, or these malignant insinuations should have been dissipated before his just judgment, as mists before the sun. I felt on his death, with my countrymen, that "verily a great man hath fallen this day in Israel."

BARBARA TUCHMAN

Lord Salisbury[1]

The last government in the Western world to possess all the attributes of aristocracy in working condition took office in England in June of 1895. Great Britain was at the zenith of empire when the Conservatives won the General Election of that year, and the Cabinet they formed was her superb and resplendent image. Its members represented the greater landowners of the country who had been accustomed to govern for generations. As its superior citizens they felt they owed a duty to the State to guard its interests and manage its affairs. They governed from duty, heritage, and habit—and, as they saw it, from right.

The Prime Minister was a Marquess and lineal descendant of the father and son who had been chief ministers to Queen Elizabeth

1. Chapter I of *The Proud Tower*, 1966.

and James I. The Secretary for War was another Marquess who traced his inferior title of Baron back to the year 1181, whose great-grandfather had been Prime Minister under George III and whose grandfather had served in six cabinets under three reigns. The Lord President of the Council was a Duke who owned 186,000 acres in eleven counties, whose ancestors had served in government since the Fourteenth Century, who had himself served thirty-four years in the House of Commons and three times refused to be Prime Minister. The Secretary for India was the son of another Duke whose family seat was received in 1315 by grant from Robert the Bruce and who had four sons serving in Parliament at the same time. The President of the Local Government Board was a pre-eminent country squire who had a Duke for brother-in-law, a Marquess for son-in-law, an ancestor who had been Lord Mayor of London in the reign of Charles II, and who had himself been a Member of Parliament for twenty-seven years. The Lord Chancellor bore a family name brought to England by a Norman follower of William the Conqueror and maintained thereafter over eight centuries without a title. The Lord Lieutenant for Ireland was an Earl, a grandnephew of the Duke of Wellington and a hereditary trustee of the British Museum. The Cabinet also included a Viscount, three Barons, and two Baronets. Of its six commoners, one was a director of the Bank of England, one was a squire whose family had represented the same county in Parliament since the Sixteenth Century, one—who acted as Leader of the House of Commons—was the Prime Minister's nephew and inheritor of a Scottish fortune of £4,000,000, and one, a notable and disturbing cuckoo in the nest, was a Birmingham manufacturer widely regarded as the most successful man in England.

Besides riches, rank, broad acres, and ancient lineage, the new Government also possessed, to the regret of the Liberal Opposition and in the words of one of them, "an almost embarrassing wealth of talent and capacity." Secure in authority, resting comfortably on their electoral majority in the House of Commons and on a permanent majority in the House of Lords, of whom four-fifths were Conservatives, they were in a position, admitted the same opponent, "of unassailable strength."

Enriching their ranks were the Whig aristocrats who had seceded from the Liberal party in 1886 rather than accept Mr. Gladstone's[2] insistence on Home Rule for Ireland. They were for the most part great landowners who, like their natural brothers the Tories, regarded union with Ireland as sacrosanct. Led by the Duke of

2. William Gladstone, Prime Minister in 1886, defeated in the general election of that year.

Devonshire, the Marquess of Lansdowne, and Mr. Joseph Chamberlain, they had remained independent until 1895, when they joined with the Conservative party, and the two groups emerged as the Unionist party, in recognition of the policy that had brought them together. With the exception of Mr. Chamberlain, this coalition represented that class in whose blood, training, and practice over the centuries, landowning and governing had been inseparable. Ever since Saxon chieftains met to advise the King in the first national assembly, the landowners of England had been sending members to Parliament and performing the duties of High Sheriff, Justice of the Peace, and Lord Lieutenant of the Militia in their own counties. They had learned the practice of government from the possession of great estates, and they undertook to manage the affairs of the nation as inevitably and unquestionably as beavers build a dam. It was their ordained role and natural task.

But it was threatened. By a rising rumble of protest from below, by the Radicals of the Opposition who talked about taxing unearned increment on land, by Home Rulers who wanted to detach the Irish island from which so much English income came, by Trade Unionists who talked of Labor representation in Parliament and demanded the legal right to strike and otherwise interfere with the free play of economic forces, by Socialists who wanted to nationalize property and Anarchists who wanted to abolish it, by upstart nations and strange challenges from abroad. The rumble was distant, but it spoke with one voice that said Change, and those whose business was government could not help but hear.

Planted firmly across the path of change, operating warily, shrewdly yet with passionate conviction in defense of the existing order, was a peer who was Chancelor of Oxford University for life, had twice held the India Office, twice the Foreign Office, and was now Prime Minister for the third time. He was Robert Arthur Talbot Gascoyne-Cecil, Lord Salisbury, ninth Earl and third Marquess of his line.

Lord Salisbury was both the epitome of his class and uncharacteristic of it—except insofar as the freedom to be different was a class characteristic. He was six feet four inches tall, and as a young man had been thin, ungainly, stooping, and shortsighted, with hair unusually black for an Englishman. Now sixty-five, his youthful lankiness had turned to bulk, his shoulders had grown massive and more stooped than ever, and his heavy bald head with full curly gray beard rested on them as if weighted down. Melancholy, intensely intellectual, subject to sleepwalking and fits of depression which he called "nerve storms," caustic, tactless, absent-minded, bored by society and fond of solitude, with a penetrating, skeptical, questioning mind, he had been called the Hamlet of English politics. He was above the conventions and refused to live in Downing Street.[3] His devotion was to religion, his interest in science. In his own home he attended private chapel every morning before breakfast, and had fitted up a chemical laboratory where he conducted solitary experiments. He harnessed the river at Hatfield for an electric power plant on his estate and strung up along the old beams of his home one of England's first electric light systems, at which his family threw cushions when the wires sparked and sputtered while they went on talking and arguing, a customary occupation of the Cecils.

Lord Salisbury cared nothing for sport and little for people. His aloofness was enhanced by shortsightedness so intense that he once failed to recognize a member of his own Cabinet, and once, his own butler. At the close of the Boer War he picked up a signed photograph of King Edward and, gazing at it pensively, remarked, "Poor Buller [referring to the Commander-in-Chief at the start of the war], what a mess he made of it." On another occasion he was seen in prolonged military conversation with a minor peer under the impression that he was talking to Field Marshal Lord Roberts.

For the upper-class Englishman's alter ego, most intimate companion and constant preoccupation, his horse, Lord Salisbury had no more regard. Riding was to him purely a means of locomotion to which the horse was "a necessary but extremely inconvenient adjunct." Nor was he addicted to shooting. When Parliament rose he did not go north to slaughter grouse upon the moors or stalk deer in Scottish forests, and when protocol required his attendance upon royalty at Balmoral, he would not go for walks and "positively refused," wrote Queen Victoria's Private Secretary, Sir Henry Ponsonby, "to admire the prospect or the deer." Ponsonby was told to have his room in the dismal castle kept "warm"—a minimum temperature of sixty degrees. Otherwise he retired for his holidays to France, where he owned a villa at Beaulieu on the Riviera and where he could exercise his fluent French and lose himself in *The Count of Monte Cristo*, the only book, he once told Dumas *fils*,[4] which allowed him to forget politics.

His acquaintance with games was confined to tennis, but when elderly he invented his own form of exercise, which consisted in riding a tricycle through St. James's Park in the early mornings or along paths cemented for the purpose in the park of his estate at Hatfield. Wearing for the occasion a kind of sombrero hat and a

3. No. 10 Downing Street is by tradition the residence of the Prime Minister.

4. Alexandre Dumas *fils* ("son"), himself a well-known writer, was the son of the author of *The Count of Monte Cristo*, Alexandre Dumas *père* ("father").

short sleeveless cloak with a hole in the middle in which he resembled a monk, he would be accompanied by a young coachman to push him up the hills. At the downhill slopes, the young man would be told to "jump on behind," and the Prime Minister, with the coachman's hands on his shoulders, would roll away, cloak flying and pedals whirring.

Hatfield, twenty miles north of London in Hertfordshire, had been the home of the Cecils for nearly three hundred years since James I had given it, in 1607, to his Prime Minister, Robert Cecil, first Earl of Salisbury, in exchange for a house of Cecil's to which the King had taken a fancy. It was the royal residence where Queen Elizabeth had spent her childhood and where, on receiving news of her accession, she held her first council, to swear in William Cecil, Lord Burghley, as her Chief Secretary of State. Its Long Gallery, with intricately carved paneled walls and gold-leaf ceiling, was 180 feet in length. The Marble Hall, named for the black and white marble floor, glowed like a jewel case with painted and gilded ceiling and Brussels tapestries. The red King James Drawing Room was hung with full-length family portraits by Romney and Reynolds and Lawrence. The library was lined from floor to gallery and ceiling with 10,000 volumes bound in leather and vellum. In other rooms were kept the Casket Letters of Mary Queen of Scots, suits of armor taken from men of the Spanish Armada, the cradle of the beheaded King, Charles I, and presentation portraits of James I and George III. Outside were yew hedges clipped in the form of crenelated battlements, and the gardens, of which Pepys[5] wrote that he never saw "so good flowers, nor so great gooseberries as big as nutmegs." Over the entrance hall hung flags captured at Waterloo and presented to Hatfield by the Duke of Wellington, who was a constant visitor and devoted admirer of the Prime Minister's mother, the second Marchioness. In her honor Wellington wore the hunt coat of the Hatfield Hounds when he was on campaign. The first Marchioness was painted by Sir Joshua Reynolds and hunted till the day she died at eighty-five, when, half-blind and strapped to the saddle, she was accompanied by a groom who would shout, when her horse approached a fence, "Jump, dammit, my Lady, jump!"

It was this exceptional person who reinvigorated the Cecil blood, which after Burghley and his son, had produced no further examples of superior mentality. Rather, the general mediocrity of succeeding generations had been varied only, according to a later Cecil, by instances of "quite exceptional stupidity." But the second Mar

5. Samuel Pepys, seventeenth-century government official, whose *Diary* (1660–69) affords an intimate and detailed account of his own affairs and of the life of his time.

quess proved a vigorous and able man with a strong sense of public duty who served in several mid-century Tory cabinets. His second son, another Robert Cecil, was the Prime Minister of 1895. He in turn produced five sons who were to distinguish themselves. One became a general, one a bishop, one a minister of state, one M.P. for Oxford, and one, through service to the government, won a peerage in his own right. "In human beings as in horses," Lord Birkenhead was moved to comment on the Cecil record, "there is something to be said for the hereditary principle."

At Oxford in 1850 the contemporaries of young Robert Cecil agreed that he would end as Prime Minister either because or in spite of his remorselessly uncompromising opinions. Throughout life he never bothered to restrain them. His youthful speeches were remarkable for their virulence and insolence; he was not, said Disraeli,[6] "a man who measures his phrases." A "salisbury" became a synonym for a political imprudence. He once compared the Irish in their incapacity for self-government to Hottentots and spoke of an Indian candidate for Parliament as "that black man." In the opinion of Lord Morley his speeches were always a pleasure to read because "they were sure to contain one blazing indiscretion which it is a delight to remember." Whether these were altogether accidental is open to question for though Lord Salisbury delivered his speeches without notes, they were worked out in his head beforehand and emerged clear and perfect in sentence structure. In that time the art of oratory was considered part of the equipment of a statesman and anyone reading from a written speech would have been regarded as pitiable. When Lord Salisbury spoke, "every sentence," said a fellow member, "seemed as essential, as articulate, as vital to the argument as the members of his body to an athlete."

Appearing in public before an audience about whom he cared nothing, Salisbury was awkward; but in the Upper House, where he addressed his equals, he was perfectly and strikingly at home. He spoke sonorously, with an occasional change of tone to icy mockery or withering sarcasm. When a recently ennobled Whig took the floor to lecture the House of Lords in high-flown and solemn Whig sentiments, Salisbury asked a neighbor who the speaker was and on hearing the whispered identification, replied perfectly audibly, "I thought he was dead." When he listened to others he could become easily bored, revealed by a telltale wagging of his leg which seemed to one observer to be saying, "When will all this be over?" Or sometimes, raising his heels off the floor, he would set up a sustained quivering of his knees and legs which could last for half an hour at a time. At home, when made restless by visitors, it shook

6. Benjamin Disraeli, Earl of Beaconsfield, Prime Minister 1868 and 1874–80.

the floor and made the furniture rattle, and in the House his colleagues on the front bench complained it made them seasick. If his
legs were at rest his long fingers would be in motion, incessantly
twisting and turning a paper knife or beating a tattoo on his knee
or on the arm of his chair.

He never dined out and rarely entertained beyond one or two
political receptions at his town house in Arlington Street and an
occasional garden party at Hatfield. He avoided the Carlton, official
club of the Conservatives, in favor of the Junior Carlton, where a
special luncheon table was set aside for him alone and the library
was hung with huge placards inscribed SILENCE. He worked from
breakfast to one in the morning, returning to his desk after dinner
as if he were beginning a new day. His clothes were drab and often
untidy. He wore trousers and waistcoat of a dismal gray under a
broadcloth frock coat grown shiny. But though careless in dress, he
was particular about the trimming of his beard and carefully
directed operations in the barber's chair, indicating "just a little
more off here" while "artist and subject gazed fixedly in the mirror
to judge the result."

Despite his rough tongue and sarcasms, Salisbury exerted a personal charm upon close colleagues and equals which, as one of
them said, "was no small asset in the conduct of affairs." He gave
detailed attention to party affairs and even sacrificed his exclusiveness for their sake. Once he astonished everyone by accepting an
invitation to the traditional dinner for party supporters given by
the Leader of the House of Commons. He asked to be given in
advance biographical details about each guest. At the dinner the
Prime Minister charmed his neighbor at table, a well-known agri-
culturist, with his expert knowledge of crop rotation and stock-
breeding, chatted amiably afterward with every guest in turn, and
before leaving, beckoned to his Private Secretary, saying "I think I
have done them all, but there was someone I have not identified
who, you said, made mustard."

Mr. Gladstone, though in political philosophy his bitterest antagonist, acknowledged him "a great gentleman in private society." In
private life he was delightful and sympathetic and a complete contrast to his public self. In public acclaim, Salisbury was uninter-
ested, for—since the populace was uninstructed—its opinions, as
far as he was concerned, were worthless. He ignored the public and
neither possessed nor tried to cultivate the personal touch that
makes a political leader a recognizable personality to the man in
the street and earns him a nickname like "Pam" or "Dizzy" or the
"Grand Old Man." Not in the press, not even in *Punch*, was Lord
Salisbury ever called anything but Lord Salisbury. He made no
attempt to conceal his dislike for mobs of all kinds, "not excluding

the House of Commons." After moving to the Lords, he never returned to the Commons to listen to its debates from the Peers' Gallery or chat with members in the Lobby, and if compelled to allude to them in his own House, would use a tone of airy contempt, to the amusement of visitors from the Commons who came to hear him. But this was merely an outward pose designed to underline his deep inner sense of the patrician. He was not rank-conscious; he was indifferent to honors or any other form of recognition. It was simply that as a Cecil, and a superior one, he was born with a consciousness in his bones and brain cells of ability to rule and saw no reason to make any concessions of this prescriptive right to anyone whatever.

Having entered the House of Commons in the customary manner for peers' sons, from a family-controlled borough in an uncontested election at the age of twenty-three, and, during his fifteen years in the House of Commons, having been returned unopposed five times from the same borough, and having for the last twenty-seven years sat in the House of Lords, he had little personal experience of vote-getting. He regarded himself not as responsible *to* the people but as responsible *for* them. They were in his care. What reverence he felt for anyone was directed not down but up—to the monarchy. He revered Queen Victoria, who was some ten years his senior, both as her subject and, with chivalry toward her womanhood, as a man. For her he softened his brusqueness even if at Balmoral he could not conceal his boredom.

She in turn visited him at Hatfield and had the greatest confidence in him, giving him, as she told Bishop Carpenter, "if not the highest, an equal place with the highest among her ministers," not excepting Disraeli. Salisbury, who was "bad on his legs at any time," was the only man she ever asked to sit down. Unlike in every quality of mind except in their strong sense of rulership, the tiny old Queen and the tall, heavy, aging Prime Minister felt for each other mutual respect and regard.

In unimportant matters of state as in dress, Salisbury was inclined to be casual. Once when two clergymen with similar names were candidates for a vacant bishopric, he appointed the one not recommended by the Archbishop of Canterbury, and this being sorrowfully drawn to his attention, he said, "Oh, I daresay he will do just as well." He reserved high seriousness for serious matters only, and the most serious to him was the maintenance of aristocratic influence and executive power, not for its own sake, but because he believed it to be the only element capable of holding the nation united against the rising forces of democracy which he saw "splitting it into a bundle of unfriendly and distrustful fragments."

Class war and irreligion were to him the greatest evils and for this reason he detested Socialism, less for its menace to property than for its preaching of class war and its basis in materialism, which meant to him a denial of spiritual values. He did not deny the need of social reforms, but believed they could be achieved through the interplay and mutual pressures of existing parties. The Workmen's Compensation Act, for one, making employers liable for work-sustained injuries, though denounced by some of his party as interference with private enterprise, was introduced and passed with his support in 1897.

He fought all proposals designed to increase the political power of the masses. When still a younger son, and not expecting to succeed to the title, he had formulated his political philosophy in a series of some thirty articles which were published in the *Quarterly Review* in the early 1860's, when he was in his thirties. Against the growing demand at that time for a new Reform law to extend the suffrage, Lord Robert Cecil, as he then was, had declared it to be the business of the Conservative party to preserve the rights and privileges of the propertied class as the "single bulwark" against the weight of numbers. To extend the suffrage would be, as he saw it, to give the working classes not merely a voice in Parliament but a preponderating one that would give to "mere numbers a power they ought not to have." He deplored the Liberals' adulation of the working class "as if they were different from other Englishmen" when in fact the only difference was that they had less education and property and "in proportion as the property is small the danger of misusing the franchise is great." He believed the workings of democracy to be dangerous to liberty, for under democracy "passion is not the exception but the rule" and it was "perfectly impossible" to commend a farsighted passionless policy to "men whose minds are unused to thought and undisciplined to study." To widen the suffrage among the poor while increasing taxes upon the rich would end, he wrote, in a complete divorce of power from responsibility; "the rich would pay all the taxes and the poor make all the laws."

He did not believe in political equality. There was the multitude, he said, and there were "natural" leaders. "Always wealth, in some countries birth, in all countries intellectual power and culture mark out the man to whom, in a healthy state of feeling, a community looks to undertake its government." These men had the leisure for it and the fortune, "so that the struggles for ambition are not defiled by the taint of sordid greed. . . . They are the aristocracy of a country in the original and best sense of the word. . . . The important point is, that the rulers of a country should be taken from among them," and as a class they should retain that "political preponderance to which they have every right that superior fitness can confer."

So sincere and certain was his conviction of that "superior fitness" that in 1867 when the Tory Government espoused the Second Reform Bill, which doubled the electorate and enfranchised workingmen in the towns, Salisbury at thirty-seven flung away Cabinet office within a year of first achieving it rather than be party to what he considered a betrayal and surrender of Conservative principles. His party's reversal, engineered by Disraeli in a neat enterprise both to "dish the Whigs" and to meet political realities, was regarded with abhorrence by Lord Cranborne (as Lord Robert Cecil had then become, his elder brother having died in 1865). Though it might ruin his career he resigned as Secretary for India and in a bitter and serious speech spoke out in the House against the policy of the party's leaders, Lord Derby and Mr. Disraeli. He begged the members not to do for political advantage what would ultimately destroy them as a class. "The wealth, the intelligence, the energy of the community, all that has given you that power which makes you so proud of your nation and which makes the deliberations of this House so important, will be numerically absolutely overmatched." Issues would arise in which the interests of employers and employed would clash and could only be decided by political force, "and in that conflict of political force you are pitting an overwhelming number of employed against a hopeless minority of employers." The outcome would "reduce to political insignificance and extinction the classes which have hitherto contributed so much to the greatness and prosperity of their country."

A year later, on his father's death, he entered the House of Lords as third Marquess of Salisbury. In 1895, after the passage of nearly thirty years, his principles had not shifted an inch. With no belief in change as improvement, nor faith in the future over the present, he dedicated himself with "grim acidity" to preserving the existing order. Believing that "rank, without the power of which it was originally the symbol, was a sham," he was determined, while he lived and governed England, to resist further attack on the power of that class of which rank was still the visible symbol. Watchful of approaching enemies, he stood against the coming age. The pressures of democracy encircled, but had not yet closed in around, the figure whom Lord Curzon described as "that strange, powerful, inscrutable, brilliant, obstructive deadweight at the top."

QUESTIONS

1. This is a description of a man whose views most people today would regard as outmoded or reprehensible. What does the author do to make the description sympathetic?

2. The wealth of anecdote certainly enlivens the description; does it serve any historical purpose?
3. What is Lord Salisbury's attitude toward "birth"? What is the author's attitude?

NATHANIEL HAWTHORNE

Abraham Lincoln[1]

Of course, there was one other personage, in the class of statesmen, whom I should have been truly mortified to leave Washington without seeing; since (temporarily, at least, and by force of circumstances) he was the man of men. But a private grief had built up a barrier about him, impeding the customary free intercourse of Americans with their chief magistrate; so that I might have come away without a glimpse of his very remarkable physiognomy, save for a semi-official opportunity of which I was glad to take advantage. The fact is, we were invited to annex ourselves, as supernumeraries, to a deputation that was about to wait upon the President, from a Massachusetts whip factory, with a present of a splendid whip.

Our immediate party consisted only of four or five (including Major Ben Perley Poore, with his note-book and pencil), but we were joined by several other persons, who seemed to have been lounging about the precincts of the White House, under the spacious porch, or within the hall, and who swarmed in with us to take the chances of a presentation. Nine o'clock had been appointed as the time for receiving the deputation, and we were punctual to the moment; but not so the President, who sent us word that he was eating his breakfast, and would come as soon as he could. His appetite, we were glad to think, must have been a pretty fair one; for we waited about half an hour in one of the antechambers, and then were ushered into a reception-room, in one corner of which sat the Secretaries of War and of the Treasury, expecting, like ourselves, the termination of the Presidential breakfast. During this interval there were several new additions to our group, one or two of whom were in a working-garb, so that we formed a very miscellaneous collection of people, mostly unknown to each other, and without any common sponsor, but all with an equal right to look our head servant in the face.

By and by there was a little stir on the staircase and in the passage-way, and in lounged a tall, loose-jointed figure, of an exaggerated Yankee port and demeanor, whom (as being about the homeliest man I ever saw, yet by no means repulsive or disagreeable) it was impossible not to recognize as Uncle Abe.

1. From an article in *The Atlantic Monthly*, July, 1862.

Unquestionably, Western man though he be, and Kentuckian by birth, President Lincoln is the essential representative of all Yankees, and the veritable specimen, physically, of what the world seems determined to regard as our characteristic qualities. It is the strangest and yet the fittest thing in the jumble of human vicissitudes, that he, out of so many millions, unlooked for, unselected by any intelligible process that could be based upon his genuine qualities, unknown to those who chose him, and unsuspected of what endowments may adapt him for his tremendous responsibility, should have found the way open for him to fling his lank personality into the chair of state—where, I presume, it was his first impulse to throw his legs on the council-table, and tell the Cabinet Ministers a story. There is no describing his lengthy awkwardness, nor the uncouthness of his movement; and yet it seemed as if I had been in the habit of seeing him daily, and had shaken hands with him a thousand times in some village street; so true was he to the aspect of the pattern American, though with a certain extravagance which, possibly, I exaggerated still further by the delighted eagerness with which I took it in. If put to guess his calling and livelihood, I should have taken him for a country school-master as soon as anything else. He was dressed in a rusty black frock coat and pantaloons, unbrushed, and worn so faithfully that the suit had adapted itself to the curves and angularities of his figure, and had grown to be an outer skin of the man. His hair was black, still unmixed with gray, stiff, somewhat bushy, and had apparently been acquainted with neither brush nor comb that morning, after the disarrangement of the pillow; and as to a nightcap, Uncle Abe probably knows nothing of such effeminacies. His complexion is dark and sallow, betokening, I fear, a insalubrious atmosphere around the White House; he has thick black eyebrows and an impending brow; his nose is large, and the lines about his mouth are very strongly defined.

The whole physiognomy is as coarse a one as you would meet anywhere in the length and breadth of the States; but, withal, it is redeemed, illuminated, softened, and brightened by a kindly though serious look out of his eyes, and an expression of homely sagacity, that seems weighted with rich results of village experience. A great deal of native sense; no bookish cultivation, no refinement; honest at heart, and thoroughly so, and yet, in some sort, sly—at least, endowed with a sort of tact and wisdom that are akin to craft, and would impel him, I think, to take an antagonist in flank, rather than to make a bull-run at him right in front. But, on the whole, I like this sallow, queer, sagacious visage, with the homely human sympathies that warmed it; and, for my small share in the matter, would as lief have Uncle Abe for a ruler as any man whom it would have been practicable to put in his place.

Immediately on his entrance the President accosted our member of Congress, who had us in charge, and, with a comical twist of his face, made some jocular remark about the length of his breakfast. He then greeted us all round, not waiting for an introduction, but shaking and squeezing everybody's hand with the utmost cordiality, whether the individual's name was announced to him or not. His manner towards us was wholly without pretence, but yet had a kind of natural dignity, quite sufficient to keep the forwardest of us from clapping him on the shoulder and asking him for a story. A mutual acquaintance being established, our leader took the whip out of its case, and began to read the address of presentation. The whip was an exceedingly long one, its handle wrought in ivory (by some artist in the Massachusetts State Prison, I believe), and ornamented with a medallion of the President, and other equally beautiful devices; and along its whole length there was a succession of golden bands and ferrules. The address was shorter than the whip, but equally well made, consisting chiefly of an explanatory description of these artistic designs, and closing with a hint that the gift was a suggestive and emblematic one, and that the President would recognize the use to which such an instrument should be put.

This suggestion gave Uncle Abe rather a delicate task in his reply, because, slight as the matter seemed, it apparently called for some declaration, or intimation, or faint foreshadowing of policy in reference to the conduct of the war, and the final treatment of the Rebels. But the President's Yankee aptness and not-to-be-caughtness stood him in good stead, and he jerked or wiggled himself out of the dilemma with an uncouth dexterity that was entirely in character; although, without his gesticulation of eye and mouth—and especially the flourish of the whip, with which he imagined himself touching up a pair of fat horses—I doubt whether his words would be worth recording, even if I could remember them. The gist of the reply was, that he accepted the whip as an emblem of peace, not punishment; and, this great affair over, we retired out of the presence in high good humor, only regretting that we could not have seen the President sit down and fold up his legs (which is said to be a most extraordinary spectacle), or have heard him tell one of those delectable stories for which he is so celebrated. A good many of them are afloat upon the common talk of Washington, and are certainly the aptest, pithiest, and funniest little things imaginable; though, to be sure, they smack of the frontier freedom, and would not always bear repetition in a drawing-room, or on the immaculate page of the *Atlantic*.[2]

2. This passage was one of those omitted from the article as originally published, and the following note was appended to explain the omission, which had been indicated by a line of points:
"We are compelled to omit two or three pages, in which the author describes the interview, and gives his idea of the personal appearance and deportment of the President. The sketch appears to have been written in a benign spirit, and perhaps conveys a not inaccurate impression of its august subject; but it lacks *reverence*, and it pains us to see a gentleman of ripe age, and who has spent years under the corrective influence of foreign institutions, falling into the characteristic and most ominous fault of Young America."

Good Heavens! what liberties have I been taking with one of the potentates of the earth, and the man on whose conduct more important consequences depend than on that of any other historical personage of the century! But with whom is an American citizen entitled to take a liberty, if not with his own chief magistrate? However, lest the above allusions to President Lincoln's little peculiarities (already well known to the country and to the world) should be misinterpreted, I deem it proper to say a word or two in regard to him, of unfeigned respect and measurable confidence. He is evidently a man of keen faculties, and, what is still more to the purpose, of powerful character. As to his integrity, the people have that intuition of it which is never deceived. Before he actually entered upon his great office, and for a considerable time afterwards, there is no reason to suppose that he adequately estimated the gigantic task about to be imposed on him, or, at least, had any distinct idea how it was to be managed; and I presume there may have been more than one veteran politician who proposed to himself to take the power out of President Lincoln's hands into his own, leaving our honest friend only the public responsibility for the good or ill success of the career. The extremely imperfect development of his statesmanly qualities, at that period, may have justified such designs. But the President is teachable by events, and has now spent a year in a very arduous course of education; he has a flexible mind, capable of much expansion, and convertible towards far loftier studies and activities than those of his early life; and if he came to Washington a backwoods humorist, he has already transformed himself into as good a statesman (to speak moderately) as his prime minister.[3]

3. Presumably the Secretary of State, William H. Seward.

QUESTIONS

1. In one sentence summarize Hawthorne's attitude toward Lincoln in the first seven paragraphs.
2. What is the basic pattern of the opening sentence of the fifth paragraph? Find other examples of this pattern. What is their total impact on Hawthorne's description?
3. In his final paragraph Hawthorne seeks to prevent misunderstanding by stressing his respect for and confidence in Lincoln. Is there anything in the paragraph which runs counter to that expression? To what effect?
4. In the footnote to the seventh paragraph the editor of The Atlantic Monthly explains his omission of the first seven paragraphs. On the evidence of this statement what sort of a person does the editor seem to be? Is there anything in the omitted paragraphs that would tend to justify his decision? Is the full description superior to the last paragraph printed alone? Explain.
5. Describe someone you know with a strong personality that has contrasting characteristics.

DEE BROWN
The War for the Black Hills[1]

Not long after Red Cloud and Spotted Tail and their Teton peoples settled down on their reservations in northwestern Nebraska, rumors began to fly among the white settlements that immense amounts of gold were hidden in the Black Hills. *Paha Sapa*, the Black Hills, was the center of the world, the place of gods and holy mountains, where warriors went to speak with the Great Spirit and await visions. In 1868 the Great Father considered the hills worthless and gave them to the Indians forever by treaty. Four years later white miners were violating the treaty. They invaded *Paha Sapa*, searching the rocky passes and clear-running streams for the yellow metal which drove white men crazy. When Indians found these crazy white men in their sacred hills, they killed them or chased them out. By 1874 there was such a mad clamor from gold-hungry Americans that the Army was ordered to make a reconnaissance into the Black Hills. The United States government did not bother to obtain consent from the Indians before starting on this armed invasion, although the treaty of 1868 prohibited entry of white men without the Indians' permission.

During the Moon of Red Cherries, more than a thousand pony soldiers marched across the Plains from Fort Abraham Lincoln to the Black Hills. They were the Seventh Cavalry, and at their head rode General George Armstrong Custer, the same Star Chief who in 1868 had slaughtered Black Kettle's Southern Cheyennes on the Washita. The Sioux called him Pahuska, the Long Hair, and because they had no warning of his coming, they could only watch from afar as the long columns of blue-uniformed cavalrymen and canvas-covered supply wagons invaded their sacred country.

When Red Cloud heard about the Long Hair's expedition, he protested: "I do not like General Custer and all his soldiers going into the Black Hills, as that is the country of the Oglala Sioux." It was also the country of the Cheyennes, Arapahos, and other Sioux tribes. The anger of the Indians was strong enough that the Great Father, Ulysses Grant, announced his determination "to prevent all invasion of this country by intruders so long as by law and treaty it is secured to the Indians."[2]

But when Custer reported that the hills were filled with gold "from the grass roots down," parties of white men began forming like summer locusts, crazy to begin panning and digging. The trail

---

1. From *Bury My Heart at Wounded Knee*, 1971. (All footnotes are Brown's.)   2. New York *Herald*, August 27 and September 25, 1874.

that Custer's supply wagons had cut into the heart of *Paha Sapa* soon became the Thieves' Road.

Red Cloud was having trouble that summer with his reservation agent, J. J. Saville, over the poor quality of rations and supplies being issued to the Oglalas. Preoccupied as he was, Red Cloud failed to assess the full impact upon the Sioux of Custer's intrusion into the Black Hills, especially upon those who left the reservations every spring to hunt and camp near the hills. Like many other aging leaders, Red Cloud was too much involved with petty details, and he was losing touch with the younger tribesmen.

In the autumn following Custer's expedition, the Sioux who had been hunting in the north began returning to the Red Cloud agency. They were angry as hornets over the invasion of *Paha Sapa*, and some talked of forming a war party to go back after the miners who were pouring into the hills. Red Cloud listened to the talk, but advised the young men to be patient; he was sure the Great Father would keep his promise and send soldiers to drive out the miners. In the Moon of Falling Leaves, however, something happened that made Red Cloud realize just how angry his young men were at the Long Hair's soldiers. On October 22 agent Saville sent some of his white workmen to cut a tall pine and bring the trunk back to the stockade. When the Indians saw the pine pole lying on the ground they asked Saville what it was to be used for. A flagpole, the agent told them; he was going to fly a flag over the stockade. The Indians protested. Long Hair Custer had flown flags in his camps across the Black Hills; they wanted no flags or anything else in their agency to remind them of soldiers.

Saville paid no attention to the protests, and next morning he put his men to work digging a hole for the flagpole. In a few minutes a band of young warriors came with axes and began chopping the pole to pieces. Saville ordered them to stop, but they paid no attention to him, and the agent strode across to Red Cloud's office and begged him to stop the warriors. Red Cloud refused; he knew the warriors were only expressing their rancor over the Long Hair's invasion of the Black Hills.

Infuriated, Saville now ordered one of his workmen to ride to the Soldiers' Town (Fort Robinson) and request a company of cavalrymen to come to his aid. When the demonstrating warriors saw the man riding toward the fort, they guessed his mission. They rushed for their tepee camps, armed and painted themselves for battle, and went to intercept the cavalrymen. There were only twenty-six Bluecoats led by a lieutenant; the warriors encircled them, fired their guns into the air, and yelled a few war cries. The lieutenant (Emmet Crawford) betrayed no fear. Through the great cloud of dust thrown up by the milling warriors, he kept his men moving steadily toward the agency. Some of the younger warriors began riding in close, colliding their ponies with the troopers' mounts, determined to precipitate a fight.

This time it was not another troop of cavalry which came galloping to Lieutenant Crawford's rescue, but a band of agency Sioux led by Young-Man-Afraid-of-His-Horses, son of Old-Man-Afraid. The agency Indians broke through the ring of warriors, formed a protective wall around the Bluecoats, and escorted them on to the stockade. The belligerent warriors were still so angry, however, that they tried to burn down the stockade, and only the persuasive oratory of Red Dog and Old-Man-Afraid-of-His-Horses stopped the demonstration.

Again Red Cloud refused to interfere. He was not surprised when many of the protesters packed up, dismantled their tepees, and started back north to spend the winter off the reservation. They had proved to him that there were still Sioux warriors who would never take lightly any invasion of *Paha Sapa*, yet apparently Red Cloud did not realize that he was losing these young men forever. They had rejected his leadership for that of Sitting Bull and Crazy Horse, neither of whom had ever lived on a reservation or taken the white man's handouts.

By the spring of 1875, tales of Black Hills gold had brought hundreds of miners up the Missouri River and out upon the Thieves' Road. The Army sent soldiers to stop the flow of prospectors. A few were removed from the hills, but no legal action was taken against them, and they soon returned to prospect their claims. General Crook (the Plains Indians called him Three Stars instead of Gray Wolf) made a reconnaissance of the Black Hills, and found more than a thousand miners in the area. Three Stars politely informed them that they were violating the law and ordered them to leave, but he made no effort to enforce his orders.

Alarmed by the white men's gold craze and the Army's failure to protect their territory, Red Cloud and Spotted Tail made strong protests to Washington officials. The Great Father's response was to send out a commission "to treat with the Sioux Indians for the relinquishment of the Black Hills." In other words, the time had come to take away one more piece of territory that had been assigned to the Indians in perpetuity. As usual, the commission was made up of politicians, missionaries, traders, and military officers. Senator William B. Allison of Iowa was the chairman. Reverend Samuel D. Hinman, who had long endeavored to replace the Santees' religion and culture with Christianity, was the principal missionary. General Alfred Terry represented the military. John Collins, post trader at Fort Laramie, represented the commercial interests.

To ensure representation of nonagency as well as agency Indians, runners were sent to invite Sitting Bull, Crazy Horse, and other "wild" chiefs to the council. Half-breed Louis Richard took the government letter to Sitting Bull and read it to him. "I want you to go and tell the Great Father," Sitting Bull responded, "that I do not want to sell any land to the government." He picked up a pinch of dust and added: "Not even as much as this."[3] Crazy Horse was also opposed to the selling of Sioux land, especially the Black Hills. He refused to attend the council, but Little Big Man would go as an observer for the free Oglalas.

If the commissioners expected to meet quietly with a few compliant chiefs and arrange an inexpensive trade, they were in for a rude surprise. When they arrived at the meeting place—on White River between the Red Cloud and Spotted Tail agencies—the Plains for miles around were covered with Sioux camps and immense herds of grazing ponies. From the Missouri River on the east to the Bighorn country on the west, all the nations of the Soux and many of their Cheyenne and Arapaho friends had gathered there—more than twenty thousand Indians.

Few of them had ever seen a copy of the treaty of 1868, but a goodly number knew the meaning of a certain clause in that sacred document: "No treaty for the cession of any part of the reservation herein described . . . shall be of any validity or force . . . unless executed and signed by at least *three-fourths of all the adult male Indians,* occupying or interested in the same."[4] Even if the commissioners had been able to intimidate or buy off every chief present, they could not have obtained more than a few dozen signatures from those thousands of angry, well-armed warriors who were determined to keep every pinch of dust and blade of grass within their territory. On September 20, 1875, the commission assembled under the shade of a large tarpaulin which had been strung beside a lone cottonwood on the rolling plain. The commissioners seated themselves on chairs facing the thousands of Indians who were moving restlessly about in the distance. A troop of 120 cavalrymen on white horses filed in from Fort Robinson and drew up in a line behind the canvas shelter. Spotted Tail arrived in a wagon from his agency, but Red Cloud had announced that he would not be there. A few other chiefs drifted in, and then suddenly a cloud of dust boiled up from the crest of a distant rise. A band of Indians came galloping down upon the council shelter. The warriors were dressed for battle, and as they came nearer they swerved to encircle the commissioners, fired their rifles skyward, and gave out a few whoops before trotting off to form a line immediately in the rear of the cavalrymen. By this time a second band of Indians was approaching, and thus tribe by tribe the Sioux warriors came in, making their demonstrations of power, until a great circle of several thousand Indians enclosed the

3. Gilbert, Hila. *"Big Bat" Pourier.* Sheridan, Wyoming, Mills Company, 1968, p. 43.   4. Kappler, Charles J. *Indian Affairs, Laws and Treaties.* Vol. 2, p. 1002.

council. Now the chiefs came forward, well satisfied that they had given the commissioners something strong to think about. They sat in a semicircle facing the nervous white men, eager to hear what they would have to say about the Black Hills.

During the few days that the commissioners had been at Fort Robinson observing the mood of the Indians, they recognized the futility of trying to buy the hills and had decided instead to negotiate for the mineral rights. "We have now to ask you if you are willing to give our people the right to mine in the Black Hills," Senator Allison began, "as long as gold or other valuable minerals are found, for a fair and just sum. If you are so willing, we will make a bargain with you for this right. When the gold or other valuable minerals are taken away, the country will again be yours to dispose of in any manner you may wish."

Spotted Tail took this proposal as a ludicrous joke. Was the commissioner asking the Indians to *lend* the Black Hills to the white men for a while? His rejoinder was to ask Senator Allison if he would lend him a team of mules on such terms.

"It will be hard for our government to keep the whites out of the hills," Allison continued. "To try to do so will give you and our government great trouble, because the whites that may wish to go there are very numerous." The senator's ignorance of the Plains Indians' feeling for the Powder River country was displayed in his next proposal: "There is another country lying far toward the setting sun, over which you roam and hunt, and which territory is yet unceded, extending to the summit of the Bighorn Mountains. . . . It does not seem to be of very great value or use to you, and our people think they would like to have the portion of it I have described."[5]

While Senator Allison's incredible demands were being translated, Red Dog rode up on a pony and announced that he had a message from Red Cloud. The absent Oglala chief, probably anticipating the greed of the commissioners, requested a week's recess to give the tribes time to hold councils of their own in which to consider all proposals concerning their lands. The commissioners considered the matter and agreed to give the Indians three days for holding tribal councils. On September 23 they would expect definite replies from the chiefs.

The idea of giving up their last great hunting ground was so preposterous that none of the chiefs even discussed it during their councils. They did debate very earnestly the question of the Black Hills. Some reasoned that if the United States government had no intention of enforcing the treaty and keeping the white miners out, then perhaps the Indians should demand payment—a great deal of mon-

5. U.S. Commissioner of Indian Affairs. Report, 1875, p. 187.

ey—for the yellow metal taken from the hills. Others were determined not to sell at any price. The Black Hills belonged to the Indians, they argued; if the Bluecoat soldiers would not drive out the miners, then the warriors must.

On September 23 the commissioners, riding in Army ambulances from Fort Robinson and escorted by a somewhat enlarged cavalry troop, again arrived at the council shelter. Red Cloud was there early, and he protested vigorously about the large number of soldiers. Just as he was preparing to give his preliminary speech to the commissioners, a sudden commotion broke out among the warriors far in the distance. About three hundred Oglalas who had come in from the Powder River country trotted their ponies down a slope, occasionally firing off rifles. Some were chanting a song in Sioux:

> The Black Hills is my land and I love it
> And whoever interferes
> Will hear this gun.[6]

An Indian mounted on a gray horse forced his way through the ranks of warriors gathered around the canvas shelter. He was Crazy Horse's envoy, Little Big Man, stripped for battle and wearing two revolvers belted to his waist. "I will kill the first chief who speaks for selling the Black Hills!" he shouted. He danced his horse across the open space between the commissioners and the chiefs.[7]

Young-Man-Afraid-of-His-Horses and a group of unofficial Sioux policemen immediately swarmed around Little Big Man and moved him away. The chiefs and the commissioners, however, must have guessed that Little Big Man voiced the feelings of most of the warriors present. General Terry suggested to his fellow commissioners that they board the Army ambulances and return to the safety of Fort Robinson.

After giving the Indians a few days to calm down, the commissioners quietly arranged a meeting with twenty chiefs in the headquarters building of the Red Cloud agency. During three days of speech making, the chiefs made it quite clear to the Great Father's representatives that the Black Hills could not be bought cheaply, if at any price. Spotted Tail finally grew impatient with the commissioners and asked them to submit a definite proposal in writing.

The offer was four hundred thousand dollars a year for the mineral rights; or if the Sioux wished to sell the hills outright the price would be six million dollars payable in fifteen annual installments. (This was a markdown price indeed, considering that one Black Hills mine alone yielded more than five hundred million dollars in gold.)

Red Cloud did not even appear for the final meeting, letting

6. Gilbert, p. 43.
7. Mills, Anson, *My Story*, Washington,   D.C., 1918, p. 168.

Spotted Tail speak for all the Sioux. Spotted Tail rejected both offers, firmly. The Black Hills were not for lease or for sale.

The commissioners packed up, returned to Washington, reported their failure to persuade the Sioux to relinquish the Black Hills, and recommended that Congress disregard the wishes of the Indians and appropriate a sum fixed "as a fair equivalent of the value of the hills." This forced purchase of the Black Hills should be "presented to the Indians as a finality," they said.[8]

Thus was set in motion a chain of actions which would bring the greatest defeat ever suffered by the United States Army in its wars with the Indians, and ultimately would destroy forever the freedom of the northern Plains Indians:

November 9, 1875: E. T. Watkins, special inspector for the Indian Bureau, reported to the Commissioner of Indian Affairs that Plains Indians living outside reservations were fed and well armed, were lofty and independent in their attitudes, and were therefore a threat to the reservation system. Inspector Watkins recommended that troops be sent against these uncivilized Indians "in the winter, the sooner the better, and *whip* them into subjection."[9]

November 22, 1875: Secretary of War W. W. Belknap warned of trouble in the Black Hills "unless something is done to obtain possession of that section for the white miners who have been strongly attracted there by reports of rich deposits of the precious metal."[9a]

December 3, 1875: Commissioner of Indian Affairs Edward P. Smith ordered Sioux and Cheyenne agents to notify all Indians off reservations to come in and report to their agencies by January 31, 1876, or a "military force would be sent to compel them."

February 1, 1876: The Secretary of the Interior notified the Secretary of War that the time given the "hostile Indians" to come in to their reservations had expired, and that he was turning them over to the military authorities for such action as the Army might deem proper under the circumstances.[1]

February 7, 1876: The War Department authorized General Sheridan, commanding the Military Division of the Missouri, to commence operations against the "hostile Sioux," including the bands under Sitting Bull and Crazy Horse.

February 8, 1876: General Sheridan ordered generals Crook and Terry to begin preparations for military operations in the direction of the headwaters of the Powder, Tongue, Rosebud, and Bighorn rivers, "where Crazy Horse and his allies frequented."[2]

---

8. U.S. Commissioner of Indian Affairs. Report, 1875, p. 199.
9. U.S. Congress. 44th. 1st session. House Executive Document 184, pp. 8–9.
9a. U.S. Secretary of War. Report, 1875, p. 21.

1. U.S. Congress. 44th. 1st session. House Executive Document 184, pp. 10, 17–18.
2. U.S. Secretary of War. Report, 1876, p. 441.

Once this machinery of government began moving, it became an inexorable force, mindless and uncontrollable. When runners went out from the agencies late in December to warn the non-agency chiefs to come in, heavy snows blanketed the northern Plains. Blizzards and severe cold made it impossible for some couriers to return until weeks after the January 31 deadline; it would have been impossible to move women and children by ponies and travois. Had a few thousand "hostiles" somehow managed to reach the agencies, they would have starved there. On the reservations during the late winter, food supplies were so short that hundreds of Indians left in March to go north in search of game to supplement their meager government rations.

In January a courier found Sitting Bull camped near the mouth of the Powder. The Hunkpapa chief sent the messenger back to the agent, informing him that he would consider the order to come in, but could not do so until the Moon When the Green Grass Is Up.

Crazy Horse's Oglalas were in winter camp near Bear Butte, where the Thieves' Road came into the Black Hills from the north. During the spring it would be a good place to make up raiding parties to go against the miners violating *Paha Sapa*. When agency couriers made their way through the snow to Crazy Horse, he told them politely that he could not come until the cold went away. "It was very cold," a young Oglala remembered afterward, "and many of our people and ponies would have died in the snow. Also, we were in our own country and were doing no harm."[3]

The January 31 ultimatum was little short of a declaration of war against the independent Indians, and many of them accepted it as that. But they did not expect the Bluecoats to strike so soon. In the Moon of the Snowblind, Three Stars Crook came marching north from Fort Fetterman along the old Bozeman Road, where ten years before Red Cloud had begun his stubborn fight to keep the Powder. River country inviolate.

About this same time, a mixed band of Northern Cheyennes and Oglala Sioux left Red Cloud agency to go to the Powder River country, where they hoped to find a few buffalo and antelope. About the middle of March they joined some nonagency Indians camped a few miles from where the Little Powder runs into the Powder. Two Moon, Little Wolf, Old Bear, Maple Tree, and White Bull were the Cheyenne leaders. Low Dog was the Oglala chief; and some of the warriors with him were from Crazy Horse's village farther north.

Without warning, at dawn on March 17, Crook's advance column under Colonel Joseph J. Reynolds attacked this peaceful

3. Neihardt, John G. *Black Elk Speaks.* Lincoln, University of Nebraska Press, 1961, p. 90.

camp. Fearing nothing in their own country, the Indians were asleep when Captain James Egan's white-horse troop, formed in a company front, dashed into the tepee village, firing pistols and carbines. At the same time, a second troop of cavalry came in on the left flank, and a third swept away the Indians' horse herd.

The first reaction from the warriors was to get as many women and children as possible out of the way of the soldiers, who were firing recklessly in all directions. "Old people tottered and hobbled away to get out of reach of the bullets singing among the lodges," Wooden Leg said afterward. "Braves seized whatever weapons they had and tried to meet the attack." As soon as the noncombatants were started up a rugged mountain slope, the warriors took positions on ledges or behind huge rocks. From these places they held the soldiers at bay until the women and children could escape across the Powder.

"From a distance we saw the destruction of our village," Wooden Leg said. "Our tepees were burned with everything in them. . . . I had nothing left but the clothing I had on." The Bluecoats destroyed all the pemmican and saddles in the camp, and drove away almost every pony the Indians owned, "between twelve and fifteen hundred head."[4] As soon as darkness fell, the warriors went back to where the Bluecoats were camped, determined to recover their stolen horses. Two Moon succinctly described what happened: "That night the soldiers slept, leaving the horses to one side; so we crept up and stole them back again, and then we went away."[5]

Three Stars Crook was so angry at Colonel Reynolds for allowing the Indians to escape from their village and recover their horses that he ordered him court-martialed. The Army reported this foray as "the attack on Crazy Horse's village," but Crazy Horse was camped miles away to the northeast. That was where Two Moon and the other chiefs led their homeless people in hopes of finding food and shelter. They were more than three days making the journey; the temperature was below zero at night; only a few had buffalo robes; and there was very little food.

Crazy Horse received the fugitives hospitably, gave them food and robes, and found room for them in the Oglala tepees. "I'm glad you are come," he said to Two Moon after listening to accounts of the Bluecoats plundering the village. "We are going to fight the white man again."

"All right," Two Moon replied. "I am ready to fight. I have

4. Marquis, Thomas B. *Wooden Leg, a Warrior Who Fought Custer.* Lincoln, University of Nebraska Press, 1957, pp. 165, 168. De Barthe, Joe. *Life and Adventures of Frank Grouard.* Norman, University of Oklahoma Press, 1958, p. 98.

5. Garland, Hamlin. "General Custer's Last Fight as Seen by Two Moon." *McClure's Magazine,* Vol. 11, 1898, p. 444.

fought already. My people have been killed, my horses stolen; I am satisfied to fight."[6]

In the Geese Laying Moon, when the grass was tall and the horses strong, Crazy Horse broke camp and led the Oglalas and Cheyennes north to the mouth of Tongue River, where Sitting Bull and the Hunkpapas had been living through the winter. Not long after that, Lame Deer arrived with a band of Minneconjous and asked permission to camp nearby. They had heard about all the Bluecoats marching through the Sioux hunting grounds and wanted to be near Sitting Bull's powerful band of Hunkpapas should there be any trouble.

As the weather warmed, the tribes began moving northward in search of wild game and fresh grass. Along the way they were joined by bands of Brulés, Sans Arcs, Blackfoot Sioux, and additional Cheyennes. Most of these Indians had left their reservations in accordance with their treaty rights as hunters, and those who had heard of the January 31 ultimatum either considered it as only another idle threat of the Great Father's agents or did not believe it applied to peaceful Indians. "Many young men were anxious to go for fighting the soldiers," said the Cheyenne warrior Wooden Leg. "But the chiefs and old men all urged us to keep away from the white men."[7]

While these several thousand Indians were camped on the Rosebud, many young warriors joined them from the reservations. They brought rumors of great forces of Bluecoats marching from three directions. Three Stars Crook was coming from the south. The One Who Limps (Colonel John Gibbon) was coming from the west. One Star Terry and Long Hair Custer were coming from the east.

Early in the Moon of Making Fat, the Hunkpapas had their annual sun dance. For three days Sitting Bull danced, bled himself, and stared at the sun until he fell into a trance. When he rose again, he spoke to his people. In his vision he had heard a voice crying: "I give you these because they have no ears." When he looked into the sky he saw soldiers falling like grasshoppers, with their heads down and their hats falling off. They were falling right into the Indian camp. Because the white men had no ears and would not listen, Wakantanka the Great Spirit was giving these soldiers to the Indians to be killed.[8]

A few days later a hunting party of Cheyennes sighted a column of Bluecoats camped for the night in the valley of the Rosebud. The hunters rode back to camp, sounding the wolf howl of danger. Three Stars was coming, and he had employed mercenary Crows and Shoshones to scout ahead of his troops.

6. *Ibid.*, p. 445.
7. Marquis, p. 185.
8. Vestal, Stanley. *Sitting Bull, Cham-* *pion of the Sioux*. Norman, University of Oklahoma Press, 1957, pp. 150–51.

The different chiefs sent criers through their villages and then held hasty councils. It was decided to leave about half the warriors to protect the villages while the others would travel through the night and attack Three Stars's soldiers the next morning. About a thousand Sioux and Cheyennes formed the party. A few women went along to help with the spare horses. Sitting Bull, Crazy Horse, and Two Moon were among the leaders. Just before daylight they unsaddled and rested for a while; then they turned away from the river and rode across the hills.

Three Stars's Crow scouts had told him of a great Sioux village down the Rosebud, and the general started these mercenaries out early that morning. As the Crows rode over the crest of a hill and started down, they ran into the Sioux and Cheyenne warriors. At first the Sioux and Cheyennes chased the Crows in all directions, but Bluecoats began coming up fast, and the warriors pulled back.

For a long time Crazy Horse had been waiting for a chance to test himself in battle with the Bluecoats. In all the years since the Fetterman fight at Fort Phil Kearny, he had studied the soldiers and their ways of fighting. Each time he went into the Black Hills to seek visions, he had asked Wakantanka to give him secret powers so that he would know how to lead the Oglalas to victory if the white men ever came again to make war upon his people. Since the time of his youth, Crazy Horse had known that the world men lived in was only a shadow of the real world. To get into the real world, he had to dream, and when he was in the real world everything seemed to float or dance. In this real world his horse danced as if it were wild or crazy, and this was why he called himself Crazy Horse. He had learned that if he dreamed himself into the real world before going into a fight, he could endure anything.

On this day, June 17, 1876, Crazy Horse dreamed himself into the real world, and he showed the Sioux how to do many things they had never done before while fighting the white man's soldiers. When Crook sent his pony soldiers in mounted charges, instead of rushing forward into the fire of their carbines, the Sioux faded off to their flanks and struck weak places in their lines. Crazy Horse kept his warriors mounted and always moving from one place to another. By the time the sun was in the top of the sky he had the soldiers all mixed up in three separate fights. The Bluecoats were accustomed to forming skirmish lines and strong fronts, and when Crazy Horse prevented them from fighting like that they were thrown into confusion. By making many darting charges on their swift ponies, the Sioux kept the soldiers apart and always on the defensive. When the Bluecoats' fire grew too hot, the Sioux would draw away, tantalize a few soldiers into pursuit, and then turn on them with a fury.

The Cheyennes also distinguished themselves that day, especially in the dangerous charges. Chief-Comes-in-Sight was the bravest of all, but as he was swinging his horse about after a charge into the soldiers' flank the animal was shot down in front of a Bluecoat infantry line. Suddenly another horse and rider galloped out from the Cheyennes' position and swerved to shield Chief-Comes-in-Sight from the soldiers' fire. In a moment Chief-Comes-in-Sight was up behind the rider. The rescuer was his sister Buffalo-Calf-Road-Woman, who had come along to help with the horse herds. That was why the Cheyennes always remembered this fight as the Battle Where the Girl Saved Her Brother. The white men called it the Battle of the Rosebud.

When the sun went down, the fighting ended. The Indians knew they had given Three Stars a good fight, but they did not know until the next morning that they had whipped him. At first daylight, Sioux and Cheyenne scouts went out along the ridges, and they could see the Bluecoat column retreating far away to the south. General Crook was returning to his base camp on Goose Creek to await reinforcements or a message from Gibbon, Terry, or Custer. The Indians on the Rosebud were too strong for one column of soldiers.

After the fight on the Rosebud, the chiefs decided to move west to the valley of the Greasy Grass (Little Bighorn). Scouts had come in with reports of great herds of antelope west of there, and they said grass for the horses was plentiful on the nearby benchlands. Soon the camp circles were spread along the west bank of the twisting Greasy Grass for almost three miles. No one knew for certain how many Indians were there, but the number could not have been smaller than ten thousand people, including three or four thousand warriors. "It was a very big village and you could hardly count the tepees," Black Elk said.[9]

Farthest upstream toward the south was the Hunkpapa camp, with the Blackfoot Sioux nearby. The Hunkpapas always camped at the entrance, or at the head end of the circle, which was the meaning of their name. Below them were the Sans Arcs, Minneconjous, Oglalas, and Brulés. At the north end were the Cheyennes.

The time was early in the Moon When the Chokecherries Are Ripe, with days hot enough for boys to swim in the melted snow water of the Greasy Grass. Hunting parties were coming and going in the direction of the Bighorns, where they had found a few buffalo as well as antelope. The women were digging wild turnips out on the prairies. Every night one or more of the tribal circles held dances, and some nights the chiefs met in councils. "The chiefs of the different tribes met together as equals," Wooden Leg said. "There was only one who was considered as being above all the others. This was Sitting Bull. He was recognized as the one old man chief of all the camps combined."[1]

9. Neihardt, p. 106. 1. Marquis, p. 205.

Sitting Bull did not believe the victory on the Rosebud had fulfilled his prophecy of soldiers falling into the Indian camp. Since the retreat of Three Stars, however, no hunting parties had sighted any Bluecoats between the Powder and the Bighorn.

They did not know until the morning of June 24 that Long Hair Custer was prowling along the Rosebud. Next morning scouts reported that the soldiers had crossed the last high ridge between the Rosebud and the Indian camp and were marching toward the Little Bighorn.

The news of Custer's approach came to the Indians in various ways:

"I and four women were a short distance from the camp digging wild turnips," said Red Horse, one of the Sioux council chiefs. "Suddenly one of the women attracted my attention to a cloud of dust rising a short distance from camp. I soon saw that the soldiers were charging the camp. To the camp I and the women ran. When I arrived a person told me to hurry to the council lodge. The soldiers charged so quickly that we could not talk. We came out of the council lodge and talked in all directions. The Sioux mount horses, take guns, and go fight the soldiers. Women and children mount horses and go, meaning to get out of the way."[2]

Pte-San-Waste-Win, a cousin of Sitting Bull, was one of the young women digging turnips that morning. She said the soldiers were six to eight miles distant when first sighted. "We could see the flashing of their sabers and saw that there were very many soldiers in the party." The soldiers first seen by Pte-San-Waste-Win and other Indians in the middle of the camp were those in Custer's battalion. These Indians were not aware of Major Marcus Reno's surprise attack against the south end of camp until they heard rifle fire from the direction of the Blackfoot Sioux lodges. "Like that the soldiers were upon us. Through the tepee poles their bullets rattled. ... The women and children cried, fearing they would be killed, but the men, the Hunkpapa and Blackfeet, the Oglala and Minneconjou, mounted their horses and raced to the Blackfoot tepees. We could still see the soldiers of Long Hair marching along in the distance, and our men, taken by surprise, and from a point whence they had not expected to be attacked, went singing the song of battle into the fight behind the Blackfoot village."[3]

Black Elk, a thirteen-year-old Oglala boy, was swimming with his companions in the Little Bighorn. The Sun was straight above and was getting very hot when he heard a crier shouting in the Hunkpapa camp: "The chargers are coming! They are charging! The chargers are coming!" The warning was repeated by an Oglala crier,

2. U.S. Bureau of American Ethnology. Annual Report, 19th, 1888–89, p. 564.

3. McLaughlin, James. *My Friend the Indian.* Boston, Houghton Mifflin Co., 1910, pp.168–69.

and Black Elk could hear the cry going from camp to camp northward to the Cheyennes.[4]

Low Dog, an Oglala chief, heard this same warning cry. "I did
not believe it. I thought it was a false alarm. I did not think it possible that any white man would attack us, so strong as we were. . . .
Although I did not believe it was a true alarm, I lost no time getting ready. When I got my gun and came out of my lodge the
attack had begun at the end of the camp where Sitting Bull and the
Hunkpapas were."

Iron Thunder was in the Minneconjou camp. "I did not know
anything about Reno's attack until his men were so close that the
bullets went through the camp, and everything was in confusion.
The horses were so frightened we could not catch them."

Crow King, who was in the Hunkpapa camp, said that Reno's
pony soldiers commenced firing at about four hundred yards' distance. The Hunkpapas and Blackfoot Sioux retreated slowly on foot
to give the women and children time to go to a place of safety.
"Other Indians got our horses. By that time we had warriors
enough to turn upon the whites."[5]

Near the Cheyenne camp, three miles to the north, Two Moon
was watering his horses. "I washed them off with cool water, then
took a swim myself. I came back to the camp afoot. When I got
near my lodge, I looked up the Little Bighorn toward Sitting Bull's
camp. I saw a great dust rising. It looked like a whirlwind. Soon a
Sioux horseman came rushing into camp shouting: 'Soldiers come!
Plenty white soldiers!' "

Two Moon ordered the Cheyenne warriors to get their horses,
and then told the women to take cover away from the tepee village.
"I rode swiftly toward Sitting Bull's camp. Then I saw the white
soldiers fighting in a line [Reno's men]. Indians covered the flat.
They began to drive the soldiers all mixed up—Sioux, then soldiers,
then more Sioux, and all shooting. The air was full of smoke and
dust. I saw the soldiers fall back and drop into the riverbed like buffalo fleeing."[6]

The war chief who rallied the Indians and turned back Reno's
attack was a muscular, full-chested, thirty-six-year-old Hunkpapa
named Pizi, or Gall. Gall had grown up in the tribe as an orphan.
While still a young man he distinguished himself as a hunter and
warrior, and Sitting Bull adopted him as a younger brother. Some
years before, while the commissioners were attempting to persuade
the Sioux to take up farming as a part of the treaty of 1868, Gall
went to Fort Rice to speak for the Hunkpapas. "We were born
naked," he said, "and have been taught to hunt and live on the

4. Neihardt, pp. 108–09.   *Times,* August 18, 1881.
5. *Leavenworth* (Kansas) *Weekly*   6. Garland, p. 446.

game. You tell us that we must learn to farm, live in one house, and take on your ways. Suppose the people living beyond the great sea should come and tell you that you must stop farming and kill your cattle, and take your houses and lands, what would you do? Would you not fight them?"[7] In the decade following that speech, nothing changed Gall's opinion of the white man's self-righteous arrogance, and by the summer of 1876 he was generally accepted by the Hunkpapas as Sitting Bull's lieutenant, the war chief of the tribe.

Reno's first onrush caught several women and children in the open, and the cavalry's flying bullets virtually wiped out Gall's family. "It made my heart bad," he told a newspaperman some years later. "After that I killed all my enemies with the hatchet." His description of the tactics used to block Reno was equally terse: "Sitting Bull and I were at the point where Reno attacked. Sitting Bull was big medicine. The women and children were hastily moved downstream. . . . The women and children caught the horses for the bucks to mount them; the bucks mounted and charged back Reno and checked him, and drove him into the timber."[8]

In military terms, Gall turned Reno's flank and forced him into the woods. He then frightened Reno into making a hasty retreat which the Indians quickly turned into a rout. The result made it possible for Gall to divert hundreds of warriors for a frontal attack against Custer's column, while Crazy Horse and Two Moon struck the flank and rear.

Meanwhile Pte-San-Waste-Win and the other women had been anxiously watching the Long Hair's soldiers across the river. "I could hear the music of the bugle and could see the column of soldiers turn to the left to march down to the river where the attack was to be made. . . . Soon I saw a number of Cheyennes ride into the river, then some young men of my band, then others, until there were hundreds of warriors in the river and running up into the ravine. When some hundreds had passed the river and gone into the ravine, the others who were left, still a very great number, moved back from the river and waited for the attack. And I knew that the fighting men of the Sioux, many hundreds in number, were hidden in the ravine behind the hill upon which Long Hair was marching, and he would be attacked from both sides."[9]

Kill Eagle, a Blackfoot Sioux chief, later said that the movement of Indians toward Custer's column was "like a hurricane . . . like bees swarming out of a hive." Hump, the Minneconjou comrade of Gall and Crazy Horse during the old Powder River days, said the

7. Robinson, D. W. "Editorial Notes on Historical Sketch of North and South Dakota." *South Dakota Historical Collections*, Vol. I, 1902, p. 151.

8. *St. Paul* (Minnesota) *Pioneer Press*, July 18, 1886.

9. McLaughlin, pp. 172-73.

first massive charge by the Indians caused the long-haired chief and his men to become confused. "The first dash the Indians made my horse was shot from under me and I was wounded—shot above the knee, and the ball came out at the hip, and I fell and lay right there." Crow King, who was with the Hunkpapas, said: "The greater portion of our warriors came together in their front and we rushed our horses on them. At the same time warriors rode out on each side of them and circled around them until they were surrounded."[1] Thirteen-year-old Black Elk, watching from across the river, could see a big dust whirling on the hill, and then horses began coming out of it with empty saddles.

"The smoke of the shooting and the dust of the horses shut out the hill," Pte-San-Waste-Win said, "and the soldiers fired many shots, but the Sioux shot straight and the soldiers fell dead. The women crossed the river after the men of our village, and when we came to the hill there were no soldiers living and Long Hair lay dead among the rest. . . . The blood of the people was hot and their hearts bad, and they took no prisoners that day."[2]

Crow King said that all the soldiers dismounted when the Indians surrounded them. "They tried to hold on to their horses, but as we pressed closer they let go their horses. We crowded them toward our main camp and killed them all. They kept in order and fought like brave warriors as long as they had a man left."[3]

According to Red Horse, toward the end of the fighting with Custer, "these soldiers became foolish, many throwing away their guns and raising their hands, saying, 'Sioux, pity us; take us prisoners.' The Sioux did not take a single soldier prisoner, but killed all of them; none were alive for even a few minutes."[4]

Long after the battle, White Bull of the Minneconjous drew four pictographs showing himself grappling with and killing a soldier identified as Custer. Among others who claimed to have killed Custer were Rain-in-the-Face, Flat Hip, and Brave Bear. Red Horse said that an unidentified Santee warrior killed Custer. Most Indians who told of the battle said they never saw Custer and did not know who killed him. "We did not know till the fight was over that he was the white chief," Low Dog said.[5]

In an interview given in Canada a year after the battle, Sitting Bull said that he never saw Custer, but that other Indians had seen and recognized him just before he was killed. "He did not wear his long hair as he used to wear it," Sitting Bull said. "It was short, but it was the color of the grass when the frost comes. . . . Where the

1. New York *Herald*, September 24, 1876. Easterwood, T. J. *Memories of Seventy-Six.* Dundee, Oregon, 1880, p. 15.

2. McLaughlin, p. 175.

3. *Leavenworth* (Kansas) *Weekly Times*, August 18, 1881.

4. U.S. Bureau of American Ethnology. Annual Report, 10th, 1888–89, p. 565.

5. *Leavenworth* (Kansas) *Weekly Times*, August 18, 1881.

last stand was made, the Long Hair stood like a sheaf of corn with all the ears fallen around him."[6] But Sitting Bull did not say who killed Custer.

An Arapaho warrior who was riding with the Cheyennes said that Custer was killed by several Indians. "He was dressed in buckskin, coat and pants, and was on his hands and knees. He had been shot through the side, and there was blood coming from his mouth. He seemed to be watching the Indians moving around him. Four soldiers were sitting up around him, but they were all badly wounded. All the other soldiers were down. Then the Indians closed in around him, and I did not see any more."[7]

Regardless of who had killed him, the Long Hair who made the Thieves' Road into the Black Hills was dead with all his men. Reno's soldiers, however, reinforced by those of Major Frederick Benteen, were dug in on a hill farther down the river. The Indians surrounded the hill completely and watched the soldiers through the night, and next morning started fighting them again. During the days, scouts sent out by the chiefs came back with warnings of many more soldiers marching in the direction of the Little Bighorn.

After a council it was decided to break camp. The warriors had expended most of their ammunition, and they knew it would be foolish to try to fight so many soldiers with bows and arrows. The women were told to begin packing, and before sunset they started up the valley toward the Bighorn Mountains, the tribes separating along the way and taking different directions.

When the white men in the East heard of the Long Hair's defeat, they called it a massacre and went crazy with anger. They wanted to punish all the Indians in the West. Because they could not punish Sitting Bull and the war chiefs, the Great Council in Washington decided to punish the Indians they could find—those who remained on the reservations and had taken no part in the fighting.

On July 22 the Great Warrior Sherman received authority to assume military control of all reservations in the Sioux country and to treat the Indians there as prisoners of war. On August 15 the Great Council made a new law requiring the Indians to give up all rights to the Powder River country and the Black Hills. They did this without regard to the treaty of 1868, maintaining that the Indians had violated the treaty by going to war with the United States. This was difficult for the reservation Indians to understand, because they had not attacked United States soldiers, nor had Sitting Bull's followers attacked them until Custer sent Reno charging through

6. New York *Herald*, November 16, 1877.
7. Graham, W. A. *The Custer Myth.* Harrisburg, Pa., Stackpole Co., 1953, p. 110.

the Sioux villages.

To keep the reservation Indians peaceful, the Great Father sent out a new commission in September to cajole and threaten the chiefs and secure their signatures to legal documents transferring the immeasurable wealth of the Black Hills to white ownership. Several members of this commission were old hands at stealing Indian lands, notably Newton Edmunds, Bishop Henry Whipple, and the Reverend Samuel D. Hinman. At the Red Cloud agency, Bishop Whipple opened the proceedings with a prayer, and then Chairman George Manypenny read the conditions laid down by Congress. Because these conditions were stated in the usual obfuscated language of lawmakers, Bishop Whipple attempted to explain them in phrases which could be used by the interpreters.

"My heart has for many years been very warm toward the red man. We came here to bring a message to you from your Great Father, and there are certain things we have given to you in his exact words. We cannot alter them even to the scratch of a pen. . . . When the Great Council made the appropriation this year to continue your supplies they made certain provisions, three in number, and unless they were complied with no more appropriations would be made by Congress. Those three provisions are: First, that you shall give up the Black Hills country and the country to the north; second, that you shall receive your rations on the Missouri River; and third, that the Great Father shall be permitted to locate three roads from the Missouri River across the reservation to that new country where the Black Hills are. . . . The Great Father said that his heart was full of tenderness for his red children, and he selected this commission of friends of the Indians that they might devise a plan, as he directed them, in order that the Indian nations might be saved, and that instead of growing smaller and smaller until the last Indian looks upon his own grave, they might become as the white man has become, a great and powerful people."[8]

To Bishop Whipple's listeners, this seemed a strange way indeed to save the Indian nations, taking away their Black Hills and hunting grounds, and moving them far away to the Missouri River. Most of the chiefs knew that it was already too late to save the Black Hills, but they protested strongly against having their reservations moved to the Missouri. "I think if my people should move there," Red Cloud said, "they would all be destroyed. There are a great many bad men there and bad whiskey; therefore I don't want to go there."[9]

No Heart said that white men had already ruined the Missouri River country so that Indians could not live there. "You travel up

8. U.S. Congress. 44th. 2nd session. Senate Executive Document 9, pp. 5, 31.   9. New York *Herald* 33, September 23, 1876.

and down the Missouri River and you do not see any timber," he declared. "You have probably seen where lots of it has been, and the Great Father's people have destroyed it."

"It is only six years since we came to live on this stream where we are living now," Red Dog said, "and nothing that has been promised us has been done." Another chief remembered that since the Great Father promised them that they would never be moved they had been moved five times. "I think you had better put the Indians on wheels," he said sardonically, "and you can run them about whenever you wish."

Spotted Tail accused the government and the commissioners of betraying the Indians, of broken promises and false words. "This war did not spring up here in our land; this was was brought upon us by the children of the Great Father who came to take our land from us without price, and who, in our land, do a great many evil things. . . . This war has come from robbery—from the stealing of our land."[1] As for moving to the Missouri, Spotted Tail was utterly opposed, and he told the commissioners he would not sign away the Black Hills until he could go to Washington and talk to the Great Father.

The commissioners gave the Indians a week to discuss the terms among themselves, and it soon became evident that they were not going to sign anything. The chiefs pointed out that the treaty of 1868 required the signatures of three-fourth of the male adults of the Sioux tribes to change anything in it, and more than half of the warriors were in the north with Sitting Bull and Crazy Horse. In reply to this the commissioners explained that the Indians off the reservations were hostiles; only friendly Indians were covered by the treaty. Most of the chiefs did not accept this. To break down their opposition, the commissioners dropped strong hints that unless they signed, the Great Council in its anger would cut off all rations immediately, would remove them to the Indian Territory in the south, and the Army would take all their guns and horses.

There was no way out. The Black Hills were stolen; the Powder River country and its herds of wild game were gone. Without wild game or rations, the people would starve. The thought of moving far away to a strange country in the south was unbearable, and if the Army took their guns and ponies they would no longer be men.

Red Cloud and his subchiefs signed first, and then Spotted Tail and his people signed. After that the commissioners went to agencies at Standing Rock, Cheyenne River, Crow Creek, Lower Brulé, and Santee, and badgered the other Sioux tribes into signing. Thus did *Paha Sapa*, its spirits and its mysteries, its vast pine forests, and

1. U.S. Congress. 44th. 2nd session. 38–40, 66. Senate Executive Document 9, pp. 8,

its billion dollars in gold pass forever from the hands of the Indians into the domain of the United States.

Four weeks after Red Cloud and Spotted Tail touched pens to the paper, eight companies of United States cavalry under Three Fingers Mackenzie (the Eagle Chief who destroyed the Kiowas and Comanches in Palo Duro Canyon) marched out of Fort Robinson into the agency camps. Under orders of the War Department, Mackenzie had come to take the reservation Indians' ponies and guns. All males were placed under arrest, tepees were searched and dismantled, guns collected, and all ponies were rounded up by the soldiers. Mackenzie gave the women permission to use horses to haul their goods into Fort Robinson. The males, including Red Cloud and the other chiefs, were forced to walk to the fort. The tribe would have to live henceforth at Fort Robinson under the guns of the soldiers.

Next morning, to degrade his beaten prisoners even further, Mackenzie presented a company of mercenary Pawnee scouts (the same Pawnees the Sioux had once driven out of their Powder River country) with the horses the soldiers had taken from the Sioux.

Meanwhile, the United States Army, thirsting for revenge, was prowling the country north and west of the Black Hills, killing Indians wherever they could be found. In late summer of 1876, Three Stars Crook's reinforced column ran out of rations in the Heart River country of Dakota, and started a forced march southward to obtain supplies in the Black Hills mining camps. On September 9, near Slim Buttes, a forward detachment under Captain Anson Mills stumbled upon American Horse's village of Oglalas and Minneconjous. These Indians had left Crazy Horses's camp on Grand River a few days before and were moving south to spend the winter on their reservation. Captain Mills attacked, but the Sioux drove him back, and while he was waiting for Three Stars to arrive, all the Indians escaped except American Horse, four warriors, and fifteen women and children, who were trapped in a cave at the end of a small canyon.

When Crook came up with the main column, he ordered soldiers to positions from which they could fire volleys into the mouth of the cave. American Horse and his four warriors returned the fire, and after some hours of continuous dueling, two Bluecoats were dead and nine wounded. Crook then sent a scout, Frank Grouard, to ask the Indians to surrender. Grouard, who had lived with the Sioux, spoke to them in their language. "They told me they would come out if we would not kill them, and upon receiving this promise, they came out." American Horse, two warriors, five women, and several children crawled out of the cave; the others were dead or too badly wounded to move. American Horse's groin had been ripped open by buckshot. "He was holding his entrails in his hands as he came out," Grouard said. "Holding out one of his bloodstained hands, he shook hands with me."[2]

Captain Millls had found a little girl, three or four years old, hiding in the village. "She sprang up and ran away like a young partridge," he said. "The soldiers caught her and brought her to me." Mills comforted her and gave her some food, and then he asked his orderly to bring her along when he went down to the cave where the soldiers were dragging out the Indian casualties. Two of the dead were women, bloody with many wounds. "The little girl began to scream and fought the orderly until he placed her on the ground, when she ran and embraced one of these squaws, who was her mother. I told Adjutant Lemly I intended to adopt this little girl, as I had slain her mother."

A surgeon came to examine American Horse's wound. He pronounced it fatal, and the chief sat down before a fire, holding a blanket over his bullet-torn abdomen, until he lost consciousness and died.

Crook ordered Captain Mills to ready his men for a resumption of the march to the Black Hills. "Before starting," Mills said, "Adjutant Lemly asked me if I really intended to take the little girl. I told him I did, when he remarked, 'Well, how do you think Mrs. Mills will like it?' It was the first time I had given that side of the matter a thought, and I decided to leave the child where I found her."[3]

While Three Stars was destroying American Horse's village, some of the Sioux who had escaped made their way to Sitting Bull's camp and told him about the attack. Sitting Bull and Gall, with about six hundred warriors, immediately went to help American Horse, but they arrived too late. Although Sitting Bull launched an attack on Crook's soldiers, his warriors had so little ammunition that the Bluecoats held them off with rearguard actions while the main column marched on to the Black Hills.

When the soldiers were all gone, Sitting Bull and his warriors went into American Horse's devastated village, rescued the helpless survivors, and buried the dead. "What have we done that the white people want us to stop?" Sitting Bull asked. "We have been running up and down this country, but they follow us from one place to another."[4]

In an effort to get as far away from the soldiers as possible, Sitting Bull took his people north along the Yellowstone, where buffalo could be found. In the Moon of Falling Leaves, Gall went out with a hunting party and came upon an Army wagon train traveling through the Yellowstone country. The soldiers were taking supplies

2. De Barthe, pp. 157–58.
3. Mills, pp. 171–72.
4. U.S. Secretary of the Interior. Report, 1877, p. 724.

to a new fort they were building where Tongue River flowed into the Yellowstone (Fort Keogh, named for Captain Myles Keogh, who was killed at the Little Bighorn).

Gall's warriors ambushed the train near Glendive Creek and captured sixty mules. As soon as Sitting Bull heard about the wagon train and the new fort, he sent for Johnny Brughiere, a half-breed who had joined his camp. Brughiere knew how to write, and Sitting Bull told him to put down on a piece of paper some words he had to say to the commander of the soldiers:

I want to know what you are doing on this road. You scare all the buffalo away. I want to hunt in this place. I want you to turn back from here. If you don't, I will fight you again. I want you to leave what you have got here, and turn back from here. I am your friend.

—SITTING BULL[5]

When Lieutenant Colonel Elwell Otis, commanding the wagon train, received the message, he sent a scout with a reply to Sitting Bull. The soldiers were going to Fort Keogh, Otis said, and many more soldiers were coming to join them. If Sitting Bull wanted a fight, the soldiers would give him one.

Sitting Bull did not want a fight; he wanted only to be left alone to hunt buffalo. He sent a warrior out with a white flag, asking for a talk with the soldier chief. By this time Colonel Nelson Miles and more soldiers had overtaken the train. As Miles had been searching for Sitting Bull since the end of summer, he immediately agreed to a parley.

They met on October 22 between a line of soldiers and a line of warriors. Miles was escorted by an officer and five men, Sitting Bull by a subchief and five warriors. The day was very cold, and Miles was wearing a long coat trimmed with bear fur. From the first moment of his appearance, he was Bear Coat to the Indians.

There were no preliminary speeches, no friendly smokes of the pipe. With Johnny Brughiere interpreting, Bear Coat began the parley by accusing Sitting Bull of always being against the white man and his ways. Sitting Bull admitted that he was not for the whites, but neither was he an enemy to them as long as they left him alone. Bear Coat wanted to know what Sitting Bull was doing in the Yellowstone country. The question was a foolish one, but the Hunkpapa answered it politely; he was hunting buffalo to feed and clothe his people. Bear Coat then made passing mention of a reservation for the Hunkpapas, but Sitting Bull brushed it aside. He would spend the winter in the Black Hills, he said. The parley ended with nothing resolved, but the two men agreed to meet again the next day.

5. U.S. War Department. Military Division of the Missouri. Record of Engagements with Hostile Indians. 1882, p. 62.

The second meeting quickly became a succession of disagreements. Sitting Bull began by saying that he had not fought the soldiers until they came to fight him, and promised that there would be no more fighting if the white men would take their soldiers and forts out of the Indians' country. Bear Coat replied that there could be no peace for the Sioux until they were all on reservations. At this, Sitting Bull became angry. He declared that the Great Spirit had made him an Indian but not an agency Indian, and he did not intend to become one. He ended the conference abruptly, and returned to his warriors, ordering them to scatter because he suspected that Bear Coat's soldiers would try to attack them. The soldiers did open fire, and once again the Hunkpapas had to start running up and down the country.

By springtime of 1877 Sitting Bull was tired of running. He decided there was no longer room enough for white men and the Sioux to live together in the Great Father's country. He would take his people to Canada, to the land of the Grandmother, Queen Victoria. Before he started, he searched for Crazy Horse, hoping to persuade him to bring the Oglalas to the Grandmother's land. But Crazy Horse's people were running up and down the country trying to escape the soldiers, and Sitting Bull could not find them.

In those same cold moons, General Crook was also looking for Crazy Horse. This time Crook had assembled an enormous army of infantry, cavalry, and artillery. This time he took along enough rations to fill 168 wagons and enough powder and ammunition to burden the backs of 400 pack mules. Three Stars's mighty column swept through the Powder River country like a swarm of grizzly bears, mauling and crushing all Indians in its path.

The soldiers were looking for Crazy Horse, but they found a Cheyenne village first, Dull Knife's village. Most of these Cheyennes had not been in the Little Bighorn battle, but had slipped away from Red Cloud agency in search of food after the Army took possession there and stopped their rations. General Crook sent Three Fingers Mackenzie against this village of 150 lodges.

It was in the Deer Rutting Moon, and very cold, with deep snow in the shaded places and ice-crusted snow in the open places. Mackenzie brought his troopers up to attacking positions during the night, and struck the Cheyennes at first daylight. The Pawnee mercenaries went in first, charging on the fast ponies Mackenzie had taken from the reservation Sioux. They caught the Cheyennes in their lodges, killing many of them as they came awake. Others ran out naked into the biting cold, the warriors trying to fight off the Pawnees and the onrushing soldiers long enough for their women and children to escape.

Some of the best warriors of the Northern Cheyennes sacrificed their lives in those first furious moments of fighting; one of them was Dull Knife's oldest son. Dull Knife and Little Wolf finally managed to form a rear guard along the upper ledges of a canyon, but their scanty supply of ammunition was soon exhausted. Little Wolf was shot seven times before he and Dull Knife broke away to join their women and children in full flight toward the Bighorns. Behind them Mackenzie was burning their lodges, and after that was done he herded their captured ponies against the canyon wall and ordered his men to shoot them down, just as he had done to the ponies of the Comanches and Kiowas in Palo Duro Canyon.

For Dull Knife's Cheyennes, their flight was a repetition of the flight of Two Moon's Cheyennes after the surprise attack in March by the Eagle Chief, Reynolds. But the weather was colder; they had only a few horses, and scarcely any blankets, robes, or even moccasins. Like Two Moon's people, they knew only one sanctuary— Crazy Horse's village on Box Elder Creek.

During the first night of flight, twelve infants and several old people froze to death. The next night, the men killed some of the ponies, disemboweled them, and thrust small children inside to keep them from freezing. The old people put their hands and feet in beside the children. For three days they tramped across the frozen snow, their bare feet leaving a trail of blood, and then they reached Crazy Horse's camp.

Crazy Horse shared food, blankets, and shelter with Dull Knife's people, but warned them to be ready to run. The Oglalas did not have enough ammunition left to stand and fight. Bear Coat Miles was looking for them in the north, and now Three Stars Crook was coming from the south. To survive, they would have to keep running up and down the country.

In the Moon of Popping Trees, Crazy Horse moved the camp north along the Tongue to a hiding place not far from the new Fort Keogh, where Bear Coat was wintering his soldiers. Cold and hunger became so unbearable for the children and old people that some of the chiefs told Crazy Horse it was time to go and parley with Bear Coat and find out what he wanted them to do. Their women and children were crying for food, and they needed warm shelters they would not have to run away from. Crazy Horse knew that Bear Coat wanted to make prisoners of them on a reservation, but he agreed that the chiefs should go if they wished to do so. He went with the party, about thirty chiefs and warriors, to a hill not far from the fort. Eight chiefs and warriors volunteered to ride down to the fort, one of them carrying a large white cloth on a lance. As they neared the fort, some of Bear Coat's mercenary Crows came charging out. Ignoring the truce flag, the Crows fired point-blank into the Sioux. Only three of the eight escaped alive. Some of the Sioux watching from the hill wanted to ride out and seek revenge on the Crows, but Crazy Horse insisted that they hurry back to camp. They would have to pack up and run again. Now that Bear Coat knew there were Sioux nearby, he would come searching through the snow for them.

Bear Coat caught up with them on the morning of January 8 (1877) at Battle Butte, and sent his soldiers charging through foot-deep snow. Crazy Horse had but little ammunition left to defend his people, but he had some good warrior chiefs who knew enough tricks to mislead and punish the soldiers while the main body of Indians escaped through the Wolf Mountains toward the Bighorns. Working in concert, Little Big Man, Two Moon, and Hump decoyed the troops into a canyon. For four hours they kept the soldiers—who were encumbered with bulky winter uniforms—stumbling and falling over ice-covered cliffs. Snow began sifting down during the engagement, and by early afternoon a blizzard was raging. This was enough for Bear Coat. He took his men back to the warmth of Fort Keogh.

Through the screen of sleety snow, Crazy Horse and his people made their way to the familiar country of the Little Powder. They were camped there in February, living off what game they could find, when runners brought news that Spotted Tail and a party of Brulés were coming from the south. Some of the Indians in the camp thought that perhaps Spotted Tail at last had tired of being told what to do on his reservation and was running away from the soldiers, but Crazy Horse knew better.

During the cold moons, Three Stars Crook had taken his men out of the snow into Fort Fetterman. While he was waiting for spring, he paid a visit to Spotted Tail and promised him that the reservation Sioux would not have to move to the Missouri River if the Brulé chief would go as a peace emissary to Crazy Horse and persuade him to surrender. That was the purpose of Spotted Tail's visit to Crazy Horse's camp.

Just before Spotted Tail arrived, Crazy Horse told his father that he was going away. He asked his father to shake hands with Spotted Tail and tell him the Oglalas would come in as soon as the weather made it possible for women and children to travel. Then he went off to the Bighorns alone. Crazy Horse had not made up his mind yet whether he would surrender; perhaps he would let his people go while he stayed in the Powder River country alone—like an old buffalo bull cast out of the herd.

When Spotted Tail arrived, he guessed that Crazy Horse was avoiding him. He sent messengers out to find the Oglala leader, but Crazy Horse had vanished in the deep snows. Before Spotted Tail returned to Nebraska, however, he convinced Big Foot that he should surrender his Minneconjous, and he received promises from

Touch-the-Clouds and three other chiefs that they would bring their people to the agency early in the spring.

On April 14 Touch-the-Clouds, with a large number of Minneconjous and Sans Arcs from Crazy Horse's village, arrived at the Spotted Tail agency and surrendered. A few days before this happened, Three Stars Crook had sent Red Cloud out to find Crazy Horse and promise him that if he surrendered he could have a reservation in the Powder River country. On April 27 Red Cloud met Crazy Horse and told him of Three Stars's promise. Crazy Horse's nine hundred Oglalas were starving, the warriors had no ammunition, and their horses were thin and bony. The promise of a reservation in the Powder River country was all that Crazy Horse needed to bring him in to Fort Robinson to surrender.

The last of the Sioux war chiefs now became a reservation Indian, disarmed, dismounted, with no authority over his people, a prisoner of the Army, which had never defeated him in battle. Yet he was still a hero to the young men, and their adulation caused jealousies to arise among the older agency chiefs. Crazy Horse remained aloof, he and his followers living only for the day when Three Stars would make good his promise of a reservation for them in the Powder River country.

Late in the summer, Crazy Horse heard that Three Stars wanted him to go to Washington for a council with the Great Father. Crazy Horse refused to go. He could see no point in talking about the promised reservation. He had seen what happened to chiefs who went to the Great Father's house in Washington; they came back fat from the white man's way of living and with all the hardness gone out of them. He could see the changes in Red Cloud and Spotted Tail, and they knew he saw and they did not like him for it.

In August news came that the Nez Percés, who lived beyond the Shining Mountains, were at war with the Bluecoats. At the agencies, soldier chiefs began enlisting warriors to do their scouting for them against the Nez Percés. Crazy Horse told the young men not to go against those other Indians far away, but some would not listen, and allowed themselves to be bought by the soldiers. On August 31, the day these former Sioux warriors put on their Bluecoat uniforms to march away, Crazy Horse was so sick with disgust that he said he was going to take his people and go back north to the Powder River country.

When Three Stars heard of this from his spies, he ordered eight companies of pony soldiers to march to Crazy Horse's camp outside Fort Robinson and arrest him. Before the soldiers arrived, however, Crazy Horse's friends warned him they were coming. Not knowing what the soldiers' purpose was, Crazy Horse told his people to scatter, and then he set out alone to Spotted Tail agency to seek refuge with his old friend Touch-the-Clouds.

The soldiers found him there, placed him under arrest, and informed him they were taking him back to Fort Robinson to see Three Stars. Upon arrival at the fort, Crazy Horse was told that it was too late to talk with Three Stars that day. He was turned over to Captain James Kennington and one of the agency policemen. Crazy Horse stared hard at the agency policeman. He was Little Big Man, who not so long ago had defied the commissioners who came to steal *Paha Sapa*, the same Little Big Man who had threatened to kill the first chief who spoke for selling the Black Hills, the brave Little Big Man who had last fought beside Crazy Horse on the icy slopes of the Wolf Mountains against Bear Coat Miles. Now the white men had bought Little Big Man and made him into an agency policeman.

As Crazy Horse walked between them, letting the soldier chief and Little Big Man lead him to wherever they were taking him, he must have tried to dream himself into the real world, to escape the darkness of the shadow world in which all was madness. They walked past a soldier with a bayoneted rifle on his shoulder, and then they were standing in the doorway of a building. The windows were barred with iron, and he could see men behind the bars with chains on their legs. It was a trap for an animal, and Crazy Horse lunged away like a trapped animal, with Little Big Man holding on to his arm. The scuffling went on for only a few seconds. Someone shouted a command, and then the soldier guard, Private William Gentles, thrust his bayonet deep into Crazy Horse's abdomen.

Crazy Horse died that night, September 5, 1877, at the age of thirty-five. At dawn the next day the soldiers presented the dead chief to his father and mother. They put the body of Crazy Horse into a wooden box, fastened it to a pony-drawn travios, and carried it to Spotted Tail agency, where they mounted it on a scaffold. All through the Drying Grass Moon, mourners watched beside the burial place. And then in the Moon of Falling Leaves came the heartbreaking news: the reservation Sioux must leave Nebraska and go to a new reservation on the Missouri River.

Through the crisp dry autumn of 1877, long lines of exiled Indians driven by soldiers marched northeastward toward the barren land. Along the way, several bands slipped away from the column and turned northwestward, determined to escape to Canada and join Sitting Bull. With them went the father and mother of Crazy Horse, carrying the heart and bones of their son. At a place known only to them they buried Crazy Horse somewhere near Chankpe Opi Wakpala, the creek called Wounded Knee.

Song of Sitting Bull

A warrior
I have been
Now
it is all over.
A hard time
I have.

QUESTIONS

1. Explain why Brown uses the Indian names for the months, for Custer, etc.
2. Compare one of the Indians' speeches (e.g., Gall's, pp. 840–841) with one of the white men's speeches (e.g., Bishop Whipple's, p. 844). If the way a person uses language can be taken as an index to his character, what can you deduce about the character of each man?
3. Judging from "Politics and the English Language" (pp. 168–180), what do you think George Orwell's comment on Bishop Whipple's speech (p. 844) might be?
4. Look closely at Brown's descriptions of the commission (p. 844) and of the reaction to Long Hair's defeat. Can you sense Brown's attitude in each case? How is that attitude conveyed?
5. In describing the events which led up to the climactic battle, Brown says that once the "machinery" of the white man's government began moving, "it became an inexorable force, mindless and uncontrollable" (p. 834). Discuss the definition of government implied by this description. Was any analogous development taking place among the Indians?
6. Look at Macaulay's discussion of history and the ideal historian (pp. 912–913). Then test Brown's account against Macaulay's standards. Does it contain a satisfactory blend of "Reason" and "Imagination"?
7. Evaluate Brown's choice of sources. Do the sources seem reliable? Well balanced? Why haven't more sources with the white man's point of view been included?
8. On pp. 840–841 Gall gives a defense of the life style of the Indians when they are asked by the commissioners to change their ways and take up farming. Is this a good argument to defend a life style against those who wish to change it?

CHIEF SEATTLE
Address[1]

The Governor made a fine speech, but he was outranged and out-classed that day. Chief Seattle, who answered on behalf of the Indians, towered a foot above the Governor. He wore his blanket like the toga of a Roman senator, and he did not have to strain his famous voice, which everyone agreed was audible and distinct at a distance of half a mile.

Seattle's oration was in Duwamish. Doctor Smith, who had learned the language, wrote it down; under the flowery garlands of his translation the speech rolls like an articulate iron engine, grim with meanings that outlasted his generation and may outlast all the generations of men. As the amiable follies of the white race become less amiable, the iron rumble of old Seattle's speech sounds louder and more ominous.

Standing in front of Doctor Maynard's office in the stumpy clearing, with his hand on the little Governor's head, the white invaders about him and his people before him, Chief Seattle said:

"Yonder sky that has wept tears of compassion upon my people for centuries untold, and which to us appears changeless and eternal, may change. Today is fair. Tomorrow may be overcast with clouds. My words are like the stars that never change. Whatever Seattle says the great chief at Washington can rely upon with as much certainty as he can upon the return of the sun or the seasons. The White Chief says that Big Chief at Washington sends us greetings of friendship and goodwill. That is kind of him for we know he has little need of our friendship in return. His people are many. They are like the grass that covers vast prairies. My people are few. They resemble the scattering trees of a storm-swept plain. The great, and—I presume—good, White Chief sends us word that he wishes to buy our lands but is willing to allow us enough to live comfortably. This indeed appears just, even generous, for the Red Man no longer has rights that he need respect, and the offer may be wise also, as we are no longer in need of an extensive country. . . . I will not dwell on, nor mourn over, our untimely decay, nor reproach our paleface brothers with hastening it, as we too may have been somewhat to blame.

"Youth is impulsive. When our young men grow angry at some real or imaginary wrong, and disfigure their faces with black paint,

1. In 1854, Governor Isaac Stevens, Commissioner of Indian Affairs for the Washington Territory, proffered a treaty to the Indians providing for the sale of two million acres of their land to the federal government. This address is the reply of Chief Seattle of the Duwampo tribe. The translator was Henry A. Smith.

it denotes that their hearts are black, and then they are often cruel and relentless, and our old men and old women are unable to restrain them. Thus it has ever been. Thus it was when the white men first began to push our forefathers further westward. But let us hope that the hostilities between us may never return. We would have everything to lose and nothing to gain. Revenge by young men is considered gain, even at the cost of their own lives, but old men who stay at home in times of war, and mothers who have sons to lose, know better.

"Our good father at Washington—for I presume he is now our father as well as yours, since King George has moved his boundaries further north—our great good father, I say, sends us word that if we do as he desires he will protect us. His brave warriors will be to us a bristling wall of strength, and his wonderful ships of war will fill our harbors so that our ancient enemies far to the northward—the Hydas and Tsimpsians—will cease to frighten our women, children, and old men. Then in reality will he be our father and we his children. But can that ever be? Your God is not our God! Your God loves your people and hates mine. He folds his strong and protecting arms lovingly about the paleface and leads him by the hand as a father leads his infant son—but He has forsaken His red children —if they really are his. Our God, the Great Spirit, seems also to have forsaken us. Your God makes your people wax strong every day. Soon they will fill the land. Our people are ebbing away like a rapidly receding tide that will never return. The white man's God cannot love our people or He would protect them. They seem to be orphans who can look nowhere for help. How then can we be brothers? How can your God become our God and renew our prosperity and awaken in us dreams of returning greatness? If we have a common heavenly father He must be partial—for He came to his paleface children. We never saw Him. He gave you laws but He had no word for His red children whose teeming multitudes once filled this vast continent as stars fill the firmament. No; we are two distinct races with separate origins and separate destinies. There is little in common between us.

"To us the ashes of our ancestors are sacred and their resting place is hallowed ground. You wander far from the graves of your ancestors and seemingly without regret. Your religion was written upon tables of stone by the iron finger of your God so that you could not forget. The Red Man could never comprehend nor remember it. Our religion is the traditions of our ancestors—the dreams of our old men, given them in solemn hours of night by the Great Spirit; and the visions of our sachems; and it is written in the hearts of our people.

"Your dead cease to love you and the land of their nativity as soon as they pass the portals of the tomb and wander way beyond the stars. They are soon forgotten and never return. Our dead never forget the beautiful world that gave them being.

"Day and night cannot dwell together. The Red Man has ever fled the approach of the White Man, as the morning mist flees before the morning sun. However, your proposition seems fair and I think that my people will accept it and will retire to the reservation you offer them. Then we will dwell apart in peace, for the words of the Great White Chief seem to be the words of nature speaking to my people out of dense darkness.

"It matters little where we pass the remnant of our days. They will not be many. A few more moons; a few more winters—and not one of the descendants of the mighty hosts that once moved over this broad land or lived in happy homes, protected by the Great Spirit, will remain to mourn over the graves of a people once more powerful and hopeful than yours. But why should I mourn at the untimely fate of my people? Tribe follows tribe, and nation follows nation, like the waves of the sea. It is the order of nature, and regret is useless. Your time of decay may be distant, but it will surely come, for even the White Man whose God walked and talked with him as friend with friend, cannot be exempt from the common destiny. We may be brothers after all. We will see.

"We will ponder your proposition, and when we decide we will let you know. But should we accept it, I here and now make this condition that we will not be denied the privilege without molestation of visiting at any time the tombs of our ancestors, friends and children. Every part of this soil is sacred in the estimation of my people. Every hillside, every valley, every plain and grove, has been hallowed by some sad or happy event in days long vanished. . . . The very dust upon which you now stand responds more lovingly to their footsteps than to yours, because it is rich with the blood of our ancestors and our bare feet are conscious of the sympathetic touch. . . . Even the little children who lived here and rejoiced here for a brief season will love these somber solitudes and at eventide they greet shadowy returning spirits. And when the last Red Man shall have perished, and the memory of my tribe shall have become a myth among the White Men, these shores will swarm with the invisible dead of my tribe, and when your children's children think themselves alone in the field, the store, the shop, upon the highway, or in the silence of the pathless woods, they will not be alone. . . . At night when the streets of your cities and villages are silent and you think them deserted, they will throng with the returning hosts that once filled and still love this beautiful land. The White Man will never be alone.

"Let him be just and deal kindly with my people, for the dead are not powerless. Dead, did I say? There is no death, only a change of worlds."

THEODORA KROEBER

Ishi[1]

The story of Ishi begins for us early in the morning of the twenty-ninth day of August in the year 1911 and in the corral of a slaughter house. It begins with the sharp barking of dogs which roused the sleeping butchers. In the dawn light they saw a man at bay, crouching against the corral fence—Ishi.

They called off the dogs. Then, in some considerable excitement, they telephoned the sheriff in Oroville two or three miles away to say that they were holding a wild man and would he please come and take him off their hands. Sheriff and deputies arrived shortly, approaching the corral with guns at the ready. The wild man made no move to resist capture, quietly allowing himself to be handcuffed.

The sheriff, J. B. Webber, saw that the man was an Indian, and that he was at the limit of exhaustion and fear. He could learn nothing further, since his prisoner understood no English. Not knowing what to do with him, he motioned the Indian into the wagon with himself and his deputies, drove him to the county jail in Oroville, and locked him up in the cell for the insane. There, sheriff Webber reasoned, while he tried to discover something more about his captive he could at least protect him from the excited curiosity of the townspeople and the outsiders who were already pouring in from miles around to see the wild man.

The wild man was emaciated to starvation, his hair was burned off close to his head, he was naked except for a ragged scrap of ancient covered-wagon canvas which he wore around his shoulders like a poncho. He was a man of middle height, the long bones, painfully apparent, were straight, strong, and not heavy, the skin color somewhat paler in tone than the full copper characteristic of most Indians. The black eyes were wary and guarded now, but were set wide in a broad face, the mouth was generous and agreeably molded. For the rest, the Indian's extreme fatigue and fright heightened a sensitiveness which was always there, while it masked the usual mobility and expressiveness of the features.

It should be said that the sheriff's action in locking Ishi up was neither stupid nor brutal given the circumstances. Until Sheriff Webber took the unwonted measure of keeping them out by force people filled the jail to gaze through the bars of his cell at the captive. Later, Ishi spoke with some diffidence of this, his first contact with white men. He said that he was put up in a fine house where

1. Prologue and Chapter I of *Ishi in Two Worlds*, 1961.

he was kindly treated and well fed by a big chief. That he would eat nothing and drink nothing during his first days of captivity Ishi did not say. Such was the case; nor did he allow himself to sleep at first. Quite possibly it was a time of such strain and terror that he suppressed all memory of it. Or he may have felt that it was unkind to recall his suspicions which proved in the event groundless, for Ishi expected in those first days to be put to death. He knew of white men only that they were the murderers of his own people. It was natural that he should expect, once in their power, to be shot or hanged or killed by poisoning.

Meanwhile, local Indians and half-breeds as well as Mexicans and Spaniards tried to talk to the prisoner in Maidu, Wintu, and Spanish. Ishi listened patiently but uncomprehendingly, and when he spoke it was in a tongue which meant no more to the Indians there than to the whites.

The story of the capture of a wild Indian became headline news in the local valley papers, and reached the San Francisco dailies in forms more or less lurid and elaborated. The story in the *San Francisco Call* was accompanied by a picture, the first of many to come later. In another newspaper story, a Maidu Indian, Conway by name, "issued a statement" that he had conversed with the wild man. Conway's moment of publicity was brief since the wild man understood nothing of what he said.

These accounts were read by Professors Kroeber and Waterman, anthropologists at the University of California, who were at once alerted to the human drama behind the event and to its possible importance, the more particularly because it recalled to them an earlier episide on San Nicolas Island, one of the Channel Islands of the Pacific Ocean some seventy miles offshore from Santa Barbara.

In 1835, the padres of Mission Santa Barbara transferred the San Nicolas Indians to the mainland. A few minutes after the boat, which was carrying the Indians, had put off from the island, it was found that one baby had been left behind. It is not easy to land a boat on San Nicolas; the captain decided against returning for the baby; the baby's mother jumped overboard, and was last seen swimming toward the island. Half-hearted efforts made to find her in subsequent weeks were unsuccessful: it was believed that she had drowned in the rough surf. In 1853, eighteen years later, seal hunters in the Channel waters reported seeing a woman on San Nicolas, and a boatload of men from Santa Barbara went in search of her. They found her, a last survivor of her tribe. Her baby, as well as all her people who had been removed to the Mission, had died. She lived only a few months after her "rescue" and died without anyone having been able to communicate with her, leaving to posterity this skeletal outline of her grim story, and four words which

someone remembered from her lost language and recorded as she
said them. It so happens that these four words identify her language as having been Shoshonean, related to Indian languages of
the Los Angeles area, not to those of Santa Barbara.

Another reason for the anthropologists' particular interest in the
wild man was that three years earlier, in 1908, some surveyors working a few miles north of Oroville had surprised and routed a little
band of Indians. After hearing of this incident, Waterman with
two guides had spent several weeks in an unsuccessful search for
the Indians: the wild man of Oroville might well be one of them.

On August 31, 1911, Kroeber sent the following telegram:
"Sheriff Butte County. Newspapers report capture wild Indian
speaking language other tribes totally unable understand. Please
confirm or deny by collect telegram and if story correct hold Indian
till arrival Professor State University who will take charge and be
responsible for him. Matter important account aboriginal history."

The sheriff's office must have confirmed the report promptly:
Waterman took the train to Oroville the same day. That he and
Kroeber correctly "guessed" Ishi's tribe and language was no *tour
de force* of intuition. The guess was based on field work with
Indians all up and down California; they knew that Oroville was
adjacent to country which formerly belonged to the Yana Indians;
presumably the strange Indian would be a Yana. He might even be
from the southernmost tribe of Yana, believed to be extinct. If this
were true, neither they nor anyone so far as they knew could speak
his language. But if he were a Northern or Central Yana, there
were files of expertly recorded vocabularies for those dialects from
two old Yanas, Batwi, called Sam, and Chidaimiya, called Betty
Brown.

With a copy of Batwi's and Chidaimiya's vocabularies in his
pocket, Waterman arrived in Oroville where he identified himself
to Sheriff Webber and was taken to visit the wild man. Waterman
found a weary, badgered Indian sitting in his cell, wearing the
butcher's apron he had been given at the slaughter house, courteously making what answer he could in his own language to a barrage of questions thrown at him in English, Spanish, and assorted
Indian from a miscellaneous set of visitors.

Waterman sat down beside Ishi, and with his phonetically transcribed list of Northern and Central Yana words before him, began
to read from it, repeating each word, pronouncing it as well as he
knew how. Ishi was attentive but unresponding until, discourag-
ingly far down the list, Waterman said *siwini* which means yellow
pine, at the same time tapping the pine framework of the cot on
which they sat. Recognition lighted up the Indian's face. Waterman said the magic word again; Ishi repeated it after him, correct-

ing his pronounciation, and for the next moments the two of them
banged at the wood of the cot, telling each other over and over,
siwini, siwini!

With the difficult first sound recognition achieved, others followed. Ishi was indeed one of the lost tribe, a Yahi; in other words,
he was from the southernmost Yana. Waterman was learning that
the unknown Yahi dialect differed considerably but not to the
point of unintelligibility from the two northern ones of his list.
Together he and Ishi tried out more and more words and phrases:
they were beginning to communicate. After a while Ishi ventured
to ask Waterman, *I ne ma Yahi?* "Are you an Indian?" Waterman
answered that he was. The hunted look left Ishi's eyes—here was a
friend. He knew as well as did his friend that Waterman was not
an Indian. The question was a tentative and subtle way of reassuring and being reassured, not an easy thing to do when the meaningful shared sounds are few. Between meetings with Ishi, Waterman wrote to Kroeber from Oroville:

> This man [Ishi] is undoubtedly wild. He has pieces of deer thong in
> place of ornaments in the lobes of his ears and a wooden plug in the
> septum of his nose. He recognizes most of my Yana words and a fair
> proportion of his own seem to be identical [with mine]. Some of his,
> however, are either quite different or else my pronunciation of them is
> very bad, because he doesn't respond to them except by pointing to his
> ears and asking to have them repeated. "No!" *k'u'i*—it is not—is one.
> "Yes!" *ähä*, pleases him immensely. I think I get a few endings that don't
> occur in Northern Yana on nouns, for example. Phonetically, he has
> some of the prettiest cracked consonants I ever heard in my life. He will
> be a splendid informant, especially for phonetics, for he speaks very
> clearly. I have not communicated with him successfully enough to get
> his story, but what can I expect? He has a yarn to tell about his woman,
> who had a baby on her back and seems to have been drowned, except
> that he is so *cheerful* about it.

Waterman misunderstood. In the excitement and relief of
having someone to talk to, Ishi poured out confidences and recol-
lections which Waterman could by no means comprehend even
with the aid of an elaborate pantomime. Ishi's seeming pleasure
was not in the recollected event, but was rather a near hysteria
induced by human interchange of speech and feelings too long
denied.

Waterman's letters continue:

> We had a lot of conversation this morning about deer hunting and
> making acorn soup, but I got as far as my list of words would take me.
> If I am not mistaken, he's full of religion—bathing at sunrise, putting out
> pinches of tobacco where the lightning strikes, etc. I'll try rattlesnake on
> him when I got back after lunch. It was a picnic to see him open his
> eyes when he heard Yana from me. And he looked over my shoulder at
> the paper in a most mystified way. He knew at once where I got my

inspiration....We showed him some arrows last night, and we could hardly get them away from him. He showed us how he flaked the points, singed the edges of the feathering, and put on the sinew wrappings.

Even before Waterman had established a thin line of communication with Ishi, the sheriff had become convinced that his prisoner was neither insane nor dangerous. There were no charges against him; he did not properly belong in jail. The question was, what in place of the shelter of the jail was there for him? Waterman offered to take him to San Francisco. Phones and telegraph wires were kept busy for the next forty-eight hours between Oroville and San Francisco, where the University's Museum of Anthropology then was, and between the museum and Washington, D.C.

While these negotiations were going forward, the sheriff, at Waterman's suggestion, sent a deputy to Redding to find and bring back with him the old man, Batwi, to act as interpreter-companion to Ishi. Batwi came, and although he patronized Ishi outrageously, he was for the present a help. He and Ishi could communicate in Yana, not without some difficulty, but quite fully. Meanwhile, the Indian Bureau in Washington telegraphed permission for Ishi to go to the University's museum whose staff was to be responsible for him at least until there was opportunity for fuller investigation. The sheriff of Butte County was greatly relieved; he at once made out a receipt of release from the jail to the University. This remarkable document seems not to have survived the years of moving and storing in odd corners which has been the fate of the museum files and specimens.

In any case, Waterman, Batwi, and Ishi, with the release and government permission, left Oroville on Labor Day, September 4, arriving in San Francisco somewhat before midnight. There remained to Ishi four years and seven months of life, years which were to pass within the shelter of the museum walls at the Affiliated Colleges, or in the hospital next door when he was sick.

Ishi was the last wild Indian in North America, a man of Stone Age culture subjected for the first time when he was past middle age to twentieth-century culture. He was content that it should be so, participating as fully as he could in the new life. Before examining more closely those astounding few years and what one Stone Age man contributed in so short a time to our understanding of man as such, let us go back to the years of childhood, young manhood, and middle age—almost a whole lifetime. These were years spent by him without experience or understanding of a way of life other than that of a tiny fugitive band of fewer than a dozen souls at most, opposing their ancient Yahi skills and beliefs to an unknown but hostile outside world.

There came the time—months, perhaps two or three years before August, 1911—when Ishi was the only one remaining of the little band, violence from without, old age and illness from within, having brought death to the others.

Ishi's arrival at the slaughter house was the culmination of unprecedented behavior on his part. A few days earlier, without hope, indifferent whether he lived or died, he had started on an aimless trek in a more or less southerly direction which took him into country he did not know. Exhaustion was added to grief and loneliness. He lay down in the corral because he could go no farther. He was then about forty miles from home, a man without living kin or friends, a man who had probably never been beyond the borders of his own tribal territory.

Our task is to piece together all that is known of Ishi's life before that day: from his own account of it; from what was learned of it on a camping trip with him in his own home country; and from the miscellany of rumor and fact and speculation as reported by surveyors, ranchers, rangers, and other white residents of Butte and Tehama counties. It is an episodic story, incomplete, and loosely strung across lacunae of time, ignorance, and events too painful for Ishi to relive in memory.

That Ishi should have crossed the boundaries of his homeland, and continued on into the unknown, means to be sure that he had also reached and crossed certain physical and psychic limits. But to begin to understand how profoundly disturbed he must have been, we must know how aberrant such behavior was, not for Ishi the man merely, but for Ishi the Yahi. His life becomes more of a piece if we step back from it, as from the detail of a face or feature in a painting, to focus briefly on the whole of the canvas, bringing its background and pattern into perspective. To understand Ishi's values and behavior and belief, and his way of life, we must know in a broad and general way something of his heritage: the land and people of Indian California.

The stubborn and enduring land of California has changed less than its people. From an airplane the "colored counties" are seen spread out like a giant relief map. Mount Shasta looms to the north, Mount Whitney to the south; the Sierra Nevada forms a wall to the east; and beyond Whitney, where the Sierra appears to go underground, the desert takes over. There are the long interior valleys; and there are the tumbled, rough, and wooded Coast Ranges through which rivers and creeks break to the sea. Below, incredible, lies the vast and varied land, its mountains and deserts empty and mute today, while over the accessible valleys and coastal plains a congested and diverse population clusters close to a few centers like wasps around heavy-hanging nests. A constant stream of automobiles, looking from the air like lines of black ants on the march, fills the passes over the Sierra barrier, moving westward to the favored spots. The hills are empty except for lumbering operations wherever there is a good stand of trees; the mining towns of the Mother Lode and the old rancherias are shabby and deserted, or have been taken over by "summer people." The banks of rivers and creeks are empty save for sporadic invasions of fishermen; and the desert is without human occupants except for a citified overflow which follows in the wake of air-cooling installations, swimming pools, and motels.

What would an air view have revealed in the days of the gold rush? The same lines of black ants moving in the same westerly direction over the same passes, on horseback, and in covered wagons drawn by oxen, traveling more slowly than today's immigrants but with the same doggedness as these later ones, heading in part for the same centers, in part stopping in the hill country where ranches, mining camps, and saw and grist mills were scattered along streams and in the forests.

Hovering over the same land, but continuing our flight back in time, we view another trek, this one on foot or on mule and horseback, coming up from the south, northward along the rim of the sea. The time is the 'seventies of the eighteenth century, and the travelers, Spaniards pushing out of Mexico, keeping a sharp eye for a sheltered and sunny and likely spot for mission, rancheria, or presidio as they move slowly on.

If we take a last backward flight in time, the Spaniard is no longer seen. This is the time before his coming; the golden land belongs wholly and undisputedly to its native sons and daughters. No lines of black ants move over the high passes or come up from the south in this view. Indeed, we must fly low to see the narrow trails meandering beside a stream, or across country to an oak flat, or up into the hills. At first there seem to be neither houses nor people, but presently a frame with surf fish strung on it to dry on a sunny beach, a clearing in the trees, a thin blue wisp of smoke from a wood fire, serve to guide the eyes to the weathered roof of a low redwood house, to an earth-covered circular house, to a thatched house, to a brush shelter. We see an old woman tending the fire outside a house, a man spearing fish beside a stream, a half-grown boy paddling downstream in a dugout canoe. A young woman, her baby in a basket carrier on her back, gathers wild iris on a hillside; a hunter brings down a deer with bow and arrow. These people step noiselessly over the ground barefoot or in soft deerskin moccasins, and their naked or near-naked copper-colored bodies blend in semicamouflage against the colors of the earth. Such clothes as they wear, a skirt of shredded bark, a buckskin breechclout, an occasional fur or feather cape, also blend into the natural background. Their voices, whether in ordinary conversation, or in song or prayer or mourning cry, are light-toned, neither harsh nor loud.

The high mountains are empty. But people are living in the hills as far up as oak trees grow and wherever manzanita and other berries are abundant, and wherever there are deer; along fish-filled streams; and where a river flows into the sea; and on the desert Even so unlikely a place as Death Valley has men who call it home.

Back on the ground and again in the twentieth century, we turn to maps and estimates and reports to learn something more of these ancestral peoples whom we have glimpsed distantly through time.

We have seen that they lived on parts of the land which modern men do not find habitable or attractive, although at no place were their numbers large. The population of Indian California was small: over the whole of the state there were probably no more than a hundred and fifty thousand people, perhaps as many as two hundred and fifty thousand. (In 1860, ten years after the beginning of the gold rush, the white population of the state was already three hundred and ninety thousand.) There are, to be sure, estimates of the pre-conquest population of California which run higher, but the archaeological remains from village and burial sites point to numbers close to those given here. There is no evidence, as there is in the Southwest, in Mexico, in Yucatan of the Mayas, that a once much more numerous people suffered disaster and decimation. Nor do the histories, legends, myths, or stories of any California Indians speak of ancient wholesale famine as do the old as well as the modern chronicles of China and India.

These one or two hundred and fifty thousand native people constituted twenty-one known nationalities, or small nations, which were in turn further separated into subnationalities, and these again into tribes or tribelets to a total number of more than two hundred and fifty—exactly how many more can never be known because of the obliteration in modern times of whole peoples and cultures by Spaniard and Anglo-Saxon alike without record of tribal name or affiliation. Many of these subgroups were of course few in number and inhabited only a small area. Their numbers were almost unbelievably small beside the territorial and population figures for modern nations, but they were nonetheless true nations in their stubbornly individual and boundaried separateness and distinctiveness one from another.

One of these nationalities was the Yana. There were probably no more than three thousand of Ishi's people, perhaps only two thousand—not many to constitute a nation to be sure, but more people than live today along the favorite streams and on the village sites of the ancient Yana. And few in number as they were, even by California standards, the Yana followed the current pattern of culture fragmentation in being further sub-subdivided into four groups: Northern, Central, Southern, and Yahi (Ishi's group), each with its own geographic boundaries, its own dialect, and its own set of specializations and peculiarities of custom.

There were and are, for the whole of Indian North America, six great linguistic superfamilies, each made up of numbers of separate stocks or families of speech. Each family usually consists of several languages which differ so much one from another that their common origin can be determined only by comparative linguistics study; the superfamilies are even more varied than the large Indo-European stock or family with its Romance and Germanic and Slavic and Hindi divisions. Of the six superfamilies, five were represented in California, and contained among them twenty-one basic languages which were, for the most part, as mutually unintelligible as are German and French; and many of them were even more unlike than these two. But this is not yet the whole of the story, since the twenty-one languages further separated and elaborated themselves into a hundred and thirteen known dialects. These dialects varied, some of them, only so much as New Orleans English from the English of Boston; others so greatly that to know one would not make the other accessible, as with Swedish and German. Only parts of the Sudan and the island of New Guinea offer so much language variety within comparable areas. Or, to demonstrate the congestion of tongues another way, there are twice as many Indian languages on record as there are counties in California today.

We know that such extreme linguistic differentiation takes time. Spoken language is in a sense always changing, since each speaker of his tongue imprints on it his imperceptibly individual voice and accent and choice or rejection of particular words and usages, but the changing is as drops of water on the stone of fixed grammatical form. Ishi's California must indeed have been an old and long-settled land.

Remains of Dawn Man or of some Dawn-like man, his bones or his stones, are proclaimed from time to time as having been found on the Pacific slope, but if Dawn Man or any of his near relations once lived in California, they have yet to be rediscovered. California's first people so far as is presently known were American Indians, ancestors of today's Indians and in no significant way different from them. And they have been in California a long time; by our standards of mobility and compared with our brief history, immemorially long.

The Yana have probably been in northern California for three or four thousand years. There are those who would double this figure, but in the present state of knowledge three thousand years as a minimum is a tentative, conservative figure arrived at, surprisingly, by way of a recently accepted branch of language study known as glottochronology. Put simply, glottochronology is a study of the rate at which the meaning of words changes, and the inferences to be drawn from such changes. It began with analyses of old and documented languages such as Sanskrit, Anglo-Saxon, or Chinese, comparing the old language in each case with its living descendants, to find the rate of change from cognate to new terms of the same basic meaning. Rates of change studied thus far vary little one from another, and their average, used as the norm of change, is applied to comparisons of pairs of other related languages to find the time which has elapsed since their separation or first differentiation. A technique for learning the history of a language thus becomes a technique also for learning something of a people's political or culture history.

Yana belongs to the Hokan superfamily, one of the six superfamilies of North America. The glottochronology of Hokan confirms and sharpens other evidence that Hokan-speaking people were old in California. Apparently Ishi's ancestors were occupying wide stretches of the upper Sacramento Valley and its tributaries at a time when there was a single Hokan language. At some time, three or four thousand years ago, this single language fragmented into ten or a dozen separate languages within the same geographical territory and amongst the original speakers of Hokan.

There is no evidence of other people having disputed the territory and its occupation with the ancestral Hokans; it is to be presumed that they lived freely in the open valley, going up into the hills, which to Ishi were a year-round home, only seasonally in the course of following the deer from valley to hills to mountains. There must have been a wide dispersal of Hokan-speakers as part of the drama of change which resulted in the appearance of many new languages within the old Hokan mold. This may well have been the time of the greatest creative florescence of the Yana and other Hokan peoples.

After two or three thousand years, "barbarians" from outside, Wintun or others, who were by then stronger and more numerous then the older population, engaged in one of their own thrusts of history making, invaded Yana country, occupied the richer parts of it, and pushed the smaller, older population back into the hills.

We turn now to archaeology to decipher a curiously half-lit corroboration of this early Yana history. Paynes Cave on Antelope Creek and Kingsley Cave on Mill Creek, both in Ishi's own country, and some smaller village and cemetery sites closeby have been excavated and their bones and tools studied. Charred wood, bone, and other substances from these presumably old and undisturbed sites have been tested and assigned absolute as well as relative dates, within one or two hundred years of exactness, by measuring their carbon fourteen content against that of recent, similar material. This is a satisfactory dating technique, over long periods, because carbon fourteen is an unstable compound which decomposes at the rate of 50 per cent in fifty-five hundred years. This dating is supplemented by a comparison of styles and any changes in styles over time. Together, the two lines of evidence, which in this case converge reasonably, suggest that the Yana territory of Ishi's lifetime and of the gold rush era had been occupied only occasionally a thousand years ago, but continuously since then. In other words, it would seem to have been not much more than a millenium ago that the Yana surrendered their valley holdings to become truly and wholly a hill people.

But we must leave scientific measurement and historical reconstruction to its specialists, and move on, closer to Ishi's time, realizing meanwhile that it is the scientist and the historian who remind us that the pace of the ancient world was no doubt pedestrian as compared with the modern world with its lightning changes, but that wherever there is life there is change. History was being made by Ishi's ancestors and their enemies as surely as it is today: languages came into being and spread and shrank and died; peoples migrated and made a way of life which was dominant and which then receded. The telescopic view into the old world cannot be made sharp, except perhaps when we hear a momentary echo of old Hokan in Ishi's recorded voice and Yahi speech, or when we hold in our hands an "old-fashioned" stone knife whose style was abandoned for something "new" a thousand years ago. The focus may be fuzzy; it is at least a look at a world in flux and motion, never wholly static; contoured and stereoscopic, never flat; even as our own moving, changing world.

What, then, of the Digger Indians who are supposed to have been the aborigines of California, to have spoken a guttural language, and to have managed barely to maintain a miserable existence by eating the roots which they dug from the unfriendly land with that most generic of tools, the wooden digging stick? Alas, the Diggers are a frontier legend, like the Siwash Indians of the Northwest, Siwash being a blanket term growing out of a mis-hearing of the word *sauvage*, the French trappers' designation for Indian. Nor was there a Digger language amongst all the babel of tongues.

There is another frontier legend which dies hard: that the hills and streams and valleys of California yielded a grudging and sorry living to their native sons and daughters. The Spaniards and Mexicans did not so misunderstand the golden land, in part because they were never wholly detached from the soil in thinking or occupation, and in part because California is not unlike much of Mexico and Spain. The Forty-niners, veteran contenders against mountains, high plains, and deserts, were without interest in the land as such, which appeared to them inhospitable, dry, barren. In the course of their continental trek, they had come to look upon food not as something to be grown or harvested, but as meat to be shot on the hoof, and as flour, sugar, coffee, and beans to be carried as part of one's pack and replaced in "Frisco" or Sacramento or at some other urban center.

The legend may have been prolonged in defiance of known fact through inertia, legends easily becoming habits which are hard to break, and through its usefulness in salving a not quite good conscience over the taking of land and lives. If the land was lean and the lives miserable then the wrong done was so much the less, or no wrong at all.

The term Digger continued to be used to refer to Indians other than those one knew. I have heard my grandmother, who came to Amador County to teach school in the early 1850's, and became a rancher's wife, speak affectionately and correctly of her Miwok Indian neighbors, and disapprovingly of the strange Digger Indians who from time to time used to wander in from a distance asking for work or perhaps only for food. Digger remains to this day a term of derogation, like "nigger."

Digger also defines, however crudely and inadequately, one occupation of California Indians which the Forty-niners must have seen over and over again. The Indians did no planting, being hunters, fishermen, gatherers and harvesters of grains and seeds and fruits and roots which grew wild in their natural habitat and uncultivated state—diggers if you will. The digging stick was used, customarily in the hands of women, who were forever going off into the hills or meadows for maidenhair and sword ferns, for squaw grass and pine root, for redbud and hazel, and for all the stems and plants and grasses which they wanted for making baskets. And the digging stick, as will be seen, helped them in season to get some of the fresh vegetables of which they were fond. Only the aberrant Mohaves and Yumas, who live on the Colorado River, have always been agriculturists of sorts. That is, they planted many of their food stuffs—not like the hard-working and true farmers of the Southwest: the Hopi, Zuni, and Rio Grande pueblo Indians—but like the people of ancient Egypt, by dropping the seeds of corn and beans and squash into the red ooze exposed by the seasonal flooding and retreat of the river, and allowing the crops to grow under the blazing sun with a minimum of attention from the planters. But the Colorado River Indians were different also—and fortunate—in having no Forty-niners.

We have seen that the varied land once supported separate little nations, rather like Greek city states at least in size, in enclaves of inland valley or rough hill-country or woods or desert or along streams or beside the sea. And we have seen that these village states set themselves off further one from another by a growth of language barrier. The peoples differed in physical type, some being broad and stocky with round faces, some slim and tall with high-bridged noses, but none resembled the Plains or woodland Indians. Some lived better than others, and with more leisure; some buried their dead while others practiced cremation. Customs and beliefs varied from tribelet to tribelet, but nonetheless underlying their differences was a certain characteristic "set," a profile of a life which, broadly speaking, fits all of them and fits no Indians east of the Sierra Nevada. It was anciently a different world, from the crest of the Sierra westward to the Pacific Ocean, as indeed it continues in oddly telling ways to be different today.

In some part, larger or smaller depending upon how one weighs it, the differences ancient and modern are born of the climate which is Mediterranean and subtropical. For the Indians this meant that during many months of each year outdoor living with only the lightest of shelters was comfortable, and that in most seasons they wore no clothes at all, a little front apron of bark and the ubiquitous brimless round basketry hat satisfying the requirements of modesty for a woman, while a man wore nothing at all except perhaps a deerskin breechclout. The buckskin shirt and leggings to be found to the east were not needed here and did not exist; an ample apron or skirt of buckskin for the women and grass or buckskin sandals with a wildcat or rabbit or feather cloak thrown over the shoulders when it was cold did very well for both men and women and completed their wardrobes except for beads and other ornaments, and ritual and dance regalia.

This was the area where, for whatever reason, basketry design was most elaborated, and the possibilities of baskets as utensils were most exploited to the almost total neglect of wood and pottery. Baskets were used for carrying and for storing all sorts of food and materials; they were the only cooking utensils; and they were the trays, plates, bowls, and mugs of dining. The creative impulse found expression most usually in basketry; also in the intricate fashioning of feather capes and headdresses; and in occasional beautifully wrought obsidian knives made from a single obsidian flake. These knives, two, three, or four feet long and correspondingly heavy, were held to be sacred and reserved for ceremonial use.

The great staple food of the California Indian was acorn flour made into mush or bread. The acorn, of which some half dozen or more edible varieties were recognized, meant to Indians what rice means to Cantonese Chinese, or maize to Mexicans. After acorns came salmon, fresh or dried and in large variety; and after salmon, deer meat, again fresh or dried. Other fish were of course eaten, and game larger and smaller than deer, and for the coastal people there was added all the rich variety of seafood. Ducks and geese were much liked. Pine nuts, hazel nuts, buckeye, manzanita berries, wild raspberry, huckleberry, plum, grape, elderberry, barberry, and thimbleberry were enjoyed in season, and some of them were dried and stored. There were sage and tarweed and clarkia seeds, and a host of other seeds small and large and, in season, the earth-oven roasted roots of the camas, annis, tiger lily, and brodiaea were a welcome addition. Certain grubs and worms were roasted as delicacies; also grasshoppers as in modern Mexico. Snakes were not eaten, nor, so far as is known, were frogs.

But far deeper than food preferences and response to climate is the psychological set of the California cultures. To judge by their descendants, the ancestral California Indians who made the Far West their permanent home had found their way in the first place, and stayed on, in order to realize an ideal of a separatist and static arrangement of life. The most conspicuous feature of this life, at least to our view, is the preference for a small world intimately and minutely known, whose utmost boundaries were within reach by boat or on foot, a few days journey at most. Outside worlds were known to exist, of course. A man knew certain of his neighbors, sometimes when the neighbor's tongue had dialectic relation to his own so close that communication came readily, or sometimes when two worlds shared adjoining stretches of the same river, for example, and were similar enough in their ways to feel some identification even though they spoke different languages, as with the Yurok and Karok Indians along the Klamath River. But anything, everything that belonged within a man's own world, including its corpus of legendary event going back to the most ancient times, was better known and was more important than any person, place, or happening across the border.

By and large, no one voluntarily left his own and familiar world for a strange one. It was terrifying and dangerous to enter a community as a stranger. You were properly suspect, the inference being that your own people had put pressure on you to leave because of some crime you were guilty of. At best you would be without family or friends or influence or status, and forced to learn to speak a foreign language, if you were allowed to remain at all. There was always the chance that you would be killed, or ordered to move on.

The California Indian was, in other words, a true provincial. He was also an introvert, reserved, contemplative, and philosophical. He lived at ease with the supernatural and the mystical which were pervasive in all aspects of life. He felt no need to differentiate mystical truth from directly evidential or "material" truth, or the supernatural from the natural: one was as manifest as the other within his system of values and perceptions and beliefs. The promoter, the boaster, the aggressor, the egoist, the innovator, would have been looked at askance. The ideal was the man of restraint, dignity, rectitude, he of the Middle Way. Life proceeded within the limits of known and proper pattern from birth through death and beyond. Its repetitive rhythm was punctuated with ritual, courtship, dance, song, and feast, each established according to custom going back to the beginning of the world, an event which, along with subsequent events having to do with setting the way of life, was well known and fully recounted in the peoples' oral but elaborate and specific histories.

It was not an easy life, but it was a good one. The hunting and fishing and gathering, the endless labor of preparation of foods and hides, the making of baskets, tools, and implements and the always vexing problem of storage, required the industry and skill of both sexes and of young and old; but there was some choice and there was seasonal and ritual variety. There were lean times, but the lean like the fat times were shared with family, friends, and tribe. Life was as it had always been.

ERIC HOFFER

The Role of the Undesirables

In the winter of 1934, I spent several weeks in a federal transient camp in California. These camps were originally established by Governor Rolph in the early days of the Depression to care for the single homeless unemployed of the state. In 1934 the federal government took charge of the camps for a time, and it was then that I first heard of them.

How I happened to get into one of the camps is soon told. Like thousands of migrant agricultural workers in California I then followed the crops from one part of the state to the other. Early in

1934 I arrived in the town of El Centro, in the Imperial Valley. I had been given a free ride on a truck from San Diego, and it was midnight when the truck driver dropped me on the outskirts of El Centro. I spread my bedroll by the side of the road and went to sleep. I had hardly dozed off when the rattle of a motorcycle drilled itself into my head and a policeman was bending over me saying, "Roll up, Mister." It looked as though I was in for something; it happened now and then that the police got overzealous and rounded up the freight trains. But this time the cop had no such thought. He said, "Better go over to the federal shelter and get yourself a bed and maybe some breakfast." He directed me to the place.

I found a large hall, obviously a former garage, dimly lit, and packed with cots. A concert of heavy breathing shook the thick air. In a small office near the door, I was registered by a middle-aged clerk. He informed me that this was the "receiving shelter" where I would get one night's lodging and breakfast. The meal was served in the camp nearby. Those who wished to stay on, he said, had to enroll in the camp. He then gave me three blankets and excused himself for not having a vacant cot. I spread the blankets on the cement floor and went to sleep.

I awoke with dawn amid a chorus of coughing, throat-clearing, the sound of running water, and the intermittent flushing of toilets in the back of the hall. There were about fifty of us, all colors and ages, all of us more or less ragged and soiled. The clerk handed out tickets for breakfast, and we filed out to the camp located several blocks away, near the railroad tracks.

From the outside the camp looked like a cross between a factory and a prison. A high fence of wire enclosed it, and inside were three large sheds and a huge boiler topped by a pillar of black smoke. Men in blue shirts and dungarees were strolling across the sandy yard. A ship's bell in front of one of the buildings announced breakfast. The regular camp members—there was a long line of them—ate first. Then we filed in through the gate, handing our tickets to the guard.

It was a good, plentiful meal. After breakfast our crowd dispersed. I heard some say that the camps in the northern part of the state were better, that they were going to catch a northbound freight. I decided to try this camp in El Centro.

My motives in enrolling were not crystal clear. I wanted to clean up. There were shower baths in the camp and wash tubs and plenty of soap. Of course I could have bathed and washed my clothes in one of the irrigation ditches, but here in the camp I had a chance to rest, get the wrinkles out of my belly, and clean up at leisure. In short, it was the easiest way out.

A brief interview at the camp office and a physical examination were all the formalities for enrollment.

There were some two hundred men in the camp. They were the kind I had worked and traveled with for years. I even saw familiar faces—men I had worked with in orchards and fields. Yet my predominant feeling was one of strangeness. It was my first experience of life in intimate contact with a crowd. For it is one thing to work and travel with a gang, and quite another thing to eat, sleep, and spend the greater part of the day cheek by jowl with two hundred men.

I found myself speculating on a variety of subjects: the reasons for their chronic bellyaching and beefing—it was more a ritual than the expression of a grievance; the amazing orderliness of the men; the comic seriousness with which they took their games of cards, checkers, and dominoes; the weird manner of reasoning one overheard now and then. Why, I kept wondering, were these men within the enclosure of a federal transient camp? Were they people temporarily hard up? Would jobs solve all their difficulties? Were we indeed like the people outside?

Up to then I was not aware of being one of a specific species of humanity. I had considered myself simply a human being—not particularly good or bad, and on the whole harmless. The people I worked and traveled with I knew as Americans and Mexicans, whites and Negroes, Northerners and Southerners, etc. It did not occur to me that we were a group possessed of peculiar traits, and that there was something—innate or acquired—in our makeup which made us adopt a particular mode of existence.

It was a slight thing that started me on a new track.

I got to talking to a mild-looking, elderly fellow. I liked his soft speech and pleasant manner. We swapped trivial experiences. Then he suggested a game of checkers. As we started to arrange the pieces on the board, I was startled by the sight of his crippled right hand. I had not noticed it before. Half of it was chopped off lengthwise, so that the horny stump with its three fingers looked like a hen's leg. I was mortified that I had not noticed the hand until he dangled it, so to speak, before my eyes. It was, perhaps, to bolster my shaken confidence in my powers of observation that I now began paying close attention to the hands of the people around me. The result was astounding. It seemed that every other man had had his hand mangled. There was a man with one arm. Some men limped. One young, good-looking fellow had a wooden leg. It was as though the majority of the men had escaped the snapping teeth of a machine and left part of themselves behind.

It was, I knew, an exaggerated impression. But I began counting the cripples as the men lined up in the yard at mealtime. I found thirty (out of two hundred) crippled either in arms or legs. I immediately sensed where the counting would land me. The simile preceded the statistical deduction: we in the camp were a human junk pile.

I began evaluating my fellow tramps as human material, and for the first time in my life I became face-conscious. There were some good faces, particularly among the young. Several of the middle-aged and the old looked healthy and well preserved. But the damaged and decayed faces were in the majority. I saw faces that were wrinkled, or bloated, or raw as the surface of a peeled plum. Some of the noses were purple and swollen, some broken, some pitted with enlarged pores. There were many toothless mouths (I counted seventy-eight). I noticed eyes that were blurred, faded, opaque, or bloodshot. I was struck by the fact that the old men, even the very old, showed their age mainly in the face. Their bodies were still slender and erect. One little man over sixty years of age looked a mere boy when seen from behind. The shriveled face joined to a boyish body made a startling sight.

My diffidence had now vanished. I was getting to know everybody in the camp. They were a friendly and talkative lot. Before many weeks I knew some essential fact about practically everyone.

And I was continually counting. Of the two hundred men in the camp there were approximately as follows:

Cripples	30
Confirmed drunkards	60
Old men (55 and over)	50
Youths under twenty	10
Men with chronic diseases, heart, asthma, TB	12
Mildly insane	4
Constitutionally lazy	6
Fugitives from justice	4
Apparently normal	70

(The numbers do not tally up to two hundred since some of the men were counted twice or even thrice—as cripples and old, or as old and confirmed drunks, etc.)

In other words: less than half the camp inmates (seventy normal, plus ten youths) were unemployed workers whose difficulties would be at an end once jobs were available. The rest (60 per cent) had handicaps in addition to unemployment.

I also counted fifty war veterans, and eighty skilled workers representing sixteen trades. All the men (including those with chronic diseases) were able to work. The one-armed man was a wizard with the shovel.

I did not attempt any definite measurement of character and intelligence. But it seemed to me that the intelligence of the men in the camp was certainly not below the average. And as to character, I found much forbearance and genuine good humor. I never came across one instance of real viciousness. Yet, on the whole, one would hardly say that these men were possessed of strong characters. Resistance, whether to one's appetites or to the ways of the world, is a chief factor in the shaping of character; and the average tramp is, more or less, a slave of his few appetites. He generally takes the easiest way out.

The connection between our makeup and our mode of existence as migrant workers presented itself now with some clarity.

The majority of us were incapable of holding onto a steady job. We lacked self-discipline and the ability to endure monotonous, leaden hours. We were probably misfits from the very beginning. Our contact with a steady job was not unlike a collision. Some of us were maimed, some got frightened and ran away, and some took to drink. We inevitably drifted in the direction of least resistance—the open road. The life of a migrant worker is varied and demands only a minimum of self-discipline. We were now in one of the drainage ditches of ordered society. We could not keep a footing in the ranks of respectability and were washed into the slough of our present existence.

Yet, I mused, there must be in this world a task with an appeal so strong that were we to have a taste of it we would hold on and be rid for good of our restlessness.

My stay in the camp lasted about four weeks. Then I found a haying job not far from town, and finally, in April, when the hot winds began blowing, I shouldered my bedroll and took the highway to San Bernardino.

It was the next morning, after I had got a lift to Indio by truck, that a new idea began to take hold of me. The highway out of Indio leads through waving date groves, fragrant grapefruit orchards, and lush alfalfa fields; then, abruptly, passes into a desert of white sand. The sharp line between garden and desert is very striking. The turning of white sand into garden seemed to me an act of magic. This, I thought, was a job one would jump at—even the men in the transient camps. They had the skill and ability of the average American. But their energies, I felt, could be quickened only by a task that was spectacular, that had in it something of the miraculous. The pioneer task of making the desert flower would certainly fill the bill.

Tramps as pioneers? It seemed absurd. Every man and child in California knows that the pioneers had been giants, men of boundless courage and indomitable spirit. However, as I strode on across the white sand, I kept mulling the idea over.

Who were the pioneers? Who were the men who left their homes and went into the wilderness? A man rarely leaves a soft spot and goes deliberately in search of hardship and privation. People become attached to the places they live in; they drive roots. A change of habitat is a painful act of uprooting. A man who has made good and has a standing in his community stays put. The successful businessmen, farmers, and workers usually stayed where they were. Who then left for the wilderness and the unknown? Obviously those who had not made good: men who went broke or never amounted to much; men who though possessed of abilities were too impulsive to stand the daily grind; men who were slaves of their appetites—drunkards, gamblers, and woman-chasers; outcasts—fugitives from justice and ex-jailbirds. There were no doubt some who went in search of health—men suffering with TB, asthma, heart trouble. Finally there was a sprinkling of young and middle-aged in search of adventure.

All these people craved change, some probably actuated by the naïve belief that a change in place brings with it a change in luck. Many wanted to go to a place where they were not known and there make a new beginning. Certainly they did not go out deliberately in search of hard work and suffering. If in the end they shouldered enormous tasks, endured unspeakable hardships, and accomplished the impossible, it was because they had to. They became men of action on the run. They acquired strength and skill in the inescapable struggle for existence. It was a question of do or die. And once they tasted the joy of achievement, they craved for more.

Clearly the same types of people which now swelled the ranks of migratory workers and tramps had probably in former times made up the bulk of the pioneers. As a group the pioneers were probably as unlike the present-day "native sons"—their descendants—as one could well imagine. Indeed, were there to be today a new influx of typical pioneers, twin brothers of the forty-niners only in a modern garb, the citizens of California would consider it a menace to health, wealth, and morals.

With few exceptions, this seems to be the case in the settlement of all new countries. Ex-convicts were the vanguard in the settling of Australia. Exiles and convicts settled Siberia. In this country, a large portion of our earlier and later settlers were failures, fugitives, and felons. The exceptions seemed to be those who were motivated by religious fervor, such as the Pilgrim Fathers and the Mormons.

Although quite logical, this train of thought seemed to me then a wonderful joke. In my exhilaration I was eating up the road in long strides, and I reached the oasis of Elim in what seemed almost no time. A passing empty truck picked me up just then and we thundered through Banning and Beaumont, all the way to Riverside. From there I walked the seven miles to San Bernardino.

Somehow, this discovery of a family likeness between tramps and pioneers took a firm hold on my mind. For years afterward it kept intertwining itself with a mass of observations which on the face of them had no relation to either tramps or pioneers. And it moved me to speculate on subjects in which, up to then, I had no real interest, and of which I knew very little.

I talked with several old-timers—one of them over eighty and a native son—in Sacramento, Placerville, Auburn, and Fresno. It was not easy, at first, to obtain the information I was after. I could not make my questions specific enough. "What kind of people were the early settlers and miners?" I asked. They were a hard-working, tough lot, I was told. They drank, fought, gambled, and wenched. They were big-hearted, grasping, profane, and God-fearing. They wallowed in luxury, or lived on next to nothing with equal ease. They were the salt of the earth.

Still it was not clear what manner of people they were.

If I asked what they looked like, I was told of whiskers, broad-brimmed hats, high boots, shirts of many colors, sun-tanned faces, horny hands. Finally I asked: "What group of people in present-day California most closely resembles the pioneers?" The answer, usually after some hesitation, was invariably the same: "The Okies and the fruit tramps."

I tried also to evaluate the tramps as potential pioneers by watching them in action. I saw them fell timber, clear firebreaks, build rock walls, put up barracks, build dams and roads, handle steam shovels, bulldozers, tractors, and concrete mixers. I saw them put in a hard day's work after a night of steady drinking. They sweated and growled, but they did the work. I saw the tramps elevated to positions of authority as foremen and superintendents. Then I could notice a remarkable physical transformation: a seamed face gradually smoothed out and the skin showed a healthy hue: an indifferent mouth became firm and expressive; dull eyes cleared and brightened; voices actually changed; there was even an apparent increase in stature. In almost no time these promoted tramps looked as if they had been on top all their lives. Yet sooner or later I would meet up with them again in a railroad yard, on some skid row, or in the fields—tramps again. It was usually the same story: they got drunk or lost their temper and were fired, or they got fed up with the steady job and quit. Usually, when a tramp becomes a foreman, he is careful in his treatment of the tramps under him; he knows the day of reckoning is never far off.

In short, it was not difficult to visualize the tramps as pioneers. I reflected that if they were to find themselves in a singlehanded life-and-death struggle with nature, they would undoubtedly display persistence. For the pressure of responsibility and the heat of battle steel a character. The inadaptable would perish, and those who survived would be the equal of the successful pioneers.

I also considered the few instances of pioneering engineered from above—that is to say, by settlers possessed of lavish means, who were classed with the best where they came from. In these instances, it seemed to me, the resulting social structure was inevitably precarious. For pioneering deluxe usually results in a plantation society, made up of large landowners and peon labor, either native or imported. Very often there is a racial cleavage between the two. The colonizing activities of the Teutonic barons in the Baltic, the Hungarian nobles in Transylvania, the English in Ireland, the planters in our South, and the present-day plantation societies in Kenya and other British and Dutch colonies are cases in point. Whatever their merits, they are characterized by poor adaptability. They are likely eventually to be broken up either by a peon revolution or by an influx of typical pioneers—who are usually of the same race or nation as the landowners. The adjustment is not necessarily implemented by war. Even our old South, had it not been for the complication of secession, might eventually have attained stability without war: namely, by the activity of its own poor whites or by an influx of the indigent from other states.

There is in us a tendency to judge a race, a nation, or an organization by its least worthy members. The tendency is manifestly perverse and unfair; yet it has some justification. For the quality and destiny of a nation is determined to a considerable extent by the nature and potentialities of its inferior elements. The inert mass of a nation is in its middle section. The industrious, decent, well-to-do, and satisfied middle classes—whether in cities or on the land—are worked upon and shaped by minorities at both extremes: the best and the worst.

The superior individual, whether in politics, business, industry, science, literature, or religion, undoubtedly plays a major role in the shaping of a nation. But so do the individuals at the other extreme: the poor, the outcasts, the misfits, and those who are in the grip of some overpowering passion. The importance of these inferior elements as formative factors lies in the readiness with which they are swayed in any direction. This peculiarity is due to their inclination to take risks ("not giving a damn") and their propensity for united action. They crave to merge their drab, wasted lives into something grand and complete. Thus they are the first and most fervent adherents of new religions, political upheavals, patriotic hysteria, gangs, and mass rushes to new lands.

And the quality of a nation—its innermost worth—is made manifest by its dregs as they rise to the top: by how brave they are, how humane, how orderly, how skilled, how generous, how independent or servile; by the bounds they will not transgress in their dealings with man's soul, with truth, and with honor.

The average American of today bristles with indignation when he is told that his country was built, largely, by hordes of undesirables from Europe. Yet, far from being derogatory, this statement, if true, should be a cause for rejoicing, should fortify our pride in the stock from which we have sprung.

This vast continent with its towns, farms, factories, dams, aqueducts, docks, railroads, highways, powerhouses, schools, and parks is the handiwork of common folk from the Old World, where for centuries men of their kind had been as beasts of burden, the property of their masters—kings, nobles, and priests—and with no will and no aspirations of their own. When on rare occasions one of the lowly had reached the top in Europe he had kept the pattern intact and, if anything, tightened the screws. The stuffy little corporal from Corsica harnessed the lusty forces released by the French Revolution to a gilded state coach, and could think of nothing grander than mixing his blood with that of the Hapsburg masters and establishing a new dynasty. In our day a bricklayer in Italy, a house painter in Germany, and a shoemaker's son in Russia have made themselves masters of their nations; and what they did was to re-establish and reinforce the old pattern.

Only here, in America, were the common folk of the Old World given a chance to show what they could do on their own, without a master to push and order them about. History contrived an earth-shaking joke when it lifted by the nape of the neck lowly peasants, shopkeepers, laborers, paupers, jailbirds, and drunks from the midst of Europe, dumped them on a vast, virgin continent and said: "Go to it; it is yours!"

And the lowly were not awed by the magnitude of the task. A hunger for action, pent up for centuries, found an outlet. They went to it with ax, pick, shovel, plow, and rifle; on foot, on horse, in wagons, and on flatboats. They went to it praying, howling, singing, brawling, drinking, and fighting. Make way for the people! This is how I read the statement that this country was built by hordes of undesirables from the Old World.

Small wonder that we in this country have a deeply ingrained faith in human regeneration. We believe that, given a chance, even the degraded and the apparently worthless are capable of constructive work and great deeds. It is a faith founded on experience, not on some idealistic theory. And no matter what some anthropologists, sociologists, and geneticists may tell us, we shall go on believing that man, unlike other forms of life, is not a captive of his past—of his heredity and habits—but is possessed of infinite plasticity, and his potentialities for good and for evil are never wholly exhausted.

QUESTIONS

The following poem by Carl Sandburg speaks about "undesirables"—"rabble," "vagabonds," "hungry men." What other words might Sandburg have used for the "undesirables"? What effect do the words he uses create? Compare the terms used by Sandburg and Hoffer and determine the ways in which their words suggest similar or different attitudes toward these people.

Now the stone house on the lake front is finished and the
    workmen are beginning the fence.
The palings are made of iron bars with steel points that can
    stab the life out of any man who falls on them.
As a fence, it is a masterpiece, and will shut off the
    rabble and all vagabonds and hungry men and all
    wandering children looking for a place to play.
Passing through the bars and over the steel points will go
    nothing except Death and the Rain and To-morrow.
                —Carl Sandburg, "A Fence"

HANNAH ARENDT
Denmark and the Jews[1]

At the Wannsee Conference,[2] Martin Luther, of the Foreign Office, warned of great difficulties in the Scandinavian countries, notably in Norway and Denmark. (Sweden was never occupied, and Finland, though in the war on the side of the Axis, was one country the Nazis never even approached on the Jewish question. This surprising exception of Finland, with some two thousand Jews, may have been due to Hitler's great esteem for the Finns, whom perhaps he did not want to subject to threats and humiliating blackmail.) Luther proposed postponing evacuations from Scandinavia for the time being, and as far as Denmark was concerned, this really went without saying, since the country retained its independent government, and was respected as a neutral state, until the fall of 1943, although it, along with Norway, had been invaded by the German Army in April, 1940. There existed no Fascist or Nazi movement in Denmark worth mentioning, and therefore no collaborators. In

1. From "Deportations from Western Europe—France, Belgium, Holland, Denmark, Italy," Chapter X of *Eich-* *mann in Jerusalem,* 1963.
2. A meeting of German officials on "the Jewish question."

Norway, however, the Germans had been able to find enthusiastic supporters; indeed, Vidkun Quisling, leader of the pro-Nazi and anti-Semitic Norwegian party, gave his name to what later became known as a "quisling government." The bulk of Norway's seventeen hundred Jews were stateless, refugees from Germany; they were seized and interned in a few lightning operations in October and November, 1942. When Eichmann's office ordered their deportation to Auschwitz, some of Quisling's own men resigned their government posts. This may not have come as a surprise to Mr. Luther and the Foreign Office, but what was much more serious, and certainly totally unexpected, was that Sweden immediately offered asylum, and even Swedish nationality, to all who were persecuted. Dr. Ernst von Weizsäcker, Undersecretary of State of the Foreign Office, who received the proposal, refused to discuss it, but the offer helped nevertheless. It is always relatively easy to get out of a country illegally, whereas it is nearly impossible to enter the place of refuge without permission and to dodge the immigration authorities. Hence, about nine hundred people, slightly more than half of the small Norwegian community, could be smuggled into Sweden.

It was in Denmark, however, that the Germans found out how fully justified the Foreign Offices's apprehensions had been. The story of the Danish Jews is *sui generis,* and the behavior of the Danish people and their government was unique among all the countries in Europe—whether occupied, or a partner of the Axis, or neutral and truly independent. One is tempted to recommend the story as required reading in political science for all students who wish to learn something about the enormous power potential inherent in non-violent action and in resistance to an opponent possessing vastly superior means of violence. To be sure, a few other countries in Europe lacked proper "understanding of the Jewish question," and actually a majority of them were opposed to "radical" and "final" solutions. Like Denmark, Sweden, Italy, and Bulgaria proved to be nearly immune to anti-Semitism, but of the three that were in the German sphere of influence, only the Danes dared speak out on the subject to their German masters. Italy and Bulgaria sabotaged German orders and indulged in a complicated game of double-dealing and double-crossing, saving their Jews by a tour de force of sheer ingenuity, but they never contested the policy as such. That was totally different from what the Danes did. When the Germans approached them rather cautiously about introducing the yellow badge, they were simply told that the King would be the first to wear it, and the Danish government officials were careful to point out that anti-Jewish measures of any sort would cause their own immediate resignation. It was decisive in this whole matter that the Germans did not even succeed in introducing the vitally important distinction between native Danes of Jewish origin, of whom there were about sixty-four hundred, and the fourteen hundred German Jewish refugees who had found asylum in the country prior to the war and who now had been declared stateless by the German government. This refusal must have surprised the Germans no end, since it appeared so "illogical" for a government to protect people to whom it had categorically denied naturalization and even permission to work. (Legally, the prewar situation of refugees in Denmark was not unlike that in France, except that the general corruption in the Third Republic's civil services enabled a few of them to obtain naturalization papers, through bribes or "connections," and most refugees in France could work illegally, without a permit. But Denmark, like Switzerland, was no country *pour se débrouiller*[3].) The Danes, however, explained to the German officials that because the stateless refugees were no longer German citizens, the Nazis could not claim them without Danish assent. This was one of the few cases in which statelessness turned out to be an asset, although it was of course not statelessness per se that saved the Jews but, on the contrary, the fact that the Danish government had decided to protect them. Thus, none of the preparatory moves, so important for the bureaucracy of murder, could be carried out, and operations were postponed until the fall of 1943.

What happened then was truly amazing; compared with what took place in other European countries, everything went topsy-turvey. In August, 1943—after the German offensive in Russia had failed, the Afrika Korps had surrendered in Tunisia, and the Allies had invaded Italy—the Swedish government canceled its 1940 agreement with Germany which had permitted German troops the right to pass through the country. Thereupon, the Danish workers decided that they could help a bit in hurrying things up; riots broke out in Danish shipyards, where the dock workers refused to repair German ships and then went on strike. The German military commander proclaimed a state of emergency and imposed martial law, and Himmler thought this was the right moment to tackle the Jewish question, whose "solution" was long overdue. What he did not reckon with was that—quite apart from Danish resistance—the German officials who had been living in the country for years were no longer the same. Not only did General von Hannecken, the military commander, refuse to put troops at the disposal of the Reich plenipotentiary, Dr. Werner Best; the special S.S. units (*Einsatz-kommandos*) employed in Denmark very frequently objected to "the measures they were ordered to carry out by the central agencies"—according to Best's testimony at Nuremberg. And Best himself, an old Gestapo man and former legal adviser to Heydrich, author of a then famous book on the police, who had

3. For wangling—using bribery to circumvent bureaucratic regulations.

worked for the military government in Paris to the entire satisfaction of his superiors, could no longer be trusted, although it is doubtful that Berlin ever learned the extent of his unreliability. Still, it was clear from the beginning that things were not going well, and Eichmann's office sent one of its best men to Denmark—Rolf Günther, whom no one had ever accused of not possessing the required "ruthless toughness." Günther made no impression on his colleagues in Copenhagen, and now von Hannecken refused even to issue a decree requiring all Jews to report for work.

Best went to Berlin and obtained a promise that all Jews from Denmark would be sent to Theresienstadt[4] regardless of their category—a very important concession, from the Nazis' point of view. The night of October 1 was set for their seizure and immediate departure—ships were ready in the harbor—and since neither the Danes nor the Jews nor the German troops stationed in Denmark could be relied on to help, police units arrived from Germany for a door-to-door search. At the last moment, Best told them that they were not permitted to break into apartments, because the Danish police might then interfere, and they were not supposed to fight it out with the Danes. Hence they could seize only those Jews who voluntarily opened their doors. They found exactly 477 people, out of a total of more then 7,800, at home and willing to let them in. A few days before the date of doom, a German shipping agent, Georg F. Duckwitz, having probably been tipped off by Best himself, had revealed the whole plan to Danish government officials, who, in turn, had hurriedly informed the heads of the Jewish community. They, in marked contrast to Jewish leaders in other countries, had then communicated the news openly in the synagogues on the occasion of the New Year services. The Jews had just time enough to leave their apartments and go into hiding, which was very easy in Denmark, because, in the words of the judgment, "all sections of the Danish people, from the King down to simple citizens," stood ready to receive them.

They might have remained in hiding until the end of the war if the Danes had not been blessed with Sweden as a neighbor. It seemed reasonable to ship the Jews to Sweden, and this was done with the help of the Danish fishing fleet. The cost of transportation for people without means—about a hundred dollars per person—was paid largely by wealthy Danish citizens, and that was perhaps the most astounding feat of all, since this was a time when Jews were paying for their own deportation, when the rich among them were paying fortunes for exit permits (in Holland, Slovakia, and, later, in Hungary) either by bribing the local authorities or by negotiating "legally" with the S.S., who accepted only hard currency

---

4. A camp for certain classes of prisoners who were to receive special treatment..

and sold exit permits, in Holland, to the tune of five or ten thousand dollars per person. Even in places where Jews met with genuine sympathy and a sincere willingness to help, they had to pay for it, and the chances poor people had of escaping were nil.

It took the better part of October to ferry all the Jews across the five to fifteen miles of water that separates Denmark from Sweden. The Swedes received 5,919 refugees, of whom at least 1,000 were of German origin, 1,310 were half-Jews, and 686 were non-Jews married to Jews. (Almost half the Danish Jews seem to have remained in the country and survived the war in hiding.) The non-Danish Jews were better off than ever before, they all received permission to work. The few hundred Jews whom the German police had been able to arrest were shipped to Theresienstadt. They were old or poor people, who either had not received the news in time or had not been able to comprehend its meaning. In the ghetto, they enjoyed greater privileges than any other group because of the never-ending "fuss" made about them by Danish institutions and private persons. Forty-eight persons died, a figure that was not particularly high, in view of the average age of the group. When everything was over, it was the considered opinion of Eichmann that "for various reasons the action against the Jews in Denmark has been a failure," whereas the curious Dr. Best declared that "the objective of the operation was not to seize a great number of Jews but to clean Denmark of Jews, and this objective has now been achieved."

Politically and psychologically, the most interesting aspect of this incident is perhaps the role played by the German authorities in Denmark, their obvious sabotage of orders from Berlin. It is the only case we know of in which the Nazis met with *open* native resistance, and the result seems to have been that those exposed to it changed their minds. They themselves apparently no longer looked upon the extermination of a whole people as a matter of course. They had met resistance based on principle, and their "toughness" had melted like butter in the sun, they had even been able to show a few timid beginnings of genuine courage. That the ideal of "toughness," except, perhaps, for a few half-demented brutes, was nothing but a myth of self-deception, concealing a ruthless desire for conformity at any price, was clearly revealed at the Nuremberg Trials, where the defendants accused and betrayed each other and assured the world that they "had always been against it" or claimed, as Eichmann was to do, that their best qualities had been "abused" by their superiors. (In Jerusalem, he accused "those in power" of having abused his "obedience." "The subject of a good government is lucky, the subject of a bad government is unlucky. I had no luck.") The atmosphere had changed, and although most of them must have known that they were doomed, not a single one of them had the guts to defend the Nazi ideology. Werner Best claimed at Nuremberg that he had played a complicated double role and that it was thanks to him that the Danish officials had been warned of the impending catastrophe; documentary evidence showed, on the contrary, that he himself had proposed the Danish operation in Berlin, but he explained that this was all part of the game. He was extradited to Denmark and there condemned to death, but he appealed the sentence, with surprising results; because of "new evidence," his sentence was commuted to five years in prison, from which he was released soon afterward. He must have been able to prove to the satisfaction of the Danish court that he really had done his best.

IAN WATT

"The Bridge over the River Kwai" as Myth

The Kwai is a real river in Thailand, and nearly thirty years ago prisoners of the Japanese—including myself—really did build a bridge across it: actually, two. Anyone who was there knows that Boulle's novel, *The Bridge on the River Kwai*, and the movie based on it, are both completely fictitious. What is odd is how they combined to create a world-wide myth, and how that myth is largely the result of those very psychological and political delusions which the builders of the real bridges had been forced to put aside.

The Real Bridges

The origin of the myth can be traced back to two historical realities.

Early in 1942, Singapore, the Dutch East Indies, and the Philippines surrendered; and Japan was suddenly left with the task of looking after over two hundred thousand prisoners of war. The normal procedure is to separate the officers from the enlisted men and put them into different camps; but the Japanese hadn't got the staff to spare and left the job of organizing the prison-camps to the prisoners themselves; which in effect meant the usual chain of command. This was one essential basis for Boulle's story: prisoners of war, like other prisoners, don't normally command anyone; and so they don't have anything to negotiate with.

The other main reality behind the myth is the building of that particular bridge. Once their armies started driving towards India, the Japanese realized they needed a railway from Bangkok to Rangoon. In the summer of 1942 many trainloads of prisoners from Singapore were sent up to Thailand and started to hack a two-hundred-mile trace through the jungle along a river called the

Khwae Noi. In Thai, *Khwae* just means "stream;" *Noi* means "small." The "small stream" rises near the Burma border, at the Three Pagodas Pass; and it joins the main tributary of the Me Nam, called the Khwae Yai, or "Big Stream," at the old city of Karnburi, some eighty miles west of Bangkok. It was there that the Japanese faced the big task of getting the railway across the river. So, early in the autumn of 1942, a large construction camp was set up at a place called Tha Makham, about three miles west of Karnburi.

Like the hundred of other Japanese prison camps, Tha Makham had a very small and incompetent staff. To the Japanese the idea of being taken prisoner of war is—or was then—deeply shameful; even looking after prisoners shared some of this humiliation. Consequently, most of the Japanese staff were men who for one reason or another were thought unfit for combat duty; too old, perhaps, in disgrace, or just drunks. What was special about Tha Makham and the other camps on the Kwai was that they were also partly controlled by Japanese military engineers who were building the railway. These engineers usually despised the Japanese troops in charge of running the camps almost as much as they despised the prisoners.

The continual friction between the Japanese prison staff and the engineers directly affected our ordinary lives as prisoners. Daily routine in the camps in November 1942, when work on the Kwai bridge began, normally went like this: up at dawn; tea and rice for breakfast; and then on parade for the day's work. We might wait anything from ten minutes to half an hour for the Korean guard to count the whole parade and split it up into work groups. Then we marched to a small bamboo shed where the picks, shovels and so on were kept. Under any circumstances it would take a long time for one guard to issue tools for thousands of men out of one small shed; the delay was made worse by the fact that the tools usually belonged to the engineers, so two organizations were involved merely in issuing and checking picks and shovels. That might take another half hour, and then we would be reassembled and counted all over again before finally marching off to work.

When we had finally got out on the line, and found the right work site, the Japanese engineer in charge might be there to explain the day's task; but more probably not. He had a very long section of embankment or bridge to look after and perhaps thirty working parties in widely separate places to supervise. He had usually given some previous instructions to the particular guard at each site; but these orders might not be clear, or, even worse, they might be clear to us, but not to the guard.

There were many organizational problems. For instance, in the early days of the railway the total amount of work each man was supposed to do—moving a cubic meter of earth or driving in so many piles—was quite reasonable under normal circumstances. But the task often fell very unequally: some groups might have to carry their earth much further than others, or drive their teak piles into much rockier ground. So, as the day wore on, someone in a group with a very difficult, or impossible, assignment would get beaten up: all the guard thought about was that he'd probably be beaten up himself if the work on the section wasn't finished: so he lashed out.

Meanwhile, many other prisoners would already have finished their task, and would be sitting around waiting, or—even worse—pretending to work. The rule was that the whole day's task had to be finished, and often inspected by the Japanese engineer, before any single work party could leave the construction site. So some more prisoners would be beaten up for lying down in the shade when they were supposed to look as though there were still work to do in the sun.

At the end of the day's work an individual prisoner might well have been on his feet under the tropical sun from 7 in the morning until 7 or 8 even 9 at night, even though he'd only done three or four hours' work. He would come back late for the evening meal; there would be no lights in the huts; and as most of the guards went off duty at 6, he probably wouldn't be allowed to go down to the river to bathe, or wash his clothes.

So our lives were poisoned, not by calculated Japanese brutality, but merely by a special form of the boredom, waste of time, and demoralization which are typical of modern industrial society. Our most pressing daily problems were really the familiar trade-union issues of long portal-to-portal hours of work, and the various tensions arising from failures of communication between the technical specialists, the personnel managers, and the on-site foremen—in our case the Japanese engineers, the higher prisoner administration, and the guards.

The people best able to see the situation as a whole were probably the officer-prisoners in charge of individual working parties. (This was before officers had been forced to do manual work.) These officers, however, normally dealt only with the particular guards on their section of the line; and back at camp headquarters neither the Japanese prison staff nor the senior British officers had much direct knowledge of conditions out on the trace. But since—mainly because of a shortage of interpreters—most of the Japanese orders were handed down through Allied officers, who were in fact virtually impotent, everything tended to increase the confusion and mistrust in our own ranks.

At first the difficulties in the Bridge Camp of Tha Makham were much like those in all the others. But soon they began to change, mainly because of the personality of its senior British officer.

Colonel Philip Toosey was tall, rather young, and with one of those special English faces like a genial but sceptical bulldog. Unlike Boulle's Colonel Nicholson, he was not a career officer but a territorial.

Toosey's previous career had been managerial. Now a cotton merchant and banker, he had earlier run a factory, where he had experienced the decline of the Lancashire cotton industry, strikes, unemployment, the Depression; he'd even gone bankrupt himself. This past training helped him to see that the problem confronting him wasn't a standard military problem at all: it had an engineering side, a labor-organization side, and above all, a very complicated morale side affecting both the prisoners and their captors.

Escaping or refusing to work on a strategic bridge were both out of the question. Trying either could only mean some men killed, and the rest punished. We had already learned that in a showdown the Japanese would always win; they had the power, and no scruples about using it. But Toosey had the imagination to see that there was a shade more room for manoeuvre than anybody else had suspected—as long as the manoeuvres were of exactly the right kind. He was a brave man, but he never forced the issue so as to make the Japanese lose face; instead he first awed them with an impressive display of military swagger; and then proceeded to charm them with his apparently immovable assumption that no serious difficulty could arise between honorable soldiers whose only thought was to do the right thing.

The right thing from our point of view, obviously, was to do everything possible to increase food and medical supplies, improve working conditions, and allocate the work more reasonably. Gradually, Toosey persuaded the Japanese that things like issuing tools or allocating the day's tasks to each working party more evenly would be better handled if we did it ourselves. He also persuaded the Japanese that output would be much improved if the duties of the guards were limited entirely to preventing the prisoners from escaping. We would be responsible for our own organization and discipline. The officers in charge of working parties would supervise the construction work; while back at camp headquarters, if the Japanese engineers would assign the next day's work to Colonel Toosey, he and his staff would see how best to carry it out.

The new organization completely transformed our conditions of life. There was much less waste of time; daily tasks were often finished early in the afternoon; weeks passed without any prisoner being beaten; and the camp became almost happy.

Looked at from outside, Toosey's remarkable success obviously involved an increase in the degree of our collaboration with the enemy. But anybody on the spot knew that the real issue was not between building or not building the bridge; it was merely how many prisoners would die, be beaten up, or break down, in the process. There was only one way to persuade the Japanese to improve rations, provide medical supplies, allow regular holidays, or reduce the brutality of the guards: to convince them that the work got done better our way.

Toosey's drive and panache soon won him the confidence of the Japanese at the camp: they got about the same amount of work out of us, and their working day was much shorter too. At the same time Toosey was never accused by his fellow prisoners—as Boulle's Colonel Nicholson certainly would have been—of being "Jap-happy." Some regarded him as a bit too regimental for their taste; but, unanswerably, he delivered the goods. Eventually, in all the dozens of camps up and down the River Kwai, Toosey became a legend: he was the man who could "handle the Nips." His general strategy of taking over as much responsibility as possible (often much more than the Japanese knew), was gradually put into practice by the most successful British, American, Australian and Dutch commanders in the other camps. Even more convincingly, in 1945, when the Japanese saw defeat ahead, and finally concentrated all their officer prisoners in one camp, the vast majority of the three thousand or so allied officers collected there agitated until various senior commanding officers were successively removed and Colonel Toosey was put in charge. He remained in command until the end of the war in August 1945, when, to general consternation, all kinds of ancient military characters precipitately emerged from the wood-work to reclaim the privileges of seniority.

The Myth Begins

But Toosey, like all the other heroes—and non-heroes—of our prisoner-of-war days, would normally have been forgotten when peace finally broke out. That he left any mark on the larger world is only because a Free-French officer, Pierre Boulle, who had never known him, had never been near the railway, and was never a prisoner of the Japanese, wrote a novel called *Le Pont de la Rivière Kwai.*

The book was not in any sense intended as history. Though he took the river's real name, Boulle placed his bridge near the Burmese frontier, two hundred miles from the only actual bridge *across* the Kwai, the one at Tha Makham. And, as Boulle recounted in his fascinating but—on this topic—not very explicit autobiographical memoir, *The Sources of the River Kwai* (1966), Colonel Nicholson was based, not on any prisoner of war but on two French colonels he had known in Indo-China. Having been Boulle's comrades in arms until the collapse of France in 1941, they then sided with Vichy, and eventually punished Boulle's activities on behalf of the Allies as treason, quite blind to the notion that it was they, and not Boulle, who had changed sides.

In his novel Boulle made Nicholson's "collaboration" much more extreme: he built a better bridge than the one the Japanese had started, and in a better place. Boulle may have got the idea from the fact that the Japanese actually built two bridges over the Kwai at Tha Makham: a temporary wooden structure, which no longer survives; and another begun at the same time and finished in May, 1943, which was a permanent iron-trestle bridge on concrete piers, and still stands. Both bridges showed up clearly on Allied aerial photographs; and Boulle may have seen these photographs when he was a Free-French Intelligence officer in Calcutta during the last year of the war.

Boulle's main aim in the novel was presumably to dramatize the ironic contradictions which he had personally experienced in Indo-China. First, Nicholson embodied the paradox of how the military —like any other institutional—mind will tend to generate its own objectives, objectives which are often quite different from, and may even be contrary to, the original purposes of the institution. Secondly, there was the political paradox—the total reversals of attitude which continually occur, almost unnoticed, in our strange world of changing ideological alliances. To drive this point home Boulle also invented the Allied commandos who were sent to blow up the bridge with exactly the same patient technological expertness as had been used by their former comrades in arms who had built it.

The book's interest for the reader comes mainly from the similar but opposite efforts of the commandos and the prisoners. Like Nicholson we forget about aims because the means are absorbing; we watch how well the two jobs are being done, and it's only at the end that we wake up and realize that all this marvellous technological expertness harnessed to admirable collective effort has been leading to nothing except death; Nicholson sabotages the saboteurs, and then dies under the fire of Warden's mortar. So, finally, we see that the novel is not really about the Kwai, but about how the vast scale and complication of the operations which are rendered possible, and are even in a sense required, by modern technology tend finally to destroy human meanings and purposes. The West is the master of its means, but not of its ends.

This basic idea was lost, of course, in the movie; but there were many other elements in Boulle's narrative which gave it a more universal appeal.

First, there was the character of Nicholson, which was very little changed in the movie: an amiable fellow in his way, but egocentric; admirable, but ridiculous; intelligent, but basically infantile. Here we come back to a very ancient French myth about the English character, a stereotype which was already fully established in a book written about an English colonel by a French liaison officer after the first world war—in André Maurois' *The Silences of Colonel Bramble*. The infantile and egocentric side of Nicholson's character is essential to the plot; the book is after all about a monomaniac who falls in love with a boy's hobby: to build a bridge, but not with an Erector set, and not for toy trains.

The audience, of course, gets caught up in the hobby too; perhaps because it fulfills the greatest human need in the modern world: being able to love one's work. Along the Kwai there had been a daily conflict between the instinct of workmanship and disgust with what one was being forced to do: people would spend hours trying to get a perfect alignment of piles, and then try to hide termites or rotten wood in an important joint. These sabotage games weren't really very significant; but they expressed a collective need to pretend we were still fighting the enemy, and to resist any tendency to see things the Japanese way. We were always on the lookout for people becoming what we called "Jap-happy"; and if anyone had started talking about "my bridge," like Nicholson, he'd have been replaced at once.

Neither the novel nor the film even hint at these conflicting impulses; and so the question arises, "How can Boulle's shrewd and experienced mind ever have imagined that Nicholson could plausibly get away with his love affair for a Japanese bridge?"

There are at least three possible reasons. First, Boulle himself was born in Avignon, site of the world's most famous ruined bridge. Secondly, he was trained as an engineer and presumably shared the mystique of his profession. These were two positive motives for loving bridges; and there was also the general intellectual and political context of the post-war world. Boulle's first collection of short stories, *Tales of the Absurd*, expressed not only a sense that history had arrived at a meaningless dead-end, but the whole Existential perspective on the human condition in general; all political causes and individual purposes were equally fictitious and ridiculous. Boulle certainly intended *The Bridge on the River Kwai* to have the same implication; as we can see from his epigraph, taken from Conrad's *Victory*: "No, it was not funny; it was, rather, pathetic; he was so representative of all the past victims of the Great Joke. But it is by folly alone that the world moves, and so it is a respectable thing on the whole. And besides, he was what one would call a good man."

The Movie

Boulle's book was published in 1952 and sold about 6,000 copies annually in France until 1958. That year sales leaped to 122,000—

the movie had come out. Later, the film's success caused the book to be translated into more than twenty languages, and to sell millions of copies; it also, of course, created the myth.

Hollywood has been a great creator of myths, but they have usually been personal—myths of individual actors, such as Charlie Chaplin or Humphrey Bogart, or of character-types, such as the cowboy or the private eye. The Hungarian producer, Sam Spiegel, and the English director, David Lean, turned a little river in Thailand that is not marked in most atlases into a household word.

So great a success obviously presupposes a very complete adaptation to the tastes of the international cinema public: and this adaptive process can be seen in the differences between the book and the movie, which is even further from what really happened on the railway. Of course, one can't fairly blame the movie for not showing the real life of the prisoner-of-war camps along the Kwai, if only because that life was boring even to those who lived it. On the other hand, using the name of an actual river suggested an element of authenticity; and the movie's version of events at the bridge certainly seemed to the survivors a gross insult on their intelligence and on that of their commanders. When news of the film's being made came out, various ex-prisoner-of-war associations, led, among other people, by Colonel Toosey, protested against the movie's distortion of what had actually happened; since the name of the river was fairly well known, people were bound to think there was an element of truth in the film. But history had given Sam Spiegel a lot of free publicity, and he refused even to change the film's title. This was vital, not only for the aura of historical truth at the box-office, but for the growth of the myth; since, in the curious limbo of mythic reality, collective fantasies need to be anchored on some real name of a place or a person.

The movie's air of pseudo-reality was also inevitably enforced by its medium. No one reading Boulle could have failed to notice from his style alone that the book aimed at ironic fantasy, rather than detailed historical realism; but the camera can't help giving an air of total visual authenticity; and the effect of this technical authenticity tends to spread beyond the visual image to the substance of what is portrayed. Every moviegoer knows in some way that—whenever he can check against his own experience—life isn't really like that; but he forgets it most of the time, especially when the substance of what he sees conforms to his own psychological or political point of view.

Politically, the movie gave no inkling of the unpleasant facts about the terrible poverty and disease along the real river Kwai. Instead, the audience must have taken away some vague impression that the poor jungle villagers of South-East Asia all have perfect complexions, and fly elaborately lovely kites. They don't. Equally unrealistically, the movie suggested that beautiful Thai girls don't have any boyfriends until some handsome white man comes along. Much more dangerously, the movie incidentally promoted the political delusion—less common now than in 1958—that the people of these poor villages are merely marking time until they are given an opportunity to sacrifice their lives on behalf of the ideology of the Western powers. All these are examples of the colonialist attitudes which were also present in the central idea of the novel: although the Japanese had beaten the Allies in a campaign that, among other things, showed a remarkable command of very difficult engineering and transport problems, Boulle presented them as comically inferior to their captives as bridge builders. Both the novel and the movie, in fact, contained as a primary assumption the myth of white superiority whose results we have seen most recently in that same Vietnam that Boulle had known.

In the movie the bridge itself, of course, also had to be transformed into a symbol of Western engineering mastery. The form and color of those two giant cantilevers had a poised serenity which almost justified Nicholson's infatuation; but it was totally beyond the technical means and the military needs of the actual bridges over the Kwai; and its great beauty soon made one forget the sordid realities of the war and the prison camp. What actually happened was that the movie-makers went to Thailand, took one look at the Kwai, and saw it wouldn't do. The area wasn't particularly interesting— too flat, and not at all wild; there was already a bridge over the river —the real one; and in any case there wasn't any accommodation in the little provincial town of Karnburi to match the splendors of the Mount Lavinia Hotel in Ceylon, where most of the movie was eventually shot.

All this is a normal, perhaps inevitable, part of making movies; and one's only legitimate objection is that ultimately the pseudo-realism of Hollywood has the accidental effect of making millions of people think they are seeing what something is really like when actually they are not.

The biggest departure of the movie both from history and from the novel, was the blowing up of the bridge, which distorted reality in a rather similar direction. The movie credits read "Screenplay by Pierre Boulle, Based on His Novel." Actually, though Boulle got an Oscar for the screenplay, he took only a "modest" part in the preliminary discussions of the screenplay with Spiegel and Lean; and the real writer—who couldn't then be named—was Carl Foreman, who had been blacklisted by Hollywood during the McCarthy era. Pierre Boulle eventually approved their final version; but only after he'd objected to many of their changes, and especially to the one which contradicted his whole purpose: that in the movie the bridge was blown up. He was told that the audience would have watched the screen "for more than two hours . . . in the hope and expectation" of just that big bang; if it didn't happen "they would feel frustrated"; and anyway it was quite impossible to pass up "such a sensational bit of action." So, on March 12, 1957, a beautiful bridge that had cost a quarter of a million dollars to build was blown up with a real train crossing it.

Building a bridge just to blow it up again so that the movie public won't feel frustrated was an unbelievably apt illustration of Boulle's point about how contemporary society employs its awesome technological means in the pursuit of largely derisory ends.

Boulle's readers had been made to think about that; not so the moviegoers. Their consciences were kept quiet by a well-intentioned anti-war message—the killing of the terrified young Japanese soldier, for example—while they were having a rip-roaring time. But, as we all know, you can't have it both ways. You can't turn an exotic adventure-comedy into a true film about war just by dunking it in blood. The film only seemed to take up real problems; at the end a big explosion showed that there was no point in thinking things over—when things will work out nicely anyway, why bother?

In the movie of the *Bridge on the River Kwai*, then, historical and political and psychological reality became infinitely plastic to the desires of the audience. All over the world audiences gratefully responded; and in the end they even caused the myth to be reincarnated where it had begun.

Reincarnation on the Kwai

The decisive phase of a myth is when the story wins a special status for itself; when people begin to think of it, not exactly as history, but as something which, in some vague way, really happened; and then, later, the fiction eventually imposes itself on the world as literally true. The earliest signs of this are normally the erection of shrines, and the beginning of pilgrimages; but the process of reincarnation is only complete when whatever is left of the truth which conflicts with the myth's symbolic meaning is forgotten or transformed. All this has begun to happen to the myth of the Kwai.

After the war ended, in August 1945, and the last train had evacuated the sad remnants of the Japanese army in Burma, silence at last descended on the railway. Robbers furtively stole the telegraph wire; termites ate away the wooden sleepers of the line and the timbers of the bridges; the monsoon rains washed away parts of the embankment; and sensing that all was normal again, the wild elephants (which few prisoners had ever seen) once again emerged from the jungle, and, finding the railway trace a convenient path, leaned against whatever telegraph poles inconvenienced their passage. By the time that, in 1946, the Thai government bought the Kwai railway from the Japanese for about $4,000,000, its track was on the way to being derelict.

Eventually it was decided to keep the railway going only as far up as a place called Nam Tok, some hundred miles above the bridge over the Kwai. Nam Tok was probably chosen as terminus because there are beautiful waterfalls nearby, waterfalls that are very famous in Thai history and legend. In 1961 the whole area was scheduled as a National Park; and now three trains a day carry villagers and tourists up to see the sights.

When I visited Nam Tok in 1966 I found that, just at the end of the embankment, the local villagers had set up a little shrine. On the altar table, in front of the little gilded image of the local tutelary deity, or *Chao Tee*, there were the usual propitiatory offerings, flowers, incense-sticks, fruit, sweets, candles, paper garlands; but in the place of honor were two rusty old iron spikes—the kind we had used to fasten the rails to the wooden ties.

There are also other and much vaster shrines near the Tha Makham bridge: an Allied cemetery for 6,982 Australian, British and Dutch prisoners of war; a Roman Catholic chapel just opposite; a Chinese burial ground for a few of the Asiatic forced-laborers of whom over a hundred thousand died along the Kwai; and a Japanese Memorial to all the casualties of the railway, including their own. All these shrines are much visited, as the fresh flowers and incense sticks testify: the Japanese Ambassador regularly lays a wreath at the Japanese Memorial; and there is an annual commemoration service in the Allied cemetery.

There are also other kinds of pilgrim. In Bangkok, "Sincere Travel Service," for instance, advertises

Tour No. 11 Daily: 7:30 a.m. Whole day soft drinks and lunch provided. The Bridge over River Kwai and the notorious 'Death Railway' of World War fame is at Karnburi. The tourists will definitely have the joy of their life when cruising along the *real River Kwai* on the way to pay a visit to the Chungkai War Memorial Cemetery, then follows a delicious lunch by the Bridge Over River Kwai and see the real train rolling across it. All inclusive rate: US $20.—per person minimum 2 persons.

The world-wide diffusion of Boulle's novel through the cinema, then, has left its mark on the Kwai. Outside the Karnburi cemetery there stands today a road sign which reads: "Bridge over the River Kwai 2.590 kilometers." It points to a real bridge; but it is only worth pointing to because of the bridge the whole world saw in the movie.

In a recent pictorial guide to Thailand there is an even more striking example of how the power of the myth is beginning to transform reality. The book gives a fine photograph of what is actually the Wang Pho viaduct along a gorge some fifty miles further up the line; but the caption reads "Bridge on the River Kwai." Some obscure need, disappointed by the failure of the real bridge *over* the river Kwai to live up to the beauty of the one in the movie, has relocated the home of the myth, and selected the most spectacular view along the railway as a more appropriate setting.

The Myth and the Reality

The myth, then, is established. What does it mean?

When *The Bridge on the River Kwai* was first televised it drew the largest TV audience ever recorded. Millions of people must have responded to it because—among other things—it expressed the same delusions as are responsible for much unreal political thinking. There was, as I've already said, the colonial myth—the odd notion that the ordinary people of South-East Asia instinctively love the white strangers who have come to their lands, and want to sacrifice themselves on their behalf. There was also the implication of the blowing-up of the bridge—however muddled we may be about our political aims, advanced high-explosive technology will always come out on top in the end. The Big Bang theory of war, of course, fitted in very nicely with the consoling illusion of a world of Friendly (and militarily backward) Natives.

The theory, and the illusion, have one fatal weakness: they clash with what Sartre calls *"la force des choses."*[1] What happened to the real bridge illustrates this very neatly.

In the summer of 1944 the new American long-range bombers, the B 29's, started flying over the Kwai, and bombing the bridges. To anyone who knows any military history, what happened was absolutely predictable. Quite a lot of people, mainly prisoners, were killed; but eventually the bombers got some direct hits, and two spans of the steel bridge fell into the river. While it was being repaired, the low wooden bridge was put back into use; and when that, too, was damaged, it was easily restored by the labor of the prisoners in the nearby camps. Japanese military supplies weren't delayed for a single day. If you can build a bridge, you can repair it; in the long run, bombing military targets is only significant if the target can later be captured and held.

The Allied command in Ceylon knew this very well. They bombed the Kwai railway then because their armies were advancing in Burma and preparing to attack Thailand: but this vital context is absent from the novel and the film. Actually there were also Allied commandos in the bridge area at the time: not to blow up the bridge, though, but to link up with the Thai resistance, and help liberate prison camps once the invasion started. Boulle probably

---

1. The force of things as they are.

knew this, since he called his commandos Force 316, whereas the real ones were Force 136. Still, Boulle's novel certainly undercuts the Big Bang theory, and one imagines that he found in its blind destructive credulity a folly that wasn't exclusively military. Since 1866, and Nobel's invention of dynamite, all kinds of individuals and social groups have attributed magical powers to dynamite; they've refused to see that the best you can expect from explosives is an explosion.

The Big Bang theory of war is rather like the colonial myth, and even the schoolboy dream of defying the adult world; all three are essentially expressions of what Freud called the childish delusion of the omnipotence of thought. The myth of the Kwai deeply reflects this delusion, and shapes it according to the particular values of contemporary culture.

Hollywood, the advertising industry, Existentialism, even the current counter-culture are alike in their acceptance or their exploitation of the delusion of the omnipotence of thought. From this come many of their other similarities: that they are ego-centered, romantic, anti-historical; that they all show a belief in rapid and absolute solutions of human problems. They are all, in the last analysis, institutional patterns based on the posture of anti-institutionalism.

These basic assumptions of the myth are perhaps most obvious in the kernel of the story, which the movie made much more recognizable as a universal fantasy, the schoolboy's perennial dream of defying the adult world. Young Nicholson cheeks the mean old headmaster, called Saito: he gets a terrible beating, but the other students kick up such a row about it that Saito just has to give in. Confrontation tactics win out; and Nicholson is carried back in triumph across the playground. In the end, of course, he becomes the best student-body president Kwai High ever had.

I don't know if anything like this—total rebellion combined with total acceptance—has ever occurred in any educational institution; but I am forced to report that nothing like it ever happened in the prison-camps along the Kwai. There, all our circumstances were hostile to individual fantasies; surviving meant accepting the intractable realities which surrounded us, and making sure that our fellow prisoners accepted them too.

No one would even guess from the novel or the film that there were any wholly intractable realities on the Kwai. Boulle proposes a simple syllogism: war is madness; war is fought by soldiers; therefore, soldiers are mad. It's a flattering notion, no doubt, to non-soldiers, but it happens not to be true; and it's really much too easy a way out to delude ourselves with the belief that wars and injustices are caused only by lunatics, by people who don't see things as we see them.

Neither the novel nor the film admits that certain rational distinctions remain important even under the most difficult or confusing circumstances. They seem instead to derive a peculiar satisfaction from asserting that in a world of madness the weakness of our collective life can find its salvation only in the strength of madmen. There is no need to insist on the authoritarian nature of this idea, but it does seem necessary to enquire why these last decades have created a myth which totally subverts the stubbornness of facts and of the human will to resist unreason.

The basic reason is presumably the widespread belief that institutions are at the same time immoral, ridiculous, and unreal, whereas individuals exist in a world whose circumstances are essentially tractable. A prisoner-of-war camp has at least one thing in common with our modern world in general: both offer a very limited range of practical choices. No wonder the public acclaimed a film where, under the most limiting circumstances imaginable, one solitary individual managed to do just what he planned to do. Of course his triumph depended on making everything else subservient to his fantasy; and if our circumstances on the Kwai had been equally pliable, there would have been no reason whatever for Toosey or anybody else to act as they did.

It's probably true that at the beginning of our captivity many of us thought that at last the moment had arrived for revolt, if not against the Japanese, at least against our own military discipline and anything else that interfered with our individual liberty. But then circumstances forced us to see that this would be suicidal. We were terribly short of food, clothes, and medicine; theft soon became a real threat to everyone; and so we had to organize our own police. At first it seemed too ridiculous, but not for long. When cholera broke out, for instance, whole camps of Asiatic laborers were wiped out, whereas in our own camps nearby, with an effective organization to make sure everyone used the latrines and ate or drank only what had been boiled, we often had no deaths, even though we had no vaccine.

In the myth, then, the actual circumstances of our experience on the Kwai were overwhelmed by the deep blindness of our culture both to the stubbornness of reality and to the continuities of history. It was surely this blindness which encouraged the public, in accepting the plausibility of Nicholson's triumph, to assert its belief in the combined wickedness, folly, and unreality of institutions—notably of those which were in conflict on the Kwai: the Japanese and their prisoners.

It isn't only on the walls of the Sorbonne that we can see the slogan "It is forbidden to forbid." It is written on all individuals at birth, in the form "It is forbidden to forbid me"; and this text has been adopted to their great profit by the movie and advertising industries: by Hollywood, in the version "You don't get rich by saying no to dreams," and by Madison Avenue in the version "Tell 'em they're suckers if they don't have everything they want."

The movie, incidentally, added one apt illustration of this slogan which had no basis whatever in Boulle or reality. No one wants to be a prisoner; you don't have to be; and so William Holden escapes, easily. On the Kwai, hundreds tried; most of them were killed; no one succeeded.

Among today's pilgrims to the present cemeteries on the Kwai, an increasing number come from the American forces in Thailand and Vietnam. When I leafed through the Visitors' Book, one entry caught my eye. A private from Apple Creek, Wisconsin, stationed at Da Nang, had been moved to write a protest that made all the other banal pieties look pale: "PEOPLE are STUPID."

Stupid, among other things, because they are mainly led by what they want to believe, not by what they know. It's easier to go along with the implication of the movie, and believe that a big bang—anywhere—will somehow end the world's confusion and our own fatigue. It would undoubtedly end it, but only in larger cemeteries for the victims of the last Great Joke.

Vietnam has been a painful lesson in the kinds of mythical thinking which *The Bridge on the River Kwai* both reflected and reinforced; we seem now to be slowly recovering from some of the political forms of the omnipotence-of-thought fantasy. Recently, I observed that the main audience reaction to the movie was ironical laughter.

If we can accept the notion that in all kinds of spheres some individual has to be responsible for the organization and continuity of human affairs, we should perhaps look again at the man without whom the myth would not have come into being. Along the Kwai, Colonel Toosey was almost universally recognized for what he was —a hero of the only kind we could afford then, and there. For he was led, not by what he wanted to believe, but by what he knew: he knew that the world would not do his bidding; that he could not beat the Japanese; that on the Kwai—even more obviously than at home—we were for the most part helpless prisoners of coercive circumstance. But he also knew that if things were as intractable as they looked, the outlook for the years ahead was hopeless: much death, and total demoralization, for the community he found himself in. The only thing worth working for was the possibility that tenacity and imagination could find a way by which the chances of decent survival could be increased. It was, no doubt, a very modest objective for so much work and restraint—two of Conrad's moral imperatives that Boulle didn't quote, incidentally; but in our circumstances then on the Kwai, the objective was quite enough to be getting on with; as it is here, now.

WILLIAM B. WILLCOX

The Excitement of Historical Research

Research in history, as in other fields, is hard work. It has its high moments, as teaching does, but exacts a much heavier price in drudgery and monotony. Why, then, are so many university teachers of history also researchers? Although they have many motives, the one that seems to me the strongest is curiosity. If the historian were asked why he wants to tackle a particular research problem, he might well answer in the often quoted words of a British mountaineer, when asked a generation ago why he wanted to tackle Everest: "because it's there." The problem is there, and its mere existence is a challenge. The historian, like the mountaineer, must of course decide which of many challenges will be worth his time and effort; and here he has little information to guide him. His decision, for all the hard thought that goes into it, rests essentially on hunch. He cannot predict the size of his problem, or the extent to which it will be soluble, or the value of solving it. But uncertainty is the spice of research. Exploration means reaching into the unknown, and the explorer who knows in advance what he will find is not an explorer.

An aspect of the past may appear from a distance picayune, and prove on investigation to be quite the contrary. Take for example the way in which work horses were harnessed in Merovingian times, a subject that scarcely appears calculated to fire the imagination. But appearance is deceptive. From earliest times until the Dark Ages, research disclosed, the power of the horse to pull a wagon or plough had been limited by his harness, which pressed upon his windpipe; the harder he pulled, the smaller his air supply and the less his strength. In the Merovingian period some unknown genius designed a new kind of harness that put the strain on the horse's shoulders; the animal was then free to breathe, and his efficiency went up. A mere rearrangement of leather straps augmented the basic source of power on the land, increased agricultural productivity, and so contributed to the slow beginnings of medieval civilization.

This example suggests a number of points about the nature of research. One, already mentioned, is that the importance of a problem cannot be predicted in advance. A second is that the problem is almost never tidily solved: some questions, such as the identity of the man who designed the new harness, remain unanswered for lack of evidence. A third is that the subject under investigation has no inherent limits, and must be limited arbitrarily. The investigator in this case establishes that increased horsepower was a factor in raising agricultural yield; his next logical step is to consider what other factors were at work, how they were interrelated, and for how long they operated—in other words to explore the whole economic history of the Dark and Middle Ages. This is too large a field for intensive research. Somewhere a line must be drawn, but where?

The line does not draw itself, for history is all of a piece. Studying a particular fragment of it out of context falsifies the nature of the fragment, and studying the entire context is impossible. Between the two extremes the researcher must find his own mean, by setting such limits as his interests and sense of feasibility suggest; but these limits are his own. They are not determined by any logic inherent in his problem, and they are likely to change as his investigation progresses and grows toward an end that he may never have anticipated. Take for illustration my own experience. It is with a narrow area of history, but one that I believe contains pitfalls and surprises that are not essentially different from those in many other areas.

The Clements Library of the University of Michigan has a large collection of manuscripts relating to the British side of the War of Independence. When I came to the University years ago, I knew next to nothing about the war; but the wealth of the Clements material, and the fact that no one else had explored it, were a challenge. From that mass of documents a subject or subjects for research would surely emerge. What form the research would eventually take was unimportant; all that mattered was to begin. I was like an archeologist who confronts a site, knowing approximately when it was inhabited but nothing more, and who cannot tell whether he will find disconnected fragments or the integrated complex of a city.

The more I learned about the British military effort in America, the subject with which most of the manuscripts deal, the more insistently one question obtruded itself: how did Britain manage to lose the war? She began it with many advantages—uncontested sea power, troops that were better than the American and generals that were at least no worse, a government that for all its muddle-headedness knew more than the Continental Congress did about how to conduct a war. Even French intervention in 1778 was not conclusive, and by the summer of 1781 the issue was still apparently hanging in the balance. Then the British suddenly blundered through to defeat at Yorktown, a failure that seemed to be anything but predetermined. What factors, then, brought it about?

The question in its entirety was too large, too ramified, for manuscript research. Such diverse factors were involved as American and French planning, the political weakness of Lord North's administration, the enormous logistic difficulties that confronted the bureaucrats of Whitehall; and these factors, along with many others of equal importance, I could not explore on my own. I had to depend on the often meager findings of those who had already explored them, and limit my search for original material to that which bore on the British war effort in America itself. This was both an arbitrary and a necessary limitation.

Even when the field was so narrowly circumscribed, however, it proved to be too broad for productive research. Such matters as the organization of the British army and navy, the details of tactics and logistics, and the administrative routine that engrossed the attention of headquarters should all have been grist for my mill. I knew nothing about them, however, and digging out the requisite information would have meant years of tedious work. I consequently restricted myself still further, to those factors that clearly affected the strategic planning of the British high command. I was no longer asking why Britain lost the war, but why her principal officers in America contributed as much to losing it as they patently did. Even though a definitive answer was impossible, the question was small enough to be explored. Such a partial study of the losers' side of the war could not be expected to produce dramatic results. It might, however, at least modify accepted views of the conflict as a whole.

Historical research rarely does more. In most cases it leaves the accepted views intact, but suggests their inadequacy by introducing alongside them some ingredient that they do not cover. Any subsequent interpretation of the events in question, if it is to include this new ingredient, must be a more complex synthesis than its predecessors, and hence may be expected to approximate more nearly the infinite complexity of the events themselves. The aim of historical research is not to upset the scholarly applecart, in short, but to go on adding to the number of apples in it, until someone is forced to design a bigger cart.

My own research soon produced a kind of apple that I had not anticipated. British strategic planning in America turned out to be not a single problem but two distinct problems, which had for their focus the two successive commanders in chief of the army, Sir William Howe (1775-78) and Sir Henry Clinton (1778-82). The two men were poles apart, but each in his way was an enigma; and the strategy of each was inseparable from his personality. To pursue my quest I had to become in some degree a biographer, and I had to decide which general to concentrate upon. The choice was obvious. Howe served for four years and then disappeared from the scene in 1778, and few of his papers have been preserved. Clinton served for seven years, as second in command under Howe and then as commander in chief, and few of his papers have been lost; they fill almost three hundred volumes in the Clements Library. A study of

Sir Henry would cover the whole British side of the war, and could be amply documented.

Another consideration strengthened the case for focusing on Clinton. I had already discovered that one of Britain's serious difficulties in America was the feuding that went on between her senior officers, and that as an instigator of feuds Clinton towered head and shoulders over all his fellows. The record of his altercations is fantastic, and their effect on the war was incalculable. When he was commander in chief, to take the major example, he was progressively on worse and worse terms with his opposite number in the navy and with his second in command, Lord Cornwallis, until by the summer of 1781 these two quarrels had paralyzed cooperation between the two services and disrupted the army command. Sir Henry was not solely to blame, for the officers with whom he tangled were no models of tact. But they did get on reasonably well with most other men most of the time, whereas he kept their animosity at fever pitch for months and even years on end. By doing so he helped to ruin his own career and lose the war for Britain.

Clinton thus became the focus of my inquiry. He offered an approach, in biographical and manageable terms, to the otherwise unwieldy problem of why the British failed. A biography, furthermore, might do more than merely exhume an obscure general: it could be a case study of personality as a causal factor in history. For Sir Henry was in himself a cause of Britain's defeat—not the sole or even the major cause, but one that was significant, that had not been seriously studied before, and for which the evidence was voluminous. It is obvious that great men, when they have power in moments of crisis, help to mold events. It is perhaps less obvious that in the same circumstances little men do the same, for the very reason that they are little: they fail to meet the demands that the crisis makes upon them, and their failure contributes to the outcome. Louis XVI's shortcomings, for example, affected the course of the French Revolution. Clinton's shortcomings affected the course of the American, in less important but equally real ways; and I set myself to define and evaluate those ways as best I could.

Although my field of inquiry was established and its limits apparently set, I soon discovered that research can develop as unpredictably as if it had a life of its own. Clinton's role in the war could not be defined, much less evaluated, without a clear understanding of why he behaved as he did; and some significant aspects of his behavior proved to be beyond my comprehension. His inveterate feuding, which time after time defeated his own best interests as well as those of the service, was only one case in point. Another was his ambivalence about sticking to his post: for more than four years he tried unsuccessfully to resign; and then, when he had permission and good reason to quit, he clung to the command as if his life depended on it—and at the same time refused to exert the authority that it gave him. He was the rationalist *par excellence* in some areas, such as military planning; in others he behaved with an irrationality that I could not understand.

These contrasting sides of his character came out in his handling of evidence. He left behind him lengthy memoirs of his campaigns, the only general on either side who did. In most of what he wrote he adhered scrupulously to the facts, insofar as they can be established from other sources; but at rare moments he took off into fantasy. The most striking example has to do with the British disaster at Yorktown. In his account of that campaign, written not long afterward and intended for publication, Sir Henry asserted that the government had ordered him not to interfere with Lord Cornwallis, but to support the Earl and his army in Virginia. To prove this assertion Clinton cited the specific words of the command that he said he had received from the King's Minister in Whitehall. Here was what looked like established fact, and for years historians accepted it as such.

Sir Henry's behavior during the actual campaign, however, suggested that he had received no such order. Until the eve of Yorktown he tried to interfere in Virginia, by withdrawing troops from there to New York; and neither his words nor his actions indicated that he was flouting a royal command. Where, furthermore, was the original command to be found? It was not in any letter from the Minister that Clinton kept among his papers (and this letter, of all others, he might have been expected to keep), or in the Minister's copies of his outgoing dispatches. This negative discovery posed a nice question: when is a fact in history not a fact? The Minister *may* have issued the order, which *may* be in a letter that is not extant or has not yet come to light; no amount of historical research can prove that a document never existed, and that a quotation from that document is false. But in this case the probability is overwhelming that Clinton, looking back on the campaign, manufactured out of whole cloth a command from his King.

Sir Henry, if so, was not merely misremembering the past, as other men have done, in a way that cleared him of blame for what had happened; he was introducing into the record a specific and cardinal charge against the government. He was also planning to publish the charge at a time when those whom he accused were still alive to refute him. If the accusation was false, in other words, he was planning to gamble his reputation on a foolishly palpable lie. Everything else that I knew of the man convinced me that he was neither a gambler nor a fool nor a liar. The only tenable explanation, therefore, was that he believed what he said—and what all the evidence indicated was untrue. Here was an impasse: either I was deceived in thinking that Sir Henry had fabricated his claim, or in some way that defied analysis he had deceived himself into thinking that his fabrication was fact.

The second alternative seemed much the more likely. I had already observed in Clinton a habit of self-deception, and I assumed that this episode was an extreme example of it. He was patently unaware that his quarrels, and his refusal to give up or exert the authority of his position, defeated his own best interests; he asserted instead that he had sound reason for what I was convinced was unreasonable conduct, just as he believed that he had received what I was convinced was a nonexistent royal command. His conscious self seemed to have put out a smoke screen of rationalization, behind which he acted from motives so far below consciousness that he could not even discern them, let alone understand them.

I could dimly discern, but was no more able to understand than he had been, for the historian is trained to hunt for motivation within the broad limits of the rational. He assumes that men acted from what by his as well as their lights was rational cause, and that if he has sufficient information he can formulate a highly probable conjecture about what the cause was. His psychological insight amounts to the application of common sense, and he is helpless when the men with whom he is dealing did not behave sensibly. He is not equipped to make even a conjecture about motives that were irrational and hence unconscious. If he does conjecture, with nothing to go on, he is indulging in mere guesswork. If instead he labels behavior as odd or aberrant and leaves it at that, he is confessing failure, because the whole purpose of this kind of research is to uncover the wellsprings of conduct.

The historical discipline as applied to biography has inherent limitations, which I was discovering by bumping into them. Just when my inquiry was far enough advanced to be exciting, it was unexpectedly demanding analytic tools that I could not provide. To continue the quest I had to have help, and I had the great good fortune to get it from Professor Frederick Wyatt, chief of the Psychological Clinic of the University of Michigan, a colleague with psychoanalytic training and a humanist's interest in history. We collaborated for a number of years on the puzzle of Clinton's behavior, in an effort to discover whether teamwork between our two disciplines could produce a fuller understanding of an historical figure than either discipline could produce alone.

We hoped to arrive at a theory of Clinton's personality that was plausible by our different canons and broad enough to include the irrational as well as rational aspects of his conduct. Our evidence would not, we knew, permit us to build a theory that was not merely plausible but demonstrable; evidence in history, as in psychotherapy, is almost never so obliging. The most we could expect was to resolve the apparent contradictions in the evidence we had, by bringing all of it together into a single, consistent pattern of behavior. This pattern would be our theory, and it would "solve" the problem in the sense that it would establish a relationship between what had seemed to be disparate sides of Sir Henry's character.

Our methodological difficulties were considerable, and for me they were educational. My colleague, like any psychotherapist, wanted to probe into Clinton's childhood, a subject about which the manuscripts were almost silent. The little that they did tell us, Wyatt insisted, should be compared with the norms of child-rearing in aristocratic families of the time; what were those norms? Again I did not know, or know where to find out; I was learning how fragmentary is a specialist's information about his period. We were forced to abandon this line of inquiry and try another—to examine the adult Clinton, about whom we had abundant information, in search of grounds for inference about Clinton the child.

Here we made progress. Sir Henry as a middle-aged general manifested—in his quarreling, his refusal to resign, his illusion that the government had been to blame for Yorktown—a form of behavior that is familiar to the modern clinical psychologist. It was the behavior now recognized as typical of the man who has never outgrown his childhood conflict with his parents, particularly with his father. The unresolved conflict endures: the child as adult longs to exercise paternal authority himself, and at the same time dreads to exercise it because he is trespassing on his father's preserve. Sir Henry showed the symptoms of this conflict so clearly and fully that we did not need to know the childhood roots of the conflict itself; we could assume their existence. What mattered to us was not the cause but the result—the consistency with which the adult Clinton continued to act out his difficulties with parents who by then had long been dead. To certain situations he responded, not sensibly, but with an almost predictable regularity; and his way of responding indicated an ambivalence that he could neither recognize nor control.

The consistency provided us with a pattern, or theory, that satisfied the requirements with which we had begun. How it satisfied them cannot be explained in brief compass, but we found that virtually all the irrational aspects of Sir Henry's behavior could be related to his basic internal struggle about exercising authority. Elements in his character that had hitherto seemed to me irreconcilable, because some were highly effective and others were self-defeating, fitted together as parts of a whole; and a man who had looked like a bundle of anomalies became a coherent person. We do not yet claim to have resolved every contradiction, to know Sir

Henry through and through; such a claim would be ridiculous. But we do believe that he has become intelligible enough to us to permit an evaluation of the role he played.

This has been a long illustration, and what does it illustrate? In the first place, that historical research is fluid, especially in its early stages. The inquirer begins with unknown material and no idea of what will come out of it. Even when some salient questions emerge to provide him a focus, it is not yet precise; considerations of time and his own interests, as much as of the material itself, determine how his problem develops. After it seems to have taken final shape (as when I decided on a biographical study of Clinton), new and unexpected questions can change the shape again. This evolutionary process may not come to an end of itself; and in that case the researcher, unless he wants to spend his life on one subject, must choose the moment for calling a halt.

My experience illustrates, in the second place, the problem of selecting evidence. On the one hand no project, however ambitiously designed, can embrace all the available and relevant data; arbitrary limits must be set, and even within them much relevant material receives only cursory treatment. On the other hand, once these limits are demarcated, no amount of digging will unearth all the data that the researcher wants; some areas about which he is curious, such as Clinton's childhood, remain obscure and conjectural. Research involves a series of choices, to emphasize this and neglect that, to go on digging or to stop; and few of the choices are logically satisfying. The specialist is not, as the old cliché would have it, one who learns more and more about less and less. He is one who is able to work out his own criteria for finishing a particular job, and to make his choices accordingly.

I have tried to illustrate, in the third place, the elusive quality of evidence. Historical "facts" are not facts in the sense that they can be empirically verified; they are merely the testimony of one or more observers about what happened. All testimony is suspect, because it depends upon whether the person giving it was in a position to know, whether he was calm or intelligent or objective enough to report accurately, and so on. Some "facts" such as dates—when the Declaration of Independence was signed, or when the firing stopped at Yorktown—can be established beyond reasonable doubt because many observers agree. But these are the historian's rudimentary data, which are about as important to him as the multiplication table is to a mathematician. The more significant data are those that bear on what people did and why they did it, and here the difficulties arise.

Even what people did can rarely be determined with complete assurance. The famous nineteenth-century German historian, Ranke, believed that the past can be reconstructed as it actually was, *wie es eigentlich gewesen.* Most historians today would disagree, because they recognize that they will never know enough, however profuse their evidence. A case in point is Clinton's role in the Yorktown campaign. We know a great deal about it, but we cannot know for sure whether the government curtailed his authority and therefore his responsibility. The evidence is *almost* conclusive. Yet, as long as it is not entirely so, a marginal chance remains that this fragment of the past was in actual fact quite different from what we think it was.

When the historian moves from considering people's actions to considering their motives for acting, he must become even more tentative. The reason lies not only in the nature of his evidence but also in human nature; for about motivation, of the living as much as of the dead, opinions always differ. Listen to a group of reporters today discussing what impels President Johnson or General de Gaulle to a given line of action, and you will hear as many interpretations as there are interpreters; or try to explain precisely why a friend reached an important decision, and see how many of his other friends will agree with you. When our contemporaries' reasons for acting as they do are controversial, sometimes even mysterious, to those about them, it would be surprising if the motives of historical figures were easier to penetrate.

The best evidence about the nature of motivation in a man long dead is what was said about him at the time. Most of what was said was not written down, and much of what was written down has not survived; mere chance selects for the historian a small fraction of the original evidence, and with this fraction he must work. It consists in comments, which are sure to be hard to interpret, on the behavior of the man in question. Comments that he made on himself are valuable, but have a built-in bias. Contemporaries' comments are also biased, and in conflicting ways: no two observers, in the past as in the present, who look at the same person see the same person. Clinton, for instance, changes slightly when he is viewed through the eyes of each of his few friends and admirers, and greatly when viewed through those of his numerous enemies; the motives that these men perceived in him run the gamut from whole-souled concentration on winning the war to pride, vanity, and a love for the fleshpots of power. The historian must move cautiously through testimony that is colored by the likes and dislikes of those who created it, and must weigh and evaluate, select and discard, to reach an opinion of his own. He can at most hope that that opinion, though fallible, will be better informed and more dispassionate than those of the men who provide him with his data.

All this may sound as if historical research were merely a system of guesswork, which might be defined, like the famous definition of logic, as "an organized method of going wrong with confidence."

There is, however, another side to the coin. If the historian does not know the truth about the past—and he certainly does not—he should have a better approximation of the truth than contemporaries had. They were imprisoned in their time as we are in ours, and they could not fully grasp the significance of what was happening before their eyes; they were also imprisoned in space, and could not grasp the significance of distant events. Take Clinton for illustration. He never spoke of the American Revolution because he did not know that there was one; he could not see the rebellion as revolutionary. Neither could he see the far-away troubles in Whitehall that impeded the war effort; he believed that the government was willfully neglecting him. The historian does not wear such blinders but has a broad perspective, and it reveals to him developments in time and space that were hidden from the men with whom he is dealing. He can never be entirely sure of what they did, let alone of why they did it; yet he can have a deeper understanding than they had.

Understanding, which comes in part from the historian's remoteness in time, comes also from the nature of his concern with the past. That concern is a blend of involvement and detachment, and the first is harder to achieve than the second. Involvement means using his imagination to become engaged with the people he is studying, so that as far as he can he sees through their eyes and views their controversies as they viewed them. He rarely takes sides, if only because he sees both sides at once; but the issues and the protagonists are almost as real to him as those of his own day. Unless he can achieve this feat of imagination, can enter into his period even while he is remote from it, his perspective upon it may be worse than useless. Suppose, for instance, that he is utterly incapable of imagining himself into another era; he must then impose upon it, *faute de mieux*, the presuppositions, values, and standards of judgment of his own society. These are certain to be inapplicable, and any conclusions to which they lead him are certain to be askew.

Detachment without involvement, in such an extreme case, leads the historian to distort the past by fitting it to the measure of his present, much as Procrustes distorted guests by fitting them to the measure of his bed. But involvement without detachment can also lead to distortion, although of a different kind; and here the biographer is in particular danger. No man, the saying goes, is a hero to his valet; neither should any man be a hero to his biographer, who ought to know him as well as the valet does. The man's foibles and complexities, virtues and shortcomings, should become so familiar to the biographer that he sees his subject not primarily as great or small but as alive, a person in his own right. When a biographer succumbs instead to hero-worship (or, more rarely, the inverted form that might be called villain-worship), his involvement has triumphed over his detachment. Where he should have assessed the evidence in its entirety, with all its shadings from white to black, he has selected in a way to bring out only the whites or blacks; and the resultant picture has the unreality of the oversimplified. This is the art of the cartoonist, not of the historian.

Research is not the only way to discover how to blend detachment with involvement; a few historians understand their discipline by instinct. Most, however, acquire understanding through research. They learn that they cannot work their way laboriously into a period without discarding many of their twentieth-century preconceptions and modifying the others. The more ambiguities and pitfalls they find in their evidence, the more gaps in their knowledge of what they thought were familiar events, the more complexities in the process of causation, the safer they are from the temptation to treat the past in Procrustean fashion. They remain objective, but experience teaches them to be cautious and tentative in their conclusions. The thundering ultimates of a Spengler or a Toynbee are not for them.

Exploring the past is a never-ending activity. The historian in each generation hunts for new evidence and reinterprets existing evidence, to provide fresh details and a fresh perspective. However stimulating the perspective may be at the moment; it will not remain indefinitely fresh; it is based on incomplete and conflicting data, and is likely to contain at most a kernel of lasting value. Few of the questions that the data raise can be settled once and for all, either because the evidence is lacking or because the questions are too large in their implications. Any segment of history, no matter how narrowly defined in time and space, is set in a context that is limitless and therefore cannot be entirely known. Although each researcher hopes to know a little more of it, to throw a little more light on the mystery of why a particular set of men acted as they did, he realizes that the mystery will remain, and that for all his efforts he will find only a partial approximation of truth.

Yet he cannot let the mystery alone, and involvement with it brings its own reward. His research may be narrow in scope, transient in value, riddled with unanswerable questions; it is still inherently exciting. It has no scale: any problem offers as sure an approach as any other to the underlying historical process, and demands the researcher's full powers of analysis and empathy. In his analytic function he is the rationalist, perhaps even the scientist. In his empathic function he is the artist, and it is research as art that redeems the drudgery of data-gathering.

This form of art is as exigent as any other. It requires its practitioner to enter into the past, to meet people who are very much alive yet different from him in ways that he can imperfectly apprehend, to view them objectively for what they were, and then to portray them in all their vitality. This is so large an assignment that his reach, he knows, will exceed his grasp; and why should it not? Just as the subject matter of research fascinates him because he will never be able to do it full justice, so does the art of research. The requirements of that art are too stringent for his comfort: they deny him the illusion that he has nothing more to learn, and keep him always reaching for what he cannot quite grasp. His own particular creativity is therefore at full stretch, and that is perhaps as near to pure joy as an academic can come.

THOMAS BABINGTON MACAULAY

History

To write history respectably—that is, to abbreviate dispatches, and make extracts from speeches, to intersperse in due proportion epithets of praise and abhorrence, to draw up antithetical characters of great men, setting forth how many contradictory virtues and vices they united, and abounding in *withs* and *withouts*—all this is very easy. But to be a really great historian is perhaps the rarest of intellectual distinctions. Many scientific works are, in their kind, absolutely perfect. There are poems which we would be inclined to designate as faultless, or as disfigured only by blemishes which pass unnoticed in the general blaze of excellence. There are speeches, some speeches of Demosthenes particularly, in which it would be impossible to alter a word without altering it for the worse. But we are acquainted with no history which approaches to our notion of what a history ought to be—with no history which does not widely depart, either on the right hand or on the left, from the exact line.

The cause may easily be assigned. This province of literature is a debatable land. It lies on the confines of two distinct territories. It is under the jurisdiction of two hostile powers; and, like other districts similarly situated, it is ill-defined, ill-cultivated, and ill-regulated. Instead of being equally shared between its two rulers, the Reason and the Imagination, it falls alternately under the sole and absolute dominion of each. It is sometimes fiction. It is sometimes theory.

History, it has been said, is philosophy teaching by examples. Unhappily, what the philosophy gains in soundness and depth the examples generally lose in vividness. A perfect historian must possess an imagination sufficiently powerful to make his narrative affecting and picturesque. Yet he must control it so absolutely as to content himself with the materials which he finds, and to refrain from supplying deficiences by additions of his own. He must be a profound

and ingenious reasoner. Yet he must possess sufficient self-command
to abstain from casting his facts in the mold of his hypothesis. Those
who can justly estimate these almost insuperable difficulties will not
think it strange that every writer should have failed, either in the
narrative or in the speculative department of history.

CICELY V. WEDGWOOD
Literature and the Historian

The modern historian is compelled by all the influences of the
time to approach literature with a certain diffidence. On the one
side he hears the echoes of those warnings uttered by scholars
against the delusions of fine writing and the cultivation of history as
an art. He may uneasily recall the statement of that great and
human scholar J. B. Bury that 'history is a science, neither more nor
less,' or the dictum of Professor York Powell in his inaugural lecture
at Oxford in the 1890's that 'style has no more to do with history
than it has with law or astronomy.'

On the other side he may feel the silent reservations of his fellow
writers, the poets, the novelists, the literary critics, and sometimes
of the public. For history, by comparison, appears uncreative, the
fruit rather of study than of inspiration. Dr. Johnson declared that
'in historical composition all the greatest powers of the human
mind are quiescent . . . there is no exercise of invention. Imagination is not required in any high degree.'

The historian can, however, take heart from the undeniable fact
that history had a secure place among the muses from classical
antiquity, which was not seriously questioned until after the scientific revolution of the seventeenth and eighteenth centuries: a revolution which, in western Europe, so thoroughly shook up men's
ideas and values that equilibrium has never fully been regained.

If he has the good fortune to write in English he can further seek
reassurance in contemplating that long alliance between history and
literature which has been, and still is, one of the glories of the English-speaking peoples. The tradition stretches back five centuries
past Gibbon, Clarendon, Bacon, Raleigh, to the Berners translation
of Froissart: it has been upheld and renewed in the twentieth century on both sides of the Atlantic.

It is a tradition distinguished by writing of many different kinds
—vivid narrative and lucid exposition, dramatic projection of character, or reflective analysis. The English language has many moods
and the historian makes use of them all.

I should like to call a few passages to mind, but with this warning—that of all prose, historical prose lends itself least well to this

process of selection. History being the record of human action is a richly variegated material, and it is not easy to give a true impression of the stuff by snipping off an inch or two for a pattern.

Here none the less are some passages. First a piece of direct narrative from Berners's translation of Froissart describing Wat Tyler's march on London[1]—surely one of the best accounts of a popular rising every written, so fearful in its straight simplicity.

"In the morning on Corpus Christi day, King Richard heard mass in the Tower of London, and all his lords, and then he took his barge with the Earl of Salisbury, the Earl of Warwick, the Earl of Oxford and certain knights, and so rowed down along the Thames to Rotherhithe whereas was descended down the hill a ten thousand men to see the King and to speak with him. And when they saw the King's barge coming they began to shout and make such a cry, as though all the devils of hell had been among them . . . And when the King and his lords saw the demeanour of the people, the best assured of them were in dread; and so the King was counselled by his barons not to take any landing there but so rowed up and down the river. And the King demanded of them what they would, and said how he was come thither to speak with them, and they said all with one voice: 'We would that you should come a-land and then we shall show you what we lack.' Then the Earl of Salisbury answered for the King and said: 'Sirs, ye be not in such order or array that the King ought to speak with you.' And then the King was counselled to return again to the Tower of London and so he did.

"And when these people saw that, they were inflamed with ire and returned to the hill where the great band was, and there showed them what answer they had and how the King was returned to the Tower of London. Then they cried all with one voice, 'Let us go to London', and so they took their way thither; and in their going they beat down abbeys, and houses of advocates and men of the court, and so came into the suburbs of London which were greater and fair and there beat down diverse fair houses . . . There were many within the city of their accord, and so they drew together and said 'Why do we not let these good people enter into the city? They are our fellows, and that they do is for us.' So therewith the gates were opened and then these people entered into the city and went into houses and sat down to eat and drink. They desired nothing but it was incontinent brought to them, for every man was ready to make them good cheer and to give them meat and drink to appease them."

Now, to leap the centuries, and try a different manner and a different subject, here is Macaulay's dramatic portrait of Thomas Wentworth, Earl of Strafford:[2]

"But Wentworth—whoever names him without thinking of those harshly dark features, ennobled by their expression into more than the majesty of an antique Jupiter; of that brow, that eye, that cheek, that lip wherein, as in a chronicle, are written the events of many stormy and disastrous years, high enterprise accomplished, frightful dangers braved, power unsparingly exercised, suffering unshrinkingly borne; of that fixed look,

---

1. Tyler led a peasant rebellion in 1381; the march on London occurred in June of that year.

2. Chief advisor to King Charles I of England from 1637 to 1640.

so full of severity, of mournful anxiety, of deep thought, of dauntless resolution, which seems at once to forbode and to defy a terrible fate, as it lowers on us from the canvas of Van Dyck? ...

"He was the first Englishman to whom a peerage was a sacrament of infamy, a baptism into the communion of corruption. As he was the earliest of that hateful list, so was he also by far the greatest; eloquent, sagacious, adventurous, intrepid, ready of invention, immutable of purpose, in every talent which exalts or destroys nations pre-eminent, the lost Archangel, the Satan of the Apostasy ..."

Differences in style reveal differences in temperament; after the generous heat of Macaulay the cool irony of Edward Gibbon:

"It is a very honourable circumstance for the morals of the primitive Christians, that even their faults, or rather errors, were derived from an excess of virtue. The bishops and doctors of the Church, whose evidence attests, and whose authority might influence, the professions, the principles, and even the practice of their contemporaries, had studied the scripture with less skill than devotion and they often received, in the most literal sense, those rigid precepts of Christ and the apostles to which the prudence of succeeding commentators has applied a looser and more figurative mode of interpretation. Ambitious to exalt the perfection of the gospel above the wisdom of philosophy, the zealous fathers have carried the duties of self mortification, of purity and of patience, to a height which it is scarcely possible to attain, and much less to preserve in our present state of weakness and corruption. A doctrine so extraordinary and so sublime must inevitably command the veneration of the people; but it was ill calculated to obtain the suffrage of those worldly philosophers who, in the conduct of this transitory life, consult only the feelings of nature and the interest of society."

To come to the present century, here is G. M. Trevelyan in the mature manner of his social history, which never approaches the cynicism of Gibbon. He is describing the manners of the early eighteenth century:

"It was the privilege of all gentlemen, from a Duke downwards, to wear swords, and to murder one another by rule. As soon as men were well drunk of an evening they were apt to quarrel, and as soon as they quarrelled they were apt to draw their swords in the room, and if manslaughter was not committed on the spot, to adjourn to the garden behind the house, and fight it out that night with hot blood and unsteady hand. If the company were not wearing swords, the quarrel might be slept upon and forgotten or arranged in the sober morning. The wearing of swords, though usual in London, as being like the full-bottomed wig a part of full dress, was fortunately not common in the depths of the country among the uncourtly but goodnatured rural squires, whose bark was often worse than their bite. And even at Bath, Beau Nash employed his despotic power to compel the fashionable world to lay aside their swords when they entered his domain: in this he did as good service to the community as in teaching the country bumpkins to discard their top boots and coarse language at the evening assemblies and dances. During his long supremacy as Master of the Ceremonies, nearly covering the reigns of Anne and the first two Georges, Nash did perhaps as much as any other person even in the Eighteenth Century to civilize the neglected manners of mankind."

Last of all, here is another portrait in the grand manner, from a living writer:

"There now appeared upon the ravaged scene an Angel of Deliverance, the noblest patriot of France, the most splendid of her heroes, the most beloved of her saints, the most inspiring of all her memories, the peasant Maid, the ever shining, ever glorious Joan of Arc. In the poor remote hamlet of Domremy, on the fringe of the Vosges Forest, she served at the inn. She rode the horses of travellers, bare back, to water. She wandered on Sundays into the woods, where there were shrines and a legend that some day from these oaks would arise one to save France. In the fields where she tended her sheep the saints of God, who grieved for France, rose before her in visions. St. Michael himself appointed her, by right divine, to command the armies of liberation. Joan shrank at first from the awful duty, but when he returned attended by St. Margaret and St. Catherine, patronesses of the village church, she obeyed their command. There welled in the heart of the Maid a pity for the realm of France, sublime, perhaps miraculous, certainly invincible . . ."

That of course, is from Sir Winston Churchill's *History of the English-Speaking Peoples*.

The literary achievement is splendid, but in spite of all, the chill of scholarly criticism strikes to the bone. It cannot be denied that the literary historians are open to criticism for failures of perception and failures of scholarship which can at times be traced directly to their literary technique. Macaulay's denunciation of Strafford is noble in sound and volume, inspired in its range of images. But, by striking off so splendid a phrase as 'the Satan of the Apostasy', Macaulay introduced a Miltonic grandeur into our vision of the man and the epoch, which makes it hard to bring the mind down again to the sober and pedestrian level on which alone historical inquiry can be safely pursued, and just estimates made of persons and things.

I would not willingly forgo Macaulay's splendid phrase, but a great power over words and images can and does intoxicate, and the historian has chosen a branch of literature in which the utmost sobriety is usually advisable. It is not quite always advisable because there is the delicate and subtle problem of historic imagination: the power to move, or to give the impression of moving, from one epoch into another, the capacity to feel and think the thoughts of another time. This is a gift of literary imagination, and at its highest it sometimes resembles a state, if not of intoxication, then of possession. Thomas Carlyle is more frequently and more strenuously possessed by this kind of imagination than any other British historian. He ceases to be a recorder of the scene and becomes himself an actor, or more truly a disembodied spirit, restlessly moving from the mind of one character to another. He makes nothing of travelling two hundred years on the thunderclouds of his imagination to give a helping hand to Cromwell and his men at the Battle of Dunbar.[3]

"The night is wild and wet . . . the Harvest Moon wades deep among clouds of sleet and hail. Whoever has a heart for prayer, let him pray now, for the wrestle of death is at hand. Pray,—and withal keep his powder dry! And be ready for extremities, and quit himself like a man! . . . the hoarse sea moans bodeful, swinging low and heavy against those whinstone bays; the sea and the tempests are abroad, all else asleep but we,— and there is ONE that rides on the wings of the wind.

"About four o'clock comes order to my pudding headed Yorkshire friend, that his regiment must mount and march straightway . . . Major Hodgson riding along heard, he says, 'a Cornet praying in the night'; a company of poor men, I think, making worship there, under the void Heaven, before battle joined; Major Hodgson turned aside to listen for a minute and worship and pray along with them; haply his last prayer on Earth, as it might prove to be. But no . . . the Heavens in their mercy I think have opened us a way of deliverance!—The Moon gleams out, hard and blue, riding among hail clouds; and over St. Abb's Head, a streak of dawn is rising . . . The Scots too . . . are awake; thinking to surprise us; there is their trumpet sounding, we heard it once; and Lambert who was to lead the attack is not here. The Lord General is impatient; behold Lambert at last! The trumpets peal, shattering with fierce clangour Night's silence; the cannons awaken along all the line: 'The Lord of Hosts! The Lord of Hosts!' On, my brave ones, on!'"

It is difficult to be sure whether the Lord General, who leads these praying troops to victory at the first streak of dawn after a stormy night, is in truth Oliver Cromwell, or a renegade Scot called Thomas Carlyle. The imaginative leap is complete. Carlyle has written himself and thought himself into the very heart of the scene. Without this extraordinary achievement of personal projection, English history as well as English literature would be the poorer for what is, by and large, a masterly interpretation of the Puritan mind in general and of Oliver Cromwell in particular.

But such imaginative fervour can be very unsafe; the slightest slip in scholarship makes it at once appear ridiculous. It is the measure of Carlyle's greatness that, although he did make mistakes, he emerges none the less as one of the great masters. But the dangers of his method, in these days of more searching scholarship, are apparent. The writer who trusts too deeply in his imaginative powers to recreate the past falls into an error as dangerous and more ridiculous than the writer who resists the imaginative impulse altogether.

Exuberance of imagination, whether about words or phrases or the interpretation of the past, can betray the writer into exaggerations and errors when he is working within the strict limits of history. On the other hand, the measured and restricted manner, the

3. Cromwell routed a Scottish army at Dunbar in September 1650.

urbane, well-bred style of Edward Gibbon for instance, is not fitted to illuminate the darker or the higher reaches of the human spirit or to give more than a brilliant surface account of their manifestations. The *Decline and Fall*[4] is the greatest masterpiece of historical writing in the English language; there are moments at which that clear, emphatic, and witty style stands between the author and the full interpretation of his subject. Gibbon's style, which reflects his mind, forces him to make light of things too complicated and too illogical or too sublime to be accommodated in the balanced framework of his sentences. But much of history, and much of human thought, is complicated and illogical, and some of it is sublime.

There is no literary style which may not at some point add to or take away something from the ascertainable outline of truth, which it is the task of scholarship to excavate and reestablish. The ability to light upon a splendid phrase, the imaginative power to breathe life into the names and actions of people long dead, may be misleading in one way; the clear, logical, and moderated manner, the epigrammatic, the concise, and the witty, may be as misleading in another.

It was partly, though not entirely, because the literary historians could sometimes be shown to have sacrificed the demands of scholarship to the demands of style that an open antagonism to literary treatment grew up among historical scholars in the later nineteenth century. Hence the dictum that style has no more to do with history than with law or astronomy. A gentler compromise was reached by Sir Charles Firth when he argued that the clear presentation of history is a necessary part of the historian's work; some art, he declared, was essential to this task and should be cultivated. History could not stand alone as a pure science. This point of view, modified by the temperamental leanings of individuals towards science or towards art, is now fairly generally held by academic historians.

The relationship of science to art in history is admitted; but the exact nature of that relationship remains undefined and possibly indefinable. Is literature the constant helpmeet and partner of scholarship, or is it the poor relation asked down for a few days once a year to assist at some necessary social occasion and help to hand round the drinks? Is the literary presentation of his work something which only begins to concern the historian when the work of scholarship is done, or is it something always present to his mind?

This problem can best be answered by negative arguments. The reaction against literature was mistaken and harmful, but it was not unreasonable or causeless. The great popular success of certain works of history which were, and are, also works of literature created a popular demand for history which was satisfied—had to be

---

4. *The Decline and Fall of the Roman Empire.*

satisfied, the laws of supply and demand being what they are—by writers and historians of lesser value than those who had created the demand. The genius of a Macaulay, the vision of a J. R. Green are not given to everyone. Moreover it is a commonplace in all the arts, not in literature alone, that the style of a master, copied, diffused, ultimately parodied by imitators, can damage the reputation of the master and the art in question. Macaulay was well aware of this: 'My manner, is I think, and the world thinks, on the whole a good one,' he wrote, 'but it is very near to a bad manner indeed, and those characteristics of my style which are most easily copied are the most questionable.' The same could be said of Gibbon, whose manner, badly imitated, had a stultifying effect on English histori- cal style for generations. In our own time, in the narrower field of biography, the imitators of Lytton Strachey managed by their smart-aleck antics to obscure for a long decade what was really valu- able in the new approach to biography.

When bad popular work came flooding in to fill the demand created by good work it was not remarkable that the more austere and conscientious historians revolted against the popular treatment of history, and came not to distinguish very clearly between popular history and literary history. The revolt against the literary treatment of history was really a revolt against popularization, in which writers of vision and power were indiscriminately condemned, along with their inferior imitators.

Furthermore, history has followed the same curve during the last two to three generations as many other branches of knowledge. First a great increase in available information and evidence led to the development of new and more precise techniques of research. Then technical advances and ever-widening fields of inquiry led to over- confidence in man's capacity to attain exact knowledge. This was followed by the dismaying discovery that men know less by knowing more. A profusion of evidence means conflicting evidence. By and large, over the whole field, doubt and uncertainty increase with the increase of information. The flow and meaning of events, the rela- tion of cause to effect are no longer clear. Historians have dug out information about the structure of society or its economic founda- tions, the physical conditions or the spiritual preoccupations of our forefathers, which modify or revolutionize, or merely confuse, the once accepted versions of the past. Scholars of great perception and integrity disagree fundamentally on the construction to be put on the always increasing evidence available. What we once thought was progress, we are now constrained to regard as regress. In the interpretation of certain epochs, and indeed in our attitude to the whole story of man, we scarcely know any more if we are coming or going. When a philosopher historian of the scope and vision of Pro- fessor Toynbee arises to suggest an overall pattern, the specialist scholars, who are writhing like Laocoon in the toils of their more detailed research, wrench themselves free of their devouring doubts for just long enough to shoot him as full of arrows as Saint Sebastian.[5]

Historical thinking is slowly and painfully going through very much the same process of questioning, destruction, and ultimate enlightenment that fell upon the natural sciences three hundred years ago. The old certainties are gone, the new are uncreated.

When so much is to be done and so much seems at stake—for we all have to believe that our own particular interest is of great importance to the world—is it to be wondered at that the mere creation of literature, this apparently irrelevant additional element in the historian's task, should seem of lesser importance to the research student, and the exact relationship of literature to history be left undefined?

It is only fair to the historian of today to remember that he thinks and works against this background of shifting values, of fluid knowledge and fluid opinions. This is very different from the atmosphere of more definite opinions, more rigid moral standards, and much more limited historical knowledge against which the classics of literary history were produced in the past.

The reaction against literary history was not causeless. Scholars had some grounds for thinking that historians with a strong literary gift were betrayed at times into sacrificing exactitude of statement to beauty of language, to minimizing or enhancing the historic picture by the qualities of individual style.

This is true. But the converse is not true. The historian who cultivates literary style can make mistakes, but there is no opposite guarantee that the historian with no literary style will make none. That is the great fallacy. Good writing is no guarantee of good scholarship; but neither is bad writing. The austere instinct which prompted the historians of fifty years ago to concentrate exclusively on discovery and regard the cultivation of writing as irrelevant, was a wrong instinct. There have been scholars of great distinction and valuable influence, who were bad writers. But they are rare. The sense of form, the capacity to weigh and to use words correctly, the shaping of sentences, and the structure and presentation of a scene, a fact, or an exposition are the natural concomitants of the clear, inquiring, disciplined, and imaginative mind which is needed for historical research. But most talents are the better for cultivation. The scholar who cultivates—as he must—the patience, the self-discipline, the spirit of inquiry, the open mind, the exactitude, and the strong but controlled imagination which are all necessary for research, will almost certainly find some of these qualities—equally

5. A third-century martyr usually depicted in Renaissance art as a youth pierced by arrows.

important for the writer—reflected in his handling of the English language when he comes to set down his conclusions. In the same way, the writer who cultivates these qualities in his writing will find his perceptions sharpened and his ideas clearer when he turns to research.

J. B. Bury, who so sternly proclaimed that history was 'a science, neither more nor less', wrote himself with lucidity, ease, and distinction. The gritty, awkward and disjointed manner which marred a good deal of serious historical writing in the early years of this century frequently reflects the slow-moving, awkward, and short-sighted approach of the writers, not only to the beauties and possibilities of the English language but to the possibilities and beauties of historical inquiry. The close relationship between clear thinking and good writing is illustrated time and again by the work of the great scholars. This fact has been obscured by the common confusion between literary history and popular history. Properly speaking, all history which is written with style and distinction belongs to English literature; it need not necessarily be 'popular' in the sense that millions can read and understand it. In other branches of literature, the universal genius who speaks to all hearts and all ages, who does not become obscure by reason of contemporary allusions or turns of phrase that reflect passing fashions, is very rare—a Shakespeare, a Tolstoy. But no one would expect millions to read and appreciate the poems of John Donne, or the prose of C. M. Doughty. These are more specialized tastes; but such writing belongs none the less to the great heritage of literature.

In history alone the term 'literary' has associations with the idea of popularity. It is assumed that good writing in history will occur most often, if not exclusively, in history which is directed towards a large public. But this does not follow. Much of the best historical writing of the last fifty years—and that in spite of the self-denying ordinance against literature passed by some of the practitioners themselves—has come from scholarly specialists, with little or no interest in reaching a large public or being acclaimed as literary figures. For the expressive, explicit, and exact use of words you would go far to find the equal of F. W. Maitland writing on the development of English law and institutions fifty years ago; and in this field today the great scholars, medieval or modern, Sir Maurice Powicke, Sir Lewis Namier have a precision, elegance, and clarity in the exposition of their themes which make many popular historians look slapdash and slipshod.

Anyone interested in modern English style would do well to turn, from time to time, away from the avowedly literary works, be they novels or criticism or literary history or that great field for fine writing so popular today, the travel book, and look into the pages of the learned periodicals. The subjects may be unappealing to the general reader but the manner in which they are treated is often an example of good style—cool, clear, reflective, and economical—in striking contrast to the average of modern popular writing, with its slack structure, careless and inattentive use of metaphors and images, and vocabulary corrupted by the stale-picturesque.

The practice of the finest scholars bears out the thesis that literature and scholarship, so far from being radically opposed to each other, are natural allies. Literary sensibility and literary technique are something more than pleasing additional graces to be cultivated by the historian if and when he has time. They are valuable to him not only in his final task of communicating his thoughts to the reading public, but from the very inception of his work; they will guide, help, and illuminate the whole process of historical inquiry.

The literary treatment of history is not a superficial thing; it goes to the root of the subject. Admittedly, it has its superficial aspects. For instance, the literary historian will often take note of superficial details which are irrelevant to the march of events and which would be rightly disregarded by a scholar dealing with, say, the evolution of ministerial responsibility or the fluctuations of wages in the fifteenth-century woollen industry. The literary historian will almost automatically make a note of any authentic details he can discover which are likely to enhance the reality of what he is describing or help the inward eye of the reader: the colour of a general's cloak or a woman's hair, the brightness or dullness of the weather, the hangings on the wall, the flowers in the garden—all things of very little consequence in themselves. In this respect the literary treatment of history is indeed merely an innocent and pleasing additional elegance. But this elegance can be used with wonderful skill and imagination, as for instance in Lytton Strachey's famous account of the dying Queen Victoria.[6]

"Yet, perhaps, in the secret chambers of consciousness, she had her thoughts too. Perhaps her fading mind called up once more the shadows of the past to float before it and retraced for the last time the vanished visions of that long history—passing back and back, through the cloud of years, to older and ever older memories, to the spring woods at Osborne so full of primroses for Lord Beaconsfield—to Lord Palmerston's queer clothes and high demeanour, and Albert's face under the green lamp, and Albert's first stag at Balmoral, and Albert in his blue and silver uniform, and the Baron coming in through a doorway, and Lord M. dreaming at Windsor with the rooks cawing in the elm trees, and the Archbishop of Canterbury on his knees in the dawn, and the old King's turkey-cock ejaculations, and Uncle Leopold's soft voice at Claremont, and Lehzen with the globes, and her mother's feathers sweeping down towards her, and a great old repeater watch of her father's in its tortoise-shell case, and a yellow rug, and some friendly flounces of sprigged muslin, and the trees and the grass at Kensington."

6. In 1901.

Here the details are accurate visual details assembled from many sources; slight in themselves, they have been selected, organized, and related to the story of the dying Queen in such a way as to illuminate what the author felt to be the essentials of her life and personality. Strachey's treatment can be compared with another closing passage, equally famous, written sixty years earlier—Motley's last lines on William the Silent.[7]

"He went through life bearing the load of a people's sorrows upon his shoulders with a smiling face. Their name was the last word upon his lips, save the simple affirmative with which the soldier who had been battling for the right all his lifetime commended his soul in dying 'to his great Captain, Christ'. The people were grateful and affectionate, for they trusted the character of their 'Father William', and not all the clouds which calumny could collect ever dimmed to their eyes the radiance of that lofty mind to which they were accustomed, in their darkest calamities, to look for light. As long as he lived, he was the guiding star of a brave nation, and when he died the little children cried in the streets."

This passage from Motley's *Rise of the Dutch Republic* illustrates a further, and more significant, stage in the marriage between literary or aesthetic sensibility and historical enquiry. In the passage about the death of Queen Victoria, Strachey has selected from the thousands of small background details that he had accumulated about his subject a striking few that light up, here and there, the personal experiences of the Queen's lifetime. He is giving us here not history but conjecture based on historical knowledge; he is making, with considerably greater discretion and restraint, the imaginative leap that Carlyle made at the Battle of Dunbar.

Motley does not depart from the stricter historical treatment of his theme. He conjectures nothing as to the state of William the Silent's mind in his last moments; he tells the facts and he sums up the impression objectively from contemporary evidence. Yet his summing up, like Strachey's more frankly imaginative flight, has the effect of poetry, the effect of striking through the surface facts to some deeper, less expressible truth about life and death and politics and the human heart.

The secret of Motley's great passage lies most of all in that last sentence: 'As long as he lived he was the guiding star of a brave nation, and when he died the little children cried in the streets.' The first part of the sentence is almost rhetorical, a sentence very well fitted to the old-fashioned idea of the dignity of history with its 'guiding star' and 'brave nation'—fine words but generalized and not particular to Motley or to the occasion; it is the last sentence, with its entirely simple statement of fact—'and when he died the little children cried in the streets'—which like a sudden beam of

7. Prince William of Orange led the Dutch in a rebellion against their Span- ish rulers from 1567 to 1584.

sunset light through clouds, streaming over the landscape, illuminates the whole of the preceding passage and tells us more about William the Silent as a ruler and as a leader than many piled-up paragraphs.

It has this effect because it is not a *rhetorical* phrase but an *historical* phrase; by the time the reader has got so far with Motley's *Dutch Republic* he knows his author well enough to understand that this is no flourish but a documented fact. He need not even consult the footnote to be reassured that these children were actually seen by someone walking in the streets of Delft at the time.

But—and this is the crux of the matter—this particular detail in a contemporary letter *might* have been missed by an historian less sensitive than Motley to aesthetic and literary values. The documentation of the epoch is very rich; there is a great deal to read and to digest; and in the mass of material it is not easy to hit upon the significant detail. By the significant detail I mean something much more than the picturesque detail. It is a superficial gift, though a useful one, to be able to pick out the vivid additional stage directions that may be found among the evidence—the picturesque touches. But it is a gift of a deeper kind to seize unfailingly on the kind of detail which illuminates to the core of an event. This is in part a literary gift, or rather it arises from the sharpening of perception which comes from literary training and the study and appreciation of literature.

It is not only in detail that the study and appreciation of literature, and the constant practice of history as an art, can be helpful to history as a science. The writer who approaches his task with some conception of the value and significance of form in writing or —more elementary still if you like—some idea of the sequence and flow of words and thoughts, some natural feeling for the relationship of words to form, will not fall into the danger of heaping up facts, and making a narrow, dry, unilluminating catalogue instead of an interpretation of his subject. If he has always in his mind a consciousness of the necessity of linking his material together, he will be a better historian as well as a better writer, for the problem of historical interpretation is largely a problem of finding out and establishing the correct relationship between facts; of restoring sequences of cause and effect whether in the lives of individuals or in much broader connections. In all this, the sense of form and structure, which has to be cultivated by the writer, is of equal importance to the historian.

The contention is one which cannot perhaps be proved except by negative evidence. History which is unimpeachable as scholarship should have lasting value regardless of its quality as writing. But when we look at the great works of scholarship which have lasted it is astonishing how rare it is to find one that reveals a writer devoid of literary skill and judgment.

Style in history is an index to the mind, and the great scholar, whether he cultivates it or not, is rarely without the natural gift. Fine writing may be the business only of the historian who has chosen to write of wide themes for a wide public. But good writing is almost the concomitant of good history. Literature and history were joined long since by the powers which shaped the human brain; we cannot put them asunder.

QUESTIONS

1. *What reasons does Wedgwood give for the movement away from literary history in the twentieth century?*
2. *How does Wedgwood regard Bury's statement that "history is a science, neither more nor less" and Powell's assertion that "style has no more to do with history than it has with law or astronomy"? What is her view of the relationship between literary style and the writing of history?*

EDWARD HALLETT CARR

The Historian and His Facts[1]

What is history? Lest anyone think the question meaningless or superfluous, I will take as my text two passages relating respectively to the first and second incarnations of *The Cambridge Modern History*. Here is Acton in his report of October 1896 to the Syndics of the Cambridge University Press on the work which he had undertaken to edit:

> It is a unique opportunity of recording, in the way most useful to the greatest number, the fullness of the knowledge which the nineteenth century is about to bequeath.... By the judicious division of labor we should be able to do it, and to bring home to every man the last document, and the ripest conclusions of international research.
>
> Ultimate history we cannot have in this generation; but we can dispose of conventional history, and show the point we have reached on the road from one to the other, now that all information is within reach, and every problem has become capable of solution.[2]

And almost exactly sixty years later Professor Sir George Clark, in his general introduction to the second *Cambridge Modern History*, commented on this belief of Acton and his collaborators that it would one day be possible to produce "ultimate history," and went on:

> Historians of a later generation do not look forward to any such prospect. They expect their work to be superseded again and again. They consider

1. Chapter I of *What is History?*, 1961.
2. *The Cambridge Modern History: Its Origin, Authorship and Production* (Cambridge University Press, 1907), pp. 10-12 [This and the following footnotes are Carr's].

that knowledge of the past has come down through one or more human minds, has been "processed" by them, and therefore cannot consist of elemental and impersonal atoms which nothing can alter.... The exploration seems to be endless, and some impatient scholars take refuge in scepticism, or at least in the doctrine that, since all historical judgments involve persons and points of view, one is as good as another and there is no "objective" historical truth.[3]

Where the pundits contradict each other so flagrantly the field is open to enquiry. I hope that I am sufficiently up-to-date to recognize that anything written in the 1890's must be nonsense. But I am not yet advanced enough to be committed to the view that anything written in the 1950's necessarily makes sense, Indeed, it may already have occurred to you that this enquiry is liable to stray into something even broader than the nature of history. The clash between Acton and Sir George Clark is a reflection of the change in our total outlook on society over the interval between these two pronouncements. Acton speaks out of the positive belief, the clear-eyed self-confidence of the later Victorian age; Sir George Clark echoes the bewilderment and distracted scepticism of the beat generation. When we attempt to answer the question, What is history?, our answer, consciously or unconsciously, reflects our own position in time, and forms part of our answer to the broader question, what view we take of the society in which we live. I have no fear that my subject may, on closer inspection, seem trivial. I am afraid only that I may seem presumptuous to have broached a question so vast and so important.

The nineteenth century was a great age for facts. "What I want," said Mr. Gradgrind in *Hard Times*, "is Facts. . . . Facts alone are wanted in life." Nineteenth-century historians on the whole agreed with him. When Ranke in the 1830's, in legitimate protest against moralizing history, remarked that the task of the historian was "simply to show how it really was [*wie es eigentlich gewesen*]" this not very profound aphorism had an astonishing success. Three generations of German, British, and even French historians marched into battle intoning the magic words, "*Wie es eigentlich gewesen*" like an incantation—designed, like most incantations, to save them from the tiresome obligation to think for themselves. The Positivists, anxious to stake out their claim for history as a science, contributed the weight of their influence to this cult of facts. First ascertain the facts, said the positivists, then draw your conclusions from them. In Great Britain, this view of history fitted in perfectly with the empiricist tradition which was the dominant strain in British philosophy from Locke to Bertrand Russell. The empirical theory of knowledge presupposes a complete separation between subject and object. Facts, like sense-impressions, impinge

3. *The New Cambridge Modern History*, I (Cambridge University Press, 1957), pp. xxiv-xxv.

on the observer from outside, and are independent of his consciousness. The process of reception is passive: having received the data, he then acts on them. *The Shorter Oxford English Dictionary*, a useful but tendentious work of the empirical school, clearly marks the separateness of the two processes by defining a fact as "a datum of experience as distinct from conclusions." This is what may be called the common-sense view of history. History consists of a corpus of ascertained facts. The facts are available to the historian in documents, inscriptions, and so on, like fish on the fishmonger's slab. The historian collects them, takes them home, and cooks and serves them in whatever style appeals to him. Acton, whose culinary tastes were austere, wanted them served plain. In his letter of instructions to contributors to the first *Cambridge Modern History* he announced the requirement "that our Waterloo must be one that satisfies French and English, German and Dutch alike; that nobody can tell, without examining the list of authors where the Bishop of Oxford laid down the pen, and whether Fairbairn or Gasquet, Liebermann or Harrison took it up."[4] Even Sir George Clark, critical as he was of Acton's attitude, himself contrasted the "hard core of facts" in history with the "surrounding pulp of disputable interpretation"[5]—forgetting perhaps that the pulpy part of the fruit is more rewarding than the hard core. First get your facts straight, then plunge at your peril into the shifting sands of interpretation—that is the ultimate wisdom of the empirical, common-sense school of history. It recalls the favorite dictum of the great liberal journalist C. P. Scott: "Facts are sacred, opinion is free."

Now this clearly will not do. I shall not embark on a philosophical discussion of the nature of our knowledge of the past. Let us assume for present purposes that the fact that Caesar crossed the Rubicon and the fact that there is a table in the middle of the room are facts of the same or of a comparable order, that both these facts enter our consciousness in the same or in a comparable manner, and that both have the same objective character in relation to the person who knows them. But, even on this bold and not very plausible assumption, our argument at once runs into the difficulty that not all facts about the past are historical facts, or are treated as such by the historian. What is the criterion which distinguishes the facts of history from other facts about the past?

What is a historical fact? This is a crucial question into which we must look a little more closely. According to the common-sense view, there are certain basic facts which are the same for all historians and which form, so to speak, the backbone of history—the fact, for example, that the Battle of Hastings was fought in 1066. But this view calls for two observations. In the first place,

4. Acton: *Lectures on Modern History* (London: Macmillan & Co., 1906), p. 318.

5. Quoted in *The Listener* (June 19, 1952), p. 992.

it is not with facts like these that the historian is primarily concerned. It is no doubt important to know that the great battle was fought in 1066 and not in 1065 or 1067, and that it was fought at Hastings and not at Eastbourne or Brighton. The historian must not get these things wrong. But when points of this kind are raised, I am reminded of Housman's remark that "accuracy is a duty, not a virtue."[6] To praise a historian for his accuracy is like praising an architect for using well-seasoned timber or properly mixed concrete in his building. It is a necessary condition of his work, but not his essential function. It is precisely for matters of this kind that the historian is entitled to rely on what have been called the "auxiliary sciences" of history—archaeology, epigraphy, numismatics, chronology, and so forth. The historian is not required to have the special skills which enable the expert to determine the origin and period of a fragment of pottery or marble, or decipher an obscure inscription, or to make the elaborate astronomical calculations necessary to establish a precise date. These so-called basic facts which are the same for all historians commonly belong to the category of the raw materials of the historian rather than of history itself. The second observation is that the necessity to establish these basic facts rests not on any quality in the facts themselves, but on an *a priori* decision of the historian. In spite of C. P. Scott's motto, every journalist knows today that the most effective way to influence opinion is by the selection and arrangement of the appropriate facts. It used to be said that facts speak for themselves. This is, of course, untrue. The facts speak only when the historian calls on them: It is he who decides to which facts to give the floor, and in what order or context. It was, I think, one of Pirandello's characters who said that a fact is like a sack—it won't stand up till you've put something in it. The only reason why we are interested to know that the battle was fought at Hastings in 1066 is that historians regard it as a major historical event. It is the historian who has decided for his own reasons that Caesar's crossing of that petty stream, the Rubicon, is a fact of history, whereas the crossing of the Rubicon by millions of other people before or since interests nobody at all. The fact that you arrived in this building half an hour ago on foot, or on a bicycle, or in a car, is just as much a fact about the past as the fact that Caesar crossed the Rubicon. But it will probably be ignored by historians. Professor Talcott Parsons once called science "a selective system of cognitive orientations to reality."[7] It might perhaps have been put more simply. But history is, among other things, that. The historian is necessarily selective. The belief in a hard core of historical facts

6. M. Manilius: *Astronomicon: Liber Primus*, 2nd ed. (Cambridge University Press, 1937), p. 87.
7. Talcott Parsons and Edward A. Shils: *Toward a General Theory of Action*, 3rd ed. (Cambridge, Mass.: Harvard University Press, 1954), p. 167.

existing objectively and independently of the interpretation of the historian is a preposterous fallacy, but one which it is very hard to eradicate.

Let us take a look at the process by which a mere fact about the past is transformed into a fact of history. At Stalybridge Wakes in 1850, a vendor of gingerbread, as the result of some petty dispute, was deliberately kicked to death by an angry mob. Is this a fact of history? A year ago I should unhesitatingly have said "no." It was recorded by an eyewitness in some little-known memoirs;[8] but I had never seen it judged worthy of mention by any historian. A year ago Dr. Kitson Clark cited it in his Ford lectures in Oxford.[9] Does this make it into a historical fact? Not, I think, yet. Its present status, I suggest, is that it has been proposed for membership of the select club of historical facts. It now awaits a seconder and sponsors. It may be that in the course of the next few years we shall see this fact appearing first in footnotes, then in the text, of articles and books about nineteenth-century England, and that in twenty or thirty years' time it may be a well established historical fact. Alternatively, nobody may take it up, in which case it will relapse into the limbo of unhistorical facts about the past from which Dr. Kitson Clark has gallantly attempted to rescue it. What will decide which of these two things will happen? It will depend, I think, on whether the thesis or interpretation in support of which Dr. Kitson Clark cited this incident is accepted by other historians as valid and significant. Its status as a historical fact will turn on a question of interpretation. This element of interpretation enters into every fact of history.

May I be allowed a personal reminiscence? When I studied ancient history in this university many years ago, I had as a special subject "Greece in the period of the Persian Wars." I collected fifteen or twenty volumes on my shelves and took it for granted that there, recorded in these volumes, I had all the facts relating to my subject. Let us assume—it was very nearly true—that those volumes contained all the facts about it that were then known, or could be known. It never occurred to me to enquire by what accident or process of attrition that minute selection of facts, out of all the myriad facts that must have once been known to somebody, had survived to become *the* facts of history. I suspect that even today one of the fascinations of ancient and mediaeval history is that it gives us the illusion of having all the facts at our disposal within a manageable compass: the nagging distinction between the facts of history and other facts about the past vanishes because the few known facts are all facts of history. As Bury, who had worked in both periods, said, "the records of ancient and mediaeval

8. Lord George Sanger: *Seventy Years a Showman* (London: J. M. Dent & Sons, 1926), pp. 188-9.

9. These will shortly be published under the title *The Making of Victorian England*.

history are starred with lacunae."[1] History has been called an enormous jig-saw with a lot of missing parts. But the main trouble does not consist of the lacunae. Our picture of Greece in the fifth century B.C. is defective not primarily because so many of the bits have been accidentally lost, but because it is, by and large, the picture formed by a tiny group of people in the city of Athens. We know a lot about what fifth-century Greece looked like to an Athenian citizen; but hardly anything about what it looked like to a Spartan, a Corinthian, or a Theban—not to mention a Persian, or a slave or other non-citizen resident in Athens. Our picture has been preselected and predetermined for us, not so much by accident as by people who were consciously or unconsciously imbued with a particular view and thought the facts which supported that view worth preserving. In the same way, when I read in a modern history of the Middle Ages that the people of the Middle Ages were deeply concerned with religion, I wonder how we know this, and whether it is true. What we know as the facts of mediaeval history have almost all been selected for us by generations of chroniclers who were professionally occupied in the theory and practice of religion, and who therefore thought it supremely important, and recorded everything relating to it, and not much else. The picture of the Russian peasant as devoutly religious was destroyed by the revolution of 1917. The picture of mediaeval man as devoutly religious, whether true or not, is indestructible, because nearly all the known facts about him were preselected for us by people who believed it, and wanted others to believe it, and a mass of other facts, in which we might possibly have found evidence to the contrary, has been lost beyond recall. The dead hand of vanished generations of historians, scribes, and chroniclers has determined beyond the possibility of appeal the pattern of the past. "The history we read," writes Professor Barraclough, himself trained as a mediaevalist, "though based on facts, is, strictly speaking, not factual at all, but a series of accepted judgments."[2]

But let us turn to the different, but equally grave, plight of the modern historian. The ancient or mediaeval historian may be grateful for the vast winnowing process which, over the years, has put at his disposal a manageable corpus of historical facts. As Lytton Strachey said in his mischievous way, "ignorance is the first requisite of the historian, ignorance which simplifies and clarifies, which selects and omits."[3] When I am tempted, as I sometimes am, to envy the extreme competence of colleagues engaged in writing ancient or mediaeval history, I find consolation in the reflection that they are so competent mainly because they are so ignorant of their sub-

1. John Bagnell Bury: *Selected Essays* (Cambridge University Press, 1930, p. 52.)
2. Geoffrey Barraclough: *History in a Changing World* (London; Basil Blackwell & Mott, 1955), p. 14.
3. Lytton Strachey: Preface to *Eminent Victorians*.

ject. The modern historian enjoys none of the advantages of this built-in ignorance. He must cultivate this necessary ignorance for himself—the more so the nearer he comes to his own times. He has the dual task of discovering the few significant facts and turning them into facts of history, and of discarding the many insignificant facts as unhistorical. But this is the very converse of the nineteenth-century heresy that history consists of the compilation of a maximum number of irrefutable and objective facts. Anyone who succumbs to this heresy will either have to give up history as a bad job, and take to stamp-collecting or some other form of antiquarianism, or end in a madhouse. It is this heresy, which during the past hundred years has had such devastating effects on the modern historian, producing in Germany, in Great Britain, and in the United States a vast and growing mass of dry-as-dust factual histories, of minutely specialized monographs, of would-be historians knowing more and more about less and less, sunk without trace in an ocean of facts. It was, I suspect, this heresy—rather than the alleged conflict between liberal and Catholic loyalties—which frustrated Acton as a historian. In an early essay he said of his teacher Döllinger: "He would not write with imperfect materials, and to him the materials were always imperfect."[4] Acton was surely here pronouncing an anticipatory verdict on himself, on that strange phenomenon of a historian whom many would regard as the most distinguished occupant the Regius Chair of Modern History in this university has ever had—but who wrote no history. And Acton wrote his own epitaph in the introductory note to the first volume of the *Cambridge Modern History*, published just after his death, when he lamented that the requirements pressing on the historian "threaten to turn him from a man of letters into the compiler of an encyclopedia."[5] Something had gone wrong. What had gone wrong was the belief in this untiring and unending accumulation of hard facts as the foundation of history, the belief that facts speak for themselves and that we cannot have too many facts, a belief at that time so unquestioning that few historians then thought it necessary—and some still think it unnecessary today—to ask themselves the question: What is history?

The nineteenth-century fetishism of facts was completed and justified by a fetishism of documents. The documents were the Ark of the Covenant in the temple of facts. The reverent historian approached them with bowed head and spoke of them in awed tones. If you find it in the documents, it is so. But what, when we get down to it, do these documents—the decrees, the treaties,

4. Quoted in George P. Gooch: *History and Historians in the Nineteenth Century* (London: Longmans, Green & Company, 1952), p. 385. Later Acton said of Döllinger that "it was given him to form his philosophy of history on the largest induction ever available to man" (*History of Freedom and Other Essays* [London: Macmillan & Co., 1907], p. 435).
5. *The Cambridge Modern History*, I (1902), p. 4.

the rent-rolls, the blue books, the official correspondence, the private letters and diaries—tell us? No document can tell us more than what the author of the document thought—what he thought had happened, what he thought ought to happen or would happen, or perhaps only what he wanted others to think he thought, or even only what he himself thought he thought. None of this means anything until the historian has got to work on it and deciphered it. The facts, whether found in documents or not, have still to be processed by the historian before he can make any use of them: the use he makes of them is, if I may put it that way, the processing process.

Let me illustrate what I am trying to say by an example which I happen to know well. When Gustav Stresemann, the Foreign Minister of the Weimar Republic, died in 1929, he left behind him an enormous mass—300 boxes full—of papers, official, semi-official, and private, nearly all relating to the six years of his tenure of office as Foreign Minister. His friends and relatives naturally thought that a monument should be raised to the memory of so great a man. His faithful secretary Bernhardt got to work; and within three years there appeared three massive volumes, of some 600 pages each, of selected documents from the 300 boxes, with the impressive title *Stresemanns Vermächtnis*.[6] In the ordinary way the documents themselves would have moldered away in some cellar or attic and disappeared for ever; or perhaps in a hundred years or so some curious scholar would have come upon them and set out to compare them with Bernhardt's text. What happened was far more dramatic. In 1945 the documents fell into the hands of the British and the American governments, who photographed the lot and put the photostats at the disposal of scholars in the Public Record Office in London and in the National Archives in Washington, so that, if we have sufficient patience and curiosity, we can discover exactly what Bernhardt did. What he did was neither very unusual nor very shocking. When Stresemann died, his Western policy seemed to have been crowned with a series of brilliant successes—Locarno, the admission of Germany to the League of Nations, the Dawes and Young plans and the American loans, the withdrawal of allied occupation armies from the Rhineland. This seemed the important and rewarding part of Stresemann's foreign policy; and it was not unnatural that it should have been over-represented in Bernhardt's selection of documents. Stresemann's Eastern policy, on the other hand, his relations with the Soviet Union, seemed to have led nowhere in particular; and, since masses of documents about negotiations which yielded only trivial results were not very interesting and added nothing to Stresemann's reputation, the process of selection could be more rigorous. Strese-

6. *Stresemann's Legacy.*

mann in fact devoted a far more constant and anxious attention to relations with the Soviet Union, and they played a far larger part in his foreign policy as a whole, than the reader of the Bernhardt selection would surmise. But the Bernhardt volumes compare favorably, I suspect, with many published collections of documents on which the ordinary historian implicitly relies.

This is not the end of my story. Shortly after the publication of Bernhardt's volumes, Hitler came into power. Stresemann's name was consigned to oblivion in Germany, and the volumes disappeared from circulation: many, perhaps most, of the copies must have been destroyed. Today *Stresemanns Vermächtnis* is a rather rare book. But in the West Stresemann's reputation stood high. In 1935 an English publisher brought out an abbreviated translation of Bernhardt's work—a selection from Bernhardt's selection; perhaps one third of the original was omitted. Sutton, a well-known translator from the German, did his job competently and well. The English version, he explained in the preface, was "slightly condensed, but only by the omission of a certain amount of what, it was felt, was more ephemeral matter . . . of little interest to English readers or students."[7] This again is natural enough. But the result is that Stresemann's Eastern policy, already under-represented in Bernhardt, recedes still further from view, and the Soviet Union appears in Sutton's volumes merely as an occasional and rather unwelcome intruder in Stresemann's predominantly Western foreign policy. Yet it is safe to say that, for all except a few specialists, Sutton and not Bernhardt—and still less the documents themselves—represents for the Western world the authentic voice of Stresemann. Had the documents perished in 1945 in the bombing, and had the remaining Bernhardt volumes disappeared, the authenticity and authority of Sutton would never have been questioned. Many printed collections of documents gratefully accepted by historians in default of the originals rest on no securer basis than this.

But I want to carry the story one step further. Let us forget about Bernhardt and Sutton, and be thankful that we can, if we choose, consult the authentic papers of a leading participant in some important events in recent European history. What do the papers tell us? Among other things they contain records of some hundreds of Stresemann's conversations with the Soviet ambassador in Berlin and of a score or so with Chicherin.[8] These records have one feature in common. They depict Stresemann as having the lion's share of the conversations and reveal his arguments as invariably well put and cogent, while those of his partner are for the most part scanty, confused, and unconvincing. This is a familiar characteristic

---

7. *Gustav Stresemann: His Diaries, Letters, and Papers* (London: Macmillan & Co.; 1935), I.

8. Soviet foreign minister 1918-28 [Editor's note].

of all records of diplomatic conversations. The documents do not tell us what happened, but only what Stresemann thought had happened. It was not Sutton or Bernhardt, but Stresemann himself, who started the process of selection. And, if we had, say, Chicherin's records of these same conversations, we should still learn from them only what Chicherin thought, and what really happened would still have to be reconstructed in the mind of the historian. Of course, facts and documents are essential to the historian. But do not make a fetish of them. They do not by themselves constitute history; they provide in themselves no ready-made answer to this tiresome question: What is history?

At this point I should like to say a few words on the question of why nineteenth-century historians were generally indifferent to the philosophy of history. The term was invented by Voltaire, and has since been used in different senses; but I shall take it to mean, if I use it at all, our answer to the question: What is history? The nineteenth century was, for the intellectuals of Western Europe, a comfortable period exuding confidence and optimism. The facts were on the whole satisfactory; and the inclination to ask and answer awkward questions about them was correspondingly weak. Ranke piously believed that divine providence would take care of the meaning of history if he took care of the facts; and Burckhardt with a more modern touch of cynicism observed that "we are not initiated into the purposes of the eternal wisdom." Professor Butterfield as late as 1931 noted with apparent satisfaction that "historians have reflected little upon the nature of things and even the nature of their own subject."[9] But my predecessor in these lectures, Dr. A. L. Rowse, more justly critical, wrote of Sir Winston Churchill's *The World Crisis*—his book about the First World War— that, while it matched Trotsky's *History of the Russian Revolution* in personality, vividness, and vitality, it was inferior in one respect: it had "no philosophy of history behind it."[1] British historians refused to be drawn, not because they believed that history had no meaning, but because they believed that its meaning was implicit and self-evident. The liberal nineteenth-century view of history had a close affinity with the economic doctrine of *laissez-faire*—also the product of a serene and self-confident outlook on the world. Let everyone get on with his particular job, and the hidden hand would take care of the universal harmony. The facts of history were themselves a demonstration of the supreme fact of a beneficent and apparently infinite progress towards higher things. This was the age of innocence, and historians walked in the Garden of Eden, without a scrap of philosophy to cover them, naked and unashamed before the

---

9. Herbert Butterfield: *The Whig Interpretation of History* (London: George Bell & Sons, 1931), p. 67.

1. Alfred L. Rowse: *The End of an Epoch* (London: Macmillan & Co., 1947), pp. 282-3.

god of history. Since then, we have known Sin and experienced a Fall; and those historians who today pretend to dispense with a philosophy of history are merely trying, vainly and self-consciously, like members of a nudist colony, to recreate the Garden of Eden in their garden suburb. Today the awkward question can no longer be evaded. * * *

During the past fifty years a good deal of serious work has been done on the question: What is history? It was from Germany, the country which was to do so much to upset the comfortable reign of nineteenth-century liberalism, that the first challenge came in the 1880's and 1890's to the doctrine of the primacy and autonomy of facts in history. The philosophers who made the challenge are now little more than names: Dilthey is the only one of them who has recently received some belated recognition in Great Britain. Before the turn of the century, prosperity and confidence were still too great in this country for any attention to be paid to heretics who attacked the cult of facts. But early in the new century, the torch passed to Italy, where Croce began to propound a philosophy of history which obviously owed much to German masters. All history is "contemporary history," declared Croce,[2] meaning that history consists essentially in seeing the past through the eyes of the present and in the light of its problems, and that the main work of the historian is not to record, but to evaluate; for, if he does not evaluate, how can he know what is worth recording? In 1910 the American philosopher, Carl Becker, argued in deliberately provocative language that "the facts of history do not exist for any historian till he creates them."[3] These challenges were for the moment little noticed. It was only after 1920 that Croce began to have a considerable vogue in France and Great Britain. This was not perhaps because Croce was a subtler thinker or a better stylist than his German predecessors, but because, after the First World War, the facts seemed to smile on us less propitiously than in the years before 1914, and we were therefore more accessible to a philosophy which sought to diminish their prestige. Croce was an important influence on the Oxford philosopher and historian Collingwood, the only British thinker in the present century who has made a serious contribution to the philosophy of history. He did not live to write the systematic treatise he had planned; but his published and unpublished papers on the subject were collected after his death in a volume entitled *The Idea of History*, which appeared in 1945.

2. The context of this celebrated aphorism is as follows: "The practical requirements which underlie every historical judgment give to all history the character of 'contemporary history,' because, however remote in time events thus recounted may seem to be, the history in reality refers to present needs and present situations wherein those events vibrate" (Benedetto Croce: *History as the Story of Liberty* [London: George Allen & Unwin, 1941], p. 19).

3. *Atlantic Monthly* (October 1928), p. 528.

The views of Collingwood can be summarized as follows. The philosophy of history is concerned neither with "the past by itself" nor with "the historian's thought about it by itself," but with "the two things in their mutual relations." (This dictum reflects the two current meanings of the word "history"—the enquiry conducted by the historian and the series of past events into which he enquires.) "The past which a historian studies is not a dead past, but a past which in some sense is still living in the present." But a past act is dead, *i.e.* meaningless to the historian, unless he can understand the thought that lay behind it. Hence "all history is the history of thought," and "history is the re-enactment in the historian's mind of the thought whose history he is studying." The reconstitution of the past in the historian's mind is dependent on empirical evidence. But it is not in itself an empirical process, and cannot consist in a mere recital of facts. On the contrary, the process of reconstitution governs the selection and interpretation of the facts: this, indeed, is what makes them historical facts. "History," says Professor Oakeshott, who on this point stands near to Collingwood, "is the historian's experience. It is 'made' by nobody save the historian: to write history is the only way of making it."[4]

This searching critique, though it may call for some serious reservations, brings to light certain neglected truths.

In the first place, the facts of history never come to us "pure," since they do not and cannot exist in a pure form: they are always refracted through the mind of the recorder. It follows that when we take up a work of history, our first concern should be not with the facts which it contains but with the historian who wrote it. Let me take as an example the great historian in whose honor and in whose name these lectures were founded. Trevelyan, as he tells us in his autobiography, was "brought up at home on a somewhat exuberantly Whig tradition"[5]; and he would not, I hope, disclaim the title if I described him as the last and not the least of the great English liberal historians of the Whig tradition. It is not for nothing that he traces back his family tree, through the great Whig historian George Otto Trevelyan, to Macaulay, incomparably the greatest of the Whig historians. Dr. Trevelyan's finest and maturest work *England under Queen Anne* was written against that background, and will yield its full meaning and significance to the reader only when read against that background. The author, indeed, leaves the reader with no excuse for failing to do so. For if, following the technique of connoisseurs of detective novels, you read the end first, you will find on the last few pages of the third volume the best summary known to me of what is nowadays called the Whig interpretation of history; and you will see that what Trevelyan is trying

4. Michael Oakeshott: *Experience and Its Modes* (Cambridge University Press, 1933), p. 99.

5. G. M. Trevelyan: *An Autobiography* (London: Longmans, Green & Company, 1949), p. 11.

to do is to investigate the origin and development of the Whig tradition, and to roof it fairly and squarely in the years after the death of its founder, William III. Though this is not, perhaps, the only conceivable interpretation of the events of Queen Anne's reign, it is a valid and, in Trevelyan's hands, a fruitful interpretation. But, in order to appreciate it at its full value, you have to understand what the historian is doing. For if, as Collingwood says, the historian must re-enact in thought what has gone on in the mind of his *dramatis personae*, so the reader in his turn must re-enact what goes on in the mind of the historian. Study the historian before you begin to study the facts. This is, after all, not very abstruse. It is what is already done by the intelligent undergraduate who, when recommended to read a work by that great scholar Jones of St. Jude's, goes round to a friend at St. Jude's to ask what sort of chap Jones is, and what bees he has in his bonnet. When you read a work of history, always listen out for the buzzing. If you can detect none, either you are tone deaf or your historian is a dull dog. The facts are really not at all like fish on the fishmonger's slab. They are like fish swimming about in a vast and sometimes inaccessible ocean; and what the historian catches will depend partly on chance, but mainly on what part of the ocean he chooses to fish in and what tackle he chooses to use—these two factors being, of course, determined by the kind of fish he wants to catch. By and large, the historian will get the kind of facts he wants. History means interpretation. Indeed, if, standing Sir George Clark on his head, I were to call history "a hard core of interpretation surrounded by a pulp of disputable facts," my statement would, no doubt, be one-sided and misleading, but no more so, I venture to think, than the original dictum.

The second point is the more familiar one of the historian's need of imaginative understanding for the minds of the people with whom he is dealing, for the thought behind their acts: I say "imaginative understanding," not "sympathy," lest sympathy should be supposed to imply agreement. The nineteenth century was weak in mediaeval history, because it was too much repelled by the superstitious beliefs of the Middle Ages and by the barbarities which they inspired, to have any imaginative understanding of mediaeval people. Or take Burckhardt's censorious remark about the Thirty Years' War: "It is scandalous for a creed, no matter whether it is Catholic or Protestant, to place its salvation above the integrity of the nation."[6] It was extremely difficult for a nineteenth-century liberal historian, brought up to believe that it is right and praiseworthy to kill in defense of one's country, but wicked and wrongheaded to kill in defense of one's religion, to enter into the state of mind of those who fought the Thirty Years' War. This difficulty is

6. Jacob Burckhardt: *Judgments on History and Historians* (London: S. J. Reginald Saunders & Company, 1958), p. 179.

particularly acute in the field in which I am now working. Much of what has been written in English-speaking countries in the last ten years about the Soviet Union, and in the Soviet Union about the English-speaking countries, has been vitiated by this inability to achieve even the most elementary measure of imaginative under-standing of what goes on in the mind of the other party, so that the words and actions of the other are always made to appear malign, senseless, or hypocritical. History cannot be written unless the his-torian can achieve some kind of contact with the mind of those about whom he is writing.

The third point is that we can view the past, and achieve our understanding of the past, only through the eyes of the present. The historian is of his own age, and is bound to it by the conditions of human existence. The very words which he uses—words like democracy, empire, war, revolution—have current connotations from which he cannot divorce them. Ancient historians have taken to using words like *polis* and *plebs* in the original, just in order to show that they have not fallen into this trap. This does not help them. They, too, live in the present, and cannot cheat themselves into the past by using unfamiliar or obsolete words, any more than they would become better Greek or Roman historians if they deliv-ered their lectures in a *chlamys* or a *toga*. The names by which suc-cessive French historians have described the Parisian crowds which played so prominent a role in the French revolution—*les sans-culottes, le peuple, la canaille, les bras-nus*—are all, for those who know the rules of the game, manifestos of a political affiliation and of a particular interpretation. Yet the historian is obliged to choose: the use of language forbids him to be neutral. Nor is it a matter of words alone. Over the past hundred years the changed balance of power in Europe has reversed the attitude of British his-torians to Frederick the Great. The changed balance of power within the Christian churches between Catholicism and Protestantism has profoundly altered their attitude to such figures as Loyola, Luther, and Cromwell. It requires only a superficial knowledge of the work of French historians of the last forty years on the French revolution to recognize how deeply it has been affected by the Russian revolu-tion of 1917. The historian belongs not to the past but to the pres-ent. Professor Trevor-Roper tells us that the historian "ought to love the past."[7] This is a dubious injunction. To love the past may easily be an expression of the nostalgic romanticism of old men and old societies, a symptom of loss of faith and interest in the present or future.[8] *Cliché* for *cliché*, I should prefer the one about freeing one-

7. Introduction to Burckhardt: *Judgments on History and Historians*, p. 17.

8. Compare Nietzsche's view of his-tory: "To old age belongs the old man's business of looking back and casting up his accounts, of seeking consolation in the memories of the past, in historical culture" (*Thoughts Out of Season* [London: Macmillan & Co., 1909], II, pp. 65-6).

self from "the dead hand of the past." The function of the historian is neither to love the past nor to emancipate himself from the past, but to master and understand it as the key to the understanding of the present.

If, however, these are some of the sights of what I may call the Collingwood view of history, it is time to consider some of the dangers. The emphasis on the role of the historian in the making of history tends, if pressed to its logical conclusion, to rule out any objective history at all: history is what the historian makes. Collingwood seems indeed, at one moment, in an unpublished note quoted by his editor, to have reached this conclusion:

> St. Augustine looked at history from the point of view of the early Christian; Tillemont, from that of a seventeenth-century Frenchman; Gibbon, from that of an eighteenth-century Englishman; Mommsen, from that of a nineteenth-century German. There is no point in asking which was the right point of view. Each was the only one possible for the man who adopted it.[9]

This amounts to total scepticism, like Froude's remark that history is "a child's box of letters with which we can spell any word we please."[1] Collingwood, in his reaction against "scissors-and-paste history," against the view of history as a mere compilation of facts, comes perilously near to treating history as something spun out of the human brain, and leads back to the conclusion referred to by Sir George Clark in the passage which I quoted earlier, that "there is no 'objective' historical truth." In place of the theory that history has no meaning, we are offered here the theory of an infinity of meanings, none any more right than any other—which comes to much the same thing. The second theory is surely as untenable as the first. It does not follow that, because a mountain appears to take on different shapes from different angles of vision, it has objectively either no shape at all or an infinity of shapes. It does not follow that, because interpretation plays a necessary part in establishing the facts of history, and because no existing interpretation is wholly objective, one interpretation is as good as another, and the facts of history are in principle not amenable to objective interpretation. I shall have to consider at a later stage what exactly is meant by objectivity in history.

But a still greater danger lurks in the Collingwood hypothesis. If the historian necessarily looks at his period of history through the eyes of his own time, and studies the problems of the past as a key to those of the present, will he not fall into a purely pragmatic view of the facts, and maintain that the criterion of a right interpretation is its suitability to some present purpose? On this hypothesis, the facts of history are nothing, interpretation is everything. Nietzsche

9. Robin G. Collingwood: *The Idea of History* (London: Oxford University Press; 1946), p. xii.

1. James Anthony Froude: *Short Studies on Great Subjects* (1894), I, p. 21.

had already enunciated the principle: "The falseness of an opinion is not for us any objection to it. . . . The question is how far it is life-furthering, life-preserving, species-preserving, perhaps species-creating."[2] The American pragmatists moved, less explicitly and less wholeheartedly, along the same line. Knowledge is knowledge for some purpose. The validity of the knowledge depends on the validity of the purpose. But, even where no such theory has been professed, the practice has often been no less disquieting. In my own field of study, I have seen too many examples of extravagant interpretation riding roughshod over facts, not to be impressed with the reality of this danger. It is not surprising that perusal of some of the more extreme products of Soviet and anti-Soviet schools of historiography should sometimes breed a certain nostalgia for that illusory nineteenth-century heaven of purely factual history.

How then, in the middle of the twentieth century, are we to define the obligation of the historian to his facts? I trust that I have spent a sufficient number of hours in recent years chasing and perusing documents, and stuffing my historical narrative with properly footnoted facts, to escape the imputation of treating facts and documents too cavalierly. The duty of the historian to respect his facts is not exhausted by the obligation to see that his facts are accurate. He must seek to bring into the picture all known or knowable facts relevant, in one sense or another, to the theme on which he is engaged and to the interpretation proposed. If he seeks to depict the Victorian Englishman as a moral and rational being, he must not forget what happened at Stalybridge Wakes in 1850. But this, in turn, does not mean that he can eliminate interpretation, which is the life-blood of history. Laymen—that is to say, non-academic friends or friends from other academic disciplines—sometimes ask me how the historian goes to work when he writes history. The commonest assumption appears to be that the historian divides his work into two sharply distinguishable phases or periods. First, he spends a long preliminary period reading his source and filling his notebooks with facts: then, when this is over, he puts away his sources, takes out his notebooks, and writes his book from beginning to end. This is to me an unconvincing and unplausible picture. For myself, as soon as I have got going on a few of what I take to be the capital sources, the itch becomes too strong and I begin to write—not necessarily at the beginning, but somewhere, anywhere. Thereafter, reading and writing go on simultaneously. The writing is added to, subtracted from, re-shaped, cancelled, as I go on reading. The reading is guided and directed and made fruitful by the writing: the more I write, the more I know what I am looking for, the better I understand the significance and relevance of what I find. Some historians probably do all this preliminary writing in their

2. Nietzsche: *Beyond Good and Evil*, Chapter 1.

head without using pen, paper, or typewriter, just as some people play chess in their heads without recourse to board and chess-men: this is a talent which I envy, but cannot emulate. But I am convinced that, for any historian worth the name, the two processes of what economists call "input" and "output" go on simultaneously and are, in practice, parts of a single process. If you try to separate them, or to give one priority over the other, you fall into one of two heresies. Either you write scissors-and-paste history without meaning or significance; or you write propaganda or historical fiction, and merely use facts of the past to embroider a kind of writing which has nothing to do with history.

Our examination of the relation of the historian to the facts of history finds us, therefore, in an apparently precarious situation, navigating delicately between the Scylla of an untenable theory of history as an objective compilation of facts, of the unqualified primacy of fact over interpretation, and the Charybdis of an equally untenable theory of history as the subjective product of the mind of the historian who establishes the facts of history and masters them through the process of interpretation, between a view of history having the center of gravity in the past and the view having the center of gravity in the present. But our situation is less precarious than it seems. We shall encounter the same dichotomy of fact and interpretation again in these lectures in other guises—the particular and the general, the empirical and the theoretical, the objective and the subjective. The predicament of the historian is a reflection of the nature of man. Man, except perhaps in earliest infancy and in extreme old age, is not totally involved in his environment and unconditionally subject to it. On the other hand, he is never totally independent of it and its unconditional master. The relation of man to his environment is the relation of the historian to his theme. The historian is neither the humble slave, nor the tyrannical master, of his facts. The relation between the historian and his facts is one of equality, of give-and-take. As any working historian knows, if he stops to reflect what he is doing as he thinks and writes, the historian is engaged on a continuous process of molding his facts to his interpretation and his interpretation to his facts. It is impossible to assign primacy to one over the other.

The historian starts with the provisional selection of facts and a provisional interpretation in the light of which that selection has been made—by others as well as by himself. As he works, both the interpretation and the selection and ordering of facts undergo subtle and perhaps partly unconscious changes through the reciprocal action of one or the other. And this reciprocal action also involves reciprocity between present and past, since the historian is part of the present and the facts belong to the past. The historian and the facts of history are necessary to one another. The historian without his facts is rootless and futile; the facts without their historian are dead and meaningless. My first answer therefore to the question, What is history?, is that it is a continuous process of interaction between the historian and his facts, an unending dialogue between the present and the past.

QUESTIONS

1. Carr begins with a question but does not answer it until the last sentence. What are the main steps of the discussion leading to his answer? The answer takes the form of a definition: which is the most important of the defining words?
2. In his discussion of the facts of history, Carr distinguishes between a "mere fact about the past" and a "fact of history." Into which category should go Bruno Bettelheim's encounter with the infirmary guard (pp. 72–74)?
3. If you were commissioned to write a history of the semester or of a particular group during the semester, what would be your most important "facts of history"?

C. VANN WOODWARD
The Age of Reinterpretation

Innumerable influences have inspired the reinterpretation of history. The most common of late would appear to have been those originating within the intellectual community, or within the historical guild itself, rather than with the impact of historical events. Influences of the predominant sort include new theories, new methods, and new sources. Of special importance in recent years has been the example of other disciplines and sciences, old ones such as philosophy and biology with new theories, or new ones such as psychology and sociology with new approaches to old problems.

With no intended disparagement for prevailing and recent types of revision, the present essay concerns itself almost exclusively with reinterpretations that are inspired by historical events and have little to do with new theories, new methods, or new disciplines. The suggested opportunities for reinterpretation are, in fact, related to historical events so recent that nearly all of them have occurred since the summer of 1945. As responsible human beings we are rightly concerned first of all with the impact of these events upon the present and immediate future. But as historians we are, or we should be, concerned with their effect upon our view of the past as well. These events have come with a concentration and violence for which the term "revolution" is usually reserved. It is a revolution, or perhaps a set of revolutions, for which we have not yet found a name. My thesis is that these developments will and should raise new questions about the past and affect our reading of large areas of history, and my belief is that future revisions may be extensive enough to justify calling the coming era of historiography an age of reinterpretation. The first illustration happens to come mainly from American history, but this should not obscure the broader scope of the revolution, which has no national limitations.

Throughout most of its history the United States has enjoyed a remarkable degree of military security, physical security from hostile attack and invasion. This security was not only remarkably effective, but it was relatively free. Free security was based on nature's gift of three vast bodies of water interposed between this country and any other power that might constitute a serious menace to its safety. There was not only the Atlantic to the east and the Pacific to the west, but a third body of water, considered so impenetrable as to make us virtually unaware of its importance, the Arctic Ocean and its great ice cap to the north. The security thus provided was free in the sense that it was enjoyed as a bounty of nature in place of the elaborate and costly chains of fortifications and even more expensive armies and navies that took a heavy toll of the treasuries of less fortunate countries and placed severe tax burdens upon the backs of their people. The costly navy that policed and defended the Atlantic was manned and paid for by British subjects for more than a century, while Americans enjoyed the added security afforded without added cost to themselves. In 1861 the United States was maintaining the second largest merchant marine in the world without benefit of a battle fleet. At that time there were only 7,600 men in the United States Navy as compared with more than ten times that number in the British Navy.[1]

Between the second war with England and World War II, the United States was blessed with a security so complete and so free that it was able virtually to do without an army and for the greater part of the period without a navy as well. Between the world war that ended in 1763 and the world wars of the twentieth century the only major military burdens placed upon the people were occasioned not by foreign threats but by domestic quarrels, the first to establish independence for the American colonies and the second to thwart independence for the southern states. After each of these civil wars, as after all the intervening wars, Americans immediately dismantled

---

1. During Andrew Jackson's administration Alexis de Tocqueville described the situation in the following terms: "The President of the United States is the commander-in-chief of the army, but of an army composed of only six thousand men; he commands the fleet, but the fleet reckons but few sails; he conducts the foreign relations of the Union, but the United States are a nation without neighbors. Separated from the rest of the world by the ocean, and too weak as yet to aim at the dominion of the seas, they have no enemies, and their interests rarely come into contact with those of any other nation of the globe." *Democracy in America*, tr. Henry Reeve (2 vols.; New York, 1904), I, 120 [Woodward's note].

their military establishment. They followed the same procedure after every succeeding war, down to World War II, and even after that they carried demobilization to dangerous extremes before reversing the policy.

The end of the era of free security has overtaken Americans so suddenly and swiftly that they have not brought themselves to face its practical implications, much less its bearing upon their history. Conventional aircraft and jet propulsion had shrunk the time dimension of the Atlantic and Pacific from weeks to hours by the mid-fifties. But before military adjustment could be properly made to that revolution, the development of ballistic missiles shrank the two oceans further from hours to minutes. In the same period the hitherto impenetrable Arctic Ocean has not only been navigated by atomic-powered submarines under the ice cap, but has been shrunk in time width to dimensions of minutes and seconds by which we now measure the other oceans. The age of security and the age of free security ended almost simultaneously.

The proposition was advanced before a meeting of the American Historical Association in 1893 that "the first period of American history," a period of four centuries, was brought to an end by the disappearance of free land. Perhaps it is not premature to suggest that another epoch of American history was closed even more suddenly sixty years later by the disappearance of free security. It may be objected that security was never completely free and that the period when it came nearest to being so did not last very long. But one can reasonably ask as much latitude to speak in comparative and relative terms about free security as the theorists of free land enjoyed in their generalizations. Land was of course never completely free either, and the period when it came nearest to being so only dated from the Homestead Act of 1862, less than three decades before the end of the frontier era. In a comparative sense land may nevertheless be said to have been relatively free for a much longer period. In similar terms security may also be said to have been free until quite recently.

Military expenditures of the federal government have, of course, increased greatly and almost continuously since the last decade of the eighteenth century. Until very recently, however, they have not increased so rapidly as the government's nonmilitary expenditures. During the first century of the Republic's history, save in war years, annual military expenditures rarely came to as much as 1 per cent of the gross national product, returned to that level a few years after World War I, and remained there until the Great Depression cut production back drastically. In the decade preceding Pearl Harbor, the percentage of federal expenditures devoted to military purposes fell lower than ever before in our history.[2]

Another measure of free security is the small demand that military service has made upon national manpower. Before World War I, apart from actual war periods and their immediate aftermath, it was an extremely rare year in which as many as 1 per cent of the total male population between the ages of twenty and thirty-nine saw military service. Between Reconstruction and the Spanish-American War there was no year in which as many as one-half of 1 per cent served in the armed forces.[3] The handful of men who made up the regular army during the nineteenth century were not employed in patrolling frontiers against foreign invasion, but chiefly in coping with a domestic police problem posed by the Indians. Upon the outbreak of the Civil War the United States army numbered a few more than sixteen thousand men, and 183 of its 198 companies were spread among seventy-nine posts on the Indian frontier. The remaining fifteen companies were available for "defense" of the Canadian and Atlantic frontiers, and the incipient Confederate frontier.[4] The southern constabulary that patrolled the slaves was organized on military lines, but like the regular army it was concerned with a domestic police problem.

The contrast between free security and security costs of the present era scarcely requires emphasis. Military expenditures in 1957 and the years since have amounted to 10 per cent of the gross national product. By way of comparison, military expenditures in the 1880's were never over four-tenths of 1 per cent. In spite of the vast increase of the gross national product during the last century, military costs have increased far faster and now represent ten to twenty times the percentage of the gross national product they represented in the peace years of the previous century.[5] Not counting payments to veterans, they now account for nearly 70 per cent of the federal budget. The more advanced and improved military

2. M. Slade Kendrick, *A Century and a Half of Federal Expenditures,* Occasional Paper 48, National Bureau of Economic Research (New York, 1955), pp. 10–12, 28, 38, 40–42. For comparisons between military appropriations of the United States and other powers, 1820–1937, see Quincy Wright, *A Study of War* (2 vols.; Chicago, 1942), I, 666–72, Appendix XXII, esp. Tables 58, 59, and 60. The significant index of comparison is the proportion between military appropriations and national income. That proportion rose in the United States from 0.8 in 1914 to 1.5 in 1937, while in the same years it stood in Great Britain at 3.4 and 5.7; in France at 4.8 and 9.1; in Japan at 4.8 and 28.2; in Germany at 4.6 and 23.5; and in Russia at 6.3 and 26.4. This was the only period for which figures are given for all these powers [Woodward's note].

3. Kendrick, *A Century and a Half of Federal Expenditures,* pp. 89-90. Before 1865 only white males of military age are included in these figures [Woodward's note].

4. Theodore Ropp, *War in the Modern World* (Durham, 1959), p. 157 [Woodward's note].

5. Simon Kuznets in Committee for Economic Development, *Problems of United States Economic Development* (2 vols.; New York, 1958), I, 29 [Woodward's note].

machinery paradoxically requires more instead of less manpower, both military and civilian. The Department of Defense and its branches employ more civilian workers now than did the entire federal government before the Great Depression. Indications are that we are only at the beginning instead of the culmination of expansion in costs and manpower for military purposes and that future expenditures will be larger still.

If historians waited until the disappearance of free land to recognize fully the influence of the frontier-and-free-land experience on American history, perhaps the even more sudden and dramatic disappearance of free security will encourage them to recognize the effect of another distinguishing influence upon our national history. I am not prepared to make any claims about the comparative importance of the two themes, nor do I wish to make or inspire any exaggerations of the influence of free security. But if the influence of free land may be considered significant in the shaping of American character and national history, it is possible that the effect of free security might profitably be studied for contributions to the same ends.

Certain traits that Americans generally regard as desirable, such as democracy, individualism, self-reliance, inventiveness, have been attributed in some measure to the frontier-and-free-land experience. It might be that the sunnier side of the national disposition—the sanguine temperament, the faith in the future,[6] what H. G. Wells once called our "optimistic fatalism"—is also related to a long era of habituation to military security that was effective, reliable, and virtually free. Optimism presupposes a future that is unusually benign and reliably congenial to man's enterprises. Anxieties about security have kept the growth of optimism within bounds among other peoples, but the relative absence of such anxieties in the past has helped, along with other factors, to make optimism a national philosophy in America. The freedom of American youth from the long period of training in military discipline that left its mark upon the youth of nations where it was a routine requirement could hardly have failed to make some contribution to the distinctiveness of national character.

Free security is related at various points to the development of the American economy. So long as an economy of scarcity prevailed in the land the gross national product was not far above the level of subsistence. While the margin was narrow, the demands of an expensive military establishment could have consumed so large a proportion of the surplus above subsistence as to retard seriously the formation of capital. Relative immunity from this drain, on the other hand, enlarged opportunities for the formation of capital and

6. Boyd C. Shafer, "The American Heritage of Hope," *Mississippi Valley Historical Review*. XXXVII (Dec. 1950), 422–50 [Woodward's note].

the increase of productivity. Free security was certainly related to light taxes and a permissive government, and they in turn had much to do with the development of the famous American living standard.

Not all the historic influences of free security have been so benign. Tocqueville's classic study of the national character attributes to democracy some familiar patterns of military conduct that might be profitably re-examined in the light of the free security thesis. Tocqueville finds, for example, that "the private soldiers remain most like civilians" in a democracy, that they chafe under discipline with "a restless and turbulent spirit," and that they are "ever ready to go back to their homes" when the fighting is over. With regard to the officer corps he observes that "among a democratic people the choicer minds of the nation are gradually drawn away from the military profession, to seek by other paths distinction, power, and especially wealth." He adds that "among democratic nations in time of peace the military profession is held in little honor and indifferently followed. This want of public favor is a heavy discouragement to the army."[7] Tocqueville may be correct in suggesting democracy as one explanation for these attitudes and patterns of behavior, but no explanation of American attitudes is complete that neglects a national disposition to look upon security as a natural right. What a people half consciously comes to regard as a free gift of nature they are with difficulty persuaded to purchase at high cost in treasure, inconvenience, and harsh discipline. To reward with high honors, prestige, and secure status the professional military men who insist upon these sacrifices in time of peace comes hard to such people.

The heritage of free and easy security can also be detected behind the disposition to put living standard, private indulgence, and wasteful luxury ahead of vital security requirements. The same heritage can almost certainly be discerned at work in the tendency to plunge into wars first and prepare for them later. The historic background of security might help to explain, even if it cannot excuse, the irresponsibility of political leaders who make foreign commitments, coin bellicose slogans, and indulge in wild threats and promises without first providing the military means to back them up.

There are other aspects of American history besides demagogic diplomacy and military shortcomings that are not to be fully understood without reference to the history of free security. Among these surely is the American Civil War. The United States is the only major country since Cromwellian England that could afford the doubtful luxury of a full-scale civil war of four years without incurring the evils of foreign intervention and occupation. Had such evils

7. Tocqueville, *Democracy in America*, II, 761–68 [Woodward's note].

been as much a foregone conclusion as they have been among other nations, it is doubtful that Americans would have proved as willing as they were to fall upon each other's throats.

It is doubtful, also, that Americans could have developed and indulged with the freedom they have their peculiar national attitudes toward power, had it not been for their special immunity from the more urgent and dire demands for the employment of power to assure national security and survival. Having this relative immunity, they were able to devise and experiment with elaborate devices to diffuse and atomize power. They divided it among the states and later among business corporations. They used such devices as checks and balances, separation of powers, and division of powers to deadlock power and to thwart positive action for long periods. The experience probably encouraged the tendency to regard power as bad in itself and any means of restraining or denying it as a positive good.

The national myth that America is an innocent nation in a wicked world is associated to some degree in its origins and perpetuation with the experience of free security. That which other nations had of necessity to seek by the sword and defend by incurring the guilt of using it was obtained by the Americans both freely and innocently, at least in their own eyes. They disavowed the engines and instruments of the power they did not need and proclaimed their innocence for not using them, while at the same time they passed judgment upon other nations for incurring the guilt inevitably associated with power. "We lived for a century," writes Reinhold Niebuhr, "not only in the illusion but in the reality of innocency in our foreign relations. We lacked the power in the first instance to become involved in the guilt of its use." But we sought to maintain the innocence of our national youth after acquiring power that was incompatible with it. We first concealed from ourselves the reality of power in our economic and technological might, but after it became undeniable, and after military strength was added to it, as Niebuhr says, "we sought for a time to preserve innocency by disavowing the responsibilities of power."[8] The urge to return to a free security age of innocence and the flight from responsibility and from the guilt of wielding power may be traced in elaborate efforts to maintain neutrality, in desperate struggles for isolationism and "America First," as well as in the idealistic plans of religious and secular pacifists.

So long as free land was fertile and arable, and so long as security was not only free but strong and effective, it is no wonder that the world seemed to be America's particular oyster. Now that both free

8. Reinhold Niebuhr, *The Irony of American History* (New York, 1952), p. 35 [Woodward's note].

land and free security have disappeared, it is not surprising that the American outlook has altered and the prospect has darkened. The contrast with the past was even sharper in the case of free security than in the instance of free land, for the transition was almost immediate from a security that was both free and effective to an attempt at security that was frightfully costly and seemed terrifyingly ineffective. The spell of the long past of free security might help to account for the faltering and bewildered way in which America faced its new perils and its new responsibilites.

This discussion leads naturally to a second and more extensive field of opportunity for reinterpretation, that of military history. In this field there are no national limitations and few limits of time and period. Military subjects have traditionally occupied a large share of the historian's attention, a disproportionate share in the opinion of some critics. Yet the military historian is now faced with the challenge of relating the whole history of his subject to the vast revolution in military weapons and strategic theory that has occurred in the past fifteen years. Primarily this revolution involves two phases: first, explosives, and second, the means of delivering them upon a target. Both phases were inaugurated toward the end of World War II.

The revolution in explosives began when the primitive A-bomb was exploded by American forces over Hiroshima on August 6, 1945.[9] This was the first and, so far, the last such weapon but one ever fired in anger. That event alone marked the lurid dawn of a new age. But the entirely unprecedented pace of change in the weapons revolution has swept us far beyond that primitive dawn and broken the continuity of military tradition and history. Since 1945 we have passed from bombs reckoned in kilotons of TNT to those computed in megatons, the first of which was the hydrogen bomb exploded at Bikini on March 1, 1954, less than a decade after the A-bomb innovation. The twenty kiloton atomic bomb dropped over Nagasaki in 1945 had a thousand times the explosive power of the largest blockbuster used in World War II, but the twenty megaton thermonuclear bomb represents a thousand-fold increase over the Nagasaki bomb. One bomb half the twenty megaton size is estimated by Henry A. Kissinger to represent *"five times the explosive power of all the bombs dropped on Germany during the five years of war and one hundred times those dropped on Japan."*[1] And according to Oskar Morgenstern, "One single bomb can harbor a force greater than all the explosives used by all belligerents in

9. Two rival dates for the opening of the nuclear age are December 2, 1942, when Enrico Fermi established a chain reaction in the Chicago laboratory, and July 16, 1945, when the test bomb was exploded in New Mexico [Woodward's note].

1. Henry A. **Kissinger**, *Nuclear Weapons and Foreign Policy* (New York, 1957), pp. 70–71. Italics in the original [Woodward's note].

World War II or even greater than all the energy ever used in any form in all previous wars of mankind put together."[2] But this would still not appear to be the ultimate weapon, for it is now said that a country capable of manufacturing the megaton bomb is conceivably capable, should such madness possess it, of producing a "begaton" bomb. Reckoned in billions instead of millions of tons of TNT, it would presumably represent a thousand-fold increase, if such a thing is conceivable, over the megaton weapon.

The revolution in the means of delivering explosives upon targets, like the revolution in explosives, also began during World War II. Before the end of that war, the jet-propelled aircraft, the snorkel submarine, the supersonic rocket, and new devices for guiding ships, aircraft, or missiles were all in use. But also as in the case of the revolution in explosives, the revolution in agents of delivery accelerated at an unprecedented pace during the fifteen years following the war. The new jet aircraft became obsolescent in succeeding models before they were in production, sometimes before they came off the drafting boards. The snorkel submarine acquired atomic power and a range of more than fifty thousand miles without refueling. The expansion of rockets in size, range, and speed was even more revolutionary. The German V-2 in use against London during the last year of the war had a range of only about two hundred miles and a speed of only about five times that of sound. The intermediary range ballistic missile, capable of carrying a thermonuclear warhead, has a range of around fifteen hundred miles, and the intercontinental missile with similar capabilities has a range in excess of five thousand miles and flies at a rate on the order of twenty times the speed of sound. To appreciate the pace and extent of the revolution in agents of delivery, one should recall that in the long history of firearms, military technology was only able to increase the range of cannon from the few hundred yards of the primitive smoothbore to a maximum of less than eighty miles with the mightiest rifled guns. Then in less than fifteen years ranges became literally astronomical.

In all these measurements and samples of change in military technology it should be kept in mind that the revolution is still in progress and in some areas may well be only in its beginning stages. The line between the intercontinental rockets and some of the space rockets would seem to be a rather arbitrary one. The race for the development of the nuclear-powered plane may produce a craft capable of ranges limited in a practical way only by the endurance of the crew. The technological breakthrough has become a familiar phenomenon of the military revolution, and there is no justification for the assumption that we have seen the last of these developments.

2. Oskar Morgenstern, *The Question of National Defense* (New York, 1959), p. 10 [Woodward's note].

To seek the meaning of this revolution in a comparison with that worked by the advent of firearms is misleading. The progress of the revolution brought on by gunpowder, first used in military operations in the early fourteenth century was glacial by comparison. Only very gradually did the gun replace the sword, the arrow, the spear, and the battering ram. Flintlocks did not arrive until the seventeenth century, field artillery of significance until the eighteenth century, and it was not until the middle of the last century, more than five hundred years after the first military use of gunfire, that the era of modern firearms really opened. Military doctrine changed even more slowly.

The nuclear revolution is of a different order entirely. If strategic bombing with theromonuclear weapons occurs on an unrestricted scale now entirely possible with existing forces, it is quite likely to render subsequent operation of armies, navies, and air forces not only superfluous but unfeasible. It is not simply that huge concentrations of forces such as were used in major amphibious and land operations in the last world war presented a vulnerable target themselves. Of more elemental importance is the fact that such armies, navies, and air forces require thriving industrial economies and huge bases and cannot operate when the cities of their home territories are smoking craters and their ports and bases are piles of radioactive rubble. As for the military effectiveness of survivors in the home territory, according to Bernard Brodie, 'the *minimum* destruction and disorganization that one should expect from an unrestricted thermonuclear attack in the future is likely to be too high to permit further meaningful mobilization of war-making capabilities over the short term."[3] Faith in the wartime potential of the American industrial plant would appear to be another casualty of the revolution.

Historic changes in weapons, tactics, and strategy between one war and the next, or even one century or one era and the next in the past, become trivial in importance by comparison with the gulf between the preatomic and the nuclear age of strategic bombing. We are now able to view the past in a new perspective. We can already see that the vast fleets that concentrated off the Normandy beaches and at Leyte Gulf, or the massed armies that grappled in the Battle of the Bulge or across the Russian steppes, or for that matter the old-fashioned bomber squadrons that droned back and forth across the English Channel year after year dropping what the air force now contemptuously calls "iron bombs" were more closely related to a remote past than to a forseeable future. They did not, as they seemed at the time, represent the beginning of a new age of

3. Bernard Brodie, *Strategy in the Missile Age* (Princeton, 1959), p. 167. See also pp. 147–49 on the comparison with the firearms revolution [Woodward's note].

warfare. They represented instead the end of an old age, a very old age.

This is not to assume that unrestricted nuclear war is the only type of military operations that are any longer conceivable, nor that wars of limited objectives, limited geographic area, and limited destructiveness are no longer possible. To make such assumptions, indeed, would be either to despair of the future of civilized man or to subscribe to the theory that national differences will thenceforth be settled without resort to force. Even assuming that limited wars may still be fought with "conventional" weapons, tactics, and strategy of the old era, there will still be an important difference setting them apart from prenuclear wars. Where major powers are directly or indirectly involved, at least, limited wars will be fought under an umbrella of nuclear power. The effects of that conditioning environment have yet to be tested, but it can scarcely be assumed that they will be inconsiderable.

Instead of making military history irrelevant or unimportant, the sudden transition from the old to the new age of warfare should actually enhance the role of the historian. We stand desperately in need of historical reinterpretation. The men who now have responsibility for determining policy, strategy, and tactics in the new age of warfare are inevitably influenced by their experience and training grounded on an earlier age of warfare and an outmoded interpretation of its history. The fact is that many of the precepts, principles, and values derived from past experience in wars can be tragically misleading in the new age. These include some of the so-called "unchanging principles of war" that are imbibed during training and discipline until they become almost "second nature" to the professional military man. Traditions that associate the new type of war with honor, valor, and glory are no longer quite relevant. The sacred doctrine of concentration and mass, applied at the critical point, has lost its traditional meaning.

The age-old assumption of a commander's freedom of choice once war was started can no longer be made. In previous ages, one could start a war and assume that his objectives, methods, or degree of commitment could be altered according to changing prospects of success or failure, or according to whether probable gains outweighed probable losses. Even as late as World War II one could still approach the abyss of barbarism or annihilation, take a look and turn back, settle for an armistice or a compromise, and bide one's time. Once resort is made to unrestricted nuclear war, there is no turning back.

The underpinnings of logic that have served historically to justify resort to war as the lesser of several evils have shifted or, in their traditional form, quite disappeared. Victory has been deprived of its historical meaning in total war with the new weapons, for the "victor" is likely to sustain such devastation as to lack the means of imposing his will upon the "vanquished." And yet to accomplish this end, according to Karl von Clausewitz, is the only rational motive of war. Democratic participation or consent in a war decision is rendered most unmeaningful at the very time popular involvement in the devastation of war has reached an unprecedented maximum.

The history of war and man's attitudes about it should be re-examined in the light of these developments. Attention has already been profitably directed in particular to the question of how and why total war came to appear the "normal" type of conflict between major powers.[4] Such investigation might reveal how military planning became divorced from political planning and war became an end in itself rather than a means of achieving more or less rational political ends. Given the destructive military capabilities presently at the disposal of major powers, it would seem to be more interesting than it has ever been before to learn how and why powers have been willing at some times in history to wage wars with more limited objectives than unconditional surrender, total victory, or complete annihilation of the enemy.

That mankind should have carried the values and precepts of the age of firearms into the thermonuclear age represents a far greater anachronism than the one represented by his carrying the values and precepts of the age of chivalry into the age of firearms. Anachronisms are pre-eminently the business of historians. The historic service that Cervantes performed with mockery in 1605, when he published the first volume of *Don Quixote,* three centuries after the advent of firearms, cannot with safety be deferred that long after the advent of nuclear weapons. Lacking a Cervantes, historians might with their own methods help to expose what may well be the most perilous anachronism in history.

On a grander scale, a third field of opportunity for historical reinterpretation has opened up since 1945. Too complex to be attributed to an event, it might better be ascribed to an avalanche of events, or a combination of avalanches. These avalanches go under such names as the collapse of Western imperialism, the revolt of the colored peoples of Asia and Africa, the rise of Eastern nationalism, the westward advance of the frontier of Russian hegemony, and the polarization of power between the Russian and American giants. All these developments and more have contributed to the

4. See, for example, Robert E. Osgood, *Limited War: The Challenge to American Strategy* (Chicago, 1957), and John U. Nef, *War and Human Progress: An Essay on the Rise of Industrial Civilization* (Cambridge, 1950) [Woodward's note].

shrinkage of Europe in power and relative importance, and thus to what is probably the greatest of all opportunities for historical reinterpretation.

In recent years historians and other scholars have coined some striking phrases to describe Europe's plight: "the political collapse of Europe," "the un-making of Europe," "farewell to European history," "the passing of the European age," "the end of European history."[5] The tone of despair echoed from one of these phrases to another may well be called in question by the remarkable economic recovery and cultural resilience of Europe since 1945. Crane Brinton is to an extent justified in taking to task the prophets of doom and calling attention to the rising birth rate, the material prosperity, and the intellectual activity in postwar Europe.[6] The end of European supremacy is not necessarily the end of Europe. The present argument, however, is not addressed to the question of the extent of cultural malaise in Europe nor to the validity of any of several cyclical theories of history. The point is simply one of relative power and influence, and no evidence so far presented disturbs the conclusion that an age of European pre-eminence in the world has come to a close. That age did not end overnight, nor does the explanation lie wholly in events of the last decade and a half, but awareness of the implications for history are only beginning to sink in.

Now that European power has dwindled or quite disappeared in Asia, Africa, and former insular dependencies, and now that Europe itself has become the theater for operations of non-European powers, their military bases, and power rivalries, the spell of an agelong European dominance begins to lift. It is difficult to realize how recently it was commonly assumed in informed circles that the world was the proper theater for European enterprises and adventures, that world leadership was a European prerogative, that trends and fashions in arts, ideas, and sciences were as a matter of course set in Europe, that European political hegemony and economic ascendancy were taken for granted, and that history of any consequence was a commodity stamped "Made in Europe." The corollaries of these assumptions were that non-Europeans, apart from a few societies composed primarily of peoples of European stock, stood in perpetual tutelage to Europe, that non-European cultures were decadent, arrested, primitive, or permanently inferior, and that progress was defined as successful imitation of the preferred European way of doing things.

5. Hajo Holborn, *The Political Collapse of Europe* (New York, 1951); Oscar Halecki, *The Limits and Divisions of European History* (New York, 1950); Alfred Weber, *Farewell to European History or the Conquest of Nihilism* (New Haven, 1948); Eric Fischer, *The Passing of the European Age* (Cambridge, 1948); Geoffrey Barraclough, *History in a Changing World* (Norman, 1956) [Woodward's note].

6. Crane Brinton, *The Temper of Western Europe* (Cambridge, 1953) [Woodward's note].

The significance of all this for historiography lies in the fact that much of the history still read and believed and taught was written while these assumptions prevailed, and written by historians, non-European as well as European, who shared them. Three of the most productive and influential generations of historians in the whole history of Western culture, those between the Napoleonic Wars and World War I, coincided in time with the crest of European ascendancy and presumption. The generation between the world wars of the twentieth century generally shared the same assumptions. The contribution they made to the enrichment of historical scholarship is invaluable and should be cherished. But in so far as it rests on a set of assumptions no longer tenable, their work would seem to stand in need of extensive revision and reinterpretation.

On the need for reinterpretation of the history of Europe itself it might be the prudent thing for an American historian to rely on the judgment of European historians, several of whom have already expressed themselves on the subject. Geoffrey Barraclough, for example, believes that "a total revision of European history [is] imperative." In this connection he has written, "Ever since the end of the war [of 1939–1945] a change has come over our conceptions of modern history. We no longer feel that we stand four square in a continuous tradition, and the view of history we have inherited . . . seems to have little relevance to our current problems and our current needs." In his opinion the trouble is that "we are dealing with a conception of European history which is out of focus and therefore misleading, because of the false emphasis and isolated prominence it gives to Western Europe, and which therefore needs revising not merely in its recent phases, but at every turn from the early middle ages onward."[7]

American historians will also have some reinterpreting to do, for in this as in so much of American cultural life, ideas were shaped by European examples and models. It should go without saying that American civilization is European derived. But the models of Europe-centered world history would seem to have restrained American historians from exploring the influence of their country upon European history and that of the world in general. There have been a few exceptions to the rule. One exception is R. R. Palmer, *The Age of the Democratic Revolution*, which demonstrates that an age traditionally called European shows the profound impact of the American Revolution on Europe. Another suggestive interpretation of the American influence on European history is Walter P. Webb, *The Great Frontier*, and yet another is Halvdan Koht, *The American Spirit in Europe*. Other neglected American themes of European history remain to be explored. The influence of European

---

7. Barraclough, *History in a Changing World*, pp. 9, 135, 178 [Woodward's note].

immigration on American history has received much attention. But the impact upon Europe itself of the emigration of 35,000,000 Europeans in the century between the Napoleonic Wars and World War I remains to be acknowledged except in a few countries and has still to receive its just share of attention in the pages of European history. The importance of the West as a safety valve for American society has undoubtedly been exaggerated. But the significance of America as a safety valve for Europe and the effect of the closing of that valve after World War I remain to be fully assessed. Apart from the United States, other offshoots and overseas establishments of European powers, including those in South America, Australia, and the British Commonwealth countries, will inevitably discover that they have not been merely on the receiving end of the line of influence, but have had their own impact upon European and world history.

The same assumptions of Europocentric history have very largely shaped the interpretation of Asiatic, African, and other non-European history as well, for Europe successfully marketed its historiography abroad, along with its other cultural products, in remote and exotic climates. We may depend on it that the new opportunities for reinterpretation will not be lost upon New Delhi, Cairo, Tokyo, and Djakarta, to say nothing of Peking and Moscow. Already an Indian historian, K. M. Panikkar, has defined the period of European pre-eminence in the Orient as "the Vasco Da Gama Epoch of Asian History." It began with the arrival of Da Gama at Calicut in 1498 and ended abruptly four and a half centuries later "with the withdrawal of British forces from India in 1947 and of the European navies from China in 1949." In the time dimensions of the Orient this could be regarded as only one of several episodes that have temporarily interrupted the flow of ancient civilizations. Relations between East and West continue and even increase in many ways, but, as Panikkar says, "the essential difference is that the basis of relationship has undergone a complete change . . . a revolutionary and qualitative change. . . ." The Indian historian concludes that "vitally important historical results may flow from this new confrontation" between East and West.[8]

One of the historical results to flow from the confrontation between East and West should be a new and revised view of world history. The ethnocentric, or Europocentric, view that has been held for so long a time in the West can hardly be expected to survive the sweeping change in East-West relationships. The "new confrontation" of which the Hindu historian writes is another event of the present that necessitates many reinterpretations of the past.

8. K. M. Panikkar, *Asia and Western Dominance: A Survey of the Vasco Da Gama Epoch of Asian History, 1498–* 1945 (London, 1953), pp. 11, 15 [Woodward's note].

Three fields for historical reinterpretation have been suggested: the first occasioned by the end of the age of free and effective security in America, the second by the end of an age of mass warfare, and the third by the end of the age of European hegemony. These subjects have been suggested to illustrate, not to exhaust, the list of possibilities for historical reinterpretation opened up since 1945. A complete list would not only be beyond the limits of this paper, but beyond the range of present vision. The need for reinterpretation is not always made immediately apparent by revolutionary events, while on the other hand such a need may easily be exaggerated by lack of sufficient perspective.

It may be noted that the ideological war between the Communist and the non-Communist worlds, which occupies so large a share of public attention at present, has not been mentioned. It could well be that the cold war and the triumphs that Russia and her allies have scored will upset more comfortable and traditional interpretations of history than the events we have listed above. It is even more probable, if we prove as myopic about our own times as historians have proved in the past, that we have overlooked or underestimated events that in future times will be accounted of far more historical significance than the noisier events we have noted. In such a situation the experienced historian will always take account of two powerful historical forces: the unforeseen and the unforeseeable. It may well turn out that new satellites for the earth will prove of more historical consequence than new satellites for earthly powers.

At least two objections to the proposal of reinterpreting history in the light of present events, however revolutionary, may be readily foreseen. The first is that the past is inviolable, that it is or should be unaffected by the present, and that it is the duty of the historian to guard its inviolability rather than to invade it with present preoccupations. But this would be to take an unhistorical view of historiography. Every major historical event has necessitated new views of the past and resulted in reinterpretations of history. This was surely true of the Reformation, of the discovery and exploration of the New World, of the Industrial Revolution, and of political upheavals such as the democratic and the Communist revolutions. These events did not leave the past inviolate, nor the traditional interpretations of it sacrosanct. There is no reason to believe that present and future revolutions will do so.

A second objection may be that if the revolutionary changes used as illustrations represent such a drastic and sharp break with the past, they render history irrelevant and useless to the needs and concerns of the present and future: that history is bypassed by events and reduced to antiquarianism. The answer to this objection is that if history is bypassed and rendered irrelevant and antiquarian, it will be due in large measure to the view that historians take of their own craft. Writing nearly half a century ago with regard to the disappearance of free land and its consequences in America, J. Franklin Jameson asked, "Can it be supposed that so great and so dramatic a transition . . . shall have no effect upon the questions which men ask concerning the past? Nothing can be more certain than that history must be prepared to respond to new demands. I do not think so ill of my profession as to suppose that American historians will not make gallant and intelligent attempts to meet the new requirements."[9]

The new demands and requirements to which Jameson urged historians to respond now come faster, more insistently, and in more momentous form than ever before. The historian, along with others, may be called upon soon to adjust his views to another age of discovery and exploration, one that transcends earthly limits. He is already confronted with a "population explosion" for which there is no precedent, not even a helpful analogy, and little but misleading counsel from classical theorists. In science and technology it is the age of the "breakthrough," when the curve of expansion suddenly becomes vertical on many fronts. Informed men of science speak of the possibility of tapping the ocean for unlimited food supplies, of curing the incurable diseases, of controlling the weather, and of developing limitless and virtually costless sources of power. Historical thought is involved as soon as men confront change with anachronistic notions of the past. Anachronism, to repeat, is the special concern of the historian. If historians assume an intransigent attitude toward reinterpretation, they will deserve to be regarded as antiquarians and their history as irrelevant. The historian who can contemplate a single nuclear bomb that harbors more destructive energy and fury than mankind has managed to exert in all previous wars fom the siege of Troy to the fall of Berlin and conclude that it has "no effect upon the questions which men ask concerning the past" would seem to be singularly deficient in historical imagination.

The present generation of historians has a special obligation and a unique opportunity. Every generation, of course, has a unique experience of history. "I had the advantage," wrote Goethe, "of being born in a time when the world was agitated by great movements, which have continued during my long life." But it is doubtful that any previous generation has witnessed quite the sweep and scope of change experienced by those who have a living memory of the two world wars of the twentieth century and the events that have followed. They carry with them into the new order a personal

9. J. Franklin Jameson, "The Future Uses of History" (1913), reprinted in American Historical Review, LXV (Oct. 1959), 69 [Woodward's note].

experience of the old. Americans among them will remember a time when security was assumed to be a natural right, free and unchallengeable. Among them also will be men of many nations who manned the ships and fought the battles of another age of warfare. And nearly all of this generation of historians will have been educated to believe that European culture was Civilization and that non-European races, if not natively inferior, were properly under perpetual tutelage. They will be the only generation of historians in history who will be able to interpret the old order to the new order with the advantage and authority derived from firsthand knowledge of the two ages and participation in both.

The historian sometimes forgets that he has professional problems in common with all storytellers. Of late he has tended to forget the most essential one of these—the problem of keeping his audience interested. So long as the story he had to tell contained no surprises, no unexpected turn of events, and lacked the elemental quality of suspense, the historian found his audience limited mainly to other historians, or captive students. While the newly dawned era adds new problems of its own to the historian's burden, it is lavish with its gifts of surprise and suspense for the use of the storyteller. If there are any readily recognizable characteristics of the new era, they are the fortuitous, the unpredictable, the adventitious, and the dynamic—all of them charged with surprise.

The new age bears another and more ominous gift for the historian, one that has not been conspicuous in historical writings since the works of the Christian fathers. This gift is the element of the catastrophic. The Church fathers, with their apocalyptic historiography, understood the dramatic advantage possessed by the storyteller who can keep his audience sitting on the edge of eternity. The modern secular historian, after submitting to a long cycle of historicism, has at last had this dramatic advantage restored. The restoration, to be sure, arrived under scientific rather than apocalyptic auspices. But the dramatic potentials were scarcely diminished by placing in human hands at one and the same time the Promethean fire as well as the divine prerogative of putting an end to the whole drama of human history.

Of one thing we may be sure. We come of an age that demands a great deal of historians. Of such a time Jacob Burckhardt once wrote, "The historical process is suddenly accelerated in terrifying fashion. Developments which otherwise take centuries seem to flit by like phantoms in months or weeks, and are fulfilled."[1] He could hardly have phrased a more apt description of our own time. It is doubtful that any age has manifested a greater thirst for historical

1. Jacob Burckhardt, *Force and Freedom* (New York, 1955), p. 238 [Woodward's note].

meaning and historical interpretation and therefore made greater demands upon the historian. What is required is an answer to the questions about the past and its relation to the present and future that the accelerated process of history raises. If historians evade such questions, people will turn elsewhere for the answers, and modern historians will qualify for the definition that Tolstoi once formulated for academic historians of his own day. He called them deaf men replying to questions that nobody puts to them. If on the other hand they do address themselves seriously to the historical questions for which the new age demands answers, the period might justly come to be known in historiography as the age of reinterpretation.

QUESTIONS

1. Woodward has indicated several changes in the world since 1945 which in his view call for a reinterpretation of history. What are these changes? Would you modify his list, or add anything further to it?
2. What several sources of discontent with modern historiography does Woodward identify? How valid are they?
3. It is said that many students today consider history irrelevant. Does Woodward's essay offer any reasons for this attitude? Does it propose any reasons for a change of that attitude?

On Science

JOHN LIVINGSTON LOWES
Time in the Middle Ages[1]

We live in terms of *time*. And so pervasive is that element of our consciousness that we have to stand, as it were, outside it for a moment to realize how completely it controls our lives. For we think and act perpetually, we mortals who look before and after, in relation to hours and days and weeks and months and years. Yesterday and to-morrow, next week, a month from now, a year ago, in twenty minutes—those are the terms in which, wittingly or automatically, we act and plan and think. And to orient ourselves at any moment in that streaming continuum we carry watches on our wrists, and put clocks about our houses and on our public towers, and somewhere in our eye keep calendars, and scan time-tables when we would go abroad. And all this is so utterly familiar that it has ceased to be a matter of conscious thought or inference at all. And—to come to the heart of the business—unless we are mariners or woodsmen or astronomers or simple folk in lonely places, we never any longer reckon with the *sky*. Except for its bearing on the weather or upon our moods, or for contemplation of its depths of blue or fleets of white, or of the nightly splendor of its stars, we are oblivious of its influence. And therein lies the great gulf fixed between Chaucer's century and ours.

For Chaucer and his contemporaries, being likewise human, also lived in terms of time. But their calendar and time-piece was that sky through which moved immutably along predestined tracks the planets and the constellations. And no change, perhaps, wrought by the five centuries between us is more revealing of material differences than that shift of attitude towards "this brave o'erhanging firmament," the sky. And it is that change, first of all, that I wish, if I can, to make clear.

1. From Chapter I, "Backgrounds and Horizons," of *Geoffrey Chaucer*, 1934.

There could be, I suspect, no sharper contrast than that between the "mysterious universe" of modern science, as interpreters like Eddington and Jeans have made even laymen dimly perceive it, and the nest of closed, concentric spheres in terms of which Chaucer and his coevals thought. The structure of that universe may be stated simply enough. Its intricacies need not concern us here. About the earth, as the fixed center, revolved the spheres of the seven then known planets, of which the sun and the moon were two. Beyond these seven planetary spheres lay the sphere of the fixed stars. Beyond that in turn, and carrying along with it in its "diurnal sway" the eight spheres which lay within it, moved the *primum mobile,* a ninth sphere with which, to account for certain planetary eccentricities, the Middle Ages had supplemented the Ptolemaic system. We must think, in a word, of Chaucer's universe as geocentric— the "litel erthe," encompassed by "thilke speres thryes three."[2] As an interesting fact which we have learned, we know it; to conceive it as reality demands an exercise of the imagination. And only with that mental *volte-face* accomplished can we realize the cosmos as Chaucer thought of it.

Now the order of succession of the planetary spheres had far-reaching implications. Starting from the earth, which was their center, that succession was as follows: Moon, Mercury, Venus, Sun, Mars, Jupiter, Saturn. And implicit in that order were two fundamental consequences—the astrological status of the successive hours of the day, and the sequence of the days of the week. The two phenomena stood in intimate relation, and some apprehension of each is fundamental to an understanding of the framework of conceptions within which Chaucer thought, and in terms of which he often wrote.

There were, then, in the first place—and this is strange to us— two sorts of *hours,* with both of which everybody reckoned. There were the hours from midnight to midnight, which constituted the "day natural"—the hours, that is, with which we are familiar—and these, in Chaucer's phrase, were "hours equal," or "hours of the *clock.*" But there were also the hours which were reckoned from sunrise to sunset (which made up "day artificial"), and on from sunset to sunrise again. And these, which will most concern us, were termed "hours inequal," or "hours of the *planets.*" And they were the hours of peculiar significance, bound up far more closely with human affairs than the "hours of the clock." It is worth, then, a moment's time to get them clear.

They were termed "inequal" for an obvious reason. For the periods between sunrise and sunset, and sunset and sunrise, respectively, change in length with the annual course of the sun, and the length of their twelfths, or hours, must of necessity change too. Between

2. "Those spheres thrice three."

the equinoxes, then, it is clear that the inequal hours will now be longer by day than by night, now longer by night than by day. And only twice in the year, at the equinoxes, will the equal hours and the inequal hours—the hours of the clock and the hours of the planets—be identical. Moreover, each of the inequal hours (and this is of the first importance) was "ruled" by one of the seven planets, and it was as "hours of the planets" that the "hours inequal" touched most intimately human life. And that brings us at once to the days of the week, and their now almost forgotten implications. Why, to be explicit, is to-day Saturday? And why to-morrow Sunday? To answer those two questions is to arrive at one of the determining concepts of Chaucer's world.

Let me first arrange the seven planets in their order, starting (to simplify what follows) with the outermost. Their succession will then be this: Saturn, Jupiter, Mars, Sun, Venus, Mercury, Moon. Now Saturn will rule the first hour of the day which, for that reason, bears his name, and which we still call *Saturday*. Of that day Jupiter will rule the second hour, Mars the third, the Sun the fourth, Venus the fifth, Mercury the sixth, the Moon the seventh, and Saturn again, in due order, the eighth. Without carrying the computation farther around the clock it is obvious that Saturn will also rule the fifteenth and the twenty-second hours of the twenty-four which belong to his day. The twenty-third hour will then be ruled by Jupiter, the twenty-fourth by Mars, and the twenty-fifth by the Sun. But the twenty-fifth hour of one day is the first hour of the next, and accordingly the day after Saturn's day will be the Sun's day. And so, through starry compulsion, the next day after Saturday *must* be Sunday. In precisely the same fashion—accomplished most quickly by remembering that each planet must rule the twenty-second hour of its own day—the ruling planet of the first hour of each of the succeeding days may readily be found. And their order, so found, including Saturn and the Sun, is this: Saturn, Sun, Moon, Mars, Mercury, Jupiter, Venus—then Saturn again, and so on *ad libitum*. And the days of the week will accordingly be the days of the seven planets in that fixed order.

Now Saturn's day, the Sun's day, and the Moon's day are clearly recognizable in their English names of Saturday, Sunday, and Monday. But what of the remaining four—to wit, the days of Mars, Mercury, Jupiter, and Venus, which we call Tuesday, Wednesday, Thursday, and Friday? French has preserved, as also in Lundi, the planetary designations: Mardi (*Martis dies*), Mercredi (*Mercurii dies*), Jeudi (*Jovis dies*), and Vendredi (*Veneris dies*). The shift of the names in English is due to the ousting, in those four instances, of the Roman pantheon by the Germanic. Tiw, Woden, Thor, and Frig (or Freya) have usurped the seats of Mars, Mercury, Jupiter, and Venus, and given their barbarous names to the days. And in France a fourth, even more significant substitution has taken place. For the sun's day is in French *dimanche*, and *dimanche* is *dominica dies*, the Lord's day. And so between Saturn's planet and Diana's moon is memorialized, along with Mercury and Jupiter and Venus and Mars, the second Person of the Christian Trinity. The ancient world has crumbled, and its detritus has been remoulded into almost unrecognizable shapes. But half the history of Europe and of its early formative ideas is written in the nomenclature of the week. And that nomenclature depends in turn upon the succession of the planetary hours. And it was in terms of those hours that Chaucer and his contemporaries thought.

In the *Knight's Tale*, to be specific, Palamon, Emily, and Arcite go to pray, each for the granting of his own desire, to the temples respectively of Venus, Diana, and Mars. And each goes, as in due observance of ceremonial propriety he must, in the hour of the planet associated with the god to whom he prays. Palamon goes to the temple of Venus, "And *in hir houre* he walketh forth." A few lines earlier that hour has been stated in everyday terms: it was "The Sonday night, er day bigan to springe . . . Although it nere nat day by houres two"—two hours, that is, before sunrise. The day that was springing after Sunday night was Monday, and the hour of Monday's sunrise is the hour of the Moon. And the hour two hours earlier, in which Palamon walked forth, was the hour ruled by Venus, to whose temple he was on the way. And Emily and Arcite, as the tale goes on, performed their pilgrimages at similarly reckoned hours. To Chaucer and his readers all this was familiar matter of the day, as instantly comprehensible as are now to us the hours which we reckon by the clock. For us alas! it has become a theme for cumbrous exposition, because the hours of the planets have vanished, with the gods whose names they bore. All that is left of them is the time-worn and wonted sequence of the seven designations of the days.

Nothing, indeed, is more characteristic of the period in which Chaucer wrote than the strange, twisted mythology, transmogrified and confused, which emerged from the association of the planets and the gods. Not even Ovid had conceived such metamorphoses.[3] For the gods were invested with the attributes of planets, and as such became accountable for the most bizarre occurrences, and kept amazing company. Under the aegis of Mars, to take one instance only, were enrolled the butchers, hangmen, tailors, barbers, cooks, cutlers, carpenters, smiths, physicians, and apothecaries—a band about as "martial" as Falstaff's Thomas Wart and Francis Feeble.[4] And so, in "the temple of mighty Mars the rede" in the *Knight's Tale*, there were depicted, together with the "open werre" which

3. Ovid's *Metamorphoses* includes poetical renderings of myths dealing with the transformation of men and women into birds, flowers, trees, etc.
4. Recruits in Shakespeare's *Henry IV, Part 2*.

was his by virtue of his godhead, the disastrous chances proceeding from his malign ascendancy as planet—the corpse in the bushes with cut throat, the nail driven, like Jael's, into the temple,[5] the sow eating the child in the cradle, the cook scalded in spite of his long ladle. And from among the members of what Chaucer twice calls Mars' "divisioun" there were present—together with the pick-purse, and "the smyler with the knyf under the cloke"—the barber and the butcher and the smith. And in the next paragraph Mars becomes again "this god of armes"—god of war and wicked planet inextricably interfused.

Moreover, as the day and week were conceived in terms of planetary sequence, so the year stood in intricate relation to the *stars*. The sun, with the other planets, moved annually along the vast starry track across the sky which then, as now, was called the zodiac —so called, as Chaucer lucidly explains to "litel Lowis" in the *Treatise on the Astrolabe*, because (and his etymology is sound) "*zodia* in langage of Greek sowneth [signifies] 'bestes' . . . and in the zodiak ben the twelve signes that han names of bestes." These twelve signs, as everybody knows, are Aries, Taurus, Gemini, Cancer, Leo, Virgo, Libra, Scorpio, Sagittarius, Capricornus, Aquarius, Pisces—or, to follow Chaucer's praiseworthy example and translate, Ram, Bull, Twins, Crab, Lion, Virgin, Scales, Scorpion, Archer, Goat, Water-carrier, Fishes. There they were, "eyrish bestes," as Chaucer calls them in a delightful passage that will meet us later, and along their celestial highway passed, from one sign to another, and from house to house, the seven eternal wanderers. To us who read this—though not to countless thousands even yet—the twelve constellations of the zodiac are accidental groupings, to the eye, of infinitely distant suns. To Chaucer's century they were strangely living potencies, and the earth, in the words of a greater than Chaucer, was "this huge stage . . . whereon the stars in secret influence comment." Each sign, with its constellation, had its own individual efficacy or quality—Aries, "the colerik hote signe"; Taurus, cold and dry; and so on through the other ten. Each planet likewise had its own peculiar nature—Mars, like Aries, hot and dry; Venus hot and moist; and so on through the other five. And as each planet passed from sign to sign, through the agency of the successive constellations its character and influence underwent change. Chaucer in the *Astrolabe* put the matter in its simplest terms: "Whan an hot planete cometh in-to an hot signe, then encresseth his hete; and yif a planete be cold, thanne amenuseth [diminishes] his coldnesse, by -cause of the hote signe." But there was far more to it than that. For these complex planetary changes exercised a determining influence upon human beings and their affairs. Arcite behind prison bars

5. See Judges iv, 17-22.

cries out:

> Som wikke aspect or disposicioun
> Of Saturne, *by sum constellacioun,*
> Hath yeven us this.

And "the olde colde Saturnus" names the constellation:

> Myn is the prison in the derke cote...
> *Whyl I dwelle in the signe of the Leoun.*

The tragedy of Constance, as the Man of Law conceived it, comes about because Mars, at the crucial moment, was in his "derkest hous." Mars gave, on the other hand, the Wife of Bath, as she avers, her "sturdy hardinesse," because Mars, at her birth, was in the constellation Taurus, which was, in astrological terminology, her own "ascendent." And since the constellation Taurus was also the "night house" of Venus, certain other propensities which the wife displayed had been thrust upon her, as she cheerfully averred, by the temporary sojourn of Mars in Venus's house, when she was born.

But the march of the signs along the zodiac touched human life in yet another way. "Everich of thise twelve signes," Chaucer wrote again to his little Lewis, "hath respecte to a certein parcelle of the body of a man and hath it in governance; as Aries hath thyn heved, and Taurus thy nekke and thy throte. Gemini thyn armholes and thyn armes, and so forth." And at once one recalls Sir Toby Belch and Sir Andrew Aguecheek in *Twelfth Night*. "Shall we not set about some revels?" asks Sir Andrew. "What shall we do else?" replies Sir Toby. "Were we not born under Taurus?" "Taurus!" exclaims Sir Andrews, "that's sides and heart." "No, sir," retorts Sir Toby, "it is legs and thighs." And you may still pick up, in the shops of apothecaries here and there, cheaply printed almanacs, designed to advertise quack remedies, in which the naked human figure is displayed with lines drawn from each of the pictured zodiacal signs— Ram, Bull, Crab, Scorpion—to the limbs or organs, legs, thighs, sides, or heart, which that particular sign (in Chaucerian phrase) "hath in governance." It is not only in worn stone and faded parchments that strange fragments of the elder world survive.

QUESTIONS

1. Arrange the steps of Lowes' explanation of medieval time in a different order. Is your order superior to Lowes' or inferior? By what criteria?
2. When the advertising man and the engineer from the electronics laboratory become suburban gardeners, why may they have to reckon with the sky and neglect their watches and calendars?

3. List some ways in which the abstractions of watch and calendar (and time table) "rule" our lives. This list will be a selection from the particulars of daily life. What generalizations about our society will these particulars justify? Does our society, as focused in these generalizations, have a mythology—a set of hypothetical or typical characters going through hypothetical or typical experiences?

KONRAD Z. LORENZ
The Taming of the Shrew[1]

Though Nature, red in tooth and claw,
With ravine, shrieked against his creed.
TENNYSON, *In Memoriam*

All shrews are particularly difficult to keep; this is not because, as we are led proverbially to believe, they are hard to tame, but because the metabolism of these smallest of mammals is so very fast that they will die of hunger within two or three hours if the food supply fails. Since they feed exclusively on small, living animals, mostly insects, and demand, of these, considerably more than their own weight every day, they are most exacting charges. At the time of which I am writing, I had never succeeded in keeping any of the terrestrial shrews alive for any length of time; most of those that I happened to obtain had probably only been caught because they were already ill and they died almost at once. I had never succeeded in procuring a healthy specimen. Now the order Insectivora is very low in the genealogical hierarchy of mammals and is, therefore, of particular interest to the comparative ethologist. Of the whole group, there was only one representative with whose behavior I was tolerably familiar, namely the hedgehog, an extremely interesting animal of whose ethology Professor Herter of Berlin has made a very thorough study. Of the behavior of all other members of the family practically nothing is known. Since they are nocturnal and partly subterranean animals, it is nearly impossible to approach them in field observation, and the difficulty of keeping them in captivity had hitherto precluded their study in the laboratory. So the Insectivores were officially placed on my program.

First I tried to keep the common mole. It was easy to procure a healthy specimen, caught to order in the nursery gardens of my father-in-law, and I found no difficulty in keeping it alive. Immediately on its arrival, it devoured an almost incredible quantity of

1. Chapter 9 of *King Solomon's Ring: New Light on Animal Ways*, 1952.

earthworms which, from the very first moment, it took from my hand. But, as an object of behavior study, it proved most disappointing. Certainly, it was interesting to watch its method of disappearing in the space of a few seconds under the surface of the ground, to study its astoundingly efficient use of its strong, spade-shaped fore-paws, and to feel their amazing strength when one held the little beast in one's hand. And again, it was remarkable with what surprising exactitude it located, by smell, from underground, the earthworms which I put on the surface of the soil in its terrarium. But these observations were the only benefits I derived from it. It never became any tamer and it never remained above ground any longer than it took to devour its prey; after this, it sank into the earth as a submarine sinks into the water. I soon grew tired of procuring the immense quantities of living food it required and, after a few weeks, I set it free in the garden.

It was years afterwards, on an excursion to that extraordinary lake, the Neusiedlersee, which lies on the Hungarian border of Austria, that I again thought of keeping an insectivore. This large stretch of water, though not thirty miles from Vienna, is an example of the peculiar type of lake found in the open steppes of Eastern Europe and Asia. More than thirty miles long and half as broad, its deepest parts are only about five feet deep and it is much shallower on the average. Nearly half its surface is overgrown with reeds which form an ideal habitat for all kinds of water birds. Great colonies of white, purple, and grey heron and spoonbills live among the reeds and, until a short while ago, glossy ibis were still to be found here. Greylag geese breed here in great numbers and, on the eastern, reedless shore, avocets and many other rare waders can regularly be found. On the occasion of which I am speaking, we, a dozen tired zoologists, under the experienced guidance of my friend Otto Koenig, were wending our way, slowly and painfully, through the forest of reeds. We were walking in single file, Koenig first, I second, with a few students in our wake. We literally left a wake, an inky-black one in pale grey water. In the reed forests of Lake Neusiedel, you walk knee deep in slimy, black ooze, wonderfully perfumed by sulphureted-hydrogen–producing bacteria. This mud clings tenaciously and only releases its hold on your foot with a loud, protesting plop at every step.

After a few hours of this kind of wading you discover aching muscles whose very existence you had never suspected. From the knees to the hips you are immersed in the milky, clay-colored water characteristic of the lake, which, among the reeds, is populated by myriads of extremely hungry leeches conforming to the old pharmaceutical recipe, "*Hirudines medicinales maxime affamati.*"[2] The

2. "In medicine, the hungriest leech is best."

rest of your person inhabits the upper air, which here consists of clouds of tiny mosquitoes whose bloodthirsty attacks are all the more exasperating because you require both your hands to part the dense reeds in front of you and can only slap your face at intervals. The British ornithologist who may perhaps have envied us some of our rare specimens will perceive that bird watching on Lake Neusiedel is not, after all, an entirely enviable occupation.

We were thus wending our painful way through the rushes when suddenly Koenig stopped and pointed mutely towards a pond, free from reeds, that stretched in front of us. At first, I could only see whitish water, dark blue sky and green reeds, the standard colors of Lake Neusiedel. Then, suddenly, like a cork popping up on to the surface, there appeared, in the middle of the pool, a tiny black animal, hardly bigger than a man's thumb. And for a moment I was in the rare position of a zoologist who sees a specimen and is not able to classify it, in the literal sense of the word: I did not know to which class of vertebrates the object of my gaze belonged. For the first fraction of a second I took it for the young of some diving bird of a species unknown to me. It appeared to have a beak and it swam on the water like a bird, not in it as a mammal. It swam about in narrow curves and circles, very much like a whirligig beetle, creating an extensive wedge-shaped wake, quite out of proportion to the tiny animal's size. Then a second little beast popped up from below, chased the first one with a shrill, bat-like twitter, then both dived and were gone. The whole episode had not lasted five seconds.

I stood open-mouthed, my mind racing. Koenig turned round with a broad grin, calmly detached a leech that was sticking like a leech to his wrist, wiped away the trickle of blood from the wound, slapped his cheek, thereby killing thirty-five mosquitoes, and asked, in the tone of an examiner, "What was that?" I answered as calmly as I could, "water shrews," thanking, in my heart, the leech and the mosquitoes for the respite they had given me to collect my thoughts. But my mind was racing on: water shrews ate fishes and frogs which were easy to procure in any quantity; water shrews were less subterranean than most other insectivores; they were the very insectivore to keep in captivity. "That's an animal I must catch and keep," I said to my friend. "That is easy," he responded. "There is a nest with young under the floor mat of my tent." I had slept that night in his tent and Koenig had not thought it worthwhile to tell me of the shrews; such things are, to him, as much a matter of course as wild little spotted crakes feeding out of his hand, or as any other wonders of his queer kingdom in the reeds.

On our return to the tent that evening, he showed me the nest. It contained eight young which, compared with their mother, who rushed away as we lifted the mat, were of enormous size. They were considerably more than half her length and must each have weighed well between a fourth and a third of their dam: that is to say, the whole litter weighed, at a very modest estimate, twice as much as the old shrew. Yet they were still quite blind and the tips of their teeth were only just visible in their rosy mouths. And two days later when I took them under my care, they were still quite unable to eat even the soft abdomens of grasshoppers, and in spite of evident greed, they chewed interminably on a soft piece of frog's meat without succeeding in detaching a morsel from it. On our journey home, I fed them on the squeezed-out insides of grasshoppers and finely minced frog's meat, a diet on which they obviously throve. Arrived home in Altenberg, I improved on this diet by preparing a food from the squeezed-out insides of mealworm larvae, with some finely chopped small, fresh fishes, worked into a sort of gravy with a little milk. They consumed large quantities of this food, and their little nest-box looked quite small in comparison with the big china bowl whose contents they emptied three times a day. All these observations raise the problem of how the female water shrew succeeds in feeding her gigantic litter. It is absolutely impossible that she should do so on milk alone. Even on a more concentrated diet my young shrews devoured the equivalent of their own weight daily and this meant nearly twice the weight of a grown shrew. Yet, at that time of their lives, young shrews could not possibly engulf a frog or a fish brought whole to them by their mother, as my charges indisputably proved. I can only think that the mother feeds her young by regurgitation of chewed food. Even thus, it is little short of miraculous that the adult female should be able to obtain enough meat to sustain herself and her voracious progeny.

When I brought them home, my young watershrews were still blind. They had not suffered from the journey and were as sleek and fat as one could wish. Their black, glossy coats were reminiscent of moles, but the white color of their underside, as well as the round, streamlined contours of their bodies, reminded me distinctly of penguins, and not, indeed, without justification: both the streamlined form and the light underside are adaptations to a life in the water. Many free-swimming animals, mammals, birds, amphibians and fishes, are silvery-white below in order to be invisible to enemies swimming in the depths. Seen from below, the shining white belly blends perfectly with the reflecting surface film of the water. It is very characteristic of these water animals that the dark dorsal and the white ventral colors do not merge gradually into each other as is the case in "counter-shaded" land animals whose coloring is calculated to make them invisible by eliminating the contrasting shade on their undersides. As in the killer whale, in dolphins, and in penguins, the white underside of the watershrew is divided from the dark upper side by a sharp line which runs, often in very decorative curves, along the animal's flank. Curiously enough, this borderline between black and white showed considerable variations in individuals and even on both sides of one animal's body. I welcomed this, since it enabled me to recognize my shrews personally.

Three days after their arrival in Altenberg my eight shrew babies opened their eyes and began, very cautiously, to explore the precincts of their nest-box. It was now time to remove them to an appropriate container, and on this question I expended much hard thinking. The enormous quantity of food they consumed and, consequently, of excrement they produced, made it impossible to keep them in an ordinary aquarium whose water, within a day, would have become a stinking brew. Adequate sanitation was imperative for particular reasons; in ducks, grebes, and all waterfowl, the plumage must be kept perfectly dry if the animal is to remain in a state of health, and the same premise may reasonably be expected to hold good of the shrew's fur. Now water which has been polluted soon turns strongly alkaline and this I knew to be very bad for the plumage of waterbirds. It causes saponification of the fat to which the feathers owe their waterproof quality, and the bird becomes thoroughly wet and is unable to stay on the water. I hold the record, as far as I know hitherto unbroken by any other birdlover, for having kept dabchicks alive and healthy in captivity for nearly two years, and even then they did not die but escaped, and may still be living. My experience with these birds proved the absolute necessity of keeping the water perfectly clean; whenever it became a little dirty I noticed their feathers beginning to get wet, a danger which they anxiously tried to counteract by constantly preening themselves. I had, therefore, to keep these little grebes in crystal clear water which was changed every day, and I rightly assumed that the same would be necessary for my water shrews.

I took a large aquarium tank, rather over a yard in length and about two feet wide. At each end of this, I placed two little tables, and weighed them down with heavy stones so that they would not float. Then I filled up the tank until the water was level with the tops of the tables. I did not at first push the tables close against the panes of the tank, which was rather narrow, for fear that the shrews might become trapped underwater in the blind alley beneath a table and drown there; this precaution, however, subsequently proved unnecessary. The water shrew which, in its natural state, swims great distances under the ice, is quite able to find its way to the open surface in much more difficult situations. The nest-box, which was placed on one of the tables, was equipped with a sliding shutter, so that I could imprison the shrews whenever the container had to be cleaned. In the morning, at the hour of general cage-cleaning, the shrews were usually at home and asleep, so that the procedure caused them no appreciable disturbance. I will admit that I take great pride in devising, by creative imagination, suitable containers for animals of which nobody, myself included, has had any previous experience, and it was particularly gratifying that the contraption described above proved so satisfactory that I never had to alter even the minutest detail.

When first my baby shrews were liberated in this container they took a very long time to explore the top of the table on which their nest-box was standing. The water's edge seemed to exert a strong attraction; they approached it ever and again, smelled the surface and seemed to feel along it with the long, fine whiskers which surround their pointed snouts like a halo and represent not only their most important organ of touch but the most important of all their sensory organs. Like other aquatic mammals, the water shrew differs from the terrestrial members of its class in that its nose, the guiding organ of the average mammal, is of no use whatsoever in its underwater hunting. The water shrew's whiskers are actively mobile like the antennae of an insect or the fingers of a blind man.

Exactly as mice and many other small rodents would do under similar conditions, the shrews interrupted their careful exploration of their new surroundings every few minutes to dash wildly back into the safe cover of their nest-box. The survival value of this peculiar behavior is evident: the animal makes sure, from time to time that it has not lost its way and that it can, at a moment's notice, retreat to the one place it knows to be safe. It was a queer spectacle to see those podgy black figures slowly and carefully whiskering their way forward and, in the next second, with lightning speed, dash back to the nest-box. Queerly enough, they did not run straight through the little door, as one would have expected, but in their wild dash for safety they jumped, one and all, first onto the roof of the box and only then, whiskering along its edge, found the opening and slipped in with a half somersault, their back turned nearly vertically downward. After many repetitions of this maneuver, they were able to find the opening without feeling for it; they "knew" perfectly its whereabouts yet still persisted in the leap onto the roof. They jumped onto it and immediately vaulted in through the door, but they never, as long as they lived, found out that the leap and vault which had become their habit was really quite unnecessary and that they could have run in directly without this extraordinary detour. We shall hear more about this dominance of path habits in the water shrew presently.

It was only on the third day, when the shrews had become thoroughly acquainted with the geography of their little rectangular island, that the largest and most enterprising of them ventured into the water. As is so often the case with mammals, birds, reptiles, and fishes, it was the largest and most handsomely colored male which played the role of leader. First he sat on the edge of the water and thrust in the fore part of his body, at the same time frantically paddling with his forelegs but still clinging with his hind ones to the board. Then he slid in, but in the next moment took fright, scampered madly across the surface very much after the manner of a frightened duckling, and jumped out onto the board at the opposite end of the tank. There he sat, excitedly grooming his belly with one hind paw, exactly as coypus and beavers do. Soon he quieted down and sat still for a moment. Then he went to the water's edge a second time, hesitated for a moment, and plunged in; diving immediately, he swam ecstatically about underwater, swerving upward and downward again, running quickly along the bottom, and finally jumping out of the water at the same place as he had first entered it.

When I first saw a water shrew swimming I was most struck by a thing which I ought to have expected but did not: at the moment of diving, the little black and white beast appears to be made of silver. Like the plumage of ducks and grebes, but quite unlike the fur of most water mammals, such as seals, otters, beavers or coypus, the fur of the water shrew remains absolutely dry under water, that is to say, it retains a thick layer of air while the animal is below the surface. In the other mammals mentioned above, it is only the short, woolly undercoat that remains dry, the superficial hair tips becoming wet, wherefore the animal looks its natural color when underwater and is superficially wet when it emerges. I was already aware of the peculiar qualities of the waterproof fur of the shrew, and, had I given it a thought, I should have known that it would look, under water, exactly like the air-retaining fur on the underside of a water beetle or on the abdomen of a water spider. Nevertheless the wonderful, transparent silver coat of the shrew was, to me, one of those delicious surprises that nature has in store for her admirers.

Another surprising detail which I only noticed when I saw my shrews in the water was that they have a fringe of stiff, erectile hairs on the outer side of their fifth toes and on the underside of their tails. These form collapsible oars and a collapsible rudder. Folded and inconspicuous as long as the animal is on dry land, they unfold the moment it enters the water and broaden the effective surface of the propelling feet and of the steering tail by a considerable area.

Like penguins, the water shrews looked rather awkward and ungainly on dry land but were transformed into objects of elegance and grace on entering the water. As long as they walked, their strongly convex underside made them look pot-bellied and reminiscent of an old, overfed dachshund. But under water, the very same protruding belly balanced harmoniously the curve of their back and gave a beautifully symmetrical streamline which, together with their silver coating and the elegance of their movements, made them a sight of entrancing beauty.

When they had all become familiar with the water, their container was one of the chief attractions that our research station had to offer to any visiting naturalists or animal lovers. Unlike all other mammals of their size, the water shrews were largely diurnal and, except in the early hours of the morning, three or four of them were constantly on the scene. It was exceedingly interesting to watch their movements upon and under the water. Like the whirligig beetle, Gyrinus, they could turn in an extremely small radius without diminishing their speed, a faculty for which the large rudder surface of the tail with its fringe of erectile hairs is evidently essential. They had two different ways of diving, either by taking a little jump as grebes or coots do and working their way down at a steep angle, or by simply lowering their snout under the surface and paddling very fast till they reached "planing speed," thus working their way downward on the principle of the inclined plane—in other words, performing the converse movement of an ascending airplane. The water shrew must expend a large amount of energy in staying down since the air contained in its fur exerts a strong pull upwards. Unless it is paddling straight downwards, a thing it rarely does, it is forced to maintain a constant minimum speed, keeping its body at a slightly downward angle in order not to float to the surface. While swimming under water the shrew seems to flatten, broadening its body in a peculiar fashion, in order to present a better planing surface to the water. I never saw my shrews try to cling by their claws to any underwater objects, as the dipper is alleged to do. When they seemed to be running along the bottom, they were really swimming close above it, but perhaps the smooth gravel on the bottom of the tank was unsuitable for holding on to and it did not occur to me then to offer them a rougher surface. They were very playful when in the water and chased one another loudly twittering on the surface, or silently in the depths. Unlike any other mammal, but just like water birds, they could rest on the surface; this they used to do, rolling partly over and grooming themselves. Once out again, they instantly proceeded to clean their fur—one is almost tempted to say "preen" it, so similar was their behavior to that of ducks which have just left the water after a long swim.

Most interesting of all was their method of hunting under water. They came swimming along with an erratic course, darting a foot or so forward very swiftly in a straight line, then starting to gyrate in looped turns at reduced speed. While swimming straight and swiftly their whiskers were, as far as I could see, laid flat against their head, but while circling they were erect and bristled out in all directions, as they sought contact with some prey. I have no reason to believe that vision plays any part in the water shrew's hunting, except perhaps in the activation of its tactile search. My shrews may have noticed visually the presence of the live tadpoles or little fishes which I put in the tank, but in the actual hunting of its prey the animal is exclusively guided by its sense of touch, located in the wide-spreading whiskers on its snout. Certain small free-swimming species of catfish find their prey by exactly the same method. When these fishes swim fast and straight, the long feelers on their snout are depressed but, like the shrew's whiskers, are stiffly spread out when the fish becomes conscious of the proximity of potential prey; like the shrew, the fish then begins to gyrate blindly in order to establish contact with its prey. It may not even be necessary for the water shrew actually to touch its prey with one of its whiskers. Perhaps, at very close range, the water vibration caused by the movements of a small fish, a tadpole or a water insect is perceptible by those sensitive tactile organs. It is quite impossible to determine this question by mere observation, for the action is much too quick for the human eye. There is a quick turn and a snap and the shrew is already paddling shorewards with a wriggling creature in its maw.

In relation to its size, the water shrew is perhaps the most terrible predator of all vertebrate animals, and it can even vie with the invertebrates, including the murderous Dytiscus larva. It has been reported by A. E. Brehm that water shrews have killed fish more than sixty times heavier than themselves by biting out their eyes and brain. This happened only when the fish were confined in containers with no room for escape. The same story has been told to me by fishermen on Lake Neusiedel, who could not possibly have heard Brehm's report. I once offered to my shrews a large edible frog. I never did it again, nor could I bear to see out to its end the cruel scene that ensued. One of the shrews encountered the frog in the basin and instantly gave chase, repeatedly seizing hold of the creature's legs; although it was kicked off again it did not cease in its attack and finally, the frog, in desperation, jumped out of the water and onto one of the tables, where several shrews raced to the pursuer's assistance and buried their teeth in the legs and hindquarters of the wretched frog. And now, horribly, they began to eat the frog alive, beginning just where each one of them happened to have hold of it; the poor frog croaked heartrendingly, as the jaws of the shrews munched audibly in chorus. I need hardly be blamed for bringing this experiment to an abrupt and agitated end and putting the lacerated frog out of its misery. I never offered the shrews large prey again but only such as would be killed at the first bite or two. Nature can be very cruel indeed; it is not out of pity that most of the larger predatory animals kill their prey quickly. The lion has to finish off a big antelope or a buffalo very quickly indeed in order not to get hurt itself, for a beast of prey which has to hunt daily cannot afford to receive even a harmless scratch in effecting a kill; such scratches would soon add up to such an extent as to put the killer out of action. The same reason has forced the python and other large snakes to evolve a quick and really humane method of killing the well-armed mammals that are their natural prey. But where there is no danger of the victim doing damage to the killer, the latter shows no pity whatsoever. The hedgehog which, by virtue of its armor, is quite immune to the bite of a snake, regularly proceeds to eat it, beginning at the tail or in the middle of its body, and in the same way the water shrew treats its innocuous prey. But man should abstain from judging his innocently-cruel fellow creatures, for even if nature sometimes "shrieks against his creed," what pain does he himself not inflict upon the living creatures that he hunts for pleasure and not for food?

The mental qualities of the water shrew cannot be rated very high. They were quite tame and fearless of me and never tried to bite when I took them in my hand, nor did they ever try to evade it, but, like little tame rodents, they tried to dig their way out if I held them for too long in the hollow of my closed fist. Even when I took them out of their container and put them on a table or on the floor, they were by no means thrown into a panic but were quite ready to take food out of my hand and even tried actively to creep into it if they felt a longing for cover. When, in such an unwonted environment, they were shown their nest-box, they plainly showed that they knew it by sight and instantly made for it, and even pursued it with upraised heads if I moved the box along above them, just out of their reach. All in all, I really may pride myself that I have tamed the shrew, or at least one member of that family.

In their accustomed surroundings, my shrews proved to be very strict creatures of habit. I have already mentioned the remarkable conservatism with which they persevered in their unpractical way of entering their nest-box by climbing onto its roof and then vaulting, with a half turn, in through the door. Something more must be said about the unchanging tenacity with which these animals cling to their habits once they have formed them. In the water shrew, the path habits, in particular, are of a really amazing immutability; I hardly know another instance to which the saying, "As the twig is bent, so the tree is inclined," applies so literally.

In a territory unknown to it, the water shrew will never run fast except under pressure of extreme fear, and then it will run blindly along, bumping into objects and usually getting caught in a blind alley. But, unless the little animal is severely frightened, it moves, in strange surroundings, only step by step, whiskering right and left all the time and following a path that is anything but straight. Its course is determined by a hundred fortuitous factors when it walks that way for the first time. But, after a few repetitions, it is evident that the shrew recognizes the locality in which it finds itself and that it repeats, with the utmost exactitude, the movements which it performed the previous time. At the same time, it is noticeable that the animal moves along much faster whenever it is repeating what it has already learned. When placed on a path which it has already traversed a few times, the shrew starts on its way slowly, carefully whiskering. Suddenly it finds known bearings, and now rushes forward a short distance, repeating exactly every step and turn which it executed on the last occasion. Then, when it comes to a spot where it ceases to know the way by heart, it is reduced to whiskering again and to feeling its way step by step. Soon, another burst of speed follows and the same thing is repeated, bursts of speed alternating with very slow progress. In the beginning of this process of learning their way, the shrews move along at an extremely slow average rate and the little bursts of speed are few and far between. But gradually the little laps of the course which have been "learned by heart" and which can be covered quickly begin to increase in length as well as in number until they fuse and the whole course can be completed in a fast, unbroken rush.

Often, when such a path habit is almost completely formed, there still remains one particularly difficult place where the shrew always loses its bearings and has to resort to its senses of smell and touch, sniffing and whiskering vigorously to find out where the next reach of its path "joins on." Once the shrew is well settled in its path habits it is as strictly bound to them as a railway engine to its tracks and as unable to deviate from them by even a few centimeters. If it diverges from its path by so much as an inch, it is forced to stop abruptly, and laboriously regain its bearings. The same behavior can be caused experimentally by changing some small detail in the customary path of the animal. Any major alteration in the habitual path threw the shrews into complete confusion. One of their paths ran along the wall adjoining the wooden table opposite to that on which the nest box was situated. This table was weighted with two stones lying close to the panes of the tank, and the shrews, running along the wall, were accustomed to jump on and off the stones which lay right in their path. If I moved the stones out of the runway, placing both together in the middle of the table, the shrews would jump right up into the air in the place where the stone should have been; they came down with a jarring bump, were obviously disconcerted and started whiskering cautiously right and left, just as they behaved in an unknown environment. And then they did a most interesting thing: they went back the way they had come, carefully feeling their way until they had again got their bearings. Then, facing round again, they tried a second time with a rush and jumped and crashed down exactly as they had done a few seconds before. Only then did they seem to realize that the first fall had not been their own fault but was due to a change in the wonted pathway, and now they proceeded to explore the alteration, cautiously sniffing and bewhiskering the place where the stone ought to have been. This method of going back to the start, and trying again always reminded me of. a small boy who, in reciting a poem, gets stuck and begins again at an earlier verse.

In rats, as in many small mammals, the process of forming a path habit, for instance in learning a maze, is very similar to that just described; but a rat is far more adaptable in its behavior and would not dream of trying to jump over a stone which was not there. The preponderance of motor habit over present perception is a most remarkable peculiarity of the water shrew. One might say that the animal actually disbelieves its senses if they report a change of environment which necessitates a sudden alteration in its motor habits. In a new environment a water shrew would be perfectly able to see a stone of that size and consequently to avoid it or to run over it in a manner well adapted to the spatial conditions; but once a habit is formed and has become ingrained, it supersedes all better knowledge. I know of no animal that is a slave to its habits in so literal a sense as the water shrew. For this animal the geometric axiom that a straight line is the shortest distance between two points simply does not hold good. To them, the shortest line is always the accustomed path and, to a certain extent, they are justified in adhering to this principle: they run with amazing speed along their pathways and arrive at their destination much sooner than they would if, by whiskering and nosing, they tried to go straight. They will keep to the wonted path, even though it winds in such a way that it crosses and recrosses itself. A rat or mouse would be quick to discover that it was making an unnecessary detour, but the water shrew is no more able to do so than is a toy train to turn off at right angles at a level crossing. In order to change its route, the water shrew must change its whole path habit, and this cannot be done at a moment's notice but gradually, over a long period of time. An unnecessary, loop-shaped detour takes weeks and weeks to become a little shorter, and after months it is not even approximately straight. The biological advantage of such a path habit is obvious: it compensates the shrew for being nearly blind and enables it to run exceedingly fast without wasting a minute on orientation. On the other hand it may, under unusual circumstances, lead the shrew to destruction. It has been reported, quite plausibly, that water shrews have broken their necks by jumping into a pond which had been recently drained. In spite of the possibility of such mishaps, it would be shortsighted if one were simply to stigmatize the water shrew as stupid because it solves the spatial problems of its daily life in quite a different way from man. On the contrary, if one thinks a little more deeply, it is very wonderful that the same result, namely a perfect orientation in space, can be brought about in two so widely divergent ways: by true observation, as we achieve it, or, as the water shrew does, by learning by heart every possible spatial contingency that may arise in a given territory.

Among themselves, my water shrews were surprisingly good-natured. Although, in their play, they would often chase each other, twittering with a great show of excitement, I never saw a serious fight between them until an unfortunate accident occurred: one morning, I forgot to reopen the little door of the nest-box after cleaning out their tank. When at last I remembered, three hours had elapsed—a very long time for the swift metabolism of such small insectivores. Upon the opening of the door, all the shrews rushed out and made a dash for the food tray. In their haste to get out, not only did they soil themselves all over but they apparently discharged, in their excitement, some sort of glandular secretion, for a strong, musk-like odor accompanied their exit from the box. Since they appeared to have incurred no damage by their three hours' fasting, I turned away from the box to occupy myself with other things. However, on nearing the container soon afterwards, I heard an unusually loud, sharp twittering and, on my hurried approach, found my eight shrews locked in deadly battle. Two were even then dying and, though I consigned them at once to separate cages, two more died in the course of the day. The real cause of this sudden and terrible battle is hard to ascertain but I cannot help suspecting that the shrews, owing to the sudden change in the usual odor, had failed to recognize each other and had fallen upon each other as they would have done upon strangers. The four survivors quietened down after a certain time and I was able to reunite them in the original container without fear of further mishap.

I kept those four remaining shrews in good health for nearly seven months and would probably have had them much longer if the assistant whom I had engaged to feed them had not forgotten to do so. I had been obliged to go to Vienna and, on my return in the late afternoon, was met by that usually reliable fellow who turned pale when he saw me, thereupon remembering that he had forgotten to feed the shrews. All four of them were alive but very weak; they ate greedily when we fed them but died nonetheless within a few hours. In other words, they showed exactly the same symptoms as the shrews which I had formerly tried to keep; this confirmed my opinion that the latter were already dying of hunger when they came into my possession.

To any advanced animal keeper who is able to set up a large tank, preferably with running water, and who can obtain a sufficient supply of small fish, tadpoles, and the like, I can recommend the water shrew as one of the most gratifying, charming, and interesting objects of care. Of course it is a somewhat exacting charge. It will eat raw chopped heart (the customary substitute for small live prey) only in the absence of something better and it cannot be fed exclusively on this diet for long periods. Moreover, really clean water is indispensable. But if these clear-cut requirements be fulfilled, the water shrew will not merely remain alive but will really thrive, nor do I exclude the possibility that it might even breed in captivity.

QUESTIONS

1. Lorenz discusses a field trip and some other matters before he reports his laboratory observations. What is the effect of this organization?
2. What features of the shrew's behavior does Lorenz select for special emphasis? What conclusions does he draw about these features?
3. Though this is mainly a report of his observations, Lorenz includes matters which are not necessary to the report of strictly controlled observation of the shrew's habits. Indicate some of the places where his discussion moves beyond strict reporting. Characterize the roles he assumes in these passages. Do these other roles or revelations of personality compromise or support his claim to being a scientist?

JOHN D. STEWART

Vulture Country

Spain is the stronghold of the vultures. There are four listed species in Europe, two common and two rare; if they are anywhere, they are in Spain. The bearded vulture and the black survive there, the Egyptian flourishes, and the great griffon swarms. The further south you go the more numerous they become, until you reach the hot grazing plains of Andalusia. There, summer and winter through, they hang in hordes in the roofless sky, for Andalusia is the vulture country.

There are three essential qualities for vulture country: a rich supply of unburied corpses, high mountains, a strong sun. Spain has the first of these, for in this sparsely populated and stony land it is not customary, or necessary, to bury dead animals. Where there are vultures in action such burial would be a self-evident waste of labor, with inferior sanitary results. Spain has mountains, too, in no part far to seek; and the summer sun is hot throughout the country. But it is hottest in Andalusia, and that is the decisive factor.

The sun, to the vulture, is not just something which makes life easier and pleasanter, a mere matter of preference. His mode of life is impossible without it. Here in Andalusia the summer sun dries up every pond and lake and almost every river. It drives the desperate frogs deep into the mud cracks and forces the storks to feed on locusts. It kills the food plants and wilts the fig trees over the heads of the panting flocks. Andalusia becomes like that part of ancient Greece, "a land where men fight for the shade of an ass."

All animals, both tame and wild, weaken in these circumstances, and the weakest go to the wall and die. The unpitying sun glares down on the corpses and speeds their putrefaction, rotting the hide and softening the sinews and the meat, to the vulture's advantage. But the sun plays a still greater part in his life. Its main and vital function, for him, is the creation of thermal currents in the atmosphere, for without these he would be helpless.

The vulture must fly high—high enough to command a wide territory, for, except at times of catastrophe, dead animals are never thick on the ground. His task is to soar to ten thousand feet, more or less, two or three times in a day, and to hang there and keep constant survey. A male griffon weighs up to sixteen pounds, so that to hoist himself up to that necessary viewpoint would call for fifty-three thousand calories, the equivalent of fifty pounds of meat. To find and eat three times his own weight in a day is clearly impossible; a short cut must be made. In the dawn of any day, in Andalusia, you may see the vulture discovering that short cut.

The eagles, buzzards, kites, and falcons are already on the wing, quartering the plain fast and low, seeking reptiles and small game. But the vulture sits on a crag and waits. He sees the sun bound up out of the sierra, and still he waits. He waits until the sun-struck rocks and the hard earth heat up and the thermal currents begin to rise. When the upstream is strong enough, he leaps out from the cliff, twists into it and without one laborious wingbeat, spirals and soars.

By the time the vulture reaches his station, a half hour later and maybe more, the sun is blazing down on the plain and betraying every detail to his telescopic eye, and the updraft is strengthening as the day approaches its zenith. His ceiling for this day is fixed by two factors. One is the strength and buoyancy of his chosen thermal, which will vary with the strength of the sun and the behavior of the upper winds. But the more important factor, for it fixes his horizontal bearings as well, is the distribution of neighboring vultures in the sky, his colleagues and competitors.

He cocks his head from side to side and checks their various positions. There they hang, dotted across the clear sky at intervals of a mile or so—at the corners of one-mile squares. Height and lateral distances all adjusted, the vulture settles, circling slowly on his invisible support, and begins his long and lonely vigil.

This griffon vulture, which I select from the four species as being by far the most prevalent and typical, is almost sure to be a male. The female rarely leaves her nest from early March, when she lays her rough white egg, until August, when her huge poult is fledged and flying. The father has to feed and carry for all three.

At first glance, from below, he appears as one great wing, ten feet from tip to tip and two feet broad. His tail is square and very short, which is all it needs to be, for there are no sharp or sudden quirks in his flight that would call for a strong rudder. His movements are premeditated, stressless, and leisurely, for his energy must be conserved at all costs and never wasted on aerobatics.

The vulture's head and neck, too, protrude very little in front of his wing plane, and this distinguishes his flight silhouette from the eagle's. His neck is, in fact, some two feet long, but since it is bare—and must be bare—he folds it back into his collar to keep it warm. His head, apart from its nakedness, is like an eagle's; his yellow claws, which never kill and rarely carry, are shorter and not so strong. His plumage is a uniform sandy color, faded and tattered by work and waiting and, perhaps, by old age. It is relieved only by his coffee-colored ruff and the broad black primary wing feathers fingering the air.

The vulture sails in silence, for no vocal signals could serve him at such a distance from his fellows. He croaks, growls, and whistles only in his family circle, and at his feasts. He circles by almost imperceptible adjustments of his wing planes, aided by slight twists of his tail. But his head is in constant and active movement. He swivels it from one side to the other, bringing each eye in turn to bear on the earth. Then he bends his neck to right or left to check on one of his neighbors to north, south, east or west.

The whole vulture network is interdependent. Each vulture can give and receive two signals or, as the scientists call them, "visual stimuli." Circling means "Nothing doing"; dropping, or its resultant hole in the sky, calls "Come here!" Like all other vultures, he rests reassured by the first and is rapidly and relentlessly drawn by the second.

It is demonstrable how, with a special density of nerve endings on his retina, the vulture can see a small animal from a great height. Many other birds—gannets, for example—have the same propensity. Their eyesight is surprising only when we compare it with the poor standards of our own. But a mystery remains: how does the bird know that the animal is dead? The sense of smell is to be ruled out straightway. It is impossible that it would operate at such a distance, even allowing for the upward current of air. Birds are not, generally, well endowed in this respect, and in the vulture's case this may be especially fortunate.

No book, no expert, could answer this question for me, and I carried it through the vulture country for years, the one tantalizing imponderable, the broken link. Then, one hot afternoon, I lay down beside an old swineherd in the shade of a cork oak on the foothills overlooking the great plan of La Janda. For fifty years, he told me, he had watched pigs on that plain—the pigs, yes, and the vultures. I put my problem to him.

The swineherd's theory is not to be proved, but it is a wise one and I shall hold it until I find a better. No, he said, it is not the white belly skin that distinguishes the dead animals. White fur may fix the vulture's eye, but it does not offer him evidence of death. All herds and flocks, said the old man, lie down together and at one time. They have their place and their hour of rest. When a vulture sees an animal lying alone and apart, he is bound to notice it. The next time he crosses, the same image strikes his eye and startles him again. Over and over again he marks it and waits and watches; but now, alerted, he watches it more closely.

The next day the animal is still there; his attention is fixed upon it now, so he circles a little lower, his eye riveted, seeking the slightest movement of limb or lung. He sees none, but he continues to wait, said the old man. It takes him two days, at least, to confirm death. He goes on circling, but lower. He becomes more engrossed, and more sure. The other vultures note his behavior and move over a little in the sky. Every time he falls, they move closer. Now he is very low. He seeks the heaving of the flanks or eye movements; he sees neither. At some point, perhaps, he receives a visual stimulus in some death sign—the protruding tongue or the wide and whitened eye. Then he falls quickly, landing heavily at a little distance from the corpse.

The swineherd and I watched the first vulture land. We watched him sidling and circling the dead goat standing erect to see better, wing tips trailing, naked neck stretched to the full, head swiveling rapidly to bring alternate eyes to bear. He hopped closer and paused, peering intently. If he could smell, even as well as we, his doubts would have been over. But he stood there, irresolute, famished yet fearful, with his bill open and his wings ready for use.

Then a big shadow swept across the brown grass, and the vulture glanced upwards. His involuntary signal had been answered, and a tall column of vultures wheeled overhead. He hopped to close quarters, stretched forward, pecked the corpse, and leapt back. He watched it for a second more; no movement. Then he croaked once, as though to bless himself, and threw himself on the body. He struck his heavy beak into the flank, flapped for balance, and thrust backwards with feet and wings to strip the hide from the ribs and belly.

Almost immediately there were eight more vultures at the corpse, and we saw that all of them sought and fought for the same place. Their aim was to penetrate, their object the viscera. Watching them thrusting their long necks deep into the belly cavity and withdrawing them befouled and bloodstained, I saw why those necks must be bare. Yes, said the swineherd, and that is the one part the vulture cannot reach to clean. His mate may clean it for him later, for pure greed, but if he had feathers there he would have maggots in them.

Now sixteen more vultures swept down, landing heavily in their haste and flap-hopping to the feast—the second square from the sky pattern. The corpse was covered, submerged in a heaving, struggling mass of broad brown wings. A new column wheeled above us, circling lower. There should be twenty-four up there, I reckoned. There were twenty-three.

The latecomers landed on nearby trees, including ours, and their weight bent thick limbs to the ground. From points four miles distant, we could expect thirty-four more, and at the height of the carnival I counted just short of one hundred birds.

A mule lasts two hours, said the old man, and an ox, three. This goat became bones in the sun in half an hour.

As the hundred fed, or hoped and waited, many more vultures circled high above, assessing the situation and the prospects and treasuring their altitude. Toward the end, when the feasters scattered and exposed the small skeleton, the watchers flapped and drifted wearily away to resume their distant stations. But they had fulfilled their function. They had marked the spot and drawn the Egyptian vultures and the kites.

Now the little Egyptian vultures landed daintily and dodged nimbly through the throng of giants. They are bare on the face and throat only, with well-feathered head and neck, and so, perforce, they are cleaner feeders. The dirty work has been done; now the long and delicate beak comes into play. The Egyptian vultures attack the skull, the large joints, and the crevices of the pelvic girdle—all parts inaccessible to the griffon's heavy beak. They extract brains, membranes, and the spinal cord, and clip out tendons and ligaments. They dodge out through the encircling griffons with their spoils, gobble them swiftly, and dance back for more. The griffons, gorged with meat and panting in the sun, pay them scant attention.

Finally, when all but the whistling kites have left the scene, comes the great solitary bearded vulture, the fierce lammergeier. His whole head is feathered, so he despises carrion. He lives aloof from all the rest of the vulture tribe, but they serve his interests, so he keeps them within sight. The old swineherd calls him *Quebrantahuesos*—the bone smasher—and Aeschylus noted him, long ago, for the same behavior. The lammergeier seizes the largest bones, carries them high, in his claws, and drops them on the rocks. Then he swoops down and rakes out the marrow.

Like an eagle, he can kill as well as carry with his claws, and he has not the true vulture's patient, soaring habit. He attacks flocks and herds and carries off the lambs and kids and piglets. After his work has been done nothing will remain except an empty skull and some small bones, which the ants and carrion beetles pick and polish.

Our griffon, first on the scene, will not be the first to leave it. He is sure to have gorged himself with his advantage. Crop, throat, and neck distended, he squats back on his tail, with his wings spread to steady him and his beak hanging open. From time to time he chokes and belches and gags, and it is an hour, maybe, before the meat subsides in him.

When he is ready, the griffon runs and leaps across the plain, thrashing heavily with his big wings, and labors into the air. He finds a thermal, circles in it to his altitude, then slips sideways and sweeps gently across the sierra to his distant nest.

The griffon vultures are gregarious in nesting, with colonies throughout the mountains at fairly regular intervals of thirty miles. They are said to pair for life. Certainly they return every year to the same nest. In January they begin to repair the nest, a broad and battered saucer of strong branches, topped with twigs and grass. They are careless builders, and many nests have bare rock protruding in them. No attempt is made to cover it. The egg is laid in late February and incubated for forty days. The new chick is bare and blue-skinned and looks as though he might become a dragon, but soon he sprouts white down and begins to assert the characteristics of his race. In a month he is voracious, and by the end of April he will demand four pounds of meat every day. Before he is fledged he will need eight pounds. Providentially, his demands coincide with the heyday of death.

When the male vulture arrives at the nest he settles on a nearby ledge, vomits, and sorts out the result with his beak. The female helps with this assessment, feeding herself hungrily on the larger relics. Then she offers her gape and crop to her cowering, whistling infant. The chick gobbles madly. With vultures it can never be "little and often," for animals die irregularly, as they must, so the birds, young and old, must gorge to the neck when opportunity offers. That is their instinct and their nature.

A male vulture with family responsibilities cannot rest for long. Now that his load is delivered and eaten, he is likely to be the hungriest of the family. This, too, is as it should be, for the hunger sends him out and up again, however little daylight may remain, to circle in the sky until the sunset reddens the sierra.

Time was when the summer drought killed thousands of beasts

every year and the floods of winter hundreds more. Nowadays there are fewer casualties, but the vultures still have a fairly constant food supply in the charnel gorges, which lie below most mountain villages.

Grazalema, Arcos, Casares, and a hundred more were built, for protection from the raiding Moors, on the edge of the precipice. All dead and dying animals, as well as all the garbage of the town, are simply pushed over the cliff and left to the birds. There is a bird in Andalusia for every class and size of refuse. From the escarpment you can watch all the scavengers of the air, soaring below you or fighting on the feast. The great black vulture may be here, the griffon and Egyptian for sure, and two kinds of kites. The cunning ravens and carrion crows wait on the outskirts, dashing in to snatch their choice. Clouds of choughs and jackdaws wheel and cry above them.

There is a new feeding ground in the unfenced highways of Andalusia. As motor traffic increases, these offer more and more dead dogs, cats, kids, pigs, and rabbits. If you are abroad at dawn, it is a common thing to run down a vulture intent on scraping a dead dog off the asphalt. Even so, with an apparently limitless population of these great birds, each looking for some thirty pounds of meat every day, one wonders how they flourish.

Their wonderful feeding system has, it seems to me, one fatal flaw. They can signal "Food here," but not how much. At the feast which I have described only some succeeded in feeding at all, and only two or three ate their fill. A majority came the distance and lost their height for little or for nothing.

In Africa, also vulture country, there is no such difficulty, for there all the game is big game, and every funeral is worth attending. It may be that some of our Andalusian vultures go there in the winter. Certainly our vulture population increases here, but that is because the vultures from further north crowd in as the heat decreases and the air currents weaken in their homelands. Fortunately, there is a seasonal food supply ready for them all, for it is the time of birth, with all its failures and fatalities. After the winter storms, too, the torrents offer up their toll of corpses. And in winter, each bird has only himself to feed. But you would not doubt, if you knew the constant panic for food which dominates him summer and winter alike, that the vulture leads a competitive and anxious life. He has strong forces for survival. It is held—and we know it to be true of eagles—that the vulture has a very long life. If this longevity is a fact, then the solitary chick each year may add up to a good replacement rate.

The nest is inaccessible, and the hen guards it constantly against the only possible natural enemy—other vultures or raptors. So the survival rate must be high as is proved by the evident increase toward saturation point.

At times, lying on my back on the plain with binoculars trained on the sky, I have seen vultures circling in two or three layers, each one high above the other. What can this mean? A hungry duplication, or triplication, hopelessly covering the same feeding ground and using the only available thermals? Or the opposite—idle and well-fed reserves standing by for surplus?

No one can tell me. But here in the vulture country there are no birds more spectacular, more fascinating to watch and to study. In time we may find out the last of their secrets. I lie on the plains and keep on watching them. And they, I know, keep on watching me.

QUESTIONS

1. *On page 981 Stewart explains the vulture's aerodynamics. What is the crucial problem and how does the bird's genetic "design" permit him to solve it?*
2. *The feast which is concluded on page 985 might reasonably be taken as the climax of the essay, but in fact Stewart goes on to do more. What does his continuation add to the essay?*
3. *Why do the vultures keep watching Stewart and what are the implications of that last sentence?*

BERTON ROUECHÉ
A Game of Wild Indians

During the second week in August, 1946, an elderly man, a middle-aged woman, and a boy of ten dragged themselves, singly and painfully, into the Presbyterian Hospital, in the Washington Heights section of Manhattan, where their trouble was unhesitatingly identified as typhoid fever. This diagnosis was soon confirmed by laboratory analysis, and on Thursday morning, August 15th, a report of the outbreak was dutifully telephoned to the Department of Health. It was received and recorded there, in accordance with the routine in all alarms of an epidemiological nature, by a clerk in the Bureau of Preventable Diseases named Beatrice Gamso. Miss Gamso is a low-strung woman and she has spent some thirty callousing years in the Health Department, but the news gave her a turn. She sat for an instant with her eyes on her notes. Then, steadying herself with a practiced hand, she swung around to her typewriter and set briskly about dispatching copies of the report to all administrative officers of the Department. Within an hour, a reliable investigator from the Bureau was on his way to Washington Heights. He was presently followed by one of his colleagues, a Department public-health nurse, several agents from the Bureau of Food and Drugs, and an inspector from the Bureau of Sanitary Engineering.

Typhoid fever was among the last of the massive pestilential fevers to yield to the probings of medical science, but its capitulation has been complete. It is wholly transparent now. Its clinical manifestations (a distinctive rash and a tender spleen, a fiery fever and a languid pulse, and nausea, diarrhea, and nosebleed), its cause (a bacillus known as *Eberthella typhosa*), and its means of transmission have all been clearly established. Typhoid is invariably conveyed by food or drink contaminated with the excreta of its victims. Ordinarily, it is spread by someone who is ignorant, at least momentarily, of his morbid condition. One reason for such unawareness is that for the first several days typhoid fever tends to be disarmingly mild and indistinguishable from the countless fleeting malaises that dog the human race. Another is that nearly five per cent of the cases become typhoid carriers, continuing indefinitely to harbor a lively colony of typhoid bacilli in their systems. The existence of typhoid carriers was discovered by a group of German hygienists in 1907. Typhoid Mary Mallon, a housemaid and cook who was the stubborn cause of a total of fifty-three cases in and around New York City a generation ago, is, of course, the most celebrated of these hapless menaces. About seventy per cent, by some unexplained, physiological fortuity, are women. The names of three hundred and eighty local carriers are currently on active file in the Bureau of Preventable Diseases. They are called on regularly by public-health nurses and are permanently enjoined from any employment that involves the handling of food. More than a third of all the cases that occur here are traced to local carriers but, because of the vigilance of the Health Department, rarely to recorded carriers; new ones keep turning up. Most of the rest of the cases are of unknown or out-of-town origin. A few are attribuable to the products of polluted waters (clams and oysters and various greens).

The surveillance of carriers is one of several innovations that in little more than a generation have forced typhoid fever into an abrupt tractability throughout most of the Western world. The others include certain refinements in diagnostic technique, the institution of public-health measures requiring the chlorination of city-supplied water and proscribing the sale of unpasteurized milk, and the development of an immunizing vaccine. Since late in the nineteenth century, the local incidence of typhoid fever has dropped from five or six thousand cases a year to fewer than fifty, and it is very possible that it may soon be as rare as smallpox. Banishment has not, however, materially impaired the vigor of *Eberthella typhosa*. Typhoid fever is still a cruel and withering affliction. It is always rambunctious, generally prolonged, and often fatal. It is also one of the most explosive of communicable diseases. The month in which it is most volcanic is August.

The investigator who led the sprint to Washington Heights that August morning in 1946 was Dr. Harold T. Fuerst, an epidemiologist, and he and Dr. Ottavio J. Pellitteri, another epidemiologist, handled most of the medical inquiry. One afternoon, when I was down at the Bureau, they told me about the case. Miss Gamso sat at a desk nearby, and I noticed after a moment that she was following the conversation with rapt attention. Her interest, it turned out, was entirely understandable. Typhoid-fever investigations are frequently tedious, but they are seldom protracted. It is not unusual for a team of experienced operatives to descry the source of an outbreak in a couple of days. Some cases have been riddled in an afternoon. The root of the trouble on Washington Heights eluded detection for almost two weeks, and it is probable that but for Miss Gamso it would never have been detected at all.

"I got to Presbyterian around eleven," Dr. Fuerst told me. "I found a staff man I knew, and he led me up to the patients. It was typhoid, all right. Not that I'd doubted it, but it's routine to take a look. And they were in bad shape—too miserable to talk. One— the woman—was barely conscious. I decided to let the questioning go for the time being. At least until I'd seen their histories. A clerk in the office of the medical superintendent dug them out for me. Pretty skimpy—name, age, sex, occupation, and address, and a few clinical notations. About all I got at a glance was that they weren't members of the same family. I'd hoped, naturally, that they would be. That would have nicely limited the scope of the investigation. Then I noticed something interesting. They weren't a family, but they had a little more in common than just typhoid. For one thing, they were by way of being neighbors. One of them lived at 502 West 180th Street, another at 501 West 178th Street, and the third at 285 Audubon Avenue, just around the corner from where it runs through the five-hundred block of West 179th Street. Another thing was their surnames. They were different, but they weren't dissimilar. All three were of Armenian origin. Well, Washington Heights has an Armenian colony—very small and very clannish. I began to feel pretty good. I didn't doubt for a minute that the three of them knew each other. Quite possibly they were friends. If so, it was reasonable to suppose that they might recently have shared a meal. It wasn't very likely, of course, that they had been the only ones to share it. Ten-year-old boys don't usually go out to meals without their parents. Maybe there had been a dozen in on it. It could even have been some sort of national feast. Or a church picnic. Picnic food is an ideal breeding ground for the typhoid organism. It can't stand cooking, but it thrives in raw stuff—ice cream and mayonnaise and so on. And if a carrier had happened to have a hand in the arrangements . . . I decided we'd do well to check and see if there was an Armenian carrier on our list."

"We found one, all right," Dr. Pellitteri said. "A widow named Christos—she died a year or two ago—who lived on West 178th Street."

"To be sure, we had only three cases," Dr. Fuerst went on. "But I didn't let that bother me. I've never known an outbreak of typhoid in which everybody who was exposed got sick. There are always a certain number who escape. They either don't eat whatever it is that's contaminated or they have a natural or an acquired immunity. Moreover, the incubation period in typhoid—the time it takes for the bug to catch hold—varies with the individual. Ten days is about the average, but it can run anywhere from three to thirty. In other words, maybe we had seen only the vanguard. There might be more to come. So in the absence of anything better, the Armenian link looked pretty good. I called the Bureau and told Bill Birnkrant—he was acting director at the time—what I thought, and he seemed to think the same. He said he'd start somebody checking. I went back upstairs for another try at the patients."

"That's when the rest of us began to come into the picture," Dr. Pellitteri said. "My job was the recent social life of the Armenian colony. Ida Matthews, a public-health nurse, took the carrier angle. Neither of us had much luck. The file listed twelve carriers in Washington Heights. As I remember, the only Armenian was Mrs. Christos. At any rate, the nurse picked her first. I remember running into Miss Matthews somewhere on Audubon toward the end of that first afternoon. She told me what progress she had made. None. Mrs. Christos was old and sick, and hadn't been out of her apartment for a month. Miss Matthews said there was no reason to doubt the woman's word, as she had a good reputation at the Department—very coöperative, obeyed all the rules. Miss Matthews was feeling pretty gloomy. She'd had high hopes. Well, I knew how she felt. I'd hit nothing but dead ends myself. Our patients didn't seem to be friends. Apparently, they just knew each other. The priest at the Gregorian church in the neighborhood— Holy Cross Armenian Apostolic, on West 187th Street—knew of no recent feasts or festivals. He hadn't heard of any unusual amount of illness in the parish, either. No mysterious chills and fevers. And the Armenian doctors in the neighborhood said the same. They had seen nothing that resembled typhoid except the cases we already had. Before I gave up for the day, I even got in touch with an Armenian girl who used to work at the Department. The only thing I could think of at the moment was a check of the Armenian restaurants. When I mentioned that, she burst out laughing. It seems Armenians don't frequent Armenian restaurants. They prefer home cooking."

"I got Pellitteri's report the next morning," Dr. Fuerst said. "And Miss Matthews'. I was back at the hospital, and when I called Birnkrant, he gave me the gist of them. I can't say I was greatly surprised. To tell the truth, I was relieved. The Armenian picnic I'd hypothesized the day before would have created a real mess. Because the hospital had reported two new cases. Two women. They lived at 500 West 178th Street and 611 West 180th Street, but they weren't Armenians. One was Italian. The other was plain American. So we were right back where we started. Only, now we had five cases instead of three, and nothing to tie them together but the fact that they all lived in the same neighborhood. And had the same brand of typhoid. There are around a dozen different strains, you know, which sometimes complicates matters. About the only thing Birnkrant and I could be sure of was that the feast theory—any kind of common gathering—was out. I'd had a word with the new patients. They had never even heard of each other. So the link had to be indirect. That gave us a number of possibilities. The source of infection could be water—either drinking water or a swimming pool. Or it could be commercial ice. Or milk. Or food. Drinking water was a job for Sanitary Engineering. The others, at the moment, were up to us—meaning Pellitteri and me. They were all four conceivable. Even ice. You can find a precedent for anything and everything in the literature on typhoid. But just one was probable. That was food. Some food that is sold already prepared —like potato salad or frozen custard—or one that is usually eaten raw. All we had to do was find out what it was, and where they got it, and how it got that way. Birnkrant and I figured out the area involved. It came to roughly four square blocks. I don't know if you know that part of Washington Heights. It's no prairie. Every building is a big apartment house, and the ground floors of most are stores. At least a fourth have something to do with food."

"I was in the office when Fuerst called," Dr. Pellitteri said. "Before he hung up, I got on the phone and we made the necessary arrangements about questioning the patients and their families— who was to see who. Then I took off. I wasn't too pessimistic. The odds were against a quick answer, but you never know. It was just possible that they all bought from the same store. Well, as it happened, they did. In a way. The trouble was it wasn't one store. It was practically all of them. Fuerst had the same experience. We ended up at the office that evening with a list as long as my arm— half a dozen fruit-vegetable stands, four or five groceries, a market that sold clams, and an assortment of ice-cream parlors and confectioneries and delicatessens. Moreover, we couldn't even be sure the list included the right store. Most people have very strange memories. They forget and they imagine. You've got to assume that most of the information they give you may be either incomplete or inaccurate, or both. But there *was* a right store—we knew that. Sanitary Engineering had eliminated drinking water, and we had been able to rule out swimming and milk and ice. Only one of the group ever went swimming, all but one family had electric refrigerators, and none of them had drunk unpasteurized milk. It had to be contaminated food from a store. That much was certain."

"It was also certain that we had to have some help," Dr. Fuerst said, "Pellitteri and I could have handled a couple of stores. Or even, at a pinch, three or four. But a dozen or more—it would take us weeks. Let me give you an idea what an investigation like that involves. You don't just walk in the store and gaze around. You more or less take it apart. Every item of food that could conceivably cause trouble is examined, the physical setup is inspected for possible violations of the Sanitary Code, and all employees and their families are interviewed and specimens taken for laboratory analysis. So we needed help, and, of course, we got it. Birnkrant had a conference with the Commissioner the next morning and they talked it over, and the result was an engineer and another nurse and a fine big team from Food and Drugs. Very gratifying."

"And Miss Matthews," Dr. Pellitteri said. "We had her back again. She had finally finished with her carriers. They were all like the first. None had violated any of the rules."

"As expected," Dr. Fuerst said. "The average carrier is pretty coöperative. Well, that was Saturday. By Monday, we had made a certain amount of progress. We hadn't found anything yet, but the field was narrowing down. And all of a sudden we got a little nibble. It came from a confectionery called Pop's, on 178th Street, around noon. Pop's had been well up on our list. They sold ice cream made on the premises, and the place was a neighborhood favorite. Which meant it got a very thorough going over. But we were about ready to cross it off—everything was in good shape, including the help—when it developed that the place had just changed hands. Pop had sold out a week before, and he and his wife, who'd helped him run it, were on the way to California. Needless to say, Pop's went back on the list, and at the top. Also, somebody did some quick checking. Pop and his wife were driving, and their plan was to spend a few days with friends in Indianapolis. That gave us a chance. We called Birnkrant and he called Indianapolis—the State Health Department. They were extremely interested. Naturally. They said they'd let us know."

Dr. Fuerst lighted a cigarette. "Then we got a jolt," he said. "Several, in fact. The first was a call from the hospital. Four new cases. That brought the total up to nine. But it didn't stay there long. Tuesday night, it went to ten. I don't mind saying that set us back on our heels. Ten cases of typhoid fever in less than a week in one little corner of the city is almost unheard of in this day and age. The average annual incidence for the whole of Washington Heights is hardly half a case. That wasn't the worst of it, though. The real blow was that tenth case. I'll call him Jones. Jones didn't fit in. The four Monday cases, like the three Armenians and the Italian and the American, all lived in that one four-block area. Jones didn't. He lived on 176th Street, but way over west, almost on Riverside Drive. An entirely different neighborhood. I had a word with Jones the first thing Wednesday morning. I remember he worked for the post office. That's about all I learned. He hardly knew where he was. When I left the hospital, I called on his wife. She wasn't much help, either. She did all the family marketing, she told me, and she did it all within a block or two of home. That was that. She was very definite. On the other hand, there was Mr. Jones. He had typhoid, which doesn't just happen, and it was the same strain as all the rest. So either it was a very strange coincidence or she was too upset to think. My preference, until proved otherwise, was the latter. I found a phone, and called Birnkrant and gave him the latest news. He had some news for me. Indianapolis had called. They had located Pop and his wife and made the usual tests. The results were negative."

"I don't know which was the most discouraging," Dr. Pellitteri said. "Jones, I guess. He meant more work—a whole new string of stores to check. Pop had been ninety per cent hope. He merely aroused suspicion. He ran a popular place, he sold homemade ice cream, and when the epidemic broke, he pulled out. Or so it appeared from where we stood. It hurt to lose him. Unlikely or not, he had been a possibility—the first specific lead of any kind that we had been able to find in a week of mighty hard work. During the next few days, it began to look more and more like the last. Until Friday evening. Friday evening we got a very excited call from the laboratory. It was about a batch of specimens we had submitted that morning for analysis. One of them was positive for *E. typhosa.* The man's name doesn't matter. It didn't even then. What did matter was his occupation. He was the proprietor of a little frozen-custard shop—now extinct—that I'll call the Jupiter. The location was interesting, too. It was a trifle outside our area, but still accessible, and a nice, easy walk from the Joneses'. Food and Drugs put an embargo on the Jupiter that night. The next morning, we began to take it apart."

"I missed that," Dr. Fuerst said. "I spent Saturday at the hospital. It was quite a day. We averaged a case an hour. I'm not exaggerating. When I finally left, the count was nine. Nine brand-new cases. A couple of hours later, one more turned up. That made twenty, all told. Fortunately, that was the end. Twenty was the grand total. But, of course, we didn't know that then. There was no reason to believe they wouldn't just keep coming."

"The rest of us had the same kind of day," Dr. Pellitteri said. "Very disagreeable. There was the owner of the Jupiter—poor devil. You can imagine the state he was in. All of a sudden, he was out of business and a public menace. He didn't even know what a typhoid carrier was. He had to be calmed down and instructed. That was the beginning. It got worse. First of all, the Jupiter was as clean as a whistle. We closed it up—had to, under the circumstances—and embargoed the stock, but we didn't find anything. That was peculiar. I can't explain it even now. He was either just naturally careful or lucky. While that was going on, we went back to the patients and questioned them again. Did they know the Jupiter? Were they customers? Did they ever buy anything there? We got one yes. The rest said no. Emphatically. If there had been a few more yeses—even three or four—we might have wondered. But they couldn't all be mistaken. So the Jupiter lead began to look pretty wobbly. Then the laboratory finished it off. They had a type report on the Jupiter organism. It wasn't the E. *typhosa* we were looking for. It was one of the other strains. That may have been some consolation to Mr. Jupiter. At least, he didn't have an epidemic on his conscience. But it left us uncomfortably close to the end of our rope. We had only a handful of stores still to check. If we didn't find the answer there, we were stumped. We didn't. We crossed off the last possibility on Tuesday morning, August 27th. It was Number Eighty. We'd examined eighty stores and something like a thousand people, and all we had to show for it was a new carrier."

"Well, that was something," Dr. Fuerst said. "Even if it was beside the point. But we also had another consolation. None of the patients had died. None was going to. They were all making excellent progress."

"That's true enough," Dr. Pellitteri said. "But we couldn't claim much credit for that." He paused, and shifted around in his chair. "About all we can take any credit for is Miss Gamso, here," He smiled. "Miss Gamso saved the day. She got inspired."

Miss Gamso gave me a placid look. "I don't know about inspired " she said. "It was more like annoyed. I heard them talking —Dr. Birnkrant, and these two, and all the rest of them—and I read the reports, and the days went by and they didn't seem to be getting anywhere. That's unusual. So it was irritating. It's hard to explain, but I got to thinking about that carrier Mrs. Christos. There were two things about her. She lived with a son-in-law who was a known food handler. He was a baker by trade. Also, where she lived was right in the middle of everything—519 West 178th Street. That's just off Audubon. And Audubon is the street where practically all our cases did most of their shopping. Well, there was one store in particular—a fruit-and-vegetable market called

Tony's—on almost everybody's list. The address was 261 Audubon Avenue. Then I really got a brainstorm. It was right after lunch on Tuesday, August 27th. I picked up the telephone and called the bureau that registers house numbers at the Borough President's office, and I asked them one question. Did 519 West 178th Street and 261 Audubon Avenue happen by any chance to be the same building? They asked me why I wanted to know. I wasn't talking, though. I just said was it, in a nice way, and the man finally said he'd see. When he came back, I was right. They were one and the same. I was so excited I thought I'd burst. Dr. Pellitteri was sitting right where he is now. He was the first person I saw, so I marched straight over and told him. He kind of stared at me. He had the funniest expression." Miss Gamso smiled a gentle smile. "I think he thought I'd gone crazy."

"I wouldn't say that," Dr. Pellitteri said. "I'll admit, however, that I didn't quite see the connection. We'd been all over Tony's— it was almost our first stop—and there was no earthly reason to question Miss Matthews' report on Mrs. Christos. The fact that they occupied the same building was news to me. To all of us, as I recall. But what if they did? Miss Gamso thought it was significant or suspicious or something. The point escaped me. When she mentioned the son-in-law, though, I began to get a little more interested. We knew him, of course—anybody who lives with a carrier is a potential cause of trouble—and checked on him regularly. But it was just possible that since our last checkup he had become infected. That happens. And although we hadn't found him working in any of the stores, he could have come and gone a couple of weeks before we started our investigation. At any rate, it was worth looking into. Almost anything was, by then. I went up that afternoon. I walked past Tony's on the way to 519. There wasn't any doubt about their being in the same building. Tony's is gone now, like Mrs. Christos, but the way it was then, his front door was about three steps from the corner, and around the corner about three more steps was the entrance to the apartments above. The Christos flat was on the fifth floor—Apartment 53. Mrs. Christos and her son-in-law were both at home. They let me in and that's about all. I can't say they were either one delighted to see me. Or very helpful. She couldn't add anything to what she had already told Miss Matthews. The son-in-law hardly opened his mouth. His last regular job, he said, had been in January, in a cafeteria over in Astoria. Since then, he'd done nothing but odd jobs. He wouldn't say what, when, or where. I couldn't completely blame him. He was afraid that if we got to questioning any of his former employers, they'd never take him on again. When I saw how it was, I arranged for a specimen, and, for the moment, let it go at that. There was no point in getting rough until we knew for sure. I told him to sit tight. If he was positive, I'd be back in a hurry. I got the report the next day. He wasn't. He was as harmless as I am. But by then it didn't matter. By that time, it was all over. To tell the truth, I had the answer before I ever left the building."

Dr. Pellitteri shook his head. "I walked right into it," he said. "It was mostly pure luck. What happened was this. On the way out, I ran into the superintendent—an elderly woman. I was feeling two ways about the son-in-law—half sympathetic and half suspicious. It occurred to me that the superintendent might have some idea where he'd been working the past few weeks. So I stopped and asked. She was a sour old girl. She didn't know and didn't care. She had her own troubles. They were the tenants, mainly. She backed me into a corner and proceeded to unload. The children were the worst, she said—especially the boys. Always thinking up some new devilment. For example, she said, just a few weeks ago, toward the end of July, there was a gang of them up on the roof playing wild Indians. Before she could chase them off, they'd stuffed some sticks down one of the plumbing vent pipes. The result was a stoppage. The soil pipe serving one whole tier of apartments blocked and sprang a leak, and the bathroom of the bottom apartment was a nice mess. I hadn't been paying much attention until then. But at that point—Well, to put it mildly, I was fascinated. Also, I began to ask some questions. I wanted to know just what bathroom had flooded. The answer was Apartment 23. What were the other apartments in that tier? They were 33, 43, and 53. What was underneath Apartment 23? A store—Tony's Market, on the corner. Then I asked for a telephone. Birnkrant's reaction was about what you'd expect. Pretty soon, a team from Sanitary Engineering arrived. They supplied the details and the proof. Tony stored his fruits and vegetables in a big wooden walk-in refrigerator at the rear of his store. When Sanitary Engineering pulled off the top, they found the soil pipe straight overhead. The leak had been repaired almost a month before, but the sawdust insulation in the refrigerator roof was still damp from the waste that had soaked through. It wasn't Tony's fault. He hadn't known. It wasn't anybody's fault. It was just one of those things. So that was that."

"Not entirely," Dr. Fuerst said. "There was still Jones to account for. It wasn't necessary. The thing was settled. But I was curious. I had a talk with him the next day. We talked and talked. And in the end, he remembered. He was a night walker. Every evening after dinner, he went out for a walk. He walked all over Washington Heights, and usually, somewhere along the line, he stopped and bought something to eat. It was generally a piece of fruit. As I say, he finally remembered. One night, near the end of July, he was walking down Audubon and he came to a fruit stand and he bought an apple. On the way home, he ate it."

QUESTIONS

1. *"Typhoid is invariably conveyed..."* (p. 988). *If you change invariably to all, you have the major premise of a syllogism: All typhoid is conveyed ... victims. On August 15 the Bureau of Preventable Diseases was given a minor premise: Three people in Washington Heights have typhoid. What is the conclusion of this syllogism and how did it govern the entire investigation?*
2. *What is the relation of the bureau's file of carriers to this syllogism?*
3. *How does Roueché's narrative correspond to the process of investigation? What is the effect of his narrative?*
4. *How far did methodical or systematic investigation get the bureau? What else was necessary to complete the investigation?*

ROBERT ARDREY

From Territory to Nation[1]

The lemur did not invent the society of outward antagonism. He merely applied an ancient behavioral solution to the new primate problem of life in the light of day. To find its evolutionary origins one must go an astonishingly long way back.

Protozoa, as we all know, are one-celled creatures, and their history must date from the first billion years of emergent life. One kind of protozoa are known as slime molds. They are of the size and general appearance of a white blood cell, and they feed on bacteria such as one finds in moist soil. They divide every three or four hours, and so a population multiplies rapidly. Just about the time, however, when growing numbers have exhausted the food supply in a given area, the single-cell creatures enter the second phase of their life cycle. They begin to form societies. Around a founder cell others will bunch in a growing aggregate, clinging together until they have formed a sausage-shaped slug visible to the naked eye. Now this social slug of individual beings begins to behave as a single organism, and it will even move toward warmth or toward light with precision of direction. At last a portion of the community will differentiate themselves and form a stalk which they stiffen with a secretion. Then others will crawl on top of the stalk and form a sphere of cells each containing a spore, the seed of a new generation.

It sounds like something out of science fiction, but it is not. It is simply a way of life that was worked out a billion-odd years ago and

1. From *The Territorial Imperative.* This is the second section of the chapter on the nation; the first section described the work of Jean-Jacques Petter in Madagascar on lemur groups unified by a common antagonism to groups on adjoining territories.

that still works. How it works defies the imagination—or, more accurately, gives some slight evidence as to how little we know about living processes. One aspect, however, of the social behavior of slime molds has yielded to laboratory investigation. It is what I define as a society of outward antagonism founded on the defense of a social territory.

Investigators have been puzzling over the behavior of slime molds ever since their discovery in 1935. An American scientist began wondering if there could be some form of communication between cells. Placed in a culture dish, they distributed themselves so evenly in their first phase of life that it seemed they repelled each other. (We should call it individual distance.) Then when the time came for aggregation, it was as if a new signal went out and all obeyed. An investigator named Arndt, working in Germany, made the striking observation that the number of fruiting societies in a given area was independent of the number of individuals. In other words, if you had a thousand protozoa in an area, they might form ten groups of a hundred each. But if you had ten thousand, they would still form ten groups. The societies were somehow a function of space, not numbers.

Only recently an American biologist, John Tyler Bonner of Princeton University, has demonstrated that in a given species of slime molds, the size of the social territory is a constant. And he has proved what had been suspected for some time, that the means of social defense is a gas which repels other groups to a given distance and at the same time attracts the clan. Charcoal absorbs gas. By placing charcoal in his culture, Bonner reduced territory size so that four times as many social aggregates crowded the area.

I do not happen to know of an earlier example of the society of outward antagonism, isolated and unified by the defense of a social territory. Ants and termites do something like it. Since early in the century, when the study of social insects was in high fashion, it has been known that every colony has its own peculiar odor, and that a worker, for example, returning to the wrong colony will be smelled by guards, recognized, and instantly attacked. It was thought for a while that the difference in odor might arise from different sources of food supply. Recently, however, a colleague of Wynne-Edwards at Aberdeen, D. I. Wallis, has shown that in ant colonies the familiar, attractive odor of a social partner and the strange, repellent odor of the foreigner must at least in part be genetically determined.

We must be always wary of conclusions drawn from the ways of the social insect, since their evolutionary track lies so far from ours. But when we find a familiar behavior pattern in a common ancestral type, the protozoa, a creature so remote, so lost in the tides of animate beginnings, then an honest man must take a deep breath and ask of himself, What came first, the cart or the horse? What ultimately preceded which, body or behavior? We know today that it is a behavioral adaptation that as a rule precedes and gives selective value to bodily change. But has natural selection for two billion years chosen among increasingly complex anatomical possibilities to fulfill increasingly complex behavior patterns? Or did these complex patterns exist from the near-beginning in creatures so simple that they lacked any apparent anatomical structures to maintain them?

These are questions of philosophical note which before this inquiry closes we may perhaps be enabled to ask with sharper precision. In the meanwhile we must give our attention to a question of more immediate concern to the human circumstance: Why have students of men failed to gain from students of the animal any notion concerning the biological origins of the nation? When the true lemur, possessing nothing but the anatomical rudiments of our Eocene primate dawn, introduced a social organization which men in their time would so intricately explore, he was merely picking up a ticket written a billion or so years earlier by the brainless, nerveless, sexless, almost formless one-celled protozoa. It passes all logic to believe that if the society integrated by its outward antagonisms has a history so venerable in the transactions of animals, it could have no bearing on the passages of men. But the question, seemingly so innocent, directs an ultimate earthquake at the more inflexible structures of contemporary thought; and in all responsibility we must inform ourselves, as fully as the new biology at present permits us, concerning the implications of the social territory and the consequences which its discovery brought to the development of the territorial concept.

I have traced the ponderings of science from the days of Aristotle and Zeno down through Altum and Moffat and Howard to David Lack and his curiosity about the private territory as a reinforcement for the pair bond. In those years, however, we find few observations of any but birds. Eagles and falcons, robins and nightingales, moor hens and meadow warblers were the messengers to bring us word that between a living being and the space he occupies there is a mysterious tie beyond habit or mere familiarity. If our observations of territory were limited, it was because insects and birds, until the 1930's, were very nearly the only wild beings that man had ever studied. Territory remained a form of behavior peculiar to the ornithologist's notebook.

There were exceptions, of course. In 1912 a French psychologist published his *La Génèse des instincts.* From studies of laboratory rats Pierre Hachet-Souplet recorded a pessimistic conclusion that

neither reason nor justice could ever contravene "la loi de terri-
toire." I have in my notes no earlier speculation concerning territory
and the human being. And one must wonder whether the French
psychologist retained his pessimism when two years later the taxicabs of Paris headed for the Marne.[2]

There was another remarkable study of a non-bird made so early
that its significance was lost. A. S. Pearse of the University of Wisconsin spent years watching that unlikely animal, the fiddler crab,
in such unlikely locations as Manila Bay, the Massachusetts coast,
and the flooded mangrove swamps of Colombia. He published his
observations in 1913, the year after Hachet-Souplet's. Half a century later his fiddler crabs may startle us; then, lacking frame of
reference, they earned small attention.

The fiddler crab is a belligerent little animal who lives on the
beach and digs burrows in the sand or mud. When high tide flows,
he retreats into his burrow and plugs up the opening. Pearse
watched thirteen species and found the same behavior in all. Each
individual lives his life near his burrow door, cleaning and scraping
the sand about it. Seldom will he move more than a yard or two
away, and Pearse established twelve yards as the roving limit. It is
the smaller area only that he defends, however, and the fiddler will
chase or fight off any intruder on his tiny estate. So vicious is his
defense that if a crab is removed experimentally to any distance
along a crowded beach, his return will be a harrowing affair. He
must cross the territories of others, and he will be attacked by every
crab along the way. The chances are better than fair that he will
lose a claw, if not his life.

"Each fiddler's hand is against every man," wrote Pearse, and it is
almost literally true. One claw of the fiddler is overdeveloped to
huge size, sometimes a third of total body weight. This claw is
called the chela. It is a brilliantly colored display object, and during
the mating season, whenever a female passes, every male in the
colony will stand by his burrow frantically waving his chela, often
adding to the excitement by squatting and rising as he waves.
Throughout the nonbreeding season, however, such diversion is
lacking, and then the male fiddler crab finds other uses for his
chela. David Lack concluded that fighting is what a robin likes best
of all. So does the fiddler crab, but his fighting is highly formalized.
Two will meet on a boundary and lock chelae precisely as two men
shake hands. The object of the action is simplicity itself: by a
sudden wrench to break the other crab's claw off.

Ornithology was naturally unaware of Pearse's crabs, as it was
unaware of the unreasonable rats in a Paris laboratory. Interpreta-

2. When the Germans threatened
Paris, taxicabs took French troops to   the first battle of the Marne.

tions of territory continued to be based entirely on the behavior of birds. And the interpretations—whether the food theory, or the dispersal of breeding pairs, or the natural selection of superior males, or reinforcement of the pair bond—all referred to the competition of individual males and in one way or another to reproduction. But then, in 1934, the American zoologist G. K. Noble brought in the fence lizard and the upsetting news that the female has a territory of her own which she defends against all comers, including males. How such behavior promoted successful reproduction was hard to say.

Many years later the way of a female lizard would be explored in sharper detail by the young Rhodesian all-around scientist C. K. Brain. In *African Genesis* I described the anthropological ingenuities which he applied to the australopithecines, the South African man-apes, and today he is curator of anthropology at South Africa's Transvaal Museum. But there was a period in Brain's career when he wearied of ancient dating, of the tools and fossil memories of small-brained proto-men, and he turned to the Kalahari desert and the chameleon. I could understand his fascination, in a way. On one of his returns from the Kalahari he showed me among other lively reptile samples a creature as upsetting to a layman as is a female proprietor to birdmen. When you looked into one ear of the deplorable creature you saw daylight coming in the other.

The young Rhodesian's confirmation of Noble's observation concerned the female of a common chameleon species who defends a solitary property against all others, female or male, with such vigor as to raise the question, How does she ever mate? By experiment Brain found the answer. The male displays by puffing out his throat. On that throat is a yellow mark which serves to make the female only worse-tempered than ever. But when the sexual season comes around, the yellow fades. She admits him to her property, and they mate. Then the yellow mark returns and she throws him out.

Brain's detailed observations were unnecessary, thirty years earlier, to lend credibility to the fence lizard. G. Kingsley Noble was curator of experimental biology at the American Museum of Natural History and his authority could not be ignored. Ponderous questions were raised for which ornithology had no answer. The female fence lizard's territorial defense most definitely did *not* reinforce a pair bond, did *not* serve to select worthy from unworthy mates, was *not* an expression of male sexual pugnacity, and could by no means be interpreted as protecting the welfare of offspring. Having laid her fertilized eggs, she would from that point on lose all interest in future generations. Then what was the selective value to the species? Brain's later demonstration showed that lizard territory could be definitely anti-sexual, since only by suspension of the behavior could mating take place.

The next non-bird man to complicate ornithology's interpretations was W. H. Burt, whose domain spread through the fields and the woodlands and the brushy river bottoms of southern Michigan, and whose castle was the University of Michigan's zoology department. Burt watched rodents: wood mice, deer mice, pine voles and lemming voles, ground squirrels and flying squirrels, chipmunks. Although he left no book about them, Burt might almost be described as the Eliot Howard[3] of the mouse world.

Rats and mice have always entered the literature of human analogy, and perhaps that is why with Burt's studies one entertains for the first time clear-cut statements of human implication. The bird inhabits the sky, and we do not tend to identify ourselves with a creature so disdainful of human limitation. Eliot Howard may have blurted to a servant girl that territory is everything; but he did not say it in public. The Michigan zoologist, however, did not hesitate to state his conviction that what was true of mice was true of men. Territory for a rodent meant security against the predator. When you live a life of marsh hawks and foxes, then the days will be fairest for those who know their homelands best.

The Muries[4] had a six-week-old deer mouse who homed two miles to the area of her nest. Burt found similar capacities in wood mice. How they got home was as inexplicable as ever, but what they did when they got there was evident. They disappeared. On its own property a small rodent knows every hole, every tunnel, every hiding place. Burt found that a wood mouse released on its own territory would vanish within twenty feet.

Security from the predator is seldom a territorial function in the lives of birds. But in the lives of rodents as in the lives of men its value is universal. One's imagination may spring to the fortified border, the castle, the drawbridge; to the walled town on an Italian hill; to the barrier of living thorns about an African kraal; to the ancestral cave. Or it may spring no farther than to the striving market place and the quiet chair by the fire. No thoughtful observer of the territorial ways of vulnerable man could fail to recognize in them the ways of the vulnerable wood mouse. I have no doubt but that Burt in his time was accused of anthropomorphism by devotees of human uniqueness wielding vocabularies more pretentious than precise. It is an anthropomorphism to attribute to the animal the capacities of man. What Burt was stating was quite the opposite, for he was attributing to man the capacities of the animal.

3. A British ornithologist, author of *Territory in Bird Life.*

4. Naturalists who investigated the homing habits of deer-mice in Wyoming.

W. H. Burt was one of the most significant contributors to the concept of territory, and in another field he came into conflict with his contemporaries. A chipmunk, he noted, will vigorously drive away any intruder who comes within fifty yards of her nest. But she will forage for food for a hundred yards or more beyond, ignoring there the same intruder whom she drove away from her nest's vicinity. The defended area, said Burt, is the territory; the foraging area is the home range.

The distinction between territory and range met opposition, since it minimized the economic importance of territory. As we see in instance after instance, there is an allure about the economic principle as there is about the sexual principle, for each provides simple answers: that an answer may be untrue is less formidable than that it be complicated. Fortunately for Burt's distinction, a biologist named Kenneth Gordon was at about the same time watching golden-mantled ground squirrels in the Far West. At two widely separated locations, one in Oregon, one in Colorado, their territorial behavior was identical. A proprietor would chase an intruder for about one hundred feet. But he would forage for nuts and cones to a much greater distance, and there, like the Michigan chipmunks, he would ignore the same individual whom earlier he had pursued. Burt's distinction between range and territory prevailed, and is today accepted widely in science.

While W. H. Burt brought both cleaner definitions and broader horizons to the territorial concept, his rodents and Noble's lizards thoroughly messed up those simpler interpretations drawn only from the life of birds. One principle, however, seemed to remain intact: that whatever the function territory may provide, it remains a competition between individuals and must somehow relate to individual selection. Then the American psychologist C. R. Carpenter returned from Panama with the news that howling monkeys defend as a group a social territory. The last principle was demolished. When five years later, in 1939, Noble at a symposium in Washington casually referred to a territory as "a defended area," biology leaped at the phrase. Problems of function and motivation were relegated to pigeonholes. From that day to this, biology as a whole asks but one question of a territory: is it defended? Defense defines it. Variability became the final description.

Ray Carpenter is a tall, quiet, scholarly man with a touch of Woodrow Wilson about him. And I should find it as difficult to visualize the late American President up to his armpits in an Asian swamp or ducking fecal matter showered down on him by large black belligerent monkeys in a Central American rain forest as I do this elegant academic gentleman in the bifocal glasses. Carpenter today is professor of psychology at Pennsylvania State University, and he lives in a low-flung modern house in a neighboring wood-land alive with civilized squirrels and accustomed birds of soft-spoken manner. For a quarter of a century Carpenter's central preoccupation has been with university administration and the mental acrobatics of contemporary man. Yet for almost ten pre-vious years his normal home was the jungle, his normal circle of acquaintance the jungle's temperamental citizens. A full quarter-century before Petter went to Madagascar, Carpenter went to Panama to initiate the modern study of primates in a state of nature.

At the time—and it was not so very long ago, for I must recall that I myself had already completed my formal education—there existed nowhere on earth a body of information acceptable to sci-ence which revealed the behavior of apes or monkeys in the wild. The amateur South African naturalist Eugène Marais had at the turn of the century lived for three years with a troop of baboons in the northern Transvaal, but his observations were regarded as unre-liable and besides had not yet been translated from Afrikaans. Another South African, S. L. Zuckerman, had published his *Social Life of Monkeys and Apes,* and it was regarded as definitive. But according to the modern authority of K. R. L. Hall and Irven DeVore, Zuckerman's monumental study had included but a few days of experience in the field, and had otherwise been based entirely on observations in the London zoo. In large part, what sci-ence knew about the behavior of primates, that zoological family of which we are a part, had been obtained in zoos and laboratories. Under such conditions, so little did the behavior of apes and mon-keys resemble our own that we came to the logical conclusion that the human way was of our own making and owed little to animal inheritance. Schools of psychology were set in motion to explain our nature in terms of the conditioned reflex. Trends in anthropol-ogy and the social sciences went their cultural or environmentalist ways. Then in 1934 Carpenter made his first return to civilization bearing under his arm a clap of thunder: our information was false.

For two years the American psychologist had been watching howling monkeys on an island in the Panama Canal's Gatun Lake. Barro Colorado Island is almost 4000 acres in extent, and at the time of Carpenter's study it was divided between twenty-eight clans, each defending a social territory and living in total hostility with its neighbors. Only three clans were so small as to include but a single mature male; in all others the males ranged from two to five and the females from two to ten. Carpenter recorded their sexual relations and the care of their young, their social organiza-tion and means of communication, and their remarkable systems of group territorial defense. The sum he published in his classic monograph *Behavior and Social Relations of the Howling Monkey.*

The first of those assumptions which his study demolished was the scientific *idée fixe*—one of such influence on the work of Sigmund Freud—that the primate is obsessed with sex and that it is sexual attraction which holds primate troops together. The assumption of a sexual obsession had offered scientific justification for the romantic tenet that love is all, for the psychological tenet that sexual energy is the fuel of the human mechanism, and for the more everyday conclusion that when you come down to it nothing matters much except fornication. The assumption that sexual attraction is the magnet drawing together the adults of a primate society had consequences even more far-reaching: Since human society is most obviously *not* held together by such a sexual magnet, then our forms of social life must be unique to man, created by man, and subject entirely to human manipulation according to our vision of human good. Anything, in a word, is possible. This is the premise of most contemporary sociology. It is also the premise that left the social sciences without other than sentimental defense against such totalitarian glimpses of the human good as fascism and communism. If anything was possible, then these were too.

The sexual assumption lies today in ruins. Mason's study of the callicebus shows the year-around integrity of the family group *except* during the sexual season. Petter's ancient lemurs, unlike most of the later monkeys and apes, retain the general mammal characteristic of seasonal heat and rut; yet their societies show an all-season solidarity. The same has been shown for the rhesus and the related Japanese monkey. Recent studies of less seasonal primates like the gorilla, the baboon, and the chimpanzee offer not a gleam of evidence to support the obsolete assumption that sex is the central preoccupation of the primate and the central force holding together his society. Yet that obsolete assumption remains today the cornerstone of most psychology, most anthropology, and very nearly all of sociology.

The assumption was, of course, rendered obsolete in 1934 by Carpenter's observations of the howling monkey. But he went further to demonstrate that it is the troop itself which is the focus of primate life. In his howler clans sexual jealousy was nonexistent. No male asserted a sexual monopoly over females, and sexual activity was an amiable entertainment in which all males shared all females. But the troop was another matter. No jealousy, neglect of young, defiance of leadership, or failure of communication could exist at the cost of the clan's welfare. Years later S. L. Washburn and Irven DeVore would record that a baboon without its troop is a dead baboon. So it was with Carpenter's howlers. On rare occasions he spotted a solitary male in the forest. But the wandering male was usually one who out of persistent conflict with his fellow males had elected to leave his clan. Someday after further persistent efforts he would join another clan, or failing, he would die alone. Few so failed. A howler without a clan is a man without a country, and what is true of men and howlers is universally true of primate species.

Finally, Carpenter's careful observations showed that the mechanism isolating and integrating the howler clan is its defense of a social territory. The territories of the callicebus, the sifaka, the black lemur are small, the borders cleanly delimited. The territories of howler clans are large, the borders vague. But clans have only to sight each other in this no man's land and total warfare breaks out. Rage shakes the forest. That rage, however, takes none but vocal expression. The howler is equipped with a voice box of dismaying dimension from which emerge cries of discouraging proportion. Black lemurs raise their voices in unison in their *cri du soir*; howler clans raise their deafening voices both morning and night as a warning against intruders. Should intrusion occur, these voices joined will be the artillery of battle. And strictly in accord with the territorial principle, the home team will always win, the visiting team will always withdraw.

The howler clan is what I should call a society of most perfect outward antagonism which has achieved a most perfect inward amity. So different from the *noyau*,[5] the biological nation spends its aggressive energies on enemies foreign, wastes none on enemies domestic. Within the howler society as within the society of the black lemur there reigns a kind of democratic tranquillity. Leadership is present, but authority is restrained. Differences of opinion are settled with a mumble and a grunt. While the female is never dominant, still her status is remarkably high. And as for offspring, they are the joint responsibility of all adults in the troop. All males, in response to a special cry, will go to the rescue of a young one who falls from a tree; all males with concerted action will defend it against the advance of a predator.

Such observations were impossible so long as we drew our conclusions from the behavior of animals in the zoo. There no natural society is possible. There no fear of the predator, no pressure of hunger, no boundary disputes with neighboring bands, not even the inconveniences of bad weather can absorb primate energy. If he seems absorbed by sex, it is simply because his captive life presents him with no other outlet for his energies. Our conclusions concerning the nature of the primate, from which we came to such

5. An animal group which bases its unity on mutual antagonism within the group.

dubious conclusions concerning the nature of man, were based on the behavior of bored, deprived, essentially neurotic animals. Carpenter presented a preliminary review of his new findings at a meeting in 1933. "You're wrong," said a dominant figure in the old biology. "I've only reported what I saw," said Carpenter. "Then you've seen wrong," said the dominant biologist.

Carpenter went back to his rain forests. In succeeding years he added major studies of that small, lithe ape, the gibbon, in Thailand, and of the rhesus monkey both in India and in a free-ranging colony which he established on an island off Puerto Rico, together with lesser studies of the red spider monkey in Panama and of that great ape, the orangutan, in Sumatra. Through the mass and variety of his experience he established standardized, objective, quantitative techniques for the difficult task of observing and recording the behavior of animals in a state of nature. In a sense he imposed the mathematics of the laboratory on the confusion of the jungle, and there are few studies made in the wild today that do not in part found their techniques on those established by Carpenter in the 1930's.

The ultimate importance of his work, of course, was less to the natural sciences than to the social sciences, less to the study of the animal than to the study of man. More recent observation might reveal primate species integrated by other than the social territory. More recent studies might reveal species in which social amity is far less perfect than is achieved by the howling monkey or the gibbon. But Carpenter's discoveries bridged the unbridged gap between man and his primate cousins, and made not only possible but compulsory a consideration of all animate life as an evolutionary whole.

What then was the impact of his discoveries on world science and world thought? The impact may be summarized briefly.

The studies were completed about 1940. When I published *African Genesis* in 1961, all were out of print, some could be obtained in specialized libraries such as those of the British Museum, several existed only as single remaining copies in a file at Carpenter's home. All since, it is pleasant to note, have been reprinted in a single volume, *Naturalistic Behavior of Nonhuman Primates*, by the Pennsylvania State University Press.

Among students of animal behavior, W. C. Allee was one who immediately grasped the whole significance of Carpenter's work, and in his article on animal sociology in the *Encyclopaedia Britannica* he discusses it at length. Little other discussion appeared, however, in reference works available to the layman.

Anyone would assume that political scientists, confronted as they are with nations and nationalism, with inspiring dreams of world federation and with the less inspiring agonies of the United

Nations, would find among their numbers at least a few crackpot souls for whom the animal's social territory carries significance. If there exists such a political scientist, then I admire him. I happen myself to be unaware that the nation as a biological expression has ever entered our lengthiest debates.

One would assume likewise that anthropology, the science of man, would have been revolutionized by Carpenter's findings. For Sir Arthur Keith, anthropology's most famous figure and one of the founders of the science, such a revolution came about. We shall return to Keith later. It is sufficient here to note that when in 1948, at the age of eighty-two, he published his masterwork, *A New Theory of Human Evolution*, he recorded that Carpenter's social territory had been a catalyst for his thinking. The book exists, however, virtually unread.

There are certain anthropologists who in the past few years have found new inspiration in ethology's investigations of animal behavior and paleontology's startling illuminations cast on the human emergence. It would be an exaggeration, though, to state that the name of C. R. Carpenter had made deep inroads on the science as a whole. In 1965, for example, the American Association of Physical Anthropologists held its annual meeting at Carpenter's home university. An official report of the conference was written by an anthropologist from the neighboring University of Pennsylvania and published in *Science*, the organ of the American Association for the Advancement of Science. Passing reference was made to the address on primate behavior delivered at the annual dinner by "Clarence S. Carpenter."

Within the specialized, developing field of ethology, of course, Carpenter's name correctly spelled traveled far. But even there something was strangely missing. When in 1960 I was completing field and reference research for my own book, I faced a mystifying absence of further material on wild primates. Niels Bolwig, the previous year, had published observations of chacma baboons drawn to the garbage pails of a camp in South Africa's Kruger Park. The conditions seemed to me artificial. A Japanese group had begun observations of semi-wild macaques frequenting traditional temple areas, but their preliminary reports had not come my way. For lack of further material I made a wrong guess or two: I underrated primate social ingenuity and presumed that he would always found his society on territory; and I overrated the probable importance of the family as his social building block.

While I was finishing my work, the vanguard of a new generation of primate students was already at theirs. Petter was in Madagascar, K. R. L. Hall in the Cape of Good Hope watching baboons, George Schaller was in the high mists of Congo volcanoes with his mountain gorillas, Jane Goodall was beginning her observations of the savannah chimpanzee near Lake Tanganyika, Adriaan Kortlandt his of forest chimpanzees lingering near a Congo plantation. The following year, too late for my book, Washburn and DeVore gave us the first of the new publications, their superb account of the social life of the baboon. But this was simply the opening wave; then came the flood: K. R. L. Hall on the patas monkey as well as the baboon, Schaller on the orangutan as well as the gorilla, Stuart A. Altmann on the rhesus in Puerto Rico, Charles H. Southwick on the rhesus in India, Stephen Gartlan as well as Brain on vervet monkeys, V. Reynolds on the forest chimp, H. Kummer and F. Kurt on the hamadryas baboon, Mason on the callicebus, Phyllis Jay on langurs, Ellefson on the gibbon in Malaya. Today, one suspects, there must be hardly a bush or a clump of vines that does not shelter a scientist, or a monkey or ape who is not busily engaged in making notes on the remarkable behavior of man.

The primate, in a scientific twinkling, became fashionable. And we may hold the legitimate suspicion, I believe, that a turn so worldwide, so spontaneous, so spectacular, has registered like a fever thermometer some change in the public temper. Monkeys and apes are the most controversial of animals, suffering as they do the misfortune of being closely related to man. And when men abruptly embrace them—it is a guess—we are seeing the first step of a rebellion, probably as yet unconscious, some first symptom of a profound dissatisfaction with all the old answers.

We shall be unwise, however, if we forget that twenty years earlier, when Ray Carpenter last emerged from the rain forest, no scientist took his place beneath the trees. He brought drama, but he played to an empty house. To believe that the sciences are rigidly objective and unswayed by the winds of intellectual fashion, of public mood, of political temper, of personal prejudice, is to go forth into the human storm clad only in trust's most innocent winding sheet. To believe that a scientist is unaffected by public disapproval, unaffected by the regard or disregard of professional colleagues, unaffected by the lack or abundance of funds for his work, is to characterize the scientist as an unperson. We, the laymen of the world, provide the milieu from which the scientist must draw his sustaining breath. You and I, we laymen, provide the freedom and the inhibitions, the receptivity and the intolerance, the affluence and the poverty, the honors and the oblivion which direct our sciences toward this goal, dissuade them from that. And it was you and I, whether we knew it or not, who in the critical year of 1940 and the decades thereafter failed to encourage our sciences to investigate further certain possibilities perhaps remote: that man and the monkey have more in common than mere anatomy; that our infant species is not as yet divorced from evolutionary processes; that nations, human as well as animal, obey the laws of the territorial imperative.

It has been an expensive failure.

QUESTIONS

1. What is the significance of the question Ardrey poses on page 999, "What ultimately preceded which, body or behavior?" What is Ardrey's thesis and why is it significant?
2. Early in his discussion, before he sets out the implications of the slime mold's behavior, Ardrey concedes that we should be wary of drawing conclusions about humans from the behavior of non-human life. Does he maintain that diffidence throughout? Does the need for such diffidence diminish when primates are the subject of investigation?
3. Ardrey wrote plays before he turned to biological subjects, and he has been accused of letting drama intrude upon science. Assuming that personal conflict is an important element in drama, can you see anything "dramatic" about Ardrey's approach to scientific investigation?
4. Ardrey dates our failure to encourage certain kinds of scientific investigation from the year 1940. Can you think of any historical reasons for that failure? What is the irony?

NAOMI WEISSTEIN

Psychology Constructs the Female, or, The Fantasy Life of the Male Psychologist
(With Some Attention to the Fantasies of His Friends, the Male Biologist and the Male Anthropologist)

It is an implicit assumption that the area of psychology which concerns itself with personality has the onerous but necessary task of describing the limits of human possibility. Thus when we are about to consider the liberation of women, we naturally look to psychology to tell us what "true" liberation would mean: what would give women the freedom to fulfill their own intrinsic natures. Psychologists have set about describing the true natures of women with a certainty and a sense of their own infallibility rarely found in the secular world. Bruno Bettelheim, of the University of Chicago, tells us that

We must start with the realization that, as much as women want to be good scientists or engineers, they want first and foremost to be womanly companions of men and to be mothers.[1]

1. Bruno Bettelheim, "The Commitment Required of a Woman Entering a Scientific Profession in Present-Day American Society," *Woman and the Scientific Professions,* MIT Symposium on American Women in Science and Engineering, 1965 [Weisstein's note].

Erik Erikson of Harvard University, upon noting that young women often ask whether they can "have an identity before they know whom they will marry, and for whom they will make a home," explains somewhat elegiacally that

Much of a young woman's identity is already defined in her kind of attractiveness and in the selectivity of her search for the man (or men) by whom she wishes to be sought...[2]

Mature womanly fulfillment, for Erikson, rests on the fact that a woman's

... somatic design harbors an "inner space" destined to bear the offspring of chosen men, and with it, a biological, psychological, and ethical commitment to take care of human infancy.[3]

Some psychiatrists even see the acceptance of woman's role by women as a solution to societal problems. "Woman is nurturance ... ," writes Joseph Rheingold (1964), a psychiatrist at the Harvard Medical School, " . . . anatomy decrees the life of a woman . . . when women grow up without dread of their biological functions and without subversion by feminist doctrine, and therefore enter upon motherhood with a sense of fulfillment and altruistic sentiment, we shall attain the goal of a good life and a secure world in which to live it."[4]

These views from men who are assumed to be experts reflect, in a surprisingly transparent way, the cultural consensus. They not only assert that a woman is defined by her ability to attract men, they see no alternative definitions. They think that the definition of a woman in terms of a man is the way it should be; and they back it up with psychosexual incantation and biological ritual curses. A woman has an identity if she is attractive enough to obtain a man, and thus, a home; for this will allow her to set about her life's task of "joyful altruism and nurturance."

Business certainly does not disagree. If views such as Bettelheim's and Erikson's do indeed have something to do with real liberation for women, then seldom in human history has so much money and effort been spent on helping a group of people realize their true potential. Clothing, cosmetics, home furnishings, are multi-million dollar businesses: if you don't like investing in firms that make weaponry and flaming gasoline, then there's a lot of hard cash in "inner space." Sheet and pillowcase manufacturers are concerned to fill this inner space:

Mother, for a while this morning, I thought I wasn't cut out for married life. Hank was late for work and forgot his apricot juice and walked out

2. Erik Erikson, "Inner and Outer Space: Reflections on Womanhood," *Daedalus*, 93 (1964), 582–606 [Weisstein's note].

3. *Ibid.* [Weisstein's note].

4. Joseph Rheingold, *The Fear of Being a Woman* (New York: Grune & Stratton, 1964), p. 714 [Weisstein's note].

without kissing me, and when I was all alone I started crying. But then the postman came with the sheets and towels you sent, that look like big bandana handkerchiefs, and you know what I thought? That those big red and blue handkerchiefs are for girls like me to dry their tears on so they can get busy and do what a housewife has to do. Throw open the windows and start getting the house ready, and the dinner, maybe clean the silver and put new geraniums in the box. *Everything to be ready for him when he walks through that door.*[5]

Of course, it is not only the sheet and pillowcase manufacturers, the cosmetics industry, the home furnishings salesmen who profit from and make use of the cultural definitions of man and woman. The example above is blatantly and overtly pitched to a particular kind of sexist stereotype: the child nymph. But almost all aspects of the media are normative, that is, they have to do with the ways in which beautiful people, or just folks, or ordinary Americans, should live their lives. They define the possible; and the possibilities are usually in terms of what is male and what is female. Men and women alike are waiting for Hank, the Silva Thins man, to walk back through that door.

It is an interesting but limited exercise to show that psychologists and psychiatrists embrace these sexist norms of our culture, that they do not see beyond the most superficial and stultifying media conceptions of female nature, and that their ideas of female nature serve industry and commerce so well. Just because it's good for business doesn't mean it's wrong. What I will show is that it *is wrong*; that there isn't the tiniest shred of evidence that these fantasies of servitude and childish dependence have anything to do with women's true potential; that the idea of the nature of human possibility which rests on the accidents of individual development of genitalia, on what is possible today because of what happened yesterday, on the fundamentalist myth of sex organ causality, has strangled and deflected psychology so that it is relatively useless in describing, explaining or predicting humans and their behavior.

It then goes without saying that present psychology is less than worthless in contributing to a vision which could truly liberate— men as well as women.

The central argument of my paper, then, is this. Psychology has nothing to say about what women are really like, what they need and what they want, essentially because psychology does not know. I want to stress that this failure is not limited to women; rather, the kind of psychology which has addressed itself to how people act and who they are has failed to understand, in the first place, why people act the way they do, and certainly failed to understand what might make them act differently.

---

5. Fieldcrest advertisement in the *New Yorker*, 1965. My italics. [Weisstein's note].

The kind of psychology which has addressed itself to these questions divides into two professional areas: academic personality research, and clinical psychology and psychiatry. The basic reason for failure is the same in both these areas: the central assumption for most psychologists of human personality has been that human behavior rests on an individual and inner dynamic, perhaps fixed in infancy, perhaps fixed by genitalia, perhaps simply arranged in a rather immovable cognitive network. But this assumption is rapidly losing ground as personality psychologists fail again and again to get consistency in the assumed personalities of their subjects.[6] Meanwhile, the evidence is collecting that what a person does and who she believes herself to be, will in general be a function of what people around her expect her to be, and what the overall situation in which she is acting implies that she is. Compared to the influence of the social context within which a person lives, his or her history and "traits," as well as biological makeup, may simply be random variations, "noise" superimposed on the true signal which can predict behavior.

Some academic personality psychologists are at least looking at the counter evidence and questioning their theories; no such corrective is occurring in clinical psychology and psychiatry: Freudians and neo-Freudians, nudie-marathonists and touchy-feelies, classicists and swingers, clinicians and psychiatrists, simply refuse to look at the evidence against their theory and practice. And they support their theory and practice with stuff so transparently biased as to have absolutely no standing as empirical evidence.

To summarize: the first reason for psychology's failure to understand what people are and how they act is that psychology has looked for inner traits when it should have been looking for social context; the second reason for psychology's failure is that the theoreticians of personality have generally been clinicians and psychiatrists, and they have never considered it necessary to have evidence in support of their theories.

Theory without Evidence

Let us turn to this latter cause of failure first: the acceptance by psychiatrists and clinical psychologists of theory without evidence. If we inspect the literature of personality, it is immediately obvious that the bulk of it is written by clinicians and psychiatrists, and that the major support for their theories is "years of intensive clinical experience." This is a tradition started by Freud. His "insights" occurred during the course of his work with his patients. Now there

6. J. Block, "Some Reasons for the Apparent Inconsistency of Personality," *Psychological Bulletin*, 70 (1968), 210–212 [Weisstein's note].

is nothing wrong with such an approach to theory *formulation*; a person is free to make up theories with any inspiration that works: divine revelation, intensive clinical practice, a random numbers table. But he/she is not free to claim any validity for his/her theory until it has been tested and confirmed. But theories are treated in no such tentative way in ordinary clinical practice. Consider Freud. What he thought constituted evidence violated the most minimal conditions of scientific rigor. In *The Sexual Enlightenment of Children*,[7] the classic document which is supposed to demonstrate empirically the existence of a castration complex and its connection to a phobia, Freud based his analysis on the reports of the father of the little boy, himself in therapy, and a devotee of Freudian theory. I really don't have to comment further on the contamination in this kind of evidence. It is remarkable that only recently has Freud's classic theory on the sexuality of women—the notion of the double orgasm—been actually tested physiologically and found just plain wrong. Now those who claim that fifty years of psychoanalytic experience constitute evidence enough of the essential truths of Freud's theory should ponder the robust health of the double orgasm. Did women, until Masters and Johnson,[8] believe they were having two different kinds of orgasm? Did their psychiatrists badger them into reporting something that was not true? If so, were there other things they reported that were also not true? Did psychiatrists ever learn anything different than their theories had led them to believe? If clinical experience means anything at all, surely we should have been done with the double orgasm myth long before the Masters and Johnson studies.

But certainly, you may object, "years of intensive clinical experience" is the only reliable measure in a discipline which relies for its findings on insight, sensitivity, and intuition. The problem with insight, sensitivity, and intuition, is that they can confirm for all time the biases that one started with. People used to be absolutely convinced of their ability to tell which of their number were engaging in witchcraft. All it required was some sensitivity to the workings of the devil.

Years of intensive clinical experience is not the same thing as empirical evidence. The first thing an experimenter learns in any kind of experiment which involves humans is the concept of the "double blind". The term is taken from medical experiments, where one group is given a drug which is presumably supposed to change behavior in a certain way, and a control group is given a placebo. If the observers or the subjects know which group took which drug, the result invariably comes out on the positive side for the new drug.

7. Sigmund Freud, *The Sexual Enlightenment of Children* (New York: Collier Books, 1963) [Weisstein's note].

8. W. H. Masters and V. E. Johnson, *Human Sexual Response* (Boston: Little, Brown, 1966) [Weisstein's note].

Only when it is not known which subject took which pill is validity remotely approximated. In addition, with judgments of human behavior, it is so difficult to precisely tie down just what behavior is going on, let alone what behavior should be expected, that one must test again and again the reliability of judgments. How many judges, blind, will agree in their observations? Can they replicate their own judgments at some later time? When, in actual practice, these judgment criteria are tested for clinical judgments, then we find that the judges cannot judge reliably, nor can they judge consistently: they do no better than chance in identifying which of a certain set of stories were written by men and which by women; which of a whole battery of clinical test results are the products of homosexuals and which are the products of heterosexuals,[9] and which, of a battery of clinical test results *and* interviews (where questions are asked such as "Do you have delusions?"[1]) are products of psychotics, neurotics, psychosomatics, or normals. Lest this summary escape your notice, let me stress the implications of these findings. The ability of judges, chosen for their clinical expertise, to distinguish male heterosexuals from male homosexuals on the basis of three widely used clinical projective tests—the Rorschach, the TAT, and the MAP—was *no better than chance*. The reason this is such devastating news, of course, is that sexuality is supposed to be of fundamental importance in the deep dynamic of personality; if what is considered gross sexual deviance cannot be caught, then what are psychologists talking about when they, for example, claim that at the basis of paranoid psychosis is "latent homosexual panic"? They can't even identify what homosexual anything is, let alone "latent homosexual panic."[2] More frightening, expert clinicians cannot be consistent on what diagnostic category to assign to a person, again on the basis of both tests and interviews; a number of normals in the Little and Schneidman study were described as psychotic, in such categories as "schizophrenic with homosexual tendencies" or "schizoid character with depressive trends." But most disheartening, when the judges were asked to rejudge the test protocols some weeks later, their diagnoses of the same subjects on the basis of the same protocol differed markedly from their initial judgments. It is obvious that even simple descriptive conventions

9. E. Hooker, "Male Homosexuality in the Rorschach," *Journal of Projective Techniques*, 21 (1957), 18–31 [Weisstein's note].

1. K. B. Little and E. S. Schneidman, "Congruences among Interpretations of Psychological Test and Anamnestic Data," *Psychological Monographs*, 73 (1959), 1–42 [Weisstein's note].

2. It should be noted that psychologists have been as quick to assert absolute truths about the nature of homosexuality as they have about the nature of women. The arguments presented in this paper apply equally to the nature of homosexuality; psychologists know nothing about it; there is no more evidence for the "naturalness" of heterosexuality. Psychology has functioned as a pseudo-scientific buttress for patriarchal ideology and patriarchal social organization: women's liberation and gay liberation fight against a common victimization [Weisstein's note].

in clinical psychology cannot be consistently applied; if clinicians were as faulty in recognizing food from non-food, they'd poison themselves and starve to death. That their descriptive conventions have any explanatory significance is therefore, of course, out of the question.

As a graduate student at Harvard some years ago, I was a member of a seminar which was asked to identify which of two piles of a clinical test, the TAT, had been written by males and which by females. Only four students out of twenty identified the piles correctly, and this was after one and a half months of intensively studying the differences between men and women. Since this result is below chance—that is, the result would occur by chance about four out of a thousand times—we may conclude that there *is* finally a consistency here; students are judging knowledgeably within the context of psychological teaching about the differences between men and women; the teachings themselves are simply erroneous.

You may argue that the theory may be scientifically "unsound" but at least it cures people. There is no evidence that it does. In 1952, Eysenck[3] reported the results of what is called an "outcome of therapy" study of neurotics which showed that, of the patients who received psychoanalysis the improvement rate was 44 percent; of the patients who received psychotherapy the improvement rate was 64 percent; and of the patients who received no treatment at all the improvement rate was 72 percent. These findings have never been refuted; subsequently, later studies have confirmed the negative results of the Eysenck study.[4] How can clinicians and psychiatrists, then, in all good conscience, continue to practice? Largely by ignoring these results and being careful not to do outcome-of-therapy studies. The attitude is nicely summarized by Rotter:[5] "Research studies in psychotherapy tend to be concerned more with pyschotherapeutic procedure and less with outcome. ... To some extent, it reflects an interest in the psychotherapy situation as a kind of personality laboratory." Some laboratory.

The Social Context

Thus, since we can conclude that because clinical experience and

3. H. J. Eysenck, "The Effects of Psychotherapy: An Evaluation," *Journal of Consulting Psychology*, 16 (1952), 319–324 [Weisstein's note].

4. F. Barron and T. Leary, "Changes in Psychoneurotic Patients with and without Psychotherapy," *Journal of Counseling Psychology*, 19 (1955); A. E. Bergin, "The Effects of Psychotherapy: Negative Results Revisited," *Journal of Counseling Psychology*, 10 (1963); R. D. Cartwright and J. L. Vogel, "A Comparison of Changes in Psychoneurotic Patients During Matched Periods of Therapy and No-therapy," *Journal of Counseling Psychology*, 24 (1960); C. B. Truax, "Effective Ingredients in Psychotherapy: An Approach to Unraveling the Patient-Therapist Interaction," *Journal of Counseling Psychology*, 10 (1963); E. Powers and H. Witmer, *An Experiment in the Prevention of Delinquency* (New York: Columbia University Press, 1951) [Weisstein's note].

5. J. B. Rotter, "Psychotherapy," *Annual Review of Psychology*, 11 (1960), 381–414 [Weisstein's note].

tools can be shown to be worse than useless when tested for consistency, efficacy, agreement, and reliability, we can safely conclude that theories of a clinical nature advanced about women are also worse than useless. I want to turn now to the second major point in my paper, which is that, even when psychological theory is constructed so that it may be tested, and rigorous standards of evidence are used, it has become increasingly clear that in order to understand why people do what they do, and certainly in order to change what people do, psychologists must turn away from the theory of the causal nature of the inner dynamic and look to the social context within which individuals live.

Before examining the relevance of this approach to the question of women, let me first sketch the groundwork for this assertion.

In the first place, it is clear[6] that personality tests never yield consistent predictions; a rigid authoritarian on one measure will be an unauthoritarian on the next. But the reason for this inconsistency is only now becoming clear, and it seems overwhelmingly to have much more to do with the social situation in which the subject finds him/herself than with the subject him/herself.

In a series of brilliant experiments, Rosenthal and his co-workers[7] have shown that if one group of experimenters has one hypothesis about what they expect to find, and another group of experimenters has the opposite hypothesis, both groups will obtain results in accord with their hypotheses. The results obtained are not due to mishandling of data by biased experimenters; rather, somehow, the bias of the experimenter creates a changed environment in which subjects actually act differently. For instance, in one experiment, subjects were to assign numbers to pictures of men's faces, with high numbers representing the subject's judgment that the man in the picture was a successful person, and low numbers representing the subject's judgment that the man in the picture was an unsuccessful person. Prior to running the subjects, one group of experimenters was told that the subjects tended to rate the faces high; another group of experimenters was told that the subjects tended to rate the faces low. Each group of experimenters was instructed to follow precisely the same procedure: they were required to read to subjects a set of instructions, and to say *nothing else.* For the 375 subjects run, the results showed clearly that those subjects who performed the task with experimenters who expected high ratings gave high ratings, and those subjects who performed the task with experimenters who expected low ratings gave low ratings. How did this

6. J. Block, *op. cit.* [Weisstein's note].

7. R. Rosenthal and L. Jacobson, *Pygmalion in the Classroom: Teacher Expectation and Pupil's Intellectual Development* (New York: Holt, Rinehart & Winston, 1968); R. Rosenthal, *Experimenter Effects in Behavioral Research* (New York: Appleton-Century Crofts, 1966) [Weisstein's note].

happen? The experimenters all used the same words; it was something in their conduct which made one group of subjects do one
thing, and another group of subjects do another thing.[8]

The concreteness of the changed conditions produced by expectation is a fact, a reality: even with animal subjects, in two separate
studies,[9] those experimenters who were told that rats learning
mazes had been especially bred for brightness obtained better learning from their rats than did experimenters believing their rats to
have been bred for dullness. In a very recent study, Rosenthal and
Jacobson (1968) extended their analysis to the natural classroom
situation. Here, they tested a group of students and reported to the
teachers that some among the students tested "showed great promise." Actually, the students so named had been selected on a
random basis. Some time later, the experimenters retested the group
of students: those students whose teachers had been told that they
were "promising" showed real and dramatic increments in their IQs
as compared to the rest of the students. Something in the conduct
of the teachers towards those who the teachers believed to be the
"bright" students, made those students brighter.

Thus, even in carefully controlled experiments, and with no outward or conscious difference in behavior, the hypotheses we start
with will influence enormously the behavior of another organism.
These studies are extremely important when assessing the validity of
psychological studies of women. Since it is beyond doubt that most
of us start with notions as to the nature of men and women, the
validity of a number of observations of sex differences is questionable, even when these observations have been made under carefully
controlled conditions. Second, and more important, the Rosenthal
experiments point quite clearly to the influence of social expectation. In some extremely important ways, people are what you expect
them to be, or at least they behave as you expect them to behave.
Thus, if women, according to Bettelheim, want first and foremost
to be good wives and mothers, it is extremely likely that this is what
Bruno Bettelheim, and the rest of society, want them to be.

There is another series of brilliant social psychological experiments which point to the overwhelming effect of social context.
These are the obedience experiments of Stanley Milgram[1] in which
subjects are asked to obey the orders of unknown experimenters,

8. I am indebted to Jesse Lemisch for
his valuable suggestions in the interpretation of these studies [Weisstein's note].
  9. R. Rosenthal and K. L. Fode, "The
Effect of Experimenter Bias on the Performance of the Albino Rat," Harvard
University, unpublished manuscript
1961; R. Rosenthal and R. Lawson, "A
Longitudinal Study of the Effects of Experimenter Bias on the Operant Learning
of Laboratory Rats," Harvard University, unpublished manuscript, 1961 [Weis-
stein's note].
  1. Stanley Milgram, "Some Conditions
of Obedience and Disobedience to Authority," *Human Relations,* 18 (1965),
57–76; "Liberating Effects of Group
Pressures," *Journal of Personality and
Social Psychology,* 1 (1965), 127–134
[Weisstein's note]. See "A Behavioral
Study of Obedience," (pp. 293–307) in
this volume.

orders which carry with them the distinct possibility that the subject is killing somebody.

In Milgram's experiments, a subject is told that he/she is administering a learning experiment, and that he/she is to deal out shocks each time the other "subject" (in reality, a confederate of the experimenter) answers incorrectly. The equipment appears to provide graduated shocks ranging upwards from 15 volts through 450 volts; for each of four consecutive voltages there are verbal descriptions such as "mild shock," "danger, severe shock," and, finally, for the 435- and 450-volt switches, a red XXX marked over the switches. Each time the stooge answers incorrectly, the subject is supposed to increase the voltage. As the voltage increases, the stooge begins to cry in pain; he/she demands that the experiment stop; finally, he/she refuses to answer at all. When he/she stops responding, the experimenter instructs the subject to continue increasing the voltage; for each shock administered the stooge shrieks in agony. Under these conditions, about 62½ percent of the subjects administered shocks that they believed to be possibly lethal.

No tested individual differences between subjects predicted how many would continue to obey, and which would break off the experiment. When forty psychiatrists predicted how many of a group of 100 subjects would go on to give the lethal shock, their predictions were orders of magnitude below the actual percentages; most expected only one-tenth of one per cent of the subjects to obey to the end.

But even though *psychiatrists* have no idea how people will behave in this situation, and even though individual differences do not predict which subjects will obey and which will not, it is easy to predict when subjects will be obedient and when they will be defiant. All the experimenter has to do is change the social situation. In a variant of Milgram's experiment, two stooges were present in addition to the "victim"; these worked along with the subject in administering electric shocks. When these two stooges refused to go on with the experiment, only 10 percent of the subjects continued to the maximum voltage. This is critical for personality theory. It says that behavior is predicted from the social situation, not from the individual history.

Finally, an ingenious experiment by Schachter and Singer[2] showed that subjects injected with adrenalin, which produces a state of physiological arousal in all but minor respects identical to that which occurs when subjects are extremely afraid, became euphoric when they were in a room with a stooge who was acting euphoric, and became extremely angry when they were placed in a room with

2. S. Schachter and J. E. Singer, "Cognitive, Social, and Physiological Determinants of Emotional State," *Psychological Review*, 63 (1962), 379–399 [Weisstein's note].

a stooge who was acting extremely angry.

To summarize: If subjects under quite innocuous and non-coercive social conditions can be made to kill other subjects and under other types of social conditions will positively refuse to do so; if subjects can react to a state of physiological fear by becoming euphoric because there is somebody else around who is euphoric, or angry because there is somebody else around who is angry; if students become intelligent because teachers expect them to be intelligent, and rats run mazes better because experimenters are told the rats are bright, then it is obvious that a study of human behavior requires, first and foremost, a study of the social contexts within which people move, the expectations as to how they will behave, and the authority which tells them who they are and what they are supposed to do.

Biologically Based Theories

Biologists also have at times assumed they could describe the limits of human potential from their observations not of human, but of animal behavior. Here, as in psychology, there has been no end of theorizing about the sexes, again with a sense of absolute certainty surprising in "science." These theories fall into two major categories.

One category of theory argues that since females and males differ in their sex hormones, and sex hormones enter the brain,[3] there must be innate behavioral differences. But the only thing this argument tells us is that there are differences in physiological state. The problem is whether these differences are at all relevant to behavior.

Consider, for example, differences in levels of the sex hormone testosterone. A man who calls himself Tiger[4] has recently argued[5] that the greater quantities of testosterone found in human males as compared with human females (of a certain age group) determine innate differences in aggressiveness, competitiveness, dominance, ability to hunt, ability to hold public office, and so forth. But Tiger demonstrates in this argument the same manly and courageous refusal to be intimidated by evidence which we have already seen in our consideration of the clinical and psychiatric tradition. The evidence does not support his argument, and in most cases, directly contradicts it. Testosterone level does not seem to be related to hunting ability, dominance, or aggression, or competitive-

3. D. A. Hamburg and D. T. Lunde, "Sex Hormones in the Development of Sex Differences in Human Behavior," in *The Development of Sex Differences*, ed. Maccoby (Stanford: Stanford University Press, 1966), pp. 1–24 [Weisstein's note].

4. H. N. G. Schwarz-Belkin claims that the name was originally Mouse, but this may be a reference to an earlier L. Tiger (putative). See "Les Fleurs Du Mal," in *Festschrift fir Piltdown* (New York: Ponzi Press, 1914) [Weisstein's note].

5. Lionel Tiger, "Male Dominance? Yes. A Sexist Plot? No," *New York Times Magazine*, sec. N, Oct. 25, 1970 [Weisstein's note].

ness. As Storch[6] has pointed out, all normal *male mammals* in the reproductive age group produce much greater quantities of testosterone than females; yet many of these males are neither hunters nor are they aggressive (e.g. rabbits). And, among some hunting mammals, such as the large cats, it turns out that more hunting is done by the female than the male. And there exist primate species where the female is clearly more aggressive, competitive, and dominant than the male.[7] Thus, for some species, being female, and therefore, having less testosterone than the male of that species means hunting more, or being more aggressive, or being more dominant. Nor does having *more* testosterone preclude behavior commonly thought of as "female"; there exist primate species where females do not touch infants except to feed them; the males care for the infants at all times.[8] So it is not clear what testosterone or any other sex-hormonal difference means for differences in nature, or sex-role behavior.

In other words, one can observe identical types of behavior which have been associated with sex (e.g. "mothering") in males and females, despite known differences in physiological state, i.e. sex hormones, genitalia, etc. What about the converse to this? That is, can one obtain differences in behavior given a single physiological state? The answer is overwhelmingly yes, not only as regards non-sex-specific hormones (as in the Schachter and Singer experiment cited above), but also as regards gender itself. Studies of hermaphrodites with the same diagnosis (the genetic, gonadal, hormonal sex, the internal reproductive organs, and the ambiguous appearances of the external genitalia were identical) have shown that one will consider oneself male or female depending simply on whether one was defined and raised as male or female:[9]

There is no more convincing evidence of the power of social interaction on gender-identity differentiation than in the case of congenital hermaphrodites who are of the same diagnosis and similar degree of hermaphroditism but are differently assigned and with a different postnatal medical and life history. (Money, 1970, p. 743).

Thus, for example, if out of two individuals diagnosed as having the adrenogenital syndrome of female hermaphroditism, one is raised as a girl and one as a boy, each will act and identify her/himself accordingly. The one raised as a girl will consider herself a girl; the one raised as a boy will consider himself a boy; and each will conduct her/himself successfully in accord with that self-definition.

6. M. Storch, "Reply to Tiger," unpublished manuscript, 1970 [Weisstein's note].

7. G. D. Mitchell, "Paternalistic Behavior in Primates," *Psychological Bulletin*, 71 (1969), 399–417 [Weisstein's note].

8. *Ibid.* [Weisstein's note].

9. J. Money, "Sexual Dimorphism and Homosexual Gender Identity," *Psychological Bulletin* 6 (1970), 425–440 [Weisstein's note].

So, identical behavior occurs given different physiological states; and different behavior occurs given an identical physiological starting point. So it is not clear that differences in sex hormones are at all relevant to behavior.

The other category of theory based on biology, a reductionist theory, goes like this. Sex-role behavior in some primate species is described, and it is concluded that this is the "natural" behavior for humans. Putting aside the not insignificant problem of observer bias (for instance, Harlow, of the University of Wisconsin, after observing differences between male and female rhesus monkeys, quotes Laurence Sterne to the effect that women are silly and trivial, and concludes that "men and women have differed in the past and they will differ in the future"[1]), there are a number of problems with this approach.

The most general and serious problem is that there are no grounds to assume that anything primates do is necessarily natural, or desirable in humans, for the simple reason that humans are not non-humans. For instance, it is found that male chimpanzees placed alone with infants will not "mother" them. Jumping from hard data to ideological speculation, researchers conclude from this information that *human* females are necessary for the safe growth of human infants. It would be reasonable to conclude, following this logic, that it is quite useless to teach human infants to speak, since it has been tried with chimpanzees and it does not work.

One strategy that has been used is to extrapolate from primate behavior to "innate" human preference by noticing certain trends in primate behavior as one moves phylogenetically closer to humans. But there are great difficulties with this approach. When behaviors from lower primates are directly opposite to those of higher primates, or to those one expects of humans, they can be dismissed on evolutionary grounds—higher primates and/or humans grew out of that kid stuff. On the other hand, if the behavior of higher primates is counter to the behavior considered natural for humans, while the behavior of some lower primate is considered the natural one for humans, the higher primate behavior can be dismissed also, on the grounds that it has diverged from an older, prototypical pattern. So either way, one can select those behaviors one wants to prove innate for humans. In addition, one does not know whether the sex-role behavior exhibited is dependent on the phylogenetic rank, or on the environmental conditions (both physical and social) under which different species live.

Is there then any value at all in primate observations as they relate to human females and males? There is a value but it is limited: its function can be no more than to show some extant examples of

---

1. H. F. Harlow, "The Heterosexual Affectional System in Monkeys," *American Psychologist*, 17 (1962), 1–9 [Weisstein's note].

diverse sex-role behavior. It must be stressed, however, that this is an extremely limited function. The extant behavior does not begin to suggest all the possibilities, either for non-human primates or for humans. Bearing these caveats in mind, it is nonetheless interesting that if one inspects the limited set of observations of existing non-human primate sex-role behaviors, one finds, in fact, a much larger range of sex-role behavior than is commonly believed to exist. "Biology" appears to limit very little; the fact that a female gives birth does not mean, even in non-humans, that she necessarily cares for the infant (in marmosets, for instance, the male carries the infant at all times except when the infant is feeding[2]); "natural" female and male behavior varies all the way from females who are much more aggressive and competitive than males (e.g. Tamarins[3]) and male "mothers" (e.g. Titi monkeys, night monkeys, and marmosets[4]) to submissive and passive females and male antagonists (e.g. rhesus monkeys).

But even for the limited function that primate arguments serve, the evidence has been misused. Invariably, those primates have been cited which exhibit exactly the kind of behavior that the proponents of the biological fixedness of human female behavior wish were true for humans. Thus, baboons and rhesus monkeys are generally cited: males in these groups exhibit some of the most irritable and aggressive behavior found in primates, and if one wishes to argue that females are naturally passive and submissive, these groups provide vivid examples. There are abundant counter examples, such as those mentioned above;[5] in fact, in general, a counter example can be found for every sex-role behavior cited, including, as mentioned in the case of marmosets, male "mothers."

But the presence of counter examples has not stopped florid and overarching theories of the natural or biological basis of male privilege from proliferating. For instance, there have been a number of theories dealing with the innate incapacity in human males for monogamy. Here, as in most of this type of theorizing, baboons are a favorite example, probably because of their fantasy value: the family unit of the hamadryas baboon, for instance, consists of a highly constant pattern of one male and a number of females and their young. And again, the counter examples, such as the invariably monogamous gibbon, are ignored.

An extreme example of this maiming and selective truncation of the evidence in the service of a plea for the maintenance of male privilege is a recent book, *Men in Groups* by Tiger.[6] The central

2. Mitchell, *op. cit.* [Weisstein's note].
3. *Ibid.* [Weisstein's note].
4. *Ibid.* (All these are lower-order primates, which makes their behavior with reference to humans unnatural, or more natural; take your choice.) [Weisstein's note].
5. *Ibid.* [Weisstein's note].
6. Lionel Tiger, *Men in Groups* (New York: Random House, 1969) [Weisstein's note].

claim of this book is that females are incapable of "bonding" as in "male bonding." What is "male bonding"? Its surface definition is simple: " . . . a particular relationship between two or more males such that they react differently to members of their bonding units as compared to individuals outside of it."[7] If one deletes the word male, the definition, on its face, would seem to include all organisms that have any kind of social organization. But this is not what Tiger means. For instance, Tiger asserts that females are incapable of bonding; and this alleged incapacity indicates to Tiger that females should be restricted from public life. Why is bonding an exclusively male behavior? Because, says Tiger, it is seen in male primates. All male primates? No, very few male primates. Tiger cites two examples where male bonding is seen: rhesus monkeys and baboons. Surprise, surprise. But not even all baboons: as mentioned above, the hamadryas social organization consists of one-male units; so does that of the gelada baboon.[8] And the great apes do not go in for male bonding much either. The "male bond" is hardly a serious contribution to scholarship; one reviewer for *Science* has observed that the book " . . . shows basically more resemblance to a partisan political tract than to a work of objective social science," with male bonding being " . . . some kind of behavioral phlogiston."[9]

In short, primate arguments have generally misused the evidence; primate studies themselves have, in any case, only the very limited function of describing some possible sex-role behavior; and at present, primate observations have been sufficiently limited so that even the range of possible sex-role behavior for non-human primates is not known. This range is not known since there is only minimal observation of what happens to behavior if the physical or social environment is changed. In one study,[1] different troops of Japanese macaques were observed. Here, there appeared to be cultural differences: males in 3 out of the 18 troops observed differed in the amount of their aggressiveness and infant-caring behavior. There could be no possibility of differential evolution here; the differences seemed largely transmitted by infant socialization. Thus, the very limited evidence points to some plasticity in the sex-role behavior of non-human primates; if we can figure out experiments which massively change the social organization of primate groups, it is possible that we might observe great changes in behavior. At present, however, we must conclude that given a constant physical environment, non-human primates do not change their social conditions by themselves very much and thus the "innateness" and fixedness of

7. *Ibid.*, pp. 19–20 [Weisstein's note].
8. Mitchell, *op. cit.* [Weisstein's note].
9. M. H. Fried, "Mankind Excluding Women," *Science*, 165 (1969), 883–884 [Weisstein's note].

1. J. Itani, "Paternal Care in the Wild Japanese Monkey *Macaca fuscata*," in *Primate Social Behavior*, ed. Southwick (Princeton: Van Nostrand, 1963) [Weisstein's note].

their behavior is simply not known. Thus, even if there were some way, which there isn't, to settle on the behavior of a particular primate species as being the "natural" way for humans, we would not know whether or not this were simply some function of the present social organization of that species. And finally, once again it must be stressed that even if non-human primate behavior turned out to be relatively fixed, this would say little about our behavior. More immediate and relevant evidence, e.g. the evidence from social psychology, points to the enormous plasticity in human behavior, not only from one culture to the next, but from one experimental group to the next. One of the most salient features of human social organization is its variety; there are a number of cultures where there is at least a rough equality between men and women.[2] In summary, primate arguments can tell us very little about our "innate" sex-role behavior; if they tell us anything at all, they tell us that there is no one biologically "natural" female or male behavior, and that sex-role behavior in non-human primates is much more varied than has previously been thought.

Conclusion

In brief, the uselessness of present psychology (and biology) with regard to women is simply a special case of the general conclusion: one must understand the social conditions under which humans live if one is going to attempt to explain their behavior. And, to understand the social conditions under which women live, one must understand the social expectations about women.

How are women characterized in our culture, and in psychology? They are inconsistent, emotionally unstable, lacking in a strong conscience or superego, weaker, "nurturant" rather then productive, "intuitive" rather than intelligent, and, if they are at all "normal," suited to the home and the family. In short, the list adds up to a typical minority group stereotype of inferiority:[3] if they know their place, which is in the home, they are really quite lovable, happy, childlike, loving creatures. In a review of the intellectual differences between little boys and little girls, Eleanor Maccoby[4] has shown that there are no intellectual differences until about high school, or, if there are, girls are slightly ahead of boys. At high school, girls begin to do worse on a few intellectual tasks, such as arithmetic reasoning, and beyond high school, the achievement of women now measured in terms of productivity and accomplishment drops off

2. Margaret Mead, *Male and Female: A Study of the Sexes in a Changing World* (New York: William Morrow, 1949) [Weisstein's note].

3. H. M. Hacker, "Women as a Minority Group," *Social Forces*, 30 (1951), 60–69 [Weisstein's note].

4. Eleanor E. Maccoby, "Sex Differences in Intellectual Functioning," in *The Development of Sex Differences*, ed. Maccoby (Stanford: Stanford University Press, 1966), pp. 25–55 [Weisstein's note].

even more rapidly. There are a number of other, non-intellectual tests which show sex differences; I choose the intellectual differences since it is seen clearly that women start becoming inferior. It is no use to talk about women being different but equal; all of the tests I can think of have a "good" outcome and a "bad" outcome. Women usually end up at the "bad" outcome. In light of social expectations about women, what is surprising is that little girls don't get the message that they are supposed to be stupid until high school; and what is even more remarkable is that some women resist this message even after high school, college, and graduate school.

My paper began with remarks on the task of the discovery of the limits of human potential. Psychologists must realize that it is they who are limiting discovery of human potential. They refuse to accept evidence, if they are clinical psychologists, or, if they are rigorous, they assume that people move in a context-free ether, with only their innate dispositions and their individual traits determining what they will do. Until psychologists begin to respect evidence, and until they begin looking at the social context within which people move, psychology will have nothing of substance to offer in this task of discovery. I don't know what immutable differences exist between men and women apart from differences in their genitals; perhaps there are some other unchangeable differences; probably there are a number of irrelevant differences. But it is clear that until social expectations for men and women are equal, until we provide equal respect for both men and women, our answers to this question will simply reflect our prejudices.

B. F. SKINNER
What Is Man?[1]

As a science of behavior follows the strategy of physics and biology, the autonomous agent to which we have traditionally attributed behavior is replaced by the environment—the environment in which the species evolved and in which the behavior of the individual is shaped and maintained.

Take, for example, a "cognitive" activity, *attention*. A person responds to only a small part of the stimuli impinging upon him. The traditional view is that he himself determines which stimuli are to be effective—by paying attention to them. Some kind of inner gatekeeper allows some stimuli to enter and keeps all others out. A sudden or strong stimulus may break through and "attract" attention, but the person himself is otherwise in control. An analysis of

1. From *Beyond Freedom and Dignity*, 1971.

the environmental circumstances reverses the relation. The kinds of stimuli that break through by "attracting attention" do so because they have been associated in the evolutionary history of the species or the personal history of the individual with important—e.g., dangerous—things. Less forceful stimuli attract attention only to the extent that they have figured in contingencies of reinforcement.

We can arrange contingencies that insure that an organism—even such a simple organism as a pigeon—will attend to one object and not to another, or to one property of an object, such as its color, and not to another, such as its shape. The inner gatekeeper is replaced by the contingencies that the person has been exposed to and that select the stimuli he reacts to.

Face

In the traditional view a person perceives the world around him and acts upon it to make it known to him. It has even been argued that the world would not exist if no one perceived it. The action is exactly reversed in an environmental analysis. There would, of course, be no perception if there were no world to perceive, but we would not perceive an existing world if there were no appropriate contingencies.

We say that a baby perceives his mother's face and knows it. Our evidence is that the baby responds in one way to his mother's face and in other ways to other faces or other things. He makes this distinction not through some mental act of perception but because of prior contingencies. Some of these may be contingencies of survival. The face and facial expressions of the human mother have been associated with security, warmth, food and other important things during both the evolution of the species and the life of the child.

The role of the environment is particularly subtle when what is known is the knower himself. If there is no external world to initiate knowing, must we not then say that the knower himself acts first? This is, of course, the field of consciousness or awareness which a scientific analysis of behavior is often accused of ignoring. The charge is a serious one and should be taken seriously.

Man is said to differ from the other animals mainly because he is "aware of his own existence." He knows what he is doing; he knows that he has had a past and will have a future; he alone follows the classical injunction, "Know thyself." Any analysis of human behavior that neglected these facts would be defective indeed. And some analyses do. "Methodological behaviorism" limits itself to what can be observed publicly; mental processes may exist, but their nature rules them out of scientific consideration. The "behaviorists" in political science and many logical positivists in philosophy have followed a similar line. But we can study self-observation, and we must include it in any reasonably complete account of human behavior.

Rather than ignore consciousness, an experimental analysis of behavior has put much emphasis on certain crucial issues. The question is not whether a man can know himself but what he knows when he does so.

Skin

The problem arises in part from the indisputable fact of privacy: a small part of the universe is enclosed within a human skin. It would be foolish to deny the existence of that private world, but it is also foolish to assert that because it is private its nature is different from the world outside. The difference is not in the stuff that composes the private world but in its accessibility. There is an exclusive intimacy about a headache or heartache that has seemed to support the doctrine that knowing is a kind of possession.

The difficulty is that although privacy may bring the knower closer to what he knows, it interferes with the process through which he comes to know anything. As we have seen, contingencies under which a child learns to describe his feelings are necessarily defective; the verbal community cannot use the same procedures for this that it uses to teach a child to describe objects. There are, of course, natural contingencies under which we learn to respond to private stimuli, and they generate behavior of great precision; we could not walk if we were not stimulated by parts of our own body. But very little awareness is associated with this kind of behavior and, in fact, we behave in these ways most of the time without being aware of the stimuli to which we are responding. We do not attribute awareness to other species that obviously use similar private stimuli. To "know" private stimuli is more than to respond to them.

Help

The verbal community specializes in self-descriptive contingencies. It asks: What did you do yesterday? Why did you do that? How do you feel about that? The answers help persons adjust to each other effectively. And it is because such questions are asked that a person responds to himself and his behavior in the special way called knowing or being aware. Without the help of a verbal community all behavior would be unconscious. Consciousness is a social product. It is not only *not* the special field of autonomous man, it is not within the range of a solitary man.

And it is not within the range of accuracy of anyone. The privacy that seems to confer intimacy upon self-knowledge makes it impossible for the verbal community to maintain precise contingencies. Introspective vocabularies are by nature inaccurate, and that is one reason why they have varied so widely among schools of philosophy and psychology. Even a carefully trained observer runs into trouble when he studies new private stimuli.

Aware

Theories of psychotherapy that emphasize awareness assign a role to autonomous man that is the function of contingencies of reinforcement. Awareness may help if the problem is in part a lack of awareness, and "insight" into one's condition may help if one then takes remedial action. But awareness or insight alone is not always enough, and may be too much. One need not be aware of one's behavior or the conditions controlling it in order to behave effectively—or ineffectively.

The extent to which a man *should* be aware of himself depends upon the importance of self-observation for effective behavior. Self-knowledge is valuable only to the extent that it helps to meet the contingencies under which it has arisen.

Think

Perhaps the last stronghold of autonomous man is the complex "cognitive" activity called thinking. Because it is complex, it has yielded only slowly to explanation in terms of contingencies of reinforcement. We say that a person *forms a concept or an abstraction,* but all we see is that certain kinds of contingencies of reinforcement have brought a response under the control of a single property of a stimulus. We say that a person *recalls* or *remembers* what he has seen or heard, but all we see is that the present occasion evokes a response, possibly in weakened or altered form, acquired on another occasion. We say that a person *associates* one word with another, but all we observe is that one verbal stimulus evokes the response previously made to another. Rather than suppose that it is therefore autonomous man who forms concepts or abstractions, recalls or remembers, and associates, we can put matters in good order simply by noting that these terms do not refer to forms of behavior.

A person may take explicit action, however, when he solves a problem. The creative artist may manipulate a medium until something of interest turns up. Much of this can be done covertly, and we are then likely to assign it to a different dimensional system; but it can always be done overtly, perhaps more slowly but also often more effectively, and with rare exceptions it must have been learned in overt form. The culture constructs special contingencies to promote thinking. It teaches a person to make fine discriminations by making differential reinforcement more precise. It teaches techniques to use in solving problems. It provides rules that make it unnecessary to expose a person to the contingencies from which the rules derive, and it provides rules for finding rules.

Self-control or self-management is a special kind of problem-solving that, like self-knowledge, raises all the issues associated with privacy. It is always the environment that builds the behavior with which we solve problems, even when the problems are found in the private world inside the skin. We have not investigated the matter of self-control in a very productive way, but the inadequacy of our analysis is no reason to fall back on a miracle-working mind. If our understanding of contingencies of reinforcement is not yet sufficient to explain all kinds of thinking, we must remember that the appeal to mind explains nothing at all.

Inside

In shifting control from autonomous man to the observable environment we do not leave an empty organism. A great deal goes on inside the skin, and physiology will eventually be able to tell us more about it. It will explain why behavior indeed relates to the antecedent events of which we can show it to be a function.

People do not always correctly understand the assignment. Many physiologists regard themselves as looking for the "physiological correlates" of mental events. They regard physiological research as simply a more scientific version of introspection. But physiological techniques are not, of course, designed to detect or measure personalities, feelings, or thoughts. At the moment neither introspection nor physiology supplies very adequate information about what is going on inside a man as he behaves, and since they are both directed inward they have the same effect of diverting attention from the external environment.

Much of the misunderstanding about an inner man comes from the metaphor of storage. Evolutionary and environmental histories change an organism, but they are not stored within it. Thus we observe that babies suck their mothers' breasts and can easily imagine that a strong tendency to do so has survival value, but much more is implied by a "sucking instinct" regarded as something a baby possesses that enables it to suck. The concept of "human nature" or "genetic endowment" is dangerous when we take it in that sense. We are closer to human nature in a baby than in an adult, or in a primitive culture than in an advanced one, in the sense that environmental contingencies are less likely to have obscured the genetic endowment, and it is tempting to dramatize that endowment by implying that earlier stages have survived in concealed form: man is a naked ape. But anatomists and physiologists will not find an ape, or for that matter, instincts. They will find anatomical and physiological features that are the product of an evolutionary history.

Sin

It is often said too that the personal history of the individual is stored within him as a "habit." The cigarette habit is talked of as being something more than the behavior said to show that a person possesses it. But the only other information we have is about the reinforcers and the schedules of reinforcement that make a person smoke a great deal. The contingencies are not stored; they simply leave a person changed.

The issue has had a curious place in theology. Does man sin because he is sinful, or is he sinful because he sins? Neither question points to anything very useful. To say that a man is sinful because he sins is to give an operational definition of sin. To say that he sins because he is sinful is to trace his behavior to a supposed inner trait. But whether a person engages in the kind of behavior called sinful depends upon circumstances not mentioned in either question. The sin assigned as an inner possession (the sin a person "knows") is to be found in a history of reinforcement.

Self

It is the nature of an experimental analysis of human behavior to strip away the functions previously assigned to autonomous man and transfer them one by one to the controlling environment. The analysis leaves less and less for autonomous man to do. But what about man himself? Is there not something about a person—a self —that is more than a living body?

A self is a repertoire of behavior appropriate to a given set of contingencies, and a substantial part of the conditions to which a person is exposed may play a dominant role. Under other conditions a person may sometimes report, "I'm not myself today" or "I couldn't have done what you said I did, because that's not like me." The identity conferred upon a self arises from the contingencies responsible for the behavior.

Split

Two or more repertoires generated by different sets of contingencies compose two or more selves. A person possesses one repertoire appropriate to his life with his friends and another appropriate to his life with his family. A problem of identity arises when a person finds himself with family and friends at the same time.

Self-knowledge and self-control imply two selves in this sense. The self-knower is almost always a product of social contingencies, but the self that is known may come from other sources. The controlling self (the conscience or superego) is of social origin, but the

controlled self is more likely to be the product of genetic suscepti-
bilities to reinforcement (the id or the Old Adam). The controlling
self generally represents the interests of others; the controlled self
the interests of the individual.

Stranger

The picture that emerges from a scientific analysis is not of a
body with a person inside but of a body that *is* a person in the
sense that it displays a complex repertoire of behavior. The picture
is, of course, unfamiliar. The man we thus portray is a stranger, and
from the traditional point of view he may not seem to be a man at
all.

C. S. Lewis put it bluntly: "Man is being abolished."

There is clearly some difficulty in identifying the man to whom
Lewis referred. He cannot have meant the human species; far from
being abolished, it is filling the earth. Nor are individual men growing less effective or productive. What is being abolished is autonomous man—the inner man, the homunculus, the possessing demon,
the man defended by the literatures of freedom and dignity.

His abolition is long overdue. Autonomous man is a device we
use to explain what we cannot explain in any other way. We constructed him from our ignorance, and as our understanding
increases, the very stuff of which he is composed vanishes. Science
does not dehumanize man, it de-homunculizes him, and it must do
so if it is to prevent the abolition of the human species.

To man *qua* man we readily say good riddance. Only by dispossessing autonomous man can we turn to the real causes of human
behavior—from the inferred to the observed, from the miraculous
to the natural, from the inaccessible to the manipulable.

Purpose

It is often said that in doing so we must treat the man who survives as a mere animal. "Animal" is a pejorative term—but only
because "man" has been made spuriously honorific. Joseph Wood
Krutch argued that the traditional view supports Hamlet's exclamation "How like a god!" while Pavlov emphasized "How like a dog!"
But that was a step forward. A god is the archetypal pattern of an
explanatory fiction, of a miracle-working mind, of the metaphysical.
Man is much more than a dog, but like a dog he is within range of
a scientific analysis.

An important role of autonomous man has been to give direction
to human behavior, and it is often said that in dispossessing an
inner agent we leave man without a purpose: "Since a scientific psychology must regard human behavior objectively, as determined by
necessary laws, it must represent human behavior as unintentional."
But "necessary laws" would have this effect only if they referred

exclusively to antecedent conditions. Intention and purpose refer to selective consequences, the effects of which we can formulate in "necessary laws." Has life, in all the forms in which it exists on the surface of the earth, a purpose? And is this evidence of intentional design? The primate hand evolved *in order that* the primate could more successfully manipulate things, but its purpose was to be found not in a prior design but rather in the process of selection. Similarly, in operant conditioning—when a pianist acquires the behavior of playing a smooth scale, for example—we find the purpose of the skilled movement of the hand in the consequences that follow it. In neither the evolution of the human hand nor in the acquired use of the hand is any prior intention or purpose at issue.

There is a difference between biological and individual purpose in that the latter can be felt. No one could have felt the purpose in the development of the human hand, but a person can in a sense feel the purpose with which he plays a smooth scale. But he does not play a smooth scale *because* he feels the purpose of doing so; what he feels is a by-product of his behavior and of its consequences. The relation of the human hand to the contingencies of survival under which it evolved is, of course, out of reach of personal observation; the relation of the behavior to contingencies of reinforcement that have generated it is not.

Control

As a scientific analysis of behavior dispossesses autonomous man and turns the control he has been said to exert over to the environment, the individual may seem particularly vulnerable. He is henceforth to be controlled by the world around him, and in large part by other men. Is he not then simply a victim? Certainly men have been victims, as they have been victimizers, but the word is too strong. It implies despoliation, which is by no means an essential consequence of interpersonal control. But even under benevolent control is the individual not helpless—"at a dead end in his long struggle to control his own destiny"?

It is only autonomous man who has reached a dead end. Man himself may be controlled by his environment, but it is an environment almost wholly of his own making. The physical environment of most persons is largely man-made—the walls that shelter them, the tools they use, the surfaces they walk on—and the social environment is obviously man-made. It generates the language a person speaks, the customs he follows, and the behavior he exhibits with respect to the ethical, religious, governmental, economic, educational and psychotherapeutic institutions that control him.

The evolution of a culture is in fact a kind of gigantic exercise in self-control. As the individual controls himself by manipulating the world he lives in, so the human species has constructed an environment in which its members behave in a highly effective way. Mistakes have been made, and we have no assurance that the environment man has constructed will continue to provide gains that outstrip the losses. But man as we know him, for better or for worse, is what man has made of man.

Roles

This will not satisfy those who cry "Victim!" C. S. Lewis protested: ". . . the power of man to make himself what he pleases . . . means . . . the power of some men to make other men what they please." This is inevitable in the nature of cultural evolution. We must distinguish the controlling self from the controlled self even when they are both inside the same skin, and when control is exercised through the design of an external environment, the selves are, with minor exceptions, distinct.

The person who, purposely or not, introduces a new cultural practice is only one among possibly billions it will affect. If this does not seem like an act of self-control, it is only because we have misunderstood the nature of self-control in the individual.

When a person changes his physical or social environment "intentionally"—that is, in order to change human behavior, possibly including his own—he plays two roles: one as a controller, as the designer of a controlling culture, and another as the controlled, as the product of a culture. There is nothing inconsistent about this; it follows from the nature of the evolution of a culture, with or without intentional design.

The human species probably has undergone little genetic change in recorded time. We have only to go back a thousand generations to reach the artists of the caves of Lascaux. Features bearing directly on survival (such as resistance to disease) change substantially in a thousand generations, but the child of one of the Lascaux artists transplanted to the world of today might be almost indistinguishable from a modern child.

Man has improved himself enormously in the same period of time by changing the world he lives in. Modern religious practices developed over a hundred generations and modern government and law developed in fewer than a hundred. Perhaps no more than 20 generations have been needed to produce modern economic practices, and possibly no more than four or five to produce modern education, psychotherapy, and the physical and biological technologies that have increased man's sensitivity to the world around him and his power to change that world.

Change

Man has "controlled his own destiny," if that expression means anything at all. The man that man has made is the product of the culture man has devised. He has emerged from two quite different processes of evolution: biological and cultural. Both may now accelerate because both are subject to intentional design. Men have already changed their genetic endowment by breeding selectively and by changing contingencies of survival, and for a long time they have introduced cultural practices as cultural mutations. They may now begin to do both with a clearer eye to the consequences.

Stage

The individual is the carrier of both his species and his culture. Cultural practices like genetic traits are transmitted from individual to individual. Even within the most regimented culture every personal history is unique. But the individual remains merely a stage in a process that began long before he came into existence and will long outlast him. He has no ultimate responsibility for a species trait or a cultural practice, even though it was he who underwent the mutation or introduced the practice that became part of the species or culture.

Even if Lamarck had been right in supposing that the individual could change his genetic structure through personal effort, we should have to point to the environmental circumstances responsible for the effort, as we shall have to do when geneticists begin to change the human endowment. And when an individual engages in the intentional design of a cultural practice, we must turn to the culture that induces him to do so and supplies the art or science he uses.

End

One of the great problems of individualism, seldom recognized as such, is death—the inescapable fate of the individual, the final assault on freedom and dignity. Death is one of those remote events that are brought to bear on behavior only with the aid of cultural practices. What we see is the death of others, as in Pascal's famous metaphor: "Imagine a number of men in chains, all under sentence of death, some of whom are each day butchered in the sight of others; those remaining see their own condition in that of their fellows, and looking at each other with grief and despair await their turn. This is an image of the human condition."

Some religions have made death more important by picturing a future existence in heaven or hell, but the individualist has a special reason to fear death: it is the prospect of personal annihilation. The individualist can find no solace in reflecting upon any contribution that will survive him. He has refused to be concerned for the survival of his culture and is not reinforced by the fact that the culture will long survive him. In the defense of his own freedom and dignity he has denied the contributions of the past and must therefore relinquish all claim upon the future.

Pictures

Science probably has never demanded a more sweeping change in a traditional way of thinking about a subject, nor has there ever been a more important subject. In the traditional picture a person perceives the world around him, selects features to be perceived, discriminates among them, judges them good or bad, changes them to make them better (or worse), and may be held responsible for his action and justly rewarded or punished for its consequences. In the scientific picture a person is a member of a species shaped by evolutionary contingencies of survival, displaying behavioral processes that bring him under the control of the environment in which he lives, and largely under the control of a social environment that he and millions of others like him have constructed and maintained during the evolution of a culture. The direction of the controlling relation is reserved: a person does not act upon the world; the world acts upon him.

It is difficult to accept such a change simply on intellectual grounds and nearly impossible to accept its implications. The reaction of the traditionalist is usually described in terms of feelings. One of these, to which the Freudians have appealed in explaining the resistance to psychoanalysis, is wounded vanity. Freud himself expounded, as Ernest Jones said, "the three heavy blows which narcissism or self-love of mankind has suffered at the hands of science. The first was cosmological and was dealt by Copernicus; the second was biological and was dealt by Darwin; the third was psychological and was dealt by Freud."

But what are the signs or symptoms of wounded vanity, and how shall we explain them? What people do about a scientific picture of man is to call it wrong, demeaning and dangerous, to argue against it, and to attack those who propose or defend it. These are signs of wounded vanity only to the extent that the scientific formulation destroys accustomed reinforcers. If a person can no longer take credit or be admired for what he does, then he seems to suffer a loss of dignity or worth, and behavior previously reinforced by credit or admiration will undergo extinction. Extinction often leads to aggressive attack.

Futility

Another effect of the scientific picture has been described as a loss of faith or "nerve," as a sense of doubt or powerlessness, or as discouragement, depression, or despondency. A person is said to feel that he can do nothing about his own destiny, but what he feels is a weakening of old responses that are no longer reinforced.

Another effect is a kind of nostalgia. Old repertoires break through as traditionalists seize upon and exaggerate similarities between present and past. They call the old days the good old days, when people recognized the inherent dignity of man and the importance of spiritual values. These fragments of outmoded behavior tend to be wistful—that is, they have the character of increasingly unsuccessful behavior.

Rainbow

These reactions to a scientific conception of man are, of course, unfortunate. They immobilize men of good will, and anyone concerned with the future of his culture will do what he can to correct them. No theory changes what it is a theory about. We change nothing because we look at it, talk about it, or analyze it in a new way. Keats drank confusion to Newton for analyzing the rainbow, but the rainbow remained as beautiful as ever and became for many even more beautiful.

Man has not changed because we look at him, talk about him, and analyze him scientifically. His achievements in science, government, religion, art and literature remain as they have always been, to be admired as one admires a storm at sea or autumn foliage or a mountain peak, quite apart from their origins and untouched by a scientific analysis. What does change is our chance of doing something about the subject of a theory. Newton's analysis of the light in a rainbow was a step in the direction of the laser.

Perils

The traditional conception of man is flattering; it confers reinforcing privileges. It is therefore easy to defend and difficult to change. It was designed to build up the individual as an instrument of countercontrol, and it did so effectively, but in such a way as to limit future progress.

We have seen how the literatures of freedom and dignity, with their concern for autonomous man, have perpetuated the use of punishment and condoned the use of only weak nonpunitive techniques. It is not difficult to demonstrate a connection between the unlimited right of the individual to pursue happiness and the catastrophes threatened by unchecked breeding, the unrestrained affluence that exhausts resources and pollutes the environment, and the imminence of nuclear war.

Physical and biological technologies have alleviated pestilence and famine and the painful, dangerous and exhausting features of daily life, and a behavioral techology can begin to alleviate other kinds of ills. In the analysis of human behavior it is just possible that we are slightly beyond Newton's position in the analysis of light, for we are beginning to make technological applications, and there are wonderful possibilities—all the more wonderful because traditional approaches have been so ineffective.

It is hard to imagine a world in which people live together with-out quarreling, maintain themselves by producing the food, shelter and clothing they need, enjoy themselves and contribute to the enjoyment of others in art, music, literature and games, consume only a reasonable part of the resources of the world and add as little as possible to its pollution, bear no more children than they can raise decently, continue to explore the world around them and dis-cover better ways of dealing with it, and come to know themselves and the world around them accurately and comprehensively. Yet all this is possible. We have not yet seen what man can make of man.

QUESTIONS

1. *What does Skinner say to indicate that he expects disagreement? Does he make any concessions in his address to his readers that would suggest an effort to win over those who disagree with him?*
2. *Is Skinner an optimist or a pessimist?*
3. *Is Skinner hard to read because his ideas are strange and disturbing or because his writing is bad? Does Orwell offer any help in answer-ing this question?*

CHARLES SANDERS PEIRCE
The Fixation of Belief[1]

That which determines us, from given premises, to draw one in-ference rather than another, is some habit of mind, whether it be constitutional or acquired. The habit is good or otherwise, according as it produces true conclusions from true premises or not; and an inference is regarded as valid or not, without reference to the truth or falsity of its conclusion specially, but according as the habit which determines it is such as to produce true conclusions in general or not. The particular habit of mind which governs this or that inference may be formulated in a proposition whose truth depends on the validity of the inferences which the habit determines; and such a formula is called a *guiding principle* of inference. Suppose, for example, that we observe that a rotating disk of copper quickly comes to rest when placed between the poles of a magnet, and we infer that this will happen with every disk of copper. The guiding principle is, that what is true of one piece of copper is true of another. Such a guiding principle with regard to copper would be much safer than with regard to many other substances—brass, for example.

1. The first in a series of papers, "Illustrations of the Logic of Science," published by Peirce in *The Popular Science Monthly*, 1877-1878.

A book might be written to signalize all the most important of these guiding principles of reasoning. It would probably be, we must confess, of no service to a person whose thought is directed wholly to practical subjects, and whose activity moves along thoroughly-beaten paths. The problems which present themselves to such a mind are matters of routine which he has learned once for all to handle in learning his business. But let a man venture into an unfamiliar field, or where his results are not continually checked by experience, and all history shows that the most masculine intellect will ofttimes lose his orientation and waste his efforts in directions which bring him no nearer to his goal, or even carry him entirely astray. He is like a ship in the open sea, with no one on board who understands the rules of navigation. And in such a case some general study of the guiding principles of reasoning would be sure to be found useful.

The subject could hardly be treated, however, without being first limited; since almost any fact may serve as a guiding principle. But it so happens that there exists a division among facts, such that in one class are all those which are absolutely essential as guiding principles, while in the others are all which have any other interest as objects of research. This division is between those which are necessarily taken for granted in asking whether a certain conclusion follows from certain premises, and those which are not implied in that question. A moment's thought will show that a variety of facts are already assumed when the logical question is first asked. It is implied, for instance, that there are such states of mind as doubt and belief—that a passage from one to the other is possible, the object of thought remaining the same, and that this transition is subject to some rules which all minds are alike bound by. As these are facts which we must already know before we can have any clear conception of reasoning at all, it cannot be supposed to be any longer of much interest to inquire into their truth or falsity. On the other hand, it is easy to believe that those rules of reasoning which are deduced from the very idea of the process are the ones which are the most essential; and, indeed, that so long as it conforms to these it will, at least, not lead to false conclusions from true premises. In point of fact, the importance of what may be deduced from the assumptions involved in the logical question turns out to be greater than might be supposed, and this for reasons which it is difficult to exhibit at the outset. The only one which I shall here mention is, that conceptions which are really products of logical reflection, without being readily seen to be so, mingle with our ordinary thoughts, and are frequently the causes of great confusion. This is the case, for example, with the conception of quality. A quality as such is never an object of observation. We can see that a thing is blue or green, but the quality of being blue and the quality of being green are not things which we see; they are products of logical reflection. The truth is, that common-sense, or thought as it first emerges above the level of the narrowly practical, is deeply imbued with that bad logical quality to which the epithet *metaphysical* is commonly applied; and nothing can clear it up but a severe course of logic.

We generally know when we wish to ask a question and when we wish to pronounce a judgment, for there is a dissimilarity between the sensation of doubting and that of believing.

But this is not all which distinguishes doubt from belief. There is a practical difference. Our beliefs guide our desires and shape our actions. The Assassins, or followers of the Old Man of the Mountain, used to rush into death at his least command, because they believed that obedience to him would insure everlasting felicity. Had they doubted this, they would not have acted as they did. So it is with every belief, according to its degree. The feeling of believing is a more or less sure indication of there being established in our nature some habit which will determine our actions. Doubt never has such an effect.

Nor must we overlook a third point of difference. Doubt is an uneasy and dissatisfied state from which we struggle to free ourselves and pass into the state of belief; while the latter is a calm and satisfactory state which we do not wish to avoid, or to change to a belief in anything else.[2] On the contrary, we cling tenaciously, not merely to believing, but to believing just what we do believe.

Thus, both doubt and belief have positive effects upon us, though very different ones. Belief does not make us act at once, but puts us into such a condition that we shall behave in a certain way, when the occasion arises. Doubt has not the least effect of this sort, but stimulates us to action until it is destroyed. This reminds us of the irritation of a nerve and the reflex action produced thereby; while for the analogue of belief, in the nervous system, we must look to what are called nervous associations—for example, to that habit of the nerves in consequence of which the smell of a peach will make the mouth water.

The irritation of doubt causes a struggle to attain a state of belief. I shall term this struggle *inquiry*, though it must be admitted that this is sometimes not a very apt designation.

The irritation of doubt is the only immediate motive for the struggle to attain belief. It is certainly best for us that our beliefs should be such as may truly guide our actions so as to satisfy our desires; and this reflection will make us reject any belief which does not seem to have been so formed as to insure this result. But it will only do so by creating a doubt in the place of that belief.

2. I am not speaking of secondary effects occasionally produced by the interference of other impulses [Peirce's note].

With the doubt, therefore, the struggle begins, and with the cessation of doubt it ends. Hence, the sole object of inquiry is the settlement of opinion. We may fancy that this is not enough for us, and that we seek, not merely an opinion, but a true opinion. But put this fancy to the test, and it proves groundless; for as soon as a firm belief is reached we are entirely satisfied, whether the belief be true or false. And it is clear that nothing out of the sphere of our knowledge can be our object, for nothing which does not affect the mind can be the motive for a mental effort. The most that can be maintained is, that we seek for a belief that we shall *think* to be true. But we think each one of our beliefs to be true, and, indeed, it is mere tautology to say so.

That the settlement of opinion is the sole end of inquiry is a very important proposition. It sweeps away, at once, various vague and erroneous conceptions of proof. A few of these may be noticed here.

1. Some philosophers have imagined that to start an inquiry it was only necessary to utter a question or set it down upon paper, and have even recommended us to begin our studies with questioning everything! But the mere putting of a proposition into the interrogative form does not stimulate the mind to any struggle after belief. There must be a real and living doubt, and without this all discussion is idle.

2. It is a very common idea that a demonstration must rest on some ultimate and absolutely indubitable propositions. These, according to one school, are first principles of a general nature; according to another, are first sensations. But, in point of fact, an inquiry, to have that completely satisfactory result called demonstration, has only to start with propositions perfectly free from all actual doubt. If the premises are not in fact doubted at all, they cannot be more satisfactory than they are.

3. Some people seem to love to argue a point after all the world is fully convinced of it. But no further advance can be made. When doubt ceases, mental action on the subject comes to an end; and, if it did go on, it would be without a purpose.

If the settlement of opinion is the sole object of inquiry, and if belief is of the nature of a habit, why should we not attain the desired end, by taking any answer to a question which we may fancy, and constantly reiterating it to ourselves, dwelling on all which may conduce to that belief, and learning to turn with contempt and hatred from anything which might disturb it? This simple and direct method is really pursued by many men. I remember once being entreated not to read a certain newspaper lest it might change my opinion upon free-trade. "Lest I might be entrapped by its fallacies and misstatements," was the form of expression. "You are not," my friend said, "a special student of political econ-

omy. You might, therefore, easily be deceived by fallacious arguments upon the subject. You might, then, if you read this paper,
be led to believe in protection. But you admit that free-trade is
the true doctrine; and you do not wish to believe what is not true."
I have often known this system to be deliberately adopted. Still
oftener, the instinctive dislike of an undecided state of mind,
exaggerated into a vague dread of doubt, makes men cling spas-
modically to the views they already take. The man feels that, if
he only holds to his belief without wavering, it will be entirely
satisfactory. Nor can it be denied that a steady and immovable faith
yields great peace of mind. It may, indeed, give rise to inconveniences, as if a man should resolutely continue to believe that
fire would not burn him, or that he would be eternally damned if
he received his *ingesta* otherwise than through a stomach-pump. But
then the man who adopts this method will not allow that its inconveniences are greater than its advantages. He will say, "I hold
steadfastly to the truth, and the truth is always wholesome." And
in many cases it may very well be that the pleasure he derives from
his calm faith overbalances any inconveniences resulting from its
deceptive character. Thus, if it be true that death is annihilation,
then the man who believes that he will certainly go straight to
heaven when he dies, provided he have fulfilled certain simple
observances in this life, has a cheap pleasure which will not be
followed by the least disappointment. A similar consideration
seems to have weight with many persons in religious topics, for we
frequently hear it said, "Oh, I could not believe so-and-so, because
I should be wretched if I did." When an ostrich buries its head in
the sand as danger approaches, it very likely takes the happiest
course. It hides the danger, and then calmly says there is no danger;
and, if it feels perfectly sure there is none, why should it raise its
head to see? A man may go through life, systematically keeping out
of view all that might cause a change in his opinions, and if he
only succeeds—basing his method, as he does, on two fundamental
psychological laws—I do not see what can be said against his doing
so. It would be an egotistical impertinence to object that his procedure is irrational, for that only amounts to saying that his method
of settling belief is not ours. He does not propose to himself to
be rational, and, indeed, will often talk with scorn of man's weak
and illusive reason. So let him think as he pleases.

But this method of fixing belief, which may be called the
method of tenacity, will be unable to hold its ground in practice.
The social impulse is against it. The man who adopts it will find
that other men think differently from him, and it will be apt to
occur to him, in some saner moment, that their opinions are quite
as good as his own, and this will shake his confidence in his belief.
This conception, that another man's thought or sentiment may be

equivalent to one's own, is a distinctly new step, and a highly important one. It arises from an impulse too strong in man to be suppressed, without danger of destroying the human species. Unless we make ourselves hermits, we shall necessarily influence each other's opinions; so that the problem becomes how to fix belief, not in the individual merely, but in the community.

Let the will of the state act, then, instead of that of the individual. Let an institution be created which shall have for its object to keep correct doctrines before the attention of the people, to reiterate them perpetually, and to teach them to the young; having at the same time power to prevent contrary doctrines from being taught, advocated, or expressed. Let all possible causes of a change of mind be removed from men's apprehensions. Let them be kept ignorant, lest they should learn of some reason to think otherwise than they do. Let their passions be enlisted, so that they may regard private and unusual opinions with hatred and horror. Then, let all men who reject the established belief be terrified into silence. Let the people turn out and tar-and-feather such men, or let inquisitions be made into the manner of thinking of suspected persons, and, when they are found guilty of forbidden beliefs, let them be subjected to some signal punishment. When complete agreement could not otherwise be reached, a general massacre of all who have not thought in a certain way has proved a very effective means of settling opinion in a country. If the power to do this be wanting, let a list of opinions be drawn up, to which no man of the least independence of thought can assent, and let the faithful be required to accept all these propositions, in order to segregate them as radically as possible from the influence of the rest of the world.

This method has, from the earliest times, been one of the chief means of upholding correct theological and political doctrines, and of preserving their universal or catholic character. In Rome, especially, it has been practiced from the days of Numa Pompilius[3] to those of Pius Nonus.[4] This is the most perfect example in history; but wherever there is a priesthood—and no religion has been without one—this method has been more or less made use of. Wherever there is an aristocracy, or a guild, or any association of a class of men whose interests depend or are supposed to depend on certain propositions, there will be inevitably found some traces of this natural product of social feeling. Cruelties always accompany this system; and when it is consistently carried out, they become atrocities of the most horrible kind in the eyes of any rational man. Nor should this occasion surprise, for the officer of a society does not

3. The legendary second king of Rome (715-672 B.C.), supposed to be the founder of nearly all the early religious institutions of Rome.

4. Pope, 1846-1878, foe of modernism, proclaimer of the important dogma of the Immaculate Conception, first pope to be regarded infallible.

feel justified in surrendering the interests of that society for the sake of mercy, as he might his own private interests. It is natural, therefore, that sympathy and fellowship should thus produce a most ruthless power.

In judging this method of fixing belief, which may be called the method of authority, we must, in the first place, allow its immeasurable mental and moral superiority to the method of tenacity. Its success is proportionately greater; and, in fact, it has over and over again worked the most majestic results. The mere structures of stone which it has caused to be put together—in Siam, for example, in Egypt, and in Europe—have many of them a sublimity hardly more than rivaled by the greatest works of Nature. And, except the geological epochs, there are no periods of time so vast as those which are measured by some of these organized faiths. If we scrutinize the matter closely, we shall find that there has not been one of their creeds which has remained always the same; yet the change is so slow as to be imperceptible during one person's life, so that individual belief remains sensibly fixed. For the mass of mankind, then, there is perhaps no better method than this. If it is their highest impulse to be intellectual slaves, then slaves they ought to remain.

But no institution can undertake to regulate opinions upon every subject. Only the most important ones can be attended to, and on the rest men's minds must be left to the action of natural causes. This imperfection will be no source of weakness so long as men are in such a state of culture that one opinion does not influence another—that is, so long as they cannot put two and two together. But in the most priestridden states some individuals will be found who are raised above that condition. These men possess a wider sort of social feeling; they see that men in other countries and in other ages have held to very different doctrines from those which they themselves have been brought up to believe; and they cannot help seeing that it is the mere accident of their having been taught as they have, and of their having been surrounded with the manners and associations they have, that has caused them to believe as they do and not far differently. And their candor cannot resist the reflection that there is no reason to rate their own views at a higher value than those of other nations and other centuries; and this gives rise to doubts in their minds.

They will further perceive that such doubts as these must exist in their minds with reference to every belief which seems to be determined by the caprice either of themselves or of those who originated the popular opinions. The willful adherence to a belief, and the arbitrary forcing of it upon others, must, therefore, both be given up, and a new method of settling opinions must be adopted, which shall not only produce an impulse to believe, but shall also decide what proposition it is which is to be believed. Let the action of natural preferences be unimpeded, then, and under their influence let men, conversing together and regarding matters in different lights, gradually develop beliefs in harmony with natural causes. This method resembles that by which conceptions of art have been brought to maturity. The most perfect example of it is to be found in the history of metaphysical philosophy. Systems of this sort have not usually rested upon any observed facts, at least not in any great degree. They have been chiefly adopted because their fundamental propositions seemed "agreeable to reason." This is an apt expression; it does not mean that which agrees with experience, but that which we find ourselves inclined to believe. Plato, for example, finds it agreeable to reason that the distances of the celestial spheres from one another should be proportional to the different lengths of strings which produce harmonious chords. Many philosophers have been led to their main conclusions by considerations like this; but this is the lowest and least developed form which the method takes, for it is clear that another man might find Kepler's theory, that the celestial spheres are proportional to the inscribed and circumscribed spheres of the different regular solids, more agreeable to *his* reason. But the shock of opinions will soon lead men to rest on preferences of a far more universal nature. Take, for example, the doctrine that man only acts selfishly—that is, from the consideration that acting in one way will afford him more pleasure than acting in another. This rests on no fact in the world, but it has had a wide acceptance as being the only reasonable theory.

This method is far more intellectual and respectable from the point of view of reason than either of the others which we have noticed. But its failure has been the most manifest. It makes of inquiry something similar to the development of taste; but taste, unfortunately, is always more or less a matter of fashion, and accordingly metaphysicians have never come to any fixed agreement, but the pendulum has swung backward and forward between a more material and a more spiritual philosophy, from the earliest times to the latest. And so from this, which has been called the *a priori* method, we are driven, in Lord Bacon's phrase, to a true induction. We have examined into this *a priori* method as something which promised to deliver our opinions from their accidental and capricious element. But development, while it is a process which eliminates the effect of some casual circumstances, only magnifies that of others. This method, therefore, does not differ in a very essential way from that of authority. The government may not have lifted its finger to influence my convictions; I may have been left outwardly quite free to choose, we will say, between monogamy and polygamy, and, appealing to my conscience only, I may have concluded that the latter practice is in itself licentious. But when I come to see that the chief obstacle to the spread of

Christianity among a people of as high culture as the Hindus has been a conviction of the immorality of our way of treating women, I cannot help seeing that, though governments do not interfere, sentiments in their development will be very greatly determined by accidental causes. Now, there are some people, among whom I must suppose that my reader is to be found, who, when they see that any belief of theirs is determined by any circumstance extraneous to the facts, will from that moment not merely admit in words that that belief is doubtful, but will experience a real doubt of it, so that it ceases to be a belief.

To satisfy our doubts, therefore, it is necessary that a method should be found by which our beliefs may be caused by nothing human, but by some external permanency—by something upon which our thinking has no effect. Some mystics imagine that they have such a method in a private inspiration from on high. But that is only a form of the method of tenacity, in which the conception of truth as something public is not yet developed. Our external permanency could not be external, in our sense, if it was restricted in its influence to one individual. It must be something which affects, or might affect, every man. And, though these affections are necessarily as various as are individual conditions, yet the method must be such that the ultimate conclusion of every man shall be the same. Such is the method of science. Its fundamental hypothesis, restated in more familiar language, is this: There are real things, whose characters are entirely independent of our opinions about them; those realities affect our senses according to regular laws, and, though our sensations are as different as our relations to the objects, yet, by taking advantage of the laws of perception, we can ascertain by reasoning how things really are, and any man, if he have sufficient experience and reason enough about it, will be led to the one true conclusion. The new conception here involved is that of reality. It may be asked how I know that there are any realities. If this hypothesis is the sole support of my method of inquiry, my method of inquiry must not be used to support my hypothesis. The reply is this: (1) If investigation cannot be regarded as proving that there are real things, it at least does not lead to a contrary conclusion; but the method and the conception on which it is based remain ever in harmony. No doubts of the method, therefore, necessarily arise from its practice, as is the case with all the others. (2) The feeling which gives rise to any method of fixing belief is a dissatisfaction at two repugnant propositions. But here already is a vague concession that there is some *one* thing to which a proposition should conform. Nobody, therefore, can really doubt that there are realities, or, if he did, doubt would not be a source of dissatisfaction. The hypothesis, therefore, is one which every mind admits. So that the social impulse does not cause me to doubt it. (3) Everybody uses the scientific method about a great many things, and only ceases to use it when he does not know how to apply it. (4) Experience of the method has not led me to doubt it, but, on the contrary, scientific investigation has had the most wonderful triumphs in the way of settling opinion. These afford the explanation of my not doubting the method or the hypothesis which it supposes; and not having any doubt, nor believing that anybody else whom I could influence has, it would be the merest babble for me to say more about it. If there be anybody with a living doubt upon the subject, let him consider it.

To describe the method of scientific investigation is the object of this series of papers. At present I have only room to notice some points of contrast between it and other methods of fixing belief.

This is the only one of the four methods which presents any distinction of a right and a wrong way. If I adopt the method of tenacity and shut myself out from all influences, whatever I think necessary to doing this is necessary according to that method. So with the method of authority: the state may try to put down heresy by means which, from a scientific point of view, seem very ill-calculated to accomplish its purposes; but the only test *on that method* is what the state thinks, so that it cannot pursue the method wrongly. So with the *a priori* method. The very essence of it is to think as one is inclined to think. All metaphysicians will be sure to do that, however they may be inclined to judge each other to be perversely wrong. The Hegelian system recognizes every natural tendency of thought as logical, although it be certain to be abolished by counter-tendencies. Hegel thinks there is a regular system in the succession of these tendencies, in consequence of which, after drifting one way and the other for a long time, opinion will at last go right. And it is true that metaphysicians get the right ideas at last; Hegel's system of Nature represents tolerably the science of that day; and one may be sure that whatever scientific investigation has put out of doubt will presently receive *a priori* demonstration on the part of the metaphysicians. But with the scientific method the case is different. I may start with known and observed facts to proceed to the unknown; and yet the rules which I follow in doing do may not be such as investigation would approve. The test of whether I am truly following the method is not an immediate appeal to my feelings and purposes, but, on the contrary, itself involves the application of the method. Hence it is that bad reasoning as well as good reasoning is possible; and this fact is the foundation of the practical side of logic.

It is not to be supposed that the first three methods of settling opinion present no advantage whatever over the scientific method. On the contrary, each has some peculiar convenience of its own. The *a priori* method is distinguished for its comfortable conclusions. It is the nature of the process to adopt whatever belief we are inclined to, and there are certain flatteries to the vanity of man which we all believe by nature, until we are awakened from our pleasing dream by some rough facts. The method of authority will always govern the mass of mankind; and those who wield the various forms of organized force in the state will never be convinced that dangerous reasoning ought not to be suppressed in some way. If liberty of speech is to be untrammeled from the grosser forms of constraint, then uniformity of opinion will be secured by a moral terrorism to which the respectability of society will give its thorough approval. Following the method of authority is the path of peace. Certain non-conformities are permitted; certain others (considered unsafe) are forbidden. These are different in different countries and in different ages; but, wherever you are, let it be known that you seriously hold a tabooed belief, and you may be perfectly sure of being treated with a cruelty less brutal but more refined than hunting you like a wolf. Thus, the greatest intellectual benefactors of mankind have never dared, and dare not now, to utter the whole of their thought; and thus a shade of *prima facie* doubt is cast upon every proposition which is considered essential to the security of society. Singularly enough, the persecution does not all come from without; but a man torments himself and is oftentimes most distressed at finding himself believing propositions which he has been brought up to regard with aversion. The peaceful and sympathetic man will, therefore, find it hard to resist the temptation to submit his opinions to authority. But most of all I admire the method of tenacity for its strength, simplicity, and directness. Men who pursue it are distinguished for their decision of character, which becomes very easy with such a mental rule. They do not waste time in trying to make up their minds what they want, but, fastening like lightning upon whatever alternative comes first, they hold to it to the end, whatever happens, without an instant's irresolution. This is one of the splendid qualities which generally accompany brilliant, unlasting success. It is impossible not to envy the man who can dismiss reason, although we know how it must turn out at last.

Such are the advantages which the other methods of settling opinion have over scientific investigation. A man should consider well of them; and then he should consider that, after all, he wishes his opinions to coincide with the fact, and that there is no reason why the results of these three methods should do so. To bring about this effect is the prerogative of the method of science. Upon such considerations he has to make his choice—a choice which is far more than the adoption of any intellectual opinion, which is one of the ruling decisions of his life, to which, when once made, he is bound to adhere. The force of habit will sometimes cause a man to hold on to old beliefs, after he is in a condition to see that they have no sound basis. But reflection upon the state of the case will overcome these habits, and he ought to allow reflection its full weight. People sometimes shrink from doing this, having an idea that beliefs are wholesome which they cannot help feeling rest on nothing. But let such persons suppose an analogous though different case from their own. Let them ask themselves what they would say to a reformed Mussulman who should hesitate to give up his old notions in regard to the relations of the sexes; or to a reformed Catholic who should still shrink from reading the Bible. Would they not say that these persons ought to consider the matter fully, and clearly understand the new doctrine, and then ought to embrace it, in its entirety? But, above all, let it be considered that what is more wholesome than any particular belief is integrity of belief, and that to avoid looking into the support of any belief from a fear that it may turn out rotten is quite as immoral as it is disadvantageous. The person who confesses that there is such a thing as truth, which is distinguished from falsehood simply by this, that if acted on it will carry us to the point we aim at and not astray, and then, though convinced of this, dares not know the truth and seeks to avoid it, is in a sorry state of mind indeed.

Yes, the other methods do have their merits: a clear logical conscience does cost something—just as any virtue, just as all that we cherish, costs us dear. But we should not desire it to be otherwise. The genius of a man's logical method should be loved and reverenced as his bride, whom he has chosen from all the world. He need not contemn the others; on the contrary, he may honor them deeply, and in doing so he only honors her the more. But she is the one that he has chosen, and he knows that he was right in making that choice. And having made it, he will work and fight for her, and will not complain that there are blows to take, hoping that there may be as many and as hard to give, and will strive to be the worthy knight and champion of her from the blaze of whose splendors he draws his inspiration and his courage.

QUESTIONS

1. Why does Peirce distinguish between doubt and belief on p. 1040?
2. What are the four methods of inquiry? Which of the four most closely describes the development of Peirce's argument?
3. Would Peirce restrict application of the method of science to the natural sciences? Would he consider as scientific Milgram's "Behavioral Study of Obedience" (pp. 293–307)? Arendt's study of "Denmark and the Jews" (pp. 881–886)?
4. In the next-to-last paragraph the last sentence separates the subject noun from its verb by six clauses. Does Peirce gain or lose by this? Explain.

5. *This essay says little about religion directly, yet many of Peirce's remarks implicitly convey a decided attitude toward the subject. What is that attitude, and in which passages is it most clearly conveyed?*

THOMAS S. KUHN
The Route to Normal Science[1]

In this essay, 'normal science' means research firmly based upon one or more past scientific achievements, achievements that some particular scientific community acknowledges for a time as supplying the foundation for its further practice. Today such achievements are recounted, though seldom in their original form, by science textbooks, elementary and advanced. These textbooks expound the body of accepted theory, illustrate many or all of its successful applications, and compare these applications with exemplary observations and experiments. Before such books became popular early in the nineteenth century (and until even more recently in the newly matured sciences), many of the famous classics of science fulfilled a similar function. Aristotle's *Physica*, Ptolemy's *Almagest*, Newton's *Principia* and *Opticks*, Franklin's *Electricity*, Lavoisier's *Chemistry*, and Lyell's *Geology*—these and many other works served for a time implicitly to define the legitimate problems and methods of a research field for succeeding generations of paracitioners. They were able to do so because they shared two essential characteristics. Their achievement was sufficiently unprecedented to attract an enduring group of adherents away from competing modes of scientific activity. Simultaneously, it was sufficiently open-ended to leave all sorts of problems for the redefined group of practitioners to resolve.

Achievements that share these two characteristics I shall henceforth refer to as 'paradigms,' a term that relates closely to 'normal science.' By choosing it, I mean to suggest that some accepted examples of actual scientific practice—examples which include law, theory, application, and instrumentation together—provide models from which spring particular coherent traditions of scientific research. These are the traditions which the historian describes under such rubrics as 'Ptolemaic astronomy' (or 'Copernican'), 'Aristotelian dynamics' (or 'Newtonian'), 'corpuscular optics' (or 'wave optics'), and so on. The study of paradigms, including many that are far more specialized than those named illustratively above, is what mainly prepares the student for membership in the particular scientific community with which he will later practice. Because he

1. From *The Structure of Scientific Revolutions*, 1962. (All notes are Kuhn's.)

there joins men who learned the bases of their field from the same concrete models, his subsequent practice will seldom evoke overt disagreement over fundamentals. Men whose research is based on shared paradigms are committed to the same rules and standards for scientific practice. That commitment and the apparent consensus it produces are prerequisites for normal science, i.e., for the genesis and continuation of a particular research tradition.

Because in this essay the concept of a paradigm will often substitute for a variety of familiar notions, more will need to be said about the reasons for its introduction. Why is the concrete scientific achievement, as a locus of professional commitment, prior to the various concepts, laws, theories, and points of view that may be abstracted from it? In what sense is the shared paradigm a fundamental unit for the student of scientific development, a unit that cannot be fully reduced to logically atomic components which might function in its stead? There can be a sort of scientific research without paradigms, or at least without any so unequivocal and so binding as the ones named above. Acquisition of a paradigm and of the more esoteric type of research it permits is a sign of maturity in the development of any given scientific field.

If the historian traces the scientific knowledge of any selected group of related phenomena backward in time, he is likely to encounter some minor variant of a pattern here illustrated from the history of physical optics. Today's physics textbooks tell the student that light is photons, i.e., quantum-mechanical entities that exhibit some characteristics of waves and some of particles. Research proceeds accordingly, or rather according to the more elaborate and mathematical characterization from which this usual verbalization is derived. That characterization of light is, however, scarcely half a century old. Before it was developed by Planck, Einstein, and others early in this century, physics texts taught that light was transverse wave motion, a conception rooted in a paradigm that derived ultimately from the optical writings of Young and Fresnel in the early nineteenth century. Nor was the wave theory the first to be embraced by almost all practitioners of optical science. During the eighteenth century the paradigm for this field was provided by Newton's *Opticks*, which taught that light was material corpuscles. At that time physicists sought evidence, as the early wave theorists had not, of the pressure exerted by light particles impinging on solid bodies.[2]

These transformations of the paradigms of physical optics are scientific revolutions, and the successive transition from one paradigm to another via revolution is the usual developmental pattern of mature science. It is not, however, the pattern characteristic of the

2. Joseph Priestley, *The History and Present State of Discoveries Relating to Vision, Light, and Colours* (London, 1772), pp. 385-90.

period before Newton's work, and that is the contrast that concerns us here. No period between remote antiquity and the end of the seventeenth century exhibited a single generally accepted veiw about the nature of light. Instead there were a number of competing schools and sub-schools, most of them espousing one variant or another of Epicurean, Aristotelian, or Platonic theory. One group took light to be particles emanating from material bodies; for another it was a modification of the medium that intervened between the body and the eye; still another explained light in terms of an interaction of the medium with an emanation from the eye; and there were other combinations and modifications besides. Each of the corresponding schools derive strength from its relation to some particular metaphysic, and each emphasized, as paradigmatic observations, the particular cluster of optical phenomena that its own theory could do most to explain. Other observations were dealt with by *ad hoc* elaborations, or they remained as outstanding problems for further research.[3]

At various times all these schools made significant contributions to the body of concepts, phenomena, and techniques from which Newton drew the first nearly uniformly accepted paradigm for physical optics. Any definition of the scientist that excludes at least the more creative members of these various schools will exclude their modern successors as well. Those men were scientists. Yet anyone examining a survey of physical optics before Newton may well conclude that, though the field's practitioners were scientists, the net result of their activity was something less than science. Being able to take no common body of belief for granted, each writer on physical optics felt forced to build his field anew from its foundations. In doing so, his choice of supporting observation and experiment was relatively free, for there was no standard set of methods or of phenomena that every optical writer felt forced to employ and explain. Under these circumstances, the dialogue of the resulting books was often directed as much to the members of other schools as it was to nature. That pattern is not unfamiliar in a number of creative fields today, nor is it incompatible with significant discovery and invention. It is not, however, the pattern of development that physical optics acquired after Newton and that other natural sciences make familiar today.

The history of electrical research in the first half of the eighteenth century provides a more concrete and better known example of the way a science develops before it acquires its first universally received paradigm. During that period there were almost as many views about the nature of electricity as there were important electrican experimenters, men like Haukshee, Gray, Desaguliers, Du Fay,

---

3. Vasco Ronchi, *Histoire de la lumière*, trans. Jean Taton (Paris, 1956), chaps. i-iv.

Nollett, Watson, Franklin, and others. All their numerous concepts of electricity had something in common—they were partially derived from one or another version of the mechanico-corpuscular philosophy that guided all scientific research of the day. In addition, all were components of real scientific theories, of theories that had been drawn in part from experiment and observation and that partially determined the choice and interpretation of additional problems undertaken in research. Yet though all the experiments were electrical and though most of the experimenters read each other's works, their theories had no more than a family resemblance.[4]

One early group of theories, following seventeenth-century practice, regarded attraction and frictional generation as the fundamental electrical phenomena. This group tended to treat repulsion as a secondary effect due to some sort of mechanical rebounding and also to postpone for as long as possible both discussion and systematic research on Gray's newly discovered effect, electrical conduction. Other "electricians" (the term is their own) took attraction and repulsion to be equally elementary manifestations of electricity and modified their theories and research accordingly. (Actually, this group is remarkably small—even Franklin's theory never quite accounted for the mutual repulsion of two negatively charged bodies.) But they had as much difficulty as the first group in accounting simultaneously for any but the simplest conduction effects. Those effects, however, provided the starting point for still a third group, one which tended to speak of electricity as a "fluid" that could run through conductors rather than as an "effluvium" that emanated from non-conductors. This group, in its turn, had difficulty reconciling its theory with a number of attractive and repulsive effects. Only through the work of Franklin and his immediate successors did a theory arise that could account with something like equal facility for very nearly all these effects and that therefore could and did provide a subsequent generation of "electricians" with a common paradigm for its research.

Excluding those fields, like mathematics and astronomy, in which the first firm paradigms date from prehistory and also those, like biochemistry, that arose by division and recombination of specialties already matured, the situations outlined above are historically typical. Though it involves my continuing to employ the unfortunate simplification that tags an extended historical episode with a single and somewhat arbitrarily chosen name (e.g., Newton or Franklin),

---

4. Duane Roller and Duane H. D. Roller, *The Development of the Concept of Electric Charge*: *Electricity from the Greeks to Coulomb* ("Harvard Case Histories in Experimental Science," Case 8; Cambridge, Mass., 1954); and I. B. Cohen, *Franklin and Newton*: *An Inquiry into Speculative Newtonian Experimental Science and Franklin's Work in Electricity as an Example Thereof* (Philadelphia, 1956), chaps. vii–xii.

I suggest that similar fundamental disagreements characterized, for example, the study of motion before Aristotle and of statics before Archimedes, the study of heat before Black, of chemistry before Boyle and Boerhaave, and of historical geology before Hutton. In parts of biology—the study of heredity, for example—the first universally received paradigms are still more recent; and it remains an open question what parts of social science have yet acquired such paradigms at all. History suggests that the road to a firm research consensus is extraordinarily arduous.

History also suggests, however, some reasons for the difficulties encountered on the road. In the absence of a paradigm or some candidate for paradigm, all of the facts that could possibly pertain to the development of a given science are likely to seem equally relevant. As a result, early fact-gathering is a far more nearly random activity than the one that subsequent scientific development makes familiar. Futhermore, in the absence of a reason for seeking some particular form of more recondite information, early fact-gathering is usually restricted to the wealth of data that lie ready to hand. The resulting pool of facts contains those accessible to casual observation and experiment together with some of the more esoteric data retrievable from established crafts medicine, calendar making, and metallurgy. Because the crafts are one readily accessible source of facts that could not have been casually discovered, technology has often played a vital role in the emergence of new sciences.

But though this sort of fact-collecting has been essential to the origin of many significant sciences, anyone who examines, for example, Pliny's encyclopedic writings or the Baconian natural histories of the seventeenth century will discover that it produces a morass. One somehow hesitates to call the literature that results scientific. The Baconian "histories" of heat, color, wind, mining, and so on, are filled with information, some of it recondite. But they juxtapose facts that will later prove revealing (e.g., heating by mixture) with others (e.g., the warmth of dung heaps) that will for some time remain too complex to be integrated with theory at all.[5] In addition, since any description must be partial, the typical natural history often omits from its immensely circumstantial accounts just those details that later scientists will find sources of important illumination. Almost none of the early "histories" of electricity, for example, mention that chaff, attracted to a rubbed glass rod, bounces off again. That effect seemed mechanical, not electrical.[6] Moreover, since the casual fact-gatherer seldom possesses the time or the

5. Compare the sketch for a natural history of heat in Bacon's *Novum Organum*, Vol. VIII of *The Works of Francis Bacon*, ed. J. Spedding, R. L. Ellis, and D. D. Heath (New York, 1869), pp. 179–203.

6. Roller and Roller, *op. cit.*, pp. 14, 22, 28, 43. Only after the work recorded in the last of these citations do repulsive effects gain general recognition as unequivocally electrical.

tools to be critical, the natural histories often juxtapose descriptions like the above with others, say, heating by antiperistasis (or by cooling), that we are now quite unable to confirm.[7] Only very occasionally, as in the cases of ancient statics, dynamics, and geometrical optics, do facts collected with so little guidance from pre-established theory speak with sufficient clarity to permit the emergence of a first paradigm.

This is the situation that creates the schools characteristic of the early stages of a science's development. No natural history can be interpreted in the absence of at least some implicit body of intertwined theoretical and methodological belief that permits selection, evaluation, and criticism. If that body of belief is not already implicit in the collection of facts—in which case more than "mere facts" are at hand—it must be externally supplied, perhaps by a current metaphysic, by another science, or by personal and historical accident. No wonder, then, that in the early stages of the development of any science different men confronting the same range of phenomena, but not usually all the same particular phenomena, describe and interpret them in different ways. What is surprising, and perhaps also unique in its degree to the fields we call science, is that such initial divergences should ever largely disappear.

For they do disappear to a very considerable extent and then apparently once and for all. Furthermore, their disappearance is usually caused by the triumph of one of the pre-paradigm schools, which, because of its own characteristic beliefs and pre-conceptions, emphasized only some special part of the too sizable and inchoate pool of information. Those electricians who thought electricity a fluid and therefore gave particular emphasis to conduction provide an excellent case in point. Led by this belief, which could scarcely cope with the known multiplicity of attractive and repulsive effects, several of them conceived the idea of bottling the electrical fluid. The immediate fruit of their efforts was the Leyden jar, a device which might never have been discovered by a man exploring nature casually or at random, but which was in fact independently developed by at least two investigators in the early 1740's.[8] Almost from the start of his electrical researches, Franklin was particularly concerned to explain that strange and, in the event, particularly revealing piece of special apparatus. His success in doing so provided the most effective of the arguments that made his theory a paradigm, though one that was still unable to account for quite all the known cases of electrical repulsion.[9] To be accepted as a paradigm, a theory

7. Bacon, *op. cit.*, pp. 235, 337, says, "Water slightly warm is more easily frozen than quite cold." For a partial account of the earlier history of this strange observation, see Marshall Clagett, *Giovanni Marliani and Late Medieval Physics* (New York, 1941), chap. iv.

8. Roller and Roller, *op. cit.*, pp. 51–54.

9. The troublesome case was the mutual repulsion of negatively charged bodies, for which see Cohen, *op. cit.*, pp. 491–94, 531–43.

must seem better than its competitors, but it need not, and in fact never does, explain all the facts with which it can be confronted.

What the fluid theory of electricity did for the subgroup that held it, the Franklinian paradigm later did for the entire group of electricians. It suggested which experiments would be worth performing and which, because directed to secondary or to overly complex manifestations of electricity, would not. Only the paradigm did the job far more effectively, partly because the end of interschool debate ended the constant reiteration of fundamentals and partly because the confidence that they were on the right track encouraged scientists to undertake more precise, esoteric, and consuming sorts of work.[1] Freed from the concern with any and all electrical phenomena, the united group of electricians could pursue selected phenomena in far more detail, designing much special equipment for the task and employing it more stubbornly and systematically than electricians had ever done before. Both fact collection and theory articulation became highly directed activities. The effectiveness and efficiency of electrical research increased accordingly, providing evidence for a societal version of Francis Bacon's acute methodological dictum: "Truth emerges more readily from error than from confusion."[2]

We shall be examining the nature of this highly directed or paradigm-based research in the next section, but must first note briefly how the emergence of a paradigm affects the structure of the group that practices the field. When, in the development of a natural science, an individual or group first produces a synthesis able to attract most of the next generation's practitioners, the older schools gradually disappear. In part their disappearance is caused by their members' conversion to the new paradigm. But there are always some men who cling to one or another of the older views, and they are simply read out of the profession, which thereafter ignores their work. The new paradigm implies a new and more rigid definition of the field. Those unwilling or unable to accommodate their work to it must proceed in isolation or attach themselves to some other

1. It should be noted that the acceptance of Franklin's theory did not end quite all debate. In 1759 Robert Symmer proposed a two-fluid version of that theory, and for many years thereafter electricians were divided about whether electricity was a single fluid or two. But the debates on this subject only confirm what has been said above about the manner in which a universally recognized achievement unites the profession. Electricians, though they continued divided on this point, rapidly concluded that no experimental tests could distinguish the two versions of the theory and that they were therefore equivalent. After that, both schools could and did exploit all the benefits that the Franklinian theory provided (*ibid.*, pp. 543–46, 548–54).

2. Bacon, *op. cit.*, p. 210.

group.[3] Historically, they have often simply stayed in the departments of philosophy from which so many of the special sciences have been spawned. As these indications hint, it is sometimes just its reception of a paradigm that transforms a group previously interested merely in the study of nature into a profession or, at least, a discipline. In the sciences (though not in fields like medicine, technology, and law, of which the principal *raison d'être* is an external social need), the formation of specialized journals, the foundation of specialists' societies, and the claim for a special place in the curriculum have usually been associated with a group's first reception of a single paradigm. At least this was the case between the time, a century and a half ago, when the institutional pattern of scientific specialization first developed and the very recent time when the paraphernalia of specialization acquired a prestige of their own.

The more rigid definition of the scientific group has other consequences. When the individual scientist can take a paradigm for granted, he need no longer, in his major works, attempt to build his field anew, starting from first principles and justifying the use of each concept introduced. That can be left to the writer of textbooks. Given a textbook, however, the creative scientist can begin his research where it leaves off and thus concentrate exclusively upon the subtlest and most esoteric aspects of the natural phenomena that concern his group. And as he does this, his research communiqués will begin to change in ways whose evolution has been too little studied but whose modern end products are obvious to all and oppressive to many. No longer will his researches usually be embodied in books addressed, like Franklin's *Experiments . . . on Electricity* or Darwin's *Origin of Species*, to anyone who might be interested in the subject matter of the field. Instead they will usually appear as brief articles addressed only to professional colleagues, the men whose knowledge of a shared paradigm can be assumed and who prove to be the only ones able to read the papers addressed to them.

3. The history of electricity provides an excellent example which could be duplicated from the careers of Priestley, Kelvin, and others. Franklin reports that Nollet, who at mid-century was the most influential of the Continental electricians, "lived to see himself the last of his Sect, except Mr. B.—his Eleve and immediate Disciple" (Max Farrand [ed.], *Benjamin Franklin's Memoirs* [Berkeley, Calif., 1949], pp. 384–86). More interesting, however, is the endurance of whole schools in increasing isolation from professional science. Consider, for example, the case of astrology, which was once an integral part of astronomy. Or consider the continuation in the late eighteenth and early nineteenth centuries of a previously respected tradition of "romantic" chemistry. This is the tradition discussed by Charles C. Gillispie in "The *Encyclopédie* and the Jacobin Philosophy of Science: A Study in Ideas and Consequences," *Critical Problems in the History of Science,* ed. Marshall Clagett (Madison, Wis., 1959), pp. 255–89; and "The Formation of Lamarck's Evolutionary Theory," *Archives internationales d'histoire des sciences,* XXXVII (1956), 323–38.

Today in the sciences, books are usually either texts or retrospective reflections upon one aspect or another of the scientific life. The
scientist who writes one is more likely to find his professional reputation impaired than enhanced. Only in the earlier, pre-paradigm,
stages of the development of the various sciences did the book ordinarily possess the same relation to professional achievement that it
still retains in other creative fields. And only in those fields that still
retain the book, with or without the article, as a vehicle for research
communication are the lines of professionalization still so loosely
drawn that the layman may hope to follow progress by reading the
practitioners' original reports. Both in mathematics and astronomy,
research reports had ceased already in antiquity to be intelligible to
a generally educated audience. In dynamics, research became similarly esoteric in the latter Middle Ages, and it recaptured general
intelligibility only briefly during the early seventeenth century when
a new paradigm replaced the one that had guided medieval
research. Electrical research began to require translation for the
layman before the end of the eighteenth century, and most other
fields of physical science ceased to be generally accessible in the
nineteenth. During the same two centuries similar transitions can
be isolated in the various parts of the biological sciences. In parts of
the social sciences they may well be occurring today. Although it
has become customary, and is surely proper, to deplore the widening
gulf that separates the professional scientist from his colleagues in
other fields, too little attention is paid to the essential relationship
between that gulf and the mechanisms intrinsic to scientific advance.

Ever since prehistoric antiquity one field of study after another
has crossed the divide between what the historian might call its
prehistory as a science and its history proper. These transitions to
maturity have seldom been so sudden or so unequivocal as my necessarily schematic discussion may have implied. But neither have they
been historically gradual, coextensive, that is to say, with the entire
development of the fields within which they occurred. Writers on
electricity during the first four decades of the eighteenth century
possessed far more information about electrical phenomena than had
their sixteenth-century predecessors. During the half-century after
1740, few new sorts of electrical phenomena were added to their lists.
Nevertheless, in important respects, the electrical writings of Caven-
dish, Coulomb, and Volta in the last third of the eighteenth century
seem further removed from those of Gray, Du Fay, and even Franklin than are the writings of these early eighteenth-century electrical
discoverers from those of the sixteenth century.[4] Sometime between

4. The post-Franklinian developments
include an immense increase in the sensitivity of charge detectors, the first reliable and generally diffused techniques
for measuring charge, the evolution of
the concept of capacity and its relation
to a newly refined notion of electric tension, and the quantification of electro-

1740 and 1780, electricians were for the first time enabled to take the foundations of their field for granted. From that point they pushed on to more concrete and recondite problems, and increasingly they then reported their results in articles addressed to other electricians rather than in books addressed to the learned world at large. As a group they achieved what had been gained by astronomers in antiquity and by students of motion in the Middle Ages, of physical optics in the late seventeenth century, and of historical geology in the early nineteenth. They had, that is, achieved a paradigm that proved able to guide the whole group's research. Except with the advantage of hindsight, it is hard to find another criterion that so clearly proclaims a field a science.

static force. On all of these see Roller and Roller, *op. cit.*, pp. 66–81; W. C. Walker, "The Detection and Estimation of Electric Charges in the Eighteenth Century," *Annals of Science*, I (1936), 66–100; and Edmund Hoppe, *Geschichte der Elektrizität* (Leipzig, 1884), Part I, chaps. iii–iv.

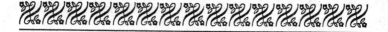

Prose Forms: Parables

[When we read a short story or a novel, we are less interested in
the working out of ideas than in the working out of characters and
their destinies. In Dickens' Great Expectations, for example, Pip the
hero undergoes many triumphs and defeats in his pursuit of success,
only to learn finally that he has expected the wrong things, or the
right things for the wrong reasons; that the great values in life are
not always to be found in what the world calls success. In realizing
this meaning we entertain, with Dickens, certain concepts or ideas
that organize and evaluate the life in the novel, and that ultimately
we apply to life generally. Ideas are there not to be exploited discursively, but to be understood as the perspective which shapes the
direction of the novel and our view of its relation to life.

When ideas in their own reality are no longer the primary interest
in writing, we have obviously moved from expository to other forms
of prose. The shift need not be abrupt and complete, however; there
is an area where the discursive interest in ideas and the narrative
interest in characters and events blend. In allegory, for example, abstract ideas are personified. "Good Will" or "Peace" may be shown
as a young woman, strong, confident, and benevolent in her bearing
but vulnerable, through her sweet reasonableness, to the single-
minded, fierce woman who is "Dissension." Our immediate interest
is in their behavior as characters, but our ultimate interest is in the
working out, through them, of the ideas they represent. We do not
ask that the characters and events be entirely plausible in relation
to actual life, as we do for the novel; we are satisfied if they are consistent with the nature of the ideas that define their vitality.

Ideas themselves have vitality, a mobile and dynamic life with
a behavior of its own. The title of the familiar Negro spiritual "Sometimes I Feel Like a Motherless Child," to choose a random instance,
has several kinds of "motion" as an idea. The qualitative identity of
an adult's feelings and those of a child; the whole burgeoning possibility of all that the phrase "motherless child" can mean; the subtle
differences in meaning—the power of context—that occur when it is
a Negro who feels this and when it is a white; the speculative possibilities of the title as social commentary or psychological analysis;
the peculiar force of the ungrammatical "like"—these suggest something of the "life" going on in and around the idea. Definition,

analogy, assumption, implication, context, illustration are some of
the familiar terms we use to describe this kind of life.

There is, of course, another and more obvious kind of vitality
which an idea has: its applicability to the affairs of men in everyday
life. Both the kind and extent of an idea's relevance are measures of
this vitality. When an essayist wishes to exploit both the life in an
idea and the life it comprehends, he often turns to narration, because
there he sees the advantage of lifelike characters and events, and of
showing through them the liveliness of ideas in both the senses we
have noted. Ideas about life can be illustrated in life. And, besides,
people like stories. The writer's care must be to keep the reader's
interest focused on the ideas, rather than on the life itself; otherwise,
he has ceased being essentially the essayist and has become the short-
story writer or novelist.

The parable and the moral fable are ideal forms for his purpose.
In both, the idea is the heart of the composition; in both the ideas
usually assume the form of a lesson about life, some moral truth of
general consequence to men; and in both there are characters and
actions. Jesus often depended on parables in his teaching. Simple,
economical, pointed, the parables developed a "story," but more
importantly, applied a moral truth to experience. Peter asked Jesus
how often he must forgive the brother who sins against him, and
Jesus answered with the parable of the king and his servants, one of
whom asked and got forgiveness of the king for his debts but who
would not in turn forgive a fellow servant his debt. The king, on
hearing of this harshness, retracted his own benevolence and punished the unfeeling servant. Jesus concluded to Peter, "So likewise
shall my heavenly Father do also unto you, if ye from your hearts
forgive not every one his brother their trespasses." But before this
direct drawing of the parallel, the lesson was clear in the outline of
the narrative.

Parables usually have human characters; fables often achieve a
special liveliness with animals. In March's "The Fisherman and the
Hen," the old hen is clearly just a chicken, clucking, picking at
worms, scratching the ground. But when the fisherman has struck her
to steal her worm for bait, and the old hen, responding to his compassion for having wronged her, gets another worm in order to be
struck and so to be fondled afterwards, the old hen is almost magically transformed into a peculiar psychological truth about human behavior. The story creates its own interest as a story, but by its end
the reader realizes that the story exists for the sake of an idea—and
that its relevance is a lesson about himself.

The writer will be verging continually on strict prose narrative
when he writes the parable or fable, but if he is skillful and tactful,
he will preserve the essayist's essential commitment to the definition
and development of ideas in relation to experience.]

ANONYMOUS: The Whale[1]

The whale is the largest of all the fishes in the sea. If you saw
one floating on the surface, you would think it was an island rising
from the sea sands. When he is hungry, this huge fish opens his
mouth and sends forth a breath—the sweetest thing on earth—
from his gaping jaws. Other fish, enticed by this sweetness, draw
near and hover in his mouth, happy in their ignorance of his deception. The whale then snaps shut his jaws, sucking in all these fish.
He thus traps the little fish; the great he cannot ensnare.

This fish lives near the bottom of the sea until the time when
equinoctial storms stir up all the waters, as winter struggles to sup-
plant summer, and the sea bottom becomes so turbulent that he
cannot stay there. Then he leaves his home and rises to the surface,
where he lies motionless. In the midst of the storm, ships are tossed
about on the sea. The sailors fearing death and hoping to live, look
about them and see this fish. They think he is an island, and,
overjoyed, they head their ships for him and drop anchor. They
step ashore and, striking sparks from stone and steel into their tinder,
they make a fire on this marvel, warm themselves, and eat and drink.
The fish soon feels the fire and dives to the bottom, drawing the
sailors down with him. He kills them all without leaving a wound.

Application: The devil is determined and powerful, with the
craftiness of witches. He makes men hunger and thirst after sinful
pleasures and draws them to him with the sweetness of his breath.
But whoever follows him finds only shame. His followers are the
men of little faith; men of great faith he cannot ensnare, for they
are steadfast, body and soul, in true belief. Whoever listens to the
devil's teachings will at last regret it bitterly; whoever anchors his
hope on the devil will be drawn down by him to the gloomy depths
of hell.

1. From *A Bestiary*, an anonymous thirteenth-century English work, translated
by Alan B. and Lidie M. Howes.

PLATO: The Allegory of the Cave[1]

And now, I said, let me show in a figure how far our nature is
enlightened or unenlightened: Behold! human beings living in
an underground den, which has a mouth open towards the light
and reaching all along the den; here they have been from their childhood, and have their legs and necks chained so that they cannot
move, and can only see before them, being prevented by the chains
from turning round their heads. Above and behind them a fire
is blazing at a distance, and between the fire and the prisoners

1. From Book VII of *The Republic*.

there is a raised way; and you will see, if you look, a low wall built along the way, like the screen which marionette players have in front of them, over which they show the puppets.

I see.

And do you see, I said, men passing along the wall carrying all sorts of vessels, and statues and figures of animals made of wood and stone and various materials, which appear over the wall? Some of them are talking, others silent.

You have shown me a strange image, and they are strange prisoners.

Like ourselves, I replied; and they see only their own shadows, or the shadows of one another, which the fire throws on the opposite wall of the cave?

True, he said; how could they see anything but the shadows if they were never allowed to move their heads?

And of the objects which are being carried in like manner they would only see the shadows?

Yes, he said.

And if they were able to converse with one another, would they not suppose that they were naming what was actually before them?

Very true.

And suppose further that the prison had an echo which came from the other side, would they not be sure to fancy when one of the passers-by spoke that the voice which they heard came from the passing shadow?

No question, he replied.

To them, I said, the truth would be literally nothing but. the shadows of the images.

That is certain.

And now look again, and see what will naturally follow if the prisoners are released and disabused of their error. At first, when any of them is liberated and compelled suddenly to stand up and turn his neck round and walk and look towards the light, he will suffer sharp pains; the glare will distress him and he will be unable to see the realities of which in his former state he had seen the shadows; and then conceive some one saying to him, that what he saw before was an illusion, but that now, when he is approaching nearer to being and his eye is turned towards more real existence, he has a clearer vision—what will be his reply? And you may further imagine that his instructor is pointing to the objects as they pass and requiring him to name them—will he not be perplexed? Will he not fancy that the shadows which he formerly saw are truer than the objects which are now shown to him?

Far truer.

And if he is compelled to look straight at the light, will he not have a pain in his eyes which will make him turn away to take refuge

in the objects of vision which he can see, and which he will conceive
to be in reality clearer than the things which are now being shown
to him?

True, he said.

And suppose once more, that he is reluctantly dragged up a steep
and rugged ascent, and held fast until he is forced into the presence
of the sun himself, is he not likely to be pained and irritated?
When he approaches the light his eyes will be dazzled and he will
not be able to see anything at all of what are now called realities.

Not all in a moment, he said.

He will require to grow accustomed to the sight of the upper
world. And first he will see the shadows best, next the reflections
of men and other objects in the water, and then the objects themselves; then he will gaze upon the light of the moon and the stars
and the spangled heaven; and he will see the sky and the stars by
night better than the sun or the light of the sun by day?

Certainly.

Last of all he will be able to see the sun, and not mere reflections
of him in the water, but he will see him in his own proper place,
and not in another; and he will contemplate him as he is.

Certainly.

He will then proceed to argue that this is he who gives the season
and the years, and is the guardian of all that is in the visible world,
and in a certain way the cause of all things which he and his fellows
have been accustomed to behold?

Clearly, he said, he would first see the sun and then reason about
him.

And when he remembered his old habitation, and the wisdom of
the den and his fellow-prisoners, do you not suppose that he would
felicitate himself on the change, and pity them?

Certainly, he would.

And if they were in the habit of conferring honors among themselves on those who were quickest to observe the passing shadows
and to remark which of them went before, and which followed after,
and which were together; and who were therefore best able to draw
conclusions as to the future, do you think that he would care for
such honors and glories, or envy the possessors of them? Would he
not say with Homer,

> Better to be the poor servant of a poor master,

and to endure anything, rather than think as they do and live after
their manner?

Yes, he said, I think that he would rather suffer anything than
entertain these false notions and live in this miserable manner.

Imagine once more, I said, such an one coming suddenly out of the sun to be replaced in his old situation; would he not be certain to have his eyes full of darkness?

To be sure, he said.

And if there were a contest, and he had to compete in measuring the shadows with the prisoners who had never moved out of the den, while his sight was still weak, and before his eyes had become steady (and the time which would be needed to acquire this new habit of sight might be very considerable) would he not be ridiculous? Men would say of him that up he went and down he came without his eyes; and that it was better not even to think of ascending; and if any one tried to loose another and lead him up to the light, let them only catch the offender, and they would put him to death.

No question, he said.

This entire allegory, I said, you may now append, dear Glaucon, to the previous argument; the prison-house is the world of sight, the light of the fire is the sun, and you will not misapprehend me if you interpret the journey upwards to be the ascent of the soul into the intellectual world according to my poor belief, which, at your desire, I have expressed—whether rightly or wrongly God knows. But, whether true or false, my opinion is that in the world of knowledge the idea of good appears last of all, and is seen only with an effort; and, when seen, is also inferred to be the universal author of all things beautiful and right, parent of light and of the lord of light in this visible world, and the immediate source of reason and truth in the intellectual; and that this is the power upon which he who would act rationally either in public or private life must have his eye fixed.

I agree, he said, as far as I am able to understand you.

Moreover, I said, you must not wonder that those who attain to this beatific vision are unwilling to descend to human affairs; for their souls are ever hastening into the upper world where they desire to dwell; which desire of theirs is very natural, if our allegory may be trusted.

Yes, very natural.

And is there anything surprising in one who passes from divine contemplations to the evil state of man, misbehaving himself in a ridiculous manner; if, while his eyes are blinking and before he has become accustomed to the surrounding darkness, he is compelled to fight in courts of law, or in other places, about the images or the shadows of images of justice, and is endeavouring to meet the conceptions of those who have never yet seen absolute justice?

Anything but surprising, he replied.

Any one who has common sense will remember that the bewilderments of the eyes are of two kinds, and arise from two causes, either from coming out of the light or from going into the light, which is true of the mind's eye, quite as much as of the bodily eye; and he who remembers this when he sees any one whose vision is perplexed and weak, will not be too ready to laugh; he will first ask whether that soul of man has come out of the brighter life, and is unable to see because unaccustomed to the dark, or having turned from darkness to the day is dazzled by excess of light. And he will count the one happy in his condition and state of being, and he will pity the other; or, if he have a mind to laugh at the soul which comes from below into the light, there will be more reason in this than in the laugh which greets him who returns from above out of the light into the den.

That, he said, is a very just distinction.

JONATHAN SWIFT: The Spider and the Bee[1]

Things were at this crisis, when a material accident fell out. For, upon the highest corner of a large window, there dwelt a certain spider, swollen up to the first magnitude by the destruction of infinite numbers of flies, whose spoils lay scattered before the gates of his palace, like human bones before the cave of some giant. The avenues of his castle were guarded with turnpikes and palisadoes, all after the modern way of fortification. After you had passed several courts, you came to the center, wherein you might behold the constable himself in his own lodgings, which had windows fronting to each avenue, and ports to sally out upon all occasions of prey or defense. In this mansion he had for some time dwelt in peace and plenty, without danger to his person by swallows from above, or to his palace by brooms from below, when it was the pleasure of fortune to conduct thither a wandering bee, to whose curiosity a broken pane in the glass had discovered itself, and in he went; where expatiating a while, he at last happened to alight upon one of the outward walls of the spider's citadel; which, yielding to the unequal weight, sunk down to the very foundation. Thrice he endeavored to force his passage, and thrice the center shook. The spider within, feeling the terrible convulsion, supposed at first that nature was approaching to her final dissolution; or else that Beelzebub,[2] with all his legions, was come to revenge the death of many thousands of his subjects, whom his enemy had slain and devoured. However, he at length valiantly resolved to issue forth, and meet his fate. Meanwhile the bee had acquitted himself of his toils, and posted securely at some distance, was employed in cleansing his

---

1. From *The Battle of the Books.*   2. The Hebrew god of flies. Pate MS.

wings, and disengaging them from the ragged remnants of the cobweb. By this time the spider was adventured out, when beholding the chasms, and ruins, and dilapidations of his fortress, he was very near at his wit's end; he stormed and swore like a madman, and swelled till he was ready to burst. At length, casting his eye upon the bee, and wisely gathering causes from events (for they knew each other by sight), "A plague split you," said he, "for a giddy son of a whore. Is it you, with a vengeance, that have made this litter here? Could you not look before you, and be d——nd? Do you think I have nothing else to do (in the devil's name) but to mend and repair after your arse?" "Good words, friend," said the bee (having now pruned himself, and being disposed to droll) "I'll give you my hand and word to come near your kennel no more; I was never in such a confounded pickle since I was born." "Sirrah," replied the spider, "if it were not for breaking an old custom in our family, never to stir abroad against an enemy, I should come and teach you better manners." "I pray have patience," said the bee, "or you will spend your substance, and for aught I see, you may stand in need of it all, towards the repair of your house." "Rogue, rogue," replied the spider, "yet methinks you should have more respect to a person, whom all the world allows to be so much your betters." "By my troth," said the bee, "the comparison will amount to a very good jest, and you will do me a favor to let me know the reasons that all the world is pleased to use in so hopeful a dispute." At this the spider, having swelled himself into the size and posture of a disputant, began his argument in the true spirit of controversy, with a resolution to be heartily scurrilous and angry, to urge on his own reasons, without the least regard to the answers or objections of his opposite, and fully predetermined in his mind against all conviction.

"Not to disparage myself," said he, "by the comparison with such a rascal, what art thou but a vagabond without house or home, without stock or inheritance, born to no possession of your own, but a pair of wings and a drone-pipe? Your livelihood is an universal plunder upon nature; a freebooter over fields and gardens; and for the sake of stealing will rob a nettle as easily as a violet. Whereas I am a domestic animal, furnished with a native stock within myself. This large castle (to show my improvements in the mathematics) is all built with my own hands, and the materials extracted altogether out of my own person."

"I am glad," answered the bee, "to hear you grant at least that I am come honestly by my wings and my voice; for then, it seems, I am obliged to Heaven alone for my flights and my music; and Providence would never have bestowed on me two such gifts, without designing them for the noblest ends. I visit indeed all the flowers and blossoms of the field and the garden; but whatever I collect from thence enriches myself, without the least injury to their beauty, their smell, or their taste. Now, for you and your skill in architecture and other mathematics, I have little to say: in that building of yours there might, for aught I know, have been labor and method enough, but by woful experience for us both, 'tis too plain, the materials are naught, and I hope you will henceforth take warning, and consider duration and matter as well as method and art. You boast, indeed, of being obliged to no other creature, but of drawing and spinning out all from yourself; that is to say, if we may judge of the liquor in the vessel by what issues out, you possess a good plentiful store of dirt and poison in your breast; and, tho' I would by no means lessen or disparage your genuine stock of either, yet I doubt you are somewhat obliged for an increase of both, to a little foreign assistance. Your inherent portion of dirt does not fail of acquisitions, by sweepings exhaled from below; and one insect furnishes you with a share of poison to destroy another. So that in short, the question comes all to this—which is the nobler being of the two, that which by a lazy contemplation of four inches round, by an overweening pride, feeding and engendering on itself, turns all into excrement and venom, produces nothing at last, but flybane and a cobweb; or that which, by an universal range, with long search, much study, true judgment, and distinction of things, brings home honey and wax."

JAMES THURBER: The Glass in the Field

A short time ago some builders, working on a studio in Connecticut, left a huge square of plate glass standing upright in a field one day. A goldfinch flying swiftly across the field struck the glass and was knocked cold. When he came to he hastened to his club, where an attendant bandaged his head and gave him a stiff drink. "What the hell happened?" asked a sea gull. "I was flying across a meadow when all of a sudden the air crystallized on me," said the goldfinch. The sea gull and a hawk and an eagle all laughed heartily. A swallow listened gravely. "For fifteen years, fledgling and bird, I've flown this country," said the eagle, "and I assure you there is no such thing as air crystallizing. Water, yes; air, no." "You were probably struck by a hailstone," the hawk told the goldfinch. "Or he may have had a stroke," said the sea gull. "What do you think, swallow?" "Why, I—I think maybe the air crystallized on him," said the swallow. The large birds laughed so loudly that the goldfinch became annoyed and bet them each a dozen worms that they couldn't follow the course he had flown across the field without encountering the hardened atmosphere. They all took his bet; the swallow went along to watch. The sea gull, the eagle, and the hawk decided to fly together over the route the goldfinch indicated. "You come, too," they said to the swallow. "I—I—well, no," said the swallow. "I don't think I will." So the three large birds took off together and they hit the glass together and they were all knocked cold.

Moral: He who hesitates is sometimes saved.

WILLIAM MARCH: The Fisherman and the Hen

When he reached the brook where he intended to fish, an angler found he had left his bait at home, but after considering matters, he thought he might be able to catch grasshoppers and use them instead. He got down on his hands and knees, but try as he would, he wasn't successful. He had about abandoned the idea of getting bait that way, when he saw an old hen in the grass, seeking her breakfast. As he watched, he realized the old hen, despite her infirmities, was a better grasshopper-catcher than he, for almost at once she pounced on a large, lively one and held it in her bill.

The fisherman crept toward the old hen, hoping to take the grasshopper from her before she could swallow it, but the hen, guessing his intention, flushed her wings and ran through the grass. She might have escaped if the fisherman had not thrown a stick at her. He caught her squarely and she fell in the weeds, her tail feathers twitching from side to side.

He pulled the half-swallowed grasshopper from her throat, put it in his pocket, and turned away; but noticing how pathetic the old hen looked there in the grass, he picked her up and stroked her head. "Poor old thing!" he said. "I'm sorry for what I did just now!" He lifted her higher and rubbed his cheek against her wings. "I was a brute to hit you so hard," he said.

It was the first time the old hen had had any affection in years, and she lay back in the fisherman's arms, making a clucking sound in her throat, until he put her down and went back to his fishing. Shortly thereafter, he dismissed the incident from his mind, being engaged with his own pleasures, so he was somewhat puzzled when he heard a soft, seductive noise behind him. He turned, and there was the old hen with another grasshopper in her beak. When she saw she had his attention, she moved away slowly, glancing back at him over her shoulder, awaiting his blow with resignation, since an old hen will put up with anything if you'll give her a little affection now and then.

WILLIAM MARCH: The Unique Quality of Truth

When the old scholar heard that Truth was in the country, he decided to find her, as he had devoted his life to studying her in all her forms. He set out immediately, and at last he came upon the cottage in the mountains where Truth lived alone. He knocked on the door, and Truth asked what he wanted. The scholar explained who he was, adding that he had always wanted to know her and had wondered a thousand times what she really was like.

Truth came to the door soon afterwards, and the scholar saw that the pictures he had formed of her in his imagination were wrong. He had thought of Truth as a gigantic woman with flowing hair who sat nobly on a white horse, or, at the very least, as a sculptured heroic figure with a wide white brow and untroubled eyes. In reality, Truth was nothing at all like that; instead, she was merely a small shapeless old woman who seemed made of some quivering substance that resembled india rubber.

"All right," said the old lady in a resigned voice. "What do you want to know?"

"I want to know what you are."

The old lady thought, shook her head, and answered, "That I don't know. I couldn't tell you to save my life."

"Then have you any special quality that makes you an individual?" asked the scholar. "Surely you must have some characteristic that is uniquely yours."

"As a matter of fact, I have," said the old lady; then, seeing the question on the scholar's lips, she added, "I'll show you what I mean. It's easier than trying to explain."

The shapeless old woman began to bounce like a rubber ball, up and down on her doorstep, getting a little higher each time she struck the floor. When she was high enough for her purpose, she seized the woodwork above her door and held on; then she said, "Take hold of my legs and walk back the way you came, and when you know what my unique quality is, shout and let me know."

The old scholar did as he was told, racking his brains in an effort to determine what quality it was that distinguished Truth. When he reached the road, he turned around, and there in the distance was Truth still clinging to the woodwork above her door.

"Don't you see by this time?" she shouted. "Don't you understand now what my particular quality is?"

"Yes," said the old scholar. "Yes, I do."

"Then turn my legs loose and go on home," said Truth in a small petulant voice.

THE BOOK OF SAMUEL: Thou Art the Man[1]

And it came to pass, after the year was expired, at the time when kings go forth to battle, that David sent Joab, and his servants with him, and all Israel; and they destroyed the children of Ammon, and beseiged Rabbah. But David tarried still at Jerusalem.

And it came to pass in an eveningtide, that David arose from off his bed, and walked upon the roof of the king's house: and from the roof he saw a woman washing herself; and the woman was very beautiful to look upon. And David sent and enquired after the woman. And one said, Is not this Bathsheba, the daughter of Eliam, the wife of Uriah the Hittite? And David sent messengers, and took her; and she came in unto him, and he lay with her; for she was purified from her uncleanness: and she returned unto her house. And the woman conceived, and sent and told David, and said, I am with child.

And David sent to Joab, saying, Send me Uriah the Hittite. And Joab sent Uriah to David. And when Uriah was come unto him, David demanded of him how Joab did, and how the people did, and how the war prospered. And David said to Uriah, Go down to thy house, and wash thy feet. And Uriah departed out of the king's house, and there followed him a mess of meat from the king. But Uriah slept at the door of the king's house with all the servants of his lord, and went not down to his house. And when they had told David, saying, Uriah went not down unto his house, David said unto Uriah, Camest thou not from thy journey? why then didst thou not go down unto thine house? And Uriah said unto David, The ark, and Israel, and Judah, abide in tents; and my lord Joab, and the servants of my lord, are encamped in the open fields; shall I then go into mine house, to eat and to drink, and to lie with my wife? as thou livest, and as thy soul liveth, I will not do this thing. And David said to Uriah, Tarry here to day also, and to morrow I will let thee depart. So Uriah abode in Jerusalem that day, and the morrow. And when David had called him, he did eat and drink before him; and he made him drunk: and at even he went out to lie on his bed with the servants of his lord, but went not down to his house.

And it came to pass in the morning, that David wrote a letter to Joab, and sent it by the hand of Uriah. And he wrote in the letter, saying, Set ye Uriah in the forefront of the hottest battle,

1. II Samuel xi and xii. 1-7.

and retire ye from him, that he may be smitten, and die. And it came to pass, when Joab observed the city, that he assigned Uriah unto a place where he knew that valiant men were. And the men of the city went out, and fought with Joab: and there fell some of the people of the servants of David; and Uriah the Hittite died also. Then Joab sent and told David all the things concerning the war; and charged the messenger, saying, When thou hast made an end of telling the matters of the war unto the king, and if so be that the king's wrath arise, and he say unto thee, Wherefore approached ye so nigh unto the city when ye did fight? knew ye not that they would shoot from the wall? Who smote Abimelech the son of Jerubbesheth? did not a woman cast a piece of millstone upon him from the wall, that he died in Thebez? why went ye nigh the wall? then say thou, Thy servant Uriah the Hittite is dead also.

So the messenger went, and came and shewed David all that Joab had sent him for. And the messenger said unto David, Surely the men prevailed against us, and came out unto us into the field, and we were upon them even unto the entering of the gate. And the shooters shot from off the wall upon thy servants; and some of the king's servants be dead, and thy servant Uriah the Hittite is dead also. Then David said unto the messenger, Thus shalt thou say unto Joab, Let not this thing displease thee, for the sword devoureth one as well as another: make thy battle more strong against the city, and overthrow it: and encourage thou him.

And when the wife of Uriah heard that Uriah her husband was dead, she mourned for her husband. And when the mourning was past, David sent and fetched her to his house, and she became his wife, and bare him a son. But the thing that David had done displeased the Lord.

And the Lord sent Nathan unto David. And he came unto him, and said unto him, There were two men in one city; the one rich, and the other poor. The rich man had exceeding many flocks and herds: but the poor man had nothing, save one little ewe lamb, which he had bought and nourished up: and it grew up together with him, and with his children; it did eat of his own meat, and drank of his own cup, and lay in his bosom, and was unto him as a daughter. And there came a traveller unto the rich man, and he spared to take of his own flock and of his own herd, to dress for the wayfaring man that was come unto him; but took the poor man's lamb, and dressed it for the man that was come to him. And David's anger was greatly kindled against the man; and he said to Nathan, As the Lord liveth, the man that hath done this thing shall surely die: and he shall restore the lamb fourfold, because he did this thing, and because he had no pity.

And Nathan said to David, Thou art the man.

MATTHEW: Parables of the Kingdom[1]

Then shall the kingdom of heaven be likened unto ten virgins, which took their lamps, and went forth to meet the bridegroom.

And five of them were wise, and five *were* foolish.

They that *were* foolish took their lamps, and took no oil with them:

But the wise took oil in their vessels with their lamps.

While the bridegroom tarried, they all slumbered and slept.

And at midnight there was a cry made, Behold, the bridegroom cometh; go ye out to meet him.

Then all those virgins arose, and trimmed their lamps.

And the foolish said unto the wise, Give us of your oil; for our lamps are gone out.

But the wise answered, saying, *Not so*; lest there be not enough for us and you: but go ye rather to them that sell, and buy for yourselves.

And while they went to buy, the bridegroom came; and they that were ready went in with him to the marriage: and the door was shut.

Afterward came also the other virgins, saying, Lord, Lord, open to us.

But he answered and said, Verily I say unto you, I know you not.

Watch therefore, for ye know neither the day nor the hour wherein the Son of man cometh.

For *the kingdom of heaven is* as a man travelling into a far country, *who* called his own servants, and delivered unto them his goods.

And unto one he gave five talents, to another two, and to another one; to every man according to his several ability; and straightway took his journey.

Then he that had received the five talents went and traded with the same, and made *them* other five talents.

And likewise he that *had received* two, he also gained other two.

But he that had received one went and digged in the earth, and hid his lord's money.

After a long time the lord of those servants cometh, and reckoneth with them.

And so he that had received five talents came and brought other five talents, saying, Lord, thou deliveredst unto me five talents: behold, I have gained beside them five talents more.

His lord said unto him, Well done, *thou* good and faithful servant: thou hast been faithful over a few things, I will make thee

1. Matthew xxv.

ruler over many things: enter thou into the joy of thy lord.

He also that had received two talents came and said, Lord, thou deliveredst unto me two talents: behold, I have gained two other talents beside them.

His lord said unto him, Well done, good and faithful servant; thou hast been faithful over a few things, I will make thee ruler over many things: enter thou into the joy of thy lord.

Then he which had received the one talent came and said, Lord, I knew thee that thou art an hard man, reaping where thou hast not sown, and gathering where thou hast not strawed:

And I was afraid, and went and hid thy talent in the earth: lo, *there* thou hast *that is* thine.

His lord answered and said unto him, *Thou* wicked and slothful servant, thou knewest that I reap where I sowed not, and gather where I have not strawed:

Thou oughtest therefore to have put my money to the exchangers, and *then* at my coming I should have received mine own with usury.

Take therefore the talent from him, and give *it* unto him which hath ten talents.

For unto every one that hath shall be given, and he shall have abundance: but from him that hath not shall be taken away even that which he hath.

And cast ye the unprofitable servant into outer darkness: there shall be weeping and gnashing of teeth.

When the Son of man shall come in his glory, and all the holy angels with him, then shall he sit upon the throne of his glory:

And before him shall be gathered all nations: and he shall separate them one from another, as a shepherd divideth *his* sheep from the goats:

And he shall set the sheep on his right hand, but the goats on the left.

Then shall the King say unto them on his right hand, Come, ye blessed of my Father, inherit the kingdom prepared for you from the foundation of the world:

For I was an hungred, and ye gave me meat: I was thirsty, and ye gave me drink: I was a stranger, and ye took me in:

Naked, and ye clothed me: I was sick, and ye visited me: I was in prison, and ye came unto me.

Then shall the righteous answer him, saying, Lord, when saw we thee an hungred, and fed *thee?* or thirsty, and gave *thee* drink?

When saw we thee a stranger, and took *thee* in? or naked, and clothed thee?

Or when saw we thee sick, or in prison, and came unto thee?

And the King shall answer and say unto them, Verily I say unto you, Inasmuch as ye have done *it* unto one of the least of these my brethren, ye have done *it* unto me.

Then shall he say also unto them on the left hand, Depart from me, ye cursed, into everlasting fire, prepared for the devil and his angels:

For I was an hungred, and ye gave me no meat: I was thirsty, and ye gave me no drink.

I was a stranger, and ye took me not in: naked, and ye clothed me not: sick, and in prison, and ye visited me not.

Then shall they also answer him, saying, Lord, when saw we thee an hungred, or athirst, or a stranger, or naked, or sick, or in prison, and did not minister unto thee?

Then shall he answer them, saying, Verily I say unto you, Inasmuch as ye did *it* not to one of the least of these, ye did *it* not to me.

And these shall go away into everlasting punishment: but the righteous into life eternal.

FRANZ KAFKA: Parable of the Law[1]

"Before the Law stands a doorkeeper. To this doorkeeper there comes a man from the country who begs for admittance to the Law. But the doorkeeper says that he cannot admit the man at the moment. The man, on reflection, asks if he will be allowed, then, to enter later. 'It is possible,' answers the doorkeeper, 'but not at this moment.' Since the door leading into the Law stands open as usual and the doorkeeper steps to one side, the man bends down to peer through the entrance. When the doorkeeper sees that, he laughs and says: 'If you are so strongly tempted, try to get in without my permission. But note that I am powerful. And I am only the lowest doorkeeper. From hall to hall, keepers stand at every door, one more powerful than the other. And the sight of the third man is already more than even I can stand.' These are difficulties which the man from the country has not expected to meet, the Law, he thinks, should be accessible to every man and at all times, but when he looks more closely at the doorkeeper in his furred robe, with his huge pointed nose and long thin Tartar beard, he decides that he had better wait until he gets permission to enter. The doorkeeper gives him a stool and lets him sit down at the side of the door. There he sits waiting for days and years. He makes many attempts to be allowed in and wearies the doorkeeper with his importunity. The doorkeeper often engages him in brief conversation, asking him about his home and about other matters, but the questions are put quite impersonally, as great men put questions, and always conclude with the statement that the man cannot be allowed

1. From the chapter, "In the Cathedral," of *The Trial* (1925).

to enter yet. The man, who has equipped himself with many things for his journey, parts with all he has, however valuable, in the hope of bribing the doorkeeper. The doorkeeper accepts it all, saying, however, as he takes each gift: 'I take this only to keep you from feeling that you have left something undone.' During all these long years the man watches the doorkeeper almost incessantly. He forgets about the other doorkeepers, and this one seems to him the only barrier between himself and the Law. In the first years he curses his evil fate aloud; later, as he grows old, he only mutters to himself. He grows childish, and since in his prolonged study of the doorkeeper he has learned to know even the fleas in his fur collar, he begs the very fleas to help him and to persuade the doorkeeper to change his mind. Finally his eyes grow dim and he does not know whether the world is really darkening around him or whether his eyes are only deceiving him. But in the darkness he can now perceive a radiance that streams inextinguishably from the door of the Law. Now his life is drawing to a close. Before he dies, all that he has experienced during the whole time of his sojourn condenses in his mind into one question, which he has never yet put to the doorkeeper. He beckons the doorkeeper, since he can no longer raise his stiffening body. The doorkeeper has to bend far down to hear him, for the difference in size between them has increased very much to the man's disadvantage. 'What do you want to know now?' asks the doorkeeper, 'you are insatiable.' 'Everyone strives to attain the Law,' answers the man, 'how does it come about, then, that in all these years no one has come seeking admittance but me?' The doorkeeper perceives that the man is nearing his end and his hearing is failing, so he bellows in his ear: 'No one but you could gain admittance through this door, since this door was intended for you. I am now going to shut it.' "

"So the doorkeeper deceived the man," said K. immediately, strongly attracted by the story. "Don't be too hasty," said the priest, "don't take over someone else's opinion without testing it. I have told you the story in the very words of the scriptures. There's no mention of deception in it." "But it's clear enough," said K., "and your first interpretation of it was quite right. The doorkeeper gave the message of salvation to the man only when it could no longer help him." "He was not asked the question any earlier," said the priest, "and you must consider, too, that he was only a doorkeeper, and as such fulfilled his duty." "What makes you think he fulfilled his duty?" asked K. "He didn't fulfill it. His duty might have been to keep all strangers away, but this man, for whom the door was intended, should have been let in." "You have not enough respect for the written word and you are altering the story," said the priest. "The story contains two important statements made by the doorkeeper about admission to the Law, one at the beginning, the other at the end. The first statement is: that he cannot admit the man at the moment, and the other is: that this door was intended only for the man. If there were a contradiction between the two, you would be right and the doorkeeper would have deceived the man. But there is no contradiction. The first statement, on the contrary, even implies the second. One could almost say that in suggesting to the man the possibility of future admittance the doorkeeper is exceeding his duty. At that time his apparent duty is only to refuse admittance and indeed many commentators are surprised that the suggestion should be made at all, since the doorkeeper appears to be a precisian with a stern regard for duty. He does not once leave his post during these many years, and he does not shut the door until the very last minute; he is conscious of the importance of his office, for he says: 'I am powerful'; he is respectful to his superiors, for he says: 'I am only the lowest doorkeeper'; he is not garrulous, for during all these years he puts only what are called 'impersonal questions'; he is not to be bribed, for he says in accepting a gift: 'I take this only to keep you from feeling that you have left something undone'; where his duty is concerned he is to be moved neither by pity nor rage, for we are told that the man 'wearied the doorkeeper with his importunity'; and finally even his external appearance hints at a pedantic character, the large, pointed nose and the long, thin, black, Tartar beard. Could one imagine a more faithful doorkeeper? Yet the doorkeeper has other elements in his character which are likely to advantage anyone seeking admittance and which make it comprehensible enough that he should somewhat exceed his duty in suggesting the possibility of future admittance. For it cannot be denied that he is a little simple-minded and consequently a little conceited. Take the statements he makes about his power and the power of the other doorkeepers and their dreadful aspect which even he cannot bear to see—I hold that these statements may be true enough, but that the way in which he brings them out shows that his perceptions are confused by simpleness of mind and conceit. The commentators note in this connection: 'The right perception of any matter and a misunderstanding of the same matter do not wholly exclude each other.' One must at any rate assume that such simpleness and conceit, however sparingly manifest, are likely to weaken his defense of the door; they are breaches in the character of the doorkeeper. To this must be added the fact that the doorkeeper seems to be a friendly creature by nature, he is by no means always on his official dignity. In the very first moments he allows himself the jest of inviting the man to enter in spite of the strictly maintained veto against entry; then he does not, for instance, send the man away, but gives him, as we are told, a stool and lets him sit down beside the door. The patience with which he endures the man's appeals during so many years, the brief conversations, the acceptance of the gifts, the politeness with which he allows the man to curse loudly in his presence the fate for which he himself is responsible—all this lets us deduce certain feelings of pity. Not every doorkeeper would have acted thus. And finally, in answer to a gesture of the man's he bends down to give him the chance of putting a last question. Nothing but mild impatience—the doorkeeper knows that this is the end of it all—is discernible in the words: 'You are insatiable.' Some push this mode of interpretation even further and hold that these words express a kind of friendly admiration, though not without a hint of condescension. At any rate the figure of the doorkeeper can be said to come out very differently from what you fancied." "You have studied the story more exactly and for a longer time than I have," said K. They were both silent for a little while. Then. K. said: "So you think the man was not deceived?" "Don't misunderstand me," said the priest, "I am only showing you the various opinions concerning that point. You must not pay too much attention to them. The scriptures are unalterable and the comments often enough merely express the commentators' despair. In this case there even exists an interpretation which claims that the deluded person is really the doorkeeper." "That's a farfetched interpretation," said K. "On what is it based?" "It is based," answered the priest, "on the simple-mindedness of the doorkeeper. The argument is that he does not know the Law from inside, he knows only the way that leads to it, where he patrols up and down. His ideas of the interior are assumed to be childish, and it is supposed that he himself is afraid of the other guardians whom he holds up as bogies before the man. Indeed, he fears them more than the man does, since the man is determined to enter after hearing about the dreadful guardians of the interior, while the doorkeeper has no desire to enter, at least not so far as we are told. Others again say that he must have been in the interior already, since he is after all engaged in the service of the Law and can only have been appointed from inside. This is countered by arguing that he may have been appointed by a voice calling from the interior, and that anyhow he cannot have been far inside, since the aspect of the third doorkeeper is more than he can endure. Moreover, no indication is given that during all these years he ever made any remarks showing a knowledge of the interior, except for the one remark about the doorkeepers. He may have been forbidden to do so, but there is no mention of that either. On these grounds the conclusion is reached that he knows nothing about the aspect and significance of the interior, so that he is in a state of delusion. But he is deceived also about his relation to the man from the country, for he is inferior to the man and does not know it. He treats the man instead as his own subordinate, as can be recognized from many details that must be still fresh in your mind. But, according to this view of the story, it is just as clearly indicated that he is really subordinated to the man. In the first place, a bondman is always subject to a free man. Now the man from the country is really free, he can go where he likes, it is only the Law that is closed to him, and access to the Law is forbidden him only by one individual, the doorkeeper. When he sits down on the stool by the side of the door and stays there for the rest of his life, he does it of his own free will; in the story there is no mention of any compulsion. But the doorkeeper is bound to his post by his very office, he does not dare go out into the country, nor apparently may he go into the interior of the Law, even should he wish to. Besides, although he is in the service of the Law, his service is confined to this one entrance; that is to say, he serves only this man for whom alone the entrance is intended. On that ground too he is inferior to the man. One must assume that for many years, for as long as it takes a man to grow up to the prime of life, his service was in a sense an empty formality, since he had to wait for a man to come, that is to say someone in the prime of life, and so he had to wait a long time before the purpose of his service could be fulfilled, and, moreover, had to wait on the man's pleasure, for the man came of his own free will. But the termination of his service also depends on the man's term of life, so that to the very end he is subject to the man. And it is emphasized throughout that the doorkeeper apparently realizes nothing of all this. That is not in itself remarkable, since according to this interpretation the doorkeeper is deceived in a much more important issue, affecting his very office. At the end, for example, he says regarding the entrance to the Law: 'I am now going to shut it,' but at the beginning of the story we are told that the door leading into the Law always stands open, and if it always stands open, that is to say at all times, without reference to life or death of the man, then the doorkeeper cannot close it. There is some difference of opinion about the motive behind the doorkeeper's statement, whether he said he was going to close the door merely for the sake of giving an answer, or to emphasize his devotion to duty, or to bring the man into a state of grief and regret in his last moments. But there is no lack of agreement that the doorkeeper will not be able to shut the door. Many indeed profess to find that he is subordinate to the man even in knowledge, toward the end, at least, for the man sees the radiance that issues from the door of the Law while the doorkeeper in his official position must stand with his back to the door, nor does he say anything to show that he has perceived the change." "That is well argued," said K., after repeating to himself in a low voice several passages from the priest's exposition. "It is well argued, and I am inclined to agree that the doorkeeper is deceived. But that has not made me abandon my former opinion, since both conclusions are to some extent compatible. Whether the doorkeeper is clear-sighted or deceived does not dispose of the matter. I said the man is deceived. If the doorkeeper is clear-sighted, one might have doubts about that, but if the doorkeeper himself is deceived, then his deception must of necessity be communicated to the man. That makes the doorkeeper not, indeed, a deceiver, but a creature so simple-minded that he ought to be dismissed at once from his office. You mustn't forget that the doorkeeper's deceptions do himself no harm but do infinite harm to the man." "There are objections to that," said the priest. "Many aver that the story confers no right on anyone to pass judgment on the doorkeeper. Whatever he may seem to us, he is yet a servant of the Law; that is, he belongs to the Law and as such is beyond human judgment. In that case one must not believe that the doorkeeper is subordinate to the man. Bound as he is by his service, even only at the door of the Law, he is incomparably greater than anyone at large in the world. The man is only seeking the Law, the doorkeeper is already attached to it. It is the Law that has placed him at his post; to doubt his dignity is to doubt the Law itself." "I don't agree with that point of view," said K., shaking his head, "for if one accepts it, one must accept as true everything the doorkeeper says. But you yourself have sufficiently proved how impossible it is to do that." "No," said the priest, "it is not necessary to accept everything as true, one must only accept it as necessary." "A melancholy conclusion," said K. "It turns lying into a universal principle."

Zen Parables

Muddy Road

Tanzan and Ekido were once traveling together down a muddy road. A heavy rain was still falling.

Coming around a bend, they met a lovely girl in a silk kimono and sash, unable to cross the intersection.

"Come on, girl," said Tanzan at once. Lifting her in his arms, he carried her over the mud.

Ekido did not speak again until that night when they reached a lodging temple. Then he no longer could restrain himself. "We monks don't go near females," he told Tanzan, "especially not young and lovely ones. It is dangerous. Why did you do that?"

"I left the girl there," said Tanzan. "Are you still carrying her?"

A Parable

Buddha told a parable in a sutra:

A man traveling across a field encountered a tiger. He fled, the tiger after him. Coming to a precipice, he caught hold of the root of a wild vine and swung himself down over the edge. The tiger sniffed at him from above. Trembling, the man looked down to where, far below, another tiger was waiting to eat him. Only the vine sustained him.

Two mice, one white and one black, little by little started to gnaw away the vine. The man saw a luscious strawberry near him. Grasping the vine with one hand, he plucked the strawberry with the other. How sweet it tasted!

Learning to Be Silent

The pupils of the Tendai school used to study meditation before Zen entered Japan. Four of them who were intimate friends promised one another to observe seven days of silence.

On the first day all were silent. Their meditation had begun auspiciously, but when night came and the oil lamps were growing dim one of the pupils could not help exclaiming to a servant: "Fix those lamps."

The second pupil was surprised to hear the first one talk. "We are not supposed to say a word," he remarked.

"You two are stupid. Why did you talk?" asked the third.

"I am the only one who has not talked," concluded the fourth pupil.

OSCAR WILDE: The Doer of Good

It was night-time, and He was alone.

And He saw afar off the walls of a round city, and went towards the city.

And when He came near He heard within the city the tread of the feet of joy, and the laughter of the mouth of gladness, and the loud noise of many lutes. And He knocked at the gate and certain of the gate-keepers opened to Him.

And He beheld a house that was of marble, and had fair pillars of marble before it. The pillars were hung with garlands, and within and without there were torches of cedar. And He entered the house.

And when He had passed through the hall of chalcedony and the hall of jasper, and reached the long hall of feasting, He saw lying on a couch of sea-purple one whose hair was crowned with red roses and whose lips were red with wine.

And He went behind him and touched him on the shoulder, and said to him:

"Why do you live like this?"

And the young man turned round and recognized Him, and made answer, and said: "But I was a leper once, and you healed me. How else should I live?"

And He passed out of the house and went again into the street.

And after a little while He saw one whose face and raiment were painted and whose feet were shod with pearls. And behind her came slowly, as a hunter, a young man who wore a cloak of two colours. Now the face of the woman was as the fair face of an idol, and the eyes of the young man were bright with lust.

And He followed swiftly and touched the hand of the young man, and said to him: "Why do you look at this woman and in such wise?"

And the young man turned round and recognized Him, and said: "But I was blind once, and you gave me sight. At what else should I look?"

And He ran forward and touched the painted raiment of the woman, and said to her: "Is there no other way in which to walk save the way of sin?"

And the woman turned round and recognized Him, and laughed, and said: "But you forgave me my sins, and the way is a pleasant way."

And He passed out of the city.

And when He had passed out of the city, He saw, seated by the roadside, a young man who was weeping.

And he went towards him and touched the long locks of his hair, and said to him: "Why are you weeping?"

And the young man looked up and recognized Him, and made answer: "But I was dead once, and you raised me from the dead. What else should I do but weep?"

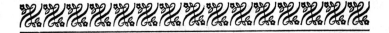

On Religion

ELDRIDGE CLEAVER
A Religious Conversion, More or Less[1]

Folsom Prison, September 10, 1965

Once I was a Catholic. I was baptized, made my first Communion, my Confirmation, and I wore a Cross with Jesus on it around my neck. I prayed at night, said my Rosary, went to Confession, and said all the Hail Marys and Our Fathers to which I was sentenced by the priest. Hopelessly enamored of sin myself, yet appalled by the sins of others, I longed for Judgment Day and a trial before a jury of my peers—this was my only chance to escape the flames which I could feel already licking at my feet. I was in a California Youth Authority institution at the time, having transgressed the laws of man—God did not indict me that time; if He did, it was a secret indictment, for I was never informed of any charges brought against me. The reason I became a Catholic was that the rule of the institution held that every Sunday each inmate had to attend the church of his choice. I chose the Catholic Church because all the Negroes and Mexicans went there. The whites went to the Protestant chapel. Had I been a fool enough to go to the Protestant chapel, one black face in a sea of white, and with guerrilla warfare going on between us, I might have ended up a Christian martyr—St. Eldridge the Stupe.

It all ended one day when, at a catechism class, the priest asked if anyone present understood the mystery of the Holy Trinity. I had been studying my lessons diligently and knew by heart what I'd been taught. Up shot my hand, my heart throbbing with piety (pride) for this chance to demonstrate my knowledge of the Word. To my great shock and embarrassment, the Father announced, and it sounded like a thunderclap, that I was lying, that no one, not even the Pope, understood the Godhead, and why else did I think

1. From *Soul on Ice*, 1968.

they called it the *mystery* of the Holy Trinity? I saw in a flash, stung to the quick by the jeers of my fellow catechumens, that I had been used, that the Father had been lying in wait for the chance to drop that thunderbolt, in order to drive home the point that the Holy Trinity was not to be taken lightly.

I had intended to explain the Trinity with an analogy to 3-in-1 oil, so it was probably just as well.

QUESTIONS

1. Why does Cleaver use the title he does, especially the word "conversion" in combination with a seeming contradiction in the qualification "more or less"?
2. How would Cleaver's account have differed in tone and style if he had been describing a "real" conversion?
3. What attitude does the phrase "sentenced by the priest" reveal? Does Cleaver use the phrase flippantly, objectively, seriously, humorously, or in some other way?
4. Explore the possibilities of Cleaver's analogy of the Trinity to 3-in-1 oil. Could it have been developed appropriately? Why does Cleaver say it was "probably just as well" he didn't use it?
5. From the way Cleaver describes his past attitude—"hopelessly enamored of sin myself, yet appalled by the sins of others"—what do you deduce his present attitude toward sin to be?

JAMES THURBER
The Owl Who Was God

Once upon a starless midnight there was an owl who sat on the branch of an oak tree. Two ground moles tried to slip quietly by, unnoticed. "You!" said the owl. "Who?" they quavered, in fear and astonishment, for they could not believe it was possible for anyone to see them in that thick darkness. "You two!" said the owl. The moles hurried away and told the other creatures of the field and forest that the owl was the greatest and wisest of all animals because he could see in the dark and because he could answer any question. "I'll see about that," said a secretary bird, and he called on the owl one night when it was again very dark. "How many claws am I holding up?" said the secretary bird, "Two," said the owl, and that was right. "Can you give me another expression for 'that is to say' or 'namely'?" asked the secretary bird. "To wit," said the owl. "Why does a lover call on his love?" asked the secretary bird. "To woo," said the owl.

The secretary bird hastened back to the other creatures and reported that the owl was indeed the greatest and wisest animal in the world because he could see in the dark and because he could answer any question. "Can he see in the daytime, too?" asked a red fox. "Yes," echoed a dormouse and a French poodle. "Can he see in the daytime, too?" All the other creatures laughed loudly at this silly question, and they set upon the red fox and his friends and drove them out of the region. Then they sent a messenger to the owl and asked him to be their leader.

When the owl appeared among the animals it was high noon and the sun was shining brightly. He walked very slowly, which gave him an appearance of great dignity, and he peered about him with large, staring eyes, which gave him an air of tremendous importance. "He's God!" screamed a Plymouth Rock hen. And the others took up the cry "He's God!" So they followed him wherever he went and when he began to bump into things they began to bump into things, too. Finally he came to a concrete highway and he started up the middle of it and all the other creatures followed him. Presently a hawk, who was acting as outrider, observed a truck coming toward them at fifty miles an hour, and he reported to the secretary bird and the secretary bird reported to the owl. "There's danger ahead," said the secretary bird. "To wit?" said the owl. The secretary bird told him. "Aren't you afraid?" He asked. "Who?" said the owl calmly, for he could not see the truck. "He's God!" cried all the creatures again, and they were still crying "He's God!" when the truck hit them and ran them down. Some of the animals were merely injured, but most of them, including the owl, were killed.

Moral: You can fool too many of the people too much of the time.

ROBERT GRAVES

Mythology[1]

Mythology is the study of whatever religious or heroic legends are so foreign to a student's experience that he cannot believe them to be true. Hence the English adjective "mythical," meaning "incredible"; and hence the omission from standard European mythologies of all Biblical narratives even when closely paralleled by myths from Persia, Babylonia, Egypt, and Greece, and of all hagiological legends. * * *

Myth has two main functions. The first is to answer the sort of awkward questions that children ask, such as: "Who made the world? How will it end? Who was the first man? Where do souls go after death?" The answers, necessarily graphic and positive, confer enormous power on the various deities credited with the creation and care of souls—and incidentally on their priesthoods.

1. Introduction to the *Larousse Encyclopedia of Mythology*, 1959.

The second function of myth is to justify an existing social system and account for traditional rites and customs. The Erechtheid clan of Athens, who used a snake as an amulet, preserved myths of their descent from King Erichthonius, a man-serpent, son of the Smith-god Hephaestus and foster-son of the Goddess Athene. The Ioxids of Caria explained their veneration for rushes and wild asparagus by a story of their ancestress Perigune, whom Theseus the Erechtheid courted in a thicket of these plants; thus incidentally claiming cousinship with the Attic royal house. The real reason may have been that wild asparagus stalks and rushes were woven into sacred baskets, and therefore taboo.

Myths of origin and eventual extinction vary according to the climate. In the cold North, the first human beings were said to have sprung from the licking of frozen stones by a divine cow named Audumla; and the Northern afterworld was a bare, misty, featureless plain where ghosts wandered hungry and shivering. According to a myth from the kinder climate of Greece, a Titan named Prometheus, kneading mud on a flowery riverbank, made human statuettes which Athene—who was once the Libyan Moon-goddess Neith—brought to life, and Greek ghosts went to a sunless, flowerless underground cavern. These afterworlds were destined for serfs or commoners; deserving nobles could count on warm, celestial mead halls in the North, and Elysian Fields in Greece.

Primitive peoples remodel old myths to conform with changes produced by revolutions, or invasions and, as a rule, politely disguise their violence: thus a treacherous usurper will figure as a lost heir to the throne who killed a destructive dragon or other monster and, after marrying the king's daughter, duly succeeded him. Even myths of origin get altered or discarded. Prometheus' creation of men from clay superseded the hatching of all nature from a world-egg laid by the ancient Mediterranean Dove-goddess Eurynome—a myth common also in Polynesia, where the Goddess is called Tangaroa.

A typical case-history of how myths develop as culture spreads: Among the Akan of Ghana, the original social system was a number of queendoms, each containing three or more clans and ruled by a Queen-mother with her council of elder women, descent being reckoned in the female line, and each clan having its own animal deity. The Akan believed that the world was born from the all-powerful Moon-goddess Ngame, who gave human beings souls, as soon as born, by shooting lunar rays into them. At some time or other, perhaps in the early Middle Ages, patriarchal nomads from the Sudan forced the Akans to accept a male Creator, a Sky-god named Odomankoma, but failed to destroy Ngame's dispensation. A compromise myth was agreed upon: Odomankoma created the world with hammer and chisel from inert matter, after which

Ngame brought it to life. These Sudanese invaders also worshipped the seven planetary powers ruling the week—a system originating in Babylonia. (It had spread to Northern Euope, bypassing Greece and Rome, which is why the names of pagan deities—Tuisto, Woden, Thor, and Frigg—are still attached to Tuesday, Wednesday, Thursday, and Friday.) This extra cult provided the Akan with seven new deities, and the compromise myth made both them and the clan gods bisexual. Towards the end of the fourteenth century A.D., a social revolution deposed Odomankoma in favor of a Universal Sun-god, and altered the myth accordingly. While Odomankoma ruled, a queendom was still a queendom, the king acting merely as a consort and male representative of the sovereign Queen-mother, and being styled "Son of the Moon": a yearly dying, yearly resurrected, fertility godling. But the gradual welding of small queendoms into city-states, and of city-states into a rich and populous nation, encouraged the High King—the king of the dominant city-state—to borrow a foreign custom. He styled himself "Son of the Sun," as well as "Son of the Moon," and claimed limitless authority. The Sun, which, according to the myth, had hitherto been reborn every morning from Ngame, was now worshipped as an eternal god altogether independent of the Moon's life-giving function. New myths appeared when the Akan accepted the patriarchal principle, which Sun-worship brought in; they began tracing succession through the father, and mothers céased to be the spiritual heads of households.

This case-history throws light on the complex Egyptian corpus of myth. Egypt, it seems, developed from small matriarchal Moon-queendoms to Pharaonic patriarchal Sun-monarchy. Grotesque animal deities of leading clans in the Delta became city-gods, and the cities were federated under the sovereignty of a High King (once a "Son of the Moon"), who claimed to be the Son of Ra the Sun-god. Opposition by independent-minded city-rulers to the Pharaoh's autocratic sway appears in the undated myth of how Ra grew so old and feeble that he could not even control his spittle; the Moon-goddess Isis plotted against him and Ra retaliated by casting his baleful eye on mankind—they perished in their thousands. Ra nevertheless decided to quit the ungrateful land of Egypt, whereupon Hathor, a loyal Cow-goddess, flew him up to the vault of Heaven. The myth doubtless records a compromise that consigned the High King's absolutist pretensions, supported by his wife, to the vague realm of philosophic theory. He kept the throne, but once more became, for all practical purposes, an incarnation of Osiris, consort of the Moon-goddess Isis—a yearly dying, yearly resurrected fertility godling.

Indian myth is highly complex, and swings from gross physical abandon to rigorous asceticism and fantastic visions of the spirit world. Yet it has much in common with European myth, since Aryan invasions in the second millennium B.C. changed the religious system of both continents. The invaders were nomad herdsmen, and the peoples on whom they imposed themselves as a military aristocracy were peasants. Hesiod, an early Greek poet, preserves a myth of pre-Aryan "Silver Age" heroes: "divinely created eaters of bread, utterly subject to their mothers however long they lived, who never sacrificed to the gods, but at least did not make war against one another." Hesiod put the case well: in primitive agricultural communities, recourse to war is rare, and goddess-worship the rule. Herdsmen, on the contrary, tend to make fighting a profession and, perhaps because bulls dominate their herds, as rams do flocks, worship a male Sky-god typified by a bull or a ram. He sends down rain for the pastures, and they take omens from the entrails of the victims sacrificed to him.

When an invading Aryan chieftain, a tribal rainmaker, married the Moon-priestess and Queen of a conquered people, a new myth inevitably celebrated the marriage of the Sky-god and the Moon. But since the Moon-goddess was everywhere worshipped as a triad, in honor of the Moon's three phases—waxing, full, and waning—the god split up into a complementary triad. This accounts for three-bodied Geryon, the first king of Spain; three-headed Cernunnos, the Gallic god; the Irish triad, Brian, Iuchar, and Iucharba, who married the three queenly owners of Ireland; and the invading Greek brothers Zeus, Poseidon, and Hades, who, despite great opposition, married the pre-Greek Moon-goddess in her three aspects, respectively as Queen of Heaven, Queen of the Sea, and Queen of the Underworld.

The Queen-mother's decline in religious power, and the goddesses' continual struggle to preserve their royal prerogatives, appears in the Homeric myth of how Zeus ill-treated and bullied Hera, and how she continually plotted against him. Zeus remained a Thunder-god, because Greek national sentiment forbad his becoming a Sun-god in Oriental style. But his Irish counterpart, a thunder-god named The Dagda, grew senile at last and surrendered the throne to his son Bodb the Red, a war-god—in Ireland, the magic of rainmaking was not so important as in Greece.

One constant rule of mythology is that whatever happens among the gods above reflects events on earth. Thus a father-god named "The Ancient One of the Jade" (Yu-ti) ruled the pre-revolutionary Chinese Heaven: like Prometheus, he had created human beings from clay. His wife was the Queen-mother, and their court an exact replica of the old Imperial Court at Pekin, with precisely the same functionaries: ministers, soldiers, and a numerous family of the gods' sisters, daughters, and nephews. The two annual sacrifices paid by the Emperor to the August One of the Jade—at the winter solstice when the days first lengthen and at the Spring equinox when they become longer than the nights—show him to have once been a solar god. And the theological value to the number 72 suggests that the cult started as a compromise between Moon-goddess worship and Sun-god worship. 72 means three-times-three, the Moon's mystical number, multipled by two-times-two-times-two, the Sun's mystical number, and occurs in solar-lunar divine unions throughout Europe, Asia, and Africa. Chinese conservatism, by the way, kept these gods dressed in ancient court-dress, making no concessions to the new fashions which the invading dynasty from Manchuria had introduced.

In West Africa, whenever the Queen-mother, or King, appointed a new functionary at Court, the same thing happened in Heaven, by royal decree. Presumably this was also the case in China; and if we apply the principle to Greek myth, it seems reasonably certain that the account of Tirynthian Heracles' marriage to Hera's daughter Hebe, and his appointment as Celestial Porter to Zeus, commemorates the appointment of a Tirynthian prince as vizier at the court of the Mycenaean High King, after marriage to a daughter of his Queen, the High Priestess of Argos. Probably the appointment of Ganymede, son of an early Trojan king, as cup-bearer to Zeus, had much the same significance: Zeus, in this context, would be more likely the Hittite king resident at Hattusas.

Myth, then, is a dramatic shorthand record of such matters as invasions, migrations, dynastic changes, admission of foreign cults, and social reforms. When bread was first introduced into Greece—where only beans, poppyseeds, acorns, and asphodel roots had hitherto been known—the myth of Demeter and Triptolemus sanctified its use; the same event in Wales produced a myth of "The Old White One," a Sow-goddess who went around the country with gifts of grain, bees, and her own young; for agriculture, pig breeding and beekeeping were taught to the aborigines by the same wave of neolithic invaders. Other myths sanctified the invention of wine.

A proper study of myth demands a great store of abstruse geographical, historical, and anthropological knowledge, also familiarity with the properties of plants and trees, and the habits of wild birds and beasts. Thus a Central American stone sculpture, a Toad-god sitting beneath a mushroom, means little to mythologists who have not considered the worldwide association of toads with toxic mushrooms or heard of a Mexican Mushroom-god, patron of an oracular cult; for the toxic agent is a drug, similar to that secreted in the sweat glands of frightened toads, which provides magnificent hallucinations of a heavenly kingdom.

Myths are fascinating and easily misread. Readers may smile at the picture of Queen Maya and her prenatal dream of the Buddha descending upon her disguised as a charming white baby elephant—he looks as though he would crush her to pulp—when "at once all nature rejoiced, trees burst into bloom, and musical instruments played of their own accord." In English-speaking countries, "white elephant" denotes something not only useless and unwanted, but expensive to maintain; and the picture could be misread there as indicating the Queen's grave embarrassment at the prospect of bearing a child. In India, however, the elephant symbolizes royalty—the supreme God Indra rides one—and white elephants (which are not albinos, but animals suffering from a vitiliginous skin disease) are sacred to the Sun, as white horses were for the ancient Greeks, and white oxen for the British druids. The elephant, moreover, symbolizes intelligence, and Indian writers traditionally acknowledge the Elephant-god Ganesa as their patron; he is supposed to have dictated the *Mahabharata*.

Again, in English, a scallop shell is associated either with cookery or with medieval pilgrims returning from a visit to the Holy Sepulcher; but Aphrodite the Greek Love-goddess employed a scallop shell for her voyages across the sea, because its two parts were so tightly hinged together as to provide a symbol of passionate sexual love—the hinge of the scallop being a principal ingredient in ancient love-philters. The lotus-flower sacred to Buddha and Osiris has five petals, which symbolize the four limbs and the head; the five senses; the five digits; and, like the pyramid, the four points of the compass and the zenith. Other esoteric meanings abound, for myths are seldom simple, and never irresponsible.

RONALD A. KNOX
The Nature of Enthusiasm[1]

I have called this book *Enthusiasm*, not meaning thereby to name (for name it has none) the elusive thing that is its subject. I have only used a cant term, pejorative, and commonly misapplied, as a label for a tendency. And, lest I should be accused of setting out to mystify the reader, I must proceed to map out, as best I may, the course of this inquiry. There is, I would say, a recurrent situation in Church history—using the word "church" in the widest sense—where an excess of charity threatens unity. You have a clique, an *élite*, of Christian men and (more importantly) women, who are trying to live a less worldly life than their neighbors; to be more attentive to the guidance (directly felt, they would tell you) of the Holy Spirit. More and more, by a kind of fatality, you see them draw apart from their co-religionists, a hive ready to swarm. There is

1. From Chapter I of *Enthusiasm*, 1950.

provocation on both sides; on the one part, cheap jokes at the expense of over-godliness, acts of stupid repression by unsympathetic authorities; on the other, contempt of the half-Christian, ominous references to old wine and new bottles, to the kernel and the husk. Then, while you hold your breath and turn away your eyes in fear, the break comes; condemnation or secession, what difference does it make? A fresh name has been added to the list of Christianities.

The pattern is always repeating itself, not in outline merely but in detail. Almost always the enthusiastic movement is denounced as an innovation, yet claims to be preserving, or to be restoring, the primitive discipline of the Church. Almost always the opposition is twofold; good Christian people who do not relish an eccentric spirituality find themselves in unwelcome alliance with worldlings who do not relish any spirituality at all. Almost always schism begets schism; once the instinct of discipline is lost, the movement breeds rival prophets and rival coteries, at the peril of its internal unity. Always the first fervors evaporate; prophecy dies out, and the charismatic is merged in the institutional. "The high that proved too high, the heroic for earth too hard"—it is a fugal melody that runs through the centuries.

If I could have been certain of the reader's goodwill, I would have called my tendency "ultrasupernaturalism." For that is the real character of the enthusiast; he expects more evident results from the grace of God than we others. He sees what effects religion can have, does sometimes have, in transforming a man's whole life and outlook; these exceptional cases (so we are content to think them) are for him the average standard of religious achievement. He will have no "almost-Christians," no weaker brethren who plod and stumble, who (if the truth must be told) would like to have a foot in either world, whose ambition is to qualify, not to excel. He has before his eyes a picture of the early Church, visibly penetrated with supernatural influences; and nothing less will serve him for a model. Extenuate, accommodate, interpret, and he will part company with you.

Quoting a hundred texts—we also use them but with more of embarrassment—he insists that the members of his society, saved members of a perishing world, should live a life of angelic purity, of apostolic simplicity; worldly amusements, the artifices of a polite society, are not for them. Poor human nature! Every lapse that follows is marked by pitiless watchers outside the fold, creates a harvest of scandal within. Worse still, if the devout circle has cultivated a legend of its own impeccability; we shall be told, in that case, that actions which bring damnation to the worldling may be inculpable in the children of light. We must be prepared for strange alternations of rigorism and antinomianism as our history unfolds itself.

Meanwhile, it must not be supposed that the new birth which the enthusiast preaches can be limited to a mere reformation of manners. It involves a new approach to religion; hitherto this has been a matter of outward forms and ordinances, now it is an affair of the heart. Sacraments are not necessarily dispensed with; but the emphasis lies on a direct personal access to the Author of our salvation, with little of intellectual background or of liturgical expression. The appeal of art and music, hitherto conceived as a ladder which carried human thought upwards, is frowned upon as a barrier which interferes with the simplicity of true heart-worship. An inward experience of peace and joy is both the assurance which the soul craves for and its characteristic prayer-attitude. The strength of this personal approach is that it dominates the imagination, and presents a future world in all the colours of reality. Its weakness—but we are not concerned here to criticize—is an anthropocentric bias; not God's glory but your own salvation preoccupies the mind, with some risk of scruples, and even of despair.

But the implications of enthusiasm go deeper than this; at the root of it lies a different theology of grace. Our traditional doctrine is that grace perfects nature, elevates it to a higher pitch, so that it can bear its part in the music of eternity, but leaves it nature still. The assumption of the enthusiast is bolder and simpler; for him, grace has destroyed nature, and replaced it. The saved man has come out into a new order of being, with a new set of faculties which are proper to his state; David must not wear the panoply of Saul. Especially, he decries the use of human reason as a guide to any sort of religious truth. A direct indication of the Divine will is communicated to him at every turn, if only he will consent to abandon the "arm of flesh"—Man's miserable intellect, fatally obscured by the Fall. If no oracle from heaven is forthcoming, he will take refuge in sortilege; anything, to make sure that he is leaving the decision in God's hands. That God speaks to us through the intellect is a notion which he may accept on paper, but fears, in practice, to apply.

A new set of faculties, and also a new status; man saved becomes, at last, fully man. It follows that "the seed of grace," God's elect people, although they must perforce live cheek by jowl with the sons of perdition, claim another citizenship and own another allegiance. For the sake of peace and charity, they will submit themselves to every ordinance of man, but always under protest; worldly governments, being of purely human institution, have no real mandate to exercise authority, and sinful folk have no real rights, although, out of courtesy, their fancied rights must be respected. Always the enthusiast hankers after a theocracy, in which the anomalies of the present situation will be done away, and the righteous bear rule openly. Disappointed of this hope, a group of sectaries will sometimes go out into the wilderness, and set up a little theocracy of their own, like Cato's senate at Utica. The American continent has more than once been the scene of such an adventure; in these days, it is the last refuge of the enthusiast.

QUESTIONS

1. What devices does Knox use in constructing his definition of enthusiasm?
2. What explanation does Knox imply for the fact that "enthusiasm" is regarded as a pejorative term?
3. What does Knox mean by "ominous references to old wine and new bottles, to the kernel and the husk"?
4. What illustrations might Knox give for his last sentence?

NICHOLAS OF CUSA

The Icon of God[1]

If I strive in human fashion to transport you to things divine, I must needs use a comparison of some kind. Now among men's works I have found no image better suited to our purposes than that of an image which is omnivoyant—its face, by the painter's cunning art, being made to appear as though looking on all around it. There are many excellent pictures of such faces—for example, that of the archeress in the market-place of Nuremberg; that by the eminent painter, Roger, in his priceless picture in the governor's house at Brussels; the Veronica in my chapel at Coblenz, and, in the castle of Brixen, the angel holding the arms of the Church, and many others elsewhere. Yet, lest ye should fail in the exercise, which requireth a figure of this description to be looked upon, I send for your indulgence such a picture as I have been able to procure, setting forth the figure of an omnivoyant, and this I call the icon of God.

This picture, brethren, ye shall set up in some place, let us say, on a north wall, and shall stand round it, a little way off, and look upon it. And each of you shall find that, from whatsoever quarter he regardeth it, it looketh upon him as if it looked on none other. And it shall seem to a brother standing to eastward as if that face looketh toward the east, while one to southward shall think it looketh toward the south, and one to westward, toward the west. First, then, ye will marvel how it can be that the face should look on all and each at the same time. For the imagination of him standing to eastward cannot conceive the gaze of the icon to be turned unto any other quarter, such as west or south. Then let the brother who stood to eastward place himself to westward and he will find its gaze fastened on him in the west just as it was afore in the east. And, as

1. Preface to *The Vision of God*.

he knoweth the icon to be fixed and unmoved, he will marvel at the motion of its immovable gaze.

If now, while fixing his eye on the icon, he walk from west to east, he will find that its gaze continuously goeth along with him, and if he return from east to west, in like manner it will not leave him. Then will he marvel how, being motionless, it moveth, nor will his imagination be able to conceive that it should also move in like manner with one going in a contrary direction to himself. If he wish to experiment on this, he will cause one of his brethren to cross over from east to west, still looking on the icon, while he himself moveth from west to east; and he will ask the other as they meet if the gaze of the icon turn continuously with him; he will hear that it doth move in a contrary direction, even as with himself, and he will believe him. But, had he not believed him, he could not have conceived this to be possible. So by his brother's showing he will come to know that the picture's face keepeth in sight all as they go on their way, though it be in contrary directions; and thus he will prove that that countenance, though motionless, is turned to east in the same way that it is simultaneously to west, and in the same way to north and to south, and alike to one particular place and to all objects at once, whereby it regardeth a single movement even as it regardeth all together. And while he observeth how that gaze never quitteth any, he seeth that it taketh such diligent care of each one who findeth himself observed as though it cared only for him, and for no other, and this to such a degree that one on whom it resteth cannot even conceive that it should take care of any other. He will also see that it taketh the same most diligent care of the least of creatures as of the greatest, and of the whole universe.

GERARD MANLEY HOPKINS
The Fall of God's First Kingdom

A.M.D.G.[1]

FOR SUNDAY EVENING JAN. 25 1880, SEPTUAGESIMA SUNDAY, AT ST. FRANCIS XAVIER'S, LIVERPOOL—on *the Fall of God's First Kingdom*—"Every kingdom divided against itself shall be made desolate and every city (commonwealth) or house divided against itself shall not stand (Matt. xii 25)."

I am to speak tonight of the fall of God's first kingdom, of the Fall of Man. Those of you who have heard this month's evening sermons will understand how this comes now in due course. God entered in the beginning into a contract with man that they two

---

1. Abbreviation for *Ad Maiorem Dei Gloriam*, "for the greater glory of God."

should make one commonwealth for their common good, which was that God might be glorified in man and man in God; God was the sovereign in this commonwealth and kingdom and man the subject; God by his providence, his laws and appointments and man by his obedience and execution of them undertook to bring this good about; both parties were bound by justice and in justice lived, which in man was called original justice, but lasted / [2] not long. It ended with the Fall, of which I am now to speak.

Before God was king of man he was king of angels and before man fell angels had fallen. Then man was made that he might fill the place of angels. But Satan, who had fallen through pride and selflove, resolved that through pride and selflove man should be brought to fall and that, whereas a breach had been made in God's kingdom in heaven, God's kingdom on earth should be broken utterly to pieces. And as he could not do it by force he would do it by fraud. Now the wise assailant attacks the weakest spot, therefore Satan tempted Eve the woman.

He chose his disguise, he spoke by the serpent's mouth; he watched his time, he found Eve alone. And here some say she should have been warned when she heard a dumb beast speaking reason. But of this we cannot be sure: St. Basil says that all the birds and beasts spoke in Paradise: not of course that they were not dumb and irrational creatures by nature then as now, but if a black spirit could speak by them so could a white and it may be that the angels made use of them as instruments to sing God's praises and to entertain man. Neither would Satan needlessly alarm the woman, rather than that he would invisibly have uttered voices in the air. But when she heard what the serpent said, *then* she should have taken alarm. So then to listen to a serpent speaking might be no blame; but how came Eve to be alone? for God had said of Adam /*It is not good for man to be alone: let us make him a helpmate like himself*/; and Eve was without the helpmate not like only but stronger than herself. She was deceived and Adam, as St. Paul tells us, was not nor would have been. Then why was Eve alone?

Now, I know, my brethren, that the Scripture does not tell us this and we cannot with certainty answer the question, but yet it is useful to ask it because it throws a great light on what God's first kingdom was and how it came to fall. Take notice then that, besides those things which we must do whether we like or no, which we cannot help doing, such as breathe, eat, and sleep, there are three sorts of things that we may lawfully do, that are right in us, that we are within our rights in doing. The first are *our bounden duties*, as to hear mass on Sunday: these God commands. The second are *what God sanctions* but does not command nor in any special way

2. This sign is used throughout the sermon as a rhetorical notation for phrasing to be used in its delivery.

approve, as to amuse ourselves. The third are what God does not command but specially approves when done, as to hear mass on a week-day: these are called works *of supererogation.* All these are good, not only the things God commands and the things he specially approves and accepts but also the things he only sanctions, for he sanctions nothing but what is good, that is to say / nothing but what is in itself harmless and which his sanction then makes positively good, and when a man says / *I do this because I like it and God allows me* / he submits himself to God as truly as if it were a duty and he said / *I do this because God wills it and commands me.* But though all are good they are not equally good; far from that. In the things God sanctions and we do for our own pleasure the whole good, the only good, comes from God's sanction and our submission to his sovereign will; for that he may reward us, but not for anything else: for the rest, we are doing our own pleasure and our own pleasure is our work's reward. But when we do what God commands or what God specially approves, then he is ready to reward us not only for our submission of ourselves to his sovereign will but also for the work done, for the pains taken; for we were doing *his* pleasure, not our own. Now you will easily understand, indeed you know, that it is the mark of a truly good will to do the good God approves of but does not bind us to, to do, in other words, works of supererogation: it shews that good is loved of itself and freely. And it is the mark of a cold heart, of poor will, I will not say a bad one, to do nothing that God especially approves, only what he commands or else sanctions: it shews that there is little love of good for good's sake. And though no one can be lost but for sin, yet those who do the least good they lawfully can are very likely indeed to fall into doing *less than that least* and so to sin. Now if this applies to us now / very strongly does it apply to man unfallen. For Adam and Eve though they were in God's kingdom not sovereign but subject, yet they were king and queen of all this earth, they were like vassal princes to a sovereign prince, God's honor was more in their hands than it is in any one of ours; we are but ourselves, they represented mankind, they represented the commons in God's commonwealth; if I dishonor God today one of you may make up by honoring him, but if they left him unhonored who was to honor him? the beasts and birds and fishes? When Adam obeyed God / mankind was obeying its sovereign; when Adam offered God of his own free will unbidden sacrifice / mankind was all engrossed in a work of supererogation, in giving God fresh glory; when Adam was doing his own pleasure / mankind was in its duty indeed but God's honor was not growing, the commonwealth was idle. Now, brethren, with this thought turn to Eve's temptation and look for what shall appear there.

Eve was alone. It was no sin to be alone, she was in her duty,

God had given her freedom and she was wandering free, God had made her independent of her husband and she need not be at his side. Only God had made her for Adam's companion; it was her office, her work, the reason of her being to companion him and she was not doing it. There is no sin, but there is no delicacy of duty, no zeal for the sovereign's honor, no generosity, no supererogation. And Adam, he too was alone. He had been commanded to dress and keep Paradise. What flower, what fruitful tree, what living thing was there in Paradise so lovely as Eve, so fruitful as the mother of all flesh, that needed or could repay his tendance and his keeping as she? There was no sin; yet at the one fatal moment when of all the world care was wanted care was not forthcoming, the thing best worth keeping was unkept. And Eve stood by the forbidden tree, which God had bidden them not to eat of, which *she* said God had bidden them not even touch; she neither sinned nor was tempted to sin by standing near it, yet she would go to the very bounds and utmost border of her duty. To do so was not dangerous of itself, as it would be to us. When some child, one of Eve's poor daughters, stands by a peachtree, eyeing the blush of color on the fruit, fingering the velvet bloom upon it, breathing the rich smell, and in imagination tasting the sweet juice, the nearness, the mere neighborhood is enough to undo her, she looks and is tempted, she touches and is tempted more, she takes and tastes. But in Eve there was nothing of this; she was not mastered by concupiscence, *she* mastered *it*. There she stood, beautiful, innocent, with her original justice *and with nothing else*, nothing to stain it, but nothing to heighten and brighten it: she felt no cravings, for she was mistress of herself and would not let them rise; she felt no generous promptings, no liftings of the heart to give God glory, for she was mistress of herself and gave them no encouragement. Such was Eve before her fall.

Now, brethren, fancy, as you may, that rich tree all laden with its shining fragrant fruit and swaying down from one of its boughs, as the pythons and great snakes of the East do now, waiting for their prey to pass and then to crush it, swaying like a long spray of vine or the bine of a great creeper, not terrible but beauteous, lissome, marked with quaint streaks and eyes or flushed with rainbow colors, the Old Serpent. We must suppose he offered her the fruit, as though it were the homage and the tribute of the brute to man, of the subject to his queen, presented it with his mouth or swept it from the boughs down before her feet; and she declined it. Then came those studied words of double meaning the Scripture tells us of: *What! and has God forbidden you to eat of the fruit of Paradise?* Now mark her answer: you would expect her to reply: No, but of this one fruit only: he has given us free leave for all the trees in Paradise excepting one—but hear her: *Of the fruit of the trees in Paradise we do eat*—no mention of God's bounty here, it is all their freedom, what they do: "we do eat"—*but the fruit of the tree in the midst of Paradise*—as though she would say / of the best fruit of all—*God has commanded us not to eat of, nor so much as touch it, or we shall die*: then she remembers God when it is question of a stern and threatening law. She gave her tempter the clue to his temptation—that God her sovereign was a tyrant, a sullen lawgiver; that God her lord and landlord was envious and grudging, a rackrent; that God her father, the author of her being was a shadow of death. The serpent took the hint and bettered it. Well was he called subtle: he does not put her suggestion into words and make it blacker; she would have been shocked, she would have recoiled; he gives the thing another turn, as much as to say: Why yes, God would be all this if you took his law according to the letter. No no; what does "death" mean? you will not die: you will die to ignorance, if you will, and wake to wisdom: *God knows, on the day you eat of it your eyes will be opened and you will be as gods, knowing good and evil.* And with these words he dealt three blows at once against God's kingdom— at God as a lawgiver and judge, at God as an owner or proprietor, at God as a father; at God as a lawgiver and judge, for the Serpent said / God has made this the tree of the knowledge of good and evil, that is / which shall decide for him whether to call you good or evil, good if you keep from it, evil if you touch it: be your own lawgivers and judges of good and evil; be as God yourselves, be divinely independent, why not? make it *good* to try the tree, *evil* to leave it untasted; at God as a proprietor, for as owner of man and the earth and all therein and sovereign of the commonwealth God had given the other trees of Paradise to his subjects but reserved this one to the crown: the Serpent advised them to trespass boldly on these rights and seize crown-property; and at God as a father, for God like a fatherly providence found them food and forbad them poison: the Serpent told them the deadly poison was life-giving food. It was enough: Eve would judge for herself. She *saw that the tree was good to eat*, that it was *not* poison, it was the food of life—and here was the pride of life; *that it was beautiful to the eyes*, a becoming object to covet and possess—and here was the desire of the eyes; *and that it was delightful to behold*, that is / sweet and enjoyable in imagination even and forecast, how much more in the eating and the reality!—and here was the desire of the flesh; she freely yielded herself to the three concupiscences; *she took and eat* of this devil's-sacrament; she rebelled, she sinned, she fell.

She fell, but still God's kingdom was not fallen yet, because it turned upon the man's obedience, not the woman's. Then came the meeting between the husband and the wife and she learnt that she was deceived and undone. Then her husband must share her lot for better and worse; this selfish and fallen woman would drag her husband in her fall, as she had had no thought of God's honor in her innocence, so in her sin she had no charity for her husband: she had so little love for him that she said, if he loved her he must share her lot. Most dearly he loved her, and she stood before him now lovely and her beauty heightened by distress, a thing never seen before in Paradise, herself a Tree of Knowledge of Good and Evil and offering him its fruit; herself a Tree of Life, the mother of all flesh to be. For he thought his hope of offspring would go with her. He was wrong: God, who gave back to Abraham for his obedience his all but sacrificed son, would have given back to Adam for his obedience his fallen wife; but he did not pause to make an act of hope. He listened to her voice. He left his heavenly father and clave to his wife and they two were in one fallen flesh; for her he took the stolen goods and harbored the forfeit person of the thief, rebelling against God, the world's great landlord, owner of earth and man, who had bestowed upon him Paradise, who had bestowed upon him the body of his wife; for her he eat the fatal fruit, making a new contract, a new commonwealth with Eve alone, and rebelling against God his lawgiver and judge. With that the contract with God was broken, the commonwealth undone, the kingdom divided and brought to desolation. God was left upon his throne but his subject had deserted to the enemy, God was left with his rights but the tenant had refused him payment, God was left a father but his children were turned to children of wrath. Then followed the disinheriting of the disobedient son; then followed the first and most terrible of evictions, when Cherubim swayed the fiery sword and man was turned from Paradise; then followed the judgment of death and the execution of the sentence which we feel yet. *Wretched men that we are, who shall deliver us from this body of death? The grace of God through Jesus Christ our Lord* (Rom. vii 24, 25.). *For the wages of sin are death, but the grace of God is eternal life in Christ Jesus our Lord* (ib. vi 23.), *a blessing etc.*

L. D. S.[3]

3. Abbreviation for *Laus Deo Semper*, "glory to God for ever."

QUESTIONS

1. Compare Hopkins' account of the fall with the account in Genesis iii. How far does Hopkins' account go beyond the brief recital of the facts in Genesis? What justification does Hopkins have in Genesis for his interpretation? Does he add anything to it?
2. Hopkins speaks of God in the first part of his sermon as a "king" or "sovereign" who "entered . . . into a contract with man" and then later has Eve refer to Him as a "tyrant," a "sullen lawgiver,"

and a "landlord . . . a rackrent." What are the differences in connotation and denotation of these various metaphors for God? How
does Hopkins use them to develop the central idea of his sermon?
3. What is the importance for the discourse of the threefold
classification of "things that we may lawfully do"? What other
examples might be given for each category?
4. Does Hopkins give Eve's case a fair hearing? Explain.
5. Hopkins said that when he delivered this sermon he was required
(presumably by his superiors in the church) to "leave out or
reword all passages speaking of God's kingdom as falling." How
would these omissions affect the central idea and the forcefulness
of the sermon?

JOHN DONNE

Let Me Wither

Let me wither and wear out mine age in a discomfortable, in an
unwholesome, in a penurious prison, and so pay my debts with my
bones, and recompense the wastefulness of my youth, with the beg-
gary of mine age; Let me wither in a spittle under sharp, and foul,
and infamous diseases, and so recompense the wantonness of my
youth, with that loathsomeness in mine age; yet if God withdraw
not his spiritual blessings, his grace, his patience, If I can call my
suffering his doing, my passion his action, All this that is temporal,
is but a caterpiller got into one corner of my garden, but a mildew
fallen upon one acre of my corn; The body of all, the substance of
all is safe, as long as the soul is safe. But when I shall trust to that,
which we call a good spirit, and God shall deject, and impoverish,
and evacuate that spirit, when I shall rely upon a moral constancy, and God shall shake, and enfeeble, and enervate, destroy
and demolish that constancy; when I shall think to refresh my self
in the serenity and sweet air of a good conscience, and God shall
call up the damps and vapors of hell itself, and spread a cloud of
diffidence, and an impenetrable crust of desperation upon my conscience; when health shall fly from me, and I shall lay hold upon
riches to succor me, and comfort me in my sickness, and riches
shall fly from me, and I shall snatch after favor, and good
opinion, to comfort me in my poverty; when even this good opinion
shall leave me, and calumnies and misinformations shall prevail
against me; when I shall need peace, because there is none but thou,
O Lord, that should stand for me, and then shall find, that all the
wounds that I have, come from thy hand, all the arrows that stick in
me, from thy quiver; when I shall see, that because I have given my
self to my corrupt nature, thou hast changed thine; and because I·
am all evil toward thee, therefore thou hast given over being good

toward me; When it comes to this height, that the fever is not in the humors, but in the spirits,[1] that mine enemy is not an imaginary enemy, fortune, nor a transitory enemy, malice in great persons, but a real, and an irresistible, and an inexorable, and an everlasting enemy, The Lord of Hosts himself, The Almighty God himself, the Almighty God himself only knows the weight of this affliction, and except he put in that *pondus gloriae*, that exceeding weight of an eternal glory, with his own hand, into the other scale, we are weighed down, we are swallowed up, irreparably, irrevocably, irrecoverably, irremediably.

1. Not in one of the four chief fluids of the body or "humors" (blood, yellow bile, phlegm, and black bile), but in the more subtle fluids.

QUESTIONS

Both Hopkins and Donne are more famous as poets than as preachers, yet all that any author writes will in one way or another bear the stamp of his thought and personality. Read the following poems, one by Donne, one by Hopkins, and compare the poems to sermons. Does the conception of God suggested by each poem resemble that in the sermon by the same author? Do the poems accomplish any of the same purposes as the sermons? Are the sermons "poetic" in any way? What differences arise from the fact that in the sermons both are speaking to congregations, in the poems both are addressing God?

Thou art indeed just, Lord, if I contend
With thee; but, sir, so what I plead is just.
Why do sinners' ways prosper? and why must
Disappointment all I endeavour end?
    Wert thou my enemy, O thou my friend,
How wouldst thou worse, I wonder, than thou dost
Defeat, thwart me? Oh, the sots and thralls of lust
Do in spare hours more thrive than I that spend,
Sir, life upon thy cause. See, banks and brakes
Now, leavèd how thick! lacèd they are again
With fretty chervil, look, and fresh wind shakes
Them; birds build—but not I build; no, but strain,
Time's eunuch, and not breed one work that wakes.
Mine, O thou lord of life, send my roots rain.
                                              —GERARD MANLEY HOPKINS

Batter my heart, three person'd God; for, you
As yet but knocke, breathe, shine, and seeke to mend.
That I may rise, and stand, o'erthrow mee, and bend
Your force, to breake, blowe, burn and make me new.
I, like an usurpt towne, to another due,
Labour to admit you, but Oh, to no end,
Reason your viceroy in mee, mee should defend,
But is captiv'd, and proves weake or untrue.

Yet dearely I love you, and would be loved faine,
But am bethroth'd unto your enemie;
Divorce mee, untie, or breake that knot againe,
Take mee to you, imprison mee, for I
Except you enthrall mee, never shall be free,
Nor ever chast, except you ravish mee.

—JOHN DONNE

JONATHAN EDWARDS

Sinners in the Hands of an Angry God[1]

Their foot shall slide in due time.[2]
—DEUT. xxxii. 35

In this verse is threatened the vengeance of God on the wicked unbelieving Israelites, who were God's visible people, and who lived under the means of grace; but who, notwithstanding all God's wonderful works towards them, remained (as ver. 28.)[3] void of counsel, having no understanding in them. Under all the cultivations of heaven, they brought forth bitter and poisonous fruit; as in the two verses next preceding the text. The expression I have chosen for my text, *Their foot shall slide in due time*, seems to imply the following things, relating to the punishment and destruction to which these wicked Israelites were exposed.

1. That they were always exposed to *destruction*; as one that stands or walks in slippery places is always exposed to fall. This is implied in the manner of their destruction coming upon them, being represented by their foot sliding. The same is expressed, Psalm lxxiii. 18. "Surely thou didst set them in slippery places; thou castedst them down into destruction."

2. It implies that they were always exposed to sudden unexpected destruction. As he that walks in slippery places is every moment liable to fall, he cannot foresee one moment whether he shall stand or fall the next; and when he does fall, he falls at once without warning: Which is also expressed in Psalm lxxiii. 18, 19. "Surely thou didst set them in slippery places; thou castedst them down into destruction. How are they brought into desolation as in a moment!"

3. Another thing implied is, that they are liable to fall of *themselves*, without being thrown down by the hand of another; as he

1. Only the first part of the sermon is printed here; the "application" is omitted.
2. The complete verse reads: "To me belongeth vengeance, and recompence; their foot shall slide in due time: for the day of their calamity is at hand, and the things that shall come upon them make haste." It occurs in the middle of a long denunciatory "song" spoken by Moses to the Israelites.
3. Verse 28: "For they are a nation void of counsel, neither is there any understanding in them."

that stands or walks on slippery ground needs nothing but his own weight to throw him down.

4. That the reason why they are not fallen already, and do not fall now, is only that God's appointed time is not come. For it is said, that when that due time, or appointed time comes, *their foot shall slide.* Then they shall be left to fall, as they are inclined by their own weight. God will not hold them up in these slippery places any longer, but will let them go; and then, at that very instant, they shall fall into destruction; as he that stands on such slippery declining ground, on the edge of a pit, he cannot stand alone, when he is let go he immediately falls and is lost.

The observation from the words that I would now insist upon is this—"There is nothing that keeps wicked men at any one moment out of hell, but the mere pleasure of God"—By the *mere* pleasure of God, I mean his *sovereign* pleasure, his arbitrary will, restrained by no obligation, hindered by no manner of difficulty, any more than if nothing else but God's mere will had in the least degree, or in any respect whatsoever, any hand in the preservation of wicked men one moment. The truth of this observation may appear by the following considerations.

1. There is no want of *power* in God to cast wicked men into hell at any moment. Men's hands cannot be strong when God rises up. The strongest have no power to resist him, nor can any deliver out of his hands. He is not only able to cast wicked men into hell, but he can most easily do it. Sometimes an earthly prince meets with a great deal of difficulty to subdue a rebel, who has found means to fortify himself, and has made himself strong by the numbers of his followers. But it is not so with God. There is no fortress that is any defense from the power of God. Though hand join in hand, and vast multitudes of God's enemies combine and associate themselves, they are easily broken in pieces. They are as great heaps of light chaff before the whirlwind; or large quantities of dry stubble before devouring flames. We find it easy to tread on and crush a worm that we see crawling on the earth; so it is easy for us to cut or singe a slender thread that any thing hangs by: thus easy is it for God, when he pleases, to cast his enemies down to hell. What are we, that we should think to stand before him, at whose rebuke the earth trembles, and before whom the rocks are thrown down?

2. They *deserve* to be cast into hell; so that divine justice never stands in the way, it makes no objection against God's using his power at any moment to destroy them. Yea, on the contrary, justice calls aloud for an infinite punishment of their sins. Divine justice says of the tree that brings forth such grapes of Sodom, "Cut it down, why cumbereth it the ground?" Luke xiii. 7. The sword of divine justice is every moment brandished over their heads, and it is

nothing but the hand of arbitrary mercy, and God's mere will, that holds it back.

3. They are already under a sentence of *condemnation* to hell. They do not only justly deserve to be cast down thither, but the sentence of the law of God, that eternal and immutable rule of righteousness that God has fixed between him and mankind, is gone out against them, and stands against them; so that they are bound over already to hell. John iii. 18. "He that believeth not is condemned already." So that every unconverted man properly belongs to hell; that is his place; from thence he is, John viii. 23. "Ye are from beneath:" And thither he is bound; it is the place that justice, and God's word, and the sentence of his unchangeable law assign to him.

4. They are now the objects of that very same *anger* and wrath of God, that is expressed in the torments of hell. And the reason why they do not go down to hell at each moment, is not because God, in whose power they are, is not then very angry with them; as he is with many miserable creatures now tormented in hell, who there feel and bear the fierceness of his wrath. Yea, God is a great deal more angry with great numbers that are now on earth; yea, doubtless, with many that are now in this congregation, who it may be are at ease, than he is with many of those who are now in the flames of hell.

So that it is not because God is unmindful of their wickedness, and does not resent it, that he does not let loose his hand and cut them off. God is not altogether such an one as themselves, though they may imagine him to be so. The wrath of God burns against them, their damnation does not slumber; the pit is prepared, the fire is made ready, the furnace is now hot, ready to receive them; the flames do now rage and glow. The glittering sword is whet, and held over them, and the pit hath opened its mouth under them.

5. The *devil* stands ready to fall upon them, and seize them as his own, at what moment God shall permit him. They belong to him; he has their souls in his possession, and under his dominion. The scripture represents them as his goods, Luke xi. 12. The devils watch them; they are ever by them at their right hand; they stand waiting for them, like greedy hungry lions that see their prey, and expect to have it, but are for the present kept back. If God should withdraw his hand, by which they are restrained, they would in one moment fly upon their poor souls. The old serpent is gaping for them; hell opens its mouth wide to receive them; and if God should permit it, they would be hastily swallowed up and lost.

6. There are in the souls of wicked men those hellish *principles* reigning, that would presently kindle and flame out into hell fire, if it were not for God's restraints. There is laid in the very nature of carnal men, a foundation for the torments of hell. There are those

corrupt principles, in reigning power in them, and in full possession of them, that are seeds of hell fire. These principles are active and powerful, exceeding violent in their nature, and if it were not for the restraining hand of God upon them, they would soon break out, they would flame out after the same manner as the same corruptions, the same enmity does in the hearts of damned souls, and would beget the same torments as they do in them. The souls of the wicked are in scripture compared to the troubled sea, Isa. lvii. 20. For the present, God restrains their wickedness by his mighty power, as he does the raging waves of the troubled sea, saying, "Hitherto shalt thou come, but no further;" but if God should withdraw that restraining power, it would soon carry all before it. Sin is the ruin and misery of the soul; it is destructive in its nature; and if God should leave it without restraint, there would need nothing else to make the soul perfectly miserable. The corruption of the heart of man is immoderate and boundless in its fury; and while wicked men live here, it is like fire pent up by God's restraints, whereas if it were let loose, it would set on fire the course of nature; and as the heart is now a sink of sin, so if sin was not restrained, it would immediately turn the soul into a fiery oven, or a furnace of fire and brimstone.

7. It is no security to wicked men for one moment, that there are no visible means of death at hand. It is no security to a natural man, that he is now in health, and that he does not see which way he should now immediately go out of the world by any accident, and that there is no visible danger in any respect in his circumstances. The manifold and continual experience of the world in all ages, shows this is no evidence, that a man is not on the very brink of eternity, and that the next step will not be into another world. The unseen, unthought-of ways and means of persons going suddenly out of the world are innumerable and inconceivable. Unconverted men walk over the pit of hell on a rotten covering, and there are innumerable places in this covering so weak that they will not bear their weight, and these places are not seen. The arrows of death fly unseen at noon-day; the sharpest sight cannot discern them. God has so many different unsearchable ways of taking wicked men out of the world and sending them to hell, that there is nothing to make it appear, that God had need to be at the expense of a miracle, or go out of the ordinary course of his providence, to destroy any wicked man, at any moment. All the means that there are of sinners going out of the world, are so in God's hands, and so universally and absolutely subject to his power and determination, that it does not depend at all the less on the mere will of God, whether sinners shall at any moment go to hell, than if means were never made use of, or at all concerned in the case.

8. Natural men's prudence and care to preserve their own lives,

or the care of others to preserve them, do not secure them a moment. To this, divine providence and universal experience do also bear testimony. There is this clear evidence that men's own wisdom is no security to them from death; that if it were otherwise we should see some difference between the wise and politic men of the world, and others, with regard to their liableness to early and unexpected death: but how is it in fact? Eccles. ii. 16. "How dieth the wise man? even as the fool."

9. All wicked men's pains and *contrivance* which they use to escape hell, while they continue to reject Christ, and so remain wicked men, do not secure them from hell one moment. Almost every natural man that hears of hell, flatters himself that he shall escape it; he depends upon himself for his own security; he flatters himself in what he has done, in what he is now doing, or what he intends to do. Every one lays out matters in his own mind how he shall avoid damnation, and flatters himself that he contrives well for himself, and that his schemes will not fail. They hear indeed that there are but few saved, and that the greater part of men that have died heretofore are gone to hell; but each one imagines that he lays out matters better for his own escape than others have done. He does not intend to come to that place of torment; he says within himself, that he intends to take effectual care, and to order matters so for himself as not to fail.

But the foolish children of men miserably delude themselves in their own schemes, and in confidence in their own strength and wisdom; they trust to nothing but a shadow. The greater part of those who heretofore have lived under the same means of grace, and are now dead, are undoubtedly gone to hell; and it was not because they were not as wise as those who are now alive: it was not because they did not lay out matters as well for themselves to secure their own escape. If we could speak with them, and inquire of them, one by one, whether they expected, when alive, and when they used to hear about hell, ever to be the subjects of that misery: we doubtless, should hear one and another reply, "No, I never intended to come here: I had laid out matters otherwise in my mind; I thought I should contrive well for myself: I thought my scheme good. I intended to take effectual care; but it came upon me unexpected; I did not look for it at that time, and in that manner; it came as a thief: Death outwitted me: God's wrath was too quick for me. Oh, my cursed foolishness! I was flattering myself, and pleasing myself with vain dreams of what I would do hereafter; and when I was saying, Peace and safety, then suddenly destruction came upon me."

10. God has laid himself under *no* obligation, by any promise to keep any natural man out of hell one moment. God certainly has made no promises either of eternal life, or of any deliverance or

preservation from eternal death, but what are contained in the covenant of grace, the promises that are given in Christ, in whom all the promises are yea and amen. But surely they have no interest in the promises of the covenant of grace who are not the children of the covenant, who do not believe in any of the promises, and have no interest in the Mediator of the covenant.

So that, whatever some have imagined and pretended about promises made to natural men's earnest seeking and knocking, it is plain and manifest, that whatever pains a natural man takes in religion, whatever prayers he makes, till he believes in Christ, God is under no manner of obligation to keep him a moment from eternal destruction.

So that thus it is that natural men are held in the hand of God, over the pit of hell; they have deserved the fiery pit, and are already sentenced to it; and God is dreadfully provoked, his anger is as great towards them as to those that are actually suffering the executions of the fierceness of his wrath in hell, and they have done nothing in the least to appease or abate that anger, neither is God in the least bound by any promise to hold them up one moment; the devil is waiting for them, hell is gaping for them, the flames gather and flash about them, and would fain lay hold on them, and swallow them up; the fire pent up in their own hearts is struggling to break out: and they have no interest in any Mediator, there are no means within reach that can be any security to them. In short, they have no refuge, nothing to take hold of; all that preserves them every moment is in the mere arbitrary will, and uncovenanted, unobliged forbearance of an incensed God.

QUESTIONS

1. Trace the steps by which Edwards gets from his text to his various conclusions about man's state. Are they all logical? What assumptions does he add to those implied by the text in developing his argument? (Before answering these questions you will probably want to check the entire context of the text in Deuteronomy xxxii.)
2. What kinds of evidence does Edwards use in supporting his argument? Are they equally valid?
3. How do the concrete details, the imagery, and the metaphors that Edwards uses contribute to the effectiveness of his argument?
4. One might make the assumption that a society's conception of hell reflects, at least indirectly, some of that society's positive values. What positive values are reflected in Edwards' picture of hell?
5. What can you deduce about the nature of the congregations that Edwards and Hopkins (pp. 1094–1099) are preaching to? About differences between the two men?
6. One of his pupils described Edwards' delivery: "His appearance

in the desk was with a good grace, and his delivery easy, natural and very solemn. He had not a strong, loud voice, but appeared with such gravity and solemnity, and spake with such distinctness and precision, his words were so full of ideas, set in such a plain and striking light, that few speakers have been so able to demand the attention of an audience as he. His words often discovered a great degree of inward fervor, without much noise or external emotion, and fell with great weight on the minds of his hearers. He made but little motion of his head or hands in the desk, but spake as to discover the motion of his own heart, which tended in the most natural and effectual manner to move and affect others." Would this manner of delivery be effective for the sermon printed here? Explain.

SÖREN KIERKEGAARD
The Knight of Faith

I candidly admit that in my practice I have not found any reliable example of the knight of faith, though I would not therefore deny that every second man may be such an example. I have been trying, however, for several years to get on the track of this, and all in vain. People commonly travel around the world to see rivers and mountains, new stars, birds of rare plumage, queerly deformed fishes, ridiculous breeds of men—they abandon themselves to the bestial stupor which gapes at existence, and they think they have seen something. This does not interest me. But if I knew where there was such a knight of faith, I would make a pilgrimage to him on foot, for this prodigy interests me absolutely. I would not let go of him for an instant, every moment I would watch to see how he managed to make the movements, I would regard myself as secured for life, and would divide my time between looking at him and practicing the exercises myself, and thus would spend all my time admiring him. As was said, I have not found any such person, but I can well think him. Here he is. Acquaintance made, I am introduced to him. The moment I set eyes on him I instantly push him from me, I myself leap backwards, I clasp my hands and say half aloud, "Good Lord, is this the man? Is it really he? Why, he looks like a tax collector!" However, it is the man after all. I draw closer to him, watching his least movements to see whether there might not be visible a little heterogeneous fractional telegraphic message from the infinite, a glance, a look, a gesture, a note of sadness, a smile, which betrayed the infinite in its heterogeneity with the finite. No! I examine his figure from tip to toe to see if there might not be a cranny through which the infinite was peeping. No! He is solid through and through. His tread? It is vigorous, belonging entirely to finiteness; no smartly dressed townsman who walks out to Fresberg on a Sunday afternoon treads the ground more firmly, he belongs entirely to the world, no Philistine more so. One can discover nothing of that aloof and superior nature whereby one recognizes the knight of the infinite. He takes delight in everything, and whenever one sees him taking part in a particular pleasure, he does it with the persistence which is the mark of the earthly man whose soul is absorbed in such things. He tends to his work. So when one looks at him one might suppose that he was a clerk who had lost his soul in an intricate system of bookkeeping, so precise is he. He takes a holiday on Sunday. He goes to church. No heavenly glance or any other token of the incommensurable betrays him; if one did not know him, it would be impossible to distinguish him from the rest of the congregation, for his healthy and vigorous hymn singing proves at the most that he has a good chest. In the afternoon he walks to the forest. He takes delight in everything he sees, in the human swarm, in the new omnibuses, in the water of the Sound; when one meets him on the Beach Road one might suppose he was a shopkeeper taking his fling, that's just the way he disports himself, for he is not a poet, and I have sought in vain to detect in him the poetic incommensurability. Toward evening he walks home, his gait is as indefatigable as that of the postman. On his way he reflects that his wife has surely a special little warm dish prepared for him, e.g. a calf's head roasted, garnished with vegetables. If he were to meet a man like-minded, he could continue as far as East Gate to discourse with him about that dish, with a passion befitting a hotel chef. As it happens, he hasn't four pence to his name, and yet he fully and firmly believes that his wife has that dainty dish for him. If she had it, it would then be an invidious sight for superior people and an inspiring one for the plain man, to see him eat; for his appetite is greater than Esau's. His wife hasn't it—strangely enough, it is quite the same to him. On the way he comes past a building site and runs across another man. They talk together for a moment. In the twinkling of an eye he erects a new building, he has at his disposition all the powers necessary for it. The stranger leaves him with the thought that he certainly was a capitalist, while my admired knight thinks, "Yes, if the money were needed, I dare say I could get it." He lounges at an open window and looks out on the square on which he lives; he is interested in everything that goes on, in a rat which slips under the curb, in the children's play, and this with the nonchalance of a girl of sixteen. And yet he is no genius, for in vain I have sought in him the incommensurability of genius. In the evening he smokes his pipe; to look at him one would swear that it was the grocer over the way vegetating in the twilight. He lives as carefree as a ne'er-do-well, and yet he buys up the acceptable time at the dearest price, for he does not do the least thing except by virtue of the absurd. And yet, and yet—actually I could become dubious over it, for envy if for no other reason—this man has made and every instant is making the movements of infinity. With infinite resignation he has drained the cup of life's profound sadness, he knows the bliss of the infinite, he senses the pain of renouncing everything, the dearest things he possesses in the world, and yet finiteness tastes to him just as good as to one who never knew anything higher, for his continuance in the finite did not bear a trace of the cowed and fearful spirit produced by the process of training; and yet he has the sense of security in enjoying it, as though the finite life were the surest thing of all. And yet, and yet the whole earthly form he exhibits is a new creation by virtue of the absurd. He resigned everything infinitely, and then he grasped everything again by virtue of the absurd. He constantly makes the movements of infinity, but he does this with such correctness and assurance that he constantly gets the finite out of it, and there is not a second when one has a notion of anything else. It is supposed to be the most difficult task for a dancer to leap into a definite posture in such a way that there is not a second when he is grasping after the posture, but by the leap itself he stands fixed in that posture. Perhaps no dancer can do it—that is what this knight does. Most people live dejectedly in wordly sorrow and joy; they are the ones who sit along the wall and do not join in the dance. The knights of infinity are dancers and possess elevation. They make the movements upward, and fall down again; and this too is no mean pastime, nor ungraceful to behold. But whenever they fall down they are not able at once to assume the posture, they vacillate an instant, and this vacillation shows that after all they are strangers in the world. This is more or less strikingly evident in proportion to the art they possess, but even the most artistic knights cannot altogether conceal this vacillation. One need not look at them when they are up in the air, but only the instant they touch or have touched the ground—then one recognizes them. But to be able to fall down in such a way that the same second it looks as if one were standing and walking, to transform the leap of life into a walk, absolutely to express the sublime in the pedestrian—that only the knight of faith can do—and this is the one and only prodigy.

SIMONE WEIL
Spiritual Autobiography[1]

P.S. To Be Read First.

This letter is fearfully long—but as there is no question of an answer—especially as I shall doubtless have gone before it reaches you—you have years ahead of you in which to read it if you care to. Read it all the same, one day or another.

From Marseilles, about May 15 [1942]

Father,[2]

Before leaving I want to speak to you again, it may be the last time perhaps, for over there I shall probably send you only my news from time to time just so as to have yours.

I told you that I owed you an enormous debt. I want to try to tell you exactly what it consists of. I think that if you could really understand what my spiritual state is you would not be at all sorry that you did not lead me to baptism. But I do not know if it is possible for you to understand this.

You neither brought me the Christian inspiration nor did you bring me to Christ; for when I met you there was no longer any need; it had been done without the intervention of any human being. If it had been otherwise, if I had not already been won, not only implicitly but consciously, you would have given me nothing, because I should have received nothing from you. My friendship for you would have been a reason for me to refuse your message, for I should have been afraid of the possibilities of error and illusion which human influence in the divine order is likely to involve.

I may say that never at any moment in my life have I 'sought for God.' For this reason, which is probably too subjective, I do not like this expression and it strikes me as false. As soon as I reached adolescence, I saw the problem of God as a problem the data of which could not be obtained here below, and I decided that the only way of being sure not to reach a wrong solution, which seemed to me the greatest possible evil, was to leave it alone. So I left it alone. I neither affirmed nor denied anything. It seemed to me useless to solve the problem, for I thought that, being in this world, our business was to adopt the best attitude with regard to the problems of this world, and that such an attitude did not depend upon the solution of the problem of God.

This held good as far as I was concerned at any rate, for I never

---

1. From *Waiting for God*, 1951.
2. The Reverend Father Perrin, a Dominican who had endeavored to bring Simone Weil into the Roman Catholic Church.

hesitated in my choice of an attitude; I always adopted the Christian attitude as the only possible one. I might say that I was born, I grew up, and I always remained within the Christian inspiration. While the very name of God had no part in my thoughts, with regard to the problems of this world and this life I shared the Christian conception in an explicit and rigorous manner, with the most specific notions it involves. Some of these notions have been part of my outlook for as far back as I can remember. With others I know the time and manner of their coming and the form under which they imposed themselves upon me.

For instance I never allowed myself to think of a future state, but I always believed that the instant of death is the center and object of life. I used to think that, for those who live as they should, it is the instant when, for an infinitesimal fraction of time, pure truth, naked, certain, and eternal enters the soul. I may say that I never desired any other good for myself. I thought that the life leading to this good is not only defined by a code of morals common to all, but that for each one it consists of a succession of acts and events strictly personal to him, and so essential that he who leaves them on one side never reaches the goal. The notion of vocation was like this for me. I saw that the carrying out of a vocation differed from the actions dictated by reason or inclination in that it was due to an impulse of an essentially and manifestly different order; and not to follow such an impulse when it made itself felt, even if it demanded impossibilities, seemed to me the greatest of all ills. Hence my conception of obedience; and I put this conception to the test when I entered the factory and stayed on there, even when I was in that state of intense and uninterrupted misery about which I recently told you. The most beautiful life possible has always seemed to me to be one where everything is determined, either by the pressure of circumstances or by impulses such as I have just mentioned and where there is never any room for choice.

At fourteen I fell into one of those fits of bottomless despair that come with adolescence, and I seriously thought of dying because of the mediocrity of my natural faculties. The exceptional gifts of my brother, who had a childhood and youth comparable to those of Pascal, brought my own inferiority home to me. I did not mind having no visible successes, but what did grieve me was the idea of being excluded from that transcendent kingdom to which only the truly great have access and wherein truth abides. I preferred to die rather than live without that truth. After months of inward darkness, I suddenly had the everlasting conviction that any human being, even though practically devoid of natural faculties, can penetrate to the kingdom of truth reserved for genius, if only he longs for truth and perpetually concentrates all his attention upon its attainment. He thus becomes a genius too, even though for lack of talent his genius cannot be visible from outside. Later on, when the strain of headaches caused the feeble faculties I possess to be invaded by a paralysis, which I was quick to imagine as probably incurable, the same conviction led me to persevere for ten years in an effort of concentrated attention that was practically unsupported by any hope of results.

Under the name of truth I also included beauty, virtue, and every kind of goodness, so that for me it was a question of a conception of the relationship between grace and desire. The conviction that had come to me was that when one hungers for bread one does not receive stones. But at that time I had not read the Gospel.

Just as I was certain that desire has in itself an efficacy in the realm of spiritual goodness whatever its form, I thought it was also possible that it might not be effective in any other realm.

As for the spirit of poverty, I do not remember any moment when it was not in me, although only to that unhappily small extent compatible with my imperfection. I fell in love with Saint Francis of Assisi as soon as I came to know about him. I always believed and hoped that one day Fate would force upon me the condition of a vagabond and a beggar which he embraced freely. Actually I felt the same way about prison.

From my earliest childhood I always had also the Christian idea of love for one's neighbor, to which I gave the name of justice—a name it bears in many passages of the Gospel and which is so beautiful. You know that on this point I have failed seriously several times.

The duty of acceptance in all that concerns the will of God, whatever it may be, was impressed upon my mind as the first and most necessary of all duties from the time when I found it set down in Marcus Aurelius under the form of the *amor fati* of the Stoics. I saw it as a duty we cannot fail in without dishonoring ourselves.

The idea of purity, with all that this word can imply for a Christian, took possession of me at the age of sixteen, after a period of several months during which I had been going through the emotional unrest natural in adolescence. This idea came to me when I was contemplating a mountain landscape and little by little it was imposed upon me in an irresistible manner.

Of course I knew quite well that my conception of life was Christian. That is why it never occurred to me that I could enter the Christian community. I had the idea that I was born inside. But to add dogma to this conception of life, without being forced to do so by indisputable evidence, would have seemed to me like a lack of honesty. I should even have thought I was lacking in honesty had I considered the question of the truth of dogma as a problem for myself or even had I simply desired to reach a conclusion on this subject. I have an extremely severe standard for intellectual honesty, so severe that I never met anyone who did not seem to fall short of it in more than one respect; and I am always afraid of failing in it myself.

Keeping away from dogma in this way, I was prevented by a sort of shame from going into churches, though all the same I like being in them. Nevertheless, I had three contacts with Catholicism that really counted.

After my year in the factory, before going back to teaching, I had been taken by my parents to Portugal, and while there I left them to go alone to a little village. I was, as it were, in pieces, soul and body. That contact with affliction had killed my youth. Until then I had not had any experience of affliction, unless we count my own, which, as it was my own, seemed to me, to have little importance, and which moreover was only a partial affliction, being biological and not social. I knew quite well that there was a great deal of affliction in the world, I was obsessed with the idea, but I had not had prolonged and first-hand experience of it. As I worked in the factory, indistinguishable to all eyes, including my own, from the anonymous mass, the affliction of others entered into my flesh and my soul. Nothing separated me from it, for I had really forgotten my past and I looked forward to no future, finding it difficult to imagine the possibility of surviving all the fatigue. What I went through there marked me in so lasting a manner that still today when any human being, whoever he may be and in whatever circumstances, speaks to me without brutality, I cannot help having the impression that there must be a mistake and that unfortunately the mistake will in all probability disappear. There I received forever the mark of a slave, like the branding of the red-hot iron the Romans put on the foreheads of their most despised slaves. Since then I have always regarded myself as a slave.

In this state of mind then, and in a wretched condition physically, I entered the little Portuguese village, which, alas, was very wretched too, on the very day of the festival of its patron saint. I was alone. It was the evening and there was a full moon over the sea. The wives of the fishermen were, in procession, making a tour of all the ships, carrying candles and singing what must certainly be very ancient hymns of a heart-rending sadness. Nothing can give any idea of it. I have never heard anything so poignant unless it were the song of the boatmen on the Volga. There the conviction was suddenly borne in upon me that Christianity is pre-eminently the religion of slaves, that slaves cannot help belonging to it, and I among others.

In 1937 I had two marvelous days at Assisi. There, alone in the little twelfth-century Romanesque chapel of Santa Maria degli Angeli, an incomparable marvel of purity where Saint Francis often used to pray, something stronger than I was compelled me for the first time in my life to go down on my knees.

In 1938 I spent ten days at Solesmes, from Palm Sunday to Easter Tuesday, following all the liturgical services. I was suffering from splitting headaches; each sound hurt me like a blow; by an extreme effort of concentration I was able to rise above this wretched flesh, to leave it to suffer by itself, heaped up in a corner, and to find a pure and perfect joy in the unimaginable beauty of the chanting and the words. This experience enabled me by analogy to get a better understanding of the possibility of loving divine love in the midst of affliction. It goes without saying that in the course of these services the thought of the Passion of Christ entered into my being once and for all.

There was a young English Catholic there from whom I gained my first idea of the supernatural power of the sacraments because of the truly angelic radiance with which he seemed to be clothed after going to communion. Chance—for I always prefer saying chance rather than Providence—made of him a messenger to me. For he told me of that existence of those English poets of the seventeenth century who are named metaphysical. In reading them later on, I discovered the poem of which I read you what is unfortunately a very inadequate translation. It is called "Love".[3] I learned it by heart. Often, at the culminating point of a violent headache, I make myself say it over, concentrating all my attention upon it and clinging with all my soul to the tenderness it enshrines. I used to think I was merely reciting it as a beautiful poem, but without my knowing it the recitation had the virtue of a prayer. It was during one of these recitations that, as I told you, Christ himself came down and took possession of me.

In my arguments about the insolubility of the problem of God I had never foreseen the possibility of that, of a real contact, person to person, here below, between a human being and God. I had

---

3. **By George Herbert:**

> Love bade me welcome: yet my soul drew back,
>   Guilty of dust and sin.
> But quick-eyed Love, observing me grow slack
>   From my first entrance in,
> Drew nearer to me, sweetly questioning
>   If I lacked anything.
>
> "A guest," I answered, "worthy to be here":
>   Love said, "You shall be he."
> "I, the unkind, ungrateful? Ah, my dear,
>   I cannot look on thee."
> Love took my hand, and smiling did reply,
>   "Who made the eyes but I?"
>
> "Truth, Lord; but I have marred them; let my shame
>   Go where it doth deserve."
> "And know you not," says Love, "who bore the blame?"
>   "My dear, then I will serve."
> "You must sit down," says Love, "and taste my meat."
>   So I did sit and eat.

vaguely heard tell of things of this kind, but I had never believed in them. In the *Fioretti* the accounts of apparitions rather put me off if anything, like the miracles in the Gospel. Moreover, in this sudden possession of me by Christ, neither my senses nor my imagination had any part; I only felt in the midst of my suffering the presence of a love, like that which one can read in the smile on a beloved face.

I had never read any mystical works because I had never felt any call to read them. In reading as in other things I have always striven to practice obedience. There is nothing more favorable to intellectual progress, for as far as possible I only read what I am hungry for at the moment when I have an appetite for it, and then I do not read, I *eat*. God in his mercy had prevented me from reading the mystics, so that it should be evident to me that I had not invented this absolutely unexpected contact.

Yet I still half refused, not my love but my intelligence. For it seemed to me certain, and I still think so today, that one can never wrestle enough with God if one does so out of pure regard for the truth. Christ likes us to prefer truth to him because, before being Christ, he is truth. If one turns aside from him to go toward truth, one will not go far before falling into his arms.

After this I came to feel that Plato was a mystic, that all the *Iliad* is bathed in Christian light, and that Dionysus and Osiris are in a certain sense Christ himself; and my love was thereby redoubled.

I never wondered whether Jesus was or was not the Incarnation of God; but in fact I was incapable of thinking of him without thinking of him as God.

In the spring of 1940 I read the *Bhagavad-Gita*. Strange to say it was in reading those marvelous words, words with such a Christian sound, put into the mouth of an incarnation of God, that I came to feel strongly that we owe an allegiance to religious truth which is quite different from the admiration we accord to a beautiful poem; it is something far more categorical.

Yet I did not believe it to be possible for me to consider the question of baptism. I felt that I could not honestly give up my opinions concerning the non-Christian religions and concerning Israel—and as a matter of fact time and meditation have only served to strengthen them—and I thought that this constituted an absolute obstacle. I did not imagine it as possible that a priest could dream of granting me baptism. If I had not met you, I should never have considered the problem of baptism as a practical problem.

During all this time of spiritual progress I had never prayed. I was afraid of the power of suggestion that is in prayer—the very power for which Pascal recommends it. Pascal's method seems to me one of the worst for attaining faith.

Contact with you was not able to persuade me to pray. On the contrary I thought the danger was all the greater, since I also had to beware of the power of suggestion in my friendship with you. At the same time I found it very difficult not to pray and not to tell you so. Moreover I knew I could not tell you without completely misleading you about myself. At that time I should not have been able to make you understand.

Until last September I had never once prayed in all my life, at least not in the literal sense of the word. I had never said any words to God, either out loud or mentally. I had never pronounced a liturgical prayer. I had occasionally recited the *Salve Regina*,[4] but only as a beautiful poem.

Last summer, doing Greek with T——, I went through the Our Father word for word in Greek. We promised each other to learn it by heart. I do not think he ever did so, but some weeks later, as I was turning over the pages of the Gospel, I said to myself that since I had promised to do this thing and it was good, I ought to do it. I did it. The infinite sweetness of this Greek text so took hold of me that for several days I could not stop myself from saying it over all the time. A week afterward I began the vine harvest. I recited the Our Father in Greek every day before work, and I repeated it very often in the vineyard.

Since that time I have made a practice of saying it through once each morning with absolute attention. If during the recitation my attention wanders or goes to sleep, in the minutest degree, I begin again until I have once succeeded in going through it with absolutely pure attention. Sometimes it comes about that I say it again out of sheer pleasure, but I only do it if I really feel the impulse.

The effect of this practice is extraordinary and surprises me every time, for, although I experience it each day, it exceeds my expectation at each repetition.

At times the very first words tear my thoughts from my body and transport it to a place outside space where there is neither perspective nor point of view. The infinity of the ordinary expanses of perception is replaced by an infinity to the second or sometimes the third degree. At the same time, filling every part of this infinity of infinity, there is silence, a silence which is not an absence of sound but which is the object of a positive sensation, more positive than that of sound. Noises, if there are any, only reach me after crossing this silence.

Sometimes, also, during this recitation or at other moments, Christ is present with me in person, but his presence is infinitely more real, more moving, more clear than on that first occasion when he took possession of me.

I should never have been able to take it upon myself to tell you

4. "Hail, Holy Queen," an antiphon the end of the canonical hours.
sung in the Roman Catholic Church at

all this had it not been for the fact that I am going away. And as I am going more or less with the idea of probable death, I do not believe that I have the right to keep it to myself. For after all, the whole of this matter is not a question concerning me myself. It concerns God. I am really nothing in it all. If one could imagine any possibility of error in God, I should think that it had all happened to me by mistake. But perhaps God likes to use castaway objects, waste, rejects. After all, should the bread of the host be moldy, it would become the Body of Christ just the same after the priest had consecrated it. Only it cannot refuse, while we can disobey. It sometimes seems to me that when I am treated in so merciful a way, every sin on my part must be a mortal sin. And I am constantly committing them.

I have told you that you are like a father and brother at the same time to me. But these words only express an analogy. Perhaps at bottom they only correspond to a feeling of affection, of gratitude and admiration. For as to the spiritual direction of my soul, I think that God himself has taken it in hand from the start and still looks after it.

That does not prevent me from owing you the greatest debt of gratitude that I could ever have incurred toward any human being. This is exactly what it consists of.

First you once said to me at the beginning of our relationship some words that went to the bottom of my soul. You said: "Be very careful, because if you should pass over something important through your own fault it would be a pity."

That made me see intellectual honesty in a new light. Till then I had only thought of it as opposed to faith; your words made me think that perhaps, without my knowing it, there were in me obstacles to the faith, impure obstacles, such as prejudices, habits. I felt that after having said to myself for so many years simply: "Perhaps all that is not true," I ought, without ceasing to say it —I still take care to say it very often now—to join it to the opposite formula, namely: "Perhaps all that is true," and to make them alternate.

At the same time, in making the problem of baptism a practical problem for me, you have forced me to face the whole question of the faith, dogma, and the sacraments, obliging me to consider them closely and at length with the fullest possible attention, making me see them as things toward which I have obligations that I have to discern and perform. I should never have done this otherwise and it is indispensable for me to do it.

But the greatest blessing you have brought me is of another order. In gaining my friendship by your charity (which I have never met anything to equal), you have provided me with a source of the most compelling and pure inspiration that is to be found among human things. For nothing among human things has such power to keep our gaze fixed ever more intensely upon God, than friendship for the friends of God.

Nothing better enables me to measure the breadth of your charity than the fact that you bore with me for so long and with such gentleness. I may seem to be joking, but that is not the case. It is true that you have not the same motives as I have myself (those about which I wrote to you the other day), for feeling hatred and repulsion toward me. But all the same I feel that your patience with me can only spring from a supernatural generosity.

I have not been able to avoid causing you the greatest disappointment it was in my power to cause you. But up to now, although I have often asked myself the question during prayer, during Mass, or in the light of the radiancy that remains in the soul after Mass, I have never once had, even for a moment, the feeling that God wants me to be in the Church. I have never even once had a feeling of uncertainty. I think that at the present time we can finally conclude that he does not want me in the Church. Do not have any regrets about it.

He does not want it so far at least. But unless I am mistaken I should say that it is his will that I should stay outside for the future too, except perhaps at the moment of death. Yet I am always ready to obey any order, whatever it may be. I should joyfully obey the order to go to the very center of hell and to remain there eternally. I do not mean, of course, that I have a preference for orders of this nature. I am not perverse like that.

Christianity should contain all vocations without exception since it is catholic. In consequence the Church should also. But in my eyes Christianity is catholic by right but not in fact. So many things are outside it, so many things that I love and do not want to give up, so many things that God loves, otherwise they would not be in existence. All the immense stretches of past centuries, except the last twenty are among them; all the countries inhabited by colored races; all secular life in the white peoples' countries; in the history of these countries, all the traditions banned as heretical, those of the Manicheans and Albigenses for instance; all those things resulting from the Renaissance, too often degraded but not quite without value.

Christianity being catholic by right but not in fact, I regard it as legitimate on my part to be a member of the Church by right but not in fact, not only for a time, but for my whole life if need be.

But it is not merely legitimate. So long as God does not give me the certainty that he is ordering me to do anything else, I think it is my duty.

I think, and so do you, that our obligation for the next two or three years, an obligation so strict that we can scarcely fail in it without treason, is to show the public the possibility of a truly incarnated Christianity. In all the history now known there has never been a period in which souls have been in such peril as they are today in every part of the globe. The bronze serpent[5] must be lifted up again so that whoever raises his eyes to it may be saved.

But everything is so closely bound up together that Christianity cannot be really incarnated unless it is catholic in the sense that I have just defined. How could it circulate through the flesh of all the nations of Europe if it did not contain absolutely everything in itself? Except of course falsehood. But in everything that exists there is most of the time more truth than falsehood.

Having so intense and so painful a sense of this urgency, I should betray the truth, that is to say the aspect of truth that I see, if I left the point, where I have been since my birth, at the intersection of Christianity and everything that is not Christianity.

I have always remained at this exact point, on the threshold of the Church, without moving, quite still, ἐν ὑπομένη[6] (it is so much more beautiful a word than *patientia*!); only now my heart has been transported, forever, I hope, into the Blessed Sacrament exposed on the altar.

You see that I am very far from the thoughts that H——, with the best of intentions, attributed to me. I am far also from being worried in any way.

If I am sad, it comes primarily from the permanent sadness that destiny has imprinted forever upon my emotions, where the greatest and purest joys can only be superimposed and that at the price of a great effort of attention. It comes also from my miserable and continual sins; and from all the calamities of our time and of all those of all the past centuries.

I think that you should understand why I have always resisted you, if in spite of being a priest you can admit that a genuine vocation might prevent anyone from entering the Church.

Otherwise a barrier of incomprehension will remain between us, whether the error is on my part or on yours. This would grieve me from the point of view of my friendship for you, because in that case the result of all these efforts and desires, called forth by your charity toward me, would be a disappointment for you. Moreover, although it is not my fault, I should not be able to help feeling guilty of ingratitude. For, I repeat, my debt to you is beyond all measure.

I should like to draw your attention to one point. It is that there

---

5. "And Moses made a serpent of brass, and put it upon a pole, and it came to pass, that if a serpent had bit- ten any man, when he beheld the serpent of brass, he lived" (Numbers xxi.9).

6. "To abide patiently."

is an absolutely insurmountable obstacle to the Incarnation of Christianity. It is the use of the two little words *anathema sit*.[7] It is not their existence, but the way they have been employed up till now. It is that also which prevents me from crossing the threshold of the Church. I remain beside all those things that cannot enter the Church, the universal repository, on account of those two little words. I remain beside them all the more because my own intelligence is numbered among them.

The Incarnation of Christianity implies a harmonious solution of the problem of the relations between the individual and the collective. Harmony in the Pythagorean sense; the just balance of contraries. This solution is precisely what men are thirsting for today

The position of the intelligence is the key to this harmony, because the intelligence is a specifically and rigorously individual thing. This harmony exists wherever the intelligence, remaining in its place, can be exercised without hindrance and can reach the complete fulfillment of its function. That is what Saint Thomas says admirably of all the parts of the soul of Christ, with reference to his sensitiveness to pain during the crucifixion.

The special function of the intelligence requires total liberty, implying the right to deny everything, and allowing of no domination. Wherever it usurps control there is an excess of individualism. Wherever it is hampered or uneasy there is an oppressive collectivism, or several of them.

The Church and the State should punish it, each one in its own way, when it advocates actions of which they disapprove. When it remains in the region of purely theoretical speculation they still have the duty, should occasion arise, to put the public on their guard, by every effective means, against the danger of the practical influence certain speculations might have upon the conduct of life. But whatever these theoretical speculations may be, the Church and the State have no right either to try to stifle them or to inflict any penalty material or moral upon their authors. Notably, they should not be deprived of the sacraments if they desire them. For, whatever they may have said, even if they have publicly denied the existence of God, they may not have committed any sin. In such a case the Church should declare that they are in error, but it should not demand of them anything whatever in the way of a disavowal of what they have said, nor should it deprive them of the Bread of Life.

A collective body is the guardian of dogma; and dogma is an object of contemplation for love, faith, and intelligence, three strictly individual faculties. Hence, almost since the beginning, the individual has been ill at ease in Christianity, and this uneasiness

---

7. "Let there be anathema" (a ban, curse, or excommunication).

has been notably one of the intelligence. This cannot be denied.

Christ himself who is Truth itself, when he was speaking before an assembly such as a council, did not address it in the same language as he used in an intimate conversation with his well-beloved friend, and no doubt before the Pharisees he might easily have been accused of contradiction and error. For by one of those laws of nature, which God himself respects, since he has willed them from all eternity, there are two languages that are quite distinct although made up of the same words; there is the collective language and there is the individual one. The Comforter whom Christ sends us, the Spirit of truth, speaks one or other of these languages, whichever circumstances demand, and by a necessity of their nature there is not agreement between them.

When genuine friends of God—such as was Eckhart to my way of thinking—repeat words they have heard in secret amidst the silence of the union of love, and these words are in disagreement with the teaching of the Church, it is simply that the language of the market place is not that of the nuptial chamber.

Everybody knows that really intimate conversation is only possible between two or three. As soon as there are six or seven, collective language begins to dominate. That is why it is a complete misinterpretation to apply to the Church the words "Wheresoever two or three are gathered together in my name, there am I in the midst of them." Christ did not say two hundred, or fifty, or ten. He said two or three. He said precisely that he always forms the third in the intimacy of the tête-à-tête.

Christ made promises to the Church, but none of these promises has the force of the expression "Thy Father who seeth in secret." The word of God is the secret word. He who has not heard this word, even if he adheres to all the dogmas taught by the Church, has no contact with truth. The function of the Church as the collective keeper of dogma is indispensable. She has the right and the duty to punish those who make a clear attack upon her within the specific range of this function, by depriving them of the sacraments.

Thus, although I know practically nothing of this business, I incline to think provisionally that she was right to punish Luther.

But she is guilty of an abuse of power when she claims to force love and intelligence to model their language upon her own. This abuse of power is not of God. It comes from the natural tendency of every form of collectivism, without exception, to abuse power.

The image of the Mystical Body of Christ[8] is very attractive. But I consider the importance given to this image today as one of the most serious signs of our degeneration. For our true dignity is not to

---

8. The Church as the community of those baptized into the life of Christ.

be parts of a body, even though it be a mystical one, even though it be that of Christ. It consists in this, that in the state of perfection, which is the vocation of each one of us, we no longer live in ourselves, but Christ lives in us; so that through our perfection Christ in his integrity and in his indivisible unity, becomes in a sense each one of us, as he is completely in each host. The hosts are not a *part* of his body.

This present-day importance of the image of the Mystical Body shows how wretchedly susceptible Christians are to outside influences. Undoubtedly there is real intoxication in being a member of the Mystical Body of Christ. But today a great many other mystical bodies, which have not Christ for their head, produce an intoxication in their members that to my way of thinking is of the same order.

As long as it is through obedience, I find sweetness in my deprivation of the joy of membership in the Mystical Body of Christ. For if God is willing to help me, I may thus bear witness that without this joy one can nevertheless be faithful to Christ unto death. Social enthusiasms have such power today, they raise people so effectively to the supreme degree of heroism in suffering and death, that I think it is as well that a few sheep should remain outside the fold in order to bear witness that the love of Christ is essentially something different.

The Church today defends the cause of the indefeasible rights of the individual against collective oppression, of liberty of thought against tyranny. But these are causes readily embraced by those who find themselves momentarily to be the least strong. It is their only way of perhaps one day becoming the strongest. That is well known.

You may perhaps be offended by this idea. You are not the Church. During the periods of the most atrocious abuse of power committed by the Church, there must have been some priests like you among the others. Your good faith is not a guarantee, even were it shared by all your Order. You cannot foresee what turn things may take.

In order that the present attitude of the Church should be effective and that she should really penetrate like a wedge into social existence, she would have to say openly that she had changed or wished to change. Otherwise who could take her seriously when they remembered the Inquisition? My friendship for you, which I extend through you to all your Order, makes it very painful for me to bring this up. But it existed. After the fall of the Roman Empire, which had been totalitarian, it was the Church that was the first to establish a rough sort of totalitarianism in Europe in the thirteenth century, after the war with the Albigenses. This tree bore much fruit.

And the motive power of this totalitarianism was the use of those two little words: *anathema sit.*

It was moreover by a judicious transposition of this use that all the parties which in our own day have founded totalitarian regimes were shaped. This is a point of history I have specially studied.

I must give you the impression of a Luciferian pride in speaking thus of a great many matters that are too high for me and about which I have no right to understand anything. It is not my fault. Ideas come and settle in my mind by mistake, then, realizing their mistake, they absolutely insist on coming out. I do not know where they come from, or what they are worth, but, whatever the risk, I do not think I have the right to prevent this operation.

Good-by, I wish you all possible good things except the cross; for I do not love my neighbor as myself, you particularly, as you have noticed. But Christ granted to his well-beloved disciple, and probably to all that disciple's spiritual lineage, to come to him not through degradation, defilement, and distress, but in uninterrupted joy, purity, and sweetness. That is why I can allow myself to wish that even if one day you have the honor of dying a violent death for Our Lord, it may be with joy and without any anguish; also that only three of the beatitudes (*mites, mundo corde, pacifici*[9]) will apply to you. All the others involve more or less of suffering.

This wish is not due only to the frailty of human friendship. For, with any human being taken individually, I always find reasons for concluding that sorrow and misfortune do not suit him, either because he seems too mediocre for anything so great or, on the contrary, too precious to be destroyed. One cannot fail more seriously in the second of the two essential commandments. And as to the first, I fail to observe that, in a still more horrible manner, for every time I think of the crucifixion of Christ I commit the sin of envy.

Believe more than ever and forever in my filial and tenderly grateful friendship.

SIMONE WEIL

9. "The meek, the pure in heart, the peace-makers" (Matthew v. 5, 8, 9).

QUESTIONS

1. Weil's account is in the form of a letter to a Catholic priest. In what ways does that fact influence the organization, style, and tone of the piece? Do you think the letter was originally meant to be published? Why or why not?

2. Weil describes "three contacts with Catholicism that really counted." How were these experiences different from each other? What effects of them can you find in attitudes described in other parts of the piece? Why didn't Weil join the Catholic Church?

3. Compare Weil's religious experiences with the religious experience

described by Watts in "The Answer of Religion" pp. 1174–1190.

4. What is Weil's objection to "the two little words anathema sit" ("let there be anathema")? What is the objection to the "image of the Mystical Body of Christ"? How are these objections related to Weil's other views?

5. Both Weil and Sartre (pp. 1156–1165) speak against some traditional religious ideas or beliefs. Are the bases for their objections to certain aspects of traditional religion in any ways the same? Explain.

6. Weil speaks of the differences between "the collective language and . . . the individual one," the "language of the market place" and "that of the nuptial chamber." What is the significance of these differences? Which kind of language does Weil appear to use most throughout the piece?

PAUL TILLICH

The Riddle of Inequality

> For to him who has will more be given; and from him
> who has not, even what he has will be taken away.
> —MARK iv. 25

One day a learned colleague called me up and said to me with angry excitement: "There is a saying in the New Testament which I consider to be one of the most immoral and unjust statements ever made!" And then he started quoting our text: "To him who has will more be given," and his anger increased when he continued: "and from him who has not, even what he has will be taken away." We all, I think, feel offended with him. And we cannot easily ignore the offense by suggesting what *he* suggested—that the words may be due to a misunderstanding of the disciples. It appears at least four times in the gospels with great emphasis. And even more, we can clearly see that the writers of the gospels felt exactly as we do. For them it was a stumbling block, which they tried to interpret in different ways. Probably none of these explanations satisfied them fully, for with this saying of Jesus, we are confronted immediately with the greatest and perhaps most painful riddle of life, that of the inequality of all beings. We certainly cannot hope to solve it when neither the Bible nor any other of the great religions and philosophies was able to do so. But we can do two things: We can show the breadth and the depth of the riddle of inequality and we can try to find a way to live with it, even if it is unsolved.

I

If we hear the words, "to him who has will more be given," we ask ourselves: What *do* we have? And then we may find that much is given to us in terms of external goods, of friends, of intellectual gifts and even of a comparatively high moral level of action. So we can expect that more will be given to us, while we must expect that those who are lacking in all that will lose the little they already have. Even further, according to Jesus' parable, the one talent they have will be given to us who have five or ten talents. We shall be richer because they will be poorer. We may cry out against such an injustice. But we cannot deny that life confirms it abundantly. We cannot deny it, but we can ask the question, do we *really* have what we believe we have so that it cannot be taken from us? It is a question full of anxiety, confirmed by a version of our text rendered by Luke. "From him who has not, even what he *thinks* that he has will be taken away." Perhaps our having of those many things is not the kind of having which is increased. Perhaps the having of few things by the poor ones is the kind of having which makes them grow. In the parable of the talents, Jesus confirms this. Those talents which are used, even with a risk of losing them, are those which we really have; those which we try to preserve without using them for growth are those which we do not really have and which are being taken away from us. They slowly disappear, and suddenly we feel that we have lost these talents, perhaps forever.

Let us apply this to our own life, whether it is long or short. In the memory of all of us many things appear which we had without having them and which were taken away from us. Some of them became lost because of the tragic limitations of life; we had to sacrifice them in order to make other things grow. We all were given childish innocence; but innocence cannot be used and increased. The growth of our lives is possible only because we have sacrificed the original gift of innocence. Nevertheless, sometimes there arises in us a melancholy longing for a purity which has been taken from us. We all were given youthful enthusiasm for many things and aims. But this also cannot be used and increased. Most of the objects of our early enthusiasm must be sacrificed for a few, and the few must be approached with soberness. No maturity is possible without this sacrifice. Yet often a melancholy longing for the lost possibilities and enthusiasm takes hold of us. Innocence and youthful enthusiasm: we had them and had them not. Life itself demanded that they were taken from us.

But there are other things which we had and which were taken from us, because we let them go through our own guilt. Some of us had a deep sensitivity for the wonder of life as it is revealed in nature. Slowly under the pressure of work and social life and the lure of cheap pleasures, we lose the wonder of our earlier years when we felt intense joy and the presence of the mystery of life through the freshness of the young day or the glory of the dying day, the majesty of the mountains or the infinity of the sea, a flower breaking through the soil or a young animal in the perfection of its movements. Perhaps we try to produce such feelings again, but we are empty and do not succeed. We had it and had it not, and it has been taken from us.

Others had the same experience with music, poetry, the great novels and plays. One wanted to devour all of them, one lived in them and created for oneself a life above the daily life. We *had* all this and did not have it; we did not let it grow; our love towards it was not strong enough and so it was taken from us.

Many, especially in this group, remember a time in which the desire to learn to solve the riddles of the universe, to find truth has been the driving force in their lives. They came to college and university, not in order to buy their entrance ticket into the upper middle classes or in order to provide for the preconditions of social and economic success, but they came, driven by the desire for knowledge. They had something and more could have been given to them. But in reality they did not have it. They did not make it grow and so it was taken from them and they finished their academic work in terms of expendiency and indifference towards truth. Their love for truth has left them and in some moments they are sick in their hearts because they realize that what they have lost they may never get back.

We all know that any deeper relation to a human being needs watchfulness and growth, otherwise it is taken away from us. And we cannot get it back. This is a form of having and not having which is the root of innumerable human tragedies. We all know about them. And there is another, the most fundamental kind of having and not having—our having and losing God. Perhaps we were rich towards God in our childhood and beyond it. We may remember the moments in which we felt his ultimate presence. We may remember prayers with an overflowing heart, the encounter with the holy in word and music and holy places. We had communication with God; but it was taken from us because we had it and had it not. We did not let it grow, and so it slowly disappeared leaving an empty space. We became unconcerned, cynical, indifferent, not because we doubted about our religious traditions—such doubt belongs to being rich towards God—but because we turned away from that which once concerned us infinitely.

Such thoughts are a first step in approaching the riddle of inequality. Those who have, receive more if they really have it, if they use it and make it grow. And those who have not, lose what they have because they never had it really.

II

But the question of inequality is not yet answered. For one now asks: Why do some receive more than others in the very beginning, before there is even the possibility of using or wasting our talents? Why does the one servant receive five talents and the other two and the third one? Why is the one born in the slums and the other in a well-to-do suburban family? It does not help to answer that of those to whom much is given much is demanded and little of those to whom little is given. For it is just this inequality of original gifts, internal and external, which arouses our question. Why is it given to one human being to gain so much more out of his being human than to another one? Why is so much given to the one that much *can* be asked of him, while to the other one little is given and little *can* be asked? If this question is asked, not only about individual men but also about classes, races and nations, the everlasting question of political inequality arises, and with it the many ways appear in which men have tried to abolish inequality. In every revolution and in every war, the will to solve the riddle of inequality is a driving force. But neither war nor revolution can remove it. Even if we imagine that in an indefinite future most social inequalities are conquered, three things remain: the inequality of talents in body and mind, the inequality created by freedom and destiny, and the fact that all generations before the time of such equality would be excluded from its blessings. This would be the greatest possible inequality! No! In face of one of the deepest and most torturing problems of life, it is unpermittably shallow and foolish to escape into a social dreamland. We have to live now; we have to live this our life, and we must face today the riddle of inequality.

Let us not confuse the riddle of inequality with the fact that each of us is a unique incomparable self. Certainly our being individuals belongs to our dignity as men. It is given to us and must be used and intensified and not drowned in the gray waters of conformity which threaten us today. One should defend every individuality and the uniqueness of every human self. But one should not believe that this is a way of solving the riddle of inequality. Unfortunately, there are social and political reactionaries who use this confusion in order to justify social injustice. They are at least as foolish as the dreamers of a future removal of inequality. Whoever has seen hospitals, prisons, sweatshops, battlefields, houses for the insane, starvation, family tragedies, moral aberrations should be cured from any confusion of the gift of individuality with the riddle of inequality. He should be cured from any feelings of easy consolation.

III

And now we must make the third step in our attempt to penetrate the riddle of inequality and ask: Why do some use and increase what was given to them, while others do not, so that it is taken from them? Why does God say to the prophet in our Old Testament lesson that the ears and eyes of a nation are made insensible for the divine message?

Is it enough to answer: Because some use their freedom responsibly and do what they ought to do while others fail through their own guilt? Is this answer, which seems so obvious, sufficient? Now let me first say that it *is* sufficient if we apply it to ourselves. Each of us must consider the increase or the loss of what is given to him as a matter of his own responsibility. Our conscience tells us that we cannot put the blame for our losses on anybody or anything else than ourselves.

But if we look at others, this answer is not sufficient. On the contrary: If we applied the judgment which we *must* apply to anyone else we would be like the Pharisee in Jesus' parable. You cannot tell somebody who comes to you in distress about himself: Use what has been given to you; for he may come to you just because he is unable to do so! And you cannot tell those who are in despair about what they are: Be something else; for this is just what despair means—the inability of getting rid of oneself. You cannot tell those who did not conquer the destructive influences of their surroundings and were driven into crime and misery that they should have been stronger; for it was just of this strength they had been deprived by heritage or environment. Certainly they all are men, and to all of them freedom is given; but they all are also subject to destiny. It is not up to us to condemn them because they were free, as it is not up to us to excuse them because they were under their destiny. We cannot judge them. And when we judge ourselves, we must be conscious that even this is not the last word, but that we like them are under an ultimate judgment. In it the riddle of inequality is eternally answered. But this answer is not ours. It is our predicament that we must ask. And we ask with an uneasy conscience. Why are they in misery, why not we? Thinking of some who are near to us, we can ask: Are we partly responsible? But even if we are, it does not solve the riddle of inequality. The uneasy conscience asks about the farthest as well as about the nearest: Why they, why not we?

Why has my child, or any of millions and millions of children, died before even having a chance to grow out of infancy? Why is my child, or any child, born feeble-minded or crippled? Why has my friend or relative, or anybody's friend or relative, disintegrated in his mind and lost both his freedom and his destiny? Why has my son or daughter, gifted as I believe with many talents, wasted them and been deprived of them? And why does this happen to any parent at all? Why have this boy's or this girl's creative powers been broken by a tyrannical father or by a possessive mother?

In all these questions it is not the question of our own misery which we ask. It is not the question: Why has this happened to *me?*

It is not the question of Job which God answers by humiliating him and then by elevating him into communion with him. It is not the old and urgent question: Where is the divine justice, where is the divine love towards me? But it is almost the opposite question: Why has this *not* happened to me, why has it happened to the other one, to the innumerable other ones to whom not even the power of Job is given to accept the divine answer? Why—and Jesus has asked the same question—are many called and few elected?

He does not answer; he only states that this is the human predicament. Shall we therefore cease to ask and humbly accept the fact of a divine judgment which condemns most human beings away from the community with him into despair and self-destruction? Can we accept the eternal victory of judgment over love? We cannot; and nobody ever could, even if he preached and threatened in these terms. As long as he could not see himself with complete certainty as eternally rejected, his preaching and threatening would be self-deceiving. And who could see himself eternally rejected?

But if this is not the solution of the riddle of inequality at its deepest level, can we trespass the boundaries of the Christian tradition and listen to those who tell us that this life does not decide about our eternal destiny? There will be occasions in other lives, as our present life is determined by previous ones and what we have achieved or wasted in them. It is a serious doctrine and not completely strange to Christianity. But if we don't know and never will know what each of us has been in the previous or future lives, then it is not really *our* destiny which develops from life to life, but in each life it is the destiny of someone else. This answer also does not solve the riddle of inequality.

There is no answer at all if we ask about the temporal and eternal destiny of the single being separated from the destiny of the whole. Only in the unity of all beings in time and eternity can a humanly possible answer to the riddle of inequality be found. *Humanly* possible does not mean an answer which removes the riddle of inequality, but an answer with which we can live.

There is an ultimate unity of all beings, rooted in the divine life from which they come and to which they go. All beings, non-human as well as human, participate in it. And therefore they all participate in each other. We participate in each other's having and we participate in each other's not-having. If we become aware of this unity of all beings, something happens. The fact that others have-not changes in every moment the character of my having: It undercuts its security, it drives me beyond myself, to understand, to give, to share, to help. The fact that others fall into sin, crime and misery changes the character of the grace which is given to me: It makes me realize my own hidden guilt, it shows to me that those who suffer for their sin and crime, suffer also for me; for I am guilty of their guilt—at least in the desire of my heart—and ought to suffer as they do. The awareness that others who *could* have become fully developed human beings and never *have*, changes my state of full humanity. Their early death, their early or late disintegration, makes my life and my health a continuous risk, a dying which is not yet death, a disintegration which is not yet destruction. In every death which we encounter, something of us dies; in every disease which we encounter, something of us tends to disintegrate.

Can we live with this answer? We can to the degree in which we are liberated from the seclusion within ourselves. But nobody can be liberated from himself unless he is grasped by the power of that which is present in everyone and everything—the eternal from which we come and to which we go, which gives us to ourselves and which liberates us *from* ourselves. It is the greatness and the heart of the Christian message that God—as manifest in the Cross of the Christ—participates totally in the dying child, in the condemned criminal, in the disintegrating mind, in the starving one and in him who rejects him. There is no extreme human condition into which the divine presence would not reach. This is what the Cross, the most extreme of all human conditions, tells us. The riddle of inequality cannot be solved on the level of our separation from each other. It is eternally solved in the divine participation in all of us and every being. The certainty of the divine participation gives us the courage to stand the riddle of inequality, though finite minds cannot solve it. Amen.

HENRY SLOANE COFFIN
What Crucified Christ?[1]

Some years ago a well-known British journalist, the late W. T. Stead, after witnessing the Passion Play at Oberammergau, came away saying to himself: "This is the story which has transformed the world." And he seemed to hear an echo from the Bavarian hills about him: "Yes, and will transform it."

Each generation stresses particular aspects of the Gospel; and it must be confessed that in our day, and especially in those circles where Christianity is interpreted in terms of contemporary thought, the cross does not hold the central place in preaching. With many men the Incarnation has taken the place formerly occupied by the Atonement, and the character of Jesus is proclaimed as the supreme revelation of God and the ideal for man. In other circles it has been the religious experience of Jesus which is oftenest preached, and men are bidden follow His way of life with God and man. In still other quarters it is His teaching which is dwelt on and men are

1. Chapter 1 of *The Meaning of the Cross* (1931).

enlisted as devotees of the Kingdom of God. But the cross, while it is mentioned as a significant unveiling of Jesus' character, or as the most draining ordeal for which He drew on spiritual resources, or as the climax of His devotion to His cause, is seldom preached as a redemptive act. Indeed few of those who have accepted the current liberal theology devote many sermons to the cross of Christ. They feel themselves incapable of treating the theme.

There are various reasons for this. Our exaggerated individualism renders it difficult for us to think of One bearing the sins of others. Our easy optimism makes us think lightly of sin as an obsession of minds which hold unwholesome views of man and of God. Above all, the luxurious circumstances in which modern American Christians have found themselves have dulled our capacities for appreciating sacrifice. We have surrounded ourselves with conveniences and comforts, and we have tried to banish pain. The tortured form of One spiked on a beam of wood and done to death does not belong in our mental picture. Our ideals and manner of life are incompatible with this tragic and heroic symbol. Preachers have felt an unreality in attempting to explore with their people the meaning of the crucifixion.

This neglect of the cross has had something to do with the lack of transforming power in our message. No one can look complacently upon the present condition of our churches. Hundreds of them are barely holding on: they make no gains from the lives about them. In hundreds more, where there is bustle and stir, the activity is about trifles, and lives are not radically altered nor their communities made over. In very few does one find comrades of the conscience of Christ. In most the majority of communicants show no marks of the Lord Jesus in the purposes to which they devote themselves, in their attitudes towards their neighbors, in the opinions which they hold on public questions. Ministers can count on their fingers the number of their people ready to give themselves for an advance of the Kingdom. The wealth in Christian hands in this country is fabulous, but almost all Church Boards are crippled for want of support. More money is taken in at the gates of a single champion prizefight than a million Church members contribute in a whole year to the spread of the Gospel throughout the world. Above all repentance—a fundamental Christian experience— "repentance unto life" as the Westminster divines termed it—is a saving grace seldom seen. That which has most moved other centuries to repentance unto life has been the preaching of Christ crucified. Commenting upon Dwight L. Moody's insistence upon the efficacy of the sacrifice of Christ to do away with sin, Gamaliel Bradford writes:

To some of us, at any rate, whether we can accept this doctrine or not, it seems that the enormous, unparalleled growth and power and majesty of Christianity in the last nineteen hundred years depend upon it.

One would not harshly criticize brethren in the ministry who have shrunk from the word of the cross. We preachers are pitiable men, doomed to be haunted week after week with a sense of the insufficiency of our treatment of subjects obviously too high for us, and on which we are still constrained to speak. We become most abysmally aware of our incompetence when we attempt to set forth the meaning of the suffering and death of the Son of Man. John Milton, who had marvelously celebrated the birth of Jesus in the "Ode on the Morning of Christ's Nativity," attempted a sequel upon the Passion, but after a few exquisite stanzas he ceased in despair, and the fragment is published with the significant note:

This Subject the Author finding to be above the years he had when he wrote it, and nothing satisfied with what was begun, left it unfinished.

And years do not of themselves mature us to deal with this theme. Happily we discover that sermons which seriously try to interpret that supreme event possess a moving power out of proportion to the wisdom of their content.

How are we to preach Christ crucified? We want an interpretation of the cross for our generation which shall move to repentance and faith. In order to remain in close touch with reality, suppose we begin with two questions of history: First, How came it that the Life which subsequent centuries have looked up to as the best ever lived on our earth seemed so intolerable to the dominant groups of His day that they executed Him? Second, Why did Jesus force the issue that made His execution inevitable?

Let us attempt to answer the first question in this initial chapter remembering that we are not attempting a doctrine of the cross for classroom discussion, but for general presentation. How came it that He whom succeeding generations have revered as the best of men was put to death as a criminal? Who were the crucifiers of Christ?

First and foremost the religious leaders whom Church folk respected. It is a tribute to the force conferred by religious conviction that believing men are so often the prime movers in momentous occurrences, both in the blackest crimes and in the brightest triumphs of mankind. Faith, like fire, empowers its possessors whether for woe or for weal. We must not forget that there was ardent faith in God and conscientious loyalty to Him in the Pharisees who contrived the cruel death of our earth's divinest figure. Like one of their own school, they verily thought themselves under compulsion to act as they did.

That is why Church folk should study them carefully. Who were they? The successors of a brave and patriotic company of stalwart believers who had saved the Jewish faith when foreign conquerors attempted to compromise and wreck it by introducing their own customs and worship. They were known for that essential element in vital religion—detachment: they were called Separatists, Pharisees. They were the heirs of a noble army of martyrs. They knew and honored the Bible as the Law of God. They reverenced the scholars who had spent their lives in explaining it and applying it to life. They were the backbone of the synagogues throughout the land. They prayed; they believed in God's present government of His world and in His immediate control of events. They thought His angelic messengers spoke in the consciences of devout folk and watched for good over their steps. They looked forward to the resurrection of the righteous and their life in the Messiah's everlasting kingdom. They were intense lovers of home and country: in their households there was family religion, and boys, like Saul of Tarsus, were brought up to become devotees and leaders of the Church. They supplied the candidates for the ministry—the scribes who studied and interpreted the Torah. They furnished the missionaries who had enthusiasm to compass sea and land for a single proselyte, and had built up around the syngagogues of the whole Mediterranean world companies of the God-fearing who had espoused the faith of Israel.

Men who sincerely try to order their lives by God's will usually work out a system of obligations, to which they hold themselves and seek to hold others. Now some matters can readily be embodied in rules—keeping the Sabbath, observing sacred festivals and fasts, adopting methodical times and habits of prayer, setting aside a tenth of one's gains for religious purposes. And some matters cannot be thus codified—having clean thoughts and generous sympathies, being conciliatory, honoring every human being, however unadmirable, as kin to God, serving him as his heavenly Father understandingly cares for him. And matters which can be incorporated in rules tend to be stressed above those which cannot be precisely defined. And when men have their beliefs and duties clearly stated, and are earnestly living by them, they are not apt to distinguish between more and less important items in their religious code: all of it is precious to them. They do not wish any of it changed. Sincere religion is inherently conservative. It deals with tested values.

Jesus scandalized them by disregarding practices which they considered God's Law. He broke the Sabbath shockingly. When asked to speak in the synagogues, His addresses upset many in the congregation. He associated with disreputable people—with loose women and with unpatriotic profiteering farmers of revenue. He touched the academic pride of their scholars: how should a carpenter correct their explanation of Scriptures which they had spent their lives in studying and for which they had the authority of recognized experts? Many of them had never heard Him for themselves, and at second or tenth hand, when the intervening hands are unfriendly, His sayings and doings appeared even more insufferable. From the outset He was surrounded in their minds with an atmosphere of suspicion. They sent spies to watch Him, and spies have a way of hearing what they fancy they are sent to hear. The Pharisees felt themselves guardians of the faith of Israel. Their fathers had fought and bled for it; their own lives were wrapped up in it; they were holding it in the dark days of Roman dominion for their children and children's children. Could they allow this Innovator, this Charlatan who made preposterous claims for Himself, to go on deceiving simple folk and perhaps wreck the Church? Quite apart from the embittering encounters Jesus had with some of them— encounters which may have been colored in our gospels by the subsequent strife between the Synagogue and the growing Christian Church, there was enough difference between His faith and life and theirs to rouse determined antagonism. In loyalty to God they must put an end to His mischievous career.

A second group were the inheritors of a lucrative commercial privilege—the aristocratic Sadducean priests who controlled the Temple area. They also were churchmen, but in comparison with the Pharisees, their religion was a subordinate and moderate interest. It was an inheritance which they cherished with an antiquarian's regard for its more primitive form. Their thought of Deity was of a remote and unaggressive Being, who left men to work out their own affairs, who certainly did not interfere or help by sending angelic spirits. God wished from Israel a seemly recognition in the maintenance of the time-honored ceremonies. For the rest they were broadminded. Their predecessors had welcomed the culture and customs of the Greeks, and they probably had a much more tolerant attitude in religion than the Pharisees. One might have picked up a Greek poem or drama in their homes; they were interested in the on-goings of the larger world; and after the manner of cultivated liberals they smiled in superior fashion on the narrow preoccupations of scribes with the details of the religious code. They were much more concerned with politics and finance than with religion. So long as Jesus remained in Galilee, they may never have heard of Him; or if some rumor of Him came to their ears, they would pay little attention to it. The alarm of the Pharisees over His teaching would have seemed to them a petty squabble which was no concern of theirs.

But when Jesus invaded the Temple precincts and created a commotion by overturning the tables of the money-changers, these gentlemen were roused. Here was a dangerous social Radical. Doubtless their leasing of space for booths in the outer court of the Temple had been criticized before, and there was popular talk over the prices of doves and lambs, and grumbling at the rate of exchange for the half-shekel. But this was the usual proletarian murmuring. Did they not provide a public convenience in these business arrangements? Were they not assisting worshippers in their religious duties? Did not the ancient Law clearly enjoin that the Temple tax should be paid in a particular coin? And must not someone supply facilities for exchanging the various currencies which pilgrims brought with them from all over the Empire for the proper silver piece? Was not four per cent a moderate broker's fee for such an exchange? The idea of this upcountry Agitator appearing and, without a word to anybody in authority, making this disturbance in the Temple court, and infecting the populace with the absurd notion that there should be no charge for perfectly legitimate ecclesiastical business! Where did He think animals for sacrifice would be procured? What did He consider a reasonable charge for exchange, if He called four per cent robbery? Who was He, anyhow, to take upon Himself to reform the financial methods of men whose forebears had derived their incomes unquestioned from these leases? His attack was a reflection not only upon them, but upon their honored fathers. Annas and Caiaphas had never seen the court of the Temple without booths and stalls; it was to them part of the natural order of things that cattle and doves should be sold there and money exchanged. Further they had been born to the tradition that the sacred area of the Temple belonged to the hereditary priesthood, and that they were to derive their support from its ceremonies. How could they understand the indignant feelings of Jesus? The charge, which the false witnesses brought, that He had threatened to destroy the Temple, may have had some slight basis in fact. Such statements are seldom made out of whole cloth. Jesus may have expressed the feeling that, if this Temple made with hands were destroyed, real religion might not lose much. That would disturb these gentlemen in their family sentiment, in their inherited faith, in their economic interests.

And they were politicians with a keen eye for the political situation. At the moment they were on fair terms with the Roman Empire and were allowed some freedom in the management of local affairs. A demagogue of this sort, as Caiaphas remarked, might stir up a political mess, and embroil them with the Roman authorities. Could they risk allowing Him to go on?[2]

A third figure among the crucifiers is the representative of imperialistic government. He seems to have been impressed by Jesus—more impressed than the scribes or the priests. We pity him as part of a system which our age feels to be inherently faulty. In theory at least we do not believe in one people governing another. It is bad for both peoples. It creates such attitudes as one sees in this scene—the priests fawning upon the governor and Pilate overbearing toward them and insulting the nation by the derisive title he orders nailed above the Victim on the cross. But among imperialistic peoples few have understood their business as well as the Romans. They probably kept Judaea in better order than any native leader could have kept it. They governed brutally, but there are still many who think that inferiors must be made to know their place. Jesus had been struck with their haughty attitude: "Ye know that the rulers of the Gentiles lord it." It may have been partially a patriot's unwillingness to speak against His own countrymen before an overlord which sealed His lips in the judgment hall.

All our narratives agree that the governor was most reluctant to execute this Prisoner. He suggested expedient after expedient to obviate it. He tried everything except the direct course of following his conscience and seeking to deal justly towards the Man before him. The system of which he was a part entangled him. Rome asked her procurators to keep the tribute flowing steadily from their provinces and to maintain quiet. No governor wished complaints lodged against him with his superiors. Pilate had to live with these priests, and in the end it seemed easier to let them have their way with this Peasant from Galilee. He was poor and insignificant, and to this day justice is never the same for the unfriended sons of poverty as for the wealthy and influential. Paul, claiming his rights as a Roman citizen, was to have days in court his Master could not command.

To the last Pilate was uncomfortable about the case. He did his best to shift responsibility—on Herod, on the crowd, on the priests. But the priests knew their man and played skillfully upon his loyalties and his fears. The fourth evangelist makes them say: "If thou

---

2. Doctor L. P. Jacks has said of our contemporary churches: "The gravamen of the charge against the Church is not so much that there are definite abuses in its corporate life as that there is a general atmosphere of acquiescence in all that is worldly and conventional. No one knows exactly what ideal of life the Church stands for, unless that it is that of a kindly and good-natured toleration of things as they are, with a mild desire that they may grow better in time, so far as that is compatible with the maintenance of existing vested interests." That is the position of the Sadducee; and Jesus touched it at its most sensitive point when He assailed vested interests [Coffin's note].

release this man, thou art not Cæsar's friend." Fidelity to Cæsar was both a Roman's patriotism and his religion. They were appealing to Pilate's principles, and they won their point. Pilate washed his hands, but throughout the centuries his name has been coupled with this event as responsible for it on the lips of thousands who repeat "crucified under Pontius Pilate."

A fourth figure among crucifiers, although he is hardly a decisive factor, is a man of the gay world—Herod Antipas. A scion of an able family, born to wealth and position, brought up in Rome at the imperial court, admitted to the fashionable society of the capital in the golden age of Augustus, a member of the smart set, he knew all about the latest delicacies of the table, had a keen eye for a beautiful dancer, and surrounded by boon companions lived for pleasure. Like many in similar circumstances in contemporary America he had a shabby marital record, having become infatuated with his half-brother's wife, for whom he divorced his own wife and whom he stole from her husband. But divorces even of this sordid variety were not bad form then, any more than they are among ourselves today, and bad form was the only taboo Herod revered. He had a reputation for political shrewdness, and he had burnt his fingers in handling one prophet, John, and was wary of repeating the blunder. Jesus dreaded what He called "the leaven of Herod"—loose morals, lavish outlay, and sharp politics. He had spoken of this tetrarch as "that fox." Now these two were face to face.

Herod displayed a man-of-the-world's versatility in asking Him "many questions"—one wonders what they were. He was clever and was pleased to display his knowledge of religious fine points before his companions and before the priests. It was a chance to impress them. But Herod could make nothing of Jesus. And Jesus could make nothing of Herod. He had borne witness to His Messiahship before Caiaphas and the Sanhedrin; He had admitted His kingship to Pontius Pilate; but He had not a syllable to utter to Antipas. The tetrarch had heard of him as a wonder-worker and craved the chance to see Him do something startling. But Jesus' mighty works are not tricks to entertain and astonish. Herod had a conscience; could not Jesus appeal to that with some piercing story such as Nathan told adulterous David?[3] Did the Saviour ever confront a needier sinner? But He had not a word for him.

Herod was apparently "past feeling," and Jesus gave him up. This clownish roysterer and his cronies could think of nothing to do with their disappointing Prisoner but tog Him out in mock finery and make game of Him. Fancy the mind of Jesus while this

3. See "Thou Art the Man" (pp. 1071–1072).

went on! It cost Pilate some struggle to condemn Him; but when He was sent away from the tetrarch's palace, Herod had been laughing at Him as a buffoon, and was now smiling at his own shrewdness in outwitting the governor, and handing his awkward case back to him.

A fifth figure among the crucifiers is a disillusioned idealist. We have no reason to think that the man of Kerioth did not enlist in the cause of Jesus from the same high motives as the other disciples. If anything it was harder for him, the only Judaean in the group, than for Galileans. He heard all that they heard and he shared all that they shared, and, like them, he was disappointed. He had looked for a different issue. Jesus outdistanced his ideals; he fancied that Jesus did not measure up to his ideals and he grew critical. With many the attempt "to go beyond themselves and wind themselves too high" is followed by a reaction. What he had hoped for, and hoped for immediately, did not happen, and Judas became bitter. He felt himself duped. The confident attitude of Jesus as He set His face to what seemed to Judas folly and defeat, irritated him. He was no longer the reasonable man he had been. It was that perhaps which led the disciples in retrospect to recall that the devil entered into him. They felt that he was at war with himself. And in such plight men not infrequently turn on those to whom they have been most warmly attached. Their disgust with themselves they are apt to vent on those who make them uncomfortable. Iago says of Cassio: "He hath a daily beauty in his life that makes me ugly." Jesus became hateful to Judas Iscariot. There may be a shred of truth in the theories which make his betrayal of the Master an attempt to force His hand, and compel Him to assume his power.

For what was it that Judas betrayed to the priests? Obviously not merely the spot where their police could arrest Jesus. That was not worth paying for. The police could follow him and find out His haunts. Probably Judas betrayed, as many modern interpreters think, the secret of Jesus' Messiahship, which was talked of in the inner circle but not published abroad. That was not clear to the priests or to the public even after the entry amid hosannas, for the shouts of a crowd are not evidence. Now they had a basis for trial, so Judas was in a sense forcing Jesus to declare Himself. But our narratives imply that Judas did it vindictively, not affectionately.

Disillusioned idealists become sour and cynical. And in cynicism consciences unravel: Judas may easily have grown careless in handling the money in his custody. Avarice cannot have been the main motive in the betrayal, but greed has a place in most ignoble stories. Very trifling sums induce people still to hideous crimes. When a man is embittered, he is capable of anything, and it was a cynic who drove the shabby bargain with the chief priests and went out with thirty pieces of silver jingling in his purse and a betrayed Master on his conscience.

A sixth factor among the crucifiers is a crowd. The individuals who composed it were decent men, kind to their families and neighbors, and personally they would not have been cruel to this Prophet from Galilee. They had a prejudice against Him, and that prejudice was worked up until they were fused into a howling mob. In such a mass a man is lifted out of himself, loses control of his feelings, and his passions surge unchecked and augmented by the passions of the throng around him. He becomes a thousand times himself emotionally. Shakespeare's Bassanio speaks of

> The buzzing pleased multitude
> Whose every something being blent together
> Turns to a wild of nothing save of joy.

And the reverse is true when the crowd is prejudiced and their every something being blended together turns to a wild of nothing save of cruelty.

A crowd, being emotionally intense, is very suggestible. A catchword will set it off. Our propagandists and advertisers have taught us how we can be worked on in masses by names, phrases, pictures. And crowds are much more readily suggestible to the more primitive and coarser sentiments than to the finer. Man is a thinly varnished savage at best, lump him together in throngs and the varnish melts at the touch. When Pilate appeared unwilling to grant the priests' request, the crowd was swayed by nationalism; the priests were their own, and the governor the representative of the hated oppressor. They had a traditional right to claim clemency for a prisoner at the Passover. They will use it, and natural self-assertion impels them not to ask for One whom Pilate would gladly let them have. A suggestion is given them—Barabbas, a popular revolutionary of the crude type—a slogan for the emotions of a crowd.

Jesus can hardly have been popular. How much better "copy" for our own press Barabbas would be than the Teacher of Nazareth! Besides Barabbas is the nationalistic type Pilate would least like to release. Mobs feel and scarcely think. Could these men as individuals have calmly weighed Jesus and Barabbas, the result might have been different; but they were atingle with their cruder instincts. And a crowd which takes to shouting works itself to a violent pitch, and when thwarted can become fiendishly brutal. The spectators who packed the tiers of the Coliseum, turned down their thumbs at some fallen gladiator and yelled themselves hoarse demanding his death, would not have done anything of the sort by themselves. Each man in the crowd has lost his sense of personal responsibility. It is what men do in a social set, a political party, an economic group, a nation, a religious assembly, that is likely to be least moral and most diabolically savage. Pilate did his weak best not to execute Jesus; Herod found loutish amusement in Him, but showed no desire for His blood; Judas wished Him out of his way, but jail would have satisfied him; the crowd, with their tribal feelings roused—the instincts of the hunting pack—shouted "Crucify Him, crucify Him!"

A seventh factor among the crucifiers was a guard of soldiers. Jesus never spoke harshly of the military profession. One of His rare compliments was paid to an officer who had expressed his faith in terms of soldierly obedience. And probably it was in extenuation of the legionaries charged with the grim details of His execution that He prayed: "Father, forgive them, for they know not what they do." But it was by men prepared for their task by military discipline that He was done to death at Golgotha.

That system is deliberately planned to depersonalize those whom it trains. They are educated not to decide for themselves, but to give machine-like response to a command. Such a system, while it has noble associations with courage, loyalty, honor, and self-effacement, counteracts that which Christianity tries hardest to create—a reasoning conscience. The soldiers who scourged Jesus and spiked His hands and feet to the beams of the cross never thought what they were doing—they were victims of a discipline which had crucified their moral judgments.

Their occupation was held in high honor as the typical and most essential patriotic service. Rome ruled by physical might. She believed in awing inferior peoples and encouraged her soldiers to strike terror into them. The scourging which Pilate ordered—"the terrible preface," as it was called, to capital punishment—was forbidden for Roman citizens, but it was customary for provincials. A small guard was ordered to inflict on Jesus this appalling indignity in public—stripping Him, binding Him to a stake in a stooping position with hands behind Him, and beating Him with thongs at the ends of which were leaden balls or sharp-pointed bones.

And when that prostrating ordeal was over they took Him for further maltreatment to the privacy of the guardroom. Brutal mockery of the condemned was allowed the soldiers in order to maintain their *morale*. All the finer feelings must be overcome in those whose trade is iron and blood. And privacy seems to be an inevitable temptation to men with fellow-beings in their power. Schoolboys, jailors, keepers of the weak in mind or body, generation after generation, have to be watched against outbreaks of savagery to their victims. It was expected of the soldiers—a crude comic interlude of their rough day. But in fairness to these systematically hardened men let us recall that when the Prisoner was uplifted on the cross, slowly bleeding to death in agony, educated and revered religious leaders, professors of divinity, vented their detestation of Him with gibes. Theological animosity renders men as callous as professional hangmen.

Perhaps more so, for these soldiers had to restrain themselves from feeling by gambling at the foot of the cross. They had to sit by while the crucified writhed, and groaned, and cried, in their prolonged misery. It is not surprising that they resorted to the excitement of playing dice as a mental relief. They are typical representatives of callings into which men cannot put themselves—their minds and consciences and hearts. Such callings rob those who engage in them of moral vitality and make them fit agents of tragic occurrences like Calvary.

But there is still an eighth factor without which the crucifixion would not have taken place—the public. Behind the chief actors in the drama at Golgotha we see thousands of obscure figures—the populace of the city. One fancies them getting up in the morning and hearing rumors of a case on before the governor. The city, crowded with Passover pilgrims, would be more excitable and talkative than usual, and news of events at the palace, involving the Sanhedrin, would spread rapidly. Then, as people were in the midst of their morning's work, they would catch sight of that sinister procession tramping through the streets on the way to the place of execution outside the city wall. We can overhear such remarks as "Hello! another hanging today? Who's to be hung? Those two bandits? Who's the third prisoner? That Prophet from Galilee? Oh, they got Him very quickly, didn't they?" And as prisoners and guards filed past, the day's work was resumed.

Behind all earth's tragedies there is a public whose state of mind has much to do with the central event. Even under the least democratic government the authorities dare not go more than a certain distance without the popular will. The thousands of uncaring nobodies, to whom what was done with Jesus was a matter of indifference, gave scribes and priests and governor their chance. These obscure folk felt themselves without responsibility. What had they to do with this Prophet from the north country who had ridden into the city, hailed by a crowd of provincial pilgrims? Possibly it was of them that Jesus was thinking—the public of the capital city—when He said: "O Jerusalem, Jerusalem, that killeth the prophets."

The public is never of one mind; it represents various shades of opinion and feeling—sympathetic, hostile, indifferent; and all shades were there in Jerusalem. But if enough of its inhabitants had really cared about Jesus, He would never have been crucified. The chief handicap of the public is ignorance. The mass of the dwellers in Jerusalem knew next to nothing about the Prophet from Galilee. But Jesus did not weep over them merely because of their lack of information. Religious capitals, like cathedral towns, are proverbially hard to move. Religion was an old story to those who lived in the neighborhood of the venerable Temple and were familiar with the figures of the great doctors of the Law. They were complacent in sacred traditions of the past and not open to fresh incomings of the Most High. Jesus wept over their apathy. To Him it seemed that even unfeeling stones must respond to One who so manifestly represented God. They did not know the things which belonged to peace because they did not wish to know them. Jerusalem slew the Son of God not only because He had won the sharp ill-will of the powerful few, but also because the many did not want to be bothered with Him. And the public of Jerusalem, who thought the fate of this Stranger none of their business, had to bear the doom with their as-yet-unborn children; for judgment brings home social obligations and convinces us that by a myriad unsuspected cords men are tied up in one bundle of life in cities, in nations, in races, and in a world of men. These thousands of citizens of Jerusalem never went through the form of washing their hands, like Pilate. They were unaware of any accountability for this execution. But history with its destruction of the city rendered its verdict upon them.

Such a survey of the factors which crucified Jesus—and a course rather than a single sermon is obviously necessary to treat them with sufficient explicitness—forces men to think. This was the world which executed the Life subsequent generations until this hour revere as the best earth has seen. And plainly it is the world in which we still live. All these forces are present and active in our society—religious intolerance, commercial privilege, political expediency, pleasure-loving irresponsibility, unfaithfulness, the mob spirit, militarism, public apathy. These are perennial evils. They are deep-seated in the very structure of human society. The forms of political and economic and ecclesiastical organization may alter, but these remain under all forms. We should find them in a socialist republic or a communist state, as surely as in an imperial despotism or a capitalist regime. Moreover, they act and react upon each other. The priests help Judas to his treachery and incite the mob; Pilate stimulates the priests to play politics; the political methods of both governor and religious leaders keep the public morally indifferent; their sinister motives interweave into a corporate force for evil. Together they make up what Jesus called "the power of darkness," the satanic kingdom.

It is significant that the national and ecclesiastical capital is the slayer of the prophets. Evil organizes itself with this inherent solidarity and possesses a group—a church, a nation, a race. These forces were present in the villages and towns of Galilee, but they came to a focus where the organization of the Jewish Church and the Jewish nation had its seat, and where the representative of imperial government exercised his power. Wickedness is a racial force. It propagates itself generation after generation. Jesus recognized the unity of the factors with which He was struggling with similar factors, which had always been present in the life of His people, when He spoke of this generation which was crucifying Him having upon it "all the righteous blood shed on earth," from the blood of Abel on the first pages of the Jewish Bible to the blood of Zachariah recorded on its last pages. Evil spreads itself laterally, building up a corporate force of wickedness, and passes itself on from age to age, linking the generations in a solidarity of sin.

When we examine the factors which slew Jesus, we recognize them at once as contemporaries. We can attach modern names to them. There is nothing abnormal or unusual about these men who rear the cross: they are acting true to type—a type which recurs century after century throughout history. They are average folk. We must not blacken their characters. John Stuart Mill, whose ethical judgments are singularly dispassionate, says of them:

They were not worse than men commonly are, but rather the contrary, men who possessed in a full, or somewhat more than a full measure the religious, moral, and patriotic feelings of their people; the very kind of men who in all times, our own included, have every chance of passing through life blameless and unspotted.

We can think of no more high-minded young man than the student of Gamaliel, Saul of Tarsus, and we know how cordially he approved the course taken by the leaders of Israel in putting Jesus out of the way.

We can easily multiply from history and literature men far more villainous—a Caesar Borgia or an Iago, for instance. Indeed we can find more depraved figures in almost any community, if we look for them. But the purpose of Jesus and the purposes of even good people clash. The inevitableness of the crucifixion is brought home to us. The issue between the motives of Jesus and those of the mass of mankind is thrown into light. They are irreconcilable. Life is a desperately real struggle between mutually destroying forces. If the motives of Jesus prevail, the factors that slew Him will cease to be. If the motives of Caiaphas and Pilate, of the mob, the soldiers, and the public prevail—there is an execution: "Away with such a fellow from the earth."

There are three crosses on Calvary: on two of them society is trying to rid itself of predatory bandits, on the third it placed One whom it considered also its enemy, perhaps a worse enemy since He was placed on the central cross. We level up with our standards of right, and we also level down. He who is above the conscience of the community is as likely to be slain as he who is below. This is our world; this is the society in which we move; these are the types of people with whom we associate; this is the public to which we belong. The slayers of Jesus are our relatives, kinsmen in thought and feeling. A sense of complicity in what they did comes upon us. We are bound up with them in this bundle of human life. The corporate evil which dominated first-century Palestine and moved these men to kill their Best dominates our world and is compassing similar fell results. Trails of blood lead to our doors. Wretched men that we are, who shall deliver us out of this social body of death?

And these factors are not only about us, they are also within us. As we scan these men who sent Jesus to His death—devout Pharisee and conservative Sadducee, Roman politician and false friend, emotional mob and unthinking soldiers, the host of indifferent or approving faces of the public behind them—their motives and feelings have been and are our own. You may recall in Hawthorne's *Mosses from an Old Manse* the scene where, going through the virtuoso's collection, he nearly falls over a huge bundle, like a peddler's pack, done up in sackcloth and very securely strapped and corded. " 'It is Christian's burden of sin,' said the virtuoso. 'O pray, let me see it,' cried I. 'For many a year I have longed to know its contents.' 'Look into your own conscience and memory,' replied the virtuoso. 'You will there find a list of whatever it contained.' " It is so with the motives of those who planned and carried out the death of Jesus. We do not need to ask: "Lord, is it I?" We are aware of belonging in this same realm of darkness, and of having dealt with His brethren very much as He was dealt with. As we think of ourselves, we shudder—"God, be merciful to me, a sinner."

Men speak of the absence of the sense of sin in our time. It has never been vigorous in any age, save as some judgment of history or the disturbing presence of the ideal has created it. We have witnessed a judgment on a colossal scale in the World War—a judgment upon our entire civilization. Some of us said to ourselves, feeling mankind in the grip of overmastering social forces of passion and greed and brutality: "Now is your hour and the power of darkness." And we know ourselves a long way yet from redemption from the motives which brought it on. Underneath the ease and comfort of our day there is restless discontent. Some of it is crassly materialistic—the common envy of the have-nots for the haves, the craving of the have-littles to have more. But souls are never satisfied with things. Life is in relationships, human and divine, in purposes. And men are dissatisfied with the quality of life. To take them to Calvary and show them the factors which nailed Jesus on the cross is to uncover for them a far more terrible world than they dreamed they were in, and to uncover for them themselves.

This gives us an inkling of Jesus' reason for putting Himself into men's hands and letting them do with Him as they would. His broken and bleeding body on the cross is the exposure of a murderous world. The Crucified becomes one with the unrecognized and misused and cruelly treated in every age. The nail-pierced Figure on Calvary haunts our race as a symbol of what is forever taking place generation after generation, and of what each of us has his part in.

Readers of Ibsen's drama *Emperor and Galilean* will recall how Julian is made to ask—

Where is He now? Has He been at work elsewhere since that happened at Golgotha?

I dreamed of Him lately. I dreamed that I had subdued the whole world. I ordained that the memory of the Galilean should be rooted out on earth; and it was rooted out. Then the spirits came and ministered to me, and bound wings on my shoulders, and I soared aloft into infinite space, till my feet rested on another world.

It was another world than mine. Its curve was vaster, its light more golden, and many moons circled around it. Then I looked down at my own earth—the Emperor's earth that I had made Galileanless—and I thought that all that I had done was very good.

But behold there came a procession by me on the strange earth where I stood. There were soldiers and judges and executioners at the head of it and weeping women followed. And lo, in the midst of the slow-moving array, was the Galilean, alive and bearing a cross on His back. Then I called to Him and said, "Whither away, Galilean?" And He turned His face to me and smiled, nodded slowly and said, "To the place of the skull."

Where is He now? What if that at Golgotha, near Jerusalem, was but a wayside matter, a thing done as it were in passing! What if He goes on and on, and suffers and dies, and conquers, again and again, from world to world!

It is a vivid way of picturing the solidarity of the worlds of every generation, each offering its Golgotha. It is there that men come to themselves and realize their plight and the plight of society. Walter Pater said that "the way to perfection is through a series of disgusts." To let men see the factors which enact the tragedy outside the wall of Jerusalem is to disgust them with their world and with themselves. If some protest that this is not a wholesome state of mind, one may answer in the words of that robust thinker, Walter Bagehot: "So long as men are very imperfect, a sense of great imperfection should cleave to them." It is a necessary part of the process towards genuine healthy-mindedness. When they realize what caused the torture and execution of Jesus, they cry, "O not that! Such a world is intolerable!" And made conscious that they are builders of such worlds, and that their hands are stained, they hunger and thirst after righteousness.

QUESTIONS

1. Indicate each of the principal groups and figures who, by Coffin's account, contributed to the crucifixion of Christ. What leading motive does Coffin ascribe to each? How does Coffin show these motives to be perennial ones, operative now as then? Why does he do so?

2. Examine each of the transitions Coffin makes. How does he proceed from one part to another in his essay? How does he relate part to part? What order of progression is discernible in the essay?

3. Coffin accords the Pharisees considerable praise. Why? What does he imply to be the essential fault of the Pharisees? In what respects does he compare and contrast the Pharisees and Sadducees?

4. Coffin refers (p. 1144) to the "motives of Jesus," but he does not delineate these or discuss them in full. To what extent has he indirectly indicated them in his account of the principal groups and figures contributing to the crucifixion?

5. Consider Coffin's title. Why has he asked precisely that question? Might he just as well have given as title "Who Crucified Christ?" Explain.

EMILY DICKINSON
Letter to Her Cousins

November, 1882

DEAR COUSINS

I hoped to write you before, but mother's dying almost stunned my spirit.

I have answered a few inquiries of love, but written little intuitively. She was scarcely the aunt you knew. The great mission of pain had been ratified—cultivated to tenderness by persistent sorrow, so that a larger mother died than had she died before. There was no earthly parting. She slipped from our fingers like a flake gathered by the wind, and is now part of the drift called "the infinite."

We don't know where she is, though so many tell us.

I believe we shall in some manner be cherished by our Maker—that the One who gave us this remarkable earth has the power still farther to surprise that which He has caused. Beyond that all is silence. . . .

Mother was very beautiful when she had died. Seraphs are solemn artists. The illumination that comes but once paused upon her features, and it seemed like hiding a picture to lay her in the grave; but the grass that received my father will suffice his guest, the one he asked at the altar to visit him all his life.

I cannot tell how Eternity seems. It sweeps around me like a sea. . . . Thank you for remembering me. Remembrance—mighty word.

"Thou gavest it to me from the foundation of the world."

Lovingly,
EMILY

THOMAS HENRY HUXLEY
Letter to Charles Kingsley

14 Waverly Place, Sept. 23, 1860

MY DEAR KINGSLEY

I cannot sufficiently thank you, both on my wife's account and my own, for your long and frank letter, and for all the hearty sympathy which it exhibits—and Mrs. Kingsley will, I hope, believe that we are no less sensible of her kind thought of us. To myself your letter was especially valuable, as it touched upon what I thought even more than upon what I said in my letter to you.

My convictions, positive and negative, on all the matters of which you speak, are of long and slow growth and are firmly rooted. But the great blow which fell upon me seemed to stir them to their foundation, and had I lived a couple of centuries earlier I could have fancied a devil scoffing at me and them—and asking me what profit it was to have stripped myself of the hopes and consolations of the mass of mankind? To which my only reply was and is—Oh devil! truth is better than much profit. I have searched over the grounds of my belief, and if wife and child and name and fame were all to be lost to me one after the other as the penalty, still I will not lie.

And now I feel that it is due to you to speak as frankly as you have done to me. An old and worthy friend of mine tried some three or four years ago to bring us together—because, as he said, you were the only man who would do me any good. Your letter leads me to think he was right, though not perhaps in the sense he attached to his own words.

To begin with the great doctrine you discuss. I neither deny nor affirm the immortality of man. I see no reason for believing in it, but, on the other hand, I have no means of disproving it.

Pray understand that I have no *a priori* objections to the doctrine. No man who has to deal daily and hourly with nature can trouble himself about *a priori* difficulties. Give me such evidence as would justify me in believing anything else, and I will believe that. Why should I not? It is not half so wonderful as the conservation of force, or the indestructibility of matter. Whoso clearly appreciates all that is implied in the falling of a stone can have no difficulty about any doctrine simply on account of its marvelousness.

But the longer I live, the more obvious it is to me that the most sacred act of a man's life is to say and to feel, "I believe such and such to be true." All the greatest rewards and all the heaviest penalties of existence cling about that act.

The universe is one and the same throughout; and if the condition of my success in unraveling some little difficulty of anatomy or physiology is that I shall rigorously refuse to put faith in that which does not rest on sufficient evidence, I cannot believe that the great mysteries of existence will be laid open to me on other terms.

It is no use to talk to me of analogies and probabilities. I know what I mean when I say I believe in the law of the inverse squares, and I will not rest my life and my hopes upon weaker convictions. I dare not if I would.

Measured by this standard, what becomes of the doctrine of immortality?

You rest in your strong conviction of your personal existence, and in the instinct of the persistence of that existence which is so strong in you as in most men.

To me this is as nothing. That my personality is the surest thing I know—may be true. But the attempt to conceive what it is leads me into mere verbal subtleties. I have champed up all that chaff about the ego and the non-ego, about noumena and phenomena, and all the rest of it, too often not to know that in attempting even to think of these questions, the human intellect flounders at once out of its depth.

It must be twenty years since, a boy, I read Hamilton's essay on the unconditioned, and from that time to this, ontological speculation has been a folly to me. When Mansel took up Hamilton's argument on the side of orthodoxy (!) I said he reminded me of nothing so much as the man who is sawing off the sign on which he is sitting, in Hogarth's picture. But this by the way.

I cannot conceive of my personality as a thing apart from the phenomena of my life. When I try to form such a conception I discover that, as Coleridge would have said, I only hypostatize a word, and it alters nothing if, with Fichte, I suppose the universe to be nothing but a manifestation of my personality. I am neither more nor less eternal than I was before.

Nor does the infinite difference between myself and the animals alter the case. I do not know whether the animals persist after they disappear or not. I do not even know whether the infinite difference between us and them may not be compensated by *their* persistence and *my* cessation after apparent death, just as the humble bulb of an annual lives, while the glorious flowers it has put forth die away.

Surely it must be plain that an ingenious man could speculate without end on both sides, and find analogies for all his dreams. Nor does it help me to tell me that the aspirations of mankind—that my own highest aspirations even—lead me toward the doctrine of immortality. I doubt the fact, to begin with, but if it be so even, what is this but in grand words asking me to believe a thing because I like it.

Science has taught to me the opposite lesson. She warns me to be careful how I adopt a view which jumps with my preconceptions, and to require stronger evidence for such belief than for one to which I was previously hostile.

My business is to teach my aspirations to conform themselves to fact, not to try and make facts harmonize with my aspirations.

Science seems to me to teach in the highest and strongest manner the great truth which is embodied in the Christian conception of entire surrender to the will of God. Sit down before fact as a little child, be prepared to give up every preconceived notion, follow humbly wherever and to whatever abysses nature leads, or you shall learn nothing. I have only begun to learn content and peace of mind since I have resolved at all risks to do this.

There are, however, other arguments commonly brought forward in favor of the immortality of man, which are to my mind not only delusive but mischievous. The one is the notion that the moral government of the world is imperfect without a system of future rewards and punishments. The other is: that such a system is indispensable to practical morality. I believe that both these dogmas are very mischievous lies.

With respect to the first, I am no optimist, but I have the firmest belief that the Divine Government (if we may use such a phrase to express the sum of the "customs of matter") is wholly just. The more I know intimately of the lives of other men (to say nothing of my own), the more obvious it is to me that the wicked does *not* flourish nor is the righteous punished. But for this to be clear we must bear in mind what almost all forget, that the rewards of life are contingent upon obedience to the *whole* law—physical as well as moral—and that moral obedience will not atone for physical sin, or *vice versa*.

The ledger of the Almighty is strictly kept, and every one of us has the balance of his operations paid over to him at the end of every minute of his existence.

Life cannot exist without a certain conformity to the surrounding universe—that conformity involves a certain amount of happiness in excess of pain. In short, as we live we are paid for living.

And it is to be recollected in view of the apparent discrepancy between men's acts and their rewards that Nature is juster than we. She takes into account what a man brings with him into the world, which human justice cannot do. If I, born a bloodthirsty and savage brute, inheriting these qualities from others, kill you, my fellow-men will very justly hang me, but I shall not be visited with the horrible remorse which would be my real punishment if, my nature being higher, I had done the same thing.

The absolute justice of the system of things is as clear to me as any scientific fact. The gravitation of sin to sorrow is as certain as that of the earth to the sun, and more so—for experimental proof of the fact is within reach of us all—nay, is before us all in our own lives, if we had but the eyes to see it.

Not only, then, do I disbelieve in the need for compensation, but I believe that the seeking for rewards and punishments out of this life leads men to a ruinous ignorance of the fact that their inevitable rewards and punishments are here.

If the expectation of hell hereafter can keep me from evil-doing, surely *a fortiori* the certainty of hell now will do so? If a man could be firmly impressed with the belief that stealing damaged him as much as swallowing arsenic would do (and it does), would not the dissuasive force of that belief be greater than that of any based on mere future expectations?

And this leads me to my other point.

As I stood behind the coffin of my little son the other day, with my mind bent on anything but disputation, the officiating minister read, as a part of his duty, the words, "If the dead rise not again, let us eat and drink, for tomorrow we die." I cannot tell you how inexpressibly they shocked me. Paul had neither wife nor child, or he must have known that his alternative involved a blasphemy against all that was best and noblest in human nature. I could have laughed with scorn. What! because I am face to face with irreparable loss, because I have given back to the source from whence it came, the cause of a great happiness, still retaining through all my life the blessings which have sprung and will spring from that cause, I am to renounce my manhood, and, howling, grovel in bestiality? Why, the very apes know better, and if you shoot their young, the poor brutes grieve their grief out and do not immediately seek distraction in a gorge.

Kicked into the world a boy without guide or training, or with worse than none, I confess to my shame that few men have drunk deeper of all kinds of sin than I. Happily, my course was arrested in time—before I had earned absolute destruction—and for long years I have been slowly and painfully climbing, with many a fall, towards better things. And when I look back, what do I find to have been the agents of my redemption? The hope of immortality or of future reward? I can honestly say that for these fourteen years such a consideration has not entered my head. No, I can tell you exactly what has been at work. *Sartor Resartus* led me to know that a deep sense of religion was compatible with the entire absence of theology. Secondly, science and her methods gave me a resting place independent of authority and tradition. Thirdly, love opened up to me a view of the sanctity of human nature, and impressed me with a deep sense of responsibility.

If at this moment I am not a worn-out, debauched, useless carcass of a man, if it has been or will be my fate to advance the cause of science, if I feel that I have a shadow of a claim on the love of those about me, if in the supreme moment when I looked down into my boy's grave my sorrow was full of submission and without bitterness, it is because these agencies have worked upon me, and not because I have ever cared whether my poor personality shall remain distinct for ever from the All from whence it came and whither it goes.

And thus, my dear Kingsley, you will understand what my position is. I may be quite wrong, and in that case I know I shall have to pay the penalty for being wrong. But I can only say with Luther, "*Gott helfe mir, Ich kann nichts anders.*"[1]

I know right well that 99 out of 100 of my fellows would call me atheist, infidel, and all the other usual hard names. As our laws stand, if the lowest thief steals my coat, my evidence (my opinions being known) would not be received against him.

But I cannot help it. One thing people shall not call me with justice, and that is—a liar. As you say of yourself, I too feel that I lack courage; but if ever the occasion arises when I am bound to speak, I will not shame my boy.

I have spoken more openly and distinctly to you than I ever have to any human being except my wife.

If you can show me that I err in premises or conclusion, I am ready to give up these as I would any other theories. But at any rate you will do me the justice to believe that I have not reached my conclusions without the care befitting the momentous nature of the problems involved.

And I write this the more readily to you, because it is clear to me that if that great and powerful instrument for good or evil, the Church of England, is to be saved from being shivered into fragments by the advancing tide of science—an event I should be very sorry to witness, but which will infallibly occur if men like Samuel of Oxford are to have the guidance of her destinies—it must be by the efforts of men who, like yourself, see your way to the combination of the practice of the Church with the spirit of science. Understand that all the younger men of science whom I know intimately are *essentially* of my way of thinking. (I know not a scoffer or an irreligious or an immoral man among them, but they all regard orthodoxy as you do Brahmanism.) Understand that this new school of the prophets is the only one that can work miracles, the only one that can constantly appeal to nature for evidence that it is right, and will constantly appeal to nature for evidence that it is right, and you will

---

1. "God help me, I can do no other."

comprehend that it is of no use to try to barricade us with shovel hats and aprons, or to talk about our doctrines being "shocking."

I don't profess to understand the logic of yourself, Maurice, and the rest of your school, but I have always said I would swear by your truthfulness and sincerity, and that good must come of your efforts. The more plain this was to me, however, the more obvious the necessity to let you see where the men of science are driving, and it has often been in my mind to write to you before.

If I have spoken too plainly anywhere, or too abruptly, pardon me, and do the like to me.

My wife thanks you very much for your volume of sermons. Ever yours very faithfully,

T. H. HUXLEY

GEORGE SANTAYANA
Classic Liberty

When ancient peoples defended what they called their liberty, the word stood for a plain and urgent interest of theirs: that their cities should not be destroyed, their territory pillaged, and they themselves sold into slavery. For the Greeks in particular liberty meant even more than this. Perhaps the deepest assumption of classic philosophy is that nature and the gods on the one hand and man on the other, both have a fixed character; that there is consequently a necessary piety, a true philosophy, a standard happiness, a normal art. The Greeks believed, not without reason, that they had grasped these permanent principles better than other peoples. They had largely dispelled superstition, experimented in government, and turned life into a rational art. Therefore when they defended their liberty what they defended was not merely freedom to live. It was freedom to live well, to live as other nations did not, in the public experimental study of the world and of human nature. This liberty to discover and pursue a natural happiness, this liberty to grow wise and to live in friendship with the gods and with one another, was the liberty vindicated at Thermopylae by martyrdom and at Salamis by victory.

As Greek cities stood for liberty in the world, so philosophers stood for liberty in the Greek cities. In both cases it was the same kind of liberty, not freedom to wander at hazard or to let things slip, but on the contrary freedom to legislate more precisely, at least for oneself, and to discover and codify the means to true happiness. Many of these pioneers in wisdom were audacious radicals and recoiled from no paradox. Some condemned what was most Greek: mythology, athletics, even multiplicity and physical motion. In the heart of those thriving, loquacious, festive little ant-hills, they preached impassibility and abstraction, the unanswerable scepticism of silence. Others practised a musical and priestly refinement of life, filled with metaphysical mysteries, and formed secret societies, not without a tendency to political domination. The cynics railed at the conventions, making themselves as comfortable as possible in the role of beggars and mocking parasites. The conservatives themselves were radical, so intelligent were they, and Plato wrote the charter[1] of the most extreme militarism and communism, for the sake of preserving the free state. It was the swan-song of liberty, a prescription to a diseased old man to become young again and try a second life of superhuman virtue. The old man preferred simply to die.

Many laughed then, as we may be tempted to do, at all those absolute physicians of the soul, each with his panacea. Yet beneath their quarrels the wranglers had a common faith. They all believed there was a single solid natural wisdom to be found, that reason could find it, and that mankind, sobered by reason, could put it in practice. Mankind has continued to run wild and like barbarians to place freedom in their very wildness, till we can hardly conceive the classic assumption of Greek philosophers and cities, that true liberty is bound up with an institution, a corporate scientific discipline, necessary to set free the perfect man, or the god, within us.

Upon the dissolution of paganism the Christian church adopted the classic conception of liberty. Of course, the field in which the higher politics had to operate was now conceived differently, and there was a new experience of the sort of happiness appropriate and possible to man; but the assumption remained unchallenged that Providence, as well as the human soul, had a fixed discoverable scope, and that the business of education, law, and religion was to bring them to operate in harmony. The aim of life, salvation, was involved in the nature of the soul itself, and the means of salvation had been ascertained by a positive science which the church was possessed of, partly revealed and partly experimental. Salvation was simply what, on a broad view, we should see to be health, and religion was nothing but a sort of universal hygiene.

The church, therefore, little as it tolerated heretical liberty, the liberty of moral and intellectual dispersion, felt that it had come into the world to set men free, and constantly demanded liberty for itself, that it might fulfil this mission. It was divinely commissioned to teach, guide, and console all nations and all ages by the self-same means, and to promote at all costs what it conceived to be human perfection. There should be saints and as many saints as possible. The church never admitted, any more than did any sect of ancient philosophers, that its teaching might represent only an

1. The reference is to Plato's *Republic*.

eccentric view of the world, or that its guidance and consolations might be suitable only at one stage of human development. To waver in the pursuit of the orthodox ideal could only betray frivolity and want of self-knowledge. The truth of things and the happiness of each man could not lie elsewhere than where the church, summing up all human experience and all divine revelation, had placed it once for all and for everybody. The liberty of the church to fulfil its mission was accordingly hostile to any liberty of dispersion, to any radical consecutive independence, in the life of individuals or of nations.

When it came to full fruition this orthodox freedom was far from gay; it was called sanctity. The freedom of pagan philosophers too had turned out to be rather a stiff and severe pose; but in the Christian dispensation this austerity of true happiness was less to be wondered at, since life on earth was reputed to be abnormal from the beginning, and infected with hereditary disease. The full beauty and joy of restored liberty could hardly become evident in this life. Nevertheless a certain beauty and joy did radiate visibly from the saints; and while we may well think their renunciations and penances misguided or excessive, it is certain that, like the Spartans and the philosophers, they got something for their pains. Their bodies and souls were transfigured, as none now found upon earth. If we admire without imitating them we shall perhaps have done their philosophy exact justice. Classic liberty was a sort of forced and artificial liberty, a poor perfection reserved for an ascetic aristocracy in whom heroism and refinement were touched with perversity and slowly starved themselves to death.

Since those days we have discovered how much larger the universe is, and we have lost our way in it. Any day it may come over us again that our modern liberty to drift in the dark is the most terrible negation of freedom. Nothing happens to us as we would. We want peace and make war. We need science and obey the will to believe, we love art and flounder among whimsicalities, we believe in general comfort and equality and we strain every nerve to become millionaires. After all, antiquity must have been right in thinking that reasonable self-direction must rest on having a determinate character and knowing what it is, and that only the truth about God and happiness, if we somehow found it, could make us free. But the truth is not to be found by guessing at it, as religious prophets and men of genius have done, and then damning every one who does not agree. Human nature, for all its substantial fixity, is a living thing with many varieties and variations. All diversity of opinion is therefore not founded on ignorance; it may express a legitimate change of habit or interest. The classic and Christian synthesis from which we have broken loose was certainly premature, even if the only issue of our liberal

experiments should be to lead us back to some such equilibrium.
Let us hope at least that the new morality, when it comes, may
be more broadly based than the old on knowledge of the world, not
so absolute, not so meticulous, and not chanted so much in the
monotone of an abstracted sage.

JEAN-PAUL SARTRE

Existentialism

Man is nothing else but what he makes of himself. Such is the first
principle of existentialism. It is also what is called subjectivity, the
name we are labeled with when charges are brought against us. But
what do we mean by this, if not that man has a greater dignity than
a stone or table? For we mean that man first exists, that is, that
man first of all is the being who hurls himself toward a future and
who is conscious of imagining himself as being in the future. Man
is at the start a plan which is aware of itself, rather than a patch of
moss, a piece of garbage, or a cauliflower; nothing exists prior to
this plan; there is nothing in heaven; man will be what he will have
planned to be. Not what he will want to be. Because by the word
"will" we generally mean a conscious decision, which is subsequent
to what we have already made of ourselves. I may want to belong to
a political party, write a book, get married; but all that is only a
manifestation of an earlier, more spontaneous choice that is called
"will." But if existence really does precede essence, man is responsible for what he is. Thus, existentialism's first move is to make every
man aware of what he is and to make the full responsibility of his
existence rest on him. And when we say that a man is responsible
for himself, we do not only mean that he is responsible for his
own individuality, but that he is responsible for all men.

The word "subjectivism" has two meanings, and our opponents
play on the two. Subjectivism means, on the one hand, that an individual chooses and makes himself; and, on the other, that it is
impossible for man to transcend human subjectivity. The second
of these is the essential meaning of existentialism. When we say
that man chooses his own self, we mean that every one of us does
likewise; but we also mean by that that in making this choice he
also chooses all men. In fact, in creating the man that we want to
be, there is not a single one of our acts which does not at the same
time create an image of man as we think he ought to be. To choose
to be this or that is to affirm at the same time the value of what we
choose, because we can never choose evil. We always choose the
good, and nothing can be good for us without being good for all.

If, on the other hand, existence precedes essence, and if we grant
that we exist and fashion our image at one and the same time, the

image is valid for everybody and for our whole age. Thus, our responsibility is much greater than we might have supposed, because it involves all mankind. If I am a workingman and choose to join a Christian trade union rather than be a Communist, and if by being a member.I want to show that the best thing for man is resignation, that the kingdom of man is not of this world, I am not only involving my own case—I want to be resigned for everyone. As a result, my action has involved all humanity. To take a more individual matter, if I want to marry, to have children, even it this marriage depends solely on my own circumstances or passion or wish, I am involving all humanity in monogamy and not merely myself. Therefore, I am responsible for myself and for everyone else. I am creating a certain image of man of my own choosing. In choosing myself, I choose man.

This helps us understand what the actual content is of such rather grandiloquent words as anguish, forlornness, despair. As you will see, it's all quite simple.

First, what is meant by anguish? The existentialists say at once that man is anguish. What that means is this: the man who involves himself and who realizes that he is not only the person he chooses to be, but also a lawmaker who is, at the same time, choosing all mankind as well as himself, cannot help escape the feeling of his total and deep responsibility. Of course, there are many people who are not anxious; but we claim that they are hiding their anxiety, that they are fleeing from it. Certainly, many people believe that when they do something, they themselves are the only ones involved, and when someone says to them, "What if everyone acted that way?" they shrug their shoulders and answer, "Everyone doesn't act that way." But really, one should always ask himself, "What would happen if everybody looked at things that way?" There is no escaping this disturbing thought except by a kind of double-dealing. A man who lies and makes excuses for himself by saying "not everybody does that," is someone with an uneasy conscience, because the act of lying implies that a universal value is conferred upon the lie.

Anguish is evident even when it conceals itself. This is the anguish that Kierkegaard called the anguish of Abraham. You know the story: an angel has ordered Abraham to sacrifice his son; if it really were an angel who has come and said, "You are Abraham, you shall sacrifice your son," everything would be all right. But everyone might first wonder, "Is it really an angel, and am I really Abraham? What proof do I have?"

There was a madwoman who had hallucinations; someone used to speak to her on the telephone and give her orders. Her doctor asked her, "Who is it who talks to you?" She answered, "He says it's God." What proof did she really have that it was God? If an angel comes to me, what proof is there that it's an angel? And if I hear voices, what proof is there that they come from heaven and not from hell, or from the subconscious, or a pathological condition? What proves that they are addressed to me? What proof is there that I have been appointed to impose my choice and my conception of man on humanity? I'll never find any proof or sign to convince me of that. If a voice addresses me, it is always for me to decide that this is the angel's voice; if I consider that such an act is a good one, it is I who will choose to say that it is good rather than bad.

Now, I'm not being singled out as an Abraham, and yet at every moment I'm obliged to perform exemplary acts. For every man, everything happens as if all mankind had its eyes fixed on him and were guiding itself by what he does. And every man ought to say to himself, "Am I really the kind of man who has the right to act in such a way that humanity might guide itself by my actions?" And if he does not say that to himself, he is masking his anguish.

There is no question here of the kind of anguish which would lead to quietism, to inaction. It is a matter of a simple sort of anguish that anybody who has had responsibilities is familiar with. For example, when a military officer takes the responsibility for an attack and sends a certain number of men to death, he chooses to do so, and in the main he alone makes the choice. Doubtless, orders come from above, but they are too broad; he interprets them, and on this interpretation depend the lives of ten or fourteen or twenty men. In making a decision he cannot help having a certain anguish. All leaders know this anguish. That doesn't keep them from acting; on the contrary, it is the very condition of their action. For it implies that they envisage a number of possibilities, and when they choose one, they realize that it has value only because it is chosen. We shall see that this kind of anguish, which is the kind that existentialism describes, is explained, in addition, by a direct responsibility to the other men whom it involves. It is not a curtain separating us from action, but is part of action itself.

When we speak of forlornness, a term Heidegger was fond of, we mean only that God does not exist and that we have to face all the consequences of this. This existentialist is strongly opposed to a certain kind of secular ethics which would like to abolish God with the least possible expense. About 1880, some French teachers tried to set up a secular ethics which went something like this: God is a useless and costly hypothesis; we are discarding it; but, meanwhile, in order for there to be an ethics, a society, a civilization, it is essential that certain values be taken seriously and that they be considered as having an *a priori* existence. It must be obligatory, *a priori*, to be honest, not to lie, not to beat your wife, to have children, etc., etc. So we're going to try a little device which will make it possible to show that values exist all the same, inscribed in a heaven of ideas, though otherwise God does not exist. In other words—and this, I believe, is the tendency of everything called reformism in France— nothing will be changed if God does not exist. We shall find ourselves with the same norms of honesty, progress, and humanism, and we shall have made of God an outdated hypothesis which will peacefully die off by itself.

The existentialist, on the contrary, thinks it very distressing that God does not exist, because all possibility of finding values in a heaven of ideas disappears along with Him; there can no longer be an *a priori* Good, since there is no infinite and perfect consciousness to think it. Nowhere is it written that the Good exists, that we must be honest, that we must not lie; because the fact is we are on a plane where there are only men. Dostoievsky said, "If God didn't exist, everything would be possible." That is the very starting point of existentialism. Indeed, everything is permissible if God does not exist, and as a result man is forlorn, because neither within him nor without does he find anything to cling to. He can't start making excuses for himself.

If existence really does precede essence, there is no explaining things away by reference to a fixed and given human nature. In other words, there is no determinism, man is free, man is freedom. On the other hand, if God does not exist, we find no values or commands to turn to which legitimize our conduct. So, in the bright realm of values, we have no excuse behind us, nor justification before us. We are alone, with no excuses.

That is the idea I shall try to convey when I say that man is condemned to be free. Condemned, because he did not create himself, yet, in other respects is free; because, once thrown into the world, he is responsible for everything he does. The existentialist does not believe in the power of passion. He will never agree that a sweeping passion is a ravaging torrent which fatally leads a man to certain acts and is therefore an excuse. He thinks that man is responsible for his passion.

The existentialist does not think that man is going to help himself by finding in the world some omen by which to orient himself. Because he thinks that man will interpret the omen to suit himself. Therefore, he thinks that man, with no support and no aid, is condemned every moment to invent man. Ponge, in a very fine article, has said, "Man is the future of man." That's exactly it. But if it is taken to mean that this future is recorded in heaven, that God sees it, then it is false, because it would really no longer be a future. If it is taken to mean that, whatever a man may be, there is a future to be forged, a virgin future before him, then this remark is sound. But then we are forlorn.

To give you an example which will enable you to understand forlornness better, I shall cite the case of one of my students who came to see me under the following circumstances: his father was on bad terms with his mother, and, moreover, was inclined to be a collaborationist; his older brother had been killed in the German offensive of 1940, and the young man, with somewhat immature but generous feelings, wanted to avenge him. His mother lived alone with him, very much upset by the half-treason of her husband and the death of her older son; the boy was her only consolation.

The boy was faced with the choice of leaving for England and joining the Free French forces—that is, leaving his mother behind —or remaining with his mother and helping her to carry on. He was fully aware that the woman lived only for him and that his going off—and perhaps his death—would plunge her into despair. He was also aware that every act that he did for his mother's sake was a sure thing, in the sense that it was helping her to carry on, where-as every effort he made toward going off and fighting was an uncertain move which might run aground and prove completely useless; for example, on his way to England he might, while passing through Spain, be detained indefinitely in a Spanish camp; he might reach England or Algiers and be stuck in an office at a desk job. As a result, he was faced with two very different kinds of action: one, concrete, immediate, but concerning only one individual; the other concerned an incomparably vaster group, a national collectivity, but for that very reason was dubious, and might be interrupted en route. And, at the same time, he was wavering between two kinds of ethics. On the one hand, an ethics of sympathy, of personal devotion; on the other, a broader ethics, but one whose efficacy was more dubious. He had to choose between the two.

Who could help him choose? Christian doctrine? No. Christian doctrine says, "Be charitable, love your neighbor, take the more rugged path, etc., etc." But which is the more rugged path? Whom should he love as a brother? The fighting man or his mother? Which does the greater good, the vague act of fighting in a group, or the concrete one of helping a particular human being to go on living? Who can decide *a priori?* Nobody. No book of ethics can tell him. The Kantian ethics says, "Never treat any person as a means, but as an end." Very well, if I stay with my mother, I'll treat her as an end and not as a means; but by virtue of this very fact, I'm running the risk of treating the people around me who are fighting, as means; and, conversely, if I go to join those who are fighting, I'll be treating them as an end, and, by doing that, I run the risk of treating my mother as a means.

If values are vague, and if they are always too broad for the con-crete and specific case that we are considering, the only thing left for us is to trust our instincts. That's what this young man tried to do; and when I saw him, he said, "In the end, feeling is what counts. I ought to choose whichever pushes me in one direction. If I feel that I love my mother enough to sacrifice everything else for her—my desire for vengeance, for action, for adventure—then I'll stay with her. If, on the contrary, I feel that my love for my mother isn't enough, I'll leave."

But how is the value of a feeling determined? What gives his feeling for his mother value? Precisely the fact that he remained with her. I may say that I like so-and-so well enough to sacrifice a certain amount of money for him, but I may say so only if I've done it. I may say "I love my mother well enough to remain with her" if I have remained with her. The only way to determine the value of this affection is, precisely, to perform an act which confirms and defines it. But, since I require this affection to justify my act, I find myself caught in a vicious circle.

On the other hand, Gide has well said that a mock feeling and a true feeling are almost indistinguishable; to decide that I love my mother and will remain with her, or to remain with her by putting on an act, amount somewhat to the same thing. In other words, the feeling is formed by the acts one performs; so, I cannot refer to it in order to act upon it. Which means that I can neither seek within myself the true condition which will impel me to act, nor apply to a system of ethics for concepts which will permit me to act. You will say, "At least, he did go to a teacher for advice." But if you seek advice from a priest, for example, you have chosen this priest; you already knew, more or less, just about what advice he was going to give you. In other words, choosing your adviser is involving yourself. The proof of this is that if you are a Christian, you will say, "Consult a priest." But some priests are collaborating, some are just marking time, some are resisting. Which to choose? If the young man chooses a priest who is resisting or collaborating, he has already decided on the kind of advice he's going to get. Therefore, in coming to see me he knew the answer I was going to give him, and I had only one answer to give: "You're free, choose, that is, invent." No general ethics can show you what is to be done; there are no omens in the world. The Catholics will reply, "But there are." Granted —but, in any case, I myself choose the meaning they have.

When I was a prisoner, I knew a rather remarkable young man who was a Jesuit. He had entered the Jesuit order in the following way: he had had a number of very bad breaks; in childhood, his father died, leaving him in poverty, and he was a scholarship student at a religious institution where he was constantly made to feel that he was being kept out of charity; then, he failed to get any of the honors and distinctions that children like; later on, at about eighteen, he bungled a love affair; finally, at twenty-two, he failed in military training, a childish enough matter, but it was the last straw.

This young fellow might well have felt that he had botched everything. It was a sign of something, but of what? He might have taken refuge in bitterness or despair. But he very wisely looked upon all this as a sign that he was not made for secular triumphs, and that only the triumphs of religion, holiness, and faith were open to him. He saw the hand of God in all this, and so he entered the order. Who can help seeing that he alone decided what the sign meant?

Some other interpretation might have been drawn from this series of setbacks; for example, that he might have done better to turn carpenter or revolutionist. Therefore, he is fully responsible for the interpretation. Forlornness implies that we ourselves choose our being. Forlornness and anguish go together.

As for despair, the term has a very simple meaning. It means that we shall confine ourselves to reckoning only with what depends upon our will, or on the ensemble of probabilities which make our action possible. When we want something, we always have to reckon with probabilities. I may be counting on the arrival of a friend. The friend is coming by rail or streetcar; this supposes that the train will arrive on schedule, or that the streetcar will not jump the track. I am left in the realm of possibility; but possibilities are to be reckoned with only to the point where my action comports with the ensemble of these possibilities, and no further. The moment the possibilities I am considering are not rigorously involved by my action, I ought to disengage myself from them, because no God, no scheme, can adapt the world and its possibilities to my will. When Descartes said, "Conquer yourself rather than the world," he meant essentially the same thing.

The Marxists to whom I have spoken reply, "You can rely on the support of others in your action, which obviously has certain limits because you're not going to live forever. That means: rely on both what others are doing elsewhere to help you, in China, in Russia, and what they will do later on, after your death, to carry on the action and lead it to its fulfillment, which will be the revolution. You even *have* to rely upon that, otherwise you're immoral." I reply at once that I will always rely on fellow-fighters insofar as these comrades are involved with me in a common struggle, in the unity of a party or a group in which I can more or less make my weight felt; that is, one whose ranks I am in as a fighter and whose movements I am aware of at every moment. In such a situation, relying on the unity and will of the party is exactly like counting on the fact that the train will arrive on time or that the car won't jump the track. But, given that man is free and that there is no human nature for me to depend on, I cannot count on men whom I do not know by relying on human goodness or man's concern for the good of society. I don't know what will become of the Russian revolution; I may make an example of it to the extent that at the present time it is apparent that the proletariat plays a part in Russia that it plays in no other nation. But I can't swear that this will inevitably lead to a triumph of the proletariat. I've got to limit myself to what I see.

Given that men are free and that tomorrow they will freely decide what man will be, I cannot be sure that, after my death, fellow-fighters will carry on my work to bring it to its maximum perfection. Tomorrow, after my death, some men may decide to set up Fascism, and the others may be cowardly and muddled enough to let them do it. Fascism will then be the human reality, so much the worse for us.

Actually, things will be as man will have decided they are to be. Does that mean that I should abandon myself to quietism? No. First, I should involve myself; then, act on the old saw, "Nothing ventured, nothing gained." Nor does it mean that I shouldn't belong to a party, but rather that I shall have no illusions and shall do what I can. For example, suppose I ask myself, "Will socialization, as such, ever come about?" I know nothing about it. All I know is that I'm going to do everything in my power to bring it about. Beyond that, I can't count on anything. Quietism is the attitude of people who say, "Let others do what I can't do." The doctrine I am presenting is the very opposite of quietism, since it declares, "There is no reality except in action." Moreover, it goes further, since it adds, "Man is nothing else than his plan; he exists only to the extent that he fulfills himself; he is therefore nothing else than the ensemble of his acts, nothing else than his life."

According to this, we can understand why our doctrine horrifies certain people. Because often the only way they can bear their wretchedness is to think, "Circumstances have been against me. What I've been and done doesn't show my true worth. To be sure, I've had no great love, no great friendship, but that's because I haven't met a man or woman who was worthy. The books I've written haven't been very good because I haven't had the proper leisure. I haven't had children to devote myself to because I didn't find a man with whom I could have spent my life. So there remains within me, unused and quite viable, a host of propensities, inclinations, possibilities, that one wouldn't guess from the mere series of things I've done."

Now, for the existentialist there is really no love other than one which manifests itself in a person's being in love. There is no genius other than one which is expressed in works of art; the genius of Proust is the sum of Proust's works; the genius of Racine is his series of tragedies. Outside of that, there is nothing. Why say that Racine could have written another tragedy, when he didn't write it? A man is involved in life, leaves his impress on it, and outside of that there is nothing. To be sure, this may seem a harsh thought to someone whose life hasn't been a success. But, on the other hand, it prompts people to understand that reality alone is what counts, that dreams, expectations, and hopes warrant no more than to define a man as a disappointed dream, as miscarried hopes, as vain expectations. In other words, to define him negatively and not positively. However, when we say, "You are nothing else than your life," that does not imply that the artist will be judged solely on the basis of his works of art; a thousand other things will contribute toward summing him up. What we mean is that a man is nothing else than a series of undertakings, that he is the sum, the organization, the ensemble of the relationships which make up these undertakings.

When all is said and done, what we are accused of, at bottom, is not our pessimism, but an optimistic toughness. If people throw up to us our works of fiction in which we write about people who are soft, weak, cowardly, and sometimes even downright bad, it's not because these prople are soft, weak, cowardly, or bad; because if we were to say, as Zola did, that they are that way because of heredity, the workings of environment, society, because of biological or psychological determinism, people would be reassured. They would say, "Well, that's what we're like, no one can do anything about it." But when the existentialist writes about a coward, he says that this coward is responsible for his cowardice. He's not like that because he has a cowardly heart or lung or brain; he's not like that on account of his physiological make-up; but he's like that because he has made himself a coward by his acts. There's no such thing as a cowardly constitution; there are nervous constitutions; there is poor blood, as the common people say, or strong constitutions. But the man whose blood is poor is not a coward on that account, for what makes cowardice is the act of renouncing or yielding. A constitution is not an act; the coward is defined on the basis of the acts he performs. People feel, in a vague sort of way, that this coward we're talking about is guilty of being a coward, and the thought frightens them. What people would like is that a coward or a hero be born that way. . . .

From these few reflections it is evident that nothing is more unjust than the objections that have been raised against us. Existentialism is nothing else than an attempt to draw all the consequences of a coherent atheistic position. It isn't trying to plunge man into despair at all. But if one calls every attitude of unbelief despair, like the Christians, then the word is not being used in its original sense. Existentialism isn't so atheistic that it wears itself out showing that God doesn't exist. Rather, it declares that even if God did exist, that would change nothing. There you've got our point of view. Not that we believe that God exists, but we think that the problem of His existence is not the issue. In this sense existentialism is optimistic, a doctrine of action, and it is plain dishonesty for Christians to make no distinction between their own despair and ours˙and then to call us despairing.

QUESTIONS

1. What are some of the methods or devices Sartre uses to define existentialism? Why does he use more than one method or device? Compare the techniques that Sartre uses with those Knox uses in defining enthusiasm (pp. 1090–1093) or those Highet uses in defining Zen (pp. 1165–1174).
2. What is the significance of the words "if existence really does precede essence"? What does this mean? What is the force of "if"? Why does Sartre repeat the words later in the essay?
3. Why does Sartre use three separate terms—anguish, forlornness, despair? What, if any, are the differences among them?
4. Sartre makes a distinction between treating "any person as a means . . . [and] as an end" (p. 1161). What are the implications of this distinction?
5. Sartre says that the "coward is responsible for his cowardice," since man "is defined on the basis of the acts he performs." Does this notion of responsibility agree with that of Henry Sloane Coffin in "What Crucified Christ?" (pp. 1131–1146)?

GILBERT HIGHET

The Mystery of Zen

The mind need never stop growing. Indeed, one of the few experiences which never pall is the experience of watching one's own mind, and observing how it produces new interests, responds to new stimuli, and develops new thoughts, apparently without effort and almost independently of one's own conscious control. I have seen this happen to myself a hundred times; and every time it happens again, I am equally fascinated and astonished.

Some years ago a publisher sent me a little book for review. I read it, and decided it was too remote from my main interests and too highly specialized. It was a brief account of how a young German philosopher living in Japan had learned how to shoot with a bow and arrow, and how this training had made it possible for him to understand the esoteric doctrines of the Zen sect of Buddhism. Really, what could be more alien to my own life, and to that of everyone I knew, than Zen Buddhism and Japanese archery? So I thought, and put the book away.

Yet I did not forget it. It was well written, and translated into good English. It was delightfully short, and implied much more than it said. Although its theme was extremely odd, it was at least highly individual; I had never read anything like it before or since.

It remained in my mind. Its name was *Zen in the Art of Archery*, its author Eugen Herrigel, its publisher Pantheon of New York. One day I took it off the shelf and read it again; this time it seemed even stranger than before and even more unforgettable. Now it began to cohere with other interests of mine. Something I had read of the Japanese art of flower arrangement seemed to connect with it; and then, when I wrote an essay on the peculiar Japanese poems called *haiku*, other links began to grow. Finally I had to read the book once more with care, and to go through some other works which illuminated the same subject. I am still grappling with the theme; I have not got anywhere near understanding it fully; but I have learned a good deal, and I am grateful to the little book which refused to be forgotten.

The author, a German philosopher, got a job teaching philosophy at the University of Tokyo (apparently between the wars), and he did what Germans in foreign countries do not usually do: he determined to adapt himself and to learn from his hosts. In particular, he had always been interested in mysticism—which, for every earnest philosopher, poses a problem that is all the more inescapable because it is virtually insoluble. Zen Buddhism is not the only mystical doctrine to be found in the East, but it is one of the most highly developed and certainly one of the most difficult to approach. Herrigel knew that there were scarcely any books which did more than skirt the edge of the subject, and that the best of all books on Zen (those by the philosopher D. T. Suzuki) constantly emphasize that Zen can never be learned from books, can never be studied as we can study other disciplines such as logic or mathematics. Therefore he began to look for a Japanese thinker who could teach him directly.

At once he met with embarrassed refusals. His Japanese friends explained that he would gain nothing from trying to discuss Zen as a philosopher, that its theories could not be spread out for analysis by a detached mind, and in fact that the normal relationship of teacher and pupil simply did not exist within the sect, because the Zen masters felt it useless to explain things stage by stage and to argue about the various possible interpretations of their doctrine. Herrigel had read enough to be prepared for this. He replied that he did not want to dissect the teachings of the school, because he knew that would be useless. He wanted to become a Zen mystic himself. (This was highly intelligent of him. No one could really penetrate into Christian mysticism without being a devout Christian; no one could appreciate Hindu mystical doctrine without accepting the Hindu view of the universe.) At this, Herrigel's Japanese friends were more forthcoming. They told him that the best way, indeed the only way, for a European to approach Zen mysticism was to learn one of the arts which exemplified it.

He was a fairly good rifle shot, so he determined to learn archery; and his wife co-operated with him by taking lessons in painting and flower arrangement. How any philosopher could investigate a mystical doctrine by learning to shoot with a bow and arrow and watching his wife arrange flowers, Herrigel did not ask. He had good sense.

A Zen master who was a teacher of archery agreed to take him as a pupil. The lessons lasted six years, during which he practiced every single day. There are many difficult courses of instruction in the world: the Jesuits, violin virtuosi, Talmudic scholars, all have long and hard training, which in one sense never comes to an end; but Herrigel's training in archery equaled them all in intensity. If I were trying to learn archery, I should expect to begin by looking at a target and shooting arrows at it. He was not even allowed to aim at a target for the first four years. He had to begin by learning how to hold the bow and arrow, and then how to release the arrow; this took ages. The Japanese bow is not like our sporting bow, and the stance of the archer in Japan is different from ours. We hold the bow at shoulder level, stretch our left arm out ahead, pull the string and the nocked arrow to a point either below the chin or sometimes past the right ear, and then shoot. The Japanese hold the bow above the head, and then pull the hands apart to left and right until the left hand comes down to eye level and the right hand comes to rest above the right shoulder; then there is a pause, during which the bow is held at full stretch, with the tip of the three-foot arrow projecting only a few inches beyond the bow; after that, the arrow is loosed. When Herrigel tried this, even without aiming, he found it was almost impossible. His hands trembled. His legs stiffened and grew cramped. His breathing became labored. And of course he could not possibly aim. Week after week he practiced this, with the Master watching him carefully and correcting his strained attitude; week after week he made no progress whatever. Finally he gave up and told his teacher that he could not learn: it was absolutely impossible for him to draw the bow and loose the arrow.

To his astonishment, the Master agreed. He said, "Certainly you cannot. It is because you are not breathing correctly. You must learn to breathe in a steady rhythm, keeping your lungs full most of the time, and drawing in one rapid inspiration with each stage of the process, as you grasp the bow, fit the arrow, raise the bow, draw, pause, and loose the shot. If you do, you will both grow stronger and be able to relax." To prove this, he himself drew his massive bow and told his pupil to feel the muscles of his arms: they were perfectly relaxed, as though he were doing no work whatever.

Herrigel now started breathing exercises; after some time he combined the new rhythm of breathing with the actions of drawing and shooting; and, much to his astonishment, he found that the whole thing, after this complicated process, had become much easier. Or rather, not easier, but different. At times it became quite unconscious. He says himself that he felt he was not breathing, but being breathed; and in time he felt that the occasional shot was not being dispatched by him, but shooting itself. The bow and arrow were in charge; he had become merely a part of them.

All this time, of course, Herrigel did not even attempt to discuss Zen docrine with his Master. No doubt he knew that he was approaching it, but he concentrated solely on learning how to shoot. Every stage which he surmounted appeared to lead to another stage even more difficult. It took him months to learn how to loosen the bowstring. The problem was this. If he gripped the string and arrowhead tightly, either he froze, so that his hands were slowly pulled together and the shot was wasted, or else he jerked, so that the arrow flew up into the air or down into the ground; and if he was relaxed, then the bowstring and arrow simply *leaked* out of his grasp before he could reach full stretch, and the arrow went nowhere. He explained this problem to the Master. The Master understood perfectly well. He replied, "You must hold the drawn bowstring like a child holding a grownup's finger. You know how firmly a child grips; and yet when it lets go, there is not the slightest jerk—because the child does not think of itself, it is not self-conscious, it does not say, 'I will now let go and do something else,' it merely acts instinctively. That is what you must learn to do. Practice, practice, and practice, and then the string will loose itself at the right moment. The shot will come as effortlessly as snow slipping from a leaf." Day after day, week after week, month after month, Herrigel practiced this; and then, after one shot, the Master suddenly bowed and broke off the lesson. He said "Just then it shot. Not you, but *it*." And gradually thereafter more and more right shots achieved themselves; the young philosopher forgot himself, forgot that he was learning archery for some other purpose, forgot even that he was practicing archery, and became part of that unconsciously active complex, the bow, the string, the arrow, and the man.

Next came the target. After four years, Herrigel was allowed to shoot at the target. But he was strictly forbidden to aim at it. The Master explained that even he himself did not aim; and indeed, when he shot, he was so absorbed in the act, so selfless and unanxious, that his eyes were almost closed. It was difficult, almost impossible, for Herrigel to believe that such shooting could ever be effective; and he risked insulting the Master by suggesting that he ought to be able to hit the target blindfolded. But the Master accepted the challenge. That night, after a cup of tea and long meditation, he went into the archery hall, put on the lights at one end and left the target perfectly dark, with only a thin taper burning in front of it. Then, with habitual grace and precision, and with that strange, almost sleepwalking, selfless confidence that is the heart of Zen, he shot two arrows into the darkness. Herrigel went out to collect them. He found that the first had gone to the heart of the bull's eye, and that the second had actually hit the first arrow and splintered it. The Master showed no pride. He said, "Perhaps, with unconscious memory of the position of the target, I shot the first arrow; but the second arrow? *It* shot the second arrow, and *it* brought it to the center of the target."

At last Herrigel began to understand. His progress became faster and faster; easier, too. Perfect shots (perfect because perfectly unconscious) occurred at almost every lesson; and finally, after six years of incessant training, in a public display he was awarded the diploma. He needed no further instruction: he had himself become a Master. His wife meanwhile had become expert both in painting and in the arrangement of flowers—two of the finest of Japanese arts. (I wish she could be persuaded to write a companion volume, called *Zen in the Art of Flower Arrangement*; it would have a wider general appeal than her husband's work.) I gather also from a hint or two in his book that she had taken part in the archery lessons. During one of the most difficult periods in Herrigel's training, when his Master had practically refused to continue teaching him—because Herrigel had tried to cheat by *consciously* opening his hand at the moment of loosing the arrow—his wife had advised him against that solution, and sympathized with him when it was rejected. She in her own way had learned more quickly than he, and reached the final point together with him. All their effort had not been in vain: Herrigel and his wife had really acquired a new and valuable kind of wisdom. Only at this point, when he was about to abandon his lessons forever, did his Master treat him almost as an equal and hint at the innermost doctrines of Zen Buddhism. Only hints he gave; and yet, for the young philosopher who had now become a mystic, they were enough. Herrigel understood the doctrine, not with his logical mind, but with his entire being. He at any rate had solved the mystery of Zen.

Without going through a course of training as absorbing and as complete as Herrigel's, we can probably never penetrate the mystery. The doctrine of Zen cannot be analyzed from without: it must be lived.

But although it cannot be analyzed, it can be hinted at. All the hints that the adherents of this creed give us are interesting. Many are fantastic; some are practically incomprehensible, and yet unforgettable. Put together, they take us toward a way of life which is utterly impossible for westerners living in a western world, and nevertheless has a deep fascination and contains some values which we must respect.

The word Zen means "meditation." (It is the Japanese word, corresponding to the Chinese Ch'an and the Hindu Dhyana.) It is the central idea of a special sect of Buddhism which flourished in China during the Sung period (between A.D. 1000 and 1300) and entered Japan in the twelfth century. Without knowing much about it, we might be certain that the Zen sect was a worthy and noble one, because it produced a quantity of highly distinguished art, specifically painting. And if we knew anything about Buddhism itself, we might say that Zen goes closer than other sects to the heart of Buddha's teaching: because Buddha was trying to found, not a religion with temples and rituals, but a way of life based on meditation. However, there is something eccentric about the Zen life which is hard to trace in Buddha's teaching; there is an active energy which he did not admire, there is a rough grasp on reality which he himself eschewed, there is something like a sense of humor, which he rarely displayed. The gravity and serenity of the Indian preacher are transformed, in Zen, to the earthy live-liness of Chinese and Japanese sages. The lotus brooding calmly on the water has turned into a knotted tree covered with spring blossoms.

In this sense, "meditation" does not mean what we usually think of when we say a philosopher meditates: analysis of reality, a long-sustained effort to solve problems of religion and ethics, the logical dissection of the universe. It means something not divisive, but whole; not schematic, but organic; not long-drawn-out, but imme-diate. It means something more like our words "intuition" and "realization." It means a way of life in which there is no division between thought and action; none of the painful gulf, so well known to all of us, between the unconscious and the conscious mind; and no absolute distinction between the self and the external world, even between the various parts of the external world and the whole.

When the German philosopher took six years of lessons in archery in order to approach the mystical significance of Zen, he was not given direct philosophical instruction. He was merely shown how to breathe, how to hold and loose the bowstring, and finally how to shoot in such a way that the bow and arrow used him as an instrument. There are many such stories about Zen teachers. The strangest I know is one about a fencing master who undertook to train a young man in the art of the sword. The relationship of teacher and pupil is very important, almost sacred, in the Far East; and the pupil hardly ever thinks of leaving a master or objecting to his methods, however extraordinary they may seem. Therefore this young fellow did not at first object when he was made to act as a servant, drawing water, sweeping floors, gathering wood for the fire, and cooking. But after some time he asked for more direct instruction. The master agreed to give it, but produced no swords. The routine went on just as before, except that every now and then the master would strike the young man with a stick. No matter what he was doing, sweeping the floor or weeding in the garden, a blow would descend on him apparently out of nowhere; he had always to be on the alert, and yet he was constantly receiving unexpected cracks on the head or shoulders. After some months of this, he saw his master stooping over a boiling pot full of vegetables; and he thought he would have his revenge. Silently he lifted a stick and brought it down; but without any effort, without even a glance in his direction, his master parried the blow with the lid of the cooking pot. At last, the pupil began to understand the instinctive alertness, the effortless perception and avoidance of danger, in which his master had been training him. As soon as he had achieved it, it was child's play for him to learn the management of the sword: he could parry every cut and turn every slash without anxiety, until his opponent, exhausted, left an opening for his counterattack. (The same principle was used by the elderly samurai for selecting his comrades in the Japanese motion picture *The Magnificent Seven*.)

These stories show that Zen meditation does not mean sitting and thinking. On the contrary, it means acting with as little thought as possible. The fencing master trained his pupil to guard against every attack with the same immediate, instinctive rapidity with which our eyelid closes over our eye when something threatens it. His work was aimed at breaking down the wall between thought and act, at completely fusing body and senses and mind so that they might all work together rapidly and effortlessly. When a Zen artist draws a picture, he does it in a rhythm almost the exact reverse of that which is followed by a Western artist. We begin by blocking out the design and then filling in the details, usually working more and more slowly as we approach the completion of the picture. The Zen artist sits down very calmly; examines his brush carefully; prepares his own ink; smooths out the paper on which he will work; falls into a profound silent ecstasy of contemplation—during which he does not think anxiously of various details, composition, brushwork, shades of tone, but rather attempts to become the vehicle through which the subject can express itself in painting; and then, very quickly and almost unconsciously, with sure effortless strokes, draws a picture containing the fewest and most effective lines. Most of the paper is left blank; only the essential is depicted, and that not completely. One long curving line will be enough to show a mountainside; seven streaks will become a group of bamboos bending in the wind; and yet, though technically incomplete, such pictures are unforgettably clear. They show the heart of reality.

All this we can sympathize with, because we can see the results. The young swordsman learns how to fence. The intuitional painter produces a fine picture. But the hardest thing for us to appreciate is that the Zen masters refuse to teach philosophy or religion directly, and deny logic. In fact, they despise logic as an artificial distortion of reality. Many philosophical teachers are difficult to understand because they analyze profound problems with subtle intricacy: such is Aristotle in his *Metaphysics*. Many mystical writers are difficult to understand because, as they themselves admit, they are attempting to use words to describe experiences which are too abstruse for words, so that they have to fall back on imagery and analogy, which they themselves recognize to be poor media, far coarser than the realities with which they have been in contact. But the Zen teachers seem to deny the power of language and thought altogether. For example, if you ask a Zen master what is the ultimate reality, he will answer, without the slightest hesitation, "The bamboo grove at the foot of the hill" or "A branch of plum blossom." Apparently he means that these things, which we can see instantly without effort, or imagine in the flash of a second, are real with the ultimate reality; that nothing is more real than these; and that we ought to grasp ultimates as we grasp simple immediates. A Chinese master was once asked the central question, "What is the Buddha?" He said nothing whatever, but held out his index finger. What did he mean? It is hard to explain; but apparently he meant "Here. Now. Look and realize with the effortlessness of seeing. Do not try to use words. Do not think. Make no efforts toward withdrawal from the world. Expect no sublime ecstasies. Live. All *that* is the ultimate reality, and it can be understood from the motion of a finger as well as from the execution of any complex ritual, from any subtle argument, or from the circling of the starry universe."

In making that gesture, the master was copying the Buddha himself, who once delivered a sermon which is famous, but was hardly understood by his pupils at the time. Without saying a word, he held up a flower and showed it to the gathering. One man, one alone, knew what he meant. The gesture became renowned as the Flower Sermon.

In the annals of Zen there are many cryptic answers to the final question, "What is the Buddha?"—which in our terms means "What is the meaning of life? What is truly real?" For example, one master, when asked "What is the Buddha?" replied, "Your name is Yecho." Another said, "Even the finest artist cannot paint him." Another said, "No nonsense here." And another answered, "The mouth is the gate of woe." My favorite story is about the monk who said to a Master, "Has a dog Buddha-nature too?" The Master replied, "Wu"—which is what the dog himself would have said.

Now, some critics might attack Zen by saying that this is the creed of a savage or an animal. The adherents of Zen would deny that—or more probably they would ignore the criticism, or make some cryptic remark which meant that it was pointless. Their position—if they could ever be persuaded to put it into words—would be this. An animal is instinctively in touch with reality, and so far is living rightly, but it has never had a mind and so cannot perceive the Whole, only that part with which it is in touch. The philosopher sees both the Whole and the parts, and enjoys them all. As for the savage, he exists only through the group; he feels himself as part of a war party or a ceremonial dance team or a ploughing-and-sowing group or the Snake clan; he is not truly an individual at all, and therefore is less than fully human. Zen has at its heart an inner solitude; its aim is to teach us to live, as in the last resort we do all have to live, alone.

A more dangerous criticism of Zen would be that it is nihilism, that its purpose is to abolish thought altogether. (This criticism is handled, but not fully met, by the great Zen authority Suzuki in his *Introduction to Zen Buddhism*.) It can hardly be completely confuted, for after all the central doctrine of Buddhism is—Nothingness. And many of the sayings of Zen masters are truly nihilistic. The first patriarch of the sect in China was asked by the emperor what was the ultimate and holiest principle of Buddhism. He replied, "Vast emptiness, and nothing holy in it." Another who was asked the searching question "Where is the abiding-place for the mind?" answered, "Not in this dualism of good and evil, being and non-being, thought and matter." In fact, thought is an activity which divides. It analyzes, it makes distinctions, it criticizes, it judges, it breaks reality into groups and classes and individuals. The aim of Zen is to abolish that kind of thinking, and to substitute—not unconsciousness, which would be death, but a consciousness that does not analyze but experiences life directly. Although it has no prescribed prayers, no sacred scriptures, no ceremonial rites, no personal god, and no interest in the soul's future destination, Zen is a religion rather than a philosophy. Jung points out that its aim is to produce a religious conversion, a "transformation": and he adds, "The transformation process is incommensurable with intellect." Thought is always interesting, but often painful; Zen is calm and painless. Thought is incomplete; Zen enlightenment brings a sense of completeness. Thought is a process; Zen illumination is a state. But it is a state which cannot be defined. In the Buddhist scriptures there is a dialogue between a master and a pupil in which the pupil tries to discover the exact meaning of such a state. The master says to him, 'If a fire were blazing in front of you, would you know that it was blazing?'

"Yes, master."

"And would you know the reason for its blazing?"

"Yes, because it had a supply of grass and sticks."

"And would you know if it were to go out?"

"Yes, master."

"And on its going out, would you know where the fire had gone? To the east, to the west, to the north, or to the south?"

"The question does not apply, master. For the fire blazed because it had a supply of grass and sticks. When it had consumed this and had no other fuel, then it went out."

"In the same way," replies the master, "no question will apply to the meaning of Nirvana, and no statement will explain it."

Such, then, neither happy nor unhappy but beyond all divisive description, is the condition which students of Zen strive to attain. Small wonder that they can scarcely explain it to us, the unilluminated.

QUESTIONS

1. What difficulties does Highet face in discussing Zen? How does he manage to give a definition in spite of his statement that Zen "cannot be analyzed"?
2. Why does Highet describe the training in archery in such detail?
3. On page 1173 Highet says that "Zen is a religion rather than a philosophy." How has he led up to this conclusion? What definitions of "religion" and "philosophy" does he imply?
4. By what means does Highet define "meditation"? Would other means have worked as well? Explain.
5. To what extent is Zen "the creed of a savage or an animal"? How does Highet go about refuting this charge?

ALAN W. WATTS

The Answer of Religion[1]

The oldest answers in the world to the problem of happiness are found in religion, for the kind of happiness we are considering belongs to the deepest realms of the human spirit. But this should not lead us to suppose that it is something remote from familiar experience, something to be sought out in supernatural spheres far beyond the world which we know through our five senses. The world of the spirit is so often understood in an almost materialistic way, as a locality infinite in space containing things that are eternal in·

1. From *The Meaning of Happiness*, 1940. (All notes are Watts's.)

terms of time.[2] It is thought to be a world corresponding in form and substance to our own, save that its forms and substances are constructed of spirit instead of matter, and its operation governed by different laws, for nothing changes—all things are everlasting. To understand the world of the spirit in this way is to make it wholly different from the world in which we live, and when religion is concerned with this kind of spiritualism a great gulf appears between the world of the spirit and the world of everyday experience, contact with the former being possible only in a disembodied condition, as after death, or in a state of consciousness where we acquire a new set of senses, spiritual senses that can perceive things to which material vision is not attuned.

This view of spirituality is so common in religion that many people believe salvation to lie utterly beyond our present life, being something for which earthly existence is only a preparation and which will be inherited when we have passed beyond the grave or when, even though still living, our thoughts have ascended to a higher sphere so that we are in this world but not of it. It is probable, however, that this idea has arisen because so much religious teaching is presented in the form of allegory; spiritual truths are presented in terms of time and space for purposes of simplification. Heaven and hell are removed in time to the life after death and in place to a *different* world-order; eternity is represented as unending time, which is not eternity but everlastingness. This kind of simplification may have its uses, but in many ways it is an unnecessary complication for the conception has greater value if we think of heaven and hell as here and now, and of eternity as the timeless, eternal Now.

Religion as a Denial of Life

However, this is one of the main trends of thought in religion as generally understood, besides which there is yet another believing that spiritual happiness is attainable on earth but in a somewhat utopian and materialistic way. Both of these trends exist in Christianity, some holding that "on this earth we have no continuing home, therefore we seek one to come," and others working for the establishment of the "kingdom of heaven on earth." The Christian holding the former opinion feels that he can never be at home in this world which he regards a kind of anteroom to the life hereafter, a place of trial and temptation where God tests the fitness of His children to enter His kingdom. At the same time he will thank his Lord for all the blessings of this earth, for the pleasures which

2. A remarkable analysis of this confusion is the first chapter of Nicolas Berdyaev's *Freedom and the Spirit* (London, 1935), esp. p. 15. "Spirit," he writes, "is by no means opposed to flesh; rather, flesh is the incarnation and symbol of spirit."

give him joy as well as for the pains which give opportunities to learn wisdom. Yet he is not content with those pleasures, and because they are so fleeting he regards them as mere hints of the glories of paradise which shall endure forever and ever.

But in modern Christianity especially there is another element which existed in olden times, though in a different form. An article of the Apostles' Creed is the belief in the resurrection of the body,[3] the belief that the world to come is not only a spiritual but also a condition of life where the physical world has been recreated by spiritual power. It is said that God will create a new heaven and a new earth, and that "the kingdom of this world shall become the Kingdom of Our Lord and of His Christ." The modern Christian is apt to regard this teaching in rather a different way, for whereas his ancestors viewed it as something which would happen only at the last day when all the dead would rise from their graves, the modern view is rather that the kingdom of heaven on earth is something which man may create by the Grace of God here and now. Hence the increasing interest of the churches in idealistic politics. Morality becomes something to be practiced, not only to insure salvation in the world to come, but to improve the lot of mankind in the world as it is. For Christianity has become linked to the idea of progress, and the churches are the foremost advocates of peace, of social service, and of political and economic justice.

But both among Christians and among followers of other religions there are those who feel that such ideals are rather naive, either because they seem impossible of achievement or else because they do not seem very desirable. Spiritual happiness, as they understand it, has little to do with either material well-being or everlasting glory in a paradise of heavenly music and streets of pure gold. But they share the same suspicion of the world as it is, believing the highest illumination of the spirit unattainable in the flesh or under the particular limitations of the senses which compel us to view life as a transient alternation of pleasure and pain.

For many centureis there has been a tendency of this kind in the religions of the East, of which the most notable example is Hinayana Buddhism—the type of Buddhism with which the West is most familiar. The Hinayana takes the most gloomy view of the world of any religion, and seeks escape from it by the quickest possible means to a stage which is not exactly complete annihilation, but a kind of vague, infinite consciousness from which all personality, all sense of individual identity, and all diversity of form have been removed. In this state there is no pain because there is no pleasure, and no death

---

3. A refreshingly different interpretation of this doctrine will be found in   Berdyaev, *ibid.*, pp. 40–41.

because there is no longer anyone to die. The gist of its teaching is that when you realize that your personal self does not exist, then you are free of suffering, for suffering can arise only when there is a person to suffer. The same may be said of pleasure, with the result that the Hinayana ideal is a state of tastelessness which is held to be the highest attainable bliss.

A similar ideal might be found by a casual examination of the teaching of Hindu Vedanta as expressed in the Upanishads. For it seems as if the supreme aspiration of the Hindu yogin is to become merged into the infinite Brahman, the one reality of which all diverse forms are illusory expressions. In common with the Hinayana Buddhist, he finds the world unsatisfying because of the impermanence of its glories. Therefore he fights against all those things in himself which move him to seek happiness in the pleasures of the world, learning to see the changing forms of life as a web of delusion hiding the face of God. To him all things are God; mountains, trees, rivers, men, and beasts only seem to be what they are because of the limitations of his own senses. Once those limitations are overcome, the world of diverse form vanishes and there remains only the vast and void infinitude of Brahman in whom is eternal rest and bliss.

Such ideas are frequent in Eastern thought, although they do not represent its deepest meaning. To most of us they are abstract and incomprehensible. Nevertheless, countless religious people maintain that the end and aim of our life here on earth is an eternal condition whose characteristics may be described in one of the following ways. First, a state beyond death wherein the beauties of life are greatly magnified and all its pains and limitations overcome. Second, a state in this life wherein earthly pains and limitations have been overcome by the exercise of human reason and skill, inspired by the Grace of God. Third, a state attainable either in the body or out of it where human consciousness has been raised above the limits imposed upon it by the personal self and its five senses, wherein all diversity of form, all pairs of opposites, have been merged into the infinite and formless divine essence from which they originally came.

Abolishing the Universe

All these three have certain elements in common. There is a distaste for the world as it is, implying that the wrong is not so much in the external world as in one's own imperfect self, which is either doomed to live in this world on account of those imperfections or else which sees that world falsely, being deluded by imperfect senses. There is also the hope for an eternal state in which good things are made permanent or abolished altogether along with the evil. And, most significant of all, there is the implication that one of these religious states is the ultimate purpose of our earthly existence, from which it must follow that appropriate religious activities are fundamentally the only worth-while pursuits for mankind. All other pursuits must therefore be considered subordinate and ephemeral, and in this view art, literature, music, politics, science, drama, exploration, and sport become vain and empty unless they are regarded simply as means of keeping body and soul together in reasonable comfort, or unless they are used for specifically religious purposes. Apart from these two uses they become simply the trimmings of life, the mere gilt on the pill, mere "relaxations" to assuage in as harmless a manner as possible our carnal nature lest its sufferings become too great for us to bear.

The direction of this kind of religion is even more apparent when we consider the various ways and means prescribed for attaining such ideals. Among civilized peoples there are two principal ways of approach to the religious ideal, both of which have various common elements. Both are founded on the idea that the search for spiritual happiness in worldly pleasures is a snare because those pleasures are impermanent; they do, perhaps, impart a certain happiness, but because that happiness is entirely dependent on external circumstances it disappears as soon as those circumstances change. But there is something in man which makes it exceedingly hard for him to avoid the pursuit of earthly pleasures, and this tendency religion attempts to vanquish by a strongly hostile attitude to them. Hence the general antipathy in religion to all that pertains to the senses, and especially to the most elementary and important of earthly pleasures which are to be found in the sexual functions.

The first of the two ways of approach to the religious ideal is found mainly in Christianity. It is the way of mortification of the flesh in order that the eyes may be turned from the snares of the world to the eternal glories of the world beyond. By prayer, fasting, and acts of charity, by abstinence from fleshly delights, man may make himself fit to receive, feel and rejoice in the Grace of God which senses deluded by earthly things cannot appreciate. If the senses are coarsened by carnal pleasures, man becomes incapable of entering either now or hereafter into that realm of supernatural glory to which the Grace of God belongs. By its light he is not illumined but burned because of his impurities, for only those things which have been refined of all evil can exist within it.

The second way is similar in most respects, save that it is a way of self-development, wherein the individual relies not on God, but on his own power of willing. It is found in Buddhism and Vedanta, and consists of exercises in mortification and meditation whose object is similarly to refine the senses, to turn them away from the snares of the world and finally to root out from the soul the sense of personal identity and self-sufficiency and its desire to find happiness in the forms of life.

Obviously we are discussing some of the more extreme forms of religious theory and practice; generally speaking, their outward forms have been increasingly modified in the course of years. But there has been little change in the underlying philosophy, which amounts virtually to the complete denial of life as we understand it. For according to this kind of teaching the world of the senses has been made for the sole purpose of encompassing the human soul with a variety of snares. Even the "highest" delights of the senses such as are to be found in the arts are "trimmings," and the less refined joys of eating and sex are just tolerated in so far as they are used only for the purpose of maintaining and reproducing life. Today the harsh attitude of religion to these things has been appreciably softened, but this softening is rather a concession to human nature than an attempt to alter the fundamental premises of religious doctrine. And a mere concession to human nature it will remain while so many types of religious philosophy regard the material and spiritual worlds as irreconcilably opposed.

The problem is important because it affects the usefulness of religion to the greater part of mankind. The belief is still generally prevalent that those who wish to "go furthest" in religion must practice extremes of fasting and chastity and other forms of cumbersome discipline to acquire the necessary spiritual sensitivity for making contact with states of consciousness and mystical insight which less refined senses can no more experience than a jaded palate can taste the subtleties of a fine wine. But this refining and exaltation of consciousness by means of asceticism is obviously a vocation for the very few, for even if it were practicable for the majority it would not be altogether desirable to have the world converted into a vast Tibet. It would be wiser to heed the warning of Lucretius, "*Tantum religio potuit suadere malorum*," or "Too much religion is apt to encourage evil."

But if the highest illumination of the spirit is only attainable by such means, of what use is religion to the ordinary run of mankind? It may encourage them to a greater morality; it may even teach them to love one another, though the course of history does not suggest that there has been much success in this. It may also give them a sense of the reality of a Father God to whom they can pray as "a very present help in time of trouble." But this does not begin to exhaust the possibilities of religion because it comes nowhere near to the real essentials of religion; it scarcely touches what is called "religious experience," without which doctrines, rites, and observances are the emptiest shells. It cannot be assumed that because most religious people are moral, moral people are therefore religious. As Wilde said, "When I am happy I am always good, but when I am good I am seldom happy," and this becomes more true than ever if by happiness we mean the state that arises from religious experience.

The Religious Experience

Religious experience is something like artistic or musical inspiration, though inspiration is a word that through misuse has unfortunate associations; religious experience is not "uplift" or flighty emotionalism. Strictly speaking, a composer is inspired when melody emerges from the depths of his mind, how or why we do not know. To convey that melody to others he writes it down on paper, employing a technical knowledge which enables him to name the notes which he hears in his mind. This fact is important: his technical knowledge does not *create* the tune in his mind; it simply provides him with a complicated alphabet, and is no more the source of music than the literary alphabet and the rules of grammar are the sources of men's ideas. If he is writing a symphony he will want to orchestrate his melody, but to do this he does not look up the books on harmony and orchestration to find out what combinations of notes he is advised by the the rules to put together. He has heard the whole symphony in his mind with every instrument playing its independent part, and his knowledge of orchestration and harmony simply enables him to tell which is which. What music teachers call the "rules" of harmony are just observations on the harmonies most usually used by such people as Bach and Beethoven. Bach and Beethoven did not use them because they were in the rules but because they liked their sound, and if people's tastes change so that they like other sounds then the old harmonic forms are replaced. It is necessary for a composer to study harmony in order that he may be able to identify chords which he hears in his mind, but he does not use his knowledge to *construct* chords unless he is a mere imitator of other people. In the same way, language is used not to create thoughts but to express them, and mastery of prose does not make a great thinker. The spiritual genius works in the same way as the musical genius. He has a wider scope because his technique of expression, his alphabet, is every possible human activity. For some reason there arises in his soul a feeling of the most profound happiness, not because of some special event, but because of the whole of life. This is not necessarily contentment or joy; it is rather that he feels himself completely united to the power that moves the universe, whatever that may be. This feeling he expresses in two ways, firstly by living a certain kind of life, and secondly by translating his feelings into the form of thoughts and words.

People who have not had this feeling make observations on his actions and words, and from them formulate the "rules" of religious morality and theology. But this involves a strange distortion, for as a rule the observer goes about his work in the wrong way. When the mystic says, "I feel united with God," the observer is interested primarily in the statement as a revelation of the existence of God, and goes on to consult the mystic's other sayings to find out what kind of God this is and in what manner He behaves. He is interested only secondarily in the mystic's feelings as a feeling, and it occurs to him only as an afterthought that it might be possible for himself to feel united with God. Whereat he proceeds to achieve this by trying to think in the same way as the mystic; that is to say, he takes the mystic's *ideas* and substitutes them for his own. He also tries to behave in the same way, imitating the mystic's actions. In other words, he tries to perform a kind of sympathetic magic, and in imitating the mystic's external forms deceives himself and others into thinking that he is really like him. But the important thing about the mystic was his feeling, not his ideas and actions, for these were only reflections of the feeling, and a reflection existing without a light is a sham. Therefore just as great technical proficiency will not make a creative genius in music, morality, theology, and discipline will not make a genius in religion, for these things are results of religious experience, not causes, and by themselves can no more produce it than the tail can be made to wag the dog.

The Spiritual Irrelevance of Occultism

This is not the only example of confused thought in searching for religious experience. The other, which we have already mentioned, is the opposition made between the spiritual and the material. Much depends, of course, on the precise meaning given to the word "spirit," but it should certainly not be confused with the word "psychic" and many things described as spiritual are clearly psychic. There is no definite rule as to how these words should be used, so to be explicit we have to make our own rules. And the spiritual, in the sense in which it is used here, is no more opposed to the material than white is opposed to long. The opposite of white is black, and of long, short; white things are no more necessarily short than material things are unspiritual. But we can say that the material and the psychic are opposed, if only in the sense that they are opposite ends of the same stick. Psychic things belong to the world explored by occultism and "psychic science"—telepathy, clairvoyance, mind-reading, and all those phenomena which appear to require sixth or seventh senses whose development seems unquestionably to be assisted by ascetic practices. The so-called spiritual realms inhabited by departed souls, angels, elementals, and demons, and the source of beatific visions, would be most correctly described as psychic if we are to allow that such things have actual, objective existence. And this world is the logical opposite of the material world because it belongs in the same category; it contains forms and substances, even though its substance may be of a wholly different order from what we understand as matter. People who are in touch with this world, however, are not necessarily spiritual people; they may have unusual faculties of perception and be familiar with the beings and ways of a more glorious world than our own, but this is a matter of *faculty* and *knowledge*, not of spirituality. The technique of living employed by such people is more highly evolved than that of ordinary men, just as the technique of the opera is more complicated than that of pure drama. Opera involves not only acting but singing, playing music, and sometimes dancing, but this does not make it a greater art.

Spirituality belongs in the same category as happiness and freedom, and strictly speaking there is no such thing as the spiritual *world*. If psychic people are to be believed, there is a psychic *world*, and because it is a world entry into it is simply an enlargement of experience. But experience as such never made anyone either free or happy, and in so far as freedom and happiness are concerned with experience the important thing is not experience itself but what is learned from it. Some people learn from experience and others do not; some learn much from a little, others learn little from much. "Without going out of my house, " said the Chinese sage Lao Tzu, "I know the whole universe." For the spiritual is in no way divided from the material, nor from the psychic, not from any other aspect of life. To find it, it is not necessary to go from one state of consciousness to another, from one set of senses to another or from one world to another. Such journeying about in the fields of experience takes you neither toward it nor away from it. In the words of the Psalmist:[4]

Whither shall I go from Thy spirit? Or whither shall I flee from Thy presence?
If I ascend up into heaven, Thou art there: if I make my bed in hell, behold, Thou art there.
If I take the wings of the morning, and dwell in the uttermost parts of the sea; even there shall thy hand lead me, and thy right hand shall hold me.
If I say, Surely the darkness shall cover me; even the night shall be light about me.
Yea, the darkness hideth not from Thee; but the night shineth as the day: the darkness and the light are both alike to Thee.

4. Psalm 139:7–12.

In fact the spiritual world, if we must use the term, is this world and all possible worlds, and spiritual experience is what we are experiencing at this moment and at any moment—if we look at it in the right way.

Union with Life

This is the difference between religious or spiritual experience and artistic inspiration; both are analogous, but the latter is particularized. The artist or musician has a special type of creative genius; he creates pictures or music, for his genius is a specialized gift. But the spiritual genius is not a specialist, for he does not just paint or compose creatively: he *lives* creatively, and his tools are not confined to brush, pen or instrument; they are all things touched by his hand. This is not to say that when he takes up a brush he can paint like Leonardo or that when he takes hammer and chisel he can work like a master-mason. Spiritual experience involves neither technical proficiency nor factual knowledge; it is no short-cut to things that must ordinarily be mastered by pains and practice. Nor is spiritual experience necessarily expressed in any *particular* mode of life; its presence in any given individual cannot be judged by measurement in accordance with certain standards. It can only be felt intuitively, for creative living is not always outwardly distinguishable from any other kind of living; in fact, spiritual people are often at pains to appear as normal as possible. At the same time, although spiritual people may do exactly the same things as others, one feels that their actions are in some way different. There is a story of a Buddhist sage who was about to speak to his disciples when he found that he wanted more light. He pointed to a curtain covering one of the windows and instantly two of the disciples went and rolled it up, whereat the sage remarked, "One of them is right, but the other is wrong."[5]

In itself, spirituality is purely an inner experience; it has no necessary effect whatsoever on one's outward behavior judged from the standards of efficiency and worldly-wisdom. This is not to say, however, that it is something absolutely private and personal, finding no expression that others can see. For spirituality is a deep sense of inner freedom based on the realization that one's self is in complete union and harmony with life, with God, with the Self of the universe or whatever that principle may be called. It is the realization that that union has existed from all times, even though one did not know it, and that nothing in all the world nor anything that oneself can do is able to destroy it. It is thus the sense that the whole might of the universe is at work in one's every thought and action,

5. *Mu-mon-kwan,* xxvi.

however trivial and small. In fact this is true of all men and all things, but only the spiritual man really knows it and his realization gives a subtly different quality to his life; all that he does becomes strangely alive, for though its outward appearance is perhaps the same as before it acquires a new meaning. It is this which other people notice, but if he has the gift for teaching they will see it in other ways as well. By his words as well as his deeds and his personal "atmosphere" they will understand that this realization has awakened in him a tremendous love for life in all its aspects.

Prose and the logic of philosophy cannot explain this love; one might as well try to describe a beautiful face by a mathematical account of its measurements and proportions. It is a mixture of the joy of freedom, a childlike sense of wonder, and the inner sensation of absolute harmony with life as in the rhythm of an eternal dance such as the Hindus portray in the interlocked figures of Shiva and his bride.[6] In one sense you feel that your life is not lived by you at all; the power of the universe, fate and destiny, God Himself are directing all your motions and all your responsibilities are blown to the winds. In another sense you feel free to move as you wish; you seem to be moving life with the same vast power with which life moves you, and your littlest acts become filled with gigantic possibilities. Indeed, physicists tell us that the stars are affected when we lift a single finger. The result of these two feelings is that you no longer distinguish between what you do to life and what life does to you; it is as if two dancers moved in such perfect accord that the distinction between lead and response vanished, as if the two became one and the same motion. By the whirling, ever-changing movement of this dance you are carried along without pause, but not like a drunken man in a torrent, for you as much as life are the source of the movement. And this is real freedom; it includes both freedom to move and to be moved; action and passivity are merged, and in spirituality as well as in marriage this is the fulfillment of love.

The Spirituality of Everyday Life

All this, however, does not take place in the ecstasy of trance, in some abstract state of consciousness where all shapes and substances have become merged into a single infinite essence. The spiritual man does not perform his ordinary activities as one in a dream, letting his surface thoughts and deeds run on mechanically. He can become just as much absorbed in the usual affairs of the world as anyone else, but in a certain way he sanctifies them for under his hands sharpening a pencil becomes as much a religious act as prayer or meditation. Indeed, he can afford to become absorbed in

---

6. See Zimmer, *Kunstform und Yoga* (Berlin, 1926).

everyday affairs almost more than others, and he can do so with a certain zest and abandon for to him ordinary human thoughts and activities are as much included in the dance of the spirit as is anything else. This, indeed, is much of his secret, for he knows that spirituality does not consist in thinking always about the spiritual as such. His world is not divided into "water-tight compartments" and his religion is not a special form of thought and activity, for the spiritual and the material are not separated.

But because a man does not occupy himself with the ordinary pursuits of mankind, this is no indication that he lacks spiritual understanding. He is free to follow whatever occupation he pleases—monk, philosopher, lawyer, clerk, or tradesman, but from the spiritual point of view a priest is not necessarily more holy than a truckdriver. Furthermore, to obtain spiritual experience it is not essential to "vex your mournful minds with pious pains," to spend years in the study of theology, to retire from the world, to become a vegetarian and teetotaler, to practice mental acrobatics and seek out "higher realms" of consciousness, to abstain from sexuality, or to develop such peculiar gifts as "fourth-dimensional vision." Certainly these things are necessary for the professional philosopher or for that particular type of *scientist* whose field of research is the psychic world. If we are going to find out how our present senses may be developed, how we can tap sources of nervous energy as yet unused, how we can understand time in terms of space and see past and future at once, how we can transfer thought or how we can acquire the faculty of immovable concentration, then indeed we have to go in training even more rigorously than the professional athlete. To acquire psychic faculties you must practice just as much as if you wanted to hold the world's record for sprinting or to be able to walk on hot coals without being burned.

The Nonessentials of Religion

Religion as we understand it includes many things which do not strictly belong to it, because in olden times it had to fulfill functions which have now been taken over by scientists, doctors, and lawyers. At one time the major preoccupation of so-called religion was the study and manipulation of the unknown and the unseen; as these things become known and seen they passed out of the hands of priests. But when priests were considered the wisest of all men they were expected to have answers to all the problems which others did not understand. They were expected to know the causes of disease, the behavior and influence of the stars, the origin of such natural phenomena as thunder, storms, and famines, not to mention the more remote questions of what happens after death and whether there are gods and angels.

Many of these problems have now been taken over by science,

though we are still ignorant of the life after death and still have not objective evidence of the existence of "supernatural" beings. Therefore the priests are still the authorities on such matters even though they remain legitimate objects of scientific inquiry and have no essential connection with religion. The day may come when science, physical or psychic, will be able to answer these questions, and some scientists imagine that there will then be no further need for religion, having no clear idea of what religion is. This is not exactly their fault, for religious people seldom understand the true function of religion and still waste thought and energy in a war with science based on wholly false premises.

If it could be proved objectively and scientifically that there was a life after death and that supernatural beings do exist this would have about as much religious significance as the discovery of a new continent, of the existence of life on Mars, or of the uses of electricity. It would be neither more nor less than an addition to human experience and knowledge. It would not necessarily be an addition to human wisdom, and this is the province of religion. For wisdom is not factual knowledge nor mere quantity and range of experience, nor even facility in the uses of knowledge and experience. Wisdom is a quality of the psychological or spiritual relationship between man and his experience. When that relationship is wise and harmonious man's experiences set him free, but when it is unwise and discordant his experiences bind him.

Religion alone can deal with that relationship, and this is its essential function. For what do we find left in religion when its *quasi*-scientific aspect is removed? There is the whole, vast problem of love or spiritual union which is contained in the question, "How can I learn to love life, whose source and essence we call God? How can I learn to be united with it in all its expressions, in living and dying, in love and fear, in the outer world of circumstances and in the inner world of thought and feeling, so that in union with it I may find freedom?" Now science cannot teach any kind of love, not even the love between man and woman, for who ever learned to love his wife out of a psychological textbook on matrimony? Morality, which religion would teach as having supernatural sanctions, is just the expression of love; it follows it as a consequence and does not precede it as a cause. The will of God as expressed in morality is not a ukase which we should merely obey, for the purpose of His will is not that there should be morality, but that there should be love, and morality is just the "outward and visible sign of an inward and spiritual grace."

In so far as religion has diverged from its main purpose into psychism, morality for its own sake, speculative theology, concern for the life after death, and attempts to awaken spirituality by imitating its expressions, it has also put itself out of touch with people who have no desire to be religious specialists. Those who cannot feel that man's principal concern should lie outside this world, who feel that salvation has nothing to do with removal to another realm of experience or with mere obedience to a moral law—such people can find little assistance from religion as usually taught, and to-day they constitute a very large proportion of intelligent men and women. For the nineteenth-century conflict between religion and science was, for those whose eyes were open, a stripping-off of nonessentials from religion, but unfortunately official religion seldom saw it in this way. It clung to supernaturalism, which, rightly or wrongly, rationalist science had discredited, and continued to make it the keystone of spirituality.

But this kind of religion does not encourage the type of love upon which spirituality is founded. We have seen that its technique is imitative and thus unlikely to produce genuine, first-hand religious experience; we have also seen that its contempt of this world and its concentration on the life hereafter has little to do with the essentials of religion. This is not all, for not only has it little to do with such essentials; it is also a decided hindrance to spiritual growth because it encourages a "love" of God on a false basis. God is loved not because He has given us *this* world, but because He is said to have promised a much better world in the life after death. His gift to us of this world is therefore declined without thanks—an effrontery which is softened by describing this world as a place of trial for fitness to enter the world to come, on the principle that if you refuse God's first gift, you will get His second.

The "Higher Sensuality"

But if God created this world only as a temporary place of trial, He seems to have taken a wholly unnecessary amount of trouble in its construction. He gave us senses which as yet we have hardly begun to develop to their full potentialities, and yet religion warns us against those senses as if they were given us simply as a sop to embellish life with such superficial trimmings as art, literature, music, and athletics so that in playing with them we may have a little relaxation from the more important task of fitting ourselves for the hereafter. But there is a way of looking at things whereby these "trimmings" become the main business of life, and religion the means to their fulfillment, on the principle that religion was made for life and not life for religion. For the contempt of the world of the senses is peculiarly like the fable of the sour grapes. Man burned his fingers at the game of pleasure, and instead of learning to play it aright was filled with fear and relegated pleasure to the realms of the Devil and his vanities, crying:

> The earthly hope men set their hearts upon
> Turns ashes, or it prospers, and anon,
>   Like snow upon the Desert's dusky face,
> Lighting a little hour or two, is gone.

But the whole point about the beauties of the earth is that they would be intolerable if they did not change and vanish. A woman is not less beautiful and desirable because she grows old and white; if she had eternal youth she would be a monster, as many women are who refuse to accept the different beauties of old age and death. For the beauty of life is not in any one of its stages but in the whole movement from birth to death, and if this movement is in any way resisted or interrupted there come unhappiness, maladjustment and neurotic disease. Those who look pitiful and hideous in their old age are only so because years rankle them, because they have not accepted the rhythm of their life and go forward to old age with regretful glances behind at lost glories.

Certainly all pleasures are transient; otherwise we should cease to appreciate them, but if this be made the excuse for refusing to enjoy them, one must suspect that man's ideas of happiness are horribly confused. The secret of the enjoyment of pleasure is to know when to stop. Man does not learn this secret easily, but to shun pleasure altogether is cowardly avoidance of a difficult task. For we have to learn the art of enjoying things *because* they are impermanent. We do this every time we listen to music. We do not seize hold of a particular chord or phrase and shout at the orchestra to go on playing it for the rest of the evening; on the contrary, however much we may like that particular moment of music, we know that its perpetuation would interrupt and kill the movement of the melody. We understand that the beauty of a symphony is less in these musical moments than in the whole movement from beginning to end. If the symphony tries to go on too long, if at a certain point the composer exhausts his creative ability and tries to carry on for just the sake of filling in the required space of time, then we begin to fidget in our chairs, feeling that he has denied the natural rhythm, has broken the smooth curve from birth to death, and that though a pretense at life is being made it is in fact a living death.

The Problem of Pain

But by itself this philosophy of "higher sensuality" is inadequate, for life is not like a musical masterpiece in certain respects. We may find all of a musical masterpiece beautiful; from the sensual point of view life is only beautiful in parts; it has also ugliness, pain, and horror, and hence the love for a God who will remove these things in the world to come. But this, too, is an avoidance of the problem. For the attitude of ordinary religion to both the pleasures and the pains of this world is negative. Pleasure is suspected, and in the everlasting life pain is not.

But we must now ask whether it is not possible that greater heights of spirituality may be attained by a positive attitude to pleasure and pain in this world. If this is possible, it is clear that religion has no special concern with the life after death and that spirituality has nothing whatever to do with retiring from this world. No one can deny the existence of a life after death, but that it should be a more spiritual life than this one is a wholly unreasonable assumption. If it is true that we are physically reincarnated on this earth or another, the whole picture is changed. But if orthodox Christianity is right in its belief that we have only one material life, then the next life will be psychic because according to our definition there can be no such thing as a spiritual world, spirituality being a quality of life and not a kind of existence in the same category as the material and the psychic.

Spirituality is therefore a way of living in whatever world one happens to be, and is in no way separable from the actual process of living in that world. In other words, there is no difference between religion and ordinary, everyday life; religious ideas and practices (which are no more religion itself than any other activities) exist solely to promote a positive and loving attitude toward ordinary life and what it stands for, namely, God. Unless one happens to be a religious specialist, which is not necessarily the same thing as spiritual person, religious practices are not ends in themselves. They are means to a fuller and greater life *in this world*, involving a positive and constructive attitude to pleasure and pain alike, and thus an increasing ability to learn happiness and freedom from every possible kind of expereience. In this sense, religion is union with life; whether that life is the present life of physical form, of thought and feeling with brain and soul, or whether it is a future life of purely psychic substance is beside the point. These are only different grades of existence; they are not different grades of spirituality, for the same spiritual laws apply in every grade of existence, and when one has learned union with one of them, one has discovered the secret of union with any of them.

We have suggested that the secret of this union lies in a positive attitude toward the world in which we live. To repeat the question which religion has to answer, we want to discover how we can learn to be united with life in all its expressions, in living and dying, in love and fear, in the outer world of circumstance and in the inner world of thought and feeling, so that in union with it we may find freedom and happiness. To be united with life in all its expressions may seem a large demand to make on oneself, for those expressions include disease, pain, death, madness, and all the horrors which man can devise, wittingly or unwittingly, for his fellow-creatures. In fact the "nub" of the whole problem is the acceptance of the dark side of life, for this is the very occasion of our unhappiness. "Acceptance" may seem a weak word for a positive attitude of love, but it is used because the type of love in question is relaxed. It is positive but not aggressive; it grows in its own way and is not forced. Therefore we may say that it is not enough to *tolerate* the dark side of life; acceptance in this sense is much more than a "let it be" with a resigned shrug of the shoulders. Let us call it "creative acceptance," though because this phrase smacks overmuch of philosophical jargon we will write the noun and only remember its qualifying adjective. This is perhaps wise in another way, for a truth oddly comes out of a play on words: to be genuine, acceptance must be unqualified.

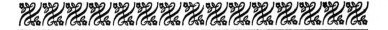

Notes on Composition

Saying Something That Matters

There is no point in the hard labor of writing unless you expect to *do* something to somebody—perhaps add to his store of information, perhaps cause him to change his mind on some issue that you care about. Determining just what that something is is half the battle; hence the importance of knowing your main point, your central purpose in writing, your **thesis**. It may seem that this step—perhaps in the form of a "thesis sentence" or exact statement of the main point—is inevitably prior to everything else in writing, but in actual practice the case is more complicated. Few good writers attain a final grasp of their thesis until they have tried setting down their first halting ideas at some length; to put it another way, you discover more precisely what it is you have to say in the act of trying to say it. Formulating and refining upon a thesis sentence as you work your way through a piece of writing helps you see what needs to be done at each stage; the finished piece, though, instead of announcing its thesis in any one sentence, may simply imply it by the fact of its unity, the determinate way the parts hang together. There is probably no single sentence in Hannah Arendt's "Denmark and the Jews" (p. 881) that will serve satisfactorily to represent the entire essay in miniature, yet clearly such a sentence could be formulated: Open resistance frankly based on ethical principle achieved a success in Denmark out of all proportion to the Danes' capacity to attain their ends by force. But whether you state the main point or leave it to be inferred, you need to decide what your piece is about, what you want to say about it, why, and to whom.

Sometimes a thesis will rest on a good many **assumptions**, related ideas that the writer may not mention but depends upon his reader to understand and agree to (if he is an honest writer) or to overlook and hence fail to reject (if his real purpose is to mislead). Stanley Milgram (p. 293) appears to assume that practicing deception on another person and even causing him considerable suffering are justifiable in the name of scientific inquiry.

We may feel that the question is highly ambiguous, or we may disagree sharply. But even if we decide, finally, that we can live with Milgram's assumption, we shall have acquired a fuller understanding of what he is saying, and of our own relationship to it, for having scrutinized what is being taken for granted. The habit of scrutiny guards us against the careless or cunning writer whose unstated assumptions may be highly questionable. The same habit, turned on our own minds when we become writers, can save us from the unthinking use of assumptions that we would be hard pressed to defend.

Some theses lend themselves to verification by laboratory methods or the like; they deal with **questions of fact.** The exact order of composition of Shakespeare's plays could conceivably be settled finally if new evidence turned up. Whether or not the plays are great literature, on the other hand, is a **question of opinion;** agreement (though not hard to reach in this instance) depends on the weighing of arguments rather than on tests or measurements. Not that all theses can be neatly classified as assertions either of fact or of opinion (consider "Shakespeare's influence has been greater than Newton's"); still the attempt to classify his own effort can help a writer understand what he is doing.

Sometimes a writer addresses himself more specifically to his readers' **understanding,** sometimes he addresses himself chiefly to their **emotions.** Although the processes of thinking and of feeling are almost always mixed, still it is obvious that a description of a chemical process and a description of a candidate you hope to see elected to office will differ considerably in tone and emphasis. Accordingly you need to give some thought to the kind of result you hope to produce: perhaps simply an addition of information, perhaps a change of attitude, perhaps a commitment of the will to action.

The Means of Saying It

No worthwhile thesis comes without work, and the work of arriving at a thesis is much like the work of writing itself—developing, elaborating, refining upon an idea that is perhaps at first hazy. For convenience the process may be divided into setting bounds, or defining; marshaling evidence; and drawing conclusions.

DEFINING in a broad sense may be thought of as what you do to answer the question "What do you mean?" It sets bounds by doing two things to an idea: grouping it with others like it and showing how it differs from those others. "An island is a tract of land" (like a lot or prairie or peninsula) "completely surrounded by water and too small to be called a continent" (and therefore different from a lot, etc.). This process of classifying and distinguishing may take many forms, depending on the kind of thing you are dealing with and your reason for doing so. (Artifacts, for example, can hardly be defined without reference to purpose; a lock is a device *for securing* a door; a theodolite is an instrument used *to measure* horizontal or vertical angles.) Some of the standard methods are these: by giving **examples,** pointing to an instance as a short way of indicating class and individual characteristics ("*That* is a firebreak"; "A liberal is a man like Jefferson") ; by **negating,** explaining what your subject is *not*—i.e., process of elimination ("Love vaunteth not itself, is not puffed up"); by **comparing and contrasting,** noting the resemblances and differences between your subject and something else ("A magazine is sometimes as big as a book but differs in binding and layout") ; by **analyzing,** breaking down a whole into its constituent parts ("A play may be seen as exposition, rising action, and denouement"); by seeking a **cause** of the thing in question or an **effect** that it has produced ("Scurvy is the result of a dietary deficiency and often leads to anemia"); or by attributing to a thing an **end** or **means**, seeing it as a way of fulfilling purpose or as the fulfillment of a purpose ("Representation is the end of the electoral system and the means to good government").

When we turn to specimens of writing, we see immediately that the various methods of defining may serve not only for one-sentence "dictionary" definitions but also as methods of organizing paragraphs or even whole essays, where unfolding the subject is in a sense "defining" it, showing where its boundaries lie. Carl Becker (p.773) begins with a broad idea of democracy that would include virtually all governments, then by considering several negative examples refines his definition until all governments that are not democracies are excluded. Thomas De Quincey (p.185) explains what he means by the "literature of knowledge" and the "literature of power" through an extended comparison in which each is made to clarify the other. Charles Sanders Peirce (p.1038), examining the process by which doubt is converted to belief, produces an illuminating four-part analysis. The choice of method in the above examples, it will be noted, is not random; each author selects according to his purpose in writing, and what suits one purpose exactly might be exactly wrong for another.

MARSHALING EVIDENCE. Once you have said what you mean, the next question is likely to be "How do you know?" Marshaling evidence may be thought of as what you do to answer that question. Where the matter at hand involves questions of fact, **factual evidence** will be most directly appropriate. (A diary, a letter—perhaps a cryptogram hidden in the text—might prove even to die-hard Baconians that Shakespeare himself did in fact write the plays which have been credited to him). Writers on scientific subjects inevitably draw chiefly on facts, often intricately arrayed, to support their conclusions. But it should not be assumed that factual evidence turns up mainly in scientific writing. William Willcox's account (p.901) of the character of Sir Henry Clinton, commander-in-chief of the British army in America during the latter stages of the Revolutionary War, is obviously based largely on facts in the form of historical documents, and even the preacher John Donne, arguing that the arrow of temptation often overtakes us simply because we cannot bring ourselves to walk resolutely away from it (p.579), plainly appeals to facts with which most of us are only too familiar.

Factual evidence is generally thought to carry more weight than any other kind, though the force of a fact is greatly diminished if it is not easily verifiable or attested to by reliable witnesses. Where factual evidence is hard to come by (consider the problems of proving that Bacon did not write Shakespeare's plays), the opinion of **authorities** is often invoked, on the assumption that the men most knowledgeable in a field are most likely to judge truly in a particular case. The testimony of authorities is relevant, of course, not only in questions of fact but also in questions of opinion. William G. Perry, Jr. (p.239), arguing for the student who "bulled" his way through an examination, implicitly invokes college professors *en masse* as authority for the idea that "bull" is closer than might be supposed to the goal of a liberal education. In general, however, the appeal to authority in matters of opinion has lost the rhetorical effectiveness it once had, perhaps because there is less agreement as to who the reliable authorities are.

As changes in the nature of the question draw in a larger and larger number of "authorities," evidence from authority shades into what might be called "the **common consent** of mankind," those generalizations about human experience that large numbers of readers can be counted upon to accept and that often find expression in proverbs or apothegms: "Risk no more than you can afford to lose" and "The first step toward Hell is halfway there." Such generalizations, whether proverbial or not, are a common ground on which writer and reader meet in agreement. The writer's task is to find and present the ones applicable to his particular thesis and then demonstrate that applicability.

DRAWING CONCLUSIONS. One of the ways of determining the consequences of thought—that is, drawing conclusions—is the process of applying generalizations (**deduction**): "If we should risk no more than we can afford to lose, then we had better not jeopardize the independence of our universities by seeking federal aid." Another way of arriving at conclusions is the process of **induction**, which consists in forming generalizations from a sufficient number of observed instances: "Since universities *A, B,* and *C* have been accepting federal aid through research grants for years without loss of independence, it is probably safe for any university to do so." Typically deduction and induction work reciprocally, each helping to supply for the other the materials upon which inference operates. We induce from experience that green apples are sour; we deduce from this generalization that a particular green apple is sour. A third kind of inference, sometimes regarded as only a special kind of deduction or induction, is **analogy**, the process of concluding that two things which resemble each other in one way will resemble each other in another way also: "Federal aid has benefited mental hospitals enormously, and will probably benefit universities just as much." An analogy proves nothing, although it may help the reader see the reasonableness of an idea and is often extremely valuable for purposes of illustration, since it makes an unknown clearer by relating it to a known.

Turning to our essays, we can see something of the variety of ways in which these three kinds of inference manifest themselves in serious writing: Thomas Jefferson deducing from certain self-evident truths the inescapable conclusion that the colonies should declare their independence of Great Britain (p. 769); Wallace Stegner arguing from a series of particular instances to the general conclusion that a community may be judged by what it throws away (p. 6); a New Testament parable adumbrating the kingdom of heaven by likening it to ten virgins (p. 1073).

Such a list of examples suggests that in good writing the conclusions the writer draws, the consequences of his thought, are "consequential" in more than one sense: not only do they follow logically from the evidence he has considered, they are also *significant;* they relate directly or indirectly to aspects of our lives that we care about. To the questions suggested earlier as demands for definition and evidence, then, we must add a third. "What do you mean?" calls for precision yet admits answers vast in scope. "How do you know?" trims the vastness down to what can be substantiated but may settle for triviality as the price of certainty. The appropriate question to raise finally, then, is simply "So what?" and the conclusions we as writers draw need to be significant enough to yield answers to that question. We have come full circle back to the idea of saying something that matters.

And the Style

One theory of style in writing sees form and content as distinct: style is the way a thing is said, the thing itself an unchanging substance that can be decked out in various ways. Mr. Smith not only *died,* he *ceased to be,* he *passed away,* he *croaked,* he *was promoted to glory*—all mean "the same thing." According to a second theory, however, they are ways of saying different things: variations in **diction** imply variations in reference. To say that Smith *ceased to be* records a privative and secular event; to say that he *was promoted to glory* (a Salvation Army expression) rejoices in an event of a different order altogether. Content and form in this view are inseparable; a change in one is a change in the other.

In **metaphor** we can see that the two theories, instead of contradicting each other, are more like the two sides of a coin: when one idea is expressed in terms of another, it is the same and yet not the same. To view the passage from life to death as if it were a promotion from one military rank to a higher one is to see a common center of reference and widening circles of association at the same time. This seeing *as if* opens up a whole range of expression, since many meanings reside in the relationship between the two parts of a comparison rather than in either part by itself. John Selden's country bumpkin (p.269), "who said, if he were King, he would live like a lord, and have * * * a whip that cried Slash," expressed metaphorically a personal realization of power that would have been diminished or altered by any other means of expression.

But style is by no means dependent on diction and metaphor alone. Grammatical relationships yield a host of stylistic devices, most of which can be described in terms of **repetition and variation**. Repetition may exist at every level; as commonly understood, its chief application is to the word (including the pronoun as a word-substitute), but the same principle governs the use of parallelism (repetition of a grammatical structure) within and between sentences, even between paragraphs. Failure to observe that principle—that similarity in idea calls for similarity in form—can be detected wherever a change in form implies that a distinction is being made when actually none is relevant to the context: "Their conversation was interrupted by dinner, but they resumed their discussion afterwards"; "She rolled out the dough, placed it over the pie, and pricked holes in it. She also trimmed off the edge." The corollary of the principle of appropriate repetition is the principle of appropriate variation—that difference in idea calls for difference in form. For every failure to repeat when repetition is called for there is a corresponding failure to vary when variation is called for: "Their discussion was interrupted when class discussion of the day's assignment began"; "It had been raining for many days near the river. It had been rising steadily toward the top of the levee." Failures of this sort, which suggest a similarity in idea or parallelism in thought where none exists, often strike the ear as a lack of euphony or appropriate rhythm: "A boxer must learn to react absolutely instantly"; "The slingshot was made of strips of inner tubes of tires of cars." The principle of appropriate variation applies, too, to sentences as wholes: if a separate sentence is used for each detail, or if every sentence includes many details, the reader may be given a false impression of parallelism or equality of emphasis. Here again variation may be a way to avoid misleading grammatical indications of meaning. In a writer like Samuel Johnson (p. 183), who works deliberately for a high degree of parallelism, correspondence between repetition and sameness of meaning, or variation and difference of meaning, is perhaps most conveniently illustrated.

All stylistic techniques come together to supply an answer to the question "Who is behind these words?" Every writer establishes an impression of himself—a persona—through what he says and the way he says it, and the quality of that impression obviously has much to do with his reader's willingness to be convinced. Honesty and straightforwardness come first—though the honesty of an ignoramus and the straightforwardness of a fool are unlikely to win assent. Some more sophisticated approaches to the adoption of a persona employ irony: the author assumes a character that the reader can see is at odds with his real intention. Whether direct or ironic, the chosen role must be suited to both the subject and the writer himself, who may want to try out several roles to see what each implies. Is he an expert or a humble seeker after truth, a wry humorist or a gadfly deliberately exacerbating hidden guilt? Even within the same general circumstances (in this case the academic world), William G. Perry, Jr. (p.239) is one sort of a person, John Livingston Lowes (p. 961) clearly another. A self will be revealed in every phrase the writer sets down—even in details of spelling, grammar, and punctuation, which, if ineptly handled, may suggest to his readers a carelessness that destroys their confidence.

Authors

[*An* * *indicates the source of a selection in this anthology.
Only a few of each author's works are cited.*]

William Alfred (1922–)
Harvard professor of English, poet, and dramatist; author of *Hogan's Goat*, a play based on Irish politics in Brooklyn.

Maya Angelou (1924–)
American actress, journalist, television script writer, and civil rights worker; author of **I Know Why the Caged Bird Sings, Just Give Me a Cool Drink of Water 'fore I Die.*

Robert Ardrey (1908–)
American zoologist, playwright, and novelist; author of *Thunder Rock, *The Territorial Imperative, African Genesis.*

Hannah Arendt (1906–)
German-born American political analyst (New School for Social Research); author of *The Origins of Totalitarianism, The Human Condition, *Eichmann in Jerusalem, On Revolution, On Violence, Men in Dark Times, Crises of the Republic.*

Matthew Arnold (1822–1888)
English man of letters, poet, and literary critic; author of *Poems, Essays in Criticism, *Culture and Anarchy, Literature and Dogma.*

Roger Ascham (1515–1568)
English scholar, tutor of Queen Elizabeth I; author of **Toxophilus* and *The Scholemaster.*

W(ystan) H(ugh) Auden (1907–)
English-born American poet, playwright, critic; author of *In Time of War, The Sea and the Mirror, Poems, *The Dyer's Hand;* with Christopher Isherwood, of *Ascent of F-6, The Dog Beneath the Skin* (plays); with Louis MacNeice, of *Letters from Iceland.*

Sir Francis Bacon (1561–1626)
English politician, statesman, and philosopher; author of **Essays, Advancement of Learning, *New Organon, New Atlantis.*

James Baldwin (1924–)
American essayist and novelist; Harlem-bred, one-time expatriate in Paris, political activist for civil rights causes; author of *Go Tell It on the Mountain, Another Country, Tell Me How Long the Train's Been Gone* (novels), **Notes of a Native Son, Nobody Knows My Name, the Fire Next Time, Going to Meet the Man, No Name in the Street* (commentaries).

Margaret Culkin Banning (1891–)
American novelist; author of *Too Young to Marry, Out in Society, *Letters to Susan, The Case for Chastity.*

(Arthur) Owen Barfield (1898–)
British literary critic; author of *History in English Words, Poetic Diction, Saving the Appearances.*

Carl Becker (1873–1945)
American historian (Cornell); author of *Progress and Power, The Declaration of Independence, *Modern Democracy.*

Saul Bellow (1915–)
American novelist, story writer (University of Chicago); author of *Herzog, Mr. Sammler's Planet, The Adventures of Augie March, Dangling Man, Mosby's Memoirs and Other Stories.*

Henri Bergson (1859–1941)
French philosopher; author of *The Two Sources of Morality and Religion, Time and Free Will, *On Laughter.*

Bruno Bettelheim (1903–)
Austrian-born American psychologist (University of Chicago) and psychoanalyst; author of *Love Is Not*

Enough, *The Informed Heart, The Empty Fortress, Children of the Dream.

Ambrose Bierce (1842–1914?)
American short-story writer and journalist; author of Tales of Soldiers and Civilians, The Cynic's Word Book (retitled *The Devil's Dictionary).

Peter Binzen (1922–)
English-born American editor, journalist, and educator (Philadelphia Bulletin); author of *Whitetown, U.S.A.

William Blake (1757–1827)
English poet, artist, and engraver; author of Songs of Innocence, Songs of Experience, *The Marriage of Heaven and Hell, the Book of Thel.

Ronald Blythe (1922–).
English historian and writer; author of Akenfield: Portrait of an English Village, The Age of Illusion.

Laura Bohannan (1922–)
American anthropologist (University of Illinois, Chicago Circle); author of Return to Laughter (as Elizabeth Bowen), Tiv Economy (with Paul Bohannan), Tiv of Central Nigeria.

Wayne C. Booth (1921–)
American literary critic, dean (University of Chicago); author of The Rhetoric of Fiction.

Jacob Bronowski (1908–)
British critic and statesman, senior fellow and trustee of Salk Institute for Biological Studies; author of The Poet's Defence, The Common Sense of Science, Science and Human Values, The Identity of Man, Nature and Knowledge.

Dee (Alexander) Brown (1908–)
American historian and writer; author of *Bury My Heart at Wounded Knee, The Galvanized Yankees, Grierson's Raid.

Harrison Brown (1917–)
American geochemist (California Institute of Technology); author of The Challenge of Man's Future, The Next Hundred Years, Community of Fear (with James Real), Must Destruction Be Our Destiny?

Jerome S. Bruner (1915–)
American psychologist (Harvard University); author of The Process of Education, Toward a Theory of Instruction, Processes of Cognitive

Growth, The Relevance of Education.

(John) Anthony Burgess (Wilson) (1917–)
Author of A Clockwork Orange, Re Joyce, The Novel Now, MF, Tremor of Intent, Enderby, The Long Day Wanes: A Trilogy, The Wanting Seed, Urgent Copy, The Worm and the Ring.

Samuel Butler (1835–1902)
English sheep farmer, biologist, composer, writer; author of Erewhon, Erewhon Revisited, Evolution Old and New, Unconscious Memory, *The Notebooks of Samuel Butler, The Way of All Flesh.

H(erbert) J(ames) Campbell (1934–)
English physiologist (Institute of Psychiatry at DeCrespigny Park); author of Correlative Physiology of the Nervous System.

Thomas Carlyle (1795–1881)
Scots essayist, historian; author of *Sartor Resartus; The French Revolution; On Heroes, Hero-Worship, and the Heroic in History; History of Frederick the Great.

Edward Hallett Carr (1892–)
English historian (Cambridge), journalist, and statesman; author of The Romantic Exiles; The Bolshevik Revolution, 1917-1923; *What Is History?

(Arthur) Joyce (Lunel) Cary (1888–1957)
Anglo-Irish novelist, poet, and political philosopher; author of Aissa Saved, The Horse's Mouth, Mister Johnson, The Captive and the Free (novels), A Case for African Freedom, Power in Men, The Process of Real Freedom (commentaries).

Lord Chesterfield (1694–1773)
Philip Dormer Stanhope, fourth earl; English statesman and diplomat, well-known letter writer (*Letters to His Son).

John Ciardi (1916–)
American poet and editor (Saturday Review); author of An Alphabestiary (poems), From Time to Time (poems), In the Stoneworks (poems), Other Skies (poems), Person to Person (poems), How Does A Poem Mean?

Robert Claiborne (1919–)
American writer on science and medi-

cine; author of *Time*; *Drugs*; *Climate, Man, and History*.

Sir Kenneth Clark (1902–)
English art historian and critic; author of *Landscape into Art, The Nude, Leonardo da Vinci, Looking at Pictures, Civilisation.*

Eldridge Cleaver (1935–)
Black American revolutionary, journalist, social critic; former Minister of Information of the Black Panther Party; currently in exile in Algeria; author of *Soul on Ice.*

Samuel Langhorne Clemens (1835–1910)
"Mark Twain"; American humorist, novelist, essayist, journalist; author of *Life on the Mississippi, The Innocents Abroad, *Roughing It, The Adventures of Tom Sawyer, The Adventures of Huckleberry Finn.*

Henry Sloane Coffin (1877–1954)
American clergyman and educator; president, Union Theological Seminary; author of *The Meaning of the Cross, Religion Yesterday and Today.*

Robert Coles (1929–)
American psychiatrist (Harvard University); author of *Children of Crisis, Still Hungry in America, The Image Is You, The Wages of Neglect, Uprooted Children, Drugs and Youth, Erik Erikson: The Growth of His Work, *The Middle Americans, The South Goes North.*

Clarence Darrow (1857–1938)
American attorney and politician; identified with many prominent cases, including defenses of labor leaders and the Scopes trial; author of *An Eye for an Eye; Crime: Its Cause and Treatment; The Story of My Life.*

Thomas De Quincey (1785–1859)
English essayist and literary journalist; author of *Confessions of an English Opium Eater, *Autobiographic Sketches.*

Bernadette Devlin (1947–)
Irish member of the British House of Commons and Catholic civil rights leader in Protestant-dominated Northern Ireland; author of *The Price of My Soul.*

Emily Dickinson (1830–1886)
American poet; a New England recluse whose poetry was published almost entirely posthumously.

Joan Didion (1934–)
American essayist, story writer, novelist, and journalist (*Life*); author of *Play It as It Lays, *Slouching Towards Bethlehem, Run River.*

John Donne (1573–1631)
English poet and clergyman, Dean of St. Paul's Cathedral, founder and chief exemplar of the Metaphysical School in English poetry; author of *Songs and Sonnets, Devotions upon Emergent Occasions.*

W(illiam) E(dward) B(urghardt) Du Bois (1868–1963)
American author, editor, and teacher; a founder of the National Association for the Advancement of Colored People; relentless exponent of the complete equality of the Negro in America; author of *The Suppression of the African Slave Trade, The Souls of Black Folk, John Brown, Black Reconstruction, Dusk of Dawn, The Black Flame (A Trilogy).*

John Earle (1601?–1665)
English churchman, Bishop of Salisbury; author of *Microcosmographie*, a series of character sketches.

Jonathan Edwards (1703–1758)
American Puritan preacher and theologian in Massachusetts Bay Colony.

Loren Eiseley (1907–)
American anthropologist and historian of science (University of Pennsylvania); author of *The Immense Journey, Darwin's Century, The Firmament of Time, The Mind as Nature, Francis Bacon and the Modern Dilemma, The Unexpected Universe, The Invisible Pyramid, *The Night Country.*

Ralph Ellison (1914–)
American novelist, story writer, social critic; author of *Invisible Man, *Shadow and Act.*

Cecil S. Emden (1889–)
British literary critic and legal authority (Oxford University); author of *Oriel Papers, *The People and the Constitution, Poets in Their Letters.*

Ralph Waldo Emerson (1803–1882)
American essayist, poet, expositor of the intellectual movement known as Transcendentalism; author of *Na-

ture, Representative Men, English Traits.

Desiderius Erasmus (1465–1536)
Dutch humanist-scholar, satirist; author of *The Praise of Folly, Colloquies, *The Education of a Christian Prince.*

Erik H. Erikson (1902–   )
German-born American psychoanalyst (Harvard University); author of *Young Man Luther, Identity and the Life Cycle, *Insight and Responsibility, Identity: Youth and Crisis, Childhood and Society, Gandhi's Truth* (Pulitzer Prize, 1970).

E(dward) M(organ) Forster (1879–1970)
English novelist and essayist; author of **The Longest Journey, Howard's End, A Passage to India, Maurice* (novels), *Aspects of the Novel, *Two Cheers for Democracy* (criticism).

Benjamin Franklin (1706–1790)
American statesman, delegate to the Continental Congress and Constitutional Convention, ambassador to France during the American Revolution, inventor, newspaper publisher, and practical philosopher; author of **Poor Richard's Almanack, *Autobiography.*

Paul A. Freund (1908–   )
American lawyer (Harvard Law School); author of *On Understanding the Supreme Court, The Supreme Court in the United States, History of the Supreme Court* (editor-in-chief).

Erich Fromm (1900–   )
German-born American psychoanalyst; author of *Psychoanalysis and Religion, The Sane Society, Sigmund Freud's Mission, The Dogma of Christ and Other Essays on Religion, Psychology and Culture, The Heart of Man.*

Robert Frost (1874–1963)
American poet, lecturer, teacher.

Christopher Fry (1907–   )
English playwright and translator; author of the plays *The Boy with a Cart, The Dark Is Light Enough, The Lady's Not for Burning, Venus Observed, A Yard of Sun.*

Northrop Frye (1912–   )
Canadian literary critic (University of Toronto); author of *Anatomy of Criticism, Design for Learning, *The Educated Imagination.*

Thomas Fuller (1608–1661)
English clergyman, historian, gazetteer, biographer; author of **The Holy State and the Profane State, Church History of Britain, The Worthies of England.*

Edward Gibbon (1737–1794)
English historian; author of **History of the Decline and Fall of the Roman Empire.*

Emma Goldman (1869–1940)
Russian-born American anarchist, editor, and propagandist; author of *Anarchism and Other Essays, *Living My Life, My Disillusionment in Russia.*

Herb Goro
American photographer; author of **The Block.*

Robert Graves (1895–   )
British man of letters; author of *The White Goddess, The Greek Myths, Collected Poems, Love Respelt.*

Garrett James Hardin (1915–   )
American biologist (University of California at Santa Barbara); author of *Nature and Man's Fate; Population, Evolution and Birth Control; Biology: Its Principles and Implications.*

Nathaniel Hawthorne (1804–1864)
American novelist, short-story writer, essayist; author of *Twice-told Tales, Mosses from an Old Manse, The Scarlet Letter, The House of the Seven Gables.*

William Hazlitt (1778–1830)
English essayist, critic; author of *Characters of Shakespeare's Plays; English Comic Writers; Table Talk, or Original Essays on Men and Manners; *Characteristics.*

Ernest Hemingway (1898–1961)
American novelist and story writer. Pulitzer and Nobel Prizes; author of *The Sun Also Rises, A Farewell to Arms, *Death in the Afternoon, For Whom the Bell Tolls, The Old Man and the Sea.*

Gilbert Highet (1906–   )
Scots-born American classicist and teacher (Columbia); author of *The Classical Tradition, The Art of Teaching, The Anatomy of Satire, *Talents and Geniuses.*

Eric Hoffer (1902–   )
American longshoreman and social critic; author of *The True Believer, The Passionate State of Mind, The*

Ordeal of Change.

John Caldwell Holt (1923–)
American educator; author of *How Children Fail, How Children Learn, Underachieving School, What Do I Do Monday?*

Gerard Manley Hopkins (1844–1889)
English Jesuit, poet, essayist.

David Hume (1711–1776)
Scots philosopher, historian; author of *Essays Moral and Political, *Enquiry Concerning Human Understanding, History of Great Britain.*

Thomas Henry Huxley (1825–1895)
English biologist, popularizer of science; author of *Evolution and Ethics, Scientific Memoirs, *Darwiniana.*

Ada Louise Huxtable
American architectural critic (*New York Times*); author of *The Architecture of New York, *Will They Ever Finish Bruckner Boulevard?, Pier Luigi Nervi.*

George Jackson (1942–1971)
American political revolutionary; 1960-1970, inmate of Soledad Prison (second-degree robbery); 1970, accused, with two other inmates, of killing a prison guard; 1971, killed in an alleged escape attempt; author of *Soledad Brother: The Prison Letters of George Jackson.*

Jane Jacobs (1916–)
American editor and sociologist; author of *The Death and Life of Great American Cities.*

William James (1842–1910)
American philosopher and pioneer psychologist (Harvard), pragmatist, brother of Henry James; author of *Principles of Psychology, The Varieties of Religious Experience, Pragmatism.*

Thomas Jefferson (1743–1826)
Third President of the United States, first Secretary of State, founder of the University of Virginia, drafter of the *Declaration of Independence and the statute of Virginia for religious freedom, founder of the Democratic party; also renowned for his talents as an architect and inventor.

Samuel Johnson (1709–1784)
English lexicographer, critic, moralist; journalist (*The Idler, *The Rambler*); author of *A Dictionary of the English Language, Lives of the Poets;* subject of Boswell's *Life.*

Carl Gustav Jung (1875–1961)
Swiss psychiatrist; a founder of analytic psychology; author of *Analytical Psychology, The Undiscovered Self, Man and His Symbols, *Modern Man in Search of a Soul, Psychology and Religion, A Theory of Psychoanalysis.*

Pauline Kael (1919–)
American movie critic (*New Yorker*); author of *Going Steady, Kiss Kiss Bang Bang* (movie reviews), *I Lost It at the Movies* (essays).

Franz Kafka (1883–1924)
Czech novelist and short-story writer; author of *The Trial, The Castle, Amerika.*

Alan S. Katz, M.D.
American psychiatrist; chief psychiatrist at Brown University's Student Health Service.

Ellen Keniston
American psychologist.

Kenneth Keniston (1930–)
American psychiatrist (Yale University Medical School); author of *The Uncommitted: Alienated Youth in American Society, Youth and Dissent: The Rise of a New Opposition, Young Radicals: Note on Committed Youth.*

X. J. Kennedy (1929–)
Pseudonym of Joseph C. Kennedy; poet, critic, professor of English (Tufts); author of *Nude Descending a Staircase; Introduction to Poetry.*

John F. Kerry (1943–)
American Yale University graduate and Vietnam veteran.

Sören Kierkegaard (1813–1855)
Danish theologian and philosopher; author of *Fear and Trembling, Either/Or, Philosophical Fragments.*

Martin Luther King, Jr. (1929–1968)
American Negro clergyman and civil rights leader; president, Southern Christian Leadership Conference; Nobel Peace Prize, 1964; author of *Stride Toward Freedom* and *Why We Can't Wait.*

Ronald Knox (1888–1957)
English Roman Catholic prelate; author of *The Belief of Catholics; The Body in the Silo; Let Dons Delight; *Enthusiasm, a Chapter in the History of Religion.*

Theodora Kroeber (1897–)
American anthropologist; author of

The Inland Whale, *Ishi in Two Worlds, Alfred Kroeber: A Personal Configuration.

Joseph Wood Krutch (1893–1970)
American literary and social critic; author of The Modern Temper, The Measure of Man, Human Nature and the Human Condition.

Thomas Kuhn (1922–   )
American historian of science (Princeton University); author of The Copernican Revolution, Planetary Astronomy in the Development of Western Thought, *The Structure of Scientific Revolutions.

Charles Lamb (1775–1834)
English essayist, critic; author of *Essays of Elia and, with his sister, Mary, Tales from Shakespeare.

Susanne K. Langer (1895–   )
American philosopher and educator (Connecticut College); author of The Practice of Philosophy, An Introduction to Symbolic Logic, Feeling and Form, *Problems of Art.

François, duc de la Rochefoucauld (1613–1680)
French moralist; author of Memoirs, *Reflections or Sentences and Moral Maxims.

Aldo Leopold (1886–1948)
American conservationist; author of The Chase Journal, Game Management, A Sand County Almanac.

C. S. Lewis (1898–1963)
English literary scholar and critic, novelist, theologian; author of A Preface to Paradise Lost, The Screwtape Letters, Mere Christianity, *Miracles.

Abraham Lincoln (1809–1865)
Sixteenth president of the United States; lawyer, congressman, celebrated for his debates with Stephen Douglas on the question of slavery's extension. His voluminous state papers include the Emancipation Proclamation, the Gettysburg Address, the Second Inaugural.

Walter Lippmann (1889–1971)
American political philosopher and journalist-statesman; author of Public Opinion, A Preface to Morals, The New Imperative, The Public Philosophy, The Communist World and Ours.

Thomas V. LoCicero (1940–   )
Writer and teacher; author of *Murder in the Synagogue.

Konrad Lorenz (1903–   )
Austrian-born German scientist; director of Max Planck Institute for Physiology of Behavior; author of *King Solomon's Ring and So kam der Mensch auf den Hund (Thus Came the Man to the Dog).

John Livingston Lowes (1867–1945)
American literary critic, scholar, and teacher (Harvard); author of *Geoffrey Chaucer, The Road to Xanadu.

Thomas Babington Macaulay (1800–1859)
English historian, member of Parliament and first Baron Macaulay; author of History of England, Lays of Ancient Rome.

Niccolò Machiavelli (1469–1527)
Florentine statesman and political philosopher during the reign of the Medici; author of The Art of War, History of Florence, Discourses on Livy, *The Prince.

Katherine Mansfield (1888–1923)
Pseudonym of Kathleen Beauchamp; New Zealand-born English short-story writer; author of Bliss, The Garden Party, The Dove's Nest.

William March (1893–1954)
Pseudonym of William Edward March Campbell; American businessman, novelist, short-story writer, fabulist; author of Company K, The Little Wife and Other Stories, Some Like Them Short, *99 Fables.

Matthew
One of the twelve Apostles of Christ, author of *The Gospel According to St. Matthew.

W. Somerset Maugham (1874–1965)
English novelist, dramatist, short-story writer; author of Of Human Bondage (novel), The Moon and Sixpence (novel), The Circle (play), *The Summing Up (autobiography).

Margaret Mead (1901–   )
American anthropologist (American Museum of Natural History and Columbia); author of Coming of Age in Samoa, *Male and Female, New Lives for Old, Continuities in Cultural Evolution, and Keep Your Powder Dry.

Stanley Milgram (1933–   )
American social psychologist (Yale).

Toni Morrison (1931–   )
American writer; author of *The Bluest Eye.

William G(amwell) Moulton (1914–)
American linguist; author of *A Linguist's Guide to Language, The Sounds of English and German, Spoken German* (with Jenni Karding Moulton).

Wolfgang Amadeus Mozart (1756–1791)
Austrian composer; composed in all forms of his art.

John Henry Newman (1801–1890)
English Catholic prelate and cardinal; author of *Tracts for the Times, *The Idea of a University, Apologia pro Vita sua.*

Huey P. Newton (1942–)
Black American revolutionary; co-founder and Minister of Defense of the Black Panther Party.

Nicholas of Cusa (c. 1400–1464)
German Catholic prelate (bishop and cardinal) and philosopher, argued in favor of church councils over the pope and for the principle of consent as the basis of government; author of *De concordantia catholica, De docta ignorantia, *De visione Dei (The Vision of God).*

George Orwell (1903–1950)
Pseudonym of Eric Blair; English novelist, essayist, and social commentator, satirist of totalitarianism; author of *Down and Out in Paris and London, Homage to Catalonia, *Nineteen Eighty-Four, Animal Farm.*

Henry F. Ottinger (1941–)
Instructor of English (University of Missouri).

Walter Pater (1839–1894)
English man of letters, interpreter of Renaissance humanism; author of *Studies in the History of the Renaissance, Marius the Epicurean, Appreciations.*

Donald R. Pearce (1917–)
Canadian professor of English (Santa Barbara); author of *Journal of a War: Northwest Europe, 1944–1945* and *In the President's and My Opinion.*

Charles Sanders Peirce (1839–1914)
American philosopher, scientist, and logician; author of *Chance, Love, and Logic; Essays in the Philosophy of Science; Values in a Universe of Chance.*

William G. Perry, Jr. (1913–)
American educator, director of the Bureau of Study Counsel at Harvard.

Plato (427?–347 B.C.)
Greek philosopher, pupil and friend of Socrates, teacher of Aristotle, founder of the Academy, proponent of an oligarchy of intellectuals based on the assumption that virtue is knowledge; author of *The Republic.*

Adrienne Rich (1929–)
American poet (City College of New York); author of *A Change of World, The Diamond Cutters, Necessities of Life, Snapshots of a Daughter-in-Law, Leaflets, The Will to Change.*

Berton Rouché (1911–)
American journalist (*New Yorker*), chronicler of medical history; author of *Eleven Blue Men, The Incurable Wound, The Neutral Spirit.*

Samuel
The subject of two books of the Old Testament; leader of Israel, anointer of Saul and of David.

Stanley Sanders (1942–)
American lawyer.

George Santayana (1863–1952)
American philosopher (Harvard), author of *The Life of Reason, The Realm of Essence, The Realm of Truth,* and *Soliloquies in England.*

Jean-Paul Sartre (1905–)
French philosopher, playwright, novelist, story writer, social and literary critic, Nobel Prize winner; author of *Existentialism, Existentialism and Humanism, No Exit, The Wall, Imagination, Of Human Freedom, The Problem of Method, The Words, The Transcendence of the Ego.*

Peter Schrag (1931–)
German-born American editor and writer; author of *Voices in the Classroom, Out of Place in America, Village School Downtown.*

Allan Seager (1906–1968)
American novelist and short-story writer, professor of English (University of Michigan); author of *Amos Berry, Hilda Manning, *A Frieze of Girls, The Glass House* (a biography of Theodore Roethke).

Chief Seattle (19th century)
American Indian, chief of the Du-

wampo tribe in Washington Territory.

John Selden (1584–1654)
English politician, jurist, Oriental scholar, and member of Parliament; author of many political tracts and works on law and *Table Talk.*

George Bernard Shaw (1856–1950)
Irish playwright and essayist; author of the plays *Saint Joan, *Man and Superman, *Major Barbara, Caesar and Cleopatra.*

Neil Simon (1927–   )
American playwright; author of *Barefoot in the Park, Last of the Red Hot Lovers, The Odd Couple, Plaza Suite, Star-Spangled Girl, The Prisoner of Second Avenue.*

B(urrhus) F(rederic) Skinner (1904–   )
American psychologist (Harvard); inventor of the Skinner box, an artificial environmental system for the control and study of behavior; author of *Science and Human Behavior, Walden Two, Beyond Freedom.*

Logan Pearsall Smith (1865–1946)
American social critic and humorist; author of *All Trivia, More Trivia, Stories and Essays.*

Wallace Stegner (1909–   )
American essayist, novelist, professor of English (Stanford); author of *Remembering Laughter, The Women on the Wall, Beyond the Hundredth Meridian, A Shocking Star, *Wolf Willow, All the Little Live Things,* and *Gathering of Zion: The Story of the Mormon Trail.*

John Steinbeck (1902–1969)
American novelist, columnist; Nobel Prize winner, 1963; author of *In Dubious Battle, Of Mice and Men, The Grapes of Wrath* (Pulitzer Price, 1939), *East of Eden, *Journal of a Novel: The East of Eden Letters.*

Jonathan Swift (1667–1745)
Irish satirist, poet, and churchman; author of *Gulliver's Travels, A Tale of a Tub, *The Battle of the Books.*

John D. Stewart (1930–   )
English essayist, fiction writer, dramatist, civil servant, contributor to English and American magazines.

Laurence Sterne (1713–1768)
English. cleric, novelist, and humorist; author of *Tristram Shandy, A Sentimental Journey, Sermons.*

(Louis) Studs Terkel (1912–   )
American actor, interviewer, and writer; author of *Hard Times: An Oral History of the Great Depression, Division Street: America.*

Theophrastus (c. 371–287 B.C.)
Greek philosopher, naturalist, and successor to Aristotle; author of *Characters, Metaphysics, On Plants.*

Dylan Thomas (1914–1953)
Welsh poet, story writer, radio-script writer, and broadcaster; author of *Collected Poems (1934–1952), Under Milk Wood* (verse drama), *Adventures in the Skin Trade and Other Stories, Portrait of the Artist as a Young Dog* (autobiographical sketches).

Henry David Thoreau (1817–1862)
American philosopher, essayist, naturalist, poet, disciple of Emerson, foremost exponent of self-reliance; author of *Walden,* "Civil Disobedience," *Journals.*

Thucydides (c. 460–400 B.C.)
Greek historian; author of *The Peloponnesian War.*

James Thurber (1894–1963)
American humorist, cartoonist, social commentator (*New Yorker*), playwright; author of *My Life and Hard Times; *Fables for Our Time; *Men, Women, and Dogs; The Beast in Me and Other Animals.*

Paul Tillich (1886–1965)
German-born American theologian; author of *The Interpretation of History, The Shaking of the Foundations, Systematic Theology, The Dynamic of Faith, Christianity and the Encounter of the World Religions.*

Barbara Tuchman (1912–   )
American writer and historian; author of the *Zimmerman Telegram; The Guns of August; *The Proud Tower; Stilwell and the American Experience in China, 1911–1945.*

John Updike (1932–   )
American novelist, story writer, poet; author of *Rabbit, Run; The Centaur; Of the Farm; Couples; Bech; Rabbit Redux* (novels); *The Same Door; Pigeon Feathers; The Music School* (stories).

Ernest van den Haag (1914–   )
Dutch-born American sociologist (New School for Social Research); author or co-author of *The Fabric of Society, Education as an Indus-*

try, Passion and Social Constraint, The Jewish Mystique.

Verta Mae (1938–   )
Black American writer; author of *Vibration Cooking* and *Thursdays and Every Other Sunday Off.*

Ian P(ierre) Watt (1917–   )
English-born American professor of English (Stanford University); author of *The Rise of the Novel.*

Alan W. Watts (1915–   )
English-born American philosopher and editor; author of *The Legacy of Asia and Western Man, The Supreme Identity, Myth and Ritual in Christianity, *The Meaning of Happiness, Beyond Theology, The Book, Does It Matter?*

Cicely V(eronica) Wedgwood (1910–   )
English historian (University College, London); author of *The Thirty Years War, William the Silent, The King's Peace, The King's War, Poetry and Politics, *Truth and Opinion; Historical Essays, Seventeenth Century Literature, Milton and His World.*

Simone Weil (1909–1943)
French essayist, poet, philosopher; author of *Waiting for God; Gravity and Grace; The Need for Roots; Oppression and Liberty; On Science, Necessity and the Love of God.*

Naomi Weisstein (1939–   )
American psychologist (Loyola University, Chicago); author of numerous papers on perception, cognition, information science, memory, and the psychology of differences between men and women.

Edward Weston (1886–1958)
American photographer; author of *The Daybooks.*

E. B. White (1899–   )
American essayist, journalist, editor

(*New Yorker*); author of *One Man's Meat, *The Wild Flag, *The Second Tree from the Corner.*

Oscar Wilde (1856–1900)
Irish wit, dramatist, poet, story writer, critic; author of *The Picture of Dorian Gray* (novel), *The Importance of Being Earnest* (play).

William B. Willcox (1907–   )
American historian (Yale University); author of *Gloucestershire: A Study in Local Government, Star of Empire: A Study of Britain as a World Power, Portrait of a General: Sir Henry Clinton in the War of Independence.*

Roger Williams (c. 1603–1683)
English clergyman, exiled from Massachusetts Bay Colony for advocating separation of church and state, founder of Rhode Island.

William Edward Wilson (1906–   )
American professor of English (Indiana University); author of *Big Knife: The Story of George Rogers Clark.*

Tom Wolfe (1931–   )
American essayist, story writer, social critic; author of *The Kandy-Kolored Tangerine-Flake Streamline Baby, The Pump House Gang, Radical Chic and Mau-Mauing the Flak Catcher.*

C(omer) Vann Woodward (1908–   )
American historian (Yale University); author of *Origins of the New South, Reunion and Reaction, The Burden of Southern History, The Strange Career of Jim Crow, American Counterpoint.*

Virginia Woolf (1882–1942)
English novelist, essayist, and critic; author of *Mrs. Dalloway, To the Lighthouse* (novels), *The Common Reader, Granite and Rainbow, *The Second Common Reader* (essays).

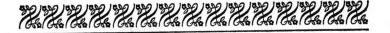

Alphabetical Index